Practical .NET2 and C#2

By Patrick Smacchia

Paradoxal Press

PUBLISHED BY
Paradoxal Press
9981 Avondale Rd. NE
Redmond, WA 98052
Unites States of America
http://www.ParadoxalPress.com
info@ParadoxalPress.com

Copyright ©2005-2006 by Patrick Smachia.

All rights reserved. No part of this book may be reproduced or transmitted in any form or by any means, electronic or mechanical, including photocopying, recording, or by any information storage or retrieval system without written permission from Paradoxal Press, except for the inclusion of brief quotations in a review.

The Paradoxal Press logo and related trade dress are trademarks of Paradoxal Press and may not be used without written permission.

Educational facilities, companies, and organizations interested in multiple copies or licensing of this book should contact the publisher for quantity discount information. Training manuals, CD-ROMs, and portions of this book can be tailored for specific needs.

ISBN-10: 0-9766132-2-0
ISBN-13: 978-0-9766132-2-0

Library of Congress Control Number: 2005910166

Printed in the United States of America

President, Paradoxal Press: Sebastien St-Laurent
Copy Editor: Nicole St-Laurent
Interior Layout: Sebastien St-Laurent
Cover Designer: Sebastien St-Laurent
Indexer: Patrick Smacchia

Contents at a Glance

PART I - The .NET2 Platform   9
  1. Introduction to .NET...1
  2. Assembly, module, IL language.....................................11
  3. Build, deploy and configure your .NET applications 39
  4. The CLR (Common Language Runtime)................................71
  5. Processes, threads and synchronization 109
  6. Security...153
  7. Reflection, late binding, attributes...........................193
  8. Interoperability between .NET and native code..................219

PART II - The C#2 Language   255
  9. Fundamental concepts of the language...........................257
  10. The .NET 2 type system from a C#2 point of view...............281
  11. Classes and objects 327
  12. Inheritance, polymorphism and abstraction.....................367
  13. Generics..387
  14. Unsafe code, exceptions, anonymous methods, iterators 417

PART III - The .NET2 Framework   469
  15. Collections 469
  16. Base Classes 497
  17. Input/Output and Streams 523
  18. Windows Forms Application....................................551
  19. ADO.NET 2..585
  20. Transactions...615
  21. XML..631
  22. .NET Remoting..653
  23. ASP.NET 2 713
  24. Introduction to web services development with .NET 819

Appendix   841
Index   858

Table Of Contents

Preface xi
About this book xi
How the book is organized xi
Who this book is for? xii
Support xiii
Acknowledgments xiii

1. Introduction to .NET 1
What is .NET? 1
History 2
.NET outside Microsoft and Windows 4
Links on .NET 5

PART I - The .NET2 Platform 9

2. Assembly, module, IL language 11
Assemblies, modules and resource files 11
Dissecting a module 12
Analysis of an assembly with the ildasm.exe and Reflector tools 15
Assembly Attributes and Versioning 19
Strong named assemblies 22
Internationalization/localization and satellite assemblies 27
Introduction to the IL language 33

3. Build, deploy and configure your .NET applications 39
Building your applications with MSBuild 39
MSBuild: Target, Task, Property, Item and Condition 39
Advanced MSBuild 43
Configuration files 46
Assembly deployment: XCopy vs. GAC 51
Publisher policy assemblies 53
Introduction to .NET application deployment 55
Deploying an application with a cab file 57
Deploying an application with the MSI technology 59
Deploying an application with the ClickOnce technology 62
Deploying and application with the No Touch Deployment (NTD) technology 68
What if the .NET runtime is not installed on the target machine? 69

4. The CLR (Common Language Runtime) 71
Application Domains (AppDomain) 71
Loading the CLR inside a Windows process with the runtime host...............76
Profiling the execution of your .NET applications.............................83
Locating and loading assemblies 83
Resolving types at runtime..89
JIT compilation (Just In Time) 90
The garbage collector (GC) and the managed heap 95
Facilities to make your code more reliable................................102
CLI and CLS 107

5. Processes, threads and synchronization 109
Introduction 109
Processes..109
Threads..112
Introduction to resource access synchronization..........................117
Synchronization with volatile fields and the Interlocked class...............119
Synchronization with System.Threading.Monitor and the lock keyword........120
Synchronizing with win32 objects: mutex, events and semaphores 126
Synchronizing using the System.Threading.ReaderWriterLock class 130
Synchronizing using the SynchronizationAttribute attribute 132
The CLR's threadpool 137
Timers...139
Calling a method asynchronously 141
Threads-resources affinities 145
Introduction to execution context 149

6. Security...153
Introduction to Code Access Security (CAS)................................153
CAS: Evidences and permissions 155
CAS: Granting permissions from evidences by applying security policies 160
CAS: The FullTrust permission..164
CAS: Imperative permission check from the source code 164
CAS: Declarative permissions check using attributes 168
CAS: Facilities to test and debug your mobile code........................169
CAS: The isolated storage permission.....................................170
.NET, Windows users and roles 170
.NET and access control to Windows resources 174
.NET and roles 179
.NET and cryptography: symmetric algorithms 181
.NET and cryptography: asymmetric algorithms (public/private keys)...........183
The Data Protection API (DPAPI) 187
Authenticating your assemblies with the Authenticode and X.509 certificates 191

7. Reflection, late binding, attributes 193
Reflection 193
Late bindings 197
Attributes 206
Dynamically building an assembly and using it on the fly 212

8. Interoperability between .NET and native code 219
P/Invoke 219
Introduction to interoperability with the C++/CLI language 225
.NET and win32 Handles 229
Using COM objects from .NET code 230
Wrapping a .NET object into a COM Callable Wrapper (CCW) 238
Introduction to COM+ 244
Overview of the COM+ enterprise services 245
Harnessing COM+ services in .NET classes 247

PART II - The C#2 Language 255

9. Fundamental concepts of the language 257
Organizing your source code 257
Compilation Steps 259
The preprocessor 260
The csc.exe compiler 264
The aliases 266
Comments and automatic documentation 269
Identifiers 271
Control Structures 272
The Main() method 278

10. The .NET 2 type system from a C#2 point of view 281
The storage of objects in memory 281
Reference types vs. Value types 283
The Common Type System (CTS) 285
The System.Object class 287
Comparing objects 288
Cloning an object 290
Boxing and Unboxing 292
Primitive types 295
Operations on primitive types 299
Structures 303
Enumerations 305
Strings 308
Delegate classes and delegate objects 313
Nullable types 319
Partial types 325

11. Classes and objects...327
Introduction...327
Vocabulary...327
Class definition...328
Fields...329
Methods...330
Properties...337
Indexer...339
Events...340
Nested types...345
Encapsulation and visibility...345
The this keyword...347
Constructors...348
Object finalization and destruction...350
Static members...356
Operator overloading...358

12. Inheritance, polymorphism and abstraction...367
Objective: code reuse...367
Class inheritance...368
Virtual methods and polymorphism...371
Abstraction...375
Interfaces...377
Virtual and abstract properties, events and indexers...383
The is and as operator...384
Solutions for code reuse...386

13. Generics...387
A C#1 problem and how to solve it with .NET 2 generics...387
.NET 2 generics: the big picture...390
Type parameter constraints...392
Members of generic types...395
Operators and generics...399
Casting and generics...401
Inheritance and generics...403
Generic methods...404
Delegates, events and generics...407
Reflection, attributes, IL and generics...409
Generics in the .NET 2 framework...414

14. Unsafe code, exceptions, anonymous methods, iterators ..417

Pointers and unsafe code 417
Using pointers in C# 418
Handling errors with exceptions 423
Exception objects and defining custom exception classes 425
Catch and finally blocks 428
Exceptions thrown from a constructor or from a finalizer 430
Exception handling and the CLR 432
Exception handling and Visual Studio. 434
Guidelines on exception management 434
Anonymous methods. 436
The C#2 compiler and anonymous methods 440
Advanced uses of anonymous methods. 446
C#1 iterators 448
C#2 iterators. 451
The C#2 compiler and iterators 456
Advanced use of C#2 iterators 459

PART III - The .NET2 Framework 469

15. Collections 469

Iterating through the items of a collection with the 'foreach' and 'in' keywords. . . .469
Arrays 471
Sequences. 478
Dictionaries 484
Sorting items of a collection 489
Functors as a mean to work with collections 492
Correspondence between System.Collections.Generic and System.Collections . . .496

16. Base Classes. 497

Math 497
Time, date and duration 499
Drives, directories, files and paths. 503
Registry. 508
Debugging 510
Traces 513
Regular expressions. 517
Console 520

17. Input/Output and Streams 523
Introduction to streams 523
Reading and writing files 525
Harnessing TCP/IP with sockets 530
Getting information about network interfaces and status 537
HTTP and FTP clients. 538
Coding an HTTP server with the HttpListener class over HTTP.SYS. 540
Support for mails protocols (SMTP and MIME) 542
Buffering and compressing data streams 543
Reading and writing data on the serial port. 545
Support for secure communication protocols: SSL, NTLM and Kerberos. 546

18. Windows Forms Application 551
Windows user interfaces. 551
Introduction to Windows Forms development 553
Facilities to develop Windows Forms applications 558
Standard controls. 563
Creating custom controls 565
Viewing and editing data 570
Windows Forms and localization. 576
GDI+ 576

19. ADO.NET 2 585
Introduction to databases. 585
Introduction to ADO.NET 586
Connections and data providers 590
Working in connected mode with DataReader 597
Working in unconnected mode with DataSet 600
Typed DataSet 606
Bridges between the connected and the unconnected modes 609
Bridges between objects and the relational data. 610
Functionalities specific to the SQL Server data provider 612

20. Transactions 615
Introduction to transactions 615
System.Transactions 619
Advanced usage of System.Transactions. 624
Facilities for implementing a custom RM. 626

21. XML 631

Introduction 631
Introduction to XSD, XPath, XSLT and XQuery. 633
Approaches to traverse and edit an XML document 636
The cursor approach with the XmlReader and XmlWriter classes 636
The tree/DOM approach using the XmlDocument class. 639
Traversing and editing an XML document using XPath 641
Transforming an XML document using a XSLT stylesheet 644
Bridges between relational data and XML documents 644
Bridges between objects and XML documents (XML serialization) 648
Visual Studio and XML 651

22. .NET Remoting 653

Introduction 653
Marshaling By Reference (MBR) 655
Marshalling By Value (MBV) and binary serialization 657
The ObjectHandle class. 658
Object activation 660
Well-Known Object activation (WKO) 661
Client Activated Object (CAO) 664
The factory design pattern and the soapsuds.exe tool 667
Life cycle of Well-Know and Client Activated Objects 670
Configuring .NET Remoting 672
Deployment of a .NET Remoting server. 677
Securing a .NET Remoting channel 679
Proxy and message 679
Channel. 690
.NET context. 700
Summary 711

23. ASP.NET 2 713
Introduction...713
ASP.NET: The big picture 714
ASP.NET application source code............................719
Compilation and deployment models 723
Web forms and controls 725
Page life cycle..734
ASP.NET application configuration (Web.Config files) 737
HTTP Pipeline 740
State and session management 745
The provider design pattern................................750
Error handling 750
Trace, diagnostic and event management 752
Validation of input data 754
User controls 757
Caching..762
Data sources...771
Viewing and editing data 776
Master pages 786
ASP.NET 2 and localization.................................791
Site navigation..792
Security...794
Personalization and user profiles..........................802
Styles, Themes and Skins 805
WebParts...808

24. Introduction to web services development with .NET . . .819
Introduction...819
Developing a simple web service 822
Testing and debugging a web service 824
Creating a .NET client of a web service 825
Asynchronous calls and Message Exchange Patterns 828
Using a web service from a .NET Remoting client 828
SOAP messages..829
Web services contracts and the WSDL language 832
Introduction to WSE and to WS-* specifications 836
WS-* specifications not yet supported by WSE 838
Introduction to WCF (Windows Communication Framework) 840

Appendix 841
Appendix A: keywords of the C#2 language 841
Appendix B : .NET 2 enhancements. 844
Appendix C: Introduction to design patterns. 854
Appendix D: Tools for the .NET 2 platform. 856

Index 858

Preface

About this book

The .NET **MSDN** documentation from *Microsoft* is vast and focuses on the details of each member of thousands of types. It also contains several articles in regards to the use of various parts of .NET. As a developer, I know how much the use of MSDN is fundamental when developing using *Microsoft* technologies. However, because of the volume of this documentation, it is difficult to get a global view of the features offered by .NET. From my own experience, new ideas and concepts are better acquired from a book. Yes, we could print the thousands of pages contained in MSDN but it would be hard to carry them around to read calmly in a garden or on your couch.

This book was conceived with the vision of being used conjointly with MSDN. The goal is not to enumerate the thousands of members within the thousands of .NET types but to rather explain and illustrate with concise and usable examples the multiple facets of the .NET platform, the C# language and the .NET framework. I hope that this book will give you a good insight into the motivations behind the technology and that it will carry you through the unbeaten paths to the discovery of modern software programming.

How the book is organized

Part I: The .NET platform

The first part of this book describes the underlying architecture of the .NET platform. It is in this part that you will find answers to questions such as:

- What are the links between the execution of a .NET application and the underlying operating system?
- What is the structure of the files produced by the compilation of my programs?
- How are security and resource access managed?
- How can I draw from all this to improve the quality and performance of my applications?
- How can I take advantage of code already developed for *Windows* from my .NET applications?

Part II: The C#2 language and the C# 2/C++ comparison

The second part completely describes the C#2 language. This language is much closer to Java than C++. Hence, I made an effort to describe the similarities and differences between C++ and C# for each facet of the C# language. I hope that this approach will quickly answer most of the questions developers migrating from C++ might have.

Part III: The .NET framework

The third part describes the base classes of the .NET framework. The functionality of these classes can be separated into the following categories:

Collections.

The classic base classes for mathematical operations, dates and durations, folders and files, traces and debugging, regular expressions, console.

The management of I/O using data streams.

The development of graphical applications with *Windows Forms 2*.

The management of databases using *ADO.NET 2*.

The management of transactions.

The creation and manipulation of XML documents.

Distributed object applications using .NET Remoting.

The development of web applications using ASP.NET 2.

Web services.

Notes on the organization

This plan allows you to constantly have a good idea of where you are through your reading. However, it is obvious that such a vast technology has many facets which transcend this organization. For example, we have chosen to explain how to synchronize concurrent resource access in the first part since this topic is based on the underlying notions of threads and processes which are closed to platform. However, classes dedicated to synchronization are also part of the .NET framework and could have been also introduced in the third part. Finally, the C# language contains specialized keywords to simplify the use of some of these classes and therefore, this subject could also have been partially covered in the second part.

This book contains several internal references which I hope, should help you navigate through the different subjects discussed.

Who this book is for?

This book addresses itself to you as soon as you have an interest in developing under .NET, whether you are a student, professional or amateur developer, teacher, architect or technical team leader.

Each chapter has been designed to be read in a linear way but this is by no means the same for the book in its totality. The first part, the .NET platform, is considered as the most difficult but also as the most fundamental part (and according to me the most interesting one). It is simply not possible to develop properly using .NET without having some good knowledge of the underlying platform.

The **beginner** can start by learning the C# language and the object development technologies, all while discovering the possibilities of .NET.

The **reader which is experienced in other technologies** should benefit from the explanations concerning the numerous innovative features offered by .NET.

The **reader experienced with .NET 1** can use Appendix B, which references all the new features brought by .NET 2 covered in this book.

Support

This book is supported on the following site: `http://www.PracticalDOT.Net/`

There, you can download the examples found in this book. We believe that quite often, a well written sample be more valuable than a long discussion on the details of a topic. This book contains 647 examples where 523 listings are in C# and a hundred are dedicated to ASP.NET 2. They are all available online at `http://www.PracticalDOT.Net/`.

You can also contact us with your comments and feedback on this title by writing to *Paradoxal Press*: 9981 Avondale Rd. NE, Redmond WA 98052

Email: `info@ParadoxalPress.com`

Acknowledgments

First of all, I wish to thank my friend, **Eli Ane** for her support which gave me so much during the authoring of this title. I have also greatly appreciated the support of **Francis**, **France**, **Michel**, **Christine**, **Mathieu**, **Julien**, **Andrée**, **Patrick**, **Marie-Laure** and **Philippe**.

A thank goes to **Sébastien St Laurent** of *Paradoxal Press* for his professionalism and his great help in translating and publishing this book. Thank you also to **Xavier Cazin** of *O'Reilly France* who has supported and helped me with this project since the beginnings of .NET.

My gratitude also goes to those who have proofread and to my friends for their valuable advice:

Alain Metge, 18 years of experience. Responsible for the southern France highway software architecture.

Dr. Bertrand Le Roy, 8 years of experience, participated for 3 years at the conception of ASP.NET technologies with *Microsoft Corporation*.

Bruno Boucard, 18 years of experience, architect/trainer at the *Société Générale* bank for 8 years. *Microsoft Informed Architect*.

Frédéric De Lène Mirouze (aka. Améthyste), web development specialist, 20 years of experience, collaborates with *ELF*, *Glaxo*, *Nortel*, *Usinor*. *MCAD.NET*.

Jean-Baptiste Evain, 3 years of experience, specialist in the Common Language Infrastructure, contributor to *Mono* and *AspectDNG*.

Laurent Desmons, 10 years of experience, architect and .NET consultant, collaborates with *Péchiney*, *Arcelor*, *Sollac*. *MCSD.NET*.

Matthieu Guyonnet-Duluc, 4 years of experience, commercial developer with *France Télécom*.

Dr Michel Futtersack, Master of Computing Conference, *René Descartes University*, teaching for more than 10 years in OOP conception and programming.

Nicolas Frelat, .NET consultant with 4 years of experience. Early adopter of the .NET 2 platform.

Olivier Girard, 6 years of experience, EAI specialist, architect at *Banque de France*.

Patrick Philippot, freelanceer, 30 years of experience (with 19 at *IBM*), .NET MVP `www.mainsoft.fr`.

Sami Jaber, 8 years of experience, trainer and senior consultant with *Valtech*, collaborates with Airbus and webmaster for `www.dotnetguru.org`.

Sébastien Ros, 7 years of experience, O/R mapping specialist, author of the *DTM* tool, CTO of *Evaluant* www.evaluant.com.

Sébastien Vaucouleur, 8 years of experience, language specialist, collaborates with *Bull*, *Fujitsu*, research assistant at *ETH university* (Zurich).

Thibaut Barrère, freelanceer, J2EE/.NET/C++ platform specialist, programming since 1984 and has recently collaborated with *Calyon*, *PPR/Redoute* and *MCS*. Open source contributor on *CruiseControl.Net*, *NAnt* and *TestDriven.Net*.

Thomas Gil, 8 years of experience, *Aspect Oriented Programing* specialist, chief of the *AspectDNG* project, consultant and independent trainer, co-webmaster of www.dotnetguru.org.

Vincent Canestrier, previous teacher at *Conservatoire National des Arts et Métiers*, previous technical director at *Cap Gemini Ernst & Young*.

I also wish to thank **Brian Grunkemeyer**, **Florin Lazar, Krzysztof Cwalina** and **Michael Marucheck**, all engineers at *Microsoft Corp*, for all their great answers to my questions.

Finally, I wish to thank you to have chosen this title. I sincerely hope that it will help you get all your tasks accomplished.

I
Introduction to .NET

What is .NET?

The Microsoft software development platform

Under the .NET name is the main development platform from *Microsoft*. This topic is vast and covers numerous specifications as the format of components, the programming languages, the standard classes and tools. In addition to specifications *Microsoft* provides an implementation dedicated for the *Windows* platform. With .NET we talk about the current generation of software development in the *Microsoft* world, which supersedes the era of COM/win32/C++/VB/ASP.

The .NET name has been chosen from the fact that the internet, and networks in general are more commonly used by software. Applications are more and more interconnected. Based on this fact, the .NET technology presents facilities to enable the communication of applications which we will discuss in chapters 22 and 24. To facilitate the interoperation of applications in a heterogeneous playing field, the .NET platform also bases itself on a strong use of XML at all levels.

Little by little, all *Microsoft* products are exposing their APIs using .NET types. For example, *SQL Server 2005* allows the injection of .NET code executed within the DBMS process which manages the data. The API for *Windows Vista,* the next version of *Windows*, is partly provided as .NET types. The web page construction technology, named ASP.NET is now privileged by the IIS 7.0 web server. The *Office* suite presents a programming model based on .NET which supersedes the old VBA model.

A set of specifications

The .NET platform bases itself on numerous specifications, some maintained by organisms other than *Microsoft*. These specifications define languages such as C#, VB.NET and IL. They also cover data exchange protocols such as the SOAP format. Some other implementation initiatives of these specifications are in process. .NET is already partly available on several operating systems other than *Microsoft* ones. .NET is a new era in the world of software development, comparable to the C era, the C++ era and the Java era. It is interesting to note that this phenomenon seems to happen periodically, about every 7 years. With each new era, developer productivity increases because of the introduction of new ideas and applications are more user friendly and can process more data due to the increase in hardware performance. The consequence is that the industry adopts these new technologies to develop software of better quality while reducing their development costs.

.NET: The big picture

The .NET technology is composed mainly of three parts:

- An extensible set of development languages including **C#** and **VB.NET**. These languages must respect a specification named **CLS** (*Common Language Specification*). The base types used by these languages must also respect a specification named **CTS** (*Common Type System*).

- A set of base classes usable from programs developed in these languages. We sometimes use the term **BCL** (*Base Class Library*) to reference them. This is what we will call the **.NET framework** throughout this book.

- A software layer respecting a specification named **CLI** (*Common Language Infrastructure*). It is responsible for the execution of .NET applications. This layer only knows one language named **IL** (*Intermediate Language*). This software is responsible during the execution of an application, of the compilation of the IL code into machine code. Consequently, the languages supported by .NET each must have a compiler which will produce IL code. Microsoft's implementation of the CLI is named **CLR** (*Common Language Runtime*).

In parallel to these three parts, there are several tools facilitating the development of .NET applications. We can mention *Visual Studio* which is an IDE (*Integrated Development Environment*) allowing you to work with C#, VB.NET and C++/CLI languages. The list of these tools is available in the article named **.NET Framework Tools** on **MSDN**. Most of these tools are described throughout this book and enumerated in Appendix D.

The plan of this book bases itself mostly on these three parts:

```
┌─────────────────────────────────────────────┐ ┌───────┐
│  CLS (Common language Specification)        │ │       │
│  C#, VB.NET, managed C++, JScript,...       │ │       │
├─────────────────────────────────────────────┤ │       │
│  BCL (Base Class Library)                   │ │       │
│  ADO.NET, Forms, XML, ASP.NET etc           │ │ Tools │
├─────────────────────────────────────────────┤ │       │
│  CLI implementation                         │ │       │
│  (Common Language Infrastructure)           │ │       │
│  CLR (Common Language Runtime)              │ │       │
└─────────────────────────────────────────────┘ └───────┘
```

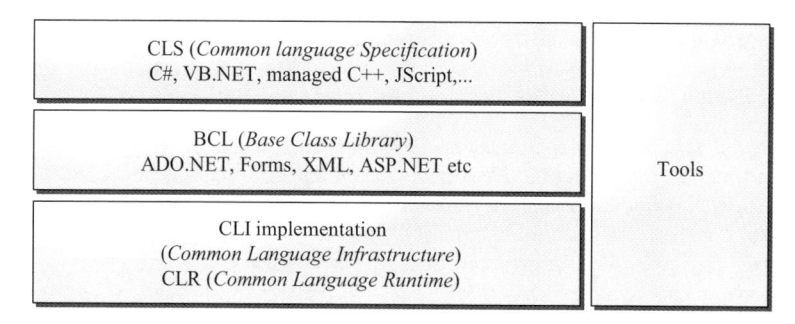

Figure 1-1 .NET: The big picture

History

The past

Since 1998, the team in charge of developing the *MTS* (*Microsoft Transaction Server*) product wished to develop a new product to solve some of the problems with the COM technology. These problems mostly concerned the strong coupling between COM and the underlying operating ystem as well as the complexities in using this technology, especially at the level of its deployment and maintenance.

In parallel, the *Java* community was gaining grounds in the software development scene. More and more enterprises were seduced by the concept of a virtual machine allowing the execution of applications on most systems without any additional work. In addition, the Java classes were much easier to use than MFC (*Microsoft Foundation Classes*) mostly because of the absence of pointers which significantly improved developer productivity. As of June 2000, *Microsoft* announced that it was currently developing a new technology which would include a new language named C#. On February 13th 2002 was published the first usable version of .NET. This event was decisive in the history of *Microsoft* and more generally, in the world of software development.

Amongst the engineers in charge of this project, we can mention *Anders Hejlsberg*, one of the co-founders of *Borland*. This Danish engineer, designer of the *Turbo Pascal* and *Delphi* languages, was hired by *Microsoft* in 1996 to work on the *WFC* (*Windows Foundation Classes*), which are the classes used by the Java virtual machine developed by *Microsoft*. Quickly, he was placed in the team that was going to produce what is known today as the CLR and the C# language.

In March 2003, version 1.1 of .NET was released. It contains more classes on the theme of data providers (Oracle and ODBC), security (cryptography), IP v6 technology and XML/XSLT technologies. .NET 1.1 contains tools for the developers of applications under *Windows CE* (Pocket PC, smart phone…). The 1.1 version of the .NET framework also contains the J# language, destined to help Java developers migrate to .NET.

The present

At the end of 2005, *Microsoft* published version 2 of .NET which is the main topic of this book. The number of base types has more than doubled; now covering several aspects neglected by versions 1.x. Improvements and optimizations has appeared in the virtual machine in charge of executing .NET applications as well to the level of the languages. A list of the new features covered by this title is present in Appendix B.

The development tools, and most importantly *Visual Studio* are much more complete and user friendly. It is now a general opinion that the quality of tools plays a major role in the assessment of a software development platform.

In parallel, we can see the beginning of the formalization of two methodologies already present in other development platforms: *eXtreme Programming* (or *XP* not to confuse with *Windows XP*) and model based development.

XP consists in rationalizing the methodologies used to develop an information system by better coordinating the activities of all the involved parties. The idea is to face efficiently the different unexpected changes which will inevitably happen while developing software. For this, we sometimes refer to an *agile* methodology. The agility comes from a certain number of constraints. You must first be listening to your client by providing them often and regularly testable versions. You must also facilitate the communication and the sharing of information between the members of a team using flexible tools available in different versions, each one adapted to a specific function. The human factor is central in XP. Other principles are also put in place such as the conception of a set of automated tests which are executed regularly to catch as early as possible regressions and bugs. This set of tests is in generally executed after a complete compilation of the application from the most recent sources. The concept of *daily build* hints that such a compilation be done on a daily basis, generally during the night. All these idea are easy to put in place thanks to the new *Team System* components of *Visual Studio 2005*.

The model based development consists in automatically generating the code of an application from a model. This model is expressed in a high level language, specially adapted to the functional needs of the application and hence really expressive. We talk of DSL (*Domain Specific Language*). The advantage of this approach is to allow a team to work on sources close to the specifications, reducing the number of refinement cycles and also reducing the complexity of the code. *Visual Studio 2005* offers specialized extensions for the conception and exploitation of DSLs. These extensions also offer the visualization of your C# or VB.NET source code in the form of diagrams in the spirit of UML.

The future

Microsoft will release *Windows Vista* in 2006. This will mark a decisive turn for the .NET platform since for the first time, the .NET execution environment will be part of an operating system. Numerous new .NET types will be offered by *Windows Vista* to give access to the features of this operating system directly to your .NET code. Of this, we can mention the new graphical application framework named *WPF* (*Windows Presentation Framework*) and the new distributed application framework named *WCF* (*Windows Communication Framework*) which we discuss briefly at page 840.

Later in 2007 maybe even in 2008, *Microsoft* will publish the 3.0 version of .NET (code-named *Orcas*). This version will mostly be focused on the advanced integration of the technologies introduced by *Windows Vista* in the framework and *Visual Studio*. For the moment, only the C# team has started to discuss their work on the 3 version of the language. They are focusing on a framework allowing the extension of the language and are working on an extension specialized to the writing of requests on sources of data (object, relational or XML). Lambda expressions which are in the same spirit of anonymous methods in C#2 but more practical, will integrate themselves into these requests. Other new features are planned such as anonymous types, the implicit typing of variables as well as an efficient syntax for the initialization of objects and arrays.

Three to four years later, version 4 of .NET will be released (code-named *Hawaii*) but not information is available at the moment.

.NET outside Microsoft and Windows

The ECMA organization and .NET

In October 2000, *Microsoft*, *Intel* and *Hewlett-Packard* proposed to the *ECMA* (*European Computer Manufacturer's Association*) to standardize a subset of .NET. This subset includes the C# language and the CLI. The ECMA has accepted the request and created a technical committee to complete the standard.

This means that *Microsoft* does not hold the full ownership of C# and the CLI and the *Redmond* giant has tolerated until now that other organizations implement these specifications. For more information and to obtain the official publication of these specifications, please consult the following URLs:

http://www.ecma-international.org/
http://www.msdn.microsoft.com/net/ecma/
http://www.ecma-international.org/publications/standards/Ecma-334.htm   *(C#2 specification)*
http://www.ecma-international.org/publications/standards/Ecma-335.htm   *(CLI specification)*

The W3C consortium

On May 9th 2000, *Microsoft* and 10 other companies such as *IBM*, *Hewlett Packard*, *Compaq* and *SAP* proposed to the W3C consortium to maintain the SOAP standard. The SOAP standard defines a message format based on XML. Web services can communicate by using SOAP messages. The idea behind standardizing this format is to make web services completely independent of a platform or enterprise. We discuss the SOAP format in more details at page 829. For more information, consult http://www.w3.org/TR/SOAP.

Since then, a certain number of specifications aiming to extend the functionality of web services have been submitted to the W3C. Some are currently being implemented while others are still being approved (see page 820 and 838).

The Mono project

On July 9th 2001, the *Ximian* enterprise, founded by *Miguel de Icaza*, has announced that it would be developing an *open source* implementation of .NET. The reason behind this is that their engineers estimate that .NET represents the best software development technology at the moment. The name of this project is *Mono*.

In mid-2003, *Novell* bought out *Ximian* and took over the Mono project. On June 30th 2004, version 1.0 of the project has been released. Mono should shortly be available for the 2 versions of .NET and C#.

The Mono project includes a C# compiler (distributed under the *GPL General Public License*), an implementation of most .NET libraries (distributed under the *MIT/X11* License) as well as a virtual machine which implements the CLI (distributed under *LGPL Lesser GPL*). All this is compatible under *Windows*, *Linux* and several other *UNIX* based operating systems such as *Mac OS X*. The homepage for the project is `http://www.mono-project.com`.

Despite the shadow that the Mono project can cast on the commercial version of .NET by *Microsoft*, they are not necessarily against this initiative. *John Montgomery*, *Microsoft* manager for .NET said: *"...The fact that Ximian is doing this work is great. It's a validation of the work we've done, and it validates our standards activities. Also, it has caused a lot of eyeballs in the open source community to be directed to .Net, which we appreciate..."*. The software giant seems to agree that the *open source* world has an opportunity to use .NET. This represents more potential clients for products developed around .NET.

The Microsoft SSCLI project (Rotor)

The *Shared Source CLI* project (also named *SSCLI* or *Rotor*) by *Microsoft* aims at distributing source code implementing the CLI and certain parts of the .NET framework. The SSCLI project is mostly distributed for academic purposes in order to allow students and researchers to introduce themselves and work on the internals of a modern virtual machine (GC, JIT compilation ...). However, you can use this code to understand the inner workings of .NET and to debug your applications but it cannot be used for commercial purposes.

The SSCLI is several million lines of code, a C# compiler, a JScript compiler and includes several tools. A 2 version should be available shortly after the release of .NET 2. The central parts of the framework (such as XML and .NET Remoting) are supported but other important domains such as ADO.NET, ASP.NET and Windows Form are not implemented by SSCLI.

Contrarily to *Microsoft's* commercial implementation of .NET, the SSCLI can function on several other operating systems than *Windows*. Currently, you can use the SSCLI on the following operating systems *FreeBSD*, *Mac OS X* and *Windows*. This is possible because internally, the SSCLI does not directly call the win32 API. The project uses an API close to win32 named *PAL* (*Platform Abstraction Layer*).

The official page for the project is: `http://msdn.microsoft.com/net/sscli`

You can also browse the source files directly online at: `http://dotnet.di.unipi.it/SharedSourceCli.aspx`

Links on .NET

We propose several links to the main sites oriented towards .NET development. As time goes by, I plan on making more resources available on my site `http://www.smacchia.com` and `http://www.PracticalDOT.net/` in regards to .NET development.

Web sites

Here is the list of the main .NET related sites:

http://www.msdn.microsoft.com
http://www.gotdotnet.com
http://msdn.microsoft.com/msdnmag
http://www.theserverside.net
http://www.dotnet247.com
http://www.15seconds.com
http://www.codeproject.com
http://www.eggheadcafe.com
http://www.devx.com
http://channel9.msdn.com
http://dotnet.sys-con.com
http://dotnet.oreilly.com http://www.ondotnet.com
http://www.dotmugs.ch
http://www.asp.net
http://www.grimes.demon.co.uk
http://dotnetjunkies.com
http://www.codeguru.com
http://www.franklins.net
http://www.c-sharpcorner.com   http://www.csharp-corner.com
http://www.devhood.com
http://www.developer.com
http://www.4guysfromrolla.com   (ASP.NET)
The download section of the site http://www.idesign.net

Newsgroup

On the msnews.microsoft.com server:

microsoft.public.dotnet.framework
microsoft.public.dotnet.framework.adonet
microsoft.public.dotnet.framework.aspnet
microsoft.public.dotnet.framework.clr
microsoft.public.dotnet.framework.performance
microsoft.public.dotnet.framework.remoting
microsoft.public.dotnet.framework.sdk
microsoft.public.dotnet.framework.webservices
microsoft.public.dotnet.general
microsoft.public.dotnet.languages.csharp

Blogs

Finally, here are a few blogs offering great information on software development using the .NET technologies:

Aaron Skonnard (XML) http://pluralsight.com/blogs/aaron/default.aspx
BCL Team http://blogs.msdn.com/bclteam/
Bart De Smet (Various) http://blogs.bartdesmet.net/bart/
Benjamin Mitchell (Web services, eXtreme Programming) http://benjaminm.net/
Bertrand Le Roy (ASP.NET) http://weblogs.asp.net/bleroy/

Bob Beauchemin (ADO.NET SQL Server) http://www.sqlskills.com/blogs/bobb/
Brad Abrams (BCL, design) http://blogs.msdn.com/brada/default.aspx
Carl Franklin (various) http://weblogs.asp.net/cfranklin
Charles Petzold (WPF) http://www.charlespetzold.com/blog/blog.xml
Chris Brumme (CLR) http://blogs.msdn.com/cbrumme/
Chris Sells (Windows Form, various) http://www.sellsbrothers.com/
Clemens Vaster (SOA, design, various) http://staff.newtelligence.net/clemensv/
Dave Broman (CLR profiling API) http://blogs.msdn.com/davbr/
David M. Kean (FxCop, Windows Installer, various) http://davidkean.net/
Dino Esposito (ASP.NET) http://weblogs.asp.net/despos/
Don Box (WCF, various) http://www.pluralsight.com/blogs/dbox/default.aspx
Eric Gunnerson (C#, various) http://blogs.msdn.com/ericgu/
Frans Bouma (Various) http://weblogs.asp.net/fbouma
Fritz Onion (ASP.NET) http://pluralsight.com/blogs/fritz/default.aspx
Florin Lazar (Transactions) http://blogs.msdn.com/florinlazar/
Fredrik Normén (ASP.NET) http://fredrik.nsquared2.com/default.aspx
Jim Johnson (Transactions) http://pluralsight.com/blogs/jimjohn
John Papa (Various) http://codebetter.com/blogs/john.papa/
Junfeng Zhang (GAC, versioning, CLR) http://blogs.msdn.com/junfeng/
Keith Brown (Security) http://pluralsight.com/blogs/keith/default.aspx
Krzysztof Cwalina (Design) http://blogs.msdn.com/kcwalina/
Martin Fowler (Architecture, pattern) http://martinfowler.com/bliki/
Matt Pietrek (Win32, Windows) http://blogs.msdn.com/matt_pietrek/
Michele Leroux Bustamante (Various) http://www.dasblonde.net/
Miguel de Icaza (Mono) http://tirania.org/blog/
Miha Markic (Various) http://cs.rthand.com/blogs/blog_with_righthand/default.aspx
Mike Stall (Debug) http://blogs.msdn.com/jmstall/
Mike Taulty (Various) http://mtaulty.com/blog
Mike Woodring (Various) http://pluralsight.com/blogs/mike/default.aspx
MSDN summarized blog (Various) http://blogs.msdn.com/
Pluralsight summarized blog (Various) http://pluralsight.com/blogs/default.aspx
Rick LaPlante (VSTS) http://blogs.msdn.com/rickla/
Rico Mariani (Performance, GC) http://blogs.msdn.com/ricom/
Rockford Lhotka (Design, various) http://www.lhotka.net/WeBlog/
Sahil Malik (ADO.NET, transactions) http://codebetter.com/blogs/sahil.malik/
Sam Gentile (Various) http://samgentile.com/blog/
Sanjay Shetty (.NET Compact framework) http://sanjayshetty.blogspot.com/
Scott Guthrie (ASP.NET) http://weblogs.asp.net/scottgu/
Soma Somasegar (*Microsoft* developer division lead) http://blogs.msdn.com/somasegar/
Ted Neward (Various) http://blogs.tedneward.com/
TheServerSide blog (Various) http://www.theserverside.net/blogs/index.tss
Thinktecture blog (WCF, .NET Remoting) http://blogs.thinktecture.com/
Valery Pryamikov (Security) http://www.harper.no/valery/
Wesner Moise (various, undocumented subjects) http://wesnerm.blogs.com/net_undocumented/
William Ryan (Various) http://www.msmvps.com/blog/williamryan/default.aspx
William Tay (Various) http://www.softwaremaker.net/blog/

The .NET2 Platform

2

Assembly, module, IL language

Assemblies are the .NET equivalent to `.exe` and `.dll` files in *Windows*. They are the *components* of the .NET platform.

Assemblies, modules and resource files

Assemblies and modules

An assembly is a logical unit which is defined by multiple files called *modules*. All of the files used to make an assembly must be in the same folder.

We have a tendency to consider that an assembly is a physical unit (i.e. one assembly = one file) since **the majority of assemblies have a single module**. This stems from the fact that the *Visual Studio* environment does not have the capabilities to generate multi-module assemblies. As we will illustrate, to obtain multi-module assemblies, you must make the effort of working with command-line tools such as the C# compiler `csc.exe` as described at page 264, or the tool named `al.exe` described at page 30.

Amongst the modules in an assembly, there is a *main module* which plays a special role since:

- Every assembly contains one and only one.
- Consequently, a single module assembly is the same as its main module.
- In the case of a multi-module assembly, it is always the main module that is first taken into consideration by the CLR. The main module of a multi-module assembly references the other modules. This means that the user of an assembly only needs to know about the main module.

The main module is a file with a `.exe` or `.dll` extension, depending on whether the assembly is an executable or a library. A module which isn't the main module is a file with a `.netmodule` extension.

Resource files

In addition to compiled .NET code, a module can physically contain other types of resources such as bitmaps or XML documents. Such resources can also be contained in their source file (for example file with the `.jpg` or `.xml` extensions) and are referenced by the assembly. In this case, we say that the referenced files are *resource files* of the assembly. In this chapter, you can see how the use of resources constitutes as an efficient technique for the globalization of an application.

Assemblies, modules, types and resources

The following figure uses an UML notation to summarize the relationship between assemblies, modules, types and resources. You can see that a same module can be contained in multiple assemblies and that a same type can be contained in multiple modules. We strongly recommend that you avoid these two techniques of code reuse and to take advantage of library assemblies instead.

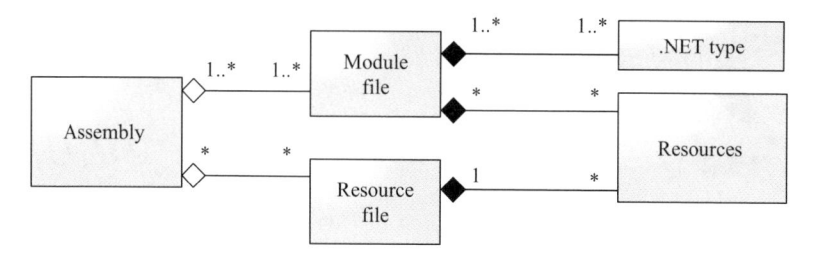

Figure 2-1: UML diagram: Assemblies, Modules, and Resources

Why would you be interested in a multi-module assembly?

You may wonder what is the advantage of taking an assembly and breaking it into multiple modules. In fact, this feature is rarely used. We have identified three cases where the use of this functionality can bring forth real advantages:

- The old saying that software spends 80% of its time in 20% of the code is still true today. If we isolate the big portion of the unused code into separate modules, these modules may never be used. In most cases, we will save on the resources required to load the complete assembly in memory. These resources are RAM memory, disk access but also bandwidth if the assembly is stored on a remote machine.
- A resource file will only be loaded when the application will really need it. If an application is running in English, we then benefit from not loading the French resources.
- If an assembly is developed by multiple developers, it is possible that some prefer VB.NET and others prefer C#. In this case, each module can be developed in a different language. Obviously, you should avoid such an odd situation.

The ILMerge tool

Know that you can also merge several assemblies together into .exe or .dll file. To accomplish this, you can use the ILMerge tool which is distributed freely by *Microsoft* and can be downloaded online. The functionality of this tool can also be exploited through a documented API. Note that this tool can also properly take into account signed assemblies when completing a merge.

Dissecting a module

Introduction to Portable Executable files (PE files)

A *PE file* (PE stands for *Portable Executable*) is a file which is executable by the *Windows* operating system. A PE file generally comes with an .exe or .dll extension. The first bytes in a PE file forms a header which can be interpreted by *Windows* when the executable is launched. These bytes contain information such as the smallest *Windows* version number on which the executable can be used or if the executable is a windowed or a console application.

The format of a PE file is optimized not to degrade performance. With the exception of a few bytes, the rest of the file is an image of how the executable will be stored in memory and exploited by *Windows* during its execution. This is why PE files are sometimes called *image files*.

Modules are also PE files as the .NET platform takes advantage of *Windows* services to execute applications. We explain at page 76 how the CLR is loaded by *Windows* during the start of a .NET application.

You may also have heard of the *PE/COFF* format (stands for *Common Object File Format*). The format is used by the C++ compiler when it links *object files*. The COFF extension to the PE/COFF format is ignored by the.NET platform.

Structure of a module

Each module contains a *CLR header* which contains the CLR version for which this assembly was compiled. This header also contains a reference to the managed entry point if the module contains one.

The main module of an assembly has also a section called the *manifest* which contains, among other things, references to other modules and resource files of the assembly. The data contained in the manifest is sometimes called *assembly metadata*.

Each module also contains a section which completely describes its content (types, type members, type dependencies, resources…). The self-descriptive information contained in this section is called *metadata*.

Finally, the module contains the compiled .NET IL code as well as other resources. The following diagram represents the physical structure of a module.

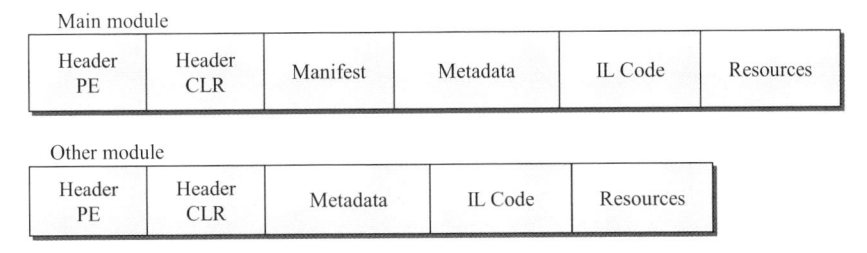

Figure 2-2: Structure of a module

Structure of the manifest

The manifest contains self-descriptive information for an assembly. There are four types of self-descriptive information and the manifest contains a table for each of them:

- *AssemblyDef*: This table has single entry which contains:
    Name of the assembly (without extension and path);
    The version of the assembly;
    The culture of the assembly;
    Flags describing certain characteristics of the assembly;
    A reference to a hashing algorithm;
    The public key of the publisher (which can be null);
  All these entries are detailed in the following pages.
- *FileDef*: This table contains an entry for each module and resource file of the assembly (except for the main module). Each entry includes the filename (with extension), flags describing the properties of the file and a *hash value* of the file.

- *ManifestResourceDef*: This table contains one entry for each type and each resource in the assembly. Each entry contains an index to the *FileDef* table to define in which file type or resource is defined. In the case of a type, the entry also contains an offset indicating where they type is physically located in the file. A consequence is that each compilation of a module implies the reconstruction of the manifest, hence the compilation of the main module.
- *ExportedTypeDef*: This table contains one entry for each type which is to be visible outside of the assembly. Each entry contains the name of the type, an index towards the *FileDef* table and an offset indicating where the type is physically located in the file. For the sake of efficiency, all types visible outside of the assembly defined within the main module are not repeated in this table. In fact, we will see that these types are already described in the metadata section.

Structure of the type metadata section

The type metadata is stored in tables. There exist three kinds of metadata tables for types: the definition tables, the reference tables and the pointer tables.

Definition tables

Each definition table contains information in regards to one type of element for the module (i.e. a table referencing the methods of all classes, a table referencing all the classes, etc.). We will not detail all the possible tables here but here is a list of the most important ones:

- *ModuleDef*: This table contains a single entry which defines the current module. This entry contains the name of the file with extension but without its path.
- *TypeDef*: This table contains one entry for each type defined in the module. Each entry contains the name of the type, the base type, flags for the type (`public`, `internal`, `sealed` etc), and indexes referencing the members of the types in the metadata tables *MethodDef*, *FieldDef*, *PropertyDef*, *EventDef*, ...
- *MethodDef*: This table contains one entry for each method defined in the module. Each entry contains the name of the method, flags for the method (`public`, `abstract`, `sealed`,...), an offset allowing the method to be located in the IL code and a reference to the signature of the method which is contained in a binary form in a heap called the *#blob* which we'll describe a little later.

There is also a table for the fields (*FieldDef*), one for the properties (*PropertyDef*), one for events (*EventDef*) etc. The definition of these tables is standard and each of them is coded with an identification byte. For example, all the *MethodDef* tables in .NET modules has a table number of 6.

Reference tables

The reference tables contain information on the elements referenced by the module. The referenced elements can be defined in other modules of the same assembly or as part of other assemblies. Here are a few commonly used reference tables:

- *AssemblyRef*: This table contains an entry for each assembly referenced in the module (i.e. each assembly which contains at least one element referenced in the module. Each entry contains the four components of a strong name that is: the name of the assembly (without path or extension), the version number, the culture and the public key token (may be null if there isn't one).
- *ModuleRef*: This table contains one entry for each module of the current assembly referenced in this module (i.e. each module which contains at least one element referenced in the module). Each entry contains the name of the module with its extension.

- *TypeRef*: This table contains one entry for each type referenced in the module. Each entry contains the name of the type and a reference to where it is defined. If the type is defined in this module or another module of the same assembly, the reference indicates an entry of the *ModuleRef* table. If the type is defined in another assembly, the reference indicated an entry to the *AssemblyRef* table. If the type is encapsulated within another type, the reference points towards an entry in the *TypeRef* table.
- *MemberRef*: This table contains one entry for each member referenced in the module. A member can, for example, be a method, a field or a property. Each entry contains the name of the member, its signature and a reference to the *TypeRef* table.

The definition of these tables is also standard and each table is coded with a byte. For example, all *MemberRef* tables in a .NET module are identified with the number 10.

Pointer tables

The pointer table allows the compilation to reference the code not yet known (a little like a declaration in C++). By changing the order of the definition of elements in your code, you can reduce the content of these tables. Here we can mention the following tables: *MethodPtr*, *ParamPtr* or *FieldPtr*.

Heaps

In addition to these tables, the metadata section contains four heaps named *#Strings*, *#Blob*, *#US* and *#GUID*.

- The *#Strings* heap contains character strings such as the name of methods. This means that elements of tables such as *MethodDef* or *MemberRef* do not contain actual strings but references to the element of the *#String* heap.
- The *#Blob* heap contains binary information such as the method signatures stored in a binary format. This means that element from the *MethodDef* or *MemberRef* tables do not contain signatures but contains references to the *#Blob* heap.
- The *#US* (for *User String*) contains character strings defined directly within the code.
- The *#GUID* heap contains the GUID defined and used in the program. A GUID is a 16 byte constant used to name a resource. The particularity of a GUID is that they can be generated by tools such as `guidgen.exe` in a way almost certain to guarantee its uniqueness. GUID are most commonly used in the COM technology.

Type metadata is very important in the .NET architecture. This information is referenced by the metadata tokens within the IL code which we will discuss at page 37. This section presents an example which underlines the importance of the tables and heaps in the type metadata section. The type metadata is also used by the notion of .NET attributes (described at page 206) and the reflection mechanism (described at page 193).

The #~ heap

Certain documents refer sometimes to a heap named #~. This special heap in fact contains all the metadata tables, including the manifest if it is a main module.

Analysis of an assembly with the ildasm.exe and Reflector tools

Building of the assembly to analyze

Here, we will create an assembly with:
- A main module `Foo1.exe`.
- A module `Foo2.netmodule`.
- A resource file `Image.jpg`.

Place in a same folder both C# source files (Foo1.cs and Foo2.cs) as well as the image file named Image.jpg.

Example 2-1   *Foo2.cs*
```
namespace Foo {
   public class Bar {
      public override string ToString() {
         return "Hi from Foo2";
      }
   }
}
```

Example 2-2   *Foo1.cs*
```
using System;
using System.Reflection;
[assembly: AssemblyCompany("ParadoxalPress")]
namespace Foo {
   class Program {
      public static void Main(string[] argv) {
         Console.WriteLine("Hi from Foo1");
         Bar b = new Bar();
         Console.WriteLine( b );
      }
   }
}
```

Since we wish to construct an assembly with more than one module, we have no choice other than to use the csc.exe command line compiler as the *Visual Studio* environment cannot handle multi-module assemblies. The csc.exe is described at page 264.

Create the files Foo2.netmodule and Foo1.exe by typing, in order, the following command (the csc.exe compiler can be found in the folder <WINDOWS-INSTALL-FOLDER>\Microsoft.NET\Framework\v2.*):

```
> csc.exe /target:module Foo2.cs
> csc.exe /Addmodule:Foo2.netmodule /LinkResource:Image.jpg  Foo1.cs
```

Launch the Foo1.exe executable and the program displays the following on the console:

```
Hi from Foo1
Hi from Foo2
```

Analysis of a module using ildasm.exe

We can analyze the contents of an assembly or module using the ildasm.exe tool supplied with the .NET development environment. *Ildasm* means IL code disassembler and the tool can be found at <VisualStudio-Install-Folder>\SDK\v2.0\Bin. Load the Foo1.exe file with ildasm.exe:

Analysis of an assembly with the ildasm.exe and Reflector tools

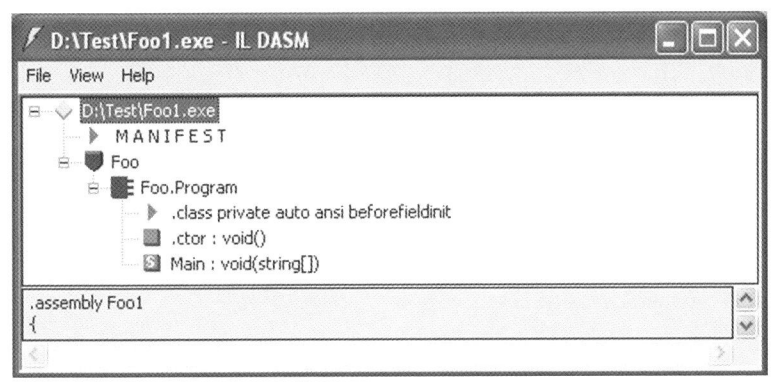

Figure 2-3: General view of ildasm

View of the manifest

By double clicking on the manifest, the following text appears in a new window (note that some comments have been removed for clarity):

```
.module extern Foo2.netmodule
.assembly extern mscorlib   {
  .publickeytoken = (B7 7A 5C 56 19 34 E0 89 )
  .ver 2:0:0:0
}
.assembly Foo1   {
  .custom instance void
  [mscorlib]System.Reflection.AssemblyCompanyAttribute::.ctor(string) =
  ( 01 00 0E 4C E2 80 99 65 6E 74 72 65 70 72 69 73   65 00 00 ) //
  // ...ParadoxalPress..
  .custom instance void [mscorlib]System.Runtime.CompilerServices.
  CompilationRelaxationsAttribute::.ctor(int32) =
     ( 01 00 08 00 00 00 00 00 )
  .hash algorithm 0x00008004
  .ver 0:0:0:0
}
.file Foo2.netmodule
    .hash = (80 CC 15 14 E2 AB E0 AF D6 BD 55 B9 1B 02 61 10  B4 CF AA 94 )
.file nometadata Image.JPG
    .hash = (0D 84 86 DE 03 E0 05 68 9D 38 F4 B0 B6 19 66 BB  3D 73 76 06 )
.class extern public Foo.UneClasse   {
    .file Foo2.netmodule
    .class 0x02000002
}
.mresource public Image.jpg    {
    .file Image.JPG at 0x00000000
}
.module Foo1.exe
// MVID: {3C680D21-A6C8-4151-A2A6-9B20B8FDDF27}
.imagebase 0x00400000
.file alignment 0x00000200
.stackreserve 0x00100000
.subsystem 0x0003       // WINDOWS_CUI
.corflags 0x00000001    //   ILONLY
// Image base: 0x04110000
```

We clearly see that `Foo2.netmodule` and `Image.jpg` files are referenced. We can also notice that another assembly is referenced. This assembly is `mscorlib` which contains base .NET types including the `object` class. This means that all .NET assemblies will reference the `mscorlib` assembly. More information on this assembly can be found at page 76.

Analysis of the Foo.Program class

By double clicking on the `Foo.Program` class, we obtain the description of this class in a new window:

```
.class private auto ansi beforefieldinit Foo.Program
       extends [mscorlib]System.Object   {
} // end of class Foo.Program
```

We can clearly see the flags associated with the `Program` class (`private`...) and that this class is derived from the `System.Object` class.

Analysis of the Main() method's IL code

By double clicking, for example, on the `Main()` method, we obtain the IL code for this method in a new window. We will briefly describe the IL language at the end of this chapter:

```
.method public hidebysig static void  Main(string[] argv) cil managed{
   .entrypoint
   // Code size       31 (0x1f)
   .maxstack  1
   .locals init (class [.module Foo2.netmodule]Foo.UneClasse V_0)
   IL_0000:  ldstr      "Bonjour de Foo1"
   IL_0005:  call       void [mscorlib]System.Console::WriteLine(string)
   IL_000a:  nop
   IL_000b:  newobj ...
          ... instance void [.module Foo2.netmodule]Foo.UneClasse::.ctor()
   IL_0010:  stloc.0
   IL_0011:  ldloc.0
   IL_0012:  call       void [mscorlib]System.Console::WriteLine(object)
   IL_0017:  nop
   IL_0018:  call       int32 [mscorlib]System.Console::Read()
   IL_001d:  pop
   IL_001e:  ret
} // end of method Program::Main
```

ildasm.exe's options

The `ildasm.exe` tools has some interesting features such as the visualization of the binary IL code (*Show Byte* option) or the presentation of the equivalent C# code (option *Show Source Lines* option).

With version 2 of `ildasm.exe` certain options are accessible by default which required the /adv command line option to use with version 1.0. These features include statistics in regards to the byte size of each section in an assembly and the display of information on the metadata of the assembly.

Using `ildasm.exe` you can essentially '*reverse engineer*' an assembly. You can extract information such as the IL code of a method or the name of the elements in an assembly (classes, methods...). However, source code comments are not stored in the assembly and cannot be recovered using `ildasm.exe`.

The Reflector tool

For many years, the Reflector tool developed by *Lutz Roeder* has dethroned `ildasm.exe` and has become the best tool to analyze .NET assemblies. This tool can be downloaded for free at `http://www.aisto.com/roeder/dotnet/`. Here is a screenshot of our previous example being processed by Reflector:

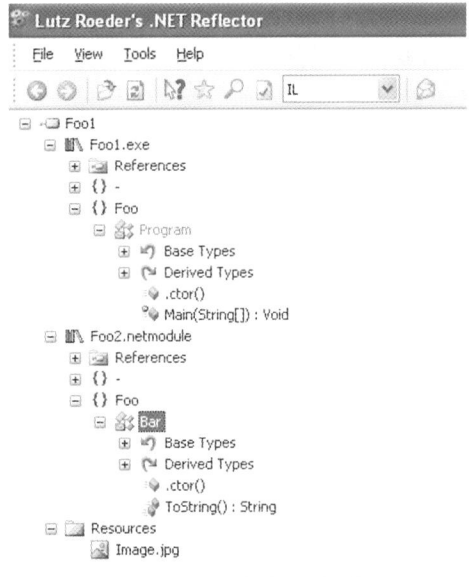

Figure 2-4: General view of Reflector

In addition to an easy to use interface, Reflector offers a set of functionalities which is very interesting and unavailable in `ildasm.exe`. For example:

- The decompilation in C# or VB.NET of the IL code in an assembly. For example, the decompilation in VB.NET of our `Program.Main()` method gives:

    ```
    Public Shared Sub Main(ByVal argv As String())
          Console.WriteLine("Hi from Foo1")
          Dim classe1 As New Bar
          Console.WriteLine(classe1)
          Console.Read
    End Sub
    ```
- The possibility of locally constructing the call graph for an element in an assembly;
- Several *addins* such as *statement graph* by *Jonathan de Halleux*, which allows you to decompile a method into a graphical representation, *Reflector Diff* by *Sean Hederman* which allows you to show the differences between two versions of an assembly or *file disassembler* by *Denis Bauer* which allows reconstructing the source code of an application from its assemblies. One advantage of *file disassembler* is that it allows the migration of an application from VB.NET to C# for example.

Assembly attributes and versioning

Assembly standard attributes

For this section, you need to be familiar with the notion of .NET attributes. If you do not know what a .NET attribute is, we recommend you read the section found at page 206.

You have the possibility of using certain attributes of the .NET framework to add information to your assembly such as a version number. These attributes must be declared a source file of your assembly after the `using` declarations but before your program elements. If you are building projects under the *Visual Studio* environment, the attributes relative to an assembly are, by default, located in the file named *AssemblyInfo.cs*.

To use this, the code in Example 2-2 uses the `AssemblyCompanyAttribute` attribute which allows you to specify the name of company name who constructed the assembly. If you take a look at the properties of the main module `Foo1.exe`, you can see that `ParadoxalPress` is visible as shown in the following screenshot:

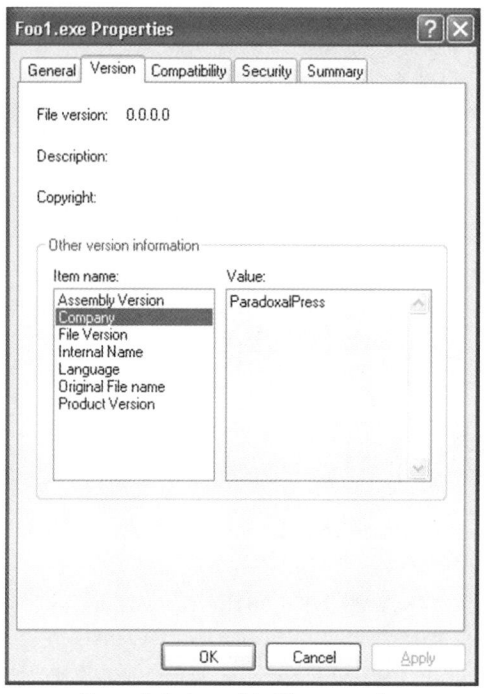

Figure 2-5: Assembly file properties:

Here is a list of the most commonly used assembly attributes:

- Information attributes:

    `AssemblyCompany`: associates with the assembly the name of the software company who developed it;

    `AssemblyProduct`: associates with the assembly the name of the product to which it belongs;

    `AssemblyTitle`: assigns a name to the assembly;

    `AssemblyDescription`: associates a description to the assembly;

    `AssemblyFileVersion`: associates a version number to the file produced by the compiler;

    `AssemblyInformationalVersion`: associates the version number of the product.

- The attributes used in the construction of a strong name (we will discuss a little later what is the definition of a strong named assembly):

    `AssemblyVersion`: specifies the version number of the assembly used to define its strong name;

    `AssemblyCulture`: specifies the culture of the assembly;

AssemblyKeyFile: specifies the .snk (*strong name key*) file generated by the sn.exe tool;

AssemblyFlags: specifies if the assembly can be executed side-by-side. We discuss the notion of side-by-side execution at page 52. If side-by-side execution is authorized, this attribute specifies if such execution can within a same AppDomain, same process or only on the same machine.

- Attributes relative to the use of the assembly within a COM+ application. This includes the ApplicationID, Application-Name and ApplicationActivation attributes.

In the **MSDN** article called **Setting Assembly Attributes** you can get more detailed information on the attributes which apply to assemblies.

Versioning assemblies

A version number is composed of four distinct elements:

- The major number;
- The minor number;
- The compilation number;
- The revision number.

You can set the version number of an assembly using the AssemblyVersion attribute. It is possible to use the star character within this attribute to let the compiler set the compilation and revision numbers, for example "2.3.*". In this case, the compilation number is defined as the number of days elapsed since January 1st 2000 and the revision number will be the number of seconds elapsed in the day (divided by two since 24*60*60=86400 and 86400 > 65536). The process of using a dating mechanism to version assemblies is useful to obtain a version number which is always increasing and is always different.

There exists three types of version numbers for a same assembly and this has been a source of confusion. Only the assembly version number is used by the CLR to allow several versions to co-exist side-by-side. The other version numbers which are the product version (set with Assembly InformationalVersion) and the file version number (set with AssemblyFileVersion) are only for informational purposes.

When you think that multiple assemblies will need to use the same version number, you can ensure this by making sure each project references that same file with the versioning attribute. However, know that if you do encounter this need, it may be a good idea to merge your assemblies into a single assembly.

The definition of the rule used for versioning assemblies is a sensitive subject and must be seriously reflected. There is no perfect solution as the rules depend on the business model of each company and may vary depending on whether an assembly is used by one or multiple products and whether it is used by external clients or inside the company. Here are a few recommendations:

- The major number: incremented each time a significant set of features have been added.
- The minor number: incremented when functionality has slightly changed or that a member visible outside the assembly (such as a protected method within a public class) has changed or when a major bug has been addressed.
- The compilation number: incremented every time the product is recompiled with the intent for use outside the enterprise (generally for small bug fixes).
- The revision number: incremented at every compilation.

Friend assemblies

Quite often when developing a framework containing multiple assemblies, you will encounter the following problem: you wish the types defined in one assembly of the framework be accessible from the code of other assemblies of the framework without them being available to the code which uses the framework. None of the type visibility levels in the CLR (public and internal) can resolve this problem. In this situation, you must make use of the assembly attribute named `System.Runtime.CompilerServices.InternalsVisibleToAttribute`. This attribute allows you to specify assemblies which can access non-public types within the assembly for which you specify the attribute. We say that these are *friend assemblies* to the assembly which contains the non-public types.

The use of this attribute allows you to specify zero, one or many components of the strong name of an assembly depending on which versions of the assembly you wish to "*be friends*":

```
using System.Runtime.CompilerServices;
...
[assembly:InternalsVisibleTo("AsmFriend1")]
[assembly:InternalsVisibleTo("AsmFriend2,PublicKeyToken=0123456789abcdef")]
[assembly:InternalsVisibleTo("AsmFriend3,Version=1.2.3.4")]
...
```

Strong named assemblies

Introduction

Over the past few years, the *Windows* operating system offers a technology called *Authenticode* which allows the authentication of an executable file. This means that when you execute a program on your machine, you can be certain that this program has been developed by a company in which you trust. We discuss this technology in greater details at page 191.

The *strong name* technology that we will describe in this section can potentially be used to authenticate a .NET assembly in the case of big organizations such as *Microsoft* or *ECMA*. However, it is mostly destined to name assembly in a unique way. The feature is unique as of before .NET, we only used the filenames to identify deployment units. With .NET, when an assembly evolves to new versions, there are multiple files with the same name but with different versions. There is a special folder which is used to store multiple version of the same assembly which is called the GAC (we discuss it further at page 51).

Practically, an assembly becomes strong named when it is digitally signed. When an assembly has a strong name, this name can be formatted as a string containing the following four pieces of information:

- The name of the file;
- The public token of the digital key (all these terms are explained below);
- The version of the assembly as specified with the `AssemblyVersion`, attribute as described in the previous section;
- The culture of the assembly that we will detail in the following section.

The name is strong in the sense that it allows an assembly to be identified in a unique way. This uniqueness is guaranteed by the public token key component.

A strong name is also supposed to make an assembly impossible to falsify. However, *Richard Grimes* describes a method (at the following URL `http://www.grimes.demon.co.uk/workshops/fusionWSCrackThree.htm`) which allows someone to crack the strong naming of an assembly. This method bases itself on a bug in the 1.1 version of the CLR which has been fixed in version 2.0. To our knowledge, there are no known security flaws as of yet in .NET 2.

Strong named assemblies 23

Before we take a closer look at how a strong named assembly can be created, we recommend that you familiarize yourself with the notions of public/private keys and *digital signatures* presented at page 185. By applying a digital signature to their assemblies, an author or an enterprise can authenticate it. *Microsoft* and the ECMA organization each have a public/private key pair used to identify their assemblies.

The sn.exe tool

The first step for a developer or enterprise who desires to create strong named assemblies is to create a public/private key pair. This operation uses several complex mathematical algorithms. Thankfully, the .NET framework puts to our disposal the sn.exe tool (sn for *strong name*) that will accomplish this task for you. This tool can create a .snk file (for *strong name key*) which contains a public/private key pair by using the –k option. For example:

```
C:\Test>sn.exe -k MyKeys.snk

Microsoft (R) .NET Framework Strong Name Utility  Version 2.0.50727
Copyright (C) Microsoft Corporation. All rights reserved.

Key pair written to MyKeys.snk

C:\Test>
```

sn.exe allows also the visualization of the public and private key contained in a .snk file using the –tp option:

```
C:\Test>sn.exe -tp MyKeys.snk

Microsoft (R) .NET Framework Strong Name Utility  Version 2.0.50727
Copyright (C) Microsoft Corporation. All rights reserved.

Public key is
0702000000240000525341320004000001000100**51a7dadde83cf10e8b7c6cd99e4d062b1aca
430e11db76365ab29d6c31fc93a7bea6def9d7b2e8a7c568b0d5ada5e8e131cb98ea3e9a8762
36b33b362e433fdd62bb4c5cc5ea23f1dfa76d35b5412d812f66d03e079009ea76462392663b
c08ab5f937524e794948532c679db5eda50210f8a8b2b8b186fcb342859c48ea76d6**09d108b1
957d3888f75b270cf85029ede8437c36b4ae59342c5fa7aacdb453c7465cc7027405930627a5
b153e5f48cdd0375840bf6feaa3548aa421ab5138fb095efa5d581ae61bd9248ac97293ee69b
139ef9ae79d907c5cf2c194adf7c2723e269b5eef55157c4095fccf436d7db1893aed8c63d57
e9d5eba5c1dd88f8bda81b6c74b77899071823c85c862254865337d2b70d545d17de9b847152
7bbd54d4e1bd6cb6b53fed9135c9c7b1b1af2b27ab0414b423b61334c9c1adb0700145ba1354
848b081e09e8a860d24fb9ea6c48ac2657f19ff1fab37a177744c377d9d7d09f34498901f443
9bc6754b4ac0efcc4d84a6c22a05c2eecaec3f7fabf8b45555d4788eaeda815cf743001477a8
c31c24c04b4016f4ef3401617e22441b95ca78265a0a6133150ca03c2886d4e3893f9d1dc6a3
e2d8770a63b8fbd0db52d8176bbda6e1f4074d9dfda916cf316294f0499eade4aa47d1b78062
7ab6fb7beb5aa484129062d3152e6b6585c865d319018727c1a34866484018f5f1c0ab0bf2b3
5e63a8a3bbf7a0b6aeeb110f4b162426a977dc2034adf08ec41cc5d20f2d6beac92a1619aff0
e25030e30a02570426a977dc2034adf08ec41cc5d20f2d6beac92a1619aff0e25030e30a0257
eb9ad74eba0f2aba90b18789ae99f8da72

Public key token is f2bf46103b24f5f0
```

In fact, this tool displays the public key (displayed in bold) and then the private key. The term '*public key is:*' is wrong. What is presented as being the public key token is a hashing value of the public/private key pair. However, if *Microsoft* made this choice of terminology it is because they suppose that most of the time the delayed signature is used (which we will discuss a little later). In this case, the term takes its entire signification.

During the creation of a public/private key pair with the sn.exe tool, the public key measures 32 header bytes + 128 bytes and the private key measures 436 bytes.

Public key tokens

The public key being so large and difficult to manipulate, the .NET platform associates a *public key token* to each public key. A public key token is a coded number of eight bytes. This number is calculates from the public key using a hashing algorithm. It identifies, in an almost unique way, the public key while being easier to manipulate due to its smaller size. Public key tokens have been created for the following reasons:

- To reduce the size of strong names (which use the token instead of the complete public key).
- To reduce the size of assemblies which reference several strong named assemblies.

An assembly signed with a public key that has a token of **b03f5f7f11d50a3a**, is guaranteed to have been produced by *Microsoft*. On the other hand, an assembly signed with a token of **b77a5c561934e089**, is guaranteed to have been produced by the *ECMA* organization. These affirmations would not be true anymore if some day, these private keys were cracked.

Signing an assembly

To assign a strong name to an assembly, you can use the options **/keycontainer** and **/keyfile** of the **csc.exe** compiler or use the project *properties > Signing > Sign the assembly* of *Visual Studio 2005*.

You can also use the **AssemblyKeyFile** assembly attribute in the source code of your main module. This attribute accepts an argument which is the name of the **.snk** file. For example:

```
[AssemblyKeyFile("MyKeys.snk")]
```

When this attribute is added, the compiler signs the assembly but emits a warning letting you know that the first two techniques are preferred.

When an assembly must be signed by one of these three techniques, the compiler includes a digital signature and the public key within the body of the assembly. The algorithm used to hash the content of the assembly is named SHA-1 (*Secure Hash Algorithm*). You can also use another hashing algorithm such as the well known MD5 (MD stands for *Message Digest*) through the use of the **AssemblyAlgorithmId** assembly attribute which takes a value from the **AssemblyHashAlgorithm** enumeration. The size of a hashing value created by the SHA-1 algorithm is 20 bytes. But this size can vary based on the algorithm used.

The compiler encrypts an assembly using the private key hashing value and then obtains a RSA digital signature for the assembly. The public key is inserted inside the *AssemblyDef* table of the manifest while the digital signature is inserted into a special part of the CLR header. Here is a diagram describing the signature process for an assembly:

A concrete example

Here is the code for an assembly named **Foo1**:

Example 2-3   *Foo1.cs*
```
using System;
namespace Foo {
   class Program {
      public static void Main( string[] argv ){
         Console.WriteLine( "Hi from Foo1" );
      }
   }
}
```

Strong named assemblies

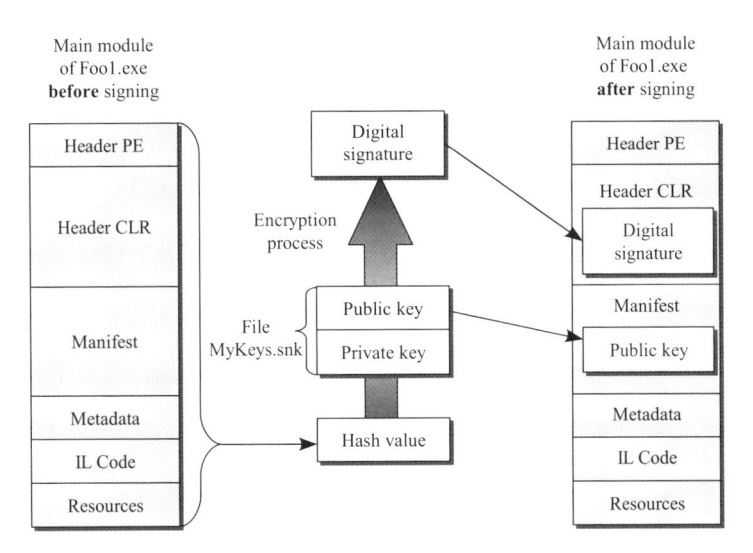

Figure 2-6: Signing an assembly

Let us compile and sign this assembly using `MyKeys.snk`:

```
>csc.exe /keyfile:MyKeys.snk Foo1.cs
```

Analyzing the manifest of the `Foo1.exe` assembly using the `ildasm.exe` tool (for clarity, we have removed a few comments):

```
.assembly extern mscorlib   {
  .publickeytoken = (B7 7A 5C 56 19 34 E0 89 )          // .z\V.4..
  .ver 2:0:0:0
}
.assembly Foo1   {
  .custom instance void
  [mscorlib]System.Reflection.AssemblyKeyFileAttribute::.ctor(string) =
     ( 01 00 08 43 6C 65 73 2E 73 6E 6B 00 00 ) // ...Cles.snk..
  [mscorlib]System.Diagnostics.DebuggableAttribute::.ctor
     (bool, bool) = ( 01 00 00 01 00 00 )

  .publickey = (   00 24 00 00 04 80 00 00 94 00 00 00 06 02 00 00
                   00 24 00 00 52 53 41 31 00 04 00 00 01 00 01 00
                   51 A7 DA DD E8 3C F1 0E 8B 7C 6C D9 9E 4D 06 2B
                   1A CA 43 0E 11 DB 76 36 5A B2 9D 6C 31 FC 93 A7
                   BE A6 DE F9 D7 B2 E8 A7 C5 68 B0 D5 AD A5 E8 E1
                   31 CB 98 EA 3E 9A 87 62 36 B3 3B 36 2E 43 3F DD
                   62 BB 4C 5C C5 EA 23 F1 DF A7 6D 35 B5 41 2D 81
                   2F 66 D0 3E 07 90 09 EA 76 46 23 92 66 3B C0 8A
                   B5 F9 37 52 4E 79 49 48 53 2C 67 9D B5 ED A5 02
                   10 F8 A8 B2 B8 B1 86 FC B3 42 85 9C 48 EA 76 D6 )
  .hash algorithm 0x00008004
  .ver 0:0:0:0
}
.module Foo1.exe
// MVID: {5DD7C72B-D1C1-49BB-AB33-AF7DA5617BD1}
.imagebase 0x00400000
```

```
.file alignment 512
.stackreserve 0x00100000
.subsystem 0x00000003
.corflags 0x00000009
// Image base: 0x03240000
```

The public key is definitely the same as the one we have seen earlier during the analysis of the MyKeys.snk file. The ildasm.exe tool does not allow us to visualize the public key token nor the digital signature. The sn.exe tool allows us to visualize the public key token with the –T option:

```
C:\Code\CodeDotNet\ModuleTest>sn.exe -T Foo1.exe

Microsoft (R) .NET Framework Strong Name Utility  Version 2.0.50727
Copyright (C) Microsoft Corporation. All rights reserved.

Public key token is c64b742bd612d74a
```

The mscorlib assembly is referenced and its public key token is also known. This is normal since this token has an integral part within the strong name of the assembly. In fact, the public key token has been created for the referencing of other assemblies. Since the size of the public key is 128 bytes, the size of assemblies referencing many other assemblies would have been too large without the use of the public key token technique.

A strong named assembly cannot reference another assembly which isn't strongly named. However, an assembly without a strong name may reference a strong named assembly.

In the case where an assembly is composed of multiple modules, all modules other than the main one do not have a public key. However, during the compilation of the main module, the compiler will calculate a hashing value for each module. These values are integrated into the *FileDef* table of the manifest. These values are then taken into account during the calculation of the hashing value for the main module. Using this trick, the modules part of a strong named assembly are also named in a unique way and cannot be falsified (in .NET 2) without the need to integrate a digital signature.

Delayed signing of an assembly

The use of a digital signature to prevent assemblies from being falsified is a great feature that is offered by .NET. However, the implementation of this technique requires access to files containing the public/private key pairs to everybody which is susceptible of compiling a strong named assembly within a company. In a large enterprise like *Microsoft*, there tens of thousands! No doubt that after a certain time an employee may leak the private key on the internet. The only way to mitigate this risk is to limit the number of employees which have access to the private key. .NET has a *delayed signature* mechanism designed to deal with this situation. In practice, an assembly is compiled and tested and is signed only before it is packaged and deployed to clients. Within a large enterprise, only one or few employees are skilled to do to this manipulation. The delayed signature mechanism requires three steps:

- First of all, you must construct a .snk file which only contains the public key. To accomplish this, you can use the –p option.

```
C:\Code>sn -p MyKeys.snk MyPublicKey.snk

Microsoft (R) .NET Framework Strong Name Utility  Version 2.0.50727
Copyright (C) Microsoft Corporation. All rights reserved.

Public key written to MyPublicKey.snk

C:\Code>
```

- The `MyPublicKey.snk` file is distributed to developers who use it during development instead of the `Keys.snk` file (in the `AssemblyKeyFile` attribute). The `AssemblyDelaySign` is also initialized with the `true` value to enable delayed signing. The compiler understands that it must not sign the main module. However, the compiler will reserve the necessary space for the signature in the main module, insert the public key in the manifest and compute the hashing values for modules without manifests.
- Then the development teams supply assemblies ready to package and deploy, all that needs to be done is run `sn.exe` tool using the –R option.

```
C:\Code>sn.exe -R Foo1.exe MyKeys.snk

Microsoft (R) .NET Framework Strong Name Utility  Version 2.0.50727
Copyright (C) Microsoft Corporation. All rights reserved.

Assembly 'Foo1.exe' successfully re-signed

C:\Code>
```

You can also delay the signing of an assembly through the compiler by using a combination of the `/delaysign`, `/keycontainer` and `/keyfile` options.

The delayed signing technique can also be used to sign assemblies which have been modified after compilation, for example, with an *Aspect Oriented Programming* tool such as *AspectDNG*.

Internationalization/localization and satellite assemblies

Cultures and localization

Certain applications must be used by users from different nationalities who use different languages. All that can be presented to the user of an application (character strings, images, animations, sounds, dates, numerical format, etc) must be supplied for each *culture* supported by the application. This process is called *globalization* or *internationalization* or *localization* of the application.

A culture is an association of a country and language such as "en-US" for United States English and "fr-CA" for French Canadian. A list of all standard cultures part of the .NET framework can be found in the entry **CultureInfo Class** on **MSDN**.

We have seen that a culture can be specified as part of the strong name of an assembly. However, you are required to use a neutral culture for any assembly containing code. In practice, the character string passed to the `CultureInfo` attribute must be empty. To index resources based on a culture, you need to create an assembly for each culture which only contains resources. These particular assemblies are the main subject of this section and are commonly called *satellite assemblies*.

Resource files

In practice, to take advantage of string resources or resources stored in a binary format (images, animations, sounds…) within an assembly, you need to follow these four steps:

1. Edit the resource file in a human readable format (such as `.txt` or `.resx`);
2. Convert the resource file into a binary form suited for the use in an application (file with a `.resources` extension);
3. Include the `.resources` in an assembly (satellite or not);
4. Use the resources in your code by using the `System.Resources.ResourceManager` class. Quite often, you will create a class which encapsulates access to the resources.

We will start by showing you how to do these manipulations by hand and we will then show you how you can achieve the same through the *Visual Studio 2005* environment which greatly automates this process.

A specific resource file targets a single culture. There are three formats of resource file, used during different steps of the development process:

- Resource files with a `.txt` extension:

    These files associate identifiers to various strings aimed for a specific culture. For example, here is such a file destined at an English culture:

    Example 2-4   *MyRes.txt*
    ```
    Bonjour = Hello!
    AuRevoir = Bye...
    ```

- Resource files with a `.resx` extension:

    These files are of XML format and also associate various identifiers to strings destined to a specific culture. The difference with `.txt` files is that a `.resx` file can also associate identifiers to resources stored in a binary form. In a `.resx` file, the binary information is converted into a UNICODE form using the *Base64* encoding. The utility named `resxgen.exe` can be used to convert such resources (for example, an image in `bmp` or `jpg` format) into a `.resx` file. The use of *Visual Studio 2005* greatly simplifies the visualization, the editing and maintenance of `.resx`.

- Resource files with a `.resources` extension:

    These file are logically equivalent to `.resx` files with the difference being that the data is stored in a binary form. These are the files which are integrated to the assemblies during the compilation process.

As we have explained, a single `.resources` can be integrated into an assembly. The `resgen.exe` tool, which can be used through the command line, allows the construction of a resource file in one of those formats from a resource in another format. `resgen.exe` knows the format of the source and destination file from their filename. Here is a usage example:

```
>resgen.exe MyRes.txt MyRes.resources
```

> Do not convert a `.resx` or `.resources` resource file which contains at least one resource which isn't a string to a `.txt` file.

Using resources from your code

The `System.Resources.ResourceManager` class must be used to take advantage of resources based on the current culture. However, in general, we prefer using a class generated by the `resgen.exe` tool which encapsulates access to this class. The source file of such a class can be generated from a resource file with an extension of .txt, `.resx` or `.ressources` by using the `/str` option:

```
>resgen.exe MyRes.resources /str:cs
```

The `/str:cs` option lets the tool know that we wish to generate a C# source file. We could also have used `/str:vb` to obtain a VB.NET file. Here is an excerpt from such a file:

MyRes.cs
```
internal class MyRes {
   private static System.Resources.ResourceManager resourceMan;
   private static System.Globalization.CultureInfo resourceCulture;
   ...
```

MyRes.cs
```
    internal static System.Resources.ResourceManager ResourceManager {
      get {
        if ((resourceMan == null)) {
          System.Resources.ResourceManager temp = new
            System.Resources.ResourceManager("MyRes",
                                    typeof(MyRes).Assembly);
          resourceMan = temp;
        }
        return resourceMan;
      }
    }
    internal static global::System.Globalization.CultureInfo Culture {
      get { return resourceCulture; } set{ resourceCulture = value; } }
...
    internal static string Bonjour {
      get{return ResourceManager.GetString("Bonjour", resourceCulture);}}
...
    internal static string AuRevoir {
      get {return ResourceManager.GetString(
            "AuRevoir", resourceCulture); } }
}
```

As you can see, in addition to encapsulating access to the `ResourceManager` class, the `MyRes` class also exposes properties which allow access to the resources in a typed manner. All that is left is to use these properties to access our resources. The following program displays 'hello':

Example 2-5 *Program.cs*
```
class Program {
   static void Main() {
      System.Console.WriteLine( MyRes.Bonjour );
   }
}
```

It is interesting to compare this code to the code needed by a program which doesn't use our generated class:

Example 2-6 *Program.cs*
```
using System.Resources;
class Program {
   static void Main() {
      ResourceManager rm = new ResourceManager( "MyRes" ,
                                    typeof(MyRes).Assembly);
      System.Console.WriteLine( rm.GetString("Bonjour") );
   }
}
```

The `ResourceManager` class presents several overloaded versions of the `GetString()` method. In addition, the class presents the more general `GetObject()` method which can be used to load strings. This method can also be used to load resources stored in a binary format. For example:

```
...
   System.Drawing.Bitmap image = (Bitmap) rm.GetObject("AnImage");
   string s = (string) rm.GetObject("Bonjour");
...
```

When using the class generated with `resgen.exe`, a property of type `System.Drawing.Bitmap` is supplied to access image resources.

```
...
    System.Drawing.Bitmap image = MyRes.AnImage;
...
```

Now lets take a look at the compilation of this program. In the case where the assembly contains code, you have to precise the name of the .resources files during the compilation of the assembly. The `csc.exe` compiler provides the `/resource` and `/linkresource` options for this purpose. For example:

```
>csc.exe /resource:MyRes.resources,MyRes.resources Program.cs MyRes.cs
```

The syntax of this option uses a comma to separate the name of the resource files (to the left) from the logical name (to the right) which will be used in the code of the assembly to identify the file. Note that the `/resource` option physically copy the content of the resources contained in the resource file to the body of the compiled module. You can also use the `/linkresource` option to reference a resource file from the main module.

Building a satellite assembly

We have just seen how you can encapsulate resources in an assembly and how you can use them. Up until now, we have not used a specific culture. The resources we have used so far were relative to a neutral culture. This is the default culture when no other culture is specified. Let us now look at the notion of satellite assembly and how you can diversify the culture of an application.

The `al.exe` tool (`al` stands for *assembly linker*), usable from the command line, permits the production of a library assembly (i.e. an assembly where the main module is a `.dll` file) from one or many modules. `al.exe` allows you to construct assemblies such as satellite assemblies which only contain resources. At page 54, we explain that this tool can also be used for the creation of publisher policy assemblies.

A specific satellite assembly contains resources destined to a single culture. Here is an example of how you can use `al.exe` tool to build a satellite assembly. Note the use of the `/c` option to specify the culture (here we use Spanish from Spain):

```
>al.exe /out:es-ES\Program.Resources.dll /c:es-ES /embed:es-ES\MyRes.es-
ES.resources
```

We use as an input to `al.exe` the /embed option with a file named `MyRes.es-ES.ressources`. This file was generated with the `resgen.exe.tool` from the following MyRes.es-ES.txt file:

Example 2-7 *MyRes.es-ES.txt*
```
Bonjour = Hola!
AuRevoir = Adiós...
```

The /embed option makes sure that the content of `MyRes.es-ES.ressources` is physically embedded in the `Program.Ressources.dll` file.

Deploy and harness satellite assemblies

The `System.Resources.ResourceManager` class knows how to deal with satellite assemblies and is capable of loading the proper assembly at run-time. The culture that is used is the one specified in the CultureInfo `Thread.CurrentUICulture{get;set}` property of the current thread. To benefit from this service, it is necessary to conform to a few rules:

Internationalization/localization and satellite assemblies

- The name of the main module of a satellite assembly (the one produced using `al.exe`) must be [name of the assembly manipulating the resources].Resources.dll.
- A satellite assembly corresponding to culture xx-XX must be located in the sub-folder named xx-XX (relative to where the assembly with the code manipulating the resource is located). We notice that the satellite assemblies relative to a same assembly all have the same name but are located in separate sub-folders.

These rules are illustrated through the organization of the files in our example:

```
\Program.exe                    // file built by csc.exe
\es-ES\Program.Resources.dll    // file built by al.exe
...
```

If the following program is executed in the above context it will display 'hola!':

Example 2-8 *Program.cs*

```
class Program {
   static void Main() {
      MyRes.Culture = new System.Globalization.CultureInfo("es-ES");
      System.Console.WriteLine( MyRes.Bonjour );
   }
}
```

By analyzing the code of the `MyRes` class generated by `resgen.exe`, we see that the search for resources is not done with the culture specified in the `Thread.CurrentUICulture` property but using the `MyRes.Culture` property (which corresponds to the field `MyRes.resourceCulture`). We can rewrite this program without using the `MyRes` class as follows:

Example 2-9 *Program.cs*

```
using System.Resources;     // For the ResourceManager class.
using System.Threading;     // For the Thread class.
using System.Globalization; // For the CultureInfoclass.
class Program {
   static void Main() {
      Thread.CurrentThread.CurrentUICulture = new CultureInfo("es-ES");
      ResourceManager rm = new ResourceManager( "MyRes" ,
                                       typeof(MyRes).Assembly);
      System.Console.WriteLine(rm.GetString("Bonjour"));
   }
}
```

The previous programs work if the satellite assembly `Program.Resources.dll` of the es-ES culture is located in the GAC. As with all assembly located in the GAC, such an assembly must have a strong name. The assemblies from one culture are differentiated from other assemblies through their strong name.

During the compilation of `Program.exe` you do not need to reference the satellite assemblies. This means that it is possible to provide additional satellite assemblies after the compilation of your program. For this, you need to make sure the application retrieves which culture it must execute. This can, for example, be done from a configuration file or from user preferences in your application.

Avoid raising exceptions when a resource can't be found

It is strongly recommended to include a resource file corresponding to the neutral culture in the assembly containing the code. Hence, during execution, if the satellite assembly corresponding to the current culture is not found or if the assembly is missing the translation of certain resources, the `ResourceManager` will fallback by pulling the resource value from the neutral culture. If this resource cannot be found, an exception will be raised.

To protect yourself against missing satellite assemblies, you can verify its existence by using the `ResourceManager.GetResourceSet()` method. For example:

Example 2-10 *Program.cs*
```
using System ;
using System.Globalization; // For the CultureInfo class.
class Program {
   static void Main() {
      CultureInfo spainCulture = new CultureInfo("es-ES");
      if( MyRes.ResourceManager.GetResourceSet(
                   spainCulture , true, false )!= null ) {
        MyRes.Culture = spainCulture;
        Console.WriteLine(MyRes.Bonjour);
      }
      else
         Console.WriteLine("Satellite assembly es-ES not found!");
   }
}
```

Visual Studio and satellite assemblies

Now that you understand the role of satellite assemblies and the use of tools such as `resgen.exe` and `al.exe` we can show you how to use *Visual Studio 2005* to simplify the globalization process of an assembly.

By default, a *Visual Studio 2005* project does not contain any resource files but you can easily add one through the *Project › Add › New Item… › Resources file* menu option. A new resource file with the `.resx` is then added to your project. During the compilation of the project, this file will automatically be converted into a .resources file which will be integrated into the compiled assembly or satellite assembly based on whether *Visual Studio* can determine the referenced culture based on its name. For example, a project named `MyProject` which contains the following resource files:

```
...
Res1.resx
Res1.en-US.resx
Res1.fr-FR.resx
Res2.resx
Res2.es-ES.resx
```

…compiles into:

```
~/MyProject.exe              contains Res1.resources and Res2.resources
~/en-US/MyProject.Resources.dll   contains Res1.en-US.resources
~/fr-FR/MyProject.Resources.dll   contains Res1.fr-FR.resources
~/es-ES/MyProject.Resources.dll   contains Res2.es-ES.resources
```

By default, a source file named `XXX.designer.cs` is associated with each resource `XXX.resx` file added to a project. This source file contains a class named [Project Name].XXX similar to the class generated using the /str option of `resgen.exe`. In general, only resource files relative to the neutral culture (i.e. Res1.resx and Res2.resx in our example) need such a class. Also know that you can deactivate the generation of these source files by putting an empty string (instead of `ResXFileCodeGenerator`) in the *file properties for* `XXX.resx` *› Custom Tool.*

Visual Studio 2005 contains a built-in editor for `.resx` resource files which can be used to easily add identifier/string or identifier/file pairs. In the second case, the file can be an image, icon, sound, text or any other binary data.

At page 576, we describe the functionality within *Visual Studio* 2005 which allows the easy localization of *Windows Forms 2.0* applications. At page 791, we also describe how you can use *Visual Studio 2005* to localize ASP.NET 2 web applications.

Culture and string formatting

The formatting of certain user interface elements such as dates or numbers can depend on the culture. The .NET framework uses the value of the `CultureInfo Thread.CurrentCulture{get;set}` to determine which culture to use during a formatting operation. For example, the following program...

Example 2-11
```
using System.Threading;     // For the Thread class.
using System.Globalization; // For the CultureInfo class.
class Program {
   static void Main() {
      Thread.CurrentThread.CurrentCulture = new CultureInfo("en-US");
      System.Console.WriteLine(System.DateTime.Now.ToString());
      Thread.CurrentThread.CurrentCulture = new CultureInfo("fr-FR");
      System.Console.WriteLine(System.DateTime.Now.ToString());
   }
}
```
...outputs the following:

```
6/20/2005 10:54:10 PM
20/06/2005 22:54:10
```

Introduction to the IL language

We have seen that assemblies contain code which is written in the IL language (*Intermediate Language*). The IL language is a complete object-oriented language on its own and constitutes the smallest common denominator between all .NET languages.

You must know that certain documentation, such as the ones by *Microsoft*, use the term *MSIL language* to name the *Microsoft* implementation of the IL language. Other documentations may use the term *CIL* (*Common Intermediate Language*) to represent the IL language. The IL language itself has been entirely specified by the ECMA organization and you can find complete specs and documentation on their website.

The `ildasm.exe` and `Reflector` tools presented earlier allow the visualization of IL code contained within a module. We will take a look at (and discuss) some IL code although a complete presentation of the IL language are outside the scope of this book. We think it is a good idea for .NET developers to have an idea of what the IL language looks like. For Java developers, you might be reminded of *bytecodes*.

You can compile your own sources written in IL into assembly with the help of the `ilasm.exe` compiler which is included with the .NET framework (do not confuse it with `ildasm.exe`).

Understand that although its resemblance to machine language, the IL language it not supported by any processor (for the moment at least). IL code is compiled at execution into a target machine language which is dependant on the machine's processor. This mechanism is described in more details at page 90. The idea of using an intermediate between the high-level language and machine language is not new and has been exploited for a long time on other platforms such as Java.

The stack and its specialized IL instructions

To understand this section, it is necessary to have assimilated the notion of execution unit (i.e. the notion of threads) presented at page 112.

As with many other languages, IL is a *stack* based language. The stack is a contiguous memory space which has the particularity of having a single access point which is called the top of the stack. As with a stack of plates, you can only add or remove plates from the top of the stack. In computer science, stacks do not contain plates but typed values.

A stack belongs to a thread. For each operand of an operation executed by a thread (arithmetic operation, function call…) a copy of its value must be made to the top of the stack.

In IL, the stack is managed by the CLR who plays the role of a virtual processor. This is why in Java, the equivalent to the CLR is named 'virtual machine'. The CLR does not function exactly like a classic processor. Most processors work using a stack and a set of registers while the CLR only works using a stack.

Example 1: local variables and the stack

The code of following C# method…

```
...
{
   int i1 =5;
   int i2 =6;
   int i3 = i1+i2;
}
...
```

…produces this IL code:

```
    .maxstack  2
    .locals ([0] int32 i1,
             [1] int32 i2,
             [2] int32 i3)
IL_0000:  ldc.i4.5
IL_0001:  stloc.0
IL_0002:  ldc.i4.6
IL_0003:  stloc.1
IL_0004:  ldloc.0
IL_0005:  ldloc.1
IL_0006:  add
IL_0007:  stloc.2
IL_0008:  ret
```

Several observations can be made:

- The fact that at no moment this method loads more than two values into the stack is saved into an attribute called `.maxstack`. The maximum stack size is then bound during compilation.
- Local variables are typed and numbered.
- Each instruction takes exactly one byte (IL_XXXX to the left represents the offset of the IL instruction relative to the start of the method).
- `ldc.i4.5` (*load constant* 5) is an IL instruction which pushes the constant value 5 onto the stack as an integer coded onto four bytes (same for 6). Understand that the integer 5 is not a parameter to this instruction. Consequently, the `ldc.i4.5` instruction is stored in a single

Introduction to the IL language

byte. For example, if we wished to store the 12345678 integer value stored as four bytes into the stack, we would need to use the `ldc.i4` instruction. This IL instruction takes in as a parameter an integer encoded into four bytes meaning that the instruction with its parameter would take five bytes. We can see that contrarily to machine languages, certain instructions of the IL language have been created specially to optimize the number of bytes used to store the IL code. In addition, with this practice, the execution speed is also increased because of the time saved when reading the parameters.

- `ldloc.N` (*load local*) is an IL instruction which pushes the value of the local variable number N to the top of the stack.
- `stloc.N` (*store local*) is an IL instruction which unstacks the number at the top of the stack and stores it in local variable number N.
- `add` is an IL instruction which unstacks two values from the top of the stack and adds them together. The result from the operation is then stored at the top of the stack. Note that the other IL instruction, `add.ovf`, tests for an overflow and raises the `OverflowException` if a failure occurs. In addition, we cannot combine all types for this operation. In the case where a combination is not supported an exception will be raised.
- `ret` (return) is an IL instruction which causes the control to return to the calling method.

In general, all IL instructions which start with `ld` load a value to the top of the stack. To each of these operations is associated a symmetrical operation which starts by `st` which unstacks the value at the top of the stack and stores it in a variable.

Example2: method calls and the stack

The stack can be seen as a piling of *stack frames*. Each call to a method corresponds to the creation on a new stack frame on the top of the stack for the current thread. Each return from a method corresponds to the destruction of the stack frame located on the top of the stack.

The C# code of the following `Main()` method…

Example 2-12

```
class Program{
   static int f(int i1, int i2){
      return i1+i2;
   }
   public static void Main(){
      int i1 =5;
      int i2 =6;
      int i3 = f(i1,i2);
   }
}
```

…produces the following IL code for the `Main()` method:

```
.maxstack  2
.locals ([0] int32 i1,
         [1] int32 i2,
         [2] int32 i3)
IL_0000:  ldc.i4.5
IL_0001:  stloc.0
IL_0002:  ldc.i4.6
IL_0003:  stloc.1
IL_0004:  ldloc.0
IL_0005:  ldloc.1
IL_0006:  call       int32 Program::f(int32,int32)
IL_000b:  stloc.2
IL_000c:  ret
```

You can see that the `i1` and `i2` values are loaded onto the stack before the call to the `Program.f()` method using the `call` instruction which:

- unstacks the arguments for the call and store them in memory;
- created a new stack frame on the top of the current thread's stack;
- executes the call to the `f()` method.

The following code is produced by the C# compile for the `f()` method:

```
.maxstack  2
.locals init ([0] int32 CS$00000003$00000000)
IL_0000:  ldarg.0
IL_0001:  ldarg.1
IL_0002:  add
IL_0003:  stloc.0
IL_0004:  br.s       IL_0006
IL_0006:  ldloc.0
IL_0007:  ret
```

The `ldarg` IL instruction is used to load the value of an argument onto the stack. Remember that arguments to the method were stored in memory by the `call` instruction. Note that the arguments are indexed from zero for a static method (such as `f()`) and from one in the case of a non-static method. In fact, during the call to a non-static method the argument indexed by zero is reserved implicitly for the reference to `this`.

The return value of a method must be the only value left on the stack frame of the method right before the call to the `ret` instruction. This instruction is used to indicate the return from the method (meaning the destruction of the stack frame for the method) but the return value at the top of the stack is kept so that the calling function can retrieve it.

Note that the following code, which does not involve any local variables, would have been used:

```
.maxstack  2
IL_0000:  ldarg.0
IL_0001:  ldarg.1
IL_0002:  add
IL_0003:  ret
```

IL instructions for comparison, branch and jump

There are several IL instructions to compare the two values at the top of the stack. Their names have been borrowed from existing machine language: `ceq` (*compare val1 equal val2*), `cgt` (*compare val1 greater than val2*), `clt` (*compare val1 less than val2*).

Let us precise that `val2` is at the top of the stack and that `val1` is right below. In addition, the `val1` and `val2` values are unstacked and an integer value (1 if the comparison is true, 0 if it is false) is added to the top of the stack.

There is also a family of IL instructions for branching. Most of them start with 'b' or 'br' and take, as a parameter, the offset of the IL instruction to branch to. The unconditional branching instruction is named `br`. All the other branching instructions are conditional, meaning that the branching will only occur if a condition is met. For example, the `brtrue` instruction will only accomplish the branching if the value at the top of the stack is non-null. The `beq` instruction only branches if the two values at the top of the stack are equal. The meaning of the instructions named `brfalse` (Branch if False), `blt` (Branch if Lower Than), `ble` (Branch if Lower or Equal), `bgt` (Branch if Greater Than), `bge` (Branch if Greater or Equal), `bne` (Branch if Not Equal) ... derive from all this.

IL as an object oriented language

Let us analyze the IL code generated from a little object oriented C# program.

Example 2-13
```
class Program {
   public override string ToString() { return "Program m_i=" + m_i; }
   int m_i = 9;
   Program(int i) { m_i = i; }
   public static void Main() {
      object obj = new Program(12);
      obj.ToString();
   }
}
```

Here is the IL code returned for the `Main()` method:

```
    .maxstack  2
    .locals init ([0] object obj)
    IL_0000:  ldc.i4.s   12
    IL_0002:  newobj     instance void Program::.ctor(int32)
    IL_0007:  stloc.0
    IL_0008:  ldloc.0
    IL_0009:  callvirt   instance string [mscorlib]System.Object::ToString()
    IL_000e:  ret
```

We see that a special IL instruction named `newobj` is used to create an object, call a constructor of its class and place a reference toward the newly created on the stack. You can also see that the call to the virtual method `Program.ToString()` (which overloads the `object.ToString()` method) is done using the `callvirt` instruction. Before this call, a reference to the object calling this method is placed on the stack. Polymorphism is then supported through the use of the `callvirt` IL instruction.

Note that at page 413 we will discuss the change to the IL language to support generic types.

Metadata tokens

The type metadata tables are often referenced by the IL code. When the IL code is disassembled by `ildasm.exe`, it places the names and signatures to the methods directly in the disassembled IL code. In fact, at the binary level, the IL code has no strings defining method referenced. To reference a method, the IL code contains four byte values which point to the type metadata table. We call these four byte values *metadata tokens*.

The first byte of a metadata references the metadata table. The other three bytes reference an element in this table. For example, the table referencing the members used by a module (the *MethodRef* table) has a reference number of 10, a metadata token to the fifth entry of this table is: 0x0A000005.

Metadata tokens can be seen by choosing the *Show token values* of `ildasm.exe`. For example, the code of the `Main()` method of the following program ...

Example 2-14
```
using System;
class Program{
   public static void Main(){
      Console.WriteLine( "Hello world!" );
   }
}
```

...contains the following IL code (seen with metadata token visualization of `ildasm.exe`):

```
.method /*06000001*/ public hidebysig static
        void  Main() cil managed
{
  .entrypoint
  // Code size       11 (0xb)
  .maxstack  1
  IL_0000:  ldstr      "Hello world!" /* 70000001 */
  IL_0005:  call       void [mscorlib/* 23000001 */]
         System.Console/* 0100000F */::WriteLine(string) /* 0A00000E */
  IL_000a:  ret
} // end of method Program::Main
```

The metadata tokens seen in this example are:

- 0x06000001: references the entry in the *MethodDef* (0x06) table representing the `Main` (0x000001) method.

- 0x70000001: references the entry to the *#userstring* (0x70) heap representing the "Hello world!" (0x000001) string.

- 0x23000001: references the entry into the *AssemblyRef* (0x23) table which represents the `mscorlib` (0x000001) assembly.

- 0x0100000F: references the entry in the *TypeRef* (0x01) table representing the `System.Console` (0x00000F) class.

- 0x0A00000E: references the entry in the *MemberRef* (0x0A) representing the `WriteLine` (0x00000F) table. Note here that the metadata for the `WriteLine` method is not in the *MethodDef* table since it is defined in another module.

3 Build, deploy and configure your .NET applications

Building your applications with MSBuild

The .NET 2 platform is delivered with a new tool named `msbuild.exe`. This tool is used to build .NET applications. It accepts XML files which describe the sequence of tasks for the build process, in the same spirit as `makefile` files. Actually, in the beginning of this project, *Microsoft* had code named the tool *XMake*. The `msbuild.exe` executable is located in the .NET installation folder `[Windows install folder]\Microsoft.NET\Framework\v2.0.50727\`. It is planned that MSBuild will be part of the *Windows Vista* operating system. Its range of action will then be increased and may be used to construct all type of applications.

Until now, to construct your .NET applications, you needed to:

- Either use the *Build* in *Visual Studio*.
- Either use the *Visual Studio* `devenv.exe` executable as a command line.
- Either use a third party tool such as the open source tool named *NAnt*, or even use batch files which called the `csc.exe` C# compiler.

MSBuild aims to unify all these techniques. Those who know NAnt will not be in unknown territory as MSBuild borrows many concepts from this tool. The main advantage of MSBuild over NAnt is that it is used by *Visual Studio 2005*. MSBuild has no dependency on *Visual Studio 2005* as it is an integral part of the .NET 2 platform. However, the `.proj`, `.csproj`, `.vbproj` etc generated by *Visual Studio 2005* to build projects are authored in the MSBuild XML format. During compilation, *Visual Studio 2005* uses the services of MSBuild. In addition, the XML format used by MSBuild is fully supported and documented. The support of MSBuild is a significant progress for *Visual Studio* since until now, it used undocumented build scripts.

MSBuild: Target, Task, Property, Item and Condition

.proj files, targets and tasks

The root element of MSBuild XML documents is `<Project>`. This element contains `<Target>` elements. These `<Target>` elements are the build units named targets. An MSBuild project can contain multiple targets and `msbuild.exe` is capable of chaining the execution of multiple targets. When you launch `msbuild.exe` through the command line, it takes as input a single `.proj` from the current folder. If multiple `.proj` files are present, you must specify to `msbuild.exe` which one to use. A single file must be specified.

An MSBuild target is a set of MSBuild tasks. Each child element to `<Target>` constitutes the definition of a task. The tasks of a target are executed in the order of their declaration. About forty types of tasks are provided by MSBuild, for example:

Task type	Description
Copy	Copies a file from a source folder to a destination folder.
MakeDir	Creates a folder.
Csc	Calls the `csc.exe` C# compiler.
Exec	Executes a system command.
AL	Calls the `al.exe` tool (*Assembly Linker*).
ResGen	Calls the `resgen.exe` tool (*Resources Generator*).

The complete list of possible tasks is available in the article named MSBuild Task Reference on MSDN. An interesting aspect of MSBuild is that each type of task is materialized by a .NET class. It is then possible to extend MSBuild with new types of tasks by supplying your own classes. We will discuss this a little later.

Let us revisit our multi-module assembly example at page 15. Let us remind you that to build this assembly constructed from three modules `Foo1.exe`, `Foo2.netmodule` and `Image.jpg` we had to execute the following two commands:

```
>csc.exe /target:module Foo2.cs
>csc.exe /Addmodule:Foo2.netmodule /LinkResource:Image.jpg Foo1.cs
```

In addition, we wanted that at the end of the construction of the assembly, the three modules be located in the `\bin` sub-folder from the current folder. Here is the MSBuild project `Foo.proj` which accomplishes the same work:

Example 3-1   *Foo.proj*
```
<Project xmlns="http://schemas.microsoft.com/developer/msbuild/2003">
  <Target Name="FooCompilation">
    <MakeDir Directories= "bin"/>
    <Copy SourceFiles="Image.jpg" DestinationFiles=".\bin\Image.jpg"/>
    <Csc Sources="Foo2.cs"        TargetType="module"
         OutputAssembly=".\bin\Foo2.netmodule" />
    <Csc Sources="Foo1.cs"        TargetType="exe"
         AddModules=".\bin\Foo2.netmodule" LinkResources="Image.jpg"
         OutputAssembly=".\bin\Foo1.exe" />
  </Target>
</Project>
```

We see that the target named `FooCompilation` is built with four tasks:

- A task of type `MakeDir` which creates the `\bin` folder;
- A task of type `Copy` which copies `Image.jpg` to the `\bin` folder;
- Two tasks of type `Csc` which invoke the `csc.exe` compiler.

To execute this build project, you need to create a folder containing the following files:

```
.\Foo.proj
.\Foo1.cs
.\Foo2.cs
.\Image.jpg
```

Go in this folder with the command window (Start Menu › *Microsoft .NET Framework SDK v2.0* › *SDK Command Prompt*) and then launch the `msbuild.exe` command. Each target must be named. By default, `msbuild.exe` only executes the first target. You can specify a list of targets separated by semi-colons using the `/target` (shortcut `/t`). You can also specify such a list using the `DefaultTarget` of the `<Project>` project. If multiple targets are specified, the order of execution is undefined.

The default behavior of MSBuild is to stop execution as soon as one of the tasks emits an error. You may wish to have a build script tolerate errors. Also, each element containing a task can contain a `ContinueOnError` attribute which is set to `false` by default but may be set to `true`.

Properties

To allow you to add parameters to control your scripts, MSBuild presents the notion of property. A property is a key/value couple defined in the `<PropertyGroup>` element. MSBuild properties work as an alias system. Each occurrence of `$(key)` in the script is replaced by the associated value. Typically, the name of the /bin folder is used in five places in our `Foo.proj` project. It constitutes a good candidate for a property:

Example 3-2   *Foo.proj*

```xml
<Project xmlns="http://schemas.microsoft.com/developer/msbuild/2003">
  <PropertyGroup>
    <OutputPath>.\bin</OutputPath>
  </PropertyGroup>
  <Target Name="FooCompilation">
    <MakeDir Directories= "$(OutputPath)"/>
    <Copy SourceFiles="Image.jpg"
          DestinationFiles="$(OutputPath)\Image.jpg"/>
    <Csc Sources="Foo2.cs"        TargetType="module"
         OutputAssembly="$(OutputPath)\Foo2.netmodule" />
    <Csc Sources="Foo1.cs"        TargetType="exe"
         AddModules="$(OutputPath)\Foo2.netmodule"
         LinkResources="Image.jpg"
         OutputAssembly="$(OutputPath)\Foo1.exe" />
  </Target>
</Project>
```

You can also use pre-defined properties defined by MSBuild such as:

Property	Description
`MSBuildProjectDirectory`	Folder hosting the current MSBuild project.
`MSBuildProjetFile`	Name of the current MSBuild project.
`MSBuildProjectExtension`	Extension of the current MSBuild project.
`MSBuildProjectFullPath`	Full path to the current MSBuild project.
`MSBuildProjectName`	Name of the current MSBuild project without the extension.
`MSBuildPath`	Folder which contains `msbuild.exe`.

During the edition of properties with Visual Studio 2005, you will notice that a certain number of keys are proposed by intellisense. `OutputPath`, for example, is such a key. You can use these keys but nothing prevents you from defining your own keys.

Items

The base behind building a project by a script is the manipulation of folders, files (source, resource, executable…) and references (to assemblies, to COM classes, to resource files…). We use the term *item* to designate these entries which constitute the entries and outputs for most of the tasks. In our example, the `Image.jpg` file is an item consumed both by the `Copy` task and the second `Csc` task. The file `Foo2.netmodule` is an item produced by the first `Csc` task and is consumed by the second `Csc` task. Let us rewrite our project using the notion of *item*:

Example 3-3 *Foo.proj*

```xml
<Project xmlns="http://schemas.microsoft.com/developer/msbuild/2003">
   <PropertyGroup><OutputPath>.\bin</OutputPath></PropertyGroup>
   <ItemGroup>
      <File_Image Include="$(OutputPath)\Image.jpg"/>
      <NetModule_Foo2 Include="$(OutputPath)\Foo2.netmodule"/>
   </ItemGroup>
   <Target Name="FooCompilation">
      <MakeDir Directories= "$(OutputPath)"/>
      <Copy SourceFiles="Image.jpg"
            DestinationFiles="@(File_Image)"/>
      <Csc Sources="Foo2.cs"         TargetType="module"
           OutputAssembly="@(NetModule_Foo2)" />
      <Csc Sources="Foo1.cs"         TargetType="exe"
           AddModules="@(NetModule_Foo2)"
           LinkResources="@(File_Image)"
           OutputAssembly="$(OutputPath)\Foo1.exe" />
   </Target>
</Project>
```

We notice the use of the @(item name) to reference an item. Moreover, an item can define a set of files through the use of the wildcard syntax. For example, the following item references all the C# files in the current folder except for Foo1.cs:

```xml
<cs_source Include=".\*.cs" Exclude=".\Foo1.cs" />
```

Conditions

We may wish that a same MSBuild project build multiple different versions. For example, it would be a shame to have to create and maintain two projects to handle the build of a Debug and a Release version of a same application. Also, MSBuild introduces the notion of condition. A Condition attribute can be added to any element of a MSBuild project (properties, item, target, task, property group, item group…). If during the execution, the condition of an element is not satisfied, the MSBuild engine will ignore it. The **MSDN** article named **MSBuild Conditions** describes the complete list of expression which can be used in a condition attribute.

In the following example, we use the condition of type *string equality compare* to make sure that our script supports both a Debug and Release mode. We also use a condition of type *test for the presence of a file or folder* to execute the MakeDir task only when needed. This condition is there purely for learning reasons as the MakeDir only executes if the folder does not already exist:

Example 3-4 *Foo.proj*

```xml
<Project xmlns="http://schemas.microsoft.com/developer/msbuild/2003">
   <PropertyGroup Condition="'$(Configuration)'=='Debug'">
      <Optimize>false</Optimize>
      <DebugSymbols>true</DebugSymbols>
      <OutputPath>.\bin\Debug</OutputPath>
   </PropertyGroup>
   <PropertyGroup Condition="'$(Configuration)'=='Release'">
      <Optimize>true</Optimize>
      <DebugSymbols>false</DebugSymbols>
      <OutputPath>.\bin\Release</OutputPath>
   </PropertyGroup>
   <ItemGroup>
...
   <Target Name="FooCompilation">
      <MakeDir Directories= "$(OutputPath)"
               Condition="!Exists('$(OutputPath)')"/>
...
```

When they are defined, the `Optimize` and `DebugSymbols` standard properties are automatically taken into account by `Csc` tasks.

Before launching this script, you must specify as a command line parameter the value of the `Configuration` property. This can be done using the `/property` (shortcut `/p`) option:

```
>msbuild /p:Configuration=Release
```

The astute reader has noticed that it is possible to use a condition to define the default value for the `Condition` property:

Example 3-5 *Foo.proj*
```
<Project xmlns="http://schemas.microsoft.com/developer/msbuild/2003">
   <PropertyGroup Condition="'$(Configuration)'==''">
      <Configuration>Debug</Configuration>
   </PropertyGroup>
   <PropertyGroup Condition="'$(Configuration)'=='Debug'">
...
```

Advanced MSBuild

Incremental build and dependencies between targets

In a real environment, the execution of an MSBuild project can take several minutes (even hours) to execute. As a side fact, did you know that since its beginning, the *Windows* operating system takes about 12 hours to build? This means the ever growing volume of code to be compiles compensates the performance increase of machines.

It is not necessarily a good thing to completely restart the build process for a minor change made on a source file for which no other components depend. Also, you can use the notion of *incremental construction*. For this, you must specify the list of input items and the output items for a target using the `Inputs` and `Outputs` attributes. If MSBuild detects that at least one of the input items is older than one of the output items, it will execute the target.

This incremental build technique forces you to partition your tasks into several targets. We have seen that if we specify multiple targets to build by MSBuild, for example with the `DefaultTargets` attribute, you can not assume any execution order. You can however specify a set of dependencies between targets using the `DependsOnTargets` attribute. MSBuild executes a target only when the totality of the targets on which it depends is executed. Naturally, the MSBuild engine will detect and emit an error when circular dependencies between targets exist:

Example 3-6 *Foo.proj*
```
<Project xmlns="http://schemas.microsoft.com/developer/msbuild/2003"
   DefaultTargets="FooCompilation">
...
   <Target Name="CreateOutputPath" Condition="!Exists('$(OutputPath)')">
      <MakeDir Directories= "$(OutputPath)"/>
   </Target>
   <Target Name="FooCompilation" DependsOnTargets="CreateOutputPath"
           Inputs="Foo2.cs;Foo1.cs"
           Outputs="@(NetModule_Foo2);$(OutputPath)\Foo1.exe">
      ...
   </Target>
</Project>
```

MSBuild transforms

You have the possibility of establishing a bijective correspondence between the input items and the output items of a target. For this, you need to use MSBuild transformations detailed in the article named **MSBuild Transforms** on **MSDN**. The advantage of using transformations is that MSBuild decides to execute the target if at least one of the input items is older than the output item which corresponds to it. Logically, such a target is going to be executed less often, hence a performance gain.

Splitting an MSBuild project on several files

We have seen that the `msbuild.exe` tool can only process a single project file for each execution. However, an MSBuild project file can import another MSBuild project file by using the `<Import>` element. In this case, all the children of the `<Project>` in the imported file are copied in place of the `<Import>` element. Our example script can then be broken into two files `Foo.proj` and `Foo.target.proj` as follows:

Example 3-7   *Foo.proj*
```
<Project xmlns="http://schemas.microsoft.com/developer/msbuild/2003"
    DefaultTargets="FooCompilation">
    <PropertyGroup Condition="'$(Configuration)'==''"> ...
    <PropertyGroup Condition="'$(Configuration)'=='Debug'"> ...
    <PropertyGroup Condition="'$(Configuration)'=='Release'"> ...
    <ItemGroup> ...
    <Import Project="Foo.target.proj"/>
</Project>
```

Example 3-8   *Foo.target.proj*
```
<Project xmlns="http://schemas.microsoft.com/developer/msbuild/2003" >
    <Target Name="CreateOutputPath">   ...
    <Target Name="FooCompilation">     ...
</Project>
```

How does Visual Studio 2005 harness MSBuild?

We have already mentioned that the files of extension `.proj`, `.csproj`, `.vbproj` etc generated by *Visual Studio 2005* to build projects are authored in the MSBuild XML format. If you analyze such a file, you will notice that no targets are explicitly specified. In fact, the project files generated by *Visual Studio 2005* import some `.targets` files which contains generic targets. For example, a file with a `.csproj` extension contains the following element:

```
<Import Project="$(MSBuildBinPath)\Microsoft.CSharp.targets" />
```

This `Microsoft.CSharp.targets` file contains two generic targets:

- A target named `CreateManifestResourceNames` which takes care of the organization of resource files (transformation of `.resx` files into `.resources`).
- A target named `CoreCompile` which contains a task named `Csc` which takes care of building C# files.

We recommend that you take a look at the `.targets` files located in the folder defined by `$(MSBuildBinPath)` which is the .NET 2 installation folder (i.e. `[Windows folder]\Microsoft.NET\Framework\v2.0.50727`).

In addition to importing such a `.targets` file, the files generated by *Visual Studio 2005* contain essentially the definition of properties and items which will be used by the generic targets.

Creating custom MSBuild tasks

Another interesting aspect of MSBuild is that each type of task materializes itself in a .NET class. This means that it is possible to extend MSBuild with new task types by supplying your own classes. Such a class must support the following constraints:

- It must implement the `ITask` interface defined in `Microsoft.Build.Framework.dll` or derive from the helper class `Task` defined in `Microsoft.Build.Utilities.dll`.
- It must implement the `bool Execute()` of the `ITask` interface. This method contains the body of the task and must return `true` if the execution succeeded.
- It can offer properties which will be set by MSBuild from attribute values in the task, before the call to `Execute()`. Only the properties marked with the `Required` must necessarily be initialized.

Here is an example of a task named `MyTouch` which updates the timestamp of the files specified with the `Files` attribute (let us mention that such a task named `Touch` is offered by the MSBuild framework):

Example 3-9 *MyTask.cs*

```
using System;
using Microsoft.Build.Framework;
using Microsoft.Build.Utilities;
namespace MyTask {
   public class MyTouch : Task {
      public override bool Execute() {
         DateTime now = DateTime.Now;
         Log.LogMessage(now.ToString() +
            " is now the new date for the following files:");
         try {
            foreach(string fileName in m_FilesNames) {
               Log.LogMessage("   " + fileName);
               System.IO.File.SetLastWriteTime(fileName, now);
            }
         }
         catch (Exception ex) {
            Log.LogErrorFromException(ex, true);
            return false;
         }
         return true;
      }
      [Required]
      public string[] Files {
         get { return (m_FilesNames); } set { m_FilesNames = value; }
      }
      private string[] m_FilesNames;
   }
}
```

Note the use of the `TaskLoggingHelper Task.Log{get;}` which allows displaying information relating to the execution of the task.

Our `MyTouch` task must be registered to all the MSBuild projects which may use it. This is done by using an element `<UsingTask>`. Here is such a script which updates the timestamps of the C# files in the current folder (the `MyTask.dll` assembly must be located in the `C:\CustomTasks\` folder):

Example 3-10 *Foo.proj*

```xml
<Project xmlns="http://schemas.microsoft.com/developer/msbuild/2003">
   <UsingTask AssemblyFile="C:\CustomTasks\MyTask.dll"
              TaskName="MyTask.MyTouch"/>
   <ItemGroup>
      <FichierSrcCs Include="*.cs"/>
   </ItemGroup>
   <Target Name="TouchTheCsFiles" >
      <MyTouch Files= "@(CsSrcFiles)"/>
   </Target>
</Project>
```

It is interesting to note that all standard tasks are declared by `<UsingTask>` elements located in the `Microsoft.Common.Tasks` file. This file is automatically and implicitly imported by `msbuild.exe` at each execution. By analyzing this file, we can see that the classes corresponding to the standard tasks are defined in the `Microsoft.Build.Tasks.dll` assembly. You can then access the code of these tasks using a tool such as *Reflector*.

Configuration files

A .NET executable assembly has the possibility of having a configuration file which can be modified after installation. The name of such a configuration file must start with the name of the module containing the manifest (including the `.exe` or `.dll` extension) to which we add the `.config` extension (for example `Foo.exe.config`). It must be placed in the same folder as the assembly.

Visual Studio offers facilities for the edition and maintenance of the configuration file of an application. You can right click on the project defining an executable assembly › *Add* › *New Item…* › *Application Configuration File* › Keep the `App.Config` name. During the compilation, *Visual Studio* will make a copy of the contents of this file to a file named `[name of the executable assembly with extension].config` located in the same folder as the produced assembly.

The machine.config file

Most of the configuration elements of a .NET application can also be declared in a file named `machine.config` which is located in the `/CONFIG` sub-folder of the .NET installation folder (`[Windows Folder]\Microsoft.NET\Framework\v2.0.50727`). The value of a parameter defined in the `machine.config` file is taken into account by a .NET application only if this value is not set in the application's own configuration file. Moreover certain configuration parameters such as the process model used by ASP.NET only really make sense at the machine level. They can then be only initialized in the `machine.config` file.

It is not recommended to modify the machine configuration file. In fact, you may inadvertently modify the behavior of applications installed on your machine. However, in the case of a production machine (a server or machine dedicated to an application), this file can constitute an efficient way to define a global configuration policy for the machine.

Standard configuration parameters

All .NET configuration file has a `<configuration>` root element:

```xml
<configuration
   xmlns="http://schemas.microsoft.com/.NetConfiguration/v2.0">
```

Here are the main sub-elements which can be found under the `<configuration>` element:

- `<appSettings>`: Contains the configuration elements specific to an application.
- `<configSections>`: Allows the definition of configuration sections that we will describe a little later.
- `<connectionStrings>`: Stores the database connection strings (see page 595).
- `<location>`: Allows the definition of ASP.NET configuration elements for each web page (see page 739).
- `<mscorlib>`: (only in machine.config) Contains a `<cryptographySettings>` element which contains the cryptographic mechanisms (see page 181).
- `<protectedData>`: Allows the definition of confidential information sections in a configuration file (see page 189).
- `<runtime>`: Contains a `<gcConcurrent>` section which allows to determine if the garbage collector executes in a concurrent way (see page 98). Contains also a section named `<assemblyBinding>` which sets the parameters of the assembly locating algorithm (see page 83).
- `<system.Data.[Data Provider]>`: Allows to specify parameters for the ADO.NET data providers (see page 596).
- `<system.Diagnostics>`: Contains information relative to traces (see page 513).
- `<system.runtime.remoting>`: Allows the configuration of .NET Remoting services and channels (see page 672).
- `<system.transactions>`: Allows the configuration of transactions (see page 623>).
- `<system.web>`: Defines the parameters used by ASP.NET. The process of configuring ASP.NET applications is a large topic to which we dedicate the section named **ASP.NET Configuration (Web.Config files)** at page 737.

Defining your own configuration parameters with the <appSettings> element

You can use the `<appSettings>` element of the configuration file of an application to store the configuration values which are specific to it. For example, suppose that the MyApp application has a parameter named MyInt:

Example 3-11 *MyApp.exe.config*
```xml
<?xml version="1.0" encoding="utf-8" ?>
<configuration
    xmlns="http://schemas.microsoft.com/.NetConfiguration/v2.0">
    <appSettings>
        <add key="MyInt" value="1234"/>
    </appSettings>
</configuration>
```

Here is the code of the MyApp application. At each execution, the code obtains the value of the MyInt parameter, multiplies it by 10 and then saves the new value:

Example 3-12 *MyApp.cs*
```csharp
using System.Configuration;
class Program {
    static void Main() {
        Configuration appCfg = ConfigurationManager.OpenExeConfiguration(
                                    ConfigurationUserLevel.None);
        AppSettingsSection appSettings = appCfg.AppSettings;
        int myInt;
        if (int.TryParse( appSettings.Settings["MyInt"].Value, out myInt)) {
            System.Console.WriteLine(myInt);
```

Example 3-12   *MyApp.cs*
```
            myInt *= 10;
            appSettings.Settings["MyInt"].Value = myInt.ToString();
            appCfg.Save();
        }
    }
}
```

If you recompile the MyApp application with *Visual Studio* and that you use the App.Config file, the value is reinitialized to 1234 since the content of the MyApp.exe.config configuration file is replaced by the content of App.Config.

It is clear that this approach presents two major disadvantages:

- The value of a parameter is not typed. We had to explicitly parse a string to obtain the value of MyInt in an integer variable.
- The name of the parameter is not verified by the compiler as it is supplied in the form of a string. This can be detrimental to productivity as developers cannot benefit from intellisense.

Defining your own configuration parameters with configuration sections

To avoid these two problems, you can use the *configuration section*. Such a section is a set of configuration parameters. Each parameter is defined either at the application level either at the level of the *Windows* user which executes the application. Hence, you can simply use this mechanism to store the preferences for each user.

The following configuration file defines a section named MySettings which contains a user configuration parameter named MyIntUsr and an application configuration parameter named MyIntApp:

Example 3-13   *MyApp.exe.config*
```
<?xml version="1.0" encoding="utf-8" ?>
<configuration
    xmlns="http://schemas.microsoft.com/.NetConfiguration/v2.0">
  <configSections>
    <sectionGroup name="userSettings"
                  type="System.Configuration.UserSettingsGroup,
                        System, Version=2.0.0.0, Culture=neutral,
                        PublicKeyToken=b77a5c561934e089" >
      <section   name="MySettings"
                 type="System.Configuration.ClientSettingsSection,
                       System, Version=2.0.0.0, Culture=neutral,
                       PublicKeyToken=b77a5c561934e089"
                 allowExeDefinition="MachineToLocalUser" />
    </sectionGroup>
    <sectionGroup name="applicationSettings"
                  type="System.Configuration.ApplicationSettingsGroup,
                        System, Version=2.0.0.0, Culture=neutral,
                        PublicKeyToken=b77a5c561934e089" >
      <section   name="MySettings"
                 type="System.Configuration.ClientSettingsSection,
                       System, Version=2.0.0.0, Culture=neutral,
                       PublicKeyToken=b77a5c561934e089" />
    </sectionGroup>
  </configSections>
  <userSettings>
```

Example 3-13   MyApp.exe.config
```
      <MySettings>
        <setting name="MyIntUsr" serializeAs="String">
          <value>1234</value>
        </setting>
      </MySettings>
    </userSettings>
    <applicationSettings>
      <MySettings>
        <setting name="MyIntApp" serializeAs="String">
          <value>4321</value>
        </setting>
      </MySettings>
    </applicationSettings>
</configuration>
```

Here is the code of the corresponding MyApp application. We see that the two problems of the previous example are solved with the introduction of a class named MySettings which derives from System.Configuration.ApplicationSettingsBase. We call such a class a *configuration section handler*. This class offers a property for each parameter. The properties relative to the user parameters are marked with the UserScopedSettingAttribute attribute while application properties are marked with the ApplicationScopedSettingAttribute attribute. We notice that the MyIntApp property does not have a set accessor. In fact, within this technique, application parameters are considered read-only:

Example 3-14   MyApp.cs
```
using System.Configuration;
class Program {
   static void Main() {
      MySettings mySettings = new MySettings();
      int myIntUsr = mySettings.MyIntUsr;
      System.Console.WriteLine(myIntUsr);
      myIntUsr *= 10;
      mySettings.MyIntUsr = myIntUsr;
      mySettings.Save();
      System.Console.WriteLine(mySettings.MyIntApp);
   }
}
class MySettings : ApplicationSettingsBase {
   [UserScopedSetting()]
   public int MyIntUsr {
      get { return (int)(this["MyIntUsr"]); }
      set { this["MyIntUsr"] = value; }
   }
   [ApplicationScopedSetting()]
   public int MyIntApp {
      get { return (int)(this["MyIntApp"]); }
   }
}
```

During the execution, the CLR uses reflection to:

- Map the name of the classes deriving from the ApplicationSettingsBase class with the name of the configuration sections.
- Map the name of the properties of these classes with the configuration parameters.

Create your own configuration sections with Visual Studio 2005

Although the advantages of using configuration sections, you may be turned off by the prospect of having to create a dedicated class and by the number of elements added to your configuration file. Thankfully, *Visual Studio 2005* offers a configuration editor which automates this extra workload.

To add a new section, you simply need to do the following: Right click on the project › *Add* › *New Items...* › *Settings File* › Supply the XXX name of the section › *OK*. A new element named XXX.settings is then added to the project. If you select this element, the configuration parameter editor appears. For each parameter, you can choose its name, its type, whether it is an application parameter or user parameter and a default value.

A XXX.Designer.cs source file is associated to the XXX.settings element. This is a generated file which contains the definition of the class named XXX which derives from ApplicationSettingBase. This definition is constantly synchronized with any modifications made in the editor. Also, as with every generated file, you must not insert your own code in there.

Notes on configuration sections

At page 189 we explain how to use the data protection API to save configuration parameters in an encrypted form.

You have the option of validating the modifications made to configuration parameters before they are actually saved out. This is explained in the article named **How to: Validate Application Settings** on **MSDN**.

It is interesting to analyze out machine.config file to notice that all standard section mentioned earlier are declared by <section> elements. For each of these sections corresponds a standard type such as ConnectionStringsSection, AppSettingsSection or ProtectedConfiguratioNSection. Example 3-2 shows how to have access to an instance of AppSettingsSection in order to modify the contents of the <appSettings> section. Note that certain of these types such as SystemDiagnosticsSection must only be used by the CLR and thus are not accessible.

The value of user parameters are not stored in the configuration file of the application but in a file named [User Name].config. This file is located in the folder specified by the static property named System.Windows.Forms.Application.LocalUserAppDataPath.

In the case of an application deployed using *ClickOnce* (presented later in this chapter), the configuration files (for the application and users) are deployed into the *ClickOnce* folder for the application (see page 68).

By default, classes derived from ApplicationSettingBase use internally the System.Configuration.LocalFileSettingsProvider to have read and write access to the configuration files. This class derives from System.Configuration.SettingsProvider. You can create your own classes derived from SettingsProvider in order to implement your own persistence mechanism for application parameters (in a database, a registry, through a web service...). You simply need to establish a link between your classes derived from ApplicationSettingBase and your classes derived from SettingsProvider by marking the parameters with the SettingsProviderAttribute attribute.

The ToolStrip control of the *Windows Form 2 framework* offers facilities to directly store it state in application parameters. This means that you must allow for the same type of facilities for your own type of controls. This is discussed further in the article named **Application Settings for Custom Controls** on **MSDN**.

Assembly deployment: XCopy vs. GAC

.NET offers two types of strategies to deploy the assemblies of an application.

- The XCopy strategy (also qualified of deployment of private assemblies) simply consists of copying the application files into a folder. Because things cannot be made any simpler, this is the strategy to use by default.
- Another strategy which must be used to deploy assemblies which are shared by multiple applications running on same machine. This strategy presents some interesting functionality such as the management of assembly versioning.

XCopy deployment

The *XCopy* assembly deployment strategy is the simplest strategy. It consists in copying all the assemblies relating to the application to deploy in a single folder. In general, developers create a folder structure. Neither the registry, or the 'Active Directory' of *Windows* are accessed by an XCopy deployment.

Not to loose any files, it is recommended to encapsulate the folder structure and all its files in a single file (for example a *cab*, *zip* or *rar* archive as we'll explain a little later). The un-installation of an application consists in the destruction of the folder structure and the change of versions implies the destruction of the folder structure and replacing it with the new one.

Those who may have already dealt with the deployment of an application under *Windows*, either as an administrator, developer or user measure the ease of use of XCopy deployments.

To access advanced functionalities such as the creation of desktop shortcuts or task bar icons, you can use the *Windows* installation service named MSI, which we will discuss further a little later.

Shared assemblies and the GAC folder

The deployment of assemblies using XCopy does not work for assemblies which are shared by multiple applications installed on the same machine. In fact, if we used this strategy for a *shared assembly*, it would be located on the hard disk for each application which uses it. Despite the space waste, this strategy has for main goal to force the change of multiple files at different locations when a shared assembly evolves. The strategy to apply for shared assembly consists to use a specialized folder made to store them. This folder is called *GAC* (*Global Assembly Cache* folder). The GAC folder is in general the following folder: `C:\Windows\Assembly\GAC`. This special folder is known by the CLR and consequently is known by all .NET applications.

> Understand that the big majority of assemblies are not shared amongst multiple applications. You will rarely encounter the need to store an assembly in the GAC.

An assembly must have a strong name to be stored in the GAC. The notion of strong name is discussed at page 22. An assembly without a strong name cannot be stored in the GAC. However, an assembly with a strong name is not necessarily required to be stored in the GAC (i.e. it can be deployed with the XCopy strategy).

Each time that a strong named assembly is loaded in a process, the verification of the validity of its digital signature must be done. However, for shared assemblies in the GAC folder, this is not necessary. In fact, when a shared assembly is added to the GAC, the validity of its digital signature is automatically verified. If the digital signature is not valid, the assembly cannot be added to the GAC folder. Thus, there is a performance gain when an assembly is loaded from the GAC.

It is interesting to notice that when you install the .NET platform on a machine, the assemblies containing the classes of the .NET framework (`System.dll`, `System.Data.dll`, `System.Security.dll`,...) are installed in the GAC. A copy of each of these assemblies exist in the .NET installation folder (i.e. `[Windows Folder]\Microsoft.NET\framework\v2.0.50727\`). If you install *Visual Studio*, it will use these copies during the analysis of references to the standard framework assemblies in a project. In fact, *Visual Studio* does not know how to reference the assemblies stored in the GAC. Only the CLR knows how to use the GAC assemblies because of a software layer named *assembly loader* which we discuss at page 83.

How does the GAC's side by side storage model solve the DLL hell problem?

If we consider it as a *Windows* folder, the GAC has an elaborate internal structure that you happily do not have to worry about. This structure is necessary due to the fact that the GAC can contain several versions of the same assembly. This particularity is called *side by side* storage of the different versions of a same assembly. When an assembly references a shared assembly, it uses its strong name. Hence, the version being part of the strong name, there is no risk of loading the wrong version.

The side by side storage resolves the problem known as *DLL hell*. This problem happens when we replace a *Windows* dynamic library (i.e. a DLL for *Dynamic Link Library*) by a newer version. The slightest compatibility problem between the different versions of the DLLs implies that applications which use the DLL and that functioned properly with the previous version may encounter execution problems with the new version. This problem is so important that a big part of the instability reputation of the *Windows* operating system comes from this. In addition to resolving the instability problems, the side by side storage minimizes the backward compatibility requirements which are often imposed by the development of a new version.

The only problem with this technique of side by side storage is the potential storage requirements needed to keep all the different versions for each assembly. For reasonably sized assemblies, this is not really a problem. But for large assemblies, it is the responsibility of the application developer to be sure to share as much data across different versions.

Side by side execution

The side by side execution of an assembly consists in authorizing the simultaneous execution of several versions of this assembly. The `AssemblyFlags` .NET attribute authorizes versions of an assembly to be executed side by side in a same application domain or in a same process or on a same machine.

It is better to avoid the side by side execution of a same assembly in an application domain or process. In fact, this feature is mostly used to allow several applications to simultaneously use an assembly, each using the version of their liking. It is somewhat clumsy to allow that such applications execute themselves within the same process or even worse, within the same application domain.

Overall, the side by side execution of an assembly, in some cases, can introduce problems which are difficult to address. These problems happen when a same resource is used simultaneously by several versions of an assembly. There is a risk that different versions of assembly may not agree on how to use the resource, leading to an unpredictable behavior.

Viewing and editing the GAC folder

To visualize the GAC from a regular explorer window, there is a shell extension named `ShFusion.dll` installed automatically during the installation of the .NET platform on a machine. This extension allows the visualization and the manipulation in an easy way of all the assemblies shared in the GAC. To use this extension, you simply need to browse to the GAC folder with a *Windows* explorer as shown in Figure 3-1:

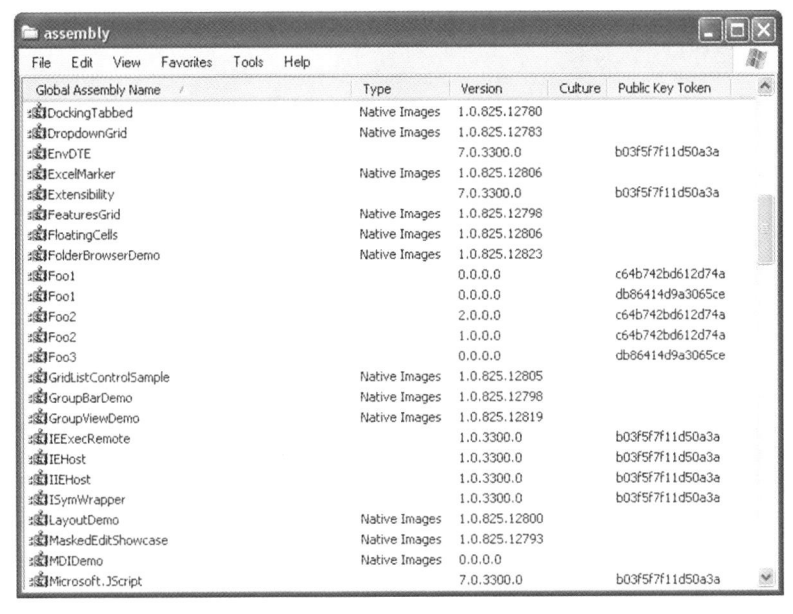

Figure 3-1: Viewing the GAC folder

The `GACUtil.exe` tool which can be used in the command line, also allows to view and edit the GAC folder. `GACUtil.exe` has numerous options described on **MSDN**. For example, the –l option allows the listing of all shared assemblies while the –i option followed by the file name of an assembly containing a manifest allows the insertion of a strong named assembly in the GAC.

> Only machine administrator can modify the GAC. You can effectively visualize and modify the internal structure of the GAC from a command line window. However, it is imperative that you never try to change the structure of the GAC folder without using the `GACUtil.exe` tool or the `ShFusion.dll` shell extension.

The *native image cache* described at page 93 is included in the GAC folder. Hence, when we visualize the GAC folder using `GacUtil.exe` or the shell extension, the native images are also visualized.

Publisher policy assemblies

The underlying problem

Despite the problem known as DLL hell, the model of sharing DLLs by multiple applications does have an advantage versus the model of sharing assemblies based on the presence of a version number in the strong name.

Suppose that a developer redistributes a new version of a shared assembly because of bug fixes. This version is fully compatible with the previous one. This new version will be installed side by side with the previous one in the GAC. However, the applications will not use this new version as the version number of to use is hardcoded in their manifest.

This problem does not exist with the classic DLL approach as the old version of the DLL is simply replaced with the new version.

The solution

We could solve this problem by recompiling and reinstalling all the applications which use the shared assembly. The recompilation would allow applications to update their manifest with the new version number of the shared assembly. Obviously, this solution is impractical and another approach must be found.

The solution proposed by *Microsoft* is to create a *publisher policy assembly*. This assembly, placed in the GAC, is there only to create a redirection on the version number of another shared assembly, which is also stored in the GAC. When an application requests version 3.3.0.0 of assembly XXX it will use version 3.3.1.0 of assembly XXX, because the publisher policy assembly associated to XXX contains information to redirect 3.3.0.0 to 3.3.1.0.

The publisher policy assembly is only a configuration file and the redirection is done by the CLR. In fact, it is the CLR which takes care of locating and loading assemblies during execution. Hence, the CLR takes into consideration for publisher policies when locating assemblies.

A publisher policy assembly concerns only a single assembly. In addition, there can be multiple publisher policy assemblies for a same assembly. In this case, only the most recent version of the publisher policy assembly will be taken into account by the CLR.

The default behavior of the CLR is to take into account publisher policy assemblies. However, for a specific application which uses a shared assembly, users can decide that the CLR should not take into account the publisher policy assemblies. This is practical in the case where a user notices that a newer version creates more problems than it solves (and we all know that these situations happen!). We will discuss at page 86 how to accomplish this manipulation.

> Understand that publisher policy assemblies are necessary when a developer has lightly modified an assembly (usually to fix bugs) and has not modified the backward compatibility. Publisher policy assemblies can only be used in this specific case.

Creating your publisher policy assemblies

Concretely, a publisher policy assembly is composed of two modules. A module is an XML configuration file with a `.config` extension which contains information on the redirections for the publisher. The other module only contains a manifest and is constructed using the `al.exe` tool which we will discuss at page 30. The XML configuration file looks as follows:

Example 3-15 *Foo2.config*

```
<configuration>
   <runtime>
      <assemblyBinding xmlns="urn:schemas-microsoft-com:asm.v1">
         <dependentAssembly>
            <assemblyIdentity name="Foo2" culture= "neutral"
                              publicKeyToken="C64B742BD612D74A" />
            <bindingRedirect oldVersion="1.0.0.0" newVersion="2.0.0.0"/>
         </dependentAssembly>
      </assemblyBinding>
   </runtime>
</configuration>
```

Notice the `<assemblyIdentity>` element which contains the elements of the strong name of the assembly on which we wish to redirect (except for the version number). The `<bindingRedirect>` element redirects the version number. This element can redirect an interval of versions to a new version with the following syntax: "`0.5.0.0-1.2.23.3`". You may also use multiple `<bindingRedirect>` elements.

Introduction to .NET application deployment 55

The creation of the module of the publisher policy assembly which contains the manifest is done as follows using the `al.exe` tool:

```
>al.exe /out:policy.1.0.Foo2.dll /version:1.0.0.0 /keyfile:MyKeys.snk /
linkresource:Foo2.config
```

- The `/out` option specifies the name of the module which will contain the manifest. This name must be formed using specific rules.

    `policy` indicates to the CLR that this is a publisher policy strategy;

    `1.0` indicates to the CLR that this publisher policy applies itself to requests of the `Foo2.dll` with a 1.0 version. Only the major and minor numbers are specified here;

    `Foo2` tells the CLR that the policy applies itself to the assembly named `Foo2.dll`.

- The `/version` option applies to the publisher policy assembly itself and not `Foo2.dll`. The CLR will always take the publisher policy with the highest version number for a specific major/minor pair.

- The `/keyfile` option specifies the public/private key pair which will be used to sign the publisher policy assembly. These keys must be the same ones used to sign `Foo2.dll` to prove to the CLR that the publisher policy does in fact come from the same publisher as `Foo2.dll`. In addition, as any shared assembly stored in the GAC, the publisher policy assembly must have a strong name and thus, must be signed.

- The `/linkresource` option specifies the name of the XML configuration file which contains the redirections for the publisher policy. Understand that `Foo2.config` becomes a module of the publisher policy assembly because of this option. Concretely, the `Foo2.config` is not physically included in the `policy.1.0.Foo2.dll` module but is logically included in the `policy.1.0.Foo2` assembly.

Introduction to .NET application deployment

The *Visual Studio 2005* development environment allows the creation of projects dedicated to the deployment of applications. Six types of deployment projects are available under *File > New > Project… > Other Project Types > Setup and Deployment*:

- **Cab Project**: Creates a cab file which assembles all the files to install and compresses them into a `.cab` file. A section in the current chapter is dedicated to the deployment using `.cab` files.
- **Smart Device Cab Project**: creates a cab file specially adapted to the deployment using *Windows CE* on machines of type *Pocket PC* or *Smart Phone*.
- **Merge Module Project**: creates a *deployment module*. Such a module can be integrated into other deployment projects. This means that a deployment module can be common to several deployment projects. Note that the notion of module here isn't the same as the notion of assembly module.
- **Setup Project**: Creates a deployment project using the MSI technology. This technology allows the execution of actions in addition to copying files. A section is dedicated on MSI a little later.
- **Web Setup Project**: Allows the deployment of a web application by installing files in virtual IIS folder. The deployment of an ASP.NET web application is a special topic and we will discuss this further at page 723.
- **Setup Wizard**: This is a step by step wizard to help the construction of one of the above deployment projects.

Since its first version, the .NET platform has offered a technology named *No Touch Deployment* (*NTD*) specially designed for the deployment of applications from the internet. This technology is always available with version 2. It has not evolved as *Microsoft* preferred creating a new technology called *ClickOnce* which is better adapted to the strong constraints of internet deployment (security, bandwidth, updates…). This technology is discussed a little later in this chapter.

There are no deployment project types for NTD and *ClickOnce*. NTD is managed through a configuration file and XCopy deployment on the server allowing the download of the application. However, we will see that *Visual Studio 2005* does offer features to allow the deployment of an application using the *ClickOnce* technology. For this, you only need that the application be represented by a *Windows Forms* or console application project.

MSI vs. .cab vs. XCopy vs. ClickOnce vs. NTD

You essentially have the choice between these techniques to deploy a .NET application which isn't an ASP.NET web application. We can divide these deployment techniques into two categories:

- The **heavy deployments** deeply impact the operating system by installing assemblies in the GAC, by registering COM classes in the registry which are usable by multiple users, which require administrative privileges to install. Clearly, only the MSI technology is adapted to the deployment of these applications. For reasons of size and security, the deployment of these applications if often done from a CD rather than through a network. The user must pay the price for such a deployment: a primary security management using authenticode (if deployed from a network), update difficulties, exposition to the DLL hell problems, delays in the delivery of a CD...

- The **light deployment** of pure .NET applications has little impact on the operating system. The four technologies *cab*, *XCopy*, *ClickOnce* and *NTD* can be considered for this type of deployment. *ClickOnce* is generally recommended because of its advanced features such as the management of security, updates and bandwidth usage. Besides for reasons of backward compatibility, there isn't really any reason for which the NTD is preferred over *ClickOnce*. The *cab* and *XCopy* technologies present the advantage of being really simple for the developer and most users are used to copy and paste files. In the case of simple deployment, the use of the *cab* technology is generally preferred as it is usually simpler to deploy a single file instead of several files.

MSI vs. ClickOnce

Here is a table which should help you decide when you are unsure between a MSI deployment and a *ClickOnce* deployment. Note that these two technologies are not mutually exclusive and it is not infrequent for the prerequisites of an application to be deployed using MSI while the functional part of the application be deployed with *ClickOnce*:

Functionality	ClickOnce	MSI
Installation of files.	x	x
Creation of program menu shortcuts.	x	x
Creation of desktop shortcuts.		x
Installation of COM classes without using the registry (see page 237).	x	x
Installation of COM classes and COM+ components.		x
File extensions associations.		x
Installation of *Windows* services.		x
Installation of assemblies in the GAC.		x
ODBC management.		x
Modifications to the registry.		x
Self-Repair		x

Introduction to .NET application deployment   57

Functionality	ClickOnce	MSI
Interaction with the user during installation.		X
Choice of the installation folder.		X
Installation for all users.		X
Special actions during installation and un-installation.		X
Manipulation of rights on *Windows* objects.		X
Installation conditions and verification of the version and state of the operating system.		X
Verification and automatic download of application updates.	X	
Advanced security management using the CAS mechanism of the CLR.	X	
Partial installation of the application on-demand.	X	
Possibility of rolling back to a previous version after the install of an update.	X	

Deploying an application with a cab file

You have the possibility of adding a deployment project which uses *cab files* to our solution as shown in Figure 3-2:

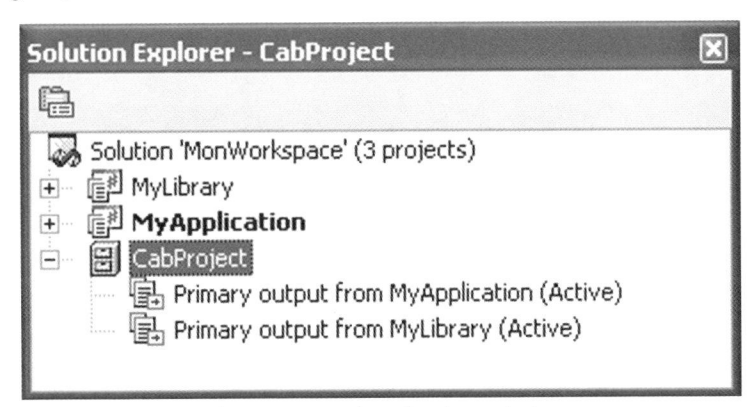

Figure 3-2: A Cab Project in a solution

You can add the files produced or contained in the other projects of the solution (*Project output*) as illustrated in Figure 3-3. Here, we have added the `MyApplication.exe` and `MyLibrary.dll` files by selecting *Primary Output* for each of these projects.

After the compilation of a cab deployment project, a file with the `.cab` extension is produced. Using an archive visualization tool, you can examine the contents of the cab file and extract the files that it contains as shown in Figure 3-4. Note that an advantage of using this type of archive is that the files contained within the archive are compressed.

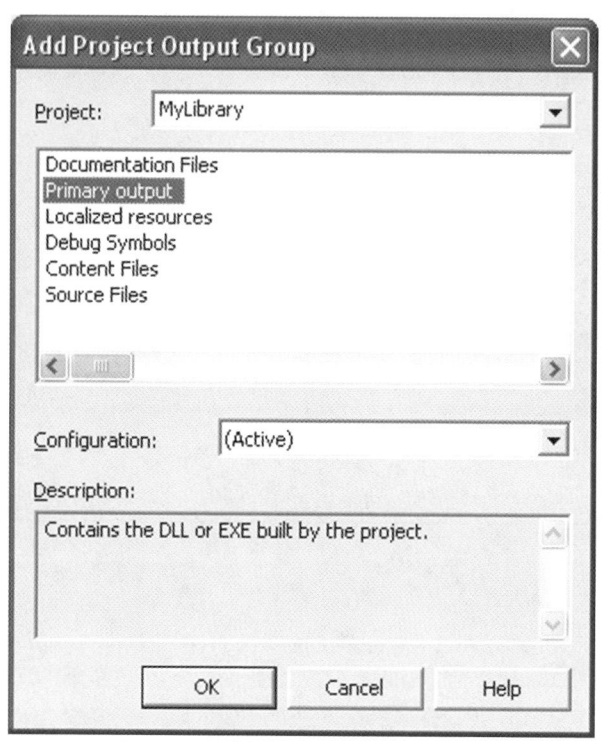

Figure 3-3: Add elements in a Cab Project

Figure 3-4: Viewing a cab file

A file with an .osd extension is contained within the cab file. This file is an XML file which describes the content of the cab file:

```
<?XML version="1.0" ENCODING='UTF-8'?>
<!DOCTYPE SOFTPKG SYSTEM "http://www.microsoft.com/standards/osd/osd.dtd">
<?XML::namespace href="http://www.microsoft.com/standards/osd/msicd.dtd"
as="MSICD"?>
<SOFTPKG NAME="CabProject" VERSION="1,0,0,0">
   <TITLE> CabProject </TITLE>
   <MSICD::NATIVECODE>
      <CODE NAME="MyApplication">
         <IMPLEMENTATION>
            <CODEBASE FILENAME="MyApplication.exe"></CODEBASE>
         </IMPLEMENTATION>
      </CODE>
   </MSICD::NATIVECODE>
   <MSICD::NATIVECODE>
      <CODE NAME="MyLibrary">
```

```
        <IMPLEMENTATION>
            <CODEBASE FILENAME="MyLibrary.dll"></CODEBASE>
        </IMPLEMENTATION>
      </CODE>
   </MSICD::NATIVECODE>
</SOFTPKG>
```

Deploying an application with the MSI technology

Add files

When you have added the setup project to your solution, you have access to the 'System File' view. This view contains three default folders: The application folder, The Desktop and the Start Menu.

The files that you will put in these folders during the construction of the setup project will be automatically copied in the corresponding folders of the target machine during installation. In general, we place in these folders the non-shared assemblies of the application and other produced files from the projects of the solution. This has been illustrated in Figure 3-5. Notice that this operation is done in the same way as it would be done with a cab deployment project.

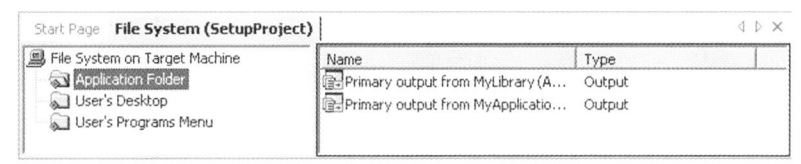

Figure 3-5: The file system view

Installing shortcuts

It is easy to add shortcuts for the desktop or start menu from the *'File System'* view. You simply need to right-click on the executable, add a shortcut and move the shortcut to the desired folder (desktop or Start Menu).

Adding a shared assembly in the GAC folder

To add a shared assembly into the GAC folder from a setup deployment project, you first must add the GAC folder to the *'File System'* view. For this, you simply need to right-click in the space reserved for the folders and to add the GAC folder, as shown in Figure 3-6. After, you simply need to add your shared assemblies to this folder. Several other special folders can also be added.

Setup project properties

There are in fact two types of setup project properties.

- The property pages accessible by using *shift-F4*. These allow to essentially manage the configuration of the setup project (Debug /Release…) and to add an *Authenticode* signature to the project.
- The setup project property window which allows the configuration of several attributes associated with the project such as its name, its culture or the publisher name as shown in Figure 3-7.

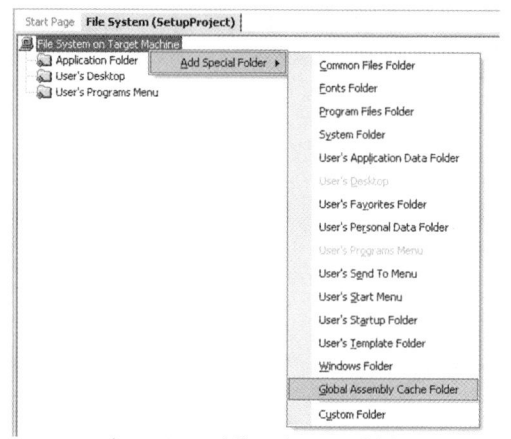

Figure 3-6: Adding the GAC folder

Figure 3-7: Setup project properties

Updating the registry

You have the possibility of adding keys relating to your application to the registry during installation. To accomplish this, you simply need to select the *Registry* view and to modify the appropriate keys as shown in Figure 3-8. Understand that most .NET applications should not use the registry.

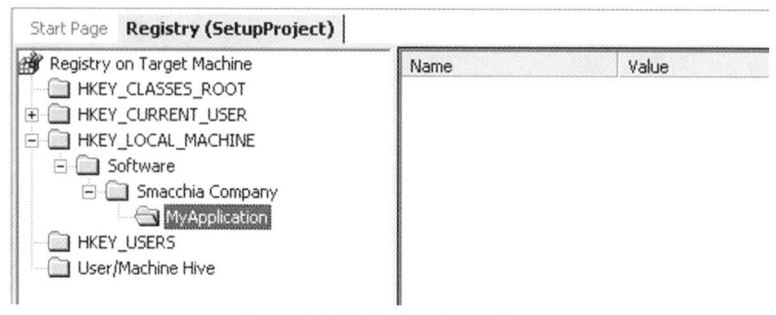

Figure 3-8: Updating the registry

Deploying an application with the MSI technology   61

Specifying custom actions to execute during installation

It can be very useful to launch an executable during the installation or un-installation of an application. For example, you may create an executable which verifies certain configuration parameters of a machine, necessary for the application to function properly. You may also wish to install a COM object during the installation and to un-register it during the uninstall process. In this particular case, you need to add the `regsvr32.exe` file to the list of installed applications. After this, you simply need to select the *Custom Actions* view and add the references as illustrated in Figure 3-9:

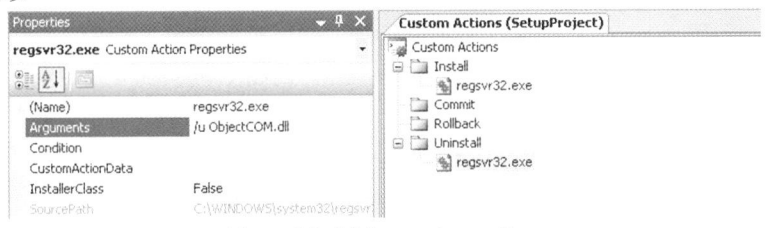

Figure 3-9: Adding custom actions

Providing a custom User Interface for installation

You can easily modify the install process by modifying the dialog windows proposed by *Visual Studio* in the *User Interface* view as illustrated in Figure 3-10. You can also add several new dialogs as shown in Figure 3-11.

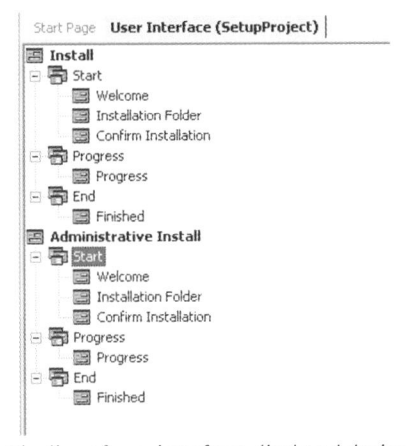

Figure 3-10: Pipeline of user interfaces displayed during installation

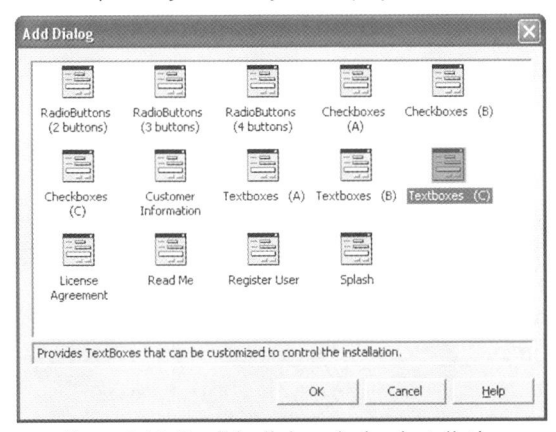

Figure 3-11: Possible dialogs during installation

Deploying an application with the ClickOnce technology

To take advantage of the *ClickOnce* technology, it is necessary to have assimilated the notions behind *Code Access Security* (CAS) discussed in chapter 6 on Security.

The deployment folder

Lets us start be describing the file structure which allows the deployment of an application using *ClickOnce*. It must be located in a deployment directory which may be a virtual IIS folder, a FTP folder, a shared network folder or even a folder on a CD. The *ClickOnce* technology requires two specific files in addition to the set of files required by the application to deploy:

- The *application manifest*: This is an XML file with an `.manifest` extension which references the files of the application and defines the set of CAS permissions necessary for its execution. Its name is the concatenation of the assembly containing the entry point to the application (including the `.exe` extension) with the `.manifest` extension.
- The *deployment manifest*: Is an XML file with an `.application.` extension which reference the application manifest file. It also contains deployment specific parameters.

These two manifest files must be digitally signed using *authenticode* to be used. This translates itself by a `<signature>` element in each of them. We discuss the *authenticode* further at page 191. You can also consult the article named **ClickOnce Deployment and Authenticode** on **MSDN**. The organization of files in the deployment folder is as follows:

```
.\MyApp_1_0_0_0.application              // Deployment manifest.
.\MyApp_1_0_0_0\MyApp.exe.manifest       // Application manifest.
.\MyApp_1_0_0_0\MyApp.exe.deploy         // Application files …
.\MyApp_1_0_0_0\MyAppClassLib.dll.deploy // … with the .deploy extension.
.\MyApp_1_0_0_0\en-US\MyApp.resources.dll.deploy
...
```

You can notice that there is a sub-folder for each version of the application. The name of this subfolder does not need to contain an indication of the version number although it is a good practice to follow. Each of these sub-folders contains the application manifest relative to the version as well as all the files to deploy for this version. A `.deploy` extension is generally added to the name of each of the files although this practice is not mandatory.

The deployment manifest is stored in the deployment folder. Since it references an application manifest that is relative to a version of the application, it is relative to a specific version of the application. Also, it is a good idea to make its name the concatenation of the name of the assembly with the entry point (without the `.exe` extension) with an indication of the version number followed by the `.application` extension. Hence, multiple deployment manifests relating to several versions of a same application can co-exist in the same deployment folder.

Preparing a ClickOnce deployment

There are several options to create the application and deployment manifest files. Here, we enumerate them from the most practical to the most tedious and error prone:

- Use the *Properties › Publish* menu in *Visual Studio 2005* on a project of type console or *Windows Forms*.
- Use the windows tool `mageui.exe` (*mage* for *Manifest Generation and Editing Tool*) available in the SDK folder of the *Visual Studio 2005* installation.
- Use the `mage.exe` command line tool available in the same folder as `mageui.exe`.
- Build the XML file by hand by using the official documentation.

Deploying an application with the ClickOnce technology 63

The `mage.exe` is peculiarly useful if you wish to integrate the creation of the manifest in an MSBuild project. The `mageui.exe` is mostly a learning tool as it allows you to obtain a precise and comprehensible view of the content of each of the manifest files. The use of these tools is described in the article named **Walkthrough: Deploying a ClickOnce Application Manually** on **MSDN**. Despite these two reasons, we recommend that you use *Visual Studio 2005* which presents the following interface:

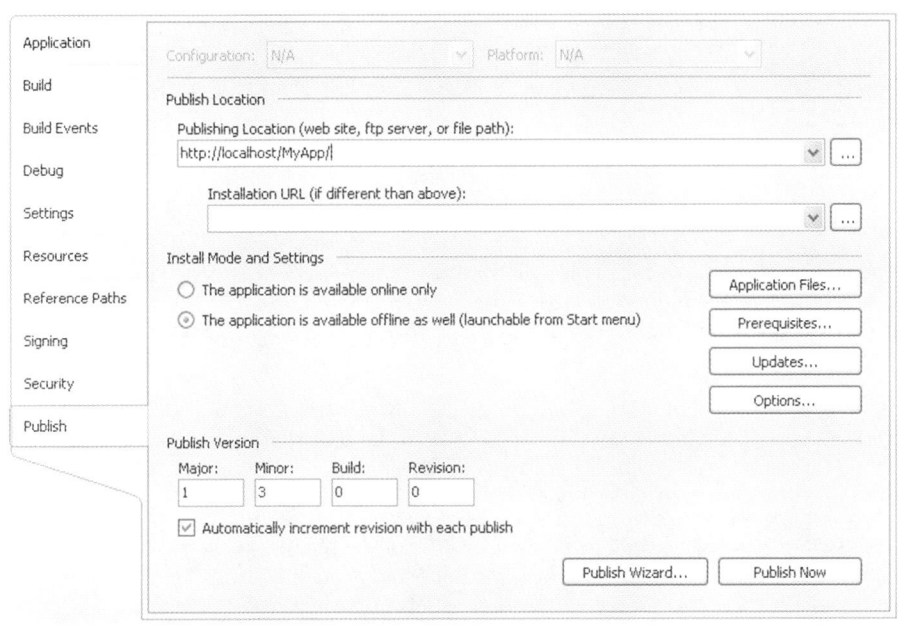

Figure 3-12: Visual Studio and ClickOnce

- **Application Files…**: Allows choosing the set of files which constitute the application. The executable assembly generated by the project is automatically part of this set. Assemblies referenced by this project, satellite assemblies generated by this project as well as all other files related to this project are part of this set. With the exception to the executable assembly, all files can be marked as a prerequisite, required or optional. In the first case, the file must be available before the installation of the application. In the second case, the file must be downloaded during the installation of the application. In the third case, the file must be part of an option group of files. These groups allow an on-demand downloading of functional parts of the application. We will come back to this a little later.

- **Prerequisites…**: Allows choosing the prerequisites to the installation of the application. Most notably, you can choose the *.NET 2.0 framework*, *SQL Server 2005 Express Edition* but also any other application, file or *framework* to be installed. *Visual Studio 2005* allows you to generate a file named `setup.exe` that is called *bootstrapper*. *ClickOnce* will offer to the client to download and execute the *bootstrapper* before the installation of the application if the machine does not have the needed pre-requisites. You can specify from where the bootstrapper must download each of the pre-requisites (deployment site, official site of the component…). Technically, the user does not need to be a machine administrator to run the *bootstrapper*. In practice, there is often a need to be administrator as the *bootstrapper* must generally install components which require an MSI installation. For more information in regards to the *bootstrapper*, read the article named **Use the Visual Studio 2005 Bootstrapper to Kick-Start Your Installation** by *Sean Draine* consultable on-line in the October 2004 edition of **MSDN Magazine**.

- **Updates…**: Allows specifying an update policy for the application. A section is dedicated on this topic a little later.

- **Options**...: Allows specifying the application parameters such as the name of the publisher, of the product, the generation of a help page, the target culture for the deployment, the use of the .deploy extension...
- **Publish Wizard**...and **Publish Now**: allows publishing the application, this means the generation of the two manifest files and the construction of the file structure that we discussed earlier. You must publish your application in a deployment folder for each supported culture. You can choose if the deployment folder will be a virtual IIS folder, a FTP folder or a standard *Windows* folder than you can then duplicate onto a CD.

This interface allows you to choose if an application is available *offline*. In this case, a shortcut to the application is installed in the program menu and the user does not need to be connected online to launch the application.

ClickOnce deployment and mobile code security

To deploy an application on a machine, you simply need to execute the deployment manifest file. In a case of a web deployment, this is generally done by the intermediary of a link to this file. In the other case, you simply need to double-click on this file (from a FTP folder, a shared network drive or a folder on a CD).

Unless the two manifest files have been signed by a X.509 certificate which is verifiable by the target machine, a dialog box will appear indicating to the user that the application that is about to be installed has been developed by an unknown publisher. The user then has the choice of continuing with the installation or not.

If the application publisher could be verified because of the certificate, the totality of permissions requested in the manifest is allowed. The same happens for an application installed from a CD. If not, a certain set of CAS can be granted by the CAS security policy. All depends on the zone from which the installation is done (*internet untrusted, internet trusted, intranet*...).

If the set of permissions described in the manifest cannot completely be granted to the application, then a dialog box appears to inform the user. If he chooses to continue with the installation, the necessary permissions as described in the application will be granted for each execution, if not the installation is aborted.

Once these two potential barriers have been passes (we are at up to three clicks now in the worst case ☺), *ClickOnce* installs the application in a folder dedicated to this application. We will discuss the topic of where this folder is located a little later. A shortcut to the application is installed in the program menu if the application is available *offline*. The application can be uninstalled from the *Add/Remove Programs* menu. The deployment manifest has the possibility of specifying that the application must be started once the installation is completed.

The application is only installed for the current user. If multiple users on a same machine need the same application, it will need to be installed for each of them in separate folders.

The application of machine security policies is only done during the installation and during the update of an application. Once an application is installed, it will use the permissions specified in the application manifest at each execution.

Contrarily to MSI, you cannot personalize the deployment process of an application when using *ClickOnce*. Practically, you cannot supply any dialogs allowing for example your users to specify the installation folder for your application. This was done to ensure a maximum level of security.

On-demand installation and download group

We have seen that a file belonging to an application can be marked as optional. In this case, it is part of a group of optional files. All the files of such a group are downloaded explicitly by the code of the application when one this file is needed for the first time. This is on-demand installation.

The *framework* represented by the `System.Deployment` namespace allows for the code of your application to download a group of files of the application that has not yet been installed. This code must be executed during the triggering of an `AppDomain.AssemblyResolve` or `AppDomain.ResourceResolve` events. We often talk of transactional installation of a group of files since they are all installed or not.

The following example exposes an executable assembly named `MyApp` which references a library assembly named `MyLib`. Let us suppose that in a *ClickOnce* deployment project, `MyLib` is part of an optional group of files named `MyGroup`. The code of the `AssemblyResolveHandler()` method is triggered during the first execution of `MyApp`, when `MyLib` is not found. The code downloads the files of the `MyGroup` group and then returns the `MyLib` assembly.

Note the necessity of the presence of the `Foo` class. If we would not be using an intermediate class to invoke `MyClass`, the JIT would compile the `Program` class before executing the `Main()` method. Hence, the `AssemblyResolve` event would be triggered even before the `AssemblyResolveHandler()` method could be registered:

Example 3-16 *MyLib.cs*

```
public class MyClass {
   public override string ToString() {
      return "Hello from MyLib.";
   }
}
```

Example 3-17 *MyApp.cs*

```
using System;
using System.Reflection;
using System.Deployment.Application;
class Program {
   public static void Main() {
      AppDomain.CurrentDomain.AssemblyResolve += AssemblyResolveHandler;
      Console.WriteLine("Hello from MyApp.");
      Foo.FooFct();
   }
   static Assembly AssemblyResolveHandler(object sender,
                                          ResolveEventArgs args) {
      if ( ApplicationDeployment.IsNetworkDeployed ) {
         // The 'CurrentDeployement' property returns null
         // when the application is not deployed hence the test
         // for the property 'IsNetworkDeployed'.
         ApplicationDeployment currentDeployment =
            ApplicationDeployment.CurrentDeployment;
         currentDeployment.DownloadFileGroup("MyGroup");
         Console.WriteLine("Downloading...");
      }
      return Assembly.Load("MyLib");;
   }
}
class Foo {
   public static void FooFct() {
      MyClass a = new MyClass();
```

Example 3-17   MyApp.cs
```
        Console.WriteLine(a);
    }
}
```

Updating an application installed with ClickOnce

The *Visual Studio 2005* tools `mageui.exe` and `mage.exe` allow you to specify the way an application deployed with *ClickOnce* manages its updates. You can specify when the application must verify if updates are available (at each execution or periodically). You can also specify when these updates must be downloaded:

- After the start of the application for the quick start up of the execution but for the updates to be taken into account during the next execution.
- Or before the start of an application to ensure that the users always execute the most recent version of the application although this may come at the expense of a slowdown at startup.

During the update of an application, the *ClickOnce* only downloads the files which have changed. This means that the set of permissions granted during the installation of an application are automatically inherited by the future updates. Finally, as soon as an application is updated once, *ClickOnce* starts storing on the machine the necessary data to potentially roll back to the previous version. This means that the user does not take any risks by updating an application as she can always elect to go back to the previous version.

Facilities to work with the CAS permission set required by an application

Visual Studio 2005 console or *Windows Forms* projects offer a menu *Properties > Security* which greatly simplifies the management of CAS permissions during the development of an application:

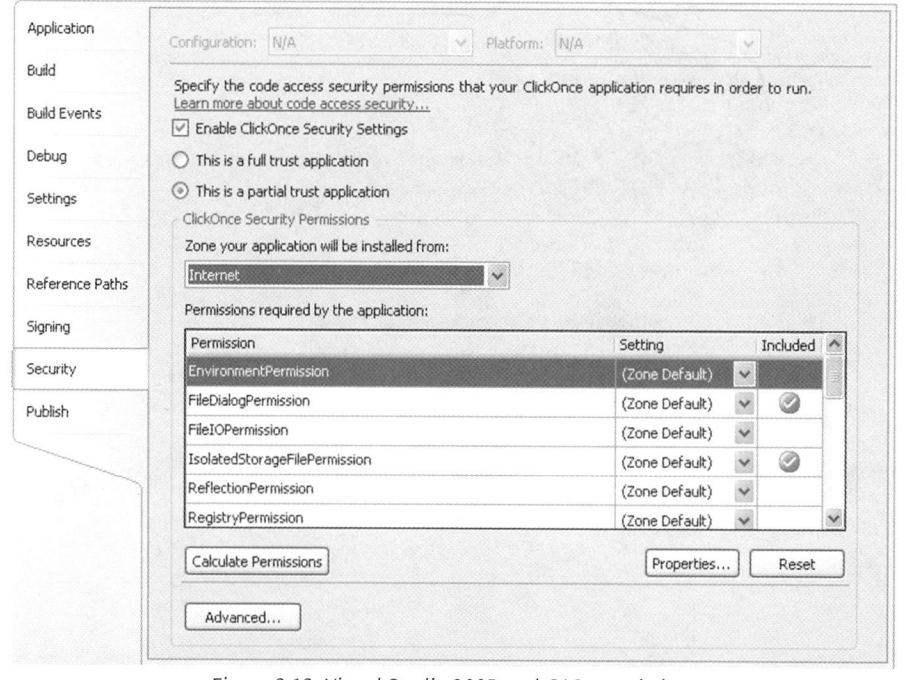

Figure 3-13: Visual Studio 2005 and CAS permissions

Deploying an application with the ClickOnce technology 67

The menu allows specifying if an application needs `FullTrust` permissions to be executed. In the second case, a grid helps you define the exact set of permissions needed by the application to execute. It is this set of permissions which will be specified in the application manifest. When one type of permission is selected, you can click the *Properties* button to obtain a window which allows the configuration of the permission.

Visual Studio 2005 helps you comparing this set with the set of permission defined by the default security policies. For this, you must chose from which zone the application will be deployed. A warning will let you know when a permissions that is not granted by default to the selected security zone. A warning means that during the installation from this zone, the *ClickOnce* will ask the user to choose if she wishes to raise the set of permission, which always leaves a bad impression!

It is difficult to determine the exact set of permissions that an application needs to execute properly. The `permcalc.exe` tool supplied with *Visual Studio 2005* allows you to determine the needed permissions by analyzing the IL code of the executable assembly as well as the code of referenced assemblies. Depending on the size of your application, this process can take some time, maybe even a few minutes. You can use this command line tool to construct the set of permissions into an XML file. This content can then be integrated into the application manifest. The *Calculate Permissions* button of the *Security* panel allows the invocation of this tool and to obtain the results directly into the permission grid.

Visual Studio 2005 allows you to debug your application within the security context defined by the set of permissions that you have defined in the *Security* menu. This feature is very practical since it is also the security context in which the application will be executed by your clients. For this, *Visual Studio 2005* generates during the compilation an assembly named `[Applicaiton name].vshost.exe` in the output folder which also contains the `[Application name].exe` assembly. It is this *VSHost* executable assembly which is launched when *Visual Studio 2005* debugs the application. It is needed to set the proper permissions before loading and executing the application.

Finally, know that *Visual Studio 2005*'s intellisense takes into account the set of permissions defined in the *Security* menu. Concretely, it will grey out the classes and methods of the *framework* which requires permissions that have not been granted.

Details on ClickOnce application installation and execution

If you open the task manager on machine which is executing an application named XXX that has been deployed with *ClickOnce*, you can notice that there isn't a current process named XXX.exe. In fact, a *ClickOnce* application which does not have `FullTrust` is executed within a process named `AppLaunch.exe`. This process takes care of the set of CAS permissions granted to the application. The added menu for an application deployed with *ClickOnce* references to a *Windows application reference* file with an `.appref-ms` extension. When such a file is opened, *Windows* executes COM objects defined in the `dfshim.dll` component which takes care of launching `AppLaunch.exe`.

During the launch of an application deployed with *ClickOnce* you can also notice the appearance of a process named `dfsvc.exe`. This is the execution engine for *ClickOnce*. This is the process which takes care of the verification and download of updates. This process automatically destroys itself after 15 minutes of inactivity.

The files of an application deployed with *ClickOnce* are installed in a sub-folder of the *ClickOnce deployed application cache*. This cache is specific to each user and has a limited size (of about 100 MB). This folder is located at `\Documents and Settings\[User Name]\Local Settings\Apps\`. The name of an application sub-folder is composed from a hashing value determined on the application during the installation. An association between this folder and the application reference file is stored in the registry. You can find this folder through the `AppDomain.CurrentDomain.BaseDirectory` which specifies the folder where the application assembly is stored. During the update of an application, a new sibling folder is created and *ClickOnce* makes sure that there are only two folders dedicated to this application: the one for the previous version and the one for the current version.

During the deployment of an application, *ClickOnce* sees the difference between the files specific to the application (essentially the structure of referenced assemblies obtained from the executable assembly and its satellite assemblies) and the data files for the application (configuration files, database files, XML files…). The data files are deployed in a sub-folder of the *ClickOnce deployed application data* (which is \Documents and Settings\[User Name]\Local Settings\Apps\ Data). This application data folder can be accessed through the string ApplicationDeployment. DataDirectory{get;} and string System.Windows.Forms.Application.LocalUserAppDa taPath{get;} properties. An application must have the proper CAS permissions for this folder for it to take advantage of the data. For this reason, you can prefer to use the isolated storage mechanism described at page 170 which requires the isolated storage permission only. Indeed, this permission is granted by default to the *internet* and *intranet* zones.

During the update of an application, the old data files are copied to the new data folder. If *ClickOnce* downloads a new version of a data file, it will overwrite the old version. However, to avoid the loss of data, the old version is copied into a sub-folder named inc.

Deploying and application with the No Touch Deployment (NTD) technology

When the .NET *framework* is installed on a machine, you can start a downloadable assembly directly from internet explorer. This feature is named *No Touch Deployment* (*NTD*).

Lets us suppose that the Foo.exe assembly which contains the following code is downloaded from the following URL: www.smacchia.com/Foo.exe. We will use the fact that the Assembly. CodeBase property contains the URL from which the assembly has been downloaded:

Example 3-18   *Foo.cs*

```
using System.Reflection;
using System.Windows.Forms;
class Program {
   static void Main() {
      Assembly asm = Assembly.GetExecutingAssembly();
      MessageBox.Show("My CodeBase is:" + asm.CodeBase);
   }
}
```

Opening internet explorer on this URL is illustrated by the following:

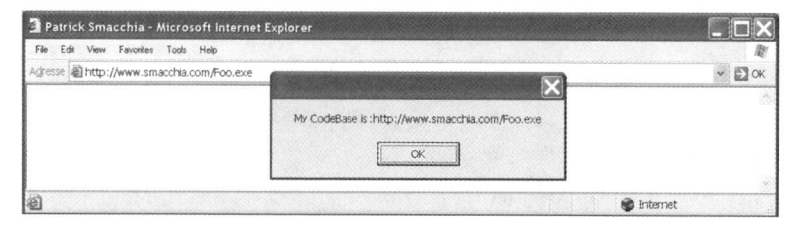

Figure 3-14: Executing an assembly downloaded from the web

You can notice that *internet explorer* did not ask your permission to download and start the assembly. In fact, the executable was deemed to be a .NET assembly and has delegated the management of security to the CLR. The CLR is hosted within the *internet explorer* process by a special run-time host introduced at page 77.

The execution of the Foo.exe assembly does not require any sensitive permissions and the CLR does interrupt its execution as the default security policy allows the execution of an assembly downloaded from the web as long as it does not require any special permissions. However, the CLR would not have allowed the execution of a sensitive operation, such as the access of a file on the hard disk or the modification of the registry, unless the security policy granted a certain trust to the www.smacchia.com site. An assembly executed from the web cannot have a strong name.

The download cache

When an assembly is downloaded for the first time from the web, it is automatically stored in the *download cache*. The download cache is a folder entirely managed by the CLR. The download cache is independent from the *internet explorer* cache as well as the various caches of the *ClickOnce* technology. The advantages of the download cache are the following:

- It avoids having to download an assembly accessible from the web each time it must be executed, hence the notion of cache.
- It allows physically isolating the assemblies downloaded from the web from other assemblies.

The download cache has two main differences in regards to the GAC folder:

- The GAC folder is global to a machine. There can only be one folder per machine. However, the CLR makes sure there is one download cache per user of a machine meaning that there can be multiple download caches on a machine.
- The CLR grants more trust to the assemblies contained in the GAC folder than to assemblies contained in the download cache.

Finally, know that the /ldl option of the gacutil.exe tool allows you to visualize the contents of the download cache:

```
C:>gacutil.exe /ldl
Microsoft (R) .NET Global Assembly Cache Utility.  Version 2.0.50727
Copyright (C) Microsoft Corporation 1998-2002. All rights reserved.
The cache of downloaded files contains the following entries:
    Foo.exe, Version=0.0.0.0, Culture=neutral, PublicKeyToken=null,
    Custom=null
Number of items = 1
```

For more information of the *No-Touch Deployment* technology, you can read the article named **No-Touch Deployment in the .NET Framework** on **MSDN**.

What if the .NET runtime is not installed on the target machine?

During the compilation of a MSI project, the compiler displays the following waning:

```
WARNING: This setup does not contain the .NET Framework which must be installed on the
target machine by running dotnetfx.exe before this setup will install. You can find
dotnetfx.exe on the Visual Studio .NET 'Windows Components Update' media. Dotnetfx.exe
can be redistributed with your setup.
```

This means that during the installation of the .NET application, the .NET *framework* will not be installed on the target machine. All .NET applications need the .NET *framework* to be installed on the machine to be executed.

The warning lets us know that to install the .NET *framework* on the target machine, you need to execute the program named **dotnetfx.exe**. This file can be freely distributed.

- **dotnetfx.exe** can be found in the folder \wcu\dotNetFramework\dotnetfx.exe if you obtained .NET from a DVD.
- **dotnetfx.exe** can be found in the folder \dotNetFramework\dotnetfx.exe if you obtained .NET from a CD.
- **dotnetfx.exe** can also be easily downloaded from the *Microsoft* site.

This file weights about 23 MB. There is such a file for each .NET version. Of course, you need the .NET 2 *framework* installed before the installation of a .NET application, no matter which deployment technology is used. In the case of a *ClickOnce* deployment we have seen that you can require the presence of the *framework* as a pre-requisite. If not, you must supply **dotnetfx.exe** for example on the CD distributed or supply a link to allow the client to download and install it.

4 The CLR (Common Language Runtime)

The CLR (*Common Language Runtime*) is the central element to the .NET platform architecture. The CLR is a software layer which manages the execution of .NET application code. The word 'manage' covers a wide range of operations needed for the execution of managed applications. Here are a few:

- Hosting of multiple applications in a single *Windows* process;
- Compilation of IL code into machine language code;
- Exception management;
- Destruction of unused objects;
- Loading of applications and assemblies;
- Resolving of types.

The CLR is conceptually close to what is commonly known as the *virtual machine* in Java.

Application Domains (AppDomain)

Introduction

An application domain (which we will commonly refer to as an *AppDomain*) can be seen as a *lightweight process*. A *Windows* process can contain many AppDomains. The notion of AppDomain is used so that a physical server can host several applications. For example, ASP.NET takes advantage of AppDomains to host, within a single process, a multitude of web applications. In fact, the *Microsoft* stress tests create up to 1000 simple web applications within a single process. The performance gain from the use of AppDomains is two fold:

- The creation of an AppDomain requires less system resources than the creation of a *Windows* process.
- AppDomains hosted in the same *Windows* process share the same resources such as the CLR, the base .NET types, the addressing space and threads.

When an assembly is executed, the CLR automatically creates a *default AppDomain* for the execution. Each AppDomain has a name and the default AppDomain has the name of the executed assembly (including the `.exe` extension).

If a single assembly is loaded within multiple AppDomains, there are two possible behaviors:

- Either the CLR will load the assembly multiple times, once for each AppDomain in the process.
- Either the CLR will load the assembly a single time outside of all the AppDomains in the process. The assembly can then be used by all the AppDomains within the process. Such an assembly is said to be *domain neutral*.

We'll see a little later in this chapter that the choice of this behavior can be configured. The default behavior being to load the assembly multiple times as needed.

Threads and AppDomains

Do not confuse the notions of 'threads' and 'application domains'.

There is no notion of ownership between the threads of a process and the AppDomains within this process. Let us remind you that this is not the case for processes since the threads belong to a single process and that each process can have one or multiple threads. In reality, a thread is not confined to a single AppDomain and that at any given time, multiple threads can execute within the context of the same AppDomain.

Let there be two AppDomains DA and DB hosted within the same process. Suppose that a method from object A, for which the assembly is contained in DA, calls a method of object B, where the assembly resides in DB. In this case, the same thread will execute both the caller and the called methods. This thread will essentially cross the boundary between the DA and DB AppDomains.

In other words, the concepts of threads and AppDomains are orthogonal.

Unloading an AppDomain

Once an assembly is loaded inside an AppDomain, you cannot unload it from this AppDomain. However, you can unload an AppDomain as a whole. This operation has some big consequences since the threads which are currently executing within the AppDomain must be aborted by the CLR and problems can occur when some of these are executing non-managed code. All managed objects within the application domain must also be garbage collected.

We recommend against having an architecture which depends on the frequent load/unload of AppDomains. We'll see that type of architecture is sometimes a necessary evil when implementing servers which require a high availability rate (99,999% of the time such as *SQL Server 2005*).

AppDomains and isolation

Isolation between AppDomains comes from the following characteristics:

- An AppDomain can be unloaded independently from other AppDomains.
- An AppDomain does not have access to assemblies and objects from other AppDomains.
- An AppDomain can have its own exception management strategy as long as it does not let an exception exit from its bounds meaning that problems from within an AppDomain will not affect the other domains within the same process.
- Each AppDomain can define its own security strategy for code access to an assembly.
- Each AppDomain can define its own rules in regard to how the CLR will locate the assemblies before loading them.

The System.AppDomain class

An instance of the `System.AppDomain` class is a reference to an AppDomain within the current process. The static property `CurrentDomain{get;}` of this class allows you to get a reference to the current AppDomain. The following example illustrates the use of this class to enumerate the assemblies loaded in the current AppDomain:

Example 4-1

```
using System;
using System.Reflection; // For the Assembly class.
class Program {
   static void Main() {
      AppDomain curAppDomain = AppDomain.CurrentDomain;
      foreach ( Assembly assembly in curAppDomain.GetAssemblies() )
         Console.WriteLine( assembly.FullName );
   }
}
```

Hosting several applications in a single process

The `AppDomain` class contains the `CreateDomain()` static method that allows the creation of a new AppDomain within the current process. This method offers multiple overloaded variations. To use this method, you must specify the following:

- (mandatory) A name for your AppDomain;
- (optional) The security rules for the CAS on this new AppDomain (with an object of type `System.Security.Policy.Evidence`);
- (optional) Information that allows the location mechanism of the CLR for this AppDomain (with an object of type `System.AppDomainSetup`).

The two important properties of a `System.AppDomainSetup` are:

- `ApplicationBase`: This property defines the base directory for the AppDomain. This directory is used by the assembly locating mechanism of the CLR when loading assemblies into this AppDomain.
- `ConfigurationFile`: This property references a configuration file for the AppDomain. This file is a XML file containing information about versioning and locating rules to be used in the AppDomain.

Now that you know how to create an application domain, we can present to you how you can load and execute an assembly within this domain by calling the `System.AppDomain.ExecuteAssembly()` method. The assembly must be an executable and the flow of execution will start at its entry point. Note that the thread calling `ExecuteAssembly()` will be executing the loaded assembly. This illustrates how a thread can cross the boundaries between AppDomains.

Here is a C# example. The first piece of code is the assembly which will be loaded by the assembly defined in the second segment of code:

Example 4-2 *AssemblyToLoad.exe*

```
using System;
using System.Threading;
public class Program {
   public static void Main() {
      Console.WriteLine(
         "Thread:{0} Hi from the domain: {1}",
         Thread.CurrentThread.Name,
         AppDomain.CurrentDomain.FriendlyName);
   }
}
```

Example 4-3 *AssemblyLoader.exe*

```
using System;
using System.Threading;
public class Program {
   public static void Main() {
      // Name the current thread.
      Thread.CurrentThread.Name = "MyThread";
      // Create an AppDomainSetup instance.
      AppDomainSetup info = new AppDomainSetup();
      info.ApplicationBase = "file:///"+ Environment.CurrentDirectory;
      // Create a new appdomain without security parameters.
      AppDomain newDomain = AppDomain.CreateDomain(
               "NewDomain", null, info);
      Console.WriteLine(
```

Example 4-3   *AssemblyLoader.exe*

```
         "Thread:{0} Calling  ExecuteAssembly() from appdomain {1}",
         Thread.CurrentThread.Name,
         AppDomain.CurrentDomain.FriendlyName );
      // Load the assembly 'AssemblyACharger.exe' inside
      // 'NewDomain' and then execute it.
      newDomain.ExecuteAssembly( "AssemblyToLoad.exe" );
      // Unload the new domain.
      AppDomain.Unload( newDomain );
   }
}
```

This example will display the following:

```
Thread:MyThread Calling ExecuteAssembly() from appdomain AssemblyLoader.exe
Thread:MyThread Hi from the domain: NewDomain
```

Note the need to add "`file:///`" to specify that the assembly is located on a local storage device. If this was not the case, we could have used "`http:///`" to load the assembly from the web.

This example also illustrates that the default name for an AppDomain is the name of the main module from the launched assembly (in this case, `AssemblyLoader.exe`).

Running some code inside the context of another AppDomain

Thanks to the instance method `AppDomain.DoCallBack()` you have the possibility of executing code of the assembly within the current AppDomain in the context of another application domain. For this, the code must be contained within a method which will be referenced through a `System.CrossAppDomainDelegate` delegate. The process is illustrated with the following example:

Example 4-4

```
using System;
using System.Threading;
public class Program {
   public static void Main() {
      Thread.CurrentThread.Name = "MyThread";
      AppDomain newDomain = AppDomain.CreateDomain( "NewDomain" );
      CrossAppDomainDelegate deleg = new CrossAppDomainDelegate(Fct);
      newDomain.DoCallBack(deleg);
      AppDomain.Unload( newDomain );
   }
   public static void Fct() {
      Console.WriteLine(
         "Thread:{0} execute Fct() inside the appdomain {1}",
         Thread.CurrentThread.Name,
         AppDomain.CurrentDomain.FriendlyName);
   }
}
```

This example displays the following:

```
Thread:MyThread execute Fct() inside the appdomain  NewDomain
```

Be aware that the possibility of 'injecting' code within an AppDomain can cause a security exception to be raised if you do not have the required security privileges.

Events of the AppDomain class

The `AppDomain` class exposes the following events:

Event.	Description
`AssemblyLoad`	Triggered when an assembly has been loaded.
`AssemblyResolve`	Triggered when an assembly to be loaded cannot be found.
`DomainUnload`	Triggered when the AppDomain is about to be unloaded.
`ProcessExit`	Triggered when the process terminates (triggered before `DomainUnload`).
`ReflectionOnly-AssemblyResolve`	Triggered when the resolution of an assembly destined to be used by the reflection mechanism fails.
`ResourceResolve`	Triggered when a resource cannot be found.
`TypeResolve`	Triggered when a type cannot be found.
`UnhandledException`	Triggered when an exception is not handled by the code in the AppDomain.

Some of these events can be used to remedy to the source of the problem that has triggered the event. The following example illustrates how to use the `AssemblyResolve` event to allow an assembly to load from a location which was not initially specified to the CLR's location mechanism:

Example 4-5

```
using System;
using System.Reflection;   // For the Assembly class.
public class Program {
   public static void Main() {
      AppDomain.CurrentDomain.AssemblyResolve += AssemblyResolve;
      Assembly.Load("AssemblyToLoad.dll");
   }
   public static Assembly AssemblyResolve( object sender,
                                    ResolveEventArgs e ) {
      Console.WriteLine("Can't find assembly : {0}", e.Name);
      return Assembly.LoadFrom(@"C:\AppDir\ThisAssemblyToLoad.dll");
   }
}
```

If the second load attempt succeeds, no exception is thrown. The name of the assembly loaded on the second attempt isn't necessarily the same as the one we initially attempted to load.

At page 432, we'll show you a program taking advantage of the `UnhandledException` event.

At page 65, we explain that classes in the `System.Deployment` namespace can make use of the `AssemblyResolve` and `ResourceResolve` events to dynamically download a group of files when an application taking advantage of the *ClickOnce* technology is run for the first time.

Sharing information between the AppDomains of a same process

Taking advantage of the `SetData()` and `GetData()` methods of the `AppDomain` class, you can store data directly within an AppDomain. As shows the following example, data within the AppDomain is indexed based on a character string:

Example 4-6

```
using System;
using System.Threading;
public class Program {
   public static void Main() {
      AppDomain newDomain = AppDomain.CreateDomain("NewDomain");
      CrossAppDomainDelegate deleg = new CrossAppDomainDelegate(Fct);
      newDomain.DoCallBack(deleg);
      // Fetch from the new appdomain the data named 'AnInteger'.
      int anInteger = (int) newDomain.GetData("AnInteger");
      AppDomain.Unload(newDomain);
   }
   public static void Fct() {
      // This method is ran inside the appdomain 'NewDomain'. It creates
      // an appdomain data named 'AnInteger' which has the value '691'.
      AppDomain.CurrentDomain.SetData("AnInteger", 691);
   }
}
```

This example shows a simple case as we are storing an integer which is a type known by all AppDomains. The .NET *Remoting* technology (which is covered in chapter 22) allows us to share data between AppDomains in a more evolved yet complex way.

Loading the CLR inside a Windows process with the runtime host

mscorsvr.dll and mscorwks.dll

Each version of the CLR is published with two DLLs:

- The `mscorsvr.dll` DLL contains a version of the CLR specially optimized for multi-processor machines ('svr' is used for 'server').
- The `mscorwks.dll` DLL contains a version of the CLR optimized for machines with a single processor ('wks' is used for 'workstation').

These two DLLs are not assemblies and consequently do not contain any IL code (and cannot be analyzed with the `ildasm.exe` tool). Each process which executes one or many .NET application will contain one of these two DLLs. We say that the process is hosting the CLR. Let us explain how this DLL is loaded into a process.

The mscorlib.dll assembly

Another DLL that plays a crucial role in the execution of .NET applications is `mscorlib.dll` which is an assembly containing implementations of all base types in the .NET *framework* (such as `System.String System.Object` or `System.Int32`). This assembly is referenced by every other .NET assembly. This reference is automatically created by every compiler producing IL code. It is an interesting task to analyze the `mscorlib` assembly using the `ildasm.exe` tool. Let us precise that the `mscorlib` resides for execution outside of all AppDomains and thus can only be loaded/unloaded once during the lifetime of a process.

Introduction to the runtime host

The fact that the CLR is not yet integrated into any operating system means that the loading of the CLR at the creation of a process must be handled by the *process* itself.

The task of loading the CLR into the process involves an entity called the *runtime host*. The runtime host being there to load the CLR, a portion if its code must be unmanaged since it is the CLR that will handle managed code. This portion of code takes care of loading the CLR, configuring it and then transferring the current thread into managed mode. Once the CLR is loaded, the runtime host has other responsibilities such dealing with untrapped exceptions. The illustration bellow illustrates the different layers of this architecture. As you can see, the CLR and the runtime host exchange data through an API:

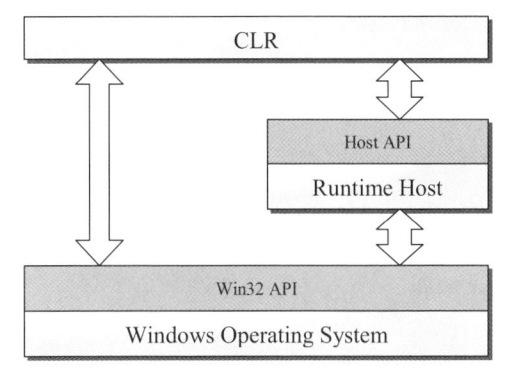

Figure 4-1: Hosting the CLR

There are several existing runtime hosts and you can even create your own. The choice of runtime host will have an impact on your application's performance and will define which functionalities are available to your application. The pre-existing runtime hosts provided by *Microsoft* are:

- The **Console** and **Winform** runtime host: The executed assembly is launched in the default AppDomain. When an assembly is implicitly loaded, it is loaded in the same domain as the referring assembly. Generally, this type of application does not need to use an AppDomain other than the default one.

- The **ASP.NET** runtime host: Create an AppDomain for each web application. A web application is identified by its ASP.NET virtual directory. If a web request is issued to an application that is already loaded, then the request is automatically routed to this AppDomain by the host.

- The **Microsoft Internet Explorer** runtime host: By default, this host creates one AppDomain for each web site visited. This allows each site to have different security levels. The CLR is only loaded once *Internet Explorer* needs to execute an assembly for the first time.

- The **SQL Server 2005** runtime host: Requests to the database can be written in IL code. The CLR is only loaded the first time that such a request must be executed. An AppDomain is created for every user/database pair. In the current chapter we will have the opportunity to come back to discuss the possibilities of this particular host that has been introduced in .NET 2.

Hosting several versions of the CLR on a single machine

The `mscorlib` assembly is strongly named meaning that many versions can co-exist side by side on the same machine. In addition, all versions of the CLR reside in the '`%windir%\Microsoft.NET\Framework`' directory. All files relating to a specific version of the .NET *framework* exist in a sub-folder named based on the version number. Since there is one directory for each version of the .NET *framework* installed on a machine, there can be multiple versions of both the `mscorsvr.dll` and `mscorwks.dll`. However, only a single version of the CLR can be loaded in each process.

The fact that you can have multiple versions of the CLR brings the existence of a small software layer which takes in as a parameter the desired version of the CLR and takes care of loading it. This code is called a *shim* and is stored in the `mscoree.dll` DLL (*MSCOREE* means *Microsoft Component Object Runtime Execution Engine*).

There can only be one shim DLL per machine and it is called through the runtime host via the `CorBindToRuntimeEx()` function. The `mscoree.dll` DLL contains COM interfaces and classes and `CorBindToRuntimeEx()` essentially creates an instance the `CorRuntimeHost` COM class for the requested version. It is through this object that you will interface with the CLR. To manipulate this object, the `CorBindToRuntimeEx()` function returns the `ICLRRuntimeHost` COM interface.

The call `CorBindToRuntimeEx()` used to create the COM objects interfacing with the CLR breaks a few fundamental COM rules: you must not call the `CoCreateInstance()` function to create your object. In addition, calling `AddRef()` and `Release()` on this interface has no effect.

Loading the CLR with the CorBindToRuntimeEx() function

Here is the prototype to the `CorBindToRuntimeEx()` which takes care of loading the shim DLL which in turns loads up the CLR:

```
HRESULT CorBindToRuntimeEx(
    LPWSTR      pwszVersion,
    LPWSTR      pwszBuildFlavor,
    DWORD       flags,
    REFCLSID    rclsid,
    REFIID      riid,
    LPVOID *    ppv);
```

This prototype is defined in the file `mscoree.h` and the code to this function is located in `mscoree.dll`.

- PwszVersion: Indicates the version of the CLR formatted as a string starting with the 'v' character (for example "v2.0.50727"). If this string is not defined (i.e. you passed null to the function), the most recent version of the CLR will be used.

- PwszBuildFlavor: This parameter indicates if you want to load the workstation (`mscorwks.dll`) version of the CLR by specifying the string "wks" or the server CLR (`mscorsvr.dll`) by specifying the string "svr". If you have a machine with a single processor the workstation version will be loader no matter which version you specify. *Microsoft* used a string parameter to allow future expansion with other new kinds of CLR.

- flags: This parameter is constructed from a set of various flags.

    By using the STARTUP_CONCURRENT_GC flag, you are indicating that you wish the *garbage collector* be executed in a concurrent mode. This mode allows a thread to complete a big part of the garbage collection work without interrupting the other threads of the application. In the case of a non-concurrent execution, the CLR often uses the application threads to execute garbage collection. The overall performance of the non-concurrent mode is better but may cause occasional lack of responsiveness from the user interface.

    We can also set other flags to indicate that we wish for assemblies to be loaded in a neutral way in regards to application domains or not. This means that all resources from the assembly will be present physically only once in the process even if multiple AppDomains load the same assembly (in the same spirit as the mapping of DLL across *Windows* applications). An assembly loaded neutrally does not belong to a specific AppDomain. This brings up the main disadvantage being that it cannot be unloaded without destroying the current process. However, the same set of security permissions must be used by each AppDomain or the assembly may be loaded

Loading the CLR inside a Windows process with the runtime host 79

multiple times. The constructor of each class in a neutrally loaded assembly is invoked for each AppDomain and a copy of every static field will exist for each domain. Internally, this is possible because of an indirection table that is managed by the CLR. This may result in a small performance loss because of the added indirection but considering the assembly will be loaded only a single time it will consume less system resources such as memory and may have some performance benefits as the assembly will only go through the JIT compiler once.

This means there is three possible flags:

STARTUP_LOADER_OPTIMIZATION_SINGLE_DOMAIN: No assemblies are loaded in a domain neutral fashion. This is the default behavior.

STARTUP_LOADER_OPTIMIZATION_MULTI_DOMAIN: All assemblies are loaded in a domain neutral fashion. No runtime hosting engine currently uses this option.

STARTUP_LOADER_OPTIMIZATION_MULTI_DOMAIN_HOST: Only shared assemblies found in the GAC are loaded domain neutral.

The mscorlib assembly is treated differently as it is always loaded neutrally.

- rclsid: The class ID (CLSID) of the COM class (coclass) that implements the CLR hosting interface desired. Only CLSID_CorRuntimeHost, CLSID_CLRRuntimeHost or null are valid values. The second value appeared with version 2.0 of .NET since new functionality was needed for the hosting of the CLR in *SQL Server 2005*.

- pwszBuildFlavor: The interface ID (IID) of the COM interface that you need. The only valid values are IID_CorRuntimeHost, IID_CLRRuntimeHost or null.

- ppv: A pointer towards the COM interface returned. This value is either of type ICorRuntimeHost or IClrRuntimeHost depending on what you have requested.

The shim only takes care of loading the CLR within the process. The lifecycle of the CLR is controlled by the unmanaged code part of the runtime host in the form of the ICLRRuntimeHost interface returned by the CorBindToRuntimeEx() function. This interface presents two methods, Start() and Stop() whose names are self-descriptive.

Creating a custom runtime host

In the majority of projects, you will not need to create your own runtime host. However, it is good to know how this can be done and it can be instructive to see how this is accomplished.

To properly understand the creation of a runtime host, you need a good understanding of the COM technology. Do not forget that the *Windows 2000/XP* operating systems still use COM as a standard communication mechanism. The CLR has the possibility of being manipulated using non-managed code via the use of COM interfaces. The ICCLRRuntimeHost plays a predominant role in accomplishing this and can be obtained through the CorBindToRuntimeEx() function. Here is the base C++ code for a runtime host:

Example 4-7

```cpp
// You need to link with the static lib mscoree.lib
// to compile this C++ file.
#include <mscoree.h>

// The import must be done on a single line.
#import <mscorlib.tlb> raw_interfaces_only …
    … high_property_prefixes("_get","_put","_putref") …
        … rename("ReportEvent","ReportEventManaged") rename_namespace("CRL")

// We use the namespace ComRuntimeLibrary.
using namespace CRL;
ICLRRuntimeHost * pClrHost = NULL;
```

Example 4-7

```
void main (void){
   // Get a COM pointer of type ICorRuntimeHost on the CLR.
   HRESULT hr = CorBindToRuntimeEx(
            NULL, // We ask for the most recent version of the CLR.
            NULL, // We ask for the workstation version of the CLR.
            0,
            CLSID_CLRRuntimeHost,
            IID_ICLRRuntimeHost,
            (LPVOID *) &pClrHost);
   if (FAILED(hr)){
      printf("Can't get a pointer of type ICLRRuntimeHost!");
      return;
   }
   printf("We got a pointer of type ICCLRRuntimeHost.\n");
   printf("Launch the CLR.\n");
   pClrHost->Start();

   // Here, we can use our COM pointer pClrHost on the CLR.

   pClrHost->Stop();
   printf("CLR stopped.\n");
   pClrHost->Release();
   printf("Bye!\n");
}
```

Let us suppose that you have an assembly named `MyManagedLib.dll` which resides in the `C:\Test` directory and is built from the following code:

Example 4-8   *MyManagedLib.cs*

```
namespace MyProgramNamespace {
   public class MyClass {
      public static int MyMethod(string s) {
         System.Console.WriteLine(s);
         return 0;
      }
   }
}
```

You can easily invoke the `Main()` method from your host as follows:

Example 4-9

```
...
   pClrHost->Start();
   DWORD retVal=0;
   hr = pClrHost->ExecuteInDefaultAppDomain(
      L"C:\\test\\MyManagedLib.dll",// Path + Asm.
      L"MyProgramNamespace.MyClass",// Full name of the type.
      L"MyMethod",                  // Name of the method to run. It must
                                    // have the signature int XXX(string).
      L"Hello from host!",          // The argument string.
      &retVal);                     // A reference to the returned value.

   pClrHost->Stop();
...
```

Tuning the CLR from a custom runtime host

One thing you need to know is that when you control the CLR through a COM object, the `ICLRRuntimeHost` is not the only interface exposed by this COM object. In fact, you can manipulate the CLR through the following COM interfaces:

- `ICLRRuntimeHost` allows you to create and unload AppDomains, manage the lifecycle of the CLR and create evidences for the CAS security mechanism.
- `ICorConfiguration` allows you to specify to the CLR certain callback interfaces to be warned of specific events. These callback interfaces are: `IGCThreadControl IGCHostControl IDebuggerThreadControl`. Events presented by these interfaces are much less fine grained than those presented by the profiling API of the CLR which we will discuss a little later.
- `ICorThreadPool` allows you to manipulate the .NET thread pool for the process and allows the modification of certain configuration parameters.
- `IGCHost` allows you to obtain information on the behavior of the *garbage collector* and to control some of its configuration parameters.
- `IValidator` allows you to validate the PE/COFF header of assemblies (used by the `peverify.exe` tool).
- `IMetaDataConverter` allows the conversion of COM metadata (i.e. tlb/tlh) into .NET metadata (used by the `tlbexp.exe` tool).

To know which methods are exposed by these interfaces, you simply need to look at the files `mscoree.h`, `ivalidator.h` and `gchost.h`. To obtain one of these interfaces from your `IClrRuntimeHost` interface, you simply need to use the well known `QueryInterface()` method as follows:

```
...
    ICorThreadpool *   pThreadPool   = NULL;
    hr = pClrHost->QueryInterface( IID_ICorThreadpool,
                                   (void**)&pThreadPool);
...
```

Characteristics of the SQL Server 2005 runtime host

As we have mentioned previously, the runtime host for *SQL Server 2005* is special because of reliability, security and performance constraints imposed by RDBMS.

The main constraint for this type of server is reliability. The three mechanisms *constrained execution region* (CER), *critical finalizer* and *critical region* (CR) have been added to the CLR to reinforce the reliability of a .NET application. We discuss them further in the current chapter.

The second constraint is security. To avoid bad user code being loaded, all user assemblies are loaded by the runtime host from the database. This implies that an initial phase involving the pre-loading of assemblies in the database by the administrator must happen. During the phase, the administrator can specify that the assembly belongs to one of the categories SAFE, EXTERNAL_ACCESS and UNSAFE based on the level of trust towards the code in the assembly. The set of permissions allowed to an assembly by the CAS mechanism will depend on this level of trust. Finally, certain functionalities of the .NET *framework* considered sensitive such as certain classes of the System. Threading namespace, cannot be used from an assembly loaded in *SQL Server 2005*.

The third constraint is performance. It is satisfied by exploiting resources in an optimal manner. In this context, the most precious resources are threads and memory pages loaded in RAM. The idea is to minimize the number of context switches between threads and to minimize the number of memory pages stored on the virtual disk.

The *context switching* is generally managed by the *preemptive multitasking* of the *Windows scheduler* which we overview at page 113. The runtime host of *SQL Server 2005* implements its own multitasking mechanism based on a *cooperative multitasking* model. In this model, the threads themselves decide when the processor can move on to another thread. One advantage is that the choice of thread switching moments are more fine since tied to the semantics of processing. Another advantage is that this model is adapted to the use of *Windows fibers*.

A fiber is a *logical thread* which also qualifies as a *lightweight thread*. A same physical thread in *Windows* can chain the execution of several fibers. The advantage is that transfer from one fiber to another is much less expensive than a regular context switch. However, when the fiber mode is used by the *SQL Server 2005* runtime host we lose the guarantee of a good relationship between the physical *Windows* threads and the threads managed by .NET. Note that a same managed thread may not be executed by the same physical thread during its whole existence. So you must remove yourself from any affinity between these two entity types. Amongst the type of affinities between a managed and physical thread controlling it are the *Thread Local Storage*, the current culture and *Windows* synchronization objects which derive from the `WaitHandle` class, mutex, semaphores or events. Note that you can communicate to the runtime host the start and end of a region which exploit this kind of affinity using the `BeginThreadAffinity()` and the `EndThreadAffinity()` methods which are part of the `Thread` class. The use of the fiber mode generally brings a performance optimization of up to 20%. (Note: *In the current version of SQL Server 2005, the fiber mode has been removed as Microsoft engineers were unsure about its reliability. This mode will be reintroduced in later versions of this product*).

The storage of memory pages is normally managed by the *Windows* virtual memory system described at page 109. The runtime host of *SQL Server 2005* wedges itself between the memory request of the CLR and the operating system mechanisms in order to maximize the available RAM. This also allows us to obtain a more predictable behavior when a memory request to the CLR fails As we will see later, this feature is essential to ensuring the reliability of servers such as *SQL Server 2005*.

All these new functionalities are accessible through an API which allows the CLR and the host to communicate. About thirty new interfaces have been planned which are listed below. It is the host responsibility to supply an object which implements the `IHostControl` interface through the `ICLRRuntimeHost.SetHostControl(IHostControl*)` method. This interface presents the method `GetHostManager(IID,[out]obj)` that is called by the CLR to obtain an object from the host for which it will delegate a responsibility such as the management of threads or the loading of assemblies. More information is available by looking at the interfaces defined in the `mscoree.h` file.

Responsibility	Interfaces implemented by the host	Interfaces implemented by the CLR
Loading of assemblies	IHostAssemblyManager IHostAssemblyStore	ICLRAssemblyReferenceList ICLRAssemblyIdentityManager
Security	IHostSecurityManager IHostSecurityContext	ICLRHostProtectionManager
Exception management	IHostPolicyManager	ICLRPolicyManager
Memory management	IHostMemoryManager IHostMalloc	ICLRMemoryNotification- Callback
Garbage collector	IHostGCManager	ICLRGCManager
Threading	IHostTaskManager IHostTask	ICLRTaskManager ICLRTask
Thread pools	IHostThreadPoolManager	

Responsibility	Interfaces implemented by the host	Interfaces implemented by the CLR
Synchronization	IHostSyncManager IHostCriticalSection IHostManualEvent IHostAutoEvent IHostSemaphore	ICLRSyncManager
I/O Completion	IHostIoCompletionManager	ICLRIoCompletionManager
Debugging		ICLRDebugManager
CLR events	IActionOnCLREvent	ICLROnEventManager

Profiling the execution of your .NET applications

This section has the goal of familiarizing you with an extremely useful functionality of the CLR allowing you to finely profile its execution. In other words, you can ask the CLR to call one of your unmanaged methods when specific events occur such as the beginning of JIT compilation or the loading of a new assembly. It is logical that these callback methods be unmanaged since they are intended to let you observe the state of the CLR and obviously you would not want the CLR to handle them.

To take advantage of the *profiling* features of the CLR, you must construct a COM class which implements the ICorProfilerCallback interface. This interface is defined in the file corprof.h which can be found in the SDK\v2.0\Include directory of your *Visual Studio* installation. The interface contains about 70 methods. Once you have implemented the ICorProfilerCallback interface, you will need to let the CLR know that you wish to use your implementation for its callbacks. To communicate the CLSID of this implementation to the CLR, you do not need to create your own runtime host. In fact, you simply need to properly set the alues of the Cor_Enable_Profiling and Cor_Profiler variables. Cor_Enable_Profiling must be set to a non-null values to let the CLR know that it must perform the profiling callbacks. And Cor_Profiler must be set to the CLSID or the ProgID of your implementation of the ICorProfilerCallback interface.

We will not fully detail this feature as the article **The .NET Profiling API and the DNProfiling Tool** by *Matt Pietrek* of the *December 2001* **MSDN Magazine** (free online) already does this. We strongly suggest that you download the code in this article and experiment with it on your own .NET applications. This will give you a much better idea of the extent of the work done by the CLR! The code in this article also demonstrates how you can use masks to only enable a specific subset of the callbacks. The necessary steps to use this code are easy:

- Register the COM class on your machine;
- open a command line window;
- set the proper environment variables using the supplies batch file;
- launch your application through a command line window.

Locating and loading assemblies

That we apply an assembly deployment model which is private or shared, it is the CLR which will locate and load assemblies for execution. More precisely, these tasks fall under the *assembly loader* of the CLR more commonly named *fusion*. The general idea is that the assembly locating process by the CLR is smart and configurable.

- The CLR is configurable in the sense that an administrator can easily move assemblies while ensuring that they can still be located by the CLR. Configurable also means that we can redirect the use of certain versions of an assembly towards another version (with two possible approaches, with a publisher policy assembly or using a configuration file as described a little later).

- The CLR is intelligent in the sense that when it cannot find an assembly in a folder, it applies an algorithm that allows it, for example, to probe in sub-folder with the same name as the assembly. The CLR is also intelligent in the sense that if an application who used to work now fails because of an assembly it cannot find anymore, it can simply rollback the offending changes.

These two constraints can be achieved through the use of the *fusion* location algorithm.

We have seen at page 11 that an assembly can be constructed from many files called modules. Here we will talk about the location process for an assembly, which is the process by which the main module of an assembly is located (the one which includes the manifest). Let us remind you that all the modules of the same assembly must be located in the same directory.

When does the CLR attempt to locate an assembly?

The location process of the CLR is often called upon when the code of an executing assembly needs to load another assembly. If the location fails, the process will issue a `System.IO.FileNotFoundException` exception. The location process is used when:

- One of the overloaded `AppDomain.Load()` is used to load an assembly into the AppDomain who called the method.
- When the CLR needs to implicitly load an assembly. This is described further in the next section when we will discuss how the CLR resolves types.

This algorithm is not used when:

- The `AppDomain.ExecuteAssembly()` method that we have discussed earlier in this chapter is called.
- When the static method `Assembly.LoadFrom()` is called.

Note that these methods do not fully adhere to the .NET philosophy as they take in a path to a file and the name of an assembly. It is recommended never to use `LoadFrom()` as it can be substituted with `Load()`. The use of the simple `AppDomain.ExecuteAssembly()` can prove to be an efficient shortcut under the right circumstances.

The location algorithm used by the CLR

The GAC

The algorithm will first look for the assembly in the GAC directory, as long as the name of the assembly is a strong name. During the search in the GAC, the user of the application can choose (through a configuration file) to use the publisher policy assembly relative to the assembly that needs to be located.

The CodeBase element

If the strong name for an assembly is not properly supplied or that the assembly cannot be found in the GAC, there is a possibility that the assembly will need to be loaded from a *URL* (*Unique Resource Locator*). This possibility is at the base of the *No Touch Deployment* mechanism described at page 68.

In fact, the configuration file for the application can have a `<codebase>` relative to an assembly to be located. In this case, this element defines a URL and will attempt to load the assembly from that location. If the assembly cannot be found at the specified URL, then the location process will fail. If the assembly to be found is defined with a strong name within the configuration file then the URL can be an internet address, an intranet address or a folder on the current machine. If the assembly to be found is not defined using a strong name, the URL can only be a sub-directory of where the application is located.

Vonage

NEW! No Credit Card Required!

Keep Your Phone Number^
Lower Your Phone Bill!

UNLIMITED
Local and Long Distance
only $24.99/month
see reverse for details

Try 1 Month FREE!
see reverse for details

30 Day Risk-Free!<
see reverse for details

Call: **1-800-694-3198**
Visit: **www.vonage.com/ring04**

Save up to $300 a Year with the New Way to Phone!‡

Try 1 Month FREE
see details below

including:

- **UNLIMITED** Local and Long Distance Calling Using Your High-Speed Internet Connection!
- **FREE** Voicemail!
- **FREE** Caller ID!
- **FREE** Call Waiting!
- **FREE** Calls to Europe!˅
  – Italy, France, Spain, UK & Ireland
  see details below for calling conditions
- **20 FREE** Premium Features in All!

UNLIMITED
Local and Long Distance Calling
only $24.99/month†

Vonage works with your existing phone!

Keep your phone number!^

Try 1 Month FREE!
see details below

Call: **1-800-694-3198**
Visit: **www.vonage.com/ring04**

Award-Winning Quality!

PC WORLD WORLD CLASS 2006
Vonage: PC World's 2006 World Class Award Winner for VOIP Service July 2006

EDITORS CHOICE NOVEMBER 2006
"Vonage's wealth of features, extensive coverage, and strong support combine to make it a solid Internet phone service."
Computer Shopper, November 2006

Vonage™

FREE MONTH OFFER ON $24.99 UNLIMITED RESIDENTIAL PLAN ONLY. PLAN FEE WAIVED BUT ALL OTHER CHARGES APPLY. NEW SUBSCRIBERS ONLY.
˅Free Calls to Europe Offer (available only with Unlimited Residential Plan) Does Not Apply To Certain Call Types, Such As Calls to Cell Phones, and is limited to Italy, France, Spain, UK and Ireland. Vonage 911 service operates differently than traditional 911. See www.vonage.com/911 for details. High-Speed Internet Required. † Rates exclude: broadband service, regulatory and activation fees and certain other charges, equipment, taxes, & shipping. International calls billed per minute. Alarms and other systems may not be compatible. Offer valid in the US only. See Terms of Service. ‡ $300 savings claim based on 7/06 survey of competing land line service providers. For complete details visit www.vonage.com/compare1. <30-day money back guarantee is refunded for activation fee, 1st month service charge, shipping charges and termination fee. Applicable only to first ordered line per account. Available only in the event of timely cancellation for subscribers who obtain a valid return authorization number from billing@vonage.com or 1-VONAGE-HELP, and return of equipment in original condition and packaging within 30 days of cancellation. Refund will not include charges for taxes, international usage, payphone calls to Vonage toll free numbers and directory assistance. Offer revocable. ^The number transfer process takes approximately 10 days on average from the time you confirm your transfer request.
©2007 Vonage.
AM070302

Locating and loading assemblies 85

Here is an extract from the configuration file of an application making use of the <codebase> element:

```
...
    <dependentAssembly>
      <assemblyIdentity name="Foo3" publicKeyToken="C64B742BD612D74A"
       culture= "en-US"/>
      <codebase version="3.0.0.0"
       href = "http://www.smacchia.com/Foo3.dll>"/>
    </dependentAssembly>
...
```

Take note that the URL contains the location of the module of the assembly containing the manifest (in this case `Foo3.dll`). If the assembly has other modules, understand that all of these modules must be downloaded from the same location (which is http://www.smacchia.com/).

When an assembly is downloaded from the web by using the <codebase> configuration element, it is stored in the download cache. Also, before you attempt to load an assembly from a URL, the *fusion* will check this cache to see if the module has already been downloaded.

The probing mechanism

If the strong name for an assembly is not properly supplied or the assembly cannot be found in the GAC folder and that the configuration file does not define a <codebase> for this assembly, then the locating algorithm will attempt to find the assembly by probing certain folders. The following example exposes this *probing* mechanism:

- Let's suppose that we wish to locate an assembly named Foo (note that we do not supply the file extension in the name).
- And also, let us assume that a configuration file element named <probing> defines, for the Foo assembly, the following paths **"Path1"** and **"Path2\Bin"**.
- The application folder is located at **"C:\AppDir\"**.
- And finally, let's assume that that no culture information was supplied with the assembly.

The search for the assembly will be accomplished in the following order:

```
C:\AppDir\Foo.dll
C:\AppDir\Foo\Foo.dll
C:\AppDir\Path1\Foo.dll
C:\AppDir\Path1\Foo\Foo.dll
C:\AppDir\Path2\Bin\Foo.dll
C:\AppDir\Path2\Bin\Foo\Foo.dll
C:\AppDir\Foo.exe
C:\AppDir\Foo\Foo.exe
C:\AppDir\Path1\Foo.exe
C:\AppDir\Path1\Foo\Foo.exe
C:\AppDir\Path2\Bin\Foo.exe
C:\AppDir\Path2\Bin\Foo\Foo.exe
```

If the assembly is a satellite assembly (i.e. it has a non-neutral culture, for example **"fr-FR"**) the folder search occurs in the following order:

```
C:\AppDir\fr-FR\Foo.dll
C:\AppDir\fr-FR\Foo\Foo.dll
C:\AppDir\Path1\fr-FR\Foo.dll
C:\AppDir\Path1\fr-FR\Foo\Foo.dll
C:\AppDir\Path2\Bin\fr-FR\Foo.dll
C:\AppDir\Path2\Bin\fr-FR\Foo\Foo.dll
```

```
C:\AppDir\fr-FR\Foo.exe
C:\AppDir\fr-FR\Foo\Foo.exe
C:\AppDir\Path1\fr-FR\Foo.exe
C:\AppDir\Path1\fr-FR\Foo\Foo.exe
C:\AppDir\Path2\Bin\fr-FR\Foo.exe
C:\AppDir\Path2\Bin\fr-FR\Foo\Foo.exe
```

The AppDomain.AssemblyResolve event

Finally, if the assembly is not found with all these steps, the CLR will trigger the `AssemblyResolve` event of the `AppDomain` class. The methods delegated to this event can return an object of type `Assembly`. This allows you to implement your own location mechanism for the assemblies. This features is notably used within the *ClickOnce* deployment technology to download group of files on-demand as discussed at page 65.

You can use the `fuslogvw.exe` tool to analyze the logs produced by the *fusion* mechanism. This tool is useful to determine the exact causes of failures when loading an assembly.

The <assemblyBinding> element of the configuration file

The configuration file for an ASM assembly can contain parameters used by the *fusion* mechanism when ASM triggers the location and loading of another assembly. The configuration file can contain a `<probing>` element which specifies one or many folders that the probing mechanism must look at. The file can also contain a `<dependentAssembly>` element for each assembly to be potentially located. Each of these `<dependentAssembly>` elements can contain the following information on how an assembly can be located:

- The `<publisherPolicy>` element determines if the eventual publisher policies for the assembly to be loaded need to be taken into account when locating the assembly.
- The `<codebase>`, element described in the previous section defines the URL from which the assembly must be downloaded from.
- The `<bindingRedirect>` element allows you to redirect the version number used in the same way as a publisher policy assembly. The publisher policy applies as to all client applications of a shared assembly but here only the application targeted by the configuration file is affected.

Here is what a configuration file may look like (notice the similarity with a publisher policy assembly XML file):

Locating and loading assemblies

Diagram of the location algorithm

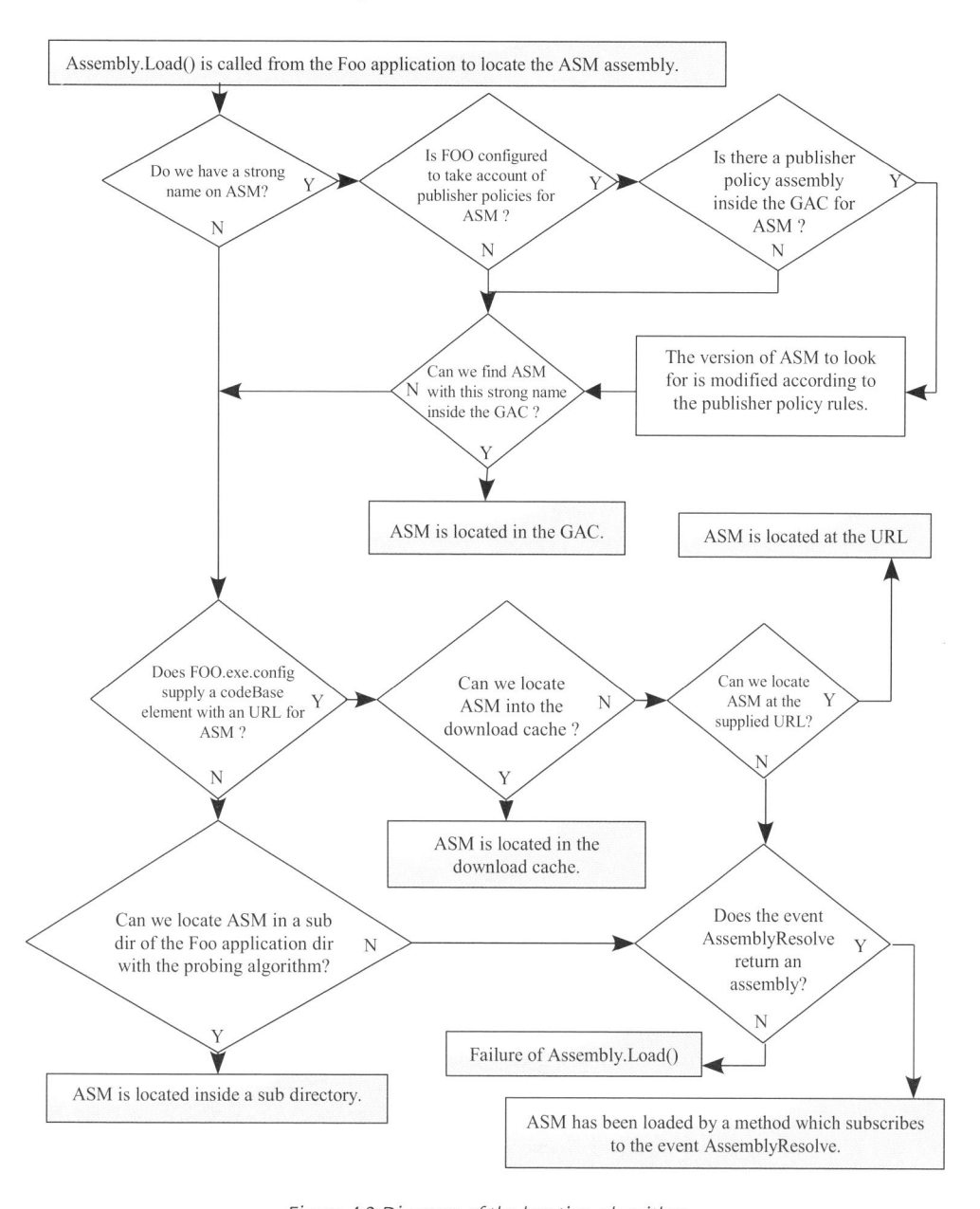

Figure 4-2: Diagram of the location algorithm

Example 4-10

```xml
<?xml version="1.0" encoding="utf-8"?>
<configuration>
   <runtime>
      <assemblyBinding xmlns="urn:schemas-microsoft-com:asm.v1">
         <probing privatePath="Path1;Path2/bin" />
         <dependentAssembly>
            <assemblyIdentity name="Foo1" culture= "neutral"
                              publicKeyToken="C64B742BD612D74A" />
            <publiherPolicy apply="no" />
            <bindingRedirect oldVersion="1.0.0.0" newVersion="2.0.0.0"/>
         </dependentAssembly>
         <dependentAssembly>
            <assemblyIdentity name="Foo2" culture= "neutral"
                              publicKeyToken="C64B742BD612D74A" />
            <codebase version="2.0.0.0"
                      href = "file:///C:/Code/Foo2.dll>"/>
         </dependentAssembly>
         <dependentAssembly>
            <assemblyIdentity name="Foo3" culture= "fr-FR"
                              publicKeyToken="C64B742BD612D74A" />
            <codebase version="3.0.0.0"
                      href = "http://www.smacchia.com/Foo3.dll>"/>
         </dependentAssembly>
      </assemblyBinding>
   </runtime>
</configuration>
```

If you do not wish to manipulate XML files, know that this information can be configured by using the .NET Framework Configuration tool accessible from: *Start menu › Configuration panel › Administrative tools › Microsoft .NET Framework 2.0 Configuration › configured assembly* menu.

The Shadow Copy mechanism

When an assembly is loaded by a process, the corresponding files are automatically locked by *Windows*. This means that you cannot update or delete the file and you can only rename it. In the case of an ASP.NET server a process can potentially host multiple applications. This behavior could be cumbersome since the process would need to be restarted each time an application needs to be updated.

Fortunately, the assembly loaded of the CLR features a mechanism called *shadow copy*. This mechanism copies assembly files in a dedicated cache folder for an application before actually loading the assembly. Hence the original files can be updated while they are being executed. ASP.NET uses this feature and periodically verifies if a loaded assembly has been updated. If it is the case, the application is restarted without loosing any requests.

The `string ShadowCopyDirectories{get;set;}` property of the `AppDomainSetup` class allows you to specify the folders which will contain the shadow copy of your assemblies.

Resolving types at runtime

Loading an assembly explicitly or implicitly

We often need to use within our code types which have been declared in other assemblies. There are two techniques to use types defined in other assemblies:

- You can rely on your compiler to early bind with the type and you rely on the CLR to load the assembly automatically when needed. This technique is called *implicit loading*.
- You can also *explicitly load* the assembly and thus late bind to the type you need to use.

In both cases, it is the responsibility of a portion of the CLR named *class loader*. The implicit loading of an assembly A is triggered at the first JIT compilation of a method using a type defined in A.

The notion of implicit loading relates to the DLL loading mechanism. In a same way, the notion of explicit loading resembles the mechanism used with COM objects through *Automation* and the well known *IDispatch* interface.

Referencing an assembly at compile time

When assembly A executes and the JIT compiles a method of A which requires a type defined in the B assembly, the B assembly is implicitly loaded by the CLR if it was referenced during the compilation process for A. For A to reference B, one of two operations must have been completed during the compilation process:

- Either you compiled A using the `csc.exe` command line compiler directly or through a compilation script. You must then use the proper `/reference` `/r` and `/lib` compiler options.
- Either you use *Visual Studio* with the *Reference > AddReference* menu option to set the proper references. Let us remind you that the *Visual Studio* environment implicitly uses the `csc.exe` compiler to generate assemblies from your C# source code. Setting the environment options essentially forces *Visual Studio* to use the `/reference` `/r` and `/lib` options of the `csc.exe` compiler.

In both cases, you must specify the assembly to load by its name (strong or not). The types as well as members within the B assembly that are referenced by the A assembly are in the *TypeRef* and *MemberRef* tables of A. In addition, the B assembly is also referenced in the *AssemblyRef* table of assembly A. An assembly can reference many other assemblies but you must avoid at all cost cyclic references (A references B which reference C which in turn references A). *Visual Studio* will detect and prevent cyclic reference. You can also use the *NDepend* tool (described at page 857) to detect cyclic assembly references.

An example

Here is an example of the whole infrastructure put in place so that the CLR can implicitly load an assembly. The first piece of code defines the assembly referenced by the second piece of code:

Example 4-11 *Code of the referenced assembly: AsmLibrary.cs*

```
using System;
namespace MyTypes {
   public class FooClass {
      public static int Sum(int a,int b){return a+b;}
   }
}
```

Example 4-12 *Code of the referencing assembly: AsmExecutable.cs*

```
using System;
using MyTypes;
class Program {
   static void Main() {
      int i = FooClass.Sum(3,4);
   }
}
```

Note the use of the `MyTypes` namespace in the referencing assembly. We could have also put the `FooClass` and `Program` classes in the same namespace or in the anonymous namespace. In this case, we could have illustrated that namespaces can spawn multiple assemblies.

It is interesting to analyze the manifest of the referencing assembly using the `ildasm.exe` tool. You can clearly see the fact that the assembly '`AsmLibrary`' is referenced. This reference takes form as an entry in the *AssemblyRef* table.

```
...
.assembly extern 'AsmLibrary'{
   .ver 0:0:0:0
}
...
```

It is also interesting to take a look at the IL code for the `Main()` method. You can clearly see that the method named `Sum()` is located in another assembly named '`AsmLibrary`':

```
.method private hidebysig static void  Main() cil managed
{
  .entrypoint
  // Code size       9 (0x9)
  .maxstack  2
  .locals init (int32 V_0)
  IL_0000:  ldc.i4.3
  IL_0001:  ldc.i4.4
  IL_0002:  call       int32
     ['AsmLibrary']MyTypes.FooClass::Sum(int32,int32)
  IL_0007:  stloc.0
  IL_0008:  ret
} // end of method Program::Main
```

JIT compilation (Just In Time)

Portable binary code

Let us remind you that .NET applications, independently of the source code language, are compiled into IL code. The IL code itself is stored in a special section of the assembly and modules. It stays in this form until the moment where the code needs to be executed.

As it name implies, the IL code (*Intermediate Language*) is an intermediate form of code between the high-level .NET languages (C#, VB.NET…) and machine code. The idea is that the compilation from IL code to a machine native form takes place during the execution of the application. This allows .NET applications to be distributed in a machine (and OS) independent form. The major point being that to distribute a .NET application across multiple operating systems, there is no need to recompile the high-level code. Hence we can say the .NET applications are *portable binary code*.

Introduction to Just In Time compilation

The compilation of IL code into machine language happens during the execution of the application. We could imagine two possible scenarios in regards to the compilation of the IL code:

- The application is completely compiled into language machine when it is launched.
- The IL instructions are interpreted one by one in the same way as an interpreted language.

None of these scenarios is used for the compilation of the IL code into machine language. An intermediate solution which is more efficient has been implemented. With this solution, the body of a method in IL language is compiled into native machine code just before the first call to the method. This is why the run-time compilation process is called *Just In Time (JIT)*. The compilation to machine language occurs just in time for the execution of the method to occur.

Diagram of the types resolving algorithm

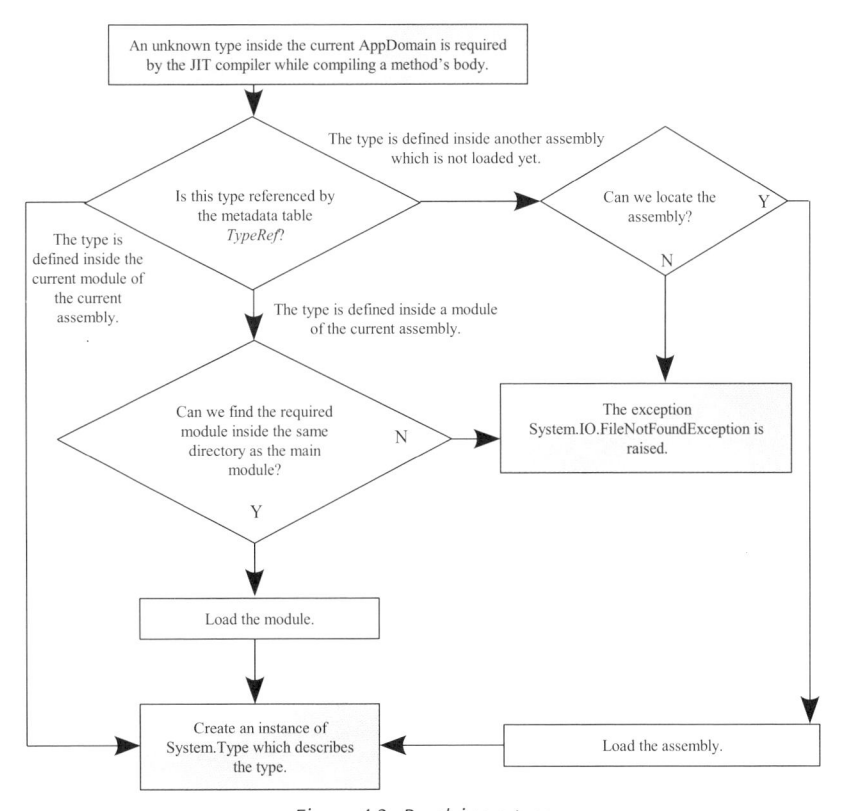

Figure 4-3: Resolving a type

Intercepting the first call with a stub

To perform JIT compilation, the CLR uses a trick commonly used in distributed architectures such as *RPC, DCOM .NET Remoting* or *Corba*. Each time a class is loaded by the CLR, a *stub* is associated to each method in the class. In a distributed architecture, the stub is a small software layer on the client which intercepts method calls to convert them into remote calls (with *DCOM* the term proxy is used). In the case of the JIT, the stub is a layer of code which will intercept the first call to the method.

This stub code essentially initiates the JIT compiler which will verify the IL code and translate into machine native instructions. The native code is then stored in the memory space of the process and then executed. Of course, the stub is then replaced with a jump to the memory address of the freshly generated code, ensuring that each method is only compiled once.

Vérification of the IL code

Before a method is compiled into native machine language, the JIT compiler does a series of validations to ensure the body of the method is valid. To determine if a method is valid, the compiler checks the flow of IL instructions and verifies the content of stack to detect invalid memory accesses. If the code fails the verification, the JIT compiler will issue an exception.

Your C# code written in safe mode is automatically translated into verifiable IL code. However, at page 417 we show that under certain circumstances, the C# compiler can produce special IL instructions which are not verifiable by the JIT compiler.

Optimisations done by the JIT compiler

The JIT compiler will perform optimizations on your code. Here are a few examples to give you an idea:

- To avoid the cost of passing parameters around, the JIT compiler can insert the body of a method into the body of the calling method. This optimization is called *inlining*. So that the cost of the optimization does not exceed the performance gains, the inlined method must meet certain conditions. The body of the function once compiled must not exceed 32 bytes, it must not catch exceptions, it must not contain loops and it cannot be a virtual function.

- The JIT compiler can set any local variable that is a reference to null once it is last used. This reduces the reference count of this object and can then give a chance that it will be garbage collected early, leaving more resources for other objects. Note that this optimization is locally deactivated when using the `System.GC.KeepAlive()` method.

- The JIT compiler can store frequently used local variables directly into the processor's registers instead of using the stack. This constitutes an optimization as access to registers is significantly more efficient than stack access. This optimization is commonly named *enregistration*.

Introduction to pitching

The compilation of methods by the JIT consumes memory since the native code for the methods must be stored. If the CLR detects that memory is running low for the application, it has the possibility of recuperating some memory by freeing the native code for certain methods. Naturally, a stub will be regenerated for these methods. This functionally is called *pitching*.

The implementation of pitching is more complex than is seems. To be efficient, the freed code must be in contiguous memory to avoid memory fragmentation. Other important problems appear in the thread stacks which contain memory addresses referencing the native code. Fortunately, all these complex consideration are hidden to the developer.

The native code of a method generated by the JIT will be destroyed when the AppDomain of its application is unloaded

JIT and JITA acronyms

For those coming from the world of COM/DCOM/COM+ the JIT acronym may remind you of the *JITA (Just In Time Activation*, described at page 245) acronym. The two mechanisms are different, have different goals and are essentially used in different technologies However, the underlying idea is the same: we mobilize resources for an entity (compilation of an IL method for JIT and activation of a COM object for JITA) only when this entity is needed (i.e. just before it is used). We often use the *lazy* adjective for such type of mechanisms.

The ngen.exe tool

Microsoft supplies a tool called `ngen.exe` which is capable of compiling assemblies before their execution. This tool functions as a standard compiler and replaces the JIT mechanism. The real name for `ngen.exe` is '*Native Image Generator*'. The `ngen.exe` tool is to be used when you notice that the JIT mechanism introduces a significant drop in performance, generally during the startup of an application. However, note that the regular compiler has access to a greater number of possible optimizations than `ngen.exe`. The use of the JIT compiler is most often preferred.

Compilation using `ngen.exe` is generally done during the installation of an application. You do not need to manipulate the new files containing the native code, called *native images*. They are automatically stored in a special directory on your machine called *native image cache*. This folder is accessible from `ngen.exe` using the `/show` and `/delete` options. This folder is also visible when a user visualizes the *global assembly cache* as the native images are included in this folder. This visualization is described at page 52.

ngen.exe option	Description
`/show` `[assembly name |folder name]`	Allows you to visualize a list of native images in the 'Native Image Cache'. If you follow this option with the name of an assembly, you will only see images with the same name, If you follow this option with the name of a folder, you will only see the images located in this folder.
`/delete` `[assembly name | folder name]`	Deletes all images contained in the 'Native Image Cache'. If you follow this option with the name of an assembly, only images with the same name will be deleted. If you follow this option with the name of a folder, only images in this folder will be deleted.
`/debug`	Produces an image which can be used by a debugger.

Many other options exist to this compiler and you can find a complete listing on MSDN in the entry Native Image Generator (Ngen.exe). Notably, some new features have been added with .NET 2.0 to support assemblies taking advantage of reflection and to automate the update of the compiled version of an assembly when dependencies have changed. For more information, take a look online in the article named NGen Revs Up Your Performance with Powerful New Features by Reid Wilkes in the April 2005 issue of **MSDN Magazine**.

Performance counters and JIT compilation

You have access to the following six performance counters of the JIT in the ".NET CLR Jit" category.

Name of the counter to be supplied as a string.	Description
"# of IL Methods JITted"	Counts the number of compiled methods. This number does not include the number of methods compiled by `ngen.exe`.
"# of IL Bytes JITted"	Counts the number of IL code bytes compiled. Pitched methods are not removed from this total.
"Total # of IL Bytes Jitted"	Counts the number of IL code bytes compiled with pitched methods accounted for in the total.
"% Time in Jit"	Percentage of time spent in the JIT compiler. This counter is updated at the end of each JIT compilation.
"IL Bytes Jitted / sec"	The average number of IL code compiled per second.
"Standard Jit Failures"	Number of times a method was determined as being non-valid and was not compiled by the JIT.

You have the choice to see the counters for all managed applications executed since the machine has booted up. This choice is done with the argument to the `PerformanceCounter Category.GetCounters()` method. In the first case, you will need to supply the character string "_Global_" as an argument to this method. In the second case, you will need to supply a string equal to the name of the process you wish to observe as an argument to this method.

These counters are particularly useful to evaluate the cost of the JIT compilation process. If this cost appears too high you may need to consider the use of the `ngen.exe` tool when deploying your application. Here is an example illustrating the use of the performance counters (note that the name of the assembly is `MyAssembly.exe`):

Example 4-13 *MyAssembly.cs*

```
using System.Diagnostics;
class Program {
   static void DisplayJITCounters() {
      PerformanceCounterCategory perfCategory
              = new PerformanceCounterCategory(".NET CLR Jit");
      PerformanceCounter[] perfCounters;
      perfCounters = perfCategory.GetCounters("MyAssembly");
      foreach(PerformanceCounter perfCounter in perfCounters)
         System.Console.WriteLine("{0}:{1}",
            perfCounter.CounterName,
            perfCounter.NextValue());
   }
   static void f() {
      System.Console.WriteLine("----> Calling  f().");
   }
   static void Main() {
      DisplayJITCounters();
      f();
      DisplayJITCounters();
   }
}
```

This program displays:

```
# of Methods Jitted:2
# of IL Bytes Jitted:108
Total # of IL Bytes Jitted:108
IL Bytes Jitted / sec:0
Standard Jit Failures:0
% Time in Jit:0
Not Displayed:0
----> Calling f().
# of Methods Jitted:3
# of IL Bytes Jitted:120
Total # of IL Bytes Jitted:120
IL Bytes Jitted / sec:0
Standard Jit Failures:0
% Time in Jit:0,02865955
Not Displayed:0
```

Let us precise that the performance counters are also available within the `perfmon.exe` tool (accessible from *Start menu › Run… › perfmon.exe*).

The garbage collector (GC) and the managed heap

Introduction to garbage collecting

In the .NET languages, the destruction of managed objects is not the responsibility of the programmer. The problem with the destruction of value types is easy to solve. The object being physically allocated on the stack of the current thread, it is automatically destroyed when the stack is emptied. The real problem exists with reference objects. To simplify the developer's task, the .NET platform provides a *garbage collector* (or commonly referred to as the *GC*) which takes care of automatically reclaiming the memory of allocated objects. This is what is called the *managed heap*.

When there are not more references to an object, it becomes inaccessible to the program since it does not need it anymore. The GC marks accessible objects. When an object is not marked this means it is not accessible by the program and must be destroyed. One problem is the fact that the GC deallocates an object only when it decides to (in general when the program needs memory). The developer has limited control over the GC. Compared to other languages such as C++, this introduces a level of uncertainty during the execution of programs. A consequence is that developers often feel frustrated by not having total control. However, with this system, recurring problems such as memory leaks are much less frequent.

> Memory leaks still exist despite the presence of the GC. In fact, a developer can introduce memory leak which keeps references towards objects which are not needed anymore (for example, a collection which is never emptied). However, the most common cause of memory leaks within .NET applications is the non deletion of unmanaged resources.

Bear in mind that the GC is a software layer in the CLR where a single instance exists for each process.

Problems encountered by the garbage collecting algorithms

Our goal here is not to do an expose on all the existing garbage collection algorithms but to make you aware of the problems that the GC designers had to face. This way, you can better understand why the algorithms described in the following sections have been chosen by *Microsoft* for their garbage collection mechanism.

You may think that the task is a simple matter or releasing an object when it is not referenced anymore. But this simplistic method can easily be made to fail. For example, imagine two objects A and B; A maintains a reference to B and B maintains a reference to A; these two objects have no other references than their mutual references. Clearly, the program does not need these objects and the GC must destroy them even though there is still a reference on each of them. The GC must use reference trees and cyclic reference detection algorithms to resolve these problems

There is another problem other than the destruction of the objects. One thing that the GC must avoid is *heap fragmentation*. After a while, when multiple allocations and deallocations occur of variously sized areas of memory, the heap can become fragmented. The memory is littered with memory spaces which are unused by the program and can lead to a wasting of valuable memory. It is the GC's task to defragment the heap to limit the consequences of memory fragmentation. There are multiple algorithms which can be used to accomplish this.

Finally, common sense and empiric approach teaches us the following rule: the older an object is the longer its lifespan, the newer an object is the shorter its lifespan. If this rule is taken into account by an algorithm where we always try to deallocate newer objects than older objects, then the garbage collection mechanism using this algorithm will benefit from a performance improvement.

The algorithm used by the .NET GC takes in consideration these problems and this temporal rule in its implementation.

The .NET GC

A *collection* of objects by the GC is automatically initiated by the CLR when memory is starting to run low. The exact algorithm used to make this decision is not documented by *Microsoft*.

The term *generation* defines the time span between two collections. Each object then belongs to the generation in which it was created. In addition, the following equation is always valid:

```
{Number of generations in process} = 1 + {number of collections in the process}.
```

Generations are numbered and the number is increased at each collection until it reaches the maximum number of generations (equal to two in the current implementation of the CLR). By convention, generation 0 is always the youngest which means that every object allocated on the heap will be part of generation 0.

A consequence of this system is that objects from the same generation occupy a contiguous area in memory as shown in Figure 4-4:

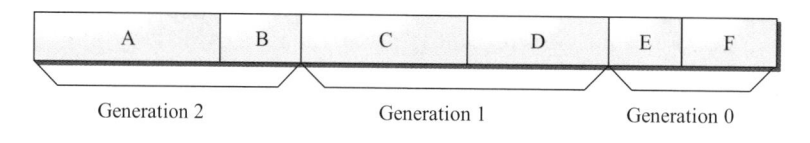

Figure 4-4: Generations

A B C D E and F are objects

Step 1: finding the root objects

The roots of the reference tree towards the *active objects* (i.e. the objects which must not be deallocated) are objects referenced by static fields, objects referenced in the process stack and objects for which the physical address (or an offset from this address) is stored in a register of the processor.

Step 2: building the tree of active objects

The GC builds the tree based on its roots by adding the objects referenced by the ones already in the tree and by repeating this process until no more references can be added. Each object referenced by the tree is marked as being active. When the algorithm encounters an object already marked as active, it is not taken into consideration again to avoid cyclic references in the tree. The GC uses the type metadata to find references contained in the object based on its class definition.

In Figure 4-5, we see that the objects A and B are the roots of the tree and that both A and B reference C. B also references E and C references F. The object D is then not marked as active.

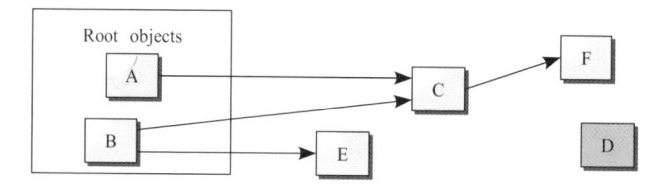

Figure 4-5: The tree of referenced objects

The garbage collector (GC) and the managed heap 97

Step 3: deallocating inactive objects

The GC linearly traverses the heap and deallocates objects which aren't marked as being active. Certain objects need that their `Finalize()` method be called in order to be physically destroyed. This method is referred to as the *finalizer*, and is defined by the `Object` class. This method must be called right before the object is destroyed if its class overrides this method. The invocation of the finalizers is taken in charge by a dedicated thread so not to overload the thread which takes care of object collection. A consequence is that the memory location of objects with finalizers will survive through a collection.

The heap is not necessarily completely traversed, either because the GC collected enough memory or because we need to do a *partial collection*. The tree traversal algorithm is significantly impacted by partial collections because it is possible that old objects (in generation 2) references newer objects (in generation 0 or 1). Although the frequency of the triggering of collections is dependant on your application, you can base yourself on the following order of magnitude: a partial collection of generation 0 every second, a partial collection of generation 1 for each 10 partial collections of generation zero and one complete collection for each 10 partial collections of generation 1.

Figure 4-6 shows that the object D is not marked as active and will consequently be destroyed.

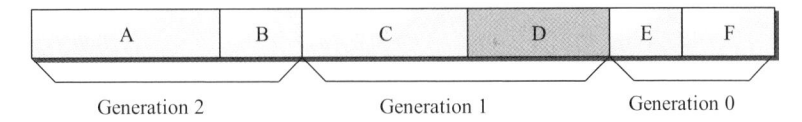

Figure 4-6: Deallocating inactive objects

Step 4: heap defragmentation

The GC defragments the heap, meaning that active objects are moved towards the bottom of heap to fill the memory voids from the deallocated objects in the previous step. The address of the top of the heap is recalculated and each generation is incremented. Older objects being towards the bottom of the heap and newer objects being at the top. In addition, active objects created at the same time are also physically close in memory. Only the new objects are often examined, meaning that it will almost always be the same memory pages which will be probed. This is done to maximize performance.

In Figure 4-7 (relating to Figure 4-6) the GC has incremented the generation number. We assume that the class for object D had no finalizer. This means that the memory for object D has been deallocated and the heap has been defragmented (E and F have been moved to fill the void left by D). Note that A and B did not see their generation number increase since they were already in generation 2.

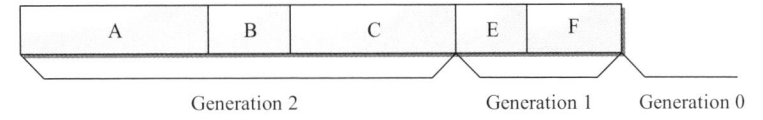

Figure 4-7: Heap defragmentation

Certain objects cannot be moved (are also said to be pinned) which means they cannot be physically moved by the GC. An object is considered to be pinned when it is referenced by unprotected or unmanaged code. For more details on this subject see page 420.

Step 5: recomputing physical addresses used by managed references

The memory addresses of certain active objects had to be modified by the previous step. The GC must then traverse the tree of active objects and update the references to the objects with their new physical memory address.

Good practices

The following good practices come from conclusions which can be drawn from the algorithm that we just described:

- Free your objects as soon as possible to avoid the promotion into a higher generation;
- Identify which objects may have a long lifespan and analyze the reasons for their lifespan so that you can attempt to reduce it. For this, we suggest that you use the *CLR Profiler* tool supplied by *Microsoft* or use the profiler supplied with *Visual Studio Team System*;
- When ever possible, avoid to reference a short lived object from a long lived object;
- Avoid implementing finalizers in your classes to that objects do not survive the collection process;
- Assign your references to `null` as soon as possible, especially before making a call to a long method.

The special heap for big objects

All objects with a size under a certain threshold are treated in the managed heap as described in the previous sections. Although this threshold is not documented by *Microsoft*, we assume an order of size in the range of 20 to 100 KB. Objects whose size is greater than this threshold are stored in a special heap for performance reasons. In fact, objects in this stack are not physically moved by the GC. A page of memory in *Windows* has a size of 4 or 8KB depending on the processor. Each of the objects in the special stack is store on an integer number of pages even if the size of the object is not an exact multiple of the page size. This leads to some minor memory waste but generally does not affect the performance. This difference in how big objects are stored is implemented transparently to the developer.

Garbage collection in a multithreaded environment

The execution of the collection process by the GC can happen with one of the application threads if it is triggered manually or using a CLR thread when it decides that collection must occur. Before starting to collect, the CLR must suspend the execution of the other application threads to avoid modifying their stacks while the collection occurs. For this, several techniques exist. We can mention the insertion of a *safe point* by the JIT compiler which allows application threads to verify if a collection is pending. Note that generation 0 of the heap is generally separated into portions (called *arenas*), one per thread, to avoid synchronization problems tied to concurrent accesses to the heap. Let us remind you that the finalizers are executed by a CLR thread dedicated to this task.

Weak references

The underlying problem

During the execution of an application, every object at a specific instant, is active, which means that the application has a reference to it or the object is inactive. When an object passes from active to inactive, which happens when the application releases the last reference to the object, there is no more possibility for the object to be accessed.

The garbage collector (GC) and the managed heap 99

In fact, there is a third intermediate stage between active and inactive. When the object is in this stage, the application can access it but the GC can also deallocate it. There is an obvious contradiction in this stage since the object can be accessed meaning it is referenced and if referenced, it cannot be destroyed. To understand this contradiction, we have to introduce the concept of a *weak reference*. When an object is referenced by a weak reference, it is both accessible by the application and deallocatable by the GC.

Why and when should you use weak references?

A developer can use a weak reference on an object if it satisfies all of the following conditions:

- The objects might be used later but we are unsure. If we are certain to reuse it later, you should be using a strong reference.
- The object can be reconstructed if needed (from a database for example). If we potentially need this object later but cannot reconstruct it, we cannot allow the GC to destroy it.
- The object is relatively large in memory (several KB). If the object is lightweight, we can keep it in memory. However, when the two previous conditions apply to a large number of lightweight objects, it is a good idea to use weak references to each of these objects.

All of this is theoretical. In practice, we say that we are using an object cache. In fact, these conditions are all fulfilled by objects contained in a cache (we talk of cache from a conceptual point of view and not of a particular implementation).

The use of caches can be considered as a natural and automatic compromise in the use of memory, processor power and network bandwidth. When a cache is too large, a portion of its cached objects are destroyed. However, under the assumption that we will need to access one of these objects later, we will need to use processing power and bandwidth to reconstruct the object as needed

To summarize, if you need to implement a cache, we recommend the use of weak references.

How to use weak references?

The use of weak references is facilitated through the use of the `System.WeakReference` class. An example is worth more than a long discussion; take a look at the following C# code:

Example 4-14

```csharp
class Program {
   public static void Main() {
      // 'obj' is a strong reference on the object
      // created by this line.
      object obj = new object();

      // 'wobj' is a weak reference on our object.
      System.WeakReference wobj = new System.WeakReference(obj);

      obj = null; // Discard the strong reference 'obj'.
      // ...
      // Here, our object might potentially be deallocated by the GC.
      // ...
      // Build a strong reference from the weak reference.
      obj = wobj.Target;
      if (obj == null) {
         // If the thread pass here, it means that the object
         // has been deallocated by the GC!
      }
      else {
         // If the thread pass here, it means that the object
```

Example 4-14

```
        // hasn't been deallocated by the GC. We can thus use it.
      }
    }
  }
}
```

The `WeakReference` class presents the method `bool IsAlive()` which returns `true` if the object part of the weak reference has been destroyed. It is also recommended to set all strong references to `null` as soon as a weak reference has been created to ensure that the strong reference is destroyed.

Short weak references and long weak references

There are two constructors for the `WeakReference` class:

```
WeakReference(object target);
WeakReference(object target, bool trackResurrection);
```

In the first constructor the `trackResurrection` parameter is implicitly set to `false`. If this parameter is set to `true`, the application can still access the object between the moment when the `Finalize()` method has been called and the moment where the memory of the object is really modified (in general by the copy of another object into this memory location during defragmentation of the heap). In this case, we say that it is a *long weak reference*. If the parameter is set to `false` the application cannot access the object as soon as the `Finalize()` method has been called. In this case we say that it is a *short weak reference*.

Although the potential gain from using long weak references, it is better to avoid using them as they are difficult to maintain. In fact, an implementation of the `Finalize()` method which does not account for long weak references could lead to the resurrection of an object in an invalid state.

Using the System.GC class to influence the GC behaviour

We can use the static methods of the `System.GC` class to modify or analyze the behavior of the GC. The idea is to improve performance of your applications. However, *Microsoft* has invested a lot of resources into optimizing the .NET GC. We recommend using the services of the `System.GC` class only when you are certain that a performance gain can be achieved by your modifications. Here are the properties and static methods of this class:

- `static int MaxGeneration{ get; }`

  This property returns the maximum number of generations in the managed heap. By default, in the current .NET implementation, this property returns 2 and is guaranteed constant during the lifetime of the application.

- `static void WaitForPendingFinalizers()`

  This method suspends the current thread until all pending finalizers have been executed.

- `static void Collect()`
  `static void Collect( int generation )`

  This method initiates the collection process by the GC. You have the possibility of triggering a partial collection since the GC will take care of objects with a generation number between `generation` and 0. The `generation` parameter can not exceed `MaxGeneration`. When a call is made to the overloaded version without a parameter, the garage collector will collect all generations.

The garbage collector (GC) and the managed heap

This method is generally invoked with a bad intent since developers hope it will solve memory problems due to bad application design (too many allocated objects, too many references between objects, memory leaks…).

It is however interesting to trigger the collection process just before the call to a critical functions that might be bothered with running low on memory or a performance drop due to an unexpected collection. In this case, it is recommended to call the methods in this order to ensure that our process will have the maximum amount of memory available:

```
// Trigger a first collection.
GC.Collect()
// Wait for all pending finalisers.
GC.WaitForPendingFinalizers()
// Trigger a second collection to get back the memory
// used by discarded objects.
GC.Collect()
```

- `static int CollectionCount( int generation )`

  Returns the number of collections done for the specified generation. This method can be used to detect if a collection has occurred during a certain time interval.

- `static int GetGeneration( object obj )`
  `static int GetGeneration( WeakReference wo )`

  Returns the generation number of an object references by either a strong reference or a weak reference.

- `static void AddMemoryPressure( long pressure )`
  `static void RemoveMemoryPressure ( long pressure )`

  The problem behind the reason for this method is that that fact that the GC does not account for unmanaged memory in its algorithms. Imagine that you have 32 instances of the `Bitmap` class which each use 32 bytes and that each of them maintain a reference to a bitmap of 6MB. Without the use of this method, the GC behaves as if only 32x32 bytes were allocated and thus might not decide that a collection is necessary. A good practice is to use theses methods during the constructors and finalizers of classes who maintain large regions of unmanaged memory. Let us mention that the class `HandleCollector` discussed at page 229 offers similar services.

- `static long GetTotalMemory( bool forceFullCollection )`

  Returns an estimate of the current managed heap size in bytes. You can refine the estimate by putting the `forceFullCollection` parameter to `true`. In this case, the method becomes blocking if a collection is currently executing. The method returns when the collection is complete or before if the wait exceeds a certain amount of time. The value returned by this function will be more exact when the GC completes its task.

- `static void KeepAlive( object obj )`

  Guarantees that `obj` will not be destroyed by the GC during the execution of the method calling `KeepAlive()`. `KeepAlive()` must be called at the end of the body of the method. You may think that this method is useless since it requires a strong reference to the object which guarantees its existence. In fact, the JIT compiler optimizes the native code by placing a local reference variable to null after its last use in a method. The `KeepAlive()` simply disables this optimization.

- `static void SuppressFinalize(object obj)`

  The `Finalize()` will not be called by the GC for the object passed as a parameter to this method. Remember however that the call to the `Finalize()` method is guaranteed by the GC for every object which has finalizer support, before the end of the process.

The `Finalize()` method should logically contain code to deallocate resources held by the object. However, we have no control over the moment of the call to `Finalize()`. Consequently, we often create a specialized method dedicated to the deallocation of resources that we call when we wish. In general, we use the `IDisposable.Dispose()` method for this exact purpose. It is within this method that you should call `SuppressFinalize()` since after its invocation, there will be no use to call `Finalize()`. More details on this subject can be found at page 350.

- `static void ReRegisterForFinalize(object obj)`

  The `Finalize()` method of the object passed in parameter will be called by the GC. In general, we use this method in two cases.

  1st case: When the `SuppressFinalize()` has already been called and that we change our mind (this should to be avoided as it indicates poor design).

  2nd case: If we call `ReRegisterForFinalize()` in the code of the `Finalize()` method, the object will survive the collection process. This can be used to analyze the behavior of the GC. However, if we keep calling `Finalize()` the program will never terminate and you must allow for a condition in which `ReRegisterForFinalize()` will not be called so that the program may terminate. In addition, if the code of such a `Finalize()` method references other objects, you must be careful as they may be destroyed by the GC without noticing it. In fact, this 'indestructible' object is not considered as active so its references to other objects are not necessarily accounted for during the construction of the reference tree.

Facilities to make your code more reliable

Asynchronous exceptions and managed code reliability

We hope that the content of the current chapter has convinced you that the execution of managed code is a major advancement. It is now time to look at the dark side of managed environment. In such an environment, expensive processes can be triggered implicitly by the CLR at almost any time during execution. This fact implies that it is impossible to predict when a lack of resources will occur. Here are a few classic examples of such expensive processes triggered by the CLR (and this list is far from being complete):

- Loading of an assembly.
- Execution of a class constructor.
- Object collection by the GC.
- JIT compilation of a class or method.
- Traversal of the CAS stack.
- Implicit boxing.
- Creation of static fields for a class whose assembly is shared by all AppDomains of a process.

A lack of resources generally translates itself by the CLR raising an exception of type `OutOfMemoryException`, `StackOverflowException` or `ThreadAbortException` on the thread executing the request. Here, we talk about *asynchronous exceptions*. This notion opposes itself to the notion of *application exception*. When an application exception is raised, it is the current code's responsibility to trap the exception and process it. For example, when you attempt to access a file, you have to be ready to catch an exception of type `FileNotFoundException`. However, when an asynchronous exception is raised by the CLR, the code currently executing cannot be held responsible. Consequently, it is not recommended to be paranoid and litter your code with try/catch/finally blocks to attempt to catch the side effects of asynchronous exceptions. The entity responsible for dealing with such exceptions is the runtime host which we have already covered in this chapter.

In the case of a console or windowed application, the raise of an asynchronous event is a rare event which generally comes from an algorithm problem (memory leak, abusive recursive calls).

Consequently, the runtime host for this application will terminate the process entirely when such an exception is not caught by the application.

The behavior is similar in the case of ASP.NET applications. In fact we notice that the various abnormal behavior detection algorithms generally detect and recycle the process often before asynchronous exceptions occur. These mechanisms are discussed at page 739.

Until the integration of the CLR in *SQL Server 2005*, asynchronous exceptions were not too problematic. The *2005* version of *SQL Server* must have a reliability of 99.999%. To be efficient, the process for *SQL Server 2005* must load a maximum amount of data in memory and limit loads of memory pages from the hard disk. The process will often flirt with the 2 or 3GB memory limit for a process. Finally, the *time out* mechanisms on the execution of request are based on the raise of the `ThreadAbortException` exception. In conclusion, when dealing with this type of server which pushes the system to its limit, asynchronous exceptions become a common thing and must not cause the process to crash.

Faced with such constraints, the CLR designers had to come up with new techniques. They constitute the subject of the current section. **Keep in mind that these techniques must be used with great wisdom, only when you develop a wide scale server that requires its own runtime host and that is likely to face asynchronous exceptions.**

Constrained Execution Regions (CER)

To avoid a whole process going down from an asynchronous exception, we have to be able to unload a specific AppDomain when such an exception happens. Here, we talk about the *application domain recycling*. The main difficulty with such recycling is to achieve it properly without leaking memory or without corrupting the general state of the process. We then need a mechanism which allows us to protect ourselves from asynchronous exceptions. Without such a mechanism is it almost impossible to guarantee that unmanaged resources held during such an exception will be deallocated properly.

The .NET 2 framework allows you to tell the CLR which portions of code where the raise of an asynchronous exception would be catastrophic. If an asynchronous exception must happen, the idea is to force the CLR to raise the exception either before or after the execution of this portion of code but not during. We call these portions of code *Constrained Execution Region*s or *CER*).

To avoid the raise of an asynchronous exception during a CER, the CLR must make a certain number of preparations before it starts the execution of this portion of code. The idea is to attempt to trigger a lack of resources if it has to happen before the execution of the CER. Typically, the CLR compiles into native code all methods which are susceptible to be executed. To know these methods, it traverses statically the graph of calls which have the CER as a root. Moreover, the CLR knows how to withhold an exception of type `ThreadAbortException` which might occur during the execution of the CER until the end of its execution.

Developers must be cautious not to allocate memory during a CER. This constraint is particularly strong as many implicit conditions can trigger the allocation of memory. Some notable examples are the use of boxing instructions, access to a multi-dimensional array or the manipulation of synchronization objects.

How to define your own CERs?

A CER is defined by a call to the static method `PrepareConstrainedRegion()` of the `System.Runtime.CompilerServices.RuntimeHelpers` class right before the declaration of a `try/catch/finally` block. All the code which can be reached by the `catch` and `finally` blocks represents a CER.

The static method `ProbeForSufficientStack()` of this class is eventually called during the call to `PrepareConstrainedRegion()`. This depends on the fact that the CER implementation of your runtime host must manage cases where the execution may exceed the maximum size of the stack for the current thread (*stack overflow*). On a x86 processor, this method attempts to reserve 48KB.

Even though the reserved memory, there is still the possibility that a *stack overflow* may occur. Also, you can follow your call to `PrepareConstrainedRegion()` by a call to `ExecuteCodeWithGuaranteedCleanup()` to indicate a method containing cleanup code to invoke if case of an overflow. Such a method is marked with the `PrePrepareMethodAttribute` attribute to specify to `ngen.exe` its special use.

The `RuntimeHelpers` class offers methods which allow developers to assist the CLR in preparing to execute a CER. You can, for example, call them in your class constructors.

- `static void PrepareMethod(RuntimeMethodHandle m)`

  The CLR traverses the graph of calls made in a CER to compile them in native code. Such a traversal cannot detect which version of a virtual method is called. Also, it is the developer's responsibility to force the compilation of the version to be called within the CER.

- `static void PrepareDelegate(Delegate d)`

  Delegates that are to be called during the execution of a CER must be prepared ahead of time by using this method.

- `static void RunClassConstructor(type t)`

  You can force the execution of a class constructor with this method. Naturally, the execution will only take place if it has not already been invoked previously.

Memory Gates

In the same spirit as the `ProbeForSufficientStack()` static method, you may need to use the class `System.Runtime.MemoryFailPoint` which is used as follows:

```
// We are about to complete an operation which required
// at most 15MB of memory.
using( new MemoryFailPoint(15) ) {
    // Complete the operation ...
}
```

Contrarily to the `ProbeForSufficientStack()` method, the quantity of memory indicated is not reserved. The constructor to this class only evaluates during its execution if such a memory request can be satisfied by the operating system without raising an `OutOfMemoryException` exception. Note that between the moment where this request is done and the execution of your code, conditions may have evolved and for example another thread may have requested a big amount of memory. Considering this weakness, this technique is generally considered to be efficient.

If it happens that the amount of memory requested is unavailable, the constructor of the `MemoryFailPoint` class will raise an exception of type `System.InsufficientMemoryException`. For this reason, we often refer to *memory gates* to designate this feature. Understand that the key distinction here is that an `InsufficientMemoryException` indicates that we're out of memory, but no corruption has occurred, so therefore this exception is safe to catch and your app can safely continue.

Reliability contracts

The .NET 2 framework exposes the `System.Runtime.ConstrainedExecution.ReliabilityContractAttribute` attribute which only applies to methods. This attribute allows you to document the level of maximal severity we can expect if an asynchronous exception happens during the execution of a marked method. These severity levels are defined by the values in the `System.Runtime.ConstrainedExecution.Consistency` enumeration:

Consistency	Description
MayCorruptProcess	The marked method may corrupt the state of the process and thus cause a crash.
MayCorruptAppDomain	The marked method may corrupt the state of an AppDomain causing it to be unloaded.
MayCorruptInstance	The marked method may corrupt the instance which it belongs to and may cause its destruction.
WillNotCorruptState	The marked method may not corrupt any state.

A second value of type `System.Runtime.ConstrainedExecution.Consistency` applies to each `ReliabilityContractAttribute` attribute. This value allows you to document if the method can fault any guarantees of an eventual CER which might execute it. Of course, if the method can corrupt the state of the process or AppDomain, it can fault these guarantees and you must then use the `Cer.None` value.

Reliability contracts constitute a means by which you can document your code. Know that they are also exploited by the CLR when it traverses the static call graph to prepare the execution of a CER. If a method without a sufficient reliability contact is encountered the tree traversal will be stopped (since we know the code is unreliable) however, the execution of the CER will still happen. This potentially dangerous behavior has been decided by *Microsoft* engineers since too few framework methods are currently annotated with a reliability contract. Note that only the following three reliability contracts are considered sufficient for CER execution:

```
[ReliabilityContract(Consistency.MayCorruptInstance, Cer.MayFail)]
[ReliabilityContract(Consistency.WillNotCorruptState, Cer.MayFail)]
[ReliabilityContract(Consistency.WillNotCorruptState, Cer.Success)]
```

Critical finalizers

The CLR considers that the class finalizer code of a class deriving from `System.Runtime.ConstrainedExecution.CriticalFinalizerObject` is a CER. Here, we are referring to a *critical finalizer*. In addition of being a CER, critical finalizers will happen together during the execution of collection, following the execution of normal finalizers. This guarantees that the most critical resources for which manage objects depend are freed last.

The mechanism of critical finalizers is exploited by the framework classes responsible for the life-cycle of a win32 handle (`System.Runtime.InteropServices.CriticalHandle` and `System.Runtime.InteropServices.SafeHandle` described at page 229).

Other classes of the framework which derive from the `CriticalFinalizerObject` class are `System.Security.SecureString` (see page 188) and `System.Threading.ReaderWriterLock` (see page 130).

Critical regions

A second reliability mechanism is in place in addition to CERs. The idea is to supply information to the CLR to it knows when a resource shared amongst multiple threads is updated. A portion of code is responsible for the update and is called a *Critical Region* or *CR*. To define the beginning and end of a critical region, you simply need to call the `BeginCriticalRegion()` and `EndCriticalRegion()` which belong to the `Thread` class.

If an asynchronous exception occurs during a critical region, the state of the shared resource may be potentially corrupted. The current thread will be destroyed but this isn't sufficient to ensure that the application can continue its execution. In fact, other threads may access the corrupted data and yield unpredictable execution. The only possible solution is to unload the whole current AppDomain and this is effectively what will happen. The behavior of propagating a thread local problem to the AppDomain is called *escalation policy*. Another inherent effect of the notion of critical region is that it will force the CLR to unload the current AppDomain if a memory allocation request fails.

If you make use of the locking classes of the *framework* (the `Monitor` class and the `lock` keywords of class `ReaderWriterLock` etc) to synchronize access to your shared resources, you do not need to explicitly define critical regions within your code as these classes make use of the `BeginCriticalRegion()` and `EndCriticalRegion()` methods. **Consequently, critical regions are mostly to be used when you develop a synchronization mechanism which isn't that common.**

CLI and CLS

Under these two acronyms are hidden the magic which allows .NET to support multiple languages. The *CLI* (*Common Language Infrastructure*) is a specification which describes the constraints followed by the CLR and assemblies. A software layer which supports the constraints of the CLI is capable of executing .NET applications. This specification was produced by the ECMA and can be found online at: `http://www.ecma-international.org/publications/standards/ECMA-335.HTM`

Constraints which must be satisfied by .NET languages

So that assemblies compiled from a language be managed by the CLR (or by a software layer supporting the CLI) and use all the classes and tools of the .NET framework, the language and its compiler must respect a set of constraints called the *CLS* (*Common Language Specification*). Amongst these constraints we can include the support for CTS types but this is not the only constraint. Constraints imposed to the languages and compilers by the CLS are numerous. Here are a few of the most common ones:

- The language must provide a syntax allowing the resolution of conflicts when a class implements two interfaces for which a method conflict exists. There is a method definition conflict when two methods, one in each interface, with the same name and signature. The CLS impose that the class must implement two distinct methods.
- Only a few primitive types are compatible with the CLS. For example, the `ushort` type present in C# is not compatible with the CLS.
- Parameter types to public methods must be CLS compliant. The notion of CLS compliant is presented a few lines below.
- An object launched in an exception must be an instance of the `System.Exception`, class or must be derived from it.

A complete list of all constraints can be found on **MSDN** in the article named '**Common Language Specification**'.

The compatibility of a language to the CLS does not need to be complete and we can observe two levels of compatibility:

- A language is said to be a *CLS consumer* if it can instantiate and use public members of classes contained within CLS compatible assemblies.
- A language is said to be a *CLS extender* if it can produce classes deriving from public classes contained within CLS compatible assemblies. This compatibility also implies consumer compatibility.

The C#, VB.NET and C++/CLI support both of theses levels of compatibility.

CLI and CLS from developer's perspective

An assembly is said to be CLS compliant if the following elements are compatible with the CLS:

- The definition of public types;
- The definition of public and protected members within public types;
- The parameters of public and protected methods.

This also means that the code of private classes and members do not need to be CLS compliant.

Developers have a vested interest into developing libraries which are CLS compliant since it makes it much easier to reuse them in the future. Fortunately, developers do not need to be a specialist about the CLS constraints to verify if their classes are CLS compatible. Using the `System.CLSCompliantAttribute` attribute, you can have the compiler verify if the elements of your applications (assemblies, classes, methods…) are compatible with the CLS. For example:

Example 4-15
```
using System;
[assembly : CLSCompliantAttribute(true)]
namespace CLSCompliantTest {
   public class Program {
      public static void Fct(ushort i ) { ushort j = i; }
      static void Main(){}
   }
}
```

The compiler will generate a warning as the type ushort, which is not CLS compatible, is used for the parameter of a public method within a public class. However, the use of the ushort type inside of the body of the Fct() method will not cause a warning.

Using the CLSCompliantAttribute, attribute you can indicate to the compiler not to test for CLS compliance for the Fct() method while testing the CLS compliance of the rest of your application as follows:

Example 4-16
```
using System;
[assembly : CLSCompliantAttribute(true)]
namespace CLSCompliantTest {
   public class Program {
      [CLSCompliantAttribute(false)]
      public static void Fct(ushort i ) { ushort j = i; }
      static void Main(){}
   }
}
```

Understand that the Fct() may not be called from code which does not know the ushort type.

5

Processes, threads and synchronization

> Here we will discuss the fundamental notions which are processes and threads, in the architecture of the *Windows NT/2000/XP* operating systems. You must keep in mind that the CLR described in the previous chapter is a software layer loaded into a process by the runtime host when a .NET assembly is launched.

Introduction

A *process* is a memory region containing resources. The process allows to the operating system to split its work amongst several *functional units*.

A process owns one or several *execution units* called *threads*. A process also owns a private virtual addressing space which can be only accessed by its own threads.

When running .NET programs, a process also contains in its memory space a software layer called the CLR. A detailed description of the CLR was done in the previous chapter. This software layer is loaded during the creation of the process by the runtime host (which is described at page 76).

A thread can only belong to a single process and can only uses the resources of this process. When a process is created by the operating system, it automatically allocates a thread called the *main thread* or *primary thread*. It is this thread which executes the runtime host, who in turn loads the CLR.

An *application* is made from one or several cooperating processes. For example, the *Visual Studio* development environment is an application which can use one process to edit the source files and another for the compilation.

Under the *Windows NT/2000/XP* operating systems, we can see at any given time all the applications and processes by launching the *task manager* tool. It is common to have about thirty processes running at the same time, even if you only have opened only a few applications. In fact, the system executes a large number of processes, for the management of the current session, for the management of the task bar and for several other tasks.

Processes

Introduction

In a 32-bits *Windows* operating system, which executes on a 32-bit processor, a process can be seen as a linear memory space of 4GB (2^32 bytes), including the addresses from `0x00000000` to `0xFFFFFFFF`. This memory space is said to be private as it cannot be accessed by the other processes. This space is divided into 2GB for the system and 2GB for the user.

If N processes run on a same machine, it is not (fortunately) necessary to have Nx4GB of RAM.

- *Windows* only allocates the memory required for each process, 4GB being the upper limit in a 32 bit environment.
- A *virtual memory* mechanism part of the system saves on the hard disk and loads on to RAM 'pieces' of the process which are called memory pages. Each page has a size of 4KB. Again, all this is transparent to the developer and user.

The System.Diagnostics.Process class

An instance of the `System.Diagnostics.Process` class references a process. The processes which can be referenced are:

- The current process in which the instance is used.
- A process on the same machine other than the current process.
- A process on a remote machine.

The methods and fields of this class allow the creation or destruction of a process, and allow you to obtain information on a process. Here, we will discuss a few of the common tasks done using this class.

Creating and destroying a child process

The program below creates a new process called *child process*. In this case, the initial process is called *parent process*. This child process executes the notepad application. The thread of the parent process waits for one second before destroying this child process. This program thus has the effect of opening and closing notepad:

Example 5-1

```
using System.Diagnostics;
using System.Threading;
class Program {
   static void Main() {
      // Create a child process which executes the 'notepad.exe'
      // application on the text file 'hello.txt'.
      Process process = Process.Start("notepad.exe", "hello.txt");
      // Sleep one second.
      Thread.Sleep(1000);
      // Destroy the child process.
      process.Kill();
   }
}
```

The `Start()` static method can use the existing *Windows* file extension associations. For example, the program would have the same behavior if we wrote:

```
Process process = Process.Start("hello.txt");
```

By default, a child process inherits the security context of its parent process. However, one overloaded version of the `Process.Start()` method allows you to launch the child process in the security context of any user assuming that you can provide the login/password pair for the user in an instance of the `System.Diagnostics.ProcessStartInfo` class.

Avoid running several simultaneous instances of the same application on a single machine

This functionality is required by several applications. In fact, it is common that is makes no sense in simultaneously running several instances of an application on a same machine.

Until now, to satisfy this constraint under *Windows*, developers most often use the *named mutex* technique described at page 127. The use of this technique to satisfy this constraint does suffer from the following drawbacks:

- There is the small, but potential, risk that the name of the mutex be used by another application, in which case this technique will not work and will create hard to detect bugs.
- This technique does not resolve the general case where we only authorize N instances of the application.

Thanks to the static methods named `GetCurrentProcess()` (which returns the current process) and `GetProcesses()` (which returns all the processes on the machine) of the `System.Diagnostics.Process` class, this problem finds an elegant and easy to implement solution using the following program:

Example 5-2

```
using System.Diagnostics;
class Program {
   static void Main() {
      if ( TestIfAlreadyRunning() ) {
         System.Console.WriteLine("This app is already running!");
      }
      else{
         // Here, the entry point of the application.
      }
   }
   static bool TestIfAlreadyRunning() {
      Process processCurrent = Process.GetCurrentProcess();
      Process[] processes = Process.GetProcesses();
      foreach ( Process process in processes )
         if ( processCurrent.Id != process.Id )
            if ( processCurrent.ProcessName == process.ProcessName )
               return true;
      return false;
   }
}
```

The `GetProcesses()` method can also return all the processes on a remote machine by indicating the name of the machine as a parameter to the method.

Terminating the current process

You can decide to terminate the current process by calling one of the `Exit(int exitCode)` or `FailFast(string message)` static methods of the `System.Environment` class.

The `Exit()` method is the best option. It will properly terminate the process and return the specified exit code to the operating system. The termination is done properly in the sense that all the finalizers of the current objects and the execution of the `finally` blocks will be done by the different threads. However, the termination of the process may take a certain amount of time.

As its name indicates, the `FailFast()` method quickly terminates the process. The precautions made by the `Exit()` method are not done. A fatal error containing the specified message is logged by the operating system. You might want to use this method if during the detection of a problem, you judge that the proper termination of this program could lead to data corruption.

Threads

Introduction

A thread includes:

- An instruction pointer which points to the instruction that is currently being executed;
- A stack;
- A set of register values, defining a part of the state of the processor executing the thread;
- A private data region.

All these elements are gathered under the name of *execution context of the thread*. The addressing space and consequently all the resources which are store there, are known of all the threads in the same process.

We will not talk about the execution of threads in *kernel mode* or in *user mode*. These two modes, used by *Windows* way before .NET, still exist. However, they are not visible from the .NET framework.

Using several threads in parallel often constitutes a natural response to the implementation of algorithms. Indeed, algorithms are often made from tasks whose execution can be done in parallel. Caution, using a large number of threads may generate a lot of *context switching*, and can eventually impair performance.

Also, we noticed that since a few years, the *Moore* law which predicted a doubling of processing speed every 18 months is not valid anymore. The frequency of processors has stagnated around 3-4GHz. This is due to physical limits which will take a certain amount of time to be surpassed. Also, to keep up with the performance race, the major processor manufacturers such as *AMD* and *Intel* are now aiming towards multi-core chip. Consequently, we can expect the proliferation of this type of architecture within the next few years. The only solution to improve the performance of an application will be to take proper advantage of multi-threading.

Managed threads vs. Windows threads

You must understand that the threads which execute .NET applications are indeed those of *Windows*. However, we say that a thread is managed when the CLR knows about it. Concretely, a thread is managed if it is created from managed code. If the thread is created by unmanaged code, it is then unmanaged itself. However, such a thread becomes managed as soon as it executes some managed code.

A managed thread distinguishes itself from an unmanaged thread by the fact that the CLR creates an instance of the `System.Threading.Thread` class to represent and manipulate it. Internally, the CLR keeps a list of all the managed threads in what is called the *ThreadStore*.

The CLR makes so that every managed thread be executed within an AppDomain at any given time. However, a thread is not necessarily tied to an AppDomain and can transition to other AppDomains over time. The notion of AppDomain is presented at page 71.

From a security point of view, the principal user of a managed thread is independent of the *Windows* principal of the underlying unmanaged thread.

Preemptive multitasking

We can ask ourselves the following question: my computer has one processor (or maybe two) and yet the task manager shows me that hundreds of threads are executing simultaneously on my machine! How is this possible?

This is possible thanks to *preemptive multitasking* which manages the scheduling of threads. Part of the *Window* kernel, called the *scheduler*, cuts up the time into portions called *quantums* (also called *time slices*). These time intervals are in the order of a few milliseconds and are not of a constant length. For each processor, every quantum is allocated to a single thread. The rapid succession of threads gives us the illusion that they are all executing simultaneously. We call *context switching* the interval between two consecutive quantums. An advantage of this method is that threads that are waiting for a *Windows* resource are not wasting quantums until the resource is available.

The 'preemptive' adjective used to qualify such a multitasking management comes from the fact that the threads are interrupted in an authoritative way by the system. For the inquiring minds, know that during the context switching, the operating system places a jump instruction to the next context switch in the code which will be executed by the next thread. This instruction is a *software interrupt*. If the thread must stop before encountering this instruction (for example, because it is waiting for a resource) this instruction is automatically removed and the context switch takes place prematurely.

The major disadvantage of preemptive multitasking is the need to protect your resources from chaotic accesses using a synchronization mechanism. There exists another model for multitasking management, called *cooperative multitasking*, where the responsibility of handing over the execution of a thread is done by the threads themselves. This model is generally deemed as dangerous as the risks of never handing over execution are big. As we explain at page 81, this mechanism is used internally to improve the performance of certain servers such as *SQL Server2005*. However, the *Windows* operating system only implements preemptive multitasking.

Priority of processes and threads

Certain tasks have a higher priority than others and require that the operating system allocates more processor time to them. For example, certain peripheral drivers taken in charge by the main processor must not be interrupted. Another category of high-priority tasks are graphical user interfaces. Indeed, the user does not like to wait for their user interface to redraw.

Those who come from the world of win32 know that the *Windows* operating system, underneath the CLR, assigns a priority number to each thread between 0 and 31. However, it is not possible in the .NET philosophy to work with these numbers because:

- They are not self-descriptive.
- Such a value is susceptible to change as time goes by.

Priority of processes

You can assign a priority to your processes using the `ProcessPriorityClass PriorityClass{get;set;}` property of the `Process` class. The `System.Diagnostics.ProcessPriorityClass` enumeration contains the following values:

Values of `ProcessPriorityClass`	Corresponding priority level
Low	4
BelowNormal	6
Normal	8
AboveNormal	10
High	13
RealTime	24

The process which owns the window in the foreground sees its priority increased by one unit if the `PriorityBoostEnabled` property of the `Process` class is set to `true` (which is its default value). This property is only accessible on an instance of the `Process` class which references a process on the same machine.

You have the possibility of changing the priority of a process by using the *task manager* tool with the following operation: *Right-click on the chosen process > Define the priority >* Choose amongst the six offered values (which are the same as in the above table).

The *Windows* operating system has an *idle process* which has a priority of 0. This priority cannot be used by any other process. By definition, the activity of processes expressed in percentage of the time is:

100% minus the time spent in the idle process.

Priority of threads

Each thread can define its own priority in relationship to the one of its process, which is set using the `ThreadPriority Priority{get;set;}` property of the `System.Threading.Thread` class. The `System.Threading.ThreadPriority` enumeration contains following values:

Value of `ThreadPriority`	Effect on the priority of the thread
Lowest	-2 units from the priority of the process
BelowNormal	−1 unit from the priority of the process
Normal	Same priority as the process
AboveNormal	+1 unit from the priority of the process
Highest	+2 units from the priority of the process

In most of your applications, you will not have to modify the priority of your processes and threads, which by default is set to `Normal`.

The System.Threading.Thread class

The CLR automatically associates an instance of the `System.Threading.Thread` to each managed thread. You can use this object to manipulate the thread from the thread itself or from another thread. You can obtain the object associated with the current thread using the `CurrentThread` static property of the `System.Threading.Thread` class:

```
using System.Threading;
...
Thread threadCurrent = Thread.CurrentThread;
```

A functionality of the `Thread` class which is practical to debug multi-threaded applications, is the possibility of naming your threads using a string:

```
threadCurrent.Name = "thread Foo";
```

Creating and joining a thread

To create a new thread in the current process, you simply need to create a new instance of the `Thread` class. The various constructors of this class take as an argument a delegate object of type `System.Threading.ThreadStart` or of type `System.Threading.ParametrizedThreadStart` which references the method which will be executed first by the created thread. The use of a delegate object of type `ParametrizedThreadStart` allows passing an object to the method which will be executed by the new thread. Some constructors of the thread class also accept an integer parameter which allows setting the maximal size of the stack in bytes for the thread. This size must be at least equal to 128KB (i.e. 131072 bytes). After an instance of type `Thread` is created, you must call the `Thread.Start()` method to actually start the thread:

Example 5-3

```
using System.Threading;
class Program {
   static void f1() { System.Console.WriteLine("f1"); }
   void f2() { System.Console.WriteLine("f2"); }
   static void f3( object obj ) { System.Console.WriteLine(
                              "f3 obj = {0}",obj); }
   static void Main() {
      // Explicitly specify the delegate class 'ThreadStart'.
      Thread t1 = new Thread( new ThreadStart(f1) );

      Program program = new Program();
      // Here, we use the C#2 facility to infer the delegate class
      // 'ThreadStart' from the definition of the 'Thread' class
      // constructor without argument.
      Thread t2 = new Thread( program.f2 );

      // Here, the C#2 compiler infer the delegate class
      // 'ParametrizedThreadStart' since the 'f3()' method
      // accept an 'object' parameter.
      Thread t3 = new Thread( f3 );

      t1.Start(); t2.Start(); t3.Start("hello");
      t1.Join();  t2.Join();  t3.Join();
   }
}
```

This program displays:

```
f1
f2
f3 obj = hello
```

In this example, we use the `Join()` method which suspends the execution of the current thread until the thread, on which the method was called, is completed. This method also exists in an overloaded form which takes in as a parameter the maximal number of milliseconds to wait for the end of the thread (i.e. a time out). This version of `Join()` returns a boolean set to `true` if the thread effectively completed within the specified timeout period.

Suspending a thread

You have the possibility of suspending the execution of a thread for a specific amount of time by using the `Sleep()` method of the `Thread` class. You can specify the sleep duration through an integer value which specifies the number of milliseconds or through an instance of the `System.TimeSpan` structure. Although that such an instance can specify the duration with a precision of a tenth of a millisecond (100 nanoseconds), the temporal granularity of the `Sleep()` method is only of one millisecond.

```
// The current thread is suspended for two seconds.
Thread.Sleep( 2000 ) ;
```

We can also suspend the activity of a thread by calling the `Suspend()` method of the `Thread` class either from the thread to suspend or from another thread. In both cases, the thread will block until another thread calls the `Resume()` method. Contrarily to the `Sleep()` method, a call to the `Suspend()` method does not immediately suspend the thread but the CLR will suspend this thread at the next safe point it encounters. The notion of safe point is discussed at page 98.

Terminating a thread

A thread can terminate itself based on several scenarios:

- It exits from the method from which its execution was started (the `Main()` method for the main thread, the method referenced by the `ThreadStart` delegate object for other threads).
- It self-terminates.
- It is terminated by another thread.

The first case being trivial, we will interest ourselves to the two other cases. In both cases, the `Abort()` method can be used (by the current thread or by an outside thread). It will cause an exception of type `ThreadAbortException` to be raised within the thread. This exception has the particularity of being automatically rethrown when it is caught by an exception handler because the thread is in a special state named `AbortRequested`. Only a call to the `Thread.ResetAbort()` static method (if we have the necessary permissions) in the exception handler can prevent this propagation.

Example 5-4   *Suicide of the main thread*

```csharp
using System;
using System.Threading;
namespace ThreadTest{
   class Program {
      static void Main() {
         Thread t = Thread.CurrentThread;
         try{
            t.Abort();
         }
         catch( ThreadAbortException ) {
            Thread.ResetAbort();
         }
      }
   }
}
```

When a thread A calls the `Abort()` on another thread B, it is recommended that A waits until B be terminated by calling `Join()` on B.

There is also the `Interrupt()` method which allows to terminate a thread when it is in a blocking state (i.e. blocked on one of the `Wait()`, `Sleep()` or `Join()` methods). This method has a different behavior depending on whether the thread to terminate is in a blocking state or not.

- If the thread to terminate is in a blocking state when `Interrupt()` is called by another thread, the `ThreadInterruptedException` exception is raised.
- If the thread to terminate is not in a blocking state when the `Interrupt()` method is called, an exception will be raised as soon as the thread enters into a blocking state. The behavior is the same if the thread calls `Interrupt()` on itself.

Foreground and background threads

The `Thread` class offers the `IsBackground{get;set}` boolean property. A *foreground thread* is a thread which prevents the termination of the process while this thread is still running. On the other hand a *background thread* is a thread which is automatically terminated by the CLR (by a call to the `Abort()` method) when there are no more *foreground threads* in the concerned process. `IsBackground` is set to `false` by default, which means that all threads are in the *foreground* state by default.

Managed thread state diagram

The `Thread` class has the `ThreadState` field of type the `System.Threading.ThreadState` enumeration type. The values of this enumeration are:

```
Aborted              AbortRequested         Background
Running              Stopped                StopRequested
Suspended            SuspendRequested       Unstarted
WaitSleepJoin
```

The description of each of these states can be found in the article named **ThreadState Enumeration** on **MSDN**. This enumeration is a *binary flag*, meaning that instances can take several values at the same time. For example, a thread can at the same time by in the `Running`, `AbortRequested` and `Background` states. The notion of binary flag is presented at page 307.

Based on what we have seen in the previous section, we can define the following simplified state diagram:

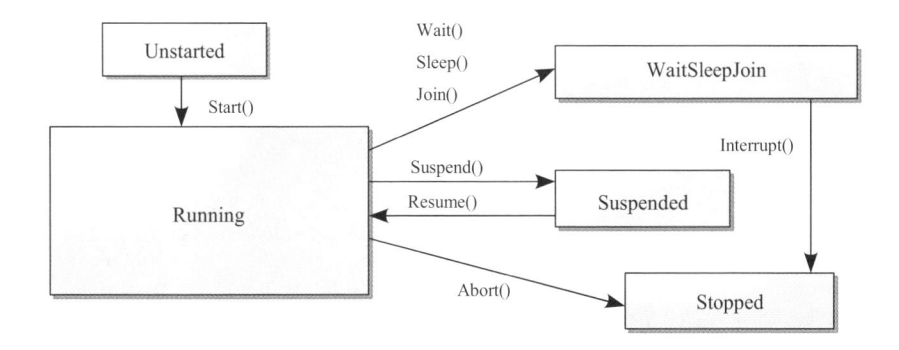

Figure 5-1: Simplified managed thread state diagram

Introduction to resource access synchronization

In computing, the *synchronization* word can be used in the case of multithreaded applications (single or multi-processor). In fact, the peculiarity of these applications is to have several execution units, where the possibility of conflicts in the access of resources. Synchronization objects are sharable between threads. The goal of a synchronization objects it to be able to block one or several threads until a condition has been met by another thread.

As we will see, there are several synchronization classes and mechanisms. Each answers to one or several specific needs and it is necessary to have properly assimilated this chapter before building a sophisticated multi-threaded application using synchronization. We have made an effort to underline the differences, especially the most subtle ones, which exists between the various mechanisms.

Properly synchronizing a program is one of the most subtle software development tasks. This subject can easily fill several books. Before diving deeper into specifics, be certain that the use of synchronization is unavoidable. Often, the use of certain simple rules can avoid the management of synchronization. Amongst these rules, let us mention the affinity rule between threads and resources that we will cover a little later.

Be aware that the difficulty in synchronizing the access to the resources of a program comes from a dilemma between a fine or coarse use of locks. If you synchronize in a coarse way the access to your resources, you simplify the code but expose yourself to bottleneck contention problems. If you synchronize too finely, your code becomes more complex to a point where it may be very tedious to maintain. You can then be exposed to *deadlocks* and *race conditions* which will be described in the following sections.

Before we start talking about the synchronization mechanisms, it is necessary to have an idea of the notions of *race conditions* and of *deadlocks*.

Race conditions

It is a situation where the actions done by various execution units chain themselves in an illogical order, causing unexpected results.

For example, a thread T modifies a resource R, releases its write access to R, retakes the read access to R and uses R as if its state was as it left it. During the time interval between when the write access is released and the read access is taken, it is possible that another thread modifies the state of R.

Another classic example of race condition is the producer/consumer model. The producer often uses the same physical memory space to store the produced information. In general, we do not forget to protect this space between concurrent accesses of the producer and consumer. We forget more often that the producer must make sure that a consumer has in fact read the old information before producing new information. If we do not take this precaution, we expose ourselves to producing information which will never be consumed.

The consequences of race conditions which are not properly managed can lead to holes in security systems. Another application can force a chain of events which was not expected by the developers. Typically, you must absolutely protect the write access to a boolean which confirms authentication. If not, it is possible that this state be modified between the moment where this bit is set by the authentication mechanism and the moment where this boolean is read to protect access to resources. Well known security holes were due to an improper management of race conditions. One of these even affected the kernel of the *Unix* operating system.

Deadlocks

This is a situation where a block occurs because two or more execution units are mutually waiting for each other. For example:

A thread T1 acquires access rights on resource R1.

A thread T2 acquires access rights on resource R2.

T1 requests the access rights to R2 and waits because T2 currently has access rights.

T2 requests the access rights to R1 and waits because T1 currently has access rights.

T1 and T2 will wait forever and we are then in a deadlock situation! There exists three main approaches to avoid this type of problem which is more subtle than most of the bugs you will encounter.

- Not authorize a thread to have access to several resources at the same time.
- Define a relationship order in the acquiring of access rights to resources. In other words, a thread cannot acquire the access rights to R2 if it has not already acquired the rights to R1. Naturally, the release of the access rights must be done in the reverse order.
- Systematically define a maximum wait time (*timeout*) for all the resource access requests and deal properly with cases where the access request fails. Almost all the .NET synchronization mechanisms offer this feature.

The first two techniques are more efficient but also more difficult to implement. In fact, they all require strong constraints which are hard to maintain during the evolution of an application. However, a failure situations will not exist with these techniques.

Large projects generally use the third approach. In fact, if the project is large, it will generally use a large number of resources. Thus, conflicts between resources will generally be rare situations, meaning that failures will also be rare. We say that such an approach is optimistic. In the same spirit, we describe at page 603 an optimistic database access model.

Synchronization with volatile fields and the Interlocked class

Volatile fields

A field of a type can be accessed by several threads. Let us suppose that these accesses are not synchronized. In this case, the several internal mechanisms of the CLR to manage code and memory make it so that there is no guarantee that a read access to the field will always load the most recent value. A field declared as volatile does give you this guarantee. In C#, a field is declared as volatile if the `volatile` keyword is used before its declaration.

Not all fields can be volatile. There is a restriction of the type of the field. For a field to be volatile, its type must be in the following list:

- A reference type (here, only accesses to references of such a type are synchronized, not the access to its members).
- A pointer (in an unsafe code block).
- `sbyte, byte, short, ushort, int, uint, char, float, bool` (`double, long` and `ulong`, as long as you are working on a 64-bit processor).
- An enumeration which uses one of the following underlying types: `byte, sbyte, short, ushort, int, uint` (`double, long` and `ulong` as long as you are working on a 64-bit processor).

As you may have noticed, only types where values or references sizes are at most the number of bytes of a native integer (four or eight depending on the underlying processor) can be volatile. This implies that concurrent accesses on a value type which is larger must be protected using the synchronization as we will discuss.

The System.Threading.Interlocked class

Experience shows that the resources which need to be protected in multithreaded situations are quite often integers. The operations most commonly done on these shared integers are increments/decrements as well as the addition of two integers. The .NET framework provides a special mechanism using the `System.Threading.Interlocked` class to accomplish these specific operations. This class offers the `Increment()`, `Decrement()` and `Add()` static methods which can be used to respectively increment, decrement and add variables of type `int` or `long` which are passed by reference. We say that the use of the `Interlocked` class makes these operations *atomic*.

The following program shows how to implement the concurrent access of two threads to an integer variable named `counter`. One thread increments it five times while the other thread decrements it five times.

Example 5-5

```
using System.Threading;
class Program {
   static long counter = 1;
   static void Main() {
      Thread t1 = new Thread(f1);
      Thread t2 = new Thread(f2);
      t1.Start(); t2.Start(); t1.Join(); t2.Join();
   }
   static void f1() {
      for ( int i = 0; i < 5; i++ ) {
         Interlocked.Increment( ref counter );
         System.Console.WriteLine( "counter++ {0}" , counter );
         Thread.Sleep( 10 );
      }
   }
   static void f2() {
      for ( int i = 0; i < 5; i++ ) {
         Interlocked.Decrement( ref counter );
         System.Console.WriteLine( "counter-- {0}" , counter );
         Thread.Sleep( 10 );
      }
   }
}
```

This program displays the following (in a non-deterministic way, which means that the display could change from an execution to another):

```
counter++ 2
counter-- 1
counter++ 2
counter-- 1
counter++ 2
counter-- 1
counter++ 2
counter-- 1
counter-- 0
counter++ 1
```

If we did not put the threads to sleep for 10 milliseconds after each modification, they would have enough time to complete their task within one quantum and there would not have been any interleaving of the operations and hence no concurrent access.

Other facilities provided by the Interlocked class

The `Interlocked` class also allows to exchange some states in an atomic way using the `Exchange()` static method. You can also use the `CompareExchange()` static method to exchange values based on a condition in an atomic way.

Synchronization with the System.Threading.Monitor class and the lock C# keyword

The fact of performing simple operations in an atomic way is without a doubt important but it is far from covering all cases where synchronization is necessary. The `System.Threading.Monitor` class allows you to make almost any portion of code executable by only one thread at the time. We call such a block of code a *critical section*.

Synchronization with the System.Threading.Monitor class and the lock C# keyword

The Enter() and Exit() methods

The `Monitor` class offers the `Enter(object)` and `Exit(object)` static methods. These methods take an object as a parameter. This object constitutes a simple mean to uniquely identify the resource which needs to be accessed in a synchronized way. When a thread calls the `Enter()` method, it waits to have the exclusive access right to the referenced object (it only waits if another thread already has this right). Once this right has been acquired and consumed, the thread releases this right by calling the `Exit()` on this same object.

> A thread can call `Enter()` several times on the same object as long as it calls `Exit()` as many times on the same object to release its exclusive access rights.
>
> A thread can also own exclusive rights on several objects at the same time, but this can lead to a deadlock situation.
>
> You must never call the `Enter()` and `Exit()` methods on an instance of a value type such as an integer!
>
> You must always call the `Exit()` in a `finally` clause in order to free all exclusive access rights no matter what happens.

If in Example 5-5, a thread must raise `counter` to its square while the other must multiply it by two, we have to replace the use of the `Interlocked` class by the use of the `Monitor` class. The code for `f1()` and `f2()` would then be:

Example 5-6

```
using System.Threading;
class Program {
   static long counter = 1;
   static void Main() {
      Thread t1 = new Thread( f1 );
      Thread t2 = new Thread( f2 );
      t1.Start(); t2.Start(); t1.Join(); t2.Join();
   }
   static void f1() {
      for (int i = 0; i < 5; i++){
         try{
            Monitor.Enter( typeof( Program ) );
            counter *= counter;
         }
         finally{ Monitor.Exit( typeof( Program ) ); }
         System.Console.WriteLine("counter^2 {0}", counter);
         Thread.Sleep(10);
      }
   }
   static void f2() {
      for (int i = 0; i < 5; i++){
         try{
            Monitor.Enter( typeof( Program ) );
            counter *= 2;
         }
         finally{ Monitor.Exit( typeof( Program ) ); }
         System.Console.WriteLine("counter*2 {0}", counter);
         Thread.Sleep(10);
      }
   }
}
```

It is tempting to write `counter` instead of `typeof(Program)` but `counter` is a static member of a value type. Notice that the square and doubling operations are not commutative and thus the final value of `counter` will not be deterministic.

The lock C# keyword

The C# language presents the `lock` keyword which is an elegant alternative to using the `Enter()` and `Exit()` methods. Our program could then be rewritten like this:

Example 5-7

```
using System.Threading;
class Program {
   static long counter = 1;
   static void Main() {
      Thread t1 = new Thread(f1);
      Thread t2 = new Thread(f2);
      t1.Start(); t2.Start(); t1.Join(); t2.Join();
   }
   static void f1() {
      for (int i = 0; i < 5; i++){
         lock( typeof(Program) ) { counter *= counter; }
         System.Console.WriteLine("counter^2 {0}", counter);
         Thread.Sleep(10);
      }
   }
   static void f2() {
      for (int i = 0; i < 5; i++){
         lock( typeof(Program) ) { counter *= 2; }
         System.Console.WriteLine("counter*2 {0}", counter);
         Thread.Sleep(10);
      }
   }
}
```

As with `for` and `if`, the blocks defined by the `lock` keyword are not required to use curly braces if they only contain a single instruction. We could have written:

```
...
lock( typeof( Program ) )
   counter *= counter;
...
```

The use of the `lock` keyword provokes the creation by the C# compiler of a `try/finally` block which allows you to anticipate any exception which might be raised. You can verify this by using one of the *Reflector* or `ildasm.exe` tool.

The SyncRoot pattern

As with the previous examples, we generally use the `Monitor` class with an instance of the `Type` class within a static method. In the same way, we will often synchronize using the `this` keyword within a non-static method. In both case, we synchronize ourselves on an object which is visible from outside of the class. This can cause problems if other parts of the code synchronize itself on these objects. To avoid such potential problems, we recommend that you use a private member named `SyncRoot` of type `object`, which is static or not depending on your needs:

Example 5-8
```
class Foo {
   private static object staticSyncRoot = new object();
   private object instanceSyncRoot = new object();
   public static void StaticFct() {
      lock ( staticSyncRoot ) { /*...*/ }
   }
   public void InstanceFct() {
      lock ( instanceSyncRoot ) { /*...*/ }
   }
}
```

The `System.Collections.ICollection` interface offers the `object SyncRoot{get;}` property. Most of the collection classes (generic or not) implement this interface. Also, you can use this property to synchronize your accesses to the elements of a collection. Here, the *SyncRoot* pattern is not really applied since the object on which we synchronize the access is not private:

Example 5-9
```
using System.Collections.Generic;
using System.Collections;
public class Program {
   public static void Main() {
      List<int> list = new List<int>();
      // ...
      lock ( ( (ICollection) list ).SyncRoot ) {
         foreach (int i in list) {
            /* ... */
         }
      }
   }
}
```

Thread-safe classes

A *thread-safe* class is a class where each instance cannot be accessed by more than one thread at the time. To create such a thread-safe class, you simply need to apply the *SyncRoot pattern* that we have seen to its methods. A good way not to burden the code of a class that we wish to be *thread-safe* is to provide a *thread-safe wrapper* derived class like this:

Example 5-10
```
class Foo {
   private class FooSynchronized : Foo {
      private object syncRoot = new object();
      private Foo m_Foo;
      public FooSynchronized( Foo foo ) { m_Foo = foo; }
      public override bool IsSynchronized { get { return true; } }
      public override void Fct1(){ lock( syncRoot ) { m_Foo.Fct1(); } }
      public override void Fct2(){ lock( syncRoot ) { m_Foo.Fct2(); } }
   }
   public virtual bool IsSynchronized { get { return false; } }
   public static Foo Synchronized(Foo foo){
      if( ! foo.IsSynchronized )
         return new FooSynchronized( foo );
      return foo;
   }
   public virtual void Fct1() { /*...*/ }
   public virtual void Fct2() { /*...*/ }
}
```

Another way is to use the `System.Runtime.Remoting.Contexts.Synchronization` attribute which we discuss a little later in this chapter.

The Monitor.TryEnter() method

```
public static bool TryEnter(object [,int] )
```

This method is similar to `Enter()` but it is non-blocking. If the exclusive access rights are already owned by another thread, this method returns immediately with a return value of `false`. We can also make a call to `TryEnter()` blocking for a limited period of time specified in milliseconds. Since the result of this method is uncertain, and that in the case where we would have acquired exclusive access rights you had to release it in a `finally` clause, it is recommended to immediately exit the calling function in the case where `TryEnter()` failed:

Example 5-11

```
using System.Threading;
class Program {
   private static object staticSyncRoot = new object();
   static void Main() {
      // Comment this line to test the case where the
      // 'TryEnter()' method returns true.
      Monitor.Enter( staticSyncRoot );
      Thread t1 = new Thread(f1);
      t1.Start(); t1.Join();
   }
   static void f1() {
      bool bOwner = false;
      try {
         if( ! Monitor.TryEnter( staticSyncRoot ) )
            return;
         bOwner = true;
         // ...
      }
      finally {
         // Don't call the 'Monitor.Exit()' if you don't own the access.
         // Keep in mind that the finally bloc will be executed
         // whatever happen.
         if( bOwner )
            Monitor.Exit( staticSyncRoot );
      }
   }
}
```

The Wait(), Pulse() and PulseAll() methods of the Monitor class

```
public static bool Wait( object [,int] )
public static void Pulse( object )
public static void PulseAll( object )
```

The `Wait()`, `Pulse()` and `PulseAll()` methods must be used together and cannot be properly understood without a small scenario. The idea is that a thread with the exclusive rights to an object decides to wait (by calling `Wait()`) until the state of the object changes. For this, this thread must accept to temporarily lose the exclusive access rights to the object in order to allow another thread to change its state. This thread must signal such a change by using the `Pulse()` method. Here is a little scenario which illustrates this in more details:

Synchronization with the System.Threading.Monitor class and the lock C# keyword

- The T1 thread which owns exclusive access to the OBJ object, calls the Wait(OBJ) method in order to register itself in a passive wait list for the OBJ object.
- With this call, T1 looses its exclusive access to OBJ. Hence, another thread T2 takes exclusive access to OBJ by calling Enter(OBJ).
- T2 eventually modifies the state of OBJ and then calls Pulse(OBJ) to indicate this modification. This call causes the first thread of the passive waiting list for OBJ (in this case T1) to move to the top of the active waiting list for OBJ. The first thread of the active list for OBJ has the guarantee that it will be the next one to have exclusive access rights to OBJ as soon as they will be released. It will then exit from its wait in the Wait(OBJ) method.
- In our scenario, T2 releases the exclusive access rights to OBJ by calling Exit(OBJ) and T1 recovers the access rights and exits from the Wait(OBJ) method.
- The PulseAll() method makes it so that the threads of the passive wait list all move to the active wait list. Notice that the threads are unblocked in the same order that they called Wait().

> If Wait(OBJ) is called by a thread who has called Enter(OBJ) several times, this thread will need to call Exit(OBJ) the same number of times to release the access rights to OBJ. Even in this case, a single call to Pulse(OBJ) by another thread will be sufficient to unblock the first thread.

The following program illustrates this functionality through two threads ping and pong which uses the access rights to a ball object in an interlaced way:

Example 5-12

```
using System.Threading;
public class Program {
   static object ball = new object();
   public static void Main() {
      Thread threadPing = new Thread( ThreadPingProc );
      Thread threadPong = new Thread( ThreadPongProc );
      threadPing.Start(); threadPong.Start();
      threadPing.Join();  threadPong.Join();
   }
   static void ThreadPongProc() {
      System.Console.WriteLine("ThreadPong: Hello!");
      lock ( ball )
         for (int i = 0; i < 5; i++){
            System.Console.WriteLine("ThreadPong: Pong ");
            Monitor.Pulse( ball );
            Monitor.Wait( ball );
         }
      System.Console.WriteLine("ThreadPong: Bye!");
   }
   static void ThreadPingProc() {
      System.Console.WriteLine("ThreadPing: Hello!");
      lock ( ball )
         for(int i=0; i< 5; i++){
            System.Console.WriteLine("ThreadPing: Ping ");
            Monitor.Pulse( ball );
            Monitor.Wait( ball );
         }
      System.Console.WriteLine("ThreadPing: Bye!");
   }
}
```

This program displays the following (in a non-deterministic way):

```
ThreadPing: Hello!
ThreadPing: Ping
ThreadPong: Hello!
ThreadPong: Pong
ThreadPing: Ping
ThreadPong: Pong
ThreadPing: Ping
ThreadPong: Pong
ThreadPing: Ping
ThreadPong: Pong
ThreadPing: Ping
ThreadPong: Pong
ThreadPing: Bye!
```

The `pong` thread does not end and remains blocked on the `Wait()` method. This results from the fact that the `pong` thread has obtained the exclusive access rights on the `ball` object second place.

Synchronizing with win32 objects: mutex, events and semaphores

The `System.Threading.WaitHandle` abstract base class offers three derived classes whose use is well known of those who have used synchronization under win32:

- The `Mutex` class (the mutex word is short for MUTual EXclusion).
- The `AutoResetEvent` class which defines an automatically reset event. The `ManualResetEvent` class which defines a manually reset event. These two classes derive from `EventWaitHandle` which represent an event in general.
- The `Semaphore` class.

The `WaitHandle` class and its derived classes have the peculiarity of overriding the `WaitOne()` method and of implementing the `WaitAll()`, `WaitAny()` and `SignalAndWait()` static methods. They respectively allow waiting for object to be signaled or that all the objects in an array be signaled, to wait for at least one object in an array to be signaled and to signal on an object while waiting for another. Contrarily to the `Monitor` and `Interlocked` classes, these classes must be instantiated to be used. So here, you must think in terms of synchronization objects and not in terms of synchronized objects. This implies that the objects passed as a parameter to the `WaitAll()`, `WaitAny()` and `SignalAndWait()` static methods are all mutex, events or semaphores.

Sharing win32 synchronization objects

It is important to note another big distinction between the synchronization models proposed by the `Monitor` class and the classes derived from `WaitHandle`. The use of the `Monitor` class is related to a single process. The use of classes derived from `WaitHandle` makes calls to unmanaged win32 objects which can be known from several processes on the same machine. For this, certain constructors of classes derived from the `WaitHandle` class allows a string argument which names the synchronization object. These classes also offer the `OpenExisting(string)` method which allows obtaining a reference to an existing named synchronization object.

You can in fact go further since the `WaitHandle` class derives from `MarshalByRefObject`. Hence, such a synchronization object can be shared amongst several processes on different machines by using the .NET Remoting technology.

Synchronizing with win32 objects: mutex, events and semaphores 127

At page 174, we explain how to use the `MutexSecurity`, `EventWaitHandleSecurity` and `SemaphoreSecurity` types of the `System.Security.AccessControl` namespace to manipulate the *Windows* access rights granted to synchronization objects.

Mutex

In terms of functionality, the use of a mutex is close to the use of the `Monitor` with a few differences:

- We can use a same mutex in several processes on a same or even remote machine.
- The use of `Monitor` does not allow waiting on several objects.
- The mutex class does not have the `Wait()`, `Pulse()` and `PulseAll()` functionalities of the `Monitor` class.

Know that instead of using a mutex inside only one process, you should consider synchronizing your access with the `Monitor` class which is more efficient.

The following program shows the use of a *named mutex* to protect the access to a resource which is shared by several processes on a same machine. The shared resource is a file in which each instance of the program writes 10 lines.

Example 5-13
```
using System.Threading;
using System.IO;
class Program {
   static void Main() {
      // The mutex created is named 'MutexTest'.
      Mutex mutexFile = new Mutex(false, "MutexTest");
      for (int i = 0; i < 10; i++){
         mutexFile.WaitOne();
         // Open the file, write 'Hello i' and then close it.
         FileInfo fi = new FileInfo("tmp.txt");
         StreamWriter sw = fi.AppendText();
         sw.WriteLine("Hello {0}", i);
         sw.Flush();
         sw.Close();
         System.Console.WriteLine("Hello {0}", i);
         // Wait one second to make obvious the sharing of mutex.
         Thread.Sleep(1000);
         mutexFile.ReleaseMutex();
      }
      mutexFile.Close();
   }
}
```

Notice the use of the `WaitOne()` method which blocks the current thread until mutex is obtained and the use of the `ReleaseMutex()` method which releases the mutex.

In this program the call to `new Mutex` does not necessarily mean the creation of a mutex but the creation of a reference to a mutex named "MutexTest". The mutex is created by the operating system only if it does not already exist. In the same way, the `Close()` method only destroys the mutex if no other process references it.

For those who are used to using the named mutex technique with win32 in order to avoid that two instance of a same program run on the same machine, know that there is a more elegant approach offered in .NET which is described at page 111.

Events

Contrarily to the synchronization mechanisms seen until now, events do not explicitly define the notion of belonging to a resource of a thread at a given time. Events are used to pass a notification from one thread to another, the notification being '*an event has occurred*'. The concerned event is associated to an instance of the two event classes named `System.Threading.AutoResetEvent` and `System.Threading.ManualResetEvent`. These two classes derive from the `System.Threading.EventWaitHandle` class. An instance of `EventWaitHandle` can be initialized with one of two `AutoReset` or `ManualReset` values from the `System.Threading.EventResetMode` enumeration meaning you do not have an explicit need to instantiate one of the derived classes directly.

Concretely, a thread waits for an event to be signaled by using the `WaitOne()` blocking method on the object that represents the event. Then another thread signals the event by using the `Set()` method on the event object thus allowing the first thread to continue its execution.

The difference between an *auto-reset event* and the *manual reset events* is that we need to call the `Reset()` method to bring the event back into a non-active state.

> The difference between a manual and automatic reset is more significant that you may think. If several threads wait on the same automatic-reset event, the event must be signaled once for each thread. In the case of a manual-reset event, you simply need to signal the event once for all the blocked threads to resume.

The following program creates two threads, t0 and t1, which increment their own counters different rates. t0 signals the events[0] event once it reaches 2 and t1 signals the events[1] event when it reaches 3. The main thread waits for both events to be signaled in order to display a message.

Example 5-14

```
using System;
using System.Threading;
class Program {
   static EventWaitHandle[] events;
   static void Main() {
      events = new EventWaitHandle[2];
      // Initial event state : false
      events[0] = new EventWaitHandle( false ,EventResetMode.AutoReset );
      events[1] = new EventWaitHandle( false ,EventResetMode.AutoReset );
      Thread t0 = new Thread( ThreadProc0 );
      Thread t1 = new Thread( ThreadProc1 );
      t0.Start(); t1.Start();
      AutoResetEvent.WaitAll( events );
      Console.WriteLine( "MainThread: Thread0 reached  2" +
                        " and Thread1 reached 3." );
      t0.Join();t1.Join();
   }
   static void ThreadProc0() {
      for ( int i = 0; i < 5; i++ ) {
         Console.WriteLine( "Thread0: {0}", i );
         if ( i == 2 ) events[0].Set();
         Thread.Sleep( 100 );
      }
   }
   static void ThreadProc1() {
      for ( int i = 0; i < 5; i++ ) {
```

Example 5-14

```
            Console.WriteLine( "Thread1: {0}", i );
            if ( i == 3 ) events[1].Set();
            Thread.Sleep( 60 );
         }
      }
   }
```

This program displays:

```
Thread0: 0
Thread1: 0
Thread1: 1
Thread0: 1
Thread1: 2
Thread1: 3
Thread0: 2
MainThread: Thread0 reached 2 and Thread1 reached 3
Thread1: 4
Thread0: 3
Thread0: 4
```

Semaphores

An instance of the `System.Threading.Semaphore` class allows you to constrain the number of simultaneous accesses to a resource. You can imagine the entry gate of a parking lot which contains only a certain number of parking spots. The gate will only open when there is room left in the parking. In the same way, an attempts to enter a semaphore using the `WaitOne()` method becomes blocking when the number of current entries reached a certain maximum number. This maximum entry number is set by the second argument of the constructors for the `Semaphore` class. The first argument defines the initial number of free entries. If the first argument is a value inferior to the second, the thread calling the constructor automatically holds a certain number of entries defined by the difference between these two values. This last remark shows that a same thread can hold several entries to a same semaphore.

The following example illustrates all this by launching 3 threads which regularly attempt to enter into a semaphore where the maximal number of entries is set to five. The main thread maintains three entries to this semaphore, forcing the 3 threads to share the remaining 2 entries.

Example 5-15

```
using System;
using System.Threading;
class Program {
   static Semaphore semaphore;
   static void Main() {
      // Initial number of free slots                         : 2.
      // Maximal number of slots used simulteanously          : 5.
      // Number of slot owned by the main thread              : 3 (5-2).
      semaphore = new Semaphore( 2, 5 );
      for ( int i = 0; i < 3; ++i ) {
         Thread t = new Thread( WorkerProc );
         t.Name = "Thread" + i;
         t.Start();
         Thread.Sleep( 30 );
      }
   }
```

Example 5-15

```
    static void WorkerProc() {
       for ( int j = 0; j < 3; j++ ) {
          semaphore.WaitOne();
          Console.WriteLine( Thread.CurrentThread.Name + ": Begin" );
          Thread.Sleep( 200 );   // Simulate a 200 milliseconds task.
          Console.WriteLine( Thread.CurrentThread.Name + ": End" );
          semaphore.Release();
       }
    }
}
```

Here is the display of the program. We see that there will never be more than 2 child threads which will be working simultaneously:

```
Thread0: Begin
Thread1: Begin
Thread0: End
Thread2: Begin
Thread1: End
Thread1: Begin
Thread2: End
Thread2: Begin
Thread1: End
Thread1: Begin
Thread2: End
Thread2: Begin
Thread1: End
Thread0: Begin
Thread2: End
Thread0: End
Thread0: Begin
Thread0: End
```

Synchronizing using the System.Threading.ReaderWriterLock class

The `System.Threading.ReaderWriterLock` class implements a *multiple read access/single write access* synchronization mechanism. Contrarily to the *exclusive access* model offered by the `Monitor` or `Mutex` classes, this mechanism takes into account the fact that a thread may require only read or write access to a resource. A read access can be obtained when there is no write access granted. A write access can be obtained when there is no other access going on. In addition, when a write access has been requested but not obtained, all new read access will be put on hold.

> When this synchronization model can be applied, it is always better to prefer it to the `Monitor` or `Mutex` classes. In fact, the exclusive access model does not allow for any simultaneous access and is thus less efficient. In addition, we can notice that applications generally access resource more often to read it than to write to it.

As with mutex and events and contrarily to the `Monitor` class, the `ReaderWriterLock` class must be instantiated in order to be used. You must then think in terms of synchronization objects and not of synchronized objects.

Synchronizing using the System.Threading.ReaderWriterLock class

Here is an example which shows the use of this class, but which does not use all of its features. Indeed, the `DowngradeFromWriterLock()` and `UpgradeToWriterLock()` methods allows to request a change of access right without having to release the current access.

Example 5-16

```
using System;
using System.Threading;
class Program {
   static int theResource  = 0;
   static ReaderWriterLock rwl = new ReaderWriterLock();
   static void Main() {
      Thread tr0 = new Thread( ThreadReader );
      Thread tr1 = new Thread( ThreadReader );
      Thread tw = new Thread( ThreadWriter );
      tr0.Start(); tr1.Start(); tw.Start();
      tr0.Join();  tr1.Join();  tw.Join();
   }
   static void ThreadReader() {
      for ( int i = 0; i < 3; i++ )
         try{
            // AcquireReaderLock() raises an
            // ApplicationException when timed out.
            rwl.AcquireReaderLock(1000);
            Console.WriteLine("Begin Read  theResource = {0}",theResource);
            Thread.Sleep(10);
            Console.WriteLine("End   Read  theResource = {0}",theResource);
            rwl.ReleaseReaderLock();
         }
         catch ( ApplicationException ) { /* ... */ }
   }
   static void ThreadWriter() {
      for (int i = 0; i < 3; i++)
         try{
            // AcquireReaderLock() raises an
            // ApplicationException when timed out.
            rwl.AcquireWriterLock(1000);
            Console.WriteLine("Begin Write theResource = {0}",theResource);
            Thread.Sleep(100);
            theResource  ++;
            Console.WriteLine("End   Write theResource = {0}",theResource);
            rwl.ReleaseWriterLock();
         }
         catch ( ApplicationException ) { /* ... */ }
   }
}
```

This program displays:

```
Begin Read   theResource = 0
Begin Read   theResource = 0
End   Read   theResource = 0
End   Read   theResource = 0
Begin Write  theResource = 0
End   Write  theResource = 1
Begin Read   theResource = 1
Begin Read   theResource = 1
End   Read   theResource = 1
End   Read   theResource = 1
Begin Write  theResource = 1
End   Write  theResource = 2
Begin Read   theResource = 2
Begin Read   theResource = 2
End   Read   theResource = 2
End   Read   theResource = 2
Begin Write  theResource = 2
End   Write  theResource = 3
```

Synchronizing using the System.Runtime.Remoting.Contexts. SynchronizationAttribute attribute

When the `System.Runtime.Remoting.Contexts.Synchronization` attribute is applied to a class, an instance of this class cannot be accessed by more than one thread at a time. We say that such a class is *thread-safe*.

> In order to obtain this behavior, the class on which the attribute is applied must be *context-bound*. In other words, it must derive from the `System.ContextBoundObject` class. The meaning of the *context-bound* term is explained at page 700.

Here is an example which exposes how to apply this behavior:

Example 5-17

```csharp
using System.Runtime.Remoting.Contexts;
using System.Threading;
[Synchronization(SynchronizationAttribute.REQUIRED)]
public class Foo : System.ContextBoundObject {
   public void DisplayThreadId() {
      System.Console.WriteLine( "Begin: ManagedThreadId = " +
                         Thread.CurrentThread.ManagedThreadId );
      Thread.Sleep( 1000 );
      System.Console.WriteLine( "End:   ManagedThreadId = " +
                         Thread.CurrentThread.ManagedThreadId );
   }
}
public class Program {
   static Foo m_Objet = new Foo();
   static void Main() {
      Thread t0 = new Thread( ThreadProc );
      Thread t1 = new Thread( ThreadProc );
      t0.Start(); t1.Start();
      t0.Join();  t1.Join();
   }
```

Synchronizing using System.Runtime.Remoting.Contexts.SynchronizationAttribute

Example 5-17
```
    static void ThreadProc() {
       for ( int i = 0; i < 2; i++ )
          m_Objet.DisplayThreadId();
    }
}
```

This program displays:

```
Begin: ManagedThreadId = 27
End:   ManagedThreadId = 27
Begin: ManagedThreadId = 28
End:   ManagedThreadId = 28
Begin: ManagedThreadId = 27
End:   ManagedThreadId = 27
Begin: ManagedThreadId = 28
End:   ManagedThreadId = 28
```

Introduction to synchronization domains

For a good reading of what follows, you must have an understanding of the following notions:

- AppDomains (described at page 71),
- .NET contexts and context-bound/context-agile objects (described at page 700),
- Message sinks (described at page 684).

A synchronization domain is an entity which is completely taken over by the CLR. Such a domain contains one or several .NET contexts and thus, contains all the objects of these contexts. A .NET context can belong to at most one synchronization domain. Moreover, the notion of a synchronization domain is finer than the notion of an AppDomain. The following figure illustrates the relations between processes, AppDomains, synchronization contexts, .NET contexts and .NET object.

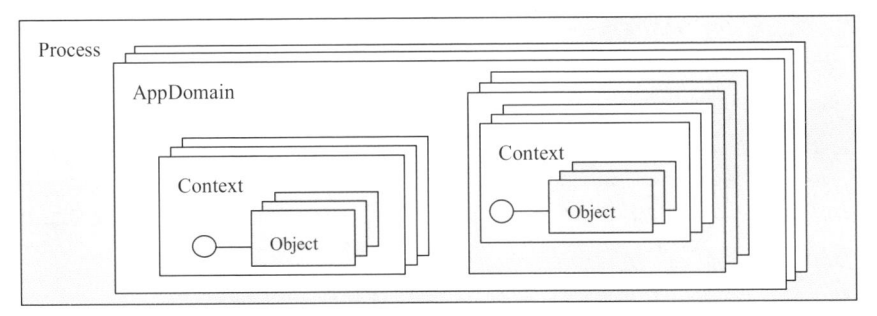

Figure 5-2: Process, AppDomain, Synchronization domain, .NET context and .NET object

Since we are talking about synchronization, and thus of *multi-threaded* applications, it is useful to remember that the notions of AppDomains and threads of a process are orthogonal. In fact, a thread can freely traverse the boundary between two AppDomains, for example, by calling an object A located in a DA AppDomain, from an object B located in the DB AppDomain. In addition, the code of an AppDomain can be executed simultaneously by zero, one or several threads.

All the interest behind a synchronization domain resides in the fact that it cannot be shared simultaneously by several threads. In other words, the methods of the objects contained in a synchronization domain cannot be simultaneously executed by several threads. This implies that at any given time, at most one thread is within the synchronization domain. We then talk of *exclusive access rights* to the synchronization domain. Again, the management of this exclusive access right is guaranteed by the CLR.

The System.Runtime.Remoting.Contexts.Synchronization and synchronization domains

You may have already guessed that the `System.Runtime.Remoting.Contexts.Synchronization` attribute is in fact used to tell the CLR when to create a synchronization domain and how to define its boundaries. These settings are done in the declaration of a `System.Runtime.Remoting.Contexts.Synchronization` attribute using one of the four following values: NOTSUPPORTED, SUPPORTED, REQUIRED or REQUIRES_NEW. Note that REQUIRED is the default value.

The membership to an AppDomain is communicated when one object creates another. Here we talk of a *creator object*, but take into account that an object can also be created within a static method. It is possible that the execution of the static method might be caused by the call from an object located in a synchronization domain. Know that in this case, the static method propagates the membership to the AppDomain and thus plays the role of a creator object. Here is the explanation of the four possible behaviors:

NOT_SUPPORTED	This parameter ensures that an instance of the class on which the Synchronization attribute is applied will **never belong** to a synchronization domain (whether or not its creator object belongs to a synchronization domain).
SUPPORTED	This parameter indicates that an instance of the class on which the Synchronization attribute is applied **does not need to belong** to a synchronization domain. However, such an instance will belong to the synchronization domain of its creator object if it is part of one. This behavior has little use as the developer must still provide another synchronization mechanism within the methods of the class. However, it can eventually allow the propagation of the membership to a synchronization domain from an object which does not need to be synchronized (this type of object is rare as it must not have any state).
REQUIRED	This parameter ensures that an instance of the class on which we apply the Synchronization attribute **will always be part of a** synchronization domain. If the creator object belongs to a synchronization domain then it will subscribe to this one. If not, a new synchronization domain is created for this new object.
REQUIRES_NEW	This parameter ensures that an instance of the class on which the Synchronization attribute is applied **will be in a new** synchronization domain (whether or not the creator object belongs to a synchronization domain).

These behaviors can be summarized as follows:

The Applied Value	Is the creator object in a synchronization domain?	The created object will reside...
NOT_SUPPORTED	No	...outside of all synchronization domain.
	Yes	
SUPPORTED	No	...outside of all synchronization domain.
	Yes	...in the synchronization domain of the creator object.
REQUIRED	No	...in a new synchronization object.
	Yes	...in the synchronization domain of the creator object.
REQUIRES_NEW	No	...in a new synchronization domain.
	Yes	

Reentrancy and synchronization domains

In a synchronization domain D, when the T1 thread which has exclusive access rights calls a method on an object located outside of D, two behaviors can be applied by the CLR:

Synchronizing using System.Runtime.Remoting.Contexts.SynchronizationAttribute

- Either the CLR authorizes another thread T2 to acquire the exclusive rights to D. In this case, it is possible that T1 may have to wait after its call outside of D for T2 to free the exclusive access rights to D. Here we say that there is *reentrancy* since T1 requests to re-enter into D.
- Either the exclusive rights to D remain allocated to T1. In this case, another thread T2 which wishes to invoke a method of an object in D will need to wait for T1 to release its exclusive access rights to D.

A call to a static method is not considered as a call outside of a synchronization domain.

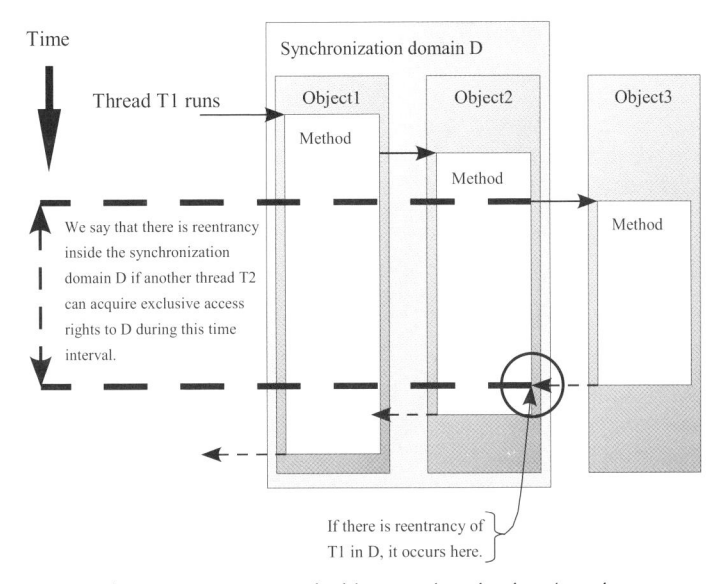

Figure 5-3: Reentrancy inside a synchronization domain

Certain constructors of the `System.Runtime.Remoting.Contexts.Synchronization` class accept a boolean as a parameter. The boolean defines if there is reentrancy when a call is made outside of the current synchronization domain. When this boolean is set to `true`, reentrancy is enabled. Note that there only needs for the synchronization attribute of the first object encountered in a synchronization domain be set to `true` for there to be reentrancy on all objects.

The following example illustrates using code the above figure:

Example 5-18

```
using System;
using System.Runtime.Remoting.Contexts;
using System.Threading;
[Synchronization( SynchronizationAttribute.REQUIRES_NEW, true )]
public class Foo1 : ContextBoundObject {
   public void DisplayThreadId() {
      Console.WriteLine( "Foo1 Begin: ManagedThreadId = " +
                         Thread.CurrentThread.ManagedThreadId );
      Thread.Sleep( 1000 );
      Foo2 obj2 = new Foo2();
      obj2.DisplayThreadId();
      Console.WriteLine( "Foo1 End:   ManagedThreadId = " +
                         Thread.CurrentThread.ManagedThreadId );
   }
}
```

Example 5-18

```
[Synchronization( SynchronizationAttribute.REQUIRED )]
public class Foo2 : ContextBoundObject {
   public void DisplayThreadId() {
      Console.WriteLine( "Foo2 Begin: ManagedThreadId = " +
                        Thread.CurrentThread.ManagedThreadId );
      Thread.Sleep( 1000 );
      Foo3 obj3 = new Foo3();
      obj3.DisplayThreadId();
      Console.WriteLine( "Foo2 End:   ManagedThreadId = " +
                        Thread.CurrentThread.ManagedThreadId );
   }
}
// We can be sure that instances of the 'Foo3' class will never reside
// in any synchronization domain.
[Synchronization( SynchronizationAttribute.NOT_SUPPORTED )]
public class Foo3 : ContextBoundObject {
   public void DisplayThreadId() {
      Console.WriteLine( "Foo3 Begin: ManagedThreadId = " +
                        Thread.CurrentThread.ManagedThreadId );
      Thread.Sleep( 1000 );
      Console.WriteLine( "Foo3 End:   ManagedThreadId = " +
                        Thread.CurrentThread.ManagedThreadId );
   }
}
public class Program {
   static Foo1 m_Objet = new Foo1();
   static void Main() {
      Thread t1 = new Thread( ThreadProc );
      Thread t2 = new Thread( ThreadProc );
      t1.Start(); t2.Start();
      t1.Join(); t2.Join();
   }
   static void ThreadProc() {
      m_Objet.DisplayThreadId();
   }
}
```

This program displays the following:

```
Foo1 Begin: ManagedThreadId = 3
Foo2 Begin: ManagedThreadId = 3
Foo1 Begin: ManagedThreadId = 4
Foo2 Begin: ManagedThreadId = 4
Foo3 Begin: ManagedThreadId = 4
Foo3 Begin: ManagedThreadId = 3
Foo3 End:   ManagedThreadId = 4
Foo2 End:   ManagedThreadId = 4
Foo1 End:   ManagedThreadId = 4
Foo3 End:   ManagedThreadId = 3
Foo2 End:   ManagedThreadId = 3
Foo1 End:   ManagedThreadId = 3
```

It is clear that if we had deactivated the reentrancy in Foo1, the display of the program would have been the following:

```
Foo1 Begin:  ManagedThreadId = 3
Foo2 Begin:  ManagedThreadId = 3
Foo3 Begin:  ManagedThreadId = 3
Foo3 End:    ManagedThreadId = 3
Foo2 End:    ManagedThreadId = 3
Foo1 End:    ManagedThreadId = 3
Foo1 Begin:  ManagedThreadId = 4
Foo2 Begin:  ManagedThreadId = 4
Foo3 Begin:  ManagedThreadId = 4
Foo3 End:    ManagedThreadId = 4
Foo2 End:    ManagedThreadId = 4
```

Reentrancy is used to optimize the management of resources as it allows to globally reduce the duration of exclusive accesses of the threads over the synchronization domains. However, by default, reentrancy is deactivated. In fact, when there is reentrancy, our understanding of the notion of synchronization domain is strongly changed. Even worse, activating reentrancy without proper justification can lead to *deadlock* situations. For these reasons, it is recommended not to take advantage of reentrancy unless needed.

Another attribute named Synchronization

The .NET framework offers another attributes with this name but that is part of a different namespace. This `System.EntrepriseServices.Synchronization` attribute has the same goal but internally uses the COM+ synchronization enterprise service. The use of the `System.Runtime.Remoting.Contexts.Synchronization` attribute is preferred for two reasons:

- Its use is more efficient.
- This mechanism supports asynchronous calls, contrarily to the COM+ version.

The notion of COM+ enterprise services is presented at page 244.

The CLR's threadpool

Introduction

The concept of *thread pool* is not new. However, the .NET framework allows you to use the thread pool more easily than with any other technology thanks to the `System.Threading.ThreadPool` class.

In a multithreaded application, most of the threads spend their time waiting for events. Generally, threads are globally under-used. In addition, the fact that you must account for the management of threads during the design of our application is an added task that you could easily live without.

The use of a thread pool resolves these problems in an elegant and efficient way. You can post tasks to the pool which takes care of distributing them to its threads. The pool is entirely responsible for:

- The creation and destruction of its threads;
- The distribution of tasks;
- The optimal use of its threads.

The developer is thus relieved from these responsibilities. Despite all these advantages, it is preferable not to use threads from the pool when:

- Your tasks must be managed using a priority system;
- Your tasks take a long time to execute (several seconds);
- Your tasks must be processed in a *STA* (*Single Apartment Thread*). In fact, the threads of a pool are of type *MTA* (*Multiple Apartment Thread*). This notion of *thread apartment*, inherent to the COM technology is detailed at page 236.

Using the thread pool

In .NET there is a single thread pool per process. This means that all the methods of the `ThreadPool` class are static since they all apply to a unique pool. The .NET framework uses this pool for asynchronous calls, asynchronous input/output needs as well as timers. Both asynchronous calls and timers are described a little later in the current chapter.

The maximal number of threads in the pool is by default 25 *worker threads* per process and 25 threads per process to handle asynchronous operations (*completion port thread* or *I/O thread*). These two limits can be modified at any time by calling the `ThreadPool.SetMaxThreads()` static method. If the maximal number of threads is reached in the pool, it will not create any new threads. If additional tasks are submitted when all threads are active, they will wait in the queue until a thread is available. However, the thread which created the tasks does not need to wait until the task is processed. You can use the thread pool in two different ways:

- By posting your own tasks and their processing methods using the `ThreadPool.QueueUserWorkItem()` static method. Once a task has been posted to the pool, it cannot be canceled.

- By creating a timer which will periodically post a predefined task and its processing method to this pool. For this, you must use the `ThreadPool.RegisterWaitForSingleObject()` static method.

Notice that processing methods are referenced using delegate objects. Each of these two methods exist in an unsafe version (`UnsafeQueueUserWorkItem()` and `UnsafeRegisterWaitForSingleObject()`). These two unsafe versions allows for the worker threads not to be in the same security context as the thread which posted the task. The use of these methods improves the performance since the stack of the thread who is posting the task is not verified during the management of the security context.

Here is an example that shows the use of user tasks (parameterized using a number and processed by the `ThreadTask()` method) and tasks which are posted periodically (without a parameter and processed by the `ThreadTaskWait()` method). The user tasks are purposefully long in order to force the pool to create new threads.

Example 5-19

```
using System.Threading;
public class Program {
   public static void Main() {
      ThreadPool.RegisterWaitForSingleObject(
         new AutoResetEvent( false ),
         // Method which represents the periodic task.
         new WaitOrTimerCallback( ThreadTaskWait ),
         null,   // No parameter for the periodic task.
         2000,   // Period = 2 seconds.
         false); // Trigger the periodic task for ever.

      // Post 3 user tasks with parameters 0,1,2.
      for ( int count = 0; count < 3; ++count )
         ThreadPool.QueueUserWorkItem(new WaitCallback(ThreadTask), count);

      // Wait 12 seconds before shutting down the process.
      // Keep in mind that threadpool threads are background.
      Thread.Sleep( 12000 );
   }
   static void ThreadTask( object obj ) {
      System.Console.WriteLine( "Thread#{0}  Task#{1}  Begin",
                Thread.CurrentThread.ManagedThreadId , obj.ToString());
```

Example 5-19
```
      Thread.Sleep( 5000 );
      System.Console.WriteLine( "Thread#{0}  Task#{1}  End",
                 Thread.CurrentThread.ManagedThreadId , obj.ToString());
   }
   static void ThreadTaskWait( object obj, bool signaled ) {
      System.Console.WriteLine("Thread#{0}   TaskWait",
                 Thread.CurrentThread.ManagedThreadId );
   }
}
```

This program displays the following (in a non-deterministic way):

```
Thread#4   Task#0   Begin
Thread#5   Task#1   Begin
Thread#6   Task#2   Begin
Thread#7   TaskWait
Thread#7   TaskWait
Thread#4   Task#0   End
Thread#5   Task#1   End
Thread#6   Task#2   End
Thread#7   TaskWait
Thread#7   TaskWait
```

Timers

Most applications contain tasks which must be executed periodically. For example, you may want to periodically verify the availability of a server. The first solution which comes to mind is to create a thread dedicated to this task which calls `Thread.Sleep()` between two executions. This implementation has the inconvenient of consuming a thread which is not used between these two executions. We will present several implementations provided by the .NET framework which are more efficient.

More specifically, the framework offers the `System.Timers.Timer`, `System.Threading.Timer` and `System.Windows.Forms.Timer` classes. The class of the `Forms` namespace must be used to execute periodical graphical tasks such as the update of data on forms or the handling of a frame-based animation. The choice between the classes of the `Timers` and `Threading` namespaces is more delicate and depends on your needs.

The System.Timers.Timer class

The `System.Timers.Timer` implementation uses the threads from the pool to execute a task. Also, you must synchronize the access to resources used by such a task.

This class presents the `double Interval{get;set;}` property which allows to set the execution period, defined in milliseconds. The `Start()` and `Stop()` methods allows to activate and deactivate the timer. You can also change the activation of the timer using the `bool Enabled{get;set;}` property.

A delegate object of type `ElapsedEventHandler` references the method which represents the tasks to be executed. This reference is represented by the `ElapsedEventHandler Elapsed` event. The signature proposed by the `ElapsedEventHandler` delegate type is as follows:

```
void ElapsedEventHandler(object sender, ElapsedEventArgs e)
```

The first argument references the timer which triggered the task. Hence, several timers can trigger a same method and you can differentiate them using this argument. In addition, since a delegate object can reference several methods, a same timer can consecutively call several methods each time it is triggered. The second argument contains the time at which the timer was triggered. You can recover it using the `DateTime ElapsedEvenArgs.SignalTime{get;}` property. The following program illustrates the use of the `System.Timers.Timer` class:

Example 5-20

```
using System.Timers;
class Program {
   static Timer Timer1 = new Timer();
   static Timer Timer2 = new Timer();
   static void Main() {
      Timer1.Interval = 1000;  // Period = 1 second.
      Timer1.Elapsed += new ElapsedEventHandler( PeriodicTaskHandler );
      Timer2.Interval = 2000;  // Period = 2 seconds.
      Timer2.Elapsed += new ElapsedEventHandler( PeriodicTaskHandler );
      Timer2.Elapsed += new ElapsedEventHandler( PeriodicTaskHandler );
      Timer1.Start(); Timer2.Start();
      System.Threading.Thread.Sleep( 5000 ); // Sleep 5 seconds.
      Timer1.Stop(); Timer2.Stop();
   }
   static void PeriodicTaskHandler( object sender, ElapsedEventArgs e ) {
      string str = ( sender == Timer1 ) ? "Timer1 " : "Timer2 ";
      str += e.SignalTime.ToLongTimeString();
      System.Console.WriteLine( str );
   }
}
```

This program displays the following:

```
Timer1 19:42:49
Timer1 19:42:50
Timer2 19:42:50
Timer2 19:42:50
Timer1 19:42:51
Timer1 19:42:52
Timer2 19:42:52
Timer2 19:42:52
Timer1 19:42:53
```

Finally, know that the `ISynchronizeInvoke Timer.SynchronizingObject` property allows you to specify the thread which must execute the task. The `ISynchronizeInvoke` interface is discussed a little later in this chapter.

The System.Threading.Timer class

The `System.Threading.Timer` class is very similar to the `System.Timers.Timer` class. This class also uses the threads from the pool to execute a task but with the exception that it does not allow you to specify which thread is to be used.

Another difference is that this class allows you to provide a *due time*. The due time defines the amount of time to delay before invoking the callback method specified when the `Timer` was constructed. You can modify the due time at any time by calling the `Change()` method. By specifying 0, you can start the timer immediately. By specifying the `System.Threading.Timer.Infinite` constant, you can stop the timer. You can also stop the timer by calling the `Dispose()` method but then you cannot restart it.

The System.Windows.Forms.Timer class

The philosophy behind the use of the `System.Windows.Forms.Timer` class is closer to the one of the `System.Timers.Timer` than the one of the `System.Threading.Timer` class. The peculiarity of this class is that it always starts its tasks with the thread dedicated to the concerned window. This comes from the fact that this implementation internally uses the `WM_TIMER` Windows message. You must not use this class to start tasks whose execution will take more than a few fractions of a second to avoid freezing the user interface. An example of the use of this class can be found in the chapter dedicated to *Windows Forms* at page 582.

Calling a method asynchronously

> To start this section it is important to have understood the notion of delegates, explained at page 313.

We say that a call to a method is synchronous when the thread on the side which triggers the call, waits for the method to be done before continuing. This behavior consumes resources as the thread is blocked during this time. During a call to a remote object, this duration can possibly be huge since the cost of a network call can take thousands of clock cycles. However, this wait is not necessary in the case where the information retrieved by the call is not consumed immediately after the call to the method. In general programming and especially in distributed architectures, it happens quite often that a call to a method completes an action and returns only information as to whether the action was successful. In this case, the program does not immediately need to know whether or not the action succeeded. We can decide to restart this action later if we learn that it has failed.

To manage this type of situation, we can use an *asynchronous call*. The idea is that the thread that makes a call to a method returns immediately without waiting for the call to be completed. In an in-process scenario, the call is immediately taken over by a thread from the pool. Later on, the program can retrieve the information returned by the asynchronous call. The asynchronous call technique is fully managed by the CLR.

The mechanism that we describe can be used in your own architectures. It is also used by the classes of the .NET framework, especially for the management of data streams in an asynchronous way or to manage asynchronous calls to remote objects, which are located in another AppDomain.

Asynchronous delegates

During an asynchronous call, you do not need to create nor manage the thread which executes the body of the method. This thread is managed by the thread pool which was described earlier.

Before using an *asynchronous delegate*, it is good to notice that all the delegate types automatically offers two methods named `BeginInvoke()` and `EndInvoke()`. The signatures of these methods are based on the signature of the delegate type which contains them. For example, the following delegate type …

```
delegate int Deleg( int a, int b );
```

…exposes the two following methods:

```
IAsyncResult BeginInvoke( int a,int b ,AsyncCallback callback, object o );
int EndInvoke( IAsyncResult result );
```

These two methods are produced by the C# compiler. However, the intellisense technology of *Visual Studio* is capable of inferring them from a delegate type in order to present them to you

To call a method in an asynchronous way, you must first reference it using a delegate object which has the same signature. Then, you simply need to call the `BeginInvoke()` method on this delegate object. As you have noticed, the compiler makes sure that the first arguments of `BeginInvoke()` are the arguments of the method to be called. The two last arguments of this method, of type `AsyncCallback` and `object`, are described a little later.

The return value of an asynchronous call can be recovered by calling the `EndInvoke()` method. There also, the compiler makes it so that the return value of `EndInvoke()` be the same as the return value of the delegate type (this type is `int` in our example). The call to `EndInvoke()` is blocking, meaning that the call will only return when the asynchronous execution is effectively done.

The following program illustrates the asynchronous call to a `WriteSum()` method.

Example 5-21
```
using System.Threading;
class Program {
   public delegate int Deleg( int a, int b );
   static int WriteSum( int a, int b ) {
      int sum = a + b;
      System.Console.WriteLine( "Thread#{0}: WriteSum() sum = {1}",
                             Thread.CurrentThread.ManagedThreadId, sum);
      return sum;
   }
   static void Main() {
      Deleg proc = WriteSum;
      System.IAsyncResult async = proc.BeginInvoke( 10, 10, null, null );
      // You can do some work here...
      int sum = proc.EndInvoke( async );
      System.Console.WriteLine( "Thread#{0}: Main()      sum = {1}",
                             Thread.CurrentThread.ManagedThreadId, sum);
   }
}
```

This program displays:

```
Thread 15: WriteSum() Sum = 20
Thread 18: Main()     Sum = 20
```

An asynchronous call is materialized by an object whose class implements the `System.IAsyncResult` interface. In this example, the underlying class is `System.Runtime.Remoting.Messaging.AsyncResult`. The `AsyncResult` object is returned by the `BeginInvoke()` method. It is passed as an argument to the `EndInvoke()` method in order to identify the asynchronous call.

If an exception is raised during an asynchronous call, it is automatically intercepted and stored by the CLR. The CLR will rethrow the exception during the call to `EndInvoke()`.

Callback method

You have the possibility of specifying a method which will be automatically called when the asynchronous call is ended. This method is called a *callback method*. A callback method is called by the same thread which executed the call to the asynchronous method.

Calling a method asynchronously 143

To use a callback method, you simply need to reference it with a delegate object of type `System.AsyncCallback` passed as the next to last argument to the `BeginInvoke()` method. This method must conform itself to this delegate type, which means that it must have a return type of void and take a single argument of type `IAsyncResult`. As shows the following example, this method must call `EndInvoke()`.

A problem can happen as the threads of the pool used to process the asynchronous calls are background threads. As with the example below, we must implement an event management mechanism which makes sure that the application does not terminate without completing the execution of the asynchronous calls. The `IAsyncResult` interface presents a synchronization object of a class which derives from `WaitHandle`, but this object is signaled as soon as the asynchronous process is done and before the callback method is called. Consequently, this object cannot be used to wait for the end of the execution of the callback methods.

Example 5-22

```
using System;
using System.Threading;
using System.Runtime.Remoting.Messaging;
class Program {
   public delegate int Deleg( int a, int b );
   // Initial state of the event: false.
   static AutoResetEvent ev = new AutoResetEvent( false );
   static int WriteSum( int a, int b ) {
      Console.WriteLine( " Thread#{0}: Sum = {1}",
                        Thread.CurrentThread.ManagedThreadId , a + b );
      return a + b;
   }
   static void SumDone(IAsyncResult async) {
      // Wait a second to simulate some work.
      Thread.Sleep( 1000 );
      Deleg proc = ( (AsyncResult) async ).AsyncDelegate as Deleg;
      int sum = proc.EndInvoke( async );
      Console.WriteLine( "Thread#{0}: Callback method sum = {1}",
                        Thread.CurrentThread.ManagedThreadId , sum );
      ev.Set();
   }
   static void Main() {
      Deleg proc = WriteSum;
      // The C#2 compiler infer a delegate object of type AsyncCallback
      // to reference the SumDone() method.
      IAsyncResult async = proc.BeginInvoke( 10, 10, SumDone , null );
      Console.WriteLine(
         "Thread#{0}: BeginInvoke() called! Wait for SumDone() completion.",
         Thread.CurrentThread.ManagedThreadId );
      ev.WaitOne();
      Console.WriteLine(
         "{0}: Bye... ", Thread.CurrentThread.ManagedThreadId );
   }
}
```

This example displays:

```
Thread#12: BeginInvoke() called! Wait for SumDone() completion.
Thread#14: Sum = 20
Thread#14: Callback method sum = 20
Thread#12: Bye...
```

If you remove this event mechanism, the example displays the following:

```
Thread#12: BeginInvoke() called! Wait for SumDone() completion.
Thread#12: Bye...
```

The application does not wait for the end of the asynchronous processing and the execution of its callback method.

Passing a state to the callback method

If you do not set it to `null`, the last parameter of the `BeginInvoke()` method represents a reference to an object which can be used both by the thread which triggers the asynchronous call as well as in the callback method. Another reference to this object is in the `AsyncState` property of the `IAsyncResult` interface. You can use it to represent a state which is set in the callback method. For example, the event of the example in the previous section can be seen as a state. Here is the previous example rewritten to use this feature:

Example 5-23
```
using System;
using System.Threading;
using System.Runtime.Remoting.Messaging;
class Program {
   public delegate int Deleg( int a, int b );
   static int WriteSum( int a, int b ) {
      Console.WriteLine( "Thread#{0}: Sum = {1}",
                        Thread.CurrentThread.ManagedThreadId , a+b);
      return a + b;
   }
   static void SumDone( IAsyncResult async ) {
      // Wait a second to simulate some work.
      Thread.Sleep( 1000 );
      Deleg proc = ( (AsyncResult) async ).AsyncDelegate as Deleg;
      int sum = proc.EndInvoke( async );
      Console.WriteLine( "Thread#{0}: Callback method sum = {1}",
                        Thread.CurrentThread.ManagedThreadId , sum );
      ( (AutoResetEvent)async.AsyncState ).Set();
   }
   static void Main() {
      Deleg proc = WriteSum;
      AutoResetEvent ev = new AutoResetEvent(false);
      IAsyncResult async = proc.BeginInvoke( 10, 10, SumDone, ev );
      Console.WriteLine(
         "Thread#{0}: BeginInvoke() called! Wait for SumDone() completion.",
         Thread.CurrentThread.ManagedThreadId );
      ev.WaitOne();
      Console.WriteLine(
         "{0}: Bye... ", Thread.CurrentThread.ManagedThreadId );
   }
}
```

One-Way calls

You have the possibility of applying the `System.Runtime.Remoting.Messaging.OneWay` attribute to any method, static or not. This attribute tells the CLR that this method does not return any information. Even if a method which returns some data (using the return parameter or using arguments defined with one of the `out` or `ref` keywords) is marked with this attribute, it does not return anything.

A method marked with the `OneWay` attribute can be called in a synchronous or asynchronous way. If an exception is raised but not caught during the execution of a method marked with the `OneWay` attribute, it is propagated if the call is synchronous. In the case of a one-way asynchronous call, the exception is not propagated. In most cases, methods marked as one-way are used in an asynchronous way.

One-way asynchronous calls generally complete ancillary tasks whose success (or failure) has no consequence on the proper execution of the application. Most of the time, we use them to communication information on the progress of an application.

Threads-resources affinities

You can greatly simplify the synchronization of the accesses to your resources by using the notion of affinity between threads and resources. The idea is that to always access a resource using the same thread. Hence, you can remove the need to protect the resource from concurrent accesses since it is never shared. The .NET framework presents several mechanisms to implement this notion of affinity.

The System.ThreadStatic attribute

By default, a static field is shared by all the threads of a process. This behavior forces the developer to synchronize all accesses to such a field. By applying the `System.ThreadStaticAttribute` attribute on a static field, you can constrain the CLR to create an instance of this static field for each thread of the process. Hence, this use of this mechanism is a good way to implement the notion of affinity between threads and resources.

It is better to avoid directly initializing such a static field during its declaration. In fact, in this case, only the thread which loads the class will complete the initialization of its own version of the field. This behavior is illustrated by the following program:

Example 5-24

```
using System.Threading;
class Program {
   [System.ThreadStatic]
   static string str = "Initial value ";
   static void DisplayStr() {
      System.Console.WriteLine("Thread#{0} Str={1}",
                               Thread.CurrentThread.ManagedThreadId , str);
   }
   static void ThreadProc() {
      DisplayStr();
      str = "ThreadProc value";
      DisplayStr();
   }
   static void Main() {
      DisplayStr();
      Thread thread = new Thread( ThreadProc );
      thread.Start();
      thread.Join();
      DisplayStr();
   }
}
```

This program displays the following:

```
Thread#1 Str=Initial value
Thread#2 Str=
Thread#2 Str=ThreadProc value
Thread#1 Str=Initial value
```

Thread local storage (TLS)

The notion of affinity between threads and resources can also be implemented with the concept of *thread local storage* (often called *TLS*). This concept is not new and exists at the level of *win32*. In fact, the .NET framework internally uses this implementation.

The concept of TLS uses the notion of a *data slot*. A data slot is an instance of the `System.LocalDataStoreSlot` class. A data slot can also be seen as an array of objects. The size of this array is always equal to the number of threads in the current process. Hence, each thread has its own slot in the data slot. This slot is invisible to the other threads. It can be used to reference an object. For each data slot, the CLR takes care of establishing a correspondence between the threads and their objects. The Thread class provides the two following methods to allow the read and write access to an object stored in a data slot:

```
static public object GetData( LocalDataStoreSlot slot );
static public void SetData( LocalDataStoreSlot slot, object obj );
```

Named data slots

You have the possibility of naming a data slot in order to identify it. The Thread class provides the following methods in order to create, obtain or destroy a named data slot:

```
static public LocalDataStoreSlot AllocateNamedDataSlot( string slotName );
static public LocalDataStoreSlot GetNamedDataSlot( string slotName );
static public void FreeNamedDataSlot( string slotName );
```

The garbage collector does not destroy named data slots. This is the responsibility of the developer.

The following program uses a named data slot in order to provide a counter to each thread of the process. This counter is incremented for each call to the `fServer()` method. This program takes advantage of the TLS in the sense where the `fServer()` method does not take a reference to the counter as a parameter. Another advantage is that the developer does not need to maintain a counter himself for each thread.

Example 5-25

```
using System;
using System.Threading;
class Program {
   static readonly int NTHREAD = 3;     // 3 threads to create.
   // 2 calls to fServer() for each thread created.
   static readonly int MAXCALL = 2;
   static readonly int PERIOD = 1000;  // 1 second between calls.
   static bool fServer() {
      LocalDataStoreSlot dSlot = Thread.GetNamedDataSlot( "Counter" );
      int counter = (int) Thread.GetData( dSlot );
      counter++;
      Thread.SetData( dSlot, counter );
      return !( counter == MAXCALL );
   }
   static void ThreadProc() {
```

Threads-resources affinities

Example 5-25

```
      LocalDataStoreSlot dSlot = Thread.GetNamedDataSlot( "Counter" );
      Thread.SetData( dSlot, (int) 0 );
      do{
         Thread.Sleep( PERIOD );
         Console.WriteLine(
            "Thread#{0} I've called fServer(), Counter = {1}",
            Thread.CurrentThread.ManagedThreadId ,
            (int)Thread.GetData(dSlot));
      } while ( fServer() );
      Console.WriteLine("Thread#{0} bye",
         Thread.CurrentThread.ManagedThreadId );
   }
   static void Main() {
      Console.WriteLine( "Thread#{0} I'm the main thread, hello world",
                        Thread.CurrentThread.ManagedThreadId );
      Thread.AllocateNamedDataSlot( "Counter" );
      Thread thread;
      for ( int i = 0; i < NTHREAD; i++ ) {
         thread = new Thread( ThreadProc );
         thread.Start();
      }
      // We don't implement a mechanism to wait for child threads
      // completion, thus, we are waiting for a while.
      Thread.Sleep( PERIOD * (MAXCALL + 1) );
      Thread.FreeNamedDataSlot( "Counter" );
      Console.WriteLine( "Thread#{0} I'm the main thread, bye.",
                        Thread.CurrentThread.ManagedThreadId );
   }
}
```

This program displays the following:

```
Thread#1 I'm the main thread, hello world
Thread#3 I've called fServer(), Counter = 0
Thread#4 I've called fServer(), Counter = 0
Thread#5 I've called fServer(), Counter = 0
Thread#3 I've called fServer(), Counter = 1
Thread#3 bye
Thread#4 I've called fServer(), Counter = 1
Thread#4 bye
Thread#5 I've called fServer(), Counter = 1
Thread#5 bye
Thread#1 I'm the main thread, bye
```

Anonymous data slots

You can call the `AllocateDataSlot()` static method of the `Thread` class to create an anonymous data slot. You are not responsible for the destruction of an anonymous data slot. However, you must make it so that an instance of the `LocalDataStoreSlot` class be visible by all the threads. Let's rewrite the previous program using the notion of an anonymous data slot:

Example 5-26

```
using System;
using System.Threading;
class Program {
   static readonly int NTHREAD = 3;    // 3 threads to create.
```

Example 5-26
```
    // 2 calls to fServer() for each thread created.
    static readonly int MAXCALL = 2;
    static readonly int PERIOD = 1000; // 1 second between calls.
    static LocalDataStoreSlot dSlot;
    static bool fServer() {
       int counter = (int) Thread.GetData( dSlot );
       counter++;
       Thread.SetData( dSlot, counter );
       return !( counter == MAXCALL );
    }
    static void ThreadProc() {
       Thread.SetData( dSlot, (int) 0 );
       do{
          Thread.Sleep(PERIOD);
          Console.WriteLine(
             "Thread#{0} I've called fServer(), Counter = {1}",
             Thread.CurrentThread.ManagedThreadId ,
             (int)Thread.GetData(dSlot));
       } while ( fServer() );
       Console.WriteLine( "Thread#{0} bye",
          Thread.CurrentThread.ManagedThreadId );
    }
    static void Main() {
       Console.WriteLine( "Thread#{0} I'm the main thread, hello world",
                          Thread.CurrentThread.ManagedThreadId );
       dSlot = Thread.AllocateDataSlot();
       for ( int i = 0; i < NTHREAD; i++ ) {
          Thread thread = new Thread( ThreadProc );
          thread.Start();
       }
       Thread.Sleep( PERIOD * (MAXCALL + 1) );
       Console.WriteLine( "Thread#{0} I'm the main thread, bye.",
          Thread.CurrentThread.ManagedThreadId );
    }
}
```

The System.ComponentModel.ISynchronizeInvoke interface

The `System.ComponentModel.ISynchronizeInvoke` interface is defined as follows:

```
public object System.ComponentModel.ISynchronizeInvoke {
      public object       Invoke( Delegate method, object[] args );
      public IAsyncResult BeginInvoke( Delegate method, object[] args );
      public object       EndInvoke( IAsyncResult result );
      public bool         InvokeRequired{ get; }
}
```

An implementation of this interface can make sure that certain methods are always executed by the same thread, in a synchronous or asynchronous way:

- In the synchronous scenario, a thread T1 calls a method M() on an object OBJ. In fact, T1 calls the `ISynchronizeInvoke.Invoke()` method by specifying a delegate object which references OBJ.M() and an array containing its arguments. Another thread T2 executed the OBJ.M() method. T1 waits for the end of the call and retrieves the information after the return of the call.

- The asynchronous scenario is different than the synchronous scenario by the fact that T1 calls the `ISynchronizeInvoke.BeginInvoke()` method. T1 does not remain blocked while T2 executes the `OBJ.M()` method. When T1 needs the information from the return of the call, it will call the `ISynchronizeInvoke.EndInvoke()` method which will provide this information if T2 completed the execution of `OBJ.M()`.

The `ISynchronizeInvoke` interface is mainly used by the framework to force the *Windows Form* technology to execute the methods of a form using the thread dedicated to the form. This constraint comes from the fact that the *Windows Form* technology is build on top of the *Windows* messages plumbing. The same kind of problem is also addressed by the `System.ComponentModel.BackgroundWorker` class which is described at page 560.

You can develop your own implementations of the `ISynchronizeInvoke` interface by inspiring yourself from the **Implementing ISynchronizeInvoke** example provided by *Juval Lowy* at the following URL `http://docs.msdnaa.net/ark_new3.0/cd3/content/Tech_System%20Programming.htm`.

Introduction to execution context

The .NET 2 framework presents new classes which allows the capture and propagation of the execution context of the current thread to another thread:

- `System.Security.SecurityContext`
  An instance of this class contains the identity of the underlying *Windows* user in the form of an instance of the `System.Security.Principal.WindowsIdentity` class as well as the state of the thread's stack in the form of an instance of the `System.Threading.CompressedStack` class. The state of the stack is mainly used by the CAS mechanism during the traversal of the stack.
- `System.Threading.SynchronizationContext`
  Allows to automatically handle some compatibility constraints amongst the various synchronization models.
- `System.Threading.HostExecutionContext`
  Allows taking into account a runtime host in the execution context of the current thread.
- `System.Runtime.Remoting.Messaging.LogicalCallContext`
  .NET Remoting allows the propagation of information through a .NET Remoting context through instances of this class. More information on this topic can be found at page 710.
- `System.Threading.ExecutionContext`
  An instance of this class contains the union of all the mentioned contexts.

Let's retake the example of page 173 which modified the security context by impersonating the `guest` *Windows* user on the current thread:

Example 5-27

```
...
   static void Main() {
      System.IntPtr pToken;
      if( LogonUser(
            "guest" ,       // login
            string.Empty,   // Windows domain
            "guest_pwd" ,   // password
            2,              // LOGON32_LOGON_INTERACTIVE
            0,              // LOGON32_PROVIDER_DEFAUT
            out pToken)) {
         WindowsIdentity.Impersonate( pToken );
```

Example 5-27

```
            DisplayContext( "Main" );
            ThreadPool.QueueUserWorkItem( Callback, null );
            CloseHandle( pToken );
        }
    }
    static void Callback(object o) { DisplayContext("Callback"); }
    static void DisplayContext( string s ) {
        System.Console.WriteLine( s+" Thread#{0} Current user is {1}",
            Thread.CurrentThread.ManagedThreadId,
            WindowsIdentity.GetCurrent().Name );
    }
...
```

This example displays the following:

```
Main Thread#1 Current user is PSMACCHIA\guest
Callback Thread#3 Current user is PSMACCHIA\guest
```

In .NET 1.1, this example would have displayed the following:

```
Main Thread#1 Current user is PSMACCHIA\guest
Callback Thread#3 Current user is PSMACCHIA\pat
```

In fact, with .NET 2 the thread pool propagates by default the context of the thread which posts the task to the thread which executes the task. This was not the case with .NET 1. The use of the `ExecutionContext.SuppressFlow()` method allows to duplicate the behavior of .NET 1 in .NET 2:

Example 5-28

```
    ...
            DisplayContext( "Main" );
            ExecutionContext.SuppressFlow();
            ThreadPool.QueueUserWorkItem( Callback, null );
    ...
```

This example displays:

```
Main Thread#1 Current user is PSMACCHIA\guest
Callback Thread#3 Current user is PSMACCHIA\pat
```

The following example shows how to programmaticaly propagate the execution context. First of all, we must capture it using the `ExecutionContext.Capture()` method. Then, we create a copy which we pass to the thread from the pool that we have requested. This thread propagates the context by calling the `ExecutionContext.Run()` method. This method takes as a parameter the execution context and a delegate object. It invokes on the current thread the method referenced by the delegate object after having set the context of the current thread:

Example 5-29

```
    ...
    static void Main() {
        ...
            WindowsIdentity.Impersonate( pToken );
            DisplayContext( "Main" );
            ExecutionContext ctx = ExecutionContext.Capture();
            ExecutionContext.SuppressFlow();
            ThreadPool.QueueUserWorkItem(
```

Introduction to execution context

Example 5-29
```
            SetContextAndThenCallback, ctx.CreateCopy() );
         CloseHandle( pToken );
      }
   }
   static void SetContextAndThenCallback( object o ) {
      ExecutionContext ctx = o as ExecutionContext;
      ExecutionContext.Run( ctx, Callback, null );
   }
   static void Callback( object o ) {
      DisplayContext( "Callback" );
   }
...
```

Without surprise, this example displays:

```
Main Thread#1 Current user is PSMACCHIA\guest
Callback Thread#3 Current user is PSMACCHIA\guest
```

6
Security

This chapter presents the different aspects of security under .NET:

- We will start by discussing the Code Access Security (CAS). The CAS technology allows measuring the level of trust that we can have on an assembly by verifying its source and ensuring it was not tampered with.
- We will then see how to measure the degree of trust that we can have in a user. The notion of user is implemented at several levels (*Windows*, ASP.NET, COM+…).
- Finally, we will discuss the various cryptographic mechanisms that the framework offers us.

Other information relative to security can be found in this book. At page 546, we will discuss the various techniques used to establish a secured connection between two machines and at page 794, we will present the security aspects of an ASP.NET web application.

Introduction to Code Access Security (CAS)

What is mobile code?

The deployment model for software has significantly improved with the increase of network bandwidth. We now download our software more frequently from the Internet and we use less and less physical media (such as CD's) for deployment. We use the *mobile code* metaphor to designate the code of this type of application which is distributed through a network.

The advantages of using a network to distribute software are numerous: immediate availability, real-time updates… However, the use of mobile code poses large security problems. In fact, a malicious user can exploit the weaknesses of the network and holes in operating systems to substitute his own code to mobile code or to transmit his mobile code onto your machine. The easiness of downloading code and software pushes us to download software which we would have not normally purchased. This means that we tend to be less picky in regards to who published the software. It is then necessary to limit the set of permissions granted to downloaded code (Can it destroy files on my computer? Can it access my network? …).

The COM technology addresses this problem in a crude manner. Before executing a COM component which has been downloaded, the user is prompted by a dialog box which gives the choice to grant or deny the execution. A certain level of trust in regards to the source of the component can be supplied through the use of a certificate mechanism but the main problem still exists: once the user has decided to execute the code, the code has all the same rights as the user.

Having a virtual machine such as the CLR allows the .NET platform to properly address this problem with a much more elegant solution. In fact, the CLR can intercept and prevent a malicious operation such as the destruction of a file before it happens. This mechanism is called *CAS* (*Code Access Security*).

The deployment of mobile code developed with .NET 2.0 is preferably done using the *ClickOnce* which we discuss in more details at page 62. A good understand of CAS is a must to take advantage of *ClickOnce*.

CAS: The big picture

.NET defines about thirty permissions which can be granted or denied to the execution of the code of an assembly. Each of these permissions defines the rules controlling access to a critical resource such as the registry, files or folders. Granting trust to an assembly means that we are granting it certain permissions needed for it to execute properly. The CAS mechanism in the CLR is used during two situations:

- During the loading of an assembly, the CLR grants it some permissions;
- When the code requests a critical operation to be executed, the CLR must verify that the assembly containing this code has the proper permissions.

Granting permissions to the code of an assembly

As with human relationships, with .NET trust must be earned. The CLR grants trust to an assembly only if it can extract a certain number of evidences. These evidences are relative to the origins and to the integrity of the data in the assembly.

The step of granting permissions to the assembly based on its evidence is completely configurable. The parameters for this step are stored in an entity named *security policy*. The information contained in a security policy looks like this: 'If the information contained in an assembly is produced by the XXX publisher then we can grant it the following set of permissions'. We will discuss how to configure the security policies. We can note that at this stage, the application has not yet been granted the permission to execute itself. In fact, it is possible that once the evidences have been looked at, this permission may not be granted. We can also mention that this permission resolution mechanism grants no permissions by default.

When a set of permissions has been granted to the assembly, the code of the assembly can modify this set and the behavior of the security management during its execution. Of course, **these modifications can never exceed the permissions which were initially granted to the assembly**.

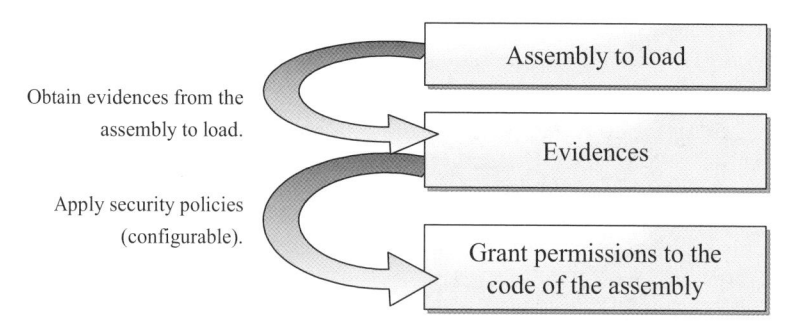

Figure 6-1: Granting permissions to the code of an assembly

Checking of permissions while running the code of an assembly

Before executing a critical operation such as an access to a file, the code of the .NET framework requests to the CLR to verify if the calling code has the appropriate permissions. The calling code is not only represented by the method which requests the operation from the .NET framework. The CLR considers the calling code as the set of methods on the stack of the current thread. The CLR verifies that all the assemblies containing this set of methods each have the required permissions. This behavior is called *stack walk*. The traversal of the stack prevents the manipulation of an assembly with a high level of trust (such as those developed by *Microsoft*) by assemblies in which we have little trust.

CAS: Evidences and permissions 155

In the following illustration, we see that the `File.OpenRead()` method request to the CLR to verify that all of the calling methods have the `FileIOPermissionAccess.Read` on a file before completing the operation. In this example, the permissions must be P3 or a `SecurityException` exception would be raised by the CLR.

We will have the chance to explain that a permission can be materialized by a .NET object and that we can call the `Demand()` on such an object in order to verify if at a specific point, the permission is granted to all callers.

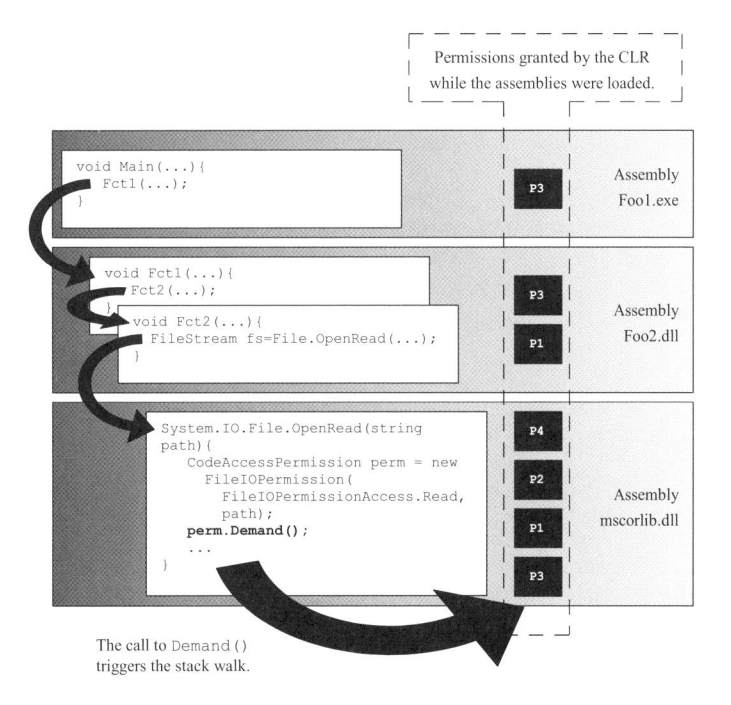

Figure 6-2: The CAS stack walk

CAS: Evidences and permissions

What is an evidence?

An evidence is a piece of information extracted from an assembly. The evidence word is used in the sense that if we extract such information from the assembly, it then proves a fact on the assembly. These facts concern the origin of an assembly and the fact this assembly has not been tampered between the moment where it was created by the compiler at the publisher and the moment where it is executed on the client's machine.

Standard kind of evidences presented by the .NET framework

Here is the list of the eight kinds of evidence that we can extract from an assembly, and thus, the list of facts which can be proved from an assembly. Each of these evidences is materialized with a class from the .NET framework which we will describe. These classes are part of the `System.Security.Policy` namespace.

- We can prove that the assembly is stored in a certain folder on the machine. This type of evidence can be represented by an instance of the `System.Security.Policy.ApplicationDirectory` class.
- We can prove that an assembly is stored in the GAC. This type of evidence can be represented by an instance of the `System.Security.Policy.Gac` class.
- We can prove than an assembly has been obtained/downloaded from a certain site (*www.smacchia.com* for example). This type of evidence can be represented by an instance of the `System.Security.Policy.Site` class.
- We can prove that an assembly has been obtained from a certain URL (*www.smacchia.com/asm/MyAssembly.dll* for example). This type of evidence can be represented by an instance of the `System.Security.Policy.Url` class.
- We can prove that an assembly has been obtained by a certain *zone*. .NET offers five zones:
    - Internet;
    - An internet site that has been added to the list of *untrusted sites* in *Internet Explorer*;
    - An internet site which has been added to the list of *trusted sited* in *Internet Explorer*;
    - Local intranet;
    - The local system storage (My Computer);

    To each of these zones corresponds a value of the `System.Security.SecurityZone` enumeration. This type of evidence can be represented by an instance of the `System.Security.Policy.Zone` class.
- If the assembly has been signed by its publisher using the Authenticode technology, we can establish an evidence from this certificate. This technology is describe at page 191. This type of evidence can be represented by an instance of the `System.Security.Policy.Publisher` class.
- If the assembly has a strong name, we can establish an evidence from this strong name. This type of evidence is represented by an instance of the `System.Security.Policy.StrongName` class. The culture component of the strong name is not taken into account in this evidence. Here is a program allowing the construction and display of the strong names of assemblies in the current AppDomain. Note that the use of the `System.Security.Permissions.StrongNamePublicKeyBlob` class to recover the public key.

Example 6-1

```
using System;
using System.Security.Permissions;
using System.Security.Policy;
using System.Reflection;
[assembly: AssemblyKeyFile("MyKeys.snk")]
class Program {
   static void DisplayStrongName(Assembly assembly) {
      AssemblyName name = assembly.GetName();
      byte[] publicKey = name.GetPublicKey();
      StrongNamePublicKeyBlob blob =new StrongNamePublicKeyBlob(publicKey);
      StrongName sn = new StrongName(blob, name.Name, name.Version);
      Console.WriteLine(sn.Name);
      Console.WriteLine(sn.Version);
      Console.WriteLine(sn.PublicKey);
   }
   static void Main() {
      Assembly[] assemblies = AppDomain.CurrentDomain.GetAssemblies();
      foreach (Assembly assembly in assemblies)
         DisplayStrongName(assembly);
   }
}
```

CAS: Evidences and permissions

- We can establish an evidence from the *hashing value* of an assembly. The hashing value of an assembly allows to verify the result of the compilation of an assembly, such as a version number except that the hashing value does not contain any temporal values like a version (for example, version 2.3 always comes after version 2.1). A small update in the code of an assembly is sufficient to completely change its hashing value. This type of evidence is represented by an instance of the `System.Security.Policy.Hash` class.

You can also add to this list, you own evidences. These must be added to the assembly before it is signed. The idea is to allow you to totally configure the security mechanism. However, the use of your own evidences is beyond the scope of this book.

An instance of the `System.Security.Policy.Evidence` class represents a collection of evidences. In fact, each instance of this class contains two evidence collections:

- One collection to store the evidence presented by the .NET framework (one of the eight described above).
- A collection to store proprietary evidences.

In practice, developers have little interest in manipulating evidence. Instances of the `Evidence` classes are manipulated internally by the .NET framework. Notably, let us remind you that such a collection of evidences is attributed to each assembly when it is loaded.

Here is a program which displays the type of evidences provided by the assemblies in the current AppDomain. To not make things more difficult, we will not display directly the evidences on the console and will only display the type of evidence:

Example 6-2   *EvidenceTest.cs*

```
using System;
using System.Reflection;
[assembly: AssemblyKeyFile("MyKeys.snk")]
class Program {
   static void DisplayEvidence( Assembly assembly ) {
      Console.WriteLine( assembly.FullName );
      foreach ( object obj in assembly.Evidence )
         Console.WriteLine("   " + obj.GetType());
   }
   static void Main() {
      Assembly[] assemblies = AppDomain.CurrentDomain.GetAssemblies();
      foreach ( Assembly assembly in assemblies )
         DisplayEvidence(assembly);
   }
}
```

This program displays:

```
mscorlib, Version=2.0.50727, Culture=neutral,
PublicKeyToken=b77a5c561934e089
   System.Security.Policy.Zone
   System.Security.Policy.Url
   System.Security.Policy.StrongName
   System.Security.Policy.Hash
PreuveTest, Version=0.0.0.0, Culture=neutral, PublicKeyToken=e0a058df80c8a007
   System.Security.Policy.Zone
   System.Security.Policy.Url
   System.Security.Policy.StrongName
   System.Security.Policy.Hash
```

Who is supplying evidences?

The *evidences* of an assembly are supplied by the CLR right before the assembly is loaded into an AppDomain:

- Either by the *runtime host of an AppDomain* right before the loading of the first assembly into the AppDomain. In this case, the assembly which contains the runtime host of the AppDomain must have obtained the meta-permission named `ControlEvidence`. In general, you do not need to worry about this if you are using a runtime host developed by *Microsoft* for which the security policy generally is granted full-trust. For the moment, *Microsoft* supplies four runtime hosts which are described at page 77.
- Either by the *class loader* right before an assembly containing the class requested is loaded into the AppDomain. The class loader is part of the CLR, it is given full trust and is granted the `ControlEvidence` meta-permission.

In all cases, the evidence retrieval mechanism requires the `ControlEvidence` meta-permission (see `SecurityPermission` in the bellow list).

Permissions

As its name implies, a *permission* allows the code to execute a certain set of actions. Some also refer to permissions as being *privileges, authorizations* or *rights*.

We will see in the following section what is the algorithm that allows obtaining the set of permissions of an assembly based on its evidences. In .NET, there are four categories of permissions: the standard permissions, the identity permissions, the meta-permissions and the custom permissions.

Standard permissions

About thirty standard permissions allow defining the totality of resources which can be exploited by an assembly. Each of these permissions is materialized by a class which derives from `System.Security.CodeAccessPermission`. This class contains methods which allow from your code to ensure that we have a permission, to request a permission to refuse to grant access... Remember that these methods do not allow obtaining a permission that a security policy does not grant. We will detail the use of these classes at the end of this section. Here is the list of standard permissions:

```
System.Security.Permissions.EnvironmentPermission
System.Security.Permissions.FileDialogPermission
System.Security.Permissions.FileIOPermission
System.Security.Permissions.IsolatedStoragePermission
System.Security.Permissions.ReflectionPermission
System.Security.Permissions.RegistryPermission
System.Security.Permissions.UIPermission
System.Security.Permissions.DataProtectionPermission
System.Security.Permissions.KeyContainerPermission
System.Security.Permissions.StorePermission
System.Security.Permissions.SecurityPermission
System.Configuration.UserSettingsPermission
System.Security.Permissions.ResourcePermissionBase
    System.Diagnostics.EventLogPermission
    System.Diagnostics.PerformanceCounterPermission
    System.DirectoryServices.DirectoryServicesPermission
    System.ServiceProcess.ServiceControllerPermission
System.Net.DnsPermission
System.Net.SocketPermission
```

```
System.Net.WebPermission
System.Net.NetworkInformation.NetworkInformationPermission
System.Net.Mail.SmtpPermission
System.Web.AspNetHostingPermission
System.Messaging.MessageQueuePermission
System.Drawing.Printing.PrintingPermission
System.Data.Common.DBDataPermission
   System.Data.OleDb.OleDbPermission
   System.Data.SqlClient.SqlClientPermission
   System.Data.Odbc.OdbcPermission
System.Data.OracleClient.OraclePermission
System.Data.SqlClient.SqlNotificationPermission
System.Transactions.DistributedTransactionPermission
```

Identity permissions

The *identity permissions* are granted by the CLR for almost each evidence provided by an assembly. The classes for identity permissions are:

```
System.Security.Permissions.PublisherIdentityPermission
System.Security.Permissions.SiteIdentityPermission
System.Security.Permissions.StrongNameIdentityPermission
System.Security.Permissions.UrlIdentityPermission
System.Security.Permissions.GacIdentityPermission
System.Security.Permissions.ZoneIdentityPermission
```

These classes also derive from `CodeAccessPermission` which allows treating them as any other permission from the code. What sets the identity permissions apart is the fact that the grant of such permission does not depend on security policy but only on the evidences provided by the assembly. This means that an identity permission does not allow to execute an action that you could not have made without it, they are only used during verifications.

Security permissions (meta-permissions)

The 'meta-permissions' or *security permissions*: These are permissions granted to the security manager itself. The list of meta-permissions is available in the article named **SecurityPermissionFlag Enumeration** on **MSDN**. We can mention the meta-permission which allow the execution of unmanaged code (value of `UnmanagedCode`), the meta-permission allowing the extraction of evidence from an assembly (discussed earlier, value of `ControlEvidence`), the meta-permission allowing the execution of unverified code (value of `SkipVerification`).... The `System.Security.Permissions.SecurityPermission`, which derives from `CodeAccessPermission`, allows the manipulation of meta-permissions from your code without allowing the self-attribution of such permissions.

> ⚠ Understand that the `UnmanagedCode` meta-permissions is a kind of super permission since it grants all other permissions giving access to the win32 API. In the same way, the `SkipVerification` meta-permission can be used in a way to bypass the verifications by the CLR. Consequently, mobile code **should never have one of the UnmanagedCode or SkipVerification permissions**.

Custom permissions

You can define your own permissions for resource access. The article named **Implementing a Custom Permission** on **MSDN** describes the use of this feature in details.

CAS: Granting permissions from evidences by applying security policies

In the current section, we will clarify what is a security policy, what such a policy is made of, which algorithm is used to apply a policy and finally, what is the default configuration of security policies.

Security policy levels

Applying a *security policy* to an assembly allows obtaining a set of permissions granted based on the evidences that the CAS system was able to obtain from the assembly.

.NET offers four security policies. The set of permissions granted to an assembly is the intersection of the set of permissions granted to each of policies. The choice of the use of an intersection instead of a union was done based on the grant and not the removal of permissions.

Security policy	Configured by...	Applies to...
Enterprise	An administrator.	To the managed code contained in the assemblies located on the machines of an enterprise.
Machine	An administrator.	To the managed code contained in the assemblies stored on the machine.
User	An administrator or the related user.	To the managed code contained in the process which executes with the rights of the specific user.
Application Domain	The host of the application domain.	To the managed code contained in the application domain.

There exists a hierarchy in security policies. Practically, they are applied one after the other in the order mentioned above (from 'enterprise' to 'application domain'). For this reason, we talk of security policy levels. The application of a security policy can impose that the security policies of the following levels are not to be applied. For example, the application of a 'machine' security policy can prevent the application of the 'user' and 'application domain' security policies. In general, we notice that most of the security rules are found in the 'machine' policy (in fact, by default, the policies at other levels generally grant all permissions).

Dissecting a security policy

A security policy is constructed as follows:

- *Code groups* stored in a tree structure,
- A list of *permission sets*,
- A list of assemblies to which the security policy grants its full trust (*policy assemblies* or *fully trusted assemblies*).

From these elements and from the evidence extracted from an assembly, we can calculate a set of permissions. Before exposing the algorithm used to accomplish this, we need to first discuss what code groups are.

A code group associates to an evidence a permissions set of the security policy. The code groups are stored in a tree structure within a security policy, this means that parent code group can have zero, one or multiple children code groups. There is no obligation of a relationship between the evidence of a child code group and the evidence of its parent, the same goes for the granted permissions. However, in order to facilitate the administration of security, it is recommended (whenever possible) to set the relation (parent children) using logical links and to define the granted permissions in a hierarchical way.

CAS: Granting permissions from evidences by applying security policies 161

To understand why the code groups are stored in a tree, we have to take a look at the algorithm used during the processing of a security policy.

The official documentation uses this vocabulary: if one of the evidences of an assembly is identical to the evidence of a code group, we say that the assembly is a member of this group. This explains why we use the code group term. The evidence of a code group allows defining a set of assemblies (or code): this group is defined by the assemblies which verify the evidence.

Know that in the case where you create custom evidences, you will also need to create custom code groups to take advantage of them.

Algorithm used to apply a security policy

- If an assembly is part of the assembly list in which the security policy has full trust, it is granted the `FullTrust` permission which we will discuss later.
- If not, the algorithm starts traversing the code groups based on the following rules:
- The algorithm verifies if the assembly is a member of each root code group.
- The child code groups are taken into account by the algorithm only if the assembly is a member of the parent code group.

    The set of permissions granted to an assembly by a security policy is the union of the set of all code groups for which the assembly is a member.

- Each code group can be marked in a way to complete the security policy to which it belongs. In this case, an assembly which belongs to this group will not evaluate the following policy levels.
- Each code group can be marked as exclusive. In this case, if an assembly belongs to this code group, it will not benefit from the permissions associated with this group.

> ⚠ If an assembly belongs to two exclusive code groups of the same security policy, no permissions will be granted to it.

Understand that here we have discussed the algorithm used to apply the security policy at a single security level. Remember that at the end, the final set of permissions is the intersection of the set of permission granted at each security level. A consequence is that an assembly to which a security policy grants full trust will not necessarily have all permissions.

Default security policy configuration

By default, the 'machine' security policy is configured with the code group structure defined in Figure 6-3. As you can see, there is a code group based on the origin of the assembly. Let us remind you that .NET zone defines the origin of an assembly and that every assembly provides evidence in regards to the zone from which it originated. Also note that by default, the 'machine' security policy has full trust in assemblies signed with the private key for which the public key token belongs to *Microsoft* or *ECMA*.

By default, all the other security policies (enterprise, user and application domain) grant full trust to all assemblies. This means that by default, everything happens as if there was only the 'machine' security policy.

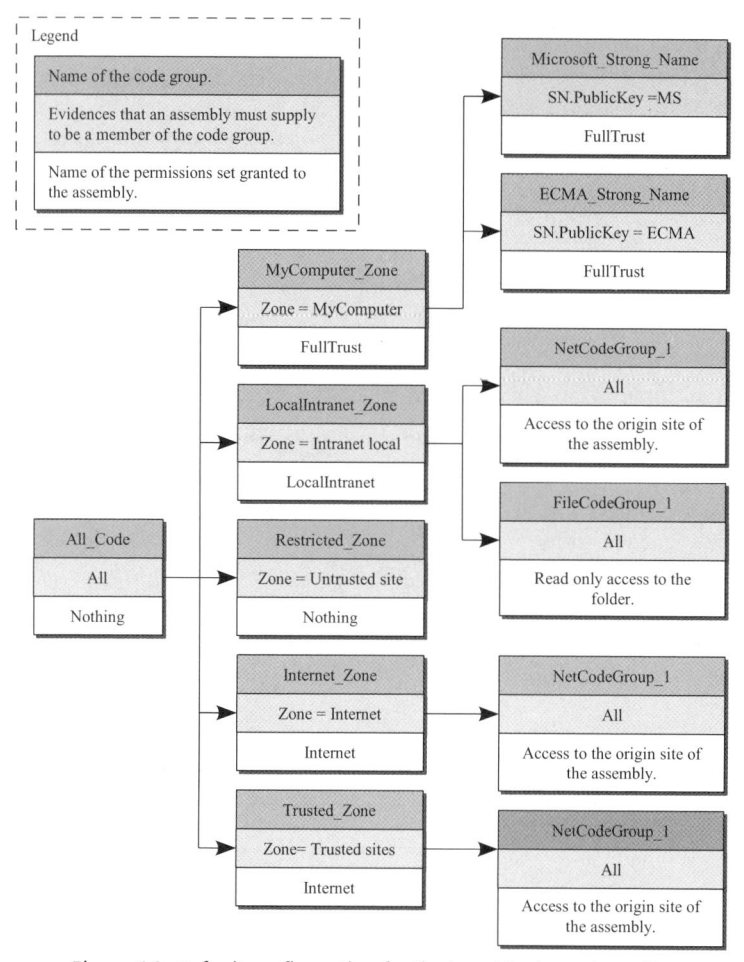

Figure 6-3: Default configuration for the 'machine' security policy

Configuring security policies

There are two tools which allow the configuration of security policies:

- The graphical configuration tool: .NET Framework Configuration Tool `mscorcfg.msc`. This tool also manages other aspects of .NET such as Remoting. You can launch this tool as follows: *Control Panel > Administrative tools > Microsoft* .NET Framework 2 Configuration.
- A command line tool: caspol.exe.

For .NET security, both these tools have the same functionality: the configuration of the 'enterprise', 'machine' and 'user' security policies for the machine. The security policy of an application domain can only be done programmatically by using the proper classes from the .NET framework.

Figure 6-4 offers a general view of `mscorcfg.msc` which allows to immediately see the notions we have just presented:

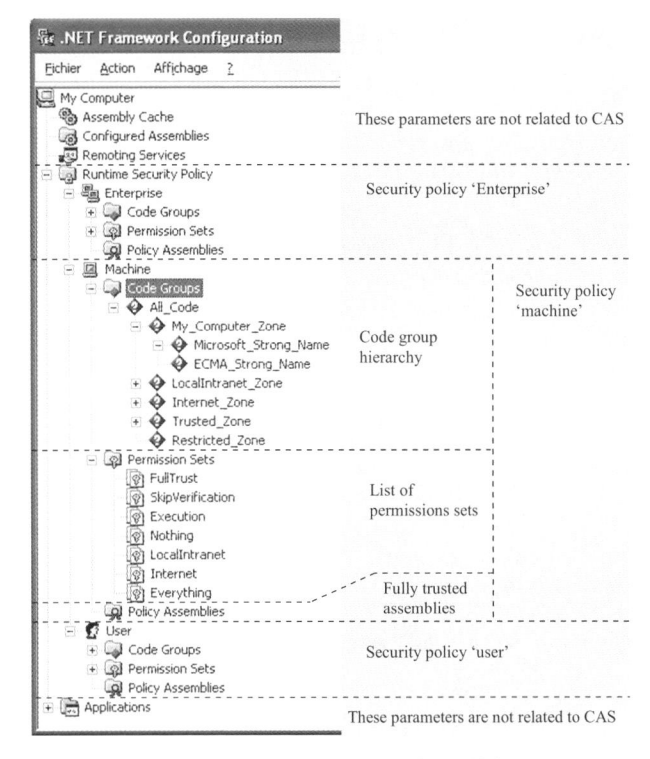

CAS: Granting permissions from evidences by applying security policies

Figure 6-4: Configuring security policies

When you are an administrator, you can do the following for each security policy (or when a user wants to configure his own security policy):

- Add/modify/delete permission sets.
- Add/remove assemblies to the list of fully trusted assemblies.
- Add/modify/delete code groups in the tree structure.
- Export or import the security policy in (of from a).msi file. This feature is available from the menu *Security Policy > Create a security policy deployment file > Open ...*
- For a given assembly, you can obtain the list of code groups (of one or all policies) to which it is a member, and the list of permissions which are granted to the assembly by the concerned policies. This functionality is available in the menu *Security policy > Evaluate an assembly...*

On a given machine, the parameters of a security policy are stored in an XML configuration file. Here is its location:

'enterprise' security policy	
Windows XP/2000/NT	%runtime install path%\ v2.050727\Config**Enterprisesec.config**
Windows 98/Me	%runtime install path%\ v2.050727\Config**Enterprisesec.config**
'machine' security policy	
Windows XP/2000/NT	%runtime install path%\ v2.050727\Config**Security.config**
Windows 98/Me	%runtime install path%\ v2.050727\Config**Security.config**
'user' security policy	
Windows XP/2000/NT	%USERPROFILE%\Application data\Microsoft\CLR security config\ v2.050727**Security.config**
Windows 98/Me	%WINDIR%*username*\CLR security config\ v2.050727\ **Security.config**

These parameters are stored for each version of the CLR. Hence, if several versions of the CLR coexist, each has its own security parameters.

The fact that these configuration parameters are stored in an XML format offers some interesting possibilities, such as the import of code groups or permission sets offered in an XML form. The three articles named **Importing a Permission Using an XML File**, **Importing a Permission Set Using an XML File** and **Importing a Code Group Using an XML File** on **MSDN** discuss this topic in details.

The options for the caspol.exe command line tool are described on **MSDN** in the article named **Code Access Security Policy Tool**. Through the various options of this tool, you will find the same functionality as presented above.

CAS: The FullTrust permission

In the previous section, we have mentioned the special permission named `FullTrust` that we could also qualify as *blind trust*. This permission essentially allows you to bypass all CAS verifications. Assemblies which have this permission consequently have access to all standard and custom permissions. From the point of view of the CAS, there are two types of assemblies: those that have `FullTrust` permission and those who don't. The CAS grants to those who don't have `FullTrust` only a *partial trust*, (*partially trusted assemblies*). In particular, the CAS grants only partial trust to assemblies that have the set of permissions named `Everything`. In fact, this set grants by default all standard permissions but does not take into account custom permissions.

By default, the code of a signed assembly can only be invoked by assemblies which have `FullTrust` permission. This comes from the fact that only signed assemblies can be placed in the GAC and they could be maliciously exploited by mobile code. In fact, unsigned assemblies present on a machine cannot be exploited by mobile code since there isn't a way to anticipate where they will be stored nor guess their implemented functionality.

This aspect of the CAS technology can become limiting but there is the possibility of deactivating it by marking your signed assembly with the `System.Security.AllowPartiallyTrustedCallersAttribute` assembly attribute. **Be aware that be doing so you are exposing your client to added risks if you largely distribute a class library marked with this attribute**. You must be certain that the distributed code cannot be hijacked. In fact, only a few specific standard assemblies from *Microsoft* are marked with this attribute.

Finally, be aware that not using this attribute is not a guarantee that you code cannot be hijacked. In fact, you could always be called from an assembly with `FullTrust` permission which itself was invoked from an assembly who does not have `FullTrust` permission.

CAS: Imperative permission check from the source code

Manually verifying permissions does not mean that you can work around a permission which was not granted as this is impossible.

We will start by showing how you can manually verify permissions from your code by calling methods specialized for this task. We will then discuss how to use attributes to allow for the declarative verification of permissions (i.e. the code of a method marked with such an attribute must have a certain permission). We will conclude with a comparison of these two approaches.

The CodeAccessPermissions and PermissionSet classes

The `CodeAccessPermission` as well as its derived classes allow you to do operations on the permissions granted to the code during its execution by using the `Demand()`, `Deny()`/`RevertDeny()`, `PermitOnly()`/`RevertPermitOnly()` and `Assert()`/`RevertAssert()` methods.

Instances of the `System.Security.PermissionSet` class represent permission collections. This class also presents the four methods mentioned above, thus allowing applying the same operation on a whole collection of permissions.

The Demand() method

The `Demand()` method verifies that the current code possess the permissions represented by the specified permission set. A traversal of the stack is then triggered in order to find the hierarchy of all the methods responsible for this call. Each method on the stack is tested for the specified permission set. If one of the methods on the stack does not have all the required permissions, a `SecurityException` is then raised. The execution of the code stops and the method from which the stack traversal originated is not executed. The following program makes sure that is has read access permission to a file:

Example 6-3

```
using System.Security;
using System.Security.Permissions;
class Program {
    static void Main() {
        string sFile = @"C:\data.txt";
        CodeAccessPermission cap =
            new FileIOPermission(FileIOPermissionAccess.Read, sFile);
        try{
            cap.Demand();
            // Read the "C:\data.txt" file.
        }
        catch ( SecurityException ){
            // The code is not allowed to read "C:\data.txt".
        }
    }
}
```

The interest in explicitly requesting permission is to anticipate an eventual denial and to adapt the behavior of your application consequently. The explicit request also allows the implementation of a more sophisticated strategy where the set of permission tested is determined based on the context such as the role of a user.

The Deny() RevertDeny() PermitOnly() and RevertPermitOnly() methods

The `Deny()` method of the `CodeAccessPermission` and `PermissionSet` classes allow to specify which permissions that our code does not need. Although most developers do not need this, it does constitute good practice. The `Deny()` method allows ensuring that the tiered code that we call will not have certain permissions. This practice also allows having a good global view of what an application uses and allows to set restrictions from the start. Here is an example which shows how to refuse the potentially dangerous permission allowing modifications to the system folders and the registry.

Example 6-4

```
using System.Security;
using System.Security.Permissions;
class Program {
   static void Main() {
      PermissionSet ps = new PermissionSet( PermissionState.None );
      ps.AddPermission( new FileIOPermission(
         FileIOPermissionAccess.AllAccess , @"C:\WINDOWS" ) );
      ps.AddPermission( new RegistryPermission(
         RegistryPermissionAccess.AllAccess , string.Empty ) );
      ps.Deny();
      // Here, we have full access to system files and registry.
      CodeAccessPermission.RevertDeny();
   }
}
```

No exception will be raised if your code did not have the permission in the first place before calling Deny().Take note that restrictions tied to the call to the Deny() method are not applied to the calling method but only to the calls made from this method. In all cases, when exiting from the calling method, all the default permissions are restored. It is also possible to cancel the permission restrictions by calling RevertDeny().

An alternative exists to the Deny()/RevertDeny() methods. The PermitOnly()/RevertPermitOnly() methods also allow to temporarily modify the set of permissions granted to the current method. The difference between these two approaches is that Deny() specifies the permissions not to grant where PermitOnly() specifies only the permissions to grant.

The Assert() and RevertAssert() methods

The Assert() method allows to specify that the caller does not need one of several permissions. For this, the Assert() method suspends the traversal of the stack for these permissions from where it was called. The method which calls Assert() must have the SecurityPermission(Assertion) meta-permissions. Also, the method must have the concerned permission(s) for the stack traversal to take place. In the other case, a call to Assert() will have no effect and no exceptions will be raised.

A call to the Assert() method can introduce vulnerabilities in the calling code but in some circumstances, its use is necessary. For example, the standard class FileStream internally uses the P/Invoke mechanism to access and all its methods suppress the traversal of the stack for the SecurityPermission(UnmanagedCode) meta-permission. Without doing this, all code accessing a file would need the SecurityPermission(UnmanagedCode) meta-permissions in addition to having FileIOPermission, which is of course unacceptable.

To suppress the traversal of the call stack to verify that all the callers have the SecurityPermission(UnmanagedCode) meta-permissions, it is recommended to flag this method (or its class) with the System.Security.SuppressUnmanagedCodeSecurityAttribute attribute rather than using the Assert() method. In fact, this attribute tells the JIT compiler that it must not produce the code to verify that all the callers have the SecurityPermission(UnmanagedCode) permission during a call to unmanaged code.

The following example suppresses the stack traversal for the registry access permissions:

Example 6-5

```
using System.Security;
using System.Security.Permissions;
class Program {
   static void Main() {
      CodeAccessPermission cap = new RegistryPermission(
         RegistryPermissionAccess.NoAccess , string.Empty );
      cap.Assert();
      // Read the registry.
      RegistryPermission.RevertAssert();
   }
}
```

You cannot call `Assert()` several times within a same method. This will cause an exception to be raised. To call the `Assert()` method several times in a row, you must call the `CodeAccessPermission.RevertAccess()` static method between each call to `Assert()`. To suppress the traversal of the call stack for several permissions in a same method you must call `Assert()` on an instance of `PermissionSet`.

To be safe, it is better to call `Assert()` only when you need it and not, for example, at the beginning of the method. In the same spirit, you should invoke `RevertAssert()` as soon as possible. In general, it is a good idea to wrap your calls within a `try/finally` block.

Finally note that contrarily to the `Deny()/RevertDeny()` methods, `PermitOnly()/RevertPermitOnly()` and `Assert()/RevertAssert()`, the `Demand()` method is the only one which does not does not influence the execution of your code.

The FromXml() and ToXml() methods

The `FromXml()` and `ToXml()` methods allow to construct and save a complex set of permissions using an XML document.

The System.Security.IPermission interface

The `System.Security.IPermission` interface allows making global operations on a set of permissions. This interface is implemented by the `PermissionSet`, `CodeAccessPermission` and its derived classes. Here is its definition:

```
public interface System.Security.IPermission {
    IPermission  Union(IPermission rhs);
    IPermission  Intersect(IPermission rhs);
    bool         IsSubsetOf(IPermission rhs);
    IPermission  Copy();
    void         Demand();
}
```

With the `IsSubsetOf()` you can calculate the inclusion relationships between permissions. For example, the permission which gives you access to the "`C:\MyDir`" folder includes the permission which gives you access to the "`C:\MyDir\MySubDir\`" folder.

Example 6-6

```
using System.Security;
using System.Security.Permissions;
class Program {
   static void Main() {
      string dir1 = @"C:\MyDir";
```

Example 6-6
```
        string dir2 = @"C:\MyDir\MySubDir";
        CodeAccessPermission cap1 = new FileIOPermission(
           FileIOPermissionAccess.AllAccess, dir1);
        CodeAccessPermission cap2 = new FileIOPermission(
           FileIOPermissionAccess.AllAccess, dir2);
        System.Diagnostics.Debug.Assert( cap2.IsSubsetOf(cap1) );
   }
}
```

You also calculate new permissions from the intersection or union of permissions with the Union() and Intersect() methods. You can then reuse the composite permissions. This type of group operation on permissions are often used by the security manager. In practice, developers have little use for this functionality.

CAS: Declarative permissions check using attributes

An alternative exists to the explicit use of the PermissionSet and CodeAccessPermission classes to manipulate permissions directly from your source code. This alternative uses standard attributes which apply to methods, types and even to a whole assembly. Each of the classes derived from the CodeAccessPermission class representing a type of permission has a standard attribute which corresponds to it. For example, the RegistryPermissionAttribute attribute represents the permissions relative to the access of the registry, exactly like the RegistryPermission class. Example 6-5 can then be rewritten as follows:

Example 6-7
```
   using System.Security.Permissions;
   class Program{
      [RegistryPermission(SecurityAction.Assert)]
      static void Main(){
         // Here, we can have access to the registry.
      }
   }
```

The values of the System.Security.Permissions.SecurityAction enumeration allows to specify the desired manipulation. We can mention that the Demand, Deny, PermitOnly and Assert values have the same effect as there synonym methods seen in the previous section. However, the SecurityAction enumeration offers values which allow operations which are not present in the CodeAccessPermission and PermissionSet classes:

SecurityAction value	Description
Inheritance-Demand	When an assembly is loaded, allows to impose that the types derived from the types on which the attribute is declared have the specified permissions.
LinkDemand	Forces the JIT compiler to verify that one or several permissions are granted to the method without regards to the permissions of the calling methods. This action is more permissive than Demand but also less expensive since it is only verified during the JIT compilations.

Attributes to tweak the granted permissions set while loading an assembly

The SecurityAction also offers the three following values, destined to be used at the assembly level. We use them to tell the CLR when an assembly is loaded, it must execute the operation on all permissions:

SecurityAction value	Description
RequestMinimum	Specifies one of multiple permissions without which the assembly cannot be loaded.
RequestOptional	Specifies one or several permissions required to correctly execute the assembly. However, the assembly is still loaded if these permissions aren't granted. Here we talk about optional permissions.
RequestRefuse	When an assembly is loaded, specifies one or several permissions that must not be granted to the assembly.

For example, an assembly which accesses a database needs the `SqlClientPermission` permissions. It may need the `RegistryPermission` permission to access certain parameters but it may be optional as the application provides default parameters. Finally, it is possible that it has no need for permissions such as `WebPermission` or `UIPermission`. The assembly should then be marked with the following permissions:

Example 6-8 *Program.cs*

```
using System.Security.Permissions;
using System.Data.SqlClient;
[assembly: SqlClientPermission( SecurityAction.RequestMinimum )]
[assembly: RegistryPermission( SecurityAction.RequestOptional )]
[assembly: UIPermission( SecurityAction.RequestRefuse )]
[assembly: System.Net.WebPermission( SecurityAction.RequestRefuse )]
class Program { public static void Main() { } }
```

The `permview.exe` tool allows you to visualize these attributes. The `permcalc.exe` tool, described on page 67 goes further and calculates the set of permissions required by an assembly.

Imperative vs. Declarative

The use of .NET attributes has the following disadvantages (compared to the use of imperative permission verifications):

- During the failure of a request or a permission related assert, you cannot trap the exception at the place where it was raised.
- Arguments passed to permissions (such as the name of a folder to manage the permissions for this folder) must be known during compilation. Generally, you cannot put in place a dynamic security logic (i.e. based only on information known during the execution such as the roles of a user).

The advantages to using attributes to manipulate permissions are:

- The possibility of having access to these attributes and to the parameters of these attribute via the assembly metadata or by using the `permview.exe` tool.
- The possibility of using some of these attributes at the assembly level.

CAS: Facilities to test and debug your mobile code

.NET 2 offers new facilities to debug your mobile code. The `System.Security.SecurityException` class offers about ten new properties allowing you to gather much more information when we trap this kind of exception. For example, the `AssemblyName FailedAssemblyInfo{get;}` contains the name of the assembly which caused the exception. Understand that this feature is a double edged sword: if such an exception is analyzed by someone with malicious intentions, it provides them as much information to allow them to exploit the vulnerabilities in your code.

At page 66, we expose the facilities offered by *Visual Studio 2005* to take into account of CAS permissions during the development of your application.

CAS: The isolated storage permission

This section has for goal of explaining a special permission that we can grant to an assembly. This is the permissions allowing for *isolated storage* which aims at solving the following problem

Giving the permission to an application to access the hard disk is sign of great trust in the application. Initially, few applications with mobile code can be given such a trust level. However, most applications need to store data in a persistent way, hence on the hard disk. This data is often activity logs or user preferences. To not authorize an application to store their data can make them unstable, yet authorizing these applications to access the hard disk can be dangerous.

Authorizing an application to make use of isolated storage consists in giving it access to a folder which is reserved for it on the hard disk. You can specify a maximum size to this folder and the application cannot access files which are outside of this folder. Two different applications will each have their own folder. The responsibility to name and locate such a folder on a machine is endorsed by the CLR. Such a folder is sometimes called a *sandbox*.

In fact, this isolated storage mechanism goes a little further than we just said. The choice of the name and location of the folder can not only be based on the identity of the assembly but also on the identity of the user executing the applications or (non-exclusively) on the identity of the application domain containing the assembly. Each of these identities are called *scope*. What this means is that the application can have multiple isolated storage folders, one for each execution context (i.e. one for each of the scope combinations). Each time that the application executes itself in the same context, it uses the same folder. The `System.IO.IsolatedStorage.IsolatedStorageFile` class offers several static methods such as `GetUserStoreForAssembly()`, `GetMachineStoreForAssembly()`, `GetMachineStoreForDomain()` and `GetMachineStoreForApplication()` allowing you to obtain the folder corresponding to the desired scope.

Here is an example showing how to access the isolated storage folder:

Example 6-9
```
using System.IO;
using System.IO.IsolatedStorage;
class Program {
  static void Main() {
    //Get a directory taking account of the current user and assembly.
    IsolatedStorageFile isf =IsolatedStorageFile.GetUserStoreForAssembly();
    IsolatedStorageFileStream isfs = new IsolatedStorageFileStream(
                  "pref.txt", FileMode.Create, isf);
    StreamWriter sw = new StreamWriter( isfs );
    sw.WriteLine("Put your preferences here...");
    sw.Close();
  }
}
```

The folder used by this program as isolated storage is shown in Figure 6-5:

.NET, Windows users and roles

Most applications offer several levels of use. For example, in a bank, all tellers using a banking application are not authorized to transfer one million dollars. Also, not all the users of such an application are authorized to configure the database access protocols. Finally, each client could be authorized to access their account (from the internet). Such an application needs to separate users between clients, basic tellers, tellers with extra responsibility and administrators. Each of these categories is called a role. For the application, each user plays zero, one or several roles. Depending on the requirements of the banking application, the developer must verify directly from the code the role of the current user. In the code, this verification is done before executing any critical operation. In this context, for the application, granting a level of trust to a user consists in determining which roles the user plays.

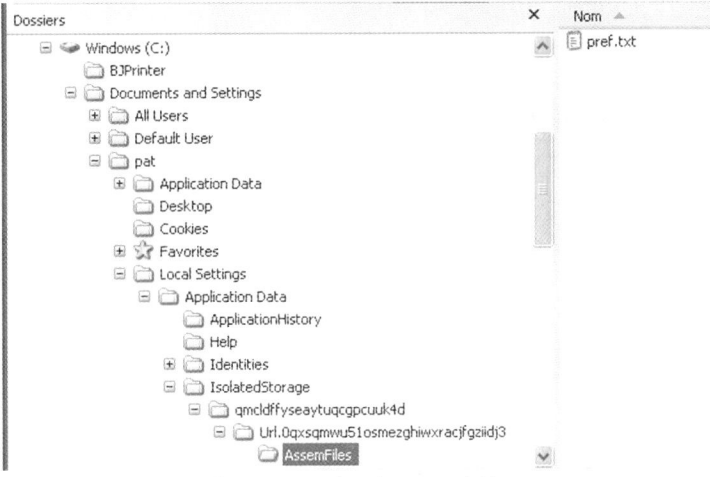

Figure 6-5: Isolated storage folder

Introduction to Windows security

The *Windows 95/98/Me* operating systems do not have a security context. However, in the *Windows NT/2000/XP/2003/Vista* all code execution is done within a security context. To each *Windows* process is associated a *Windows* identity that is called a *principal*. To simplify, you can consider that a principal is a *Windows* user. For the moment, we will consider that a thread executes itself in the context of the principal for its process. We will see that under certain conditions, this rule can be broken.

Windows associates to each of its resources (files, registry…) a set of access rules. When a thread attempts to access a *Windows* resource, *Windows* verify that the principal associated with this thread is authorized by the access rules.

Windows presents the notion of *user groups*. Each user belongs to one or several groups. The resource access rules can be configured based on users or based on user groups. Hence, an administrator can authorize or refuse access to a resource to all users of a group by specifying this group rather than having to specify N users.

Amongst the classic *Windows roles* we can mention the administrator role, the user role, the guest role… The notion of user group allows to naturally implement the concept of role played by a user. To each role corresponds a *Windows* group and a *Windows* user plays a role only if it is part of the corresponding group.

Each time a user logs in, *Windows* creates a *session logon*. A session logon is materialized by a *security token*. The principal of a process is also materialized by a security token. When a process creates a new process, the new one inherits automatically the security token of its creator and runs in the same security context. We will discuss at page 110 how the .NET framework allows you to create a process which runs in a different security context than its parent.

During startup, *Windows* automatically creates three sessions logon: the system session, the local session and the network session. This explains the fact that some applications can execute on a machine without a user being logged-in (this is often used for *Windows* services). This option is often exploited in the case of servers which are susceptible to reboot automatically.

.NET offers several namespaces and several types allowing the programmatic exploitation of the *Windows* security system. Understand that these types simply encapsulate *Win32* functions and structures dedicated to security.

The IIdentity and IPrincipal interfaces

The .NET framework presents the two following interfaces which represent the notion of identity and of principal:

```
interface System.Security.Principal.IIdentity{
   string      AuthenticationType{get;}
   bool        IsAuthenticated{get;}
   string      Name{get;}
}
interface System.Security.Principal.IPrincipal{
   IIdentity   Identity {get;}
   bool        IsInRole(string role);
}
```

While the `IIdentity` interface represents the aspect of authentication (who we are), the `IPrincipal` interface represents the authorization aspect (what are we authorized to do). These interfaces are used to manipulate the *Windows* security using the `System.Security.Principal.WindowsIdentity` and `System.Security.Principal.WindowsPrincipal` implementations. For example, the following program grabs the identity of the user associated with the underlying *Windows* security context:

Example 6-10

```
using System;
using System.Security.Principal;
class Program {
   static void Main() {
      IIdentity id = WindowsIdentity.GetCurrent();
      Console.WriteLine( "Name : " + id.Name );
      Console.WriteLine( "Authenticated? : " + id.IsAuthenticated );
      Console.WriteLine( "Authentication Type : " +id.AuthenticationType );
   }
}
```

This program displays:

```
Nom : PSMACCHIA\pat
Authenticated? : True
Authentication type : NTLM
```

The .NET framework also offers other implementations of the `IIdentity` and `IPrincipal` interfaces relating to other security mechanisms and you can supply your own implementations to develop your own security mechanisms. We can mention the `System.Web.Security.FormsIdentity` class used by ASP.NET and the `System.Web.Security.PassportIdentity` class used by the *Passport* security mechanism.

The pair of classes `System.Security.Principal.GenericIdentity` and `System.Security.Principal.GenericPrincipal` can be use as a base implementation to your own authentication/authorization mechanisms but nothing prevent you from implementing directly the `IIdentity` and `IPrincipal` interfaces.

Windows Security Identifiers (SID)

To identify the users and groups, *Windows* uses a *Security Identifier* (SID). The SIDs can be seen as big unique numbers in time and space, essentially like a GUID. The SIDs can be represented by a string formatted with *SDDL (Security Descriptor Definition Language)*) which is a non-XML textual representation format which gives some information in regards to the represented entity.

.NET, Windows users and roles

For example, we can deduce from the following SID "S-1-5-21-1950407961-2111586655-839522115-500" that it represents an administrator as it contains 500 at the end (501 would have indicated a guest).

The .NET framework .offers the three following classes where instances simply represent SIDs:

```
System.Object
   System.Security.Principal.IdentityReference
      System.Security.Principal.NTAccount
      System.Security.Principal.SecurityIdentifier
```

The `NTAccount` class allows representing the SID in a human readable form while the `SecurityIdentifier` class is used to communicate a SID to *Windows*. Each of these classes have a method named `IdentityReference Translate(Type targetType)` allowing you to obtain a different representation of a same SID.

The `WindowsIdentity` class has the `SecurityIdentifier User{get;}` property which allows you to recover the SID of the current *Windows* user. The `System.Security.Principal.WellKnownSidType` enumeration represents most *Windows* groups supplied by default. Finally, the `SecurityIdentifier` class offer the method named `bool IsWellKnown(WellKnownSidType)` which allows to verify whether the current SID belongs to the specified *Windows* group. The following example exploits all this to test if the current user is an administrator:

Example 6-11
```
using System.Security.Principal;
class Program {
   static void Main() {
      WindowsIdentity id = WindowsIdentity.GetCurrent();
      SecurityIdentifier sid = id.User;
      NTAccount ntacc = sid.Translate( typeof( NTAccount ) ) as NTAccount;
      System.Console.WriteLine( "SID:       " + sid.Value);
      System.Console.WriteLine( "NTAccount: " + ntacc.Value);
      if ( sid.IsWellKnown( WellKnownSidType.AccountAdministratorSid ) )
         System.Console.WriteLine("...is administrator.");
   }
}
```

This example displays:

```
SID:       S-1-5-21-1950407961-2111586655-839522115-500
NTAccount: PSMACCHIA\pat
...is administrator.
```

Impersonating the underlying Windows thread

By default, a *Windows* thread evolves in the security context of its process. However, from code, you can associate the context of a thread with a user by using the `WindowsIdentity.Impersonate(IntPtr jeton)` *win32* function. You must initially log-in the user and obtain a security token with the `LogonUser()` function. This user is not necessarily the user of the security context for the process. When the security context of a thread is associated to a user we say that the thread is doing an *impersonation*. This is demonstrated in the following example:

Example 6-12
```
using System.Runtime.InteropServices;
using System.Security.Principal;
class Program{
   [DllImport("Advapi32.Dll")]
```

Example 6-12

```
    static extern bool LogonUser(
       string    sUserName,
       string    sDomain,
       string    sUserPassword,
       uint      dwLogonType,
       uint      dwLogonProvider,
       out       System.IntPtr token);
[DllImport("Kernel32.Dll")]
static extern void CloseHandle( System.IntPtr token );

static void Main(){
   WindowsIdentity id1 = WindowsIdentity.GetCurrent();
   System.Console.WriteLine( "Before impersonating : " + id1.Name);
   System.IntPtr pToken;
   if( LogonUser(
         "guest" ,          // login
         string.Empty,      // Windows domain
         "guest_pwd" ,      // password
         2,                 // LOGON32_LOGON_INTERACTIVE
         0,                 // LOGON32_PROVIDER_DEFAUT
         out pToken) ) {
      WindowsIdentity.Impersonate( pToken );
      WindowsIdentity id2 = WindowsIdentity.GetCurrent();
      System.Console.WriteLine( "After impersonating  : " + id2.Name );
      // Here, the underlying Windows thread ...
      // ... has the 'guest' identity.
      CloseHandle( pToken );
   }
  }
}
```

This program displays:

```
Before impersonating  : PSMACCHIA\pat
After impersonating   : PSMACCHIA\guest
```

The `WindowsIndentity.GetCurrent()` method has an overload taking in a boolean parameter. When the boolean is set to `true`, this method returns the identity of the user only if the thread is impersonating another user. When the boolean is set to `false`, this method returns the identity of the user only if the thread is not impersonating a user.

.NET and access control to Windows resources

Introduction to Windows access control

After having introduced the notion of *Windows* users and groups we will interest ourselves to the second part of the security under *Windows*: access control to resources.

A *Windows* resource can be a file, a *Windows* synchronization object (mutex, event...), a registry entry... Each type of resource has access rights that are specific to the resource. For example, we can mention the access right allowing adding data to a file and the right to own a mutex. None of these access rights has sense outside of the context for a type of resource.

Each resource physically contains information allowing *Windows* to deduce which user has which access rights on this resource. This information is contained in a structure associated with the resource that is called a security descriptor (SD). A SD contains a SID representing the user who created or owns the resource and a list named *Discretionary Access Control List* (DACL). Although stored in a binary format, a SD can be also represented by a SDDL string.

When a thread which executes in the security context of a user attempts to obtain some access rights on a resource, *Windows* determines if it can obtain the requested rights from the DACL of the resource.

A DACL is an ordered list of *Access Control Elements* (ACE). An ACE is a structure which associates a SID to a list of access rights. A DACL contains two types of ACE:

- The ACE which grant access rights to their SID;
- The ACE that denies access rights to their SID.

When a thread tries to obtain some access rights to a resource, *Windows* makes its verdict from the SID of the thread and the DACL of the resource. The ACE are evaluated in the order that they are stored in the DACL. Each ACE grants or denies access rights when the SID of the thread is included in its SID. The set of access rights demanded are granted as soon as all the access rights have been granted during the evaluation. The access rights are all denied as soon as one of the requested access rights is denied by an ACE. Understand that the order of storage of the ACE in the DACL is relevant and that *Windows* does not necessarily evaluate all ACEs during an access right request.

For certain types of resources, *Windows* allows the inheritance of SD. This possibility can be essential, for example to the administrator wishing to set the SD of thousands of files contained in a folder with a single operation.

Each SD of a *Windows* resource contains a second list of ACE named *System Access Control List* (*SACL*). This second list is used by *Windows* to audit the access to a resource. As the ACE of a DACL, the ACE of a SACL associates to each SID a list of access rights. Contrarily to the ACE in a DACL, the ACE of a SACL contains two pieces of binary information which can be interpreted as follows:

- Does the event *one of my rights has been granted to a SID included in my SID list* event must be logged?
- Does the event *one of my rights has been denied to a SID included in my SID list* must be logged?

Clearly, the storage order of the ACEs in a SACL is irrelevant.

The new namespace named `System.Security.AccessControl` defines types allowing you to use SDs. After having presented the types dedicated to the manipulation of resource SDs specific to *Windows*, we will present types which allow the use of SD's in a generic way (i.e. independently of the type of the underlying *Windows* resource).

Using specific SDs from .NET code

The types relative to specific resources consist in a hierarchy of types representing the SD, a hierarchy representing the ACE types and enumeration representing access rights. The following classes allows the representation of security descriptors:

```
System.Object
   System.Security.AccessControl.ObjectSecurity
      System.Security.AccessControl.DirectoryObjectSecurity
         System.DirectoryServices.ActiveDirectorySecurity
      System.Security.AccessControl.CommonObjectSecurity
```

```
            Microsoft.Iis.Metabase.MetaKeySecurity
            System.Security.AccessControl.NativeObjectSecurity
               System.Security.AccessControl.EventWaitHandleSecurity
               System.Security.AccessControl.FileSystemSecurity
                  System.Security.AccessControl.DirectorySecurity
                  System.Security.AccessControl.FileSecurity
               System.Security.AccessControl.MutexSecurity
               System.Security.AccessControl.RegistrySecurity
               System.Security.AccessControl.SemaphoreSecurity
```

These classes accept specific parameters representing the ACE to fill the DACL and SACL. Note that there are classes representing the ACE of the DACL (*access rule*) and classes representing the ACE of the SACL for the audit (*audit rule*):

```
System.Object
   System.Security.AccessControl.AuthorizationRule
      System.Security.AccessControl.AccessRule
         Microsoft.Iis.Metabase.MetaKeyAccessRule
         System.Security.AccessControl.EventWaitHandleAccessRule
         System.Security.AccessControl.FileSystemAccessRule
         System.Security.AccessControl.MutexAccessRule
         System.Security.AccessControl.ObjectAccessRule
            System.DirectoryServices.ActiveDirectoryAccessRule
               System.DirectoryServices.[*]AccessRule
         System.Security.AccessControl.RegistryAccessRule
         System.Security.AccessControl.SemaphoreAccessRule
      System.Security.AccessControl.AuditRule
         Microsoft.Iis.Metabase.MetaKeyAuditRule
         System.Security.AccessControl.EventWaitHandleAuditRule
         System.Security.AccessControl.FileSystemAuditRule
         System.Security.AccessControl.MutexAuditRule
         System.Security.AccessControl.ObjectAuditRule
            System.DirectoryServices.ActiveDirectoryAuditRule
         System.Security.AccessControl.RegistryAuditRule
         System.Security.AccessControl.SemaphoreAuditRule
```

Here is the list of enumeration representing the access rights. For example, the `FileSystemRights` enumeration contains the value `AppendData` while the `MutexRights` enumeration contains the `TakeOwnership` value.

```
Microsoft.Iis.Metabase.MetaKeyRights
System.Security.AccessControl.EventWaitHandleRights
System.Security.AccessControl.FileSystemRights
System.Security.AccessControl.MutexRights
System.Security.AccessControl.RegistryRights
System.Security.AccessControl.SemaphoreRights
```

Finally, the different types of the .NET framework directly represent the concerned *Windows* resources (`System.Threading.Mutex`, `System.IO.File`...) have new constructors accepting ACLs and the new `Set/GetAccessControl()` methods which allow setting or obtaining the ACL for an instance. Here is an example illustrating all this during the creation of a file with a DACL:

Example 6-13

```
using System.Security.AccessControl;
using System.Security.Principal;
using System.IO;
class Program {
   static void Main() {
```

.NET and access control to Windows resources 177

Example 6-13
```
            // Fill the DACL.
            FileSecurity dacl = new FileSecurity();
            // Fill the DACL with an ACE.
            FileSystemAccessRule ace = new FileSystemAccessRule(
               WindowsIdentity.GetCurrent().Name,
               FileSystemRights.AppendData | FileSystemRights.ReadData,
               AccessControlType.Allow);
            dacl.AddAccessRule( ace );
            // Create a new file which has this DACL.
            System.IO.FileStream fileStream = new System.IO.FileStream(
                  @"file.bin" , FileMode.Create , FileSystemRights.Write ,
                  FileShare.None, 4096 , FileOptions.None, dacl );
            fileStream.Write( new byte[] { 0, 1, 2, 3 }, 0, 4 );
            fileStream.Close();
      }
   }
```

You can visualize the access rights to the `file.bin` as follows: *Properties of file.bin > Security > Advanced > Permission > Edit the permission granted to the principal with which you executed the program > Read permission and Append Data.*

If the security tab does not display itself, you need to do the following: *Control Panel > Folder options > View > Use simple file sharing (recommended).*

Using generic SDs from .NET code

.NET offers several types for the manipulation of SDs. The following type hierarchy allows the representation of SDs:

```
System.Object
   System.Security.AccessControl.GenericSecurityDescriptor
      System.Security.AccessControl.CommonSecurityDescriptor
      System.Security.AccessControl.RawSecurityDescriptor
```

The following type hierarchy allows the representation of ACL, DACL and SACL:

```
System.Object
   System.Security.AccessControl.GenericAcl
      System.Security.AccessControl.CommonAcl
         System.Security.AccessControl.DiscretionaryAcl
         System.Security.AccessControl.SystemAcl
      System.Security.AccessControl.RawAcl
```

The following type hierarchy allows the representation of an ACE:

```
System.Object
   System.Security.AccessControl.GenericAce
      System.Security.AccessControl.CustomAce
      System.Security.AccessControl.KnownAce
         System.Security.AccessControl.CompoundAce
         System.Security.AccessControl.QualifiedAce
            System.Security.AccessControl.CommonAce
            System.Security.AccessControl.ObjectAce
```

The example bellow shows how to create a SD, how to add ACEs to its DACL and then transform this SD into a *Windows* resource specific SD (a mutex in this case):

Example 6-14
```
using System;
using System.Security.AccessControl;
using System.Security.Principal;
class Program {
   static void Main() {
      // Create a new security descriptor.
      CommonSecurityDescriptor csd = new CommonSecurityDescriptor(
                                      false, false, string.Empty);
      DiscretionaryAcl dacl = csd.DiscretionaryAcl;
      // Add an ACE to its ACL.
      dacl.AddAccess(
         AccessControlType.Allow, // Allow OR Deny.
         WindowsIdentity.GetCurrent().Owner, // Current user.
         0x00180000, // Mask: TakeOwnerShip AND Synchronize
         //                     equivalent to
         //(int) MutexRights.TakeOwnership | (int) MutexRights.Synchronize
         InheritanceFlags.None,  // Disable ACE inheritance.
         PropagationFlags.None);

      string sSDDL = csd.GetSddlForm( AccessControlSections.Owner );
      Console.WriteLine( "Security Descriptor : " + sSDDL );

      MutexSecurity mutexSec = new MutexSecurity();
      mutexSec.SetSecurityDescriptorSddlForm( sSDDL );
      AuthorizationRuleCollection aces = mutexSec.GetAccessRules(
                                      true, true, typeof(NTAccount));
      foreach ( AuthorizationRule ace in aces ) {
         if (ace is MutexAccessRule) {
            MutexAccessRule mutexAce = (MutexAccessRule)ace;
            Console.WriteLine( "-->SID : " +
                               mutexAce.IdentityReference.Value );
            Console.WriteLine( "   Kind of access right : " +
                               mutexAce.AccessControlType.ToString());
            if (0xffffffff == (uint) mutexAce.MutexRights)
               Console.WriteLine( "   Full rights!" );
            else
               Console.WriteLine( "   Rights : " +
                               mutexAce.MutexRights.ToString());
         }
      }
   }
}
```
This example displays:
```
Security Descriptor : D:(A;;0xffffffff;;;WD)(A;;0x180000;;;LA)
-->SID : EVERYBODY
   Kind of access right : Allow
   Full rights!
-->SID : PSMACCHIA\pat
   Kind of access right: Allow
   Rights : TakeOwnership, Synchronize
```

We notice that by default, a DACL of a new SD contains an ACE which grants all rights to everyone. You can use the `CommonAcl.Purge(SecurityIdentifier)` method to remove the ACE of an SID in an ACL.

.NET and roles

In the same way that a *Windows* thread executes in a *Windows* security context, a managed thread has the possibility of executing itself in the security context of your choice. You can then exploit a user/role security mechanism other that the one in *Windows*, such as the one of ASP.NET for example. This is possible because the `Thread` class offers the `IPrincipal CurrentPrincipal {get;set;}` property. A principal can be associated to a thread in three different ways:

- Either you explicitly associate a principal to a managed thread using the `Thread.CurrentPrincipal` property.
- Either you define a *principal policy* for an AppDomain. When a managed thread will execute the code of the AppDomain, the principal policy for the domain will eventually associate a principal to the thread, except in the case where the thread has been explicitly associated a principal.
- Either you can decide that all the threads created in a domain or that penetrate into a domain without having a .NET principal will have a specific principal. To accomplish this, you simply need to use the `void AppDomain.SetThreadPrincipal(IPrincipal)` method.

These three operations require the `SecurityPermissionFlag.ControlPrincipal` meta-permission to be executed.

Defining the principal policy of an AppDomain

The following example sets the principal policy of the current application domain to `WindowsPrincipal`. This means that when a managed thread executes the code contained in an AppDomain, if it did not have a principal explicitly associated to it, then the underlying *Windows* security context is associated to it:

Example 6-15

```
using System;
using System.Security.Principal;
class Program{
   static void Main(){
      System.AppDomain.CurrentDomain.SetPrincipalPolicy(
                  PrincipalPolicy.WindowsPrincipal);
      IPrincipal pr = System.Threading.Thread.CurrentPrincipal;
      IIdentity  id = pr.Identity;
      Console.WriteLine( "Name : " + id.Name );
      Console.WriteLine( "Athenticated? : " + id.IsAuthenticated );
      Console.WriteLine( "Authentification type : "+id.AuthenticationType);
   }
}
```

This program displays:

```
Name : PSMACCHIA\pat
Authenticated? : True
Authentication type : NTLM
```

The other principal policies which are possible for an application domain are:

- No principal associated to the thread (`PrincipalPolicy.NoPrincipal`). In this case, the `Thread.CurrentPrincipal` is `null` by default.
- An unauthenticated principal associated to the thread (`PrincipalPolicy.UnauthenticatedPrincipal`). In this case, the CLR associated an unauthenticated instance of `GenericPrincipal` to the `Thread.CurrentPrincipal` property.

This last alternative constitutes the default principal policy taken by all application domains.

Checking if a user belongs to a particular role

You can verify the role of the principal of a managed thread in three different ways:

- You can use the `IsInRole()` method offered by the `IPrincipal` interface.

Example 6-16
```
using System.Security.Principal;
class Program{
   static void Main(){
      IPrincipal pr = System.Threading.Thread.CurrentPrincipal;
      if( pr.IsInRole( @"BUILTIN\Administrators" ) ){
         // Here, the principal is an administrator.
      }
      else
         System.Console.WriteLine(
            "You must be an administrator to run this program!");
   }
}
```

The attentive reader will notice that in Example 6-11 we have used another technique to verify that a *Windows* user is a member of a *Windows* group. This technique, based on the `WellKnownSidType`, is preferred in the particular case of *Windows* users and roles. The reason is that a *Windows* group varies based on the language used (for example *Administrateurs* in French, *Administrators* in English).

- You can use the `System.Security.Permissions.PrincipalPermission` class. Although that this class does not derive from `CodeAccessPermission`, it implements the `IPermission` interface. This class also offers all the classic methods allowing the manipulation of permissions (`FromXml()`, `ToXml()`...). This technique offers an advantage for developers as it allows a coherent way to manage the roles compared to the management of permissions.

Example 6-17
```
using System.Security.Permissions;
class Program{
   static void Main(){
      try{
         PrincipalPermission prPerm = new PrincipalPermission(
            null, @"BUILTIN\Administrators" );
         prPerm.Demand();
         // Here, the principal is an administrator.
      }
      catch(System.Security.SecurityException){
         System.Console.WriteLine(
            "You must be an administrator to run this program!");
      }
   }
}
```

Another advantage of this technique is that it allows you to verify multiple roles in a single operation:

Example 6-18
```
...
   PrincipalPermission prPermAdmin = new PrincipalPermission(
         null, @"BUILTIN\Administrators" );
   PrincipalPermission prPermUser = new PrincipalPermission(
         null, @"BUILTIN\Users" );
   System.Security.IPermission prPerm = prPermAdmin.Union( prPermUser );
   prPerm.Demand();
...
```

- As with permission management, you can use the `PrincipalPermission` .NET attribute:

Example 6-19
```
using System.Security.Permissions;
class Program {
    [PrincipalPermission( SecurityAction.Demand,
                         Role= @"BUILTIN\Administrators")]
    static void Main() {
        // Here, the principal is an administrator.
    }
}
```

The comparison between the technique using the `PrincipalPermission` class and the technique of using .NET attributes is discussed at page 169.

COM+ roles

COM+ is a *Microsoft* technology allowing a class (.NET or not) to use the functionalities called enterprise services. Amongst these enterprise services, there is a service of role based security management. For each component served (i.e. that uses COM+), you can associate the required roles to use the component and then assign roles to each user. The COM+ roles can be different than the *Windows* roles but in practice we often use the *Windows* roles. When an assembly contains served components, it can verify that a user belongs to a role by using the `System.EnterpriseServices.SecurityRole` attribute on the assembly or on certain classes or interfaces of the assembly. For more information on how to use the role management enterprise service and on the unification of *Windows* and COM+ roles, you can refer to the article named **Unify the Role-Based Security Models for Enterprise and Application Domains with .NET** by *Juval Lowy* available at http://msdn.microsoft.com/msdnmag/issues/02/05/rolesec/.

.NET and cryptography: symmetric algorithms

Brief introduction to symmetric algorithms

We are about to explain how Joe and Bob can exchange messages in a confidential manner using a *symmetric algorithm* of encryption. The symmetric algorithms are based on a system of key pairs. Before we can encrypt a message M, Joe and Bob must choose a symmetric algorithm and construct a pair of keys (S,P). Let's name P(M) a message M encrypted with the P key and S(M) a message M encrypted with the S key. The properties of a symmetric algorithm are as follows:

- S(P(M)) = P(S(M)) = M
- We cannot obtain M if we have P(M) without knowing the S key.
- We cannot obtain M if we have S(M) without knowing the P key.

We see that the S and P keys plays a symmetric role hence the name of symmetric algorithm. For Joe to send the message M to Bob in a confidential way, it must send one of the two versions of the encrypted message. Bob can then obtain the original message by applying the symmetric algorithm on the message encrypted with the two keys. In practice, Joe and Bob agree on which key to be used for the encryption. If another party intercepts the encrypted version of the message, he cannot decrypt the original message as he does not have the (S,P) key pair. All this is summarized in the following figure:

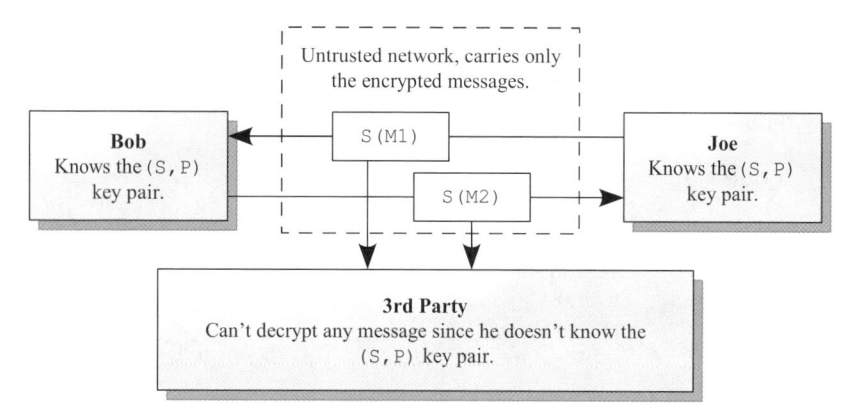

Figure 6-6: Exchanging messages encrypted with a symmetric algorithm

Symmetrical algorithms aren't secret and largely discussed in numerous publications. In the measure that the publication of an algorithm allows thousands of mathematicians to examine it for weaknesses, we can say that publishing such an algorithm participates in proving its robustness. Only the keys must be kept confidential. This is a principle of cryptography that has recently appeared, about thirty years ago.

The .NET framework and symmetric algorithms

The .NET framework offers an implementation of the most commonly known symmetric algorithms *DES*, *RC2*, *Rinjdael* and *Triple DES*. Here is the class hierarchy. Only the classes not in bold are abstract. You can then implement your own version of these algorithms.

```
System.Object
  System.Security.Cryptography.SymmetricAlgorithm
    System.Security.Cryptography.DES
      System.Security.Cryptography.DSECryptoServiceProvider
    System.Security.Cryptography.RC2
      System.Security.Cryptography.RC2CryptoServiceProvider
    System.Security.Cryptography.Rijndael
      System.Security.Cryptography.RinjdaelManaged
    System.Security.Cryptography.TripleDES
      System.Security.Cryptography.TripleDESCryptoServiceProvider
```

The *DES* (*Digital Encryption Standard*) algorithm is probably the most commonly used symmetric algorithm. The following example illustrates the use of the DESCryptoServiceProvider class to encrypt and decrypt a string. In addition to a key, we supply this algorithm an *Initialization Vector* or *IV*. An initialization vector can be seen as a random number chosen to initialize the algorithm:

Example 6-20

```
using System.Security.Cryptography;
class Program{
    static void Main() {
        string sMsg = "The message to encrypt!";
        string sEnc, sDec;
        DESCryptoServiceProvider des = new DESCryptoServiceProvider();
        System.Text.Encoding utf = new System.Text.UTF8Encoding();
        byte[] key = utf.GetBytes("12345678");
        byte[] iv = { 1, 2, 3, 4, 5, 6, 7, 8 };
```

.NET and cryptography: asymmetric algorithms (public/private keys)

Example 6-20

```
      ICryptoTransform encryptor = des.CreateEncryptor(key, iv);
      ICryptoTransform decryptor = des.CreateDecryptor(key, iv);
      {
         byte[] bMsg = utf.GetBytes(sMsg);
         byte[] bEnc = encryptor.TransformFinalBlock(bMsg, 0,
                                                      bMsg.Length);
         sEnc = System.Convert.ToBase64String(bEnc);
      }
      {
         byte[] bEnc = System.Convert.FromBase64String(sEnc);
         byte[] bDec = decryptor.TransformFinalBlock(bEnc, 0,
                                                      bEnc.Length);
         sDec = utf.GetString(bDec);
      }
      System.Console.WriteLine("Message   : " + sMsg);
      System.Console.WriteLine("Encrypted: " + sEnc);
      System.Console.WriteLine("Decrypted: " + sDec);
   }
}
```

This example displays the following:

```
Message   : The message to encrypt!
Encrypted: Z4hH+B4L8xKp7VeAChsZTu/yDmOS/YJn
Decrypted: The message to encrypt!
```

In the previous example, note that the `encryptor` and `decryptor` objects both implement the `ICryptoTransform` interface. This is a consequence of the symmetrical aspect of these algorithms.

The `DESCryptoServiceProvider` class can also be used to construct a key and an initialization vector. The previous example can be rewritten as follows to take advantage of these features:

Example 6-21

```
      ...
      des.GenerateKey();
      des.GenerateIV();
      ICryptoTransform encryptor = des.CreateEncryptor();
      ICryptoTransform decryptor = des.CreateDecryptor();
      ...
```

.NET and cryptography: asymmetric algorithms (public/private keys)

Brief introduction to asymmetric algorithm

The *symmetric algorithms* have two main flaws:

- The key pair must be known by both parties which wish to exchange messages. At some point in time, this pair must be sent to both parties on a potentially unsecured communication channel.
- A key pair is only valid for two parties. If Joe wishes to exchange encrypted messaged with Bob and Sebastian, he must then deal with two key pairs: one to exchange messages with Bob and one to exchange messages with Sebastian. We can then see potential key pair management issue.

Asymmetric algorithms solve these two problems. An asymmetric algorithm has the three properties of a symmetric algorithm, which are:

- S(P(M)) = P(S(M)) = M
- We cannot obtain M if we have P(M) without knowing the S key.
- We cannot obtain M is we have S(M) without knowing the P key.

In addition to these three properties, an asymmetric algorithm has the two following properties:

- It is easy to calculate the S key when we know the P key
- It is difficult to calculate the P key if we know the S key.

We have then introduced an asymmetry in our key pair, hence the name of this type of algorithm.

We now understand how Bob and Joe can use this type of algorithm without having to exchange keys and without having to manage a large number of keys. They simply need to each calculate a key pair that we will name (Sj,Pj) and (Sb,Pb). Bob uses the Sj key while Joe uses the Sb key. Anyone wishing to send a message M to Bob in a confidential way can use the Sb key to encrypt it. If Bob has taken care of keeping the Pb key private, he is then the only one which can decrypt Sb(M) by calculating Pb(Sb(M)). All this is summarized in the following illustration

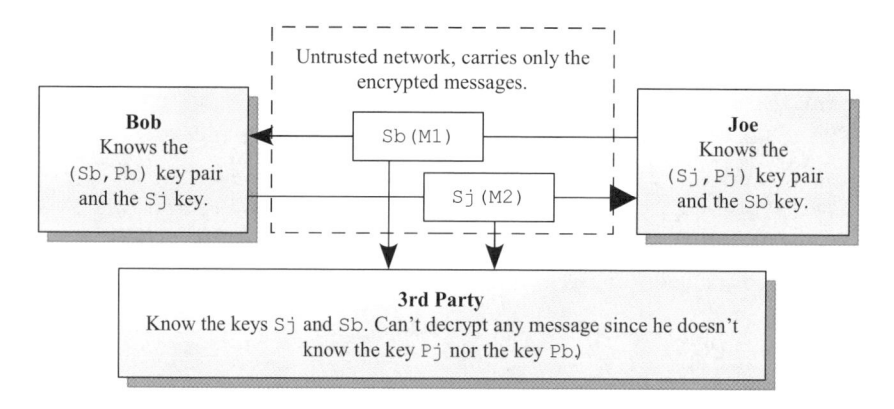

Figure 6-7: Exchanging messages encrypted with an asymmetric algorithm

We say that S is the *public key* or *shared key*. We say that P is the *private key*. We sometime also refer to these algorithms as public/private key algorithms.

However, an authentication problem still exists. Since the Sb key is known by everyone another party could easily send an encrypted message Sb(M) to Bob pretending to be Joe. This problem can be avoided using the following trick: Joe can send the encrypted message Sb(Pj(M)) to Bob. Bob can then decrypt this message since he owns the Pb and Sj keys and that Sj(Pb(Sb(Pj(M)))) = Sj(Pj(M)) = M. In other words, Bob can be certain that Joe is the sender since Joe is the only one who knows Pj.

Introduction to secure sessions

Another problem still remains: the computation cost of asymmetric algorithms is known as being about 1000 times more expensive than symmetric algorithms. In practice, secure exchange protocols use an asymmetric algorithm to exchange a key pair and then use a symmetric algorithm to encrypt the messages. The key pair of the symmetric algorithm is then only valid for one message exchange session. We then talk of *session key* and of *secure session*.

The RSA algorithm

The RSA algorithm, created in 1977, is currently the most commonly used asymmetric algorithm. The protection of bank cards and even military messages uses it. The .NET platform also uses it. The RSA name comes from the name of its inventors, *R.L. Rivest, A. Shamir* and *L.M Adelman*.

The RSA algorithm is based on a property of large prime numbers. Given two large prime numbers A and B. It is easy to calculate the product of A and B. However, when we know the AB product, it is difficult to calculate the original A and B numbers. Without going into the details of the RSA algorithm, you can consider that the pair of numbers (A,B) defines the private key while the product of A and B defines the public key.

As long as we can obtain a pair of prime numbers A and B from their product in polynomial time, the RSA algorithm will remain reliable. In fact, we have not been able to prove that there exists an algorithm which can do better than polynomial time. Most contemporary mathematicians assume that the problem will remain unsolved for several decades. However, history has shown that it is almost impossible to predict when such a mathematical problem will be resolved.

Finally, know that we use efficient statistical algorithms to calculate large prime numbers. This type of algorithm allows determining if a large number is prime with a great degree of certainty while never being 100%.

Asymmetric algorithm and digital signature

In addition to allowing you to encrypt data, the properties of the asymmetrical algorithms can also be used to digitally sign data. Digitally signing data means that someone consuming the data can absolutely be certain about the fact that the entity who produced the data has the private key. We talk about data authentication if the consumer can be certain that the entity who produced the data is the only one who has the private key.

To understand what we will discuss, it is first necessary to understand what is a *hashing value*. A hashing value is a number calculated from a set of data. This computation has the property of giving two different numbers for two distinct sets of data in an almost certain way. The .NET framework offers the `System.Security.Cryptography` namespace which implements the main hashing algorithms, which include: *SHAx*, *RIPEMD160* and *MD5*.

Lets suppose that Bob wishes to convince Joe that he is the author of the F00 file He must first calculate a hashing value x for the file. Then, Bob calculates Pb(x) from his private key. Finally, Bob integrates the Pb(x) and his public key Sb in the F00 file (for example, at the beginning of the file).

Joe already knows Sb, Bob's public key. Joe gets the F00 file and extracts Pb(x) and the public key of the file. He verifies that the key is in fact the public key from Bob. He can then calculate x using two different approaches:

- By calculating the hashing value of the F00 file (from which he removed Pb(x) and the public key).
- By calculating x from Pb(x) and the public key Sb since Sb(Pb(x))=x.

If these two calculations by Joe yield the same value, he can be sure that the author of F00 has the Pb private key. We say that Pb(x) constitutes a *digital signature* for the F00 file. If Bob was able to convince that he is the only party who has the Pb private key, Joe can be sure that the author of F00 is Bob.

However, there is one flaw in this algorithm. We have said that '*This computation has the property of giving two different numbers for two distinct sets of data in an almost certain way*'. If another party manages to find a sequence of bytes which produced the same hashing value, it can then use the previous digital signature with this new sequence of bytes. Joe will have no way of knowing that the file was not produced by the owner of the **Pb** private key However, the size of hashing values is in the order of 20 bytes meaning that there is one chance over 10 at the power of 48 that a random byte sequence would produce the same hashing value.

At page 23, we explain how the .NET platform allows to digitally sign assemblies. At page 191, we will see that this technique has been used in the *Windows* environment way before .NET to authenticate files. We will then present a technology allowing ensuring that we are the only owners of a certain private key.

The .NET framework and the RSA algorithm

The .NET framework presents two classes allowing you to use the RSA algorithm: The `RSACryptoServiceProvider` class for the encryption of data and the `DSACryptoServiceProvider` class for the digital signing of data (DSA for *Digital Signature Algorithm*). Here is the class hierarchy:

```
System.Object
    System.Security.Cryptography.AsymmetricAlgorithm
        System.Security.Cryptography.DSA
            System.Security.Cryptography.DSACryptoServiceProvider
        System.Security.Cryptography.RSA
            System.Security.Cryptography.RSACryptoServiceProvider
```

The following example exposes the use of the `RSACryptoServiceProvider` class to encrypt a string. The `ExportParameter(bool)` method allows you to retrieve the public key of the public/private key pair depending on whether it is called with `false` or `true`:

Example 6-22

```
using System.Security.Cryptography;
class Program {
    static void Main() {
        string sMsg = "The message to encrypt!";
        string sEnc, sDec;
        System.Text.Encoding utf = new System.Text.UTF8Encoding();
        RSACryptoServiceProvider rsa = new RSACryptoServiceProvider();
        RSAParameters publicKey = rsa.ExportParameters( false );
        RSAParameters publicAndPrivateKey = rsa.ExportParameters( true );
        {
            RSACryptoServiceProvider rsaEncryptor = new
                                    RSACryptoServiceProvider();
            rsaEncryptor.ImportParameters( publicKey );
            byte[] bMsg = utf.GetBytes(sMsg);
            byte[] bEnc = rsaEncryptor.Encrypt( bMsg, false );
            sEnc = System.Convert.ToBase64String( bEnc );
        }
        {
            RSACryptoServiceProvider rsaDecryptor = new
                                    RSACryptoServiceProvider();
            rsaDecryptor.ImportParameters( publicAndPrivateKey );
            byte[] bEnc = System.Convert.FromBase64String(sEnc);
            byte[] bDec = rsaDecryptor.Decrypt( bEnc, false );
            sDec = utf.GetString( bDec );
        }
        System.Console.WriteLine("Message   : " + sMsg);
        System.Console.WriteLine("Encrypted: " + sEnc);
        System.Console.WriteLine("Decrypted: " + sDec);
    }
}
```

This program displays the following:

```
Message  : The message to encrypt!
Encrypted: a4M+VBM2a6sBbMcWbxHrDTKoU3mIVQ6lLS/ZIMQRh5xesq6zXNCKAN
2GSX+Fxnt3YiBO+HrX3UPy/KE7ifRxZgq7bGNPOeyCr1Lopx5GnkcC4pXbB5/Q4fi
aUOBgamFZXRqyUlicIs6WRO91Pzjh3WdpVLMqJOkU/XkaB43JJWU=
Decrypted: The message to encrypt!
```

The Data Protection API (DPAPI)

The Data Protection API of Windows

Since *Windows 2000*, the *Windows* operating systems offer a cryptographic API named *DPAPI* (*Data Protection API*). This API is implemented in the `crypt32.dll` system DLL and has the peculiarity of using the login/password pair of the current user to manage keys. It can base itself on the identity of a process, *Windows* session or the identity of the current machine. In fact, quite often we wish to encrypt data to ensure its confidentiality at the user, process, session or machine level. In these cases, the use of DAPI avoids us from having to manage the keys.

This API is capable of managing the modifications to the password. In other words, if you store data by encrypting them for a specific user, you will be able to use them even when the password of this user has changed. This is possible due to a mechanism which stores the expired keys. For more details on this topic, read the article named **Windows Data Protection** on **MSDN**.

The System.Security.Cryptography.ProtectedData class

The following example shows how to use the `System.Security.Cryptography.ProtectedData` class to protect data at the user level. We could have used the `DataProtectionScope.LocalMachine` value to protect this data at the machine level. In this example, we use the option to add *entropy* to the encryption. This means that a process executing in the appropriate context (i.e. under the right user or the right machine) will not be able to decrypt the data if he does not know the entropy used to encrypt it. You can then consider the entropy as some kind of secondary key:

Example 6-23

```
using System.Security.Cryptography;
class Program{
    static void Main() {
        string sMsg = "The message to encrypt!";
        string sEnc, sDec;
        System.Text.Encoding utf = new System.Text.UTF8Encoding();
        byte[] entropy = new byte[] { 1, 2, 3, 4, 5, 6, 7, 8 };
        {
            byte[] bMsg = utf.GetBytes(sMsg);
            byte[] bEnc = ProtectedData.Protect(
                    bMsg , entropy , DataProtectionScope.CurrentUser);
            sEnc = System.Convert.ToBase64String(bEnc);
        }
        {
            byte[] bEnc = System.Convert.FromBase64String(sEnc);
            byte[] bDec = ProtectedData.Unprotect(
                    bEnc, entropy, DataProtectionScope.CurrentUser);
            sDec = utf.GetString(bDec);
        }
        System.Console.WriteLine("Message   : " + sMsg);
        System.Console.WriteLine("Encrypted: " + sEnc);
        System.Console.WriteLine("Decrypted: " + sDec);
    }
}
```

This example displays the following:

```
Message   : The message to encrypt!
Encrypted: AQAAANCMnd8BFdERjHoAwE/Cl+sBAAAAE/FqFZagjESaOWbU4QAizAAA
AAACAAAAAAADZgAAqAAAABAAAABtOsILXE/X13YgQnZoF54NAAAAAASAAACgAAAAEAA
AAJazQCM/SMts1IBOkGg1skYYAAAAKlWDOOMZUrfjKJ/YpLpjvDnqmRknoChKFAAAAJ
cIYBaad28dwqXOuc1oOn9KKX7P
Devrypted: The message to encrypt!
```

The System.Security.Cryptography.ProtectedMemory class

The `System.Security.Cryptography.ProtectedMemory` class allows you to protect data at a finer scope than possible with the `ProtectedData` class. The options offered by the `MemoryProtectionScope` enumeration are as follows:

- `SameProcess`: Specifies that only the code invokes within the same process that encrypted the data can decrypt it.
- `SameLogon`: Specifies that only the code within the same user context as the one who encrypted the data can decrypt it. This implies that the encryption and decryption operations must take place within the same *Windows* session.
- `CrossProcess`: Specifies that the data can be decrypted by any code executed within any process with the condition that the operating system has not restarted since the encryption operation.

The following example illustrates the use of this class. The byte size of the data to encrypt must be a multiple of 16:

Example 6-24

```
using System.Security.Cryptography;
class Program {
    static void Main() {
        string sMsg = "012345678901234567890123456789 01";
        System.Text.Encoding utf = new System.Text.UTF8Encoding();
        System.Console.WriteLine("Message   : " + sMsg);
        byte[] bMsg = utf.GetBytes(sMsg);
        ProtectedMemory.Protect( bMsg, MemoryProtectionScope.SameProcess );
        System.Console.WriteLine("Encrypted: " + utf.GetString(bMsg));
        ProtectedMemory.Unprotect( bMsg, MemoryProtectionScope.SameProcess );
        System.Console.WriteLine("Decrypted: " + utf.GetString(bMsg));
    }
}
```

This example displays the following:

```
Message   : 012345678901234567890123456789 01
Encrypted: m;SH□^"?vfn6b{m.Op%□
Decrypted: 012345678901234567890123456789 01
```

The System.Security.SecureString class

The manipulation of strings using the `String` class has several vulnerabilities if we consider that someone with malicious intentions can have access to pages of memories in a *Windows* process:

- A same character string can be duplicated in the memory of the process as the garbage collector reserves the right to move the memory location of referenced objects.
- Strings are stored in memory with no form of encryption.

The Data Protection API (DPAPI)

- The fact that strings are immutable implies that at each modification of a string, the previous version resides in memory for a duration that we cannot control.
- Another consequence of immutable of strings is that you do not have the possibility of cleaning the bytes used to store it when it is no longer needed (unless you use the technique described at page 423).

To counter this vulnerability, the .NET framework has the `System.Security.SecureString` class whose implementation is based on the DPAPI services and allows the storage of a string in an encrypted way in memory.

You can initialize an instance of `SecureString` either from a character array (that you can later set to zero) or either by building it character by character. The `Marshal` class offers several methods to recover the encrypted string within an instance of `SecureString`.

The following example shows how you can use an instance of `SecureString` to store a password entered by a user on the console. We will then display this string on the console. For the needs of this example, we convert the instance of `BSTR` containing the decrypted string into an instance of `String`. In practice, you have to avoid this manipulation. Fatally, to use a secured string, you will at some point in time have to decrypt it in memory. You must then store it in a memory area that we can destroy as soon as possible to avoid the problems with the `String` class that we discussed earlier:

Example 6-25

```
using System;
using System.Security;
using System.Runtime.InteropServices;
class Program {
   static void Main() {
      SecureString pwd = new SecureString();
      ConsoleKeyInfo nextKey = Console.ReadKey( true );
      while(nextKey.Key != ConsoleKey.Enter) {
         pwd.AppendChar( nextKey.KeyChar );
         Console.Write( "*" );
         nextKey = Console.ReadKey( true );
      }
      Console.WriteLine();
      pwd.MakeReadOnly();
      IntPtr bstr = Marshal.SecureStringToBSTR(pwd);
      // Get an instance of the Sring class
      // only for the example needs.
      try{    Console.WriteLine( Marshal.PtrToStringAuto(bstr) ); }
      finally{ Marshal.ZeroFreeBSTR(bstr); }
   }
}
```

Protect data in your configuration files

The `System.Configuration.Configuration` class allows you to store encrypted data within the configuration file of the application. The following example shows how to store an encrypted version of the `MyPassword` string in a configuration parameter named `TagPassword`. Note that only the save operation needs a special manipulation to specify that we wish to store an encrypted version. The decryption is done automatically when the configuration file is loaded:

Example 6-26

```
using System.Configuration;
class Program {
   static void Main() {
      SavePwd("MyPassword");
      System.Console.WriteLine(LoadPwd());
   }
   static void SavePwd(string pwd) {
      Configuration cfg = ConfigurationManager.OpenExeConfiguration(
                          ConfigurationUserLevel.None );
      cfg.AppSettings.Settings.Add( "TagPassword", pwd );
      cfg.AppSettings.SectionInformation.ProtectSection(
                          "RsaProtectedConfigurationProvider" );
      cfg.Save();
   }
   static string LoadPwd() {
      Configuration cfg = ConfigurationManager.OpenExeConfiguration(
                          ConfigurationUserLevel.None );
      return cfg.AppSettings.Settings["TagPassword"].Value;
   }
}
```

Here is the configuration file generated by the previous example. We see that it contains a section named `protectedData` which declares that the `appSettings` section contains some encrypted data:

```xml
<?xml version="1.0" encoding="utf-8" ?>
<configuration xmlns="http://schemas.microsoft.com/.NetConfiguration/v2.0">
    <protectedData>
        <protectedDataSections>
            <add name="appSettings"
                provider="RsaProtectedConfigurationProvider"
                inheritedByChildren="false" />
        </protectedDataSections>
    </protectedData>
    <appSettings>
        <EncryptedData Type="http://www.w3.org/2001/04/xmlenc#Element"
            xmlns="http://www.w3.org/2001/04/xmlenc#">
           <EncryptionMethod
            Algorithm="http://www.w3.org/2001/04/xmlenc#tripledes-cbc" />
           <KeyInfo xmlns="http://www.w3.org/2000/09/xmldsig#">
              ...
                 <CipherData>
                    <KeyName>Rsa Key</KeyName>
                    <CipherValue>EuZpuz7Rj(...)qalkG3VbQ=</CipherValue>
                 </CipherData>
              ...
           </KeyInfo>
             <CipherData>
                <CipherValue>5OcJLWVB(...)JHsGvLTY</CipherValue>
             </CipherData>
        </EncryptedData>
    </appSettings>
</configuration>
```

Securing data carried on a network

In the chapter relating to data streams, we will discuss at page 546 the different secure protocols which can be used to exchange data over a network.

Authenticating your assemblies with the Authenticode technology and X.509 certificates

Authenticode vs. Strong names

Way before the public distribution of the .NET platform, the *Windows* operating system used the technology known as *Authenticode* to authenticate executable files. This technology is similar to the strong name technology that we discuss at page 23 in the sense that it allows to digitally sign an assembly. However, these two technologies have different goals:

- The Authenticode technology must be used to identify the author or enterprise which constructed an executable. It allows the execution of a program without having to worry about its falsification.

- The strong name technology must be used to identify an assembly (i.e. to name in a unique way each assembly and even every version of a same assembly). It can be use to store assemblies side-by-side.

Also, these two technologies present significant differences:

- The Authenticode technology allows signing all kind of executable files, .NET assemblies as with *Windows* executable containing native code. The strong name technology is only for use with assemblies.

- The verification of the validity of an executable by the Authenticode technology is only done by *Windows* once, when we download or install the file. The verification of the strong name is done by the CLR each time a signed assembly is loaded (unless the concerned strong named assembly is stored in the GAC).

However, the main difference between these two technologies resides in the concept of certificate.

Certificates and Certificate Authorities

A *certificate* contains a public key and information in regards to its publisher. It allows you to guarantee that the public key has in fact been produced by the mentioned publisher. A certificate also contains other information such as the date where its validity ends. The strong name technology does not present a certificate. Although that some public keys are well known and allow the identification of the publisher (such as the public key for *Microsoft*) there is no standard way to determine with certitude that a public key has been fabricated by a certain publisher.

Several certificate standards exist. The Authenticode technology uses the *X.509* standard which stores certificates in files with the `.cer` extension. The *CMS/Pkcs7* standard which stores the certificates in files with the `.p7b` extension is also widely spread as it is used in the *Secure/Multipurpose Internet Mail Extensions* (*S/MIME*) protocol to sign and encrypt emails.

A file signed with Authenticode contains an X.509 certificate. *Windows* can then request to an external authority if the certificate is valid. These external authorities are named *Certificate Authorities* (*CA*). These are enterprises which have for goal to validate certifications. Some of the most common CA include organisms such as *VeriSign* or *EnTrust*. In practice, a software publisher pays a CA so that they verify their certificates to their clients. The CA is responsible to perform a set of verifications on the legitimacy of the publisher.

Root certificates

In practice, there is a mechanism allowing *Windows* to not have to systematically contact a CA during the verification of a certificate. In fact, each *Windows* system maintains a list of certificates (named *Certificate Store*). The certificates contained in this list are named *root certificates*. The list of root certificates offered by default in *Windows* is available in the article named **Microsoft Root Certificate Program Members** on **MSDN**.

You can visualize, add or remove certificates from this list using the `certmgr.exe` tool. When a software publisher asks a CA to publish their certificate, this one signs the certificate with their own certificate. If the certificate of a CA is a root certificate, *Windows* does not need to make a network access to CA in order to validate the certificate since it has all the elements needed to validate on its own.

We can imagine that the CA contacted by a publisher is of less importance. In this case, the certificate for this CA is most likely not a root certificate for the *Windows* system. However, nothing prevents this CA to request to a known CA to sign its certificate. We then see a certificate chain which in most case avoids most machines from having to contact the CA during the installation of software.

Windows, .NET and the Authenticode technology

When *Windows* installs or downloads a piece of software which does not have a certificate or where the certificate cannot be validated, it will display a dialog box asking if you authorize the execution of the program.

The CAS mechanism is capable to obtain an evidence from an assembly signed with a X.509 certificate (see page 156). You can also decide that the assemblies signed with a certificate can be executed with more (or less) permissions than the others.

The details of the creation of a certificate, the signature of an executable with a certificate and the verification of a certificate are beyond the scope of this book. All this is described in the article named **Signing and Checking Code with Authenticode** on **MSDN**.

Also know that the .NET framework offers the `System.Security.Cryptography.X509Certificates` and `System.Security.Cryptography.Pkcs` namespaces which contain types specialized in the manipulation of these standards as well as the manipulation of *Windows* certificate stores.

7 Reflection, late binding, attributes

We have discussed at page 13 about metadata and the way it is physically stored in assemblies. We will see in this chapter how they constitute the basis for the reflection and attribute mechanisms.

Reflection

The *reflection* mechanism denotes the use during execution of the type metadata of an assembly. In general, this assembly is loaded explicitly during the execution of another assembly but it can also be dynamically built.

The *reflection* word is used to show that we use the image of an assembly (like an image in a mirror). This image is made from the type metadata of the assembly. We sometimes use the term *introspection* to talk about reflection.

When do we need reflection?

We have collected a few use categories for the reflection mechanism. We discuss them in more details in the following sections of this chapter. The reflection mechanism can be used in the following cases:

- During the discovery of the types on an assembly at execution by the dynamic analysis of the type metadata. For example, the `ildasm.exe` and `Reflector` tools explicitly load the modules of an assembly and analyze its contents (see page 16).
- During the use of *late binding*. This technique involves using a class located in an assembly which is not known during compilation. The late binding technique is generally used in interpreted languages such as scripting languages.
- When we wish to use the information contained in attributes.
- When we wish to access non-public members of a class from outside this class. Of course, this practice is to avoid but it is sometimes necessary to use it if, for example, unit tests need to be completed which cannot be completed without non-public members.
- During the dynamic construction of an assembly. To use the classes of a dynamically constructed assembly we use the explicit late binding technique.

The reflection mechanism is used by the CLR and by the framework in several cases. For example, the default implementation of the `Equals()` method on a value type uses reflection to compare two instances field by field.

Reflection is also use by the CLR during the serialization of an object in order to determine which fields to serialize, or even by the garbage collector which uses it to construct the reference tree during the collection process.

What is new with .NET reflection?

The underlying idea with the reflection mechanism is not new. For a long time we have been able to dynamically analyze the content of an executable, notably using self-description information. The TLB format (described at page 230) was conceived for this exact purpose. Let us mention that data in the TLB format is produced from data in the IDL (Interface Definition Language) format. The IDL language can also be seen as a self-description language. The reflection mechanism in .NET goes much further than the TLB and IDL formats:

- It is easy to use because of certain base classes.
- It is more abstract than the TLB and IDL languages. For example, it does not use physical addresses meaning it can work both on 32 and 64 bits machines.
- Contrarily to TBL metadata, the .NET metadata is always contained in the module which it described.
- The level of detail at which the data is described goes much further than the TLB format. Concretely, we can have all the possible information on any type declared in an assembly (for example, the type of an argument to a method in a class).

The unprecedented level of detail in .NET reflection is due to the numerous base classes of .NET framework which allow extracting and using the various type metadata of an assembly contained in the AppDomain. Most of these classes can be found in the `System.Reflection` namespace and there is a class for each type of element in an assembly:

- There is a class whose instances represent assemblies (`System.Reflection.Assembly`);
- A class whose instances represent classes and structures (`System.Type`);
- A class whose instances represent the methods (`System.Reflection.MethodInfo`);
- A class whose instances represent the fields (`System.Reflection.FieldInfo`);
- A class whose instances represent the parameters to a method (`System.Reflection.ParameterInfo`).

...

Finally, these classes do not represent anything else than a way to visualize logically the totality of the type metadata. This visualization is not physical in the sense where certain elements used for the internal organization of an assembly (such as metadata tokens) are not represented.

All the classes of the `System.Reflection` namespace interact in a logical way. For example, from an instance of `System.Reflection.Assembly`, we can obtain a list of `System.Type` instances. From an instance of `System.Type`, we can obtain a table of `System.Reflection.MethodInfo` instances. From an instance of `System.Reflection.MethodInfo`, we can obtain a table of `System.Reflection.ParameterInfo` instances. All this is illustrated in Figure 7-1.

You may find it unfortunate that you cannot drill down all the way to the IL instruction level but only to the level of a byte table containing the IL body of a method. For this, you may want to use certain libraries such as *Cecil* (developed by *Jean-Baptiste Evain*), *ILReader* (developed by *Lutz Roeder*) or *Rail* (developed by the university of *Coimbra*). Know that with .NET 2, reflection knows how to handle generic types, generic methods as well as constraints on parameter types (see page 413).

Reflection

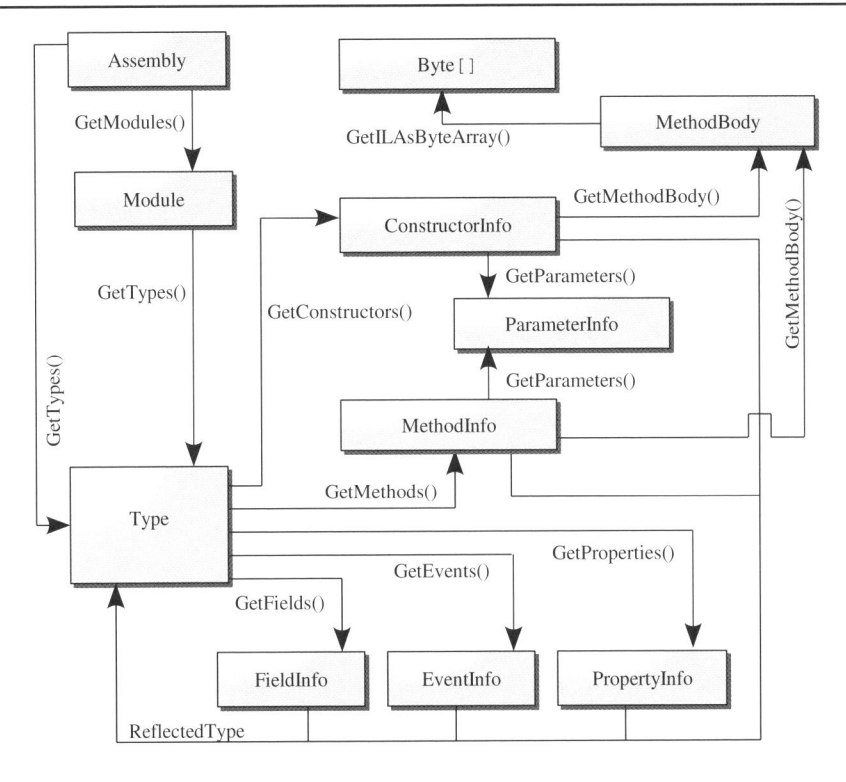

Figure 7-1: Interactions between reflection classes

Reflecting on assemblies loaded in an AppDomain

Here is an example which exposes the analysis of type metadata using classes from the `System.Reflection` namespace. In fact, here we present an assembly which analyzes its own type metadata. To obtain an instance of the `Assembly` class representing this assembly, we use the `Assembly.GetExecutingAssembly()` static method:

Example 7-1
```
using System;
using System.Reflection;
class Program{
   public static void Main(){
      Assembly assembly = Assembly.GetExecutingAssembly();
      foreach ( Type type in assembly.GetTypes() ){
         Console.WriteLine( "Class: " + type );
         foreach ( MethodInfo method in type.GetMethods() ){
            Console.WriteLine( "  Method: " + method );
            foreach ( ParameterInfo param in method.GetParameters() )
               Console.WriteLine( "    Param: " + param.GetType() );
         }
      }
   }
}
```

This program displays the following:

```
Class: Program
  Method: Void Main()
  Method: System.Type GetType()
  Method: System.String ToString()
  Method: Boolean Equals(System.Object)
     Param: System.Reflection.ParameterInfo
  Method: Int32 GetHashCode()
```

Obtaining information from metadata

The goal of the current section is to present a small program which uses the reflection mechanism to display the set of exception classes contained in the System and mscorlib assemblies. We based ourselves on the fact that all exception classes derive from System.Exception. The exception types which do not directly derive from System.Exception are marked with a star.

We could easily modify this program to display all the attribute classes of the framework basing ourselves on the fact that all these classes derive from the System. Attribute class.

Example 7-2

```csharp
using System;
using System.Reflection;
class Program {
   static void Main() {
      // Build the strong name of the 'System' assembly.
      // Its version number is the same as the one of the assembly
      // 'mscorlib' which contains the System.Object class.
      string systemAsmStrongName = "System, Culture = neutral, " +
         "PublicKeyToken=b77a5c561934e089, Version=" +
         typeof(System.Object).Assembly.GetName().Version.ToString();

      // Explicitly load the 'System' assembly for reflecting on it.
      // There is no need to load the 'mscorlib' assembly since
      // it is automatically and implicitly loaded by the CLR.
      Assembly.ReflectionOnlyLoad( systemAsmStrongName );

      // For each assembly in the current AppDomain...
      foreach (Assembly a in AppDomain.CurrentDomain.GetAssemblies()) {
         Console.WriteLine("\nAssembly:" + a.GetName().Name);

         // For each type in the assembly 'a'...
         foreach (Type t in a.GetTypes()) {
            // Treat only public classes...
            if (!t.IsClass || !t.IsPublic) continue;
            bool bDerivedException = false;
            bool bDirectInherit = true;

            // Is System.Exception a base type of 't'?
            Type baseType = t.BaseType;
            while ( baseType != null && !bDerivedException ) {
               // To find attribute classes replace the following line
               // by:  if( baseType == typeof(System.Attribute))
               if ( baseType == typeof(System.Exception) )
                  bDerivedException = true;
               else bDirectInherit = false;
               baseType = baseType.BaseType;
            }// end while
```

Example 7-2

```
            // Display the name of the class if it is an exception
            // class. Put a star if the class doesn't inherit directly
            // from System.Exception.
            if ( bDerivedException )
               if ( bDirectInherit )
                  Console.WriteLine( "  " + t );
               else
                  Console.WriteLine( "  *" + t );
         }// end foreach(Type...
      }// end foreach(Assembly...
   }// end Main
}
```

Note the use of the `Assembly.ReflectionOnlyLoad()` method in the previous example. This method allows you to tell the CLR that the loaded assembly will only be used for reflection. In consequence, the CLR will disallow the execution of the code of an assembly loaded with this method. Also, the loading of an assembly in *Reflection Only* mode is slightly faster as the CLR does not need to complete any security verifications. The `Assembly` class offers the `bool ReflectionOnly{get;}` property which allows you to know if an assembly was loaded with this method.

Late bindings

> Before starting this section, it is recommended to have a good understanding of object programming basics, especially with the notions of polymorphism. This topic is covered in chapter 12.

What does it mean to 'bind with a class'?

First of all, we have to agree on what we mean by '*bind with a class*'. We will talk of software layers rather than assemblies as this is also valid for other technologies.

A link with a class is created between the software layer which uses the class (which instantiates the class and uses its instances) and the software layer which defines the class. Concretely, this link is the correspondence between the call to the methods of the class in the using software layer and the physical location of these methods in the software layer defining the class. It is this link that allows the thread to continue its execution in the method of a class when it is called.

In general, we distinguish three types of links with a class: *early binding* created during compilation, *dynamic binding* which is partly created during compilation and *late binding* created during execution.

Early binding and dynamic binding

Early binding links are created by the compiler during the creation of an assembly based on the .NET source code. We cannot create an early binding with a virtual or abstract method. In fact, the *polymorphism* mechanism decides during execution which code to execute when a virtual or abstract method is called, based on the real class of the object on which the method was called. In this case, the link is considered as a *dynamic binding*. In other documents, dynamic binding is sometimes referred to as *implicit late binding* since they are created implicitly by the polymorphism mechanism and since they are done during the execution.

Let us now take a closer look at early bindings, those created with static methods or methods of classes which aren't virtual or abstract. If we stick to the '*linking with a class*' definition of the previous section, there is no early bindings in .NET. In fact, we have to wait for the body of a method to be processed by the JIT compiler into language machine before we can know its physical location in the process address space. This information in regards to the physical location of the method can then not be known by the compiler which creates the assembly. We have seen at page 90 that to resolve this problem, the compiler that creates the assembly inserts the corresponding metadata token corresponding to the method to call in the IL code location where the call will take place. When the body of the method is compiled by the JIT, the CLR internally stores the correspondence between the method and the physical location of the body of the method in machine language. This information is physically stored in a memory location associated to the method, called *stub*.

This realization is important because that in a language like C++, when a method is not virtual or abstract (i.e. pure virtual function in C++), the compiler computes the physical location of the body of the method in machine language. After, the compiler inserts a pointer to this memory location at each call to this method. This difference gives a strong advantage to .NET since the compilers do not have to worry about the technical details such as memory representation. The IL code is totally independent of the physical layer on which it will run.

In regards to dynamic binding, almost everything happens in the same way as with early binding. The compiler inserts the metadata token corresponding to the virtual (or abstract) method to call in the IL code location where the call is made. Here, we talk about the metadata token of the method defined in the type of the reference on which the call will take place. It is then the CLR's job to determine during the execution which method to jump to based on the exact implementation of the referenced object.

This technique is used by the compilers inserting a type metadata token for dynamic and early binding is used in the three following cases:

- When the code contained in a module calls a method within the same module.
- When the code contained in a module called a method defined in a different module of the same assembly.
- When the code contained in a module of an assembly calls a method defined in another assembly referenced during compilation. At runtime, if this assembly is not already loaded during the JIT compilation of a call to the method, the CLR will load it implicitly.

Late binding

The code of an assembly A can instantiate and use during execution a type defined in an assembly B which was not referenced during the compilation of A. We qualify this type of linking as *late binding*. We use the term 'late' in the sense that the binding is not done during the compilation but during the execution of the code. This type of binding is also explicit in the sense that the name of the method to be called must be explicitly specified as a string.

The idea of late binding is not new in the *Microsoft* development world. The *Automation* mechanism in the COM technology which uses the `IDispatch`, interface as a workaround to allow late binding from scripting languages or weakly typed languages such as VB. The notion of late binding also exists in Java.

Late binding is part of concepts which developers used to C++ have difficulty assimilating. In fact, in C++ only early and dynamic binding exists. The comprehension problem comes from the following fact: we understand that the necessary information to create a binding (i.e. the metadata tokens) are in the B assembly containing the class to call but we do not understand why the developer does not take advantage of the compiler's ability to create early and dynamic bindings by referencing the B assembly during the compilation of A. There a several reasons for this:

Late bindings 199

- The most common reason is that for some languages, there are no compilers! In a scripting language, the instructions are interpreted one by one. In this case, there can only be late binding. The use of late binding allows using the classes compiled and contained in assemblies from interpreted languages. The fact that the .NET late binding technique is readily usable makes it easy to create proprietary interpreted/dynamic languages (such as the *IronPython* language `http://www.ironpython.com/`).

- We may wish to use the late binding technique from a program written in a compiled language such as C#. The idea is that the use of late binding allows the introduction of a certain degree of flexibility in the general architecture of your application. This technique is in fact a popular design pattern named *plugin* that we will present further in the current chapter.

- Certain applications have for goal to call the code of any assembly which is given to it. The typical example for this would be the open source tool named `NUnit` which allows testing the code of any assembly by calling its methods. We will touch this subject a little deeper during the construction of a custom attribute later in this chapter.

- We must use late binding between the code of an assembly A and the classes of an assembly B if B does not exist during the compilation of A. This situation is described a little later in this chapter where we talk about the dynamic construction of assemblies.

Certain prefer the use of late binding instead of polymorphism. In fact, because during the call, only the name and the signature of the method are taken into account, the type of the object on which the method is called is irrelevant. You simply need that the implementation of the object offers a method with the proper name and signature. We personally do not recommend this use as it is permissive and does not force the designer of applications to make proper design and use abstract interfaces.

Besides the cases we have just mentioned, you will not need to use explicit late binding. Do not use them for the fun of having late binding in your application because:

- You can loose the benefit of the syntax verification done by the compiler.
- The performance of late binding is not as good as with early or dynamically bound methods (even if you use the optimizations presented a little later).
- We cannot create late binding with an obfuscated class. In fact, during the obfuscation process, the name of the class is changed in the assembly which contains it. Hence, the late binding approach cannot properly find the right class.

How to instantiate an unknown class during C# to IL compilation?

If a class or a structure is not known during compilation, we cannot instantiate it using the `new` operator. Hopefully, the .NET framework does have classes which allow the instantiation of classes not known during compilation.

Precise a type

Let's now look at the different techniques which allow the specification of a type:

- Certain methods of certain classes accept a string containing the complete name of the type (with its namespace).
- Others accept an instance of the `System.Type` class. In an AppDomain, each instance of `System.Type` represents a type and there cannot be two instances representing this type. There are several ways of obtaining an instance of `System.Type`:

    In C#, we often use the `typeof()` keyword which takes a type in as a parameter and returns the appropriate instance of `System.Type`.

    You can also use one of the overloaded `GetType()` static methods of the `System.Type` class.

If a type is encapsulated within another type, you can use on of the overloaded of the non-static methods `GetNestedType()` or `GetNestedTypes()` of the `System.Type` class.

You can also use the non-static methods named `GetType()` `GetTypes()` or `GetExportedTypes()` of the `System.Reflection.Assembly` class.

You can also use the non-static `GetType()` `GetTypes()` or `FindTypes()` methods of the `System.Relection.Module` class

Let us now suppose that the following program is compiled into the `Foo.dll` assembly. We are about to show several ways which allow the creation of an instance of the `NMFoo.Calc` class from an assembly which does not reference `Foo.dll`.

Example 7-3 *Code of the Foo.dll assembly*

```
using System;
namespace NMFoo {
   public class Calc {
      public Calc() {
         Console.WriteLine("Calc.Constructor called!");
      }
      public int Sum(int a, int b) {
         Console.WriteLine("Mathod Calc.Sum() called!");
         return a + b;
      }
   }
}
```

Use of the System.Activator class

The `System.Activator` class offers two static methods `CreateInstance()` and `CreateInstanceFrom()` which allow the creation of an instance of a class which was not known during compilation. For example:

Example 7-4

```
using System;
using System.Reflection;
class Program {
   static void Main() {
      Assembly assembly = Assembly.Load("Foo.dll");
      Type type = assembly.GetType("NMFoo.Calc");
      object obj = Activator.CreateInstance(type);
      // 'obj' is a reference toward an instance of NMFoo.Calc.
   }
}
```

Each of these methods offers several overloaded and even generics versions with the following arguments:

- A class as a string or an instance of `System.Type`;
- Optionally, the name of the assembly which contains the class;
- Optionally, the list of arguments for the constructor.

If the assembly that contains the class is not present in the AppDomain, the call to `CreateInstance()` or `CreateInstanceFrom()` will cause this assembly to be loaded. To cause the assembly to be loaded, `System.AppDomain.Load()` or `System.AppDomain.LoadFrom()` is called internally depending on whether we call `CreateInstance()` or `CreateInstanceFrom()`. A constructor for the class is chosen based on the arguments supplied. An instance of the `ObjectHandle` class that contains a marshaled object is returned. In chapter 22 about .NET remoting, we will show another use for these methods in the context of distributed applications.

Late bindings

The overload versions of `CreateInstance()` where the type is specified using an instance of `System.Type` directly returns an instance to an object.

The `System.Activator` class also has the `CreateComInstanceFrom()` method which is used to create instances of COM objects and the `GetObject()` method used to create remote objects.

Use of the System.AppDomain class

The `System.AppDomain` class has the four following non-static members named `CreateInstance()`, `CreateInstanceAndUnWrap()`, `CreateInstanceFrom()` and `CreateInstanceFromAndUnwrap()` which allows the creation of an instance of a class which is not known during compilation. For example:

Example 7-5
```
using System;
using System.Reflection;
class Program {
   static void Main() {
      object obj = AppDomain.CurrentDomain.CreateInstanceAndUnwrap(
                        "Foo.dll", "NMFoo.Calc");
      // 'obj' is a reference toward an instance of NMFoo.Calc.
   }
}
```

These methods are similar to the methods of the `System.Activator`, class discussed earlier. However, they allow you to choose the AppDomain in which we want the object to be created. In addition, the 'AndUnwarp()' versions give a direct reference to the object. This reference is obtained from an instance of `ObjectHandle`.

Use of the System.Reflection.ConstructorInfo class

An instance of the `System.Reflection.ConstructorInfo` class references a constructor. The `Invoke()` method of this class internally creates a late bind to the constructor and invokes it through this binding. Hence, they allow the creation of an instance of the type to which the constructor belongs. For example:

Example 7-6
```
using System;
using System.Reflection;
class Program {
   static void Main() {
      Assembly assembly = Assembly.Load ("Foo.dll");
      Type type = assembly.GetType("NMFoo.Calc");
      ConstructorInfo constructorInfo = type.GetConstructor( new Type[0] );
      object obj = constructorInfo.Invoke( new object[0] );
      // 'obj' is a reference toward an instance of NMFoo.Calc.
   }
}
```

Use of the System.Type class

The `InvokeMember()` non-static method of the `System.Type` class allows you to create an instance of a class not known during compilation with the condition that it is called with the `CreateInstance` value of the `BindingFlags` enumeration. For example:

Example 7-7

```
using System;
using System.Reflection;
class Program {
   static void Main() {
      Assembly assembly = Assembly.Load("Foo.dll");
      Type type = assembly.GetType("NMFoo.Calc");
      Object obj = type.InvokeMember(
        null, // Don't need to provide a name for calling a constructor.
        BindingFlags.CreateInstance,
        null, // Don't need a binder.
        null, // Don't need a target object since we build it.
        new Object[0]); // No parameters.
      // Here, 'obj' is a reference toward an instance of NMFoo.Calc.
   }
}
```

Special cases

With the methods presented earlier, you can create an instance of almost any kind of class or structure. Two special cases are to mention:

- To create an array, you must call the `CreateInstance()` static method of the `System.Array` class.
- To create a delegate object you must call the `CreateDelegate()` method of the `System.Delegate` class.

Harnessing late binds

Now that we know how to create instances of a type unknown during compilation, let us look at the creation of late bindings to the members of these types in order to use these instances. There also, is several ways to proceed.

The Type.InvokeMember() method

Let's come back to the `Type.InvokeMember()` method which we used previously to create an instance of a type not known during compilation by calling one of its constructors. Internally, this method accomplishes three tasks:

- It looks for a member of the type on which it is called that corresponds to the provided information.
- If the member is found, it creates a late bind to it.
- It uses the member (invokes it for a method, creates an instance of the object for a constructor, gets or sets the value for a field, executes the set or get accessor for a property...).

The following example shows how to invoke the `Sum()` method on our instance of the `NMFoo.Calc` class (note that during the debugging process, the debugger is able to continue into the body of a method used with late binding):

Example 7-8

```
using System;
using System.Reflection;
class Program {
   static void Main() {
      object obj = AppDomain.CurrentDomain.CreateInstanceAndUnwrap(
                           "Foo.dll", "NMFoo.Calc");
      Type type = obj.GetType();
      object[] parameters = new object[2];
```

Example 7-8

```
        parameters[0] = 7;
        parameters[1] = 8;
    int result = (int) type.InvokeMember(
                            "Sum",           // Name of the method.
                            BindingFlags.InvokeMethod,
                            null,            // Don't need a binder.
                            obj,             // The target object.
                            parameters);    // Parameters.
        // Here, the value of 'result' is 15.
    }
}
```

The most commonly used overload of the Type.InvokeMember() method is:

```
public object InvokeMember(
    string        name,         // The name of the member.
    BindingFlags  invokeAttr,   // Caracteristics supported by the
                                // member to found. (private/public,
                                // instance/static, ingnore case …)
    Binder        binder,       // Some rules to bind with the member.
    object        target,       // The target object on which
                                // the member is invoked.
    object[]      args          // Arguments of the call.
);
```

The invokeAttr parameter is a binary flag which indicates on which type of member the search will be done. To search for methods, we use the BindingFlags.InvokeMethod flag. The various flags are described on **MSDN** in the article named **BindingFlags Enumeration**.

The binder parameter is an object of type Binder which will orient InvokeMember() on how to do its search. Most of the time, this parameter can be set to null to indicate that you wish to use the default, which is System.Type.DefaultBinder. An object of type Binder provides this type of information:

- It indicates which type conversions are accepted for the arguments. In the previous example, we could have supplied two arguments of type double. Because of DefaultBinder, the call to the method would have still succeeded as it supports the conversion from double to int.

- It indicates if we are using the optional parameters in our list of parameters.

All this (especially the type conversion table) is described in more details on **MSDN** in the article named **Type.DefaultBinder Property**. You can create your own binder objects by deriving from the Binder class. However, using an instance of the DefaultBinder is sufficient in most cases.

If an exception is raised during a late binding call to a member, InvokeMember() intercepts the exception and re-throws an exception of type System.Reflection.TargetInvocation Exception. Naturally, the exception raised in the method is referenced by the InnerException property of the re-thrown exception.

Finally note that when you create a late bind, you cannot access non-public members. The System. Security.SecurityException is then generally thrown. However, if the TypeInformation bit of System.Security.Permissions.ReflectionPermissionFlags (accessible through an instance of the System.Security.Permissions.ReflectionPermission class) is set, you are allowed to access non-public members. If the MemberAccess is set, you have access to non-visible types (i.e. encapsulated in other types in a non-public way).

Link once, invoke at whim

In the same way that we have seen that an instance of the `ConstructorInfo` allows to create a late bind and to invoke a constructor, an instance of the `System.Reflection.MethodInfo` class allows to create a late bind and to invoke any method. The advantage of using the `MethodInfo` class rather than the `Type.InvokeMember()` method resides in the time saved on the search for the member at every call, hence a small optimization. The following example illustrates this:

Example 7-9

```
using System;
using System.Reflection;
class Program {
   static void Main() {
      object obj = AppDomain.CurrentDomain.CreateInstanceAndUnwrap(
                            "Foo.dll", "NMFoo.Calc");
      Type type = obj.GetType();
      // Create a late bind with the 'Sum' method.
      MethodInfo methodInfo = type.GetMethod("Sum");
      object[] parameters = new object[2];
      parameters[0] = 7;
      parameters[1] = 8;
      int result;
      // 10 calls to 'Sum'.
      for (int i = 0; i < 10; i++)
         result = (int)methodInfo.Invoke( obj, parameters );
   }
}
```

How the VB.NET compiler creates late binds behind your back

Let us make a little VB.NET side-note and observe how this language uses late binds secretly behind your back when the `Strict` option is set to `Off`. For example, the following VB.NET program...

Example 7-10   *VB.NET and late binds*

```
Option Strict Off
Module Module1
   Sub Main()
      Dim obj = AppDomain.CurrentDomain.CreateInstanceAndUnwrap(
                            "Foo.dll", "NMFoo.Calc")
      Dim result As Integer = obj.Sum(7, 8)
   End Sub
End Module
```

...is equivalent to the following C# program:

Example 7-11

```
using System;
using System.Reflection;
using Microsoft.VisualBasic.CompilerServices;
class Program {
   static void Main() {
      object obj = AppDomain.CurrentDomain.CreateInstanceAndUnwrap(
                            "Foo.dll", "NMFoo.Calc");
      object[] parameters = new object[2];
      parameters[0] = 7;
      parameters[1] = 8;
      int result = (int) LateBinding.LateGet(obj, null, "Sum",
                            parameters, null, null);
   }
}
```

Late bindings 205

This feature offered to VB.NET developers can quickly become catastrophic both for the performance or if the program is obfuscated. Hence the interest in setting the `Strict` option to `On`.

Harness interfaces: The right way to use late binding

There is another totally different way than those we have explained to use a class unknown at compile-time through the use of late binding. This approach has the major advantage of having no performance loss compared to the use of early or dynamic binding. However, you will have to constrain yourself to using a certain discipline to apply this 'recipe' (which in fact is the *design pattern* named *plugin*).

The idea is to make sure that the type unknown at compile-time implements an interface which is known by the compiler. For this, we are constrained to creating a third assembly, designated to host this interface. Let's rewrite our example with the `Calc` using three assemblies:

Example 7-12   *Code of the assembly which contains the interface (InterfaceAsm.cs)*

```
namespace NMFoo {
   public interface ICalc {
      int Sum(int a, int b);
   }
}
```

Example 7-13   *Code of the assembly which contains the target class (ClassAsm.cs)*

```
using System;
namespace NMFoo {
   public class CalcWithInterface : ICalc {
      public CalcWithInterface() {
         Console.WriteLine("Calc.Constructor called!");
      }
      public int Sum(int a, int b) {
         Console.WriteLine("Method Calc.Sum() called!");
         return a + b;
      }
   }
}
```

Example 7-14   *Code of the client assembly of the target class not known during compilation (ProgramAsm.cs)*

```
using System;
using System.Reflection;
using NMFoo;
class Program {
   static void Main() {
      ICalc obj = AppDomain.CurrentDomain.CreateInstanceAndUnwrap(
         "ClassAsm.dll", "NMFoo.CalcWithInterface") as ICalc;
      int result = obj.Sum(7, 8);
   }
}
```

Be attentive to the explicit typecasting to `ICalc` of the object returned by the `CreateInstanceAndUnwrap()` method which allows the use of a dynamic link to the `Sum()` method. We could have avoided this typecast be using the generic overload on the `Activator.CreateInstance<ICalc>()` method.

The following illustration summarizes the organization as well as the links between our three assemblies:

```
┌─────────────────────────┐
│ Assembly which contains the │      Referenced during compilation in order to
│      Program class.         │      use the ICalc interface.
└─────────────────────────┘
       ┊                                        ┌─────────────────────────┐
       ┊ Explicit loading of assembly at runtime │ Assembly which contains the │
       ┊ with AppDomain.CurrentDomain.           │      ICalc interface.       │
       ┊ CreateInstanceFromAndUnWrap()           └─────────────────────────┘
       ▼
┌─────────────────────────┐    Referenced during compilation in order to
│ Assembly which contains the │    use the ICalc interface.
│   CalcWithInterface class.  │
└─────────────────────────┘
```

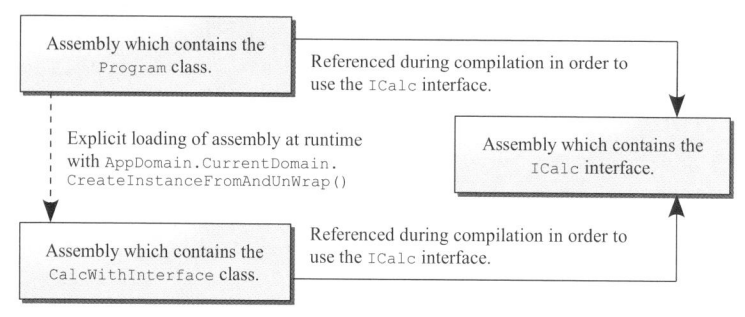

Figure 7-2: The plug-in design pattern and assemblies organization.

In the philosophy behind the *plugin* design pattern, the data necessary to the `CreateInstanceAndUnwrap()` method in order to create an instance (in this case the two strings "Foo.dll" and "NMFoo.CalcWithInterface") are generally stored in a configuration file. Then you can choose a new implementation simply by changing a configuration file without needing any recompilation.

A variant of the *plugin* design pattern consists in using an abstract class rather than an interface.

Finally, know that is it also possible to use a delegate to create a late bind with a method. Although that this approach is more efficient than the use of the `MethodInfo`, we generally prefer the use of the *plugin* design patter.

Attributes

What is an attribute?

An *attribute* is a piece of information which marks the elements of the code such as a class or a method. For example, the .NET framework provides the `System.ObsoleteAttribute` attribute which can be used to mark a method as follows (note the syntax using `[] brackets`):

```
[System.ObsoleteAttribute()]
void Fct() { }
```

The `Fct()` method is marked with the `System.ObsoleteAttribute` attribute information is inserted in the assembly during compilation. This information can then be used by the C# compiler. When it encounters a call to this method, it can then emit a warning indicating it is better to avoid a call to an obsolete method, which risks of going away in future versions. Without an attribute, you would be forced to properly document the fact that `Fct()` method is now obsolete The weakness of this approach is that you will have no guarantee that your clients will read the documentation and be aware of the fact that the method is now obsolete.

When do we need attributes?

The advantage of using attributes resides in the fact that the information that it contains is inserted into the assembly. This information can then be consumed at various times for all sorts of purposes:

- An attribute can be consumed by the compiler. The `System.ObsoleteAttribute` attribute that we have just described is a good example of how an attribute is used by the compiler. Certain standard attributes which are only destined for the compiler are not stored in the assembly. For example, the `SerializationAttribute` attribute does not directly mark a type but rather tells the compiler that the type can be serialized. Consequently, the compiler sets certain flags on the concerned type which will be consumed by the CLR during execution. Such attributes are also named *pseudo-attributes*.

Attributes

- An attribute can be consumed by the CLR during execution. For example, the .NET framework offers the `System.ThreadStaticAttribute` attribute. When a static field is marked with this attribute, the CLR makes sure that during the execution, there is only one version of this field per thread.

- An attribute can be consumed by a debugger during execution. Hence, the `System.Diagnostics.DebuggerDisplayAttribute` attribute allows personalizing the display of an element of the code (the state of an object for example) during debugging.

- An attribute can be consumed by a tool. For example, the .NET framework offers the `System.Runtime.InteropServices.ComVisibleAttribute` attribute. When a class is marked with this attribute, the `tlbexp.exe` tool generates a file which will allow this class to be consumed as if it was a COM object.

- An attribute can be consumed by your own code during execution by using the reflection mechanism to access the information. For example, it can be interesting to use such attributes to validate the value of fields in your classes. Such a field must be within a certain range. Another reference field must not be null. A string field can be at most 100 characters... Because of the reflection mechanism, it is easy to write code to validate the state of any marked fields. A little later, we will show you such an example where you can consume attributes by your own code.

- An attribute can be consumed by a user which analyses an assembly with a tool such as `ildasm.exe` or `Reflector`. Hence, you could imagine an attribute which would associate a character string to an element of your code. This string being contained in the assembly, it is then possible to consult these comments without needing to access the source code.

Things to know about attributes

- An attribute must be defined by a class which derives from `System.Attribute`.

- An instance of the attribute class is only instantiated when the reflection mechanism accesses one of its representatives. Depending on its use, an attribute class is not necessarily instantiated (as with the `System.ObsoleteAttribute` class which does not need to be used by the reflection mechanism).

- The .NET framework puts several attributes to your disposition. Certain attributes are destined to be used by the CLR. Other are consumed by the compiler or tools supplied by *Microsoft*.

- You have the possibility of creating your own attribute classes. They will then necessarily be consumed by your program as you cannot tinker the compiler or the CLR.

- By convention, the name of an attribute class is suffixed by `Attribute`. However, an attribute named XXXAttribute can be used in C# both using the XXXAttribute expression but also with the XXX expression when it marks an element of the code.

In the chapter dedicated to generics, we discuss at page 413 the rules relative to overlapping between the notion of attributes and generics.

Code elements on which you can apply attributes

Attributes apply themselves to element of your source code. Here is exactly which are the elements that you can mark using attributes. They are defined by the values of the `AttributeTargets`. enumeration.

Type of element	Scope of the attribute's effect
All	All the elements of the code: the assembly itself, classes, members of the classes, delegates, events, fields, interfaces, methods, modules, parameters, properties, return values and structures,
Assembly	The assembly itself.
Class	The classes.
Constructor	The constructors.
Delegate	The delegates.
Enum	The enumerations.
Event	The events.
Field	The fields.
GenericParameter	Generic parameters.
Interface	The interfaces.
Method	The methods.
Module	The modules.
Parameter	Method parameters.
Property	Class properties.
ReturnValue	The return values of methods.
Struct	The structures.

Some standard attributes of the .NET framework

A good understanding of an attributes comes from a good understanding of the situation in which it must be used. Hence, each standard attribute is described in the chapter which concerns it.

A few attributes relative to security management are presented at page 168.

A few attributes relative to the P/Invoke mechanism are presented at page 219.

A few attributes relative to the use of COM from .NET application are presented at page 233.

A few standard attributes relative to the serialization mechanism are described at page 657.

A few standard attributes relative to the XML serialization are presented at page 649.

A few standard attributes relative to assemblies are presented at page 19.

A few standard attributes allowing the personalization of the debugger's behavior are presented at page 510.

The `System.Runtime.Remoting.Contexts.Synchronization` attribute, which allows the implementation of a synchronization mechanism is presented at page 132.

The `ConditionalAttribute` attribute which allows to indicate to the C# compiler to conditionally compile certain methods is described at page 261.

The `ThreadStaticAttribute` attribute which is used to modify the behavior of threads in regards to static fields is described at page 145.

The `CLSCompliantAttribute` attribute which is used to indicate to the compiler if it must perform certain verifications is described at page 107.

The `ParamArrayAttribute` attribute which allows the implementation of the `params` C# keyword is presented at page 335.

The `CategoryAttribute` is presented at page 568.

Example of a custom attribute

A *custom attribute* is an attribute that you create yourself by deriving one of your classes from `System.Attribute`. As with the field validation attributes that we described at the beginning of this section, we can imagine multiple scenarios where we can benefit from using custom attributes. The example that we will presents inspires itself from the `NUnit` open-source tool.

The `NUnit` tool allow to execute and thus to test any method from any assembly. As there is no point in testing every method of an assembly, `NUnit` only executes only the methods marked with the `TestAttribute` attribute.

To implement a simplified version of this behavior, we will impose the following constrains:

- The test of a method is considered successful if it does not throw any uncaught exceptions.
- We define a `TestAttribute` which can only be applied to methods. The attribute can be configured by the number of times the method must be executed (the `int TestAttribute.nTime` property). The attribute can also be used to ignore a marked method (the `bool TestAttribute.Ignore` property).
- The `Program.TestAssembly(Assembly)` method allows the execution of all the methods contained in the assembly passed as an argument which are marked with the `TestAttribute` attribute. To simplify, we will suppose that these methods are public, non-static and do not take any arguments. We are also forced to use late binding to access the marked methods.

The following program satisfies these constraints:

Example 7-15
```
using System;
using System.Reflection;

[AttributeUsage(AttributeTargets.Method,AllowMultiple=false)]
public class TestAttribute : System.Attribute {
   public TestAttribute() {
      Console.WriteLine("TestAttribute.ctor() Default ctor.");
   }
   public TestAttribute(int nTime) {
      Console.WriteLine("TestAttribute.ctor(int)");
      m_nTime = nTime;
   }
   private int m_nTime = 1;
   private bool m_Ignore = false;
   public bool Ignore{ get { return m_Ignore; } set { m_Ignore = value; } }
   public int  nTime { get { return m_nTime; }  set { m_nTime = value; } }
}

class Program {
   static void Main() {
      // The programs reflects on itself.
      TestAssembly( Assembly.GetExecutingAssembly() );
   }
   static void TestAssembly(Assembly assembly) {
      // For each methods of each type declared in 'assembly'.
      foreach( Type type in assembly.GetTypes() ) {
         foreach( MethodInfo method in type.GetMethods() ) {
            // Get attributes of type 'TestAttribute' which mark
            // the method. Trigger the call to 'TestAttribute.ctor()'.
            object[] attributes = method.GetCustomAttributes(
                                     typeof(TestAttribute),false);
```

Example 7-15

```
                    if( attributes.Length == 1 ) {
                       // Get an instance of 'TestAttribute'.
                       TestAttribute testAttribute =attributes[0] as TestAttribute;
                       // If we shouldn't ignore the method.
                       if( ! testAttribute.Ignore ) {
                          object [] parameters = new object[0];
                          object instance = Activator.CreateInstance(type);
                          // Call the method 'nTime' times.
                          for(int i=0;i< testAttribute.nTime ; i++) {
                             try {
                                //Invoke the method with a late binds.
                                method.Invoke(instance,parameters);
                             } catch( TargetInvocationException ex ) {
                                Console.WriteLine(
                                      "The method {" + type.FullName + "." +
                                      method.Name +
                                      "} threw an exception of type " +
                                      ex.InnerException.GetType() +
                                      " during run #" + (i+1) + ".");
                             }// end catch(...
                          }// end for(...
                       }// end if( ! attribute.Ignore )
                    }// end if( attributes.Length == 1 )
                 }// end foreach(MethodInfo...
              }// end foreach(Type...
   }
}

class Foo {
   [Test()]
   public void Crash() {
      Console.WriteLine("Crash()");
      throw new ApplicationException();
   }
   int state = 0;
   [Test(4)]
   public void CrashTheSecondTime() {
      Console.WriteLine("CrashTheSecondTime()");
      state++;
      if (state == 2) throw new ApplicationException();
   }
   [Test()]
   public void DontCrash () {
      Console.WriteLine("DontCrash");
   }
   [Test(Ignore = true)]
   public void CrashButIgnored() {
      Console.WriteLine("CrashButIngnored()");
      throw new ApplicationException();
   }
}
```

This program displays:

Attributes

```
TestAttribute.ctor() Default ctor.
Crash()
The method {Foo.Crash} threw an exception of type System.ApplicationExce
ption during run #1.
TestAttribute.ctor(int)
CrashTheSecondTime()
CrashTheSecondTime()
The method {Foo.CrashTheSecondTime} threw an exception of type System.Ap
plicationException during run #2.
CrashTheSecondTime()
CrashTheSecondTime()
TestAttribute.ctor() Default ctor.
DontCrash
TestAttribute.ctor() Default ctor.
```

Let's make a few remarks.

- We mark our `TestAttribute` class with an attribute of type `AttributeUsage`. We use the `Method` value of the `AttributeTarget` enumeration to tell the compiler that the `TestAttribute` can only be applied to methods.
- We set to `false` the `AllowMultiple` property of the `AttributeUsage` class to signify that a method cannot accept multiple attributes of type `TestAttribute`. Note the special syntax used to initialize the `AllowMultiple` property. We say that `AllowMultiple` is a *named parameter*.
- We also use the named parameter syntax in the declaration of the `Test` attribute which marks the `Foo.CrashButIgnore()` method.
- We use the fact than when an exception is raised and is not caught during the execution of a method invoked through late binding, it is an exception of type `TargetInvocationException` which is recovered by the calling method. The initial exception is referenced by the `InnerException` of the recovered exception.
- To avoid breaking the code across multiple assemblies, this program tests itself (in fact, only the methods of the `Foo` class are tested since they are the only methods marked with the `TestAttribute` attribute). Here is what the organization of the assemblies would have been if we had broken up the code:

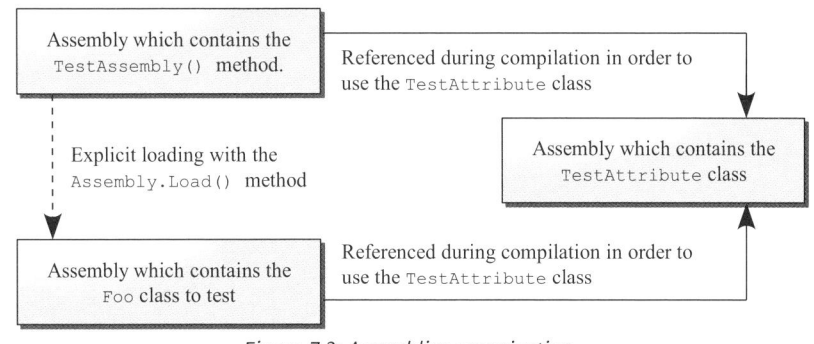

Figure 7-3: Assemblies organization.

The resemblance of this diagram with Figure 7-2 is not by chance. In both case, we use an element which is unknown during compilation by the intermediate of an element known during the compilation of all (an attribute in this case, an interface in the previous).

Conditional attributes

C#2 introduces the notion of *conditional attribute*. A conditional attribute is only taken into account by the compiler if a symbol is defined. The following example illustrates the use of conditional attributes in a project built from three files:

Example 7-16
```
[System.Diagnostics.Conditional("_TEST")]
public class TestAttribute : System.Attribute { }
```

Example 7-17
```
#define _TEST
[Test]  // The compiler marks the Foo1 class with the 'Test' attribute.
class Foo1 { }
```

Example 7-18
```
#undef _TEST
[Test]  // The compiler doesn't mark the Foo2 class with
        // the 'Test' attribute.
class Foo2 { }
```

In the example of the previous section, conditional attributes were used to generate both a debug and a release version from the same code. At page 261, we describe another use of the `Conditional` attribute.

Dynamically building an assembly and using it on the fly

The `System.Reflection.Emit` namespace offers a set of classes allowing the construction of a new assembly at run-time during the execution of another assembly. This is in fact code generation except that the code generated is not in the C# or C++ form but in a ready to use assembly. You then have the possibility of saving the assembly in a persistent way.

Why should we consider building an assembly dynamically?

When you construct an assembly using the classes of the `System.Reflection.Emit` namespace, the code is emitted directly using IL language, which is briefly described at page 33. Although that the IL language is relatively straightforward, most developers are more accustomed to the C# and VB.NET languages. For most developers, it is more difficult to generate IL code directly than to generate a C# source file which could be compiled later on. In fact, it is always preferable to generate code in a structured language such as C# or VB.NET.

But then, why would you need to dynamically generate an assembly?

There are in fact at least three main scenarios presented in more details on the **MSDN** article named **Reflection Emits Application Scenarios**:

- The execution of a script within a web browser: the idea is that a script in a web page dynamically constructs an assembly which is stored in a persistent way on the client.
- The execution of a script in an ASP.NET page: the idea is that a script in an ASP.NET page dynamically constructs an assembly which is saved in the server's cache. Hence, only the first visit to the page provokes the creation of the assembly.
- The compilation of a regular expression supplied during execution. The problem of the execution of a regular expression is representative of this type of problem which has a relatively slow general solution but much more efficient specific solutions. The idea is to construct a specific solution during execution, when the regular expression is supplied rather than offering a slower, general solution to developers. The .NET framework allows the compilation of regular expressions and all this is described at page 517. The same idea can be also found in the implementation of the `XsltCompiledTransform` class (see page 644).

Dynamically building an assembly and using it on the fly

All this may appear abstract but we are about to show you a practical example which should give you a better understanding.

A real-life problem

Introduction

The example that we will present here is based on the evaluation of a polynomial P with integer coefficients. Imagine an application where such a polynomial is given at run-time (by the user for example). Suppose that after, the application must compute this polynomial a large number of times for a wide range of values. We will show that such a practical problem has a really optimized solution by taking advantage of the dynamic creation of a new assembly at run-time.

For now, let assume that thy polynomial P input by the user is the following:

$$P(x) = 66x^3 + 83x^2 - 13735x + 30139$$

For a little piece of history, this polynomial was discovered in 1999 by the mathematicians *Dress* and *Landreau*. It has the peculiarity of taking only prime integer values between -26 et 19 (inclusive) for x. We could have used any other polynomial with integer coefficients for our example.

For our performance tests, we will evaluate P for each of these values, 10 million of times. We will only work with four byte signed integers (the `int` or `System.Int32` types in C#). For those who have forgotten some of their math, let us remind that the easiest way (in terms of operation count), is to rewrite P in the following form:

$$P(x) = 30139 + x(-13735 + x(83 + 66x))$$

This trick is called the *Hörner* method. Only three multiplications and three additions are needed to evaluate P for a certain value of x.

Solution1: The general way

Without this knowledge, the easy solution which comes to mind is:

Example 7-19

```
using System;
using System.Diagnostics;
class Program {
   static int Eval ( int x, int[] Coefs ) {
      int tmp = 0;
      int degree = Coefs.GetLength(0);
      for(int i=degree-1 ; i>= 0 ; i--)
         tmp = Coefs[i]+x*tmp;
      return tmp;
   }
   static void Main() {
      Stopwatch sw = Stopwatch.StartNew();
      int [] Coefs = {30139,-13735,83,66};
      for( int x = -26 ; x<= 19 ; x++ )
         for( int i = 0 ; i<10000000 ; i++)
            Eval (x,Coefs);
      Console.WriteLine("Duration:" + sw.Elapsed );
   }
}
```

Since we are focusing our tests on performance, there is no need to verify if integers returned by the `Eval()` method are primes.

Solution 2: The optimized way

If we did not have the constraint of defining the coefficients outside of the `Eval()` we could have rewritten the program as follows:

Example 7-20

```
using System;
using System.Diagnostics;
class Program {
   static int Eval( int x ) {
      return 30139-x*(13735-x*(83+x*66));
   }
   static void Main() {
      Stopwatch sw = Stopwatch.StartNew();
      for( int x = -26 ; x<= 19 ; x++ )
         for( int i = 0 ; i<10000000 ; i++)
            Eval(x);
      Console.WriteLine("Duration:" + sw.Elapsed );
   }
}
```

Performance benchmark between the two solutions

The duration obtained on a reference machine for the first solution (the general approach) is of 17.81 seconds. The duration obtained on the same machine for the second solution (the optimized one) is of 3.87 seconds, hence a performance gain by a factor of **4.6** compared to the first solution. Several machine instructions such the passing of a reference on the table, the search of coefficients in the table and the management of the loop have gone away in the second solution. These results show that the optimized approach to the evaluation of a specific polynomial is much more efficient than the use of a general algorithm.

Two problems can eventually skew these performance results.

- Potential problem 1: The garbage collector could activate itself during one of these tests but not in the other. We have verified that the garbage collector did not trigger it self since we use little memory in these programs.
- Potential problem 2: The JIT compiler could be sufficiently 'smart' to notice that it is not worth calling the `Eval()` since we do not use its results. We have verified that this was not the case by incrementing a global counter from `Eval()` and to verify that the performance results were similar.

An ideal third solution by creating an assembly dynamically

The problem with the optimized method versus the general method is that the coefficients in the `Eval()` method must be known during compilation. The polynomial cannot be supplied during the execution, but only when you compile. Using the dynamic construction of an assembly, we will be able to use the optimized approach which is more efficient while being able to accept the polynomial coefficients at run-time. In fact, we simply need to generate the IL code of the `Eval()` for the optimized approach.

For the polynomial given in the example of the previous section, the IL code generated by the C# compiler is the following:

Dynamically building an assembly and using it on the fly

```
  .method private hidebysig static int32  Eval(int32 x) cil managed
{
  // Code size       28 (0x1c)
  .maxstack  7
  .locals init ([0] int32 CS$00000003$00000000)
  IL_0000:  ldc.i4     0x75bb     // coef 30139 push on top of the stack
  IL_0005:  ldarg.0               // x value push on top of the stack
  IL_0006:  ldc.i4     0xffffca59 // coef -13735 push on top of the stack
  IL_000b:  ldarg.0               // x value push on top of the stack
  IL_000c:  ldc.i4.s   83         // coef 83 push on top of the stack
  IL_000e:  ldarg.0               // x value push on top of the stack
  IL_000f:  ldc.i4.s   66         // coef 66 push on top of the stack
  IL_0011:  mul                   //
  IL_0012:  add                   //    Computation of the polynomial
  IL_0013:  mul                   //    value for x with
  IL_0014:  add                   //    three additions
  IL_0015:  mul                   //    and three multiplications.
  IL_0016:  add                   //
  IL_0017:  stloc.0
  IL_0018:  br.s       IL_001a
  IL_001a:  ldloc.0
  IL_001b:  ret
} // end of method Program::Calc
```

We now simply need to be able to produce this IL code for any polynomial using the classes of the System.Reflection.Emit namespace.

> In this example, the ldarg IL instruction is used with the parameter 0 to load the first argument. If the method was not static, ldarg.0 would have represented the this reference and we would have needed to use ldarg.1 to access the first argument. From this point on the function will not be static anymore and we will then use ldarg.1 to access the first element.

Here is the code:

Example 7-21

```
using System;
using System.Reflection;
using System.Reflection.Emit;
using System.Threading;
using System.Diagnostics;

public interface IPolynome {
   int Eval(int x);
}
class Polynome {
   public IPolynome polynome;
   public Polynome(int[] coefs) {
      Assembly asm = BuildCodeInternal(coefs);
      polynome = (IPolynome)asm.CreateInstance("PolynomeInternal");
   }
   private Assembly BuildCodeInternal(int[] coefs) {
      AssemblyName asmName = new AssemblyName();
      asmName.Name = "EvalPolAsm";

      // Build an assembly dynamically.
```

Example 7-21

```
        AssemblyBuilder asmBuilder =
           Thread.GetDomain().DefineDynamicAssembly(
              asmName, AssemblyBuilderAccess.Run );

        // Add a module in the assembly.
        ModuleBuilder modBuilder =
           asmBuilder.DefineDynamicModule("MainMod");

        // Ad the 'PolynomeInternal' class in the module.
        TypeBuilder typeBuilder = modBuilder.DefineType(
              "PolynomeInternal", TypeAttributes.Public);
        typeBuilder.AddInterfaceImplementation(typeof(IPolynome));

        // Implement the int Eval(int) method
        MethodBuilder methodBuilder = typeBuilder.DefineMethod(
              "Eval",
              MethodAttributes.Public | MethodAttributes.Virtual,
              typeof(int),                  // return type
              new Type[] { typeof(int) });  // argument

        // Generate the IL code from the table of coefs.
        ILGenerator ilGen = methodBuilder.GetILGenerator();
        int deg = coefs.GetLength(0);
        for (int i = 0; i < deg - 1; i++) {
           ilGen.Emit(OpCodes.Ldc_I4, coefs[i]);
           ilGen.Emit(OpCodes.Ldarg, 1);
        }
        ilGen.Emit(OpCodes.Ldc_I4, coefs[deg - 1]);
        for (int i = 0; i < deg - 1; i++) {
           ilGen.Emit(OpCodes.Mul);
           ilGen.Emit(OpCodes.Add);
        }
        ilGen.Emit(OpCodes.Ret);

        // Indicate that the 'Eval()' method is an implementation...
        // ... of the interface method 'IPolynome.Eval()'.
        MethodInfo methodInfo = typeof(IPolynome).GetMethod("Eval");
        typeBuilder.DefineMethodOverride(methodBuilder, methodInfo);
        typeBuilder.CreateType();
        return asmBuilder;
     }
  }

  class Program {
     static void Main() {
        Stopwatch sw = Stopwatch.StartNew();
        int[] coefs = { 30139, -13735, 83, 66 };
        Polynome p = new Polynome(coefs);
        for (int x = -26; x <= 19; x++)
           for (int i = 0; i < 10000000; i++)
              p.polynome.Eval(x);
        Console.WriteLine("Duration:" + sw.Elapsed);
     }
  }
```

Dynamically building an assembly and using it on the fly

Comparing Solution3 with the Solution1 and 2

The duration obtained on the reference machine for this solution is of 4.36 seconds. This is about 1.12 times slower than the second version but the creation of the assembly is not taken into account as it consumes between 2 and 4 hundreds of a seconds. We can suppose that this small performance drop is due to the use of a non-static method which forces us to pass a reference of instance at each call to `Evalue()`. In addition, the call of a method defined in an interface is slightly more expensive than that call to a non-virtual or abstract method. In fact, the `callvirt` IL instruction is used for the call of a method in an interface and the `call` IL instruction is used for the call to a static method. Hence, the JIT compiler generates code which consumes less clock cycles for the `call` instruction than the `callvirt` instruction. This small performance drop is also due to the fact that we do not take in consideration of the fact that certain coefficients of the polynomial could have been stored in one byte (in these case, the 83 and 66 values). Hence, the compiler takes advantage of this situation to use IL instructions specially optimized to manipulate bytes stored on an integer.

However, the third solution is still **4.1** times faster than the first solution, all while respecting the same constraints (i.e. the coefficients of the polynomial are defined outside of the `Eval()` method). This is a huge gain which directly results from the dynamic creation of an assembly. We could still optimize the code even more if we took into account for null coefficients.

Technical description of the code

The interesting types from the previous examples are:

```
AssemblyName
AssemblyBuilder
ModuleBuilder
TypeBuilder
MethodBuilder
ILGenerator
MethodInfo
```

They are generally used in this order, in the same way we have done in this example. There are several other types detailed on **MSDN**. These other types mainly take care of exception management, the management of branches and the management of other elements of a class (property, events…).

The ability to store the assembly on disk

If you wanted to store the assembly on disk, you would have needed to:

- Name the module (for example `MainMod.dll`).
- Use `AssemblyBuilderAccess.RunAndSave` instead of `AssemblyBuilderAccess.Run`.
- Save the assembly with the following line of code, just before the return of the `BuildCodeInternal()` method:

    ```
    TheAsm.Save("MainMod.dll");
    ```

We can compare the IL code generated by the C# compiler and the IL code produced by our program:

The differences are due to the following facts:

- We have dynamically generated a non-static method.
- We have not used local variables compared to the code produced by the C# compiler.
- We have not used the `ldc.i4.s` optimized instruction which loaded on the stack a signed byte (between −128 and 127) into four bytes. We could have modified our program to use this instruction.

Conclusion

We have seen here a representative example of the possibilities offered by the dynamic creation of assemblies. We could have easily adapted the approach to other domains as useful as vectorial computation (matrix composition, evaluation of a quadratic…). It often happens that a same matrix, unknown ahead of time, be composed millions of times (for example to calculate the position of points in a 3D scene).

The majority of developers will never have to dynamically build an assembly but certain projects have a lot to gain from this feature.

8 Interoperability between .NET and native code/ COM/ COM+

The .NET platform offers several techniques to allow the interoperation of managed code with native code and to allow the cooperation of managed objects with COM objects. The need for such techniques is particularly present during the migration process of a C++ or VB6 application to .NET. In fact, the use of interoperability allows the migration of projects little by little.

P/Invoke

The CLR used together with certain base classes of the .NET framework allows managed code to directly call functions defined in native code. This feature is called *Platform Invoke* or *P/Invoke*. You can use this to call the functions within your own DLLs. *Microsoft* also uses the P/Invoke mechanism to call the functions within their own native DLLs.

Also note the existence of a mechanism called *internal call* which has the same result as P/Invoke. This mechanism implements the effect of certain native function calls directly (i.e. hard-coded) into the CLR. This mechanism is thus more efficient but can only be used by *Microsoft*.

The DllImport attribute

The classes allowing you to use the P/Invoke mechanism are located in the `System.Runtime.InteropServices` namespace. To call a function in a native DLL from a C# program, you must first declare this function within a C# class:

- The declaration of this function must be marked with the `System.Runtime.InteropServices.DllImport` attribute which indicates the name of the DLL.
- Use the `static` and `extern` keywords in front of the method declaration.
- Use the same name for the method as used in the DLL.
- Give a name to each argument.

An example

The following program calls the `Beep()` function which is defined in the standard (and native) `Kernel32.dll`.

Example 8-1
```
using System.Runtime.InteropServices;
class Program {
   [DllImport("Kernel32.dll")]
   public static extern bool Beep( uint iFreq, uint iDuration );
   static void Main() {
      bool b = Beep(100, 100);
   }
}
```

In certain rare cases, you cannot specify the name of the function defined in the DLL as you already have a method with the same name. It is possible to change the name of a function implemented in a native DLL like this:

Example 8-2
```
using System.Runtime.InteropServices;
class Program {
   [DllImport("Kernel32.dll", EntryPoint = "Beep")]
   public static extern bool MyBeep( uint iFreq, uint iDuration );
   static void Main() {
      bool b = MyBeep(100, 100);
   }
}
```

Calling convention

Functions implemented within native DLLs support several types of calling conventions. These calling conventions tell to the compiler how the parameters must be passed to the function. If you must use a function which has a specific calling convention, you must use the `DllImport` attribute as follows:

```
[DllImport("MaDLL.dll", CallingConvention=XXX)]
```

XXX is a value from the `System.Runtime.InteropServices.CallingConvention` enumeration. The meaning of the various values to this enumeration is detailed on **MSDN** in the article named **CallingConvention Enumeration**. By default, this value is `StdCall` which is the standard calling convention on the *Microsoft* operating systems (with the exception to *Windows CE* which uses the `Cdecl` calling convention).

Performances issues

During each call to a native DLL function, two steps are done internally. These steps are called *P/Invoke Marshalling*:

- The stack must be traversed to make sure that all calling methods have the `UnmanagedCode` permission. In order to improve performance, you can suppress this step by using the `System.Security.SuppressUnmanagedCodeSecurity` attribute on a P/Invoke method or on a class which contains P/Invoke calls. However, remember that the use of this attribute can potentially compromise security.

- A new *stack frame* which is compatible with the unmanaged stack must be created. This step is generally lightweight.

Since the second step is lightweight and that the first step can be suppressed (if security is not an issue), you can make the use of P/Invoke of little impact on performance.

Inferring the definitions of standard functions

Microsoft does not provide a managed definition of its native functions. To obtain such definitions, we recommend that you visit www.pinvoke.net.

Type conversion

The prototype for `Beep()` in the `Kernel32.dll` DLL is the following:

```
BOOL Beep(DWORD dwFreq,DWORD dwDuration);
```

To call `Beep()`, we had to convert the win32 `BOOL` type into a .NET `bool` and the win32 `DWORD` type into a .NET `uint`. Here is the conversion table of *win32* types into .NET types.

Win32 type	.NET Type	C# equivalent
LPSTR, LPCSTR, LPWSTR, LPCWSTR	System.String	string
	System.StringBuilder	
BYTE	System.Byte	byte
SHORT	System.Int16	short
WORD	System.UInt16	ushort
DWORD, UINT, ULONG	System.Int32	uint
INT, LONG	System.UInt32	uint
BOOL	System.Bool	bool
CHAR	System.Char	char
FLOAT	System.Single	float
DOUBLE	System.Double	double

We say that a type is *blittable* if its binary representation of its instances is identical in managed and native modes. Within the context of interoperability, the use of blittable types is more efficient. In the previous table, only strings are non-blittable. Multi-dimensional tables and types composed of only blittable types are also considered blittable.

Passing arguments by pointer

At page 97 we explain that the garbage collector may move the physical location of referenced objects at any time. If you were to pass the address of a reference object through a pointer to unmanaged code, you would expose yourself to the risk that the garbage collector may move the location of this reference behind your back. Fortunately, the P/Invoke mechanism is capable of detecting this situation. In this case, it will pin the object in memory and will then provide a pointer to the native code (the notion of object pinning is discussed at page 420). The object will be automatically unpinned when we return from the call. Another problem may come up. Certain native function store the pointers passed to them in order to use them in an asynchronous way after the call. For example, the `ReadFileEx()` win32 function is defined as follows:

```
BOOL ReadFileEx(
  HANDLE hFile,
  LPVOID lpBuffer,
  DWORD nNumberOfBytesToRead,
  LPOVERLAPPED lpOverlapped,
  LPOVERLAPPED_COMPLETION_ROUTINE lpCompletionRoutine
);
```

It reads data from a file in an asynchronous way. To accomplish this, it stores the `lpBuffer` and `lpOverlapped` pointers. If you invoke this function from your managed code, it is necessary to explicitly pin the buffers passed for the complete duration of the asynchronous call and not only for the call to the function.

You must be particularly careful as problems resulting from improper pinning of objects used in an asynchronous way can lead to sporadic and unpredictable behavior.

Passing strings

To pass a string during a call to a native method while using the P/Invoke method, you simply need to use the `System.String` type. Know that native functions who take strings each exist in two versions: an ANSI version suffixed with A and a UNICODE version suffixed with W. To choose between these two versions, the `DllImport` attributes offers a parameter named `CharSet` which can take the values of `Auto`, `Unicode` or `Ansi`. The `Auto` value is equivalent to the `Ansi` on the *Windows 98* and *Windows Me* operating systems. The following example shows how to pass to strings during a call to the `MessageBox()` method:

Example 8-3

```
using System.Runtime.InteropServices;
class Program {
   [DllImport("user32.dll", CharSet = ChaSet.Auto)]
   public static extern int MessageBox( System.IntPtr hWnd,
                           string text, string caption, uint type );
   static void Main() {
      MessageBox( System.IntPtr.Zero, "hello", "caption text", 0 );
   }
}
```

Fetching strings

Here we will show how to use a string returned by a function implemented in a native DLL. In unmanaged code, there are two ways to proceed:

- Either the calling code provides a memory buffer and the size of this buffer. In this case, the called function fills the buffer memory with the string to return.
- Either the calling code expects to receive a pointer from the called function. In the case, the called function allocates the memory which will be used to contain the string.

You must absolutely take into account these differences when you make calls to an unmanaged function using P/Invoke. The `GetCurrentDirectory()` function of the `Kernel32.dll` DLL is a good candidate to illustrate the first case.

```
DWORD GetCurrentDirectory( DWORD    nBufferSize, LPTSTR   lpBuffer );
```

In fact, this function takes a pointer to a buffer memory zone and its size as arguments. Here is the C# allowing calling this function. We cannot use the `string` class since the instances of this class are immutable. You must then use the `System.Text.StringBuilder` class.

Example 8-4

```
using System.Text;
using System.Runtime.InteropServices;
class Program {
   [DllImport("Kernel32.dll", CharSet = CharSet.Auto)]
   public static extern uint GetCurrentDirectory(
      uint Size,
      StringBuilder stringBuilder );
   static void Main() {
      uint size = 255;
      StringBuilder stringBuilder = new StringBuilder( (int) size );
      uint i = GetCurrentDirectory( size, stringBuilder );
      System.Console.WriteLine( stringBuilder );
   }
}
```

The `GetCommandLine()` function of the `Kernel32.dll` DLL is a good candidate to illustrate the second case.

```
            LPTSTR GetCommandLine();
```

The function returns a pointer to the string provided to the command line. If we use the `string` class as a return type, the *P/Invoke marshaller* will copy the returned string into a memory buffer allocated for this. Then, the *P/Invoke marshaller* will deallocate the original string. However, the original string must not be deallocated as it existed before the call to `GetCommandLine()` and will most likely be used later. You must then use the `IntPtr` class which allows copying the returned string into an instance of the `string` class without deallocating the original string:

Example 8-5

```csharp
using System.Runtime.InteropServices;
class Program {
   [DllImport("Kernel32.dll", CharSet = CharSet.Auto)]
   public static extern System.IntPtr GetCommandLine();
   static void Main() {
      System.IntPtr ptr = GetCommandLine();
      string sTmp = Marshal.PtrToStringAuto( ptr );
      System.Console.WriteLine( sTmp );
   }
}
```

Passing structures and unions

During the use of a structure in a P/Invoke call, you must take into account the way the fields are stored in the instances of the structure. Most of the time, the fields are stored in a sequential way in the order of their declaration. In other words, they are stored one after the other and the computation of the position of a field by the compiler is done by adding the size of all the preceding fields. However, in the case of an *union*, the fields are stored in the same location and thus all have the same position. Unions do not exist in .NET and you must use a combination of the `System.Runtime.InteropServices.StructLayout` and `System.Runtime.InteropServices.FieldOffset` attributes during the declaration of a structure destined to be used for the call of functions declared in native DLLs.

For example, the `Point` structure can be declared in C# like this:

```csharp
[StructLayout(LayoutKind.Sequential)]
public struct Point {
      public int x;
      public int y;
}
```

The `Point` structure can also be declared like this:

```csharp
[StructLayout(LayoutKind.Explicit)]
public struct Point {
      [FieldOffset(0)] public int x;
      [FieldOffset(4)] public int y;
}
```

The `_Union` union declared like this in C:

```c
union _Union {
   int   i;
   char  c;
   float f ;
}
```

...can be declared in C# like this:

```csharp
[StructLayout(LayoutKind.Explicit)]
public struct Point {
      [FieldOffset(0)] public int i;
      [FieldOffset(0)] public char c;
      [FieldOffset(0)] public float f;
}
```

Note that with the `System.Runtime.InteropServices.MarshalAs` attribute, you can tell the *P/Invoke marshaller* how to transform certain types. For example, the following win32 structure:

```
typedef struct {
    int    wStructSize;
    int    x;
    int    y;
    int    dx;
    int    dy;
    int    wMax;
    TCHAR  rgchMember[2];
} HELPWININFO;
```

...could be declared in C# like this:

```
[StructLayout(LayoutKind.Sequential)]
public struct HELPWININFO {
   int    wStructSize;
   int    x;
   int    y;
   int    dx;
   int    dy;
   int    wMax;
   [MarshalAs(UnmanagedType.ByValArry, SizeConst =2)]
   public char[] rgchMember;
}
```

Direction attributes

During the declaration of a 'P/Invoked' method, you can use the `System.Runtime.InteropServices.In` and `System.Runtime.InteropServices.Out` attributes in front of each arguments of the function. This allows you to tell the *P/Invoke marshaller* to only convert the argument only on the entry or exit of the function. By default, all arguments are converted both at the entry and exit of the function.

Delegates and unmanaged function pointers

You can invoke a function defined in a native DLL by the intermediate of a delegate fabricated from an *unmanaged function pointer*. In fact, using the `GetDelegateForFunctionPointer()` and `GetFunctionPointerForDelegate()` static methods of the `Marshal` class, the notion of delegates and function pointers becomes interchangeable:

Example 8-6

```
using System;
using System.Runtime.InteropServices;
class Program {
   internal delegate bool DelegBeep(uint iFreq, uint iDuration);
   [DllImport("kernel32.dll")]
   internal static extern IntPtr LoadLibrary(String dllname);
   [DllImport("kernel32.dll")]
   internal static extern IntPtr GetProcAddress(IntPtr hModule,
                                                String procName);
   static void Main() {
      IntPtr kernel32 = LoadLibrary( "Kernel32.dll" );
      IntPtr procBeep = GetProcAddress( kernel32, "Beep" );
      DelegBeep delegBeep = Marshal.GetDelegateForFunctionPointer(
```

Example 8-6
```
        procBeep , typeof( DelegBeep ) ) as DelegBeep;
    delegBeep(100,100);
  }
}
```

Introduction to interoperability with the C++/CLI language

In addition of exposing the P/Invoke mechanism in a transparent way, the *C++/CLI* language offers the unique possibility of creating assemblies which contain both native and managed code. It is a good time to make a little incursion into this language in order to give you a more global view that will help you decide if your interoperability needs justify its use.

The It Just Works (IJW) facility

The inner workings of the *IJW* (*It Just Works*) mechanism of the C++/CLI language is the same as the *P/Invoke* mechanism presented in the previous section: to allow the calling of native functions from managed code. At first glance, these two mechanisms are different since *IJW* does not use attributes. But from the point of view of the CLR however, both the *IJW* and *P/Invoke* mechanisms are a single feature. The IL code generated for a call using the *P/Invoke* mechanism is then equivalent to the IL code generated by the *IJW* mechanism. To convince you, let's rewrite Example 8-1 in C++/CLI:

Example 8-7
```
// compile with: /clr
#include "stdafx.h"
#include "windows.h"
int main(){
    bool b = Beep(100, 100);
}
```

The C++/CLI code can compile without the `DllImport` attribute since the compiler knows the definition of the method we wish to call through the inclusion of the proper header file. In our example, the `Beep()` method is defined in the `windows.h` header file. The visualization of the assembly produced by the C++/CLI compiler using the `ildasm.exe` tool reveals that the following static method was built:

```
.method public static pinvokeimpl(lasterr stdcall)
   int32 modopt([mscorlib]System.Runtime.CompilerServices.CallConvStdcall)
   Beep(
     uint32 modopt([Microsoft.VisualC]Microsoft.VisualC.IsLongModifier) A_0,
     uint32 modopt([Microsoft.VisualC]Microsoft.VisualC.IsLongModifier) A_1)
       native unmanaged preservesig {
   .custom instance void
       [mscorlib]System.Security.SuppressUnmanagedCodeSecurityAttribute::
       .ctor() = ( 01 00 00 00 )
 // Embedded native code
 // Disassembly of native methods is not supported.
 // Managed TargetRVA = 0x00001D92
} // end of method 'Global Functions'::Beep
```

The visualization of the assembly produced by the C# compiler for Example 8-7 gives this definition:

```
.method public hidebysig static pinvokeimpl("Kernel32.dll" winapi)
   bool Beep(uint32 iFreq,uint32 iDuration) cil managed preservesig{}
```

226   Chapter 8 - Interoperability Between .NET, Native Code, COM and COM+

From the point of view of the CLR, the two versions of the `Beep()` are to be invoked using the P/Invoke mechanism since they both use the `pinvokeimpl` flag. However, we can notice that the C++/CLI compiler has generated native code to locate the `Beep()` method contained in the `kernel32.dll` DLL while the C# version counts on the CLR to complete this operation. Notice also the use of the `SuppressUnmanagedCodeSecurity` attribute in the C++/CLI version (described at page 166) and the `IsLongModifier` modifier which solves problems due to the fact that the `long` and `int` C++/CLI keywords both refer to the `Int32` type.

Coexistence of managed and unmanaged types

In version 2 of the C++/CLI language, a type marked with `ref`, `value`, `interface` or `enum` is a managed type while a type not marked by these keywords is native. Also, a method defined after `#pragma managed` will be compiled in IL language while a method defined after `#pragma unmanaged` will be compiled in native code. The C++/CLI language allows:

- The definition of unmanaged types with methods which contains native code;
- The definition of unmanaged types with methods containing IL code;
- The definition of managed types with methods containing IL code.

The `#pragma managed` and `unmanaged` definitions must be defined outside of a type to take effect. As consequence, a type cannot at the same time contain native and managed methods. Moreover the C++/CLI language does not allow the definition of managed types with methods containing native code. All this is illustrated by the following program:

Example 8-8

```
// compile with: /clr
#include "stdafx.h"
#using <mscorlib.dll>
#pragma unmanaged
class NativeTypeNativeCode {
public:
    NativeTypeNativeCode(int state){ m_State = state; }
    int GetState(){ return m_State; }
private:
    int m_State;
};
#pragma managed
class NativeTypeILCode {
public:
    NativeTypeILCode (int state){ m_State = state; }
    int GetState(){ return m_State; }
private:
    int m_State;
};
ref class ManagedTypeILCode {
public:
    TypeGereCodeIL(int state){ m_State = state; }
    int GetState(){ return m_State; }
private:
    int m_State;
};
int main() {
    NativeTypeNativeCode * o1 = new NativeTypeNativeCode( 1 );
    int i1 = o1->GetState();
    delete o1;
    NativeTypeILCode * o2 = new NativeTypeILCode( 2 );
    int i2 = o2->GetState();
```

Example 8-8

```
        delete o2;
        ManagedTypeILCode ^ o3 = gcnew ManagedTypeILCode( 3 );
        int i3 = o3->GetState();
        return 0;
}
```

If you compile this code and that you analyze the assembly produced with the `ildasm.exe` tool, you will notice that the compiler has provided two managed types `NativeTypeILCode` and `NativeTypeNativeCode` to allow the use of the underlying native types from native code. These two managed types do not have any members and their state is stored in the native types. The native type's definition and code is stored in the binary sections of the assembly which cannot be visualized by `ildasm.exe` and `Reflector`.

We notice the presence of four static public managed methods `NativeTypeILCode.GetState(...)`, `NativeTypeILCode.{ctor}(...)`, `NativeTypeNativeCode.GetState(...)` and `NativeTypeNativeCode.{ctor}(...)`. There is no `NativeTypeNativeCode` or `NativeTypeILCode` namespace. The IL language accepts method names containing a dot. It is interesting to notice that the two `.GetState()` methods take a parameter representing the `this` reference. Also, the two methods relative to `NativeTypeILCode` contain IL code while the two methods relative to `NativeTypeNativeCode` have the `pinvokeimpl` flag, indicating a native method call using P/Invoke.

Finally, if you visualize the IL code of the `main()` method, you will see that the C++/CLI compiler uses the types of the `System.Runtime.CompilerServices` namespace to make possible the magic of the IL code used to manipulate native types.

Using managed objects from native code

The fundamental problem during the use of a managed object from native code is that you cannot use a pointer to the managed object unless you pin its memory. However, the garbage collector loses a lot of its efficiency when objects are pinned. We then had to find another approach than pointers to reference managed object from native code.

The garbage collector implements a *handle* system to deal with this situation. A handle is a four byte number. The garbage collector makes sure that each managed object has its own handle. The native code can then reference a managed object by using its handle.

A handle to an instance of the T managed type is represented in C++/CLI with the T^ expression. The .NET framework offers the `System.Runtime.InteropServices.GCHandle` managed type which serves as a bridge between managed objects and their handles. However, the native code does not have direct access to managed types. Thus, you do not have the possibility of using the `GCHandle()` managed structure nor the T^ syntax from native code.

To reference a managed object of type T from native code, you need to use an instance of `gcroot<T^>`. `gcroot<T>` is a native structure which uses *templates* in C++/CLI and where the methods are in IL. It is interesting to look at the definition of `gcroot<T>` in the `gcroot.h` file. There, you will see:

- A `_handle` field of type `void*`. This field cannot be of type `GCHandle`. In fact, a `gcroot<T>` structure is native and cannot have managed fields such as `GCHandle`.

- The methods of `gcroot<T>` can use an instance of `GCHandle` since they are compiled in IL. The bridge between an instance of `GCHandle` and the `_handle` is ensured by the static conversion operators of the `GCHandle` structure. To simplify these operations, the `gcroot<T>` type uses the two following macros:

```
__GCHANDLE_TO_VOIDPTR(x)((GCHandle::operator System::IntPtr(x)).ToPointer())
__VOIDPTR_TO_GCHANDLE(x)(GCHandle::operator GCHandle(System::IntPtr(x)))
```

- The destructor of the gcroot<T> type frees the handle. While the native code calls this destructor, it essentially indicates to the garbage collector that the underlying object can be destroyed if there are no other outstanding references to the object.

In the following example, the NativeTypeNativeCode class keeps a reference to a managed string. As you can see, the use of gcroot is reduced to strict minimum and you do not see the GCHandle structure appear.

Example 8-9

```
// compile with: /clr
#include "stdafx.h"
#include <vcclr.h>
using namespace System;
#pragma unmanaged
class NativeTypeNativeCode {
public:
   NativeTypeNativeCode( gcroot<String^> s ) {m_s = s;}
   gcroot<String^> m_s;
};
#pragma managed
int main() {
   NativeTypeNativeCode * obj = new NativeTypeNativeCode("Hello");
   Console::WriteLine( obj->m_s );
   delete obj;
}
```

To use a managed object from native code, you must develop yourself a native type with managed code which does the bridge between the two worlds. The following example shows how native code which has a reference (well a handle) to a managed instance of type string can invoke the get_Length() method on this instance:

Example 8-10

```
// compile with: /clr
#include "stdafx.h"
#include <vcclr.h>
using namespace System;
#pragma managed
class NativeTypeILCode {
public:
   static int Lentgh( gcroot<String^> s ) {
      return s->Length;
   }
};
#pragma unmanaged
class NativeTypeNativeCode {
public:
   NativeTypeNativeCode( gcroot<String^> s ) {
      m_Length = NativeTypeILCode::Lentgh(s);
   }
   int m_Length;
};
#pragma managed
int main() {
   NativeTypeNativeCode * obj = new NativeTypeNativeCode( "Hello" );
   Console::WriteLine( obj->m_Length );
   delete obj;
}
```

.NET and win32 Handles

> The handles of the garbage collector presented in the previous section are conceptually close to win32 handles that we will see. However, these two types of handles belong to completely different domains.

Introduction

An application executed under a *Windows* operating system can use system resources such as files, the registry, drivers, processes, threads, mutex, named pipes, sockets... A same system resource can be used simultaneously by several processes (for example a named muted). Thus, a system resource may not be referenced using a pointer since it does not belong in the address space of a process. A consequence of this is that *Windows* processes access system resources through the use of logical pointers named *handles*.

All win32 functions which allow the manipulation of a system resource accept a parameter of type HANDLE. A handle is a number encoded in four bytes. Each *Windows* process maintains internally an association table between the handles and the underlying system resource. This means that two system resources cannot be referenced by the same handle within a process and that two handles referencing the same resource within two distinct processes can be different four bytes numbers.

A system resource is created during the call to certain win32 functions such as CreateFile(), CreateMutex() or CreateThread(). These functions have the peculiarity of returning a handle. A call to one of these functions does not necessarily create a resource. For example, you can get a handle to an existing mutex by calling the CreateMutex() with the name of the mutex as a parameter. The CloseHandle() win32 function allows you to tell *Windows* that the calling process does not need the referenced resource anymore. *Windows* destroys a system resource when no other processes have a handle referencing it.

The *'Process/Number of handles' Windows* performance counter allows you to know the number of handles currently held by a process. The *'Handles'* column of the *task manager* tool also allows you to visualize this number in real-time.

The HandleCollector class

An instance of the System.Runtime.InteropServices.HandleCollector class allows to provide the CLR an estimate of the number of handlers currently held by the process. You can specify a minimum and maximum threshold at which the garbage collector will trigger a collection. In fact, the garbage collector has no knowledge of the amount of unmanaged memory maintained by system resource and this class allows having some control on this effect. An instance of HandleCollector can be named in a way to only be concerned with handles referencing to a certain type of resource.

The SafeHandle and CriticalHandle classes

Before .NET 2, handles were referenced from managed code by instances of IntPtr. This approach had a few problems:

- There was no type verification during compilation. For example, nothing would prevent you from passing a handle to a window (with a win32 type of HWND) to a win32 function which needed a handle to a file (with a win32 type of HFILE).
- You had no guarantees in regards to the release of a handle. An exception of type ThreadAbortException or OutOfMemory could compromise this operation.

- You were exposed to a *race condition* in regards to the closure of a handle. Nothing would prevent a thread from using a handle while another thread attempted to close it. This could also lead to a security problem named *handle-recycling attack* where malicious code could exploit a resource in the process of being closed.

The .NET framework 2 offers a way to address these problems with the `System.InteropServices.CriticalHandle` and `System.InteropServices.SafeHandle` abstract classes. The idea is to provide a non-abstract class derived from one of these types to manage the lifecycle of a handle. This class must derive from `SafeHandle` to implement a type of handle which supports reference counting. If not, this class must derive from `CriticalHandle`. Both the `SafeHandle` and `CriticalHandle` classes derive from `System.Runtime.ConstrainedExecution.CriticalFinalizer` and consequently have a critical finalizer. Critical finalizers are described in more details at page 105. Because of this, we obtain a certain guarantee in regards to the closing operation of a handle.

You can also derive from the `CriticalHandleMinusOneIsInvalid`, `SafeHandleMinusOneIsInvalid` and `SafeHandleZeroOrMinusOneIsInvalid` abstract classes whose names are self-descriptive in regards to the offered lifetime service. These classes are located in the `Microsoft.Win32.SafeHandles` namespace.

Using COM objects from .NET code

With time, the COM technology has become more and more complicated to use and understand, to a point where certain companies have specialized themselves in the development of COM components. At the beginning of the .NET project, *Microsoft* wanted to build a new technology while ignoring the constraints of backward compatibility. However, since *Microsoft* had been strongly pushing the use of the COM technology for several years, there were already millions of COM components throughout the world. It was unreasonable to require all companies to rewrite all their components under .NET, and it was necessary not to build .NET on top of COM. The only solution was to build a set of classes and tools which allowed the use of COM components directly from code developed under .NET. This is what we will be discussing here.

Type metadata and type library

Although they respond to the same need, early binding with COM classes and early binding with .NET classes are technically speaking, very different. **The main difference is that the managed .NET code needs to consult the type metadata before creating a link with a method of a .NET class** (whether the binding is early or late). This comes from the fact that the IL code uses the notion of metadata token instead of addresses/offset. Here are a few other differences:

- COM classes are only manipulated through COM interfaces.
- Arguments are passed differently.
- COM classes do not support constructors with arguments.

COM components (i.e. the COM equivalent to assemblies, DLLs in general but can also be executables) optionally offer metadata contained in what is called a *type library*. Such a library can be contained directly in the COM component or in a separate file with a `tlb` extension. In addition to the fact that a COM component is not required to have a type library, the binary format used within a type library is totally different than the format used for .NET assembly metadata.

Interop assemblies and Runtime Callable Wrapper classes (RCW)

Microsoft created the *type library importer* tool (`tlbimp.exe`) to construct an assembly directly from a COM component whose type library is available. An assembly created from `tlbimp.exe` is called an *interop assembly*. We will see in the next section how to use, from managed code, COM

Using COM objects from .NET code

components for which the type library is not available. At the end of the current section, we will show that using *Visual Studio,* you can avoid from having to directly manipulate the `tlbimp.exe` tool.

An *IDL (Interface Definition Language)* file which describes a COM component named `COMComponent` is shown below. It is clear that this COM component has a type library which contains the `CCOMClass` class. This class has a proprietary interface named `ICOMClass` which in turn contains a function named `CalcSum()` which computes the sum of the two first parameters, while returning the result in the third parameter.

COMComponent.idl

```
[
   object,
   uuid(947469B1-61EB-4010-AE29-8380C2D577E9),
   dual,
   helpstring("ICOMClass Interface"),
   pointer_default(unique)
]
interface ICOMClass: IDispatch{
   HRESULT  CalcSum([in]int a, [in]int b, [out,retval] int *pResult);
};

[ version(1.0),
   uuid(8A4F713C-910F-4EE0-8A26-B870FBE58596),
   custom(a817e7a1-43fa-11d0-9e44-00aa00b6770a,
   "{23391CA9-529E-43CF-9BF6-C636BF96BF26}"),
   helpstring("COMComponent 1.0 Type Library") ]
library COMComponent {
   importlib("stdole2.tlb");
   importlib("olepro32.dll");
   [
      version(1.0),
      uuid(1E3B6413-7E63-42B5-874D-E0A27A42190C),
      helpstring("CCOMClass Class")
   ]
   coclass CCOMClass{
      interface ICOMClass;
   };
}
```

Here is the command line to use in order to obtain an interop assembly from this COM component. `tlbimp.exe` gives us the possibility of assigning a namespace by using the `/namespace` directive. This tool has several other options presented on **MSDN** in the article named **Type Library Importer (tlbimp.exe)**.

```
>tlbimp.exe COMComponent.dll /out:AsmCOMComponent.dll /namespace:TestInterop
```

If we analyze the `AsmCOMComponent.dll` assembly using `ildasm.exe`, we see that it contains a class named `CCOMClassClass` and an interface named `ICOMClass`. The `ICOMClass` interface presents the method named `CalcSum()` and the `CCOMClassClass` class implements this interface `ICOMClass`.

The implementation of the `CalcSum()` method inside the `CCOMClassClass` class only contains code to transform the call of a .NET type into a call to the `ICOMClass.CalcSum()` COM method. In the .NET jargon, we say that the `CCOMClassClass` .NET class is a *Runtime Callable Wrapper (RCW)*. In *design patterns* (Gof) terminology, we say that such a class is an *adaptator*, since it adapts the COM class to an interface that the client can call. We can also say that `CCOMClassClass` is a *proxy* class in the sense that all the calls are intercepted, in order to process its arguments. After the interception, the calls are done on the underlying COM class.

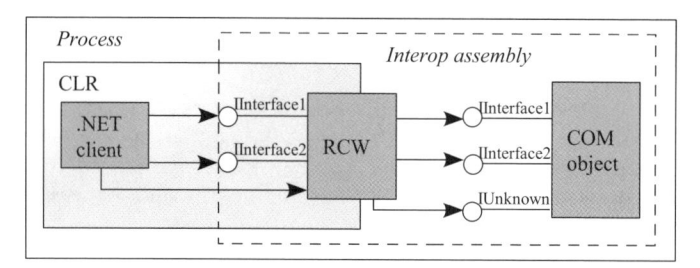

Figure 8-1: Using COM objects from .NET code

Here is the code of a C# program which uses the `AsmCOMComponent.dll` interop assembly. Naturally, we must specify during compilation that this program references the `AsmCOMComponent.dll` assembly:

Example 8-11   *DotNETClient.cs*

```
using TestInterop;
class Program {
   static void Main() {
      ICOMClass foo = new CCOMClassClass();
      int result = foo.CalcSum(2, 3);
      System.Console.WriteLine("Result :{0}", result);
   }
}
```

Note that differently to a COM class, a RCW class can be called directly without needing to pass an interface. We could have written:

```
...
   CCOMClassClass foo = new CCOMClassClass ();
   int result = foo.CalcSum(2,3);
...
```

If the COM class supports multiple proprietary interfaces, `tlbimp.exe` will generate as many .NET interfaces. Moreover, all the methods of these interfaces will be declared and accessible publicly from the RCW class.

The use of *Visual Studio* avoids you the direct use of the `tlbimp.exe` tool. You simply need to add a reference within the project directly to the COM component, exactly as if you were adding a reference to another assembly (see Figure 8-2). The interop assembly containing the RCW classes will be automatically constructed and placed in the same folder as the concerned assembly.

The interop assemblies and the COM components of a .NET application are of course part of the files you will need to deploy along with your .NET application.

Accessing COM classes of a COM component without using a type library

The .NET framework also offers the possibility of creating your own RCW to access instances of COM classes without using the type library and the `tlbimp.exe` tool. This functionality is essentially used when a COM component does not have a type library, or when a type library is not available during development.

Using COM objects from .NET code

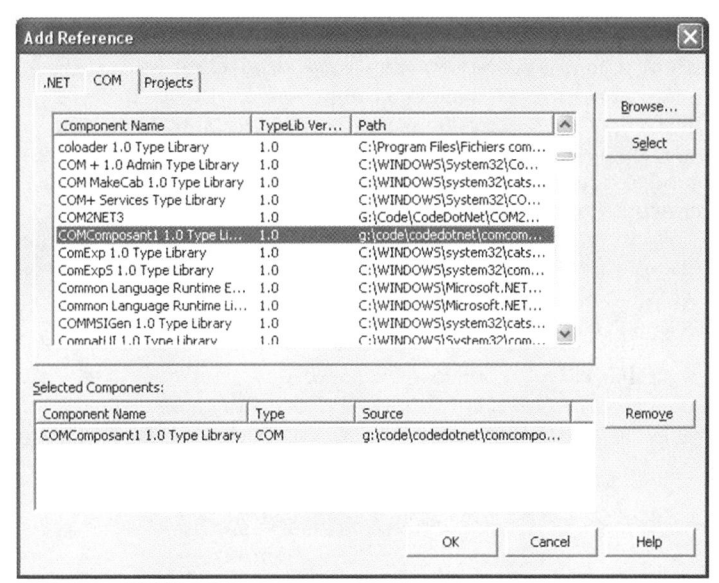

Figure 8-2: Adding a reference toward a COM component from Visual Studio

This functionality is rather cumbersome to use. You have to completely redefine each COM interfaces and COM classes that you wish to use. For each argument and return value, you must use the `System.Runtime.InteropServices.MarshalAs` attribute. For the COM component at page 231, you would need to write:

Example 8-12

```
using System;
using System.Runtime.InteropServices;
[
    ComImport,
    Guid("947469B1-61EB-4010-AE29-8380C2D577E9"),
    InterfaceType(ComInterfaceType.InterfaceIsDual)
]
public interface ICOMClass {
    [return : MarshalAs(UnmanagedType.I4)]
    int CalcSum(
        [In,MarshalAs(UnmanagedType.I4)]  int a,
        [In,MarshalAs(UnmanagedType.I4)]  int b,
        [Out,MarshalAs(UnmanagedType.I4)] out int c);
}
[
    ComImport,
    Guid("1E3B6413-7E63-42B5-874D-E0A27A42190C")
]
public class CCOMClass {}
class Program {
    static void Main() {
        ICOMClass foo = new CCOMClass() as ICOMClass;
        int result;
        foo.CalcSum( 2, 3, out result );
        System.Console.WriteLine( "Result :{0}", result );
    }
}
```

Importing an ActiveX with Visual Studio

An *ActiveX* is the term used to describe a graphical COM class. We can also use the *ActiveX control* or *OCX* terms. ActiveX controls are stored in COM components with a `.dll` or `.ocx` extension. There are a great number of ActiveX controls available freely on the internet. There are OCX controls to visualize images, animations, some OCX to traverse folders, to edit phone numbers... In addition, most graphical technologies (*Flash* by *Macromedia*, *MapPoint* by *Microsoft* ...) are generally supplied with an ActiveX control allowing its use. As you can see there is a vast choice of ActiveX controls which you can use. The good news is that *Visual Studio* allows using them within your .NET programs as easily as if they were .NET *Windows Form* controls. In the chapter dedicated on *Windows Form* we will explain how to use .NET graphical controls but let's take a look at the use of ActiveX controls in .NET forms using *Visual Studio*.

It is preferable to get the field ready and to insert a special tab within our graphical control toolbox for the import of ActiveX controls. For this, right click on this toolbox and select the '*Add Tab*' option and give a name to the new tab (for example '*ActiveX*'). Your tool box should look like the one in Figure 8-3.

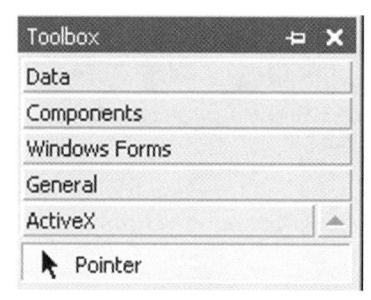

Figure 8-3: Prepare the tool box to import OCX

You can now add an ActiveX control by right clicking on the '*ActiveX*' and choosing '*Customize Toolbox...*'. You will then see the window in Figure 8-4 which allows you to add either an ActiveX control or a graphical .NET control to your tab.

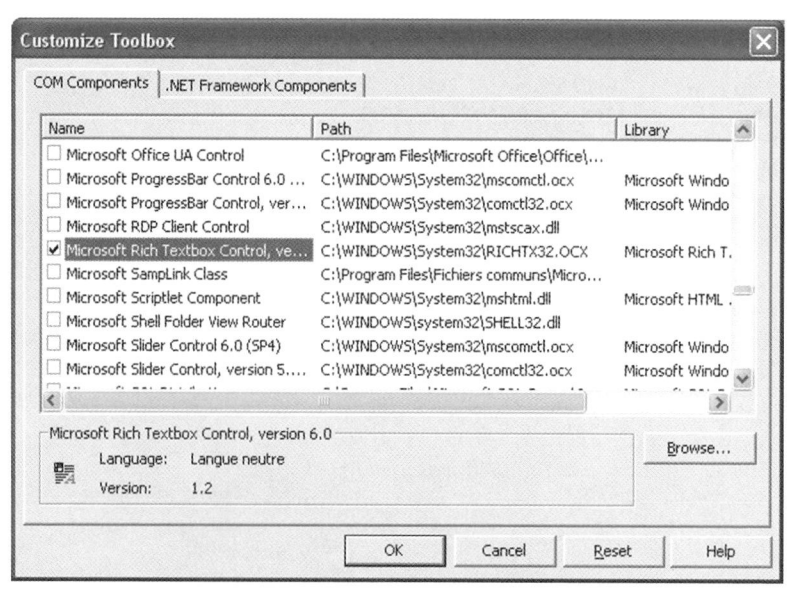

Figure 8-4: Add an OCX in the toolbox

Here we have chosen the *Microsoft Rich Textbox Control* ActiveX control which allows the display of a RTF document. When we add such a control into a *Windows Form* form, we have access to the property window for this control. Internally, an interop assembly is created, containing the needed RCW classes.

COM specificities to bear in mind while using a RCW class

Dealing with the life cycle of COM objects from .NET

The lifecycle of a COM object follows very specific rules which are completely encapsulated within the RCW classes. Notably, the call to the `CoCreateInstance()` function which allows the creation of a COM object are encapsulated. The calls to the methods of the `IUnknow` interface (`QueryInterface()` which allows to navigate the various interface, `AddRef()` and `Release()` which allow to manage the internal reference count) are also encapsulated.

A RCW class is a managed class and thus you cannot decide exactly when it will be destroyed since this is the responsibility of the garbage collector. Hence, a RCW class only destroy its underlying COM object when it is itself destroyed. From the start, you cannot decide when the destruction of a COM object will take place in your .NET program. This can be somewhat of an annoyance as the architecture behind COM objects implies that you have control on when the destruction of a COM object will take place.

The `System.Marshal.InteropServices.Marshal` interface offers the `int ReleaseComObject(object)` method to deal with this problem. This method takes as a parameter an `object` which must be the concerned RCW object. Internally, a call to this method provokes a call to the `Release()` method of the COM object and only decrements its internal reference counter. The new value for this counter is returned and you can test if the COM object is effectively destroyed by verifying that this value is in fact 0. Once the COM object is destroyed, we recommend placing all the references to the RCW to null as any use of this object will cause of `InvalidComObjectException` to be raised. For example:

```
...
    ICOMClass  foo = new CCOMClassClass();
    int result = foo.CalcSum(2,3);
    System.Runtime.InteropServices.Marshal.ReleaseComObject(foo);
    foo = null;
...
```

Dealing with COM data types from .NET

The conversion between COM and .NET data types does not pose any problems. It is however useful to mention the following conversions:

- The RCW classes convert the *Basic Strings* (*BSTR*) of COM into instances of the `System.String` class
- The RCW classes convert the *VARIANT* COM type into instances of a class derived from `object`. The .NET class of the underlying object naturally depends on the underlying type of the VARIANT and you can typecast this .NET object using the C# `as` operator.
- The RCW classes convert the *SAFEARRAY* COM type into the appropriate managed array. For example, an argument of type `SAFEARRAY(BSTR)` in a COM method becomes an argument of type `System.String[]` in the RCW class.

Dealing with COM error codes from .NET

The management of errors is radically different between .NET and COM:

- .NET manages errors through the use of exceptions which are managed by the CLR.
- COM manages errors through the use of a return value of each method of each COM interface. This return value is of type *HRESULT*. A HRESULT is a numerical value stored on four bytes which specifies if and error was produced during a call to a method on a COM object. In this case, the HRESULT contains the type of error and eventual information on the software layer which caused the error.

If a call to a method of a COM object returns an error through the HRESULT, an exception of type COMException is automatically raised by the CLR. The ErrorCode property of this exception contains the value of HRESULT.

Dealing with COM apartments from .NET

COM allows the management of the affinities between COM objects and threads through the use of *COM apartments*. Concretely, you can ensure that the methods of the instance of a COM class can only be executed by certain threads. A process can contain several COM apartments. Each COM object is contained in a process and belongs to one COM apartment. Each thread of the process also belongs to a COM apartment. If a thread from a COM apartment must make a call to a method of a COM object which is not in the same COM apartment (even in another process), the concerned COM interface must be marshaled in a way for it to be used by the client thread. This marshalling operation is necessary as the code of the methods of the COM class is always executed by the threads within the COM apartment for this object.

There are two kinds of COM apartments the *Single Thread Apartment* (*STA*) and the *Multi Thread Apartment* (*MTA*) which respectively contain one or several threads. A process can contain several STA but may only contain one MTA. During the evolution of the COM technology, the notion of STA appeared before the notion of MTA. The goal of the STA was to remove the developers from the burden of dealing with concurrent access to the resources of a COM class. In fact, in the STA mode, it is the same thread which manages calls to the different instances of a same COM class. The STA approach proved itself insufficient for certain applications and the notion of MTA had to be introduced, which gave back to the developer the responsibility of managing concurrent accesses.

The managed threads of .NET know this notion of COM apartment. More exactly, a managed thread knows if its underlying *Windows* thread is a STA or MTA. You can set the ApartmentState property of the Thread class with a value of the System.Threading.ApartmentState enumeration, which can be STA, MTA or Unknown (which is the default value). This property can be set only once during the lifetime of a managed thread.

You can also specify the COM apartment of a thread by using one of the System.STAThread or System.MTAThread attributes on the method which constitutes the entry point of the thread. For example:

```
...
[MTAThread]
public static void Main(){
}
...
```

Explicit late binding on COM classes

Way before the arrival of .NET and its reflection mechanism, the technique of explicit late binding was available on COM classes which implement the IDispatch interface. IDispatch offers the GetDispID() method which allows to get the position of the declaration of a method in an interface based on the name of the method. This position is called DISPID. IDispatch also

Using COM objects from .NET code

offers the `Invoke()` method which allows to call a method by knowing its `DISPID`. The use of these two methods allows the creation of explicit late bindings with COM classes and to invoke these methods using such bindings.

You can use the `IDisptach` late binding mechanism of COM from the explicit late binding mechanism of .NET. To use this feature with the class of the COM component from page 231 you would need to write:

Example 8-13
```
using System;
using System.Reflection;
class Program {
   static void Main() {
      Type type = Type.GetTypeFromProgID("COMComponent1.CCOMClass");
      // We could also wite :
      // Type type = Type.GetTypeFromCLSID(
      //    new System.Guid("1E3B6413-7E63-42B5-874D-E0A27A42190C"));
      Object obj = Activator.CreateInstance( type );
      Object[] args = new Object[] { 3, 4 };
      int retVal = (int) type.InvokeMember(
         "CalcSum",
         BindingFlags.InvokeMethod,
         null,
         obj,
         args);
      Console.WriteLine(retVal);
   }
}
```

Notice how we get the COM type from its PROGID or its CLSID, using one of the static methods of the `Type` class, `GetTypeFromProgID()` or `GetTypeFromCLSID()`.

Registration free COM

Windows XP as well as future *Windows* versions offer the possibility of using a COM class without needing to register it within the registry. The idea is to supply a file which contains the associations between the CLSIDs and the COM DLLs of the COM classes used for each application. During the launch of the application, *Windows* loads the data from this table. During execution, when a COM class must be loaded, *Windows* consults this table. If the COM class is not found by this technique, the standard location process using the registry is initiated.

You can use this technique named *registration free COM* (or *reg free COM*) from a .NET assembly. For this, we need to provide a file with the same name as the assembly but with a `.manifest` extension containing the association between the CLSIDs and the COM DLLs in an XML form like this (MyAsm.exe is the name of the assembly and thus the name of the file will be MyAsm.exe.manifest):

MyAsm.exe.manifest
```
<?xml version="1.0" encoding="utf-8"?>
<assembly xsi:schemaLocation="urn:schemas-microsoft-com:asm.v1
                             assembly.adaptive.xsd"
          manifestVersion="1.0"
          xmlns:asmv2="urn:schemas-microsoft-com:asm.v2"
          xmlns:xsi="http://www.w3.org/2001/XMLSchema-instance" ... >
   <assemblyIdentity name="MyAsm.exe" version="1.0.0.0" type="win32" />
   <file name="[Absolute or relative path]/MyCOMComponent.dll"
         asmv2:size="20480">
      <typelib  tlbid="{ea995c49-e5d0-4f1f-8489-31239fc9d9d0}"
                version="2.0" helpdir=""
```

```
                    resourceid="0" flags="HASDISKIMAGE" />
    <comClass clsid="{97b5534f-3b96-40a4-88b8-19a3bf4eeb2e}"
              threadingModel="Apartment"
              tlbid="{ea995c49-e5d0-4f1f-8489-31239fc9d9d0}"
              progid="MyCOMComponent.MyClass" />
    <comClass ... />
  </file>
  <file ... />
...
```

Visual Studio 2005 allows you to easily use this technique. For this, you must set the `Isolated` attribute of a COM reference to `true`. This also works if the referenced COM class is an OCX. The compilation of the project will generate the file with the `.manifest` in the output folder. It will also copy the DLLs for the needed COM components in this folder. *Reg free COM* is particularly useful if you desire to use COM classes in a project deployed using *XCopy*, for example with the *ClickOnce* technology.

Let us precise that to use this attribute, the COM classes must be registered in the registry for the machine which compiles the application. This means that it is a good idea to test this kind of application on a "virgin" machine. In fact, a misuse of *reg free COM* would not be detected on a machine on which the used COM components are registered.

Know that you can accomplish the same work as *reg free COM* by locating, loading and instantiating the COM class yourself. This is useful if you wish to deploy your application on machines running versions prior to *Windows XP*. For each COM class and COM component, you must:

- Locate the COM component DLL.
- Load it in memory using the `LoadLibrary()` win32 function
- Locate the `DllGetClassObject()` function exported by the COM DLL. For this, you must use the `GetProcAddress()` win32 function.
- Call this function to obtain a COM object implementing the `IClassFactory` COM interface.
- Call the `IClassFactory.CreateInstance()` method to create a COM object.

Wrapping a .NET object into a COM Callable Wrapper (CCW)

Introduction to CCW

In the migration process of an application to .NET, it can happen that certain components be migrated before others. It is then possible that unmanaged code needs to instantiate and use a .NET class. For this purpose, the .NET framework allows us to encapsulate a .NET class into a *COM Callable Wrapper* (*CCW*). A CCW is a COM object created and managed automatically by the CLR. Such a COM object encapsulates a .NET object, to make it usable as it were a COM object. A CCW is created during the execution by the CLR, from the metadata of the .NET class (and not from a COM type library). There exists at most one CCW per .NET object, no matter how many clients wish to use it as a COM object. A .NET object with a CCW can also be used by .NET clients. In this case, the fact that the .NET object has a CCW is transparent to the .NET clients. Figure 8-5 summaries the interaction between the unmanaged client and the .NET object using a CCW.

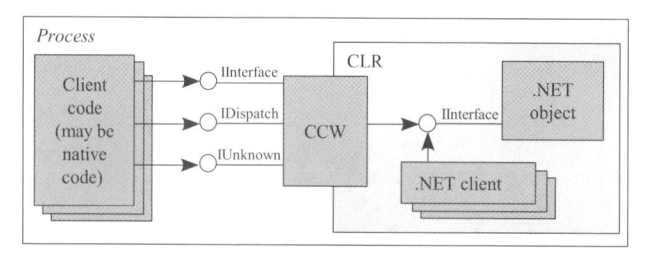

Figure 8-5 : Using a .NET object wrapped into a CCW

Wrapping a .NET object into a COM Callable Wrapper (CCW)

It is important to note that the object model proposed by COM is restrictive compared to the object model proposed by .NET. To be used as a normal COM class by the intermediate of a CCW, a .NET class must satisfy the following constraints:

- The .NET class must have a constructor without arguments, also known as a default constructor. In fact, COM does not support constructors with arguments. Amongst the constructors of the .NET class, only the default constructor can be called through the CCW.
- Only the public classes of an assembly can be encapsulated in a CCW.
- The .NET class can have static members, but they cannot be used through the intermediate of a CCW since COM does not support the notion of static members.
- Method overloading in a .NET class is not recommended as COM does not support this notion. In practice an underscore is put before the name of each overloaded method and a number is placed at the end of the name of the method.

Building a COM type library describing CCW classes from a .NET assembly

The *Type Library Exporter* `tlbexp.exe` tool allows the construction of a COM type library which describe the .NET public classes and interfaces contained in an assembly. Let's show how to use `tlbexp.exe` through a simple example. Here is the C# code:

Example 8-14   *dotNET2COM.cs*
```
namespace Test {
   public interface ICalc {
      int CalcSum(int a, int b);
   }
   public class CCalc : ICalc {
      public int CalcSum(int a, int b) {
         return a + b;
      }
   }
}
```

To produce the `dotNET2COM.dll` assembly from this C# file, you simply need to use the following command line:

```
>csc.exe -t:library dotNET2COM.cs
```

To produce a COM type library describing the CCW which encapsulated the `CCalc` and the `ICalc` interface, you need to use the following command line:

```
>tlbexp.exe dotNET2COM.dll /out:dotNET2COM.tlb
```

> Understand that the CCW is created at run-time by the CLR. During this operation, the CLR does not need a type library. The type library is only useful for the clients which need to create a COM early binding with the CCW.

We can visualize the type library for `dotNET2COM.tlb` by using the *OLE Viewer* (`oleview.exe`) tool which can be accessed from the *Tools* menu in Visual Studio .NET. It is also accessible through the command line. *OLE Viewer* has the *File > View TypeLib...* menu entry. Let us remind you that type libraries are described in a binary format and such a tool is needed to visualize them:

```
[
    uuid(824A9F5F-39AE-35BB-8741-7C4C8F7DB26C),
    version(1.0),
    custom(90883F05-3D28-11D2-8F17-00A0C9A6186D,
   dotNET2COM,
   Version=0.0.0.0,
   Culture=neutral,
   PublicKeyToken=null)
]
library dotNET2COM{
    importlib("mscorlib.tlb");
    importlib("stdole2.tlb");

    // Forward declare all types defined in this typelib
    interface ICalc;
    interface _CCalc;

    [
      odl,
      uuid(72E3095D-B243-37F0-A95A-41ABBE13E029),
      version(1.0),
      dual,
      oleautomation,
      custom(0F21F359-AB84-41E8-9A78-36D110E6D2F9, Test.ICalc)
    ]
    interface ICalc : IDispatch {
        [id(0x60020000)]
        HRESULT CalcSum( [in] long a,
                         [in] long b,
                         [out, retval] long* pRetVal );
    };

    [
      uuid(A51C81A3-4892-39EC-981A-AF77FB4CFD36),
      version(1.0),
      custom(0F21F359-AB84-41E8-9A78-36D110E6D2F9, Test.CCalc)
    ]
    coclass CCalc {
        [default] interface _CCalc;
        interface _Object;
        interface ICalc;
    };

    [
      odl,
      uuid(84181003-CCB9-3219-B373-629AF4E3B246),
      hidden,
      dual,
      oleautomation,
      custom(0F21F359-AB84-41E8-9A78-36D110E6D2F9, Test.CCalc)
    ]
    interface _CCalc : IDispatch {
    };
};
```

Several remarks can be made:

Wrapping a .NET object into a COM Callable Wrapper (CCW)   241

- The `CCalc` COM class implements the following interfaces:

    `ICalc`: This COM interface represents the `ICalc` .NET interface.

    `_Object`: This interface represents the methods of the `System.Object` that all .NET classes derive from. The `_Object` interface is defined in the `mscorlib.tlb` type library.

    `_CCalc`: This COM interface is the class interface of the `CCalc` .NET class. A class interface is supposed to represent all the public non-static members of a .NET class (including the members of the types from which the class is derived). However, in our example, this class interface contains no members. Since the use of class interfaces is not recommended, the default behavior of `tlbexp.exe` is to not insert any members in the class interface that it generates. The use of class interfaces is not recommended because it couples unmanaged clients with managed classes and not interfaces. You can however tell `tlbexp.exe` that you wish for the class interface to be completely created by using the `System.Runtime.InteropServices.ClassInterface` attribute with the `AutoDual` in your C# code For example:

    ```
    ...
        [ClassInterface(ClassInterfaceType.AutoDual)]
        public class CCalc : ICalc{
            ...
        }
    ...
    ```

    The public fields of a class with a class interface are materialized in the form of two accessors. In the same way, the accessors of properties of public interfaces are present as interface methods in the COM interfaces generated by `tlbexp.exe`.

- A class ID can be produced automatically for the `CCalc` COM class. We could have used the `System.RunTime.InteropServices.Guid` attribute to specify our own GUID within the C# code:

    ```
    ...
        [Guid("A51C81A3-4892-39EC-981A-AF77FB4CFD36")]
        public class CCalc : ICalc{
            ...
        }
    ...
    ```

- An interface ID has been produced automatically for the `ICalc` COM interface. There also, we could have use our own interface ID using the `Guid` attribute.
- The `ICalc` COM interface extends the `IDispatch` COM interface which allows the creation of explicit late bindings on a COM class.

You have the possibility of using the `System.RunTime.InteropServices.COMVisible` attribute in your .NET code on an interface, a class, method or an event in order to tell `tlbexp.exe` that the concerned entity must not be visible in a type library. For example:

```
...
    [ComVisible(false)]
    public class CCalc : ICalc{
        ...
    }
...
```

Public structures are taken into account by `tlbexp.exe`. They can then be passed as arguments to methods of classes and interfaces.

Registering CCWs on the OS

We have seen in the previous section how to build a COM type library from a .NET assembly. We will now see how you can register this type library in the registry of a *Microsoft* operating system. Let us remind you that to be useful, a COM class must be registered in the registry. This is essentially the association information between the class ID of the COM class and the file (DLL or executable) containing the implementation of the class which is stored in the registry. In fact, an application which instantiates a COM class only knows the class by its class ID and has no information in regards to the file which contains its implementation. We must then consult the registry to locate the implementation of a COM class, at least the first time that it is instantiated within an application.

To register (or unregister) the COM classes of a classic COM component, you simply need to use the tool named `regsvr32.exe`. To register (or unregister) the .NET classes of an assembly, you must use the tool named *Assembly Registration Tool* `regasm.exe` specially dedicated to this task. For example:

```
>regasm.exe dotNET2COM.dll
```

This tool can be configured using the several options described on **MSDN** in the article named **Assembly Registration Tool (Regasm.exe)**. The `/regfile` option allows to tell `regasm.exe` to generate a registry update file with a `.reg` extension. The use of the `/regfile` causes the registry not to be modified. The execution of a `.reg` file does the actual update to the registry. In a `.reg` file, the update information is encoded in a text format making it easy to consult and modify this information. For example:

```
>regasm.exe dotNET2COM.dll /regfile:dotNET2COM.reg
```

Creates the following file:

dotNET2COM.reg

```
[HKEY_CLASSES_ROOT\Test.CCalc]
@="Test.CCalc"

[HKEY_CLASSES_ROOT\Test.CCalc\CLSID]
@="{A51C81A3-4892-39EC-981A-AF77FB4CFD36}"

[HKEY_CLASSES_ROOT\CLSID\{A51C81A3-4892-39EC-981A-AF77FB4CFD36}]
@="Test.CCalc"

[HKEY_CLASSES_ROOT\CLSID\{A51C81A3-4892-39EC-981A-AF77FB4CFD36}\InprocServer32]
@="C:\WINDOWS\System32\mscoree.dll"
"ThreadingModel"="Both"
"Class"="Test.CCalc"
"Assembly"="dotNET2COM, Version=0.0.0.0, Culture=neutral, PublicKeyToken=null"
"RuntimeVersion"="v1.0.3705"

[HKEY_CLASSES_ROOT\CLSID\{A51C81A3-4892-39EC-981A-AF77FB4CFD36}\ProgId]
@="Test.CCalc"

[HKEY_CLASSES_ROOT\CLSID\{A51C81A3-4892-39EC-981A-AF77FB4CFD36}\Implemented
Categories\{62C8FE65-4EBB-45E7-B440-6E39B2CDBF29}]
```

The `InprocServer32` key, which is supposed to contain the path to the implementation of the COM class points to `mscoree.dll`. This DLL, also called a shim DLL, allows the CLR to be loaded in a process. The four components of the strong name of the assembly containing the implementation of the .NET class are specified in the `Assembly` sub-key. When an application will need the

Wrapping a .NET object into a COM Callable Wrapper (CCW)

COM class which has the ProgID of Test.Calc, it will first load the CLR (if it is not already loaded in this process) and will then use the assembly locating mechanism to find the dotNET2COM assembly.

The ThreadingModel sub-key is set to both, this means that the instances of the CCW COM class support both the STA and MTA modes. This comes from the fact that the STA and MTA models are not taken into account in .NET. The .NET objects have no affinities with threads.

By default, the ProgID of the generated COM class is *{namespace}.{class name}*. You can however specify your own ProgID by using the System.RunTime.InteropServices.ProgId attribute in your .NET code. For example:

```
...
    [ProgID("dotNET.CCalc")]
    public class CCalc : ICalc{
...
```

The regasm.exe tool also offers the /tlb option which allows the generation of a type library, exactly as with the tlbexp.exe tool.

```
>regasm.exe dotNET2COM.dll /tlb:dotNET2COM.tlb
```

The regasm.exe and tlbexp.exe tools can be used independently on the same assembly. We could worry that the unique identifiers for the classes and interfaces not be the same in the files produced by regasm.exe and in the files produced by tlbexp.exe. Fortunately, this is not the case, which leads us to believe that these unique identifiers are calculated in a deterministic way from the assembly. In practice, the unique identifiers do not change if the members of classes or interface change but they do change if the name of classes or interfaces does change.

Using a .NET assembly as a COM component

We will now present an example of unmanaged C++ code which uses out CCalc .NET class as a COM class. Thanks to the import of the dotNET2COM.tlb type library produced from the dotNET2COM.dll by using tlbexp.exe or regasm.exe, the C++ code can complete an early binding with the CCalc COM class. Here is the code:

Example 8-15
```
#include "stdafx.h"
#import "dotNET2COM.tlb"
int _tmain(int argc, TCHAR* argv[], TCHAR* envp[])
{
    int nRetCode = 0;
    // Initialize the current thread for harnessing COM.
    HRESULT hr = ::CoInitialize(NULL);
    dotNET2COM::ICalcPtr pI;
    // Create the CCW which wraps the .NET object.
    hr = pI.CreateInstance( __uuidof(dotNET2COM::CCalc) );
    // Call a method (the C++ compiler creates an early bind thanks to
    // the imported typelib dotNET2COM).
    int result = pI->CalcSum(2,3);
    // Release the CCW.
    pI = NULL;
    // Uninitialize COM on the current thread.
    ::CoUninitialize();
    return nRetCode;
}
```

.NET exception and CCW

Let's suppose that an exception is raised from the managed code of a .NET object used by native code as a COM object. In this case, the CLR has the responsibility of managing the transition between the managed code and unmanaged code. To accomplish this, it converts, as best it can, the information of the incoming exception into a HRESULT error code. The CLR uses specific rules to convert the various exception classes into different HRESULT values. For example, HRESULT COR_E_DIVIDEBYZERO is converted into a DivideByZeroException exception. All this is detailed in the article named **HRESULTs and Exceptions** on **MSDN**.

Dealing with the objects' life cycles

We will now mention a problem with the use of a .NET class as a COM object. When such an object is not used anymore, that is when the internal reference counter of the CCW COM object reaches 0, the CCW COM object is destroyed but not the underlying .NET object. This .NET object will only be destroyed when it will, at some point, be collected by the GC.

Contrarily to the use of a COM object within .NET, there is no special mechanism to force the destruction of a .NET object encapsulated within a CCW COM object. This behavior may not be wanted as the .NET object may be holding on to precious resources that need to be released as soon as possible.

A problem even more troublesome can occur if the .NET object contains references to COM objects and that the developer of the unmanaged code assumes there are no more COM objects in the process. After the destruction of the CCW object, the developer of the unmanaged code may call the CoUninitialize() to indicate he does not need the COM libraries in the current thread. However, if this thread is forced to destroy all COM objects owned by .NET objects, there will be an unpredictable behavior which will most likely lead to a crash.

To avoid the problems of resource leak and of crash, it is recommended to provide a method in the .NET class, specially provided to free all the resources held by the object. This method will need to be explicitly called by the unmanaged code.

Introduction to COM+

What is COM+?

COM+ is the term used to designate the *enterprise services* in the context of applications destined to be executed under a *Microsoft* operating system. COM+ is essentially the *Microsoft* technology to build *application servers*. A COM+ enterprise service is an evolved feature which can be added to a COM class. These features are centered on the development of transactional distributed applications. We will see the list of these features in the following section but we can mention object pooling or the bridge which allows the transition to non-*Microsoft* transactional platforms.

COM+ 1.0 has appeared with *Windows 2000*. COM+ is not a new version of COM but a new version of the *MTS* (*Microsoft Transaction Server*) technology which allows, amongst other things, the completion of distributed transactions. Compared to the MTS, we obtained much better performance with COM+ 1.0. COM+ 1.5 was released with *Windows XP* and adds a few more enterprise services to COM+ 1.0.

COM+ via .NET: Enterprise Services

It was necessary that the .NET framework offered its own application server technology. During the last few years, *Microsoft* was hard at work on the development of the .NET framework. At the same time, the COM+ was meeting the needs of several and its adoption was growing. *Microsoft* has then decided to capitalize on the use of COM+ rather than develop a new application server technology.

Each COM+ enterprise service is usable via a .NET class. The .NET framework offers a set of attributes, classes and tools allowing your own .NET classes to use the COM+ enterprise services. These attributes and classes are all located under the `System.EnterpriseServices` namespace and are implemented in the `System.EnterpriseServices.dll` assembly which is located in the GAC. The main idea is that the developer does not need to know COM+ in details to use COM+ enterprise services within their .NET classes.

Overview of the COM+ enterprise services

The complete list of COM+ enterprise services

The detailed presentation of all COM+ enterprise services is beyond the scope of this book. Here is a list of COM+ enterprise services that you can assign to your .NET classes:

- **Object pooling**;
  The idea of object pooling is to recycle objects so that they can serve several clients consecutively. The cost of the construction and destruction of an object is then divided by the number of clients served by the object. The pool holds the content of objects which are not currently serving a client.

- **Just In Time Activation (JITA)**;
  The idea behind this mechanism is to deactivate an object after the call to certain methods in order to make it usable by other clients. Let us remind you that deactivating a COM+ object means calling the `Deactivate()` method on the object, then it is put back in the instance pool for the serviced component. If such an object pool does not exist, the `Dispose()` method is called on the object and it will be destroyed by the garbage collector. To indicate that the instances of a serviced component support the JITA mechanism, you simply need to use the `System.EnterpriseServices.JustInTimeActivation` attribute in the declaration of the serviced components.

- **Distributed transactions**;
  COM+ allows using the transactional server of *Windows* named MS DTC (*Distributed Transaction Coordinator*) in order to complete distributed transactions.

- **BYOT (Bring Your Own Transaction)**
  This mechanism allows associating an existing transaction to a component which did not previously take part of this transactions. The transaction can be managed by MS DTC, but also in another transactional environment such as *TIP* (*Transaction Internet Protocol*).

- **COM Transaction Integrator (COMTI)**
  This mechanism allows you to integrate mainframes developed with the *CICS* (*Customer Information Control System*) and *IMS* (*Information Management System*) technologies of *IBM*, into classic COM objects. Under the COMTI term are grouped the tools and classes allowing this integration.

- **Compensating Resource Manager (CRMs)**
  The transactional theory applies itself, amongst other things, to relational databases. However, you must not forget that it constitutes the general theoretical framework for the protection of the integrity of resources. A CRM serviced component is a custom serviced component which

manages resources (for example, files). A CRM can participate within a distributed transaction managed by MS DTC. When a CRM participates in a transaction, it must be able to store in a temporary and in a persistent way the state of the resource before its modification in order for it to roll back the change if the transaction failed. The CRM must be capable of validating the changes (*commit*) or to cancel them (*rollback*) even if the process which manages it is destroyed during the transaction. If this process is effectively destroyed during the transaction, the *commit* or *rollback* operations must be executed once the process is restarted. Contrarily to what we may think, writing a CRM is a relatively easy task. Most of the functionality is encapsulated in the classes provided by the .NET framework.

- **XA Interoperability**
  This mechanism allows to encapsulate within a transaction managed by the *Microsoft* transaction model (*OLE Transaction*), the access to a database which supports the *XA* (*X/Open Distributed Transaction Processing, DTP*) transactional model.

- **Loosely Coupled Events**
  This mechanism allows a client of a COM+ application to be warned by the server when an event happens. It avoids for the client to regularly poll the server to see if the event happened.

- **Passing a string to the constructor of an object**
  This mechanism allows to partly address the lack of arguments on the constructor of COM classes. However, the string is the same for all instances of a serviced component. You have the possibility of modifying this string through the use of the 'Component services' tool. The classic use of this string is to provide a connection string to a database.

- **Private components**
  All the serviced components in a COM+ application are not necessarily accessed by the clients of the COM+ application. There often exist serviced components which must only be used by other serviced components, which exist within the same process and belong to the same COM+ application. To prevent a client from using such a serviced component, it must be declared as a private component.

- **Queued Components**
  This *asynchronous call* mechanism goes further than the .NET asynchronous call mechanism. Contrarily to this mechanism, the client requests are not treated directly. They are stored in a message queue. During this operation, no server object has been created. The client and the server can even be physically disconnected. All this is transparent for the client which talks through a proxy object. All this is also transparent for the server which will eventually get these requests and process them once connected to the client machine. Note that the internal queue management mechanism is the *Microsoft Message Queue* (*MSMQ*). MSMQ must be installed on both the client and server machines.

- **Role-Based Security**
  COM+ offers its own security mechanism based on the role that the calling user plays. This mechanism is different from the .NET and *Windows* role based security mechanisms.

- **SOAP Services**
  This mechanism allows publishing a serviced component as a web service. We can still continue to access it as a COM+ component.

- **Synchronization / COM+ activity**
  A *COM+ activity* is a logical call tree between instances of serviced components. This mechanism allows synchronizing the access to the instances of serviced components between multiple COM+ activities. The call interception mechanism of COM+ makes sure that you cannot have more than one COM+ activity which uses one instance of a serviced component at a time.

Do you need COM+ enterprise services?

Because COM+ is not integrated to .NET, it is better to avoid using it until whenever possible. In fact, certain functionalities are redundant between the .NET framework .NET and the COM+ enterprise services. Here are a few of the functionalities which are redundant.

.NET 2 offers a transactional development framework which is always preferred to the management of transactions using COM+. This framework is the topic of the chapter on transactions.

Quite often, the COM+ object pooling is used to avoid the construction and destruction of connections to the database for each client. Be aware that a connection pool mechanism is provided by most ADO.NET data provider (see page 595).

The COM+ JITA activation functionality of an object ('Just In Time Activation') allows to postpone the creation (or activation) of an object until the moment of its first real use by the client. The WKO mode of .NET Remoting works on this same activation model (see page 661).

The notion of COM+ asynchronous call is a little more general than the one offered by .NET which we discuss at page 141. It is more general in the sense where it allows a client to make a call even if the server cannot be reached at the moment of the call. In this case, the call is stored in a queue on the client side and will be eventually executed automatically when the server can be reached. If you do not need this functionality, it is better to stick with .NET asynchronous calls.

The notion of security role is present all at once in COM+, *Windows* and .NET. You can read more on this topic at page 179.

The possibility of authorizing at most one client to use a given instance of a component at a given time is possible in both COM+ and .NET (see page 132).

Harnessing COM+ services in .NET classes

Introduction to serviced component

A *serviced component* is a .NET class which uses one or more COM+ enterprise services. To use at least one COM+ enterprise service, a .NET class must derive from the `System.EnterpriseServices.ServicedComponent` class. A serviced component must absolutely offer one constructor without an argument, also called a default constructor.

The `ServicedComponent` class implements the `IDisposable` interface and it's `Dispose()` method. The `ServicedComponent` also presents the protected virtual component `Dispose(bool)`. If the boolean argument is set to `true`, this means that we must release all managed and unmanaged resources. If the boolean is set to `false`, this means that we must only free unmanaged resources.

Here is what the skeleton of a serviced component looks like:

Example 8-16
```
using System;
using System.EnterpriseServices;

public class BankSystem : ServicedComponent {
   public BankSystem() { }
   new public void Dispose() {
      Dispose(true);
      GC.SuppressFinalize(this);
   }
```

Example 8-16
```
   protected override void Dispose(bool bDisposing){
      // Release unmanaged resources here.
      if( bDisposing ){
         // Release managed resources here.
      }
      base.Dispose(bDisposing);
   }
}
```

Declaring the enterprise services used by a serviced component

To tell the compiler that a class derived from `ServicedComponent` uses a certain enterprise service, it must be declared with the .NET attributes corresponding to the desired services. These attributes are all defined in the `System.EnterpriseServices` namespace. For example, the `Transaction` attribute allows configuring the transactional mode used in a class. The `ObjectPooling` attribute allows you to indicate that the instances of the class are part of a pool. To use conjointly these two services and to configure them with our `BankSystem` class, you would need to declare it as follows:

```
...
[Transaction( TransactionOption.Required )]
[ObjectPooling( MinPoolSize=5, MaxPoolSize=30 )]
public class BankSystem : ServicedComponent {
...
```

COM+ contexts and serviced components

A *COM+ context* is a logical container in a process which hosts the objects that uses a same COM+ enterprise service.

> Caution, although that conceptually similar to the notion of .NET context presented at page 700, the notion of COM+ context is different. Certain documents talk of managed contexts (.NET) and of unmanaged contexts (COM+).

The internal plumbing implemented in order to use an enterprise service is relatively heavy. The notion of context allows the sharing of this plumbing amongst several objects in order to improve performance. The management of contexts is transparent to the developer. During the creation of a serviced component, COM+ takes care to verify if there already exists a context within the process which uses the same enterprise services. If this is the case, the instance of the serviced component will use this context. If not a new context with the proper enterprise service will be created.

Know that if the client of the instance of a serviced component is not in the same COM+ context, COM+ creates a *proxy* object for the client. The interest of this is that each call to the serviced component is first intercepted internally by COM+ before being executed. What COM+ does during this interception completely depends on the enterprise services used. The JITA mechanism, described a little later, constitutes an interesting example of what COM+ can do during these interceptions. Note that this proxy object mechanism is transparent to the user.

From the point of view of a developer using a .NET serviced component, the control of the use of the enterprise services is done by the intermediate of the `System.EnterpriseServices.ContextUtil` class which contains only static members. Suppose that a serviced component uses the same enterprise service of transaction management and that you wish to abort the current transaction in the code of a method. You simply need to call the `ContextUtil.SetAbort()` method. We cannot say that a .NET serviced component belongs to a COM+ context because the serviced component is managed but not the context. We rather say that a serviced component uses a context to have access to its enterprise services. Figure 8-6 illustrates all this:

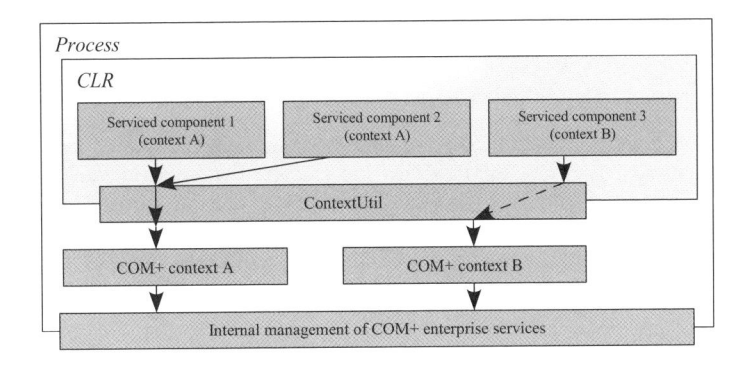

Figure 8-6: COM+ contexts and .NET serviced components

Introduction to COM+ application

A *COM+ application* is a collection of serviced components. The serviced component of a COM+ application can be defined in different assemblies. However, all the serviced components of an assembly belong to the same COM+ application. COM+ applications represent what we commonly called an *enterprise server*. The clients use the instances of the serviced components of a COM+ application and that the serviced components use the COM+ enterprise services to complete their tasks.

Several assembly attributes have been created so that you can configure the parameters of the COM+ application which will contain the assembly that you are developing. Here are the main ones:

- `ApplicationName`: specifies the name of the COM+ application. For example:

    `[assembly : ApplicationName("Bank server.")]`
- `ApplicationID`: specifies the unique identifier of the COM+ application.

    `[assembly : ApplicationID("301E31A3-E011-432b-9D7E-5643253EEE89")]`
- `Description`: gives a description of the COM+ application.

    `[assembly : Description("Allows the access to banking information.")]`
- `ApplicationAccessControl`: allows configuring the security parameters of a COM+ application.
- `ApplicationQueuing`: Allows configuring the message queues in the COM+ application.
- `ApplicationActivation`: There exist two activation modes for a COM+ application, the library activation mode and the server activation mode. The description of these modes is the topic of the next section.

If several assemblies configure the same COM+ application, a configuration value of the COM+ application will take the value specified in the last installed assembly. If a parameter of a COM+ application is not set by any assembly, it will be set to a default value during the creation of a COM+ application.

The COM+ catalog

The *COM+ catalog* is a database present in all *Microsoft* operating systems since Windows 2000. The COM+ catalog contains the configuration information of the COM+ applications which resides on the machine. The COM+ catalog is physically stored on two supports:

- Part of the information of the COM+ catalog is stored in the registry, directly with the information for the COM classes.
- Another part of the information in the COM+ catalog is stored in a series of component library files (.clb extension). These files are stored in the '%systemroot%\Registration' folder.

The format of the .clb files is not documented. It is strongly recommended not to attempt modifying or visualizing the data in the COM+ catalog by the intermediate of a tool such as regedt32.exe or even by modifying the .clb files. We will present a little later a tool specially designed for the visualization and modification of the COM+ catalog information. Figure 8-7 shows the different relationships between the COM+ catalogs, COM+ application and the serviced components installed on a machine.

Activation mode of a COM+ application

Each COM+ application has an *activation mode* which is either 'library' or 'server'.

Library activation mode (also called in process activation mode)

The 'library' activation mode indicates that assemblies containing the serviced components of a COM+ application must be loaded into the client process of the COM+ application. Figure 8-8 exposes the general architecture of the implementation of the 'library' activation mode.

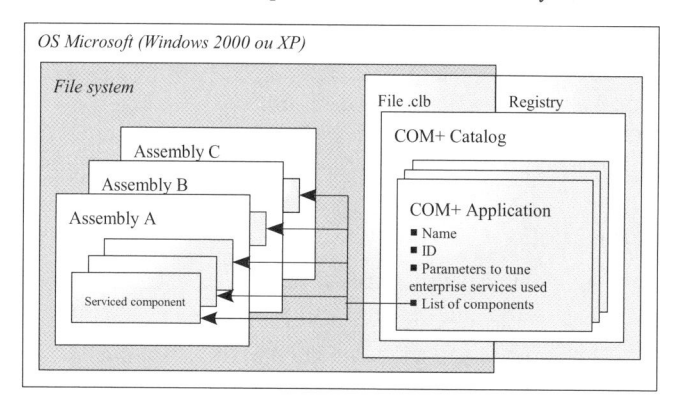

Figure 8-7: COM+ catalog and COM+ applications

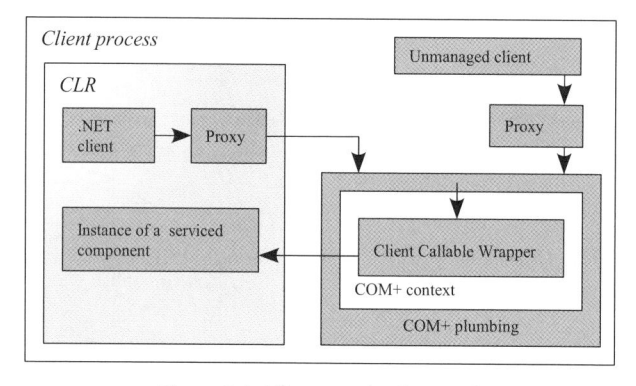

Figure 8-8: Library activation mode

Harnessing COM+ services in .NET classes 251

Server activation mode

The 'server' activation mode indicates that the assemblies containing the serviced components of a COM+ application must be loaded in a process provided to host COM+ applications. This process is launched automatically during the first use of a COM+ application. The `dllhost.exe` executable is used to launch this process. We say that such a process is a *surrogate*. For a COM+ application to be used by remote clients (i.e. which are not on the same machine) it must be activated using the 'server' mode. Figure 8-9 exposes the general architecture of the implementation of the 'server' activation mode.

Installing serviced component

The installation of serviced components of a COM+ application contained in an assembly requires this assembly to have a strong name. This means that the assembly must be digitally signed using the `sn.exe` tool. At the moment of execution, the CLR will find this assembly either in the GAC or in the current application folder.

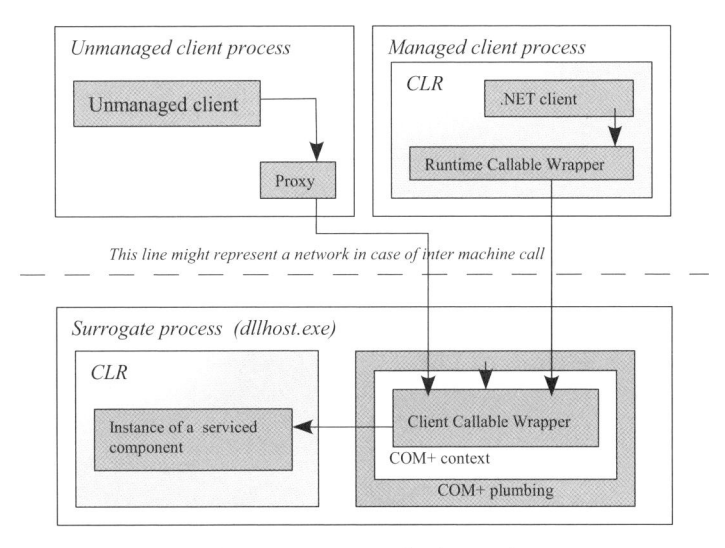

Figure 8-9: Server activation mode

Installation steps

The installation of serviced components contained in an assembly, within a COM+ application, implies the four following steps:

- Registering the serviced components in the registry so that they can be accessed like COM object. This step was described in the previous sections.
- Build a type library describing the serviced components within the assembly. This type library contains the information specified by the COM+ attributes contained in the assembly.
- Find the COM+ application which must contain the serviced components. If the COM+ application is not found, then create a new COM+ application.
- Configure the COM+ information from the information of the type library, coming from the COM+ attributes in the assembly. Parameters which are not set take default values. In addition, if the COM+ application already existed, it is possible that the value of the parameters change during the installation of a new serviced component.

252　　　　　　　　　Chapter 8 - Interoperability Between .NET, Native Code, COM and COM+

Ways to perform the installation

The `System.EnterpriseServices.RegistrationHelper` class allows the installation (or uninstallation) of the serviced components of an assembly. It allows executing the four above steps in a single transaction. After having used the `RegistrationHelper` class, you can be certain that all the steps have been successfully completed or that nothing has been modified as one of the steps has failed.

Concretely, there are three ways to install the serviced components of an assembly. Each of these ways uses directly or indirectly the `RegistrationHelper` class. Whatever way you use, only a user with administrator rights can complete this operation.

- The 'manual' way:

  You simply need to use the *Services Installation Utility* (`regsvcs.exe`) tool in the command line with the assembly containing the serviced components as a parameter. For example:

  ```
  >regsvcs.exe BankSystem.dll
  ```

  The options of the `regsvcs.exe` tool are described on **MSDN** in the article named **.NET Services Installation Tool (Regsvcs.exe)**. If the name of the COM+ application is not specified in the assembly or by using the `/appname` option of `regsvcs.exe`, the name of the COM+ application will be set to the same as the name of the assembly (without the file extension).

- The 'programmatic' way:

  You simply need to use the `RegistrationHelper` within a method of a class in an assembly. The `RegistrationHelper` presents the `InstallAssembly()` for this purpose. For example:

  Example 8-17
  ```
  using System.EnterpriseServices;
  public class Program {
     static void Main() {
        RegistrationHelper rh = new RegistrationHelper();
        string sCOMPlusAppName = "Bank server.";
        string sTypeLibName = "BankSystem.tlb";
        rh.InstallAssembly(
           "BankSystem.dll", // Name of the assembly.
           ref sCOMPlusAppName,
           ref sTypeLibName,
           InstallationFlags.CreateTargetApplication );
     }
  }
  ```

  The `CreateTargetApplication` argument indicates that a new COM+ application must be created. If this is not possible the `RegistrationException` is raised.

- The 'automatic' way:

  When a client needs a serviced component to be instantiated, the CLR verifies if the component is indeed present in a COM+ application. If this is not the case, the CLR automatically installs the assembly in a new COM+ application. Although seductive, this approach must be avoided as you cannot be certain that the first client will have administrator privileges which are needed to complete the installation.

Viewing and working with the COM+ catalog

You can visualize and manipulate the COM+ catalog, and thus the COM+ applications present on a machine by using the *snap-in* named *component services*. Figure 8-10 shows a screenshot of this tool.

Harnessing COM+ services in .NET classes 253

The 'component services' allows an administrator to modify the parameters of a COM+ application. However, it is recommended to only modify the parameters related to the installation of a COM+ application such as the security parameters.

If a COM+ application is currently being used the 'component services' tool will indicates this with a little animation. It also allows you to stop a COM+ application being used. If you change the parameters of a COM+ application, you will need to stop this application in order for the changes to take effect.

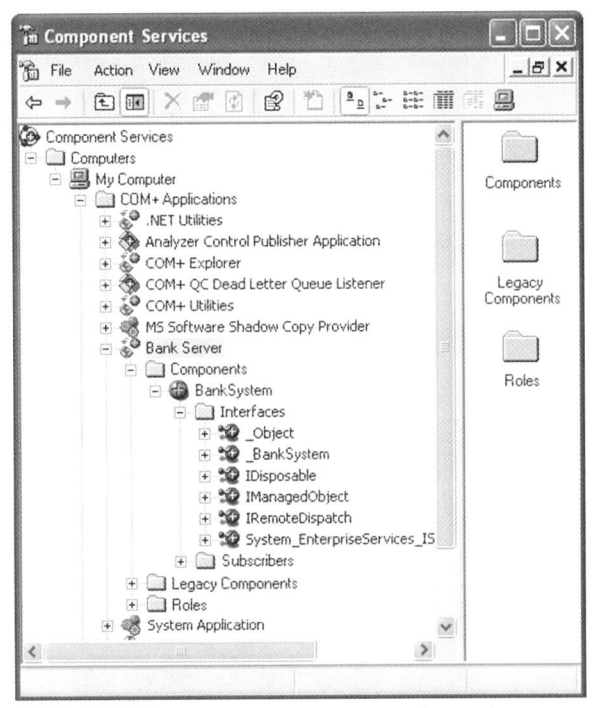

Figure 8-10: The Component Services tool

Building a client of a serviced component

From the point of view of a managed client, there is no difference between the use of a normal class and the use of the instance of a serviced component. It is recommended to use the C# syntax with the using keyword to call the Dispose() method in an implicit way. For example:

```
public class Program {
   static void Main(){
      using( BankSystem sys = new BankSystem() ){
         // Use sys here.
      } //implicit call to sys.Dispose().
   }
}
```

From the point of view of an unmanaged client, the use of a serviced component goes through the use of a COM classed defined by a *Com Callable Wrapper*.

The C#2 language and the C#2 / C++ comparison

9
Fundamental concepts of the language

Organizing your source code

C++ › C#: Although C# has a syntax similar to that of C++, namespaces play a more crucial role.

In C++, namespaces were used to avoid collision between similar identifiers. With C#, namespaces are used to replace the `#include` preprocessor directive. In fact, in C#, there are no more header (.h) files. To use a resource contained within a namespace declared in another C# file, you simply need to declare that you will be using the specific namespace. This source file can even reside in a totally separate assembly.

The possibility of using resources declared in external assemblies can also be exploited to use resources defined within libraries. For example, all the base classes of the .NET framework are accessible through the `System` namespace.

Another big difference is that the declaration and definition (the body) of a method or class cannot be separated as is possible in C++ through the use of the scope operator '::'.

Another major difference is that there is no concept of global functions within C#. The language can only define methods, which are functions declared as part of a type (class or structure).

In C#, the use of namespaces to prevent the collision of identifiers is still valid. In addition, to extend an identifier by prefixing it with its namespace is done with a dot operator and not with the C++ scope operator (which has another use under C#2).

Finally, C# also provides means of aliasing and combining namespaces.

The namespaces

A resource within your source code can be declared within a namespace. If a resource is not declared within a namespace, it will be part of the anonymous global namespace. For example, a *namespace* named `Foo` is declared as follows:

```
namespace Foo{
   // Here, you can define your resources.
}
```

You have the possibility of embedding namespaces:

```
namespace Foo1{
   // Here, you can define your resources.
   namespace Foo2{
      // Here, you can also define your resources.
      // The thorough qualification of Foo2 is Foo1.Foo2.
   }
   // Here, you can also define your resources.
}
```

You also have the option to split up namespaces to spread resources that must be within a same namespace across multiple source files. To accomplish this, you simply need to declare one or many namespaces with the same name for each affected file. Note that with partial types in C#2, a resource now has the possibility of being declared across multiple source files.

The technique behind splitting up namespaces can be even more powerful as the separation can occur across various modules (from the same or even different assemblies).

Namespaces are a means of separating source code into distinct and organized blocks, in a hierarchical way as defined by project architects.

Harnessing resources declared in a namespace

The types of resources which can be declared within a namespace are:

Type of resource	C# keyword
Namespace	namespace
Class	class
Interface	interface
Structure	struct
Enumeration	enum
Delegate Type	delegate

In a lesser way, we can also consider comments to constitute one type of resource with the main characteristic being that they will be discarded by the compiler.

To use a resource defined in the namespace B, the namespace must be declared in the beginning of the source file with the `using` keyword. For example:

Example 9-1
```
using B;
namespace A{
    class Program{
        static void Main() {}
        ClassFoo f; // Here, you can use the ClassFoo class.
    }
}
namespace B{
    using A;
    class ClassFoo{Program p;} // Here, you can use the Program class.
}
```

All resources declared within a namespace can be accessible from the code contained within the same namespace. This also includes code which belongs in the same namespace but is located in a different source file or assembly.

Note that the use of the `using` keyword is a simple commodity for the C# compiler to allow the proper association between resources and their fully qualified names without their namespace. The equivalent keyword in Java and VB.NET is `Imports/imports`. In either case, this directive does not cause anything to be physically imported or moved.

You can also take advantage of the `using` keyword to define a *namespace alias*. In general, this allows you to avoid having to continuously type in complex namespaces. For example:

```
using SysWinForm = System.Windows.Forms;
```

Of course, you will need to be aware that in this particular case, you will be obligated to use the alias before any identifier that is a member of the namespace. This is however not the case when there are no aliases and no ambiguity in regards to which namespace an identifier belongs to.

Finally, take note that C# does not expose a syntax equivalent to the following Java construct:

```
using Foo.*;
```

Structure of a C# project

The source code for a C# project is spread across one or multiple text files with a .cs extension. A project is defined as the sum of all the C# source files required by the compiler to construct an assembly. The organization of a C# project can be summarized by Figure 9-1:

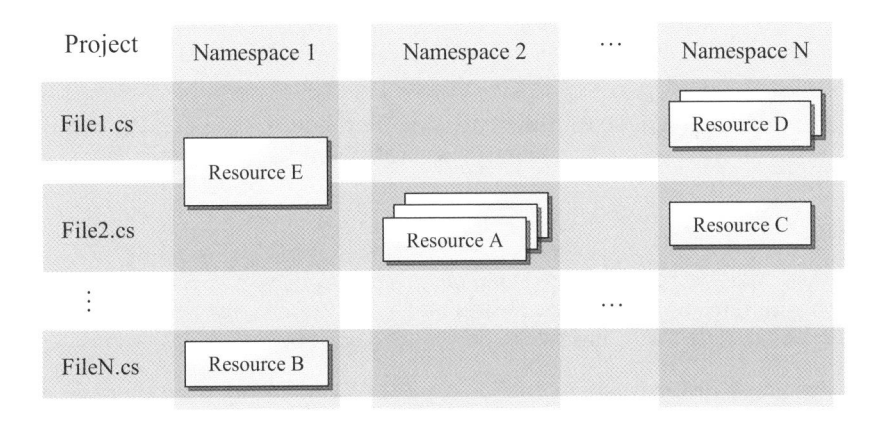

Figure 9-1 : Structural elements of a C# project

Taking into consideration the following points:

- The same namespace can be found across multiple files.
- Resources located outside of any namespace are considered part of the anonymous and global namespace.
- As demonstrated with resource E, in version 2.0 of C#, a class, structure or interface can now be declared across multiple files within a project. Of course, this applies as long as the declaration is within the same namespace.

Organizing your namespaces and your assemblies

A good coding practice is to name your assemblies with the root namespace it contains as its filename. *Microsoft* applies this rule when naming their standard system assemblies. This makes the organization of all these base classes immediately apparent to the reader: System.dll, System.Drawing.dll, System.Drawing.Design.dll, System.Runtime.Remoting.dll, System.Security.dll, etc.

Compilation Steps

C++ › C#: Note that the linking step found in C++ does not exist with C#. In fact, the compiler does not make use of intermediate .obj files.

However, the standard preprocessing and compilation steps are still present in C#. With C#, many of the C++ style preprocessing directives went away and a few new ones have been added.

C#: The compilation process takes source files written in C# and constructs an assembly from them. Details about assemblies can be found in chapter Assembly, module, IL language. The compiling process is handled by the `csc.exe` compiler and is described later on. This compiler can be executed directly from the command line or from the *Visual Studio* environment. Compiler parameters can also be defined either through command line arguments of from the development environment in the project properties.

There are two main steps to the compilation process:

- *Preprocessing* of source code files: this step generates new source files based on the preprocessor directives which can be inlined in the source code file of defined through compiler options. We'll cover the preprocessor directives a little later.
- *Compilation* of files resulting from preprocessing which results in either:
- An assembly contained in a file with a `.exe` or `.dll` extension,
- A module contained in a file with the extension `.netmodule`. Keep in mind that the *Visual Studio* environment does not know how to manage modules.

The preprocessor

C++ › C#: With C#, the `#define` preprocessor directive cannot be used to define a constant substitution. This directive can only be used to modify the source code with the use of the `#if #elif #else` and `#endif` directives.

The following predefined constants (`__LINE__` , `__FILE__`, `__DATE__`...) do not exist anymore. In addition, macros with parameters are also gone.

Note that *Visual Studio* will highlight any obsolete preprocessor code that will not be taken into account during compilation.

Because of the source code file organization with C#, the famous `#include` directive has been removed as well as the `#` and `##` string manipulation preprocessor directives.

A new `#warning` has been added to C# and is analogous to the `#error` directive. The C# language also defines the following new directives: `#line #region` and `#endregion` which we will discuss later.

C#: Source file compilation is always preceded with a file manipulation phase which is accomplished by the preprocessor. These manipulations only affect the text content of the source file and do not accomplish any compilation on the file. Note that all *preprocessor directives* are prefixed with the # character.

The preprocessor recognizes the following directives:

```
#define    #undef    #if      #elif    #else     #endif
#error     #warning  #line    #region  #endregion
#pragma warning disable       #pragma warning restore
```

Preprocessor symbols and conditional compilation

Using the `#define` directive, you can define an entity which can be used by the preprocessor to modify the source code based on the presence of this entity. This is accomplished using the `#if #elif #else` and `#endif` directives:

Example 9-2

```
#define MACRO1
using System;
public class Program {
   public static void Main() {
#if (MACRO1)
      Console.WriteLine("MACRO1 is defined.");
#elif (MACRO2)
      Console.WriteLine("MACRO2 is defined and MACRO1 is not defined.");
#else
      Console.WriteLine("MACRO2 and MACRO1 are both not defined.");
#endif
   }
}
```

As you can see, the *Visual Studio* environment grays out the lines of code which will not be accounted for during compilation However, note that symbolic constants must be defined before the use of the using directive.

Symbolic constants can also be defined through the command line compiler. For example:

```
>csc.exe prepross.cs /define:MACRO2
```

The #undef directive can be used in your code to undefine a previously defined constant. For example:

Example 9-3

```
#define MACRO1
#undef MACRO1
using System;
public class Program {
   public static void Main() {
#if (MACRO1)
      Console.WriteLine("MACRO1 is defined.");
#elif (MACRO2)
      Console.WriteLine("MACRO2 is defined and MACRO1 is not defined.");
#else
      Console.WriteLine("MACRO2 and MACRO1 are both not defined.");
#endif
   }
}
```

Preprocessor symbols and the Conditional attribute

There is an elegant (although restrictive) alternative to the use of #if #elif #else and #endif. This alternative is called ConditionalAttribute which allows the definition of a method based on the value of a symbolic constant. The advantage of this approach is that you do not need to go and comment all the calls to your method when the constant is not defined. The disadvantage however is that a few special constraints apply to the method. For example, the method must have a return type of void. A more complete list of constraints can be found in the article **The Conditional Attribute** on **MSDN**. Here is a usage example for the ConditionalAttribute attribute:

Example 9-4

```
//#define __TRACE__
class Program {
   [System.Diagnostics.Conditional("__TRACE__")]
   public static void Trace(string s) {
      System.Console.WriteLine(s);
   }
   static void Main() {
      Trace("Hello");
      System.Console.WriteLine("Bye");
   }
}
```

This code will display the following if the __TRACE__ constant is not defined.

```
Bye
```

And will display the following when __TRACE__ is defined.

```
Hello
Bye
```

The #error and #warning directives

The #error directive can be used to prevent constant definition conflicts during the compilation process by causing the compiler to generate an error on demand.

The following sample code will not compile and will display the following message: `MACRO1 and MACRO2 cannot be defined at the same time`

Example 9-5

```
#define MACRO1
#define MACRO1
#define MACRO2
#if MACRO1 && MACRO2
#error MACRO1 and MACRO2 cannot be defined at the same time
#endif
public class Program {
   public static void Main() {
#if (MACRO1)
      Console.WriteLine("MACRO1 is defined.");
#elif (MACRO2)
      Console.WriteLine("MACRO2 is defined and MACRO1 is not defined.");
#else
      Console.WriteLine("MACRO2 and MACRO1 are both not defined.");
#endif

   }
}
```

The #warning directive works in the same way except that it will not terminate the compilation process but will only generate a warning message.

The #pragma warning disable and restore directives

The `#pragma warning disable` and `#pragma warning restore` directives allow you deactivate the generation of certain warning messages by the C# compiler. The following example illustrates their use:

Example 9-6
```
class Program {
   static void Main() {
#pragma warning disable 105
   // Disable the warning CS0105 inside this bloc.
#pragma warning restore 105

#pragma warning disable
   // Disable all kinds of warnings inside this bloc.
#pragma warning restore

#pragma warning disable 105, 251
   // Disable the warning CS0105 and CS0251 inside this bloc.
#pragma warning restore 105
   // Disable only the warning CS0251 inside this bloc.
#pragma warning restore
   // Enable all kinds of warnings inside this bloc.

#pragma warning disable
   // Disable all kinds of warnings until the end of this file.
   }
}
```

The #line directive

The `#line` directive allows the developer to modify the line number (and even the filename) where an error or warning generated by the compiler will appear to come from. The example below will cause the compilation errors to appear as they are coming from line 1 in the file method Main():

Example 9-7
```
class Program {
   public static void Main() {
      #line 1 "Method Main()"
      int i == 0;   // <- ERROR : Not allowed to use the operator '=='
                    //           in this context!
   }
}
```

You must be careful when using this directive as it can have a negative effect on the development environment. Since you are changing file and line references, *Visual Studio* may not be able to locate the correct source of compilation errors especially if the new reference points to a non existent file or line.

The #region and #endregion directives

The `#region` and `#endregion` directives are practical as they allow you to stack/unstack with a click of a mouse on a specific segment of source code. This feature is used in both the *Visual Studio* IDE and *SharpDevelop*. Figure 9-2 illustrates this feature.

```
□class Program {
     static void Main(string[] args) {
         #region Code of method Main
         int j = 0;
         for ( int i = 0 ; i < 10 ; i++ )
             j += i;
         System.Console.Read();
         #endregion
     }
}

□class Program {
     static void Main(string[] args) {
         Code of method Main
     }
}
```

Figure 9-2: Illustration of the effect of the #region and #endregion directives

`#endregion` can optionally be used to end the text defined by the `#region` directive. It is also possible to embed such directives.

The csc.exe compiler

The `csc.exe` compiler can be invoked either directly from the command line, the *Visual Studio* environment or by compilation scripting engines such as *MSBuild* or *NAnt*. Compilation options are defined either through the command line or through the development environment.

Figure 9-3 illustrates the possible inputs and output files possible for `csc.exe`. Only a single file will be generated per compilation:

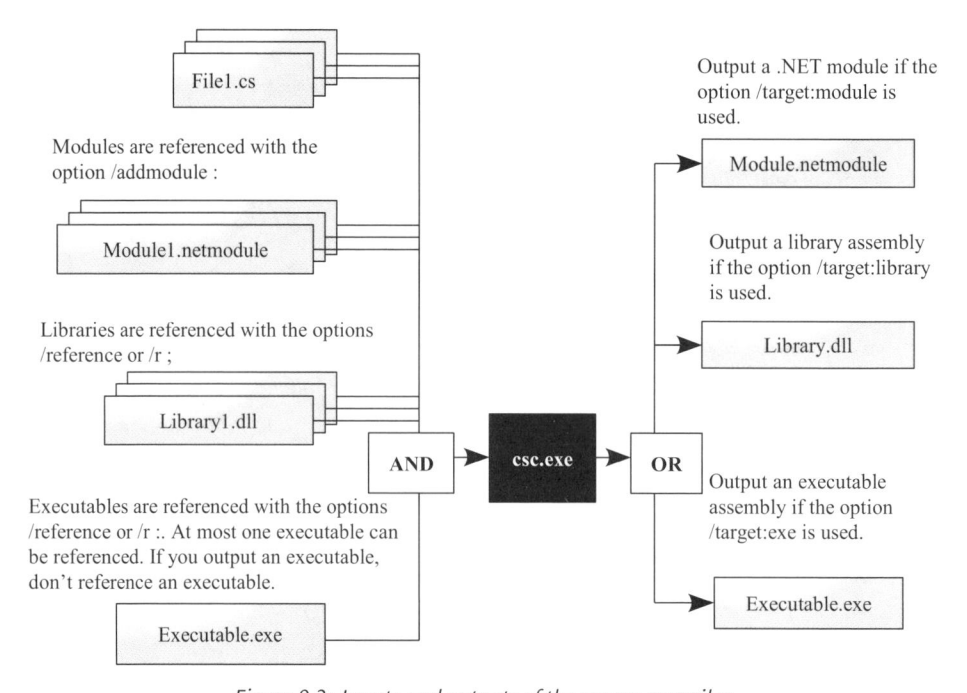

Figure 9-3: Inputs and outputs of the csc.exe compiler

Let us present some the compilation options through the use of a few examples:

- Compile `file.cs` and produce `file.exe` (note that to generate an executable, you need at least one static method named `Main()` within at least once class).

  ```
  >csc.exe file.cs
  ```

- Compile `file.cs` and produce `file.dll` (a static method named `Main()` is not required).

  ```
  >csc.exe /target:library file.cs
  ```

- Compile `file.cs` and produce `prog.exe`. The entry point function, `Main()`, belongs to the class `Prog` that is part of the `Namespace001` namespace.

  ```
  >csc.exe /out:prog.exe /main:Namespace001.Prog file.cs
  ```

- Compile all files in the current directory with a `.cs` extension with optimizations enabled. Also define the `MACRO1` and generate an executable named `prog.exe`.

  ```
  >csc.exe /out:prog.exe /define:MACRO1 /optimize *.cs
  ```

- Compile a debugging version of all `.cs` files in the current directory while not producing any warning message and generating `mod.netmodule` as an output file.

  ```
  >csc.exe /target:module /out:mod.netmodule /warn:0 /debug *.cs
  ```

- Compile all C# files in the current directory while taking in consideration the reference to the assemblies defined in the manifest for the files `lib1.dll` and `lib2.dll`.

  The `mod.netmodule` module will be part of the assembly for which the generated program manifest will be contained in `prog.exe`.

  For the compilation, the files `lib1.dll` and `lib2.dll` can be located either in the current directory or in the specified path, which is `C:\`.

  ```
  >csc.exe /lib:c:\ /r:lib1.dll;lib2.dll /addmodule:mod.netmodule /out:prog.exe
  file.cs
  ```

So far, we have demonstrated the following options:

Option	Description
/target /t	Specify the format for the compilation output. The format can be: /target:library A library (`.dll` extension) /target:module A module (`.netmodule` extension) /target:exe A console based executable (`.exe` extension). This is the default option if `target` is not specified. /target:winexe An executable running within a window (*Windows Form* type). The file extension will also be `.exe`.
/out	Specifies the output filename to be generated by the compiler.
/main /m	Specifies the class containing the entry point function `Main()`. Keep in mind that this class name must be fully qualified with the proper namespace and can only be used if you are generating an executable.
/define /d	Defines a symbolic constant.
/optimise /o	Enables code optimization (compatible with the `debug` option).
/warn /w	Specifies the warning output level which can be between 0 (no warnings) to 4 (all warnings).

266 Chapter 9 - Fundamental Concepts of the Language

Option	Description
/debug	Tells the compiler to generate debugging information which will be contained in a file of the same name as the output but with a pdb extension (*program database*). (Compatible with the optimise option).
/addmodule	References the modules uses by the compilation output (an assembly or a module). Remember that during execution, all modules of an assembly must be located in the same directory as the assembly itself.
/reference /r	Reference the assemblies (executables or libraries) used by the compiler output. You can use resources from a referenced assembly in the referencing code. In this case, the referenced assembly will be loaded when any of its resources is first used. If the compiler output is an executable, you may not reference another executable. If the compiler output is not an executable, you may only reference (at most) one executable.
/lib	Specifies the directories where the compiler will search for files referenced by the /reference or /r options. Directories will be searched in the following order: • In the current directory; • In the CLR directory; • In the directory specified by /lib ; • In the directories specified by the LIB environment variable.
/resource /linkresource	Adds resources to the assembly. The use of this option is detailed at page 30.
/unsafe	Indicates that the assembly may contain unsafe code which cannot be verified by the CLR (see page 417).
/doc	This option allows the creation and an XML file containing documentation based on information within the source code comments in the /// form. You can find an example of this later in this chapter.
/help /?	Displays the compiler help.

About thirty compiler options are available. We have presented to you only the most common and practical ones. The article **C# Compiler Options Listed by Category** on **MSDN** supplies a complete description of all compiler options.

All of these options are also available from the project properties page within the Visual Studio development environment.

The aliases

Creating an alias on namespaces and types

The using keyword can be used to define an *alias* for a namespace or type. The scope of an alias is limited to the current file if it is defined outside of any namespace. Other wise, the scope of the alias is limited to the intersection of the current block and the namespace in which the alias is defined.

Example 9-8
```
//Define the alias 'C' toward the 'System.Console' type.
using C = System.Console;
class Program{
   static void Main(){
      C.WriteLine("Hello 1");
   }
}
```

Namespaces alias qualifiers

There may be conflicts between a namespace and an alias. The following three assemblies illustrate this case:

The aliases 267

Example 9-9 *Code of Asm1.dll*
```
namespace Foo.IO{ public class Stream{} }
```

Example 9-10 *Code of Asm2.dll*
```
namespace Custom.IO{ public class Stream{} }
```

Example 9-11 *Code of Program.exe (which references Asm1.dll and Asm2.dll)*
```
using FooIO = Foo.IO;
using CusIO = Custom.IO;
class Program{
   static void Main(){
      FooIO.Stream stream1 = new FooIO.Stream();
      CusIO.Stream stream2 = new CusIO.Stream();
   }
}
```

With the use of the `FooIO` and `CusIO` aliases, you can use both `Stream` types in `Program.exe` without having to rewrite the namespaces to avoid any conflicts. However, the program will fail to compile if you modify the code for `Asm2.dll` as follows:

Example 9-12 *Code of Asm2.dll*
```
namespace Custom.IO{ public class Stream{} }
namespace FooIO{ public class Stream{} }
```

In fact, the compiler will be unable to distinguish if the `FooIO.Stream` type `FooIO.Stream` defined in `Asm2.dll` or if the `FooIO.Stream` alias of the `Foo.IO.Stream` type in `Asm1.dll` is to be used.

To avoid that the evolution of a library prevents your code from compiling you may need to use an *alias namespace qualifier* `::`. The use of the qualifier to the left of a type lets the compiler know that you are deferring to an alias. In our example, `Program.exe` must be modified as follows:

Example 9-13 *Code of Program.exe (which references Asm1.dll and Asm2.dll)*
```
using FooIO = Foo.IO;
using CusIO = Custom.IO;
class Program {
   static void Main(){
      FooIO::Stream stream1 = new FooIO::Stream();
      CusIO.Stream stream2 = new CusIO.Stream();
   }
}
```

The namespace alias qualifier technique is efficient since the scope of an alias is limited to the file in which it is defined. A change in an external assembly cannot introduce a sudden compiler error.

Global qualifiers

In certain large projects, it is possible that you will encounter a conflict between a namespace and the name of a resource. The following program will fail to compile:

Example 9-14
```
using System;
class Program {
   class System { }
   const int Console = 691;
```

Example 9-14
```
    static void Main() {
       // KO : The compiler attemps to acces Program.Console.
       Console.WriteLine("Hello 1");
       // KO : The compiler attemps to acces Program.System.
       Console.WriteLine("Hello 2");
    }
}
```

C#2 introduces the concept of a global qualifier that, when placed in front of a namespace alias qualifier, tells the compiler that we wish to use a namespace. The previous example can be rewritten as follows:

Example 9-15
```
using System;
class Program{
   class System { }
   const int Console = 691;
   static void Main(){
      global::System.Console.WriteLine("Hello 1");
      global::System.Console.WriteLine("Hello 2");
   }
}
```

Extern aliases

Extern aliases are used to allow you simultaneously use two types with the same name within the same namespace but that are declared in separate assemblies. This situation can occur if you must use two versions of the same assembly within the same program. The syntax for `extern` aliases is illustrated in the following example:

Example 9-16   *Code of Asm1.dll*
```
namespace FooIO{ public class Stream{} }
```

Example 9-17   *Code of Asm2.dll*
```
namespace FooIO{ public class Stream{} }
```

Example 9-18   *Code of Program.exe (which references Asm1.dll and Asm2.dll)*
```
extern alias AliasAsm1;
extern alias AliasAsm2;
class Program{
   static void Main(){
      AliasAsm1::FooIO.Stream stream1 = new AliasAsm1::FooIO.Stream();
      AliasAsm2::FooIO.Stream stream2 = new AliasAsm2::FooIO.Stream();
   }
}
```

You must then compile `Program.exe` like this:
```
>csc.exe /r:AliasAsm1=Asm1.dll /r:AliasAsm2=Asm2.dll Program.cs
```

You can also specify external aliases within *Visual Studio* through the `Aliases` property in the reference properties for libraries. You will notice that an assembly reference can support multiple aliases.

Finally, it is worth mentioning that the best way to use these qualifiers and aliases is to not have to use them in the first place by trying to avoid naming conflicts in your program. Being an advanced featured of C#2, most developers will not have mastered their use, making code difficult to comprehend.

Comments and automatic documentation

C++ › C#: Comments in C# and C++ are declared the same way. However, C# accepts a new type of comments destined to the documentation of your code. These new comments are declared using ///.

Comments

C#: There are three ways to add comments to a C# source file:

- Text placed between /* and */ is commented. Such a comment can spawn multiple lines of code.
- If a line contains a // marker then the text that follows on this line is commented.
- If a line contains the /// marker then the text that follows on this line is commented. In addition, this text will be part of automatically generated documentation as we will discuss a little later.

A comment using /*...*/ cannot be embedded within another /*...*/ comment. On the flipside, a comment of type // or /// can be embedded within a comment of type /*...*/.

Consequently, a good practice is to use comments of type // or /// to comment the code and to use /*...*/ to deactivate a region of code.

Using the tasks list of Visual Studio

Quite often as a developer, you will need to postpone writing a portion of code. Under *Visual Studio*, if a comment of // or /*...*/ type starts with one of the words **TODO, HACK** or **UNDONE** it will be automatically added to the list of tasks. To access this functionality, you must select *View › task list* in the menu and then select *Comments* in the combo box above the task list.

Automatic documentation

C# gives you the option to create a document based on the comments in your source code which are marked with ///. This feature is interesting for many reasons:

- As soon as a project reaches a certain size, simple code comments are not sufficient to give an overall view of the project. At this point, you will need documentation associated with the project.
- Code documentation can be a tedious and labor intensive task. Experience shows that with time many developers tend to neglect the maintenance of the project's documentation. Only big development houses who can afford a dedicated team to documentation can manage to properly keep documentation up to date.
- Developers are quite often the best people to document their own code.

The fact that technical documentation of a project is a task parallel to the development itself implies the fact that the documentation will inevitably get out of date. The possibility of automatically generating documentation based on your source code solves this problem since the task of documenting a project becomes integrated to the development process. Practically, as soon as a developer adds a new class or method, he creates the associated documentation at the same location and at the same time.

The automated documentation generation takes place in two steps:

- We must first extract and classify the information defined with /// comments in your source code. This information is then stored in an XML file. The comments contain XML markers which will be moved directly into the generated XML document. Note that *Visual Studio 2005* will help you with the creation of documentation markers through intellisense. We must also mention that the comments generating the automatic documentation will also automatically find their way to the *tooltips* in *Visual Studio* relating to the commented entities.
- Apply a style sheet to the XML file in order to obtain a readable presentation of the documentation. This style sheet is essentially a XSLT transformation which will yield a sequence of HTML files.

Figure 9-4 resumes this process:

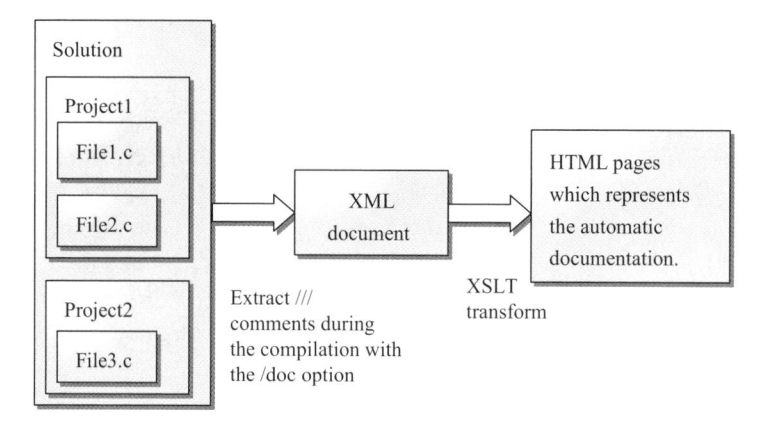

Figure 9-4: Automatic build process of documentation

Let's illustrate this in more details with an example. Look at the following C# source file...

Example 9-19

```
namespace MyNamespace {
    /// <summary>
    /// Here is my class !
    /// </summary>
    class MyClass {
        /// <summary>
        /// The entry point of the application.
        /// </summary>
        static void Main() {}
        /// <summary>
        /// The f(int) function.
        /// </summary>
        /// <param name="i">An integer!!</param>
        static void f(int i){}
    }
}
```

...produces the following XML file:

```xml
<?xml version="1.0"?>
<doc>
    <assembly>
        <name>AutomaticDocTest</name>
    </assembly>
    <members>
        <member name="T:MyNamespace.MyClass">
            <summary>
            Here is my class !
            </summary>
        </member>
        <member name="M:MyNamespace.MyClass.Main(System.String[])">
            <summary>
            The entry point of the application !
            </summary>
        </member>
        <member name="M:MyNamespace.MyClass.f">
            <summary>
            The f(int) function.
            </summary>
            <param name="i">An integer!!</param>
        </member>
    </members>
</doc>
```

Note the presence of the <summary> and <param> markers both in the C# code and the XML file. There is two ways to generate this XML file:

- You can use the /doc option of the csc.exe C# compiler:

```
>csc.exe MyFile.cs /doc:MyFileDoc.XML
```

- You can also specify in the *Visual Studio* project properties that you wish an XML documentation file to be generated. For this, you must specify the name of the XML file in the option *Xml documentation file* of the *Build* project *Properties*.

From the XML file, you can apply a style sheet to produce the final documentation in the format of your choice. *Visual Studio 2003* included a tool to produce such HTML documentation from XML files. With *Visual Studio 2005*, we recommend you use tools specialized for this task, especially NDoc which is a great freeware that you can download online.

Identifiers

Identifiers are names chosen by the developer to name resources such as namespaces, methods, classes and in fact anything which can be named in your source code.

Identifiers must obey the following rules:

- The first character must be a letter (A to Z or a to z or an accentuated UNICODE letter), the underline character _ or the @ character. The first character cannot be a number.
- The other characters are from the same set as the first character (except @) and can also contain numbers (0 to 9).
- An identifier cannot contain more than 255 characters.
- An identifier cannot be a C# keyword

Note that the C# compiler is case sensitive and will treat upper and lower case differently.

Naming conventions CamelCase and PascalCase

The *PascalCase* naming convention encourages developers to name their identifiers with lower case characters except for the first character of each word. For example: `MyVariable`, `AFunction`, `APascalCaseIdentifier`.

The *CamelCase* naming convention is similar to *PascalCase* with the exception that the first character is always lower case. For example: `myVariable`, `aFunction`, `aCamelCaseIdentifier`. The name *CamelCase* originates from the 'bumps' caused by the uppercase characters reminding us a camel. There is no relationship with the *Camel* programming language.

With C#, *Microsoft* recommends the use of the *PascalCase* naming convention for identifiers representing the name of methods, events, fields, properties, constants, namespaces, classes, structures, delegates, enumerations, interfaces and attributes.

The *CamelCase* convention must be applied to the name of variables and method parameters.

It is also recommended to prefix private instance members with `m_`, to prefix private static members with `s_` and to begin interface names with an uppercase `I`.

Control Structures

C++ › C#: In regards to control structures, there is little difference between C++ and C#. The use of the `switch` has changed a little. In addition, the loop instruction `foreach`, has been added to traverse array elements

C#: A control structure is an element of a program which is intended to change the regular course of execution. Remember that the regular execution consists of executing instructions one after the other. Control structures can generally be divided into three categories:

- *Conditionals*, execute (or not) a block of code based on a condition which is generally based on the state of variables or objects.
- *Loops*, repeat the execution of a block of code. The programmer has control as to how many iteration the loops may go through and can terminate the loop when a certain condition is met.
- *Branches* or *jumps*, allows you to redirect the execution to a specific location in your code. However, this type of control structure should generally be avoided as it impairs code readability and maintenance. In addition, it has been demonstrated that we can always work without jumps in C#.

Method calls also modify the flow of execution. They could be compared to a jump or branch but a fundamental difference is that the execution will return to the calling point once the method is finished. Because of this, we generally do not classify method calls as a type of control structure.

Conditionals (if/else, ?:, switch)

C++ › C#: In C#, it is not possible to write `if(i=1)` instead of `if(i==1)`. The assignment operator does not return a boolean. This mistake is dangerous in C++ as it cannot be detected by the compiler but can yield an incorrect execution.

The switch instruction has also gone through a few changes which we will cover later.

No other significant changes are notable for the `if`/`else` between C/C++ and C#.

Control Structures

Use of if/else

C#: A conditional presents itself under the following form:

```
if ( expression which produces a boolean )
    Block to execute if the expression produces true.
else
    Block to execute if the expression produces false.
```

The '*else block*' is optional. An instruction block can either be a single instruction or multiple instructions enclosed within curly braces. For example:

```
if (expression which produces a boolean)
    i = j*5;
else{
    // Beginning of the block to execute if the expression produces false.
    i = j*2;
    j++;
} // Ending of the block to execute if the expression produces false.
```

For new readers, you will have to pay attention when reading the code in case there is a single instruction. You can use curly braces even when there is a single instruction. In fact, it is a good practice to increase code readability to always use curly braces.

A condition is considered as an instruction, thus it is possible to embed several conditions:

```
if( expression1 which produces a boolean )
    if( expression2 which produces a boolean )
        Block to execute if both expressions produce true.
    else
        Block to execute if expression1=true and expression2=false.
else
    if( expression3 which produces a boolean )
        Block to execute if expression1=false and expression3=true.
```

This approach impedes to the quality of your code. In addition, embedded conditionals come from poor design.

Expressions which evaluates to a boolean

Here are a few examples of expressions which return a boolean:

```
bool b = true; int  i = 5; int  j = 8;
if( b )                     // if b equals to true then...
if( !b )                    // if b equals to  false then...
if( b == true )             // if b equals to true then...
if( b == false)             // if b equals to false then...
if( i )                     // if i not equals to 0 then...
if( !i )                    // if i equals to 0 then...
if( i == 4)                 // if i equals to 4 then...
if( i != 4 )                // if i not equals to 4 then...
if( i < 4)                  // if i strictly lower than 4 then...
if( i <= 4)                 // if i lower or equals to 4 then...
if( i < 4 && j > 6)         // if i strictly lower than 4 and j strictly
                            // greather than 6 then...
if( i >= 4 && i<= 6)        // if i inside the closed interval [4,6] then...
if( i < 4 || j > 6)         // if i strictly lower than 4 or j strictly
                            // greather than 6 then...
if( i < 4 || i > 6)         // if i outside of the closed interval [4,6] then...
if( i != 4 || b )           // if i not equals to 4 or b equals true then...
```

The ternary operator ?:

Take a look at the following operator:

```
condition ? Val if condition is true : Val returned if condition is false;
```

We are talking about the ternary operator ?:. In fact, it is the only operator which takes in three operands.

Here are a few examples of its use:

```
bool b = true ;
int  i = 5 ;
int  j = 8;

// k1 = i if b is true, else k = j
int k1 = b  ?  i  :  j;

// k2 = 6 if i is not equals to j, else k2 = 7
int k2 = (i!=j) ?  6 : 7;

// s="bonjour" if i is strictly lower than j, else s="hello"
string s = i<j ? "bonjour" : "hello";

// k3 = i*2 if i is greater or equal to j, else k3 = i*3
int k3 = i>=j ? i*2 : i*3;
```

The switch instruction

C++ › C#: C/C++ developers BEWARE! There are a few subtle modifications to the use of the `switch` instruction:

- You can always 'switch' on a variable of integer, boolean or enumeration types. The new feature in C# is that you can now also 'switch' on a string.
- The continuation to the next `case` statement is not done automatically so the `break` keyword is mandatory. Continuation to the next `case` statement happens automatically only when there are no instructions to the previous statement.
- You can now declare variables within a `case`, statement even if it is not enclosed by curly braces.

C#: As with the `if/else` keywords, the `switch` keyword allow you to modify the flow of execution of a program based on a variable. However, the use of the `switch` instruction is adapted to be used with discreet values such as integer, enumerations and strings. The syntax of `switch` allows you to treat multiple cases more easily than with the use of `if/else` instructions. Here is an example:

Example 9-20

```
class Program {
   static void Main() {
      int i = 6;
      switch (i){
         case 1:
            System.Console.WriteLine("i equals 1");
            break;
         case 6:
            System.Console.WriteLine("i equals 6");
            break;
         default:
            System.Console.WriteLine("i is not equals to 1 or 6");
```

Example 9-20
```
            break;
        }
    }
}
```

Two new keywords appear in this example in addition to `switch` and `case`:

- break: When execution encounters the `break` instruction, the execution goes straight to the end of the `switch` statement. Note that if a block of code within a `switch` statement contains at least a single instruction, it must be terminated with the use of a `break`, `goto` or `return` instruction. Otherwise, the compiler will generate an error.
- default: Execution will go to the block of code defined with the `default` instruction if the value of the expression cannot be matched to any of the case statements. Note that the `default` block does not necessarily need to be in the last position although most developers prefer to put it at the end.

You can also execute the same block of code for multiple values. For example:

Example 9-21
```
class Program {
   static void Main() {
      int i = 6;
      switch (i){
         case 1:
         case 3:
         case 6:
            System.Console.WriteLine("i equals 1 or 3 or 6");
            break;
         default:
            System.Console.WriteLine("i is not equals to 1, 3 or 6");
            break;
      }
   }
}
```

In this case, you must ensure that no instruction appears after `case 1:` or `case 3:`.

Finally, you can also use the `goto` instruction (which we will discuss a little later) but you are recommended not to use it. The following case illustrates how you can make your code difficult to understand with only a few lines:

Example 9-22
```
class Program {
   static void Main() {
      int i = 6; int j = 7;
      switch (i){
         case 1:
            System.Console.WriteLine("executing case 1");
            goto default;
         case 6:
            System.Console.WriteLine("executing case 6");
            if (j > 2) goto case 1;
            break;
         default:
            System.Console.WriteLine("executing default");
            break;
      }
   }
}
```

This program displays:

```
executing case 6
executing case 1
executing default
```

The types on which a `switch` statement can act are:

- The numerical types `sbyte`, `byte`, `short`, `ushort`, `int`, `uint`, `long` and `ulong`.
- Booleans of type `bool`.
- Enumerations.
- Character stings of type `string`. Note that in this case, if a `switch` instruction uses more than six `case` blocks, the C#2 compiler will make use of a hash table to reduce the number of string compares.

Loops (do, while, for, foreach)

C++ › C#: A new type of loop is present in C#, the `foreach` loops are specially adapted to traverse elements of arrays. However, we will go over all the aspects of using the `foreach` at page 469.

The three other types of loops in C/C++ `do/while`, `while` and `for` are used the same way in C#. This also applies to the `continue` and `break` keywords.

C#: We talk about loops when a block of instruction (between curly braces) or a single instruction is executed multiple times.

The while and do/while loops

With those two types of loops, the exit from the loop depends on a condition (similar to those seen in the previous section). For example:

while loop
```
int i=0;int j=8;
while( i < 6 && j > 9) {
    i++;j--;
}
```

do/while loop
```
int i=0;int j=8;
do {
    i++;j--;
}
while( i < 6 && j > 9)
```

The only difference between the two types of loops is shown in the previous example. The `do/while` loops execute at least one time the instruction block before evaluation the condition. With a `while` loop, the condition is evaluated before the execution of the block of code meaning that the execution if the code may not be executed at all depending on the condition.

The for loop

The `for` loops are used as follows:

```
for(Initialisation instructions (coma separated) ;
    Exit condition (exit if false) checked at the beginning of each loop ;
    Instructions to execute during each loop ending (coma separated) )
        Bloc to execute at each loop.
```

The condition is similar as to the conditions used in pervious sections. Here are a few examples:

```
for(int i = 1; i<=6 ; i++) ...
//---------------------------------------------------------------
int i = 3;int j=5;
for(; i<7&& j>1 ;i++ , j--)...
//---------------------------------------------------------------
for( int i =6 ; i<9 ; ) { ... i++;}
```

Control Structures

Variables declared within the initialization portion of the `for` loop must have a different name to variables outside of the loop. In addition those variables are only visible from within the scope of the loop.

The foreach loops

Loops of type `foreach` are specially adapted to the traversal of array or collection elements. Because of this, we will detail their use when we will discuss the use of arrays on page 469.

The break and continue instructions

Two instructions exist which can be used to modify the behavior of a loop (of type `while`, `do/while`, `for` or `foreach`).

- The `continue` instruction causes execution to proceed to the next iteration of the loop.
- The `break` instruction causes the execution to end the loop. This instruction is also used to terminate the current block of code within a `switch` statement.

In the case of embedded loops, these instructions will apply to the loop the closest to the instruction.

Example 9-23

```
class Program {
    static void Main() {
        for (int i = 0; i < 10; i++){
            System.Console.Write(i);
            if (i == 2) continue;
            System.Console.Write("C");
            if (i == 3) break;
            System.Console.Write("B");
        }
    }
}
```

This program displays the following:

```
0CB1CB23C
```

The use of the `break` and `continue` instructions has a tendency to make code less readable. The result from the previous code is less than obvious and thus these instructions should only be used when needed.

The `break` instruction can also be used to interrupt what we call an infinite loop. An infinite loop is a loop of type `for`, `do/while` and `while`, where the loop condition is always true. Here are a few examples of infinite loops:

```
for(;;) {...}
for(;true;) {...}
while(true) {...}
do{...}
while(true) {...}
```

Optimizing your loops

Because of the fact that the code contained within a loop is subject to multiple executions, it might be wise to try and optimize this code. Here are a few tips:

- If you notice that method calls within your loop takes many arguments, it may be more efficient to copy the code of the method inside your loop (this is called *inlining*). Note that at page 92, we will discuss how the JIT compiler of the CLR can sometimes do this optimization for you.

- If you are accessing a property of an object that you know will remain constant throughout the loop, it may be worth to cache this value into a local variable before your loop.
- Think of using the `StringBuilder` class rather than `String` to construct a character string within a loop.
- If you have the choice, use loops rather than recursion.
- If you must test multiple conditions within as the exit condition for your loop, take advantage of expression short circuiting by placing the most probably condition first.
- Although less practical, `for` loops are slightly more efficient than `foreach` loops.

When optimizing code, always attempt to quantify the gain from your optimizations. In fact, some optimizations may make the JIT compiler's life more difficult and end up being counter-productive.

The goto instruction

The `goto` branching instruction had its days of glory a long time ago. Today, the use of this instruction must be done in very specific cases. For example, the `goto` instruction can be a powerful tool within the source code of a compiler. Some praise its use within a *state machine*. But in this case, you are better off using a `switch` statement within an infinite loop.

The `goto` instruction forces the flow of execution to jump to the point defined by a particular label. This label and the `goto` must be located within the same method. In addition, the label must be visible to the `goto`, which does not necessarily mean that it must be located in the same block of code. For example, the following code will compile:

Example 9-24

```
class Program {
    static void Main() {
        int i = 0;
        goto label2;
    label1:
        i++;
        goto label3;
    label2:
        i--;
        goto label1;
    label3:
        System.Console.WriteLine(i);
    }
}
```

It is possible that the improper use of a `goto` will cause your code to use an uninitialized variable. The C# compiler will detect this and yield an error.

The Main() method

C++ › C#: As with C/C++, the entry point of an executable in C# is a method called `Main()`.

As with C/C++, the `Main()` method can return either an `int` or `void` and accept a string of characters containing the command line arguments to the executable. However, with C#, there is no longer a need to specify the length of this string.

One difference with C/C++ is that the command line argument string does not contain the name of the executable as a first argument but starts directly with the first argument.

Another difference with C/C++ is that the 'm' of `Main` is an uppercase letter and that the `Main` method must be a static member of a class and not a global function.

C#: Each assembly that can be directly executed (i.e. where the main module is an `.exe`) must contain at least one static `Main()` method in one of its classes. This method represents the *entry point to the program*, that is where the execution of the main thread of your .NET application will start once the application is initialized. Once this method returns, the process will be destroyed assuming there are not any foreground threads still executing. If the notion of threads and foreground threads are unknown to you, we will present them in more details in chapter 5.

An assembly can contain multiple `Main()` methods (each in different classes). When this case occurs, you will need to specify to the compiler which `Main()` method constitutes the entry point for the application. This can be done either with the `/main` command line option of the `csc.exe` compiler, or by changing the project property *Application > startup object* within *Visual Studio*. This feature makes it easy to debug a particular class within an application.

The `Main()` method must be static and its signature must follow the following rules:

- It must have a return type of `void` or `int`.
- It must accept an optional array or strings. The strings in the array representing the command line arguments to the application. The first string representing the first argument, the second string represents the second argument and so on.

Here are the possible definitions for the `Main()` method:

```
static void Main() {/*...*/}
static int Main() {/*...*/}
static void Main(string[] args) {/*...*/}
static int Main(string[] args) {/*...*/}
```

For example, the following program adds the numbers passed as arguments and displays the result. If no arguments are present, the program simply aborts:

Example 9-25

```
class Program {
   static void Main(string[] args) {
      if (args.Length == 0)
         System.Console.WriteLine("You didn't type any number to add.");
      else{
         long result = 0;
         foreach (string s in args)
            result += System.Int64.Parse(s);
         System.Console.WriteLine("Sum :{0}", result);
      }
   }
}
```

The information passed through the command line (as well as the environment variables) can also be accessed through the `string[] GetCommandLineArgs()` and `IDictionary GetEnvironmentVariables()` methods of the `System.Environment` class.

10

The .NET 2 type system from a C#2 point of view

C++ > C#: This chapter describes most of the big differences between C/C++ and C#.

C#: C# is a typed language, meaning that each object has one and only one type. This type if completely defined when the object is created, during execution. In C# each variable must be initialized or else the compiler will produce an error during its initialization.

The storage of objects in memory

The concepts of threads (i.e. execution units) and of process (i.e. tasks or addressing space) are required to understand this section, and more generally this chapter. These concepts are introduced at the beginning of chapter 5.

Allocating and deallocating objects

During the execution of a program, the reservation of a memory zone to contain the data relating to an object is called an *allocation*. The reverse operation of releasing this memory is called a *deallocation*. The size of this memory zone, specified in bytes, must be at least equal to the number of bytes required to store the state of the object. This number of bytes is fully defined by the implementation of the object.

At any time, a process can contain one or several threads. As an addressing space, the process contains all the memory zones allocated for all the objects of the program. As execution units, its threads can use objects.

Managed thread stack

Each Windows threads has a private memory zone that is named the stack. This memory zone is private in the sense that it should not be accessible by the other threads (although it is possible under certain special conditions). This memory zone is located in the addressing space of the process containing the thread. The thread uses the stack mainly for:

- storing the values of the arguments passed to the method which is currently being executed;
- storing the address of the native code to jump to when the method returns;
- storing objects (but not all of them).

Each thread has a privileged access to its stack. In fact, the machine instruction sets contain specialized instructions to access the stack. Also, the IL language contains several instructions dedicated to the management of the stack. Note that a stack is of a variable size and is generally bound by a maximal size in the order of MB. This limit can be fixed at thread creation time.

Managed heap

A process has generally one (but sometimes several) *heap*. It is a memory region contained in the addressing space of the process. This memory region is accessible by all the threads of the process. This means that contrarily to the stack of a thread, the heap is not specific to a particular thread. The heap is mainly used to store objects and as with stacks, its size can vary during the execution of a program. However, the maximal size of the heap is much larger than the size of the stack. In fact, it is rather uncommon that the proper execution of a program be limited by the maximum size of the heap.

Object storage: Managed thread stack vs. managed heap

A .NET object can then be stored either in the stack of a managed thread or in the managed heap. The notions of stacks and heaps must coexist as they each have their advantages:

- The advantage of the heap is that it can be much larger than a stack. In addition, it is accessible by all the threads of a process (although this is not always an advantage).
- The advantage of the stack is that the access to its data is quicker than to the heap. This gain is mostly due to IL instruction specialized for the access to the stack. This gain is also due to the fact that the access to the elements of the stack does not need to be synchronized.

It is thus a good idea to use the heap to store large object and to use the stack in order to store small objects. We will see that this is exactly the choice which was made by the designers of .NET.

Static allocation vs dynamic allocation

C++ › C#: A common point between C++ and C# is that objects can be allocated either on the stack of a thread (here we talk of a *static allocation*) either on the heap of the process (here we talk of a *dynamic allocation*). The difference between C++ and C# is in the way that allocation mode (static or dynamic) is chosen:

- In C++ the choice of the allocation mode of an object is left to the developer. A static allocation is used when the object is directly declared in the code (for example `int i=0;`). A dynamic allocation is used when the object is allocated using the `new` operator (for example `int * pi = new int(0);`).
- In C#, the choice of the allocation mode of an object is dependent on its implementation. In fact, we will see that there exist two kinds of types. The value types whose instances are statically allocated and the reference types whose instances are dynamically allocated.

Another important difference between C++ and C# is the responsibility of the deallocation of dynamically allocated objects. In C++ this responsibility falls on the developer while in C#, it falls on a software layer provided by the .NET runtime environment. This software layer is called the *garbage collector* and is the topic of the section at page 95. In both cases, this responsibility is heavy. Indeed, if dynamically allocated objects which are not used anymore are not regularly freed, the size of the heap will grow and will eventually cause problems. This type of situation is known as a *memory leak*.

The deallocation of statically allocated variables is in all cases the responsibility of the thread who owns the concerned stack. Remember mainly that **in C#, the responsibility of the developer is greatly reduced compared to C++**:

- He does not need to choose the type of allocation for its objects.
- He does not need to worry about the deallocation of its objects.

Reference types vs. Value types

C++ › C#: If you are a C++ programmer you might be confused by these notions of value/reference types. We will see that in C#, the new operator can be used for dynamic allocations but also for the static allocation of an object. A consequence is that we cannot provide the arguments of a constructor directly after the declaration of a variable. Remember that in C++, the use of the new operator is reserved for the dynamic allocations of a variable.

C#: The notion of value/reference types is fundamental, no matter which .NET language you use.

Each type in C# is either a *value type* or a *reference type*. Each object is then an instance of a value type or an instance of a reference type. An instance of a value type is *generally* allocated on the stack of a thread (static allocation) but might be stored on the heap in certain situations. An instance of a reference type is *always* allocated on the heap of the process (dynamic allocation).

We never directly manipulate reference type objects. We manipulate these objects through references. However, we always directly manipulate an object of a value type. Here is an example which illustrates this (we anticipate a little the notion of structures, which always define value types and the notion of class which always define reference types):

Example 10-1
```
// TypeVal is a value type because it's a structure.
struct TypeVal {
   public int m_i;
   public TypeVal( int i ) { m_i = i; }
}
// TypeRef is a reference type because it's a class.
class TypeRef {
   public int m_i;
   public TypeRef( int i ) { m_i = i; }
}
class Program {
   static void Main() {
      TypeVal v1 = new TypeVal(6); // Create an instance of TypeVal.
      TypeVal v2 = v1; // Here, a second instance of 'TypeVal' is
      // created and its field 'v2.i' is also equal to 6.
      // However, 'v1' and 'v2' are two different objects. We often
      // use the term 'variable' to name such instances of value type
      // stored on the stack of its creator thread.
      v2.m_i = 9;
      // Assert that 'v1.i' is equal to 6 and 'v2.i' is equal to 9.
      System.Diagnostics.Debug.Assert( v1.m_i == 6 && v2.m_i == 9 );

      TypeRef r1 = new TypeRef(6); // Create an instance of TypeRef.
      TypeRef r2 = r1; // Here, r2 si a second reference to the object
      // already referenced by r1. There is only one object and two
      // references.
      r2.m_i = 9;
      // Assert that both 'r1.i' and 'r2.i' are equal to 9.
      System.Diagnostics.Debug.Assert( r1.m_i == 9 && r2.m_i == 9 );
   }
}
```

We notice in the previous example that the new operator can be eventually used for the allocation of value type instance. However, such an instance is still statically allocated. In this case, the new operator only serves to communicate parameters to the constructor.

> Contrarily to C++, during a C# static allocation, we cannot provide constructor arguments without using the new operator. In C++, this was accepted by the compiler:
> MyType v1(6) ;
> While in C#, you must write:
> MyType v1 = new MyType(6) ;

In the case of a dynamic allocation, thus the allocation of an object of a reference type, the use of the new operator is mandatory (even if the concerned constructor does not need any arguments). We will detail shortly what are value and reference types. We can already mention that value types are the primitive types of C# (declared with the int, double, float... keywords), structures (declared using the struct keyword), enumerations (declared using the enum keyword) while reference types are classes (declared using the class keyword) and delegate types (which are special classes declared using the delegate keyword).

Instances of value types are not always stored on the stack. In fact, when a field on an instance of a class is of a value type, it is stored in the same location as the instance of the class that is on the heap. However, objects of a reference type are always stored on the heap. When a field of an instance of a structure is of a reference type, only the reference is stored in the same location as the instance of the structure (on the stack or on the heap depending on the case).

Understanding references

C++ › C#: The notion of references in C# is half way between the notion of pointers and references in C++. As with a C++ reference, a C# reference references an object, and the public members of the object are accessible using the '.' operator.

Contrarily to a C++ reference, and as with a C++ pointer, a C# reference can be null.

Contrarily to a C++ reference, and as with a C++ pointer, a C# reference can be modified. Meaning that for a given reference, the referenced object can be modified.

Contrarily to a C++ pointer, and as with a C++ reference, a C# reference does not give access to the physical space of the object (i.e to the address of the object).

C#: All classes are reference types and all reference types are a class or an interface. All classes inherit from the System.Object class that we will soon describe.

There can be a certain ambiguity between the *type*, *class* and *implementation* terms. The signification of the *type* term varies depending on the context. We talk of the *type of a reference* to indicate the class or interface which is the type of a reference. We talk of the *type of an object* to indicate its implementation. The implementation of an object designates the class or structure of which it is an instance. The *type* term is then more general and abstract than the *implementation* term which is itself more general than the *class* term.

The notion of class is a vast subject, which is the topic of the following chapter. We will here interest ourselves to the fact that the instances of classes are EXCLUSIVELY manipulated through references. Take a look at the following example:

Example 10-2

```
class Person {
   public int m_Age;
   public string m_Name;
   public Person( int age, string name ) { m_Age = age; m_Name = name; }
}
```

Example 10-2

```
class Program {
   static void Main() {
      Person ref1 = null;   // 'ref1' doesn't reference any object.
      Person ref2 = new Person(10, "Bart");
      Person ref3 = new Person(8, "Lisa");
      ref1 = ref2;          // 'ref1' references Bart.
      ref1.m_Age += 5;      // Bart gets 5 years older!
      ref1 = ref3;          // 'ref1' references Lisa.
      ref1.m_Age += 5;      // Lisa gets 5 years older!
      // Here, 'ref2.m_Age' is equal to 15. Bart is 15.
      // Here, 'ref3.m_Age' is equal to 13. Lisa is 13.
   }
}
```

A class is declared using the `class` keyword. First of all, understand that `ref1`, `ref2` and `ref3` are all three references to objects, instances of the `Person` class. In the beginning, `ref1` is initialized with the `null` keyword. This means that no object is referenced by `ref1`. At this stage, no members of `Person` can be used on `ref1`.

Two `Person` objects are then dynamically allocated on the heap since they are of a reference type. Let's call them `Bart` and `Lisa`. Contrarily to what we have seen for value types, in the case of a reference type, it is necessary to use the new operator to create `Bart` and `Lisa`. At this stage, we have two objects, `Bart` and `Lisa`, which instantiate the `Person` class. We also have three references, `ref1` which is null, `ref2` which references `Bart` and `ref3` which references `Lisa`. `ref1` is then set to reference `Bart` and `Bart` is aged by five years. `ref1` is then referenced to `Lisa` who is aged by five years also.

Finally, the `Bart` and `Lisa` objects have both been modified without using the `ref2` and `ref3` references. In addition, the `Bart` and `Lisa` objects are not directly manipulated. The syntax of C# only allows the manipulation of reference types through the use of references.

The brace at the end of the `Main()` method implies that the `Bart` and `Lisa` objects are not referenced (in fact, the `ref1`, `ref2` and `ref3` references do not exist anymore). `Bart` and `Lisa` will not be used anymore since they are not referenced anymore. Hence, these two objects are marked as inactive and will be destroyed by the garbage collector.

The Common Type System (CTS)

.NET types are not related to any programming language

An interesting aspect of the .NET platform is that the types are independent of the language in which the source code is written. This is possible because of a set of types which are common to all .NET languages. This set is named *CTS (Common Type System)*. The CTS is a specification which describes the characteristics of each type known by the CLR.

The existence of the CTS solves several well known problems from those who have developed modules written in different languages. For example, the strings of VB are represented by an instance of the BSTR type. In C++ a string is a pointer to an array of char. The consequence is that a module written in C++ used from a program written in VB must handle instances of BSTR and use conversion functions. This adds complexity to the programs and has a significant cost (even prohibitive if encoding formats such as ASCII or UNICODE are mixed).

CTS: The big picture

The CTS is mainly composed of value types, reference types and pointer types. Most of .NET languages give you the opportunity to define your own value types and reference types:

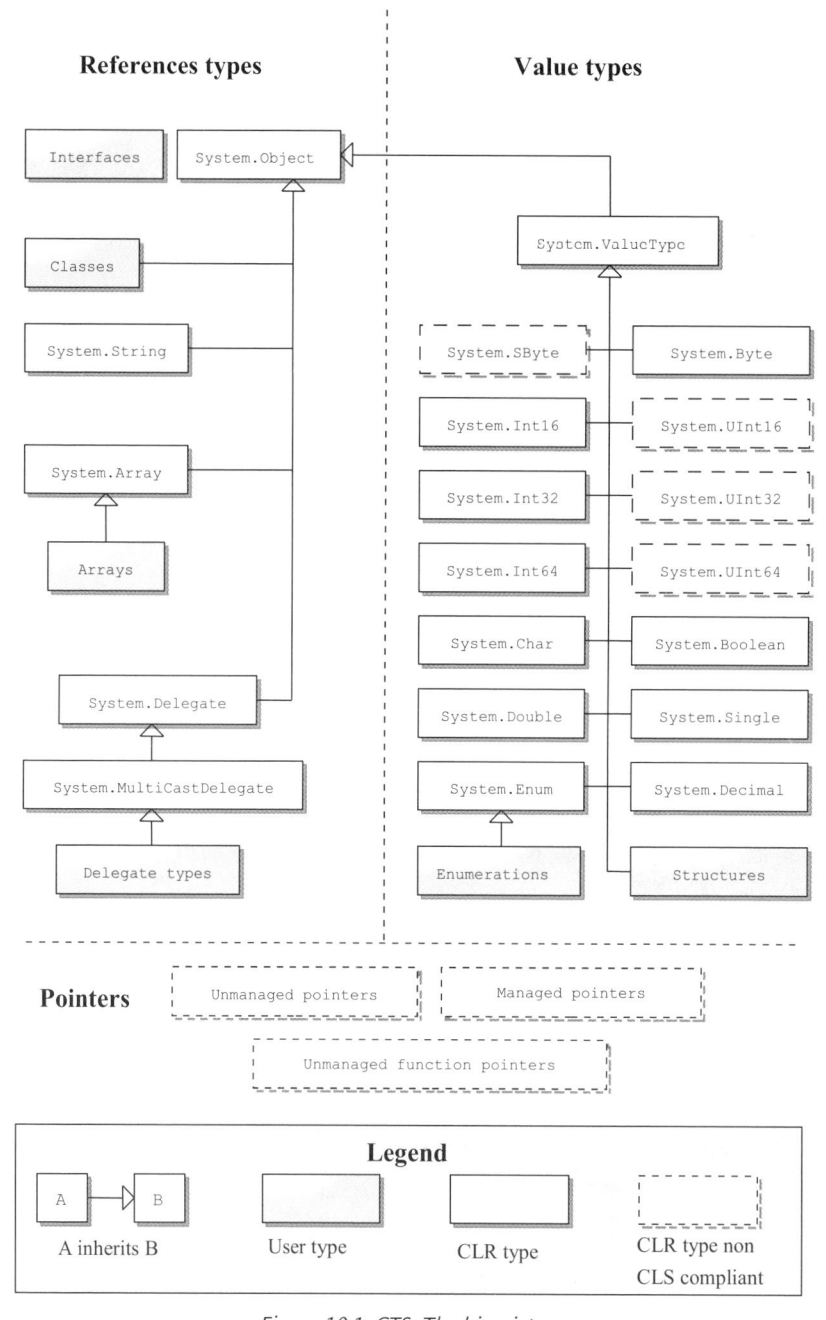

Figure 10-1: CTS: The big picture

The remainder of this chapter is dedicated to the study of the different type of the CTS that we can classify as follows:

- The *primitive types* (also called *elementary types*): These types represent integers, floating-point numbers, characters and booleans. They are value types and .NET languages generally define aliases to facilitate their use. Hence, the `System.Int16` type corresponds to the `short` alias in C# and to `Short` in VB.NET.
- The *enumerations*: These types are value types and are used to type a set of values.
- *Structures*: These types are value types. Structures and classes have similarities and differences.
- *Classes*: These types are reference types. Note that the type representing strings and the type representing arrays are respectively the `System.String` and `System.Array` (respectively described at page 308 and at page 475). Note that the use of the `Array` class takes advantage of a special syntax in C# and in VB.NET.
- The *delegate types*: These types are special classes whose instances are used to reference methods in the same spirit as C++ function pointers.
- *Pointers*: These types are special and can only be used in C# under certain conditions. We discuss this topic in the section at page 418.

The System.Object class

C++ > C#: In C#, all classes and all structures derive from the `Object` class. The methods of the `Object` class, which can be used by all classes and structures, offers object comparing, hashing and *RTTI* (*Run Time Type Information*) functionalities. The functionality the most commonly used is the possibility of redefining the `Object.ToString()` method which is supposed to return a string describing the object, a little like the << C++ operator in a data stream.

C#: The `object` keyword of the C# language is an alias towards `System.Object`. The big picture of the CTS shows that with the exception of interfaces and pointers, all .NET types automatically and implicitly inherit from the `Object` class. In regards to interfaces, we can always convert an object referenced by an interface into a reference of type `Object` because an interface is always implemented by a reference or a value type. Hence, the `Object` class plays an important role in the architecture of the .NET platform. Several standard methods accept their arguments as a reference typed by the `Object` class.

The `Object` class offers several methods. Each of these methods can thus be applied to all objects. However, it is logical to override some of the virtual methods to be able to use them. These virtual methods can be overridden within a class but also within a structure. The methods of the `Object` class are:

- `public Type GetType()`

  Returns the type of an object.

- `public virtual string ToString()`

  Returns a string which describes the object. The default behavior of this method is to return the name of the type, which is not what the developer needs most of the time. Here is an example of redefinition and use of this method:

Example 10-3
```
class Person { // The type 'Person' could be also a structure here.
   string m_Name;
   int m_Age;
   public Person(string name, int age) { m_Name = name; m_Age = age; }
   public override string ToString() {
      return "Name:" + m_Name + " Age:" + m_Age;
   }
}
class Program {
   static void Main() {
```

Example 10-3

```
        Person bart = new Person("Bart", 10);
        // The 'WriteLine()' method automatically call the
        // 'ToString()' method on the 'bart' object.
        System.Console.WriteLine( bart );
    }
}
```

This program displays:

| Name:Bart Age:10 |

`Console.WriteLine()` automatically calls the `ToString()` virtual method of objects on which it must display the state on the console. If this method is not overridden, it is the default implementation of `ToString()` of the `Object` class which is called.

- `public virtual void Finalize()`

    This method is called when the object is destroyed by the garbage collector. In C#, it is impossible to explicitly override this special method. In order to override it, you must use a special syntax which is explained at page 350.

- `protected object MemberwiseClone()`

    This method is explained a little later when we will talk about the cloning of objects.

- `public static bool ReferenceEquals(object objA, object objB)`
  `public virtual bool Equals(object obj)`
  `public virtual int GetHashCode()`

    These three methods are explained in the following section.

Comparing objects

Equivalence vs. Identity

By default, there are three ways to compare two instances of a same reference type: the use of the two '==' or '!=' operators, the use of the `Object.Equals()` instance method or the use of the `Object.ReferenceEquals()` static method. By default, the comparison is done on the references and not on the state of referenced objects. Two references are equal if they both reference the same object. This is a comparison based on *identity*.

By default, you cannot compare two instances of a same value type by using the `Object.Equals()` virtual method. The default implementation of this method compares the instances field-by-field using internally the reflection mechanism. Two instances of a value type are considered equal if all their fields' values are equal. This comparison is based on *equivalence*. The following example illustrates all this:

Example 10-4

```
  using System.Diagnostics;
  class  TypeRef { public int state; }
  struct TypeVal { public int state; }
  public class Program {
     public static void Main() {
        // Identity comparison.
        TypeRef ref1 = new TypeRef(); ref1.state = 3;
        TypeRef ref2 = new TypeRef(); ref2.state = 3;
        Debug.Assert( ref1 != ref2 );
        Debug.Assert( ! ref1.Equals( ref2 ) );
        Debug.Assert( ! object.ReferenceEquals( ref1, ref2 ));
```

Example 10-4

```
      ref2 = ref1;
      Debug.Assert( ref1 == ref2 );
      Debug.Assert( ref1.Equals(ref2) );
      Debug.Assert( object.ReferenceEquals(ref1, ref2) );

      // Equivalence comparison.
      TypeVal val1 = new TypeVal(); val1.state = 3;
      TypeVal val2 = new TypeVal(); val2.state = 3;
      Debug.Assert( val1.Equals(val2) );
      val1.state = 4;
      Debug.Assert( !val1.Equals(val2) );
   }
}
```

We will now interest ourselves to the features offered by the .NET framework to customize the comparison of objects.

Customizing equality comparison

If you wish to only redefine the equality test between two instances, it is better to both override the `Object.Equals()` method and redefine the '==' and '!=' operators. The implementation of these operators should only call the `Object.Equals()` method.

It is recommended to override the `Equals()` method and the equality operators for all value types which need to have their instances compared. You will gain in performance as the default implementation of the `Equals()` method for value types uses reflection and is therefore not efficient.

It is recommended that the implementation of `Object.Equals()` defines what we call an *equivalence relation* on the instances of the related type. To satisfy this criterion, the implementation must be:

- Reflexive: For all instances x, `x.Equals(x)` returns `true`.
- Symmetric: For all instances x and y, `x.Equals(y)` is equal to `y.Equals(x)`.
- Transitive: for all instances x, y and z, if `x.Equals(y)` and `y.Equals(z)` are both equal to `true`, then `x.Equals(z)` is equal to `true`.

It is also recommended that the overridden implementation of the `Equals()` method in a class D which is a subclass of B, calls the overridden implementation of the `Equals()` method defined in the B class if it exists.

In general, we decide to customize the equality test between two objects of a reference type to obtain an equivalence behavior. This practice is illustrated by how instances of the `System.String` class are compared. Indeed, we will see that instances of string are compared based on their equivalency.

More information concerning the redefinition of operators with C# and the `Equals()` method is available at page 359.

Equality and hash tables

If you only override the `Object.Equals()` method, you will see that the C# compiler will emit a warning recommending you to override also the `Object.GetHashCode()` method. This warning is emitted independently from whether or not you have overridden the equality operators. In fact, you only need to follow this recommendation if the instances of the concerned types can potentially be used as keys within a hash table. More information on this topic can be found at page 486.

Customizing ordering comparison

In addition to being able to compare your instances for equality, you might also wish to be able to order your instances, for example, to store them in a sorted list. In this case, you have the choice between implementing the `System.IComparable<T>` interface on the type of objects to compare or to implement the `System.Collections.Generic.IComparer<T>` interface in a dedicated class. If you implement one of these classes, it is better to provide implementations for '==', ' !=', '<', '>', '<=' and '>=' operators which just call the code for comparison.

Cloning an object

We often need to obtain a copy of an existing object, in other words, to clone an object. It is more rigorous to say that we are copying the state of one object into another object. For certain classes, cloning an instance makes no sense. For example, there would be no sense in cloning an instance of the `Thread` class.

For instances of value types, the '=' assignment operator copies the state of the source object to the destination object. The copy is done byte-by-byte.

For instances of a reference type, the '=' assignment operator copies the reference, and not the object. It is then necessary to provide a method in order to copy the state of an object of a reference type. You can implement the `object Clone()` method of the `System.ICloneable` interface which is dedicated to this task. This interface only offers a single method. Here is an example which illustrates the use of this interface:

Example 10-5

```csharp
class Article {
   public string Description;
   public int Price;
}
class Order : System.ICloneable {
   public int Quantity;
   public Article Article;
   public override string ToString() {
      return "Order: " + Quantity + " x " + Article.Description +
             "   Total cost: " + Article.Price * Quantity;
   }
   public object Clone() {
      Order clone = new Order();
      // Shallow copy
      clone.Quantity = this.Quantity;
      clone.Article = this.Article;
      return clone;
   }
}
class Program {
   static void Main() {
      Order order = new Order();
      order.Quantity = 2;
      order.Article = new Article();
      order.Article.Description = "Shoes";
      order.Article.Price = 80;
      System.Console.WriteLine( order );
      Order orderClone = order.Clone() as Order;
      orderClone.Article.Description = "Shirt";
      System.Console.WriteLine( order );
   }
}
```

Cloning an object

This example displays:

```
Order: 2 x Shoes    Total cost: 160
Order: 2 x Shirt    Total cost: 160
```

Clearly, the modification made on the article of the cloned order was reflected in the article of the original order. This is totally normal since in this program, there exists a single instance of the `Article` class. It is referenced by the two instances of the `Order` class. We say that the original order went through a *shallow copy*. The `Object` class offers the `MemberwiseClone()` protected member which does a shallow copy. Hence, we can rewrite the previous example as following without changing its meaning:

Example 10-6

```
...
class Order : System.ICloneable {
   ...
   public object Clone() {
      // Shallow copy
      return this.MemberwiseClone();
   }
}
...
```

The notion of shallow copy generally induces bugs as in general it is not considered normal that a modification on the cloned object graph had an impact on the original object graph. We may prefer the notion of *deep copy* which, as its name indicates, clones the totality of the object graph. Let's adapt our example to perform a deep copy:

Example 10-7

```
...
class Article : System.ICloneable {
   ...
   public object Clone() {
      // For the 'Article' class, shallow copy = deep copy.
      return this.MemberwiseClone();
   }
}
class Order : System.ICloneable {
   ...
   public object Clone() {
      // Deep copy.
      Order clone = new Order();
      clone.Quantity = this.Quantity;
      clone.Article = this.Article.Clone() as Article;
      return clone;
   }
}
...
```

The display of the program is now the following:

```
Order: 2 x Shoes    Total cost: 160
Order: 2 x Shoes    Total cost: 160
```

Notice that in the previous example we specify that in regards to the `Article` class, a shallow copy is equivalent to a deep copy. We may be tempted to assert that for a given class, a shallow copy is equivalent to a deep copy if and only if all its members are value types. However, the `Article` class has a `string` field which is a reference type. We will explain a little later in this chapter (at page 308) that the `String` class offers certain properties including the immutability of its instance, which makes it that quite often, the instances of this class behave the same as instances of a value type.

The `ICloneable` interface is often critiqued mainly because it does not allows its implementations to communicate to their clients whether the copy is deep or shallow, or even partially deep. The designers of the framework almost made this interface obsolete when transitioning to .NET 2. The main reason which 'saved' this interface from becoming obsolete is that it is now implemented by several standard and custom classes. Also it is not recommended to implement it unless you provide sufficient documentation. An alternative is for example a *copy constructor* which takes as a parameter the type of copy that we wish to use:

Example 10-8

```
...
class Order {
   public int Quantity;
   public Article Article;
   public override string ToString() {
      return "Order: " + Quantity + " x " + Article.Description +
         "   Total cost: " + Article.Price * Quantity;
   }
   // Default constructor.
   public Order() { }
   // Copy constructor (parameterized).
   public Order( Order original , bool bDeepCopy) {
      this.Quantity = original.Quantity;
      if( bDeepCopy )
         this.Article = original.Article.Clone() as Article;
      else
         this.Article = original.Article;
   }
}
class Program {
   static void Main() {
      ...
      Order orderClone = new Order( order , true );
      ...
   }
}
```

Another argument which is in favor of the `ICloneable` interface is that it allows to naturally implement the *prototype Gof design pattern*. This pattern allows the creation of new objects by cloning a prototype object which is referenced by a reference of type `ICloneable`.

Boxing and Unboxing

C++ › C#: Nothing similar exists in C/C++. All this directly comes from the fact that value and reference types derive from the `Object` class. There exists no such class in C/C++.

C#: Instances of a value type, local to a method, are directly stored in the stack of the thread. The thread does not need pointers nor references to the instances of these value types in order to use them.

Several methods need arguments in the form of references of type `Object`. All value types derive from the `Object` class. However, the instances of value types do not have references. A solution needed to be found in order to obtain a reference to an instance of a value type when we need it. This solution is the topic of this section, which is called *boxing*.

Boxing

Here is a practical example which exposes the problem. The `f()` method accepts a reference of type `object`. Initially, we cannot call it with an argument which does not have a reference, for example, an integer of type `int`:

Example 10-9

```
class Program {
   static void f( object o ) { }
   public static void Main() {
      int i = 9 ;
      f( i );
   }
}
```

However, this little program compiles and functions properly. The magic of boxing allowed us to obtain a reference to an instance which did not have one! The boxing operation is done in three steps:

a) A new instance of the value type is created and allocated on the heap.
b) This instance is initialized with the state of the instance on the stack. In the case of our integer, a copy of four bytes is done. We can say that our initial instance has been cloned.
c) A reference to the new instance is used instead of the instance allocated on the stack.

The IL code of this Main() method is the following:

```
.locals init ([0] int32 i)
IL_0000:  ldc.i4.s   9
IL_0002:  stloc.0
IL_0003:  ldloc.0
IL_0004:  box        [mscorlib]System.Int32
IL_0009:  call       void Program::f(object)
IL_000e:  ret
```

We see that the box instruction of the IL language is provided specially for the boxing operation. This instruction places the reference to the new instance on the top of the stack.

> We take advantage of this example to underline that the int C# keyword is an alias to the System.Int32 type.

Some dangerous issues with boxing

If you are concerned with performance, you must know that the boxing operation does not come for free. The program in Example 10-10 uses two boxing operations while the program in Example 10-11 only uses one boxing operation, and is thus more efficient. Despite the appearances, these programs do not have the same behaviors as the first program displays 'Different references' and the second displays 'Same references'. This optimization can be dangerous as it modifies the behavior of the program in a non-obvious way. We recommend that you not use such an optimization.

Example 10-10

```
class Program {
   static void f( object o1, object o2 ) {
      if ( o1 == o2 )
         System.Console.WriteLine( "Same references" );
      else
         System.Console.WriteLine( "Different references" );
   }
   public static void Main() {
      int i = 9;
      f( i, i );
   }
}
```

Example 10-11

```
class Program {
   static void f( object o1, object o2 ) {
      if ( o1 == o2 )
         System.Console.WriteLine( "Same references" );
      else
         System.Console.WriteLine( "Different references" );
   }
   public static void Main() {
      int i = 9;
      object o = i;
      f( o, o );
   }
}
```

Unboxing

The inverse operation to boxing exists and is called *unboxing*. Here is an example where unboxing is used:

Example 10-12

```
class Program {
   public static void Main() {
      int i = 9;
      object o = i;    // i is 'boxed'.
      int j = (int) o; // o is 'unboxed'.
   }
}
```

The IL code of this `Main()` method is the following:

```
   .locals init ([0] int32 i,
            [1] object o,
            [2] int32 j)
IL_0000:  ldc.i4.s    9
IL_0002:  stloc.0
IL_0003:  ldloc.0
IL_0004:  box         [mscorlib]System.Int32
IL_0009:  stloc.1
IL_000a:  ldloc.1
IL_000b:  unbox       [mscorlib]System.Int32
IL_0010:  ldind.i4
IL_0011:  stloc.2
IL_0012:  ret
```

We see that the `unbox` instruction of the IL language is specially provided for the unboxing operation. Without going into the internal details, know that the `unbox` instruction places a pointer on the stack to the boxed object which is found on the heap. It is the `ldind` IL instruction which loads on the stack, the value of the referenced object.

The instance cannot be unboxed to the specified type if it is not exactly of this type. The `InvalidCastException` exception can be raised by an unboxing operation. In addition, if the reference to unbox is null, then the `NullReferenceException` exception is raised.

In C#, the boxing and unboxing operations are implicit. Meaning that it is the C# compiler which will generate the calls to the `box` and `unbox` IL instructions when needed. This is not necessarily the case with all .NET languages.

Primitive types

C++ › C#: The types presented here are quite similar to the corresponding types in C++.

The `unsigned` keyword does not exist in C#. We use the `byte`, `ushort`, `uint` and `ulong` types to indicate unsigned integers.

The size of `long`/`ulong` is of eight bytes in C#.

In C#, the `decimal` (on 16 bytes) type represents real numbers in an exact way with a limit of 28 significant digits.

In C#, the `bool` type only accepts the `true` and `false` values. No conversion with any integer types is allowed.

In C#, the `char` type is now coded on two bytes and respects the UNICODE standard. Remember that in C++, this type is only stored on one byte and follows the ASCII standard.

C#: The C# language has several primitive types, which are all value types. Each primitive type of C# exactly corresponds to a type of the CTS. The primitive types are defined by the following keywords: `bool`, `byte`, `sbyte`, `char`, `short`, `ushort`, `int`, `uint`, `long`, `ulong`, `float`, `double` and `decimal`. The correspondence between these keywords and the primitive types of the .NET framework are defined below.

Each primitive type allows you to define constants in the source code. In fact, the developer often needs to initialize his variables of a primitive type using values of this type.

Integer types

Types

C# keywords	Corresponding CTS types.	Size (bits)	Range of values.
byte	System.Byte	8	[0 ; 255]
sbyte	System.SByte	8	[-128 ; 127]
short	System.Int16	16	[-32768 ; 32767]
ushort	System.UInt16	16	[0 ; 65635]
int	System.Int32	32	[$-2,1 \times 10^9$; $2,1 \times 10^9$]
uint	System.UInt32	32	[0 ; 4.2×10^9]
long	System.Int64	64	[$-9,2 \times 10^{18}$; $9,2 \times 10^{18}$]
ulong	System.UInt64	64	[0 ; $1,8 \times 10^{19}$]

> ⚠ The `ushort`, `uint` and `ulong` unsigned types as well as the `sbyte` signed type are not CLS compliant (meaning they are not conform to the CLS explained at page 106). Concretely, other .NET languages are not required to implement them. You must not use these types as arguments to methods which are susceptible of being called from another assembly written in another language than C#.

Defining constant integers in your C# code

By default, constants for these types can be written simply by using a base-10 number. For example:

```
int i = 1024;
```

However, you can also write such a constant as a base-16 (hexadecimal) number:

```
int i = 0X00000400;
```

Here is a little problem:

```
int  i = 1000000000;   // i = 1 billion
long j = 10 * i;       // j is not equal to 10 billions
```

What is the value of j? It is not 10 billions. In fact, the computation was done using `int` (limited to a little over two billions). The result is then of type `int`. Then the result is finally copied into a variable of type `long`. The main problem is that nothing is signaled to the developer by the compiler (unless he uses the `checked` keyword). To solve these problems, we must tell the compiler that we wish to use an 8 bytes integer values by adding L to the integer constant:

```
int  i = 1000000000 ;  // i = 1 billion
long j= 10L * i;       // j = 10 billions
```

Real types

C# keyword	Corresponding CTS types	Size	Range of values	Smallest value	Precision
float	System.Single	32	[-3,4x10^38 ; 3,4x10^38]	1,4x10^-45	7 decimals
double	System.Double	64	[-1,8x10^308; 1,8x10^308]	4,9x10^-324	15 decimals
decimal	System.Decimal	128	[-8x10^28 ; 8x10^28]	1x10^-28	28 decimals

Particularities of float and double types

The `float` type (respectively `double`) is defined by the ANSI IEEE 754 standard. All the values of 32 (respectively 64) bits does not necessarily represent a correct floating-point number. These incorrect values are represented by the `System.Single.Nan` (respectively `System.Double.Nan`) static field. Nan essentially means *Not A Number*.

The `float` (respectively `double`) type also offers two practical values which represent the positive and negative infinity. The idea is that the operation and standard functions operating on real numbers handle infinity properly. Indeterminate cases (such zero multiplied by infinity) return the `Nan` value. These values are represented by the `PositiveInfinity` and `NegativeInfinity` constant static fields.

The `Single` and `Double` types offer the following methods:

Methods	Description
`public static float/double Parse(string s)`	Same functionality as with integer types.
`public string ToString()`	Same functionality as with integer types.
`public static bool IsInfinity(float/double d)`	This static method returns `true` if the input is infinity in the proper primitive type.
`public static bool IsNan(float/double d)`	This static method returns `true` if the input is not valid in the related type.

The `single` and `double` types also offer the following constant static fields:

Field	Description
Epsilon	Smallest non-null positive value which can be represented by the concerned primitive type.
MaxValue	The greatest positive value which can be represented by the concerned primitive type (also exists for the `decimal` type).
MinValue	Opposite of `MaxValue` (also exists for the `decimal` type).

Primitive types

The decimal type

With its 28 decimals, the decimal type is very useful in financial applications where each decimal counts. It is better to avoid this type for computationally intensive applications which doesn't require such a precision as the manipulation of the `decimal` type is expensive.

Defining floating-point constants in your C# code

By default, floating-point constants are of type `double`. Here are a few examples:

```
double d1 = 10;      // OK, d1 is equal to 10
double d2 = 10.0;    // OK, d2 is equal to 10
double d3 = 10E3;    // OK, scientific notation d3 is equal to 10,000
double d4 = 10.1E3;  // OK, scientific notation d4 is equal to 10,100
double d4 = 1.1E-1;  // OK, scientific notation d5 is equal to 0.11
```

For the constant to be converted to a `float`, you must use the f or F suffix.

```
float  d1 = 1.2;         // KO, the constant is a double. A double cannot
                         // be explicitly converted to a float.
float  d2 = 1.2f;        // OK
float  d3 = (float)1.2;  // OK, there is an explicit conversion
float  d4 = 12E-1F;      // OK, there is an explicit conversion.
```

For the constant to be converted to `decimal`, it must be suffixed with m or M.

```
decimal d1 = 1.2;            // KO, the constant is a double. A double cannot
                             // be explicitly converted to a decimal.
decimal d2 = 1.2m;           // OK
decimal d3 = (decimal)1.2;   // OK, there is an explicit conversion.
decimal d4 = 12E-1m;         // OK, there is an explicit conversion.
```

The bool type

The C# keyword for this type is `bool`. A variable of this type can only take two values: `true` or `false`. The fact that the `true` value is represented by a 1 or a 0 by the CLR during execution does not concern the developer. However, you must know that an instance of `bool` is represented by a byte. If you have an array of booleans, it is preferable to use types dedicated to represent arrays of bits which are described at page 477. These types optimize the storage in memory of 8 booleans in a single byte.

The `bool` keyword is an alias for the `System.Boolean` CTS type. This structure presents the two `public static bool Parse(string s)` and `public string ToString()` methods which have been described earlier. Also note that the `Sytem.Boolean` type offers two static constant fields which are string, `FalseString` (set to "False") and `TrueString` (set to "True"). These two strings are the strings which are used by the `ToString()` and `Parse()` methods to represent `false` and `true`.

The char type

The C# keyword for this type is `char`. An instance of this type represents a character which follows the UNICODE standard. Here are a few examples of constants of type `char`:

```
char  c1 = 'A';         // The 'A' letter in UNICODE.
char  c2 = '\x41';      // The 65th character in UNICODE 'A'.
                        // (41 is the Hexadecimal value of 65).
char  c3 = (char)65;    // The 65th character in UNICODE 'A'.
char  c4 = '\u0041';    // The 65th character in UNICODE 'A'.
```

The `char` keyword represents the `System.Char` CTS type. This structure offers static methods to determine if a character is an upper case letter, lower case latter, a number... Here are a few of these methods:

Static methods of System.Char	Description
bool IsLower(char ch)	Returns true if ch is a lower case character.
bool IsUpper(char ch)	Returns true if ch is an upper case character.
bool IsDigit(char ch)	Returns true if ch is a number.
bool IsLetter (char ch)	Returns true if ch is a letter.
bool IsLetterOrDigit(char ch)	Returns true if ch is a letter or a number.
bool IsPunctuation(char ch)	Returns true if ch is a punctuation character.
bool IsWhiteSpace(char ch)	Returns true if ch is a white space.
char ToUpper(char ch)	Returns the upper cased version of ch.
char ToLower(char ch)	Returns the lower cased version of ch.

Conversions between integers and characters

The presented primitive types each offer the three following methods:

- `public static [the concerned primitive type].Parse(string s)`

    This static method parses a string in order to recover a value in the concerned primitive type. Two exceptions can be raised:

    - `FormatException` if the string does not only contain numbers with an optional '+' or '-' prefix.

    - `OverflowException` if the number represented does not fit in the interval of valid values for the concerned primitive type.

- `public bool [the concerned primitive type].TryParse(string s, out [the concerned primitive type])`

    This static method parses the string in order to recover a value of the concerned primitive type into the `out` parameter. This method returns `true` if it was successful or `false` otherwise.

- `public string [the concerned primitive type].ToString()`

    This method writes the value into a string. This method is an override of the `ToString()` method in the `Object` class.

The following example displays the "-234" string twice:

Example 10-13

```
class Program {
   static void Main() {
      string s1 = "-234";
      int i = System.Int32.Parse( s1 );
      string s2 = i.ToString();
      System.Console.WriteLine( s1 );
      System.Console.WriteLine( s2 );
   }
}
```

Operations on primitive types

C++ › C#: In C#, the modulus operator can also be applied to floating point types. In addition, the C# language provides the `checked` keyword which allows you to force the verification of all conversions and operations. An exception is raised if a problem is encountered.

Arithmetic on operands of the same primitive type

C#: The five main arithmetic operations are:

Operator	Description
+	Addition.
-	Subtraction.
*	Multiplication.
/	Division.
%	Modulus (i.e. division remainder)

The operations can be applied to all primitive types, integer or floating-point. Each of these operations accepts two operands. A writing facility is also proposed with the five following operators:

Writing facility	Equivalence
`i += j;`	`i = i+j;`
`i -= j;`	`i = i-j;`
`i *= j;`	`i = i*j;`
`i /= j;`	`i = i/j;`
`i %= j;`	`i = i%j;`

Dealing with the divide by zero issue

In regards to *divisions by zero* on an integer type and `decimal` type, the `DivideByZeroException` exception is raised.

In regards to the division by zero on the `double` and `float` types, the variable takes the NaN (Not a Number) value (and not infinity as you may think).

Dealing with overflows

An *overflow* happens when you obtain as a result of an operation a value out of the authorized range. An overflow has the following consequences:

- On variables of type `decimal`, the `OverflowException` exception is raised.
- On variables of type `double` and `float`, the variable takes the NaN (Not a Number) special value.
- On variables of integer types, the, the significant bits which have overflowed are not taken into account meaning that we will obtain an incorrect result. To deal with this dangerous default behavior, you can use the `checked` keyword:

Example 10-14
```
class Program {
   static void Main() {
      byte i = 255;
      checked {
         i += 1; // A System.OverflowException is raised.
      }
   }
}
```

The `checked` keyword can also be applied directly to an expression.

Example 10-15
```
...
```

Example 10-15

```
        byte i=255;
        i = checked( (byte)(i+1) ); //A System.OverflowException is raised.
...
```

The checked keyword cannot be applied to a class or a method. In a block of code verified using the checked keyword, you can use the unchecked keyword to switch back to the default behavior on the fly.

Operator priority

In regards to the *priority of operators*, it is defined as follows:

- + - * / have priority over %.
- + and − have the same priority.
- * and / have the same priority.
- * and / have priority over + and −.
- When two operators have the same priority, the leftmost operator of an expression has the priority. However, this has little importance since the base operations with the same priority are commutative.
- We can always increase the priority of an operator by using parenthesis.

For example:

Example 10-16

```
...
        int a = 3;
        int b = 10;
        int c = 4;
        int r1 = b+c %a;      // r1 = 11
        int r2 = (b+c)%a;     // r2 = 2
        int r3 = a*b+c;       // r3 = 34
        int r4 = a*b%c;       // r4 = 2 (30 modulus 4)
...
```

The pre and post increment/decrement operators

C++ › C#: A difference with C++ is that in C#, these operators can also be applied to floating-point types. In addition, in the case of an integer, we can deal with overflows by using the checked keyword.

C#: We can increment of decrement by one unit, a variable of an integer or floating-point primitive type using the ++ and −− operators. For example:

- `i++;` is equivalent to `i = i+1;`
- `i--;` is equivalent to `i = i-1;`

The difficulty comes from the fact that these operators can be placed either before or after the variable, which changes the order in which they are evaluated in an expression. For example:

Example 10-17

```
...
        int i = 3;
        int j = i++; // j is equal to 3 and i is equal to 4
        int k = 3;
        int l = ++k; // l is equal to 4 and i is equal to 4
...
```

Operations on primitive types 301

When we use these operators with integer types, it is possible that we will cause an overflow. As with any overflows on integer variables, an exception is not raised...

Example 10-18

```
...
    byte i = 255;
    i++;  // i is equal to 0
...
```

...unless you use the checked keyword:

Example 10-19

```
...
    byte i = 255;
    checked{ i++; } // A System.OverflowException is raised.
...
```

Arithmetic operations on different primitive types

C++ › C#: The involved primitive types being different, the behavior of the arithmetic operations between different primitive types is not the same in C++ and in C#.

C#: When an arithmetic operation is done with two operands of different primitive types, the result has a type whose range of values is at least equal or greater to these two operands' types' ranges. Here are the results from my own tests, presented in a table:

One of the two types	The other type	Returned type
Operations between integer primitive types		
sbyte byte short ushort	sbyte byte short ushort	int
sbyte byte short ushort	int	int
sbyte byte short ushort int long	uint	long
int long uint	int	long
ulong	int	Compilation error
long	long	long
ulong	ulong	ulong
ulong	long	Compilation error
Operations between integer and floating-point primitive types		
sbyte byte short ushort int uint long ulong	float	float
sbyte byte short ushort int uint long ulong	double	double
sbyte byte short ushort int uint long ulong	decimal	decimal
Operations between floating-point primitive types		
float double	decimal	Compilation error
double	float	double
float	float	Float
double	double	double
decimal	decimal	decimal

In addition, casts are authorized between any integer or floating-point types. Of course, this remains dangerous since the valid ranges of values for all these types are all different. The developer can always use the checked keyword. Hence if a value must be converted to a type where it cannot be represented, an exception of type System.OverflowException will be raised.

Example 10-20

```
...
    int i = -5;
    checked {
        byte b = (byte) i; // Exception raised. The 'byte' type can't
    }                      // represent any negative integer.
...
```

However note that is it possible to round a floating-point type into an integer type. For example, we can convert a `double` equal to 3.1415 into a `byte` with a value of 3.

When several operators are used in an expression they are executed based on the order of their priority (described a little earlier). If the primitive types of the variables are different the intermediate results will follow the rules we just discussed.

Operations on bits

C++ > C#: Nothing is new compared to C/C++ with the exception to the support for 64-bit values using the `long` and `ulong` types.

C#: Binary operations (i.e. bit-by-bit) can be done between operands of type `int`, `long`, `uint` and `ulong`. In the case of a binary operation, the variables of type `sbyte`, `short`, `byte`, `ushort` are converted to the `int` type:

Operation	Also known as	Operator
AND	Logical 'and'	&
OR	Logical 'or'	|
XOR	Logical 'exclusive or'	^
NOT	Bit inversion	~

Only the '~' operator acts on a single operand while all the other operators act on two operands. Let's go over these operations:

Bit A	Bit B	A AND B	A OR B	A XOR B
0	0	0	0	0
0	1	0	1	1
1	0	0	1	1
1	1	1	1	0

The shift operations can be made on variables of type `int`, `long`, `uint` and `ulong` thanks to the following operators:

- `<<` left shift.
- `>>` right shift.

Remember that a left shift by one position in decimal notation causes a multiplication by 10. In the same way, a left shift in a binary notation causes a multiplication by two. A right shift by one position in a binary notation causes a division by two.

Example 10-21

```
...
    uint a = 11;
    uint b = a << 2; // 'a' is not modified, 'b' is equal to 44.
    uint c = a >> 2; // 'a' is not modified, 'c' is equal to 2.
...
```

Let's precise that:

Structures 303

- If the shift is done on a variable of a signed type (i.e. `int` or `long`), the shift is arithmetic, meaning that the sign bit is not shifted.
- If the shift is done on a variable of an unsigned type (i.e. `uint` or `ulong`), the shift is done in a binary way and the result remains positive.

Structures

<u>C++ > C#:</u> In C++, structures and classes are similar notions. In C#, the base difference is that structures define value types while classes define reference types.

In C#, all structures derive from the `Object` class

Contrarily to C++, the fields of a structure are private by default. In addition, any field which we want to be declared public must be prefixed with the `public` keyword.

Contrarily to C++, structures cannot derive from any class or structures, and cannot be used as a base class of any derived class or structure.

In C#, a structure can have one or several constructors but the developer does not have the right to define a default constructor (i.e. without arguments). In addition, the field initialization syntax for constructors (: `field_name(value)`...) does not exist. Finally, the default constructor initializes all the fields to zero.

A structure can have public and private methods but they must be completely defined inside the declaration of the structure (same for classes). The '::' scope operator is not usable anymore in this context.

In C#, the possibility of using bit fields within a structure does not exist anymore.

In C#, it is not required to put a ';' at the end of the declaration of a structure (same for classes).

Finally, although this is a general difference, in C#, within a same namespace, it is not necessary to have already defined a structure in order to use it.

<u>C#:</u> In C#, a structure is declared using the `struct` keyword. The notion of structure is close to the one of a class. The common points are:

- A structure can have fields, properties, methods, delegates, events and nested types. If one of the fields is not declared using the `public` keyword it is not accessible from outside the class.

    ```
    ...
    struct Employee {
       int salary;            // This field is private.
       public string name;    // This field is public.
    }
    ...
    ```

- The members of a structure are accessible outside of the structure using the '.' dot operator.

    ```
    ...
      Employee bob;
      bob.name = "Bob";      // OK The 'name' field is public.
      bob.salary = 3000;     // KO The 'salary' field is private.
    ...
    ```

- All structures derive from the `Object` class.
- A structure can be defined:

    - Inside of another structure. It can however be instantiated outside of the encapsulating structure, if the visibility level allows;

- Inside of a class. It can however be instantiated outside of the encapsulating class if the visibility level allows;

- Outside of all classes or structures. We can then instantiate this structure anywhere within this namespace or any other code which uses this namespace.

A structure cannot be defined within a method.

- A structure can have one or several constructors but the developer is not allowed to define the default constructor (i.e. without arguments). In addition, the compiler expects all the fields of the structure to be initialized within all constructors.

```
...
struct Employee {
   int salary;
   public string name;
   Employee ( int _salary,string _name ) {
      salary = _salary;
      name = _name;
   }
}
...
```

The default constructor sets all the fields of a value type to zero and all the fields of a reference type to null.

- A structure can have methods other than constructors:

```
...
struct Employee {
   int salary;
   public string name;
   public int GetSalary() { return salary; } // This method is public.
}
...
```

However, structures and classes do have important differences:

- A structure is a value type while a class is a reference type, with all the consequences that this implies.
- Structures cannot derive from another class or structure and cannot be used as a base for any derived class or structure even though that all structures derive from the `Object` class.
- Contrarily to the fields of a class, the fields of a structure cannot be explicitly initialized in their declarations.
- The developer cannot overload the default constructor.
- Instances of structures being often stored on the stack, it is better that they not be too large. In the case of large structures, it is better to use a class.

Enumerations

C++ › C#: Enumerations in C# remain close to the enumerations in C++. There are however a few differences that you should note.

The `System.Enum` class offers functionalities which can help the manipulation of enumerations.

Enumerations in C# are ideal to replace the mechanism of binary flags in C++. Remember that in C++ the binary flag mechanism generally uses macros. Such an approach doesn't benefit from the compiler's type checking.

Enumerations

C#: An enumeration type defines a set of values. In C#, such a type is defined using the `enum` keyword. An instance of an enumeration takes its values from this set. For example:

Example 10-22

```
class Program {
  enum Maker { Renault, Ford, Toyota }
  static void Main() {
    Maker maker = Maker.Renault;
    switch ( maker ) {
      case Maker.Renault:  System.Console.WriteLine("Renault"); break;
      case Maker.Ford:     System.Console.WriteLine("Ford");    break;
      case Maker.Toyota:   System.Console.WriteLine("Toyota");  break;
    }
  }
}
```

An enumeration can be defined:

- Within a structure or a class. It can however be instantiated outside of the encapsulating class or structure if its visibility level allows;
- Outside of any class or structure. We can instantiate this enumeration anywhere within this namespace of within any code that uses this namespace.

Enumerations and integer types

The compiler considers by default that the value of an enumeration is an integer of type `int`. Consequently, every possible value within the set of values for the enumeration is associated with an integer value. As a consequence, we can:

- Explicitly cast a variable of an enumeration type into an integer type:

    ```
    ...
    int i = (int) maker;
    ...
    ```

- Increment or decrement a variable of an enumeration type:

    ```
    ...
    Maker maker  = Maker.Renault;
    Maker maker2 = maker++;
    maker2       += 2;
    ...
    ```

- Associate our own integer values to the values within the set of values for the enumeration:

    ```
    ...
    enum Maker{ Renault = 100 , Ford= Renault+1 , Toyota = 200 }
    ...
    ```

    By default, the first value is 0, then each following value is incremented by 1. It is better to define 0 as the most common value as constructors will initialize to 0 by default all the fields of an enumeration type.

- Choose any other integer than `int` to define the values of an enumeration type:

    ```
    ...
    enum MakerFR : byte { Renault , Peugeot };
    enum MakerIT : long { Fiat    , Ferrari };
    ...
    ```

All enumerations derive from the `Object` class. Consequently, the methods of this class are accessible on enumerations. Note that the `Object.ToString()` is overridden automatically for each enumeration, in a way where the returned character string corresponds to the string defining the value in the code. For example:

Example 10-23
```
class Program {
   enum Maker { Renault, Ford, Toyota }
   static void Main() {
      Maker  maker = Maker.Renault;
      string s = maker.ToString();
      System.Console.WriteLine( s );
   }
}
```
This program displays:

```
Renault
```

The System.Enum class

The `System.Enum` class derives from the `System.ValueType` class. It offers several static methods which help to handle enumeration instances. Amongst these, we can mention:

- `static string Format(Type type, object value, string format)`
  This method allows recovering a string which corresponds to the enumeration: the `format` argument must be equal to "G" or "g" to return the name (for example "Renault"). It must be "D" or "d" to return the corresponding value (for example "100").

  Example 10-24
  ```
  ...
        Maker  maker = Maker.Renault;
        string s = System.Enum.Format( typeof( Maker ) , maker , "G" );
        // Here, the string 's' is equal to "Renault".
  ...
  ```

- `static object Parse(Type type, string value, bool ingnoreCase)`
  Converts a string into a value of the enumeration. If the `ignoreCase` argument is set to `true`, this method dose not take upper/lower cases into account:

  Example 10-25
  ```
  ...
        Maker maker = (Maker) System.Enum.Parse(typeof(Maker),"ReNaUlt",true);
        // Here, 'maker' is equal to 'Maker.Renault'.
  ...
  ```
  If the string does not correspond to a value, the `ArgumentException` exception is raised.

- `string [] GetNames(Type type)`
  Returns all values names of the enumeration in an array of strings. For example:

  Example 10-26
  ```
  ...
         foreach( string s in System.Enum.GetNames( typeof(Maker) ) )
            System.Console.WriteLine(s);
  ...
  ```

- `object[] GetValues(Type type)`
  Returns all the values of the enumeration in an array of object. For example (be aware here that o references them one-by-one a boxed instance of the value of the enumeration):

  Example 10-27
  ```
  ...
         foreach( object o in System.Enum.GetValues( typeof(Maker) ) )
            System.Console.WriteLine( o.ToString() );
  ...
  ```

Bit fields (set of flags)

We can make it so that an instance of an enumeration can contain several values of the enumeration. This notion is known as *binary flag* or *flag enum*. For example:

Example 10-28

```
// Don't need more than a byte to store 3 binary flags.
[System.Flags()]
enum Flags : byte {
   Flag1 = 0x01, // The first bit is true, the others are false.
   Flag2 = 0x04, // The third bit is true, the others are false.
   Flag3 = 0x10  // The fifth bit is true, the others are false.
}
class Program {
   public static void Main() {
      // flag is equal to 10001000 (binary notation).
      Flags flag = Flags.Flag1 | Flags.Flag3;
      // (If the first bit is set) equivalent to (If Flag1 is set).
      if ( (flag & Flags.Flag1) > 0 ) { /* */ }
      // (If the 3th and 5th are set) equivalent to
      // (If Flag2 and Flag3 are set).
      if ( (flag & Flags.Flag2) > 0 && (flag & Flags.Flag3) > 0 ){ /* */ }
      System.Console.WriteLine( flag.ToString() );
   }
}
```

Notice that all bit field enumerations should be tagged with the `System.Flags` attribute. This attribute allows telling the CLR and the clients that this enumeration will be used for bit field and not as a standard enumeration. The presence of this attribute affects the results of the `ToString()` method and our example displays the following:

```
Flag1, Flag3
```

If would display the following if the `Flags` attribute was not set:

```
17
```

An example of bit field which can be found in the .NET framework is the `System.Threading.ThreadState` binary flags enumeration which is described at page 117.

Strings

The System.String class

C++ › C#: The .NET framework introduces the `System.String` class which is used to represent strings and finally breaks the traditional (and dangerous) use of `char*` and `char[]` (adios `strcpy()` and other dangerous functions). The way of using the `String` class is similar to the `string` type provided by STL in C++.

A big difference with the STL type is that in C#, an instance of the `String` class is immutable, as it cannot be modified. It constantly keeps the value which was assigned by its constructor.

Another big difference is that the convention which required terminating a string with a null character in C++ does not exist anymore in C#.

The `string` C# keyword is an alias to the `System.String` class. An instance of this class represents a character string encoded using the UNICODE standard.

The `String` class is declared as `sealed`, meaning that no other class can derive from it. In addition, the instances of the `String` class are compared using equivalence and not identity even though the `String` class is a reference type.

Instances of the `String` class are *immutable*. Meaning that a string cannot be modified once it has been created. The various string modification methods of this class always return a new instance of the `String` class containing the modified string. This behavior can have a negative impact on performance. You can use the `System.Text.StringBuilder` class which allows the direct manipulation of character strings. We discuss this class a little later.

The three previous characteristics (`sealed`, equivalence comparison and immutability) makes it so that **strings are manipulated almost as if they were instances of value types. However, keep in mind that the String type is a class and is thus a reference type**. We recommend that you review the beginning of this chapter to fully understand all that this implies (manipulation of references, storage of instances of `String` on the heap, involvement of the garbage collector ...).

Strings constants

C++ › C#: Contrarily to C++, C# offers two types of constant strings:

- Standard constant strings which are similar to C++ constant strings.
- Verbatim constant strings, which are described in the following section.

C#: Here is an example of a constant of type `string`:

```
string  s = "ABCDEFG";
```

We can introduce special characters into a string. Understand that these characters are interpreted by the C# compiler. Here is the list:

Meaning	Representation	Value
New line	\n	0x000A
Horizontal tab	\t	0x0009
Vertical tab	\v	0x000B
Backspace	\b	0x0008
Carriage return	\r	0x000D
Form feed	\f	0x000C
Backslash	\\	0x005C
Single quote	\'	0x0027
Double quote	\"	0x0022
Null	\0	0x0000

For example, the following program displays "hel\nlo":

Example 10-29

```
class Program {
   public static void Main() {
      string s = "hel\\nlo";
      System.Console.WriteLine(s);
   }
}
```

Verbatim string literals

The C# language allows the definition of a *verbatim* string literal by adding the '@' character right before the quotation mark for the start of the string. A verbatim string literal has the following peculiarities:

- It accepts all the characters as is, including the '\' backslash character but with the exception of the '"' quote character. In fact, it is used to define the end of the string.
- It accepts and takes into account linefeeds within the string. This functionality is especially useful when we generate code.

Here is an example:

Example 10-30
```
class Program {
   public static void Main() {
      string sRegular ="\\Hi\n\\How are you doing\n\\this morning?";
      string sVerbatim = @"\Hi
\How are you doing
\this morning?";
      System.Console.WriteLine( "Regular string literal :" );
      System.Console.WriteLine( sRegular );
      System.Console.WriteLine( "Verbatim string literal :" );
      System.Console.WriteLine( sVerbatim );
   }
}
```

Here is the output:

```
Regular string literal :
\Hi
\How are you doing
\this morning?
Verbatim string literal :
\Hi
\How are you doing
\this morning?
```

Working with strings

The `String` class offers several methods to help you manipulate strings. For example, we can obtain the length of a string, search for a sub-string...

Methods (all public)	Description
int Length()	Returns the number of characters.
static int Compare(string s1, string s2)	Returns 0 if s1 is equal, character-by-character to s2. If not, it computes a weight for each string and returns the difference Weight(s2)-Weight(s1). The weight is computed based on the order of characters in UNICODE.
int CompareTo(string s)	Similar to Compare() but this method is non-static. Returns Weight(instance)-Weight(argument).
static string Concat(string s1,string s2)	Returns a new string which is the concatenation of s1 and s2. Note that the s1 + s2 C# notation is equivalent.
static string Copy(string s)	Returns a new string which is equal to s.
bool StartWith(string s)	Returns true if the string represented by the current instance starts with the s string.
bool EndWith(string s)	Returns true if the string represented by the current instance ends with the s string.

Methods (all public)	Description
static string Format(string s, arguments)	Creates a string from at most four arguments. See the following section for the formatting of a string.
int IndexOf(char c)	Returns the index of the c character in the current instance. If the character is at the first position of the string, the index is 0. If the character cannot be found, the method returns –1. The LastIndexOf() method is equivalent but it scans the string starting from the end.
int LastIndexOf(char c)	
int IndexOf(char c ,int pos)	Idem, but the search starts from the pos index in the string.
int IndexOf(string s)	Idem, but the search is done for a sub-string instead of a character.
int IndexOf(string s , int pos)	Idem, but the search starts at the specified position in the string.
string Insert(int pos, string s)	Returns a new string which is the string of the current instance to which s is added at the pos position.
string PadLeft(int n)	Returns a new string which is the string represented by the current instance with n spaces added at the beginning.
string PadLeft(int n , char c)	Idem, but the padding is done using the c character.
string PadRight(int n)	Idem, but the padding is done at the end of the string using spaces.
string PadRight(int n , char c)	Idem, but the padding is done at the end of the string using the c character
string Remove(int pos, int n)	Returns a new string which is the string represented by the current instance in which we have removed n characters from the position specified by pos.
string Replace(string oldstr, string newstr)	Returns a new string which is the string represented by the current instance on which we have replaced each sub-string equal to oldstring with newstring.
string Replace(char oldchar, char newchar)	Returns a new string which is the string represented by the current instance in which we replaced each oldchar character with newchar.
string Split(char[])	Returns an array of new strings obtained from the string represented by the current instance. A character arrays is passed as an argument which defines the separators.
string SubString(int pos, int n)	Returns a new string equal to the sub-string extracted at the pos position and of n characters.
string ToLower()	Returns a new string which is the string represented by the current instance converted to lower case.
string ToUpper()	Returns a new string which is the string represented by the current instance converted to upper case.
string Trim()	Returns a new string which is the string represented by the current instance with the spaces at the beginning and end removed. TrimStart() (respectively TrimEnd()) is identical except that it only processes the beginning of the string (respectively the end of the string).
string Trim(char[])	Idem, but the characters which are removed are provided as an argument which is a character array.

Formatting strings

C++ › C#: In C/C++, the formatting of string uses markers (such as "%d") within a string provided to printf(). The markers contain information on the type of variable to display.

In C# formatting still uses markers but they are different and contain no information concerning the type. However, they contain information indicating the position in the argument list of the Format() method.

C#: This section details the use of the Format() static method of the string class:

Strings

```
static string Format( string, object );
static string Format( string, object, object );
static string Format( string, object, object, object );
static string Format( string, object[] );
static string Format( IFormatProvider, string, object[] );
```

This method is often used and offers several options. The table below illustrates several formatting examples which uses the i and d variables:

```
int i = 123;
double d = 3.1415;
string sOut = System.String.Format( Signature of Format() );
```

Signature of Format()	Value of sOut	Notes
"abcd"	"abcd"	-
"ab{0}cd",i	"ab123cd"	-
"ab{0}cd",d	"ab3,1415cd"	-
"ab{0}cd",i,d	"ab123cd"	The d argument is not used, but no error will be generated.
"ab{0}cd{1}ef",i,d	"ab123cd3.1415ef"	Use of the two arguments.
"ab{1}cd{0}ef",i,d	"ab3.1415cd123ef"	Another use of the two arguments.
"ab{0}{0}cd ",i	"ab123123cd"	Same argument is used twice
"ab{0}cd{1}ef",i	Execution ERROR	The second argument is needed.
"ab{0,6}cd",i	"ab 123cd"	i is represented by six characters aligned to the right. Three space characters are added. If the number of characters was less than the number of characters required to display i, it still would have been completely displayed.
"ab{0,-6}cd",i	"ab123 cd"	Same but with a left alignment.
"ab{0:0000}cd",i	"ab0123cd"	Displays at least four numbers, padding using zeroes.
"ab{0,6:0000}cd",i	"ab 0123cd"	Displays at least four numbers, padding with zeroes, represented with six characters with a right alignment.
"ab{0:####}cd",i	"ab123cd"	A # character to replace is not used.
"ab{0:##}cd",i	"ab123cd"	The formatting is not respected.
"ab{0:##.##}cd",d	"ab3,14cd"	At most, two decimals are displayed.
"ab{0:##.#}cd",3.14	"ab3,1cd"	Rounding down.
"ab{0:##.#}cd",3.18	"ab3,2cd"	Rounding up.
"ab{0:##%}cd",0.143	"ab14%cd"	0.143 is multiplied by 100 then rounded down. 0.147 would have produced 15%.
"ab{0:E}cd",d	"ab3,141500E+000cd"	Scientific notation.
"ab{0:X}cd",i	"ab7Bcd"	Hexadecimal representation using uppercase letters.
"ab{0:x}cd",I	"ab7bcd"	Hexadecimal representation using lowercase letters.

The System.Text.StringBuilder class

As we have seen at the beginning of the current section, instances of the String class are immutable. This fact can have a negative impact on performance as each modification to a string will allocate a new instance of String. This is even worse, if you deal with long strings.

If one of your applications often modifies strings or works with long strings, it is more efficient to use the System.Text.StringBuilder class.

In general, an instance of the StringBuilder class is built from an instance of the String class with the StringBuilder(string) constructor

To properly understand the StringBuilder class, you must first assimilate the notion of capacity of an instance of StringBuilder. For this, we will present the following properties of StringBuilder (which are all public and non-static):

- int Length{get;}
  This property returns the number of characters in the string.

- `int Capacity{get;set;}`

  This property represents the number of characters physically allocated to store the string. This number is the capacity of the instance. The value of this field is always greater or equal to the value of the Length field. It is useful to set this field to a value larger than the real size of the string. You can then prevent memory allocation operations by the garbage collector (which can be expensive), by giving yourself a margin when manipulating the string.

  Note that the value of this field is automatically increased when a string manipulation produces a result which is larger than the current capacity. The value of this increment depends on the implementation of the framework. In this situation, the current implementation by *Microsoft* doubles the capacity. If you set this field to a value inferior to the value of Length the ArgumentOutOfRangeException exception is raised.

- `int MaxCapacity{get ;}`

  This property gives the maximum capacity that a string can have. In the current *Microsoft* implementation, this field is set to Int32.MaxValue which means 2,147,483,647 characters.

The StringBuilder class offers the following methods:

- `int EnsureCapacity(int capacity)`

  Ensures that the capacity is at least equal to the value of capacity. If this is not the case, the capacity is increased. The new capacity is returned.

- `StringBuilder Append(...)`

  Adds the characters to the end of the string. This method exists in various overloaded versions.

- `StringBuilder Insert(int index,...)`

  Inserts the characters at the position specified by index. A position of 0 indicates the first character of the string. This method exists in several overloaded versions.

- `StringBuilder Remove(int startIndex, int length)`

  Removes the characters included between the startIndex position and the startIndex+length position. The ArgumentOutOfRangeException exception is raised if one of these positions is negative or exceeds the length of the string.

- `StringBuilder Replace(...old,...new,...)`

  Replaces the character(s) specified by old, with the character(s) specified by new. The search for old can also be done on a sub-string using overloaded versions of this method.

Here is a little program which illustrates all this (for each call to Program.Display(), we inserted the output value):

Example 10-31

```
class Program{
   static void Display(System.Text.StringBuilder s) {
      System.Console.WriteLine("The string : \"{0}\"",s);
      System.Console.WriteLine(" Length    : {0}", s.Length);
      System.Console.WriteLine(" Capacity  : {0}", s.Capacity);
   }
   public static void Main(){
      System.Text.StringBuilder s = new System.Text.StringBuilder("hello");
      Display(s);
      //The string : "hello"
      // Length    : 5
      // Capacity  : 16

      s.Insert( 4 , "--salut--" );
      Display(s);
      //The string : "hell--salut--o"
```

Example 10-31

```
    //  Length      : 14
    //  Capacity    : 16

    s.Capacity = 18;
    Display(s);
    //The string  : "hell--salut--o"
    //  Length     : 14
    //  Capacity   : 18

    s.Replace("salut","HELLO EVERYBODY");
    Display(s);
    //The string  : "hell--HELLO EVERYBODY--o"
    //  Length     : 24
    //  Capacity   : 36

    s.EnsureCapacity(42);
    Display(s);
    //The string  : "hell--HELLO EVERYBODY--o"
    //  Length     : 24
    //  Capacity   : 72
  }
}
```

Before using the services of the `StringBuilder` class, you must be aware that it is possible to break the immutability of an instance of the `String` if you're allowed to use unsafe code. This topic is discussed at page 423.

Delegate classes and delegate objects

Introduction

C++ › C#: C# defines the notion of delegates which is absent in C++.

However this notion is conceptually close to function and method pointers in C++. As with them, a delegate is a reference to one or several methods (static or not).

Delegates are however more powerful that function pointers, since a same delegate can reference more than one method. Also, the syntax for delegates is clearer and more user-friendly.

C#: C# allows the creation of special classes using the `delegate` keyword. We call such a class a *delegate class*. Instances of these delegate classes are called *delegate objects*.

Conceptually, a delegate object is a reference to one or several methods (static or not). We can then 'call/invoke' delegate object with the same syntax than the call to a method. This causes the call of the referenced methods. Note that the call to these methods is done by the same thread which called the delegate object. Here we talk of a synchronous call.

There are several base delegate classes defined in the .NET framework. You can find the list of these delegate classes in the article named **MulticastDelegate Hierarchy** on **MSDN**. As this article mentions, each delegate class derives from the `System.MulticastDelegate` class. This class is special. We cannot derive from it explicitly. Only the compilers of the .NET languages can build classes which derive from `MulticastDelegate`. Thanks to certain methods of the `MulticastDelegate` class, a delegate object can also be used to make asynchronous calls on a method. This concept of asynchronous delegate is the topic of another section at page 141.

> Certain books use the term delegate to sometimes talk of delegate classes or delegate objects. In this book, we made an effort to use a clear terminology and will use the delegate class or delegate type and delegate object or delegate instance terms to avoid any confusion.

Delegate objects and static methods

Here is an example which uses two delegate objects and two delegate classes:

Example 10-32

```
public class Program {
  // Definitions for delegate classes: Deleg1 and Deleg2.
  delegate void Deleg1();
  delegate string Deleg2(string s);
  static void f1() {
    System.Console.WriteLine("f1() called.");
  }
  static string f2( string s ) {
    string _s=string.Format( "f2() called with the param \"{0}\"." , s );
    System.Console.WriteLine( _s );
    return _s;
  }
  public static void Main() {
    // Create a delegate object, instance of the 'Deleg1' delegate class.
    // This object references the 'f1()' method.
    Deleg1 d1 = new Deleg1( f1 );
    // Call the 'f1()' method through the 'd1' delegate object.
    d1();
    // Create a delegate object, instance of the 'Deleg2' delegate class.
    // This object references the 'f2()' method.
    Deleg2 d2 = new Deleg2( f2 );
    // Call the 'f2("hello")' method with the 'd2' delegate object.
    string s = d2( "hello" );
  }
}
```

This program displays:

```
f1() called.
f2() called with the param "hello".
```

We use two delegate classes to properly underline the fact that a delegate object can only reference a method whose signature corresponds to the signature provided during the declaration of the delegate class. For example, the following line would have provoked a compilation error since the f1() method does not have the proper signature:

```
   Deleg2 d2  = new Deleg2( f1 );
```

The C#2 compiler can infer a delegate class

The C#2 compiler introduces a new facility which allows the possibility of inferring the type of a delegate object that we create. We can thus directly assign a method to a delegate object which is created implicitly. The previous program can be rewritten as follows:

Delegate classes and delegate objects

Example 10-33

```
public class Program {
   delegate void Deleg1();
   delegate string Deleg2( string s );
   static void f1() {
      System.Console.WriteLine("f1() called.");
   }
   static string f2(string s) {
      string _s=string.Format( "f2() called with the param \"{0}\"." , s );
      System.Console.WriteLine( _s );
      return _s;
   }
   public static void Main() {
      Deleg1 d1 = f1;  // Instead of   Deleg1 d1 = new Deleg1( f1 );
      d1();
      Deleg2 d2 = f2;  // Instead of   Deleg2 d2 = new Deleg2( f2 );
      string s = d2("hello");
   }
}
```

Do not be mistaken, this is just a syntactic facility. If you analyze the generated IL code for this example, you will see that it in fact calls the constructors of the `Deleg1` and `Deleg2` delegate classes.

Delegate objects and instance methods

We can obtain the same behavior with instance methods. Naturally, when we provide the method to reference, it must be tied to the object on which it must be called. For example:

Example 10-34

```
using System;
public class Article {
   private int m_Price = 0;
   public Article( int price ) { m_Price = price; }
   public int IncPrice( int i ) {
       m_Price += i;
       return m_Price;
   }
}
public class Program {
   public delegate int Deleg( int i );
   public static void Main() {
      // Create an article with a price of 100.
      Article article = new Article( 100 );
      // Create a delegate object that references the 'IncPrice()'
      // method on the object 'article'.
      Deleg deleg = article.IncPrice;
      int p1 = deleg( 20 );
      Console.WriteLine("Price of article: {0}", p1 );
      int p2 = deleg( -10 );
      Console.WriteLine("Price of article: {0}", p2 );
   }
}
```

This program displays the following:

```
Price of article: 120
Price of article: 110
```

Referencing several methods from a single delegate object

We can reference several methods (static or not) with the same signature using a single delegate object. In this case, the call to the delegate object will cause the successive calls to the methods by the same thread which has initiated the call. These methods are called in the same order that they have been added to the delegate object, each of them with the same arguments. For example:

Example 10-35

```csharp
using System;
public class Article {
   public int m_Price = 0;
   public Article(int price) { m_Price = price; }
   public int IncPrice(int i) {
      m_Price += i;
      return m_Price;
   }
}
public class Program {
   public delegate int Deleg(int i);
   public static void Main() {
      // Create three articles with different prices.
      Article a = new Article( 100 );
      Article b = new Article( 103 );
      Article c = new Article( 107 );
      // Assign three methods to a single delegate object.
      Deleg deleg = a.IncPrice;
      deleg += b.IncPrice;
      deleg += c.IncPrice;
      // Increment prices of the three articles in a single call
      // to the delegate object 'deleg'.
      int p1 = deleg( 20 );
      // Here, the value of 'p1' is 127 i.e the price of the third article.
      Console.WriteLine( "Prices of articles: a:{0} b:{1} c:{2}",
                         a.m_Price , b.m_Price , c.m_Price );
      // Decrement prices of the three articles in a single call.
      int p2 = deleg(-10);
      // Here, the value of 'p2' is 117.
      Console.WriteLine( "Prices of articles: a:{0} b:{1} c:{2}",
                         a.m_Price , b.m_Price , c.m_Price );
   }
}
```

This program displays:

```
Prices of articles: a:120 b:123 c:127
Prices of articles: a:110 b:113 c:117
```

If the signature returns a value in the case where there are several referenced methods, it is the value returned by the last method called by the delegate object which will be returned.

Although this example does not expose it, a single delegate object can reference both static and instance methods at the same time. Moreover, these referenced methods can be declared in several types.

The System.Delegate class

You must know that internally, when several methods are referenced from a single delegate object, an instance of the `System.Deletage` class is created for each method. In fact, an instance of the `MulticastDelegate` class can be seen as a list of instances of the `System.Delegate` class. The following example shows how to use the `Delegate` class to invoke one of the methods contained in the delegate object. Note the use of the `GetInvocationList()` method in order to obtain the list of delegates.

Example 10-36

```
using System;
public class Article {
   public int m_Price = 0;
   public Article( int price ) { m_Price = price; }
   public int IncPrice( int i ) {
      m_Price += i;
      return m_Price;
   }
}
public class Program {
   public delegate int Deleg( int I );
   public static void Main() {
      Article a = new Article( 100 );
      Article b = new Article( 103 );
      Article c = new Article( 107 );
      Deleg delegs = a.IncPrice;
      delegs += b.IncPrice;
      delegs += c.IncPrice;
      int sum = 0;
      // Get an array of several delegate objects from the delegate
      // object 'delegs'.
      Delegate[] delegArr = delegs.GetInvocationList();
      // Invoke each method referenced, one by one.
      foreach ( Deleg deleg in delegArr )
         sum += deleg(20);
      Console.WriteLine( "Price after increment: a:{0} b:{1} c:{2}",
                         a.m_Price , b.m_Price , c.m_Price);
      Console.WriteLine("Sum: {0}", sum );
   }
}
```

This example displays:

```
Price after increment: a:120 b:123 c:127
Sum: 370
```

Modifying the list of referenced methods

The previous example shows that we can add (and respectively remove) a delegate object to another delegate object of the same type with the '+=' (respectively '-=') operator. If the added delegate objects contain several method references, they will be added to the end of the reference list of the target delegate object. However, in the case of a removal, it is possible that the operation cannot be completed if the provided list does not appear in the reference list of the target delegate object. The following example illustrates this:

Example 10-37

```
using System;
public class Article {
   public int m_Price = 0;
   public Article( int price ) { m_Price = price; }
```

Example 10-37

```
      public int IncPrice( int i ) {
         m_Price += i;
         return m_Price;
      }
   }
}
public class Program {
   public delegate int Deleg(int i);
   public static void Main() {
      Article a = new Article( 100 );
      Article b = new Article( 103 );
      Article c = new Article( 107 );

      // 'deleg' references ( a.IncPrice , b.IncPrice , c.IncPrice ).
      Deleg deleg = a.IncPrice;
      Deleg deleg1 = b.IncPrice;
      deleg1 += c.IncPrice;
      deleg += deleg1;
      deleg( 10 );
      Console.WriteLine( "a:{0} b:{1} c:{2}",
                        a.m_Price , b.m_Price , c.m_Price );

      // Try to supress the sub list ( a.IncPrice , c.IncPrice )
      // that cannot be found in the delegate object 'deleg'.
      Deleg deleg2 = a.IncPrice;
      deleg2 += c.IncPrice;
      deleg -= deleg2;
      deleg(10);
      Console.WriteLine( "a:{0} b:{1} c:{2}",
                        a.m_Price , b.m_Price , c.m_Price );

      // Try to supress the sub list ( a.IncPrice , b.IncPrice )
      // that can be found in the delegate object 'deleg'.
      Deleg deleg3 = a.IncPrice;
      deleg3 += b.IncPrice;
      deleg -= deleg3;
      deleg(10);
      Console.WriteLine( "a:{0} b:{1} c:{2}",
                        a.m_Price , b.m_Price , c.m_Price);
   }
}
```

This example displays:

```
a:110 b:113 c:117
a:120 b:123 c:127
a:120 b:123 c:137
```

In the first removal attempt, the `deleg` delegate object is not modified. To determine if a removal completed properly, you can inspect the size of the array obtained from the `GetInvocationList()` method.

Nullable types

The designers of C#2 have added the concept of nullable types to deal with a weaknesses of value types versus reference types. It is then essential to have properly assimilated these two notions presented at the beginning of the current chapter before continuing.

Value types and null value paradigm

A reference is null when it does not reference any object. This is the default value taken by all references. You just need to have a glance at the code of any application to notice that developers commonly take advantage of null references. In general, the use of a null reference allows communicating some information:

- A method which must return a reference to an object returns a null reference to indicate that the requested object cannot be found. This relieves developers from having to implement a binary error code.
- When you encounter a method which accepts an argument of a reference type which can be null, this means that this argument is generally optional.
- A field of a reference type which is null can be used to indicate that the object is being initialized, updated or even deleted and that it does not have a valid state.

The notion of nullness is also commonly used within relational databases to indicate that a value in a record is not assigned. This notion can also be used to designate an optional attribute in an XML element.

Amongst the several differences between the value and reference types, we can take a look at the fact that the notion of nullness doesn't exist for value type. This generally causes several problems. For example, how to interpret a null integer value (or not yet assigned) retrieved from a database or from an XML document? Multiple solutions exist but none are fully satisfying:

- If the whole range of integer values is not usable, we create a convention. For example, a null integer value is represented by an integer equal to 0 or -1. The several disadvantages to this approach are evident: constraint to maintain everywhere in the code, possibility of changes in the range of values taken by this field…
- We create a *wrapper* structure containing two fields, an integer and a boolean, that is set to `false`, means that we have a null value. Here, we must manage an additional structure for value type and an additional state for each value.
- We create a *wrapper* class containing an integer field. Here, the disadvantage is that in addition to having to maintain a new class, we add a significant burden to the garbage collector by creating several small objects on the heap.
- We use boxing, for example by casting our integer value into a reference of type `object`. In addition to not being *type-safe*, this solution also has the disadvantage of overloading the garbage collector.

To deal with this recurring problem, the designers of C#2/.NET2 decided to provide the concept of *nullable types*.

The System.Nullable<T> structure

The .NET 2 framework offers the `System.Nullable<T>` generic structure which is defined as follows:

```
public struct System.Nullable<T> {
   public Nullable(T value);

   public static explicit operator T(  T? value );
   public static implicit operator T?( T value );

   public bool HasValue { get; }
   public T Value { get; }

   public override bool Equals( object other );
```

```
      public override int GetHashCode();
      public T GetValueOrDefault();
      public T GetValueOrDefault( T defaultValue );
      public override string ToString();
   }
```

This structure responds well to the problem of null values when the T type parameter takes the form of a value type such as int. Here is a little example which illustrates the use of this structure. The first version of Fct() uses the nullness of the string type while the second version uses the nullness of an instance of the Nullable<int> structure:

Example 10-38

```
class Foo {
   static string Fct( string s ) {
      if ( s == null )
         return null;
      return s + s;
   }
   static System.Nullable<int> Fct( System.Nullable<int> ni ) {
      if ( !ni.HasValue )
         return ni;
      return (System.Nullable<int>) ( ni.Value + ni.Value );
   }
}
```

Evolution of the C# syntax: Nullable<T> and the null keyword

The C# syntax allows you to assign and to compare null keyword to an instance of System.Nullable<T>:

```
Nullable<int> ni = null;
System.Diagnostics.Debug.Assert( ni == null );
```

These two lines are equivalent to:

```
// Call the default ctor which internally set 'Hasvalue' to false.
Nullable<int> ni = new Nullable<int>();
System.Diagnostics.Debug.Assert( !nullable1.HasValue );
```

The use of the System.Nullable<T> structure is intuitive but can quickly become blurring. It is not obvious that these two programs are equivalent (the two pieces of generated IL code are equivalent):

Example 10-39

```
class Program{
   static void Main(){
      System.Nullable<int> ni1 = 3;
      System.Nullable<int> ni2 = 3;
      bool b = ( ni1 == ni2 );
      System.Diagnostics.Debug.Assert( b );
      System.Nullable<int> ni3 = ni1 + ni2;
      ni1++;
   }
}
```

Example 10-40

```
using System;
class Program {
```

Example 10-40
```
    static void Main() {
        Nullable<int> ni1 = new Nullable<int>(3);
        Nullable<int> ni2 = new Nullable<int>(3);
        bool b = ( ni1.GetValueOrDefault() == ni2.GetValueOrDefault() ) &&
                 ( ni1.HasValue == ni2.HasValue );
        System.Diagnostics.Debug.Assert( b );
        Nullable<int> ni3 = new Nullable<int>();
        if ( ni1.HasValue && ni2.HasValue )
            ni3 = new Nullable<int>( ni1.GetValueOrDefault() +
                                     ni2.GetValueOrDefault() );
        if ( ni1.HasValue )
            ni1 = new Nullable<int>( ni1.GetValueOrDefault() + 1 );
    }
}
```

Also it might seem strange that the `ni++` instruction called on the `ni` variable which is supposed to be `null` does not cause an exception of type `NullReferenceException`.

Evolution of the C# syntax: equivalence between Nullable<T> and T?

In C#2, you can follow the name of a non-nullable value type T by a question mark. In this case, the C#2 compiler will replace all T? expressions by `Nullable<T>`. To simplify, you can imagine that this is a pre-processing which is done directly on the source code, a little like a pre-compiler. Hence, the following line…

```
int? i = null;
```

…is equivalent to:

```
Nullable<int> i = null;
```

For example, the two following methods are rigorously equivalent:

Example 10-41
```
class Foo {
    static System.Nullable<int> Fct1( System.Nullable<int> ni ) {
        if ( !ni.HasValue )
            return ni;
        return (System.Nullable<int>) ( ni.Value + ni.Value );
    }
    static int? Fct2( int? ni ){
        if (ni == null)
            return ni;
        return ni + ni;
    }
}
```

In general, equivalent instances of a nullable type mix well together:

Example 10-42
```
class Program{
    static void Main(){
        int? ni1 = null;
        int? ni2 = 9;
        int? ni3 = ni1 + ni2;  // OK, ni3 is null.
        int? ni4 = ni1 + 3;    // OK, ni4 is null.
        int? ni5 = ni2 + 3;    // OK, ni5 is equal to 12.
        ni1++;                 // OK, ni1 stays null.
        ni2++;                 // OK, ni2 is now equal to 1.
    }
}
```

However, the compiler will prevent you from implicitly converting an object of a nullable type to its underlying type. In addition, it is dangerous to do such a conversion explicitly without previously testing the value since it might raise an exception of type `InvalidOperationException`.

Example 10-43

```
class Program{
   static void Main(){
      int? ni1 = null;
      int? ni2 = 9;
      int i1 = ni1;         // KO: Cannot implicitly convert
                            //     type 'int?' to 'int.
      int i2 = ni2;         // KO: Cannot implicitly convert
                            //     type 'int?' to 'int.
      int i3 = ni1 + ni2;   // KO: Cannot implicitly convert
                            //     type 'int?' to 'int.
      int i4 = ni1 + 6;     // KO: Cannot implicitly convert
                            //     type 'int?' to 'int.
      // Compilation OK but an InvalidCastException is raised
      // at runtime since ni1 is still null at this point.
      int i5 = (int) ni1;
   }
}
```

No special treatment for bool? in C#2

Contrarily to what you may have seen in the beta version of C#2, in the final version there is not special processing of the `bool?` type by the `if`, `while` and `for` keywords. Hence, this example will not compile:

Example 10-44

```
class Program {
   static void Main() {
      bool? b = null;
      // Cannot implicitly convert type 'bool?' to bool.
      if ( b ) { /*...*/ }
   }
}
```

Nullables types and boxing/unboxing

During the conception of .NET 2.0, until the last moment, nullable types were only an artifact and did not impact the CLR. They only impacted the C#2 compiler and the `System.Nullable<T>` structure. This did pose a problem since when an instance of a nullable type was boxed it could not be null. There was then an incoherency compared to the manipulation of reference types:

```
string s = null;
object os = s;    // os is a null reference.
int?   i = null;
object oi = i;    // oi was not a null reference.
```

Under the pressure from the community, *Microsoft* engineers decided to fix this problem. Hence, the assert in the following program is verified:

Example 10-45

```
class Program{
   static void Main(){
```

Example 10-45
```
        int? ni = null;
        object o = ni;    // boxing
        System.Diagnostics.Debug.Assert( o == null );
    }
}
```

From the point of view of the CLR, an instance of a boxed value type T can be null. If it is not null, the CLR does not store any information to know if it was originated from the T or Nullable<T> types. You can then unbox such an object into any of the two types as shows the following example. However, be aware that you cannot unbox a null value:

Example 10-46
```
class Program {
    static void Main() {
        int i1 = 76;
        object o1 = i1;        // boxing of an int
        int? ni1 =(int?)o1;    // unboxing to an int?
        System.Diagnostics.Debug.Assert( ni1 == 76 );

        int? ni2 = 98;
        object o2 = ni2;       // boxing of an int?
        int i2 = (int)o2;      // unboxing to an int
        System.Diagnostics.Debug.Assert( i2 == 98 );

        int? ni3 = null;
        object o3 = ni3;       // boxing of a null int?
        int i3 = (int)o3;      // unboxing -> NullReferenceException raised!
    }
}
```

Nullable structures and enumerations

The concept of nullable type can also be used on structures and enumerations. This can however lead to crippling compilation errors which are illustrated in the following example where the Nullable<MyStruct> structure does not support the members of MyStruct.

Example 10-47
```
struct Struct {
    public Struct(int i) { m_i = i; }
    public int   m_i;
    public void Fct(){}
}
class Program {
    static void Main(){
        Struct? ns1 = null; // OK
        Struct? ns2 = new Struct?(3);  // KO: Cannot implicitly convert
                                       // type 'int' to 'Struct'.
        Struct? ns3 = new Struct?();   // OK: the default Struct.ctor()
                                       // is called.
        Struct? ns4 = new Struct(3);   // OK
        Struct? ns5 = new Struct();    // OK: the default Struct.ctor()
                                       // is called.
        ns4.m_i = 8;  // KO: System.Nullable<Struct>' does not
                      // contain a definition for 'm_i'.
        ns4.Fct();    // KO: System.Nullable<Struct>' does not
                      // contain a definition for 'Fct'.
    }
}
```

However, if the need is there, the compiler will know how to use custom definitions of operators:

Example 10-48
```
struct Struct {
   public Struct( int i ) { m_i = i; }
   public int  m_i;
   public static Struct operator +( Struct a, Struct b ) {
      return new Struct( a.m_i + b.m_i ); }
}
class Program {
   static void Main() {
      Struct? ns1 = new Struct(3);
      Struct? ns2 = new Struct(2);
      Struct? ns3 = null;
      Struct? ns4 = ns1 + ns2; // OK, ns4.m_i is equal to 5.
      Struct? ns5 = ns1 + ns3; // OK, ns5 is null.
   }
}
```

In regards to an instance of a nullable enumeration, be aware that you must explicitly get the underlying value to use it. For example:

Example 10-49
```
using System;
class Program {
   enum MyEnum { VAL1, VAL2 }
   static void Main() {
      MyEnum? e = null;
      if( e == null )
         Console.WriteLine( "e is null" );
      else
         switch( e.Value ) { //Here, we must be sure that e is not null.
            case MyEnum.VAL1: Console.WriteLine("e is equal to VAL1");
                              break;
            case MyEnum.VAL2: Console.WriteLine("e is equal to VAL2");
                              break;
         }
   }
}
```

Partial types

C#2 offers the possibility of spreading the declaration of a class, structure or interface over several source files. We often talk of *partial type* to name this feature. From now on we will use the *type defined over several source files* and *partial type definition* expressions which carry more meaning than *partial type*. Note that you cannot declare a delegate class or an enumeration over several source files.

To declare a type on several files, you must precede the class, struct or interface keyword with the partial keyword for each partial declarations. Partial definitions of a type must all belong to the same namespace.

The different source files containing the different partial definitions of a type must all be compiled at the same time. A consequence of this feature is that it cannot be use to spread a same type over one of several modules or assemblies. This limitation is a consequence of the fact that being able to define a type over several source files is just *syntactic sugar*. It only involves the C#2 compiler and has no incidence on the way that the types are contained in the assembly nor on the processing of the CLR during execution.

Defining a type on several source files generally leads to more complex code. Hence, we recommend that you use this feature only when you which to generate code. In this case, it is nice to separate the generated code from the hand-written code. *Visual Studio 2005* includes several code generators which harness this feature: *Windows Forms* (at page 555), the typed `DataSet` generator (at page 606), the web page generator (at page 721)…

Let us mention that a nested type can be defined across multiple source files. In this case, each partial definition of the nested type must be written in a partial definition of the outer type.

Type declaration elements that must be repeated in each partial declaration

The different partial definitions of a same type must all be preceded with the partial keyword. Also, if the type is generic, the definition of the parameter types must be repeated for each partial definition. The name of the parameter types as well as their position in the list must be identical for each partial definition.

Type declaration elements that can optionally be repeated in each partial declaration

The following type declaration elements can be optionally repeated in the various partial definitions of a type. They simply need to be present in a single partial declaration for them to have effect on the type as a whole. Of course, the C#2 compiler will detect and emit an error when partial definitions lead to incoherencies.

- The abstract and sealed keywords. Let us mention that a same type cannot be abstract and sealed at the same time.
- The visibility of a type.
- The base class of a type.
- The set of constraints on type parameters.

Type declaration elements that cumulate their effects when repeated in several partial declarations

The following type declaration elements can be repeated in the different partial definitions of a type. In this case, their effect is cumulative. Here also, the C# compiler will detect and emit an error for all incoherencies such as the repetition of a method in several partial declarations of a same type.

- The members. The set of members of a type defined across several source files is the union of the members of each partial definition.
- Attributes. The set of attributes which are applied to a type defined across multiple source files is the union of the attributes applied to each partial definition. In particular, the concerned type will be marked several times by a same attribute if it is marked several times in several partial definitions.
- Implemented interfaces. The set of the interfaces implemented by a type defined over several source files is the union of the interfaces declared in each partial definition.

Type declaration elements that only have a local effect on a partial declaration

Only the unsafe keyword falls into this category. It can be applied to one or several partial definitions of a same type. In this case, its effect is limited to the members which are defined in the concerned partial definition.

II

Classes and objects

Introduction

C++ > C#: C# can be considered 'more object oriented' than C++. In fact, the notion of global variable and global function does not exist in C#. Only the methods (static or not) of a class exist.

C#: The concept of *procedural programming* is build around the notion of procedures. Every program can be seen as a set of procedures calling each other.

The concept of *object oriented programming* is built around the notions of objects and classes. **A class is the implementation of a data type** (in the same spirit as an `int` or a structure). **An object is an instance of a class**.

In object programming, every program can be seen as a set of objects which interact with each other. We will discuss how C# deals with object oriented programming (OOP). However, this book is not dedicated to OOP. In fact, most of the main concepts will be summarized but this isn't sufficient to use them efficiently.

Vocabulary

C++ > C#: In C#, the word *attribute* is reserved for other notions than the one of the fields of a class. This notion of attribute is presented at page 206. In addition, we will see that C# distinguishes between the notion of field and property.

Moreover since the .NET platform possesses a garbage collector, a C# destructor is different than a C++ destructor.

C#:

A *class* is a data type. The notions of variables of a certain type and of *class instance* are similar in the sense where all processing gravitates around data. An object is an instance of a class. The notion of class defines a concept while the notion of object defines an instance of this concept. The notion of class is to the concept of automobile while the notion of object is to a particular automobile. An automobile on the road is an instance of the automobile concept.

It is interesting to underline a paradox in object oriented programming. Objects only exist during the execution and are created, managed and destroyed by the execution environment. Developers only write classes. Also, certain prefer using the *class oriented programming* terminology.

In the context of an object language such as C#, the *variable* term is used to designate an instance of a value type allocated in the body of a method and whose lifetime does not exceeds the scope of this method.

A class is constructed of several entities of different type: fields, properties, methods, events, indexers and encapsulated types. We call these entities members of the class. We will, in this chapter, have the opportunity to detail each of these entities.

Each object contains a certain quantity of information in the form of values stored in its fields. The whole set of these values is called the state of the object.

The notion of method is close to the notion of function with the exception that a method is called on an instance of its class. A method acts on the object on which it is called. It can as well read and write to the fields of an object, in addition to doing an action on the object.

An object has a lifetime which falls under the time period for which the program that hosts the object runs. An object is necessarily constructed at a certain time and destroyed later at another point in time. A method is automatically called during the construction of an object. It can, for example, initialize the object or allocate resources consumed by the object. There can be several constructors for a same class as there can be several ways to construct an object.

A method is automatically called during the destruction of an object by the garbage collector of the .NET platform. The destruction of object is a sensitive subject with .NET/C# and must absolutely be understood.

Class definition

C++ › C#: C# does not know the '::' scope resolution operator such as the one used in C++ during the definition of classes (this operator has been introduced with C#2 but for other reasons).

Consequently, the definition of a class (the body of its methods as well as the initialization of its static fields) must absolutely be done within the pair of braces after the `class` keyword.

The concept of friend classes and methods to a class, present in C++, has completely disappeared in C#. The reason is that this concept is a violation of the OOP notion of encapsulation. Note that however, the new concept of .NET 2.0 of friend assemblies is similar (presented at page 22).

Finally, the ';' character is not necessary at the end of the definition of a class.

C#: The definition of a class is done using the `class` keyword. Here is an example:

Example 11-1

```
class Program{
   // Here, you can define members of the Programm class.
   static void Main() {
      // Here, you must define the body of the Main() method.
   }
   // Here, you can define members of the Programm class.
}
```

The members of a class are entities declared in the class. There are six kinds of class members: Fields; Properties; Indexers; Methods; Events; Nested types.

With the exception of a few details, what we will mention in regards to the members of a class also applies to the members of a structure.

Member access

C++ › C#: Member access is simpler in C# than in C++. Since in C#, the allocation mode of an object (static or dynamic) is not the decision of the programmer, there is no need to make a difference between object values and references. Hence, the arrow operator '->' is not present and only the dot operator '.' is available.

Fields

C#: When a region of code accesses a member (non-static) of a class (or of a structure), we can use the dot operator '.' from an instance of this implementation to access its members. This applies whether...

- ...the member is a field, a property, a method, an event or a type.
- ...the object be a value type (a structure) or a reference type (a class).

Fields

C++ › C#: A few little differences between C# and C++.

First of all, the fields (static or not) can be initialized directly within their declaration in the class. The value of a non-static field in an object will be set just before the call to the constructor. The value of a static field will be set before the creation of any instance of the class.

However, we loose the C++ syntax used to initialize fields directly after the prototype of a constructor:

```
ctor(int field) : m_Field( field ) {}
```

The specifications of the C# compiler are less permissive than with C++. It requires that all non-static value type fields be initialized before the end of the constructor. Reference type fields which are not initialized will be automatically set to `null`.

Finally, a field can be `const`, meaning that it can only be initialized within its declaration or `readonly`, meaning that it can only be initialized within its declaration or within constructors. In both cases, the field cannot be modified after its initialization.

C#: The notion of a class field is the same as the notion of a structure field. The set of states of the non-static fields of an instance of a class represents the state of this instance. A field can be of any type (primitive, enumeration, structure, class, interface, delegate…).

When an object A contains a field that represents another object B, we say that A contains B if B is of a value type. If B is a reference type, we say that A has a *reference* on B. This distinction is important from an OOP point of view.

Initializing fields

All of the value type fields must be initialized before the object can be used and, thus before the end of the construction of the object. The fields can be initialized two ways:

- Directly during their declaration within the class (`Field1` and `Field2` in the example).
- Within a constructor of the class (`Field1` and `Field3` in the example).

Example 11-2

```
class Foo {
   int Field1 = 4;
   int Field2 = 3;
   int Field3;
   public Foo() { // A public constructor of the Foo class.
      Field1 = 7;
      Field3 = 6;
   }
}
```

We see that with `Field1` the two approaches are not incompatible. However, the initialization of `Field1` in the class is useless here since the initialization within the constructor is executed last.

Constant fields

We can make a field constant, meaning that it takes its value during its initialization (within the class or in the constructor) and then cannot be modified. C# offers two ways to make a field a constant:

- We declare it using the `const` keyword.
- We declare it using the `readonly` keyword.

`readonly` authorizes its initialization within the class or the constructor while `const` only authorizes its initialization within the class.

Example 11-3

```
class Foo {
    const     int Field1 = 4;
    readonly  int Field2 = 3;
    // A public constructor of the Foo class.
    public Foo() {
        // The C# compiler would emit an error if we initialize
        // Field1 in the body of a constructor.
        Field2 = 7;
    }
}
```

This implies that a reference type field declared with `const` must be initialized during its declaration within the class otherwise the compiler will report an error.

Another implication is that a reference type field declared with `readonly` must be initialized with an object allocation by the end of at least one of the constructors. Otherwise, the compiler will not say anything but the field will be totally useless since it will always remain `null`.

Potential problem with field initialization

The C# compiler is incapable of detecting a loop in the object aggregation/reference graph. This means that it will not see that the following program is not valid. If B instantiates an object of class A, which in turn instantiates and object of class B, the termination of the program is caused by either the overflow of the stack or the overflow of the heap.

Example 11-4

```
class Program {
    static void Main() {
        B b = new B ();
    }
}
class A {
    B m_Field = new B ();
}
class B {
    A m_Field = new A ();
}
```

Methods

C++ > C#: Several differences exist between C# and C++ in regards to methods. Note that the possibility of having constant methods (i.e. which do not modify the state of the object) in C++, does not exist in C#.

Methods 331

In C++, the passing of arguments to a method or function can be done through pointers, values or reference.

C# allows for all methods, the passing of arguments by value or reference. Under certain conditions, C# also allows the passing of arguments by pointers.

By default, C# passes value type arguments by value and reference type arguments are passed by reference.

The syntax for passing by reference a value type argument has changed.

C# introduces the feature that an argument be only 'out', i.e. we are only interested in its output value.

Finally, the default method arguments of C++ have disappeared. They are replaced by a much more powerful concept similar to the use of variable argument counts in C++ (as used with the `printf` function).

C#: An instance method of a class is a procedure which works on the objects of the class. A method can both modify the state of the objects by manipulating the fields as well as doing calculations.

Example 11-5
```
public class Article {
   public decimal Price = 10;
   public decimal Discount = 20;
   public decimal GetDiscountPrice() { // A method of the Article class.
      return Price * (100-Discount / 100);
   }
}
```

Methods are part of the class in the same respect as fields and properties. Methods play an essential role in C# and are one of the major points to master with this language.

Passing arguments by value or by reference

To understand what follows, it is preferable to have assimilated the notion of value and reference types, described at page 283.

In programming theory, there are two distinct ways to pass a variable (or an object) as arguments to a procedure:

- The *passing of arguments by reference*:

    A reference on the object is passed. This implies that the called method and the calling method both use the same object. The major consequence is that if the called method modifies the state of the object, the calling method will use the object with these modifications. In this case, we say that the called method has a *side-effect* since the overall state of the program has changed after its execution.

- The *passing of arguments by value*:

    The value (state) of the object is passes. This implies that the called method and the calling method each use a different object. The compiler takes care of creating a copy (a clone) of the object passed on the stack of the current process. This copy is only usable by the called method and is destroyed when the execution returns from the called method. The major consequence of this is that if the called method modifies the state of the object, the calling method will never see those changes.

Default C# rules

The fact that there is argument passing by value and by reference goes hand in hand with the fact that in C# each type is either a value type or a reference type. Logically, by default, C# applies this rule:

- A value type instance is passed by value to a method.
- A reference type instance is passed by reference to a method.

For example:

Example 11-6

```csharp
public class Article { public int Price = 0; }
class Program {
   static void Main() {
      int i = 10;   // 'int' is a value type.
      Article article = new Article(); // 'Article' is a reference type.
      article.Price = 10;
      fct( i, article );
      // Here, 'i' is equal to 10 and 'article.Price' is equal to 100.
   }
   static void fct( int i, Article article ) {
      // Here, the 'i' integer passed is not the same as the 'i'
      // declared in the Main() method. However, the 'article' reference
      // references the 'Article' object allocated in the Main() method.
      i = 100;
      article.Price = 100;
   }
}
```

Passing any argument by reference

C++ › C#: In C#, we can force an argument to be passed by reference, as with C++. In C#, the syntax has changed and corrects the fact that in C++, the client is not always aware that an argument is being passed by reference. In fact, in C++, the syntax of the call does not change except in the signature of the method (using '&').

In C#, this problem does not exist anymore. When an argument is passed by reference, you must use the `ref` keyword, both when declaring the method and when calling it.

C#: C# offers the possibility of forcing an argument to be passed by reference. This technique can be used for both value types and reference types. We will see right after that this technique also impacts the passing of reference type arguments. This technique uses the `ref` keyword both at the declaration of the method as well as when it is called. For example:

Example 11-7

```csharp
class Program {
   static void Main() {
      int i = 10;   // 'int' is a value type.
      fct( ref i );
      // Here, i is equal to 100.
   }
   static void fct( ref int i ) {
      // This 'i' integer is the same as the one declared in the
      // 'Main()' method.
      i = 100;
   }
}
```

Using the ref keyword with a reference type

C++ › C#: Here we will present a technique of argument passing in C#, conceptually close to the use of double pointers in C++.

C#: Passing a reference type argument by reference allows the calling method to directly act on the reference. Concretely, the calling method can modify the object that is referenced by the reference of the calling method. This is illustrated by the following example:

Example 11-8
```
public class Article { public int Price = 0; }
class Program {
   static void Main() {
      Article articleA = null;
      Article articleB = null;
      // 'Article' is a reference type.
      fct( articleA, ref articleB );
      // Here 'articleA' is still null. It doesn't reference any
      // object. 'articleB' references the object allocated in fct().
   }
   static void fct( Article articleA, ref Article articleB ) {
      if ( articleA == null )
         articleA = new Article();
      if ( articleB == null )
         articleB = new Article();
   }
}
```

As with this example, we often use this technique to delegate the allocation of one or several objects to a method. In this case, it is preferable to use the **out** argument technique, discussed a little later.

Initializing arguments

C++ › C#: The C++ compiler does not detect the explicit use of uninitialized objects or variables. This is a big problem since C++ does not initialize variables and objects implicitly. In C++, several bugs are caused by unitialized variables.

In addition, certain compilers do not respect the C++ standard and initialize to zero the memory allocated for variables. The code is then less portable as different compilers may have different behavior.

The C# compiler corrects these problems by imposing that the arguments passed to a method be initialized.

C#: C# forces the developer to initialize its value type objects before passing them to a method. This rule applies whether the argument is passed by value or by reference. In the case of a reference declared in a method, the compiler requires its initialization (with an object or with the **null** value) before passing it to a method. Here is an important example, which you need to assimilate:

Example 11-9
```
public class Article { public int Price = 0; }
class Program {
   static void Main() {
      // This value type object (variable) MUST be initialized
      // before being passed to the fct() method.
```

Example 11-9

```
        int i = 10;
        // These two references MUST be initialized
        // before being passed to the fct() method.
        Article articleA = null;
        Article articleB = new Article();
        articleB.Price = 100;
        fct(i, articleA, articleB);
    }
    static void fct(int i, Article articleA, Article articleB) {
        if (articleA == null)
            articleA = new Article();
        articleA.Price = i;
        articleB.Price = i;
    }
}
```

Out parameters

C++ › C#: In C++, to recover the result of a method, you must either use the return value or use arguments passed by reference or by pointer. In the second case, the intent of the developer to use the argument to retrieve a result is not obvious since the same syntax can also be used to pass information to a function. C# offers a more elegant syntax to solve this problem.

C#: C# allows a method to return information (for example the results from a calculation) with two different approaches:

- Directly through the use of the return parameter of the method. The problem with this approach, used in several languages, is the fact that there is a single return value. The `return` is used in the body of a method to define the contents of the return parameter. Note that there can be several uses of the `return` keyword within a method. If the method has nothing to return, it must be declared using the `void` type for the return type. In this case, it is not necessary to use the `return` keyword in the body of the method.

- C# allows for one or several parameters of the method to be return parameters. In this case, the parameters are flagged with the `out` keyword in the signature of the method and when the method is called. In addition, the arguments do not need to be initialized. The method must then initialize these parameters. It cannot use these parameters until they have been explicitly initialized.

Example 11-10

```
public class Article { public int Price = 0; }
class Program {
    static void Main() {
        int i;              // 'i' is not initialized.
        Article articleA;   // 'articleA' is not initialized.
         // 'articleB' references an object.
        Article articleB = new Article();
        articleB.Price = 100;
        fct( out i, out articleA, out articleB );
        // Here 'i', 'articleA.Price' and 'articleB.Price' are all
        // equal to 10. 'articleB' references another object, the one
        // created in 'fct()'.
    }
    static void fct(out int i, out Article a, out Article b) {
        i = 10;
        a = new Article();
```

Example 11-10

```
      b = new Article();
      a.Price = i;
      b.Price = i;
   }
}
```

The params keyword

C++ › C#: C++ allows a function to have arguments with default values. C++ also allows for a function to have a variable number of arguments. This second feature is used, for example, with the `printf()` function.

C# does not allow having default arguments. However C# does allow for a function to have a variable number of arguments. To replace the default arguments of C++, we can also overload the method but this technique is relatively heavy.

C# allows for a method to have a variable number of arguments. The syntax of this feature uses the `params` keyword. The argument which uses the `params` keyword must be the last argument of the argument list of the method. Note that C# compiles such a method using the `System.ParamArrayAttribute` attribute. During execution, the CLR then understands that the method uses this feature. Here is an example of its use:

Example 11-11

```
using System;
class Program {
   static void Main() {
      fct( "Call 1");
      fct( "Call 2", 67, 3.1415, "hello", 8 );
      fct( "Call 3", "hello", 2.7, 1729, 691, "bye" );
   }
   static void fct( string str, params object[] args ) {
      Console.WriteLine( str );
      foreach ( object obj in args ) {
         if (obj is int)         Console.WriteLine( " int:" + obj );
         else if (obj is double) Console.WriteLine( " double:" + obj );
         else if (obj is string) Console.WriteLine( " string:" + obj );
         else                    Console.WriteLine( " other type:" + obj );
      }
   }
}
```

This program displays:

```
Call 1
Call 2
 int:67
 double:3,1415
 string:hello
 int:8
Call 3
 string:hello
 double:2,7
 int:1729
 int:691
 string:bye
```

This example uses the `is` operator described in the next chapter. As you can see, this operator allows testing the type of an object. In addition, we specify that the arguments corresponding to the argument using the `params` keyword must by of type `object`. By using this trick, we can allow the type of the arguments to vary since all types inherit from the `object` type.

Method overloading

C++ › C#: The overloading of methods exists in C#, as with C++.

C#: C# allows for multiple methods of a class to have the same name. This possibility is called *overloading* a method. In this case, the list of arguments of these methods must be different from each other. Otherwise, there will be an ambiguity during a call to this method. The return argument is not taken into account by the compiler when differentiating methods with the same name. This means that the compiler will generate an error if two methods have the same name, the same list of arguments but have a different return type. However, if two methods declared within a same type have the same name and different parameters, they can have a different return type. It is however not recommended to have overloaded methods with different return types as it is generally strongly associated with the semantic of the shared name of the methods.

Other ambiguities can appear if certain of these methods accept a variable number of arguments. In this case, the C# compiler will solve the ambiguity by preferring methods without variable arguments. However, this type of ambiguity is to avoid in the first case as it makes code harder to read. For example:

Example 11-12

```
class Program {
    static void Main() {
        fct( "Call1", "hello" );    // Call overload 3.
        fct( "Call2" );             // Call overload 1.
        fct( "Call3", 10 );         // Call overload 2.
        fct( "Call4", 10, 11 );     // Call overload 4.
        fct( "Call5", 10.1 );       // Call overload 3.
    }
    // Overload 1:
    static void fct( string str ) {
        System.Console.WriteLine("overload 1");
    }
    // Overload 2:
    static void fct( string str, int I ) {
        System.Console.WriteLine("overload 2");
    }
    // Overload 3:
    static void fct( string str, params object[] Args ) {
        System.Console.WriteLine("overload 3");
    }
    // Overload 4:
    static void fct( string str, params int[] Args ) {
        System.Console.WriteLine("overload 4");
    }
}
```

At page 395, we will explain the type of ambiguities which can occur because of method overloading in a generic type.

Properties

C++ › C#: The concept of property does not exist in C++.

C#: C# allows for classes and structures to contain properties. Properties allow accessing the state of an instance using the same syntax as the access of a field, but without accessing a field directly. Access is done through special methods called property accessors. This has a double advantage:

- The user of the class wants to access the state of the object with the same syntax as the access to a field. There is no need to explicitly call a method.
- The developer of a class may want to intercept all accesses to the state of the object. For this, he uses property accessors.

There are two types of accesses to the state of an object. Also, there are two possible accessors for each property:

- For each read access to a property, the `get` accessor of the property is called. Certain documents refer to this as a *getter*.
- For each write access to a property, the `set` accessor is called. Certain documents refer to this as a *setter*.

For example:

Example 11-13
```
public class Foo {
    private int m_FieldPrivate = 10;
    public int Prop {    // An 'int' property.
        get{ return m_FieldPrivate; }
        set{ m_FieldPrivate = value; }
    }
}
public class Program {
    static void Main() {
        Foo foo = new Foo();
        foo.Prop = 56;     // The set accessor of Prop is called.
        int i = foo.Prop;  // The get accessor of Prop is called.
    }
}
```

Accessors are coded as methods with the exception that:

- They cannot be explicitly called as methods.
- In their declaration, they have no input or output arguments.

A property can be of any type (value of reference). As with this example, there is in general one property for each private field that corresponds to it.

The get accessor

The `get` accessor of a property has as a constraint of returning an object of the same type as its property (or a reference to an object of this type if it is a reference type).

A property is not obligated to implement the `set` accessor. In this case, we say that the property is *read-only*. A read-only property cannot be initialized, however it can return an object which is calculated within the `get` accessor.

Example 11-14

```
public class Foo {
   private int m_ChampPrivate = 10;
   public bool Prop { // A read only 'bool' property.
      get{ return (m_ChampPrivate >100);}
   }
}
public class Program {
   static void Main() {
      Foo foo = new Foo();
      bool b = foo.Prop;   // The get accessor is called.
   }
}
```

The set accessor

In the body of a `set` accessor, the `value` keyword represents an object of the same type as the property (or a reference if this is a reference type). It is the object (or reference) supplied during the assignment to the property.

A property is not obligated to implement the `get` accessor. In this case, we say that the property is *write-only*. However, we can compute a new state for the object which offers the property by taking into account the value passed in.

Example 11-15

```
public class Foo {
   private int m_ChampPrivate = 10;
   public int Prop { // A write only 'int' property.
      set{ m_ChampPrivate = value*2;}
   }
}
public class Program {
   static void Main() {
      Foo foo = new Foo();
      foo.Prop = 56;  // The accessor set is called.
   }
}
```

Notes on properties

A property needs to have at least one accessor. It has either a `get` accessor, a `set` accessor, or both.

It is recommended not to modify the state of an object within the `get` accessor. You must consider the `get` accessor as a way to intercept and control the access to the state of an object. For example, we can take advantage of this to keep a log of these accesses.

It is recommended not to raise uncaught exceptions from an accessor. In fact, based on the syntax, the client does not necessarily know that he is in fact calling an accessor during the access to a property. The client could then be caught off guard with an exception.

At page 347, we will explain that accessors from a same property can have different visibility levels.

Indexer

C++ › C#: As with the C++ language, the C# language allows to define the access of the array operator '[ ]' on a class. However, C# allows a much more complete definition of this operator. In fact, there can be several indexes, we can use any type for the index (including custom types) and there can be several definitions of this operator within a same class.

C#: C# allows you to consider an object as an array with one or several dimensions. In fact, C# allows the use of the [ ] operator directly after the name of an object. This operator accepts a list of one or several parameters, of any type (integer, string, objects of any class…). The parameters must be separated by commas.

Of course, a class must account for the fact that the [ ] operator can be used on its instances. For this, it declares one or several *indexers*. The indexers of a class can be considered as special properties, with a few differences:

Property	Indexer
Identified by its name.	Identified by its signature.
Accessed from its name, as with a field.	Accessed using the [ ] operator.
Can be static or not.	Cannot be static.
The get accessor does not have any parameters.	The get accessor has the list of parameters to the indexer.
The set accessor can use the implicit value parameter.	The set accessor has the list of the parameters to the indexer in addition to the implicit value parameter.

As with properties, accessors of indexers are optional, although that you need at least one per indexer. The definition of accessors allows read-only, write-only or both access modes. The parameters of indexer cannot use the ref and out keywords.

The following example exposes the syntax of indexers. We present the access to an array of persons. Persons can be accessed by their names (using a string) in read-only access. Persons can also be accessed by their index in the internal object array which stores them, with a read/write access.

Example 11-16

```
using System;
public class Persons {
   // Private array to store persons' names.
   string [] m_Names;
   // The constructor which initializes the array m_Names.
   public Persons( params string [] names ) {
      m_Names = new string[names.Length];
      // Copy the array.
      names.CopyTo(m_Names,0);
   }
   // The indexer which returns the index from the name.
   public int this[string name] {
      get{ return Array.IndexOf(m_Names,name);}
   }
   // The indexer which returns the name from the index.
   public string this[int index] {
      get{ return m_Names[index];}
      set{ m_Names[index] = value;}
   }
}
class Program {
```

Example 11-16
```
    static void Main() {
       Persons array = new Persons ("Anna" , "Ingrid" , "Maria" , "Ulrika");
       Console.WriteLine( array [1] ); // Display "Ingrid"
       int index = array["Maria"];
       array[index] = "Marie";
       Console.WriteLine( array[index] ); // Display "Marie"
    }
}
```

Often, classes which have indexers must offer the feature of being usable with the syntax of the `foreach` and `in` keywords.

Events

Introduction

C++ › C#: C# defines the notion of events, which is completely absent in C++. In C++, you must implement this plumbing yourself, for example, using the observer design pattern (Gof).

C#: C# allows an object to offer *events*. The concept of event encompasses:

- *Subscribers* to the event. These are warned each time the event is triggered. They have the possibility of subscribing or unsubscribing themselves dynamically (i.e. during the execution of the program). In C#, a subscriber is represented by a method.
- The event itself, which can be triggered at any time by the object. Internally, the event is aware of its subscribers. The responsibility of the event is to notify its subscribers when it is triggered. The event has the possibility of supplying information to its subscribers when it is triggered using the argument object to the event. In C#, events are similar to a delegate field which is a member of a class with the exception than it is declared using the `event` keyword.

The concept of event/subscriber is not new and is well known in Java. The same behavior can be obtained using the *observer design pattern* (Gof).

Events are very useful in an application with a graphical interface (*Windows Forms* and ASP.NET). In fact, each possible action on an interface (a button click, text typing, ComboBox selection...) triggers the call of the adequate method. During a mouse click, the argument of the event can, for example, be the position of the mouse on the screen. In the .NET platform, inheritance combined with events is at the base of all graphical controls.

The C# syntax

Let's suppose that we have created an event in a class called `EventName`. The names of the entities which are concerned by the event are function of the `EventName` name. An event argument is an object of a class derived from `System.EventArgs`. You thus have the possibility of creating your own event arguments by creating your own classes derived from `System.EventArgs`.

To improve code readability, it is recommended that the argument class for the `EventName` be called `EventNameEventArgs`.

Subscribers to the event are materialized using methods (static or not). The action of notifying subscribers translates itself by a call to each of these methods. These methods generally have the following signature:

- A return type of `void`.

Events

- The first argument is of type `objet`. When the method is called, this argument references the object which contains the event.
- The second argument is of type `System.EventArgs`. When a method is called, this argument references the argument to the event.

An event is a member of a class, declared using the `event` keyword. An event is an instance of the `EventNameEventHandler` delegate class. An event has the possibility of being static or not. Visibility levels apply themselves to events. Since an event is a member of a class, the declaration can be preceded with one of the following keywords:

```
new       public    protected   internal   private   static
virtual   sealed    override    abstract   extern
```

An event contains

- A delegate object which contains the references to the subscribed methods. The delegate has the same signature as the subscribed methods and must be called `EventNameEventHandler`.
- An `add` accessor which is invoked when a method subscribes to the event.
- A `remove` accessor which is invoked when a method unsubscribes to the event.

These three entities are automatically defined by the C# compiler as soon as the event is declared. You can however define your own bodies for the accessors. If you change the body of one accessor, you must also code the body of the other. In the body of an accessor, the `value` keyword designates the delegate to add or remove. For example, the two following definitions of an event are acceptable:

```csharp
// without accessor
public event ClickButtonEventHandler ClickButton;
// with accessors
private event ClickButtonEventHandler m_ClickButton;
public event ClickButtonEventHandler ClickButton{
    add    { m_ClickButton += value; }
    remove { m_ClickButton -= value; }
}
```

Note that it is rare to have to modify the `add` and `remove` accessors. However, this feature can be useful in order to restrict the visibility level of an event. Understand that possibility of using polymorphism on an event (i.e. the fact of being able to use the `virtual`, `new`, `override` and `abstract` keywords in the declaration of an event) only applies itself to the `add` and `remove` accessors.

In C#, the event is triggered by a call to its delegate. This is not the case in other .NET languages. For example, VB.NET triggers an event through the use of the `RaiseEvent` keyword which does not exist in C#. The compiler imposes that the call to the delegate must be done within the class that declares the event. Also, the class has the possibility of presenting a public method named On*EventName*() which allows the event to be triggered from outside the class.

```csharp
...
public void OnClickButton(System.EventArgs Arg){
    if(ClickButton != null )
        // Trigger the event.
        ClickButton(this,Arg);
}
...
```

A practical example

Here is an example where an object instance of the `NewsBoard` class publishes press releases throughout the USA and the world. The publication is done through the `WorldNews` and `USANews` events. The argument of a press release event (an instance of the `InfoEventArgs` class) contains the description of the press release. Finally, the instances of the `Subscriber` class have the possibility of receiving press releases by subscribing their `OnReceivingInfo()` methods.

Example 11-17

```
using System;

class Subscriber{
    private string m_Name;
    public Subscriber( string name ) { m_Name = name; }
    // Method to call when an event is triggered
    // (i.e when a news report is published).
    public void OnReceivingInfo(object sender, EventArgs e){
       NewsEventArgs info = e as NewsEventArgs;
       if( info != null ){
          Console.WriteLine( m_Name + " receives the news: " +
                           ((NewsEventArgs)e).GetBulletinInfo() );
       }
    }
}

// An instance of this class represents a news report.
class NewsEventArgs: EventArgs{
    private string m_Report;
    public string GetBulletinInfo() { return m_Report; }
    public NewsEventArgs (string report) { m_Report = report ; }
}

// The delegate class. Its instances reference subscriber methods.
public delegate void NewsEventHandler(object sender, EventArgs e);

// The class which publishes news reports by triggering events.
class NewsBoard {
    // Events used to publish news.
    public event NewsEventHandler USANews;
    public event NewsEventHandler WorldNews;
    // Methods used to trigger news publishing from outside NewsBoard.
    public void OnUSANews(NewsEventArgs newsReport) {
       if( USANews != null )
          USANews( this , newsReport );
    }
    public void OnWorldNews(NewsEventArgs newsReport) {
       if( WorldNews != null )
          WorldNews( this , newsReport );
    }
}

class Program {
   public static void Main(){
      // Create the news board.
      NewsBoard  newsBoard = new NewsBoard  ();
      // Create subscribers.
      Subscriber bob = new Subscriber("Bob");
```

Example 11-17

```
        Subscriber joe = new Subscriber("Joe");
        Subscriber max = new Subscriber("Max");
        // Link subscribers and the news board.
        newsBoard.USANews   += bob.OnReceivingInfo;
        newsBoard.USANews   += joe.OnReceivingInfo;
        newsBoard.WorldNews += joe.OnReceivingInfo;
        newsBoard.WorldNews += max.OnReceivingInfo;
        // Publish news reports by triggering events.
        newsBoard.OnUSANews(new NewsEventArgs("Oil price increases."));
        newsBoard.OnWorldNews(new NewsEventArgs("New election in France."));
        // Unsubscribe Joe.
        newsBoard.USANews -= new NewsEventHandler(joe.OnReceivingInfo );
        // Publish another news report.
        newsBoard.OnUSANews(new NewsEventArgs("Hurricane alert."));
    }
}
```

The program displays:

```
Bob receives the news: Oil price increases.
Joe receives the news: Oil price increases.
Joe receives the news: New election in France.
Max receives the news: New election in France.
Bob receives the news: Hurricane alert.
```

In this example, nothing changes if you remove the two occurrences of the **event** keyword (i.e. nothing changes if we use two delegate fields instead of two events). There are two reasons for this. The first one is that we do not use the event accessors. The second is that we do not trigger this event from outside the **NewsBoard** class. In fact, one of the advantages of the **event** keyword is to prevent the event from being triggered from outside its class. The triggering of an event is also forbidden from classes deriving from the class which defines the event, even if the event is virtual. This means that the C# compiler will generate an error if we wrote the following in the body of the **main()** method in Example 11-17:

Example 11-18

```
    public static void Main(){
        ...
        newsBoard.USANews(newsBoard, new NewsEventArgs("Oil price increases."));
        ...
    }
```

In C#, the notion of event is relatively close to the one of a delegate. The mechanism mostly allows supplying a standard framework for the management of events. Note that the VB.NET language presents several dedicated keywords for the management of events (**RaiseEvent**, **WithEvents**...).

Asynchronous event handling

When an event is triggered, you must be aware that the methods which are subscribed to the event are executed by the thread which triggers the event.

A potential problem is that certain subscribed methods may take too long to execute. Another problem is that a subscribed method may raise an exception. This exception will prevent the other subscribers which have not been yet notified from being executed and will go back to the method which triggered the event. It is clear that this poses a problem as the method which triggers an event should be decoupled from the methods subscribed to the event.

To deal with these problems, it would be practical that the subscribed method be executed in an asynchronous way (the notion of asynchronous methods is described at page 141). Also, it would be interesting that different threads execute the subscribed methods. Hence, a subscribed method which takes a long time to execute or that raises an exception does not affect the method which has triggered the event nor the execution of the other subscribed methods. The thread pool of the CLR, which is described at page 137, is specially adapted to these two constraints.

Those who understand the syntax of asynchronous calls may be tempted to directly use the `BeginInvoke()` function on the event itself. The problem with this solution is that only a single subscribed method will be executed. The proper solution, illustrated in the following example which is based on Example 11-17 requires the explicit traversal of the subscriber method list:

Example 11-19

```
...
// Methods used to trigger news publishing from outside NewsBoard.
public void OnUSANews(NewsEventArgs newsReport){
   if( USANews != null ){
      Delegate[] subscribers = USANews.GetInvocationList();
      foreach(Delegate _subscriber in subscribers ){
         NewsEventHandler subscriber = (NewsEventHandler) _subscriber;
         subscriber.BeginInvoke(this, newsReport, null, null);
      }
      // Wait a bit to allow asynchronous threads to execute
      // their tasks. Indeed, they are thread pool threads and thus,
      // they are background threads. If we don't wait,
      // threadpool threads wouldn't have the time to begin
      // their tasks.
      System.Threading.Thread.Sleep(100);
   }
}
...
```

Finally take note that there is no need to call the `EndInvoke()` method since the subscribed methods are not supposed to return any results to the method which triggered the event.

Protecting your code from exceptions raised by subscriber methods in a synchronous scenario

Invoking the methods subscribed to an event in an asynchronous way is an efficient technique to protect the code which triggered the event from exceptions raised by the subscribing methods. It is however possible of having the same level of protection when invoking subscribed methods in a synchronous way. For this, you have to invoke them one by one as shows the following example:

Example 11-20

```
...
// Methods used to trigger news publishing from outside NewsBoard.
public void OnUSANews(NewsEventArgs newsReport){
   if( USANews != null ){
      Delegate[] subscribers = USANews.GetInvocationList();
      foreach(Delegate _subscriber in subscribers ){
         NewsEventHandler subscriber = (NewsEventHandler) _subscriber;
         try{
            subscriber(this,newsReport);
         }
         catch(Exception){ /* treat the exception */ }
      }
   }
}
...
```

Encapsulation and visibility 345

Nested types

We can define a type within another type. In this case, the type defined inside the other type is referred to as a *nested type*. There are at least two main advantages to defining a type within another:

- We can restrict the visibility of the encapsulated type. This means that a type defined within a class cannot be used anywhere in the code but only where it was declared (generally only inside the outer class).
- We can access all the members of the outer class from the methods of the nested class. Here is an example to illustrate this non-trivial feature. The instance of `InnerType` have free access to the private field `m_i` of an instance of `OuterType`:

Example 11-21

```
public class OuterType {
   private int m_i = 10;
   public class InnerType {
      public void Add(OuterType foo, int i) {
         foo.m_i += i;    // Access the private field 'OuterType.m_i'.
      }
   }
}
public class Program {
   static void Main() {
      OuterType foo1 = new OuterType();
      OuterType.InnerType foo2 = new OuterType.InnerType();
      foo2.Add(foo1, 3);
      // Here, foo1.m_i is equal to 13.
   }
}
```

> Note that outside the definition of the `OuterType` class, the `InnerType` class is called `OuterType.InnerType`.

Encapsulation and visibility

Visibility of members

C++ › C#: Two new levels of visibility are introduced with C#: `internal` and `internal protected`. These new levels of visibility only relate to class members and not to structure members. Their signification is tied to the notion of assembly.

Another difference with C++ is at the syntax level. The visibility keywords (`private`, `protected` `public` or `internal`) of a member must be placed in front of every member. If none of these keywords is specified, the member is declared as `private` by default in a class as well as in a structure.

The feature in C++ of being able to derive from a base class using the `private` `protected` or `public` keywords in order to keep or restrain the visibility levels of the members of the base class in the derived class does not exist in C#. In C#, we can only keep the visibility level of the members of a base class.

C#: *Encapsulation* is a powerful concept of Object Oriented Programming which allows to control the visibility of the members of a type seen from outside its definition.

The client of a class (this is a developer which writes code that instantiates or references an instance of the class) does not have access to certain members. As a consequence it is easier to use a class since the number of visible members is reduced.

To properly understand the various *visibility levels* you must first understand the notion of assembly which is the topic of chapter 2 and the notion of derived class which is discussed in chapter 12.

There are five different visibility levels. Each class member has one (and only one) of the following visibility levels:

- The *public* visibility level: `public` keyword.

  A *public* member is accessible from anywhere in the code of the current assembly and in the code of the assemblies which reference this assembly.

- The *private* visibility level: `private` keyword.

  A *private* member defined within a type T is accessible only from T as well as from nested types of T.

- The *protected* visibility level: `protected` keyword.

  A *protected* member can only be accessed from the class that defined it and from its subclasses. This remains valid for the subclasses defined in other assemblies.

- The *internal* visibility level: `internal` keyword.

  An *internal* member can be accessed from anywhere in the code of its assembly. However, if the declaring type is used in other assemblies, members marked as internal are invisible to these other assemblies.

- The *internal protected* visibility level: `internal protected` keyword.

  An *internal protected* member can be accessed from anywhere in the code of its assembly. However, if the declaring type is used in other assemblies, a member marked as internal protected is only visible within the code of subclasses deriving from the declaring type. Note that this is the only case where two keywords can be used together to declare a visibility level.

Let's summarize all this into a table. The columns represent the visibility levels of a member of class A. The rows represent zones of code. An OK means that the zone of code has access to this member.

	public	internal protected	internal	protected	private
Methods of type A and methods of nested types of A.	OK	OK	OK	OK	OK
Methods of a subclass of A, declared in the same assembly.	OK	OK	OK	OK	
Methods of another type declared within the same assembly.	OK	OK	OK		
Methods of a subclass of A, declared in a different assembly.	OK	OK		OK	
Methods of another class declared in another assembly.	OK				

The internal and internal protected visibility levels cannot be applied to the members of a structure.

An event cannot be triggered outside of its type, no matter what its visibility level is. Even the code of a nested type of its declaring type cannot trigger an event. Only the event accessors are impacted by its visibility level.

By default, if we do not explicitly set its visibility level, a member is considered as private by the C# compiler.

Visibility of types

A type which is not nested within another type can only have the internal and public visibility levels (CAUTION, here we talk of the visibility level for the type, not its members). If no visibility level is specified explicitly for a type, the internal visibility level is used by default. At page 22, we introduce the notion of a *friend assembly*. The assemblies which are friend to another assembly have the possibility of accessing its non-public types.

Visibility of property and indexer accessors

C#2 allows the accessors of properties and indexers to have different visibility levels. To use this feature, you simply need to assign a visibility level to one of the two accessors. This visibility level must be different and more restrictive than the one of the property or the indexer. The other accessor will automatically have the visibility level of its property or indexer. In general, this feature is used to make sure that the visibility level of the `set` accessor is more restrictive than the visibility level of the `get` accessor:

Example 11-22
```
class Foo {
    public int Prop {
        get { return 5; }
        private set { }
    }
    protected string this[int index] {
        private get { return "hello"; }
        set { }
    }
}
```

This feature cannot be used on the `add` and `remove` accessors of an event.

Notes on private members

Since the private members of a class A are only accessible within this class, this means that an instance I1 of class A can access the private members of an instance I2 of the same class. You must be aware of this feature. In fact, this comes from an arbitrary choice that was made during the conception of the C# language. This choice is not necessarily the same in all object oriented languages such as *Smalltalk*.

Notes on visibility levels of the IL language

All programs written in C# will be compiled into a program written in the IL language. The IL language offers a sixth visibility level which is not supported by C#. This visibility level is *internal AND protected*. To understand its effect, imagine that the `internal protected` C# visibility level is compiled into the *internal OR protected* visibility level. If we had represented this sixth visibility level in the previous table, only the first two lines would have been marked.

The this keyword

C++ › C#: As with C++, the `this` keyword also exists in C#. In C#, this keyword can be used in non-static methods and is a reference (and not a pointer as in C++) to the current object.

C#: In all instance methods of all classes, C# allows the use of the `this` keyword. This keyword is a reference to the object on which the current method is acting. The `this` keyword thus cannot be used within static methods.

In C#, the `this` keyword allows to the arguments of a method to have names similar to the names of some fields and properties of the declaring type. Hence, in the body of the method, you must precede this name with `this` in order to access the member instead of the argument. For example:

Example 11-23

```
class Foo {
   string str;  // An instance field of the class Foo.
   void fct( string str ){  // An instance method.
      // The field 'str' gets the value of the argument 'str'.
      this.str = str;
   }
}
```

Another use of the `this` keyword is to communicate the reference of the current object to other methods, even to other classes. This type of use is generally a sign of an evolved object architecture. For example, the visitor *design pattern* (GoF) uses this feature:

Example 11-24

```
class Foo {
   void fct(){  // An instance method.
      fct2( this );
   }
   static void fct2( Foo foo ){
      // Work with the object referenced by 'foo' ...
   }
}
```

Also, the `this` keyword is used by the syntax of indexers described at page 339.

The `this` keyword can also be used within non-static methods of structures. Although that a structure is a value type, the `this` keyword still represents the current instance. In such a case, no boxing operations are done.

For those interested with the IL language, know that in IL, the `this` reference is passed as argument zero to an instance method, thus offsetting by one position the other arguments in the list.

Constructors

Declaring constructors

C++ › C#: The C# language does not have the field initialization syntax of the C++ language, which allows to accomplish this task immediately after the constructor's prototype (`ctor(int Field): m_Field(Field) {}`).

The C# compiler is less permissive and imposes that all value type fields be initialized before the end of the execution of a constructor.

We will see that the syntax used to pass arguments to the constructor of a base class from a derived class is different compared to the one in C++.

We will also see that in C#, there can be a class constructor which is invoked when the class is loaded into the application domain. This feature does not exist in C++.

The feature of casting constructor in C++ does not exist in C#. We can of course construct an object of class A from another object of class B (by defining a class A constructor which takes an object of type B as a parameter) but the syntax of C++ allowing the creation of A by typecasting:

```
explicit    A objA = (A)objB;
or implicit A objA = objB;
```

does not exist in C# and you must write:

```
A objA = new A(objB).
```

However, the overload of the casting operator is still possible in C# which still makes the same examples possible.

C#: A method is automatically called when an object is created. We call such a method a *constructor* (*ctor* in short). Syntactically, in C#, a constructor method carries the name of the class and returns nothing (note even the `void` type). There can be:

- No constructors: in this case, the C# compiler automatically provides a *default constructor*, which takes no parameters. Such a constructor is public.
- A single constructor: in this case, this will always be this constructor which will be called. The compiler will not supply a default constructor.
- Several constructors: in this case, they differ based on their signatures and we can consider the constructor as an overloaded method. The compiler will not supply a default constructor.

To summarize, from the moment where there is at least one constructor, the compiler does not provide a default constructor in the case of a class. This is illustrated in the examples of the following section.

In the case of a structure, this is different since it is forbidden to provide a constructor without arguments. The default constructor provided by the compiler is then always accessible. This is illustrated by examples in the following section.

When a constructor returns, it is imperative that all the non-static fields of value type have been initialized.

The constructors are affected by visibility levels in the same way as other methods. It is legitimate to wonder what is the use of a private or protected constructor, i.e. a constructor which cannot be accessed outside of its class. This type of use is a sign of an evolved object architecture. For example, some implementations of the *singleton design pattern* (Gof) uses this feature. Another use for a private constructor is done in a class which only contains static members. There is then no use to instantiate this class. Know that C#2 introduces a new feature which allows a class to be declared as static, which avoids the interest in such a practice.

The declaration of a constructor in a derived class can call the constructor of the base class.

Accessing constructors when creating objects

C++ > C#: Contrarily to C++, in C#, during the construction of an object using the `new` operator, it is imperative to put a pair of parenthesis to explicitly indicate that we wish to call the constructor without arguments. Let us precise that C++ does not make the distinction between these two syntaxes.

C#: A constructor is called at the creation of each object. Here is an example in the case of a structure:

Example 11-25

```
struct Article {
    public int Price;
    public Article( int price ) { this.Price = price; }        // ctor 1
```

Example 11-25

```
    public Article( double price ) { this.Price = (int)price; }// ctor 2
}
class Program {
   static void Main() {
      Article a;  // Call the default constructor of the structure.
      Article b = new Article(6);    // Call ctor 1.
      Article c = new Article(6.3);  // Call ctor 2.
   }
}
```

Here is an example in the case of a class:

Example 11-26

```
class Article {
   public int Price;
   public Article( int price ) { this.Price = price; }          // ctor 1
   public Article( double price ) { this.Price = (int)price; }  // ctor 2
   public Article() { Price = 0; }                              // ctor 3
}
class Program {
   static void Main() {
      Article a = new Article();    // Call ctor 3.
      Article b = new Article(6);   // Call ctor 1.
      Article c = new Article(6.3);// Call ctor 2.
   }
}
```

The new keyword is required to call the constructor of a reference type. For a value type, the new keyword is only required to call a constructor with arguments. If you do not use the new keyword, the default constructor is automatically called.

Object finalization and destruction

Destructor, finalizer and the Object.Finalize() method

C++ › C#: The notion of garbage collector is absent from the C/C++ standard. There are a few GC implementations for C++ but in the *Microsoft* world, they are rarely used.

Destructors, which are so commonly used and so subject to controversy in C++ (exceptions raised in a destructor, virtual destructors…) do still exist in C#. However, in C# the developer does not have full control as to the exact moment at which a destructor is called.

C#:

> For a good understanding of the current section, it is important to have assimilated the notion of garbage collector presented at page 95. Compared to C++ we will talk of finalizers rather than destructors.

In the section relating to the garbage collector, we explain that there exists a thread, created and managed by the CLR which is dedicated to call the *finalizers* of objects. The finalizer of a class is defined by overriding the Finalize() method of the Object class. Structures do not have finalizers. The CLR considers that a class which does not override this method does not have a finalizer. We have seen that the finalizer of an object is executed after its collection by the garbage collector. The memory held to store the state of the object will be freed during the following collection.

Object finalization and destruction 351

Consequently, objects which have a finalizer will survive to one more collection than others. Also, you have no control on which thread will invoke the finalizer nor at which time it will be invoked. Objects with finalizers are then globally more expensive and less practical to use.

The C# compiler prevents the direct overriding of the `Finalize()` method of the `Object` class. You are constrained of using the 'destructor syntax' which takes the name of the class prefixed with the '~' character. The following program illustrates this syntax. This program creates an instance of the `Article` class then destroys the only reference to this object and then forces the garbage collector to go through a collection:

Example 11-27

```
using System.Threading;
public class Article {
   public int m_Price;
   public Article(int price) { this.m_Price = price; }   // Constructor.
   ~Article() {   // Finalizer defined with the 'destructor syntax'.
      System.Console.WriteLine( "Thread#{0} Finalizer thread.",
         Thread.CurrentThread.ManagedThreadId );
   }
}
class Program {
   static void Main() {
      System.Console.WriteLine( "Thread#{0} Main thread.",
         Thread.CurrentThread.ManagedThreadId );
      Article a = new Article(300);
      a = null; // The Article instance is not referenced anymore.
      System.GC.Collect(); // Force a GC collection.
      System.GC.WaitForPendingFinalizers();
   }
}
```

This program displays:

```
Thread#1 Main thread.
Thread#2 Finalizer thread.
```

We will see a little later that the code of a finalizer should only contain instructions to free the unmanaged resources held by the object. It is generally dangerous to access an object from a finalizer since it is possible that this object has already been finalized. In fact, the thread dedicated to the garbage collector will invoke the finalizers in an unpredictable order.

Finally, at page 105 we describe the notion of critical finalizer which allows to add guarantees in regards to the reliability of the release of resources.

The IDisposable interface and its Dispose() method

C++ › C#: This technique aims to minimize the problems dues to the non-deterministic behavior of the garbage collector in C# and thus has no equivalent in C++.

C#: There exists a technique to allow a certain method on an object to be automatically called when we decide that we don't need it anymore. Understand that this technique is only a developer aid and does not in any way change the behavior of the garbage collector. Concretely, the concerned class must implement the `System.IDisposable` interface which only has one member, the `Dispose()` method.

Example 11-28

```
using System.Threading;
public class Article : System.IDisposable {
   public int m_Price;
   public Article( int price ) { this.m_Price = price; } // ctor
   public void Dispose() {
      System.Console.WriteLine("Thread#{0} Dispose().",
         Thread.CurrentThread.ManagedThreadId );
   }
}
class Program {
   static void Main() {
      System.Console.WriteLine("Thread#{0} Main thread.",
         Thread.CurrentThread.ManagedThreadId );
      Article a = new Article(300);
      try {
         // In this scope, you can use the object referenced by 'a'.
      }
      finally{
         a.Dispose();
      }
   }
}
```

This program displays:

```
Thread#1 Main thread.
Thread#1 Dispose().
```

Note that the client must call the `Dispose()` method from a `finally` block to avoid that an exception compromise the call to `Dispose()`.

The C# language provides a syntax using the `using` keyword to implicitly and automatically invoke the `Dispose()` method within a `try/finally` block. Hence, the `Main()` method of our program can be rewritten as follows:

Example 11-29

```
...
   static void Main() {
      System.Console.WriteLine("Thread#{0} Main thread.",
         Thread.CurrentThread.ManagedThreadId );
      Article a = new Article(300);
      using(a) {
         // In this scope, you can use the object referenced by 'a'.
         // This scope is compiled as a try block.
      } // The C# compiler compiles this end brace as a call the the
        // a.Dispose() method inside a finally block.
   }
...
```

> **CAUTION:** The use of the `using` keyword presented above has nothing to do with namespaces and aliases.

Note that a validity zone can be common to several objects of a same or different class:

Example 11-30

```
...
    static void Main() {
        System.Console.WriteLine("Thread#{0} Main thread.",
            Thread.CurrentThread.ManagedThreadId );
        Article a = new Article(300);
        Article b = new Article(400);
        using(a) using(b){
            // In this scope you can use the objects
            // referenced by 'a' and 'b'.
        } // Compiled as some calls to 'b.Dispose()' and 'a.Dispose()'
          // (in this order).
    }
...
```

The `Dispose()` methods will be called in the reverse order than the `using` blocks at the end of the validity zone (here `b.Dipose()` and then `a.Dispose()`).

For semantic reasons, you may be tempted to use a method named, for example, `Close()` instead of implementing the `IDisposable` and its `Dispose()` method. It is better to avoid this practice as the simple fact of implementing the `IDispose` interface is a standard way to expose to your clients that they must use the `Dispose()` method. There are code analyzers which are capable of detecting that `Dispose()` was not called on an object of a class which implements `IDisposable`.

However, if you opt to use a method such as `Close()` you must encapsulate the call to this method within the `Dispose()` method, as certain .NET class do. It is also important to properly documents this in order to avoid successive calls to `Close()` and `Dispose()`. Sometimes, such a practice can cause an exception to be raised.

When a class implements the `IDisposable` interface, it is recommended to prevent the call to all other methods on an object which has been 'disposed' by raising an exception of type `System.ObjectDisposedException`. To give your clients more leeway, it is also recommended to allow several calls to the `Dispose()` method on a same object. Of course, only the first call will have an effect. With these rules in mind, the `Article` class can be rewritten as follows (note the use of a private Boolean field):

Example 11-31

```
public class Article : System.IDisposable {
    public int m_Price;
    public Article( int price ) { this.m_Price = price; }

    private bool m_bDisposed = false;
    public void Fct() {
        if (m_bDisposed)
            throw new System.ObjectDisposedException("ObjectID");
        // Here, you can put the body of the 'Fct()' method.
    }
    public void Dispose() {
        if (!m_bDisposed) {
            m_bDisposed = true;
            // Here, you must release resources.
        }
    }
}
```

This implementation of `Article` has one weakness. In a multi-threaded application, it is possible that the test on `m_bDisposed` in a method takes place between the test in the `Dispose()` method and this field being set to `true` in the `Dispose()` method. For the same reasons, it is also possible that the code which releases resources within the `Dispose()` be called twice by two different threads. To solve this problem without making the whole class *thread-safe,* you can use synchronization to the access of `m_bDisposed` like this:

Example 11-32

```
public class Article : System.IDisposable {
   public int m_Price;
   public Article(int price) { this.m_Price = price; }

   private object m_SyncRootDisposed = new object();
   private bool m_bDisposed = false;
   public void Fct() {
      lock ( m_SyncRootDisposed ) {
         if ( m_bDisposed )
            throw new System.ObjectDisposedException("Name of Object");
      }
      // Here, you can put the body of the 'Fct()' method.
   }
   public void Dispose() {
      bool bOldDisposedState = true;
      lock ( m_SyncRootDisposed ) {
         if ( !m_bDisposed ) {
            bOldDisposedState = false;
            m_bDisposed = true;
         }
      }
      if ( !bOldDisposedState ) {
         // Here, you must release resources.
      }
   }
}
```

When do you need finalizer and Dispose() method ?

It is legitimate to ask yourself why and when you should use finalizers and/or a `Dispose()` method on your class. The answer in regards to finalizers is simple:

> All classes which maintain one or several unmanaged resources (such as a handle to a Windows object for example) must have a finalizer which frees these resources. We can add that it is essential that such a class always keep its unmanaged resources private. These two conditions allow guaranteeing that the unmanaged resources will be properly freed. Also, only classes must be able to handle unmanaged resources as structures do not have finalizers.

The previous remark implies that a class which does not maintain managed resources does not need a finalizer. In fact, it would serve no purpose to assign the reference type fields to null as a finalizer is strictly executed between two collections by the garbage collector and its execution implies the loss of the references contained in the fields of the concerned object. We may be tempted to implement a finalizer on a class which maintains a reference to a managed object which has a `Close()` or `Dispose()` method (such as a connection to a database). In fact, this kind of class maintains directly or indirectly through another class references to unmanaged resources. The call to the `Close()` or `Dispose()` methods do not allow to anticipate when these unmanaged resources will be freed. There is then no point in invoking these methods in a finalizer. They must be called before, using a `Dispose()` method. And this raises another question: when must we implement the `IDisposable` interface?

Object finalization and destruction   355

Part of the answer is easy: if your class maintains references to objects whose lifetime is the same as its instance and where their implementation offers a `Dispose()` or `Close()` method, then you must implement a `Dispose()` method which will in turn call the `Dispose()` and `Close()` methods of these objects. If your class does not fit within this criterion, the decision of whether or not to implement the `IDisposable` is more complicated since you will be faced with a dilemma. In one way, it is good to have a `Dispose()` method to set to null the references that you maintain to other managed objects in order to increase the chance that they will be freed during the following collection. On the other hand, implementing the `IDisposable` interface complexifies your code as well as the code of your clients. The choice must be made based on the memory requirements of your application as well as the size of the managed objects which are referenced.

When a class implements a finalizer, you may also be tempted to implement the `IDisposable` interface to allows your clients to free the resources (managed or not) earlier. In this case, we recommend that you apply the following rules:

- Apply the rules mentioned for the implementation of the `IDisposable` interface.
- Implement a `protected virtual void Dispose(bool bDisposeManagedRes)` method. Call this method from the `Dispose()` method with the `bDisposeManagedRes` parameter set to `true`. Call this method from the finalizer with `bDisposeManagedRes` set to `false`.
- In the `Dispose(bool bDisposeManagedRes)` method, free all unmanaged resources and only free managed resources if `bDisposeManagedRes` is set to `true`.
- In the `Dispose()` method, after calling the `Dispose(bool bDisposeManagedRes)` overload, call `GC.SuppressFinalize(this)`. You can then tell the garbage collector that it does not need to call the finalizer on this object.

If you apply these tips, you relieve the finalizer thread from having to free the managed resources for nothing, yet protect yourself in case a client forgets to call the `Dispose()` method. Here is a `Foo` class which follows these tips (without the synchronization to the access of `m_bDisposed`):

Example 11-33

```
public class Foo : System.IDisposable {
   public Foo() {
      // Here, you can eventually allocate resources.
   }
   private bool m_bDisposed = false;
   public void Fct() {
      if ( m_bDisposed )
         throw new System.ObjectDisposedException("Name of the objet");
      // Here, you can put the body of the 'Fct()' method.
   }
   public void Dispose() {
      Dispose( true );
      System.GC.SuppressFinalize(this);
   }
   ~Foo() { Dispose(false); }
   protected virtual void Dispose(bool bDisposeManagedRes) {
      if ( !m_bDisposed ) {
         m_bDisposed = true;
         // Here, you must release unmanaged resources.
         if ( bDisposeManagedRes ) {
            // Here, you must release managed resources.
         }
      }
   }
}
```

In the case where `Foo` is a base class which has derived classes which maintains resources, it is better to override the `Dispose(bool bDisposeManagedRes)` method since it is virtual and protected. It is interesting to note that the design of the framework classes follow these rules.

Static members

C++ › C#: In C#, there are several small syntax differences compared to static members in C++. In C#:

- We access a static member with this syntax `ClassName.StaticMemberName`. We do not need the scope resolution operator as in C++.
- We cannot access a static member through a reference to an instance of the class.

Conceptually, nothing is different with the exception of that there can be a static constructor and a class can be defined as purely static.

C#: Fields, properties, methods and events of a class all have the possibility of being declared using the `static` keyword. This keyword means that the member belongs to the class and not to instance objects as with non-static members. Static members are sometimes called *shared members*, as they are shared by all instances of the class. In fact, the VB.NET uses the `Shared` keyword instead of the `static` C# keyword. The non-static members are called *instance members*.

Members declared as static follow the same rules in regards to their visibility levels as other members. In addition, amongst all the different kind of members only nested types and indexers cannot be declared using the `static` keyword.

Static fields, properties and events

The static fields, properties or events of a class distinguish themselves by the following characteristics:

- They exist independently from the instance of the class, including if no instance of the class has been created;
- They are all shared by all instances of the class;
- They are accessible within the class by their name and from outside of the class (depending on their visibility level) using the following syntax:

    `NameOfTheClass.NameOfTheStaticField`

Fields can be initialized directly in their declaration within the class. As with the initialization of instance fields, the initialization of static fields is a subtle subject. In fact, when the class is created, the static fields are then initialized to their default value and are then initialized with their initialization value (for those who have one), in the order in which they appear in the class. Finally, the static constructor (presented a little later) is called. All this allows creating cross references as shown below, although that this practice is strongly discouraged:

Example 11-34

```
public class Program {
    static int a = b + 2;   // The 'a' initialization references 'b'.
    static int b = a + 3;   // The 'b' initialization references 'a'.
    public static void Main() {
        System.Console.WriteLine("a = {0}", a);   // a = 2
        System.Console.WriteLine("b = {0}", b);   // b = 5
    }
}
```

The example below also leads to confusion and in fact the result is different than with the preceding example. In fact, the construction of the B class is done halfway through the construction of the A class since A is called first but also uses B!

Example 11-35
```
public class A {
   static public int a = B.b + 2;
}
public class B {
   static public int b = A.a + 3;
}
public class Program {
   public static void Main() {
      System.Console.WriteLine("A.a = {0}", A.a);   // A.a = 5
      System.Console.WriteLine("B.b = {0}", B.b);   // B.b = 3
   }
}
```

Static methods

Static methods distinguish themselves by the following characteristics:

- A static method does not have access to the non-static methods, fields, properties and events of the class;
- A static method is not accessible from a reference to an object of the class,
- A static method is accessible in all methods (static or not) of the class by its name or outside of the class (depending on its visibility level) by using the following syntax:

    ```
    NameOfTheClass.NameOfTheStaticMethod()
    ```
- A static method cannot use the `this` keyword.

Class constructor (also named static constructor)

C# allows the definition of a *static constructor* sometimes also named a *class constructor* or *cctor*. As with all static methods, this method only has access to the static member and can be used, for example, to initialize them. The syntax is the same as a constructor without arguments with the exception that it is declared using the `static` keyword. A class constructor does not have a visibility level. In fact, neither the exact moment at which this constructor is called nor which thread will call it is defined by the C# specification. However, the following points from the C# specification can help you evaluating this moment:

- The static constructor is called by the CLR when it loads the type metadata for this class in the current application domain;
- The static constructor must be called before the creation of any instances of the class;
- The static constructor must be called before a static member of the class be accessed;
- The static constructor must be called after that all static fields explicitly initialized in the class definition have been initialized;
- The static constructor of a class loaded by the CLR must be called at least once during the execution of the program.

You have the possibility of forcing the call to a class constructor with the `void RunClassConstructor(type t)` static method of the `System.Runtime.CompilerServices.RuntimeHelpers` class. Naturally, the execution will only happen if the constructor has not already been called.

Here is a class which counts the number of currently valid instances, where this number is initialized in a static constructor:

Example 11-36
```
public class Article {
   static int NbArticles;      // A static field.
   static Article() {          // The class constructor.
      NbArticles = 0;
   }
   int Price = 0;              // An instance private field.
   public Article( int price ) { // The constructor.
      this.Price = price;
      NbArticles++;
   }
   ~Article() { NbArticles--; } // Finalizer.
}
```

Static classes

C#2 allows the definition of *static classes*. A static class can only contain static members. The C# compiler doesn't provide a default constructor for a static class. Since it does not have an instance constructor, a static class cannot be instantiated. Also, we cannot derive from a static class. Note that a structure cannot be static.

To define a static class, you simple need to use the `static` keyword in its definition:

Example 11-37
```
static class Program {
   static void Main() { }
}
```

Operator overloading

C++ › C#: In C#, the overload of arithmetic operators has several differences compared to C++. We can already say that the operator overloading is simpler, less permissive but also less powerful in C# than in C++.

First of all, of the fourthy (or so) operators which can be overloaded in C++, there is only about twenty in C#. Those which do not exist in C# are:

- The '+=' '%=' operators;
- The '&&' '||' operators;
- The '=' assignment operator;
- The '%' modulo operator;
- The 'new' 'delete[]' allocation and deallocation operators;
- The operators close to the language such as '->' '->*' ',' ;
- The '()' function call operator which allowed *functors* (object functions) on which a large part of STL depends on. This notion of functors can still be implemented with a different approach as we will explain at page 492.

The '[]' indexing operator has given birth to indexers presented a little earlier. The casting operators exist in C# and are described in the following section.

The syntax used to declare operators has also changed. In fact, in C++ an overload could be internal to the class (the overload method is non-static and is in the class) or external (the operator overload method is a friend function to the class). In C#, an operator overload method is a static method which must follow the rules bellow. Note that in C#, the notion of 'friendship' found in C++ does not exist.

C#: To present the operators which can be overloaded in C#, we will separate them into three categories:

- The arithmetic operators such as '+', '-'...;
- The type conversion operators which are also called casting operators;
- The comparison operators.

Arithmetic operator overloading

The C# language allows a class to overload arithmetic operators such as the plus operator '+' or the negation operator '!', by using the **operator** keyword. Concretely, when the C# compiler encounters objects of this class which are manipulated with an overloaded operator, it simply calls the method which corresponds to the operator.

A method which overloads an operator is static. As with all other static methods, it is subject to the visibility level rules. Arithmetic operators that we can overload fall into two categories:

- The *unary operators*, which only operate on a single operand. The static method which overloads a unary operator only accepts one argument of the same type as its class. In addition, it returns also a value of the same type as its class.
- The *binary operators* which operate on two operands. The static method which overloads a binary operator takes two arguments: the first is of the type of the class while the second can be of any type. It also returns a value which can be of any type.

Not all operators can be overloaded, and this is a good thing. In fact, the code quickly becomes complex when operators are overloaded unless the meaning of the operator is logical within the context of the class. Each overloadable operator has a meaning which is well known to developers. Hence, the '+' operator is used for addition. It is logical to use such an operator in a class which represents number (for example, fractional number, complex numbers or even quaternions) other mathematical objects contained in a set which can be added (matrices, vectors...) or even strings. But, what would such an operator mean in the context of a class representing a person? It is for this reason that we recommend overloading operators only when this operator makes logical sense in the semantic context of the class.

Here is the list of overloadable operators:

Overloadable unary operators.	+	-	!	~	++	--			
Overloadable binary operators.	+	-	*	/	%	&	|	^	<< >>

Some operators are both unary and binary. For example, the '-' operator can be used as a negation and also be used to subtract two operands.

The increment '++' and decrement '--' unary overloaded operator both call the same function whether they used as a prefix or a suffix. Let us remind you that that when we use these operators, the evaluation order of the operators is different depending on the operand.

Here is an example which uses operators. We create a `Distance` and a `Surface` class. Internally, values are stored using doubles and one unit represents one meter (or one square meter). We overload the '+' and '*' operators for two distances and the '++' operator to add one meter to a distance and the '/' operator:

Example 11-38
```
public class Distance {
   double m_Measure = 0.0;
   public double Measure { get { return m_Measure; }
                           set { m_Measure = value; } }
   public Distance( double d ) { m_Measure = d; }
   public static Distance operator +( Distance d1, Distance d2 ) {
      return new Distance( d1.m_Measure + d2.m_Measure );
```

Example 11-38

```
   }
   public static Surface operator *( Distance d1, Distance d2 ) {
      return new Surface( d1.m_Measure * d2.m_Measure );
   }
   public static Distance operator ++( Distance d ) {
      return new Distance( d.m_Measure++ );
   }
}
public class Surface {
   double m_Measure = 0.0;
   public double Measure {
      get { return m_Measure; }
      set { m_Measure = value; }
   }
   public Surface(double d) { m_Measure = d; }
   public static Distance operator /( Surface s, Distance d ) {
      return new Distance(s.m_Measure / d.Measure);
   }
   public static double operator /( Surface s1, Surface s2 ) {
      return s1.m_Measure / s2.m_Measure;
   }
}
class Program {
   static void Main() {
      Distance d1 = new Distance( 5.3 );
      Distance d2 = new Distance( 2.4 );
      Distance d3 = d1 + d2;
      Surface s1 = d1 * d2;
      Surface s2 = d3 * d2;
      Distance d4 = s1 / d3;
      double dQuotient = s1 / s2;
      Distance d5 = d1++;
      // Here, d5 measures 6.3 and d1 measures 5.3.
      Distance d6 = ++d1;
      // Here, d6 measures 5.3 and d1 measures 5.3.
   }
}
```

Be aware that in this code, we do not test whether the operands may be null. We accept the fact that an exception of type `NullReferenceException` will be raised automatically by the CLR.

The way we coded the '++' operator in `Distance` causes an unexpected behavior. In fact, the call to this operator returns a new `Distance` object whose distance is incremented by one. This behavior is particularly dangerous since in general, the '++' modifies the object on which it is called. A more logical way to code this operator would be:

Example 11-39

```
...
   public static Distance operator ++(Distance d) {
      d.m_Measure++;
      return d;
   }
...
      Distance d5 = d1++;
      // Here, d5 measures 6.3 and d1 measures 6.3.
      Distance d6 = ++d1;
      // Here, d6 measures 7.3 and d1 measures 7.3.
...
```

Cast operator overloading

C++ › C#: As with C++, C# allows the definition of implicit and explicit cast operators. The C# syntax requires these operators to be static.

In C#, casting constructors do not exist. Let us remind you that in C++, the casting constructors and cast operators have the same functionality. The difference comes from the fact that the casting constructors are in the destination class and that the cast operators reside in the source class. This can lead to some ambiguities when both forms co-exist. This problem is then not present in C#.

C#: The cast operator represents the construction of an instance of a destination class from an instance of a source class. C# allows the creation of your own casting operators, in other words, methods which are automatically called when you write:

    Dest objDest = objSrc;

The code of these methods essentially executes a copy of the fields and properties. There are two types of casting operators.

- The *implicit cast operator*. The following code is sufficient to cause a call to an implicit cast operator of Src to Dest, declared in Src.

      Dest objDest = objSrc;

- The *explicit cast operator*. The previous code is not sufficient to provoke a call to the explicit cast operator from Src to Dest, declared Src. In this case, the compiler generates an error and the developer must explicitly express the typecast this way:

      Dest objDest = (Dest) objSrc;

As with all operators, cast operators are static methods. They are declared in the source class and have as a name the name of the destination class. The use of the `explicit` or `implicit` keywords is mandatory.

Here is a code example where an object of the `Distance` can be implicitly cast into a `double` variable and can be explicitly cast into a `RoundedDistance` class. Note the need to take into account the fact that an input reference might be null in these operators:

Example 11-40

```
public class Distance {
   public double m_Measure = 0.0;
   public Distance(double d) { m_Measure = d; }
   public static implicit operator double( Distance d ) {
      // Take care of the case where 'd' is null.
      if ( object.ReferenceEquals( d, null ) ) {
         return 0.0;
      }
      return d.m_Measure;
   }
   public static explicit operator RoundedDistance( Distance d ) {
      if ( object.ReferenceEquals(d, null) ) {
         // You might prefer returning the null reference in this case.
         return new RoundedDistance(0);
      }
      // Here, we need to build a new object.
      return new RoundedDistance((int)d.m_Measure);
   }
}
```

Example 11-40

```
// Rounded distance means that the measure is stored on an integer.
public class RoundedDistance {
   public int m_Measure = 0;
   public RoundedDistance( int i ) { m_Measure = i; }
}
class Program {
   static void Main() {
      Distance d1 = new Distance(5.3);
      // OK the casting is implicit.
      double dbl1 = d1;
      // The explicit form is also accepted.
      double dbl2 = (double) d1;

      // Compilation error!! : the casting must be explicit.
      RoundedDistance de1 = d1;
      // OK the casting is explicit.
      RoundedDistance de2 = (RoundedDistance) d1;

      // Test the case where the source reference is null.
      Distance d2 = null;
      double dbl3 = (double)d2;
      RoundedDistance de3 = (RoundedDistance)d2;
   }
}
```

It is always preferable to declare cast operators as explicit. Otherwise, your code risks of being permissive, meaning that the compiler will have to make a choice. In the best case, it will emit an error as it does not know which choice to make. In the worst case, it will not give any warning and will make a choice which may not be what you expected. For example, imagine that an instance of the `Distance` class could be implicitly converted to an instance of the `double` type or to an instance of the `string` class. Which cast operator will the compiler choose when we wish to display this object using the `Console.WriteLine(object)` method?

Example 11-41

```
public class Distance {
   public double m_Measure = 0.0;
   public Distance(double d) { m_Measure = d; }
   public static implicit operator double( Distance d ) {
      if (object.ReferenceEquals(d, null))
         return 0.0;
      return d.m_Measure;
   }
   public static implicit operator string( Distance d ) {
      if (object.ReferenceEquals(d, null))
         return null;
      return string.Format("Distance:{0:##.##} meters", d.m_Measure);
   }
}
class Program {
   static void Main() {
      Distance d1 = new Distance(5.3);
      // Compilation error: The call is ambiguous between
      // 'Console.WriteLine(double)' and 'Console.WriteLine(string)'.
      System.Console.WriteLine( d1 );
      // OK it is not an ambiguous call.
      System.Console.WriteLine( (string) d1);
   }
}
```

Comparison operator overloading

C++ › C#: As with C++, C# allows the redefinition of the '==' and '!=' comparison operators.

However, the motivation behind these operators is different in C#. By default, the behavior of these operators on reference types is to compare whether both references point to the same object. However, we quite often wish to compare the contents. In addition, in C#, the comparison operators are not defined by default on structures, contrarily to C++.

C#: The *comparison operators* are the following:

Operator	Name	Comments
==	Equality operator.	When this operator is defined, the compiler forces the developer to provide an inequality operator.
!=	Inequality operator.	When this operator is defined, the compiler forces the developer to define an equality operator.
<=	Lesser than or equal operator.	When this operator is defined, the compiler forces the developer to also implement the greater or equal operator.
>=	Greater or equal operator.	When this operator is defined, the compiler forces the developer to implement the lesser or equal operator.
<	Lesser than operator.	When this operator is defined, the compiler forces the developer to implement the greater than operator.
>	Greater than operator.	When this operator is defined, the compiler forces the developer to also define the lesser than operator.

By default, if these operators are not overloaded, the following rules are applies depending on the nature of the operands:

- If both operands are of a primitive type or an enumeration. The compiler will first attempt to cast one of the two operands so that it is of the same type as the other. If it succeeds, the comparison operators will compare the content of both objects.
- If both operands are of the same structure type, the compiler will generate an error. The comparison of structures is not allowed by default in C#.
- If the two operands are of a reference type and that the comparison operator is for equality or inequality, the compiler will first verify that the classes of both objects are the same. This condition can be fulfilled even if the referenced types are different. In fact, inheritance, which is the topic of the next chapter, allows to an object and to a reference to this object to be of different types. If both referenced objects have the same implementation, the comparison operator will verify if the same object is referenced.
- If both operands are reference types and that the operator is not equality or inequality, an error is produced by the compiler as no other operators exist by default on reference types in C#.
- If one operand is of a value type and the other is of a reference type, the compiler will produce an error.

When you decide to overload the equality and inequality operators, it is recommended that you also override the `Equals()` method of the `Object` class. If you follow this tip, you need to make sure that the overloaded operators call the `Equals()` method, as in the following example: (more information on the `Object.Equals()` method can be found at page 288, where we explain why the compilation of the following program will generate a warning in regards to the `Object.GetHashCode()` method).

Example 11-42
```
public class Distance {
    private double m_Measure = 0.0;
    public Distance(double d) { m_Measure = d; }
    public override bool Equals( object obj ) {
```

Example 11-42
```
        Distance d = obj as Distance;
        // Check that we are effectively comparing with a Distance.
        // With the same test, handle also the case where 'obj' is null.
        if( !Distance.ReferenceEquals( d , null ) )
            // Comparison on content.
            return m_Measure == d.m_Measure;
        return false;
    }
    public static bool operator ==(Distance d1, object d2) {
        // Handle the case where one or two distances are null.
        if( Distance.ReferenceEquals( d1 , null ) ) {
            return Distance.ReferenceEquals( d2 , null );
        }
        return d1.Equals(d2);
    }
    public static bool operator !=(Distance d1, object d2) {
        return ! (d1 == d2) ;
    }
}
class Program {
    static void Main() {
        Distance d1 = new Distance(5.2);
        Distance d2 = new Distance(5.2);
        Distance d3 = new Distance(7.3);
        Distance d4 = null;
        // All the following assertions are true.
        System.Diagnostics.Debug.Assert( d1 == d2 );
        System.Diagnostics.Debug.Assert( d1 != d3 );
        System.Diagnostics.Debug.Assert( d1 != null );
        System.Diagnostics.Debug.Assert( null != d1 );
        System.Diagnostics.Debug.Assert( !(d1 == null) );
        System.Diagnostics.Debug.Assert( !(null == d1) );
        System.Diagnostics.Debug.Assert( d4 == null );
    }
}
```

As you can see when analyzing this example, overloading the == and =! operators is not an easy task:

- You must first consider the case where both references are null. By convention, two null references are considered equal.
- You must also consider the case where the other reference in the comparison is not of type Distance.
- Finally, internally, you must avoid the use of the == and != operators as they could potentially cause an infinite loop. This is why we make a call to the Object.ReferenceEquals() method.

Operator overloading and CLS

The support for operator overloading in C# is present mostly to improve code readability. Operator overloading is not *CLS Compliant*. This means that other .NET language do not support then and cannot use them. Also, if your class is destined to be used by other .NET languages, we recommend that you expose public methods with the same functionality as the operators you have overloaded. For example, if you were to overload the '+' operator in a class, we recommend that you provide an Add() static method which accomplishes the same task. Let us remind you that if you have any doubts in regards as to whether your code is CLS compliant, you can use the CLSCompliant attribute that we describe at page 107.

Here is the list of the name of substitutions given to methods in order to obtain the same functionality as an overloaded operator. These names are recommended, and the compiler allows you to use your own identifiers.

Operator	Recommended name.
Cast operators	
Implicit cast to Xxx	ToXxx
	FromXxx
Explicit cast to Xxx	ToXxx
	FromXxx
Binary arithmetic operators	
+	Add
-	Subtract
*	Multiply
/	Divide
%	Mod
^	Xor
&	BitwiseAnd
|	BitwiseOr
<<	LeftShift
>>	RightShift
Unary arithmetic operators	
+	Plus
-	Negate
++	Increment
--	Decrement
~	OnesComplement
!	Not
Comparison operators	
==	Equals
!=	Compare
<=	Compare
>=	Compare
<	Compare
>	Compare

12 Inheritance, polymorphism and abstraction

Objective: code reuse

The underlying problem

The following law is fundamental in programming:

> The complexity of a program in relation to its size grows faster than a linear function of its size.

This law is illustrated by Figure 12-1:

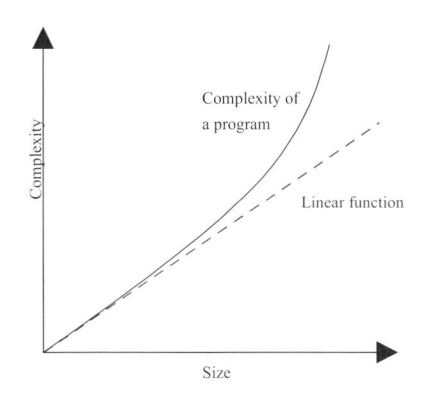

Figure 12-1: Complexity of a program

A program twice the size of another is then more than twice as complex to write, test and maintain.

This law is of course empirical. The work of a program designer is to make sure that the complexity of a program remains as close to a linear function as possible. The inheritance mechanism is an important point to help alleviate this problem but as we will see at the end of this chapter, it is not the only way.

Concretely, we can see that in a program, different classes have identical functionalities:

- In an employee management application, there may be classes for secretaries, a class for technicians and a class for the managers. All these classes have in common that an instance represents an employee with common attributes such as `Name`, `Age`, `Address`, `Salary` and the `ComputeBonus()` and `ChangeHours()` methods.

- In a drawing program, there can be a class for circles, one for rectangles and one for triangles. All these classes have in common an instance of the `Color` and `Position` attributes and the `Draw()`, `Translate()`, `Rotate()` and `Resize()` methods.
- In a middleware program which communicates using various protocols, each communication endpoint has independently of the underlying protocol, the `NBytesSent/Received`, `LastOpenDate` attributes and the `SendData()` method.

A solution: class inheritance

The idea is to reuse the similarities between various classes by gathering them in a class called a *base class* (for example `Employee`, `GeometricFigure` or `CommunicationEndPoint`).

A *derived class* is a class which *inherits* the members of a base class. Concretely, if the `Technician` class inherits from the `Employee` class, the `Technician` class inherits the `Name` and `Age` properties as well as the `ComputeBonus()` and `ChangeHours()` methods. We also say that the derived class is a specialization of the base class and that the base class of a derived class is the *super class* of this derived class.

One of the difficulties in software design is to properly notice the similarities between classes, and this as early as possible in the development cycle. The other major difficulty is to define how the object will interact with each other. Here are a few sentences you can use to confirm your intuition (this way to do is often referred as *ISA*).

- A Technician **is an** employee, a Rectangle **is a** geometrical figure, a socket **is a** communication endpoint (hence the term ISA).
- A Technician **has a** name, a Rectangle **has a** color, a socket **has a** number of bytes sent since its creation.
- A Technician **can be** evaluated, a Rectangle **can be** resized, a socket **can be** used to send a data stream.

Class inheritance

The syntax

C++ › C#: The syntax for implementation inheritance is the same between C# and C++. Conceptually there is a big difference between C# and C++ as C# does not support multiple inheritance. We will see that this lack is at least in part compensated, in C#, by the simpler concept of interfaces and the implementation of several interfaces by a class.

C#: In C#, the syntax to indicate that the `Technician` class derives from the `Employee` class is the following:

```
// The Technician class inherits the Employee class.
class Technician : Employee {  ...  }
```

A class can only inherit from a single base class. In object oriented terms, we say that C# support *simple inheritance* but not *multiple inheritance*. This is not the case with all object oriented languages. The C++ and EIFFEL languages both support multiple inheritance while Java does not.

In C#, if a class C derives from a class B, nothing prevents the class B of deriving from class A. We say that C derives indirectly from A. Also, the B class is both at the same time a derived class and a base class.

The protected and internal protected visibility levels

C++ › C#: As with C++, C# allows to protect the members of a base class. The notion of member protection is identical between both languages. Both use the `protected` keyword, and the only difference is that in C#, you have to write the keyword for every protected member. C# also adds the notion of an internal protected member (`internal protected` keyword).

C#: Let us remind you the definition of the protected and internal protected visibility levels that we presented at page 345:

- The *protected* visibility level: `protected` keyword

  A member with the *protected* visibility level defined in a type T is accessible only from the code contained in T (including the types encapsulated in T) as well as from the code which derives from T. This remains valid for the types derived from T defined in another assembly.

- The *internal protected* visibility level: `internal protected` keyword.

  A member with the *internal protected* visibility level which is defined in a type T is only accessible anywhere within the code of the current assembly. However, if the T type is used in another assembly, the members marked as internal protected are only visible within the code which derives from T. Note that this is the only case where two keywords can be combined to define a visibility level.

Class inheritance diagram

A base class can also be a derived class. All this can be illustrated in an inheritance diagram. For example:

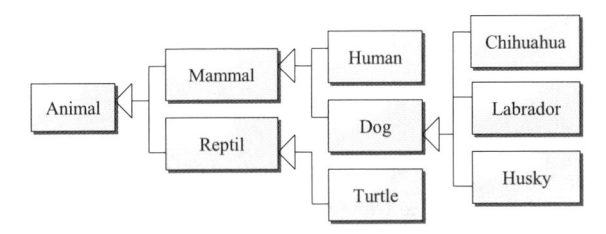

Figure 12-2: Example of a class inheritance diagram

There exists several modeling languages for object diagrams, the most common being UML (*Unified Modeling Language*). We have used the notion of class diagram of this language to represent the diagram in Figure 12-2. As you can see, in UML, a white arrow points towards the base classes and divides itself towards the derived classes.

Visual Studio 2005 offers the possibility of visualizing a class diagram similar to an UML class diagram. You can access this feature by selecting *View Class Diagram*. A `.cd` XML file is then inserted in your project. It contains the definition of your diagram. Here is an example extracted from the *Windows Forms* control hierarchy presented at page 563:

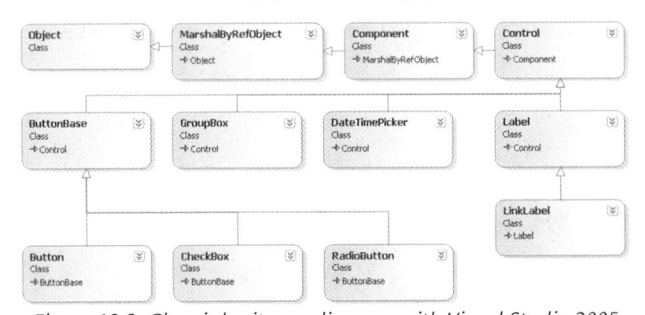

Figure 12-3: Class inheritance diagram with Visual Studio 2005

Calling a base class constructor

C++ › C#: As with C++, C# allows to explicitly call the constructor of a base class in the constructor of a derived class. As with C++, if the call is not explicitly declared, the default constructor of the base class is called. If such a constructor is not present, a compilation error occurs.

However, the syntax of the C# language is slightly different than the syntax of C++. Since there is no multiple inheritance in C#, the base class is unique. Hence, it is not necessary to specify the name of the base class. In this context, with C#, the name of the base class is

d by the **base** keyword.

C#: In C#, each constructor of a derived class calls the constructor of its base class. This call can be implicit, meaning that there is no code showing that this call must be done. In this case, it is the default constructor of the base class which will be called. If the base class does not have a default constructor (i.e. without any arguments) the compiler will generate an error. Remember the following principles:

- If the class does not declare a constructor: the compiler will automatically produce a default constructor without any arguments.
- If a class declares a single constructor: there is only a single constructor, this one. The compiler does not provide a default constructor.
- If a class declares several constructors then they differ from their signature. We say that the constructor is overloaded. The compiler does not provide a default constructor.

The call to the constructor of the base class can be done explicitly from the constructor of a derived class. For this, the **base** keyword must be used with the same syntax as in the following example:

Example 12-1

```csharp
public class Employee {
   string m_Name;
   short m_Age;
   // A constructor with the {string,short} signature.
   public Employee(string name, short age) {
      m_Name = name;
      m_Age = age;
   }
   // Default constructor.
   public Employee() {
      m_Name = "n/a";
      m_Age = 0;// <- Not needed, a 'short' is always initialized to 0.
   }
}
class Technician : Employee {   // Technician inherits Employee.
   string m_Competencies;
   // Call the ctor with the {string,short} signature.
   public Technician( string name, short age, string competencies )
      : base( name , age ) {
      m_Competencies = competencies;
   }
}
class Program {
   static void Main() {
      Technician bob = new Technician("Bob", 45, "PC install");
   }
}
```

Virtual methods and polymorphism 371

Visibility of a base class members

C++ › C#: In C# you cannot specify the visibility level that a derived class has on the members of its base class. In C# everything happens as in C++ when the visibility level is `public`.

Sealed classes

C++ › C#: Contrarily to C++, the C# language allows to clearly state that a class cannot be used as a base class.

C#: C# allows specifying that a class can never be the base class of another class. In other words, no class can derive from this one. You simply need to place the `sealed` keyword before the declaration of the class. We sometimes use the *finalized class* term to name this feature. For example:

```
sealed class Foo{  /* Here, the class' members. */ }
```

A sealed class can be a derived class. And as with all types, sealed classes derive from the `Object` class. In addition, structures can be seen as value typed sealed classes.

Virtual methods and polymorphism

C++ › C#: Note that we here talk of virtual methods, in other words a method which has an implementation in the base class. Pure virtual functions of C++ are called abstract functions in C# and we will discuss them a little later.

The concepts of polymorphisms and virtual methods are identical in C++ and C#. However, C# allows you to prevent that polymorphism applies to certain virtual methods of a derived class. In addition, there are a few little syntax differences:

- In C++, to have access to polymorphism, we often use pointers on the type of the base class on which we call the virtual methods. In C#, pointers are not popular. Most of the time we use references typed by a base class, referencing objects instances of derived classes. Note that in C++, this feature is less often used than pointers.

- In C++, a virtual method is declared using the `virtual` keyword in the first base class which implements it. The implementations of this method in the derived classes can optionally reuse this keyword to indicate that the method is virtual. The C# language resolves this problem. A virtual method is always declared using the `virtual` keyword in the first base class which implements it. In every derived class where the virtual method is overridden, you must use the `override` keyword.

A conceptual difference:

- The conceptual difference at the level of virtual methods, between C++ and C#, can be found in the fact that with C#, the developer can override a virtual method while preventing polymorphism from being applied. For this, we can use the `new` keyword instead of `override`. If we do not place any of these keywords on the method, the compiler will simply produce a warning similar to: 'you must use `new`' but during execution, everything will happen as if the method was declared using `new`. So be careful!

The underlying problem

In object oriented programming, we are often faced with the following problem: we create several objects, instances of several classes deriving from a base class, then we want to apply a base process (i.e. a process defined on the base class). The problem is that this process varies depending on the derived class. For example:

- We wish to obtain a description of all employees (base process: obtain a description of an employee no matter which type of employee it is).
- We want to draw all geometrical shapes (base process: draw a geometrical shape no matter the type of the shape).
- We wish to send data through a communication endpoint (base process: send data, no matter what is the underlying communication protocol).

A solution: virtual methods and polymorphism

It is useful to collect the objects which must go through the base process, and then to do the base process on each of them (for example in a loop).

> The beauty of this method comes from the fact that the base process applies to an object without knowing its exact type, we only know it by a reference of the type of the base class: this is an illustration of polymorphism.

What we have called a base process is essentially a *virtual method*. This is a method defined at the same time in the base class (using the `virtual` keyword) and in the derived class (using the `override` keyword).

There exist several bodies for this method, one in the base class and eventually one in each derived class. During the call to this method on a reference of the type of the base class, the proper method body is selected during the execution of the program. The notion of multiple bodies for a same function is known as *polymorphism*.

A derived class is not obligated to override the body of a virtual method of its base class. A base class which contains at least one virtual method is known as a *polymorphic class*. Also, it is possible to override the body of a virtual method using the `override sealed` keywords. In this case, this virtual method cannot be overridden in the classes derived from this class. Here, we talk of *sealed method*.

An example

Here is an example where we have:

- An `Employee` base class and two derived classes `Technician` and `Secretary`
- A base process which displays the description of the employee. This process is different depending on the class: For an `Employee` object, this process limits itself to displaying the name. For a `Techician` object, this process executes the display of the employee followed by *'Position: Technician'*. For a `Secretary` object, this process displays the employee followed by *'Position: Secretary'*.

We can illustrate this with a diagram obtained from *Visual Studio 2005*:

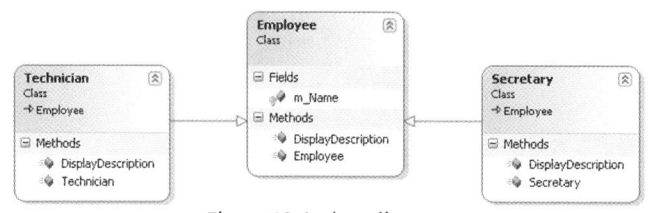

Figure 12-4: class diagram

The body of this program creates three employees put in an array of type `Employee`. Then, we apply the base process (the display of its description) for each employee referenced in the array.

Virtual methods and polymorphism

Example 12-2

```
public class Employee {
    // The field m_Name is visible from derived classes.
    protected string m_Name;
    public Employee( string name ) { m_Name = name; }
    public virtual void DisplayDescription() {
        System.Console.Write( "Name: {0}", m_Name );
    }
}
class Secretary : Employee {   // Secretary inherits Employee.
    public Secretary( string name ) : base( name ) {}
    public override void DisplayDescription() {
        // Call the Employee version of the DisplayDescription() method.
        base.DisplayDescription();
        System.Console.Write( "   Position: Secretary\n" );
    }
}
class Technician : Employee {  // Technician inherits Employee.
    public Technician( string name ) : base( name ) {}
    public override void DisplayDescription(){
        // Call the Employee version of the DisplayDescription() method.
        base.DisplayDescription();
        System.Console.Write( "   Position: Technician\n");
    }
}
class Program {
    static void Main() {
        Employee[] array = new Employee[3];
        array[0] = new Technician("Line");
        array[1] = new Secretary("Lisanette");
        array[2] = new Secretary("Anne-Mette");
        foreach( Employee employee in array )
            employee.DisplayDescription();
    }
}
```

Here is what the program displays:

```
Name: Line       Position: Technician
Name: Lisanette  Position: Secretary
Name: Anne-Mette Position: Secretary
```

The `DisplayDescription()` method is always called on a reference of type `Employee`. Yet, we can see that program executes the `DisplayDescription()` methods of `Technician` and `Secretary`. This is the magic of polymorphism. This avoids a cumbersome type testing and simplifies the maintenance of the application. Indeed, during the addition of a class derived from `Employee` (a `Manager` class for example) you would need to update the type testing, while with polymorphism, there is nothing to do for the proper `Manager.DisplayDescription()` method to be called.

The `DisplayDescription()` method call the `DisplayDescription()` method of the base class using the `base` keyword. For each of your derived classes, we recommend to verify that all your virtual methods eventually call the corresponding method in the base class. If this is not the case, then this absence generally reveal a design flaw in your object model.

Disabling polymorphism

C++ › C#: Caution, the deactivation of polymorphism is not possible in C++ while rewriting a non virtual method of a base class is allowed.

C#: C# allows to hide a method (virtual or not) of a base class in a derived class by overriding the method with the new placed in front of the method in the derived class.

Caution, in this case, polymorphism does not apply even if the method is declared as virtual in the base class. Note that if we do not place the new keyword, the compiler will simply produce a warning but the runtime behavior will be the same as if you used new. The explicit use of the new keyword is to clarify the code.

Let's take the previous example and observe the effect of using new to override a virtual method:

Example 12-3
```csharp
public class Employee{
...
}
class Secretary : Employee{   // Secretary inherits Employee.
...
}
class Technician : Employee{  // Technician inherits Employee.
   public Technician( string name ): base( name ) {}
   public new void DisplayDescription() {
      base.DisplayDescription();
      System.Console.Write( "   Position: Technician\n" );
   }
}
class Program {
   static void Main(){
      Employee[] array = new Employee[3];
      array[0] = new Technician("Line");
      array[1] = new Secretary("Lisanette");
      array[2] = new Secretary("Anne-Mette");
      foreach( Employee employee in array )
         employee.DisplayDescription();
      // Call the Technician version of the DisplayDescription() method.
      ( (Technician)array[0] ).DisplayDescription();
   }
}
```

Here is what the program displays:

```
Name: LineName: Lisanette    Position: Secretary
Name: Anne-Mette    Position: Secretary
Name: Line    Position: Technician
```

Notice that the `DisplayDescription()` method is called twice for the object describing `Line`. However, the first time, it is the `DisplayDescription()` method of `Employee` while the second time, it is the `DisplayDescription()` method of `Technician`. In the first case, we see that the polymorphism has been deactivated. In the second case, we explicitly cast our `Employee` reference to a `Technician` reference. Here also, the polymorphism is not involved. Such an explicit cast from a base class to a derived class is named a '*downcast*'. We will come back to this a little later.

Abstraction

C++ › C#: The concept of abstraction is completely similar between the C# and C++ languages. However, some syntax and vocabulary differences appear.

Pure virtual methods in C++ are called abstract methods in C# and are declared using the `abstract` keyword.

In addition, it is not sufficient anymore for a class to contain a single abstract method for it to be considered abstract. It must be declared using the `abstract` keyword. Contrarily to C++, with C#, you can have abstract classes without any abstract methods.

Despite appearances, the concept of interface exists in C++: nothing prevents to declare a class with only abstract methods and without any fields. However, C# makes this clearer by using the `interface` keyword, forcing the developer to respect the constraints of an interface.

Interfaces are important in C# since a class can implement several interfaces, which allows to partly compensate for the lack of multiple inheritance.

The underlying problem

In the example of the previous section, displaying the description of an employee (i.e. displaying his name) has a sense. It is then useful to put the code in the `DisplayDescription()` virtual method of the `Employee` base class. When the `Employee` class is instantiated, it has something to display.

It happens that we do not have any code to put in a virtual method since we do not have the necessary information at this level of the inheritance.

For example, with the `GeometricFigure` class, there is nothing to put in the `Draw()` virtual method. In fact, at this inheritance level, we do not know which type of geometric figure will be instantiated.

The same is true for the `CommunicationEndPoint` class. There is nothing to put in the `SendData()` since at this level, we do not know the underlying communication protocol.

We could always declare a virtual function with no code inside. But we need a more efficient mechanism to properly declare these base classes which do not have enough information on what they represent. Such a class wants to impose operations to its derived classes, even through there is not enough information to implement these operations, at least in part.

A solution: abstract classes and abstract methods

The solution is called *abstraction*. An *abstract class* is a class which must completely delegate the implementation of certain methods to its derived classes. We have seen that the reasons for which these methods cannot be implemented comes from a lack of information and our wish to impose these operations to the derived classes.

These methods which cannot be implemented are called *abstract methods* (or *pure virtual*). They are declared using the `abstract` keyword and must be declared within abstract classes, also declared using the `abstract` keyword.

An abstract method is only a specific virtual method and must be implemented in the derived classes using the `override` keyword (or `override sealed`). If a class deriving from an abstract class does not implement all the abstract methods, it is itself abstract.

An immediate and fundamental consequence of all this is that: **An abstract base class cannot be instantiated.**

There cannot be any instances of an abstract class but a reference can be of the type of an abstract class. Such a reference then points to an object, instance a non-abstract class which derives from this abstract class. Polymorphism is automatically put into place once a call to these virtual and abstract methods is made. Polymorphism is even more evident when it is used on abstract methods since we are certain that the body of an abstract method cannot be called since it does not exist!

Note that an abstract method cannot have a private visibility. This would in fact prevent the derived classes from being able to implement it.

An example

Here is an example where we have: an abstract base class `GeometricFigure`, two derived classes `Circle` and `Rectangle`, a base process to draw the figure.

This process varies based on the class and is abstract for `GeometricFigure` (i.e. it is not implementable in this class since we do not know how to draw anything in this class). For an object of type `Circle`, this process displays a circle based on the center and radius. For a `Rectangle` object, this process displays a rectangle based on three of its corners.

Example 12-4

```
class Point{
    public Point ( int x, int y ){ this.x = x; this.y = y; }
    int x; int y;
}
abstract class GeometricFigure{
    // As the Draw() method is abstract, it doesn't have a body.
    public abstract void Draw();
}
class Circle : GeometricFigure {
    private Point    m_Center;
    private double   m_Radius;
    public Circle( Point center, double radius ) {
        m_Center = center;
        m_Radius = radius;
    }
    public override void Draw (){
        // Draw the circle { m_Center ; m_Radius }.
    }
}
class Rectangle : GeometricFigure {
    private Point m_Vertice1, m_Vertice2, m_Vertice3;
    public Rectangle( Point s1, Point s2, Point s3 ) {
        m_Vertice1 = s1; m_Vertice2 = s2; m_Vertice3 = s3;
    }
    public override void Draw (){
        // Draw the Rectangle { m_Vertice1 ; m_Vertice2 ; m_Vertice3 }.
    }
}
class Program {
    static void Main() {
        GeometricFigure[] array = new GeometricFigure[3];
        array[0]=new Circle( new Point(0,0), 3.2 );
        array[1]=new Rectangle(new Point(0,0),new Point(0,2),new Point(1,2));
```

Example 12-4
```
        array[2]=new Circle( new Point(1,1), 4.1 );
        // Thanks to polymorphism,
        // proper versions of the Draw() method is called.
        foreach(GeometricFigure f in array )
           f.Draw();
        // Compilation error!
        // We can't instantiate an abstract class !
        GeometricFigure figure = new GeometricFigure();
    }
}
```
Note that an abstract class can have constructor, fields and properties.

Simultaneously using the abstract and override keywords

It is possible to mark a method simultaneously with these two keywords. Imagine a class C which derives from the class B which itself is derived from A which declares a method Foo() as being abstract. B can itself be an abstract class and did not implement the Foo() method. In this case, the declaration of the B.Foo() method must be preceded with the abstract override keywords. This means that the B pushes back the implementation of this method to one of its derived classes:

Example 12-5
```
abstract class A { public abstract void Foo();}
abstract class B : A { public abstract override void Foo();}
class C : B { public override void Foo() { /*...*/ } }
```

As the following example illustrates, the association of the abstract and override can also allow B to force its derived class to reimplement the Foo() method, already implemented in the A class:

Example 12-6
```
class A { public virtual void Foo() { /*...*/ } }
abstract class B : A { public abstract override void Foo();}
// The C class MUST override the Foo() method.
class C : B { public override void Foo() { /*...*/ } }
```

Interfaces

C++ › C#: An interface can bee seen as an abstract class without any fields and with only abstract methods, abstract properties, abstract events and abstract indexers. This concept can be implemented in C++, but C# goes further by offering the use of the interface keyword instead of the class keyword. This distinction is important in C# since a class can derive from several interfaces.

C#: There are special abstract classes. These classes only have abstract methods, abstract properties, abstract events and abstract indexers. The object oriented theory calls them *interfaces* or *abstractions*. We say that a class implements an interface instead of saying that a class derives from an interface. We also say that a class which implements an interface is an *implementation* of the interface. Structures can also implement interfaces but this option is dangerous as we will explain a little later.

To declare an interface in C#, you simply need to declare a class with the interface keyword instead of the class keyword. An interface can have four types of members: methods, properties, events, and indexers.

378   *Chapter 12 - Inheritane, Polymorphism and Abstraction*

Visibility levels cannot be applied to the methods of an interface. It is the responsibility of the implementing class to decide on the visibility level. In fact, we can only use the `virtual` and `public` keywords in front of the declaration of the members of an interface. The consequence of this rule is detailed in the following section. Here is an important point to mention in regards to interfaces:

> A class can eventually implement several interfaces (in addition to deriving from one base class). Also, an interface can derive from one or several other interfaces. We say that such an interface *extends* the other interfaces.

This feature allows adding your own behaviors to a class but also behaviors defined by the standard interfaces of the .NET architecture. For example, the `IEnumerator` interface allows for an object to be used by the `foreach` loop as it if were an array. Other .NET interfaces which can be used in your classes are presented in this book. We recommend starting the name of your interfaces with a capital 'I' as with the standard interfaces.

A reference can be of an interface type. In this case, we can only access the object with the behavior specified by the interface, for example:

Example 12-7
```
interface IA { void f(int i); }
interface IB { void g(double d); }
class C : IA, IB {
   public void f(int i) { System.Console.WriteLine("C.f({0})", i); }
   public void g(double d){ System.Console.WriteLine("C.g({0})", d); }
}
class Program {
   static void Main() {
      // 'obj1' is an interface-typed reference to an object.
      IA obj1 = new C();
      // 'obj2' is an interface-typed reference to an object.
      IB obj2 = new C();
      // Downcast the reference 'obj2' to a class-typed reference.
      C _obj2 = (C)obj2;
      obj1.f(5);
   }
}
```

Contrarily to classes and structures, interfaces do not derive from the `Object` class. However, since only classes and structures are capable of implementing an interface, it is allowed to call methods of the `Object` class on an interface. The following example shows that it is also allowed to typecast an interface reference into a reference of type `Object`.

Example 12-8
```
interface I {}
class C : I {}
class Program {
   static void Main() {
      I c = new C();
      c.GetHashCode();
      object o = c;
   }
}
```

Forcing a client to use an abstraction instead of an implementation

.NET gives us an unusual possibility compared to C++ and Java. You can force the clients of your class to use an abstraction (i.e. a reference of type of an interface) rather than an implementation (i.e. a reference of type of a class). This feature reveals itself extremely useful to class library developers. They have access to a technique which is an integral part of the language to force the code of their clients to be decoupled from implementations. The decoupling of the classes is one of the fundamental principals of OOP in regards to code coherency.

Here is an example, the `fct2()` method can not be called from a reference of type C but can be called from a reference of type I. In a real case, we would certainly have forced the use of the interface on all the methods offered by the interface.

Example 12-9
```
interface I {
   void fct1();
   void fct2();
}
public class C : I {
   public void fct1() { System.Console.WriteLine("fct1() called"); }
   void I.fct2() { System.Console.WriteLine("fct2() called "); }
}
public class Program {
   public static void Main() {
      C refImpl = new C();
      I refAbst = (I)refImpl;
      refAbst.fct1();   // Compilation OK
      refAbst.fct2();   // Compilation OK
      refImpl.fct1();   // Compilation OK
      refImpl.fct2();   // Compilateur error : 'C' does not contain a
                        // definition for 'fct2'
   }
}
```

Method name conflict resolution

Since a class can implement several interfaces and derive from a class, it is possible that there might be a conflict between methods with the same name and signature. To solve these conflicts, you must use the syntax presented in the previous section:

Example 12-10
```
interface IA { void f( int i ); }
interface IB { void f( int i ); }
abstract class FooBase { public abstract void f(int i); }
class FooDerived : FooBase, IA, IB {
   void IA.f( int i ) { System.Console.WriteLine("IA.f({0})", i); }
   void IB.f( int i ) { System.Console.WriteLine("IB.f({0})", i); }
   public override void f( int i ) {
      System.Console.WriteLine( "f({0})", i );
   }
}
class Program {
   static void Main() {
      FooDerived refImpl = new FooDerived();
      FooBase refAbst = (FooBase) refImpl;
      IA refA = (IA) refImpl;
```

Example 12-10
```
        IB refB = (IB) refImpl;
        refImpl.f(1);
        refAbst.f(2);
        refA.f(3);
        refB.f(4);
    }
}
```

This program displays:

```
f(1)
f(2)
IA.f(3)
IB.f(4)
```

A same class can then have several implementations for a same method. The choice of which implementation will be executed will depend on the type of the reference on which the call is made. This is one form of polymorphism.

Interface extension conflict resolution

C++ › C#: In C++, we talk about virtual inheritance when a class inherits several times from the same class. For example, suppose that the D class derives from C and B, which in turn both derive from the A class. In this case, D essentially derives twice from the A class. By using the notion of virtual inheritance, you can specify if you wish an instance of D to be built from the inheritance of two instance of A or from a single instance.

The topic of this section is close to the virtual inheritance feature in C++, although here we talk about the inheritance of multiple interfaces.

C#: A class has the possibility of implementing several interfaces which all extend the same interface. This possibility is useful when we have a UML diagram similar to the one in Figure 12-5.

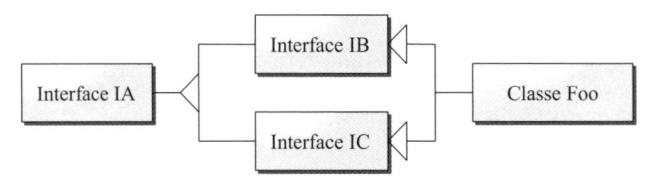

Figure 12-5: An interface extension conflict scenario

The following example illustrates this possibility and its consequences:

Example 12-11
```
    interface IA { void fa(); }
    interface IB : IA { new void fa(); void fb(); }
    interface IC : IA { new void fa(); void fc(); }
    class Foo : IB, IC {
       void IA.fa() { System.Console.WriteLine("IA.fa"); }
       void IB.fa() { System.Console.WriteLine("IB.fa"); }
       void IC.fa() { System.Console.WriteLine("IC.fa"); }
       public void fa() { System.Console.WriteLine("Foo.fa"); }
       public void fb() { System.Console.WriteLine("Foo.fb"); }
       public void fc() { System.Console.WriteLine("Foo.fc"); }
```

Example 12-11

```
   }
   class Program {
      static void Main() {
         Foo r = new Foo();  r.fa();
         IA rA = r;          rA.fa();
         IB rB = r;          rB.fa();
         IC rC = r;          rC.fa();
      }
   }
```

This program displays:

```
Foo.fa
IA.fa
IB.fa
IC.fa
```

Overriding the implementation of an interface method

You have the possibility of declaring a method of an interface implemented in a class, as virtual. It can then be overridden by a class deriving from the class which implements the interface. Here is an example to illustrate this feature:

Example 12-12

```
   interface I {
      void f(int i);
      void g(int i);
   }
   class FooBase : I {
      public virtual void f(int i) {
         System.Console.WriteLine("FooBase.f({0})", i);
      }
      public void g(int i) {
         System.Console.WriteLine("FooBase.g({0})", i);
      }
   }
   class FooDerived : FooBase {
      public override void f(int i) {
         System.Console.WriteLine("FooDerived.f({0})", i);
      }
   }
   class Program {
      static void Main() {
         FooBase   refB1 = new FooBase();
         I         refI1 = refB1;
         FooDerived refD= new FooDerived();
         FooBase   refB2 = refD;
         I         refI2 = refD;
         refB1.f(1);
         refI1.f(2);
         refD.f(3);
         refB2.f(4);
         refI2.f(5);
      }
   }
```

This program displays the following:

```
FooBase.f(1)
FooBase.f(2)
FooDerived.f(3)
FooDerived.f(4)
FooDerived.f(5)
```

Interfaces and structures

To read properly this section, it is necessary to understand what are the boxing and unboxing operations presented at page 292.

This section has the goal of making you aware of a classic problem which occurs when a structure implements an interface. If you attempt to access the members of an interface implemented by the structure from a reference to the interface you will not obtain the results you were expecting. In fact, during the typecasting of the structure towards the interface, a boxing operation is implicitly done since the interface needs a reference. To convince you, take a look at the following example:

Example 12-13

```
interface I {
   void SetState(int i);
   int GetState();
}
struct Struct : I {
   private int i;
   public void SetState(int i) { this.i = i; }
   public int GetState() { return i; }
}
class Program {
   static void Main() {
      Struct s = new Struct();
      // Here, there is an implicit boxing of the instance 's'.
      I i = (I) s;
      s.SetState(10);
      i.SetState(20);
      System.Console.WriteLine( "s.GetState() returned:" + s.GetState() );
      System.Console.WriteLine( "i.GetState() returned:" + i.GetState() );
   }
}
```

This program displays:

```
s.GetState() returned:10
i.GetState() returned:20
```

> As a general rule, it is better to avoid that a structure implements an interface. If you do not have any other option, it is better to directly call the methods of the interface from the implementation, contrarily to what is recommended for classes.

For the skeptical, the analysis with `ildasm.exe` of the IL code for the `Main()` method clearly shows that a boxing operation is done. Note that that two other boxing operations are necessary to display the value of the integer returned by the `GetState()` method:

```
.method private hidebysig static void  Main() cil managed {
  .entrypoint
  // Code size      86 (0x56)
  .maxstack  2
  .locals ([0] valuetype Struct s,
           [1] class IInterface I)
  IL_0000:  ldloca.s   s
  IL_0002:  initobj    Struct
  IL_0008:  ldloc.0
  IL_0009:  box        Struct  // <- Here, 's' is boxed.
  IL_000e:  stloc.1
  IL_000f:  ldloca.s   s
  IL_0011:  ldc.i4.s   10
  IL_0013:  call       instance void Struct::SetState(int32)
  IL_0018:  ldloc.1
  IL_0019:  ldc.i4.s   20
  IL_001b:  callvirt   instance void IInterface::SetState(int32)
  IL_0020:  ldstr      "Retour de s.GetState():"
  IL_0025:  ldloca.s   s
  IL_0027:  call       instance int32 Struct::GetState()
  IL_002c:  box        [mscorlib]System.Int32
  IL_0031:  call       string
                       [mscorlib]System.String::Concat(object,object)
  IL_0036:  call       void [mscorlib]System.Console::WriteLine(string)
  IL_003b:  ldstr      "Retour de i.GetState():"
  IL_0040:  ldloc.1
  IL_0041:  callvirt   instance int32 I::GetState()
  IL_0046:  box        [mscorlib]System.Int32
  IL_004b:  call       string
                       [mscorlib]System.String::Concat(object,object)
  IL_0050:  call       void [mscorlib]System.Console::WriteLine(string)
  IL_0055:  ret
} // end of method Program::Main
```

Virtual and abstract properties, events and indexers

Properties, events and indexers of a class have the possibility of being virtual or abstract. In fact, the underlying idea is that accessors of these members, considered as methods, can be virtual or abstract. Let us remind you that the possible accessors for a property or an indexer are `get` and `set` while for an event the accessors are `add` and `remove`.

As with virtual and abstract methods, the virtual and abstract properties, events and indexers can be:

- Overridden in a derived class with the `override` keyword. In this case, polymorphism is applied to the accessor.

- Overridden in a derived class using the `override sealed` keywords. In this case, polymorphism applies on the accessors and the member cannot be overridden in a derived class.

- Overridden in a derived class using the `new` keyword. In this case, polymorphism will not apply to the accessors.

As with abstract methods, to contain an abstract property, event or indexer, a class must be abstract. In addition, as with abstract methods, such a member cannot have a private visibility. Here is an example using virtual and abstract properties:

Example 12-14

```
abstract class FooBase {
   protected int valA = 0;
   public virtual int Prop1 {
      get { return valA; }
      set { valA = value; }
   }
   public virtual int Prop2 {
      get { return 43; }
   }
   public abstract int Prop3 {
      get;
      set;
   }
}
class FooDerived : FooBase {
   private int valB = 0;
   public override int Prop1 {
      get { return base.Prop1 * 2; }
      set { base.Prop1 = value * 2; }
   }
   public override sealed int Prop2 {
      get { return valA > valB ? valA : valB; }
   }
   public override int Prop3 {
      get { return valA + valB; }
      set { valA = value - valB; }
   }
}
```

It is not necessary to make the `FooDerived` class abstract since it does not contain any abstract members. Note the use of the **base** keyword to call the accessors defined in the base class.

The is and as operator

C++ › C#: The possibility of doing the runtime evaluation or typecasting of a type in an expression is implemented in C++ with the `typeid(expression)` operator which returns an object of type `type_info`. This feature falls into the more general aspect of *RTTI (RunTime Type Information)*.

RTTI is at the same time more easy to use in C# than C++; and is much more complete because of the type metadata and the reflection mechanism which we discuss at page 193.

The is operator

The **is** operator is used to determine during execution whether an expression can be casted into a specific type. This operator returns a boolean. Its left operand is an expression and its right operand is a type.

An object of class A deriving from class B and implementing the I1, I2, ... In, interfaces, can be used by the intermediate of:

- A reference of type A, B, I1, I2, ... In;
- A type reference, of a base class located in the hierarchy of the B base class;
- A type reference of an interface supported by one of the base classes located in the hierarchy of the base classes of A.

If the reference is null, the `is` operator returns `false`. Here is an example which illustrates the `is` keyword:

Example 12-15
```
using System;
interface IA { void f( int i ); }
interface IB { void g( int i ); }
abstract class FooBase { public abstract void h(int i); }
class FooDerived : FooBase, IA {
   public void f( int i ) { /*...*/ }
   public override void h( int i ){ /*...*/ }
}
class Program {
   static void Main() {
      IA refA = new FooDerived();
      IB refB = null;
      FooBase refAbst = null;
      FooDerived refC = null;
      // This test returns true at runtime.
      if ( refA is FooBase ) {
         refAbst = (FooBase) refA;
         // use refAbst...
      }
      // This test returns true at runtime.
      if ( refA is FooDerived ) {
         refC = (FooDerived) refA;
         // use refC...
      }
      // This test returns false at runtime.
      if ( refA is IB ) {
         refB = (IB) refA;
         // use refB...
      }
      // The C# compiler detects that 'refA' is typed with 'IA'.
      // As a consequence it emits:  'if( refA != null )'.
      if ( refA is IA ) { /*...*/ }
   }
}
```

> ⚠️ Be careful as the `is` operator is often used in situations where polymorphism would have avoided the need for this test.

The as operator

After determining during the execution if an expression can be casted into a given type with the `is` operator, most of the time we effectively do that actual cast. The `as` operator allows to complete these two operations in a single operation. If the cast cannot be done, a null reference is returned. Of course, you must always test the returned reference.

The advantage of using the `as` operator instead of the `is` operator when possible is double: the code is more readable and the performance is better. Here is the `Main()` method of the example in the previous section, rewritten to use the `as` operator:

Example 12-16

```
...
class Program {
   static void Main() {
      IA refA = new FooDerived();
      IB refB = null;
      FooBase refAbst = null;
      FooDerived refDeriv = null;
      refAbst = refA as FooBase;
      // Here, refAbst is null at runtime.
      if ( refAbst != null ) {
         // use refAbst...
      }
      refDeriv = refA as FooDerived;
      // Here, refDeriv is null at runtime.
      if ( refDeriv != null ) {
         // use refC...
      }
      refB = refA as IB;
      // Here, refB is null at runtime.
      if ( refB != null ) {
         // use refB...
      }
   }
}
```

Solutions for code reuse

Class inheritance is not the only solution for code reuse. In fact, this solution suffers from several problems often referred to using the '*Fragile Base Class*' expression. Implementation inheritance is quite often wrongly used because when most developers are taught, this mechanism is presented as the cornerstone of OOP. OOP encapsulates other principles as important which include encapsulation, object composition, abstraction using interfaces and genericity. In fact, it is almost always preferable to conjointly use interfaces and object composition in order to reuse code in a more efficient and robust way than with class inheritance.

The following chapter talks about genericity. This mechanism is introduced with C#2 and proves itself to be a powerful code reuse approach. We will see that it is particularly suited to the writing of generic algorithms such as collections which need to store objects of a same class.

For a few years, there has been a certain excitement around *Aspect Oriented Programming* (*AOP*). AOP is a code reuse technique for the implementation of the different aspects of software (synchronization, security, persistence...). Currently, the *AspectDNG* tool is the most advanced for the implementation of AOP with .NET (*home page*: http://sourceforge.net/projects/aspectdng/).

Finally, let us mention that the 3.0 version of C# will introduce a new code reuse mechanism allowing to essentially extend classes using methods defined in other classes.

One of the most elegant points of the .NET platform is that the notion of component doesn't introduce any limitation to the object model. For example, a class can derive from a class defined in another assembly and implement an interface defined in a third assembly.

13

Generics

Without any doubt, *generics* is the flagship functionality in .NET 2 from the language's perspective. After explaining what generics are, we will examine the implication of its support at the level of the C#2 language, the CLR and the framework. To start off, let us mention that all generic types and methods are *CLS compliant* and can thus be used across all CLR v2 languages.

A C#1 problem and how to solve it with .NET 2 generics

The problem of typing collection items with C#1

Let's assume that we have to implement a `Stack` class which allows stacking and unstacking elements. To simplify our code, we will assume that the stack cannot contain more than a certain number of elements. This constraint allows us to internally use a C# array. Here is an implementation of this `Stack` class:

Example 13-1

```
class Stack{
   private object[] m_ItemsArray;
   private int m_Index = 0;
   public const int MAX_SIZE = 100;
   public Stack() { m_ItemsArray = new object[MAX_SIZE]; }
   public object Pop() {
      if (m_Index ==0 )
         throw new System.InvalidOperationException(
            "Can't pop an empty stack.");
      return m_ItemsArray[--m_Index];
   }
   public void Push( object item ) {
      if(m_Index == MAX_SIZE)
         throw new System.StackOverflowException(
            "Can't push an item on a full stack.");
      m_ItemsArray[m_Index++] = item;
   }
}
```

This implementation suffers from three major problems.

- First of all, the client of the `Stack` class must explicitly cast all elements obtained from the stack. For example:

   ```
   ...
   Stack stack = new Stack();
   stack.Push(1234);
   int number = (int)stack.Pop();
   ...
   ```

- A second problem which is less obvious is from a performance perspective. We must be aware that when we use our **Stack** class with value type elements, we will implicitly perform a boxing operation when inserting elements and an unboxing operation when removing an element. This is highlighted by the following IL code:

```
L_0000: newobj instance void Stack::.ctor()
L_0005: stloc.0
L_0006: ldloc.0
L_0007: ldc.i4 1234
L_000c: box int32
L_0011: callvirt instance void Stack::Push(object)
L_0016: nop
L_0017: ldloc.0
L_0018: callvirt instance object Stack::Pop()
L_001d: unbox int32
L_0022: ldind.i4
L_0023: stloc.1
L_0024: ret
```

- Finally, a third problem comes from the fact that we can store elements of different types within a same instance of the **Stack** class. Generally, we wish to have a stack of elements with a common type. This feature can easily lead to casting errors which are only found during the execution as with the following example:

```
...
Stack stack = new Stack();
stack.Push("1234");
int number = (int)stack.Pop(); // Raise an InvalidCastException.
...
```

When a casting problem is not detected during compilation but can provoke an exception at run-time we say that the code is not *type-safe*. In software development, as well as any other discipline, the earlier an error is detected the least costly will this error be. This means that whenever possible, you must make sure to have type-safe code as this allows the detection of problems early on, at compile-time.

It is possible to implement our stack in a *type-safe* way. In fact, we could have implemented a **StackOfInt** class which describes a stack containing only integers, a **StackOfString** class which only contains strings,…

Example 13-2

```
class StackOfInt {
    private int[] m_ItemsArray;
    private int m_Index = 0;
    public const int MAX_SIZE = 100;
    public StackOfInt(){ m_ItemsArray = new int[MAX_SIZE]; }
    public int Pop() { /*...*/ return -1; }
    public void Push(int item) { /*...*/ }
}
class StackOfString {
    private string[] m_ItemsArray;
    private int m_Index = 0;
    public const int MAX_SIZE = 100;
    public StackOfString(){ m_ItemsArray = new string[MAX_SIZE]; }
    public string Pop() {/*...*/ return null; }
    public void Push(string item) {/*...*/}
}
```

Although it is *type-safe* and that is solves both the casting and performance problems, this solution is clearly unsatisfactory. It implies code duplication since the same stack logic is implemented by several classes. This means more code to maintain and hence a loss of productivity.

An ideal solution using C#2 generics

C#2 offers an elegant solution to the problem exposed in the previous section through the introduction of *generic types*. Concretely, we can implement a stack of elements of type T by giving the client the freedom to specify the T type when they instantiate the class. For example:

Example 13-3

```
class Stack<T>{
   private T[] m_ItemsArray;
   private int m_Index = 0;
   public const int MAX_SIZE = 100;
   public Stack(){ m_ItemsArray = new T[MAX_SIZE]; }
   public T Pop(){
      if (m_Index ==0 )
         throw new System.InvalidOperationException(
            "Can't pop an empty stack.");
      return m_ItemsArray[--m_Index];
   }
   public void Push(T item) {
      if(m_Index == MAX_SIZE)
         throw new System.StackOverflowException(
            "Can't push an item on a full stack.");
      m_ItemsArray[m_Index++] = item;
   }
}
class Program{
   static void Main(){
      Stack<int> stack = new Stack<int>();
      stack.Push(1234);
      int number = stack.Pop(); // Don't need any awkward cast.
      stack.Push(5678);
      string sNumber = stack.Pop();   // Compilation Error:
         // Cannot implicitly convert type 'int' to 'string'.
   }
}
```

This solution does not suffer from any of the problems discussed earlier

- The client does not need to cast an element popped from the stack.
- This solution is efficient as it does not require boxing/unboxing operations.
- The client writes *type-safe* code. There is no possibility of having a stack with various types during execution. In our example, the compiler prevents the insertion of any element which is not an int or which cannot be implicitly converted into an int.
- There is no code duplication.

Understand that in our example, the generic class is Stack<T> while T is the *parameter type* for our class. We sometimes used the *parametric polymorphism* term to talk about generics. In fact, our Stack<T> class can take several forms (Stack<int>, Stack<string> etc). It is then polymorphic and parameterized by one type. Caution, do not confuse this with the *polymorphism* of object oriented languages which allows the manipulation of various types of objects (i.e. instance objects from different classes) through a same interface.

To summarize, the Stack<T> class represents any kind of stack while the Stack class represents a stack of anything.

.NET 2 generics: the big picture

Declaring several parameter types

It can be useful to parameterize a type using several types. C#2 offers this feature. For example, as the following example shows, it is possible to implement a dictionary class which gives to the client the choice of types for both the key and the values:

```
class DictionaryEntry<K,V>{
   public K Key;
   public V Value;
}
class Dictionary<K,V>{
   private DictionaryEntry<K,V>[] m_ItemsArray;
   public void Insert( DictionaryEntry<K,V> entry ) {...}
   public V Get(K key) {...}
   ...
}
```

Open and closed generic types

A *generic type* is a type that is parameterized by one or several other types. For example Stack<T>, Stack<int>, Dictionary<K,V>, Dictionary<int,V>, Dictionary<int,string> and Stack<Stack<T>> are generic types.

An *open generic type* is a generic type for which none of its parameter types are specified. For example Stack<T> and Dictionary<K,V> are open generic types.

A *closed generic type* is a generic type for which all the type parameters are specified. For example, Stack<int>, Dictionary<int,string> and Stack<Stack<int>> are closed generic types.

A generic type is compiled into a single type within its assembly. If we were to analyze the assembly which contains the Stack<T> open generic type in a certain assembly, we notice that the compilation only produced a single class even though we may be using the following closed generic types Stack<int>, Stack<bool>, Stack<double>, Stack<string>, Stack<object> and Stack<IDispose>.

However, during execution, the CLR will create and use several versions of the Stack<T> class. More precisely, the CLR uses a same version of Stack<T> common to all the parameters of a reference type and one version of Stack<T> for each parameter of a value type.

.NET generics vs. C++ templates

C# › C++: Those of you who know C++ have certainly made a correlation between the generics in C# to the *templates* of C++. Although that the functionalities are conceptually similar, this section will explain one of the fundamental differences:

- Closed generic types generated by C++ templates are produced by the compiler and are contained in the component generated by the compiler.

- Closed generic types generated by .NET are produced during execution by the JIT compiler and the underlying generic type is only present in one form in the assembly resulting from the compilation.

In other words, the notion of an open generic type exists in C#/.NET at both the code and runtime level while in C++ it only exists at the source code level.

Source code view
Only one stack class

```
class Stack<T> {
  private T[] m_ItemsArray;
  private int m_Index = 0;
  public const int MAX_SIZE = 100;
  public Stack(){...}
  public T Pop(){...}
  public void Push(T item) {...}
}
class Program {
  static void Main(){
    Stack<int>     s1=
        new Stack<int>();
    Stack<bool>    s2=
        new Stack<bool>();
    Stack<double>  s3=
        new Stack<double>();
    Stack<string>  s4=
        new Stack<string>();
    Stack<object>  s5=
        new Stack<object>();
    Stack<IDisposable>s6=
      new Stack<IDisposable>();
    ...
  }
}
```

Compile time view
Only one stack class

- StackAsm
  - StackAsm.exe
    - References
    - { } -
      - <Module>
      - Program
      - **Stack<T>**
        - Base Types
        - Derived Types
        - .ctor()
        - Pop() : T
        - Push(T) : Void
        - m_Index : Int32
        - m_ItemsArray : T[]
        - MAX_SIZE : Int32

C# compiler

CLR JIT compiler

Runtime view
Several stack classes

Program

Stack<T> — Used for all reference type versions (here string, object and IDisposable).

Stack<int>   Stack<bool>   Stack<double>

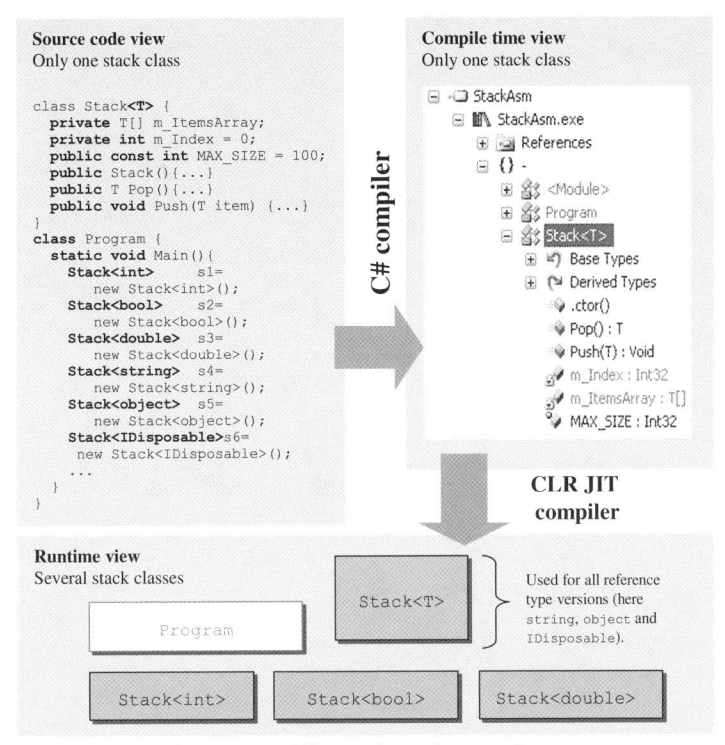

Figure 13-1: Different views of a generic type

The observation clearly shows one of the advantages of generics in C# since the size of the .NET components is actually reduced. This is not a small saving as the phenomenon known as *code-bloat*, can lead to code size problems (and that is without taking into account the avalanche of warnings produced by some C++ compilers). Also, this component based programming model offered by .NET is even more powerful with this implementation since an open generic type can be closed by a type which exists in another component.

There can still be some *code-bloat* in .NET but to a lesser extent. In fact, the generic types which are closed by the CLR will never be collected by the garbage collector or by another entity. They reside in their AppDomain until it is destroyed. In certain rare cases which can be resolved by manually unloading the AppDomain, there can be a memory bloat. A good point for generics in .NET is that a closed generic type is only created as late as possible, when it is used for the first time. In addition, the number of classes generated at runtime is bound by the number of closed generic classes used in the source code.

A similar problem which may be more cumbersome is when we use the `ngen.exe` tool to improve performance by performing the work of the JIT compiler before execution. In this case, all the closed generic types referenced in the source code will be created. The `ngen.exe` tool is incapable of distinguishing whether certain closed generic types referenced in the source code will be effectively used.

Visibility of a generic type

The visibility of a generic type is the intersection of the generic type with the visibility of the parameter types. If the visibility of all the C, T1, T2 and T3 types is set to `public`, then the visibility of C<T1,T2,T3> is also `public`; but if the visibility of only one of these types is `private`, then the visibility of C<T1,T2,T3> is `private`.

The astute reader may have realized by now that with generics, we can obtain a type of visibility which wasn't accessible in C# but know by the CLR which is `protected AND internal` (visible only in the derived classes of a same assembly, see page 345). However know that such a type is constructed during the execution by the CLR and thus does not create an incoherency in the C# language.

Example 13-4

```
internal class ClassInternal { }
public class ClassFoo{
   protected class ClassProtected { }
   public class ClassPublic<U,V> { }

   // The C# compiler checks that the
   // 'ClassPublic<ClassInternal,ClassProtected>' type is not used
   // outside this class and outside its derived classes defined in
   // the current assembly. However, you can't assign any other
   // visibility than 'private' to this field.
   private ClassPublic<ClassInternal,ClassProtected> foo;
}
```

Generic structure and interface

In addition to generic classes, C#2 allows to defining generic structures and interfaces. This feature does not require any special remarks with the exception that a type cannot implement the same generic interface with different parameter types. For example, the following program will not compile:

Example 13-5

```
interface I<T> { void Fct(); }
// Compilation Error:
// 'C<U,V>' cannot implement both 'I<U>' and 'I<V>' because they
// may unify for some type parameter substitutions.
class C<U, V> : I<U>, I<V>{
   void I<U>.Fct() { }
   void I<V>.Fct() { }
}
```

Aliases and generic types

The `using` directive can be used to create an alias on the name of a closed generic type. The scope of such a directive is to the current file if it is used outside of all namespaces. If not, it is restricted to the intersection of the current file and the namespace in which the alias is defined. For example:

```
using TelephoneDirectory = Dictionary<TelephoneNumber, string>;
class TelephoneNumber { }
class Dictionary<K, V>{ }
...
TelephoneDirectory telephoneDirectory = new TelephoneDirectory();
```

Type parameter constraints

C#2 allows you to impose *constraints* on the parameter type of a generic type. Without this feature, the generics in C#2 would be hard to exploit. In fact, it is hard to do almost anything on a parameter type of which we know nothing. We do not even know if it can be instantiated (as it can take the form of an interface or abstract case). In addition, we cannot call a specific method on an instance of such a type, we cannot compare the instances of such a type...

.NET 2 generics: the big picture

To be able to use a parameter type within a generic type, you can impose one or several constraints amongst the following:

- The constraint of having a default constructor.
- The constraint of implementing a certain interface or (non-exclusive) of deriving from a certain type.
- The constraint of being a value type or (exclusive) being a reference type.

C# › C++: The template mechanism of C++ has no need for constraints to use type parameters since these types are resolved during compilation. In this case, all attempts to use a missing member will be detected by the compiler.

Default constructor constraint

If you need to be able to instantiate an object of the parameter type within a generic, you do not have a choice but impose the default constructor constraint. Here is an example which illustrates this syntax:

Example 13-6
```
class Factory<U> where U : new() {
   public static U GetNew() { return new U(); }
}
class Program {
   static void Main(){
      int i = Factory<int>.GetNew();
      object obj = Factory<object>.GetNew();
      // Here, 'i' is equal to 0 and 'obj' references
      // an instance of the class 'object'.
   }
}
```

Derivation constraint

If you wish to use certain members of the instances of a parameter type in a generic, you must apply a derivation constraint. Here is an example which illustrates the syntax:

Example 13-7
```
interface ICustomInterface { int Fct(); }
class C<U> where U : ICustomInterface {
   public int AnotherFct(U u) { return u.Fct(); }
}
```

You can apply several interface implementation constraints and one base class inheritance constraint on a same type parameter. In this case, the base class must appear in the list of types. You can also use this constraint conjointly with the default constructor constraint. In this case, the default constructor constraint must appear last:

Example 13-8
```
interface ICustomInterface1 { int Fct1(); }
interface ICustomInterface2 { string Fct2(); }
class BaseClass{}
class C<U>
   where U : BaseClass, ICustomInterface1,  ICustomInterface2, new() {
   public string Fct(U u) { return u.Fct2(); }
}
```

You cannot use a `sealed` class or a one of the `System.Object`, `System.Array`, `System.Delegate`, `System.Enum` or `System.ValueType` class as the base class of a type parameter.

394 Chapter 13 - Generics

You also cannot use the static members of T like this:

Example 13-9
```
class BaseClass { public static void Fct(){} }
class C<T> where T : BaseClass {
   void F(){
      // Compilation Error: 'T' is a 'type parameter',
      // which is not valid in the given context.
      T.Fct();
      // Here is the right syntax to call Fct().
      BaseClass.Fct();
   }
}
```

A type used in a derivation constraint can be an open or closed generic type. Let's illustrate this using the System.IComparable<T> interface. Remember that the types which implement this interface can see their instances compared to an instance of type T.

Example 13-10
```
using System;
class C1<U> where U : IComparable<int> {
   public int Compare( U u, int i ) { return u.CompareTo( i ); }
}
class C2<U> where U : IComparable<U> {
   public int Compare( U u1, U u2 ) { return u1.CompareTo( u2 ); }
}
class C3<U,V> where U : IComparable<V> {
   public int Compare( U u, V v ) { return u.CompareTo( v ); }
}
class C4<U,V> where U : IComparable<V>, IComparable<int> {
   public int Compare( U u, int i ) { return u.CompareTo( i ); }
}
```

Note that a type used in a derivation constraint must have a visibility greater or equal to the one of the generic type which contains this parameter type. For example:

Example 13-11
```
internal class BaseClass{}
// Compilation Error: Inconsistent accessibility:
// constraint type 'BaseClass' is less accessible than 'C<T>'
public class C<T> where T : BaseClass{}
```

To be used in a generic type, certain functionalities can force you to impose certain derivation constraints. For example, if you wish to use a T type parameter in a catch clause, you must constrain T to derive from System.Exception or of one of its derived classes. Also, if you wish to use the using keyword to automatically dispose of an instance of the type parameter, it must be constraint to use the System.IDisposable interface. Finally, if you wish to use the foreach keyword to enumerate the elements of an instance of the parameter type, it must be constraint to implement the System.Collections.IEnumerable or System.Collections.Generic.IEnumerable<T> interface.

Take note that in the special case where T is constrained to implement an interface and T is a value type, the call to a member of the interface on an instance of T will not cause a boxing operation. The following example puts this into evidence:

Example 13-12
```
interface ICounter{
   void Increment();
```

Example 13-12
```
      int Val{get;}
   }
   struct Counter : ICounter {
      private int i;
      public void Increment() { i++; }
      public int Val { get { return i; } }
   }
   class C<T> where T : ICounter, new() {
      public void Fct(){
         T t = new T();
         System.Console.WriteLine( t.Val.ToString() );
         t.Increment();   // Modify the state of 't'.
         System.Console.WriteLine( t.Val.ToString() );

         // Modify the state of a boxed copy of 't'.
         (t as ICounter).Increment();
         System.Console.WriteLine( t.Val.ToString() );
      }
   }
   class Program {
      static void Main() {
         C<Counter> c = new C<Counter>();
         c.Fct();
      }
   }
```
This program displays:
```
0
1
1
```

Reference\Value type constraint

The value/reference type constraint allows constraining a parameter type to be either a value type or a reference type. This constrain must be used first in the list of constraints for a given parameter type, using the **struct** keyword to constrain to a value type and **class** keyword to constrain to a reference type. Caution, this syntax can lead to confusion since classes represent a subset of referenced types (as they also include interfaces) and structures represent a subset of value types. This constraint can be useful in certain cases where we wish to test a reference against null (as an instance of a value type cannot be null) or when we want to ensure that a parameter type used with the **lock** keyword is a reference type.

Example 13-13
```
   class C<U> where U : class, new () {
      U u = new U();
      void Fct(){ lock(u){ } }
   }
```

Members of generic types

Method overloading

Properties, constructors, methods and indexers can be overloaded in a generic class. However, there can be ambiguity when a certain combination of parameter types causes several of the overloads to have the same signature. In this case, the preference will go towards the overload with the signature which contains the least amount of parameter types. If such a method cannot be found, the compiler will emit an error letting you know about the ambiguous call. Here is an example which should clarify these rules:

Example 13-14

```csharp
interface I1<T> {}
interface I2<T> {}
class C1<U> {
   public void Fct1(U u){}      // This method can't ...
   public void Fct1(int i){}    // ... be called if 'U' is 'int'.

   public void Fct2(U u1, U u2){}      // Not ambiguous.
   public void Fct2(int i, string s){}

   public void Fct3(I1<U> a){}         // Not ambiguous.
   public void Fct3(I2<U> a){}

   public void Fct4(U a){}             // Not ambiguous.
   public void Fct4(U[] a){}
}
class C2<U,V> {
   public void Fct5(U u, V v){}        // Might be ambiguous if 'U'='V'.
   public void Fct5(V v, U u){}

   public void Fct6(U u, V v){}        // Might be ambiguous if ...
   public void Fct6(V v, U u){}        // ... 'U'='V' and 'V'!='int'.
   public void Fct6(int u, V v){}

   public void Fct7(int u, V v){}      // Might be ambiguous if ...
   public void Fct7(U u, int v){}      // ... 'U'='V'='int'.

   public void Fct8(U u, I1<V> v){}    // Might be ambiguous ...
   public void Fct8(I1<V> v, U u){}    // ... for example c2<I1<int>,int>.

   public void Fct9(U u1, I1<V> v2){}  // Not ambiguous.
   public void Fct9(V v1, U u2){}

   public void Fct10(ref U u){}        // Not ambiguous.
   public void Fct10(out V v){ v = default(V); }
}
class Program {
   static void Main(){
      C1<int> a = new C1<int>();
      a.Fct1(34); // Call 'Fct1(int i)'.
      C2<int, int> b = new C2<int, int>();
      b.Fct5(13, 14);  // Compilation Error: This call is ambiguous.
      b.Fct6(13, 14);  // Call 'Fct6(int u, V v)'.
      b.Fct7(13, 14);  // Compilation Error: This call is ambiguous.
      C2<I1<int>,int> c = new C2<I1<int>,int>();
```

Example 13-14

```
        c.Fct8(null,null);// Compilation Error: This call is ambiguous.
    }
}
```

Static fields

When a generic type contains a static field, there are as many versions during execution as there are closed generic types constructed from this generic type. This rule applies independently of the fact that the type of the static field is dependant or not on the parameter type. This rule is also applied independently of the fact that the parameter types of this generic are value or reference types. This last remark is relevant since closed generics which take reference types as parameter types all share the same implementation. All this is illustrated by the following example:

Example 13-15

```
using System;
class C<T> {
   private static int m_NInst = 0;
   public C() { m_NInst++; }
   public int NInst { get { return m_NInst; } }
}
class Program {
   static void Main() {
      C<int>    c1 = new C<int>();
      C<int>    c2 = new C<int>();
      C<int>    c3 = new C<int>();
      C<string> c4 = new C<string>();
      C<string> c5 = new C<string>();
      C<object> c6 = new C<object>();
      Console.WriteLine( "NInst C<int>    : " + c1.NInst.ToString() );
      Console.WriteLine( "NInst C<string>: " + c4.NInst.ToString() );
      Console.WriteLine( "NInst C<object>: " + c6.NInst.ToString() );
   }
}
```

This program displays:

```
NInst C<int>    : 3
NInst C<string>: 2
NInst C<object>: 1
```

Static methods

A generic type can have static methods. In this case it is necessary to resolve the parameter types when such a method is invoked. For example:

Example 13-16

```
class C<T> {
   private static T t;
   public static void ChangeState(T _t){ t = _t; }
}
class Program {
   static void Main() {
      C<int>.ChangeState(5);
   }
}
```

The `Main()` static method, which is the entry point to a program, cannot be in a generic class.

Class constructor

If a generic type contains a class constructor, it is called by the CLR when it creates each of the closed generic types. We can take advantage of this feature to add our own constraints on the parameter types. For example, we cannot strictly constrain a parameter type to not be the int type. We can take advantage of the class constructor to verify such a constraint as follows:

Example 13-17

```
using System;
class C<T> {
   static C() {
      int a=0;
      if( ( (object) default(T) != null ) && a is T )
         throw new ArgumentException("Don't use the type C<int>.");
   }
}
```

Note the null test on the default value for T. In fact, the (a is T) is true when T is of type object and when T is of type int. To eliminate the first case, we count on the fact that (object)defaut(object) will return null.

Operator overloading

Although that it can lead to hard to read code, a generic type allows the overloading of operators. There is nothing particular to mention in regards to the arithmetic and comparison operation.

However, when we define a cast operator of a Src source type to a Dest destination type, the compiler must not find an inheritance relationship between the two types when the generic type is compiled. For example:

Example 13-18

```
class C<T>{}
class D<T> : C<T>{
   public static implicit operator C<int>(D<T> val) {}  // OK
   // Compiler error: 'D<T>.implicit operator C<T>(D<T>)':
   // user-defined conversion to/from base class.
   public static implicit operator C<T>(D<T> val) {}
}
class Program{
   static void Main() {
      D<int> dd = new D<int>();  // OK
   }
}
```

A consequence of the fact that we can overload certain casting operators in a generic type makes it possible to redefine certain predefined type conversions. In the following example, if the parameter type U is the objet type we can redefine the implicit conversion operator of D<object> to object:

```
class D<U> {
   public static implicit operator U(D<U> val) { return default(U); }
}
```

In this case, two rules are applied by the CLR:

- If a predefined implicit conversion exists from the Src type to the Dest type, then any redefinition (implicit or explicit) of this conversion is ignored.

- If a predefined explicit conversion exists from the Src type to the Dest type, then all redefinitions of this explicit conversion are ignored. However, an eventual implicit redefinition of the Src to Dest conversion is used.

Nested types

A nested type within a generic type is implicitly a generic type itself. The parameter types of the nesting generic type can be freely used within the nested type. A nested type within a generic type has the possibility of having its own parameter types. In this case, there will be a closed generic type generated by the CLR for each different combination of parameter types used.

Example 13-19
```
using System;
class Outer<U> {
   static Outer(){ Console.WriteLine("Hello from Outer .cctor."); }
   public class Inner<V> {
      static Inner(){ Console.WriteLine("Hello from Inner .cctor."); }
   }
}
class Program {
   static void Main() {
      Outer<string>.Inner<int> a = new Outer<string>.Inner<int>();
      Outer<int>.Inner<int> b = new Outer<int>.Inner<int>();
   }
}
```

This program displays:

```
Hello from Inner .cctor.
Hello from Inner .cctor.
```

Operators and generics

Equality, inequality and comparison operators on parameter type instances

The equality and inequality operators can not be used with an instance or a reference of a parameter type in the following cases:

- If T has a derivation constraint of a class or T has a reference type constraint, then the equality and inequality operators can be used between a reference of type T and any other reference.
- If T does not have a value type constraint, then the equality and inequality operators can be used between a reference of type T and the null reference. If T takes the form of a value type, the equality test will be false and the inequality test will be true.

Let's illustrate these rules through the following example:

Example 13-20
```
class C<T,U,V> where T : class   where V :struct {
   public void Fct1( T t , U u , V v , object o, int i) {
      if ( t == o ) { } // OK
      if ( u == o ) { } // Compilation error.
      if ( v == o ) { } // Compilation error.
      if ( v == i ) { } // Compilation error.
      if ( u == null ) { } // OK
```

Example 13-20
```
        if ( v == null ) { } // Compilation error.
    }
    public void Fct2(T t1, U u1, V v1, T t2, U u2, V v2) {
        if ( t1 == t2 ) { } // OK
        if ( u1 == u2 ) { } // Compilation error.
        if ( v1 == v2 ) { } // Compilation error.
    }
}
```

The comparison operators <, >, <=, >= can never be used with an instance or a reference of a parameter type T.

The typeof operator and generics

The `typeof` operator used on a parameter type returns the instance of the `Type` class which corresponds to the current value of this parameter type.

The `typeof` operator used on a generic type returns the instance of the `Type` class corresponding to the set of current values for the parameter types.

This behavior is not obvious since the `Name` property of the returned types does not display the name of the parameter types.

Example 13-21
```
class C<T>{
    public static void PrintTypes(){
        System.Console.WriteLine( typeof( T ).Name );
        System.Console.WriteLine( typeof( C<T> ).Name );
        System.Console.WriteLine( typeof( C<C<T>> ).Name );
        if( typeof( C<T> ) != typeof( C<C<T>> ) ) {
            System.Console.WriteLine("Despite a similar name" +
                        " they are different instances of Type.");
        }
    }
}
class Program {
    static void Main() {
        C<string>.PrintTypes();
        C<int>.PrintTypes();
    }
}
```

This program displays:

```
String
C`1
C`1
Despite a similar name they are different instances of Type.
Int32
C`1
C`1
Despite a similar name they are different instances of Type.
```

The same is not true if we use the `FullName` property:

Example 13-22
```
    ...
    public static void PrintTypes(){
        System.Console.WriteLine( typeof( C<T> ).FullName );
        System.Console.WriteLine( typeof( C<C<T> >).FullName );
```

Example 13-22
```
    }
...
```

This program displays:

```
C`1[[System.String, mscorlib, Version=2.0.0.0, Culture=neutral,
PublicKeyToken=b77a5c561934e089]]
C`1[[C`1[[System.String, mscorlib, Version=2.0.0.0, Culture=neutral,
PublicKeyToken=b77a5c561934e089]], AsmTest, Version=1.0.0.0,
Culture=neutral, PublicKeyToken=null]]
C`1[[System.Int32, mscorlib, Version=2.0.0.0, Culture=neutral,
PublicKeyToken=b77a5c561934e089]]
C`1[[C`1[[System.Int32, mscorlib, Version=2.0.0.0, Culture=neutral,
PublicKeyToken=b77a5c561934e089]], AsmTest, Version=1.0.0.0,
Culture=neutral, PublicKeyToken=null]]
```

params and lock keywords and generics

A parameter type can be used to type a params argument in the signature of a method.

A parameter type can also be used to type the object of a lock clause. This feature presents a danger when the parameter type is a value type. You must be aware that in this case, the lock keyword will have no effect. It is actually surprising that the compiler does not force a parameter type used in a lock clause to have a constraint which forces it to be a reference type.

The default operator

In the stack example, we had considered the Pop() operation on an empty stack to be an error in the use of the Stack<T> class by the client (i.e. a violation of the contract presented by a stack). We could have weakened this contract and considered this operation as a possible event. In the first case, raising an exception is the proper behavior. In the second case, it would be better to return an empty element which the client would interpret as: there are no more elements on my stack. However, we know nothing about the type T of the element to return. If T is a reference type, we wish to return a null reference while if T is a value type such as int we wish to return 0. The default operator of C#2 allows you to obtain the default value for a type.

Example 13-23
```
class Stack<T>{
   ...
   public T Pop(){
      if (m_Index == 0)
         return default(T);
      return m_ItemsArray[--m_Index];
   }
   ...
}
```

Casting and generics

Basic rules

From now on, we will suppose that T is a parameter type. The C#2 language allows you to:

- Cast implicitly an instance of a type T (if T is a value type, else a reference of type T) to a reference of an `objet` type. If T is a value type, a boxing operation will occur.
- Cast explicitly a reference of type `objet` to an instance of type T. If T is a value type, there will be an unboxing operation.
- Cast explicitly an instance of a type T to a reference of any interface. If T is a value type, a boxing operation will occur.
- Cast explicitly a reference of any interface to an instance of the T type. If T is a value type, there will be an unboxing operation.
- In the last three cases, if the cast is not possible, an exception of type `InvalidCastException` is raised.

Other casting rules are added if we use derivation constraints:

- If T is constrained to implement the interface I, you can implicitly cast an instance from T into I or into any interface implemented by I and vice versa. If T is a value type, a boxing operation (or unboxing) will occur.
- If T is constrained to derive from the C class, you can implicitly cast an instance of T to C or into any sub-class of C and vice versa. If a custom implicit conversion exist from C to a type A then the compiler will accept an implicit conversion from T to A. If a custom explicit conversion exists from A to C then the compiler will accept an explicit conversion from A to T.

Casting and generic arrays

If T is a parameter type of a generic class and if T is constrained to derive from C then the C#2 compiler will accept to:

- Cast implicitly an array of T into an array of C. In other words, the C#2 compiler accepts to cast implicitly a reference of type T[ ] into a reference of C[ ]. We say that the C# arrays accept *covariance* on their elements.
- Cast explicitly an array of C into an array of T. In other words, the C#2 compiler accepts to explicitly cast a reference of type C[ ] to a reference of type T[ ]. We say that the C# arrays accept *contravariance* on their elements.

These two rules are illustrated by the following example:

Example 13-24
```
class C { }
class GenericClass<T> where T : C {
   T[] arrOfT = new T[10];
   public void Fct(){
      C[] arrOfC = arrOfT;
      T[] arrOfT2 = (T[]) arrOfC;
   }
}
```

There is no equivalent rule if T is constrained to implement the I interface. Also, the covariance and the contravariance are not supported on the parameter types of a generic class. In other words, if class D derives from class B, there exists no implicit conversion between a reference of type List<D> and a reference of type List<B>.

is and as operators

To avoid an exception of type `InvalidCastException` when you are not certain of a type conversion implicating a T type parameter, it is recommended to use the `is` operator to test if

Inheritance and generics 403

the conversion is possible and the as operator to attempt the conversion. Remember that the as operator returns null if the conversion is not possible. For example:

Example 13-25
```
using System.Collections.Generic;
class C<T> {
   public void Fct(T t){
      int i = t as int;  // Compilation error:
                   // The as operator must be used with a reference type.
      string s = t as string;
      if( s!= null ) { /*...*/ }
      if( t is IEnumerable<int> ){
         IEnumerable<int> enumerable = t as IEnumerable<int>;
         foreach( int j in enumerable) { /*...*/ }
      }
   }
}
```

Inheritance and generics

Basic rules

A non-generic class can inherit from a generic class. In this case, all parameter types must be resolved:

```
class B<T> {...}
class D : B<double> {...}
```

A generic class can derive from a generic class. In this case, it is optional to resolve all the parameters. However, it is necessary to repeat the constraints on the non-resolved parameter types. For example:

```
class B<T> where T : struct { }
class D1<T> : B<T> where T : struct   { }
class D2<T> : B<int> { } // Awkward: 'T' is a different parameter type.
class D3<U,V> : B<int> { }
```

Finally, know that a generic class can inherit from a non-generic class.

Overriding virtual methods of generic types

A generic base class can have abstract or virtual methods which uses or not parameter types in their signatures. In this case, the compiler forces the methods to be overridden in derived classes to use the proper parameters. For example:

Example 13-26
```
abstract class  B<T> {
   public abstract T Fct(T t);
}
class D1 : B<string>{
   public override string Fct( string t ) { return "hello"; }
}
class D2<T> : B<T>{
   public override T Fct(T t) { return default (T); }
}
// Compilation error :
// Does not implement inherited abstract member 'B<U>.Fct(U)'
class D3<T, U> : B<U> {
```

Example 13-26
```
    // Compilation error: No suitable method found to override
    public override T Fct(T t) { return default(T); }
}
```

We take advantage of this example to underline the fact that a generic class can also be abstract. This example also shows the type of compiler error that we will encounter when we do not properly use the parameter types.

It is interesting to note that the parameter types of a derived generic class can be used in the body of an overridden virtual method, even if the base class is not generic.

Example 13-27
```
class B {
   public virtual void Fct() { }
}
class D<T> : B where T : new(){
   public override void Fct() {
      T t = new T();
   }
}
```

All the rules mentioned in the current section remain valid in the implementation of generic interfaces, classes or structures.

Generic methods

Introduction

Whether that it is defined in a generic type or not, that it is static or not, a method has the possibility of defining its own parameter types. Each time such a method is invoked, a type must be provided for each parameter type. Here we talk about the concept of *generic method*.

The parameter types specific to a method can only be used within the scope of the method (i.e. the return value + signature + body of the method). In the C2<T> class of the following example, there is no correlation between the U parameter type of the Fct<U>() method and the U parameter type of the FctStatic<U>() method.

The parameter types of a method can have the same name as a parameter type for the class defining the method. In this case, the parameter type of the class is hidden within the scope of the method. In the C3<T>.Fct<T>() method of the following example, the T parameter type defined by the methods hides that T parameter type defined by the class. This practice can lead to confusion and the compiler will emit a warning when it is detected.

Example 13-28
```
class C1 {
   public U Fct<U>(U u) { return u; }
}
class C2<T> {
   public U Fct<U>(U u) { return u; }
   public static U FctStatic<U>(U u) { return u; }
}
class C3<T> {
   // Compilation warning : Type parameter ' T' has same
   // name as type parameter from outer type 'C3<T>'.
   public T Fct<T>(T t) { return t; }
}
```

Generic methods

Example 13-28
```
class Program {
    static void Main() {
        C1 c1 = new C1();
        c1.Fct<double>(3.4);
        C2<int> c2 = new C2<int>();
        c2.Fct<double>(3.4);
        c2.Fct<string>("hello");
        C3<int> c3 = new C3<int>();
        c3.Fct<double>(3.4);
    }
}
```

This feature cannot be used on operators, on `extern` methods nor on the property, indexer and event accessors.

Generic methods and constraints

A generic method can define all sorts of constrains for each of its parameter types. The syntax for this is identical to the one for the definition of constraints on generic types.

Example 13-29
```
class C {
    public int Fct<U>(U u) where U : class, System.IComparable<U> ,new(){
        if ( u == null )
            return 0;
        U unew = new U();
        return u.CompareTo( unew );
    }
}
```

Of course, a generic method cannot override the constraints on a parameter type defined on its class.

Virtual generic methods

Abstract, virtual and interface methods can also be generic. In this case, the overridding of such methods does not need to respect the name of the parameter types. When overriding a virtual or abstract generic method which has constraints on its parameter types, you must not rewrite this set of constraints. When implementing an interface method which has constraints on its parameter types, you must rewrite this set of constraints. These rules are illustrated by the following example which compiles without warning or errors:

Example 13-30
```
using System;
abstract class B {
   public virtual A Fct1<A, C>( A a, C c ) { return a; }
   public abstract int Fct2<U>(U u) where U:class,IComparable<U>,new();
}
class D1 : B {
   public override X Fct1<X, Y>( X x, Y y ) { return x; }
   public override int Fct2<U>( U u )  { return 0; }
}
interface I {
   A Fct1<A, C>( A a, C b );
   int Fct2<U>( U u ) where U : class, IComparable<U>, new();
```

Example 13-30
```
   }
   class D2 : I {
      public X Fct1<X, Y>( X x, Y y ) { return x; }
      public int Fct2<U>( U u ) where U : class, IComparable<U>, new()
      { return 0; }
   }
```

Inference of generic method parameter types

When a generic method is invoked, the C#2 compiler has the possibility of inferring the parameter types based on the types of the provided arguments to the method. Explicitly providing the parameter types for a generic method overrides the inference rules.

The inference rule does not take into account the type of the return value. However, the compiler is capable of inferring a parameter type from the elements of an array. This is illustrated by the following program:

Example 13-31
```
   class C {
      public static U Fct1<U>() { return default(U); }
      public static void Fct2<U>( U u ) { return; }
      public static U Fct3<U>( U u ) { return default(U); }
      public static void Fct4<U>( U u1, U u2 ) { return; }
      public static void Fct5<U>( U[] arrayOfU ) { return; }
   }
   class Program {
      static void Main() {
         // Compilation error: The type arguments for method
         // 'C.Fct1<U>()' cannot be inferred from the usage.
         string s = C.Fct1();

         // Compilation error: Cannot implicitly convert type
         // 'System.IDisposable' to 'string'.
         string s = C.Fct1<System.IDisposable>();
         s = C.Fct1<string>(); // OK

         C.Fct2( "hello" ); // Infer 'U' as 'string'.

         // Compilation error: The type arguments for
         // method 'C.Fct2<U>(U)' cannot be inferred from the usage.
         C.Fct2( null );

         int i = C.Fct3( 6 ); // Infer 'U' as 'int.

         double d = C.Fct3( 6 ); // Awkward: Infer 'U' as 'int' ...
                                 // ... and not as 'double'.

         // Compilation error: Cannot implicitly convert 'int'
         // to 'System.IDisposable'.
         System.IDisposable dispose = C.Fct3( 6 );

         // Infer 'U' as 'string'.
         C.Fct4( "hello", "bonjour" );

         // Compilation error: The type arguments for method
```

Example 13-31
```
        // 'C.Fct4<U>(U,U)' cannot be inferred from the usage.
        C.Fct4( 5, "bonjour" );

        C.Fct5( new int[6] ); // Infer 'U' as 'int.
    }
}
```

C#2 grammar ambiguity

There is an ambiguity in the C#2 grammar as the lesser than '<' and greater than '>' characters can be used, in certain special cases, both for the definition of the list of parameter types and as well as comparison operators. This special case is illustrated in the following example:

Example 13-32
```
class C<U,V> {
    public static void Fct1() {
        int U = 6;
        int V = 7;
        int Fct2 = 9;
        Fct3( Fct2 < U, V > (20) ); // Call Fct3(int)
        Fct3( Fct2 < U, V > 20 );   // Call Fct3(bool,bool)
    }
    public static int Fct2<A, B>( int i ) { return 0;}
    public static void Fct3( int i ) { return; }
    public static void Fct3( bool b1, bool b2 ) { return; }
}
```

The rule is that when the compiler is faced with this ambiguity, it analyzes the character located right after '>'. If this character is in the following list, then the compiler will infer a list of parameter types:

```
( ) ] > : ; , . ?
```

Delegates, events and generics

Introduction

As with all nested types, a delegate class can use the parameter types of the nesting class:

Example 13-33
```
class C<T> {
    public delegate T GenericDelegate( T t );
    public static T Fct( T t ) { return t; }
}
class Program {
    static void Main() {
        C<string>.GenericDelegate genericDelegate = C<string>.Fct;
        string s = genericDelegate( "hello" );
    }
}
```

A delegate class can also define its own parameter types as well as their constraints:

Example 13-34

```
public delegate U GenericDelegate<U>( U u ) where U : class;
class C<T> {
   public static T Fct( T t ) { return t; }
}
class Program {
   static void Main() {
      GenericDelegate<string> genericDelegate = C<string>.Fct;
      string s = genericDelegate( "hello" );
   }
}
```

Generic delegates and generic methods

When assigning a generic method to a generic delegate object, the C#2 compiler is capable of inferring the parameter types of the generic method from the parameter types of the generic delegate object. This is illustrated by the following example:

Example 13-35

```
delegate void GenericDelegateA<U>(U u);
delegate void GenericDelegateB(int i);
delegate U    GenericDelegateC<U>();
class Program {
   static void Fct1<T>(T t) { return; }
   static T    Fct2<T>() { return default(T); }
   static void Main() {
      GenericDelegateA<string> d1 = Fct1; // The compiler infers
                                          // 'Fct1<string>'.
      GenericDelegateB d2 = Fct1; // The compiler infers 'Fct1<int>'.
      GenericDelegateC<string> d3 = Fct2<string>; // OK but no inference.

      // Compilation error: The type arguments for method
      // 'Program.Fct2<T>()' cannot be inferred from the usage.
      GenericDelegateC<string> d4 = Fct2;
   }
}
```

As illustrated in this example, there is never any inference on the parameter types of a generic delegate object.

Contravariance, covariance, delegates and generics

Here, we will expose a new functionality of delegate objects which will come in handy later. In C#2, delegate objects support the notion of *contravariance* on their arguments and the notion of *covariance* on their return type. This is illustrated below:

Example 13-36

```
class Base { }
class Derived : Base { }
delegate Base DelegateType ( Derived d );
class Program{
   static Derived Handler ( Base b ) { return b as Derived; }
   static void Main() {
       // Notice that the 'Handler()' method signature is not ...
       // ... the same as the 'DelegateType' signature.
```

Example 13-36
```
      DelegateType delegateInstance = Handler;
      Base b = delegateInstance( new Derived() );
   }
}
```

It is legitimate for this program to compile properly. Think about it in terms of contract:

- The Handler(Base) method has a contract less strict on its input than the one proposed by the DelegateType(Derived) delegate class. An instance of DelegateType can then reference the Handler() method without risking an invalid *downcast*. This is contravariance.

- The Derived Handler() method has a more strict contract on its output than the one proposed by the Base DelegateType() delegate class. There also, an instance of DelegateType can reference the Handler() method without risking an invalid *downcast*. This is covariance.

Now, lets assume that the notions of covariance and of contravariance did not exist and that we wished to called the Derived Handler(Base) method through a delegate object of type Base delegate(Derived). We could in fact use a generic delegate object like this:

Example 13-37
```
class Base { }
class Derived : Base { }
delegate B DelegateType<B,D>(D d);
class Program {
   static Derived Handler(Base b){return b as Derived;}
   static void Main() {
      DelegateType<Base, Derived> delegateInstance = Handler;
      // The in reference is implitly casted from 'Derived' to 'Base'.
      // The out reference is implitly casted from 'Derived' to 'Base'.
      Base b = delegateInstance( new Derived() );
   }
}
```

Events and generic delegates

Generic delegates can be used to avoid the definition of multiple delegates in order to type events. The following example shows that with a single generic delegate class, you can type all events which take in a single 'sender' parameter and one argument:

Example 13-38
```
delegate void GenericEventHandler<U,V>( U sender, V arg );
class Publisher {
   public event GenericEventHandler<Publisher,System.EventArgs> Event;
   public void TriggerEvent() { Event(this, System.EventArgs.Empty); }
}
class Subscriber {
   public void EventHandler( Publisher sender, System.EventArgs arg ){}
}
class Program {
   static void Main() {
      Publisher publisher = new Publisher();
      Subscriber subscriber = new Subscriber();
      publisher.Event += subscriber.EventHandler;
   }
}
```

Reflection, attributes, IL and generics

Generics and the System.Type class

Remember that an instance of System.Type can be obtained either using the typeof operator or by calling the object.GetType() method. With .NET 2, an instance of System.Type can reference an opened or closed generic type.

Example 13-39

```
using System;
using System.Collections.Generic;
class Program {
    static void Main() {
        List<int> list = new List<int>();
        Type type1 = list.GetType();
        Type type2 = typeof( List<int> );
        Type type3 = typeof( List<double> );
        // type4 is an open generic type.
        Type type4 = type3.GetGenericTypeDefinition();
        System.Diagnostics.Debug.Assert( type1 == type2 );
        System.Diagnostics.Debug.Assert( type1 != type3 );
        System.Diagnostics.Debug.Assert( type3 != type4 );
    }
}
```

The System.Type class supports new methods and properties dedicated to generics:

```
public abstract class Type : System.Reflection.MemberInfo,
                             System.Runtime.InteropServices._Type,
                             System.Reflection.IReflect
{
    // Returns from a generic type a new generic Type instance based
    // on the provided parameter types.
    public virtual System.Type MakeGenericType(
                        params System.Type[] typeArgs);

    // Returns an array of Type objects which represent the parameter
    // types of a generic type.
    public virtual System.Type[] GetGenericArguments();

    // Returns an open generic type from a generic type.
    public virtual System.Type GetGenericTypeDefinition();

    // Returns true if it's an open generic type.
    public virtual bool IsGenericTypeDefinition { get; }

    // Returns true if some parameter types are not specified.
    public virtual bool ContainsGenericParameters { get; }

    // Returns true if the current type is a parameter type not
    // specified for a generic type or method.
    public virtual bool IsGenericParameter { get; }


    //------------------------------------------------------------
    // Following members can only be called on Type instances for
    // which the 'IsGenericParameter' property returns true.

    // Returns the 0-based position in the list of parameter types.
```

Delegates, events and generics

```
    public virtual int GenericParameterPosition { get; }

    // Returns the generic method which declares the parameter type.
    // Returns null if not declared in a generic method.
    public virtual System.Reflection.MethodBase DeclaringMethod { get; }

    // Returns derivation constraints on the current parameter type.
    public virtual System.Type[] GetGenericParameterConstraints();

    // Returns constraints other than the derivation ones.
    public virtual System.GenericParameterAttributes
            GenericParameterAttributes { get; }
    ...
}
```

Here is an example of the use of this class used to locate the definition of a generic type:

Example 13-40

```
using System;
using System.Reflection;
class Program {
   static void WriteTypeConstraints(Type type ){
      string[] results = new string[type.GetGenericArguments().Length];
      // For each parameter types.
      foreach (Type t in type.GetGenericArguments()) {
         // If 't' is a parameter type not specified?
         if ( t.IsGenericParameter ) {
            int pos = t.GenericParameterPosition;
            Type[] derivConstraints = t.GetGenericParameterConstraints();
            MethodBase methodBase = t.DeclaringMethod;
            GenericParameterAttributes attributes =
                     t.GenericParameterAttributes;
            results[pos] = "   where " + t.Name + ":";
            if ((GenericParameterAttributes.ReferenceTypeConstraint &
                  attributes) != 0 ) {
               results[pos] += "class,";
            }
            if((GenericParameterAttributes.
                  NotNullableValueTypeConstraint & attributes) != 0 ) {
               results[pos] += "struct,";
            }
            foreach (Type derivConstraint in derivConstraints) {
               results[pos] += derivConstraint.Name + ",";
            }
            if ((GenericParameterAttributes.
                  DefaultConstructorConstraint & attributes) != 0 ) {
               results[pos] += "new()";
            }
         } // end -- If 't' is a parameter type not specified?
      } // end -- For each parameter types.
      Console.WriteLine(type.Name);
      foreach (string result in results)
         if (result != null)
            Console.WriteLine(result);
   }

   class Bar{}
```

Example 13-40

```
   class Foo : Bar, IDisposable{ public void Dispose() {} }
   class C<U, V>
      where U : Bar, IDisposable, new()
      where V : struct {}

   static void Main() {
      WriteTypeConstraints( typeof(C<Foo,int>) );
      WriteTypeConstraints( typeof(C<Foo,int>).GetGenericTypeDefinition());
   }
}
```

This program displays:

```
C`2
C`2
   where U:Bar,IDisposable,new()
   where V:struct,ValueType,new()
```

We can see that the constraint forcing the type to be a value type actually adds the constraints of deriving from `ValueType` and of implementing a default constructor.

Generics and the System.Reflection.MethodBase and System.Reflection.MethodInfo classes

The `System.Reflection.MethodBase` and `System.Reflection.MethodInfo` (which derives from `MethodBase`) classes have evolved in order to support the concept of generic methods. Here are the new members:

```
public abstract class MethodBase :
      System.Reflection.MemberInfo,
      System.Runtime.InteropServices._MethodBase {

   // Returns an array containing type parameters of a generic method.
   public virtual System.Type[] GetGenericArguments();

   // Returns true if it's an open generic method.
   public virtual bool IsGenericMethodDefinition { get; }

   // Returns true if some parameter types are not specified.
   public virtual bool ContainsGenericParameters { get; }
   ...
}

public abstract class MethodInfo :
      System.Reflection.MemberBase,
      System.Runtime.InteropServices._MethodInfo {

   // Returns a new generic MethodInfo from a generic method
   // with the provided parameter types.
   public virtual System.Reflection.MethodInfo MakeGenericMethod(
                     params System.Type[] typeArgs);

   // Returns an open generic type from a generic type.
   public virtual System.Reflection.MethodInfo GetGenericMethodDefinition();
   ...
```

Delegates, events and generics

   }

The following program shows how to create a late bind on a generic method and how to invoke it after having resolved the parameter types:

Example 13-41

```
using System;
using System.Reflection;
class Program{
   public class Bar{}
   public class Foo : Bar, IDisposable{ public void Dispose() { } }
   public static void Fct<U, V>()
      where U : Bar, IDisposable, new()
      where V : struct {
      Console.WriteLine( typeof(U).Name );
      Console.WriteLine( typeof(V).Name );
   }
   static void Main() {
      Type typeProgram = typeof(Program);
      MethodInfo methodGenericOpen = typeProgram.GetMethod("Fct",
                  BindingFlags.Static | BindingFlags.Public);
      //  Specify parameter types.
      MethodInfo methodGenericClosed = methodGenericOpen.MakeGenericMethod(
            new Type[] { typeof(Foo), typeof(int) } );
      System.Diagnostics.Debug.Assert (
            methodGenericClosed.GetGenericMethodDefinition() ==
            methodGenericOpen );
      methodGenericClosed.Invoke (
            null,  // It is null because we call a static method.
            new object[0]); // No parameters in.
   }
}
```

This program displays:

```
Foo
Int32
```

Attributes and generics

An attribute which can be used to mark a general method can also be used on a generic method.

An attribute which can mark a general type can also be used on a generic type.

The `System.AttributeTargets` enumeration now has the new value `GenericParameter` which allows specifying that an attribute can be used to mark a parameter type. For example:

Example 13-42

```
[System.AttributeUsage(System.AttributeTargets.GenericParameter)]
public class A : System.Attribute{}
class C<[A]U, V> { }
```

An attribute class cannot be a generic class. Thus, a generic class cannot directly (or indirectly) derive from `System.Attribute`.

An attribute class can use generic types and also define generic methods:

Example 13-43
```
class C<U, V> { }
public class A : System.Attribute{
   void Fct1(C<int, string> c) { }
   void Fct2<X>() { }
}
```

The IL Language and generics

Support for generics implies changes at the CLR level but also changes within the IL language, the CTS and also in the metadata contained in assemblies.

In the body of methods of a generic type or within the scope of a generic method, the IL languages uses the !x notation to name a type parameter located at position x (0 based index) in the list of the parameter types.

New IL instructions have been added such stelem.any and ldelem.any for the access of the elements of a type parameter array (they complete the stelem.i2, ldelem.i2, stelem.i4, ldelem.i4, stelem.ref, ldelem.ref... instruction family). Certain IL instructions such as stloc.x or ldloc.x (which allows the manipulation of local variables) were already not taking into account the type of the manipulated values. They were then already ready for generics and only their interpretation by the JIT compiler has evolved.

Only two metadata tables have been added to the list of the metadata tables of an assembly containing generic types or methods:

- The GenericParam table allows the description of the parameter types.
- The GenericParamConstraint table allows the description of derivation constraints.

The value/reference and default constructor constraints are not stored in an attribute or a metadata table. They are simply contained in the name of the generic type or method. Hence, the following classes...

```
class C1<T> where T : new() {...}
class C2<T> where T : class {...}
class C3<T> where T : struct {...}
```

...as named as follows in IL code:

```
... C1<(.ctor) T> {...}
... C2<(class) T> {...}
... C3<(value type, .ctor, [mscorlib]System.ValueType) T> {...}
```

Generics in the .NET 2 framework

Object serialization and generics

It is possible to serialize and deserialize an instance of a generic type. In this case, it is required that the list of parameter types for the serialized object be identical to the parameter type list for the deserialized object. For example:

Example 13-44
```
using System;
using System.Runtime.Serialization;
using System.Runtime.Serialization.Formatters.Binary;
using System.IO;
[Serializable]
```

Generics in the .NET 2 framework

Example 13-44

```
public class C<T>{
   private T m_t;
   public T t { get { return m_t; } set { m_t = value; } }
}
class Program{
   static void Main() {
      C<int> objIn = new C<int>();
      objIn.t = 691;
      IFormatter formatter = new BinaryFormatter();
      Stream stream = new FileStream( "obj.bin", FileMode.Create,
                                      FileAccess.ReadWrite);
      formatter.Serialize(stream, objIn);
      stream.Seek(0, SeekOrigin.Begin);
      C<int> objOut = (C<int>)formatter.Deserialize( stream );
      // Here, objOut.t is equal to 691.

      // This line raises a SerializationException.
      C<long> objOut2 = (C<long>) formatter.Deserialize( stream );
      stream.Close();
   }
}
```

.NET Remoting and generics

It is possible to consume an instance of a closed generic type using the .NET Remoting technology whether you are in CAO or WKO modes:

```
// Define a generic class that can be used with .NET remoting.
public class Server<T> : MarshalByRefObject{}
...
   // Server side code
   RemotingConfiguration.RegisterActivatedServiceType(
      typeof( Serveur<int>) );
   RemotingConfiguration.RegisterWellKnownServiceType(
      typeof( Serveur<string>), "MyService",
      WellKnownObjectMode.SingleCall );
...
   // Client side code
   RemotingConfiguration.RegisterActivatedClientType(
      typeof( Serveur<int>), url );
   RemotingConfiguration.RegisterWellKnownClientType(
      typeof( Serveur<string>), url );
```

If you wish to use the client-side or server-side configuration files, you must specify the parameter types used:

```
// Server side
   <service>
      <activated
       type="ServerAssembly.Server[[System.Int32]],ServerAssembly"/>
   </service>
// Client side
   <client url="...">
      <activated
       type="ServerAssembly.Server[[System.Int32]],ServerAssembly"/>
   </client>
```

The *double square brackets* syntax allows you to specify a parameter type list:

```
type="ServeurAssembly.Serveur[[System.Int32],[System.String]],
    ServeurAssembly"
```

The `System.Activator` class also supports generics. Know that when you use this class with a generic type, you cannot use the `CreateInstance()` and `CreateInstanceFrom()` overloads in which you specify the name of the types using strings.

Collections and generics

The collection classes part of the .NET framework is the topic of chapter 15. They have been revised to take advantage of generics. The `System.Collections` namespace is supported for compatibility issues. However, there are no reasons to prefer a `System.Collections` type to a `System.Collections.Generic` type. At page 496 we provide a correspondence table between the `System.Collections` and `System.Collections.Generic` namespaces.

Domains which don't support generics

The notions of web service and serviced component (i.e. COM+, Enterprise Services) do not support the concept of generics as neither standard currently supports generics.

14 Unsafe code, exceptions, anonymous methods, iterators

We will see that C# allows suspending the verification of code by the CLR to allow developers to directly access memory using pointers. Hence with C#, you can complete, in a standard way, certain optimizations which were only possible within unmanaged development environments such as C++. These optimizations concern, for example, the processing of large amounts of data in memory such as bitmaps.

As with the C++ and Java languages, C# exposes a simple yet powerful exception management system.

We will finally see that the C#2 language adds two syntax features which are close to functional programming which, in certain specific cases, can significantly increate code readability.

Pointers and unsafe code

C++ › C#: C++ does not know the notion of code management. This is one of the advantages of C++ as it allows the use of pointers and thus allows developers to write optimized code which is closer to the target machine.

This is also a disadvantage of C++ since the use of pointers is cumbersome and potentially dangerous, significantly increasing the development effort and maintenance required.

C#: Before the .NET platform, 100% of the code executed on the *Windows* operating system was unmanaged. This means the executable contains the code directly in machine instructions which are compatible with the type of processor (i.e. machine language code). The introduction of the managed execution mode with the .NET platform is revolutionary. The main sources of hard to track bugs are detected and resolved by the CLR. Amongst these:

- *Array access overflows* (Now dynamically managed by the CLR).
- *Memory leaks* (Now mostly managed by the garbage collector).
- The use of an invalid pointer. This problem is solved in a radical way as the manipulation of pointers if forbidden in managed mode.

However, during the presentation of the CTS at page 285, we have shown that the CLR knows how to manipulate three kinds of pointers:

- *Managed pointers*. These pointers can point to data contained in the object heap managed by the garbage collector. These pointers are not used explicitly by the C# code. They are thus used implicitly by the C# compiler when it compiles methods with `out` and `ref` arguments.
- *Unmanaged function pointers*. The section at page 224 discusses the use of these pointers.
- *Unmanaged pointers*. These pointers can point to any data contained in the user addressing space of the process. The C# language allows to use this type of pointers in zones of code considered *unsafe*. The IL code emitted by the C# compiler corresponding to the zones of code which use these unmanaged pointers make use of specialized IL instructions. Their effect on

the memory of the process cannot be verified by the JIT compiler of the CLR. Consequently, a malicious user can take advantage of unsafe code regions to accomplish malicious actions. To counter this weakness, the CLR will only allow the execution of this code at run-time if the code has the `SkipVerification` CAS meta-permission

Since it allows to directly manipulating the memory of a process through the use of an unmanaged pointer, unsafe code is particularly useful to optimize certain processes on large amounts of data stored in structures. An example of optimization of image manipulation, using pointers can be found at page 580.

Compilation options to allow unsafe code

Unsafe code must be used on purpose and you must also provide the `/unsafe` option to the `csc.exe` compiler to tell it that you are aware that the code you wish to compile contains zones which will be seen as unverifiable by the JIT compiler. *Visual Studio* offers the *Build > Allow unsafe code* project property to indicate that you wish to use this compiler option.

Declaring unsafe code in C#

In C#, the `unsafe` keyword lets the compiler know when you will use unsafe code. It can be used in three situations:

- Before the declaration of a class or structure. In this case, all the methods of the type can use pointers.
- Before the declaration of a method. In this case, the pointers can be used within the body of this method and in its signature.
- Within the body of a method (static or not). In this case, pointers are only allowed within the marked block of code. For example:

```
unsafe{
    ...
}
```

Let us mention that if a method accepts at least one pointer as an argument or as a return value, the method (or its class) must be marked as unsafe, but also all regions of code calling this method must also be marked as unsafe.

Using pointers in C#

C++ > C#: The use syntax for pointers is identical in C# as in C++ except for certain particular pointers: in C#, the `int *p1,p2;` declaration makes it so `p1` is a pointer on an integer and `p2` is an integer.

Only certain types can be used as pointers.

In C#, it is necessary to pin objects in memory to use pointers on them.

C#: Each object, whether it is a value or reference type instance, has a memory address at which it is physically located in the process. This address is not necessarily constant during the lifetime of the object as the garbage collector can physically move objects store in the heap.

.NET types that support pointers

For certain types, there is a dual type, the unmanaged pointer type which corresponds to the managed type. A pointer variable is in fact the address of an instance of the concerned type. The set of types which authorizes the use of pointers limits itself to all value types, with the exception of structures with at least one reference type field. Consequently, only instances of the following types can be used through pointers: primitive types; enumerations; structures with no reference type fields; pointers.

Declaring pointers

> ⚠ A pointer might point to nothing. In this case, it is **extremely important** that its value should be set to null (0). In fact, the majority of bugs due to pointers come from pointers which are not null but which point to invalid data.

The declaration of a pointer on the `FooType` is done as follows:

```
FooType * pointeur;
```

For example:

```
long * pAnInteger = 0;
```

Note that the declaration…

```
int * p1,p2;
```

…makes it so that `p1` is a pointer on an integer and `p2` is a pointer.

Dereferencing and indirection operators

In C#, we can obtain a pointer on a variable by using the *address of* operator &. For example:

```
long anInteger = 98;
long * pAnInteger = &anInteger;
```

We can access to the object through the *indirection* operator *. For example:

```
long anInteger = 98;
long * pAnInteger = &anInteger;
long anAnotherInteger = *pAnInteger;
// Here, the value of 'anAnotherInteger' is 98.
```

The sizeof operator

The `sizeof` operator allows obtaining the size in bytes of instances of a value type. This operator can only be used in unsafe mode. For example:

```
int i = sizeof(int)      // i is equal to 4
int j = sizeof(double)   // j is equal to 8
```

Pointer arithmetic

A pointer on a type T can be modified through the use of the '++' and '--' unary operator. The '−' operator can also be used with pointers.

- The '++' operator increments the pointer by `sizeof(T)` bytes.
- The '--' operator decrements the pointer by `sizeof(T)` bytes.
- The '-' operator used between two pointers of same type T, returns a value of type `long`. This value is equal to the byte offset between the two pointers divided by `sizeof(T)`.

The comparison can also be used on two pointers of a same or different type. The supported comparison operators are:

```
==      !=      <      >      <=      >=
```

Pointer casting

Pointers in C# do not derive from the `Object` class and thus the boxing and unboxing (at page 292) does not exist on pointers. However, pointers support both implicit and explicit casting.

Implicit casts are done from any type of pointer to a pointer of type `void*`.

Explicit casts are done from:

- Any pointer type to any other pointer type.
- Any pointer type to the `sbyte`, `byte`, `short`, `ushort`, `int`, `uint`, `long`, `ulong` types (caution, we are not talking about the `sbyte*`, `byte*`, `short*`... types).
- One of `sbyte`, `byte`, `short`, `ushort`, `int`, `uint`, `long`, `ulong` types to any pointer type.

Double pointers

Let us mention the possibility of using a pointer on a pointer (although somewhat useless in C#). Here, we talk of a *double pointer*. For example:

```
long aLong = 98;
long * pALong = &aLong;
long ** ppALong = &pALong ;
```

It is important to have a naming convention for pointers and double pointers. In general the name of a pointer is prefixed with '`p`' while the name of a double pointer is prefixed with '`pp`'.

Pinned object

C++ › C#: The notion of object pinning is completely unknown to C++, since it comes from the fact that the .NET platform leaves the management of the managed heap to the garbage collector.

C#:

At page 97 we explain how the garbage collector has the possibility of physically moving the objects for which it is responsible. Objects managed by the garbage collector are generally reference type's instances while pointed objects are value type's instances. If a pointer points to a value type field of an instance of a reference type, there will be a potential problem as the instance of the reference type can be moved at any time by the garbage collector. The compiler forces the developer to use the `fixed` keyword in order to tell the garbage collector not to move reference type instances which contain a value field pointed to by a pointer. The syntax of the `fixed` keyword is the following:

Example 14-1

```
class Article { public long Price = 0;}
unsafe class Program {
   unsafe public static void Main() {
      Article article = new Article();
      fixed ( long* pPrice = &article.Price ){
         // Here, you can use the pointer 'pPrice' and the object
         // referenced by 'article' cannot be moved by the GC.
      }
      // Here, 'pPrice' is not available anymore and the object
      // referenced by 'article' is not pinned anymore.
   }
}
```

Using pointers in C# 421

If we had not used the `fixed` keyword in this example, the compiler would have produced an error as it can detect that the object referenced by the `article` may be moved during execution.

We can pin several objects of a same type in the same `fixed` block. If we need to pin objects of a several types, you will need to use nested `fixed` blocks.

You must pin objects the least often as possible, for the shortest duration possible. When objects are pinned, the work of the garbage collector is impaired and less efficient.

Variables of a value type declared as local variable in a method do not need to be pinned since they are not managed by the garbage collector.

Pointers and arrays

C++ › C#: The notion of pointers and arrays are close in C++ from the fact that elements of an array are stored in a contiguous memory area. This similarity also exists in C#.

C#: In C#, the elements of an array made from a type which can be pointed to can be accessed by using pointers. Let us precise that an array is an instance of the `System.Array` class and is stored on the managed heap by the garbage collector. Here is an example which both shows the syntax but also the overflow of the array (which is not detected at compilation or execution!) due to the use of pointers:

Example 14-2
```
using System;
public class Program {
   unsafe public static void Main() {
      // Create an array of 4 integers.
      int [] array = new int[4];
      for( int i=0; i < 4; i++ )
         array[i] = i*i;
      Console.WriteLine( "Display 6 items (oops!):" );
      fixed( int *ptr = array )
         for( int j = 0; j< 6 ; j++ )
            Console.WriteLine( *(ptr+j) );
      Console.WriteLine( "Display all items:" );
      foreach( int k in array )
         Console.WriteLine(k);
   }
}
```

Here is the display:

```
Display 6 items (oops!):
0
1
4
9
0
2042318948
Display all items:
0
1
4
9
```

Note that it is necessary to only pin the array and not each element of the array. This confirms the fact that during execution, the value type elements of an array are store in contiguous memory.

Fixed arrays

C#2 allows the declaration of an array field composed of a fixed number of primitive elements within a structure. For this, you simply need to declare the array using the `fixed` keyword and the structure using the `unsafe` keyword. In this case, the field is not of type `System.Array` but of type a pointer to the primitive type (i.e. the `FixedArray` field is of type `int*` in the following example):

Example 14-3

```
unsafe struct Foo {
   public fixed int FixedArray[10];
   public int Overflow;
}
unsafe class Program {
   unsafe public static void Main() {
      Foo foo = new Foo();
      foo.Overflow = -1;
      System.Console.WriteLine( foo.Overflow );
      foo.FixedArray[10] = 99999;
      System.Console.WriteLine( foo.Overflow );
   }
}
```

This example displays:

```
-1
99999
```

Understand that `FixedArray[10]` is a reference to the eleventh element of the array since the indexes are zero based. Hence, we assign the 99999 value to the `Overflow` integer.

Allocating memory on the stack with the stackalloc keyword

C++ › C#: C# allows, using a dedicated syntax, the allocation of an array of elements which can be pointed to on the stack. The result is the same as the static allocation of an array in C++.

C#: C# allows you to allocate on the stack an array of elements of a type which can by pointed to. The `stackalloc` keyword is used for this, with the following syntax:

Example 14-4

```
public class Program {
   unsafe public static void Main(){
      int * array = stackalloc int[100];
      for( int i = 0; i< 100 ; i++ )
         array[i] = i*i;
   }
}
```

None of the elements of the array are initialized, which means that it is the responsibility of the developer to initialize them. If there is insufficient memory on the stack, the `System.StackOverflowException` exception is raised.

The size of the stack is relatively small and we can allocate arrays containing only a few thousand elements. This array is freed implicitly when the method returns.

Strings and pointers

The C# compiler allows you to obtain a pointer of type char from an instance of the System.String class. You can use this feature to circumvent managed string immutability. Let us remind that managed string immutability allows to considerably ease their use. However, this can have a negative impact on performance. The System.StringBuiler class is not always the proper solution and it can also be useful to directly modify the characters of a string. The following example shows how to use this feature to write a method which converts a string to uppercase:

Example 14-5
```
public class Program {
   static unsafe void ToUpper( string str ) {
      fixed ( char* pfixed = str )
         for ( char* p = pfixed; *p != 0; p++ )
            *p = char.ToUpper(*p);
   }
   static void Main() {
      string str = "Hello";
      System.Console.WriteLine(str);
      ToUpper(str);
      System.Console.WriteLine(str);
   }
}
```

Handling errors with exceptions

The underlying problem: How to properly handle most of the errors which can occur at runtime?

Applications must deal with special situations independently of the program. For example:

- Accessing a file which does not exist.
- Being faced to a memory request when there is insufficient memory available.
- Accessing a server which is not available.
- Accessing a resource without the proper rights.
- The capture of an invalid parameter by the user (such as a birth date in the year 3000).

These situations are not bugs but we can call them errors, which can stop the execution of the program, unless we handle them. To handle such errors, we can test the error codes returned by methods but this approach has two drawbacks:

- The code becomes complicated as every call to a method must be followed by several tests. The tests aren't centralized and thus violate the principle of code coherency; an important principle in software design.
- The programmer must envision all possible situations during the conception of the program. She must also define the reaction of the program and how to deal with each error type. She cannot easily refactor several types of errors in the same handling code.

In fact, these drawbacks are significant. A solution had to be found to this problem: *exception management*.

Introduction to exception management in C#

C++ › C#: From the point of view of exception management, nothing major has changed compared to C++. However, we will see that several details have changed because .NET exceptions are completely managed by the CLR and not by the operating system.

C#: Here are the steps to error management:

1. An error happens;
2. The CLR, the code of the .NET framework or custom code constructs an object which contains some data that describe the error. The details of the implementation of such an object is described a little later;
3. The exception is raised with the object as its parameter;
4. Two possibilities can now occur:

    a) An exception manager catches the exception. It analyzes it and determines the possibility of executing code, for example to save the data or warning the user.

    b) No exception manager catches the exception. The execution of the program ends.

Here is an example where an exception of type `System.DivideByZeroException` is raised: (note that the division by zero of floating-point numbers does not raise an exception).

Example 14-6

```
public class Program {
    public static void Main() {
        int i = 1;
        int j = 0;
        int k = i/j;
    }
}
```

The program stops since the exception is not captured and the window in Figure 14-1 is displayed (whether the assembly has been compiled in Debug or Release mode), which offers you to debug your program:

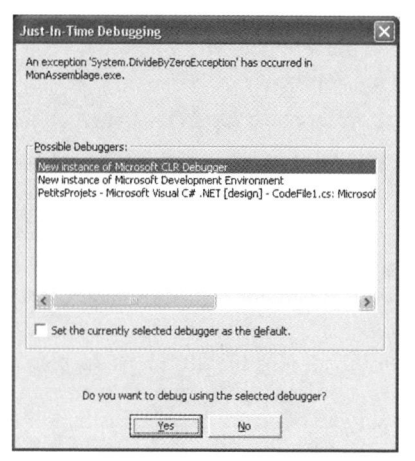

Figure 14-1: Consequence of an uncaught exception

Once you are in the Debug mode, *Visual Studio 2005* pops up a very useful assistant to help you visualize the data relating to the exception:

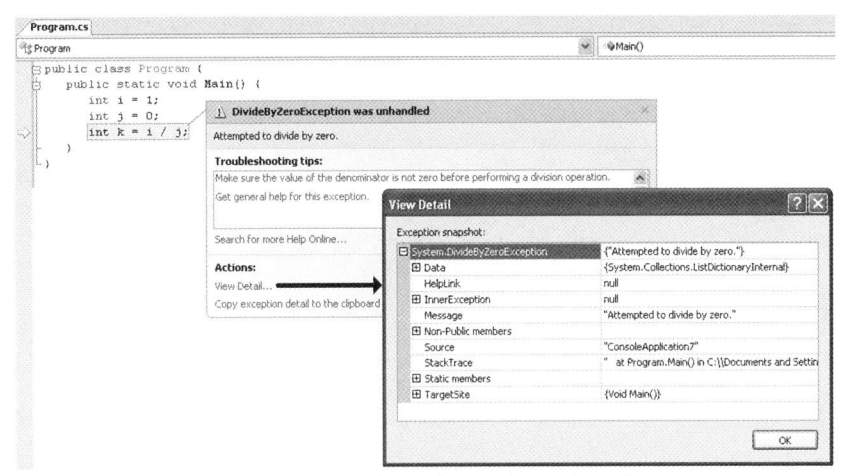

Figure 14-2: The exception assistant of Visual Studio 2005

Here is the same example where the exception is caught by an exception manager:

Example 14-7

```
using System;
public class Program {
   public static void Main(){
      try {
         int i = 1;
         int j = 0;
         int k = i/j;
      } catch( System.DivideByZeroException ) {
         Console.WriteLine("A division by zero occured!");
      }
   }
}
```

The exception being caught, the program does not stop and displays the following on the console:

```
A division by zero occured!
```

The syntax to define an exception management block is done with two keywords: `try`, `catch`. This syntax is the same as in other languages such as C++, ADA or Java. Let us mention that you can nest several `try`/`catch` blocks.

Exception objects and defining custom exception classes

C++ › C#: As with C++, in C#, an exception is represented by an object. The exception can be raised using the `throw new objet` syntax, which also exists in C++. In C++, we had the option of raising an exception without creating an object. In C#, it is required to allocate a new object for each exception explicitly raised using `throw` (except if the exception is raised in a `catch` block, where the current exception can be rethrown).

In C#, this object must be an instance of a class derived from `System.Exception`. In C++, this object can be of any type.

In addition, being a C# object, it must be allocated dynamically (which is not the case in C++).

C#: An exception is always represented by an object. This object generally contains information relative to the problem which caused the exception. This object must be an instance of a class derived from the `System.Exception` class. There are two types of classes which derive from `System.Exception`:

- Those provided by the framework which are thrown by the system but which can also be thrown by your own methods (for example, `System.DivideByZeroException` as seen previously).
- Those that you define yourself and which can only be raised from your own code.

The System.Exception class

The `System.Exception` class contains properties that you can use from custom exception classes:

- `public string Message{get;}`
  This string contains a descriptive message for the exception. This property is accessible in read only mode but can be initialized by calling the `System.Exception` constructor which accepts a string as a parameter (the property then takes the value of this parameter).

- `public string Source{get;set;}`
  This string contains the name of the object or of the application which generated the error.

- `public string HelpLink{get;set;}`
  This string contains a reference to a web page which explains the exception. You can use this if you put information regarding your own exceptions online.

- `public Exception InnerException{get;}`
  This property references an exception. It is used when a caught exception causes a new exception to be raised. The new exception references the caught exception through this property.

It is recommended to use these properties but it is not a requirement. For example, in the case of exceptions which instantiate the `System.DivideByZeroException` class:

- The `Message` property contains the "`Attempted to divide by zero.`" string.
- The `Source` property is a string equal to the name of the assembly where the exception was raised.
- The `HelpLink` property is an empty string.

Other interesting properties which are automatically initialized by the CLR can be found in this class:

- `public string StackTrace{get;}`
  Contains a representation of the call stack at the moment where the exception was raised (the most recent method being first). It is possible that this string does not contain what should logically be there because some optimizations made by the compiler sometimes modify the structure of the code. If a program is compiled in Debug mode, this string also contains the line number and file name of the instruction which raised the exception.

- `public MethodBase TargetSite{get;}`
  Returns a reference to the `MethodBase` object which references the method that raised the exception.

Defining custom exception classes

As we have mentioned, you can create your own exception using classes which derive from `System.Exception`. Actually, it is rather recommended to derive custom exception classes from `System.ApplicationException` (which itself derives from the `Exception` class). Here, for example, the definition of an exception class which could be used when an integer argument to a method is outside of a certain range.

Exception objects and defining custom exception classes

Example 14-8

```
using System;
public class IntegerOutOfRangeException : ApplicationException {
   public IntegerOutOfRangeException ( int argVal, int inf, int sup ):
      base( string.Format(
                  "The argument value {0} is out of range [{1},{2}]",
                  argVal, inf, sup ) ) { }
}
```

We could have also saved the three integer values in three fields of the class.

Throwing exception from your code

You have the option of raising an exception (custom or standard) using the `throw` C# keyword. It is necessary to represent this exception using an object, unless the exception is thrown in a `catch` block in which case the current exception is rethrown. Here is an example of the use of `throw` with our own exception class:

Example 14-9

```
using System;
public class IntegerOutOfRangeException : ApplicationException {
   public IntegerOutOfRangeException ( int argVal, int inf, int sup ):
      base( string.Format(
                  "The argument value {0} is out of range [{1},{2}]",
                  argVal, inf, sup ) ) { }
}
class Program {
   static void f( int i ){
      // Assume that 'i' must be between 10 and 50 included.
      if( i < 10 || i > 50 )
         throw new IntegerOutOfRangeException ( i , 10 , 50 );
      // Here, we can assert that 'i' is in the range [10;50].
   }
   public static void Main() {
      try {
         f(60);
      }
      catch( IntegerOutOfRangeException e ){
         Console.WriteLine( "Exception: " + e.Message );
         Console.WriteLine(
            "State of the stack when the exception has been raised:"
            + e.StackTrace);
      }
   }
}
```

The execution of this program, when compiled in Debug mode, displays the following:

```
Exception: The argument value 60 is out of range [10,50]
State of the stack when the exception has been raised:
  at Program.f(Int32 i) in d:\my documents\visual studio projects
   \test_exception\program.cs:line 11
  at Program.Main() in d:\my documents\visual studio projects
   \test_exception\program.cs:line 17
```

The execution of this same program, when run in Release mode, displays the following:

```
Exception: The argument value 60 is out of range [10,50]
State of the stack when the exception has been raised:
  at Program.f(Int32 i)
  at Program.Main()
```

You can also raise exceptions defined by the .NET framework. For example, we could have also used the `System.ArgumentOutOfRangeException` class as follows:

Example 14-10

```
public class Program {
   static void f(int i) {
      if( i < 10 || i > 50 )
         throw new System.ArgumentOutOfRangeException("i");
   }
   public static void Main() {
      try {
         f(60);
      }
      catch( System.ArgumentOutOfRangeException e ) {
         System.Console.WriteLine( "Exception: " + e.Message );
      }
   }
}
```

This program displays:

```
Exception: Specified argument was out of the range of valid values.
Parameter name: i
```

No checked exception in C#

Developers who know the Java language may be surprised by the lack of *checked exceptions* in C#. In the article at the following URL `http://www.artima.com/intv/handcuffsP.html` *Anders Hejlsberg* one of the main designers of C#, explains two potential problems caused by controlled exceptions. These happen when a large number of APIs are called and when we must maintain a new version of the application. With the absence of a solution to the problems, the C# language designers preferred not to provide such a mechanism.

Catch and finally blocks

C++ > C#: Exception handlers in the C# language are relatively similar to those of C++ with a few exceptions.

In C#, we do not use the `catch(...)` syntax to catch all exceptions but the `catch(Exception e)` syntax. The advantage is that we still have access to the exception.

The `finally` clause of C# does not exist in C++. It replaces the fact that in C++, we often release the critical resources in the destructors of statically allocated objects. This is not possible in C# as we cannot code the destructor of value types. Another problem is that in C#, the moment where a destructor is called is not determined.

Notes on catch blocks (exception handlers)

C#: An exception handler can contain zero, one or several `catch` blocks, and at most one `finally` block.

Catch and finally blocks 429

In the case where you have several `catch` clauses, the type of exceptions must be different for each block. In addition, at runtime the CLR will test if the type of the exception to catch corresponds to the type of exception handled by `catch` blocks, from the first to the last one. At most, one `catch` block will be executed.

Note that an exception thrown using an instance of the D class which is derived from B, matches both the `catch(D d)` and the `catch(B b)` clause. The consequences of this are as follows:

- In the same exception handler, the compiler will disallow `catch(D d)` blocks where D is a subclass of B, after the definition of a `catch(B b)` block. Indeed, such `catch` blocks would not have any chance of being executed.
- The `catch(System.Exception e)` block catches all exceptions since all exception classes are derived from the `System.Exception` class.
- You have the option of having a non-parameterized `catch` block. You simply need to write the `catch` keyword directly followed by the opening brace of the `catch` block. Such a block is equivalent to `catch(System.Exception)`.
- If an exception handler has a non-parameterized `catch` block, it must be the last block. The same applies to `catch(System.Exception)`. If those two blocks are present, the empty `catch` clause must be last.

finally block

If a `finally` block is present, it must be located after all `catch` blocks. The `finally` block of code is executed in all possible cases which are:

- No exception was raised in the `try` block.
- An exception was raised in the `try` block and was caught by a `catch` block.
- An exception was raised in a `try` clause and was caught by a `catch` block. An exception is then raised in this block.
- An exception was raised in the `try` block and was not caught by a `catch` block.

A `finally` clause is generally used to free critical resources (such as a database connection or an opened file) independently of whether an exception was thrown or not. Note that if an exception is raised in a `finally` block (which is not advisable) while a raised exception could not be caught by the current exception handler, this new exception replaces the previous one. For example:

Example 14-11

```
using System;
public class Program {
   public static void Main(){
      try {
         try {
            throw new ArgumentOutOfRangeException();
         }
         catch( DivideByZeroException e ) {
            Console.WriteLine( "Exception handler 1:" );
            Console.WriteLine( "Exception: " + e.Message );
         }
         finally {
            Console.WriteLine( "finally 1" );
            throw new DivideByZeroException();
         }
      }
      catch(Exception e) {
```

Example 14-11
```
            Console.WriteLine( "Exception handler 2:" );
            Console.WriteLine( "Exception: " + e.Message );
        }
        finally {
            Console.WriteLine( "finally 2" );
        }
    }
}
```

This program displays:

```
finally 1
Exception handler 2:
Exception: Attempted to divide by zero.
finally 2
```

It is often preferable to use a `finally` clause indirectly through the use of the *Dispose pattern* described at page 351.

Increasing exception semantics

When an exception bubbles up the different embedded calls, it has a tendency to loose signification as it traverses several code layers. It is then often necessary to catch the exception to throw a new one, where the content depends on the caught exception. To not loose anything of the initial exception, you can reference it directly in the new exception using the `InnerException` property of the `Sytem.Exception` class.

Exceptions thrown from a constructor or from a finalizer

C++ > C#: In C#, an exception thrown from a constructor is treated exactly like any other exceptions, and the object is not created. We will interest ourselves to the behavior of the CLR when an exception is thrown from a class constructor.

In C#, an exception raised from the `Finalize()` method and which is not caught in the constructor does not cause any major problems.

Exception thrown from an instance constructor

C#: An exception thrown from an instance constructor is treated exactly as any other exception and the object is not created. It is however recommended not to raise an exception from a constructor. Here is a program which illustrates this:

Example 14-12
```
using System;
public class Article {
   public Article() { i=3; throw new ArgumentOutOfRangeException(); }
   public Article( int j ) { i=j; }
   public int i=0;
}
public class Program {
   public static void Main() {
      Article article = new Article( 2 );
      try{
```

Exceptions thrown from a constructor or from a finalizer 431

Example 14-12
```
            article = new Article();
        } catch( Exception e ) {
            Console.WriteLine("Exception: "+e.Message);
        }
        Console.WriteLine( article.i );
    }
}
```

This program displays:

```
Exception: Specified argument was out of the range of valid values.
2
```

Understand that allocation of the second instance of `Article`, in the `try` block, has failed from the fact that an exception was thrown from the constructor without being caught.

Exception thrown from a class constructor or while initializing a static field

Calls to class constructors and the initialization of static fields are non-deterministic, meaning that the rules which define when they will be called depend on the implementation of the CLR and are not documented. More details on this topic can be found at page 357. However, an exception can be raised in one of these methods and not be caught. In this case, all happens as if an exception of type `TypeInitializationException` is raised at the place (which is not determined) in the program which triggered the call to the static constructor. In general, this location is the first instantiation of the class or where the first access to one of its static members occurs. The exception which was initially raised in the class constructor is then referenced by the `Exception.InnerException` field of the `TypeInitializationException` exception. This behavior is automatically managed by the CLR. Here is an example which illustrates this:

Example 14-13
```
using System;
public class Article {
    static  Article() {
        throw new ArgumentOutOfRangeException();
    }
}
public class Program {
    public static void Main() {
        try{
            Article article = new Article();
        }
        catch(Exception e) {
            Console.WriteLine("Exception: " + e.Message );
            Console.WriteLine("Inner Exception: "+ e.InnerException.Message );
        }
    }
}
```

This program displays the following:

```
Exception: The type initializer for "Article" threw an exception.
Inner Exception: Specified argument was out of the range of valid values.
```

Exceptions thrown from a finalizer

An uncaught exception thrown from a finalizer has for effect of immediately exiting this method within the thread dedicated to the execution of finalizers. However, the memory allocated for the object is still released by the garbage collector.

If the exception was thrown from a finalizer of a subclass, the finalizer of the base class is still executed.

It is strongly recommended not to throw exceptions from finalizers.

Exception handling and the CLR

You must understand that the CLR completely takes care of the management of .NET exceptions. It has the following responsibilities:

- The CLR has the responsibility of finding the proper the proper `catch()` block by traversing the call stack. The CLR stores information about this search in the object representing the exception. Amongst this we find the call stack of the method which leads to the exception. Hence the developer can sift through this information in order to understand the cause of the exception.

- When the exception is raised in a distributed environment, the CLR takes care of serializing and propagating the exception to the AppDomain containing the client. Be aware that there is however certain precautions to take if you wish custom exceptions to transit through .NET Remoting (more information on this topic can be found at http://www.thinktecture.com/Resources/RemotingFAQ/CustomExceptions.html).

- The CLR sometimes has the responsibility of catching an exception to rethrow another which has more meaning. For example, we have seen in the previous section that the CLR propagates a `TypeInitializationException` exception no matter what the type of the exception thrown from a class constructor. This is also the case for exception thrown from methods called using late binding invocation. Note that in this type of case, the exception initially thrown is stored in the `InnerException` property of the exception.

- At page 236 we explain that the CLR transforms `HRESULT` error codes returned by COM objects into managed exception. Also, when a managed object is considered as a COM object, the CLR produces a `HRESULT` from a managed exception which goes back into unmanaged code. We will see in the next section how the CLR deals with *Windows* native exceptions.

- At page 75 we explain that the `AppDomain` class presents the `UnhandledException` event. The following example shows how this event can be used to execute code when the CLR notices that the current process will crash because an exception was not caught. We explain in the comments the operations which are generally needed before ending the process:

Example 14-14

```
using System;
using System.Threading;
public class Program {
   public static void Main() {
      Console.WriteLine("Thread{0}: Hello world...",
                        Thread.CurrentThread.ManagedThreadId );
      AppDomain currentDomain = AppDomain.CurrentDomain;
      currentDomain.UnhandledException += UnhandledExceptionHandler;
      throw new Exception ("The exception explanation goes here.");
   }
   static void UnhandledExceptionHandler(
            object s, UnhandledExceptionEventArgs e) {
```

Exception handling and the CLR

Example 14-14

```
        Console.WriteLine("Thread{0}: UnhandledExceptionHandler: {1}",
                    Thread.CurrentThread.ManagedThreadId ,
                    (e.ExceptionObject as Exception).Message);
        // a) Save an error report.
        // b) Ask the user if he wishes to save the current state.
        // c) Ask the user if he wishes that the error report is
        //    automatically sent to the development team.
    }
}
```

The program displays this before crashing:

```
Thread1: Hello world...
Thread1: UnhandledExceptionHandler: The exception explanation goes here.
```

- At page 102 we explain advanced features specific to the CLR which allow to improve the reliability of an application which may be faced to asynchronous exceptions.

Unmanaged exceptions

Typically, the underlying *Windows* thread to a managed thread traverses managed code (which is compiled in native code) and some native code. When a managed exception happens within a block of managed code, the CLR makes sure to find the proper `catch` clause in the managed code. Regions of native code which are eventually located between the raised exception and the managed `catch` clause are unstacked normally.

Windows offers a mechanism named *Structured Exception Handling* (SEH) to manage native exceptions. A detailed description of this mechanism can be found in an article written by *Matt Pietrek* http://www.microsoft.com/msj/0197/exception/exception.aspx.

The CLR is capable of detecting when a native exception goes up into managed code. In this situation, it yields a managed exception which depends on the type of native exception intercepted:

Native exception code	Managed exception type
STATUS_FLOAT_INEXACT_RESULT	System.ArithmeticException
STATUS_FLOAT_INVALID_OPERATION	
STATUS_FLOAT_STACK_CHECK	
STATUS_FLOAT_UNDERFLOW	
STATUS_FLOAT_OVERFLOW	System.OverflowException
STATUS_INTEGER_OVERFLOW	
STATUS_FLOAT_DIVIDE_BY_ZERO	System.DivideByZeroException
STATUS_INTEGER_DIVIDE_BY_ZERO	
STATUS_FLOAT_DENORMAL_OPERAND	System.FormatException
STATUS_ACCESS_VIOLATION	System.NullReferenceException
STATUS_ARRAY_BOUNDS_EXCEEDED	System.IndexOutOfRangeException
STATUS_NO_MEMORY	System.OutOfMemoryException
STATUS_STACK_OVERFLOW	System.StackOverflowException
All other codes	System.Runtime.InteropServices.SEHException

The SEH mechanism works with an exception filter model which are registered to the thread. These filters allow telling *Windows* the native function to call when a native exception is detected on a thread. The CLR registers its own filter on each thread which executes managed code. The registered native function has the responsibility of triggering the `AppDomain.UnhandledException` event. If a thread was not created by the CLR (i.e. it was not created using a call to the `Thread.Start()` method) there is always a risk that exception filters registered on this thread by other component may interfere with the filters registered by the CLR. Also, be aware that in this particular case, the `UnhandledException` may not necessarily be triggered.

Exception handling and Visual Studio

When the *Visual Studio* environment debugs an application, it can suspend execution by returning control to the debugger when an exception (managed or not) is raised or when it is not caught. This feature can be configured by the type of exception through the *Debug Exceptions…*menu. The list of exceptions is divided into five categories:

- **C++ Exceptions**: lists the unmanaged C++ exceptions.
- **Common Language Runtime Exceptions**: lists the managed exception (categorized by their namespace).
- **Managed Debugging Assistants**: lists problematic events known by the CLR which can sometimes result into a managed exception. Hence, if you wish to confirm that such an exception is the consequence of a certain event or if you wish to be informed of such an event when it does not result into an exception, you must use this list. These events are described on **MSDN** in the article named **Diagnosing Errors with Managed Debugging Assistants**.
- **Native Run-Time Checks**: lists critical exceptions which can occur in a C/C++ program
- **Win32 Exceptions**: lists the SHE exception codes.

Visual Studio also allows you to add custom exception types to this list.

Guidelines on exception management

When should you consider throwing an exception?

The exception mechanism is generally well understood but quite often used improperly. **The base principle is that an application which functions in a normal way should not throw exceptions.** This forces us to define what an abnormal situation is. There are three types:

- Those which happen because of a problem with the execution environment but can be solved by a modification to this environment (missing file, invalid password, non-well-formed XML document, network unavailability, restricted security permissions…). Here we talk of *business exception*.
- Those which happen because of an execution environment problem which cannot be solved. For example memory hungry applications such a *SQL Server 2005* may be limited to 2 or 3GB of addressing space in a 32-bits *Windows* process. Here we talk of *asynchronous exceptions* from the fact that they are not related to the semantic of the code which raised it. To manage this type of problem, you must use advanced CLR features described at page 102. This is essentially equivalent to treating such abnormal situation as normal! **Be aware that only the large servers with push the limits of its resources should encounter asynchronous exceptions and will need to use these mechanisms.**
- Those which happen because of a bug and which can only be solved by a new version which fixes properly the bug.

What to do in exception handlers?

When you catch an exception, you can envision three scenarios:

Guidelines on exception management 435

- Either you are faced with a real problem but that you can address it by fixing the conditions which cause the problem. For this, you may need new information (invalid password › ask the user to reenter the password…).

- Either you are faced with a problem which you cannot resolve at this level. In this case, the only good approach is to rethrow the exception. It is possible that there may not be a proper exception handler and in this case, you delegate the decision to the runtime host. In console or windowed applications, the runtime host causes the whole process to terminate. Note that you can use the `AppDomain.UnhandledException` event which is triggered in this situation in order to take over the termination of the process. You can take advantage of this 'last chance' to save your data (as with *Word*) which without this would definitely lead to data loss. In an ASP.NET context, an error processing mechanism, described at page 750 is put in place.

- In theory, a third scenario can be envisioned. It is possible that the exception that was caught represents a false alarm. In practice, this never happens.

You must not catch an exception to simply log it and then rethrow it. To log exceptions and the code that they have traversed, we recommend using less intrusive approaches such as the use of specialized events of the `AppDomain` class or the analysis of the methods on the stack at the moment where the exception was thrown.

You must not release the resources that you have allocated when you catch an exception. Also be aware that in general only unmanaged resources are susceptible of causing problems (such as memory leaks). This type of code to release resources must be placed in the `finally` block or in a `Dispose()` method. In C#, the `finally` blocks are often implicitly encapsulated in a `using` block which acts on objects implementing the `IDisposable` interface.

Where should you put exception handlers?

For a specific type of exception, asking this question comes down to asking yourself at which method depth this exception must be caught and what must be done about it. By method depth, we means the number of calls embedded since the entry point (generally the `Main()` method). This means that the method representing the entry point is the least deep. The answer to these two questions depends on the semantics of an exception. Ask yourself for each type of exception, at which depth your code is more apt to be able to correct the conditions which have triggered the exception and resume the execution or to be able to properly terminate the application.

Generally, the deeper a method is, the less it must catch custom exceptions. The reason is that custom exceptions often have a signification to the business of your application. Hence, if you develop a class library, you must let exceptions which are meant to the client application bubble outside of the library.

Exceptions vs. returned error code

You may be tempted to use exceptions instead of returning error codes in your methods, in order to indicate a potential problem. You must be careful as the use of exceptions suffers from two major disadvantages:

- The code is hard to read. In fact, to understand the code, you must manually do the work of the CLR which consists in traversing the calls until you find an exception handler. Even if you properly separate your calls into layers, the code is still difficult to read.

- Exception handling by the CLR is much more expensive than simply looking at an error code.

The fundamental rule mentioned at the beginning of this section can help you make this decision: **an application which functions within normal conditions does not raise exceptions**.

Never under estimate bugs whose consequences are caught by exception handlers

An abusive use of exceptions happen when we assume that, since we catch all exceptions, those provoked by eventual bugs will also be caught. We then assume that they will prevent the application from crashing. This reasoning does not take into account the fact that the main nuisances from bugs are those which goes uncaught such as indeterminist, unexpected or false results.

Anonymous methods

The current section as well as the following section presents two new features added to the 2.0 version of the C# language. Unlike generics, these two features do not involve new IL instructions. All the magic happens at the level of the compiler.

Each of these two sections will have the same structure: a 'classic' presentation of the feature followed by a more detailed explanation of the work done by the compiler in order to explain how you can make full use of the feature.

Introduction to C#2 anonymous methods

Let's begin by enhancing some C#1 code to use C#2 anonymous methods . Here is a simple C# program that first references and then invokes a method, through a delegate:

Example 14-15
```
class Program {
    delegate void DelegateType();
    static DelegateType GetMethod(){
        return new DelegateType(MethodBody);
    }
    static void MethodBody() {
        System.Console.WriteLine("Hello");
    }
    static void Main() {
        DelegateType delegateInstance = GetMethod();
        delegateInstance();
        delegateInstance();
    }
}
```

Here is the same program rewritten using a C#2 anonymous method:

Example 14-16
```
class Program {
    delegate void DelegateType();
    static DelegateType GetMethod() {
        return delegate() { System.Console.WriteLine("Hello"); };
    }
    static void Main() {
        DelegateType delegateInstance = GetMethod();
        delegateInstance();
        delegateInstance();
    }
}
```
You should notice that:

Anonymous methods

- The `delegate` keyword has a new use in C#2. When the C#2 compiler finds the delegate keyword inside the body of a, it expects it to be followed by an anonymous method body.
- It is possible to assign an anonymous method to a delegate reference
- We understand why this feature is named anonymous method: the method defined in the body of `GetMethod()` is not named. Nevertheless, it is possible to invoke it because it is referenced by a delegate instance.

You should notice as well that it is possible to use the operator += to allow a delegate instance to reference several methods (anonymous or not):

Example 14-17

```
using System;
class Program{
   delegate void DelegateType();
   static void Main(){
      DelegateType delegateInstance = delegate() {
         Console.WriteLine("Hello"); };
      delegateInstance += delegate() { Console.WriteLine("Bonjour"); };
      delegateInstance();
   }
}
```

As you might expect this program outputs:

```
Hello
Bonjour
```

Anonymous methods can accept arguments

As shown in the following example, an anonymous method can accept arguments of any type. You can also use keywords `ref` and `out` to tune how arguments are passed to the method:

Example 14-18

```
class Program {
   delegate int DelegateType( int valTypeParam, string refTypeParam,
                              ref int refParam, out int outParam);
   static DelegateType GetMethod() {
      return delegate( int valTypeParam , string refTypeParam,
                       ref int refParam , out int outParam    ) {
         System.Console.WriteLine( "Hello valParam:{0} refTypeParam:{1}",
                                   valTypeParam, refTypeParam);
         refParam++;
         outParam = 9;
         return valTypeParam;
      }; // End of the body of the anonymous method.
   }
   static void Main() {
      DelegateType delegateInstance = GetMethod();
      int refVar = 5;
      int outVar;
      int i = delegateInstance( 1, "one", ref refVar, out outVar );
      int j = delegateInstance( 2, "two", ref refVar, out outVar );
      System.Console.WriteLine( "i:{0} j:{1} refVar:{2} outVar:{3}",
                                i, j, refVar, outVar);
   }
}
```

This program outputs:

```
Hello valParam:1 refTypeParam:one
Hello valParam:2 refTypeParam:two
i:1 j:2 refVar:7 outVar:9
```

As you can see, the returned type is not defined inside the anonymous method declaration. The returned type of an anonymous method is inferred by the C# v2 compiler from the returned type of the delegate to which it is assigned. This type is always known because the compiler forces the assignment of any anonymous method to a delegate.

An anonymous method can't be tagged with an attribute. This restriction implies that you can't use the `param` keyword in the list of arguments of an anonymous method. Indeed, using the keyword `param` forces the compiler to tag the concerned method with the `ParamArray` attribute.

Example 14-19

```csharp
using System;
class Program {
   delegate void DelegateType( params int[] arr );
   static DelegateType GetMethod() {
      // Compilation error: param is not valid in this context.
      return delegate( params int[] arr ){ Console.WriteLine("Hello");};
   }
}
```

A syntax subtlety

It is possible to declare an anonymous method without any signature, i.e. you are not compelled to write a pair of parenthesis after the keyword `delegate` if your anonymous method doesn't take any argument. In this case, your method can be assigned to any delegate instance that returns a void type and that doesn't have an out arguments. Obviously, such an anonymous method doesn't have access to the parameters that are provided through its delegate invocation.

Example 14-20

```csharp
using System;
class Program{
   delegate void DelegateType(int valTypeParam, string refTypeParam,
                              ref int refParam);
   static void Main() {
      DelegateType delegateInstance = delegate {
         Console.WriteLine( "Hello" ); };
      int refVar = 5;
      delegateInstance( 1, "one", ref refVar );
      delegateInstance( 2, "two", ref refVar );
   }
}
```

Anonymous methods and generics

As shown in the example below, an argument of an anonymous method can be of a generic type:

Example 14-21

```csharp
class Foo<T> {
   delegate void DelegateType( T t );
   internal void Fct( T t ) {
      DelegateType delegateInstance = delegate( T arg ){
```

Example 14-21
```
            System.Console.WriteLine( "Hello arg:{0}" , arg.ToString() ); };
         delegateInstance( t );
      }
   }
   class Program {
      static void Main() {
         Foo<double> inst = new Foo <double>();
         inst.Fct(5.5);
      }
   }
```

In .NET 2, a delegate type can be declared with generic arguments. An anonymous method can be assigned to a delegate instance of such a type. You just have to resolve type parameters on both side of the assignment:

Example 14-22
```
class Program{
   delegate void DelegateType<T>( T t );
   static void Main() {
      DelegateType<double> delegateInstance = delegate( double arg ) {
         System.Console.WriteLine( "Hello arg:{0}" , arg.ToString() );
      };
      delegateInstance(5.5);
   }
}
```

Use of anonymous methods in the real world

Anonymous methods are particularly suited to define 'small' methods that must be invoked through a delegate. For instance, you might use an anonymous method to code the entry point procedure of a thread:

Example 14-23
```
using System.Threading;
class Program{
   static void Main(){
      Thread thread = new Thread( delegate() {
        System.Console.WriteLine( "ManagedThreadId:{0} Hello",
                          Thread.CurrentThread.ManagedThreadId );
      } );
      thread.Start();
      System.Console.WriteLine( "ManagedThreadId:{0} Bonjour",
                          Thread.CurrentThread.ManagedThreadId );
   }
}
```

This program displays:

```
ManagedThreadId:1 Bonjour
ManagedThreadId:3 Hello
```

Another classic example of this kind of use lies in the *Windows Forms* control event callbacks:

Example 14-24
```
public class FooForm : System.Windows.Forms.Form {
   System.Windows.Forms.Button m_Button;
   public FooForm() {
      InitializeComponent();
      m_Button.Click += delegate( object sender, System.EventArgs args ) {
         System.Windows.Forms.MessageBox.Show("m_Button Clicked");
      };
   }
   void InitializeComponent()  {/*...*/}
}
```

It seems that anonymous method looks like a tiny language enhancement. It's now time to dig under the hood to realize that anonymous methods are far more complex and can be far more useful.

The C#2 compiler and anonymous methods

The easy way

As you might expect, when an anonymous method is compiled, a new method is created by the compiler in the concerned class:

Example 14-25
```
class Program {
   delegate void DelegateType();
   static void Main() {
      DelegateType delegateInstance = delegate() {
         System.Console.WriteLine("Hello"); };
      delegateInstance();
   }
}
```

The following assembly is the compiled version of the previous program (the assembly is viewed using the Reflector tool introduced at page 19):

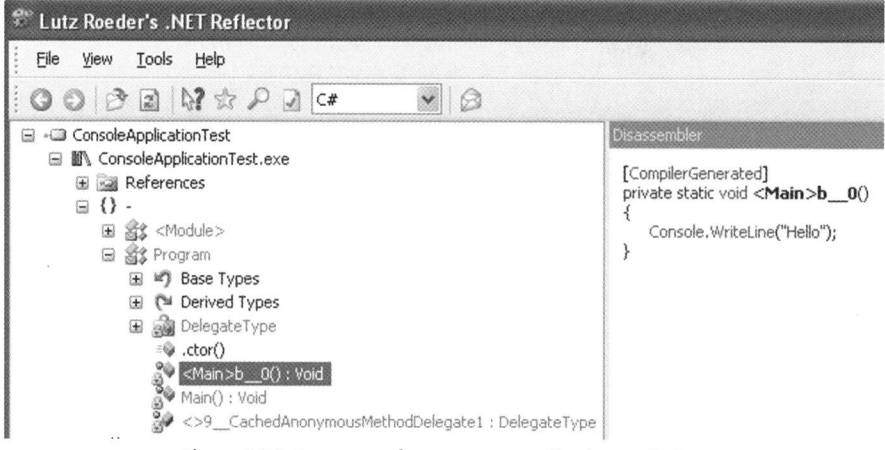

Figure 14-3: Easy way of anonymous method compilation

The C#2 compiler and anonymous methods

Indeed, a new private and static method named <Main>b__0() has been automatically generated and contains the code of our anonymous method. If our anonymous method was declared inside an instance method, the generated method would have been an instance method.

We also note that a delegate field named <>9_CachedAnonymousMethoddelegate1 of type delegateType has been generated to reference our anonymous method.

It is interesting to note that all these generated members can't be viewed with the C# intellisense because their names contain a pair of angle brackets < >. Such names are valid for the CLR syntax but incorrect for the C# syntax.

Captured local variable

To keep things clear and simple, we haven't mentioned yet the fact that an anonymous method can have access to a local variable of its outer method. Let's analyze this feature through the following example:

Example 14-26
```
class Program {
   delegate int DelegateTypeCounter();
   static DelegateTypeCounter MakeCounter(){
      int counter = 0;
      DelegateTypeCounter delegateInstanceCounter =
         delegate { return ++counter; };
      return delegateInstanceCounter;
   }
   static void Main() {
      DelegateTypeCounter counter1 = MakeCounter();
      DelegateTypeCounter counter2 = MakeCounter();
      System.Console.WriteLine( counter1() );
      System.Console.WriteLine( counter1() );
      System.Console.WriteLine( counter2() );
      System.Console.WriteLine( counter2() );
   }
}
```

This program outputs:

```
1
2
1
2
```

Think about it, it might stump you. The local variable counter seems to survive when the thread leaves the MakeCounter() method. Moreover, it seems that two instances of this 'surviving' local variable exist!

Note that in .NET 2, the CLR and the IL language haven't been tweaked to support the anonymous method feature. The interesting behavior must stem from the compiler. It's a nice example of 'syntactic sugar'. Let's analyze the assembly with the Reflector tool (see Figure 14-4).

This analysis makes things clear because:

- The compiler doesn't only create a new method as we saw in the previous section. It utterly creates a new class named <>c__DisplayClass1 in this example.
- This class has an instance method called <MakeCounter>b__0(). This method has the body of our anonymous method.

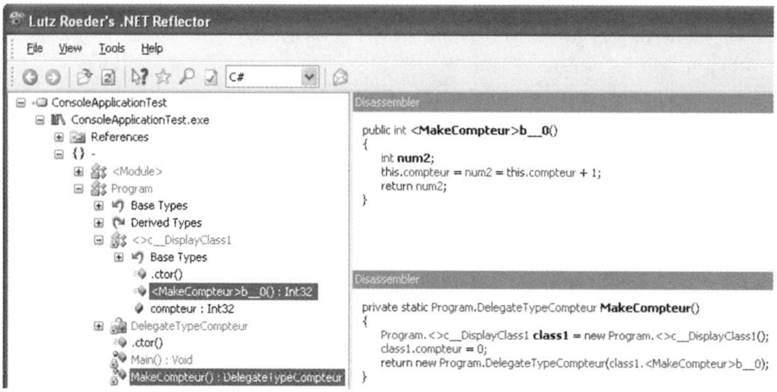

Figure 14-4: Anonymous method and captured local variable

- This class has also an instance field called `counter`. This field keeps track of the state of the local variable `counter`. We say the local variable `counter` has been **captured** by the anonymous method.
- The method instantiates the class `<>c__DisplayClass1`. Moreover it initializes the field `counter` of the created instance.

Notice that the `MakeCounter()` method doesn't have any local variable. For the `counter` variable, it uses the same field of the generated instance of the class `<>c__DisplayClass1`.

Before explaining why the compiler has this surprising behavior, let's go further to get a thorough understanding of its work.

Captured local variables and code complexity

The following example is more subtle than expected:

Example 14-27
```
using System.Threading;
class Program {
   static void Main() {
      for (int i = 0; i < 5; i++)
         ThreadPool.QueueUserWorkItem( delegate {
            System.Console.WriteLine(i); }, null);
   }
}
```

This program outputs in a non-deterministic way something like:

```
0
1
5
5
5
```

This result compels us to infer that the local variable `i` is shared amongst all threads. The execution is non-deterministic because the `Main()` method and our closure (or anonymous methods) are executed simultaneously by several threads. To make things clear, here is the decompiled code of the `Main()` method:

The C#2 compiler and anonymous methods 443

```
private static void Main(){
   bool flag1;
   Program.<>c__DisplayClass1 class1 = new Program.<>c__DisplayClass1();
   class1.i = 0;
   goto Label_0030;
Label_000F:
   ThreadPool.QueueUserWorkItem(new WaitCallback(class1.<Main>b__0), null);
   class1.i++;
Label_0030:
   flag1 = class1.i < 5;
   if ( flag1 ) {
      goto Label_000F;
   }
}
```

Notice that the fact that the value of 5 being printed indicates that the Main() method is done executing the loop when the display is done. The following version of this program has a deterministic execution:

Example 14-28

```
using System.Threading;
class Program {
   static void Main() {
      for (int i = 0; i < 5; i++){
         int j = i;
         ThreadPool.QueueUserWorkItem(delegate {
            System.Console.WriteLine(j); }, null);
      }
   }
}
```

This time, the program outputs:

```
0
1
2
3
4
```

This behavior stems from the fact that the local variable j is captured for each iteration. Here is the decompiled code of the Main() method:

```
private static void Main(){
   Program.<>c__DisplayClass1 class1;
   bool flag1;
   int num1 = 0;
   goto Label_0029;
Label_0004:
   class1 = new Program.<>c__DisplayClass1();
   class1.j = num1;
   ThreadPool.QueueUserWorkItem(new WaitCallback(class1.<Main>b__0), null);
   num1++;
Label_0029:
   flag1 = num1 < 5;
   if (flag1) {
      goto Label_0004;
   }
}
```

444   Chapter 14 - Unsafe code, exceptions, anonymous methods, iterators

This sheds light on the fact that capturing local variables with anonymous methods is not an easy thing. You should always take care when using this feature.

Note that a captured local variable is no longer a local variable. If you access such a variable with some unsafe code, you might have pin it before (with the C# keyword `fixed`).

An anonymous method accesses to an argument of the outer method

Arguments of a method can always be deemed as local variables. Therefore, C#2 allows an anonymous method to use arguments of its outer method. For instance:

Example 14-29

```
using System;
class Program {
   delegate void DelegateTypeCounter();
   static DelegateTypeCounter MakeCounter( string counterName ) {
      int counter = 0;
      DelegateTypeCounter delegateInstanceCounter = delegate{
         Console.WriteLine( counterName + (++counter).ToString() );
      };
      return delegateInstanceCounter;
   }
   static void Main() {
      DelegateTypeCounter counterA = MakeCounter("Counter A:");
      DelegateTypeCounter counterB = MakeCounter("Counter B:");
      counterA();
      counterA();
      counterB();
      counterB();
   }
}
```

This program outputs:

```
Counter A:1
Counter A:2
Counter B:1
Counter B:2
```

Nevertheless, an anonymous method can't capture an `out` or `ref` argument. This restriction is easy to understand as soon as you realize that such an argument can't be seen as a local variable. Indeed, such an argument survives the execution of the method.

An anonymous method accessing a member of the outer class

An anonymous method can access members of its outer class. The case of static member access is easy to understand since there is one and only one occurrence of any static field in the domain application. Thus, there is nothing like 'capturing' a static field.

The access to the instance of a member is less obvious. To clarify this point, remember that the `this` reference that allows access to instance members, is a local variable of the outer instance method. Therefore, the `this` reference is captured by the anonymous method. Let's analyze the following example:

Example 14-30

```
delegate void DelegateTypeCounter();
class CounterBuilder {
    string m_Name; // An instance field
    internal CounterBuilder( string name ) { m_Name = name; }
    internal DelegateTypeCounter BuildCounter( string counterName ) {
        int counter = 0;
        DelegateTypeCounter delegateInstanceCounter = delegate {
            System.Console.Write( counterName +(++counter).ToString() );
            // we could have written this.m_Name.
            System.Console.WriteLine(" Counter built by: " + m_Name);
        };
        return delegateInstanceCounter;
    }
}
class Program {
    static void Main() {
        CounterBuilder cBuilder1 = new CounterBuilder( "Factory1" );
        CounterBuilder cBuilder2 = new CounterBuilder( "Factory2" );
        DelegateTypeCounter cA = cBuilder1.BuildCounter( "Counter A:" );
        DelegateTypeCounter cB = cBuilder1.BuildCounter( "Counter B:" );
        DelegateTypeCounter cC = cBuilder2.BuildCounter( "Counter C:" );
        cA(); cA ();
        cB(); cB();
        cC(); cC();
    }
}
```

This program outputs:

```
Counter A:1 Counter built by: Factory1
Counter A:2 Counter built by: Factory1
Counter B:1 Counter built by: Factory1
Counter B:2 Counter built by: Factory1
Counter C:1 Counter built by: Factory2
Counter C:2 Counter built by: Factory2
```

Let's decompile the MakeCounter() method to expose the capture of the this reference:

```
internal DelegateTypeCounter BuildCounter(string counterName){
    CounterBuilder.<>c__DisplayClass1 class1 = new
                            CounterBuilder.<>c__DisplayClass1();
    class1.<>4__this = this;
    class1.counterName = counterName;
    class1.counter = 0;
    return new DelegateTypeCounter(class1.<BuildCounter>b__0);
}
```

Notice that the this reference cannot be captured by an anonymous method that is defined in a structure. Here is the compiler error:

Anonymous methods inside structs cannot access instance member of 'this'. Consider copying 'this' to a local variable outside the anonymous method and using the local instead.

Advanced uses of anonymous methods

Definitions: closure and lexical environment

A *closure* is a function that captures values of its lexical environment, **when** it is created at run-time. The *lexical environment* of a function is the set of variables visible **from** the concerned function.

In previous definitions, we carefully used the terms **when** and **from**. It indicates that the notion of closure pinpoints something that exists at run-time (as the concept of object). It also indicates that the notion of lexical environment pinpoints to something that exists in the code, i.e. at compile-time (as the concept of class). Consequently, you can consider that the lexical environment of a C#2 anonymous method is the class generated by the compiler. Following the same idea, you can consider that an instance of such a generated class is a closure.

The definition of a closure also implies the notion of creating a function at run-time. Mainstream *imperative languages* such as C, C++, C#1, Java or VB.NET1 don't support the ability to create an instance of a function at run-time. This feature stems from *functional languages* such as Haskell or Lisp. Thus C#2 goes beyond imperative languages by supporting closures. However, C#2 is not the first imperative language that supports closures since Perl and Ruby also have this feature.

C# › C++: The concept of closure is close to the concept of *functor* described at page 492.

Ramblings on closures

A function computes its results both from values of its arguments and from the context that surrounds its invocation. You can consider this context as a set of background data. Thus, arguments of a function can be seen as foreground data. Therefore, the decision that an input data of a function must be an argument must be taken from the relevance of the argument for the computation.

Generally, when using object languages, the context of a function (i.e. the context of an instance method) is the state of the object on which it is invoked. When programming with non object oriented imperative languages such as C, the context of a function is the values of global variables. When dealing with closures, the context is the values of captured variables when the closure is created. Therefore, as classes, closures are a way to associate behavior and data. In object oriented world, methods and data are associated thanks to the `this` reference. In functional world a function is associated with the values of captured variables. To make thinks clear:

- You can think of an object as a set of method attached to a set of data.
- You can think of a closure as a set of data attached to a function.

Using closures instead of classes

The previous section implies that some type of classes could be replaced by some anonymous methods. Actually, we already perform such replacement in our implementation of counter. The behavior is the increment of the counter while the state is its value. However, the counter implementation doesn't harness the possibility of passing arguments to an anonymous method. The following example shows how to harness closures to perform parameterized computation on the state of an object:

Example 14-31
```
class Program {
   delegate void DelegateMultiplier( ref int integerToMultipl);
   static DelegateMultiplier BuildMultiplier ( int multiplierParam ) {
      return delegate( ref int integerToMultiply ) {
         integerToMultiply *= multiplierParam;
      };
   }
   static void Main() {
      DelegateMultiplier multiplierBy8 = BuildMultiplier(8);
      DelegateMultiplier multiplierBy2 = BuildMultiplier(2);
      int anInteger = 3;
      multiplierBy8( ref anInteger );
      // Here, anInteger is equal to 24.
      multiplierBy2( ref anInteger );
      // Here, anInteger is equal to 48.
   }
}
```

Here is another example that shows how to harness closures to perform parameterized computation in order to obtain a value from the state of an object:

Example 14-32
```
using System;
class Article {
   public Article( decimal price ) { m_Price = price; }
   private decimal m_Price;
   public decimal Price { get { return m_Price; } }
}
class Program {
   delegate decimal DelegateTaxComputer( Article article );
   static DelegateTaxComputer BuildTaxComputer( decimal tax ) {
      return delegate( Article article ) {
         return ( article.Price * (100 + tax) ) / 100;
      };
   }
   static void Main(){
      DelegateTaxComputer taxComputer19_6 = BuildTaxComputer(19.6m);
      DelegateTaxComputer taxComputer5_5 = BuildTaxComputer(5.5m);
      Article article = new Article(97);
      Console.WriteLine("Price TAX 19.6% : " + taxComputer19_6(article) );
      Console.WriteLine("Price TAX  5.5% : " + taxComputer5_5(article) );
   }
}
```

Understand that all the power behind the use of closures in both previous examples comes from the fact that they prevent us from creating small classes (which are in fact created implicitly by the compiler).

Delegates and closures

By taking a closer look, we notice that the notion of a delegate used on an instance method in .NET 1.x is conceptually close to the notion of closure. In fact, such a delegate references both data (the state of the object) and a behavior. A constraint does exist: the behavior must be an instance method of the class defining the type of the this reference.

This constraint is minimized in .NET 2. Because of certain overloads of the `Delegate.CreateDelegate()` method, you can now reference the first argument of a static method in a delegate. For example:

Example 14-33
```
class Program {
   delegate void DelegateType( int writeNTime );
   // This method is public to avoid problems of reflection
   // on a non-public member.
   public static void WriteLineNTimes( string s, int nTime ) {
      for( int i=0; i<nTime; i++ )
         System.Console.WriteLine( s );
   }
   static void Main() {
      DelegateType deleg = System.Delegate.CreateDelegate(
         typeof( DelegateType ),
         "Hello",
         typeof(Program).GetMethod( "WriteLineNTimes" )) as DelegateType;
      deleg(4);
   }
}
```

This program displays:
```
Hello
Hello
Hello
Hello
```

Finally note that internally, the implementation of delegates has been completely revised in the 2.0 version of the framework and the CLR. The good news is that the invocation of a method through a delegate is now much more efficient.

Using anonymous methods to handle collections

Aat page 493 we explain how to use the syntax of anonymous methods to greatly improve the syntax needed to manipulate collections.

C#1 iterators

Enumerables, enumerators and the iterator design pattern

It is necessary to get a good understanding on what enumerables and enumerators are before covering C#1 and C#2 enumerators. An object is an *enumerable* if it contains or references a collection of objects and if elements of this collection can be enumerated with the `foreach` C# keyword. Instances of classes that implement `System.Collections.IEnumerable` are enumerables. As we'll see, there exists some enumerables that don't fulfill this condition. An object is an *enumerator* if its class implements the interface `System.Collections.IEnumerator`. Here are the definitions of these interfaces:

```
public interface System.Collections.IEnumerable {
   System.Collections.IEnumerator GetEnumerator();
}
public interface System.Collections.IEnumerator {
   object Current { get; }
   bool MoveNext();
   void Reset();
}
```

A client that wishes to enumerate items over an enumerable asks for an enumerator from the enumerable using the `IEnumerator IEnumerable.GetEnumerator()` method. Then, the client uses methods `IEnumerator.MoveNext()` and `IEnumerator.Reset()` on the enumerator to iterate over items of the collection. An enumerator is a stateful object that keeps track of an index on the collection. A client calls the get accessor of the `IEnumerator.Current` property to access the item referenced currently by the index of the iterator. If we try to represent enumerables, enumerators and their clients in an UML diagram it would look like this:

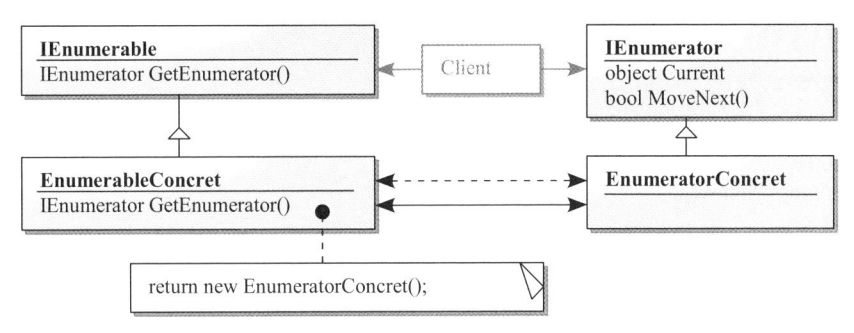

Figure 14-5: UML diagram of the iterator design pattern

We have just exactly described the *iterator design pattern* described in GoF as presented at page 854.

An example

Here is an example of implementing iterators in C#1. The `Persons` class is the enumerable class. The `PersonsEnumerator` class is the enumerator class. Note that the `Persons` class could have played both roles of enumerable and enumerator if it would have implemented both interfaces. However, we'll see that it is always preferable that each role be implemented in a dedicated class (after all, we follow a central object oriented programming tenet: one responsibility/one class).

Example 14-34

```
public class Persons : System.Collections.IEnumerable {
   private class PersonsEnumerator : System.Collections.IEnumerator {
      private int index = -1;
      private Persons P;
      public PersonsEnumerator( Persons p ){ this.P = p; }
      public bool MoveNext() {
         index++;
         return index < P.m_Names.Length;
      }
      public void Reset() { index = -1; }
      public object Current { get { return P.m_Names[index]; } }
   }
   // The method GetEnumerator() of IEnumerable.
   public System.Collections.IEnumerator GetEnumerator() {
      return new PersonsEnumerator( this );
   }
   string[] m_Names;
   // The constructor to initialize the array.
   public Persons( params string[] Names ) {
      m_Names = new string[ Names.Length ];
      // Copy the array.
      Names.CopyTo( m_Names, 0 );
   }
}
```

Example 14-34

```
      // An indexer that returns the name from the index.
      private string this[ int index ] {
         get { return m_Names[index]; }
         set { m_Names[index] = value; }
      }
   }
   class Program {
      static void Main() {
         Persons arrPersons = new Persons(
                     "Michel", "Christine", "Mathieu", "Julien");
         foreach (string s in arrPersons)
            System.Console.WriteLine(s);
      }
   }
```

It's a fairly long program to code such a simple functionality. Most of lines implement the indexer behavior of the enumerator. Hopefully, we'll see that C#2 dramatically reduces the amount of code to express the same need. This program outputs:

```
Michel
Christine
Mathieu
Julien
```

Note that the C# compiler has generated something like the following to interpret the `foreach` keyword:

Example 14-35

```
   ...
   class Program {
      static void Main() {
         Persons arrPersons = new Persons(
                     "Michel", "Christine", "Mathieu", "Julien");
         System.Collections.IEnumerator e = arrPersons.GetEnumerator();
         while ( e.MoveNext() )
            System.Console.WriteLine( (string) e.Current );
      }
   }
```

Several enumerators for a single enumerable

An enumerable class is not required to implement the `IEnumerable` interface. This responsibility can be delegated to a third class `PersonsEnumerable`, for example:

Example 14-36

```
   using System.Collections;
   public class Persons  // Doesn't implement IEnumerable!
      private class PersonsEnumerator : IEnumerator {
         ...
      }
      private class PersonsEnumerable : IEnumerable {
         private Persons m_Persons;
         internal PersonsEnumerable( Persons persons ) {
            m_Persons = persons;
         }
```

Example 14-36
```
         IEnumerator IEnumerable.GetEnumerator(){
            return new PersonsEnumerator( m_Persons );
         }
      }
      public IEnumerable InOrder{ get {return new PersonsEnumerable(this);} }
      ...
   }
   class Program {
      static void Main() {
         Persons arrPersons = new Persons(
                           "Michel", "Christine", "Mathieu", "Julien");
         foreach ( string s in arrPersons.InOrder )
            System.Console.WriteLine(s);
      }
   }
```

This way, it is easy to implement several enumerator classes that target the same enumerable class. It can be quite useful to have an enumerator `Reverse` that yields elements in the reverse order, a `Shuffle` enumerator which traverses the list in a random order or an enumerator `EvenPosOnly` that returns only items at even positions.

Drawbacks of C#1 iterators

Clearly, the C#1 syntax for iterators is too heavy compared to the functionality provided. For this reason, most developers don't use it. Moreover, with this syntax, trying to enumerate over items of a barely exotic collection (such as a binary tree) quickly becomes a nightmare.

C#2 iterators

The keyword yield return

C#2 has been enhanced with the `yield return` keyword in order to implement the iterator pattern seamlessly. Concretely, it relieves developers from the burden of implementing enumerator and enumerable classes. Here is our previous example rewritten:

Example 14-37
```
   public class Persons : System.Collections.IEnumerable{
      string[] m_Names;
      public Persons( params string[] names ){
         m_Names = new string[names.Length];
         names.CopyTo(m_Names, 0);
      }
      // The GetEnumerator() method of IEnumerable.
      public System.Collections.IEnumerator GetEnumerator(){
         foreach (string s in m_Names)
            yield return s;
      }
   }
   class Program {
      static void Main() {
         Persons arrPersons = new Persons(
                           "Michel", "Christine", "Mathieu", "Julien");
         foreach (string s in arrPersons)
            System.Console.WriteLine(s);
      }
   }
```

The behavior of the `yield return` keyword might stump you. It looks like the `yield return` keyword is returning a string but the type of the return value of the method `GetEnumerator()` is `IEnumerator`. Moreover, which class implements the `IEnumerator` returned since we don't explicitly supply such an implementation? We'll thoroughly shed light on these mysteries but it's still time to dig in C#2 iterators basics. Notice that a method can call the `yield return` keyword several times. For instance:

Example 14-38

```
public class Persons : System.Collections.IEnumerable {
   public System.Collections.IEnumerator GetEnumerator() {
      yield return "Michel";
      yield return "Christine";
      yield return "Mathieu";
      yield return "Julien";
   }
}
class Program {
   static void Main() {
      Persons arrPersons = new Persons();
      foreach (string s in arrPersons)
         System.Console.WriteLine(s);
   }
}
```

It seems that each time the thread calls `GetEnumerator()`, it branches itself just after the previous call to `yield return`. We'll soon verify that this hunch is the right one.

Iterators and generics

In a language that supports generics, it would be a drag to still use the object's `IEnumerator.Current` property. Therefore, interfaces `IEnumerable` and `IEnumerator` are both provided in a generic form in the .NET 2 framework:

```
public interface System.Collections.Generic.IEnumerable<T> :
                                         System.Collections.IEnumerable {
   System.Collections.Generic.IEnumerator<T> GetEnumerator();
}
public interface System.Collections.Generic.IEnumerator<T> :
                     System.Collections.IEnumerator, System.IDisposable {
   T Current { get; }
}
```

Notice that the interface `IEnumerator<T>` implements the `IDisposable` interface. Notice also that the method `IEnumerator.Reset()` has been removed. Thanks to generics, we can now tell the compiler that our enumerable is a collection of strings instead of a collection of object:

Example 14-39

```
using System.Collections.Generic;
using System.Collections;
public class Persons : IEnumerable<string> {
   string[] m_Names;
   public Persons(params string[] names) {
      m_Names = new string[names.Length];
      names.CopyTo(m_Names, 0);
   }
   IEnumerator<string> IEnumerable<string>.GetEnumerator() {
      return PRIVGetEnumerator();
```

```
     }
     IEnumerator IEnumerable.GetEnumerator() {
        return PRIVGetEnumerator();
     }
     private IEnumerator<string> PRIVGetEnumerator() {
        foreach (string s in m_Names)
           yield return s;
     }
  }
```

It is a shame to have to implement two versions of the GetEnumeror() method. This is a direct consequence of the fact the IEnumerable<T> implements IEnumerable. *Microsoft* engineers have made this choice to ensure that all enumerable be usable in a non generic form. In fact, several APIs only take an IEnumerable parameter while several APIs return an IEnumerable<T>. Without this trick, there would not be any implicit conversions between IEnumerable<T> and IEnumerable and developers would often have to explicitly specify such a conversion. This choice was made to the advantage to those who use enumerable classes rather than for those who develop them. As a developer, you will most often find your self in the first situation rather than the second.

Several enumerators for a single enumerable

C#2 iterators are also a good mean to implement concisely several iterators on a single enumerable. For instance:

Example 14-40
```
  public class Persons{
     string[] m_Names;
     public Persons( params string[] names ){
        m_Names = new string[names.Length];
        names.CopyTo(m_Names, 0);
     }
     public System.Collections.Generic.IEnumerable<string> Reverse {
        get {
           for (int i = m_Names.Length - 1; i >= 0; i--)
              yield return m_Names[i];
        }
     }
     public System.Collections.Generic.IEnumerable<string> PosEven {
        get {
           for (int i = 0; i < m_Names.Length ; i++,i++)
              yield return m_Names[i];
        }
     }
     public System.Collections.Generic.IEnumerable<string> Concat {
        get {
           foreach (string s in Reverse)
              yield return s;
           foreach (string s in PosEven)
              yield return s;
        }
     }
  }
  class Program {
     static void Main() {
        Persons arrPersons = new Persons(
```

Example 14-40

```
                    "Michel", "Christine", "Mathieu", "Julien");
      System.Console.WriteLine( "-->Iterator Reverse" );
      foreach ( string s in arrPersons.Reverse )
         System.Console.WriteLine( s );
      System.Console.WriteLine( "-->Iterator PosEven" );
      foreach ( string s in arrPersons.PosEven )
         System.Console.WriteLine( s );
      System.Console.WriteLine( "-->Iterator Concat" );
      foreach ( string s in arrPersons.Concat )
         System.Console.WriteLine( s );
   }
}
```

This program outputs:

```
-->Iterator Reverse
Julien
Mathieu
Christine
Michel
-->Iterator PosEven
Michel
Mathieu
-->Iterator Concat
Julien
Mathieu
Christine
Michel
Michel
Mathieu
```

The yield break keyword

You might wish to enumerate a subset of an enumerable. In this case, the `yield break` keyword is the right way to tell the client that it should stop looping.

Example 14-41

```
   ...
   public IEnumerator<string> GetEnumerator() {
      for ( int i = 0; i < 2;i++ )
         yield return m_Names[i];
      yield break;
      // Warning : Unreachable code detected.
      System.Console.WriteLine("hello");
   }
   ...
```

This program outputs:

```
Michel
Christine
```

As a consequence, the code written after a `yield break` instruction is not reachable. The C# compiler emits a warning when it encounters such unreachable code.

Syntactic constraints on yield return and yield break keywords

The `yield break` and `yield return` keywords can be used only inside the body of a method, the body of a property accessor or the body of an operator.

Whatever the kind of method that use `yield break` or `yield return` keywords, it must return one the following interfaces `System.Collections.Generic.IEnumerable<T>`, `System.Collections.IEnumerable`, `System.Collections.Generic.IEnumerator<T>` or `System.Collections.IEnumerator`.

`yield break` and `yield return` keywords can't be used in the body of an anonymous method.

`yield break` and `yield return` keywords can't be used in a `finally` block.

`yield break` and `yield return` keywords can't be used in a try block that has at least one `catch` block.

`yield break` and `yield return` keywords can't be used in a method that has `ref` or `out` arguments. More generally, a method that contains at least one of these keywords should not return any other information than the yielded item.

A recursive iterator example

The following example shows the power of C#2 iterators by enumerating the items of a non-flat collection, such as a binary tree:

Example 14-42

```
using System.Collections.Generic;
public class Node<T> {
   public Node( T item , Node<T> leftNode , Node<T> rightNode ) {
      m_Item = item;
      m_LeftNode = leftNode;
      m_RightNode = rightNode;
   }
   public Node<T> m_LeftNode;
   public Node<T> m_RightNode;
   public T m_Item;
}
public class BinaryTree<T> {
   Node<T> m_Root;
   public BinaryTree( Node<T> root ){
      m_Root = root;
   }
   public IEnumerable<T> InOrder {
      get{
         return PrivateScanInOrder( m_Root );
      }
   }
   private IEnumerable<T> PrivateScanInOrder( Node<T> root ) {
      if ( root.m_LeftNode != null ) {
         foreach ( T item in PrivateScanInOrder( root.m_LeftNode ) ) {
            yield return item;
         }
      }
      yield return root.m_Item;
      if ( root.m_RightNode != null ) {
         foreach ( T item in PrivateScanInOrder( root.m_RightNode ) ) {
```

Example 14-42

```
            yield return item;
         }
      }
   }
}

class Program {
   static void Main() {
      BinaryTree<string> binaryTree = new BinaryTree<string> (
         new Node<string>( "A",
            new Node<string>( "B" , null , null ),
            new Node<string>( "C" ,
               new Node<string>( "D" , null , null ),
               new Node<string>( "E" , null , null ) ) ) );
      foreach ( string s in binaryTree.InOrder )
         System.Console.WriteLine( s );
   }
}
```

A representation of the binary tree built by the `Main()` method is:

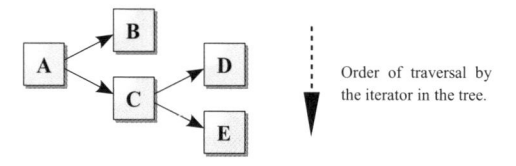

Figure 14-6: Binary tree

This program outputs:

```
B
A
D
C
E
```

The C#2 compiler and iterators

If you are a curious developer, you might be delighted by the work done by the C#2 compiler to interpret `yield break` and `yield return` keywords. This is the subject of the current section. Keep in mind that iterators are syntactic sugar. Unlike generics, no IL instructions have been added to implement iterators.

Enumerator classes are automatically built and used by the compiler

A method that uses at least one of the `yield break` or `yield return` keywords must return an enumerable or an enumerator (generic or not). In any cases, you can consider that an enumerator object is returned since the only purpose to implement an enumerable interface is to return an enumerator. If you've read the previous sections concerning anonymous methods, you might have guessed that for each method that contains at least one of the `yield break` or `yield return` keywords, the compiler builds a class that can be seen as a lexical environment.

The C#2 compiler and iterators 457

This generated class implements the four interfaces `System.Collections.Generic.IEnumerable<T>`, `System.Collections.IEnumerable`, `System.Collections.Generic.IEnumerator<T>` and `System.Collections.IEnumerator` if the concerned method returns an enumerable object. The generated class implements only the two enumerator interfaces if the concerned method returns an enumerator object. Moreover, such a method is not directly compiled. The logic contained in its body is in the `MoveNext()` method of the generated class. Let's check all these facts on a small example:

Example 14-43

```
class Foo {
    public System.Collections.Generic.IEnumerable<string> AnIterator() {
        yield return "str1";
        yield return "str2";
        yield return "str3";
    }
}
class Program {
    static void Main() {
        Foo collec = new Foo();
        foreach ( string s in collec.AnIterator() )
            System.Console.WriteLine( s );
    }
}
```

The following assembly is the compiled version of the previous program (the assembly is viewed with the tool *Reflector* introduced at page 19):

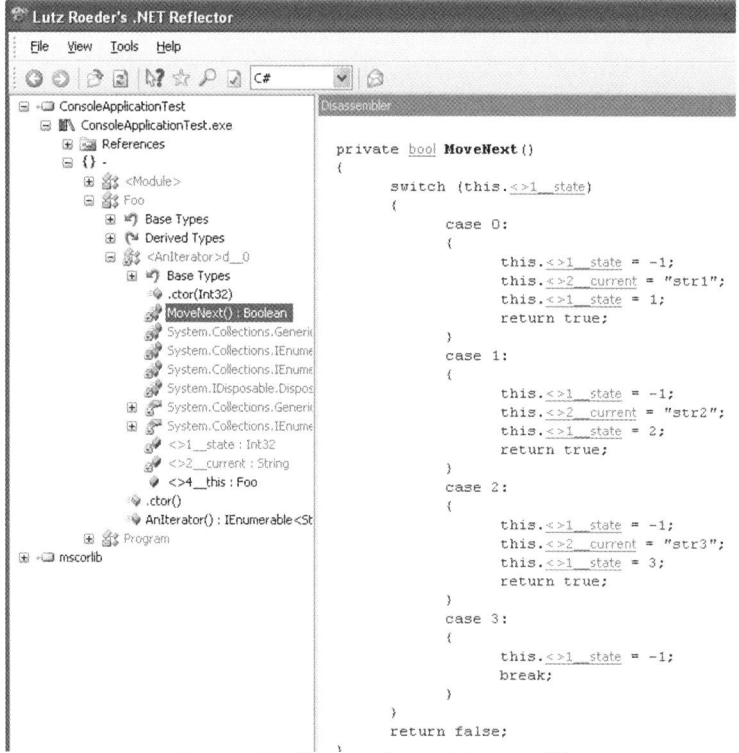

Figure 14-7: C#2 compiler and iterators (1)

To make things clear, here is the decompiled code of the Main() method. We can then check that an instance of the <AnIterator>d__0 class is created. In the previous section concerning anonymous methods, we said that such an instance is a closure. Thus in C#2, an iterator is a special kind of closure. Pay attention to the automatic and implicit use of the dispose pattern that surrounds the creation of the enumerator:

```
class Foo {
   public System.Collections.Generic.IEnumerable<string> AnIterator() {
      Foo.<AnIterator>d__0 d__1 = new Foo.<AnIterator>d__0(-2);
      d__1.<>4__this = this;
      return d__1;
   }
   ...
}
class Program {
   private static void Main() {
      Foo foo1 = new Foo();
      using (IEnumerator<string> enumerator1 =
         ( ( IEnumerator<string>)foo1.AnIterator().GetEnumerator() ) ) {
         while (enumerator1.MoveNext()) {
            string text1 = enumerator1.get_Current();
            Console.WriteLine(text1);
         }
      }
   }
}
```

Here is another example that deserves some decompilation:

Example 14-44

```
class Foo {
   public System.Collections.Generic.IEnumerable<int> AnIterator() {
      for ( int i = 0; i < 5; i++ ) {
         if( i == 3 ) yield break;
         yield return i;
      }
   }
}
class Program {
   static void Main() {
      Foo collec = new Foo();
      foreach ( int i in collec.AnIterator() )
         System.Console.WriteLine( i );
   }
}
```

The assembly exposed in Figure 14-8 is the compiled version of the previous program.

Notes on generated classes

By looking at the bodies of the MoveNext() methods of the previous example, it seems that a state machine is built by the compiler when compiling a method that contains a yield break or yield return keyword. The state of the machine is held by the two instance fields <>1__state and <>2__current of the generated class. Remember that we observed that a thread executing an iterator is able to branch itself just after the previous call to yield return. This magic is possible thanks to the <>1__state field. A switch instruction on <>1__state is inserted at the beginning of the MoveNext() method while the value of <>1__state is properly set each time the running thread is about to leave the MoveNext() method. The field <>2__current holds the value computed by the previous call to MoveNext(). Thus the type of <>2__current is the type of enumerated elements (i.e. int32 in both previous examples).

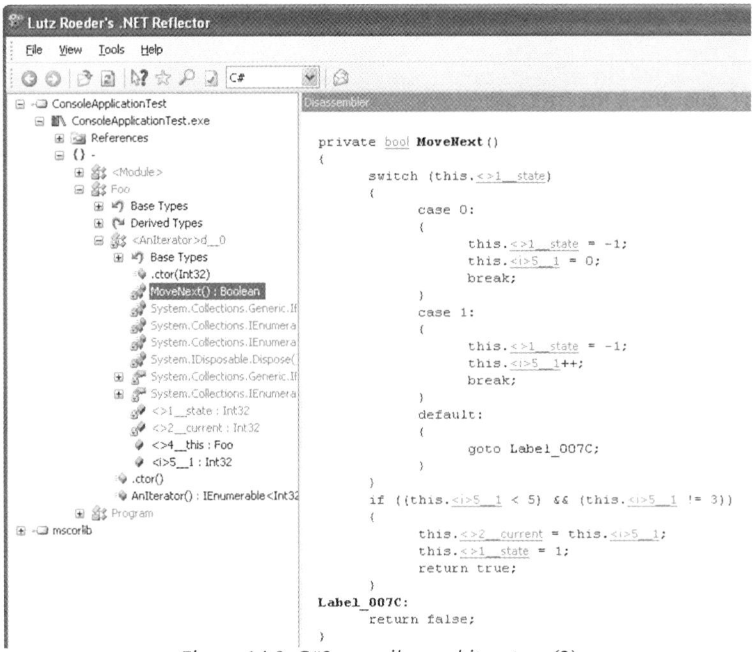

Figure 14-8: C#2 compiler and iterators (2)

Notes on generated classes

By looking at the bodies of the `MoveNext()` methods of the previous example, it seems that a state machine is built by the compiler when compiling a method that contains a `yield break` or `yield return` keyword. The state of the machine is held by the two instance fields `<>1__state` and `<>2__current` of the generated class. Remember that we observed that a thread executing an iterator is able to branch itself just after the previous call to `yield return`. This magic is possible thanks to the `<>1__state` field. A switch instruction on `<>1__state` is inserted at the beginning of the `MoveNext()` method while the value of `<>1__state` is properly set each time the running thread is about to leave the `MoveNext()` method. The field `<>2__current` holds the value computed by the previous call to `MoveNext()`. Thus the type of `<>2__current` is the type of enumerated elements (i.e. int32 in both previous examples).

If the method that contains a `yield` instruction is an instance method, the generated class has an instance field called `<>4__this`. This field references the enumerable object.

Notice that if the method that contains a `yield` instruction has some local variables or some arguments, they are captured by the compiler. For instance, in the second example the local variable `i` is captured. As a consequence, the generated class has a field named `<i>5__1`.

Advanced use of C#2 iterators

From the previous compilation analysis, we can infer two interesting differences between C#1 and C#2 iterators:

- By design, C#2 iterators support the *lazy evaluation pattern*. Concretely, the value of a yielded item is computed only when the client asks for it. When dealing with C#1 iterators, the values of all elements of an enumerable must have been computed before looping on it with a `foreach` instruction.

- C#2 iterators have no bounds on the number of items yielded. When dealing with C#1 iterators, the number of items had to be fixed before any looping with a `foreach` instruction.

We will take advantage of these properties in order to use iterators in other contexts that the iteration over the elements of an enumerable.

Definitions: coroutine and continuation

A *coroutine* is a function that resumes its execution at the point where it stopped the last time it was called, as if nothing had happened between invocations. A *subroutine* is a function that starts its execution at the beginning of its body each time it is called. Clearly, all C# methods are subroutines except methods that contain a `yield` instruction that can be considered as coroutine.

Coroutines are a specialization of closures. Indeed, values of local variables and arguments must be captured by an object between invocations to make possible the magic of resuming at the point we quit last time. Notice also that the offset of the instruction in a coroutine body where the thread will resume its course, must also be captured between invocations. The closure that captures local variables values and the captured instruction offset is called a *continuation*. Thus, a continuation is an object created behind your back. Notice that a continuation is semantically equivalent to a thread's stack frame. This last remark will be soon relevant.

Harness the power of continuations and coroutines with iterators

By coding two coroutines A and B where A calls B and B calls A, we can readily implement an infinite recursion that won't bloat the running thread's stack. This facility can be useful to develop a simplified chess game where the white treatment calls the black treatment and vice-versa. Suppose that some information must be stored by each treatment. In C#1, you would certainly design a class to store this information. In C#2 you can harness the power of continuations and coroutines to code this paradigm:

Example 14-45

```
using System;
using System.Collections;
public class Program {
   static IEnumerator White() {
      int whiteTreatmentInfo = 0;
      while ( true ) {
         Console.WriteLine( "white move, whiteTreatmentInfo=" +
                            whiteTreatmentInfo );
         whiteTreatmentInfo++;
         yield return black;
      }
   }
   static IEnumerator Black() {
      while ( true ) {
         Console.WriteLine( "black move" );
         yield return white;
      }
   }
   static IEnumerator black;
   static IEnumerator white;
   static void Main() {
      black = Black();
      white = White();
      IEnumerator enumerator = white;  // Whites begin.
```

Advanced use of C#2 iterators

Example 14-45
```
      // We dispatche 5 times.
      for ( int i = 0; i < 5; i++ ) {
         enumerator.MoveNext();
         enumerator = (IEnumerator) enumerator.Current;
      }
   }
}
```

This program outputs:

```
white move, whiteTreatmentInfo=0
black move
white move, whiteTreatmentInfo=1
black move
white move, whiteTreatmentInfo=2
```

In this example, the role of the black and white static fields is essential. Each time the White() method is called a new continuation is created. Consequently the White() method must be called only one time. The field white is used to reference the unique continuation created by the method White(). The same remark also works with the field black and the method Black().

In C#, a goto instruction and the label it references must lie in the same method body. This example shows that you can consider coroutines/continuations as a mean to implement 'goto' between methods, without any risk to bloat the thread stack.

The pipeline pattern

Iterators are perfect to implement the *pipeline pattern*, the one that you have used so many times in your console windows. For instance:

Example 14-46
```
using System.Collections.Generic;
class Program{
   static public IEnumerable<int> PipelineIntRange( int begin, int end ) {
      System.Diagnostics.Debug.Assert( begin < end );
      for( int i=begin; i<=end ; i++ )
         yield return i;
   }
   static public IEnumerable<int> PipelineMultiply( int factor ,
                                         IEnumerable<int> input ) {
      foreach ( int i in input )
         yield return i * factor;
   }
   static public IEnumerable<int> PipelineFilterModulo( int modulo ,
                                         IEnumerable<int> input ) {
      foreach ( int i in input )
         if( i%modulo == 0 )
            yield return i;
   }
   static public IEnumerable<int> PipelineJoin( IEnumerable<int> input1,
                                         IEnumerable<int> input2 ) {
      foreach ( int i in input1 )
         yield return i;
      foreach ( int i in input2 )
         yield return i;
```

Example 14-46

```
   }
   static void Main(){
      foreach (int i in PipelineJoin(
         PipelineIntRange(-4, -2), PipelineFilterModulo( 3,
                                     PipelineMultiply( 2,
                                        PipelineIntRange(1, 10) ) ) ) )
         System.Console.WriteLine(i);
   }
}
```

This program outputs:

```
-4
-3
-2
6
12
18
```

Values -4,-3 and -2 are readily understandable. Here is a schema that sheds light on values 6, 12 and 18:

```
PipelineIntRange(1,10) yields       1  2  3  4  5  6  7  8  9  10
PipelineMultiply(2) yields          2  4  6  8  10 12 14 16 18 20
PipelineFilterModulo(3) yields            6        12       18
```

If you modify `PipelineIntRange` like this...

Example 14-47

```
...
   static public IEnumerable<int> PipelineIntRange( int begin, int end ) {
      System.Diagnostics.Debug.Assert( begin < end );
      for ( int i = begin; i <= end; i++ ) {
         System.Console.WriteLine( "Yield:" + i );
         yield return i;
      }
   }
...
using System.Collections.Generic;
class Program{
   static public IEnumerable<int> PipelineIntRange( int begin, int end ) {
      System.Diagnostics.Debug.Assert( begin < end );
      for (int i = begin; i <= end; i++) {
         System.Console.WriteLine( "Yield:" + i );
         yield return i;
      }
   }
   static public IEnumerable<int> PipelineMultiply( int factor ,
                                          IEnumerable<int> input ) {
      foreach ( int i in input )
         yield return i * factor;
   }
   static public IEnumerable<int> PipelineFilterModulo( int modulo ,
                                          IEnumerable<int> input ){
      foreach ( int i in input )
         if( i%modulo == 0 )
            yield return i;
```

Example 14-47

```
    }
    static public IEnumerable<int> PipelineJoin( IEnumerable<int> input1,
                                                 IEnumerable<int> input2) {
        foreach ( int i in input1 )
            yield return i;
        foreach ( int i in input2 )
            yield return i;
    }
    static void Main(){
        foreach (int i in PipelineJoin(
            PipelineIntRange(-4, -2), PipelineFilterModulo( 3,
                                        PipelineMultiply( 2,
                                          PipelineIntRange(1, 10) ) ) ) )
            System.Console.WriteLine(i);
    }
}
```

...you get the following output:

```
Yield:-4
-4
Yield:-3
-3
Yield:-2
-2
Yield:1
Yield:2
Yield:3
6
Yield:4
Yield:5
Yield:6
12
Yield:7
Yield:8
Yield:9
18
Yield:10
```

This experience exposes the fact that items yield by an iterator are never stored somehow. As soon as an integer is yielded by `PipelineIntegerRange`, it is consumed by chained pipelines.

Continuation vs. Threading

The pipeline pattern can be seen as a way to implement the *producer/consumer* paradigm. We generally use this paradigm in a multithreaded environment. This is the second time that threads are quoted in the current section on iterators. Indeed, we saw that information bundled in a continuation is the same as those contained in a thread stack frame.

The point is that continuations can help to implement some concurrency pattern. In the following example, a producer thread is computing *Fibonacci* numbers while the main thread is a consumer that prints yielded numbers on the console:

Example 14-48

```
using System.Collections;
using System.Threading;
public class Program {
   static AutoResetEvent eventProducterDone = new AutoResetEvent( false );
   static AutoResetEvent eventConsumerDone  = new AutoResetEvent( false );
   static int currentFibo;
   static void Fibo() {
      int i1 = 1;
      int i2 = 1;
      currentFibo = 0;
      // The producer triggers the cascade.
      eventProducterDone.Set();
      while( true ) {
         // Wait that the consumer is done.
         eventConsumerDone.WaitOne();
         // Let's build a new Fibonacci number.
         currentFibo = i1 + i2;
         i1 = i2;
         i2 = currentFibo;
         // Let's signal that the new number is ready to be consumed.
         eventProducterDone.Set();
      }
   }
   static void Main() {
      Thread threadProducteur = new Thread(Fibo);
      threadProducteur.Start();
      for ( int i = 1; i < 10; i++ ) {
         // Wait that the producer is done.
         eventProducterDone.WaitOne();
         // Let's consumme.
         System.Console.WriteLine(currentFibo);
         // Let's signal that we have consumed.
         eventConsumerDone.Set();
      }
   }
}
```

Notice that the state of the producer thread (i.e. values of `i1` and `i2`) is permanently stored on its own stack. Here is the same problematic implemented with a single thread and an iterator. This time, values of `i1` and `i2` are permanently stored in the continuation that is created when calling the `Fibo()` method.

Example 14-49

```
using System.Collections.Generic;
public class Program {
   static IEnumerator<int> Fibo() {
      int i1 = 1;
      int i2 = 1;
      int currentFibo = 0;
      while ( true ) {
         currentFibo = i1 + i2;
         i1 = i2;
         i2 = currentFibo;
         // Let's signal that the new number is ready to be consumed.
         yield return currentFibo;
```

Advanced use of C#2 iterators

Example 14-49

```
         }
      }
      static void Main() {
         IEnumerator<int> e = Fibo();
         for ( int i = 1; i < 10; i++ ) {
            // Let's the producer do its job.
            e.MoveNext();
            // Let's consumme.
            System.Console.WriteLine( e.Current );
         }
      }
   }
```

This time the `i1` and `i2` values are all stored in the enumerator created by a call to the `Fibo()` method.

A limitation of C#2 iterators

Clearly, the limitation that we underline in the present section won't hamper you in most of your algorithms. It can be found while trying to do something like a 'recursive iterator'. The idea was to use an iterator that calls itself to implement the *sieve of Eratosthène*. This sieve is an algorithm that allows computing prime numbers. It is explained by the following schema:

```
2 3 4 5 6 7 8 9 10 11 12 13 14 15 16 17 |
  3   5   7   9    11    13    15    17 | 3 is prime,
                                        | 4,6,8,10,12,14,16,18 and
                                        | 20 are multiples of 2.
      5   7        11    13          17 | 5 is prime, 9 and 21
                                        | are multiples of 3.
          7        11    13          17 | 7 is prime, the list doesn't
                                        | contain any multiple of 5.
                   11    13          17 | 11 is prime, the list doesn't
                                        | contain any multiple of 7.
                         13          17 | 13 is prime, the list doesn't
                                        | contain any multiple of 11.
                                     17 | 17 is prime, the list doesn't
                                        | contain any multiple of 13.
```

The first number of each step is a prime. We remove this first number and its multiples to reach the next step. Each step yields a prime number.

The idea is to use as many pipelines as prime numbers we want. The first element of the pipeline will yield integers between 2 and N. In order to asses the number of prime numbers between 1 and N, we use the following theorem that was conjectured by *Gauss* and that was proved by *de la Vallée Poussin*. This theorem says that if P(N) is the number of prime numbers smaller than N then we have the approximation:

$$P(n) \approx \frac{n}{\ln n}$$

Here is the program:

Example 14-50

```
using System;
using System.Collections.Generic;
class Program {
```

Example 14-50

```csharp
static public IEnumerable<int> PipelineIntRange( int begin, int end ) {
    System.Diagnostics.Debug.Assert( begin < end );
    for ( int i = begin; i <= end; i++ )
        yield return i;
}
static public IEnumerable<int> PipelinePrime( IEnumerable<int> input ) {
    using ( IEnumerator<int> e = input.GetEnumerator() ) {
        e.MoveNext();
        int prime = e.Current;
        // The first number of the list is a prime.
        Console.WriteLine( prime );
        if ( prime != 0 ) {
            while ( e.MoveNext() ) {
                // Remove all multiple of the found prime.
                if ( e.Current % prime != 0 )
                    yield return e.Current;
            }
        }
    }
}
const int N = 100;
static void Main() {
    // Apply the approximation of Gauss/de la Vallée Poussin
    // to get the number of iterators.
    int N_PRIME = (int)Math.Floor( ((double)N)/Math.Log(N) );

    // Build a pipeline of N_PRIME PipelineIntegerRange chained with
    // a PipelineIntegerRange. Each call to PipelinePrime yield an
    // iterator object that we store.
    List<IEnumerable<int>> list = new List<IEnumerable<int>>();
    list.Add(PipelinePrime( PipelineIntRange( 2, N ) ) );
    for( int i=1 ; i<N_PRIME ; i++ )
        list.Add( PipelinePrime(list[i-1]) );

    // Cascade the computation among iterators by yielding every
    // numbers between 2 and N.
    foreach ( int i in list[N_PRIME-1] );
}
```

The limitation of C#2 iterators that is pinpointed here is the impossibility for an iterator object to reference and call itself. We can't use the keyword `this` in the body of the method that contains a `yield` instruction. In the case of an instance method, the keyword `this` references the current object. In the case of a static method, the compiler emits an error. It's like if the developer is not supposed to know what happens behind the scene. We could use reflection but this solution wouldn't be satisfactory.

The .NET2 Framework

15

Collections

The use of collections is fundamental in software development. We quite often need to manipulate data structured in lists, arrays, dictionaries... This chapter presents the different classes of the framework which correspond to the different needs of developers.

We will first present the similarities in the manipulation of the various types of collections. Then, we will introduce arrays, their use in C# as well as the underlying .NET platform facilities. We will then present the collections which store their elements in a certain sequence such as a list, a queue or a stack. Finally, we will focus on special collections called dictionaries.

In our discussion, we will carefully underline the differences between each implementation in order to help you choose which type of collection is best suited for your needs. You can also consult the article named **Selecting a Collection Class** on **MSDN** when you are hesitating between several types of implementations.

The set of collection types offered by the framework can be somewhat limited in the context of certain applications. For example, there is no classic implementation of sets. By searching the internet, you can surely find implementations which are directly reusable. For example, you could use the **Power Collections** *open-source* framework by **Wintellect** which fills certain gaps in the framework (http://www.wintellect.com/powercollections/).

Iterating through the items of a collection with the 'foreach' and 'in' keywords

Using the `foreach` and `in` keywords, C# has a particularly user friendly syntax to allows the traversal of the elements in a collection. The use of `foreach` and of `in` is possibly on any type which implements the `System.Collections.IEnumerable` interface.

It is your responsibility to ensure that the size of a collection does not change during the traversal of its elements. In other words, you must synchronize the access to your collections between the various threads of a program.

Using foreach and in on an array

To calculate the sum of the elements of an array containing integers, you simply need to write:

Example 15-1
```
using System;
class Program {
   static void Main() {
      int[] arr = { 1, 3, 4, 8, 2 };
      // Compute the sum of items.
      int sum = 0;
```

Example 15-1
```
        foreach ( int i in arr )
            sum += i;
        // Here the sum is equal to: 1+3+4+8+2 = 18
    }
}
```

The `foreach` keyword also allows the traversal of multi-dimensional arrays. The order in which the elements are traversed is illustrated by the following example:

Example 15-2
```
class Program {
    static void Main() {
        string[,] arr = { { "A", "B", "C" }, { "D", "E", "F" } };
        foreach ( string s in arr )
            System.Console.Write(s + ",");
    }
}
```

This program displays:
```
A,B,C,D,E,F
```

The foreach syntax on jagged arrays

The notion of jagged arrays is defined a little later in this chapter. `foreach` also allows the traversal of a jagged array. However, you must take into account that a jagged array is in fact an array of arrays. In general, we use embedded `foreach` loops to traverse the elements of a jagged array. For example:

Example 15-3
```
class Program {
    static void Main() {
        int[][] arr = new int[3][];
        arr[0] = new int[12];
        arr[1] = new int[5];
        arr[2] = new int[9];
        int sum = 0;
        foreach ( int[] arrSub in arr )
            foreach ( int i in arrSub )
                sum += i;
    }
}
```

The benefit of using `foreach` is that there is no need to know the size of the dimensions of an array in order to traverse it. There are also no risks of overflow. This benefit is even more significant when we are traversing jagged arrays.

The variable defined in the `foreach` loop can only be read. This means that in our example, we cannot assign to the `arrSub` reference nor on the `i` integer. However, we could easily call a method or a property on these objects which internally modifies their state.

Supporting the foreach syntax on your custom collection classes

C#2 supports the concept of iterator which allows to easily support the foreach and in syntax on your own classes. The concept of iterator is discussed at page 448.

Arrays

Creating and referencing an array

C# allows the creation and use of *arrays* with one or several dimensions. Here is the syntax which allows declaring a reference to a type of array:

```
int [] r1;        // r1 is a reference on an integer array of rank 1.
int [,] r2;       // r2 is a reference on an integer array of rank 2.
int [,,] r3;      // r3 is a reference on an integer array of rank 3.
double [,,,] r4;  // r4 is a reference on a double array of rank 4.
```

It is essential to understand that the `int[]`, `int[,]`, `int[,,]` and `double[,,,]` types represent classes (and thus reference types) which are constructed and managed during the execution by the CLR. In addition, each of these classes derives from the `System.Array` abstract class that we will describe a little later. This brings us to make a few remarks:

- The allocation of an array is only done when you use the `new` operator. The four lines of code **above** do not allocate a single array. They define four references, each to a specific type of array. When you create an array, the size of each dimension must be specified either statically by an integer constant or dynamically by using an integer variable. For example:

Example 15-4
```
public class Program {
   public static void Main() {
      byte i = 2;
      long j = 3;

      // 't1' references an 'integer' unidimensional array
      // that contains 6 items.
      int [] t1 = new int [6];

      // 't2' references a 'double' multi-dimensional array of rank 2
      // that contains 12 items (j=3 and 3x4=12).
      double [,] t2 = new double [j,4];

      // 't3' references an 'object' multi-dimensional array of rank 3
      // that contains 30 items (j=3 and i=2 and 3x5x2=30).
      object [,,] t3 = new object [j,5,i];
   }
}
```

- Arrays are allocated on the heap and not on the stack. The allocation of arrays on the stack is possible in certain special situations (see page 422).
- The deallocation of arrays is the responsibility of the garbage collector.
- Each type of array is derived from the `object` class since the `System.Array` class is derived from `object`.
- We do not physically copy an array when using the '=' assignment operator. With this operator, we only obtain another reference to the same array.
- The passing of an array as an argument to a method is always done by reference, even if the `ref` keyword is not used.

C# forces all the elements of an array of having the same type. However, this constraint can easily be circumvented. You simply need to specify that the elements are references to a base class (or to an interface), so that every element can be a reference to an instance of a class which derives from this base class (or interface).

Accessing array items and handling out-of-bounds access

As with most languages, the access syntax to the elements of an array is the same whether you are reading or writing. This syntax is similar to the use of indexers of a class. For example:

```
int [,] arr = new int[2,3];
arr[2,1] = 5;        // Write access.
int i = arr[2,1];    // Read access.
```

Note that as with most languages, in C#, the elements of an array are indexed with a zero-based index. This means that if the dimension of an array is an integer number N, an index on this dimension takes the 0, 1, 2..., N-1 values. In addition, the type of an index must be an integer type. Finally know that the access to the elements of an array using an index is done in constant time (i.e. independently from the number of elements in the array).

The advantage of being executed on a virtual machine such as the CLR is that it systematically verifies during the access to an element that the index specified does not exceed the bounds of the array. In the case of an overflow, an exception of type `System.IndexOutOfRangeException` is automatically raised by the CLR. For example:

```
int [,] arr = new int[2,3];
// Overflow on the first dimension. An exception is thrown.
arr[13,1] = 5;
short i = 14;
// Overflow on the second dimension. An exception is thrown.
int e = arr[0,i];
```

Jagged arrays

We define the *jagged array* term for a one dimensional array where the elements are arrays themselves. Figure 15-1 shows a jagged array of three elements where the first element is an array of 12 elements, the second an array of 5 elements and the third an array of 9 elements.

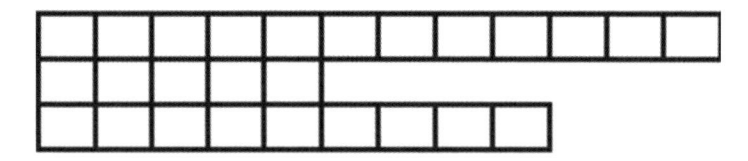

Figure 15-1: View of a jagged array

C# has an intuitive syntax for the definition of jagged arrays. For example, we could reference the above array with the following `t1` reference (assuming that elements are integers):

```
int [][] t1;
```

The creation of this array is done with the following code:

```
int [][] t1 = new int [3][];
t1[0] = new int[12];
t1[1] = new int[5];
t1[2] = new int[9];
```

Here are other examples of jagged arrays:

```
int [][,,] t1;
string [,,][][] t2;
double [][][,,][,,,] t3;
```

Arrays 473

As you may have noticed, the mental representation of jagged arrays is more complicated than the idea of a multi-dimensional array. Contrarily to multi-dimensional arrays, jagged arrays are not *'CLS compliant'*. Other languages do not necessarily implement them and their use should be constrained within a C# assembly and never use them in the arguments of methods exposed outside the assembly. However, the use of jagged arrays is more efficient than the use of multi-dimensional arrays as the IL language contains special instructions specially adapted to the manipulation of one-dimension arrays. The following example shows an optimization factor greater than 2:

Example 15-5

```
using System;
using System.Diagnostics;
class Program {
   const int N_ITERATION = 10000;
   const int N_ELEM = 100;
   static void Main() {
      int tmp = 0;

      int[][] arrayJagged = new int[N_ELEM][];
      for (int i = 0; i < N_ELEM; i++)
         arrayJagged[i] = new int[N_ELEM];
      Stopwatch sw = Stopwatch.StartNew();
      for (int k = 0; k < N_ITERATION; k++)
         for (int i = 0; i < N_ELEM; i++)
            for (int j = 0; j < N_ELEM; j++){
               tmp = arrayJagged[i][j];
               arrayJagged[i][j] = i * j;
            }
      Console.WriteLine("Jagged array: " + sw.Elapsed );

      int[,] arrayMultiDim = new int[N_ELEM, N_ELEM];
      sw = Stopwatch.StartNew();
      for (int k = 0; k < N_ITERATION; k++)
         for (int i = 0; i < N_ELEM; i++)
            for (int j = 0; j < N_ELEM; j++){
               tmp = arrayMultiDim[i, j];
               arrayMultiDim[i, j] = i * j;
            }
      Console.WriteLine("Multi-dimensional array: " + sw.Elapsed );
   }
}
```

Finally note that the CLR will detect access overflows on jagged arrays. For example:

Example 15-6

```
class Program{
    static void Main() {
        int[][] t1 = new int[3][];
        t1[0] = new int[12];
        t1[1] = new int[5];
        t1[2] = new int[9];
        int i = t1[0][7];   // OK, the access is in range.
        int j = t1[1][7];   // Out-of-range access on the second
    }                       // dimension. An IndexOutOfRangeException
}                           // is raised.
```

Initializing array items

When an array has elements of a value type, these elements are automatically created during the initialization of the array. By default, they are initialized to zero.

```
int [] arr = new int [3];
int i = arr[0];
// Here, i is equal to 0.
```

In the case of an array of elements of a reference type, the references are set to null by default. You must initialize the references one-by-one with the appropriate objects.

Example 15-7

```
class Article {
   private decimal m_Price;
   public Article(decimal price){ m_Price = price; }
}
public class Program {
   public static void Main() {
      Article [] arr = new Article[3];
      // Here, no 'Article' objects have been created yet.
      arr[0] = new Article(98.5M);
      arr[1] = new Article(190M);
      arr[2] = new Article(299.0M);
      // Here, the array 'arr' references three 'Article' objects.
   }
}
```

These remarks are valid whether or not an array is jagged. However, what follows is only valid for non-jagged arrays. C# authorizes you to write constant arrays. For example:

```
// The rank of arrVal is 2.
int [,] arrVal = { {3,4,5} , {7,8,9} };
// The rank of arrRef is 1.
Article [] arrRef =
         { new Article(98.5M), new Article(190M), new Article(299.0M) };
```

We do not specify the size of each dimension as it is implicitly known in constant arrays. This means that the compiler will detect and emit an error when a constant jagged array is created:

```
// Compilation Error.
int [][] arrVal = { {3,4} , {7,8,9} };
```

Array covariance

When there exists an inheritance relationship between the two reference types B and D (D derived from B if B is a class or D implements B if B is an interface) it is then possible to **implicitly** convert an array of type D[] into an array of type B[]. It is also possible to convert **explicitly** an array of type B[] into an array of type D[]. In this case, the CLR verifies the validity of the conversion for each element and will raise an exception of type InvalidCastException if the conversion fails. This conversion feature is called *covariance* on arrays.

Example 15-8

```
class B { }
class D1 : B { }
class D2 : B { }
public class Program {
   public static void Main() {
```

Example 15-8
```
        D2[] td2 = { new D2(), null , new D2() };
        B[]  tb  = td2;        // Implicit casting from D2[] to B[].
        D1[] td1 = (D1[])tb;   // Implicit casting from B[] to D1[].
   } // This program compile but the second cast raises an
}      // 'InvalidCastException' at runtime.
```

The System.Array class

As we have seen, each type of array is a class constructed during the execution by the CLR which derives from the `System.Array` abstract class. This allows the use of the numerous members of this class.

System.Array members

The properties of `System.Array` which are most commonly used are:

- `int Length{ get ; }`
  Returns the number of elements in the array. In jagged arrays, `Length` returns the number of sub-arrays.

- `int Rank{ get ; }`
  Returns the number of dimensions of an array. Caution, when using jagged arrays, `Rank` returns the number of dimensions of the array containing the sub-arrays.

Amongst the methods of `System.Array`, the most commonly used are:

- `int GetLength(int dimension)`
  Returns the size of the specified dimension, `dimension` being a zero-based index on the dimension of the array (i.e. specify 0 to obtain the size of the first dimension). If the dimension is negative or greater than the rank of the array, then the `IndexOutOfRange` exception is raised.

- `static void Copy(Array src, Array dest, ...)`
  `void CopyTo(Array dest, ...)`
  The various overloads of this method allow copying all the elements or a sub-sequence of elements from a one-dimensional array to another.

- `static int IndexOf<T>(Array array, T value, ...)`
  `static int LastIndexOf<T>(Array array, T value, ...)`
  The different overloads of these methods return the index of the first (or of the last) occurrence of `value` in a one-dimension array (or in a sub-sequence of elements). Caution, be aware the notion of equality varies depending on whether `T` is a value or reference type. If the specified sub-sequence is invalid, the `IndexOutOfRange` exception is raised. If `array` has more than one dimension, the `RankException` is raised.

- `static void Reverse(Array array, ...)`
  The various overloads of this method revert the sequence (or sub-sequence) of the elements of `array`. If the sequence of elements is not valid, an `IndexOutOfRange` exception is raised. If `array` has more than one dimension, the `RankException` exception is raised.

- `static int BinarySearch<T>(T[] array,T value, ... )`
  Completes a binary search for an element in a sorted array (or in a sub-sequence depending on the overload used). If `value` is found, its index is returned. If not, the returned value represents the opposite of 'index+1' of the smallest element which is greater than `value`. If `value` is greater than all elements, the returned value represents the opposite of 'size+1'. For example:

Example 15-9
```
public class Program {
   public static void Main() {
      int[] arr = new int[2];
      arr[0] = 10;
      arr[1] = 20;
      int a = System.Array.BinarySearch<int>(arr, 5);
      int b = System.Array.BinarySearch<int>(arr, 10);
      int c = System.Array.BinarySearch<int>(arr, 15);
      int d = System.Array.BinarySearch<int>(arr, 25);
      // Here,  a = -1    b = 0     c = -2    d = -3.
   }
}
```

Certain overloads of BinarySearch<T>() accept an object implementing IComparer<T> which allows the specification of the comparison operation.

New .NET 2 members of System.Array

- static void Resize<T>(ref T[] array, int newSize)
  Resizes a one-dimensional array. If the new size is greater than the original size, the new elements take the default value for the type T (0 for a value type, null for a reference type). If not, the elements at the end of the array are deleted. If the array reference is null, then this method creates a new one-dimensional array of the specified size.

- static void ConstrainedCopy(Array src, int srcIndex, Array dest, int destIndex, int length)
  This new method completes a copy of a one-dimensional or multi-dimensional array with the guarantee that the destination table is not modified if the operation fails. For this, it uses the constrained execution mechanism described at page 102. This method has a cost and must be used only when needed. In the case of the copy of a sub-sequence of multi-dimensional array, you must consider that you are dealing with one-dimensional arrays placed end-to-end.

- static IList<T> AsReadOnly(T[] array)
  Returns a reference of type IList<T> which allows access to the underlying table in a read-only mode. Caution, that it is in fact the same array. As shown in the following example, all changes in the initial array are visible from the IList<T> reference:

Example 15-10
```
using System.Collections.Generic;
public class Program {
   public static void Main() {
      int[] arr = new int[2];
      arr[0] = 10;
      arr[1] = 20;
      IList<int> arrReadOnly = System.Array.AsReadOnly(arr);
      arr[1] = 25;
      // Here 'arr[1]' is equal to 25.
      arrReadOnly[1] = 30;  // This line raises a
   }                        // NotSupportedException at runtime.
}
```

A little later, we will describe several new methods of the System.Array which allows the easy and efficient manipulation of the elements of an array.

Non zero-indexed arrays

The System.Array class offers several overloads of the CreateInstance() method. These overloads are used by the C# compiler to instantiate multi-dimensional arrays. One of these overloads is never used by the C# compiler but you can use it explicitly in order to create two-dimensional arrays which are not zero-based indexed. The following example illustrates this feature:

Example 15-11
```
public class Program {
    static void Main() {
        int[] lengths = { 4, 5 };
        int[] lowerBounds = { -2, 3 };
        double[,] arrBiDim = System.Array.CreateInstance(
            typeof(double), lengths, lowerBounds) as double[,];
        double d1 = arrBiDim[-2, 5];  // OK, indexes are valids.
        double d2 = arrBiDim[0, 0];   // KO, at runtime this line raises an
    }                                 // IndexOutOfRangeException.
}
```

The `arrBiDim` array contains 20 elements (4x5) whose coordinates are from [-2,3] to [1,7]. The example illustrates the fact that the CLR will detect any eventual overflows.

Bit arrays

The System.Collection.BitArray class

You can use the `System.Array` class to store a one-dimensional array of boolean, but the .NET framework gives you access to the `System.Collections.BitArray` class specially designed for this use. The advantages of using this class instead of `System.Array` are multiple:

- To store an array containing N booleans, the *Microsoft* implementation of the `BitArray` class needs `((N-1)/32)+1` integers (of four bytes each). In fact, booleans are stored in a compact form, at the rate of 32 booleans per integer. However, each boolean is store in one byte when you use the `Array` class to store them.

- The `BitArray` class has integer indexers. The easy element access syntax (for reading and writing) with the `[]` operator remains possible on arrays of type `BitArray`.

- The `BitArray` class offers several constructors practical for the initialization of boolean arrays.

`BitArray(int)`	The parameter specifies the number of bits in the array. All of them are initialized to `false`.
`BitArray(int,bool)`	The first parameter specifies the number of bits in the array while the second parameter specifies the initial value of the bits.
`BitArray(bool[])`	The array of type `BitArray` is initialized from an `Array` containing booleans.
`BitArray(byte[])`	The array of type `BitArray` is initialized from an `Array` containing bytes.

- The `BitArray` class also offers several practical functions for the manipulation of booleans. Here are a few of them:

`BitArray Not()`	Inverts each boolean in the array. Those set to `false` are set to `true` and vice-versa.
`Void SetAll(bool)`	Sets all the booleans in the array to the specified value.
`BitArray And(BitArray)`	Does a 'logical and' with the booleans of the array passed as a parameter. If both arrays are not of the same size, the `System.ArgumentException` exception is raised. The modified booleans are those of the array on which the method is called and a reference returned is a reference to the same array.
`BitArray Or(BitArray)`	Does a 'logical or' with the booleans of the array passed as a parameter. The same remarks as the `And()` method applies.
`BitArray Xor(BitArray)`	Does an 'exclusive or' with the booleans of the array passed as a parameter. The same remarks as the `And()` method applies.

Here is an example which shows most of the features:

Example 15-12

```
using System.Collections;
public class Program {
   public static void Main() {
      BitArray bArr1 = new BitArray (10,true);
      BitArray bArr2 = new BitArray (10,false);
      // 'bArr3' and 'bArr1' reference both the same object.
      BitArray bArr3 = bArr1.And(bArr2);
      // Here, 'bArr3[0]' and 'bArr1[0]' are both equal to false.
      bArr3[0] = true;
   } // Here, 'bArr3[0]' and 'bArr1[0]' are both equal to true.
}
```

The System.Collections.Specialized.BitVector32 structure

The `BitVector32` structure allows storing an array of exactly 32 bits. If it is better suited to your needs, use this structure as it is more efficient than the `BitArray` class. You can build an instance of `BitVector32` from another instance of `BitVector32` or from an integer. This structure offers an indexer which allows read/write access of the bits within the [0,31] interval. It also offers operations specific to the manipulation of bits using masks or using sections.

Sequences

Here we will present interfaces and then specific classes for the manipulation of arrays where the size can vary as we add or remove elements. We call such arrays *sequences*.

The System.Collections.Generic.ICollection<T> interface

```
public interface ICollection<T> : IEnumerable<T>
```

The `System.Collections.Generic.ICollection<T>` interface is implemented by all classes which represent collections. Here are the members of the `ICollection<T>` interface:

- `int Count{ get; }`
  This property returns the number of elements in a collection.
- `bool IsReadOnly{ get; }`
  This property returns `true` if the collection is accessible in read-only mode.
- `void Add( T item )`
  Adds an item to a collection.
- `void Clear()`
  Removes all the elements from the collection.
- `bool Contains( T item )`
  Returns `true` if the collection contains the specified element.
- `bool Remove( T item )`
  Removes the first occurrence of the specified element. Returns `true` if an occurrence of the specified element was removed from the collection.
- `public virtual void CopyTo( T[] array, int index )`
  Copies the elements of the collection into `array`. The array defined by `array` must have a single dimension or the `System.ArgumentException` exception will be raised.

index specifies the index of array from which the copy will begin. If the destination array is not large enough (i.e. if the array – index size is less than the number of elements in the collection), the System.ArgumentException exception is raised.

If the elements are of a reference type, it is the references to the objects which are copied and not the objects. This is what is called a *shallow copy*. Here is an example where reference type elements of a list are copied into an array:

Example 15-13

```
using System.Collections.Generic;
class Article{
   public decimal Price;
   public Article(decimal price) { this.Price = price; }
}
public class Program {
   public static void Main() {
      Article a1 = new Article( 98.5M );
      Article a2 = new Article( 190M );
      ICollection<Article> collection = new List<Article>();
      collection.Add( a1 );
      collection.Add( a2 );
      Article[] array = new Article[2];
      // Copy items from 'collection' to 'array'.
      collection.CopyTo( array , 0 );
      array[0].Price = 80M;
      decimal d = a1.Price;
      // Here, d is equal to 80.
   }
}
```

The System.Collections.Generic.IList<T> interface

```
public interface IList<T> : ICollection<T>, IEnumerable<T>
```

The System.Collections.Generic.IList<T> interface allows considering that a collection is a list. The IList<T> interface extends the ICollection<T> interface. The implementation of choice for this interface is the System.Collections.Generic.List<T> class which we will discuss in the next section. The members of the IList<T> interface are:

- int IndexOf(T item)
  Returns the index of the specified element (-1 if the element is not found).
- void Insert(int index , T item)
  This method inserts an element in the list at the position represented by the index, increasing the size of the list by one entry. If the index is not valid, the ArgumentOutOfRange-Exception exception is raised. If the insertion fails, generally because the list is read-only, the NotSupportedException exception is raised.
- void RemoveAt(int index)
  Removes the element at the position specified by the index. The ArgumentOutOfRange-Exception and NotSupportedException exceptions may be raised for the same reasons as with the previous method.
- T this[int index] { get; set; }
  Indexers allow the read and write access of the element located at the position specified by the index. The ArgumentOutOfRangeException and NotSupportedException exception can be raised for the same reasons as mentioned in the previous methods.

The System.Collections.Generic.List<T> class

The `System.Collections.ArrayList` class, commonly used in applications developed using .NET 1.x must now be abandoned and replaced with the use of the `System.Collections.Generic.List<T>` class defined as follows:

```
public class List<T> : IList<T>, ICollection<T>, IEnumerable<T>,
                      IList,    ICollection,    IEnumerable
```

This generic class was created to be optimized. Especially, the use of `List<object>` is much more efficient than the use of de `ArrayList`.

Contrarily to an instance of the `Array` class, an instance of `List<T>` has a variable number of elements. As with any compromise, the advantage of lists over arrays has a cost. The cost comes in the form of a memory allocation when the number of element in a list changes. However, as with arrays, access to the elements of a list from an index is done in a constant time (i.e. independent to the number of elements). We will see in the next section that another list model implemented by the `LinkedList<T>` class where the insertion is done in a constant time but where element access is done in a time proportional to the number of elements. You now know the key points to decide whether you should use the `Array` class, the `List<T>` class or the `LinkedList<T>` class, depending on your specific needs.

The `List<T>` class offers the following construction (the notion of capacity is explained a little later in this section):

- List<T>()
  In the *Microsoft* implementation, this default constructor creates an instance with a capacity of 0.
- List<T>(int capacity)
  This constructor creates an instance of `List<T>` with a capacity of `capacity`.
- List<T>(IEnumerable<T> collection)
  This constructor creates an instance of `List<T>` with the elements of an enumerable collection `collection`.

In addition to the members of the `IList<T>` and `ICollection<T>` interfaces, the `List<T>` class offers the following members:

- T[] ToArray()
  Equivalent to ICollection<T>.CopyTo(T[],0).
- int IndexOf(T value, ...)
  int LastIndexOf(T value, ...)
  Same behavior as the different overloads of `IndexOf()` and `LastIndexOf()` of the `Array` class, except that they are instance methods and not static methods.
- int BinarySearch(T value, ...)
  Same behavior as the various overloads of the `BinarySearch()` method in the `Array` class.
- IList<T> AsReadOnly()
  Same remarks as with the `AsReadOnly()` method of the `Array` class
- void AddRange(IEnumerable collection)
  void InsertRange(int index, IEnumerable collection)
  List<T> GetRange(int index, int count)
  void RemoveRange(int index, int count)
  These methods allows the insertion, addition, obtaining or deleting a set of contiguous elements in the list on which they are called. The difference between the insertion and the addition is that the addition is always done at the end of the list.

Capacity of a List<T> object

The capacity of an instance of List<T> can be managed through the Capacity property. The problem with collections of variable size is that the allocation/deallocation of memory during the modification of the number of elements in the collection can have a negative effect on performance. To minimize these effects, you must reduce the number of allocations/deallocations. This is possible by allocating more memory, to anticipate for future element insertions. Also, you must deallocate the memory when a certain number of elements have been removed. The same problem is discussed for the StringBuilder class at page 311.

A consequence to the use of capacity mechanism is that at a specific point in time, the number of elements contained in the list is different than the number that the list can contain without needing new allocations. The number of elements contained in the list is represented with the Count property of the ICollection interface. The number of elements that the list can contain without a new allocation is represented by the Capacity property.

The value of Capacity is by definition greater or equal to the value of Count. Also, if you attempt to assign to Capacity a value which is less to the value of Count, the ArgumentOutOfRange-Exception will be raised. Note that you can at any time remove the unused slots by calling the void TrimExcess() method. The management of the expansion of the capacity is generally left to the internal algorithms of the .NET framework as shown in the following example:

Example 15-14

```
using System.Collections.Generic;
public class Program {
   public static void Main() {
      List<int> list = new List<int>(3);
      for (int i = 0; i < 8; i++) {
         list.Add(i);
         System.Console.WriteLine("Count:{0}  Capacity:{1}",
                                  list.Count, list.Capacity );
      }
      list.TrimExcess();
      System.Console.WriteLine("Count:{0}  Capacity:{1}",
                               list.Count, list.Capacity );
   }
}
```

This example displays:

```
Count:1   Capacity:3
Count:2   Capacity:3
Count:3   Capacity:3
Count:4   Capacity:6
Count:5   Capacity:6
Count:6   Capacity:6
Count:7   Capacity:12
Count:8   Capacity:12
Count:8   Capacity:8
```

The constructor of List<T> that we use in the previous example accepts an integer value which represents the initial capacity of the list. It is clear that the *Microsoft* implementation doubles the capacity each time a new allocation is necessary. We say of the List<T> class that is has a *growth factor* of 2.

The System.ComponentModel.IBindingList and System.ComponentModel. IListSource interfaces

The *Windows Forms 2* and *ASP.NET 2* frameworks offer facilities in order to bind a data source to controls used to display the data. A data source is quite often a list of data. To bind such a list to a display control, these technologies require a class which implements `IBindingList` such as the `System.ComponentModel.BindingList<T>` class (see page 574) or a class which implements `IListSource` such as the `DataSet` class (see page 771).

The System.Collections.Generic.LinkedList<T> class

The `System.Collections.Generic.LinkedList<T>` class represents the concept of a *double linked list*. A double linked list is a collection of nodes which are bound one to the others as the links on a chain. Each node is linked to the previous and to the following node. Each node also knows about the list in which it is contained and each node contains an element of the list. A double linked list only knows about the first and last node. All this is illustrated in the following figure:

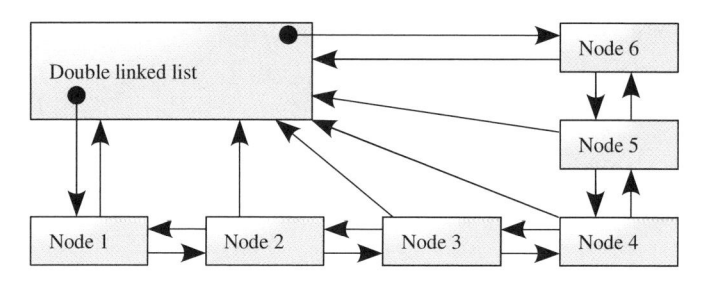

Figure 15-2: A double linked list

Consequently, access to an element is done in a time which is proportional to the number of nodes while the insertion of deletion of an element is done in constant time (i.e. independently to the number of elements in the list).

The `System.Collections.Generic.LinkedList<T>` class is defined as follows:

```
public class LinkedList<T> : ICollection<T>, IEnumerable<T>, ICollection,
   IEnumerable, ISerializable, IDeserializationCallback
```

The `System.Collections.Generic.LinkedListNode<T>` class which represents a node in the list is defined as follows:

```
public sealed class LinkedListNode<T> {
   public LinkedListNode( T value );
   public System.Collections.Generic.LinkedList<T> List { get; }
   public System.Collections.Generic.LinkedListNode<T> Next { get; }
   public System.Collections.Generic.LinkedListNode<T> Previous { get; }
   public T Value { get; set; }
}
```

Note that the `List`, `Next` and `Previous` properties have read-only access which implies that only the operations on a double linked list are allows to link a node to a list.

In addition to the methods of `ICollection<T>`, the `LinkedList<T>` presents the following members:

- void AddHead(T value)
  void AddHead(LinkedListNode<T> node)
  void AddTail(T value)
  void AddTail(LinkedListNode<T> node)
  Add an element at the head of the list using AddHead() or at the tail of the list using AddTail().
- void AddAfter(LinkedListNode<T> node, T value)
  void AddAfter(LinkedListNode<T> node,LinkedListNode<T> _node)
  void AddBefore(LinkedListNode<T> node, T value)
  void AddBefore(LinkedListNode<T> node,LinkedListNode<T> _node)
  Adds an element before or after the specified element. The InvalidOperationException exception is raised if node does not belong to the list.
- void RemoveHead()
  void RemoveTail()
  Remove the element at the head of the list using RemoveHead() or at the tail of the list using RemoveTail(). The InvalidOperationException exception is raised if the list is empty.

List of strings

You may hesitate between two implementations of a string list offered by the framework: The System.Collections.Specialized.StringCollection class (available since version 1.0) and the System.Collections.Generic.List<string> class (available only since version 2.0).

The answer is simple. You must prefer the use of the generic List<string>. Not as much for its performance (which is barely better than performance of StringCollection) but rather for coherency reasons within your code. Also, List<string> implements the generic interfaces such as IEnumerable<string> which are not supported by StringCollection.

The use of the StringCollection class only makes sense if you wish to remain coherent with code that already uses this class.

The System.Collections.Generic.Queue<T> class

The notion of *queue* is often used in programming. A queue is generally used to process messages in the order of their arrival, in the same way as a store cashier will serve its clients in the order in which they arrived. The classic term to designate this behavior is *FIFO (First In First Out)*. As with a queue at a store, we talk of the start of a queue and the end of a queue.

To reproduce such a behavior, it is recommended to use the System.Collections.Generic.Queue<T> class which is defined as follows:

```
public class Queue<T> : ICollection<T>, IEnumerable<T>,
                       ICollection,    IEnumerable
```

This class mainly offers the three following methods:

- void Enqueue(T item)
  This method adds the item to the end of the queue.
- T Dequeue()
  This method removes the element which is at the beginning of the queue and returns it. If the queue is empty, the InvalidOperationException exception is raised.
- T Peek()
  This method returns the element at the beginning of the queue without removing it. If the queue is empty, the InvalidOperationException exception is raised.

As with the `List<T>` class, the `Queue<T>` class has a capacity and implements the `TrimExcess()` method to minimize performance drops due to the allocation/deallocation produced by the changes in the size of the queue. The `Queue<T>` also offers a constructor which allows setting the initial capacity of the queue.

The System.Collections.Generic.Stack<T> class

The notion of *stack* is often used in programming. For example, each thread uses a stack to store its processing data. A stack is generally used to process messages in the order in which they are put on the stack, in the same way as a stack of files is processed. In general, we start with the file at the top of the stack. The classic term used to define this behavior is *LIFO* (*Last In First Out*). As with a stack of files, we talk of the top of a stack.

To reproduce such a behavior, it is recommended to use the `System.Collections.Generic.Stack<T>` class provided especially for this purpose and which is defined as follows:

```
public class Queue<T> : ICollection<T>, IEnumerable<T>,
                       ICollection,    IEnumerable
```

This class mainly offers the three following methods:

- `void Push(T item)`
  This method adds `item` to the top of the stack pile.
- `T Pop()`
  This method removes the element which is located on the top of the stack and returns. If the stack is empty, the `InvalidOperationException` exception is raised.
- `T Peek()`
  This method returns the element which is located at the top of the stack without removing it. If the stack is empty, the `InvalidOperationException` exception is raised.

As with the `List<T>` and `Queue<T>` classes, the `Stack<T>` class has a capacity and implements the `TrimExcess()` method to minimize performance drops due to the allocation/deallocation produced by the changes in the size of the queue. The `Stack<T>` also offers a constructor which allows setting the initial capacity of the queue.

Dictionaries

Dictionaries are collections where the elements are key/value pairs. In such a pair, the key is used to index the value. For example, in the dictionary for a language, the words are used as the keys while the definitions represent the values. In the classes we will present in this section, the keys and values can by of any type. Let us mention that a dictionary cannot contain several key/value pairs with the same key. The two main characteristics of a dictionary are:

- The quick insertion of a key/value pair.
- The quick search of a value from its key.

Speed is crucial as we use dictionaries mainly for performance reasons. To optimize the insertion and search, two families of algorithms exist. In the .NET framework, they give place to the two implementations presented in this section.

The Sytem.Collections.Generic.IDictionary<K,V> interface

The two implementations of dictionaries, that is the `System.Collections.Generic.SortedDictionary<K,V>` and `System.Collections.Generic.Dictionary<K,V>` classes, implement the `System.Collections.Generic.IDictionary<K,V>` interface which is defined as follows:

Dictionaries

```
public interface IDictionary<K, V> : ICollection<KeyValuePair<K, V>>,
                                     IEnumerable<KeyValuePair<K, V>>
```

Hence, a dictionary can be seen as a collection of instances of the `System.Collections.Generic.KeyValuePair<K,V>` structure which is defined as follows:

```
public struct KeyValuePair<K, V>{
    public K Key;
    public V Value;
}
```

The methods of the `IDictionary<K,V>` interface are:

- `void Add(K key, V value)`
  Adds the `key`/`value` pair to the dictionary. If a key/value pair already exists for this key, the `ArgumentException` exception is raised. If the underlying dictionary is in read-only mode, then the `NotSupportedException` exception is raised.

- `bool Remove(K key)`
  Removes the pair with `key` as the value for the key. If such a pair cannot be found, this method returns `false`. If the underlying dictionary is read-only, the `NotSupportedException` exception is raised.

- `bool ContainsKey(K key)`
  Returns `true` if the dictionary contains a pair indexed by `key`.

The `IDictionary<K,V>` also offers the following properties:

- `V this[ K key ] {get;set;}`
  Indexer to access in read/write the key/value pairs from a key.

- `ICollection<K> Keys {get;}`
  Returns a collection containing all the keys in the dictionary.

- `ICollection<V> Values {get;}`
  Returns a collection containing all the values of the dictionary.

The System.Collections.Generic.SortedDictionary<K,V> class

The `System.Collections.Generic.SortedDictionary<K,V>` implementation of the concept of dictionary rests on the fact that there must exist an order relationship between all the keys. The key/value elements are constantly ordered based on the ordering relation of the keys. A binary algorithm can then be used during the insertion of a key/value pair as well as when searching for a key in the dictionary. The main advantage of this algorithm is that it is more efficient since it works in logarithmic time. It is this algorithm that we intuitively apply when searching in an English dictionary for example. In this case, the order of the keys is determined based on the alphabetical order of the words in the dictionary. It only takes us a few seconds to find, amongst tens of thousands of definitions, the definition which corresponds to the desired word.

Clearly, the implementation of `SortedDictionary<K,V>` must be capable of comparing two instances of the type K. If these keys do not support the `IComparable<K>` interface or if the default `Comparer<K>.Default` compare is not well suited, you can use certain constructors of `SortedDictionary<K,V>` which accept a parameter of type `IComparer<K>`. This interface is described a little later.

The `SortedDictionary<K,V>` class is defined as follows:

```
public class SortedDictionary<K, V> : IDictionary<K, V>,
    ICollection<KeyValuePair<K, V>>, IEnumerable<KeyValuePair<K, V>>,
    IDictionary, ICollection, IEnumerable
```

In addition to the members of the `IDictionary<K,V>` interface, the `SortedDictionary<K,V>` class offers the `bool TryGetValue(K key, out V value)` which returns a value based on the provided key. If the key is found, the method returns `true`. If the key cannot be found, the method returns `false`.

The System.Collections.Generic.Dictionary<K,V> class

The implementation of the `System.Collections.Generic.Dictionary<K,V>` class is based on the concept of *hash tables* that we will describe. Hence, it does fix a few inherent problems to the implementation of the `SortedDictionary<K,V>` class:

- We do not always have an ordering relationship on all the keys of a dictionary.
- If the comparison operation for two keys is expensive, the performance of using `SortedList<K,V>` will degrade.
- The insertion and search time are generally done in a constant time within a hash table (i.e. independently on the number of elements), which is better than the logarithmic time offered by the implementation of the `SortedDictionary<K,V>`.

Here is the definition `Dictionary<K,V>` class:

```
public class Dictionary<K, V> : IDictionary<K, V>,
    ICollection<KeyValuePair<K, V>>, IEnumerable<KeyValuePair<K, V>>,
    IDictionary, ICollection, IEnumerable,
    ISerializable, IDeserializationCallback
```

Hash table

The idea of a hash table is to calculate a hash value based on the key of the dictionary, during the insertion or search. The hash value corresponding to a key is an integer. Once the key has been hashed into an integer number, we use a constant time search algorithm based on some characteristics of finite groups of prime order.

However, it can happen that two different keys have the same hash value. This is called a *collision* between the keys. To deal with this problem, the concept of a hash table introduces the notion of a *bucket*. The hash table contains several buckets indexed by the hash value. A bucket indexed with the hash value H contains all the key/value pairs for which the key generates the hash value H. This is illustrated in Figure 15-3.

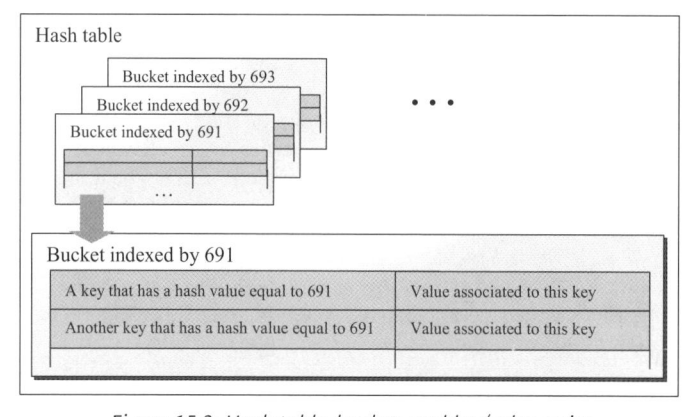

Figure 15-3: Hash table, buckets and key/value pairs

The notion of bucket is internal to the implementation of the hash table and the developer will never have to manipulate them. For the inquiring minds, know that the magic behind the search in constant time comes from an arithmetic theorem which states that the order of all elements of a finite group of prime order is equal to the order of the group. Hence, the implementation `Dictionary<K,V>` internally maintains a prime number of buckets which varies in time based on the current number of buckets. By applying this theorem, the basked in which must be contained a key with a hash value of H has for index H modulo with the current number of buckets.

With this algorithm, the insertion of a key/value pair is done in constant time if there are no collisions. The search operation is done in three steps:

- Determine the hash value for the key;
- Search for the appropriate bucket (in constant time);
- Finally, once the bucket is found, sequentially search in the bucket. This step is obviously more efficient if there is no collision (i.e. if there is only one element in the bucket).

Load factor of a hash table

We wish to sensitize you to an important detail on hash table algorithms. Based on what we have presented, in a hash table, smaller is the (number of key/value pairs) / (number of buckets) ratio, faster searches will be as the number of collisions will be reduced. Unfortunately, smaller this ration is, the more memory the hash table will consume and thus performance will suffer. This behavior is managed internally in the `Dictionary<K,V>` by what is called a *load factor*.

For each insertion of a key/value pair in a hash table, the #pairs/#buckets ratio increases. When this ratio exceeds the load factor, the number of buckets is increased to be equal to the smallest prime number which is at least double the current number of buckets.

The `Dictionary<K,V>` class is optimized and you cannot act on the load factor. It is deemed that the value 0.72 represents the optimal value for load factor.

Notice also that certain protected constructors of the `Dictionary<K,V>` class accept an initial capacity. If this capacity is not a prime number, it will be automatically set to the first prime number which is greater to this value.

The GetHashCode() method of the object class

The `object` class offers the two methods named `Equals()` and `GetHashCode()`, used on the K type by the algorithms of the `Dictionary<K,V>` class. If you decide to override the `Equals()` method on a class for which the instances are susceptible of representing the keys of a hash table, it is imperative that you also override the `GetHashCode()` method in order to satisfy the following constraint: for all instances of x and y of your type, if `x.GetHashCode()` and `y.GetHashCode()` are two different integers, then the `x.Equals(y)` and `y.Equals(x)` expressions must both return `false`. If you do not respect this constraint, you expose yourself to incorrect behavior from the hash table. To help you enforce this constraint, the C#2 compiler will emit a warning if you override the `Equals()` method without overriding the `GetHashCode()` method.

Hash values computed on strings

The default implementation of the `String.GetHashCode()` method takes into account the case of the characters but does not take into account for the culture. If you wish to configure the way that the culture is taken into account or if you do not wish to take into account the case of the characters when obtaining a hash value from a string, you must use an instance of a class derived from the `System.StringComparer` abstract class. Such an instance is obtained from one of the properties of this class such as `StringComparer CurrentCultureIgnoreCase{get;}` or `StringComparer Ordinal{get;}`. We notice that this design trick allows for the class of the framework derived from `StringComparer` to be declared as internal.

The System.Collections.Generic.IEqualityComparer<T> interface

In the case where you cannot (or do not want to) modify the class representing the keys in order to define your own hashing algorithm, you can implement the `IEqualityComparer<K>` interface in a custom class specially created for this task. This interface is defined as follows:

```
public interface IEqualityComparer<T> {
   bool  Equals(T x, T y);
   int   GetHashCode(T obj);
}
```

Certain constructors of the `Dictionary<K,V>` class accept this interface as a parameter.

Guidelines for hash algorithms

It is recommended that your hash algorithm have the following properties:

- The algorithm must have a good random distribution in order to minimize collisions.
- The algorithm must execute quickly.
- Two objects with the same state must have the same hash value.
- The calculation of the hash value must use immutable fields. These fields are initialized during the construction of the object and do not change during the lifetime of the object. If this tip is not respected, the hash value of a same object is not guaranteed of being constant with time.

An example

Here is an example where we provide our own hashing algorithm for instances of the `Person` class. Our algorithm multiplies the hash value of the string representing the name of the person with the year of birth. Note that we do not worry about overflows during the multiplication since by default integer multiplication overflows do not throw exceptions.

Example 15-15

```
using System.Collections.Generic;
class Person {
   public Person(string name, int birthYear) {
      m_Name = name;
      m_BirthYear = birthYear;
   }
   public override int GetHashCode() {
      return m_BirthYear * m_Name.GetHashCode();
   }
   public override bool Equals(object o) {
      Person person = o as Person;
      if ( person != null )
         return ( person.GetHashCode() == GetHashCode() );
      return false;
   }
   private string m_Name;
   private int m_BirthYear;
}
class Program {
   public static void Main() {
      Dictionary<Person,string> dictionary=new Dictionary<Person,string>();
      Person julien = new Person( "Julien" , 2002);
      Person mathieu = new Person( "Mathieu" , 2001);
      dictionary.Add( julien, "20 Arson st" );
      dictionary.Add( mathieu, "90 Barberis st" );
      bool b = dictionary.ContainsKey( julien );
      // Here, b is true.
   }
}
```

Iterating through the items of a dictionary

When we presented the `IDictionary<K,V>` interface, which is implemented by all dictionaries, we have seen that this interface implements the `IEnumerator<KeyValuePair<K,V>>` interface. Hence, when we traverse the elements of a dictionary, we actually enumerate the key/value pairs and not only the keys or the values. Here is an example which illustrates the traversal of the elements of a dictionary:

Example 15-16
```
using System.Collections.Generic;
class Program {
   public static void Main() {
      Dictionary<string,string> dico = new Dictionary<string,string>();
      dico.Add("France", "20 Arson st");
      dico.Add("Francis", "90 Barberis st");
      foreach ( KeyValuePair<string,string> item in dico )
         System.Console.WriteLine(item.Key + " : " + item.Value);
   }
}
```

This example displays:

```
France : 20 Arson st
Francis : 90 Barberis st
```

Thanks to the use of generic types, the traversal of dictionary elements in .NET 2 using a `foreach` loop does not use any useless *unboxing* operations which would have a performance penalty as in .NET 1.x.

Sorting items of a collection

You have the possibility of sorting the elements of a collection of type `System.Array` or `System.Collections.Generic.List<T>`. The other collections do not need to be sorted for the following reasons:

- `System.Collections.BitArray` and `System.Collections.Specialized.BitVector32`
  There is no sense in sorting bits!

- `System.Collections.Generic.Queue<T>` and `System.Collections.Generic.Stack<T>`
  These types of collections are use for the specific type of access to its elements (*FIFO* or *LIFO* access). The sort of such a collection modifies the access to the elements, and thus its purpose.

- `System.Collections.Generic.LinkedList<T>`
  If you have to sort the elements of a list, you are better off using the `List<T>` class to represent your list.

- `System.Collections.Generic.SortedDictionary<T>`
  The elements of such a collection are, by definition, sorted based on their keys. It would then be pointless to provide a sorting operation.

- `System.Collections.Generic.Dictionary<K,T>`
  This implementation uses an algorithm based on hash values of the keys to provide quick access to the elements. A sort of the elements of this collection would mess up the internal organization necessary to this collection.

There exists several sort algorithms. The algorithm used by *Microsoft* in .NET is the `QuickSort` algorithm. This algorithm executes itself in a `O(n log2(n))` time if n is the number of elements to sort. This algorithm is an unstable sort algorithm meaning that it does not necessarily preserve the initial order of initial elements with the same value.

The IComparer<T> and IComparable<T> interfaces

To allow the sorting objects, we must have a way to compare them. There are several ways to compare the instances of a class:

- Either the class implements one of the `System.IComparable` or `System.IComparable<T>` interfaces which, using the `int CompareTo(T other)` method, allows sorting the current instance in regards to the instance passed as a parameter.
- Either another class implements the `System.Collections.IComparer` or `System.Collections.Generic.IComparer<T>` interface to sort the instances of the related class (using the `int Compare(object/T,object/T)` method). In this case, this other class must be nested within the related class if it must make use of its private members. This other class is generally derived from the `System.Collections.Generic.Comparer<T>` class, which of course implements the `IComparer<T>` interface.
- Let us finally mention that certain comparison methods use a delegate of type `System.Comparison<T>` to compare the elements. This delegate is defined as follows:

```
public delegate int System.Comparison<T>(T x, T y);
```

When possible, it is preferable to use the first approach. You are however obligated to use one of the two other approaches if you do not wish (or cannot) modify the class whose instances need to be compared.

All the primitive types of the CTS representing numbers support the `IComparable` and `IComparable<T>` interfaces.

Sorting items of an array

The `System.Array` offers several overloads of the `Sort()` method in order to sort the elements. The methods not presented here only allow sorting a portion of the table. Note that the methods for sorting an array are static and it is preferable to use the generic overloads in order to obtain strong typing.

- `public static void Sort<K,V>(K[] arrayKeys, V[] arrayValues)`
  Sort `arrayValues` by using the elements of `arrayKeys` as the keys for the sort. The class of the elements of `arrayKeys` must implement the `IComparable<T>` interface:

  Example 15-17
  ```
  public class Program {
     public static void Main() {
        string[] arrNames = { "Jean", "Seb", "Eva", "Paul" };
        int[] arrKeys = { 3, 1, 6, 2 };
        System.Array.Sort<int,string>( arrKeys, arrNames );
        // Here 'arrNames' contains {"Seb","Paul","Jean","Eva"}.
        // Here 'arrKeys' contains {1,2,3,6}.
     }
  }
  ```

- `public static void Sort<T>(T[] array)`
  Sorts `array`, by assuming that the class of the elements in `array` implements the `IComparable<T>` interface. Here is a sort example on an array of integers:

  Example 15-18
  ```
  public class Program {
     public static void Main() {
        int[] arr = { 3, 1, 6, 2 };
        System.Array.Sort( arr );
        // Here 'arr' contains {1,2,3,6}.
     }
  }
  ```

Here is an example of sort on an array of elements of a custom class which implements the IComparable interface:

Example 15-19
```
using System;
class Article : IComparable<Article> {
   public decimal price;
   public Article(decimal price) { this.price = price; }
   int IComparable<Article>.CompareTo( Article other ) {
      return price.CompareTo( other.price );
   }
}
public class Program {
   public static void Main() {
      Article[] arr = { new Article(98M) , new Article(19M) ,
                        new Article(9.5M) };
      Array.Sort<Article>(arr);
      // Here, 'arr[0].price' = 9.5 ; 'arr[1].price' = 19 ;
      // 'arr[2].price' = 98
   }
}
```

- `public static void Sort<T>(T[] array, IComparer<T> comparer)`
Sorts array by using the comparer object to compare the elements. Here is the previous example rewritten with this version of Sort():

Example 15-20
```
using System.Collections.Generic;
class Article {
   public class CmpArticle : IComparer<Article>{
      int IComparer<Article>.Compare(Article a1, Article a2){
         return a1.price.CompareTo(a2.price);
      }
   }
   public decimal price;
   public Article(decimal price) { this.price = price; }
}
public class Prog{
   public static void Main(){
      Article[] arr = { new Article(98M) , new Article(19M) ,
                        new Article(9.5M) };
      System.Array.Sort<Article>( arr , new Article.CmpArticle() );
      // Here, 'arr[0].price' = 9.5 ; 'arr[1].price' = 19 ;
      // 'arr[2].price' = 98
   }
}
```

- `public static void Sort<T>(T[] array, Comparison<T> comparison)`
Sorts array by using the method referenced by the comparison delegate to compare the elements. Here is the previous example rewritten using this version of Sort():

Example 15-21
```
class Article {
   public static int MethodCmp(Article a1, Article a2){
      return a1.price.CompareTo(a2.price);
   }
   public decimal price;
   public Article(decimal price) { this.price = price; }
}
```

Example 15-21
```
public class Program {
   public static void Main(){
      Article[] arr = { new Article(98M) , new Article(19M) ,
                        new Article(9.5M) };
      System.Array.Sort<Article>( arr , Article.MethodCmp );
      //  Here, 'arr[0].price' = 9.5 ; 'arr[1].price' = 19 ;
      //  'arr[2].price' = 98
   }
}
```

Sorting the elements of an instance of List<T>

The `System.Collections.Generic.List<T>` class offers the following sort methods. Note that the sort methods on a list are all non-static.

- void Sort()
  void Sort(Comparison<T> comparison)
  void Sort(IComparer<T> comparer)
  void Sort(int index, int count, IComparer<T> comparer)
  Sorts a part of the elements of a list. This section is contained between the index and index+count elements.

Functors as a mean to work with collections

It is preferable to have assimilated the notions of iterators and of anonymous methods introduced in C#2 before reading this section.

Specialized delegate types

The `System` namespace contains four new delegate types particularly useful to manipulate and obtain information from collections:

```
namespace System {
   public delegate void Action<T> ( T obj );
   public delegate bool Predicate<T> ( T obj );
   public delegate U    Converter<T,U> ( T from );
   public delegate int  Comparison<T> ( T x, T y );
}
```

In Example 15-21, we had the chance to use an instance delegate of `Comparison<T>` to sort the elements of an array. The following example exposes four other processes which can be done on a list (a request, a calculation, a sort and a conversion), done using instances of these delegates:

Example 15-22
```
using System.Collections.Generic;
class Program {
   class Article {
      public Article(decimal price,string name){Price=price;Name=name;}
      public readonly decimal Price;
      public readonly string  Name;
   }

   static bool IsEven(int i) { return i % 2 == 0; }
   static int sum = 0;
   static void AddToSum(int i) { sum += i; }
```

Example 15-22

```csharp
    static int CompareArticle(Article x, Article y){
       return Comparer<decimal>.Default.Compare(x.Price, y.Price);
    }
    static decimal ConvertArticle(Article article){
       return (decimal)article.Price;
    }

    static void Main(){
       // Seek out every odd integers.
       // Implicitly uses a 'Predicate<T>' delegate object.
       List<int> integers = new List<int>();
       for(int i=1; i<=10; i++)
          integers.Add(i);
       List<int> even = integers.FindAll( IsEven );

       // Sum up items of the list.
       // Implicitly uses an 'Action<T>' delegate object.
       integers.ForEach( AddToSum );

       // Sort items of type 'Article'.
       // Implicitly uses a 'Comparison<T>' delegate object.
       List<Article> articles = new List<Article>();
       articles.Add( new Article(5,"Shoes") );
       articles.Add( new Article(3,"Shirt") );
       articles.Sort( CompareArticle );

       // Cast items of type 'Article' into 'decimal'.
       // Implicitly uses a 'Converter<T,U>' delegate object.
       List<decimal> artPrice =
                articles.ConvertAll<decimal>( ConvertArticle );
    }
}
```

Readers who have use the *Standard Template Library* (*STL*) of C++ will recognize the notion of *functor*. A functor is a parameterized process. Functors are particularly useful to complete a same operation on all the elements of a collection. In C++, we overloaded the parenthesis operator in order to implement the notion of functor. In .NET, a functor takes the form of a delegate instance. In fact, in the previous program, the four delegates instances created implicitly are four examples of functors.

Using anonymous methods

As shows the following example, the anonymous methods of C# can prove themselves to be particularly adapted to the implementation of functors. Note that as with the second functor, which stores the sum of the elements in an integer, a functor can encapsulate a state.

Example 15-23

```csharp
using System.Collections.Generic;
class Program {
   class Article {
      public Article(decimal price,string name){Price=price;Name=name;}
      public readonly decimal Price;
      public readonly string  Name;
   }
   static void Main(){
```

Example 15-23

```csharp
   // Seek out every odd integers.
   // Implicitly uses a 'Predicate<T>' delegate object.
   List<int> integers = new List<int>();
   for(int i=1; i<=10; i++)
      integers.Add(i);
   List<int> even =integers.FindAll( delegate(int i){ return i%2==0; });

   // Sum up items of the list.
   // Implicitly uses an 'Action<T>' delegate object.
   int sum = 0;
   integers.ForEach(delegate(int i) { sum += i; });

   // Sort items of type 'Article'.
   // Implicitly uses a 'Comparison<T>' delegate object.
   List<Article> articles = new List<Article>();
   articles.Add( new Article(5,"Shoes") );
   articles.Add( new Article(3,"Shirt") );
   articles.Sort(delegate(Article x, Article y) {
      return Comparer<decimal>.Default.Compare(x.Price,y.Price); } );

   // Cast items of type 'Article' into 'decimal'.
   // Implicitly uses a 'Converter<T,U>' delegate object.
   List<decimal> artPrice = articles.ConvertAll<decimal> (
      delegate(Article article) { return (decimal)article.Price; } );
   }
}
```

List<T> and Array classes support for functors

The use of functors is only possible on collections of type List<T> and Array. In fact, only these collections offer methods which accept functors to process their elements. These methods, which have self-descriptive names, are listed below:

```csharp
public class List<T> : ... {
   public int FindIndex(Predicate<T> match);
   public int FindIndex(int index, Predicate<T> match);
   public int FindIndex(int index, int count, Predicate<T> match);

   public int FindLastIndex(Predicate<T> match);
   public int FindLastIndex(int index, Predicate<T> match);
   public int FindLastIndex(int index, int count, Predicate<T> match);

   public List<T> FindAll(Predicate<T> match);
   public T Find(Predicate<T> match);
   public T FindLast(Predicate match);

   public bool Exists(Predicate<T> match);
   public bool TrueForAll(Predicate<T> match);

   public int RemoveAll(Predicate<T> match);
   public void ForEach(Action<T> action);
   public void Sort(Comparison<T> comparison);
   public List<U> ConvertAll<U>(Converter<T,U> converter);
   ...
}
```

Functors as a mean to work with collections 495

```
public class Array {
   public static int FindIndex<T>(T[] array, int startIndex,
                                  int count, Predicate<T> match);
   public static int FindIndex<T>(T[] array, int startIndex,
                                  Predicate<T> match);
   public static int FindIndex<T>(T[] array, Predicate<T> match);

   public static int FindLastIndex<T>(T[] array, int startIndex,
                                      int count, Predicate<T> match);
   public static int FindLastIndex<T>(T[] array, int startIndex,
                                      Predicate<T> match);
   public static int FindLastIndex<T>(T[] array, Predicate<T> match);

   public static T[] FindAll<T>(T[] array, Predicate<T> match);
   public static T Find<T>(T[] array, Predicate<T> match);
   public static T FindLast<T>(T[] array, Predicate<T> match);

   public static bool Exists<T>(T[] array, Predicate<T> match);
   public static bool TrueForAll<T>(T[] array, Predicate<T> match);

   public static void ForEach<T>(T[] array, Action<T> action);
   public static void Sort<T>(T[] array, System.Comparison<T> comparison);
   public static U[] ConvertAll<T, U>( T[] array,
                                       Converter<T, U> converter);
   ...
}
```

C#2 iterators and collections

It is easy to implement this kind of feature to all types of collection using iterators as shown by the following program (which is based on the *pipeline pattern* shown at page 461):

Example 15-24
```
using System;
using System.Collections.Generic;

class Program{
   static public IEnumerable<T> Filter<T> (
                   Predicate<T> predicate, IEnumerable<T> collection) {
      foreach (T item in collection)
         if (predicate(item))
            yield return item;
   }
   static public IEnumerable<T> Transform<T> (
                   Converter<T,T> transformer, IEnumerable<T> collection) {
      foreach (T item in collection)
         yield return transformer(item);
   }
   static public IEnumerable<U> Converter<T, U> (
                   Converter<T, U> converter, IEnumerable<T> collection) {
      foreach (T item in collection)
         yield return converter(item);
   }
   static public IEnumerable<int> PipelineIntRange( int begin, int end ) {
      System.Diagnostics.Debug.Assert( begin < end );
      for ( int i = begin; i <= end; i++ )
```

Example 15-24
```
            yield return i;
      }
      static void Main() {
         int modulo = 3;
         int factor = 2;
         foreach (string s in
            Converter<int,string>( delegate(int item) {
               return "Hello:" + item.ToString(); },
                  Filter( delegate(int item) {
                     return (item % modulo == 0); },
                       Transform( delegate(int item) {
                          return item * factor; },
                             PipelineIntRange(1, 10) ) ) ) )
            Console.WriteLine(s);
      }
   }
```

This program displays:

```
Hello:6
Hello:12
Hello:18
```

Correspondence between System.Collections.Generic and System.Collections

Here is a table which enumerates the correspondence between these two namespaces. Remember that the System.Collections namespace is only supported for backward compatibility reasons with the 1.x .NET framework and that there is no need to use it in .NET 2 specific development:

System.Collections.Generics	System.Collections
Comparer<T>	Comparer
Dictionary<K,T>	HashTable
List<T>	ArrayList
LinkedList<T>	
Queue<T>	Queue
SortedDictionary<K,T>	SortedList
SortedList<K,T>	
Stack<T>	Stack
ICollection<T>	ICollection
IComparable<T>	System.IComparable
IComparer<T>	IComparer
IDictionary<K,T>	IDictionary
IEnumerable<T>	IEnumerable
IEnumerator<T>	IEnumerator
IList<T>	IList

16

Base Classes

Math

The System.Math class

The `System.Math` class only contains fields and static methods.

There are two static fields: the two mathematical constants e ('E' static field) and π ('PI' static field). Both these fields are of type `double`.

The static methods represent the set of classical math functions, such as the trigonometric functions, logarithmic and power functions, rounding… If an input value is outside of the supported range for a specific math function, the `double.NaN` value is returned and no exception is raised (except for the `Round()` method). The behavior of these functions at infinity logically corresponds to the behavior of the corresponding math functions (thanks to the `double.NegativeInfinity` and `double.PositiveInfinity` values which can be used as an input or output depending on the function).

Here is a complete listing of these functions:

- The methods defined for several numerical types:

Type **Abs**(Type a)	This method returns the absolute value of a. Type can be any numerical signed type, floating-point or integer.
Type **Min**(Type a, Type b) Type **Max**(Type a, Type b)	These methods return the minimum (respectively the maximum) of a and of b. Type can be any numerical signed type, floating-point or integer.
int **Sign**(Type a)	This method returns the sign in the form of an integer: -1 if a is negative; 0 if a is equal to 0; 1 if a is positive. Type can be any numerical type signed, floating-point or integer.

- The trigonometric methods. All angles are specified in radians. If an argument is outside of the valid range for a specific function, the `double.NaN` value is returned.

double **Cos**(double d)	Returns the cosine of d. This method is defined for all floating-points numbers and output values are in the range [-1 ; 1].
double **Sin**(double d)	Returns the sine of d. This method is defined for all floating-points numbers and output values are in the range [-1 ; 1].
double **Tan**(double d)	Returns the tangent of d. This method is defined for all floating-points numbers (contrarily to the mathematical tangent which is not defined for certain real values).
double **Acos**(double d)	Returns the arc-cosine of d. The valid input range of floating-point numbers for this method is [-1 ; 1] and the range of return values is [0 ; π].
double **Asin**(double d)	Returns the arc-sine of d. The valid input range of floating-point numbers for this method is [-1 ; 1] and the range of return values is [-π/2 ; π/2].

double **Atan**(double d)	Returns the arc-tangent of d. This method is defined for all floating-points numbers and output values are in the range [-π/2 ; π/2]. π/2 is obtained for the `double.PositiveInfinity` value while -π/2 is obtained for the `double.NegativeInfinity` value.
double **Atan2**(double y, double x)	Returns the angle between the positive axis and the vector which connects the origin to the (x,y) point. Output values are in the range [-π ; π].
double **Cosh**(double d)	Returns the hyperbolic cosine of d. This method is defined for all floating-points numbers and the range of return values is [1; `double.PositiveInfinity`]. `double.PositiveInfinity` is obtained both for the `double.NegativeInfinity` and `double.PositiveInfinity` values.
double **Sinh**(double d)	Returns the hyperbolic sine of d. This method is defined for all floating-points numbers and the range of return values is [`double.NegativeInfinity`; `double.PositiveInfinity`]. `double.PositiveInfinity` is obtained for `double.PositiveInfinity` and `double.NegativeInfinity` is obtained for `double.NegativeInfinity`.
double **Tanh**(double d)	Returns the hyperbolic tangent of d. This method is defined for all floating-points numbers and the range of return values is [-1 ; 1]. 1 is obtained for the `double.PositiveInfinity` value and -1 is obtained for the `double.NegativeInfinity` value.

- The power, exponential and logarithmic methods:

double **Sqrt**(double d)	Returns the square root of d. The set of valid inputs include all non-null and positive floating-point numbers. If a negative value is passed, the `double.Nan` value is returned.
double **Pow**(double x,double y)	Returns x to the power of y.
double **Exp**(double d)	Returns the exponential of d (i.e. e at the power of d).
double **Log**(double d)	Returns the logarithm of d. If a negative value is used, the `double.Nan` value is returned.
double **Log**(double d,double b)	Return the base-b logarithm of d. If a negative value is used for d or b, the `double.Nan` value is returned.
double **Log10**(double d)	Returns the base-10 logarithm of d. If a negative value is used, the `double.Nan` value is returned.

- Type Round(Type d)
  Type Round(Type d, int n)
  Type is a floating-point number. The Round() methods allows to round a floating-point number to the precision specified by n. For example:

  ```
  Math.Round( 3.1415 )   // returns 3.0
  Math.Round( 3.1415,2 ) // returns 3.14
  ```

  > If n is negative, the `System.ArgumentOutOfRangeException` exception will be raised.

- double Ceiling(double d)
  double Floor(double d)

  The Floor() returns the integer part of d i.e. the largest integer which is smaller than d. In the same way, the Ceiling() method returns the integer part of d +1 i.e. the smallest integer which is greater than d.

- double IEEERemainder(double x,double y)
  Returns the x-(yQ) number where Q is equal to the quotient of x by y rounded to the closest integer. If this quotient is exactly between two integer numbers, the even integer value is used. If y is null the `double.NaN` value is returned.

Several mathematical domains as matrix computations or complex numbers are not covered by the .NET framework.

The System.Random class

The use of the `System.Random` class allows the generation of random numbers. The methods of this class are not static. In other words, this class must be instantiated to be used. The methods of this class are:

`Random()`	Constructor for a `Random` object. The seed value used by random number generation algorithm is calculated based on the current time.
`Random(int seed)`	Constructor of a `Random` object which allows you to specify the seed value.
`int Next()`	Returns a random integer number chosen in the 0 to `int.MaxValue` range.
`int Next(int a)`	Returns a random number chosen between 0 and `a-1`.
`int Next(int a,int b)`	Returns a random number chosen between `a` and `b-1`.
`double NextDouble()`	Returns a floating point random number chosen in the range of [0 ; 1.0 [.
`void NextBytes(Byte[] Tab)`	Fills the elements of the input array of bits with random numbers.

Time, date and duration

With the .NET framework, the *Microsoft* developers have access to a coherent management of temporal data. Using win32 and COM, you needed to use various classes which represented dates on four bytes (for the `CTime` or `time_t` classes) or on eight bytes (for the `COleDateTime` class). The functionalities of these classes were redundant with methods with different names and arguments.

In .NET, temporal data are principally manipulated by the use of two structures:

- The `System.DateTime` structure whose instances represent a date.
- The `System.TimeSpan` structure whose instances represent a time interval. For example, there is an operation which allows recovering an instance of `System.TimeSpan` from two instances of `System.DateTime`.

The System.DateTime structure

Dates represented by instances of `System.DateTime` are in the time interval between these two dates: midnight (beginning of the day) on January 1st 0001 and midnight (end of day) on December 31 9999.

In an instance of `System.DateTime`, internally, the date is represented by an integer of type `long` (a signed integer of eight bytes). The correspondence is of one unit for an interval of time of 100 nanoseconds. This integer is accessible using the `Ticks{get;set}` non-static property. This integer is included between the `MinValue` and `MaxValue` static constants of the `DateTime` type. The two integers correspond to the extremity dates mentioned above are 0 and 3,155,378,975,999,999,999.

In this book, we will only consider the Gregorian calendar, used in the occidental world. Know that the `System.Globalization` namespace contains in addition to the `GregorianCalendar` class, other classes which represent other calendars such as `HebrewCalendar`, `JapaneseCalendar`, `JulianCalendar`...

The `DateTime` class contains several members, static and non-static. An exhaustive list of these members can be found in the article named **DateTime Members** on **MSDN**. However, we will present a few of the most commonly used ones:

- The constructors:
  ```
  DateTime(int year, int month, int day)
  DateTime(int year, int month, int day, int hour, int minute, int second)
  DateTime(int year, int month, int day, int hour, int minute, int second, int millisec)
  DateTime(long ticks)
  ```
  year is between 1 and 9999. month is between 1 and 12. day is between 1 and 28, 29, 30 or 31 (depending on the month). hour is between 0 and 23. minute is between 0 and 59. second is between 0 and 59. millisec is between 0 and 999.

- The representations of the current time:

`static DateTime Now{get;}`	This static property returns an instance of `DateTime` which represents the current date and time. The precision of this value is of the order of the hundredth of a second.
`static DateTime Today{get;}`	This static property returns an instance of `DateTime` which represents the current date with the time initialized to midnight at the beginning of the day.
`static DateTime UtcNow{get;}`	This static property returns an instance of `DateTime` which represents the current date and time using universal time.

- Extraction of temporal information in a familiar format from an instance of `DateTime` (non-static members):

`DateTime Date{get;}`	Returns the date with the time portion initialized to midnight at the beginning of the day.
`int Day{get;}`	Between 1 and 31.
`DayOfWeek DayOfWeek{get;}`	Returns a value of the `System.DayOfWeek` enumeration which are: Sunday Monday Tuesday Wednesday Thursday Friday Saturday
`int DayOfYear{get;}`	Between 1 and 366.
`int Hour{get;}`	Between 0 and 23.
`int Millisecond{get;}`	Between 0 and 999.
`int Minute{get;}`	Between 0 and 59.
`int Month{get;}`	Between 1 and 12.
`int Second{get;}`	Between 0 and 59.
`TimeSpan TimeOfDay{get;}`	Time since midnight.
`int Year{get;}`	Between 1 and 9999.

- Operations on dates

`DateTime Add(TimeSpan dT)` `operator+`	Adds the `dT` time span to the date. The + operator is generally preferred.
`TimeSpan Subtract(DateTime date)` `operator-`	Subtracts `date` to the date represented by the instance. The − operator is generally preferred. Note that the time span returned can be negative.
`static int Compare(DateTime d1,DateTime d2)` `operator< <= > >= ==`	Returns 0 if d1 equals d2. Returns 1 if d1 is after d2. Returns -1 if d1 is before d2. The use of the comparison operators is generally preferred.
`static bool IsLeapYear(int year)`	Returns true if the specified year is a leap year.
`static int DayInMonths(int year,int month)`	Returns the number of days in the specified month. For example `DayInMonths(2000,2)` returns 29 as the year 2000 is a leap year.

- `string ToString(string format)`

  Returns a date in a string. The `format` string specifies the way that the date will be formatted. From here on, we will suppose the display of the following program (with the XXX string as a variable):

  ```
  // Tue, 15 Oct 2002 14:30:00 GMT
  DateTime d = new DateTime( 2002, 10, 15, 14, 30, 0 );
  Console.WriteLine( d.ToString( XXX ) );
  ```

Time, date and duration 501

Flags for the general representation of a date

XXX	Displays
"d"	10/15/2002
"D"	Tuesday, October 15, 2002
"f"	Tuesday, October 15, 2002 2:30 PM
"F"	Tuesday, October 15, 2002 2:30:00 PM
"g"	10/15/2002 2:30 PM
"G"	10/15/2002 2:30:00 PM
"M"	October 15
"R"	Tue, 15 Oct 2002 14:30:00 GMT
"s"	Dates formatted to be easily sorted. For example: 2002-10-15T14:30:00
"t"	2:30 PM
"T"	2:30:00 PM
"u"	2002-10-15 14:30:00Z
"U"	Tuesday, October 15, 2002 5:30:00 AM Universal time: at this date California is 9 hours behind the universal time.
"y"	October, 2002

Flags for the personalized presentation of a date

XXX	Displays
:	Separator for hour:minutes:seconds. This separator depends on the current culture chosen in *Windows*.
/	Separator for year/month/day. This separator depends on the current culture chosen in *Windows*.
y	Year, represented by a number from 0 to 99.
yy	Year, represented by a number from 00 to 99.
yyy	Year, represented by a number from 0000 to 9999.
M	Month, represented by a number from 1 to 12.
MM	Month, represented by a number from 01 to 12.
MMM	Month, represented by a three letter abbreviation in the language defined by *Windows* (For example oct.).
MMMM	Month, in the language defined by *Windows*
d	Day, represented by a number from de 1 to 31.
dd	Day, represented by a number from 01 to 31.
ddd	Month, represented by a three letter abbreviation in the language defined by *Windows* (For example sun.).
dddd	Month, in the language defined by *Windows*
h	Hour, represented by a number from 0 to 11.
hh	Hour, represented by a number from 00 to 11.
H	Hour, represented by a number from 0 to 23.
HH	Hour, represented by a number from 00 to 23.
m	Minute, represented by a number from 0 to 59.
mm	Minute, represented by a number from 00 to 59.
s	Second, represented by a number from 0 to 59.
ss	Second, represented by a number from 00 to 59.

Certain flags such as y or d have a double meaning. The following table shows how ambiguities are solved.

Example of customized presentation of dates using the flags presented in the previous table

XXX	Displays
"y/M/d h:m:s"	2/10/15 2:30:0
"yy/MM/dd HH:mm:ss"	02/10/15 14:30:00
"ddd d MMM yyy"	Tue 15 Oct 2002
"dddd d MMMM yyyy"	Tuesday 15 October 2002
"m minutes s secondes"	30 30inue0 0 0econ15e0
"m 'minutes' s 'secondes'"	30 minutes 0 secondes

- `static DateTime Parse(string s)`

    Builds a date from a character string. If the date is not valid, the `FormatException` exception is raised. If the string is empty, the `ArgumentException` exception is raised. By default, the representation of the string must the one of the current culture of *Windows*. For example, if the current culture is set to English US, you can write:

    Example 16-1

    ```
    ...
        DateTime d = DateTime.Parse( "10/15/2002 2:30:0 PM" );
        Console.WriteLine( d.ToString("G") );
    ...
    ```

    Which displays: 10/15/2002 2:30:00 PM

    If the date is represented in another culture, you can write:

    Example 16-2

    ```
    ...
        DateTime d=DateTime.Parse( "15/10/2002 14:30:0",
                    new System.Globalization.CultureInfo("en-US") );
        Console.WriteLine( d.ToString("G") );
    ...
    ```

    Which displays: 10/15/2002 2:30:00 PM

    You can also use the name of the month (abbreviated or not), for example:

    Example 16-3

    ```
    ...
        DateTime d = DateTime.Parse( "October 15 2002 2:30:0 PM" );
        Console.WriteLine( d.ToString("G") );
    ...
    ```

    Displays: 10/15/2002 2:30:00 PM

    Example 16-4

    ```
    ...
        DateTime d = DateTime.Parse( "Oct. 15 2002 2:30:0 PM" );
        Console.WriteLine( d.ToString("G") );
    ...
    ```

    Displays: 10/15/2002 2:30:00 PM

    Example 16-5

    ```
    ...
        DateTime d=DateTime.Parse( "15 octobre 2002 14:30:0",
                    new System.Globalization.CultureInfo("fr-FR") );
        Console.WriteLine( d.ToString("G"));
    ...
    ```

    Displays: 10/15/2002 2:30:00 PM

The System.TimeSpan structure

Instances of the `System.TimeSpan` structure represent duration. We showed in the previous section that such instances can be obtained from operations on dates (such as the subtraction of a date from another which returns the time span between these two dates).

The internal representation of an instance of `TimeSpan` is the same as for an instance of `DateTime`. The only difference is that such duration can be negative.

The `TimeSpan` class includes several static and non-static members. The complete list of these members can be found in the article named **TimeSpan Members** on **MSDN**. However, we will present a few of most commonly used members:

- The constructors
  `TimeSpan(int days, int hours, int minutes, int seconds)`
  `TimeSpan(int hours, int minutes, int seconds)`
  `TimeSpan(long Ticks)`
  All the arguments can take any positive or negative values.

- The extraction of temporal information in a familiar format from an instance of `TimeSpan` (non-static members):

`int Days{get;}`	Number of full days in the time span. If the time span is negative, this is the number of full negative days contained in the time span.
`Double TotalDays{get;}`	Number of days contained in the time span. The fractional part represents the remainder.
`int Hours{get;}`	Number of hours in the time span with full days taken out. The returned value is thus between 0 and 23 if the time span is positive and between 0 and –23 if the time span is negative.
`Double TotalHours{get;}`	Number of hours contained in the time span. The fractional part represents the remainder.
`int Minutes{get;}`	Number of full minutes contained in the time span with full hours taken out. The returned value is between 0 and 59 if the time span is positive and between 0 and –59 if the time span is negative.
`Double TotalMinutes{get;}`	Number of minutes contained in the time span. The fractional part represents the remainder.
`int Seconds{get;}`	Number of full seconds contained in the time span with full minutes taken out. The returned value is between 0 and 59 if the time span is positive and between 0 and –59 if the time span is negative.
`Double TotalSeconds{get;}`	Number of seconds contained in the time span. The fractional part represents the remainder.
`int Milliseconds{get;}`	Number of full milliseconds in the time span with full seconds taken out. The returned value is between 0 and 999 if the time span is positive and between 0 and –999 if the time span is negative.
`double TotalMilliseconds{get;}`	Number of milliseconds contained in the time span. The fractional part represents the remainder.
`long Ticks{get;}`	Number of 100 nanosecond intervals contained in the time span. This is thus the internal representation of the time span.

- `TimeSpan Duration()`
  Returns the duration (in an absolute value) of the time span.

- The + - != == < <= > >= operators are defined and allow to readily and logically manipulate instances of `TimeSpan`.

The System.Diagnostics.Stopwatch class

The `Sytem.Diagnostics.Stopwatch` class is specially designed to measure the elapsed time when doing performance tests. An example of the use of this class can be found at page 213.

Drives, directories, files and paths

Drives, directories (or folders) and files are an integral part of the operating system. The .NET framework offers a set of classes which allow their manipulation in a way that is independent from the underlying operating system. These classes can all be found in the `System.IO` namespace.

The management of access rights to directories and files is part of the more general framework for the management of security, which is covered on the chapter on security.

Handling drives

The .NET framework offers the `System.IO.DriveInfo` class which represents a *drive*. This class offers the `DriveInfo[] GetDrives()` static method which allows to enumerate all the available drives on the machine. When you have an instance of `DriveInfo`, the following properties let's you obtain information about the underlying drive:

Property of `DriveInfo`	Functionality
`long AvailableFreeSpace{get;}`	Returns the number of bytes free on the drive. It takes quotas into account.
`long TotalFreeSpace{get;}`	Returns the number of bytes free on the drive. Does not take quotas into account.
`string DriveFormat{get;}`	Returns the name of the file system used (NTFS, FAT32…).
`DriveType DriveType{get;}`	Returns a value of the `DriveType` which describes the type of the drive (`CDRom`, `Fixed`, `Removable`…).
`bool IsReady{get;}`	Determines if the drive is ready.
`string Name{get;}`	Returns the name of the drive.
`directoryInfo RootDirectory{get;}`	Returns the root folder of the drive.
`long TotalSize{get;}`	Returns the size in bytes of the drive.
`string VolumeLabel{get;set;}`	Returns or set the label (i.e. the name) of the drive.

This class has a constructor which accepts a string indicating the label of the drive that we wish to represent.

Handling directories

The .NET framework presents the two classes named `System.IO.Directory` and `System.IO.DirectoryInfo` which allow the manipulation of the *directory* of the operating system. Both classes support almost the same set of functionalities. In fact, they each present a different way of working with directories:

- `Directory` only contains static members. It allows working with directories without needing to instantiate an object.
- `DirectoryInfo` only contains instance members. To work with the `DirectoryInfo` class, you must instantiate it. Each instance of `DirectoryInfo` represents a directory. The `DirectoryInfo` class is derived from the `System.IO.FileSystemInfo` class which represents a file in the wide sense of the word (i.e a file or a directory).

Here are a few of the functionalities that these classes offer. For the complete list of its members, refer to **MSDN**:

Members of `Directory` or `DirectoryInfo`	Functionality

`Name`
`Attributes`
`LastAccessTime`
`LastWriteTime`
`CreationTime`
	Obtain and modify all the information relative to the directory such as its name (`Name`), its attributes (`Attributes`), the date of its last access (`LastAccessTime`), the date of its last modification (`LastWriteTime`) or its creation date (`CreationTime`).

`string Directory.GetCurrentDirectory()` `void Directory.SetCurrentDirectory(string)`	Obtain and modify the execution directory of the application.
`DirectoryInfo Directory.CreateDirectory(string)` `DirectoryInfo Directory.CreateSubdirectory(string)`	Creation of a new directory.
`void Directory.Delete(string[,bool bRecursive])` `void DirectoryInfo.Delete([bool bRecursive])`	Destruction of the directory and of its contents.
`string[] Directory.GetDirectories(string)` `DirectoryInfo[] DirectoryInfo.GetDirectories()`	Obtain the sub-directories of a directory.
`string[] Directory.GetFiles(string)` `FileInfo[] DirectoryInfo.GetFiles()`	Obtain the files contained in a directory.

Drives, directories, files and paths 505

Members of Directory or DirectoryInfo	Functionality
DirectoryInfo Directory.GetParent(string) DirectoryInfo DirectoryInfo. Parent	Obtain the parent directory of a directory.
bool Directory.Exists(string) bool DirectoryInfo.Exists	Tests if a directory exists.
void Directory.Move(string src, string dest) void DirectoryInfo.MoveTo(string src)	Moves a directory and its contents.
DirectoryInfo.Refresh()	Refresh the information contained in an instance of DirectoryInfo.

Here is an example which allows you to list the sub-directory structure of the current application. Note the recursive call to `DisplayDirectory()` and the approach used to build the indentation string:

Example 16-6
```
using System;
using System.IO;
class Program {
   static void DisplayDirectory( DirectoryInfo dir, string sIndent ) {
      Console.WriteLine( sIndent + dir.Name );
      foreach ( DirectoryInfo subDir in dir.GetDirectories() )
         DisplayDirectory( subDir, sIndent + " " );
   }
   static void Main() {
      DirectoryInfo dir=new DirectoryInfo(Directory.GetCurrentDirectory());
      DisplayDirectory( dir, string.Empty );
   }
}
```

Handling files

The .NET framework presents the two classes named `System.IO.File` and `System.IO.FileInfo` which allow to work with *files* on an operating system. Both classes support almost the same set of functionalities. In fact, they each present a different way of working with files:

- `File` only contains static members. It allows you to manipulate files without needing to create an instance of an object.
- `FileInfo` only contains instance members. To work with `FileInfo`, you must instantiate it. Each instance of `FileInfo` represents a file. `FileInfo` is derived from the `System.IO.FileSystemInfo` which represents a file in the wider sense of the word, which means files and directories.

Here is some of the functionality that they offer. For a complete listing of the members of `File` and `FileInfo`, refer to **MSDN**:

Classes which allow to work with the content of files are presented at page 525. They are part of a more general framework dedicated to the management of data streams.

Members of File or FileInfo	Functionality
Name Attributes LastWriteTime CreationTime	Obtain and modify information relative to the file such as its name (Name), its attributes (Attributes), the date of its last access (LastAccessTime), the date of its last modification (LastWriteTime) or its creation date (CreationTime).
DirectoryInfo FileInfo. Directory{get;}	Obtains the directory of a file.
bool File.Exists(string) bool FileInfo.Exists	Tests the existence of a file.
string FileInfo.Extension	Obtains the extension of a file.
long FileInfo.Length	Obtains the size of a file (in bytes).

Members of `File` or `FileInfo`	Functionality
`FileStream File.Create(string)` `FileStream File.Create()`	Creates a file.
`void File.Move(string src, string dest)` `void FileInfo.MoveTo(string)`	Moves a file.
`void File.Copy(string src, string dest,[bool bOverwrire])` `void FileInfo.CopyTo(string,[bool bOverwrire])`	Copies a file.
`void File.Delete(string)` `void FileInfo.Delete()`	Destroys a file.

Handling paths

The .NET framework offers the `System.IO.Path` class which allows the manipulation of *paths* to a file or directory, in a way which is independent of the underlying operating system. In fact, the formatting of a string representing a path depends on the underlying operating system. For example, certain operating systems represent a drive with a letter while others do not accept more than three characters for a file extension.

Paths are represented by character strings. All the members of the `Path` class are static. The class allows the manipulation of *relative paths* and of *absolute paths*.

Be cautious, in C#, the '\' character which is used to separate elements of a path must be written as "\\" in a non-*verbatim* string. Note that the `char PathSeparator` read-only property of the `Path` class represents the separation character used by the underlying operating system.

The `Path` class offers other interesting properties such as `char[] InvalidPathChars` which contain all the characters which cannot be used in a string describing a path by the underlying operating system. For the complete list of members of `Path`, refer to **MSDN**.

File System Watcher

The `System.IO.FileSystemWatcher` class allows you to intercept the events which happen to a file, to a directory or to a directory and its sub-directories. The file and folders to watch can be local or remote. However, read-only files such as those on CDs and DVDs cannot be watched.

The events of the `FileSystemWatcher` class are the following. Note that for the events to be properly intercepted, you must set the `EnableRaisingEvents` property to `true`:

- **Changed**: this event is triggered when any change happens to one of the watched objects (files or directory).
- **Created**: this event is triggered when an object (file or directory) is added in the watched directory (or one of its sub-directories).
- **Deleted**: this event is triggered when a watched object (file or directory) is destroyed.
- **Error**: internally, the `FileSystemWatcher` class contains a buffer to store the intercepted events for which the callback procedure has not yet been called. If the limit of this buffer is reached, the `Error` event is triggered. You can access and modify the size of this buffer with the `InternalBufferSize` property.
- **Renamed**: this event is triggered when a watched object (file or directory) is renamed.

You have the possibility of controlling the type of events that you wish to intercept using the following techniques:

Drives, directories, files and paths 507

- By setting the `bool IncludeSubdirectories{get;set;}` property to indicate that you also wish to watch sub-directories.
- By modifying the `string Filter{get;set;}` property of the `FileSystemWatcher` class, you can select files which are to be watched. By default, this property is set to "`*`". You can for example decide to only watch text files by assigning "`*.txt`" to this property.
- When you use the `Changed` event, you intercept the event: *the content of the file has changed*. The `NotifyFilter` property of the `FileSystemWatcher` class allows you to intercept one or several other type of changes. This property takes values from the `System.IO.NotifyFilters` binary flag:

Value of System.IO.NotifyFilters	Description
Attributs	The attributes of an object (file or directory) to watch have changed.
CreationTime	The creation date of an object (file or directory) to watch has changed.
DirectoryName	The name of a directory to watch has changed.
FileName	The name of a file to watch has changed.
LastAccess	The last access date of an object (file or directory) to watch has changed.
LastWrite	The last write access to an object (file or directory) to watch has changed.
Security	The security attributes of an object (file or directory) to watch have changed.
Size	The size of an object (file or directory) to watch has changed.

For a complete list of members of the `FileSystemWatcher` class consult **MSDN**.

The following program will watch for the changes of content, the changes of name of sub-directories and the access to all the text files located in the current directory of the application or located in one of its sub-directories:

Example 16-7
```
using System.IO;
public class Program {
    public static void Main() {
        FileSystemWatcher watcher = new FileSystemWatcher();
        watcher.Path = Directory.GetCurrentDirectory();

        watcher.NotifyFilter = NotifyFilters.LastAccess |
                               NotifyFilters.DirectoryName;

        watcher.Filter = "*.txt";
        watcher.IncludeSubdirectories = true;
        watcher.Changed += new FileSystemEventHandler( OnChange );
        watcher.EnableRaisingEvents = true;

        System.Console.WriteLine("Press \'q\' to stop the program...");
        while (System.Console.Read() != 'q' ) ;
    }

    public static void OnChange( object source, FileSystemEventArgs e ) {
        System.Console.WriteLine( "File: " + e.FullPath +
                                  " Change Type:" + e.ChangeType );
    }
}
```

Registry

Introduction

The *registry* is a database which contains most of the information consumed by the operating system. This information is extremely varied. This goes from the type of keyboard used to the preferences used by the software installed on the machine. The registry was introduced under *Windows NT 3.x*. Before, we used text files of type .ini, which had the main inconvenient of disorganizing the system. The registry aims to remove this inconvenient. You can visualize and modify the information contained in the registry using regedit.exe or regedt32.exe (under *Windows NT/200/XP* we prefer using regedt32.exe.). These editors give a hierarchical representation of the information in the registry. These are grouped as in a file system except that instead of directories, we talk of sub-keys.

It is not recommended to access the registry from your .NET applications for two reasons:

- You must never store application configuration in the registry. In fact, the XML configuration files described throughout this book were conceived especially for this. They have the advantage of being physically stored in the same directory as the application. Meaning that we can then do an XCopy deployment.

- The registry only exists under the *Microsoft* operating systems. Although that it was ported to other operating systems outside of the *Microsoft* world, its use remains marginal. If you access the registry, your application will not be easily portable to other operating systems which support .NET.

The registry structure

The hierarchy of the information contained in the registry is the following (from the most general to the most specific):

- The root keys (prefixed with HKEY_);
- The keys;
- The sub-keys;
- Value entries.

The root keys contain keys which in turn contains sub-keys. An entry is composed of three parts:

- The name of the value;
- The type of data;
- The value itself.

Each value has one of the following types. We specify the type used in the registry as well as the .NET type which is associated when reading a value from the registry from .NET code.

Type used in the registry	.NET Type	Description
REG_DWORD	System.Int32	Number encoded over four bytes. Used for the parameters of services and of drivers, memory addresses and interrupts.
REG_SZ	System.String	String in the Unicode format.
REG_MULTI_SZ	System.String[]	Array of Unicode strings.
REG_EXPAND_SZ	System.String	Expandable Unicode strings: this format is used for strings using environment variables such as %SystemRoot%.
REG_BINARY	System.Byte[]	Binary data. For example, information relating to the hardware components.

The registry hierarchy

The registry is structured with five root keys:

- HKEY_CLASSES_ROOT: Contains the following sub-keys:

    File name extensions: we find for example the .cs key which allows the association of files with the .cs extension to *Visual Studio* (or another application) by the intermediate class definition sub-keys.

    The PROGID of COM classes registered on the machine: for each PROGID we define its CLSID, and eventually attributes such as the version number of the class.

    CLSID: contains all the CLSID of all the COM classes registered on the machine. Each CLSID contains the PROGID, the path and name of the COM component file which contains the implementation of the COM class, and eventually attributes such as the execution mode of object of the class.

- HKEY_CURRENT_USER: contains the profile of the last user which opened a session on the machine. This key references the HKEY_USERS key which contains the recently used data, desktop and printer parameters, network connections and uses settings. An application can, for example, store a large quantity of information such as the size of the main window, the position of sub-windows…

- HKEY_LOCAL_MACHINE: contains the hardware and software information specific to the local machine. This data is independent of the current user. This key contains the following sub-keys:

    HARDWARE: this database is regenerated each time the system is started. It contains a description of the hardware: the data of the BIOS and of the hardware abstraction layer, parameters for SCSI and video adapters. The diagnostic program of *Windows* takes this information into account.

    SAM: security database for domains (in NT Server) and of the workgroup user accounts (in NT Workstation). The information of this key are reproduced in the HKEY_LOCAL_MACHINE\SECURITY\SAM key.

    SECURITY: the NT security sub-system draws from this sub-key the security policies and the user privileges.

    SOFTWARE: contains the data relative to the software installed on the machine.

    SYSTEM: information of the startup (services, drivers…) and the behavior of the system.

- HKEY_USERS: contains all the profile data of the current user, as well as the profile data of all the users which are connected to the machine. We also find the default profile (.DEFAULT sub-key). The policy editor allows the modification and the creation of user profiles.

- HKEY_CURRENT_CONFIG: contains the profile data for the active hardware, including the display parameters as well as hardware drivers.

Reading/writing in the registry with .NET

The Microsoft.Win32.RegistryKey class is dedicated to read/write access to the registry. Here is a little example which shows how to read the value of a key:

Example 16-8

```
// Read access to the registry key:
//HKEY_LOCAL_MACHINE/SOFTWARE/Microsoft/.NETFramework/DbgManagedDebugger
using System;
using Microsoft.Win32;
class Program {
    static void Main() {
        string[] sArr = new String[4];
```

Example 16-8
```
        sArr[0] = "HKEY_LOCAL_MACHINE";
        sArr[1] = "SOFTWARE";
        sArr[2] = "Microsoft";
        sArr[3] = ".NETFramework";

        string sSubKey = "DbgManagedDebugger";

        string sKey = sArr[0];
        RegistryKey rKey = Registry.LocalMachine;
        for ( int i = 1; i < sArr.Length; i++ ) {
           sKey += "/" + sArr[i];
           rKey = rKey.OpenSubKey( sArr[i] );
        }
        Console.WriteLine( "Key value  {0}/{1}", sKey, sSubKey );
        Console.WriteLine( rKey.GetValue( sSubKey ) );
     }
  }
```

This program displays:

```
Key value  HKEY_LOCAL_MACHINE/SOFTWARE/Microsoft/.NETFramework/
DbgManagedDebugger
C:\Program Files\Common Files\Microsoft Shared\VS7Debug\vs7jit.exe
 PID %d AP PDOM %d EXTEXT "%s" EVTHDL %d
```

Debugging

Attributes to customize the view of your objects at debug-time

The `System.Diagnostics` namespace offers attributes which allows you to customize the display of the state of your objects during debugging:

- `DebuggerDisplayAttribute`

  Applies to classes, structures, delegate types, enumerations, fields, properties and assemblies. This attribute allows the personalization of the description line provided by the debugger. This line can contain expressions between braces which can be the name of a property, field or method. Understand that such a line must remain concise:

Example 16-9
```
  using System.Diagnostics;
  [DebuggerDisplay("{Description} price:{m_Price} $")]
  class Article {
     private decimal m_Price;
     private string m_Description;
     public string Description { get{return m_Description;} }
     public Article(string description,decimal price) {
        m_Description = description;
        m_Price = price;
     }
  }
  class Program  {
     static void Main() {
        Article article = new Article( "Shoes", 120 );
     }
  }
```

Debugging

```
class Program {
    static void Main() {
        Article article = new Article("Shoes", 120);
    }
}
```

article "Shoes" price:120 $
- Description   "Shoes"
- m_Description "Shoes"
- m_Price   120

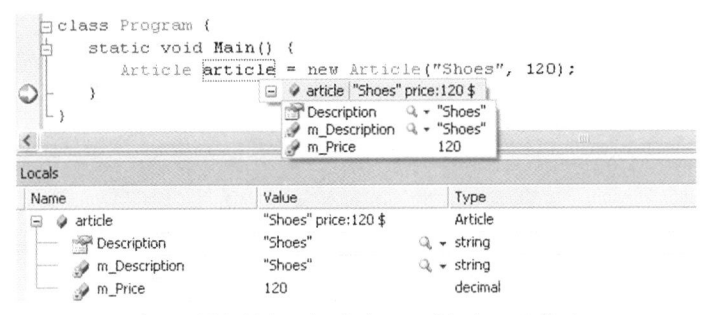

Locals

Name	Value	Type
article	"Shoes" price:120 $	Article
Description	"Shoes"	string
m_Description	"Shoes"	string
m_Price	120	decimal

Figure 16-1: Using the DebuggerDisplay attribute

- **DebuggerBrowsable**

  Applies to fields and properties. Allows to tell the debugger how it must display this property or field using one of the three values of the `DebuggerBrowsableState` enumeration which are:

  Collapsed: the debugger displays the value of the field of property when the state of the object is collapsed (this is the default behavior);

  RootHidden: the debugger does not display the value when the object is collapsed but displays the values of the sub-members of the concerned property or field;

  Never: the debugger will never display the value when the state of the object is collapsed.

- **DebuggerTypeProxyAttribute**

  Applies to structures, classes and assemblies. This attribute applied to a type T allows to specify a proxy type dedicated for displaying the state of an instance of T. Generally, this proxy type is a class nested in the T type since such a class can access all the private members of the encapsulating type:

Example 16-10

```
[System.Diagnostics.DebuggerTypeProxy( typeof( ArticleProxy ) )]
class Article {
   private class ArticleProxy {
      private Article m_Article;
      public ArticleProxy(Article article) { m_Article = article; }
      public string Price { get{ return m_Article.m_Price + " $"; } }
   }
   private decimal m_Price;
   private string m_Description;
   public Article( string description, decimal price ) {
      m_Description = description;
      m_Price = price;
   }
}
class Program  {
   static void Main() {
      Article article = new Article( "Shoes", 120 );
   }
}
```

Note the presence of the `Raw View` property which allows obtaining the default view of the state of the object:

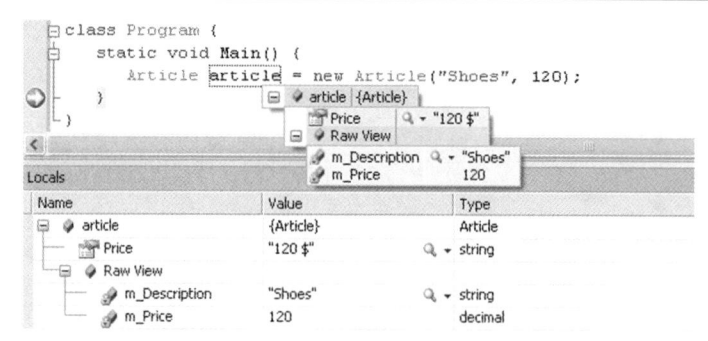

Figure 16-2: Using the DebuggerTypeProxy attribute

- DebuggerVisualizerAttribute
  Applies to structures, classes and assemblies. This attribute constitutes the corner stone of a very powerful state visualization system for objects during debugging. The idea is to draw the state of an object directly in a window using GDI+. We can thus visualize an image, a 3D object or a graph during debugging. More information on the use of this attribute can be found on **MSDN**.

Debugging Just My Code (JMC)

.NET 2 offers the possibility of specifying to the debugger the assemblies, modules or regions of code that you do not wish to debug by the intermediate of attributes declared in the `System.Diagnostics` namespace. In general, we use these attributes to not be bothered during the debugging of the code of libraries that we use. This functionality is known as *Just My Code (JMC)*. It is activated by default but you can deactivate it under *Visual Studio 2005* with *Tools › Options › Debugging › Enable Just My Code*. During the debugging, you can also decide to temporarily disable JMC by right-clicking on the *Call Stack* window and selecting the *External Code* option. Here are the related attributes:

- DebuggerHiddenAttribute
  Applies to constructors, methods and properties. This attributes allows specifying hidden code. If JMC is activated, the debugger will not enter the code of this method even if it contains a breakpoint. If a method tagged with this attribute calls a method which is not tagged with this attribute, it is still possible to debug the code of this second method. In this case, the call stack window will show `External Code` in the window.

- DebuggerStepThroughAttribute
  Applies to classes, structures, constructors and methods. This attribute is comparable to `DebuggerHiddenAttribute` except that in the described situation, instead of displaying an `External Code` stack frame in the call stack window, no stack frame will be displayed at all.

- DebuggerNonUserCodeAttribute
  Applies to classes, structures, constructors, methods and properties. This attribute is comparable to `DebuggerHiddenAttribute`.

Debugging modes

The `System.Diagnostics` namespace also presents the `DebuggableAttribute` attribute which applies to assemblies and modules. This attribute allows to specify or not the set of debugging modes that the JIT compiler must apply on the IL code of the target assembly or module. These modes are described by the `DebuggableAttribute.DebuggingModes` binary flag. We can mention the *Edit and Continue* mode, the *deactivated JIT optimization* mode, the *ignore the .pdb file information* mode or the mode which allows the production of information by the JIT compiler which establishes a link between the IL code and the generated machine code (*JIT tracking*).

Solving debugging problems

It sometimes happens that you cannot debug you application properly. *MinKwan Park* has written an excellent entry in his blog which describes several problematic situations and their solution (for now only available for .NET 2003). This article is available at `http://blogs.msdn.com/mkpark/articles/86872.aspx`.

Traces

The NET framework presents the `System.Diagnostics.Trace` and `System.Diagnostics.Debug` classes which allows you to trace the execution of a program. We sometimes talk of an execution *log* for the program. Each of these classes offer the four methods named `Write(string)`, `WriteLine(string)`, `WriteIf(bool,string)` and `WriteLineIf(bool,string)` which can, for example, be used like this:

Example 16-11
```
using System.Diagnostics;
class Program {
   static void Main() {
      Trace.Listeners.Add( new ConsoleTraceListener() );
      Trace.WriteLine( "Trace hello" );
      for( int i=0; i<5; i++ )
         Debug.WriteLineIf( i > 2, "debug i=" + i.ToString() );
   }
}
```

Here is the display of this program on the console:

```
Trace hello
debug i=3
debug i=4
```

The `Trace` class is mostly dedicated to the logging of information on the functioning of the application while the `Debug` class is destined to trace information which is useful for debugging. From this fact, they are relatively similar although they are used for different purposes. These two classes work properly only if the assembly is compiled using the `TRACE` and/or `DEBUG` symbolic constants.

Listener

Example 16-11 started with the line:

```
      Trace.Listeners.Add( new ConsoleTraceListener() );
```

This means that the *list of listeners* will contain a *listener* of type `ConsoleTraceListener`. A listener is an instance of a subclass of `System.Diagnostics.TraceListener`. The list of listeners is common to the `Debug` and `Trace` classes. When a trace is logged by one of these classes, each of the listeners of the list writes the trace using its own persistence mechanism, for example, the console for a listener of type `ConsoleTraceListener`. Other listener classes are provided by the framework (the classes in bold have been added with .NET 2.0):

```
System.Diagnostics.TraceListener
   Microsoft.VisualBasic.Logging.FileLogTraceListener
   System.Diagnostics.DefaultTraceListener
   System.Diagnostics.EventLogTraceListener
   System.Diagnostics.TextWriterTraceListener
      System.Diagnostics.ConsoleTraceListener
      System.Diagnostics.DelimitedListTraceListener
      System.Diagnostics.XmlWriterTraceListener
   System.Web.WebPageTraceListener
```

- `DefaultTraceListener`: Traces in the data stream dedicated for debugging. By default, this data stream is redirected to the output window of *Visual Studio*.
- `EventLogTraceListener`: Traces in the *Windows* event log.
- `TextWriterTraceListener`: Traces in a data stream such as a file.
- `DelimitedListTraceListener`: Traces in a data stream such as a file. At the difference of `TextWriterTraceListener`, the traces are separated by a string (such as a semi-colon) in order to be easily usable by a trace analysis program.
- `XMLWriterTraceListener`: Traces in an XML file which follows a certain XML schema.
- `WebPageTraceListener`: Used by ASP.NET. Traces directly in the web page that is being constructed.

You have the possibility of building the list of listeners through the configuration file. For example, this configuration file adds a listener of type `ConsoleTraceListener` to the list:

Example 16-12
```xml
<?xml version="1.0" encoding="utf-8" ?>
<configuration
   xmlns="http://schemas.microsoft.com/.NetConfiguration/v2.0">
    <system.diagnostics>
       <trace>
          <listeners>
             <add name="TraceOnConsole"
                  type="System.Diagnostics.ConsoleTraceListener"/>
          </listeners>
       </trace>
    </system.diagnostics>
</configuration>
```

If Example 16-11 is used conjointly with this configuration file, the listener list will contain two listeners which both trace on the console and the program will display each trace twice:

```
Trace hello
Trace hello
debug i=3
debug i=3
debug i=4
debug i=4
```

Finally, know that you can develop your own listener classes derived from `TraceListener`.

Trace source and source level

The .NET 2 framework introduces the `System.Diagnostics.TraceSource` class which allows the management of several *trace sources*. Each trace source is named and has its own list of listeners. The trace sources are active during execution only if the **TRACE** symbol is specified during compilation. In general, the trace sources are accessible from the static fields of a class visible from the whole application.

A filter system on the severity of a trace is implemented. Here is a use example of this system. Here, the filter accepts all the traces (`SourceLevels.All`) and our traces have the severity level *information* (`TraceInformation()`) and *warning* (`TraceEventType.Warning`):

Example 16-13

```
using System.Diagnostics;
class Program {
   static void Main() {
      Trace.Listeners.Add( new ConsoleTraceListener() );
      TraceSource trace1 = new TraceSource( "Trace1" );
      trace1.Listeners.Add( new ConsoleTraceListener() );
      trace1.Switch.Level = SourceLevels.All;
      trace1.TraceInformation( "Trace hello" );
      for ( int i = 0; i < 2; i++ )
         trace1.TraceData( TraceEventType.Warning, 122,
                           "debug i=" + i.ToString());
   }
}
```

This program displays the following on the console:

```
Trace1 Information: 0 : Trace hello
Trace1 Warning: 122 : debug i=0
Trace1 Warning: 122 : debug i=1
```

It would have not displayed the Trace Hello trace if we had chosen SourceLevels.Warning. The concept of *switch* can also be implemented with instance of the SourceSwitch class:

Example 16-14

```
...
      TraceSource trace1 = new TraceSource( "Trace1" );
      SourceSwitch switch1 = new SourceSwitch( "Switch1" );
      switch1.Level = SourceLevels.All;
      trace1.Switch = switch1;
...
```

A trace source can be configured after compilation thanks to the configuration file. With the following configuration file, we would only need to create a trace source named Trace1 in our code:

Example 16-15

```
<?xml version="1.0" encoding="utf-8" ?>
<configuration
  xmlns="http://schemas.microsoft.com/.NetConfiguration/v2.0">
    <system.diagnostics>
      <sources>
        <source name="Trace1" switchName="Switch1">
          <listeners>
            <add name="TraceOnConsole"
                 type="System.Diagnostics.ConsoleTraceListener" />
          </listeners>
        </source>
      </sources>
      <switches>
        <add name="Switch1" value="All" />
      </switches>
    </system.diagnostics>
</configuration>
```

Filtering trace sources

A second filtering level exists with listeners. A listener has the possibility of accepting traces issued from certain sources. Here, the filter assigned to the listener of type `ConsoleTraceListener` only accepts traces issues by a fictitious trace source named `TraceXXX` and consequently this program will display nothing:

Example 16-16

```
...
    TraceSource trace1 = new TraceSource( "Trace1" );
    ConsoleTraceListener listener = new ConsoleTraceListener();
    listener.Filter = new SourceFilter( "TraceXXX" );
    trace1.Listeners.Add( listener );
...
```

Trace indent

The `Debug` and `Trace` classes offers the `Indent()` and `Unindent()` methods which allows to increase and decrease the indentation level of your traces. Also, the `IndentSize` property defines the number of spaces for an indentation level:

Example 16-17

```
using System.Diagnostics;
class Program {
   static void Main() {
      Trace.Listeners.Add(new ConsoleTraceListener());
      Trace.IndentSize = 3;
      Trace.WriteLine( "Begin Main()" );
      fct( 2 );
      Trace.WriteLine( "End Main()" );
   }
   static void fct( int i ) {
      Trace.Indent();
      Trace.WriteLine( "Begin fct(" + i.ToString() + ")" );
      if (i > 0)
         fct(i-1);
      Trace.WriteLine( "End fct(" + i.ToString() + ")" );
      Trace.Unindent();
   }
}
```

This program displays the following on the console:

```
Begin Main()
   Begin fct(2)
      Begin fct(1)
         Begin fct(0)
         End fct(0)
      End fct(1)
   End fct(2)
End Main()
```

The `TraceSource` class does not offer this feature. The following program shows how you can work around this through an `IndentLevel` property which calculates the current indentation level from the current size of the call stack of the current thread. Hence, the display of this program is identical to the previous:

Regular expressions

Example 16-18

```
using System.Diagnostics;
class Program {
   static TraceSource trace1;
   const int IndentSize = 3;
   static string IndentLevel { get{
       StackTrace stackTrace = new StackTrace();
       return new string(' ',(stackTrace.FrameCount - 2)* IndentSize);
      }
   }
   static void Main() {
      trace1 = new TraceSource( "Trace1" );
      trace1.Listeners.Add(new ConsoleTraceListener());
      trace1.Switch.Level = SourceLevels.All;
      trace1.TraceInformation( IndentLevel + "Begin Main()");
      fct( 2 );
      trace1.TraceInformation( IndentLevel + "End Main()");
   }
   static void fct( int i ) {
      trace1.TraceInformation( IndentLevel+"Begin fct("+i.ToString()+")" );
      if (i > 0)
         fct(i-1);
      trace1.TraceInformation( IndentLevel+"End fct(" + i.ToString()+")" );
   }
}
```

Regular expressions

Introduction

Regular expressions, often named *regexp* or *regex* are a powerful tool to accomplish three major kinds of operations on strings:

- Regular expressions allow to **verify** that a string abide by certain syntax rules (for example, if an email address contains characters before and after the @ character and if the name of the server contains a valid extension such as *.com*, *.org* or *.edu*).
- Regular expressions allow to **modify** a string by replacing an element with another.
- Regular expressions allow to **extract** elements from a string.

The notion of regular expression was especially popularized with the *Unix grep* command which allows the filtering of data. The filter is itself configured using a regular expression.

We will now present a few of the main points of regular expressions.

Syntax

A regular expression presents itself as a string. Each character of this string has a specific meaning. Here are the most common:

Character(s)	Meaning
\	Cancels the meaning of a meta-character.
^	Start of a line.
.	Any character.
$	End of line.
x|y	x or y.

Character(s)	Meaning
( )	Grouping.
[xyz]	Set of character (x or y or z).
[x-z]	Character interval (x or y or z).
[^x]	All except x.

You can also specify the number of occurrences of a regular expression with the following expressions:

Character(s)	Meaning
x*	Zero, one or several occurrences of x.
x+	One or several occurrences of x.
x?	Zero or one occurrence of x.
x{n}	Exactly n occurrences of x.
x{n,}	At least n occurrences of x.
x{n,m}	At least n, but at most m occurrences of x.

Finally, there exist several practical aliases:

Character(s)	Alias for	Meaning
\n		End of line character.
\r		A line feed character.
\t		A tab.
\s	[\f\n\r\t\v]	A white space.
\S	[^\f\n\r\t\v]	Everything that isn't a white space
\d	[0-9]	A digit.
\D	[^0-9]	All but digit.
\w	[a-zA-Z0-9_]	An alphanumerical character.
\W	[^a-zA-Z0-9_]	All but an alphanumerical character.
\067	7	A character in octal notation.
\x5A	Z	A character in hexadecimal notation.

Examples

Here are a few examples of regular expression as well as their meaning:

- The regular expression below verifies if a string begins with an upper cased letter.

    [A-Z].*

- The regular expression below verifies if a string contains at least one non-alphanumerical character.

    .*[^0-9A-Za-zÀ-ÿ].*

- The regular expression below verifies is a string ends by "el" or "elle".

    .*(el|elle)

- The regular expression below verifies if a string is a date with the yyyy-mm-dd format between 1900 01-01 and 2099 12-31.

    (19|20)\d\d[- /.](0[1-9]|1[012])[- /.](0[1-9]|[12][0-9]|3[01])

.NET and regular expressions

The `System.Text.RegularExpressions.RegEx` class allows the use of regular expressions to verify a syntax rule on a string, to modify a string or to extract elements from a string. The following program shows these features:

Regular expressions

Example 16-19

```csharp
using System;
using System.Text.RegularExpressions;
public class Program {
   static void Main() {
      // Using a regexp to check that a string doesn't contains digits.
      Regex regex1 = new Regex( "^[^0-9]*$" );
      bool b = regex1.IsMatch( "ab3de" ); // b is false
      b = regex1.IsMatch( "abcde" ); // b is true

      // Replace the word 'nice' by the word 'pretty'.
      Regex regex2 = new Regex( "nice" );
      // Display 'She is pretty.'.
      Console.WriteLine( regex2.Replace( "She is nice.", "pretty" ) );

      // Extract words separated by a space.
      Regex regex3 = new Regex( "[ ]" );
      string[] words = regex3.Split(
         "Age is a very high price to pay for maturity" );
      foreach ( string word in words )
         Console.WriteLine( word );
   }
}
```

Optimizing the evaluation of regular expressions

We explain at page 212 how to optimize certain operations thanks to the generation of assemblies. Regular expressions are a good candidate for this type of optimization. Also, the `RegExp` class offers the `CompileToAssembly()` static method which easily allows to accomplish such an optimization. The following program produces an assembly named `regexp.dll` which contains the `CompiledExpressions.NoDigits` class which derives from the `RegEx` class.

Example 16-20

```csharp
using System.Reflection;
using System.Text.RegularExpressions;
public class Program {
   static void Main() {
      string sExpression = "^[^0-9]*$";
      RegexCompilationInfo info = new RegexCompilationInfo(
         sExpression,
         RegexOptions.Compiled,
         "NoDigits",
         "CompiledExpressions",
         true);
      RegexCompilationInfo[] infos = new RegexCompilationInfo[] { info };
      AssemblyName assemblyName = new AssemblyName();
      assemblyName.Name = "Regex";
      Regex.CompileToAssembly( infos, assemblyName );
   }
}
```

The following example shows how to measure the optimization factor of such a compiled regular expression:

Example 16-21
```
using System;
using System.Text.RegularExpressions;
using CompiledExpressions;
using System.Diagnostics;

public class Program {
   const int NLOOP = 1000000;
   const string str = "abcdefghijklmnopqrstuvwxyz";
   static void Main() {
      bool b;
      Regex regex1 = new Regex("^[^0-9]*$");
      Stopwatch sw = Stopwatch.StartNew();
      for ( int i = 0; i < NLOOP; i++ )
         b = regex1.IsMatch( str );
      Console.WriteLine( "Without precompile:{0}", sw.Elapsed );

      sw = Stopwatch.StartNew();
      DateTime dateDebut2 = DateTime.Now;
      NoDigits regex2 = new NoDigits();
      for ( int i = 0; i < NLOOP; i++ )
         b = regex2.IsMatch( str );
      Console.WriteLine( "With precompile:{0}", sw.Elapsed );
   }
}
```

We have done several tests with regular expression to verify that there is no digits ("^[^0-9]*$") and the regular expression to verify a date (@"(19|20)\d\d[- /.](0[1-9]|1[012])[- /.](0[1-9]|[12][0-9]|3[01])"). The test strings were the alphabet ("abcdefghijklmnopqrstuvwxyz") and a double alphabet ("abcdefghijklmnopqrstuvwxyz-abcdefghijklmnopqrstuvwxyz"). Here are the optimization factors we obtained:

Regular expression	String tested	Optimization factor
No digits	alphabet	1,21
No digits	double alphabet	1,12
Date verification	alphabet	3,99
Date verification	double alphabet	4,03

Console

The `System.Console` class allows to control the display and the capture of data on the console. All the functionalities of this class are available through static members since an application can have at most one console.

Cursor

The console supports a cursor which represents the place where the next display of data will be done.

- By default, the cursor is displayed after the last character displayed but you can set its position with the `SetCursorPosition(int column,int row)` method.
- You can obtain or modify the current position of the cursor using the `int CursorTop{get; set;}` and `int CursorLeft{get;set;}` properties.

- You can choose to make the cursor visible or not using the `int CursorVisible{get;set;}` property.
- You can obtain or set the size of the cursor using the `int CursorSize{get ;set}` property which takes values in the `[1,100]` closed interval. The size of the cursor designates the fill percentage of the rectangle for the cursor.

Display

- You can display a string where the cursor is located by calling the `Write()` method. The `WriteLine()` method forces the cursor to move to a new line after displaying the data.
- The `MoveBufferArea(int sourceLeft, int sourceTop, int sourceWidth, int sourceHeight, int targetLeft, int targetTop)` method allows you to move a block of data. The source rectangle specified must be completely visible. It is possible that part of the data be truncated if the destination rectangle is not completely contained in the visible part of the console.
- The `Clear()` method allows to erase all the data currently visible in the console and sets the cursor in the upper left corner.

Size and position

- You can modify the position of the console on the screen using the `SetWindowsPosition(int left, int top)` method. The parameters specify the number of pixels from the upper left corner of the screen. You can obtain or modify the current position of the console using the `int WindowLeft{get;set;}` and `int WindowTop{get;set;}` properties.
- You can modify the size of the console using the `SetWindowsSize(int nColumn, int nRow)` method. You can obtain or modify the size of the console (in terms of the number of rows and columns) using the `int WindowWidth{get;set;}` and `int WindowHeight{get;set;}` properties.
- You can obtain the largest number of possible rows or columns based on the screen resolution by using the `int LargestWindowWidth{get;}` and `int LargestWindowHeight{get;}` properties.
- The number of rows and columns that the console contains can exceed the size of the console. You can obtain the number of rows and columns using the `int BufferWidth{get;set;}` and `int BufferHeight{get;set;}` properties.

Color

The `Console` class allows you to modify the color of the data that you display by specifying the color using the `System.ConsoleColor` enumeration.

- The `ConsoleColor ForegroundColor{get;set;}` and `ConsoleColor BackgroundColor {get;set;}` properties allow to obtain and set the *foreground* and *background* colors of the next data to be displayed.
- You can reset the *foreground* and *background* colors to their default values by calling the `ResetColor()` method.

Data input

- You can obtain the next character typed on the keyboard by the user by calling the `int ReadKey()` method. The call to this method is blocking until a character is typed on the keyboard. After, the character corresponding to the key which was pressed is displayed on the console. You can convert the returned integer in an instance of `char` by calling the `char Convert.ToChar(int)` method. The `int ReadKey(bool)` overload does not display the character on the console when we specify `false` as an argument.

- The `bool KeyAvailable{get;}` property allows to check if the next call to the `ReadKey()` will block or not.
- The `string ReadLine()` returns the line which was input by the user. This method will block until the user presses the *Enter* key.
- The `bool TreatControlCAsInput{get;set;}` allows to control whether or not the *Ctrl-C* will be treated as a normal input or not. If you set this property to `false` you can take advantage of the `CancelPressedKey` event.
- The `bool NumberLock{get;}` and `bool CapsLock{get;}` properties allows to know if the *NumLock* and *CapsLock* keyboard modes are currently active.

Redirecting console streams

You can modify or obtain the input, output and error data streams of the console. A data stream is an instance of the `System.IO.Stream` abstract class. By default, the input data stream is the keyboard while the output and the error data streams are the console.

You can obtain one of these data streams using one of the three properties named `TextReader In{get;}`, `TextWriter Out{get;}` or `TextWriter Error{get;}`.

You can set these data streams using one of the three methods named `void SetError(TextWriter newError)`, `void SetIn(TextReader newIn)` or `void SetOut(TextWriter newOut)`.

Miscellaneous

- The `Beep()` method allows you to play a beep on the computer. An overload of this method allows specifying the frequency and duration of this beep.
- The `string Title{get;set }` property allows you to get or set the window title of the console.

17
Input/Output and Streams

The base classes of the .NET framework allowing the input/output of data can, for the most part, be found in the `System.IO` namespace.

Introduction to streams

Class hierarchy for streams

The `System.IO.Stream` class is the base class for all classes who want to do stream based inputs/outputs. The `Stream` is an abstract class. There exist three types of manipulations which can be done on a data stream:

- Read access to the data.
- Write access to the data.
- Random access to the data (*seek*). This feature allows the user to move the *cursor* forward and backwards within the stream of data. The cursor defines the location within the data stream where the next read/write operation will take place. If this feature is not supported by a data stream, the use of the `Length` and `Position` properties as well as the use of the `SetLength()` and `Seek()` methods of the `Stream` class will cause the `NotSupportedException` exception to be raised. If this property is not supported by a data stream, we say that such a stream is *forward-only*.

You can test to see which manipulations are supported by a data stream by using the `CanRead`, `CanWrite` and `CanSeek` properties of the `Stream` class. Here is the list of subclasses:

- `System.IO.FileStream`
  This class allows the representation of a data stream to a file. This type of data stream is described at page 526. It can also support all three types of accesses.
- `System.IO.IsolatedStorage.IsolatedStorageFileStream`
  This class derives from the `FileStream` class. It allows implementing *isolated storage* described at page 170, in the chapter relating to security.
- `System.Net.Sockets.NetworkStream`
  This class allows the representation of a data stream to a remote entity using sockets (see page 530). This type of data stream never supports random access.
- `System.IO.Ports.SerialPort`
  This class allows the representation of a data stream to a serial port (see page 545). This type of data stream never supports random access.

Facilities to handle streams

The .NET framework proposes an architecture which allows the addition of services to a data stream. This architecture is described at page 543. Here is the list of classes representing the services on a data stream. They are all derived from the `Stream` class:

- `System.Net.Security.AuthenticatedStream`
  The classes which are derived from this class are implementations of stream security protocols making use of authentication and encryption (see page 546).

- `System.Security.Cryptography.CryptoStream`
  This class allows the encryption of a data stream. A stream which uses this service never supports random access (see page 549).

- `System.IO.BufferedStream`
  This class is used conjointly with a data stream in order to provide buffer memory to it. The use of `BufferedStream` allows to improve performance in certain cases, such as discussed at page 544. `BufferedStream` supports all the access types of the underlying data stream.

- `System.IO.MemoryStream` and `System.IO.UnmanagedMemoryStream`
  These classes allow to obtain buffer memory which can be shared between several data streams (see page 545). The *unmanaged* version allows you to avoid a copy on the CLR heap and is thus more efficient.

- `System.IO.Compression.DeflateStream System.IO.Compression.GZipStream`
  These classes allow the compression/decompression of a data stream (see page 545).

Stream data typing

In addition to the classes which allows the representation of a data stream, the `System.IO` namespace offers several pairs of classes which allows the typing of the input or output bytes of a data stream. Each pair contains a class for input and one class for output. Here is the list of theses pair of classes:

- `System.IO.BinaryWriter` and `System.IO.BinaryReader`
  These classes allow the read and write of data encoded in a primitive .NET type from a data stream. These classes offer methods such as `short ReadInt16()`, `void Write(short)`, `double ReadDouble()` or `void Write(double)`.

- `System.IO.TextWriter` and `System.IO.TextReader`
  These classes are abstract. They are used as base classes to the classes which allow the reading and writing of characters encoded in a certain format. The presentation of these formats is the topic of the next section. These classes offer methods such as `string ReadLine()` or `void WriteLine(string)`.

- `System.IO.StringWriter` and `System.IO.StringReader`
  These classes are respectively derived from `TextWriter` and `TextReader`. They are used to read and write characters (or strings) to a (or from a) string.

- `System.IO.StreamWriter` and `System.IO.StreamReader`
  These classes are respectively derived from `TextWriter` and `TextReader`. They are used to read and write characters (or strings) encoded in a particular format, to any (or from any) type of data stream.

String encoding

The problem of *string encoding* is to associate to a character such as letter, digit or symbol a certain binary representation. One of the first standards for the encoding of characters was the 7 bit *ASCII* standard (*American Standard Code for Information Interchange*), which represented 128 characters such as the 26 lower and upper cased letters of occidental alphabet or even the 10 digits. In the ASCII standard, the 8th bit was either set to zero or used as a parity bit.

The ASCII character set is sufficient for English/US applications. Quickly, the need to represent accentuated characters for international application has appeared. Each language having a different set of characters, they could not be encoded within 256 values. There appeared various sets of 256 *OEM (Original Equipment Manufacturer)* characters. These sets are named *codepages*.

The OEM codepages are sufficient for several languages such as English, French and Spanish but cannot represent the alphabet of certain languages such as Chinese or Arabic. With this, appeared the invention of the *UNICODE* standard. This standard assigns to (almost) all possible combinations of 16 bits, a character of most alphabets as well as various common symbols. The first 256 characters of UNICODE correspond to the ones of the ISO 8859-1 codepage. UNICODE goes further than the previous formats by taking into account the fact that various processors do not manage integers in the same way. In fact, certain processors (such as the ones by *Intel*) first works with the eight least significant bits (we say that they are *little-endian*) while other work with the eight most significant bits first (we say that they are *big-endian*). A data stream being a series of bits, we must transform certain bytes for certain processors. This transformation is named *UTF (Universal Transformation Format)*. There are several UTF standards, UTF-7, UTF-8 and UTF-16.

The *UTF-8* standard is the most commonly used at the moment. It has the particularity of having a variable number of bytes in order to represent UNICODE characters. This number of bytes can go from 1 to 5. The characters represented by one byte are the 128 characters of the ASCII standard. Accentuated characters not being part of this set, they are coded on more than one byte. If a text editor supports UTF-8 encoding, it will correctly reproduce accentuated characters. If not, several symbol characters will replace each accentuated character. You may have encountered this problem before, especially when reading emails.

During the processing of a data stream relating to characters using either the `StreamWriter` or `StreamReader` classes, we have the possibility of specifying the encoding format used with one of the following classes:

```
System.Object
    System.Text.Encoding
        System.Text.ASCIIEncoding
        System.Text.UnicodeEncoding
        System.Text.UTF7Encoding
        System.Text.UTF8Encoding
```

The `Encoding` class contains methods allowing the conversion of a string from one format to another.

Reading and writing files

Simple read/write on a file

The `File` class offers six methods which allow to easily read and write into a file:

- The `ReadAllText()` and `WriteAllText()` methods allow to read or write a string from or into a file.
- The `ReadAllLines()` and `WriteAllLines()` methods allow to read or write an array of strings from or into a file.
- The `ReadAllBytes()` and `WriteAllBytes()` methods allow to read or write a byte array from or into a file.

The write methods create the file if it does not already exist and will erase the current data if the file already exists. Also, all these methods properly close the used file. The following example shows how to replicate a text file while displaying its contents on the screen:

Example 17-1
```
using System.IO;
public class Program {
   public static void Main() {
      string text = File.ReadAllText( @"G:\source\Test.txt" );
      System.Console.Write( text );
      File.WriteAllText( @"G:\source\TestCopy.txt",text );
   }
}
```

Reading and writing binary data in a file

We are about to show how to duplicate a binary file using data streams. Here are the steps to accomplish this:

- Create an input data stream for the source file using an instance of the `System.IO.FileStream` class.
- Create an output data stream for the destination file using an instance of the `FileStream` class.
- Transfer the content from the source file to the destination. You do not need to interpret the content of this file and does not need to use the data stream typing classes.

To transfer the data between an input and output data stream, we generally use a *buffer*. The buffer is a memory region which is filled by the input stream then emptied into the output stream. This fill/empty operation is done as many times as needed.

The following program copies the executable file of the current assembly to a file named `Copy.exe`, located in the folder of the application. Of course, the current application cannot be named `Copy.exe`.

Example 17-2
```
using System.IO;
public class Program {
   static readonly int bufferSize = 512;
   public static void Main() {
      // The name of the default AppDomain is equal to the...
      // ...name of the current assembly (with the extension).
      string sExe = System.AppDomain.CurrentDomain.FriendlyName;
      // Src and dest files are in the application folder.
      FileStream inStream = File.OpenRead( sExe );
      FileStream outStream = File.OpenWrite( "Copy.exe" );
      // Need a buffer.
      byte[] buffer = new System.Byte[ bufferSize ];
      int nBytesRead = 0;
      // Copy binary data.
      while ( ( nBytesRead = inStream.Read( buffer, 0, bufferSize ) ) > 0 )
         outStream.Write( buffer, 0, nBytesRead );
      // Close streams.
      inStream.Close();
      outStream.Close();
   }
}
```

Reading and writing text in a file

Here we present the copy of a text file using the `System.IO.StreamWriter` and `System.IO.StreamReader` classes. We will copy our text file line-by-line. The length of a line being unbound, we cannot use a buffer of a fixed size. For the copy of each line, we use a new string built by the `ReadLine()` method of the `StreamReader` class. We will then use the `WriteLine()` method of `StreamWriter` to copy this string into the destination file.

Each line is displayed on the console using the `WriteLine()` method of the `Console` class. A difference between these two `WriteLine()` methods is that the version of the `Console` is static while the version of the `StreamWriter` is an instance method.

Example 17-3

```
using System.IO;
public class Program {
   public static void Main() {
      StreamReader inStream = File.OpenText( @"G:\source\Test.txt" );
      StreamWriter outStream = new StreamWriter(@"G:\source\TestCopy.txt");
      // Copy lines of the source file in the destination file.
      string sTmp;
      do {
         sTmp = inStream.ReadLine();
         outStream.WriteLine( sTmp );
         System.Console.WriteLine( sTmp );
      }
      while ( sTmp != null );
      // Close streams.
      inStream.Close();
      outStream.Close();
   }
}
```

The notion of character encoding seems to be missing in this example, and yet this example works no matter what the encoding format is in the source file. In fact, if the user does not specify a specific encoding to the `StreamReader` class, it will automatically detect the encoding by analyzing the first few characters of the text file. Each type of encoding provides a special marker on the first few characters of the text file. You can obtain this marker by using the `byte[] GetPreamble()` method of the appropriate class derived from `Encoding`. For example, this marker is the three `0xEF 0xBB 0xBF` bytes for the UTF8 encoding, `0xFF 0xFE` for the UNICODE encoding and nothing for the ASCII encoding. This marker is not necessarily present in all text files and you have the option of deactivating the output of such a marker when you write in a text file using the `StreamWriter` class. In this case, the *Microsoft* implementation uses the UTF-8 encoding by default.

The `Encoding CurrentEncoding{get;}` property of the `StreamReader` class allows you to know the currently used encoding. This property is automatically set at the first read in a text file. In the same way, the `StreamWriter` offers the `Encoding Encoding{get;}` property.

Working asynchronously with streams

The processing of a data stream linearly depends on the size of the data source. The developer of an application which processes one or several data streams may have a rough idea of this size but most often, will not know ahead of time. The time required to process a data stream is thus unknown from the developer. If such a process is done by the main thread of an application, the result may be disastrous as the application may pause for an unknown amount of time. In addition, if the application has several data streams which are to be processed independently, it would be better to process them in parallel.

The asynchronous processing of a data stream solves these problems. It allows the delegation of this processing onto another thread. The developer does not need to manage this other thread as it is part of the CLR's *thread pool*. As we will see in the next example, it is easy to launch in parallel the processing of several data streams. The use of such an architecture for your application can prove itself several order of magnitude more efficient than a simple sequential processing of your streams.

The following example illustrates the parallel launch of N asynchronous processes. First of all, we create a large file of about 10MB using the `CreateBlobFile()` method. Then, NRead reads of this file are done in parallel in our loop using the `BeginRead()` method of `FileStream`. The threads designated to execute this processing are those from the thread pool. The `BeginRead()` method allows you to specify a *callback method* which will be called once the read is complete. It is the same thread that executes the read that will call this callback method. In the example, the `CallbackOnReadDone()` method is used as our callback method. The example shows how this method retrieves the data read and access information from the main thread (such as the ID of the process) using the `FileStatus` class.

Contrarily to the previous section, the memory buffer used is equal to the size of the file to read meaning we do not have to manage a buffer. In fact, the `FileStream` implementation manages its own internal buffer mechanism which is transparent to the developer. The developer can optionally set the size of this internal buffer using the constructor of the class (here we specify 4096 bytes).

Example 17-4
```
using System;
using System.IO;
using System.Threading;

public class Program {
   class FileStatus {
      public byte []    Buffer;
      public FileStream Fs;
      public int        Id;
   }

   // Size of files : almost 10 MB.
   static readonly int   NBytesPerFile = 10000000;
   static readonly int   NRead = 5;
   static string         FileName = "blob.bin";

   // Create a file of NBytesPerFile bytes.
   static void CreateBlobFile() {
      byte [] blob = new byte[ NBytesPerFile ];
      FileStream fs = new FileStream(
         FileName,
         FileMode.Create,FileAccess.Write,FileShare.None,
         4096, false);
      fs.Write( blob, 0, NBytesPerFile );
      fs.Flush();
      fs.Close();
   }

   public static void Main() {
      CreateBlobFile();
      for(int i = 0 ; i< NRead; i++ ) {
         FileStream fs = new FileStream(
            FileName,
            FileMode.Open,FileAccess.Read,FileShare.Read,
```

Reading and writing files 529

Example 17-4

```
                   // Size of the internal buffer.
                   4096,
                   true);

         // Initialize data for the callback method.
         FileStatus status = new FileStatus();

         status.Id = i;
         status.Fs = fs;
         status.Buffer = new Byte[ NBytesPerFile ];

         Console.WriteLine( "Thread #{0}: Trigger asynchronous read #{1}",
                     Thread.CurrentThread.ManagedThreadId ,i);

         // Trigger asynchronous read.
         fs.BeginRead( status.Buffer, 0, NBytesPerFile ,
                     new AsyncCallback(CallbackOnReadDone), status);
      }
      // To keep the example simple, we don't implement any
      // synchronization mecanism to wait for the end of reads
      // done by background threads.
      Thread.Sleep(10000);
   }

   // The callback method which works with read data.
   static void CallbackOnReadDone( IAsyncResult asyncResult ) {
      // Fetch read data.
      FileStatus status = asyncResult.AsyncState as FileStatus;
      byte[] data = status.Buffer;
      FileStream fs = status.Fs;

      // Close the stream used to read data.
      int nBytesRead = fs.EndRead( asyncResult );
      fs.Close();

      Console.WriteLine( "Thread #{0}: Begin work on data #{1}",
                     Thread.CurrentThread.ManagedThreadId ,status.Id);
      // Simulate working on the data for one second.
      Thread.Sleep(1000);
      Console.WriteLine( "Thread #{0}: End work on data #{1}",
                     Thread.CurrentThread.ManagedThreadId ,status.Id);
   }
}
```

This program displays the following on my machine. We see that the main thread has an ID of 8 and that the two threads involved in the asynchronous processing have an ID of 6 and 10. This behavior can vary from one execution to another and there can be between 1 and min(NRead, Number of IO threads in the pool) threads assigned to the processing of data.

```
Thread #8: Trigger asynchronous read #0
Thread #8: Trigger asynchronous read #1
Thread #6: Begin work on data #0
Thread #8: Trigger asynchronous read #2
Thread #8: Trigger asynchronous read #3
Thread #8: Trigger asynchronous read #4
Thread #6: End work on data #0
Thread #6: Begin work on data #1
Thread #7: Begin work on data #2
```

```
Thread #6: End work on data #1
Thread #6: Begin work on data #3
Thread #7: End work on data #2
Thread #6: End work on data #3
Thread #7: Begin work on data #4
Thread #7: End work on data #4
```

Harnessing TCP/IP with sockets

Introduction to sockets and TCP/IP

In this section, we will show that the manipulation of network data streams between remote machines, is similar to what we have already discussed earlier through instances of the `System.Net.Sockets.Socket` class which represents *sockets*. A detailed presentation of sockets and the TCP/IP protocol is beyond the scope of this book, but let us remind you the main points on this topic.

The *IP (Internet Protocol)* protocol offers an addressing model for a machine. The IP protocol is widely spread today. Although that it is a simplistic version, we can say that an *IP address* identifies a machine (or group of machines) over the *Internet*. An IP address is a number which is encoded over four bytes. In addition to having an IP address, each machine connected to the Internet can present up to 65536 *ports*. A port is a number encoded on two bytes which represent a point of communication on a machine. Each machine can thus offer several points of communication and an *IP address/port* represents a unique communication point on the internet. For the user of the IP protocol, all happens as if there were 65536 input/output data streams. It's the low-level network layer which takes care of multiplexing this information and transferring it over the network cable. These layers are conceptually below the IP protocol.

A socket materializes a communication endpoint on a machine. Sockets were, about 20 years ago, a set of low-level functionalities written in C. They were invented by the *Berkeley* University in California to answer to the need of communicating between machines. This set of functionality has since become standard and is encapsulated in some classes. Sockets support several communication protocols which include *UDP/IP (User Datagram Protocol)* and most especially *TCP/IP (Transfer Control Protocol)* which, as its name indicates, uses the IP protocol and its addressing mechanism.

Concretely, a process, named server, creates a socket and calls a blocking method (generally named `Accept()`) on this object in order to wait for a request. Another process, named client, creates another socket. The client can exist on the same machine or on a remote machine. The client supplies the IP address/Port pair identifying the socket of the server. Using this information, the client connects on the socket of the server, which as for effect of unblocking the server from its wait on `Accept()` and to create a data stream between the client and the server. From this point, two scenarios can happen on the server:

- Either the server completely handles the needs of the client before returning to a waiting mode by calling `Accept()`. Here we say that the server works in a synchronous way as it serves the clients one after the other.

- Either the server creates, as quickly as possible, a new socket which is handed off to a new thread which will process the needs of the client. The main server will then call `Accept()` right after the client connection. Here we say that the server works in an asynchronous way.

Of course, the use of the asynchronous approach is generally much more efficient as it minimizes the global wait time for the clients. We will present both approaches in the two following sections.

Harnessing TCP/IP with sockets 531

Working synchronously with sockets

Here we will detail a synchronous use of sockets with both the client and the server code. Surprisingly we don't use the Socket class! The .NET framework offers the System.Net.Sockets.TcpListener and System.Net.Sockets.TcpClient classes which harness the Socket class internally. The use of these classes greatly simplifies the programming of sockets using TCP/IP. For readers which are already familiar to programming with sockets, know that their use remains similar. In addition, nothing prevents you from using the Socket class if you prefer.

Server side

Our server creates a communication endpoint on port 50000 with an instance of the TcpListener class. The server then waits for a client to connect by calling the AcceptTcpClient() method. When a client connects itself, the server obtains an instance of the System.Net.Sockets.NetworkStream which represents a data stream with the client. In the ProcessClientRequest() method, the server opens a text file and copies it line-by-line to the data stream to the client. Once the file has been copied, the server closes the both the data streams for the file and the client before returning into its 'wait mode' for another client.

Note that the close operations on a stream take place within a finally clause. In fact, these are typically operations which involve the release of critical resources. We could have opted for the use of the *using/Dispose()* pattern since all the stream classes implement the IDisposable interface.

Example 17-5   *Code for sync server: Server.cs*

```csharp
using System;
using System.Net.Sockets;
using System.Net;
using System.IO;

class ProgServeur {
   static readonly ushort port = 50000;

   static void Main() {
      IPAddress ipAddress = new IPAddress( new byte[] { 127, 0, 0, 1 } );
      TcpListener tcpListener = new TcpListener( ipAddress , port );
      tcpListener.Start();

      // Each loop = send a file to a client.
      while(true) {
        try {
           Console.WriteLine( "Waiting for a client..." );
           // 'AcceptTcpClient()' is a blocking call. The thread
           // continue its course only when a client is connected.
           TcpClient tcpClient = tcpListener.AcceptTcpClient();
           Console.WriteLine( "Client connected." );
           ProcessClientRequest( tcpClient.GetStream() );
           Console.WriteLine( "Client disconnected." );
        }
        catch( Exception e ) {
           Console.WriteLine( e.Message );
        }
      }
   }
   static void ProcessClientRequest( NetworkStream networkStream ) {
      // Stream used to send data.
      StreamWriter  streamWriter = new StreamWriter( networkStream );
```

532   Chapter 17 - Input/Output and Streams

Example 17-5   Code for sync server: Server.cs

```
      // Stream used to read the file.
      StreamReader  streamReader = new StreamReader( @"C:/Text/File.txt" );

      // For each line of the file: send it to the client.
      string sTmp = streamReader.ReadLine();
      try {
         while(sTmp != null ) {
            Console.WriteLine( "Sending: {0}" , sTmp );
            streamWriter.WriteLine( sTmp );
            streamWriter.Flush();
            sTmp = streamReader.ReadLine();
         }
      }
      finally {
         // Close streams.
         streamReader.Close();
         streamWriter.Close();
         networkStream.Close();
      }
   }
}
```

Here is the display done by the server when a client connects:

Sync server display

```
Waiting for a client...
Client connected.
Sending: ###################
Sending: Here is the content...
Sending: ...of File.txt
Sending: ###################
Client disconnected.
Waiting for a client...
```

Client side

The code for the client is even simpler than the code for the server. The client creates an instance of the `TcpClient` class and provides the IP Address/Port of the server. When the client is connected, it obtains an instance of the `System.Net.Sockets.NetworkStream` class which represents a data stream to the server. The client only needs to read the data from this stream. We know that the server will send strings and the client reads them one-by-one and displays them on the console.

Example 17-6   Code for sync client: Client.cs

```
using System;
using System.Net.Sockets;
using System.IO;

class ProgClient {
   static readonly string host = "localhost";
   static readonly ushort port = 50000;
   static void Main() {
      TcpClient tcpClient;
      try {
         // Invoking the 'TcpClient' constructor raises an exception
         // if it can't connect to the server.
```

Example 17-6   Code for sync client: Client.cs

```csharp
         tcpClient = new TcpClient( host , port );
         Console.WriteLine("Connection established with {0}:{1}",host,port);
         NetworkStream networkStream = tcpClient.GetStream();
         StreamReader streamReader = new StreamReader( networkStream );
         try {
            // Each loop = a line is fetched from the server.
            string sTmp = streamReader.ReadLine();
            while( sTmp != null ) {
               Console.WriteLine( "Receiving: {0}" , sTmp );
               sTmp = streamReader.ReadLine();
            }
         }
         finally {
            // Close stream.
            streamReader.Close();
            networkStream.Close();
            Console.WriteLine( "Disconnecting from {0}:{1}", host, port);
         }
      }
      catch( Exception e ) {
         Console.WriteLine( e.Message );
         return;
      }
   }
}
```

Here is the display of the client:

Sync client display

```
Connection established with localhost:50000
Receiving: ###################
Receiving: Here is the content...
Receiving: ...of File.txt
Receiving: ###################
Disconnecting from localhost :50000
```

The IP here is "`localhost`" since we assume that the client and server reside on the same machine. In a real case, the IP address of the server would be a parameter to the client application, placed in the application configuration file or passed as a command line argument to the application. Know that instead of using an IP address, you can provide a domain name such as www.smacchia.com. The `System.Net.Dns` class allows the conversion of a domain name into an IP address and vice versa. We will not use this class here.

Working asynchronously with sockets

Server side

As in the previous section, we do not use the `Socket` class but only the `TcpListener` and `TcpClient` classes. The implementation of the asynchronous model on the server side rests on the fact that we will use the `BeginRead()` and `BeginWrite()` methods. As we have seen earlier, during the asynchronous processing of a data stream from a file using the `BeginRead()` and `BeginWrite()` methods, these methods allow the specification of a *callback method*. This callback method is automatically called at the end of each read or write operation. Also remember that this method is called by the same thread which completes the read/write operation. You do not need to manage this thread as it comes from the I/O *thread pool* of the CLR.

Contrarily to the asynchronous processing of a data stream originating from a file (Example 17-4), we do not use the possibility of sharing an object between the main thread and the thread from the pool which does the processing of the input/output. In general, the architecture which allows the asynchronous processing of remote client connections contains a class where each instance processes a client. We have named this class `ClientRequestProcessing`. An instance of this class only needs the data stream for a specific client. This stream is obtained in the same way as in the previous section by successively calling the `AcceptTcpClient()` method followed by `GetStream()`.

Our example is built in a way where the server starts by reading the data from the client. Once data has been received, it sends it back to the client. The server performs these two operations until the client stops sending data. At this time, the server stops processing this client. Of course, in a real situation, the server would not simply resend the data to the client without processing it but we attempted to create the simplest example possible.

Example 17-7   *Code for async server: Server.cs*

```
using System;
using System.Net.Sockets;
using System.Net;
using System.IO;
using System.Text;

class ProgServeur {
   static readonly ushort port = 50000;

   static void Main() {
      IPAddress ipAddress = new IPAddress( new byte[] { 127, 0, 0, 1 } );
      TcpListener tcpListener = new TcpListener( ipAddress, port );
      tcpListener.Start();

      while(true) {
         try {
            Console.WriteLine( "Main:Waiting for a client..." );
            TcpClient tcpClient = tcpListener.AcceptTcpClient();
            Console.WriteLine( "Main:Client connected." );
            ClientRequestProcessing clientRequestProcessing =
                new ClientRequestProcessing( tcpClient.GetStream() );
            clientRequestProcessing.Go();
         }
         catch( Exception e ) {
            Console.WriteLine( e.Message );
         }
      }
   }
}

// An instance of this class is created for each client.
class ClientRequestProcessing {
   static readonly int    bufferSize = 512;
   private byte []        m_Buffer;
   private NetworkStream  m_NetworkStream;
   private AsyncCallback  m_CallbackRead;
   private AsyncCallback  m_CallbackWrite;

   // The constructor initializes :
   //    - m_NetworkStream: stream to communicate with the client.
   //    - m_CallbackRead : callback procedure for read.
   //    - m_CallbackWrite: callback procedure for write.
```

Example 17-7   *Code for async server: Server.cs*

```
   //   - m_Buffer : used both for reading and writing data.
   public ClientRequestProcessing( NetworkStream networkStream ) {
      m_NetworkStream  = networkStream;
      m_CallbackRead   = new AsyncCallback( this.OnReadDone );
      m_CallbackWrite  = new AsyncCallback( this.OnWriteDone );
      m_Buffer         = new byte[ bufferSize ];
   }

   public void Go() {
      m_NetworkStream.BeginRead(
         m_Buffer, 0 , m_Buffer.Length , m_CallbackRead , null );
   }

   // This callback procedure is called when an asynchronous read
   // triggered by a call to 'BeginRead()' terminates.
   private void OnReadDone( IAsyncResult asyncResult  ) {
      int nBytes = m_NetworkStream.EndRead(asyncResult );
      // Send back the received string to the client.
      if( nBytes > 0 ){
         string s = Encoding.ASCII.GetString( m_Buffer , 0 , nBytes );
         Console.Write(
            "Async:{0} bytes received from client: {1}" , nBytes, s );
         m_NetworkStream.BeginWrite(
            m_Buffer, 0 , nBytes , m_CallbackWrite , null );
      }
      // If the client didn't send anything, the we discard him.
      else{
         Console.WriteLine( "Async:Client request processed." );
         m_NetworkStream.Close();
         m_NetworkStream = null;
      }
   }

   // This callback procedure is called when an asynchronous write
   // triggered by a call to 'BeginWrite()' terminates.
   private void OnWriteDone( IAsyncResult asyncResult  ) {
      m_NetworkStream.EndWrite( asyncResult );
      Console.WriteLine( "Async:Write done." );
      m_NetworkStream.BeginRead(
         m_Buffer, 0 , m_Buffer.Length , m_CallbackRead , null );
   }
}
```

Here is the display of the server when it is connected to the client for which we will present the code right after. Note that the server goes back to waiting before even receiving any data from the first client.

Async server display

```
Main:Waiting for a client...
Main:Client connected.
Main:Waiting for a client...
Async:21 bytes received from client: Hi from the client!
Async:Write done.
Async:21 bytes received from client: Hi from the client!
Async:Write done.
Async:21 bytes received from client: Hi from the client!
Async:Write done.
Async:Client request processed.
```

Client side

The fact that the server works asynchronously does not have any impact on the code of the client. Hence, the client is very similar to the version presented in the previous section. The difference is that here, the client does not simply wait for data coming in from the server. It sends data and receives data three times in a row. Here is the code:

Example 17-8 *Code for async client: Client.cs*

```
using System;
using System.Net.Sockets;
using System.IO;

class ProgClient {
   static readonly string host = "localhost";
   static readonly ushort port = 50000;

   static void Main() {
      TcpClient tcpClient;
      try{
         // Invoking the 'TcpClient' constructor raises an exception
         // if it can't connect to the server.
         tcpClient = new TcpClient(host,port);
         Console.WriteLine("Connection established with {0}:{1}",host,port);

         // Initialize the stream to communicate with the server
         // available for sending and receiving data.
         NetworkStream networkStream = tcpClient.GetStream();
         StreamWriter streamWriter =new StreamWriter( networkStream );
         StreamReader streamReader =new StreamReader( networkStream );
         try {
            string sSend = "Hi from the client!";
            string sReceived;
            for(int i=0;i<3;i++) {
               // Send data to the server.
               Console.WriteLine( "Client  -> Server :" + sSend );
               streamWriter.WriteLine( sSend );
               streamWriter.Flush();
               // Receiving data from the server.
               sReceived = streamReader.ReadLine();
               Console.WriteLine( "Server  -> Client :" + sReceived );
            }
         }
         finally{
            streamWriter.Close();
            streamReader.Close();
            networkStream.Close();
         }
      }
      catch(Exception e) {
        Console.WriteLine( e.Message );
        return;
      }
   }
}
```

Here is what the client displays:

Async client display

```
Connection established with localhost:50000
Client  -> Server :Hi from the client!
Server  -> Client :Hi from the client!
Client  -> Server :Hi from the client!
Server  -> Client :Hi from the client!
Client  -> Server :Hi from the client!
Server  -> Client :Hi from the client!
```

Getting information about network interfaces and status

Discovering available network interfaces

Instances of the `System.Net.NetworkInformation.NetworkInterface` represent a network interface. The `GetAllNetworkInterfaces()` static method of this class allows the listing of all the network interfaces available on the machine. For example:

Example 17-9

```csharp
using System;
using System.Net.NetworkInformation;
public class Program {
   public static void Main() {
      NetworkInterface[] nis=NetworkInterface.GetAllNetworkInterfaces();
      foreach ( NetworkInterface ni in nis ) {
         Console.WriteLine( "Name: " + ni.Name );
         Console.WriteLine( "Description: " + ni.Description );
         Console.WriteLine( "Status: "+ni.OperationalStatus.ToString() );
         Console.WriteLine( "Speed: {0} Kb", ni.Speed / 1024 );
         Console.WriteLine( "Media Acess Control (MAC):" +
                            ni.GetPhysicalAddress().ToString() );
         Console.WriteLine( "--------------------------------" );
      }
   }
}
```

Ping

You can use the `System.Net.NetworkInformation.Ping` class to determine if a remote machine is accessible through the network. In fact, this class is equivalent to the `Ping` command.

Example 17-10

```csharp
using System;
using System.Net.NetworkInformation;
public class Program {
   public static void Main() {
      using ( Ping ping = new Ping() ) {
         PingReply pingReply = ping.Send( "www.smacchia.com", 10000 );
         System.Console.WriteLine( "IP:{0} Status:{1}",
                                   pingReply.Address , pingReply.Status );
      }
   }
}
```

This class implements the `IDispose` interface. Also, the `Ping.SendAsync()` method allows to initiate an asynchronous ping. You must then subscribe to the `Ping.PingCompleted` event to be notified when the request has completed.

Event on network changes

The IP address assigned to a network interface can change from time to time, for various reasons. You may be notified of such changes by subscribing to the NetworkAddressChanged event of the System.Net.NetworkInformation.NetworkChange class.

Network activity statistics

You can programmatically access to statistics of the IP, ICMP, TCP, and UDP protocols. These statistics are the same values which can be obtained through the various options of the netstat command. For example:

Example 17-11
```
using System;
using System.Net.NetworkInformation;
public class Program {
   public static void Main() {
      IPGlobalProperties ipProp=IPGlobalProperties.GetIPGlobalProperties();
      IPGlobalStatistics ipStat = ipProp.GetIPv4GlobalStatistics();
      Console.WriteLine("Host name:" + ipProp.HostName );
      Console.WriteLine("Domain name:" + ipProp.DomainName );
      Console.WriteLine("IPv4 # packets received:"+ipStat.ReceivedPackets);
      Console.WriteLine("IPv4 # packets sent:"+ipStat.OutputPacketRequests);
      TcpConnectionInformation[] tcpConns= ipProp.GetActiveTcpConnections();
      foreach (TcpConnectionInformation tcpConn in tcpConns) {
         Console.WriteLine( "localhost:{0} <-> {1}:{2} state:{3}",
                           tcpConn.LocalEndPoint.Port,
                           tcpConn.RemoteEndPoint.Address.ToString(),
                           tcpConn.RemoteEndPoint.Port, tcpConn.State);
      }
   }
}
```

You can also obtain the statistics relative to a specific network interface by using the NetworkInterface.GetIPInterfaceProperties() method.

HTTP and FTP clients

URI

A *URI* (*Universal Resource Identifier*) is a string which can be used to locate a resource. A URI is composed of three parts;

- The first characters of a URI represent the *scheme* of the URI. Here are some of the most common schemes:

    The file scheme indicates that the resource is a file located locally or through an intranet.

    The http scheme indicates that the resource is managed by a web server. The https scheme indicates that the secure HTTP protocol (i.e. HTTP on top of the SSL protocol described a little later At page 546).

    The mailto scheme indicates that the resource is an email address.

    The ftp scheme indicates that the resource is managed by a FTP server (*File Transfer Protocol*) (the same remarks apply to ftps as with https).
- The name of the server.
- The name of the resource.

Here are a few URI examples:

```
http://www.smacchia.com/ConstructeursAutomobiles.html
ftp://ftp.lip6.fr/pub/gnu/a2ps/a2ps-4.10.4.tar.gz
file://localhost/
mailto:patrick@smacchia.com
```

As with file paths, a URI can be relative to another URI. *Relative URIs* thus does not have a scheme at the beginning of the string which represents them. The `System.Uri` class has been created for the storage and manipulation of URIs.

The WebClient class

The `System.Net.WebClient` class allows you to write or retrieve data from a URI. This data can be stored on a local file system, on an intranet or on the internet. The `WebClient` class is very practical since its implementation automatically decides which data transfer protocol to use based on the provided URI (`file`, `http`, `https`, `ftp` or `ftps`). The following example downloads an HTML page from its URI and then displays it as text on the console:

Example 17-12

```
using System.Net;
class Program {
    static void Main() {
        WebClient webClient = new WebClient();
        string s=webClient.DownloadString("http://www.microsoft.com/france");
        System.Console.Write(s);
    }
}
```

The `WebClient` class offers several methods such as `void DownloadFile(string uri,string fileName)` or `byte[] DownloadData(string uri)` to ease the download of data stored in files in a binary format. Each of these methods has a counterpart named `UploadXXX(string uri, data)` which allows you to send data to the location pointed to by the specified URI. Also note the presence of the `Stream OpenWrite(string uri)` and `Stream OpenRead(string uri)` method pair which allow the manipulation of a resource accessed at an URI through a data stream. Finally, all these methods (`DownloadXXX()` and `UpLoadXXX()`) are available in an asynchronous form which is suffixed with `Async`. In this case, the operation is completed by one of the thread of the CLR's thread pool. You can then be notified of the completion of such an operation by subscribing to an event such as `UpdloadDataCompleted` of your instance of `WebClient`.

Other classes to access resources from their URIs

The `WebClient` class is very practical but is not sufficient when you must use specific features of the underlying protocol (such as *cookies* with the HTTP protocol). The `System.Net.FileWebRequest`, `System.Net.FtpWebRequest` and `System.Net.HttpWebRequest` classes allow the completion of request taking into account transfer protocol used. All three classes derive from the `WebRequest` class. To obtain an instance of one of these classes, it is recommended to invoke the `WebRequest WebRequest.Create(string uri)` static method. From there, you can customize your request. For example, the `HttpWebRequest` class offers the `CookieContainer` property which allows the association of cookies to your request.

To complete the request, you must call the `WebResponse GetResponse()` method on the object representing your request. This method returns an instance of a class derived from `System.Net.WebResponse`, that is `System.Net.FileWebResponse`, `System.Net.FtpWebResponse` and `System.Net.HttpWebResponse`. You can then obtain the data associated with the response by calling `Stream WebResponse.GetResponseStream()`. Note that certain `BeginGetXXX()` and `EndGetXXX()` methods of the `WebRequest` allows for a request to be completed in an asynchronous way. Finally know that internally, the `WebClient` uses the classes that we have just discussed.

The following example displays on the console the content of a file downloaded from a FTP server:

Example 17-13

```
using System.Net;
using System.Text;
using System.IO;
class Program{
   static void Main(){
      FtpWebRequest ftpReq = WebRequest.Create(
         "ftp://smacchia.com/test.txt") as FtpWebRequest;
      ftpReq.Method = WebRequestMethods.Ftp.UploadFile;
      ftpReq.Credentials = new NetworkCredential( "login", "password" );
      FtpWebResponse ftpResp = ftpReq.GetResponse() as FtpWebResponse;
      StreamReader streamReader = new StreamReader(
                    ftpResp.GetResponseStream() , Encoding.ASCII );
      System.Console.WriteLine( streamReader.ReadToEnd() );
      streamReader.Close();
   }
}
```

You can define a resource cache. For this, you simply need to create an instance of the `System.Net.Cache.RequestCachePolicy` class with a value of the `System.Net.Cache.RequestCacheLevel` enumeration which specifies the type of cache desired. You can also set the global caching level using the `RequestCachePolicy WebRequest.DefaultCachePolicy{get;set;}` static property or at the level of a request by using the `RequestCachePolicy WebRequest.CachePolicy{get;set;}` instance property. More information on this topic can be found in the article named **Cache Management For Network Applications** on **MSDN**.

Coding an HTTP server with the HttpListener class over HTTP.SYS

Introduction to HTTP.SYS

The *Windows XP SP2*, *Windows Server 2003* and *Windows Vista* operating systems contain a kernel layer named *HTTP.SYS* specialized in the processing of the HTTP protocol. Until this innovation, HTTP servers executing on the *Windows* operating systems used the *Winsock* (*Windows Socket API*) layer which itself used the services of the kernel TCP/IP layer. In this model, each HTTP request required an expensive transition between the kernel and the user mode. HTTP.SYS is a layer which executes itself at the kernel level. Noteworthy, HTTP.SYS takes care of the response cache. This means that when HTTP.SYS returns a page directly from the cache, there is no need to an expensive transition to the user mode. This model is thus more efficient.

IIS (the *Windows* HTTP server) takes advantage of the HTTP.SYS layer since with version 6.0. This layer knows how to manage the routing of an HTTP request to the proper process since IIS 6.0 communicates this information to HTTP.SYS at each startup. HTTP.SYS is also capable of storing HTTP requests until the start of the process which will handle the request.

The System.Net.HttpListener class

The .NET framework 2 offers the `System.Net.HttpListener` class which allows you to take advantage of the HTTP.SYS layer to develop your own HTTP server. Of course, you cannot use this class when your application executes on an operating system which does not support HTTP.SYS. The following program shows how to use this class in order to return an HTML page which contains the current time and date as well as the requested URL. Such an HTML page is returned for each incoming HTTP request to the 8008 port which has a destination path of /`hello`:

Example 17-14
```
using System.Net;
using System.IO;
class Program {
   static void Main() {
      HttpListener httpListener = new HttpListener();
      string uri = string.Format( "http://localhost:8008/hello/" );
      httpListener.Prefixes.Add(uri);
      httpListener.Start();
      while (true) {
         // Blocking method...
         HttpListenerContext ctx = httpListener.GetContext();
         ctx.Response.ContentType = "text/html";
         TextWriter writer = new StreamWriter(
           ctx.Response.OutputStream, System.Text.Encoding.Unicode);
         writer.WriteLine(
           "<html><body><b>Page asked at {0}</b><br/>URL:{1}</body></html>",
           System.DateTime.Now, ctx.Request.Url);
         writer.Flush();
         writer.Close();
      }
   }
}
```

The start of the HTTP server is done by a call to the `Start()` method. You must first register all the URLs that your instance of `HttpListener` will process using the `Prefixes` property. HTTP.SYS supports the HTTPS protocol, meaning that you can specify a URL which uses the `https//` scheme. If a URL is already treated by HTTP.SYS, an exception will be raised when it is added. A classic error is to not specify the port number to use in your URLs. The port 80 is used by default but this port is generally already used by the IIS server if it is installed on this machine. In this case, an exception will be raised.

Once the web server is started, we enter into an infinite loop. Each iteration of the loop represents the processing of an HTTP request. The `HttpListener.GetContext()` will block until the reception of a request. The processing of a request is then materialized by an instance of `System.Web.HttpListenerContext`. We then build our page that we include in the HTTP response using the `Stream HttpListenerContext.Response.OutputStream` data stream.

In addition to the `Request` and `Response` properties, the `HttpListenerContext` class offers the property named `IPrincipal User{get;}` which specifies the *Windows* user responsible for the request if it has been authenticated. HTTP.SYS supports the four authentication modes: Anonymous connection, Digest authentication, Base authentication and *Windows* integrated authentication. These modes are described at page 795.

Processing HTTP requests asynchronously

In Example 17-14, all the HTTP requests are processed one after the other by the same thread. Clearly, this approach is not efficient. Hence, the `HttpListener` also presents the `BeginGetContext()` and `EndGetContext()` methods which allow the processing of several requests simultaneously on the thread pool of the CLR. Here is our example, rewritten to take advantage of this feature (note that for each execution of the loop, we wait one second in order to avoid that the main thread monopolizes the processor since the `BeginGetContext()` method is non-blocking):

Example 17-15

```
using System;
using System.Net;
using System.IO;
class Program {
   static void Main() {
      HttpListener httpListener = new HttpListener();
      string uri = string.Format("http://localhost:8008/hello/");
      httpListener.Prefixes.Add(uri);
      httpListener.Start();
      while (true) {
         IAsyncResult result =
            httpListener.BeginGetContext(ProcessResponse, httpListener);
         System.Threading.Thread.Sleep(1000);
      }
   }
   private static void ProcessResponse( IAsyncResult result ) {
      HttpListener httpListener = result.AsyncState as HttpListener;
      HttpListenerContext ctx = httpListener.EndGetContext(result);
      ctx.Response.ContentType = "text/html";
      TextWriter writer = new StreamWriter(
         ctx.Response.OutputStream, System.Text.Encoding.Unicode);
      writer.WriteLine(
         "<html><body><b>Page asked at {0}</b><br/>URL:{1}</body></html>",
         System.DateTime.Now, ctx.Request.Url );
      writer.Flush();
      writer.Close();
   }
}
```

Support for mails protocols (SMTP and MIME)

In .NET 2, the classes of the `System.Web.Mail` namespace are now obsolete. To send mails, you must use the `System.Net.Mail` namespace. For example, an instance of the `SmtpClient` class represents an access point to a SMTP server. Here is an example which uses this class in order to send an email:

Example 17-16

```
using System.Net;
using System.Net.Mail;
class Program {
   static void Main() {
      SmtpClient client = new SmtpClient("smtp.myserver.fr",25);
      client.Credentials = new
         NetworkCredential( "patrick.smacchia@myserver.fr", "mypwd" );
      client.Send( "patrick@smacchia.com", "target@xyz.com",
                  "my subject", "my body");
   }
}
```

The `SmtpClient` class also provides a method named `SendAsync()` and an event named `SendCompleted` which allows you to send a mail asynchronously. Facilities are also provided to communicate with a SMTP server in SSL mode.

An instance of the `MailMessage` class represent an email, an instance of the `MailAddress` class represents an email address and an instance of the `Attachment` represent an email attachment. Let's rewrite our program using these classes to send an email with the `C:\file.txt` attached:

Example 17-17
```
using System.Net;
using System.Net.Mail;
class Program {
   static void Main() {
      SmtpClient client = new SmtpClient("smtp.myserver.fr",25);
      client.Credentials = new
         NetworkCredential("patrick.smacchia@myserver.fr", "mypwd");
      MailMessage msg = new MailMessage("patrick@smacchia.com",
         "target@xyz.com", "my subject", "my body");
      msg.Attachments.Add( new Attachment( @"C:\file.txt" ) );
      client.Send( msg );
   }
}
```

The `System.Net.Mime` namespace also contains classes to support the *Multipurpose Internet Mail Exchange* (MIME) standard. This standard describes the formatting of the headers in the body of an email. These headers allow describing the way that the body of the email, as well as its attachments must be displayed. For example, certain mails are in an HTML format and contain images.

Buffering and compressing data streams

This section shows how you can tune the way that the data of a stream is written and read using services. These services are materialized by certain classes of the framework which allow, for example, to buffer or to compress/decompress the data of a stream. We will see in the following section that other classes allow the securing (i.e. authentication and/or encryption) of the data in a stream.

Applying services on streams with the decorator design pattern

The .NET framework bases itself on the design pattern GoF named *decorator* in order to implement the architecture which allows you to apply a series of services on a data stream. The idea is simple: each class representing a stream and each class representing a service is derived from the `Stream` abstract class. An instance of a class representing a service holds a reference of type `Stream` to the stream on which it acts. The client of this instance manipulates it by calling the `Read([out]buffer)` and `Write([in]buffer)` methods. The client is not necessarily aware that he is in fact manipulating a service which encapsulates the access to a string as he might be satisfied with a reference of type `Stream`. The following code snippet illustrates a use of this architecture where three services are sequentially applied to a network data stream:

```
...
   NetworkStream  networkStream = new NetworkStream( ... );
   BufferedStream bufferedStream = new BufferedStream( networkStream , ... );
   CryptoStream   cryptoStream = new CryptoStream( bufferedStream , ... );
   GZipStream     gzipStream = new GZipStream( cryptoStream , ... );
   Stream         clientStream = gzipStream as Stream;
...
   clientStream.Read( ... );
   clientStream.Write( ... );
...
```

In this example, if the code for the creation of the stream and its three services is isolated, the fact that the data from the flow is compressed/decompressed, encrypted/decrypted and then buffered is completely transparent from the point of view of the code which calls `Read()` and `Write()`. Here is a UML class of this architecture:

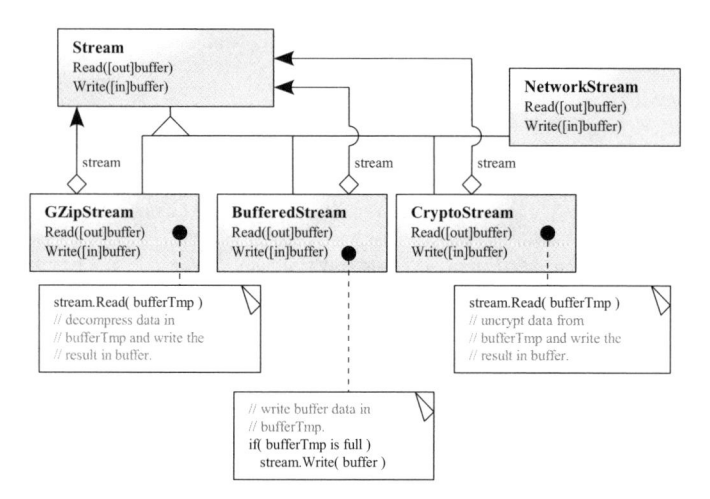

Figure 17-1: Applying a sequence of services to a stream with the decorator design pattern

Buffering streams data

The `NetworkStream` class does not manage a memory buffer. In practice, when you call one of the `Write()` or `WriteByte()` methods, the data is sent directly to the client. A big performance problem can appear if you send too much data in the form of small packets. In fact, each transmission on the network consumes a certain amount of resources independently of the number of bytes sent. If you send a lot of data in the form of small packets without waiting for a response from the client, it would be better to send all these packets at once. In other words, it would be better that several consecutive calls to the `Write()` or `WriteByte()` methods only generate a single network access. You must then manage a buffer to accept these packets as they are produced by the server and send this buffer through the network when best suited.

The `System.IO.BufferedStream` class was conceived especially with this goal in mind. This class is extremely simple to use. During the creation of an instance, you provide to the constructor a reference to an instance of `NetworkStream` to which you want to associate a buffer. The `BufferedStream` derives from the `Stream` class. As a consequence the methods offered to manipulate a data stream can be used on the instance of the buffer. The instance of `BufferedStream` transmits the data to send to the instance of `NetworkStream` only when the buffer is full. You can also force the data to be sent to the instance of `NetworkStream`, by calling the `Flush()` method on the instance of `BufferedStream`.

During the creation of an instance of `BufferedStream`, you have the option of specifying the size of the buffer. This size is the parameter on which you must play in order to obtain the best possible performance. Empirically, a size of 4KB is a good choice but you may wish to do some tests using various size.

The `BufferedStream` class can also be used to read data. Note that is not recommended to use an instance of `BufferedStream` to read and write data at the same time. Also, if you use an instance of `BufferedStream` with data always larger than the size of the buffer, it is possible that memory for the buffer never be allocated.

Reading and writing data on the serial port 545

An instance of the `System.IO.MemoryStream` class can be used in the same spirit as `BufferedStream` to improve the performance of a network data stream. The difference is that an instance of `MemoryStream` is not directly tied to an instance of `NetworkStream`. You only specify the underlying stream during the call to the `WriteTo()` method. Hence, you can send the same data contained in the same memory buffer to several clients.

The `System.IO.UnmanagedMemoryStream` unmanaged version of the `MemoryStream` class allows to avoid the copy of the data onto the CLR's object heap, which is more efficient.

Finally note that it is not necessary to use the `BufferedStream` class to use a memory buffer with an instance of `FileStream`. In fact, as we have already seen, the `FileStream` internally manages its own memory buffer.

Compressing a data stream

The new `System.IO.Compression` namespace contains the two classes named `GZipStream` and `DeflateStream` which allows the compression and decompression of a data stream using the *GZip* (RFC 1952: GZIP 4.3) and *Deflate* (RFC 1951: DEFLATE 1.3) algorithms. The following example shows how to compress a file:

Example 17-18
```
using System.IO;
using System.IO.Compression;
public class Program {
   public static void Main() {
      string sFileIn = @"C:\Test.txt";
      string sFileOut = @"C:\Test.bin";
      byte[] content = File.ReadAllBytes(sFileIn);
      FileStream fileStream = new FileStream( sFileOut,
                                  FileMode.Create, FileAccess.Write);
      GZipStream gzipStream = new GZipStream( fileStream,
                                  CompressionMode.Compress );
      gzipStream.Write(content, 0, content.Length);
      gzipStream.Close();
      fileStream.Close();
      FileInfo fileOut = new FileInfo(sFileOut);
      System.Console.WriteLine("{0} bytes before", content.Length);
      System.Console.WriteLine("{0} bytes after", fileOut.Length);
   }
}
```

It is unfortunate that we cannot simply use the `GZipStream` class to directly manipulate .zip files. Also, here is a link to the free (and open-source) *SharpZipLib* library which allows you to accomplish this: `http://www.icsharpcode.net/OpenSource/SharpZipLib/Default.aspx`

Reading and writing data on the serial port

The `System.IO.Ports.SerialPort` class allows to use a serial port in either a synchronous way or in an event based approach.

An instance of this class is not a data stream since it does not derive from `Stream`. However, the `SerialPort` class has a property named `Stream BaseStream{get;}` which provides a read/write stream to the underlying serial port. Of course, random access is not supported on such a data stream.

The `string PortName{get;set;}` property specifies the name of the underlying serial port. The `string[] GetPortNames()` static method allows you to obtain a list of all the serial ports available on the current machine.

The `ReadLine()` and `WriteLine()` methods are provided to send and receive strings. The `Encoding SerialPort.Encoding{get;set;}` property allows to set the encoding used for string.

The `SerialPort` class allows you to work at a lower level thanks to several properties which allows the manipulation of the bits of the underlying serial port.

Support for secure communication protocols: SSL, NTLM and Kerberos

Introduction to secure communication protocols

The *SSL* (*Secure Socket Layer*) protocol was originally developed by *Netscape* to secure the exchange of data on the internet. Its latest version is named *TLS* (*Transport Layer Security*). This protocol provides three services: authentication of the server, optional authentication of the user and secured exchange of data. This protocol is not tied to a particular internet protocol and can be placed underneath any of the HTTP, TCP, FTP, TELNET protocols.

The *NTLM* (*NT Lan Manager*) and *Kerberos* protocols are authentication and data securing protocols used for the exchange of data between *Windows* platforms. NTLM is supported by all *Windows* systems since *Windows 95/98* while Kerberos is only supported by the most recent version of *Windows*. If at least one of the two parties does not support Kerberos, the NTLM protocol is used by default.

Secure communication protocols and the System.Net.Security namespace

The new `System.Net.Security` namespace offers classes which allow the use of the SSL, NTLM and Kerberos protocols to secure the data from a data stream. These classes encapsulate the Win32 API relative to these protocols which is also known as *SSPI* (*Security Support Provider Interface*). The `NegociateSteam` and `SslStream` classes derive from the `AuthenticatedStream` class.

The SslStream class

The `SslStream` class is used to take advantage of the SSL protocol. Let's retake the TCP client/server code from page 531 in order to secure the TCP data stream using the SSL protocol:

Example 17-19   *Server.cs*

```
   ...
      private static X509Certificate getServerCert() {
         X509Store store = new X509Store( StoreName.My,
                                          StoreLocation.CurrentUser);
         store.Open(OpenFlags.ReadOnly);
         X509CertificateCollection certs = store.Certificates.Find(
             X509FindType.FindBySubjectName, "CN=SslSvrCertif", true);
         return certs[0];
      }
      static void ProcessClientRequest(NetworkStream networkStream) {
         SslStream streamSsl = new SslStream( networkStream );
         streamSsl.AuthenticateAsServer( getServerCert() );
         StreamWriter streamWriter = new StreamWriter( streamSsl );
```

Support for secure communication protocols: SSL, NTLM and Kerberos

Example 17-19   *Server.cs*

```
      StreamReader streamReader = new StreamReader( @"C:/Text/File.txt" );
      string sTmp = streamReader.ReadLine();
      try {
         while ( sTmp != null ) {
            Console.WriteLine( "Sending: {0}" , sTmp );
            streamWriter.WriteLine( sTmp );
            streamWriter.Flush();
            sTmp = streamReader.ReadLine();
         }
      } finally {
         streamReader.Close();
         streamWriter.Close();
         streamSsl.Close();
         networkStream.Close();
      }
   }
...
```

We see that on the server side, a new data stream of type `SslStream` places itself between the `networkStream` data stream and the `streamWriter` data stream which is used to send the data.

To create this SSL data stream, we retrieve an X509 certificate named `SslSvrCertif` which is stored in the personal folder for the current user. The fact of passing this certificate to `AuthenticateAsServer()` allows the SSL authentication of the server using this certificate. Here is the code for the client:

Example 17-20   *Client.cs*

```
...
      NetworkStream networkStream = tcpClient.GetStream();
      SslStream streamSsl = new SslStream (
         networkStream,false, ValidateSvrCertificateCallback );
      streamSsl.AuthenticateAsClient( "SslSvrCertif" );
      StreamReader streamReader = new StreamReader( streamSsl );
      try {
         string sTmp = streamReader.ReadLine();
         while ( sTmp != null ) {
            Console.WriteLine( "Receiving: {0}", sTmp );
            sTmp = streamReader.ReadLine();
         }
      } finally {
         streamReader.Close();
         streamSsl.Close();
         networkStream.Close();
         Console.WriteLine( "Deconnecting from {0}:{1}", host, port );
      }
...
   static bool ValidateSvrCertificateCallback( object sender,
                              X509Certificate certificate,
                              X509Chain chain,
                              SslPolicyErrors sslPolicyErrors ) {
      if ( sslPolicyErrors != SslPolicyErrors.None ) {
         Console.WriteLine(
            "Error validating the SSL certificate!");
         Console.WriteLine( sslPolicyErrors.ToString() );
         return false;
      } else return true;
   }
...
```

Here also, a data stream of type `SslStream` places itself between the `networkStream` network data stream and the `streamWriter` data stream used to receive the data from the server. The `ValidateSvrCertificateCallback()` method is called during the authentication of the certificate of the server. If this method returns `true`, the server is considered as being authenticated. This method is known of our `SslStream` instance since it is referenced by a delegate which is passed to its constructor.

We pass the name of the server certificate to the `AuthenticateAsClient()` method. Another overload of this method allows passing a certificate which is specific to the client for its authentication. The authentication of the client is optional with the SSL protocol and we will not use it here.

The NegociateStream class

The `NegociateStream` class is used to take advantage of the NTLM and Kerberos *Windows* protocols. Let's retake our example in order to use these protocols on a TCP data stream. The highest protection level, which is `EncryptAndSign`, is used:

Example 17-21 *Server.cs*

```
...
    static void ProcessClientRequest( NetworkStream networkStream ) {
        NegotiateStream streamAuth = new NegotiateStream( networkStream );
        streamAuth.AuthenticateAsServer(
            CredentialCache.DefaultNetworkCredentials,
            ProtectionLevel.EncryptAndSign,
            TokenImpersonationLevel.Impersonation);
        WindowsPrincipal principal = new WindowsPrincipal(
            streamAuth.RemoteIdentity as WindowsIdentity);
        // Don't process the request if the authentificated
        // Windows client is not an administrator.
        if( !principal.IsInRole( @"BUILTIN\Administrators" ) ){
           networkStream.Close();
           return;
        }

        StreamWriter streamWriter = new StreamWriter( streamAuth );
        StreamReader streamReader = new StreamReader( @"C:/Text/File.txt" );
        string sTmp = streamReader.ReadLine();
        try {
           while ( sTmp != null ) {
              Console.WriteLine( "Sending: {0}", sTmp );
              streamWriter.WriteLine( sTmp );
              streamWriter.Flush();
              sTmp = streamReader.ReadLine();
           }
        } finally {
           streamReader.Close();
           streamWriter.Close();
           streamAuth.Close();
           networkStream.Close();
        }
    }
...
```

We observe that a data stream of type `NegociateStream` wedges itself between the `networkStream` network data stream and the `streamWriter` data stream which is used to send the data. We retrieve the *Windows* user used by the client with the `IIdentity NegociateStream`.

Support for secure communication protocols: SSL, NTLM and Kerberos 549

RemoteIdentity{get;} property. The identity of this user is automatically sent to the underlying protocol (NTLM or Kerberos). If this user is not an administrator, we choose not to satisfy the request. Another alternative would have been, for example, to assign this user to the current thread during the duration of the request (impersonation) in order that all the permission verifications be done implicitly. Here, only the read permission on the C:/Text/File.txt would have been required.

Here is the code for the client. We notice that it is the identity under which this code executes itself which is sent to the server by the implementation of NegociateStream:

Example 17-22 *Client.cs*

```
...
    NetworkStream networkStream = tcpClient.GetStream();
    NegotiateStream streamAuth=new NegotiateStream( networkStream );
    streamAuth.AuthenticateAsClient(
          CredentialCache.DefaultNetworkCredentials,
          WindowsIdentity.GetCurrent().Name,
          ProtectionLevel.EncryptAndSign,
          TokenImpersonationLevel.Impersonation);
    StreamReader streamReader = new StreamReader( streamAuth );
    try {
       // Each loop = a line fetched.
       string sTmp = streamReader.ReadLine();
       while ( sTmp != null ) {
          Console.WriteLine( "Receiving: {0}", sTmp );
          sTmp = streamReader.ReadLine();
       }
    } finally {
       // Close streams.
       streamReader.Close();
       streamAuth.Close();
       networkStream.Close();
       Console.WriteLine( "Deconnecting from {0}:{1}", host, port );
    }
...
```

Encrypting data streams

The System.Security.Cryptography.CryptoStream class allows the encryption and decryption of a data stream without needing authentication. The constructor of the CryptoStream class allows you to specify which algorithm to use for the encryption and decryption by passing an instance of a class which implements the ICryptoTransform. The cryptographic algorithms are detailed at page 181.

18

Windows Forms Application

Windows user interfaces

As its name indicates, windowed user interface plays a main role within the *Windows* operating system. *Microsoft* always made sure that the development of windowed application on its operating systems be both simple and standardized. With this goal in mind, *Microsoft* distributes most of the techniques they use internally to develop their own user interfaces. This explains the coherency in the style of windows which greatly contributes to the user friendliness and hence the popularity of the *Windows* operating system.

Console applications vs. Windows applications

Before the *Windows* operating system, there was the *DOS* operating system. Under the *Windows* operating system, there are two types of applications:

- Console mode application: we execute them in a DOS style command window.
- Windowed applications: we can execute them from the command line or from an icon in an explorer.

This console/windowed application duality still exists with .NET.

- The `csc.exe` C# compiler needs to know if the executable must be produced as a console application (`/target:exe` option) or a windowed application (`/target:winexe` option).
- The *Visual Studio* development environment asks you when you create a project whether it will be a *Console Application* or a *Windows Application*.

Introduction to Windows messages

The transition from DOS to the *Windows* operating system has brought the introduction of *Windows messages*. For each event (movement of the mouse, keyboard key pressed or released…), the *Windows* operating system creates a message which it sends to the concerned application. Each message contains:

- A message identifier which indicates the type of event (mouse right click, keyboard key pressed…).
- The parameters whose type and number vary depending on the type of message (mouse position, key which was pressed…).

For each type of event corresponds a *callback procedure*. For a particular window, the developer has the possibility of writing (or rewriting) the callback procedure for a certain event (for example, a left click on a button).

In windowed application, each window has one and only one thread which waits for messages in a message queue specific to this thread. Such a thread can manage several windows. When a message arrives, the thread executes the appropriate callback procedure. The main code of such a thread is built with a loop which is executed each time a message is received. This loop generally contains a gigantic *switch* statement (with possibly hundreds of cases) which associates the callback to the events.

Evolution of Windows applications development

The evolution of windowed application development under *Windows* has always converged towards the simplification of this large switch statement. The introduction of *MFC* (*Microsoft Foundation Classes*) went in this direction. The developer only needed to create the event/callback associations which he needed. An association table was defined through C++ macros and could look like this:

```
BEGIN_MESSAGE_MAP(CDlgWizard, CDialog)
  ON_NOTIFY_EX( TTN_NEEDTEXT, 0, OnToolTips )       // Tool Tips

  ON_WM_SHOWWINDOW()      // Corresponds to the standard callback
                          // procedure 'OnShowWindow()'.

  ON_WM_MOUSEMOVE()       // Corresponds to the standard callback
                          // procedure 'OnMouseMove()'.

  ON_WM_PAINT()           // Corresponds to the standard callback
                          // procedure 'OnPaint()'.

  ON_BN_CLICKED( IDC_BN_VALIDATE, OnBnClickedValidate )
          // The button with the ID 'IDC_BN_VALIDATE' is clicked.
          // Corresponds to the custom callback procedure
          // 'OnBnClickedValidate()'.
END_MESSAGE_MAP()
```

The *Visual Studio* IDE simplified this management by allowing the placement of controls in the window through the use of a *WYSIWYG* (*What You See Is What You Get*) editor This editor automatically added the event/callback associations in the table. This editor did have the disadvantage of disallowing the manual edition of the association it had created. You needed a certain experience in order to complete these operations manually. In addition, the editor used a unique file in order to describe all the windows of an application. Several write conflicts could occur between the developers of the application.

This section is written in the past tense as for a .NET developer; 'almost' all of this is from the past. The work of a windowed application developer is greatly simplified in .NET thanks to the *Windows Forms* technology. As we will show in the following sections, the description of the content of the windows as well as the event/callback associations are very intuitive and do not make use of unnecessary code or files. This mainly implies that a windowed application can be developed without the use of a specific editor. All this can easily be done using notepad!

Introduction to the System.Windows.Forms namespace

The `System.Windows.Forms` namespace contains several classes used to create *Windows* graphical application. These classes can be split into five groups:

- The *forms:*
  These are the classes which contains the base behaviors of forms. You simply need to create a class which inherits from one of these form classes in order to create your own form. Here, we can mention the `System.Windows.Forms.Form` class which represents the base class for all forms.

- The *controls*:

    A control is an element of a form. About fifty types of classic controls are provided by the .NET framework, such as a button or a textbox. They all have the peculiarity of deriving from the `System.Windows.Forms.Control` class which describes the base behavior of a control. The following sections list all the standard control classes and explains how you can also create your own control classes.

- The *components:*

    In the domain of graphical application, components allow to add functionalities to forms and controls. For example, the `System.Windows.Forms.ToolTip` class allows adding the functionality of tooltip descriptions of controls to a form. We can also mention the functionality of menu and user help.

    The base class of all components is `System.ComponentModel.Component`. The `Control` and `Form` classes derive from the `Component` class. The notion of component is more global than the notions of controls and forms. In addition, the notion of component is not restrained only to graphical application. More details on components are available in the article named **Class vs. Component vs. Control** on **MSDN**.

    Concretely, a component is a form field. The idea of enclosing the global behavior of the form within a class, while defining the controls of the form as fields of this class is in fact a *design pattern* (Gof) named *mediator*. The advantage of this *design pattern* is that the components do not necessarily need to know about each other in order to interact with each other. This implies that the classes of components are totally decoupled.

- Common dialog windows:

    Several standard dialogs are directly encapsulated within bases classes in the .NET framework, for example, we can mention the file selection dialog, the font selection dialog, the color selection dialog or the printer setup dialog.

- Form development helper classes:

    Several types are necessary to the developers of forms. You have, for example, delegate types which represent the signatures of the callback methods or enumeration where the values define the style of controls or forms.

Introduction to Windows Forms development

We will now create a form for the conversion between miles/kilometers based on the conversion rate of 1 mile = 1.609 kilometer. For this, we will use *Visual Studio*. At the end of this section, we will show how we could have used a simple text editor such as *Notepad* and the `csc.exe` compiler to achieve the same result.

First of all, you must create a new project *Visual C# Windows Application* with the *Visual Studio* editor. You will immediately be brought to the form editor. Note that a C# class associated to this form is also created.

The form editor allows the addition of controls to your forms. You only need to choose the type of control in the toolbox and then place and size it on your form. By using two controls of type `Button`, two controls of type `TextBox` and two controls of type `Label`, we were able to create the form in Figure 18-1.

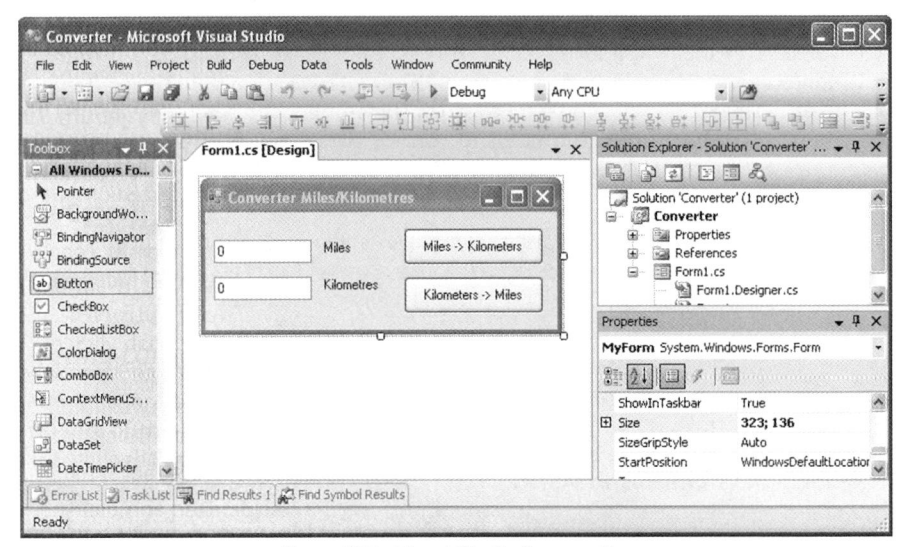

Figure 18-1: Visual Studio forms editor

You can now modify the *Text* property of the six controls of the form in order to achieve the result in the previous figure.

To access the properties of a control, you simply need to right-click on the control in the editor and to choose the *Properties* menu option or to select the control and press F4. A window similar to the one in Figure 18-2 appears and allows the edition of the properties of a control. The set of properties available is specific to each type of control (with the exception to the sub-set of properties of the `Control` class).

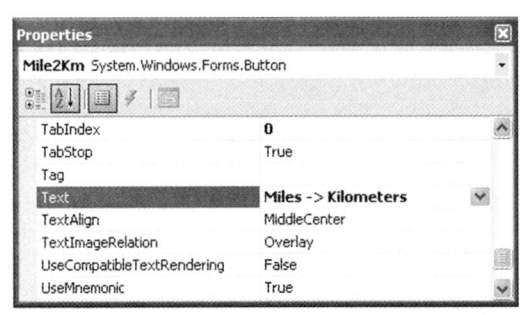

Figure 18-2: Editing the properties of a control

Each control of the form is represented by a field of the form class. The editor has added these fields automatically in the class of the form.

```
...
    public class Form1 : System.Windows.Forms.Form {
        private System.Windows.Forms.Button    Mile2Km;
        private System.Windows.Forms.Button    Km2Mile;
        private System.Windows.Forms.TextBox   TextBoxMile;
        private System.Windows.Forms.Label     Label1;
        private System.Windows.Forms.Label     Label2;
        private System.Windows.Forms.TextBox   TextBoxKm;
...
```

With *Visual Studio 2003*, a *Windows Forms* was completely defined within a single C# source file. The code generated by the IDE was separated from your code by using regions. *Visual Studio .2005* takes advantage of the concept of partial classes in C#2. By default, to each form named `FormXXX` corresponds two files: `FormXXX.cs` which contains your code and `FormXXX.Designer.cs` which contains the code generated by *Visual Studio 2005*. For the sake of simplicity, the form code examples presented in this book will be presented in a single C# file.

The name of the fields of the form referencing the controls were also modified in the property window in Figure 18-2. In the `InitializeComponent()` method of the form class, the editor has automatically added code which allows to create the controls, to position the controls and to configure their size. For example, the code added corresponding to a button is:

```
...
    //
    // Km2Mile
    //
    this.Km2Mile.Location = new System.Drawing.Point(160, 56);
    this.Km2Mile.Name     = "Km2Mile";
    this.Km2Mile.Size     = new System.Drawing.Size(96, 32);
    this.Km2Mile.TabIndex = 1;
    this.Km2Mile.Text     = "Kilometers -> Miles";
...
```

As you can see, contrarily to the management of windows using MFC, their are no superfluous lines of code and all that is related to a form is found in the class for this form.

Handling events

Each type of control offers a set of events. Here, we indeed are talking of the same event concept than the one offered by C# as we talk of the events of the class for the control. For each event of a control, you can associate a method of the form class containing the control. This method is essentially the callback function for the event. For example, a control of type `Button` offers the `Click` event which triggers a call to the associated callback method when the button is clicked. By double-clicking on the *Kilometers -> Miles* in the editor, *Visual Studio* automatically adds the following method to the form:

```
...
private void Km2Mile_Click(object sender, System.EventArgs e) {
    // To fill with your own code.
}
...
```

The editor associates this method to the `Click` event with the following code placed in the `InitializeComponent()` method after the initialization of the `Km2Mile` control:

```
...
    this.Km2Mile.Click += new System.EventHandler(this.Km2Mile_Click);
...
```

Rather than to double-click on the button in the editor, we can easily associate the events to a control of a form, through properties menu of the control as shown in Figure 18-3. Note that to access to this property sub-menu, you need to click on the icon which looks like a lightning bolt.

Finally note that the prototype of the methods which will be used as the callback procedure is an immutable event. It must be equal to the prototype of the `System.EventHandler` delegate.

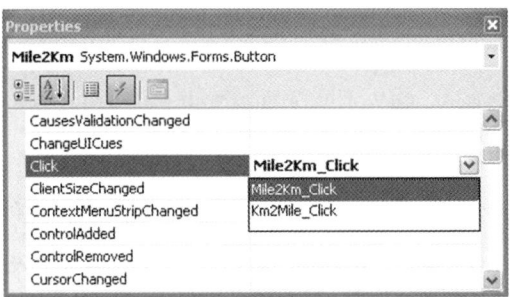

Figure 18-3: Binding methods and events of a control

Coding methods

We only have to fill the two `Km2Mile_Click()` and `Mile2Km_Click()` methods with the following code:

```
    ...
    static void Main() { Application.Run(new MyForm()); }
    const double RATE = 1.609;
    private void Mile2Km_Click( object sender,System.EventArgs e ) {
       double ditanceMile;
       if ( double.TryParse( TextBoxMile.Text, out ditanceMile ) )
          TextBoxKm.Text = ( ditanceMile * RATE ).ToString();
    }
    private void Km2Mile_Click( object sender,System.EventArgs e ) {
       double ditanceKm;
       if( double.TryParse( TextBoxKm.Text, out ditanceKm ) )
          TextBoxMile.Text = ( ditanceKm / RATE ).ToString();
    }
    ...
```

Note the use of the `double.TryParse()` method to avoid that an exception be raised in the case where an invalid floating-point number is input.

Windows Forms development without Visual Studio

We could have completely avoided using *Visual Studio* to create this windowed application. You simply need to write the following code in a C# source file (`Converter.cs` for example) then to compile this file using the `csc.exe` as follows:

```
>csc.exe /target:winexe Converter.cs
```

If we would have chosen the `/target:exe` option, the compiler would not have produced an error. The difference is that generated executable would have needed a console to execute itself. If we would have launched this executable from explorer, it would have created its own console.

It is evident that the form editor of *Visual Studio* is mostly use to visualize and adjust the look of a form. The majority of the following code is oriented around the initialization of the controls. Only the code in bold was effectively written by hand.

Example 18-1   Converter.cs

```csharp
using System.Drawing;
using System.ComponentModel;
using System.Windows.Forms;

namespace WindowsMileKm {
   public class MyForm : Form {
       private Button Mile2Km;
       private Button Km2Mile;
       private TextBox TextBoxMile;
       private Label Label1;
       private Label Label2;
       private TextBox TextBoxKm;
       public MyForm() { InitializeComponent(); }

       private void InitializeComponent() {
          this.Mile2Km = new Button();
          this.Km2Mile = new Button();
          this.Label1 = new Label();
          this.Label2 = new Label();
          this.TextBoxMile = new TextBox();
          this.TextBoxKm = new TextBox();
          this.SuspendLayout();

          // Mile2Km
          this.Mile2Km.Location = new Point(178, 14);
          this.Mile2Km.Name = "Mile2Km";
          this.Mile2Km.Size = new System.Drawing.Size(125, 32);
          this.Mile2Km.TabIndex = 0;
          this.Mile2Km.Text = "Miles -> Kilometers";
          this.Mile2Km.Click += this.Mile2Km_Click;

          // Km2Mile
          this.Km2Mile.Location = new Point(178, 56);
          this.Km2Mile.Name = "Km2Mile";
          this.Km2Mile.Size = new Size(125, 32);
          this.Km2Mile.TabIndex = 1;
          this.Km2Mile.Text = "Kilometers -> Miles";
          this.Km2Mile.Click += this.Km2Mile_Click;

          // Label1
          this.Label1.Location = new Point(104, 24);
          this.Label1.Name = "Label1";
          this.Label1.Size = new Size(68, 16);
          this.Label1.TabIndex = 3;
          this.Label1.Text = "Miles";

          // Label2
          this.Label2.Location = new Point(104, 56);
          this.Label2.Name = "Label2";
          this.Label2.Size = new Size(68, 16);
          this.Label2.TabIndex = 5;
          this.Label2.Text = "Kilometres";

          // TextBoxMile
          this.TextBoxMile.Location = new Point(8, 24);
          this.TextBoxMile.Name = "TextBoxMile";
          this.TextBoxMile.Size = new Size(88, 20);
```

Example 18-1 Converter.cs

```
            this.TextBoxMile.TabIndex = 4;
            this.TextBoxMile.Text = "0";

            // TextBoxKm
            this.TextBoxKm.Location = new Point(8, 56);
            this.TextBoxKm.Name = "TextBoxKm";
            this.TextBoxKm.Size = new Size(88, 20);
            this.TextBoxKm.TabIndex = 6;
            this.TextBoxKm.Text = "0";

            // Form1
            this.ClientSize = new Size(315, 102);
            this.Controls.AddRange(new Control[] {
                    this.TextBoxKm,
                    this.Label2,
                    this.TextBoxMile,
                    this.Label1,
                    this.Km2Mile,
                    this.Mile2Km});
            this.Name = "Form1";
            this.Text = "Converter Miles/Kilometres";
            this.ResumeLayout(false);
        }
        [System.STAThread]
        static void Main() { Application.Run(new MyForm()); }
        const double RATE = 1.609;
        private void Mile2Km_Click(object sender,System.EventArgs e){
           double ditanceMile;
           if ( double.TryParse( TextBoxMile.Text, out ditanceMile ) )
              TextBoxKm.Text = ( ditanceMile * RATE ).ToString();
        }
        private void Km2Mile_Click(object sender,System.EventArgs e){
           double ditanceKm;
           if( double.TryParse( TextBoxKm.Text, out ditanceKm ) )
              TextBoxMile.Text = ( ditanceKm / RATE ).ToString();
        }
    }
}
```

Facilities to develop Windows Forms applications

Introduction to modal/modeless dialogs

In a graphical interface, it is often a good idea to make a new window appear (which we call a dialog) to capture data or to present specific data to the user. There are two types of scenarios when the display of a new child window is a consequence of an action on the parent window:

- Either the parent window remains in the background and is frozen, until the child window is closed. In this case, we say that the dialog is *modal*. To create a modal window, you need to use the ShowDialog() of the Form class:

```
...
    MyFormClass aForm = new MyFormClass()
    // The ShowDialog() only returns when the 'AForm' form is closed.
    aForm.ShowDialog();
...
```

Facilities to develop Windows Forms applications

- Either the parent window can still be used, even if the child window is still visible. In this case, we say the child window is *modeless*. To create a modeless dialog, you must use the `Show()` method of the `Form` class:

```
...
        MyFormClass aForm = new MyFormClass()
        // The Show() method returns immediately after the creation of
        // the form.
        aForm.Show();
...
```

It is more common to use modal dialogs than modeless dialogs. In fact, modal dialogs are well adapted to the capture of data in a sequential manner. However, in certain scenarios where several windows are needed for the use of the application, modeless dialog is the appropriate alternative. For example *Visual Studio* uses several modeless dialogs, one for the view of files, one for the project view, one to display compiler messages… But understand that an application which uses too many modeless windows can confuse the user.

Mouse and keyboard events

You have the possibility of intercepting events which are produced by standard input peripherals which are the keyboard and the mouse. All the events which are presented also exist in the `Form` class.

A control intercepts the keyboard events as soon as it has the *focus* of the keyboard. A control obtains the focus:

- Either because the user has clicked on a control.
- Either because he changes the focus from one control to another by pressing TABS or SHIFTS+TAB. You can modify the order in which the focus will change from one control to another by assigning increasing values to the `TabIndex` property of your controls.

The `System.Windows.Forms.Control` class, from which inherits all the standard controls of *Windows Forms*, offers the `KeyDown`, `KeyUp`, and `KeyPress` events which provoke the call to their respective callback procedure. Of course, the event is only triggered when the control has the focus. The parameter of this event is the code of the keyboard key which was pressed.

A control intercepts the mouse events as soon as the mouse is located in the region of the control. You can however decide to capture the mouse events when the mouse is outside of the control's region if the `Capture{get;set;}` property is set to `true`.

Several mouse events are available and it is important to understand when they are triggered. Each of these events is parameterized, for example, with the mouse button on which the click is done (if there is a click) and the position of the mouse.

Event	Description
`MouseDown`	A mouse button was pressed.
`MouseUp`	A mouse button was released.
`Click`	A mouse button was clicked.
`DoubleClick`	A mouse button was double-clicked (it is better to not implement this event at the same time than the `Click` event. In this case, *Windows* calls both callback when a double-click occurs).
`MouseMove`	The mouse is moved over the control (or elsewhere if the `capture` property is set to `true`).
`MouseEnter`	The mouse enters the zone of the control.
`MouseLeave`	The mouse leaves the zone of the control.
`MouseHover`	The mouse pauses within the region of a control.
`MouseWheel`	The mouse wheel is used.

The Paint event

The Paint event and its OnPaint() callback is important in graphical applications under the *Windows* operating system. Indeed, the display of windows is not persistent. In other words if a window (or a part of the window) becomes visible while it was previously hidden, it is necessary that the thread responsible for this window redraws this part. When a window (or a part of a window) becomes visible, the *Windows* operating system sends the WM_PAINT message. Under .NET, this translates by triggering of the Paint event of the concerned form and the call to the OnPaint() callback method. Amongst the arguments of this event, there is the coordinates of the rectangle to draw. Most of the time, you do not need to take care of this event as, by default, the event is automatically transmitted to the controls which must be redrawn. However, when you use the GDI+ library or when you create your own controls, you will need to override the OnPaint() method with your own code.

Asynchronous processing

In a *Windows Forms* application, when the thread which processes the events is blocked by the execution of a long operation, the user is disappointed to see his window frozen. To solve this problem, we generally delegate the long operation either to a thread of the pool or to a thread specially dedicated for this operation.

Windows Forms 2 offers the BackgroundWorker class which allows the standardization of the development of asynchronous operations within a form. This class offers facilities to periodically notify the progress or to cancel the operation. Its use is illustrated by the following example which delegates the calculation of prime numbers by using an instance of the System.ComponentModel.BackgroundWorker class. The progress of the work is indicated by the use of a progress bar and you have the possibility of canceling the operation by using a button. In this example, only the DoWork() and IsPrime() methods are executed by a thread from the thread pool:

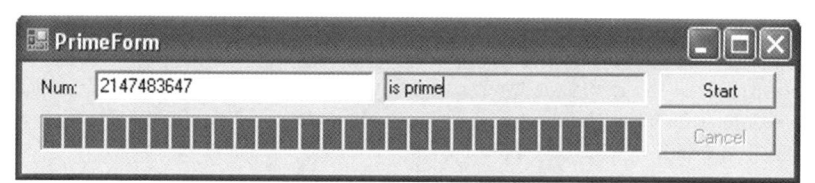

Figure 18-4: Prime number program

Example 18-2

```
...
public class PrimeForm : Form {
   public PrimeForm() {
      InitializeComponent();
      InitializeBackgoundWorker();
   }
   private void InitializeBackgoundWorker() {
      backgroundWorker.DoWork += DoWork;
      backgroundWorker.RunWorkerCompleted += Complete;
      backgroundWorker.ProgressChanged += ProgressChanged;
      backgroundWorker.WorkerReportsProgress = true;
      backgroundWorker.WorkerSupportsCancellation = true;
   }
   private void DoWork( object sender,DoWorkEventArgs e ) {
      BackgroundWorker worker = sender as BackgroundWorker;
      e.Result = IsPrime( (int) e.Argument, worker, e );
   }
   private void ProgressChanged( object sender,
```

Facilities to develop Windows Forms applications 561

Example 18-2
```
                                    ProgressChangedEventArgs e ) {
      progressBar.Value = e.ProgressPercentage;
   }
   private void Complete( object sender,RunWorkerCompletedEventArgs e ) {
      textBoxInput.Enabled = true;
      buttonStart.Enabled  = true;
      buttonCancel.Enabled = false;
      if ( e.Error != null ) //Case where an exception has been raised.
         MessageBox.Show( e.Error.Message );
      else if ( e.Cancelled )// Case of cancellation.
         textBoxResult.Text = "Processing cancelled!";
      else                   // Processing succeeded.
         textBoxResult.Text = e.Result.ToString();
   }
   private void buttonStart_Click( object sender, EventArgs e ) {
      int number = 0;
      if ( int.TryParse( textBoxInput.Text, out number ) ) {
         textBoxResult.Text   = String.Empty;
         textBoxInput.Enabled = false;
         buttonStart.Enabled  = false;
         buttonCancel.Enabled = true;
         progressBar.Value    = 0;
         backgroundWorker.RunWorkerAsync(number);
      } else textBoxResult.Text = "input invalid!";
   }
   private void buttonCancel_Click( object sender, EventArgs e ) {
      backgroundWorker.CancelAsync();
      buttonCancel.Enabled = false;
   }
   private string IsPrime( int number, BackgroundWorker worker,
                           DoWorkEventArgs e) {
      int root = ( (int)System.Math.Sqrt(number) )+1;
      int highestPercentageReached = 0;
      for ( int i = 2; i < root; i++ ) {
         if ( worker.CancellationPending ) {
            e.Cancel = true;
            return String.Empty;
         } else {
            if ( number % i == 0 )
               return "can be divided by " + i.ToString();
            int percentComplete = (int)((float)i / (float)root * 100);
            if ( percentComplete > highestPercentageReached ) {
               highestPercentageReached = percentComplete;
               worker.ReportProgress(percentComplete);
            }
         }
      }
      return "is prime";
   }
...
```

Some others featuress

The creation of graphical application with *Windows Forms* presents a large number of features other than what we have already discussed. We have tried above to select features which are trivial and non-trivial but that are often used. Here are other features, whose use is described in **MSDN**:

- A peculiarity of the `Component` class is to implement the `System.ComponentModel.IComponent` interface. This interface allows for a component to be encapsulated in an instance of a class which implements the `System.ComponentModel.IContainer` interface. A *container* is a set of components and each component knows about its container. This set of interfaces illustrates an implementation of the *mediator design pattern*. A consequence of this approach is a possibility of editing your forms in a WYSIWYG way with *Visual Studio*. To name this component/container edition feature, *Microsoft* uses the *design-time editing* term. More details on this topic can be found in the article named **Design-Time Architecture** on **MSDN**.

- The `System.Windows.Forms.MessageBox` class allows the easy display of a window with text and classic buttons:

  ```
  OK ;
  OK/Cancel ;
  Abort/Retry/Ignore ;
  Retry/Cancel ;
  Yes/No ;
  Yes/No/Cancel.
  ```

  The display is done using the `Show()` static method of this class which comes in several flavors.

- The management of *drag & drop* is done thanks to the `System.Windows.Forms.Control.DragDrop DragEnter` and `DragOver` events. Each of these events accepts a parameter of type `System.Windows.Forms.DragEnventArgs`.

- You can use different types of menus thanks to the `System.Windows.Forms.Menu` class and to its `ContextMenu, MainMenu` and `MenuItem` derived classes.

- You can use the following standard dialog classes:

  ```
  System.Windows.Forms.ColorDialog
  System.Windows.Forms.FileDialog
  System.Windows.Forms.FontDialog
  System.Windows.Forms.OpenFileDialog
  System.Windows.Forms.PageSetupDialog
  System.Windows.Forms.PrintControllerWithStatusDialog
  System.Windows.Forms.PrintDialog
  System.Windows.Forms.PrintPreviewDialog
  System.Windows.Forms.SaveFileDialog
  ```

- The `System.Windows.Forms.Timer` class allows the easy use of a *timer*. This is an object which triggers an event at a regular time interval. More detail on this can be found at page 139.

- The `System.Windows.Forms.ToolTips` class allows the display of a tooltip help window which gives information on the use of a control. To obtain this help, the user only needs to let the mouse over a control for a short amount of time. The tooltip disappears automatically after the mouse is moved or after a certain delay. All this can be configured through the properties of the class.

- The `System.Windows.Forms.Help` class allows the display of application help in HTML within a browser. This help is generally more complete than the one offered by *tooltips*. You can display the help with the `ShowHelp()` method (or the help index using `ShowHelpIndex()`). You can download the *HTML Help WorkShop* on the *Microsoft* site. This tool allows the creation of help files in a `.chm` or `.htm` format.

- The `System.Windows.Forms.ClipBoard` allows you to store and retrieve information on the *clipboard*. Never use this technique to communicate information between processes. The clipboard is strictly reserved for user data.

- The `System.Windows.Forms.NotifyIcon` class allows the development of *tray icon* applications.The application remains resident in memory and presents an icon in the *Windows* icon bar which indicates its current state. The *Windows Messenger* application is a good example of *tray icon* application.

- By calling the `Application.EnableVisualStyles()` method on the startup of a *Windows Forms* you ensure that controls with their `FlatStyle` properties set to `Standard` or `System` will have the same look as defined by the underlying operating system.

Standard controls

Hierarchy of Windows Forms 2 controls

The hierarchy of standard controls is presented below. The controls whose names are in bold are new in *Windows Forms 2*:

```
System.Object
    System.MarshalByRefObject
        System.ComponentModel.Component
            System.Windows.Forms.Control
                Microsoft.WindowsCE.Forms.DocumentList
                System.ComponentModel.Design.ByteViewer
                System.Windows.Forms.AxHost
                System.Windows.Forms.ButtonBase
                    System.Windows.Forms.Button
                    System.Windows.Forms.CheckBox
                    System.Windows.Forms.RadioButton
                System.Windows.Forms.DataGrid
                System.Windows.Forms.DataGridView
                System.Windows.Forms.DateTimePicker
                System.Windows.Forms.GroupBox
                System.Windows.Forms.Label
                    System.Windows.Forms.LinkLabel
                System.Windows.Forms.ListControl
                    System.Windows.Forms.ComboBox
                    System.Windows.Forms.ListBox
                System.Windows.Forms.ListView
                System.Windows.Forms.MdiClient
                System.Windows.Forms.MonthCalendar
                System.Windows.Forms.PictureBox
                System.Windows.Forms.PrintPreviewControl
                System.Windows.Forms.ProgressBar
                System.Windows.Forms.ScrollableControl
                    System.Windows.Forms.ContainerControl
                        System.Windows.Forms.Form
                        System.Windows.Forms.PropertyGrid
                        System.Windows.Forms.SplitContainer
                        System.Windows.Forms.ToolStripContainer
                        System.Windows.Forms.ToolStripPanel
                        System.Windows.Forms.UpDownBase
                            System.Windows.Forms.DomainUpDown
                            System.Windows.Forms.NumericUpDown
                        System.Windows.Forms.UserControl
```

```
            System.Windows.Forms.Design.ComponentTray
            System.Windows.Forms.Panel
                System.Windows.Forms.FlowLayoutPanel
                System.Windows.Forms.SplitterPanel
                System.Windows.Forms.TableLayoutPanel
                System.Windows.Forms.TabPage
                System.Windows.Forms.ToolStripContentPanel
            System.Windows.Forms.ToolStrip
                System.Windows.Forms.BindingNavigator
                System.Windows.Forms.DataNavigator
                System.Windows.Forms.MenuStrip
                System.Windows.Forms.StatusSTrip
                System.Windows.Forms.ToolStripDropDown
                    System.Windows.Forms.ToolStripDropDownMenu
                        System.Windows.Forms.ContextMenuStrip
        System.Windows.Forms.ScrollBar
            System.Windows.Forms.HScrollBar
            System.Windows.Forms.VScrollBar
        System.Windows.Forms.Splitter
        System.Windows.Forms.StatusBar
        System.Windows.Forms.TabControl
        System.Windows.Forms.TextBoxBase
            System.Windows.Forms.RichTextBox
            System.Windows.Forms.TextBox
            System.Windows.Forms.MaskedTextBox
        System.Windows.Forms.ToolBar
        System.Windows.Forms.TrackBar
        System.Windows.Forms.TreeView
        System.Windows.Forms.WebBrowserBase
            System.Windows.Forms.WebBrowser
```

We invite you to consult **MSDN** to get more details on each of these classes.

Overview of the new controls

Here is a quick overview of all the new *Windows Form 2* controls:

- The `ToolStrip`, `MenuStrip`, `StatusStrip` and `ContextMenuStrip` controls:
  These controls respectively replace the `ToolBar`, `MainMenu`, `StatusBar` and `ContextMenu` controls (which are still present for backward compatibility reasons). In addition to nicer visual style, these new controls are particularly easy to manipulate during the design of a window thanks to a consistent API. New functionality has been added such as the possibility of sharing a render between controls, the support for animated GIFs, opacity, transparency and the facility of saving the current state (position, size...) in the configuration file. The hierarchy of the classes derived from the class `System.Windows.Forms.ToolStripItem` constitutes as many elements which can be inserted in this type of control. More information on this topic can be found in the articles named **ToolStrip Technology Summary** and **ToolStrip Control Overview (Windows Forms)** on **MSDN**.

- The `DataGridView` and `BindingNavigator` controls:
  These controls are part of a new framework to develop data driven forms. This framework is the subject of the Viewing and editing data section a little later in this chapter. Know that it is now preferable to use a `DataGridView` for the display of any data table or list of objects instead of the *Windows Form 1* `DataGrid` control.

- The `FlowLayoutPanel` and `TableLayout` controls:

Creating custom controls 565

These controls allow the dynamic positioning of the child controls that it contains when the user modifies its size. The layout philosophy of the `FlowLayoutPanel` control is to list the child controls horizontally or vertically in a way where they are moved when the control is resized. This approach is similar to what we see when we resize an HTML document displayed by a browser. The layout philosophy of the `TablePanel` control is comparably to the *anchoring* mechanism where the children controls are resized based on the size of the parent control. However, here the child controls are found in the cells of a table.

- The `SplitterPanel` and `SplitContainer` controls:
  The combined use of these controls allows the easy implementation of the splitting of a window in a way which can be resized as we had with version 1.1 using the `Splitter` control.
- The `WebBrowser` control:
  This control allows the insertion of a web browser directly in a *Windows Forms* form.
- The `MaskedTextBox` control:
  This control displays a `TextBox` in which the format of the text to insert is constrained. Several type of masks are offered by default such dates or US telephone number. Of course, you can also provide your own masks.
- The `SoundPlayer` and `SystemSounds` controls:
  The `SoundPlayer` class allows you to play sounds in a `.wav` format while the `SystemSounds` class allows you to retrieve the system sounds associated with the current user of the operating system.

Creating custom controls

You have the possibility of easily creating your own graphical controls. All those who even had to create their own *ActiveX* controls will be pleasantly surprised with the simplicity of creating a graphical control with .NET. In general, a graphical control is reusable. Also, it is usually a good idea to create a shared assembly to contain the code of a control (or a set of controls). You have the possibility of inserting in your own controls:

- Standard .NET controls.
- Other custom controls.
- Your own graphical rendering using the GDI+ library, which we discuss in the last section of this chapter.

A custom control class must derive from the `System.Windows.Forms.UserControl` class.

Here, we propose a tutorial which shows how to create a graphical control which displays percentages with a bar graph. The created control contains a combination of standard controls and rendering using the GDI+ library. For more simplicity, we create the control and the form which uses it in the same assembly, but it is better to create your custom controls in a separate shared assembly. To simplify our presentation, we will use *Visual Studio*. However, a text editor would be sufficient to create such a control.

Create a new project of type *Windows Application*. Add a new user control to the project (right-click on the project, *Add* → *Add New Item… → User Control*) that we will call *PercentViewer*. The idea is that our control will resemble to the one illustrated in Figure 18-5. A client to the control can change the percentage value during the execution. A developer who is a client of the control can choose to display the grid and/or the border, during the development of the application (at *design-time*) and during execution.

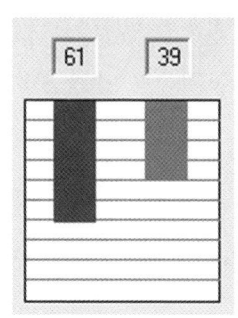

Figure 18-5: Overview of our custom control

Here is the code. Note that in the `Draw()` method, we use the classes of the GDI+ library that we will describe in the next section:

Example 18-3

```
using System.ComponentModel;
using System.Drawing;
using System.Windows.Forms;

public class PercentViewer : UserControl {
   private TextBox PercentLeft;
   private TextBox PercentRight;

   // Tune the percentage value (between 0.0 and 1.0).
   private byte m_Value = 30;
   public double Value {
      set {
         if (value < 0.0)      m_Value = 0;
         else if (value > 1.0) m_Value = 100;
         else                  m_Value = (byte)(100.0 * value);
         Draw();
      }
   }

   // Should we draw the grid ?
   private bool m_bGrid = true;
   [Category("Appearance")]
   public bool bGrid {
      set { m_bGrid = value; Draw(); }
      get { return m_bGrid; }
   }

   // Should we draw borders ?
   private bool m_bBorder = true;
   [Category("Appearance")]
   public bool bBorder {
      set { m_bBorder = value; Draw(); }
      get { return m_bBorder; }
   }

   // Constructor.
   public PercentViewer() { InitializeComponent(); }

   // Code to intialize controls.
```

Creating custom controls

Example 18-3

```
    #region Component Designer generated code
    private void InitializeComponent() {
       this.PercentLeft = new TextBox();
       this.PercentRight = new TextBox();
       this.SuspendLayout();

       // PercentLeft
       this.PercentLeft.Location = new Point( 16, 8 );
       this.PercentLeft.Name = "PercentLeft";
       this.PercentLeft.ReadOnly = true;
       this.PercentLeft.Size = new Size( 24, 20 );
       this.PercentLeft.TabIndex = 0;
       this.PercentLeft.Text = "";
       this.PercentLeft.TextAlign = HorizontalAlignment.Center;

       // PercentRight
       this.PercentRight.Location = new Point(64, 8);
       this.PercentRight.Name = "PercentRight";
       this.PercentRight.ReadOnly = true;
       this.PercentRight.Size = new Size( 24, 20 );
       this.PercentRight.TabIndex = 1;
       this.PercentRight.Text = "";
       this.PercentRight.TextAlign = HorizontalAlignment.Center;

       // PercentViewer
       this.Controls.AddRange(new Control[] { this.PercentRight,
                                              this.PercentLeft});
       this.Name = "PercentViewer";
       this.Size = new Size( 104, 168 );
       // Bind the 'PercentViewer_Paint' method with the 'Paint' event.
       this.Paint += new PaintEventHandler( this.PercentViewer_Paint );
       this.ResumeLayout( false );
    }
    #endregion

    private void Draw() {
       // Fill text boxes.
       PercentLeft.Text = m_Value.ToString();
       PercentRight.Text = (100 - m_Value).ToString();

       // Ensure that the Graphics object dispose method will be called.
       using ( Graphics g = CreateGraphics() ) {
          // Discard last display with a white-filled rectangle.
          g.FillRectangle( Brushes.White, 3, 39, 100, 101 );

          // If 'm_bBorder' is true then draw the border.
          if (m_bBorder)
             g.DrawRectangle( new Pen(Color.Black), 2, 39, 100, 101 );

          // If 'm_bGrid' is true then draw the grid.
          if (m_bGrid) {
             Pen p = new Pen(Color.Gray);
             for (int i = 1; i < 10; i++)
                g.DrawLine(p, 3, 39 + i * 10, 102, 39 + i * 10);
          }
```

Example 18-3

```
        // Draw percentage filled rectangles.
        g.FillRectangle( Brushes.Blue, 17, 40, 22, m_Value );
        g.FillRectangle( Brushes.Red, 64, 40, 22, 100 - m_Value );
      }
   }

   // Callback procedure for the 'Paint' event.
   // To keep it simple, we are redrawing everything each time.
   private void PercentViewer_Paint( object sender,PaintEventArgs e ) {
      Draw();
   }
}
```

The use of the `CategoryAttribute` attribute on the `bGrid` and `bBorder` properties allows to the client of the control to configure these properties as shown in Figure 18-6. Note that you can create your own categories using the `CategoryAttribute` attribute. You can also use the dozen of standard categories offered by *Visual Studio*. These categories are explained in details in the article named **CategoryAttribute Class** on **MSDN**.

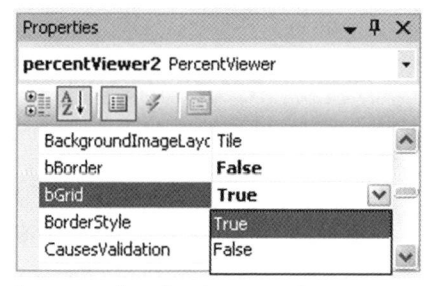

Figure 18-6: Configuration properties of an instance of a custom control with Visual Studio

Finally note that you can provide facilities in order to directly store the state of a control in the parameters of the application. Hence, it will keep the same state at each execution of the application. This feature is discussed in the article named **Application Settings for Custom Controls** on **MSDN**.

Using the custom control

Our control is used in the same way as a standard control. You simply need to reference the assembly in which the control is defined (in our example, the control is in the same assembly as the one using it, but it is not generally the case).

The client form for our control is shown in Figure 18-7. A click on the *New result!* button produces a random percentage which is displayed in three instances of the control. We have used three instances of the control to illustrate the various options of the control.

Creating custom controls

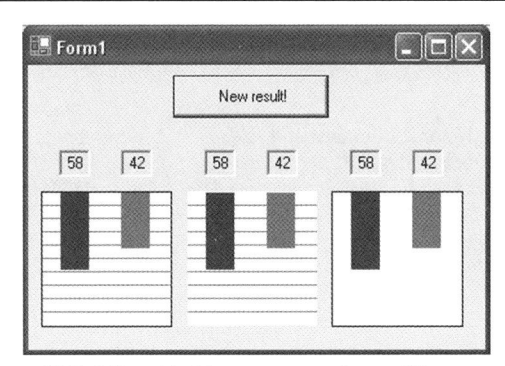

Figure 18-7: A form that harnesses our PercentViewer control

Here is the code:

Example 18-4
```
using System.Drawing;
using System.ComponentModel;
using System.Windows.Forms;

public class MyForm : Form {
    private Button NewResult;
    private PercentViewer percentViewer1;
    private PercentViewer percentViewer2;
    private PercentViewer percentViewer3;

    public MyForm() { InitializeComponent(); }

#region Windows Form Designer generated code
    private void InitializeComponent() {
        this.percentViewer1 = new PercentViewer();
        this.NewResult = new Button();
        this.percentViewer2 = new PercentViewer();
        this.percentViewer3 = new PercentViewer();
        this.SuspendLayout();

        // Result
        this.NewResult.Location = new Point(112, 8);
        this.NewResult.Name = "NewResult";
        this.NewResult.Size = new Size(120, 32);
        this.NewResult.TabIndex = 0;
        this.NewResult.Text = "New result!";
        this.NewResult.Click+= new System.EventHandler(this.NewResult_Click);

        // percentViewer1
        this.percentViewer1.bBorder = true;
        this.percentViewer1.bGrid = true;
        this.percentViewer1.Location = new Point(8, 56);
        this.percentViewer1.Name = "percentViewer1";
        this.percentViewer1.Size = new Size(104, 152);
        this.percentViewer1.TabIndex = 1;

        // percentViewer2
        this.percentViewer2.bBorder = false;
        this.percentViewer2.bGrid = true;
        this.percentViewer2.Location = new Point(120, 56);
        this.percentViewer2.Name = "percentViewer2";
```

```
            this.percentViewer2.Size = new Size(104, 144);
            this.percentViewer2.TabIndex = 2;

            // percentViewer3
            this.percentViewer3.bBorder = true;
            this.percentViewer3.bGrid = false;
            this.percentViewer3.Location = new Point(232, 56);
            this.percentViewer3.Name = "percentViewer3";
            this.percentViewer3.Size = new Size(104, 144);
            this.percentViewer3.TabIndex = 3;

            // Form1
            this.AutoScaleDimensions = new SizeF(5, 13);
            this.ClientSize = new Size(352, 214);
            this.Controls.AddRange(new Control[] {
                this.percentViewer3,
                this.percentViewer2,
                this.percentViewer1,
                this.NewResult});
            this.Name = "MyForm";
            this.Text = "MyForm";
            this.ResumeLayout(false);
        }
    #endregion
        [System.STAThread]
        static void Main() { Application.Run(new MyForm()); }

        private void NewResult_Click(object sender, System.EventArgs e) {
            // Compute a random value between 0.0 and 1.0.
            System.Random random = new System.Random();
            double d = random.NextDouble();
            percentViewer1.Value = d;
            percentViewer2.Value = d;
            percentViewer3.Value = d;
        }
}
```

Viewing and editing data

Facilities provided by Visual Studio 2005

Thanks to certain tools of *Visual Studio 2005*, it is possible to develop an evolved window for data viewing and editing as shown in Figure 18-8 in two minutes on a stopwatch. This is what is called RAD (*Rapid Application Development*).

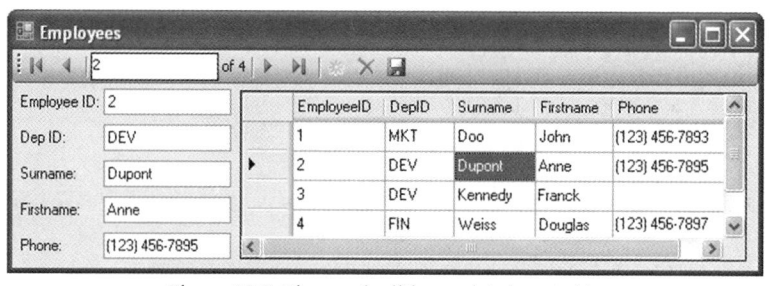

Figure 18-8: View and editing a database table

Viewing and editing data 571

Here is a little tutorial that explains how to create this window using *Visual Studio 2005*. But before this, you must have inserted the typed `DataSet` presented at page 606 into your project (it is also necessary to have assimilated the notion of typed `DataSet` before stating the next section). Also provide an empty window named `FormEmployees` in your project.

Make the *Data Source* view visible (*Data › Show Data Sources*) › Unroll the `ORGANIZATIONDataSet` data source › Select the `EMPLOYEES` node › Unroll the combo box which appears › Choose the *DataGridView* option › Drag-and-drop the `EMPLOYEES` node onto the `FormEmployees` window. *Visual Studio 2005* has now added several entities to your window:

- A typed `DataSet` of type `ORGANIZATIONDataSet` which represents the data source as well as a `TableAdapter` of type `EMPLOYEESTableAdapter`.
- A non-visual control of type `BindingSource` which represents the binding between our data source (i.e. the typed `DataSet`) and the visual controls for the presentation and edition of data.
- A visual control of type `DataGridView` which presents the list of the employees and also allows the edition of each cell.
- A visual control of type `BindingNavigator` which contains VCR-like buttons that allows the navigation of the list of employees. This control also offers a button to add a new employee, a button to delete the currently selected employee and a button to save the changes made on the employee list.

In addition to all the code necessary for the creation and edition of these controls and objects, *Visual Studio* has generated two methods which are found in the `FormEmployees.cs` source file.

```
...
private void FormEmployees_Load(object sender, EventArgs e) {
  this.eMPLOYEESTableAdapter.Fill(this.oRGANIZATIONDataSet.EMPLOYEES);
}
private void bindingNavigatorSaveItem_Click(object sender, EventArgs e){
  if ( this.Validate() ) {
    this.eMPLOYEESBindingSource.EndEdit();
    this.eMPLOYEESTableAdapter.Update(this.oRGANIZATIONDataSet.EMPLOYEES);
  } else {
    System.Windows.Forms.MessageBox.Show(this,
                "Validation errors occurred.", "Save",
                System.Windows.Forms.MessageBoxButtons.OK,
                System.Windows.Forms.MessageBoxIcon.Warning);
  }
}
...
```

It is clear that the `FormEmployees_Load()` method which is called during the loading of the window contains the code which allows to fill the `EMPLOYEES` table in our typed `DataSet` from our database. As explained at page 606, this is done be using the `TableAdapter` associated to the `EMPLOYEES` table.

It is also clear that the `bindingNavigatorSaveItem_Click()` method called when the save button of the `BindingNavigator` control is clicked, contains the code which allows to save in the database the modifications which were made. Here also, this operation is done using the `TableAdapter` associated to the `EMPLOYEES` table.

If you take a peek at the `FormEmployees.Designer.cs` file, you will notice that all can be configured including the set of buttons contained in the `BindingNavigator` control as well as the rows of the `DataGridView` control.

572   Chapter 18 - Windows Forms Applications

To obtain the window in Figure 18-8, you must now add five controls of type `Label` and five controls of type `EditBox` which allow the presentation of a detailed view of the currently selected employee. Select the EMPLOYEES node in the `ORGANIZATIONDataSet` data source > Unroll the combo box > Choose the *Details* option > Drag-and-drop the EMPLOYEES node onto the `FormEmployees` window. *Visual Studio 2005* has added ten new controls. We then obtain a master/detail view which is very practical for the edition and insertion of data in a table. Note that at page 783 we will show how to obtain a similar behavior in a web page.

It is interesting to analyze the lines of code dedicated to the creation of the bindings. They are found in the `InitializeComponent()` generated method of the `FormEmployees.Designer.cs` file. We have added some descriptive comments:

```
private void InitializeComponent() {
  ...
  // Create the 'BindingSource' object.
  this.eMPLOYEESBindingSource =
     new System.Windows.Forms.BindingSource(this.components);
  ...
  ((System.ComponentModel.ISupportInitialize)
     (this.eMPLOYEESBindingSource)).BeginInit();
  ...
  // Bind the 'BindingSource' object to the 'EMPLOYEES' table
  // of the typed DataSet.
  this.eMPLOYEESBindingSource.DataMember = "EMPLOYEES";
  this.eMPLOYEESBindingSource.DataSource = this.oRGANIZATIONDataSet;
  ...
  // Bind the 'BindingNavigator' object to the 'BindingSource' object.
  this.eMPLOYEESBindingNavigator.BindingSource=this.eMPLOYEESBindingSource;
  ...
  // Bind the 'DataGridView' object to the 'BindingSource' object.
  this.eMPLOYEESDataGridView.DataSource = this.eMPLOYEESBindingSource;
  ...

  // For each column of the 'DataGridView', specify the name of the
  // associated colum in the 'EMPLOYEES' table.
  this.dataGridViewTextBoxColumn1.DataPropertyName = "EmployeeID";
  ...
  this.dataGridViewTextBoxColumn2.DataPropertyName = "DepID";
  ...
  this.dataGridViewTextBoxColumn3.DataPropertyName = "Surname";
  ...
  this.dataGridViewTextBoxColumn4.DataPropertyName = "Firstname";
  ...
  this.dataGridViewTextBoxColumn5.DataPropertyName = "Phone";
  ...

   // Create dynamic binds between 'TextBox' objects and the typed DataSet.
   this.employeeIDTextBox.DataBindings.Add(new System.Windows.Forms.Binding(
      "Text", this.eMPLOYEESBindingSource, "EmployeeID", true));
   ...
   this.depIDTextBox.DataBindings.Add( new System.Windows.Forms.Binding(
      Text", this.eMPLOYEESBindingSource, "DepID", true));
   ...
   this.nameTextBox.DataBindings.Add( new System.Windows.Forms.Binding(
      "Text", this.eMPLOYEESBindingSource, "Surname", true));
   ...
   this.surnameTextBox.DataBindings.Add( new System.Windows.Forms.Binding(
```

Viewing and editing data

```
      "Text", this.eMPLOYEESBindingSource, "Firstname", true));
   ...
   this.telTextBox.DataBindings.Add( new System.Windows.Forms.Binding(
      "Text", this.eMPLOYEESBindingSource, "Phone", true));
   ...
   ((System.ComponentModel.ISupportInitialize)
      (this.eMPLOYEESBindingSource)).EndInit();
   ...
}
```

The BindingSource control

You can be without a control of type `BindingSource` to bind a control of type `DataGridView` directly to a data source such as a `DataTable`. The following example shows a window with a `DataGridView` filled with the content of the EMPLOYEES table and a `DataGridView` filled with the content of the DEPARTMENTS table:

Example 18-5

```
   ...
   public class MyForm : Form {
   ...
      private void Form1_Load( System.Object sender, System.EventArgs e ) {
         depDataGridView.DataSource = dSet.DEPARTMENTS;
         empDataGridView.DataSource = dSet.EMPLOYEES;
         depTableAdapter.Fill(dSet.DEPARTMENTS);
         empTableAdapter.Fill(dSet.EMPLOYEES);
      }
   ...
      private DataGridView empDataGridView;
      private DataGridView depDataGridView;
      private DEPARTMENTSTableAdapter depTableAdapter;
      private EMPLOYEESTableAdapter empTableAdapter;
      private ORGANIZATIONDataSet dSet;
   ...
```

Although that we can work without objects of type `BindingSource`, they can come in handy for several reasons:

- *By design*, they represent an indirection between the presentation controls and the data source. This indirection allows to easily choose the data source without having to change the code of a window.
- As we have seen, the `BindingNavigator`, `DataGridView` and `BindingSource` controls were designed in a way to easily collaborate.
- As we have seen, we can use a `BindingSource` control to bind the data of the presentation control during the design of the window using *Visual Studio 2005*.
- Controls of type `BindingSource` allow you to provide your own logic during the creation of a new element. More details on this can be found in the article named **How to: Customize Item Addition with the Windows Forms BindingSource** on **MSDN**.
- Thanks to the `Filter` and `Sort` properties of the `BindingSource` class, you can easily filter or sort the data of a data source before presenting it to the user.
- Controls of type `BindingSource` allow to easily harness a *one to many* relationship. Consider the relation named `Is_Employed_By` between the EMPLOYEES and DEPARTMENTS tables in our typed `DataSet` (this relationship is defined at page 589). Let's create a window with two `DataGridView` and two `BindingSource`. The first `BindingSource` is bound to the

DEPARTMENT table. The second is bound to the first one with the value of the `DataMember` property set to the name of the relationship. The second `BindingSource` is then capable of detecting the change of the department selection on the first one and applies this relationship to only display the employees of the selected department:

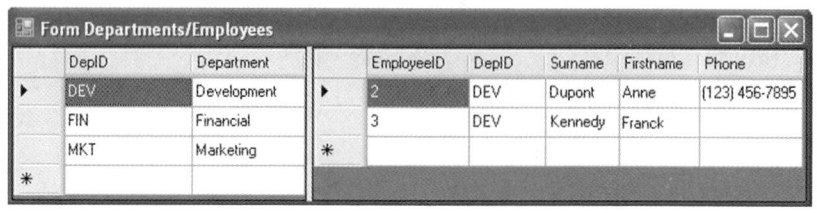

Figure 18-9: BindingSource and relations

Example 18-6

```
...
    private void Form1_Load(System.Object sender, System.EventArgs e) {
        depDataGridView.DataSource = depBindingSource;
        empDataGridView.DataSource = empBindingSource;
        depTableAdapter.Fill(dSet.DEPARTMENTS);
        empTableAdapter.Fill(dSet.EMPLOYEES);
        depBindingSource.DataSource = dSet;
        depBindingSource.DataMember = "DEPARTMENTS";
        empBindingSource.DataSource = depBindingSource;
        empBindingSource.DataMember = "Is_Employed_By";
    }
...
```

Harnessing a data source by using a BindingSource

An advantage of using instances of the `BindingSource` class is the features that it offers to abstract yourself from the type of data source used. Whatever the underlying type of data source is, the consumer of a `BindingSource` control can always use the data with the `IBindingList` interface. This interface implements the `IEnumerables`, `IList` and `ICollection` interfaces which are all implemented by `BindingSource`. In addition to the access methods of the implemented interfaces, the `IBindingList` interface offers properties to inform the client on the features supported by the source (sort, edition, insertion…), methods such as `AddNew()` to add an element or `Find()` to search for an element and the `ListChanged` event triggered each time the data is modified.

As we have seen, we can assign a data source of type `DataTable` to an object of type `BindingSource` by the intermediate of the `object DataSource{get;set;}` property. We can also assign a `DataSet` to this property at the condition that you specify the name of the table through the `string DataMember{get;set;}` property. We can also assign to this property:

- Any object which presents the `IEnumerable` interface.
- Any object representing an array (i.e. whose class derives from `System.Array`).
- An instance of the `System.Type` to specify the type of the object which can be added.
- Any object. The type of the object will be the type of the objects which can be added.

Using an object list as a data source

We have just seen that we are not constraint to be bound with an ADO.NET object such as a `DataSet` or a `DataTable`. Any type of object list can be used as a data source. This feature is essential for developing 3-Tiers or N-Tiers applications where the data is processed between the persistence layer and the presentation layer. The following example illustrates this. We have a list of

Viewing and editing data 575

objects of type `Employee` that we wish to display and edit in a `DataGridView`. This list derives from the `BindingList<Employee>` class. Therefore, we don't need an object of type `BindingSource` to bind it to the `DataGridView`. Notice that we override the `BindingList<>.AddNewCore()` method. It is automatically called by the `DataGridView` when a new employee is added. We also implement the `UserDeletingRow` event in order to detect the deletion of an employee. Finally, since our `Employe` class implements the `IEditableObject` interface, the `DataGridView` informs us about the selection of an employee by calling `BeginEdit()`, the end of the edition by calling `EndEdit()` or the cancellation of the edit by calling `CancelEdit()`. The cancellation of the edition is done when the user presses the ESC key. During the call to `EndEdit()`, the `Surname` and `Firstname` properties of the concerned employee objects have already been set to the new values input by the user.

Example 18-7

```
using System;
using System.ComponentModel;
using System.Windows.Forms;
public partial class MyForm : Form {
   private DataGridView dataGridView;
   EmployeeList list = new EmployeeList();
   public MyForm() {
      InitializeComponent();
      list.Add( new Employee( "Doo", "John" ) );
      list.Add( new Employee( "Dupont", "Anne" ) );
      dataGridView.DataSource = list;
   }
   private void InitializeComponent() {
      this.dataGridView = new System.Windows.Forms.DataGridView();
      dataGridView.Dock = DockStyle.Fill;
      dataGridView.AutoGenerateColumns = true;
      dataGridView.UserDeletingRow += UserDeletingRowHandler;
      this.Controls.Add( this.dataGridView );
   }
   protected virtual void UserDeletingRowHandler( object s,
         DataGridViewRowCancelEventArgs e) {
      if ( MessageBox.Show( "Are you sure?", string.Empty,
                      MessageBoxButtons.YesNo) == DialogResult.Yes)
         ((Employee)e.Row.DataBoundItem).Deleting();
   }
   [STAThread]
   static void Main() { Application.Run( new MyForm() ); }
}
class EmployeeList : BindingList<Employee> {
   public EmployeeList() { this.AllowNew = true; }
   protected override object AddNewCore() {
      Employee employee = new Employee( "-", "-" );
      Add( employee );
      return employee;
   }
}
public class Employee : IEditableObject {
   private string m_Surname;
   private string m_Firstname;
   public Employee(string surname, string firstname) {
      m_Surname = surname; m_Firstname = firstname;
   }
   public string Surname{  get{return m_Surname;}   set{m_Surname=value;} }
```

Example 18-7

```
    public string Firstname{get{return m_Firstname;}set{m_Firstname=value;}}
    void IEditableObject.BeginEdit() { }
    void IEditableObject.CancelEdit() { }
    void IEditableObject.EndEdit() { }
    public void Deleting() { }
}
```

Windows Forms and localization

Before starting this section, you must have read the localization section named Internationalization/ localization and satellite assemblies at page 27.

In the case of a *Windows Forms* application, *Visual Studio 2005* offers features to edit several localized version of a same window. In the properties of a window, you can find in the Design category the Localizable property which is set to false by default and Language which is set to (Default) by default. If you wish to edit several versions of a same window named XXX.cs based on several cultures, you must first set the Localizable property to true. A file named XXX.resx is then automatically associated to the window. If you select the yy-ZZ culture for the Language property of your window, *Visual Studio* will automatically allow you to edit this culture. During the first change to a control, a file named XXX.yy-ZZ.resx is then automatically associated to the window. Obviously, it contains the resource values which are specific to the yy-ZZ culture. To add controls to your window, you must reset the Language property of the window back to (Default).

It is interesting to notice that the initialization code of the controls (in the InitializeComponents() method) is different whether a window is localized or not. When a window is localized, you will notice calls to a ComponentResourceManager.ApplyRessource() method which will take care of loading the proper version of the resource during the execution based on the current culture.

GDI+

The *GDI+* library (GDI for *Graphical Device Interface*) contains several classes allowing you to accomplish all type of rendering operations: rendering of lines, curves, gradients, display images... GDI+ replaces the old GDI library used by developers under *Windows*. In addition of benefiting from the .NET object model, this library offers new features especially in regards to the support for image files and the display of gradients. The GDI+ library supports the JPG, PNG, GIF and BMP formats while the GDI library only supported the BMP format (unless you used a third party library).

The System.Drawing.Graphics class

The GDI+ allows you to draw, in other words to create all sorts of geometric shapes such as rectangles, lines and even Bezier curves. We can acquire an instance of the System.Drawing.Graphics class by calling the CreateGraphics() method of the Control or Form classes. The instances of the Graphics class constitute the support on which we can draw, in the same way that a piece of paper is the support for a drawer. For those who have already worked with GDI, the instances of this class are equivalent to instances of a *Device Context* (DC).

> ⚠ It is important to call the Dispose() method as soon as possible on all the instances of the Graphics class obtained by a call to CreateGraphics().

The System.Drawing.Pen class

In the same was as an artist needs a pen to draw a curve, the methods of the `Graphics` class used to draw lines, curves or the outline of shapes, all need an instance of the `System.Drawing.Pen`.

- The constructors of the `Pen` class accept an instance of the `System.Drawing.Color` structure to specify the color of the stroke, either an instance of the `System.Drawing.Brush` class to specify the fill type of a thick stroke.
- You can specify the thickness of the stroke using the `Width` property of the `Pen` class.
- You can indicate if you wish the stroke to be full, dashed or dotted using the `DashStyle` property of the `Pen` class.
- You can specify which type of drawing must occur at the ends of the stroke with the `StartCap` and `EndCap` properties of the `Pen` class.

For example, the following code displays a Bezier curve as shown in Figure 18-10:

Example 18-8

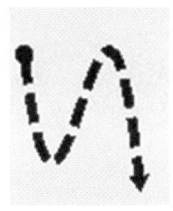

```
...
    using ( Graphics g = CreateGraphics() ) {
       Pen pen = new Pen( Color.Black );
       pen.Width = 5;
       pen.DashStyle = DashStyle.Dash;
       pen.StartCap = LineCap.RoundAnchor;
       pen.EndCap = LineCap.ArrowAnchor;
       g.DrawBezier( pen, new Point(10, 30),   new Point(30, 200),
                          new Point(50, -100), new Point(70, 100));
    }
...
```

Figure 18-10: Drawing a Bezier curve with GDI+

The System.Drawing.Brush class

In the same way that a painter needs a brush to fill a surface on a canvas, the methods of the `Graphics` class used to fill a surface need an instance of a class derived from `System.Drawing.Brush`. These derived classes are the following (note that they all are in the `System.Drawing.Drawing2D` namespace):

- `SolidBrush`: Brush to use to achieve a solid fill;
- `HatchBrush`: Brush to use to fill with a hatch patters;
- `TextureBrush`: Brush to use to fill using an image in the background;
- `LinearGradientBrush`: Brush to use in order to fill using a color gradient;
- `PathGradientBrush`: Brush to use for a color gradient fill (more elaborate than using `LinearGradientBrush`).

For example, the following code displays the pentagon in Figure 18-11, filled in a random way with a criss-cross of diagonal lines:

Example 18-9

```
...
    using ( Graphics g = CreateGraphics() ) {
      Brush brush = new HatchBrush( HatchStyle.DiagonalCross,
                                 Color.White, Color.Black);
      Point[] pts = new Point[5];
      pts[0] = new Point(50, 3);
      pts[1] = new Point(30, 100);
      pts[2] = new Point(80, 30);
      pts[3] = new Point(4, 35);
      pts[4] = new Point(70, 100);
      g.FillClosedCurve( brush, pts, FillMode.Alternate );
    }
...
```

Figure 18-11: Filling a curve using GDI+

Drawing text

The `DrawString()` method of the `Graphics` class allows the display of strings in your drawings. For example, the following code displays *hi* as shown in Figure 18-12:

Example 18-10

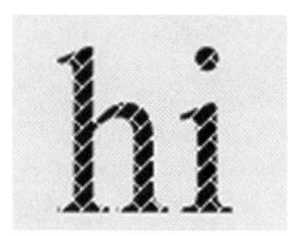

```
...
    using ( Graphics g = CreateGraphics() ) {
      Brush brush = new HatchBrush( HatchStyle.DiagonalBrick ,
                                 Color.White , Color.Black );
      g.DrawString( "hi", new Font("Times", 70), brush,
                    new Point(5, 5));
    }
...
```

Figure 18-12: Drawing text with GDI+

Handling images

The `System.Drawing.Image` abstract class is a base class of the: `System.Drawing.Bitmap` and `System.Drawing.Imaging.Metafile` classes.

Bitmaps

The `Image` class is used to load from a file, to modify, to display and to save into files, bitmap images. The image formats supported are defined by the static members of `System.Drawing.Imaging.ImageFormat`, amongst which you will find:

Static properties of ImageFormat	Associated format
Bmp	The standard bitmap image format. Let us mention that this format does not compress the image.
Gif	The GIF (*Graphic Interchange Format*) format. Let us mention that one of the characteristics of this format is the reduction of the number of colors (generally 256 colors) in order to reduce the image weight. In addition, this format allows the creation of animations.
Jpeg	The JPEG (*Joint Photo Expert Group*) format. Let us mention that this format compresses the image using a lousy algorithm. In addition, the compression rate can be configured.
Png	The W3C PNG (*Portable Network Graphics*) format. Let us mention that the particularity of this format is the compression of the image in a lossless way. It is well adapted for screenshots.
Tiff	The TIFF (*Tag Image File Format*) format.

The `PixelFormat` property of the `Image` determines the number of *bits per pixel* (*bpp*) in the image and takes values from the `System.Drawing.Imaging.PixelFormat` enumeration. In the case of pixel formats where the value of each pixel is determined from a color table (called *palette*), you must used the `Palette` of the `Image` class.

To display an image in a form or control, you simply need to use of the various overloaded version of the `DrawImage()` method in the `Graphics` class.

The transformation that you can apply to an image are limited to 'flips' (i.e. horizontal or vertical flips) and to right angle rotation. We will see in the next section how to do more complex processing on an image.

It is recommended to integrate the images in a resource file integrated to the current assembly or in a satellite assembly.

Metafile images

The `System.Drawing.Imaging.Metafile` class which is derived from the `Image` class gives you the possibility to load from a file, to build or to save in a file, images which are defined from simple operations such as lines or shapes.

The GDI library supports the *EMF* (*Enhanced Meta File*) format which can store the operations. The GDI+ library supports the *EMF+* format which allows storing all the operations of EMF, while adding a certain number of operations specific to EMF+. There is then a backward compatibility between the EMF and EMF+ formats. Here is an example of use of the `Metafile` class:

Example 18-11

```
using System.Drawing.Imaging;
...
public class Form1 : System.Windows.Forms.Form {
   private Metafile m_Metafile;
   private void OnClick1( object sender, System.EventArgs e ) {
```

Example 18-11
```
        using ( Graphics g = CreateGraphics() ) {
            System.IntPtr hDC = g.GetHdc();
            m_Metafile = new Metafile( hDC, EmfType.EmfPlusOnly );
            using ( Graphics metafilegraphic = Graphics.FromImage(m_Metafile))
            using ( Brush brush = new SolidBrush( Color.Black ) ) {
                metafilegraphic.FillEllipse( brush, 10, 10, 50, 50 );
                metafilegraphic.FillRectangle( brush, 5, 5, 10, 10 );
            }
            // You must always release the hDC or else
            // an exception will be raised.
            g.ReleaseHdc( hDC );
        }
    }
    public void OnClick2( object sender, System.EventArgs e ) {
        if( m_Metafile != null )
            using ( Graphics g = CreateGraphics() ) {
                g.DrawImage(m_Metafile, 10, 10);
            }
    }
    ...
}
...
```

Optimized image processing

The processing of an image consists into modifying its pixels based on certain mathematical operations. Each pixel is encoded using three integer values, one for red, one for green and one for blue. The range of values depends on the number of *bits per pixel*. The best image quality possible is obtained with 24 bits per pixel, a value between 0 and 255 for each component, which means a little over 16 million different colors. The human eye cannot distinguish more than 16 million colors.

We will show the image processing task which involves the inversion of the colors. Suppose that the number of bits per pixel is 24. The inversion of a color consists to assign the 255 complement to each of the three components, for each pixels of the image. Figure 18-13 shows this process applied to an image. For anecdotal purposes, know that this image is often used to test image processing algorithms. It is a photograph of *Lena Soderberg*, a Swedish playmate which was extracted from a 1972 edition of the *Playboy* magazine. Afterwards, she was actually invited to certain image processing conferences.

Figure 18-13: Lena and processed version

GDI+

With the .NET framework, there are two ways to process:

- Either we use the `SetPixel()` and `GetPixel()` methods of the `Bitmap` class. Here is an extract of code using these methods:

Example 18-12

```
...
      using ( Graphics g = CreateGraphics() ) {
         Bitmap m_Bmp = new Bitmap( "Lena.jpg" );
         g.DrawImage( m_Bmp, new Point(5, 5) );
         // Wait one second...
         System.Threading.Thread.Sleep( 1000 );
         int width = m_Bmp.Width;
         int height = m_Bmp.Height;
         Color cSrc, cDest;
         for ( int y = 0; y < height; y++ )
            for ( int x = 0; x < width; x++ ) {
               cSrc = m_Bmp.GetPixel( x, y );
               cDest=Color.FromArgb( 255-cSrc.R, 255-cSrc.G, 255-cSrc.B );
               m_Bmp.SetPixel( x, y, cDest );
            }
         g.DrawImage( m_Bmp, new Point(5, 5) );
      }
...
```

- Either we directly use pointers to access the pixels the image. **This technique is about 20 to 100 times more efficient than the previous technique depending on the process applied to the image!** This technique is a little more delicate to implement, but such an optimization is definitely worth the effort. You must take account of the following points:

    The method (or the piece of code) which completes the processing must be marked using the `unsafe` keyword to allow the manipulation of pointers (see page 417).

    You must also lock the access to the memory region of the bitmap be using the `LockBits()`/`UnlockBits()` methods of the `Bitmap` class.

Here is a source code extract which accomplishes this:

Example 18-13

```
...
   public struct StructPixel {
      public byte R; public byte G; public byte B;
   }
...
      using ( Graphics g = CreateGraphics() ) {
         Bitmap m_Bmp = new Bitmap( "Lena.jpg" );
         g.DrawImage( m_Bmp, new Point(5, 5) );
         // Wait one second...
         System.Threading.Thread.Sleep( 1000 );
         unsafe {
            int width = m_Bmp.Width;
            int height = m_Bmp.Height;
            BitmapData bmpData = m_Bmp.LockBits(
               new Rectangle( 0, 0, width, height ),
               ImageLockMode.ReadWrite,
               m_Bmp.PixelFormat );
            StructPixel* pCurrent = null;
            StructPixel* pBmp = (StructPixel*) bmpData.Scan0;
            for ( int y = 0; y < width; y++ ) {
               pCurrent = pBmp + y * height;
```

Example 18-13
```
                for ( int x = 0; x < height; x++ ) {
                    pCurrent->R = (byte) (255 - pCurrent->R);
                    pCurrent->G = (byte) (255 - pCurrent->G);
                    pCurrent->B = (byte) (255 - pCurrent->B);
                    pCurrent++;
                }
            }
            m_Bmp.UnlockBits( bmpData );
        }
        g.DrawImage(m_Bmp, new Point(5, 5));
    }
    ...
```

In this specific case, the optimization factor obtained on test done using a reference machine was of about 97!

Animation and double buffering

It is easy to create an animation by displaying different frames at the rate of several dozens times per second. To accomplish this, we generally use an instance of the `System.Windows.Forms.Timer` class which takes care of triggering a regular call to a method by the thread of the window. The following example shows how to create an animation representing a square which rotates in the center of a window:

Example 18-14
```
using System.Drawing;
using System.Windows.Forms;
using System.Drawing.Drawing2D;
public partial class AnimForm : Form {
    private float angle;
    private Timer timer = new Timer();
    public AnimForm() {
        timer.Enabled = true;
        timer.Tick += OnTimer;
        timer.Interval = 20; // 20 milliseconds => 50 images per second.
        timer.Start();
    }
    private void OnTimer( object sender, System.EventArgs e ) {
        angle ++;
        if ( angle > 359 )
            angle = 0;
        Refresh();
    }
    protected override void OnPaint( PaintEventArgs e ) {
        Graphics g = e.Graphics;
        Matrix matrix = new Matrix();
        matrix.Rotate( angle, MatrixOrder.Append );
        matrix.Translate( this.ClientSize.Width / 2,
                    this.ClientSize.Height/ 2, MatrixOrder.Append);
        g.Transform = matrix;
        g.FillRectangle( Brushes.Azure, -100, -100, 200, 200 );
    }
    [System.STAThread]
    public static void Main() {
```

Example 18-14

```
        Application.Run( new AnimForm() );
    }
}
```

If you execute this example, you will notice that the animation is not perfect. In fact, you will notice flickering in the display. This minor, yet noticeable defect is due to the lack of synchronization between the display of your screen and the display frequency of the image. Concretely, it happens that your square is displayed half-way through its construction.

To deal with this problem, we use a *double buffering* technique. With this technique you maintain two graphic buffers in memory. At any time, one of these buffers contains the last created image while the other contains the image currently being constructed. As soon as an image is created, the role of these buffers is inverted. It is easy to use this technique on your form. You only have to call the `SetStyle()` method with the proper arguments in the constructor of your form after the initialization of the components. Hence, in order to solve the flickering problem during the rotation of our square, we simply need to rewrite our example as follows:

Example 18-15

```
...
    public AnimForm() {
        ...
        timer.Start();
        SetStyle(
            ControlStyles.AllPaintingInWmPaint |
            ControlStyles.UserPaint |
            ControlStyles.OptimizedDoubleBuffer , true );
    }
    private void OnTimer( object sender, System.EventArgs e) {
...
```

It is possible that this double buffering mechanism may not be adapted to your animations. In this case, you can use the `BufferedGraphicsContext` and `BufferedGraphics` classes in order to manage programmatically these buffers. An instance of `BufferedGraphics` is obtained from the `BufferedGraphicsContext.Allocate()` method. Such an instance internally manages a buffer. You can access this buffer by using the `BufferedGraphics.Graphics{get;}` property. Once you are done drawing in this buffer, you must call `BufferedGraphics.Render()` in order to display its content on the screen:

Example 18-16

```
using System.Drawing;
using System.Windows.Forms;
using System.Drawing.Drawing2D;
public partial class AnimForm : Form {
    private float angle;
    private Timer timer = new Timer();
    private BufferedGraphics bufferedGraphics;
    public AnimForm() {
        BufferedGraphicsContext context = BufferedGraphicsManager.Current;
        context.MaximumBuffer = new Size( this.Width + 1, this.Height + 1 );
        bufferedGraphics = context.Allocate( this.CreateGraphics(),
                        new Rectangle( 0, 0, this.Width, this.Height) );
        timer.Enabled = true;
        timer.Tick += OnTimer;
        timer.Interval = 20; // 50 images per second.
        timer.Start();
```

Example 18-16

```
    }
    private void OnTimer( object sender, System.EventArgs e ) {
        angle ++;
        if (angle > 359)
            angle = 0;
        Graphics g = bufferedGraphics.Graphics;
        g.Clear( Color.Black );
        Matrix matrix = new Matrix();
        matrix.Rotate( angle, MatrixOrder.Append );
        matrix.Translate( this.ClientSize.Width / 2,
                          this.ClientSize.Height/ 2, MatrixOrder.Append );
        g.Transform = matrix;
        g.FillRectangle( Brushes.Azure, -100, -100, 200, 200 );
        bufferedGraphics.Render( Graphics.FromHwnd( this.Handle ) );
    }
    [System.STAThread]
    public static void Main() {
        Application.Run( new AnimForm() );
    }
}
```

19

ADO.NET 2

Introduction to databases

DBMS (DataBase Management System)

Almost all software uses some form of *persistence system* in the large sense of the term. For example, the *Windows* registry and even an `.ini` file can been seen as persistence systems. To manage a large volume of information, software uses *Database Management Systems* (*DBMS*) developed by third parties such as *Oracle* or *Microsoft*. We can mention the DBMS *SQL Server*, *Access*, *MySql*. Managing data does not limit itself to the storage of data. DBMS supply a number of features such as the search of data from some criteria or the protection of data. Certain developers create their own DBMS often for performance reasons sometimes from a misunderstanding of the relational model, but this practice is still marginal and debatable.

RDBMS (Relational DataBase Management System)

The first DBMS appeared at the end of the 60's within the context of the American space program. A significant progress was made in the 70's with the invention of the *relational model*. The relational model is based on a mathematical model which allows to present data in a simple way within tables.

The notion of table is relatively close to the one of *relation*. A column in a table is called an attribute of the relation and is defined by a name. The elements of an attribute take their values in a *domain* (a type in general). We have to precise for each column if it is required that every element contain a valid element (i.e. in the domain). The set of description of the columns of a table (i.e. the attributes of a relation) is called *schema of the relation*. The *rows* of a table are also called *records*. A *primary key* is the set of columns for which allow to uniquely identify a record. Often, the primary key is made of a single column.

The relational model allows avoiding information redundancy which can threaten the integrity of the table and waste resources. This important functionality is due to *foreign key*. Instead of spreading the same data in several locations of the database, we use foreign keys which allow the referencing of data. Hence, the data is not duplicated but remains accessible. Because of such a system, we can store complex structures within a database, as a data tree. Another advantage of the relational model is to ensure the integrity of the database by using *integrity constraints*. For example, if you have a table where the rows describe automobiles and another table where the rows describe brands you can enforce the following constraints: for each automobile corresponds a single brand.

The *relational algebra* offers six basic operations which act on the relations and produces relationships. These operations are the *selection*, the *projection*, the *cartesian product*, the *set union*, the *set difference*, and the *rename*. Using these operations, the client of a relational database can access the data within the database and modify them.

The SQL language

The standardized and non-procedural language named *SQL* (*Structured Query Language*) was developed to access data within a relational database by the use of requests. These requests essentially model the operations of the relational algebra. The SQL language allows performing complex requests in a few words. This set of operations on the data of the SQL language is named *DML* for *Data Manipulation Language*. We also use SQL requests to construct and modify the structure of a database (insertion of table, assignment of user privileges…). This part of the language is named *DDL* for *Data Definition Language*.

Most current DBMS are based on the relational model and support a language derived from SQL. For example, the *SQL Server* RDBMS published by *Microsoft* supports the *T-SQL* (*Transact SQL*) language which in addition to standard SQL processing allows the declaration of variables, control transactions, manage exceptions, manage XML data… The part of the language relative to these features is called *DCL* for *Data Control Language*.

The need for a distributed architecture

Applications with user interfaces which access databases are of two types:

- There are monolithic applications which encapsulate in the same executable, both the user interface and the database access code.
- Distributed applications where only the server part is capable of accessing the database. The server can be handled by ASP.NET, COM+ or even be written from scratch. Several kinds of middleware can be used between the client and the server (HTTP/SOAP, .NET Remoting…). The clients can be light (web browser) or rich (*Windows Forms* executable for example). Within the server, we name *DAL* (*Data Access Layer*) the set of code specific to the persistence management.

The choice between the two architectures for your application is fundamental. The first choice is only warranted for small applications which are unlikely to evolve.

> The choice of architecture must be done early within the lifecycle of a project.

Introduction to ADO.NET

The *ADO.NET* acronym encompasses at the same time the classes of the .NET framework used to manipulate the data contained in relational DBMS and the philosophy of use behind these classes.

Before ADO.NET, the *ADO* (*ActiveX Data Object*) technology constituted the set of classes that you needed to use to access data within databases under the *Microsoft* environment. Despite its name, ADO.NET is much more than a successor to ADO. Although both technologies have a common goal, they have significant differences. Basically ADO.NET is much more complete.

Connected mode vs unconnected mode

The notions of *disconnected mode* and of *connected mode* describe how an application works with a database. We must first introduce the notion of *connection* with a database. A connection is a resource which is initialized and used by an application to work with a database. A connection with a database can have two states of either open or closed. If an application holds an open connection with a database we say that it is connected to the database. A connection is generally initialized from a string which contains information on the type of DBMS supporting the database and/or the physical location of the database. All this is described a little later.

Introduction to ADO.NET

When an application works with ADO.NET, several illustrative cases are possible:

- An application works in connected mode if it loads data as it needs. The application stays connected to the database. The application sends its modifications to the database as they occur.
- An application works in disconnected mode in the following cases:

    If the application loads data from the database, then it disconnects itself from the database, that it uses and modifies the data and reconnects itself to the database in order to send its modifications.

    If the application loads data from a database, disconnects itself from the database and then uses the loaded data. In this case we say that the application accesses the database in a read-only mode.

    If the application gathers data from another data source (such as manual input or from an XML file) and then connects itself to a database to store the new data.

    If an application does not use a database. Mentioning this case does make sense as an application can work with the classes of ADO.NET without using a database. For example, we will see that the classes of ADO.NET are particularly useful for the presentation of XML data.

The philosophy of ADO was to work in a connected mode. It is difficult, almost impossible to create efficient servers in terms of *scalability* when we work in connected mode. Note that with ADO, we can work in disconnected mode but it does require a lot of work.

Let us mention the signification of the word *scalable*. We say than an application is *scalable* if for an increase in hardware to execute it (processor, RAM, CPUs, …) you obtain a performance gain proportional to the hardware added. In practice, we observe that the addition of hardware to execute an application does not necessarily create a performance gain. In fact, several bottlenecks still remain at various levels (*data locking, middleware*…). Only the architecture of the application can minimize the effect of these bottlenecks.

With ADO.NET, we can work either in connected or disconnected mode. Several interesting features, that we will discuss later, are available for both of these modes.

The weakness of the connected mode is that it generates several accesses to the database and more generally, it will generate several accesses to the network if the database is physically separated from the application. The weakness of the disconnected mode is that it can lead to a large consumption of memory as a part of the database is copied to memory for each client call. This weakness can be prohibitive for a server who needs to manage a large number of clients as the server needs to manipulate large amounts of data in memory.

> Although a pre-analysis is always required, it is generally more efficient to work in the disconnected mode with ADO.NET.

Data providers

A *data provider* is a software layer which allows the communication with a specific DBMS. Here are the four data providers supported by default in the .NET framework:

- The *SQL Server* DBMS has its own data provider. The classes for this data provider can be found in the `System.Data.SqlClient` namespace. This data provider works with the 7.0, 2000 and 2005 versions of *SQL Server*. Of course, features specific to one version of *SQL Server* cannot be used from this data provider if you use a previous version of the product.
- Another data provider allows you to communicate with DBMS which support the *OleDB* API. OleDB is an API allowing access to data within a DBMS using COM technology. The classes for this data provider are located within the `System.Data.OleDbClient` namespace. Note that you need to use this data provider if you wish to use previous versions than 7.0 of *SQL Server*.

- There is a .NET data provider which places itself on top of the *ODBC* (*Open DataBase Connectivity*) protocol. This managed data provider allows accessing DBMS which support the ODBC API (but not all of them, see the *Microsoft* site for more details). The classes for this provider can be found inside the `System.Data.Odbc` namespace.
- There is also a specialized .NET data provider for use with *Oracle* databases. The classes for this provider can be found in the `System.Data.OracleClient` namespace.

With the exception of the *Oracle* data provider which is found in the `System.Data.OracleClient.dll` DLL, all other providers are located in `System.Data.dll`.

ADO.NET: The big picture

Here is a global diagram (but simplified) of the ADO.NET architecture:

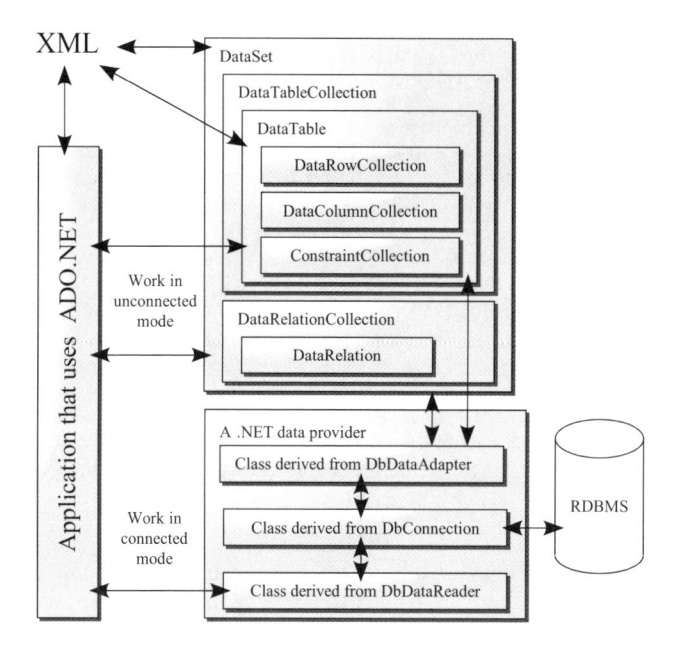

Figure 19-1: Global diagram of ADO.NET

This diagram illustrates a few key concepts of ADO.NET:

- All access to the DBMS must be done through a connection where the implementation is part of the data provider.
- The `DataSet` and `DataTable` classes allow you to work in disconnected mode. In this mode, all loading or saving of data is done through the use of an *adaptor* object. A `DataSet` is a relational data cache hosted in the current application domain during execution. You can fill a `DataSet` with data coming from a database, disconnect yourself, consume the data within the `DataSet` and eventually reconnect to the database in order to save any changes you made to the data.
- The `DataReader` class allows you to work in connected mode.
- As we will see in the next chapter which is dedicated to XML, many bridges exist between the XML document world and the relational databases world.

The DB that we'll use in our examples

In all the examples of this chapter, we will use a database named ORGANIZATION which will be managed by the *SQL Server* RDBMS. Our examples are compatible with both the 2000 and 2005 versions unless noted otherwise. We will of course use the *SQL Client* data provider which is specific to *SQL Server*. In the last section, we will describe the features which are specific to this data provider.

Our ORGANIZATION database contains the DEPARTMENTS and EMPLOYEES tables which are meant to model the internal organization of a company with the assumption that every employee belongs to a single department. The tables as well as constraints can be created with the following *T-SQL* script:

Example 19-1

```
CREATE TABLE [dbo].[EMPLOYEES] (
    [EmployeeID] [int] IDENTITY (1, 1) ,
    [DepID] [char] (3)   NOT NULL ,
    [SurName] [nvarchar] (30)   NOT NULL ,
    [FirstName] [nvarchar] (30)   NOT NULL ,
    [Phone] [nvarchar] (20)   NULL
) ON [PRIMARY]
GO
CREATE TABLE [dbo].[DEPARTMENTS] (
    [DepID] [char] (3) NOT NULL,
    [Department] [nvarchar] (30)   NOT NULL
) ON [PRIMARY]
GO
ALTER TABLE EMPLOYEES ADD CONSTRAINT Primary_ID
PRIMARY KEY (EmployeeID)
GO
ALTER TABLE DEPARTMENTS ADD CONSTRAINT Primary_DepID
PRIMARY KEY (DepID)
GO
ALTER TABLE EMPLOYEES ADD CONSTRAINT Is_Employed_By
FOREIGN KEY (DepID) REFERENCES DEPARTMENTS(DepID)
GO
```

The primary key of the EMPLOYEES table is defined by the EmployeID column. The IDENTITY (1, 1) syntax means that the integer values of this column will be automatically assigned by *SQL Server* which will use an internal counter based on the following algorithm: the internal counter is set to 1 when a row is inserted for the first time in this table; for each insertion of a new row the counter is incremented by 1. For each insertion of a new row in the EMPLOYEES, table, the value of EmployeID will take the current value of the internal counter.

The primary key for the DEPARTMENTS table is defined by the DepID column. It must be explicitly set by the user for each new row added to the table. Here is the diagram of our database:

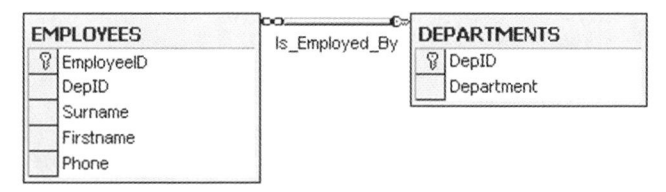

Figure 19-2: The diagram of our database

We will assume that in our examples, the initial state of the database is as follows:

DEPARTMENTS table

DepID	Department
DEV	Development
FIN	Financial
MKT	Marketing

EMPLOYEES table

EmployeeID	DepID	Surname	FistName	Phone
1	MKT	Doo	John	(123) 456-7893
2	DEV	Dupont	Anne	(123) 456-7895
3	DEV	Kennedy	Franck	
4	FIN	Weiss	Douglas	(123) 456-7897

Here is the T-SQL script which will fill our database. Notice that we let the RDBMS assign the values to `EmployeeID`:

Example 19-2

```
INSERT INTO DEPARTMENTS VALUES ('DEV','Development')
INSERT INTO DEPARTMENTS VALUES ('FIN','Financial')
INSERT INTO DEPARTMENTS VALUES ('MKT','Marketing')
GO
SET IDENTITY_INSERT EMPLOYEES OFF
GO
INSERT INTO EMPLOYEES VALUES ('MKT','Doo','John','(123) 456-7893')
INSERT INTO EMPLOYEES VALUES ('DEV','Dupont','Anne','(123) 456-7895')
INSERT INTO EMPLOYEES (DepID,Surname,Firstname) VALUES
                     ('DEV','Kennedy','Franck')
INSERT INTO EMPLOYEES VALUES   ('FIN','Weiss','Douglas','(123) 456-7897')
GO
```

The connection string that we will use to access the database is the following:

"server = localhost ; uid=sa ; pwd =; database = ORGANIZATION"

Remember to configure the *SQL Server and Windows* authentication modes to execute our examples with this connection string.

Connections and data providers

Decoupling an application and its data providers

A large number of paradigms can be found in most RDBMS: they are accessible though a connection, we can manipulate data through a SQL request... Of course, each RDBMS/data provider pair has feature relating to its own specific needs. For example, only the data provider for the SQL Server allows to obtain statistics on a connection.

In the new namespace named `System.Data.Common` ADO.NET2 offers several abstract classes which define the set of shared functionality by all RDBMS. For example, the `DbConnection` class defines the notion of a connection to a database while the `DbCommand` class defines the notion of database command Note that ADO.NET 1.x represented this set of features through interfaces such as `IDbConnection` or `IDbCommand`. These interfaces are still offered by the framework and the new corresponding abstract classes implement them. However, the new shared functionalities in ADO.NET2 are only available through these abstract classes and thus their use is recommended over the interfaces.

Connections and data providers

When an application uses data stored in a RDBMS, it is in your interest to find a way to keep your code as independent as possible (as abstract as possible) from a specific type of RDBMS. The interest in using such an approach comes from the fact that you may not know which RDBMS will be used in production. A client may want to use your application with an *Oracle* RDBMS while another may prefer a free RDBMS such as *MySQL*. This independence from a specific type of RDBMS can easily be achieved if you stick to only using the functionality common to all RDBMS. In fact, you simply need to manipulate data through the abstract classes of the `System.Data.Common` namespace that we discussed earlier. However, there is a problem: at some place in your code, you need to create the ADO.NET objects that you will manipulate. This operation implies that you need to specify which class to use. For example:

Example 19-3

```
using System.Data.Common;
using System.Data.SqlClient;
class Program {
   static void Main() {
      DbConnection cnx;
      DbCommand    cmd;
      if( /* test if we are working with SQL Server */ true ) {
         cnx = new SqlConnection(); // Here we have a dependency...
         cmd = new SqlCommand();    // ...on the SqlClient provider.
      }
      // Here, we use 'cnx' and 'cmd'. These references are not coupled
      // with the underlying data provider.
   }
}
```

To limit the effects of this problem, each data provider in ADO.NET2 presents a class derived from `System.Data.Common.DbProviderFactory`. This class exposes the following methods:

```
DbConnection CreateConnection();
DbCommand CreateCommand();
DbCommandBuilder CreateCommandBuilder();
DbConnection CreateConnection();
DbConnectionStringBuilder CreateConnectionStringBuilder();
DbDataAdapter CreateDataAdapter();
DbDataSourceEnumerator CreateDataSourceEnumerator();
DbParameter CreateParameter();
DbPermission CreatePermission();
```

At a first glance, you would need to rewrite the example as follows:

Example 19-4

```
using System.Data.Common;
using System.Data.SqlClient;
class Program {
   static void Main() {
      DbProviderFactory factory;
      if( /* test if we are working with SQL Server */ true ) {
         factory= new SqlClientFactory();
         // From here, the code is not coupled with the underlying provider.
         DbConnection cnx = factory.CreateConnection();
         DbCommand    cmd = factory.CreateCommand();
      }
   }
}
```

However, this example fails to compile as the `SqlClientFactory` does not have a public constructor. The only way to create an instance of a class derived from `DbProviderFactory` is to use the `CreateFactory()` static method of the `System.Data.Common.DbProviderFactories` class. This method can be seen as a factory of factories. The `CreateFactory()` method returns an ADO.NET object factory for the data provider if you pass the namespace of the data provider as a string. Our example can be rewritten as follows:

Example 19-5
```
using System.Data.Common;
// We don't need the System.Data.SqlClient namespace anymore !!
class Program {
   static void Main() {
      DbProviderFactory factory =
            DbProviderFactories.GetFactory( "System.Data.SqlClient" );
      //From here, the code is not coupled with the underlying provider.
      DbConnection cnx = factory.CreateConnection();
      DbCommand    cmd = factory.CreateCommand();
   }
}
```

For our example to be 100% independent from a data provider, you need to obtain the string defining the data provider from a configuration file. In order to achieve this, it is recommended to use the `providerName` attribute of an `add` element contained within the `connectionStrings` element of the configuration file. For example, the configuration file for our application may look like this:

Example 19-6   *app.exe.config*
```
<?xml version="1.0" encoding="utf-8" ?>
<configuration>
   <connectionStrings>
      <add name="My DB" providerName="System.Data.SqlClient"
           connectionString=
           "server = localhost ; uid=sa ; pwd =; database = ORGANIZATION"/>
   </connectionStrings>
</configuration>
```

The code of your application now looks like this. It is now 100% independent from any data provider:

Example 19-7   *app.cs*
```
using System.Data.Common;
using System.Configuration;
class Program {
   static void Main() {
      ConnectionStringSettings cfg =
         ConfigurationManager.ConnectionStrings["My DB"];
      DbProviderFactory factory =
         DbProviderFactories.GetFactory( cfg.ProviderName );
      DbConnection cnx = factory.CreateConnection();
      DbCommand    cmd = factory.CreateCommand();
      cnx.ConnectionString = cfg.ConnectionString;
      cmd.Connection = cnx;
   }
}
```

The architecture presented by this set of classes is known as a *design pattern* named *abstract factory*. This architecture does not prevent you from using on the fly the services specific to a data provider. For example, the following program shows how to obtain the statistics for a connection conditionally on the fact that we use a *SQL Server* data provider (the only provider which offers this option):

Connections and data providers

Example 19-8 *app.cs*

```
using System.Data.Common;
using System.Configuration;
using System.Collections;   // For IDictionary.
using System.Data.SqlClient;
class Program {
   static void Main() {
      ConnectionStringSettings cfg =
         ConfigurationManager.ConnectionStrings["My DB"];
      DbProviderFactory factory =
         DbProviderFactories.GetFactory( cfg.ProviderName );
      DbConnection cnx = factory.CreateConnection();
      IDictionary cnxStats = EventuallyGetStats( cnx );
   }
   public static IDictionary EventuallyGetStats( DbConnection cnx ) {
      if ( cnx is SqlConnection )
         return ( cnx as SqlConnection ).RetrieveStatistics();
      return null;
   }
}
```

The list of data providers is extensible. Also, each data provider available on a machine must be declared in the `machine.config` file as follows:

Example 19-9 *app.exe.config*

```
<?xml version="1.0" encoding="utf-8" ?>
<configuration>
   ...
   <system.data>
     <DbProviderFactories>
       ...
       <add name="OleDb Data Provider"
            invariant="System.Data.OleDb"
            support="BF"
            description=".Net Framework Data Provider for OleDb"
            type="System.Data.OleDb.OleDbFactory, System.Data,
                  Version=2.0.3600.0, Culture=neutral,
                  PublicKeyToken=b77a5c561934e089" />
       ...
     </DbProviderFactories>
   </system.data>
</configuration >
```

Note that a data provider specific to a web application can be declared within the corresponding `web.config` file

The string specified by the `invariant` attribute is the same as the one supplied as a parameter to the `DbProviderFactory.GetFactory()` method. The `support` attribute defines an 8 bit mask relative to the binary indicator `System.Data.Common.DbProviderSupportedClasses` specifying the features supplied by the data provider. Finally, the `type` attribute indicates the name of the factory class deriving from `DbProviderFactory` as well as the assembly which contains it. This assembly must be stored either in one of the application folders either in the GAC.

Connection strings

A *connection string* is a string which contains the necessary information to locate and connect to a database. Such a string is composed of multiple key/value pairs separated by semi-colons. For example:

```
"Data Source=Server;Database=MyDB;User ID=FOOID;Password=FOOPWD;"
"Data Source=Server; Initial Catalog=pubs;Integrated Security=SSPI;"
"SERVER = localhost ; UID=sa ; PWD =; database = ORGANIZATION"
```

Certain data must be represented in a connection string. We can mention the name of the server hosting the database or the login information for the DB user under which we want to connect. The keys attributed to this data can be different based on the data provider. For example, the OleDb data provider uses the "`Data Source`" and "`User ID`" keys while the ODBC data provider uses "`Server`" and "`UID`". The SqlClient data provider supports both these syntaxes. Certain data providers offer the possibility of building a connection string through the use of a class derived from System.Data.Common.DbConnectionStringBuilder. This possibility is illustrated by the following example which also uses the fact that a SqlClient data provider can enumerate the data sources which it can access:

Example 19-10 *app.cs*

```
using System.Data;
using System.Data.Common;
using System.Configuration;
class Program {
   static void Main() {
      Configuration cfg = ConfigurationManager.OpenExeConfiguration(
         ConfigurationUserLevel.None);
      ConnectionStringSettings cfg_cs =
         cfg.ConnectionStrings.ConnectionStrings["My DB"];
      DbProviderFactory factory =
         DbProviderFactories.GetFactory( cfg_cs.ProviderName );
      DbDataSourceEnumerator e = factory.CreateDataSourceEnumerator();
      DataTable tbl = e.GetDataSources();

      if ( tbl.Rows.Count > 0 ) {
         int userChoice = 0; // Simulate that the user choose a server.
         DataRow row = tbl.Rows[ userChoice ];
         string dataSource = row[ "ServerName" ].ToString();
         string instanceName = row[ "InstanceName" ].ToString();
         string isClustered = row[ "IsClustered" ].ToString();
         string version = row[ "Version" ].ToString();

         // Update the connection string in the config file
         // independently from the underlying data provider.
         DbConnectionStringBuilder csBuilder =
            factory.CreateConnectionStringBuilder();
         csBuilder.ConnectionString = cfg_cs.ConnectionString;
         if( csBuilder.ContainsKey( "Server" ) )
            csBuilder.Remove( "Server" );
         csBuilder.Add( "Server", dataSource );
         cfg_cs.ConnectionString = csBuilder.ConnectionString;
         cfg.Save();
      } // end line choice.
   } // end Main() method
} // end class Program
```

Connections and data providers 595

This example is particularly relevant if you use the "`Data Source`" key in the connection string within your configuration file. In fact, the associated value will be correctly updated although we use the "`Server`" string to reference it in our program.

If you would rather not use this dynamic connection string construction feature, we recommend that you take a look at `http://www.connectionstrings.com/`. This site gathers a large number of connection string examples based on most DBMS available on the market.

When you use an ODBC data provider, it is recommended to use the notion of *DSN* (*Data Source Name*) to prevent developers from having to manipulate the data contained within connection strings. A DSN is a piece of information stored in the operating system of the machine executing the application. This information associates a database to a string. For example a connection string using a DSN may look like this:

```
string s1 = "DSN=MyAppDSN";
```

In addition to is simplicity of use, a DSN offers the advantage of creating an indirection towards the database which can changed after the compilation of the application. This indirection is done independently of the underlying DBMS and independently of the physical location of the database since this data is part of the DSN. In general, we configure the DSNs of *Windows* through the *Control Panel › Administration tools › Data sources (ODBC)* menu.

How and where to store connection strings?

Connection strings have the possibility of being stored in a configuration file. This notion of configuration file is discussed in the section at page 46.

Example 19-6 illustrates a configuration file which defines a connection string within the `<connexionStrings>` element. Example 19-7 shows how the C# code of an application can access the connection strings defined in a configuration file.

Connection strings are generally considered as confidential data as they will often contain a password. The .NET 2 framework allows you to store an encrypted version of the connection string in the configuration file. This is detailed at page 189.

Connection pool

Those of you who have already dealt with writing server code accessing database know that the use of a *connection pool* can significantly increase performance. A connection pool is a collection of equivalent connections. This means that the connections are connected to the same database and that each request from a client uses one of these connections to access the data. These connections are complex objects, expensive to construct and destroy. The underlying idea behind connection pools is to recycle connections which are already open in order to globally reduce the creation, initialization and destruction cost of such connections.

The good news is that ADO.NET takes care of this connection pooling mechanism transparently to the user. A connection pool is automatically created internally for each connection string used. For example:

```
...
string sCnx = "server=localhost ;uid=sa ;pwd =;database = ORGANIZATION";
SqlConnection cnx = new SqlConnection( sCnx );
cnx.Open();
// Here the connection pool for the string 'sCnx' doesn't contain
// any connection but the current thread is using such a connection.
cnx.Close();
// Here, the connection is not discarded but it is stored in the pool
// for the string 'sCnx'.
...
```

596   Chapter 19 - ADO.NET 2.0

The internal management of a connection pool depends on the underlying data provider. Also, we recommend that you refer to the official documentation for the data provider if you wish to control this management. Know that the SqlClient data provider offers a certain number of features which allow a certain programmatic control on the pooling mechanism. For more information on this topic, read the article named **Connection Pooling for the .NET Framework Data Provider for SQL Server** on **MSDN**.

Access metadata of your data source

ADO.NET 2 offers a framework which allow the programmatic navigation of the schema of a RDBMS. By schema, we mean the set of metadata of the RDBMS such as the tables, the columns, the views, the users, the foreign keys, the indexes... Typically, such a framework allows the development of tools which present the structure of a RDBMS. *Visual Studio 2005* contains such a tool illustrated by the panel on the left of Example 19-4 (at page 607). We can see the structure of a DBMS expressed in a hierarchical way.

The problem behind such a *framework* is that it is generic in the sense that it is common to all DBMS and thus all data providers. Evidently, not all DBMS have the exact same structure. Of course, we will find some classic concepts which are common such as tables or indexes but the details are generally different. For example, there are three types of filters (also named restriction) that can apply to a request on the tables of an *Oracle* RDBMS (OWNER, TABLE_NAME, and TYPE) while there are four for a *SQL Server* RDBMS (table_catalog, table_schema, table_name and table_type).

The response to this problem generally means a less strong typing. Requests to the structure of a RDBMS are done in an untyped way by using a single method, the DataTable GetSchema() method defined in the DbConnection base class. The set of structural elements of the RDBMS satisfying a request are contained in a DataTable. If you use this method without a parameter, you will obtain what is known as the total collection of metadata. For a *SQL Server* this set is: MetaDataCollections, DataSourceInformation, DataTypes, Restrictions, ReservedWords, Users, Databases, Tables, Columns, Views, ViewColumns, ProcedureParameters, Procedures, ForeignKeys, IndexColumns, Indexes, and UserDefinedTypes. If you use this method with a string as a parameter representing one of these collections, you will obtain the set of elements within this collection. The following example illustrates this by enumerating the tables of a RDBMS:

Example 19-11

```
using System;
using System.Data.Common;
using System.Data.SqlClient;
using System.Data;
class Program {
   static void Main() {
      string sCnx =
         "server = localhost ; uid=sa ; pwd=; database = ORGANIZATION";
      using ( DbConnection cnx = new SqlConnection( sCnx ) ) {
         cnx.Open();
         DataTable tbl = cnx.GetSchema( "tables" );
         foreach ( DataRow row in tbl.Rows ) {
            foreach ( DataColumn col in tbl.Columns )
               Console.WriteLine(col.ToString()+" = "+row[col].ToString());
            Console.WriteLine();
         }
      } // end using cnx.
   }
}
```

Working in connected mode with DataReader 597

Here is an extract from the output of this example:

```
...
TABLE_CATALOG = ORGANIZATION
TABLE_SCHEMA = dbo
TABLE_NAME = EMPLOYEES
TABLE_TYPE = BASE TABLE

TABLE_CATALOG = ORGANIZATION
TABLE_SCHEMA = dbo
TABLE_NAME = DEPARTMENTS
TABLE_TYPE = BASE TABLE
...
```

Finally, a third overload of this `GetSchema()` method exists. It allows you to filter the result from the request.

More information on this topic can be found in the article named **Schemas in ADO.NET 2** by *Bob Beauchemin* on **MSDN**. The notion of restriction is detailed as well as the impact of the framework for data provider developers.

Working in connected mode with DataReader

Fetching data from database with DataReader

Here is a small console program using the `SqlReader` to retrieve the content of the EMPLOYES table. Rows are obtained from the database, one by one with a call to the `Read()` method. The connection is only closed when all the data has been processed:

Example 19-12

```
using System;
using System.Data.Common;
using System.Data.SqlClient;
class Program {
   static void Main() {
      // Connection string.
      string sCnx =
         "server = localhost ; uid=sa ; pwd =; database = ORGANIZATION";
      // The SQL request to fetch data.
      string sCmd = "SELECT * FROM EMPLOYEES";
      // Create a connection object.
      using( DbConnection cnx = new SqlConnection(sCnx) ) {
         // Create a command object.
         using( DbCommand cmd=new SqlCommand(sCmd,cnx as SqlConnection) ) {
            // Open the connection.
            cnx.Open();
            // Perform the command.
            using( DbDataReader rdr = cmd.ExecuteReader() ) {
               // Display columns #2 and #3 of the EMPLOYEES table.
               while( rdr.Read() )
                  Console.WriteLine(rdr.GetString(2)+" "+rdr.GetString(3));
            } // end using rdr.
         } // end using cmd.
      } // end using cnx.
   }
}
```

This example displays the following on the console:

```
Doo John
Dupont Anne
Kennedy Franck
Weiss Douglas
```

Most of the classes of ADO.NET implement the `IDispose` interface and can be instantiated within a `using` clause or must be manually disposed of.

The `DbProviderFactory` class does not offer the `CreateDbDataReader()` although that each data provider has a class derived from `DbDataReader`. The reason is that new instances of this class must be obtained directly through a call to the `ExecuteReader()` on a command.

Getting a scalar computed on the database side

It happens than an application need a simple scalar value computed from information contained in a database. For example, we may wish to count the number of rows in a table (COUNT), calculate a sum (SUM), an average (AVG), the minimum (MIN), the maximum (MAX), a *variance* (VAR, VARP) or *standard deviation* (STDEV, STDEVP) of values in one or multiple columns or tables. It would a tremendous waste of resources to fetch an entire table or column and do the calculation within your code. Also, the SQL language can do these calculations directly on the RDBMS side by using special keywords within a request. Here is an example of the use of the COUNT keyword, which allows retrieving the number of rows in the EMPLOYES table:

Example 19-13

```csharp
using System.Data.Common;
using System.Data.SqlClient;
class Program {
   static void Main() {
      // The SQL request to obtain the scalar.
      string sCmd = "SELECT COUNT(*) FROM EMPLOYES";
      int nEmployes;
      using( DbConnection cnx = new SqlConnection (
        "server = localhost ; uid=sa ; pwd =; database = ORGANIZATION") ) {
         cnx.Open();
         using(DbCommand cmd = new SqlCommand(sCmd,cnx as SqlConnection)) {
            nEmployes = (int) cmd.ExecuteScalar();
         } // end using cmd.
      } // end using cnx.
      System.Console.WriteLine("Total number of employees:{0}", nEmployes);
   }
}
```

Modifying data with SQL queries

Database commands come in three flavors.

- SQL command/request built on the client side and executed on the RDBMS side.
- *Stored procedure* which associate a name and parameters to a SQL request stored directly by the RDBMS. Understand that architecturally speaking, the use of stored procedures allows displacing the complexity from your code to the DBMS. The proximity of processing in a stored procedure with the data is advantageous. However, the use of stored procedures generally complexifies the global maintenance of an application especially since multiple programming languages are involved (T-SQL, C# …).
- A command which only takes into account the name of one or multiple tables. In this case, the entire content of the table will be recovered by the command.

Working in connected mode with DataReader

This type of command can be defined by the `CommandType` property of the `IDbCommand` interface. The first solution is used by default. There are principally four types of SQL command/request:

- SELECT: allows obtaining data. This type of request is generally used to fill a `DataSet` from a command and a `DataAdapter`.
- INSERT: allows the insertion of a row in a table, for example:

    ```
    INSERT INTO DEPARTMENTS VALUES ('COM','Communication')
    ```
- UPDATE: allows the modification of one or many rows in a table, for example:

    ```
    UPDATE DEPARTMENTS SET Departement='Comm' WHERE DepID = 'COM'
    ```
- DELETE: allows the deletion of one of several rows in a table, for example:

    ```
    DELETE FROM DEPARTMENTS WHERE DepID = 'COM'
    ```

To execute an INSERT, UPDATE or DELETE command, you simply need to use the `ExecuteNonQuery()` method of `IDbCommand` (note that *non query* means that we are not executing a query which will return information):

Example 19-14

```
using System.Data.Common;
using System.Data.SqlClient;
class Program {
   static void Main() {
      // SQL request to insert a row.
      string sCmd1="INSERT INTO DEPARTMENTS VALUES('COM','Communication')";

      // SQL request to modify a row.
      string sCmd2 =
       "UPDATE DEPARTMENTS SET Department='Comm' WHERE DepID = 'COM'";

      // SQL request to delete a row.
      string sCmd3 = "DELETE FROM DEPARTMENTS WHERE DepID = 'COM'";

      using ( DbConnection cnx = new SqlConnection(
        "server = localhost ; uid=sa ; pwd =; database = ORGANIZATION") ) {
         cnx.Open();
         DbCommand cmd = new SqlCommand( sCmd1, (SqlConnection) cnx );
         int nRowsAffected = (int) cmd.ExecuteNonQuery();
         cmd.CommandText = sCmd2;
         nRowsAffected = (int) cmd.ExecuteNonQuery();
         cmd.CommandText = sCmd3;
         nRowsAffected = (int) cmd.ExecuteNonQuery();
      } // end using cnx.
   }
}
```

To insert a row in the EMPLOYEES table, the SQL command would be as follows:

```
INSERT INTO EMPLOYEES VALUES ('COM','Smith','Adam','(123) 456-7899')
```

We do not initialize the `EmployeeID` field of the row inserted in the EMPLOYEES table since the value for this field is automatically computed by the RDBMS. The technique to recover this value after the insertion depends on the data provider. You can read more on this subject in the article named **Retrieving Identity or Autonumber Values** on **MSDN**.

Working in unconnected mode with DataSet

The example in this section use the database presented at page 589.

Filling a cache with data fetched from a database

Here is a small console application using the `SqlDataAdapter` and `DataSet` classes to retrieve the contents of the EMPLOYES table. We see that a `DataAdapter` object represents the set of commands coupled with a connection which is used to fill the `DataSet`. The data is then processed while the application isn't connected to the database. The `DataSet` plays the role of a disconnected cache to the database. The processing of data consists in displaying the first/last name pairs on the console:

Example 19-15

```
using System;
using System.Data;
using System.Data.Common;
using System.Data.SqlClient;
class Program {
   static void FillWithData(DataSet dSet) {
      // Create a DataAdapter to access the database.
      // It needs an SQL request and a connection string.
      using ( DbDataAdapter dAdapter = new SqlDataAdapter(
        "SELECT * FROM EMPLOYEES",
        "server = localhost ; uid=sa ; pwd =; database = ORGANIZATION" ) ) {

         // This call to the Fill() method triggers:
         //  - Open a connection with the databasr.
         //  - Execute the SQL request.
         //  - Create the EMPLOYEES table in the DataSet.
         //  - Fill the EMPLOYEES table of the DataSet
         //     with data fetched with the SQL request.
         dAdapter.Fill(dSet);
      } // end using dAdapter -> close the connection.
   }
   static void Main() {
      DataSet dSet = new DataSet();
      FillWithData(dSet);
      // Display Surname and Firstname columns of the EMPLOYEES table.
      // The index of the EMPLOYEES table in our DataSet is 0
      // since it contains only this table.
      DataTable dTable = dSet.Tables[0];
      foreach ( DataRow dRow in dTable.Rows )
         Console.WriteLine( dRow["Surname"] + " " + dRow["Firstname"] );
   }
}
```

This example displays the following:

Doo John
Dupont Anne
Kennedy Franck
Weiss Douglas

Working with relations between tables of a DataSet

An instance of the `DataSet` class can contain one or multiple tables. You have the possibility of adding relationships between the tables contained in a same `DataSet`. A relationship is done between the column of one table and the column of another table. Such a relationship is used in general to model a *'one to many'* relationship between the rows of a parent table (i.e. the table for which the column contains the primary key) and the rows of a child table (i.e. the table for which the column part of the relationship contains a foreign key). In the following example, we create a relationship between the `DepID` column of DEPARTMENTS and the `DepID` column of EMPLOYES. In fact, there is indeed a *'one to many'* relationship between departments and the employees since each employee is part of one department and a department can contain many employees. The creation of such a relationship in the `DataSet` allows the logical traversal of this data:

Example 19-16

```
using System;
using System.Data;
using System.Data.SqlClient;
class Program {
   static void Main() {
      DataSet dSet = new DataSet();
      using ( SqlConnection cnx = new SqlConnection(
         "server = localhost ; uid=sa ; pwd =; database = ORGANIZATION" ) ) {
         using ( SqlDataAdapter dAdapter = new SqlDataAdapter() ) {
            dAdapter.SelectCommand = new SqlCommand(
               "SELECT * FROM EMPLOYEES", cnx );
            dAdapter.Fill( dSet, "EMPLOYEES" );
            dAdapter.SelectCommand = new SqlCommand(
               "SELECT * FROM DEPARTMENTS", cnx );
            dAdapter.Fill( dSet, "DEPARTMENTS" );
         } // end using cnx.
      } // end using dAdapter.
      // Create a relation inside the DataSet.
      // The relation is made between the DEPARTMENTS.DepID column
      // and the EMPLOYEES.DepID column.
      DataColumn dCol1 = dSet.Tables[ "DEPARTMENTS" ].Columns[ "DepID" ];
      DataColumn dCol2 = dSet.Tables[ "EMPLOYEES" ].Columns[ "DepID" ];
      DataRelation dRelation = dSet.Relations.Add( "Is_Employed_By",
                                                   dCol1, dCol2);

      // Natural browsing of the relation 'one to many' between
      // a department and its employees.
      foreach ( DataRow dRow1 in dSet.Tables["DEPARTMENTS"].Rows ) {
         Console.WriteLine( "Department: {0}", dRow1["Department"] );
         foreach ( DataRow dRow2 in dRow1.GetChildRows(dRelation) )
            Console.WriteLine("   {0} {1}", dRow2["Surname"],
                                            dRow2["Firstname"] );
      }
   }
}
```

The program displays the following:

```
Department: Development
   Dupont Anne
   Kennedy Franck
Department: Financial
   Weiss Douglas
Department: Marketing
   Doo John
```

Storing in the database data updated inside a DataSet

When you modify the data in a `DataTable` (contained in a `DataSet` or not) the original data is preserved. This means that internally, a `DataTable` maintains both the original and modified versions of data. As a client to `DataTable`, you can only access the current data. Each row of a table (i.e. each instance of the `DataRow` class) offers a property named `DataRowState RowState{get;}` which indicates if the data has been modified:

Value of DataRowState	Description
Unchanged	The row has not been modified.
Added	The row has been added to the table.
Deleted	The row has been deleted from the table.
Modified	The data in the row has been modified.
Detached	The row has been created but is not yet part of a table.

It would be more exact to add to each of these descriptions, *'since the last call to the* `AcceptChanges()` *or* `RejectChanges()` *methods on the* `DataTable` *containing the row'*. In fact, if you call either one of these methods, the state of each row is reset to `Unchanged`. In addition, if we call `AcceptChanges()`, the rows which were in the `Deleted` state are effectively removed from the table. If we call `RejectChanges()`, the rows which were in the `Added` state are destroyed and the data that has been modified is reset to its initial state.

The call of the `AcceptChanges()` on a `DataSet` or a `DataTable` object does not mean that an access to the database will occur. Do not forget that a `DataSet` or a `DataTable` is a disconnected data cache. However, if a cache contains data extracted from a database, before accepting the changes, ou will generally need to update the database. In fact, the update operation on a database and the accepting of the changes are two distinct operations needed to be coded separately.

To update the database with the modified data of a cache, you need to reconnect yourself to the database and to complete a SQL request for each modification. To avoid having to code such a labor intensive task, the underlying data provider has the possibility of presenting a class which is capable of constructing such SQL requests by deducing them from a SELECT request. This class must derive from `System.Data.Common.DbCommandBuilder`. All this is illustrated by the following example:

Example 19-17

```
using System.Data;
using System.Data.SqlClient;
class Program {
   static string sCnx =
       "server = localhost ; uid=sa ; pwd =; database = ORGANIZATION";
   static string sCmd = "SELECT * FROM DEPARTMENTS";
   static void Main() {
      DataTable dTable = new DataTable();
      FillTableFromDB( dTable );
      ChangeDataInTable( dTable );
      SynchronizeChangesWithDB( dTable );
   }
   static void ChangeDataInTable( DataTable dTable ) {
      // Add a new department.
      dTable.Rows.Add("COM","Communication");
   }
   static void FillTableFromDB( DataTable dTable ) {
      using ( SqlDataAdapter dAdapter = new SqlDataAdapter(sCmd, sCnx) ) {
         dAdapter.Fill( dTable );
      } // end using dAdapter.
   }
```

Example 19-17

```
    static void SynchronizeChangesWithDB( DataTable dTable ) {
      using ( SqlDataAdapter dAdapter = new SqlDataAdapter(sCmd, sCnx) ) {
         // Build update commands from the select command.
         SqlCommandBuilder cmdBuilder = new SqlCommandBuilder( dAdapter );
         try {
            // Persist changes in the database.
            dAdapter.Update( dTable );
         }
         catch {
            // Here, we got an update error.
            return;
         }
         // Accept changes inside the dataset.
         dTable.AcceptChanges();
      } // end using dAdapter.
   }
}
```

Know that this principle of internally keeping the original and modified versions of data in order to facilitate the update can be found in a *design pattern* by *Martin Fowler* named *Unit Of Work*.

As this program is written, a call to the Update() method causes an access to the database for each SQL request. This technique is inefficient if you need to save a large number of changes. With ADO.NET2, classes derived from DbDataAdapter have the possibility of updating in a single database access. For this, you must set the value of the int DbDataAdapter.UpdateBatchSize {get;set;} which specifies the number of SQL requests contained in a batch.

Finally, note that the update operation is susceptible of raising an exception. The reason is that ADO.NET uses an optimistic management of concurrent accesses to a database.

Unconnected mode and optimistic/pessimistic concurrency strategies

When several users work simultaneously in disconnected mode with the same database, there is the possibility of a conflict during the modification of the database. For example, suppose that user A retrieves the phone number of *Anne Dupont* at 8:00. Now, let's suppose that a user B modifies the phone number of *Anne Dupont* at 8:05. Finally, suppose that user A decided to also change the phone number of *Anne Dupont* at 8:10, from the number he retrieved 10 minutes earlier. There will clearly be a conflict during the update of the phone number for *Anne Dupont*. What is the final phone number of *Anne Dupont*: the one of user B saved at 8:05 or the one of user A saved at 8:10?

ADO.NET manages these conflicts in an *optimistic* way. This means that no measures are taken to avoid such conflicts but if such a conflict happens, it is detected and by default the data is not modified. In our example, the phone number would keep the value saved at 8:05 and user A would be warned of such a conflict at 8:10. The management is optimistic in the sense that it assumes that conflicts will rarely happen. When a conflict is detected, an exception of type System.Data.DBConcurrenyException is raised during the call to the Update() method on the adaptor.

Theoretically, there is a technique to prevent conflicts. This technique is called *pessimistic* management of conflicts. This technique uses a locking mechanism on the rows (or even the tables) in order to synchronize accesses. The management is pessimistic in the sense that we predict that conflicts will happen often enough to impair the proper operation of an application. This locking mechanism implies that clients may have to wait before accessing data and hence a potential drop in application performance.

It is recommended that developers using ADO.NET make sure that the architecture of their database and of their applications be adapted to the use of an optimistic management policy. This constraint is weak in the sense that you simply need to minimize the cases where one or multiple users write the same data. In most real distributed systems, this constraint is satisfied *de facto*. In fact, the amount of data to manage is generally large in comparison to the number of simultaneous users. Meaning that in most cases, the odds of two users working on the same data are low.

Constraints on the tables of a DataSet

You can associate *constraints* to a table contained in a `DataSet`. These constraints serve as a safeguard. In practice, the presence of such constraints on a table provokes an exception to be raised when a modification does not respect one of the constraints. For the exception to be properly raised, you must set the `EnforceConstraints` property of the `DataSet` containing the `DataTable` to `true`.

Each constraint is represented by an instance of a class derived from `System.Data.Constraint`. Two classes derive from the `Constraint` class:

- `System.Data.UniqueConstraint`
  A constraint of this type imposes that table that we would be obtained by projecting the current table onto certain columns have different rows two by two. The columns are specified in the constraint. This type of constraint is particularly useful to ensure that we are not using a value already used as a primary key when we add a new row in the table.

- `System.Data.ForeignKeyConstraint`
  This constraint is used on a parent table when a 'one to many' relationship on primary/foreign keys exist between a parent and child table. Such a constraint allows specifying the behavior to use when a row of the parent table sees its primary key modified or when a row of the parent table is destroyed. For this, the `DeleteRule` and `UpdateRule` properties of such a constraint take their values from the `System.Data.Rule` enumeration.

    `Cascade:` the concerned rows of the child table are updated with the new value of the primary key of the parent table or deleted if the row of the primary key in the parent table is deleted. This is the default behavior.

    `None:` nothing is done on the rows of the child table.

    `SetDefault:` each value of the rows of the child table takes the default value for their respective columns (`DefaultValue` property of the `Column` class).

    `SetNull:` the corresponding values in the rows of the child tables are set to null.

The DataView class

The `System.Data.DataView` class allows the partial selection of the contents of a `DataTable` based on a certain set of criteria:

- You can decide to only visualize the rows which are in a certain state by setting the `DataRowViewState RowStateFilter{get;set;}` property. For example, the `DataRowViewState.ModifiedCurrent` value allows you to visualize the current content of each line that has been modified while the `DataRowViewState.Deleted` allows you to see the original content for each row that has been deleted.

- You can decide to apply a filter on the content of certain columns by setting the `string RowFilter{get;set;}` property. The formatting of the string representing the filter is similar to the formatting of a `WHERE` SQL clause. For more details on this formatting, read the article named **The DataColumn.Expression Property** on **MSDN**.

Working in unconnected mode with DataSet 605

- You can decide to sort the filtered rows based on the columns with the primary keys by setting the `bool ApplyDefaultSort{get;set;}` property.
- You can decide to sort the filtered rows based on the content of one or multiple columns by using the `string Sort{get;set;}` property. The sort is done in ascending order by default. You can separate the name of the columns with a semicolon and use the ASC or DESC expressions to specify either an ascending or a descending sort.

The content of a `DataView` is dynamic. In other words, it will reflect in real-time the changes made to the data underneath the `DataTable`. This peculiarity is illustrated by the following program:

Example 19-18
```
using System;
using System.Data;
using System.Data.SqlClient;
class Program {
   static string sCnx =
      "server = localhost ; uid=sa ; pwd =; database = ORGANIZATION";
   static string sCmd = "SELECT * FROM EMPLOYEES";
   static void Main() {
      DataTable dTable = new DataTable();
      using (SqlDataAdapter dAdapter = new SqlDataAdapter( sCmd, sCnx ) ) {
         dAdapter.Fill(dTable);
      } // end using dAdapter.
      DataView dView = new DataView( dTable );
      // Filter employees of development department.
      dView.RowFilter = "DepID='DEV'";

      Console.WriteLine( "--> Data Table:" );
      foreach ( DataRow dRow in dTable.Rows )
         Console.WriteLine( dRow["DepID"] + " " + dRow["Surname"] );

      Console.WriteLine( "--> Data View before transfering Weiss:" );
      for (int i = 0; i < dView.Count; i++)
         Console.WriteLine( dView[i]["DepID"] + " " + dView[i]["Surname"]);

      // Transfer 'Weiss' to the development department.
      foreach ( DataRow dRow in dTable.Rows )
         if ( ( (string)dRow["Surname"] ) == "Weiss" )
            dRow["DepID"] = "DEV";

      Console.WriteLine( "--> Data View after transfering Weiss:" );
      for (int i = 0; i < dView.Count; i++)
         Console.WriteLine( dView[i]["DepID"] + " " + dView[i]["Surname"]);
   }
}
```

This program displays the following:
```
--> Data Table:
MKT Doo
DEV Dupont
DEV Kennedy
FIN Weiss
--> Data View before transfering Weiss:
DEV Dupont
DEV Kennedy
--> Data View after transfering Weiss:
DEV Dupont
DEV Kennedy
DEV Weiss
```

With the difference to the view system provided by various RDBMS, the `DataView` does not allow the creation of a view based on the joining of tables. It also does not allow the inclusion or exclusion of specific columns.

The method named `DataTable DataView.ToTable()` allows you to build a new `DataTable` with a copy of the content from the current `DataView`.

You can add lines to a `DataView` if the `bool AllowNew{get;set;}` property is set. You can also modify the content of the existing rows if the `bool AllowEdit{get;set;}` property is set. These modifications will be reported to the underlying `DataTable` only if the `EndEdit()` method of `DataRowView` is called. More details on this topic can be found in the article named **Modifying Data Using a DataView** on **MSDN**.

If you use the sort option on one or many columns, you can use the `Find()` and `FindRows()` methods to find one or multiple rows where the value of the columns used for the sort is equal to the specified values.

The `DataView DataRowView.CreateChildView(DataRelation)` method allows obtaining a `DataView` on the rows of the child `DataTable` when you harness a relationship between tables of a `DataSet`. Of course, for this to work, the underlying `DataTable` to the `DataView` containing the source row must be the parent table of the relationship.

The `System.Data.DataViewManager` class allows the management of multiple tables within the same `DataSet`.

Typed DataSet

Now that we have introduced the notion of `DataSet`, it is time to explain that we rarely directly use `DataSet` objects. In fact, we prefer to use what is named a *typed DataSet*. The `xsd.exe` tool supplied with the framework allows the construction of a C# or VB.NET class derived from `DataSet`. This construction is done from an XSD schema or from the tables of the database. Such a generated class allows access to the data of a cache in strongly typed manner. To illustrate this notion of strong typing, here is Example 19-16 rewritten by using the typed class `ConsoleApplication1.ORGANIZATIONDataSet`:

Example 19-19

```
using System;
using System.Data;
using System.Data.Common;
using System.Data.SqlClient;
using ConsoleApplication1;  // This namespace contains the
                            // ORGANIZATIONDataSet class.
class Program {
   static void Main() {
      ORGANIZATIONDataSet dSet = new ORGANIZATIONDataSet();
      using ( SqlConnection cnx = new SqlConnection(
         "server = localhost ; uid=sa ; pwd =; database = ORGANIZATION") ) {
         using ( SqlDataAdapter dAdapter = new SqlDataAdapter() ) {
            dAdapter.SelectCommand = new SqlCommand(
               "SELECT * FROM EMPLOYEES", cnx );
            dAdapter.Fill( dSet, "EMPLOYEES" );
            dAdapter.SelectCommand = new SqlCommand(
               "SELECT * FROM DEPARTMENTS", cnx );
            dAdapter.Fill( dSet, "DEPARTMENTS" );
         } // end using dAdapter.
      } // end using cnx.
```

Example 19-19

```
    foreach(ORGANIZATIONDataSet.DEPARTMENTSRow dRow in dSet.DEPARTMENTS){
        Console.WriteLine( "Department: " + dRow.Department );
        foreach ( ORGANIZATIONDataSet.EMPLOYEESRow eRow in
                    dRow.GetEMPLOYEESRows() )
            Console.WriteLine( "   " + eRow.Surname
                              + " " + eRow.DEPARTMENTSRow.Department );
        }
    }
}
```

This example displays the following:

```
Department: Department
   Dupont Development
   Kennedy Development
Department: Financial
   Weiss Financial
Department: Marketing
   Doo Marketing
```

We can see that an instance of the ORGANIZATIONDataSet class is manipulated just as a DataSet. This is normal since it is a DataSet as the ORGANIZATIONDataSet class is derived from DataSet. We also see that the ORGANIZATIONDataSet class contains the EMPLOYEESRow and DEPARTMENTSRow nested classes which are very practical. Not only do they contain properties properly typed for every column of the underlying table, but they also contain member allowing the proper navigation based on the Is_Employed_By relationship. Finally, we see that the ORGANIZATIONDataSet offers the EMPLOYEES and DEPARTMENTS properties which allow direct access to the corresponding tables.

Creating a typed DataSet class

As we have explained, the ORGANIZATIONDataSet and its encapsulated classes were generated using the tool named xsd.exe. To avoid having to manually use this command line tool *Visual Studio* offers menus to create typed DataSet:

- Either you do: *Menu Data > Add New Data Source > Database >* and then select a database and its tables which are to be taken into account in your typed DataSet.

- Either you do: *Right click on a project > Add > New Item... > DataSet >* and then select the databases as well as the tables you wish to use in your typed DataSet through the *Server Explorer* window.

In both cases, you project contains a new file with a .xsd extension (in this case ORGANIZATIONDataSet.xsd). A source code file (in this case ORGANIZATIONDataSet.Designer.cs) is associated to this file. This file contains the code generated for the ORGANIZATIONDataSet class and its encapsulated classes.

If you wish to add functionality to one of the generated classes, you must right click on the ORGANIZATIONDataSet.xsd and select *View Code*. This action will create a new associated file named ORGANIZATIONDataSet.cs. This file contains a partial declaration of the ORGANIZATIONDataSet class. You can now use this partial declaration to add new members to the ORGANIZATIONDataSet class or its encapsulated classes. In fact, all these generated classes are declared in a partial manner. Hence, this technique allows the separation of your code and the generated code into distinct files. This has the consequence of avoiding the loss of code due to an update.

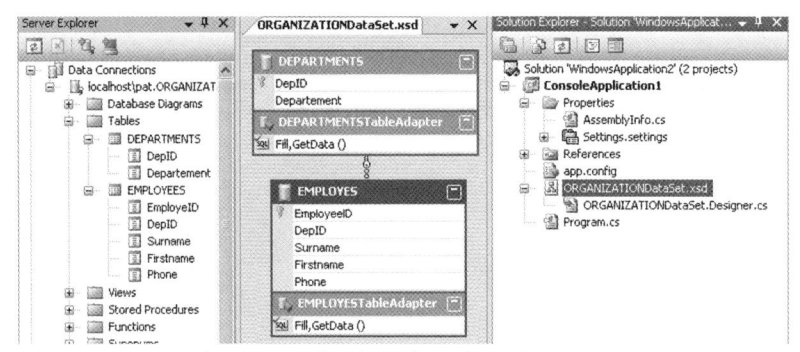

Figure 19-3: Visual Studio and typed DataSet

TableAdapter and typed SQL requests

During the generation of a typed `DataSet`, *Visual Studio* also generates typed `DataAdapter` classes in a dedicated namespace (in this case `ConsoleApplication1.ORGANIZATIONDataSetTable Adapters`). We name these classes `TableAdapter`. Let us remind you that an instance of `DataAdapter` is a set of commands coupled with a connection allowing you to fill the tables of a `DataSet`. Let us rewrite Example 19-20 using the `EMPLOYEESTableAdapter` and `DEPARTMENTSTableAdapter` classes that were generated:

Example 19-20

```
...
// The namespace which contains TableAdapters.
using ConsoleApplication1.ORGANIZATIONDataSetTableAdapters;
class Program {
   static void Main() {
      ORGANIZATIONDataSet dSet = new ORGANIZATIONDataSet();
      using (SqlConnection cnx = new SqlConnection(
         "server = localhost ; uid=sa ; pwd =; database = ORGANIZATION") ) {
         using ( EMPLOYEESTableAdapter eAdapter = new
                                       EMPLOYEESTableAdapter() ) {
            eAdapter.Connection = cnx;
            eAdapter.Fill( dSet.EMPLOYEES );
         } // end using eAdapter.
         using ( DEPARTMENTSTableAdapter dAdapter = new
                                         DEPARTMENTSTableAdapter() ) {
            dAdapter.Connection = cnx;
            dAdapter.Fill( dSet.DEPARTMENTS );
         } // end using dAdapter.
      } // end using cnx.
...
```

We note the use of the `Fill(EMPLOYEESDataTable)` and `Fill(DEPARTMENTSDataTable)` methods. These methods allow us to avoid having to write the SQL requests to select the rows of a table. We could have also used the `EMPLOYEESDataTable GetData()` and `DEPARTMENTSDataTable GetData()` methods which play the same role with the exception that they prevent you from having to create the table.

In fact, the main advantage of `TableAdapter` classes resides in the fact that they prevent us from having to write all kind of SQL requests (i.e. requests of type `SELECT`, `INSERT`, `UPDATE` and `DELETE`). The idea is to replace each request with a method of `TableAdapter`. The advantage is that the parameters to these methods are typed. A *wizard* for the creation of these methods exists. Here is how you can use it to create a new `EMPLOYEESDataTable GetEmployeesByDepID(string DepID)` method which returns a table containing the employees of a department:

Right click on ORGANIZATIONDataSet.xsd › *View designer* ›*Right click* EMPLOYEESTableAdapter › *Add Query* › *Use SQL Statements* › *Next* › *SELECT which returns Rows* (at this point you can also decide to create a *INSERT, UPDATE, DELETE* request) › *Next* › *Query Builder* › *Create the request:* SELECT EmployeeID, DepID, Surname, Firstname, Phone FROM EMPLOYEES WHERE DepID = @DepID › *OK* › *Next* › *Return a DataTable with the method named* GetEmployeesByDepID() › *Finish*

Here is an example using this method:

Example 19-21
```
using System.Data.SqlClient;
using ConsoleApplication1;
using ConsoleApplication1.ORGANIZATIONDataSetTableAdapters;
class Program {
   static void Main() {
      ORGANIZATIONDataSet.EMPLOYEESDataTable table;
      using ( SqlConnection cnx = new SqlConnection(
         "server = localhost ; uid=sa ; pwd =; database = ORGANIZATION") ) {
         using ( EMPLOYEESTableAdapter eAdapter = new
                                       EMPLOYEESTableAdapter() ) {
            table = eAdapter.GetEmployeesByDepID( "DEV" );
         } // end using eAdapter.
      } // end using cnx.
      foreach ( ORGANIZATIONDataSet.EMPLOYEESRow eRow in table )
         System.Console.WriteLine( "   " + eRow.Surname );
   }
}
```

Bridges between the connected and the unconnected modes

ADO.NET2 offers a bridge between the connected and disconnected modes. Concretely, you can fill a `DataSet` or a `DataTable` from a `DataReader`. You can also traverse the data contained in a `DataSet` or in a `DataTable` using a `DataReader`. These two options are illustrated by the following example which fills a `DataTable` with the data from the EMPLOYEES table using a `DataReader` connected to the database. In the second step, the data from the `DataTable` are read using another `DataReader` not connected to the database. All happens as if the `DataTable` was the database to which this second `DataReader` was connected to:

Example 19-22
```
using System;
using System.Data;
using System.Data.Common;
using System.Data.SqlClient;
class Program {
   static void Main() {
      DataTable dTable = new DataTable();
      using ( DbConnection cnx = new SqlConnection (
         "server = localhost ; uid=sa ; pwd =; database = ORGANIZATION")){
         using ( DbCommand cmd = new SqlCommand (
            "SELECT * FROM EMPLOYEES", (SqlConnection) cnx) ) {
            cnx.Open();
            using ( DbDataReader rdrCmd = cmd.ExecuteReader() ) {
               // Connected DataReader -> DataTable
               dTable.Load( rdrCmd, LoadOption.OverwriteChanges );
            } // end using rdrCmd.
         } // end using cmd.
```

Example 19-22

```
      } // end using cnx.
   // DataTable -> DataReader unconnected.
   using ( DbDataReader rdrTbl = dTable.CreateDataReader() ) {
      while (rdrTbl.Read())
         Console.WriteLine(rdrTbl.GetString(2)+" "+rdrTbl.GetString(3));
   } // end using rdrTbl.
   }
}
```

The Load() method of the DataTable class (which is also offered by the DataSet class) takes as a second argument a value from the LoadOption enumeration. This information indicates how to resolve update conflicts between the original and current data contained in the DataSet and the data coming in from the DataReader. The LoadOption enumeration has three possible values:

- PreserveChanges: (default value) Writes over only the original data of the DataSet with the data coming from the DataReader.
- OverwriteChanges: Writes over the original and current data of the DataSet with the data coming from the DataReader.
- Upsert: Writes over only the current data of the DataSet with the data coming from the DataReader.

Bridges between objects and the relational data

The relational model has reached its limits with the coming of object oriented languages. In fact, the relational model is not well adapted to store the state of objects instances of classes written in an object oriented language such as C#, C++ or Java.

Structural problems

When we plan on using a relational persistence model from an object oriented language, the first problem that we are confronted with is: there is no easy way to store the state of an object instance of a subclass of another class:

- Either we create a single table for the whole class hierarchy (*design pattern* by *Martin Fowler* named **Single Table Inheritance**). Although that this approach may be efficient for a small hierarchy of classes, it quickly becomes impractical when the number of classes and fields increase.
- Either you create a table for each non-abstract class (*design pattern* by *Martin Fowler* named **Concrete Table Inheritance**). This solution has the big disadvantage of being hard to maintain. If a base class changes, you must also change the structure of all tables representing the derived classes.
- Either we create a table for each class by using a system of foreign keys (*design patterns* by *Martin Fowler* named **Class Table Inheritance**). A table contains only the fields defined by the corresponding class. This approach resolves the problem of maintenance but introduces complexities in the access to the data.

Another structural problem is due to the fact that '*one to many*' and '*many to many*' relations between objects must be stored. In object oriented languages, collections are physically managed either by an object position (value type) or either by an object reference system (reference type). None of these two systems are applicable within a relational database. To solve the case of '*one to many*' relationships, we use foreign keys. To solve the problem in the case of '*many to many*' relationships, we use an association table. You must understand that all the difficulty behind the storage of relationships come from the management and maintenance of the 'foreign key/association table' and 'reference/index' systems.

Behavioral problems

Another problem encountered when we use a relational persistence model from an object oriented is behavioral. The behavior problem is related to the way objects are loaded and saved. In general, you load several states in objects, modify them and then save these new states. It is often more efficient to only partially load the state although this requires more analysis and design (*design pattern* by *Martin Fowler* named **Lazy Load**). In addition, during the processing of data by the application, it is difficult to keep track of each load. For this specific task, the ADO.NET technology offers an efficient solution which we discuss at page 602.

Three different approaches to solve these problems

There are three different approaches to solve these problems: object databases, the generation of code and reflection on an association table:

- A new generation of databases allowing the storage of object states has seen the light a few years ago. The idea is to simply store the state of the object by either serializing it or either establishing a correspondence with relational data to benefit from the efficiency of the relational request model. The use of such databases has remained marginal. A significant leap forward is happening because of *Microsoft* with *SQL Server 2005*. In fact, during execution, the RDBMS process hosts the CLR in a way which allows a certain integration between managed .NET types and the database data. For example, under certain conditions, a .NET type can directly type a column of a table (this functionality is named *User Defined Type* or *UDT*). In addition the stored procedures can be written in managed .NET code.

- If you wish to remain with a more traditional approach, you can minimize the consequences of the complexity and maintenance problems inherent to the object/relational paradigm with the automatic generation of code (*design pattern* by *Martin Fowler* named **Metadata Mapping with code generation**). With this method, the SQL code necessary to exploit and use a database as well as the software layer which tackles the database are constructed from a same description. There are less maintenance problems and a large part of the complexity can be encapsulated in the generated code.

- Another way that generated code can be used to establish a link between objects and a relational database is to allow for a correspondence table (i.e. mapping table) between the fields of the classes and the columns of the tables. During execution, we use a mapping engine to traverse such a table to establish the correspondence between the state of objects and the relational database. This is the *design pattern* by Fowler named **Metadata Mapping with reflection**.

A debate on the pros and cons of the two variants of the Metadata Mapping design pattern is available at http://www.theserverside.net/news/thread.tss?thread_id=29071.

Finally, lets us precise that one of the priorities of the designers of the 3.0 version of C# is to unify at the language level the world of data (both XML and SQL) and the world of objects. Initial work is based on the experimental language Cω (pronounced C omega) presented at http://research.microsoft.com/Comega/.

Object/relational mapping .NET tools

There are more than forty tools which address the object/relational mapping for the .NET platform. Most of them base themselves on one of the two versions of the Metadata Mapping design pattern. Some are free and open source while other must be purchased. Amongst these tools, here are some of the most popular:

- NHibernate: http://wiki.nhibernate.org/display/NH/Home
- Data Tier Modeler (DTM): http://www.evaluant.com/en/solutions/dtm/default.aspx

- OlyMars (for Olympic de Marseille, a famous French soccer team ☺) http://www.microsoft.com/france/msdn/olymars/default.mspx
- Object Broker http://sourceforge.net/projects/objectbroker/
- LLBLGen Pro http://www.llblgen.com/defaultgeneric.aspx

A more complete list can by found at http://sharptoolbox.com under the *Object-Relational mapping* category.

Microsoft planed on including such a tool with .NET 2 named *Object Space*. However, the delivery of this tool has been postponed as the project grew and will be part of the future *WinFS* data engine.

You can consult this article by *Fabrice Marguerie* which presents a certain number of criteria to consider in the choice of an OR mapping tool http://madgeek.com/Articles/ORMapping/FR/mapping.htm.

Functionalities specific to the SQL Server data provider

Asynchronous requests

The SqlClient data provider that is part of ADO.NET2 allows the execution of commands in an asynchronous way. The new thing compared to .NET vI.x is that during the execution of an asynchronous request, no threads wait for the result from the database. This new approach is more efficient than the use of a thread from the pool by using asynchronous delegate. Internally, this new feature uses a win32 asynchronous input/output mechanism supplied since *Windows 2000*. It is available on all versions of *SQL Server* supported by the SqlClient data provider, that is 7/2000/2005.

At the framework level, this feature can be exploited by using six new methods of the `SqlCommand` class:

```
BeginExecuteNonQuery()   /  EndExecuteNonQuery()
BeginExecuteReader()     /  EndExecuteReader()
BeginExecuteXmlReader()  /  EndExecuteXmlReader()
```

Although that internally, the behavior is different, these methods are used in the same way as an asynchronous delegate by using an object accessible by the `IAsyncResult` interface. The following example obtains two `DataReader` from our `ORGANIZATION` database in an asynchronous manner. Note that a connection cannot support multiple simultaneous asynchronous calls hence we are obligated to use two equivalent connections. Also note that you must specify `async=true` in the connection string so that such a connection be usable to make asynchronous calls. In fact, the support of this feature has a small negative impact on synchronous calls made to connections with the `async` flag set.

Example 19-23
```
using System.Data;
using System.Data.SqlClient;
class Program {
   static string sCnx = "server = localhost ; uid=sa ; pwd =; " +
                       "database = ORGANIZATION ; async=true";
   static string sCmd1 = "SELECT * FROM EMPLOYEES";
   static string sCmd2 = "SELECT * FROM DEPARTMENTS";
   static void Main() {
      using ( SqlConnection cnx1 = new SqlConnection(sCnx) )
      using ( SqlConnection cnx2 = new SqlConnection(sCnx) ) {
         cnx1.Open();
         SqlCommand cmd1 = new SqlCommand( sCmd1, cnx1 );
```

Functionalities specific to the SQL Server data provider

Example 19-23

```
            System.IAsyncResult ar1 = cmd1.BeginExecuteReader();
            cnx2.Open();
            SqlCommand cmd2 = new SqlCommand( sCmd2, cnx2 );
            System.IAsyncResult ar2 = cmd2.BeginExecuteReader();
            // Here, you can work with the current thread while your
            // SQL requests are executed.
            SqlDataReader rdr1 = cmd1.EndExecuteReader( ar1 );
            SqlDataReader rdr2 = cmd2.EndExecuteReader( ar2 );
            // Here, you can use rdr1 and rdr2.
         } // end using cnx1 et cnx2.
      }
}
```

Finally note that verifications are done on the parameters during the call to `BeginXxx()` which may cause an exception to be raised. Also, the execution may fail. In this case, an exception will be raised during the call to the `EndXxx()` method.

Bulk copy

The `bcp.exe` (*Bulk Copy Program*) tool delivered with *SQL Server* allows to copy or to obtain a large volume of data from a *SQL Server* database. The SqlClient provider of ADO.NET2 allows the use of the services of this tool through a new class named `System.Data.SqlClient.SqlBulkCopy`. This class allows the mass copy of data from a `DataTable`, a `DataSet` or a `DataReader` to a *SQL Server* database. The following example shows how to mass copy the content of the DEPARTMENT table from the ORGANIZATION database to the DEPARTMENT table of another database named ORGANIZATION2:

Example 19-24

```
using System.Data;
using System.Data.SqlClient;
class Program {
   static string sCnx =
       "server = localhost ; uid=sa ; pwd =; database = ORGANIZATION";
   static string sCnx2 =
       "server = localhost ; uid=sa ; pwd =; database = ORGANIZATION2";
   static void Main() {
      using (SqlConnection cnx = new SqlConnection(sCnx)) {
         SqlCommand cmd = new SqlCommand("SELECT * FROM DEPARTMENTS ",cnx);
         cnx.Open();
         SqlDataReader rdr = cmd.ExecuteReader();
         // Bulk copy of N_ROWS rows.
         using ( SqlBulkCopy bulkCopier = new SqlBulkCopy( sCnx2 ) ) {
            bulkCopier.DestinationTableName = "DEPARTMENTS";
            bulkCopier.WriteToServer( rdr );
         } // end using bulkCopier;
      } // end using cnx.
   }
}
```

The `SqlBulkCopy` class also offers the possibility of being notified on the current state of the current copy operation, the possibility of setting a *time out* on the copy operation and the possibility of defining the correspondence between the source and destination columns in the case where the schema for the tables does not identically match.

Statistics on SqlClient connections

Example 19-8 at page 592 shows how to obtain statistics about activity of a connection to a *SQL Server* RDBMS. The object returned is a dictionary where the keys represent the name of the statistics. This dictionary contains about 20 statistics such as the number of bytes sent or received. In addition to the `RetrieveStatistics()` method, the `SqlConnection` class also offers a method named `ResetStatistics()` which allows to reset the statistics of a connection.

SQL Server 2005 Express Edition

Although this product does not take integral part of the .NET framework, we still mention it as it will certainly encounter a large success from developers using .NET 2. *SQL Server 2005 Express Edition* is the successor to the free DBMS named *Microsoft SQL Server Desktop Engine* (MSDE) and *Jet*. The new version offers several advantages compared to the previous versions:

- A strong integration of the CLR. *SQL Server Express* is a simplified version of the flagship RDBMS by *Microsoft, SQL Server 2005*.
- Deployment of an application using XCopy is now possible. A database can resume itself to an .mdf file present in the tree structure of the deployed .NET application.
- The installation of *SQL Server 2005 Express Edition* can be a prerequisite to the *ClickOnce* deployment of a .NET application. No need of installing MDAC.
- Graphical tools facilitate the use of the product.
- A strong integration with *Visual Studio 2005*. This means that *SQL Server Express Edition* is automatically installed during the installation of *Visual Studio 2005*.
- Strong support for XML where it is possible to type a column of a table in XML.
- Better performance and security management.

More information on this product can be found on the *Microsoft* website.

20

Transactions

Introduction to transactions

A sequence of operations on data is said to be *transactional*, if at the end of these operations all the changes are validated (*commit*) or none of the changes are validated (*rollback*). The standard example using a transaction is the transfer of a certain amount from a bank account A to a bank account B. This operation is the result of two commands:

- Debit of the sum from account A.
- Credit of the sum to account B.

If one of the two commands fails, the other one must absolutely fail. The two commands must then be executed within a same transaction.

> Transactions are used to guarantee the integrity of a set of data after an update.

This example also illustrates the fact that commands executed within a transaction can be done on a same database or even on different databases. In fact, we can suppose that both accounts belong to the same bank, in which case the commands might be done on the same database. But if the two accounts belong to different banks, the commands will be done on different databases. We then say that the transaction is *distributed*.

The transaction theory is relatively complex. A transactional environment ideally supports four properties, called *ACID properties*:

Atomicity	All commands are completed or none are completed.
Consistency	The transaction leaves the data in a coherent state.
Isolation	Transactions are executed in an isolated way from each other.
Durable	The results are stored in a persistent way.

We will see in this section which are the features offered by the framework to complete local and distributed transactions. We will see that set of ACID properties can be reduced in order to reduce the performance burden.

Transaction Manager (TM), Resource Manager (RM) and data source

Databases only represent one use case for transactions. In fact, this concept of data update coordination can prove itself useful to other data source such as messaging queues, web services, file systems or even memory representation of data. All these data sources can participate in a transaction because of a software layer specific to each source generally named *RM* (for *Resource Manager*) that we will detail a little later.

In modern applications, the management of transactions is delegated to a software layer named *transaction manager* (or *TM*). When using a TM, an application which uses transactions has the following responsibilities:

- To request the creation of a transaction.
- To indicate which are the data sources implicated in the transaction. During this step, the RM of a data source registers itself to the TM. We then talk of the enlistment of a data source within a transaction.
- Complete the update of the data for each source during the transaction.
- Notify the TM when the update is completed.

The TM is responsible for the coordination of the work done by the RM. This coordination has for goal to guarantee the integrity of the data: either they are all updated correctly, either the transaction encountered a problem and no modification will be done on the data. To manage such coordination, from the point of view of the TM, all RMs support a same API which allows their participation within a transaction. This architecture is exposed in the following illustration:

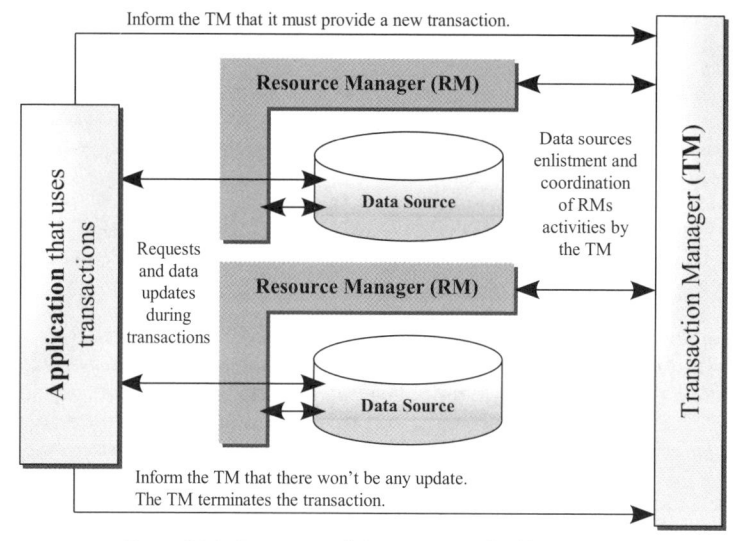

Figure 20-1: TM, RM and data source: The big picture

Introduction to distributed transactions and to 2PC algorithms

A distributed transaction implies the update of data in several RMs while respecting the ACID properties. For this, the TM implementation is commonly based on a *2 Phase Commit* or *2PC*) validation algorithm:

- In the first phase, the application enlists each data source and executes the data update requests. The TM notifies each of RMs that they participate in a distributed transaction. Each RM then executes a local transaction on its data. It contacts the TM right before the transaction is committed whether or not the update succeeded. We say that RMs are voting where each vote *success* or *fail*.
- If at least one RM votes *fail*, the TM then informs all the participating RMs that the distributed transaction has failed. Each RM must then cancel its transaction and rollback the data to its initial state. If all RMs unanimously vote *success*, then the transaction has succeeded and each RM is notified to commit the changes.

Introduction to transactions

A variant of this algorithm exists. In the first phase, when a RM sees that a local transaction has succeeded, it can commit its changes. If the distributed transaction succeeds as a whole, then there is nothing to do in the second phase. If a failure is detected, the RM must make a necessary local transaction to cannel the effect of the first transaction. Here we talk of a *recovery* data update algorithm.

As is, the 2PC algorithm is not 100% reliable. If a network failure happens between the TM and a RM halfway through the second phase, this leaves this RM in an inconsistent state. Such a situation is called *in-doubt*. The impact of these rare, but inevitable cases can be repaired using a *recovery service* (or RS) which periodically verifies if a distributed transaction has potentially corrupted data by completing in an in-doubt way. This service can attempt to automatically repair the corrupt data using the information saved by the data source during the first phase. If it fails, the recovery service can, as a last resort, informs the administrator.

There are protocols which allow for a TM to coordinate a distributed transaction between RMs. We can mention the *OleDB*, *XA* or *WS-AtomicTransaction* protocols.

After seeing the description of the 2PC algorithm, it is clear that distributed transactions are costly operations which require several communications between the various involved parties. It is thus always preferable to use a local transaction when possible.

Local transaction on a SQL Server connection

In the description of the 2PC algorithm, we have talked about local transactions. Most RDBMS natively offer the possibility to execute local transactions. The `DbConnection` class (from which derive all the other data provider connection classes of ADO.NET) exposes the `BeginTransaction()` method which returns an object of a class derived from `DbTransaction`. Most data providers encapsulate transactional support of the underlying RDBMS by overriding the `BeginTransaction()` and by specializing the `DbTransaction` class. The following example uses the relational database described at page 589. It shows how to complete a local transaction using the `SqlClient` data provider. There, we will complete two commands on our database:

- We add the *Communication* department to the `ORGANIZATION` database.
- We add an employee to this department.

These commands must be executed within a transaction. In fact, if the addition of the department fails but the addition of the employee succeeds, the database is then in an incoherent state since the employee belongs to a non-existent department. Note that in this specific case, the `FOREIGN KEY (DepID) REFERENCES DEPARTEMENTS(DepID)` referential integrity condition will prevent this type of data corruption.

Example 20-1

```
using System.Data.Common;
using System.Data.SqlClient;
class Program {
   static void Main() {
      string sCnx =
         "server = localhost ; uid=sa ; pwd =; database = ORGANIZATION";
      string sCmd1 =
         "INSERT INTO DEPARTEMENTS VALUES ('COM','Communication')";
      string sCmd2 =
    "INSERT INTO EMPLOYEES VALUES ('COM','Smith','Adam','(123) 456-7899')";
      try {
         using (SqlConnection cnx = new SqlConnection(sCnx)) {
            cnx.Open();
            DbTransaction tx = cnx.BeginTransaction();
```

Example 20-1
```
                DbCommand cmd = new SqlCommand(sCmd1, cnx);
                cmd.Transaction = tx;
                cmd.ExecuteNonQuery();
                cmd.CommandText = sCmd2;
                cmd.ExecuteNonQuery();
                tx.Commit();
                // Here, both commands have been successfully executed.
                // and the transaction is done.
            } // end using cnx.
        } catch {
            // If an exception has been raised before or during the
            // call to 'Commit()' data of the DB haven't been updated.
        }
    }
}
```

In the particular case of the *SQL Server* RDBMS, the T-SQL language offers the possibility of completing transactions (where the T stands for *Transact*). For example, the following T-SQL code allows completing both our operations in a transactional way. Note the need to test after each operation if an error has occurred:

```
BEGIN TRANSACTION
INSERT INTO DEPARTMENTS VALUES ('COM','Communication')
If @@error <> 0 GOTO ERR_HANDLER
INSERT INTO EMPLOYEES VALUES ('COM','Smith','Adam','(123) 456-7899')
If @@error <> 0 GOTO ERR_HANDLER
COMMIT TRANSACTION
RETURN

ERR_HANDLER:
    ROLLBACK TRANSACTION
    RETURN
```

In our C# program, the `SqlClient` data provider takes advantage of T-SQL to create our transactional behavior. The direct use of T-SQL is then more efficient to complete local transactions. However, the use of the data provider leads itself to the easier creation of complex transactions involving a large number of rows. Let us mention that it is better not to update too much data at once in a local transaction (in the order of a thousand rows). In fact, in the case of a massive transaction which ends in failure (or an in-doubt situation), the work needed to finalize the transaction becomes prohibitive. If your needs exceed this limit, it is better to split your transactions into smaller pieces.

The Distributed Transaction Coordinator (the DTC, the Windows TM)

Microsoft delivers a TM with its OS. This TM is named *DTC* (*Distributed Transaction Coordinator* also sometimes called *MSDTC*). It currently supports the *OleDB* and *XA* protocols. The *Windows Vista* version of DTC will also support the transactional protocols relating to *Web Services, WS-Coordination, WS-AtomicTransaction* and *WS-BusinessActivity*. *Windows Vista* will also provide RMs to allow transactional updates on *Windows* data sources such as files or the registry.

The DTC is not necessarily accessible or installed on your machine depending on the version of *Windows* you are using. You can check its presence by doing: *Start* › *Control panel* › *Administration tools* › *Component services* › *Component services* › *Computer* › *My Computer* › *Distributed Transaction Coordinator*.

Under *Windows XP SP2* the DTC is installed by default but all the options are deactivated. You can access the setup window of the DTC like this: (…) *Component services > Computer > MyComputer > Right-click Properties > MSDTC Tab.* Then you can activate all the security parameters that you need.

Under *Windows 2003* the DTC is not installed by default. To install it, you need to do the following: *Start > Control panel > Add/Suppress programs* or *Add/Suppress Windows/Components > Application server.* Then install COM+ followed by MSDTC.

If the DTC is currently executing, it is possible to list all the current transactions using the *'Transactions list'* tab and to obtain statistics on the transactions completed by the DTC using the *'Transaction statistics'* tab.

For several years now, the DTC has been usable from the COM+ technology. Since the version 1.x of .NET, developers could complete distributed transactions using the DTC. In fact, the part of the .NET framework named *Enterprise Services* (which we discuss at page 244) allows the encapsulation of the COM+ technology through a .NET API. Hence, using the 1.x versions of the framework you needed to use enterprise services in order to complete distributed transactions and the ADO.NET data providers to complete local transactions.

System.Transactions

Version 2 of the .NET framework presents a new namespace called `System.Transactions` which offers a unified transactional programming model. All assemblies which wish to use the services of this framework must reference the `Systems.Transactions.dll` assembly.

Introduction to LTM, durable RM and volatile RM

The `System.Transactions` framework contains a TM called *LTM* (*Lightweight Transaction Manager*) specialized with the management of *volatile RMs*. The characteristic of a volatile RM is that it does not need a recovery service when it participates to a 2PC transaction which leads to an in-doubt situation. Consequently, the data managed by a volatile RM is often stored in memory where an in-doubt situation does not carry the risk of permanently corrupting data. Sooner or later, the process containing the corrupted data will be restarted.

The concept of a volatile RM is opposite to the one of a *durable RM*. A durable RM is then a RM which needs a recovery service when it participates to a 2PC transaction which leads to an in-doubt situation. The data managed by a durable RM is generally stored on a hard disk, in a persistent way. Before the first phase, a durable RM which participates to a 2PC transaction must store both old and new versions of the data. If a transaction leads to an in-doubt situation, the recovery service will contact the durable RM to tell it which version of the data it must keep. The time span between the in-doubt transaction and the contact by the recovery service can be several minutes, if not hours. More details on this topic can be found in the article named **Performing Recovery** on **MSDN**.

All transactions created with `System.Transactions` are first managed by the LTM. The use of the LTM is much more efficient that the one of the DTC since all the communications between the LTM and its RMs are done within the same AppDomain.

A transaction managed by the LTM can involve several volatile RMs and at most one durable RM which can perform its task in either one or two phases depending on the algorithm used by the TM. Such a durable RM is said to be a *Promotable Single Phase Enlistment* (*PSPE*). The `System.Transactions` framework knows how to automatically delegate a transaction from the LTM to the DTC as soon as one of the following conditions is met:

- A non PSPE durable RM enrolls its data source in the transaction.
- A durable PSPE RM already participates to the transaction when a second durable RM (PSPE or not) enrolls its data source. At this time, the first durable PSPE RM must save the data to resolve any possible in-doubt situation. In other words, it transitions from the one phase mode to the two phase mode. We talk here of a *promotable enlistment*.
- The transaction is serialized to be used in another AppDomain.

All RDBMS connections are durable RMs. However, only connections to the *SQL Server 2005* RDBMS are PSPE durable RMs (for the moment).

The documentation says that a transaction is *escalated* when it is delegated from the LTM to the DTC. This transaction *escalation* is done in a completely transparent way to the client code of `System.Transactions`. It is the same classes and methods of `System.Transactions` which are used independently of whether the LTM or the DTC is used. This optimization is implicit but is a good thing to know especially if performance is an important aspect of your code. Let us precise that internally, the delegation of a transaction to the DTC does not completely eliminate the LTM from the game. It does in fact collaborate with DTC to manage volatile RMs.

Let us mention a classic misunderstanding. Understand that both the LTM and the DTC are distributed TMs. Their difference is not at the level of the number of RMs they can manage. Only the durable/durable PSPE/volatile property of the RMs participating to a transaction allows the `System.Transactions` framework to decide whether or not to implicate the DTC.

Implicit transactions with System.Transactions

Let's rewrite Example 20-1 by using the types of the `System.Transactions` namespace.

Example 20-2

```
using System.Data.Common;
using System.Data.SqlClient;
using System.Transactions;
class Program {
   static void Main() {
      string sCnx =
         "server = localhost ; uid=sa ; pwd =; database = ORGANIZATION";
      string sCmd1 =
         "INSERT INTO DEPARTMENTS VALUES ('COM','Communication')";
      string sCmd2 =
   "INSERT INTO EMPLOYEES VALUES ('COM','Smith','Adam','(123) 456-7899')";
      try {
         using (TransactionScope txScope = new TransactionScope()) {
            using (SqlConnection cnx = new SqlConnection(sCnx)) {
               cnx.Open();
               DbCommand cmd = new SqlCommand(sCmd1, cnx);
               cmd.ExecuteNonQuery();
               cmd.CommandText = sCmd2;
               cmd.ExecuteNonQuery();
               txScope.Complete();
            } // end using cnx.
         } // end using txScope, the transaction terminates here.
      } catch {
         // If an exception has been raised before or during the
         // call to 'Complete()' data of the DB haven't been updated.
      }
   }
}
```

System.Transactions

This example illustrates the fact that any connection opened during the existence of an object of type `System.Transactions.TransactionScope` is automatically and implicitly enrolled in the underlying transaction. If you execute this example on a RDBMS other than *SQL Server 2005* (using *SQL Server* 7 or 2000, for example) you will notice that a DTC transaction is created in the *'Transactions list'* tab of the DTC. In this particular case, it is more efficient to use the ADO. NET transactional model through a data provider. *Jim Johnson* discusses in a blog entry available at `http://pluralsight.com/blogs/jimjohn/archive/2005/09/13/14795.aspx` a way to detour this limitation be making a durable non-PSPE RM into a PSPE.

The following program illustrates a distributed transaction which works on two databases. The idea here is to move an employee from the `ORGANIZATION` database to the `ORGANIZATIOSN2` database. Thanks to the unified programming model of `System.Transactions`, the code of this example is similar to the one of the previous example:

Example 20-3

```
using System.Data.Common;
using System.Data.SqlClient;
using System.Transactions;
class Program {
   static void Main() {
      string sCnx1 =
         "server = localhost ; uid=sa ; pwd =; database = ORGANIZATION";
      string sCnx2 =
         "server = localhost ; uid=sa ; pwd =; database = ORGANIZATION2";
      string sCmd1 =
    "DELETE FROM EMPLOYEES WHERE Surname='Smith' AND Firstname='Adam'";
      string sCmd2 =
    "INSERT INTO EMPLOYEES VALUES ('COM','Smith','Adam','(123) 456-7899')";
      try {
         using ( TransactionScope txScope = new TransactionScope() ) {
            using ( SqlConnection cnx1 = new SqlConnection(sCnx1) ) {
               cnx1.Open();
               DbCommand cmd = new SqlCommand(sCmd1, cnx1);
               cmd.ExecuteNonQuery();
            } // end using cnx1.
            using ( SqlConnection cnx2 = new SqlConnection(sCnx2) ) {
               cnx2.Open();
               DbCommand cmd = new SqlCommand(sCmd2, cnx2);
               cmd.ExecuteNonQuery();
            } // end using cnx2.
            txScope.Complete();
         } // end using txScope, the transaction terminates here.
      } catch { }
   }
}
```

In this case, the DTC is used no matter the type of RDBMS used.

Events triggered during a transaction

You have the possibility of being notified when a transaction is completed using the `Transaction.TransactionCompleted` event. You can also be notified when transactions it escalated through the `TransactionManager.DistributedTransactionStarted` event. Let's rewrite Example 20-2 by subscribing to these events:

Example 20-4

```
...
class Program {
   static void Main() {
      ...
      try {
         using ( TransactionScope txScope = new TransactionScope() ) {
            Transaction.Current.TransactionCompleted += OnTxCompleted;
            TransactionManager.DistributedTransactionStarted +=
                                             OnDistributedTxStarted;
            using ( SqlConnection cnx1 = new SqlConnection(sCnx1) ) {
      ...
   }
   static void OnTxCompleted(object sender, TransactionEventArgs e) {
      Transaction tx = e.Transaction;
      System.Console.WriteLine("Completed! Status:" +
                       tx.TransactionInformation.Status.ToString());
   }
   static void OnDistributedTxStarted(object sender,
                                      TransactionEventArgs e) {
      Transaction tx = e.Transaction;
      System.Console.WriteLine("Distributed tx started!");
   }
}
```

System.Transactions under the hood

The magic of the automatic and implicit enrollment of a connection into a transaction is done internally thanks to the `ITransaction Transaction.Current{get;set;}` static property. The `ITransaction` interface offers methods which allow for a RM to enroll its data source in the transaction. The activation code of a RM (for example, the opening of a connection) only needs to enroll itself if the `Transaction.Current` property returns a transaction. Of course, the fact of creating an instance of `TransactionScope` initiates the internal creation of the transaction which is returned by the `Transaction.Current` property.

Let us remind you that a connection is marked as available at the level of its connection pool when it is closed (with the `Close()` or `Dispose()` method). This rule is modified when a connection is enrolled in a transaction. It is then marked as available in the connection pool when the transaction ends.

Introduction to Transaction Isolation Level (TIL)

The `TransactionScope` class offers several constructors. Some take as parameter an instance of the `TransactionOptions` structure. This instance allows configuring the *time out* of the transaction (which is of one minute by default) as well as its isolation level relative to other transactions operating on the same RMs.

The isolation level is better known under the *TIL* acronym for *Transaction Isolation Level*. Naturally, higher is the TIL, more the performance will degrade because of the stricter locking on the data. Depending on the isolation level chose, three kinds of problems can occur:

- *Dirty read*: A transaction T1 in progress may have read access to data modified by another transaction T2 in progress. This poses a problem if T2 does not commit its changes.
- *Non repeatable read*: When a transaction in progress completes a second read on some data, it is possible that the value read has changed from the fact that another transaction completed between the two reads.

- *Phantom read*: When a transaction in progress does a same request for the second time, it is possible that the set of returned rows be different than the set or rows returned with the first request. This is due to modification made and committed between the two requests by another transaction.

Here are the various isolation levels offered by the `IsolationLevel` enumeration: from the most permissive to the strictest, hence from the most efficient to the least.

TIL	Dirty read	Non repeatable read	Phantom read
`ReadUncommited`	possible	possible	possible
`ReadCommited`	impossible	possible	possible
`RepeatableRead`	impossible	impossible	possible
`Snapshot`	impossible	impossible	impossible
`Serialize`	impossible	impossible	impossible

The difference between the `Snapshot` and `Serialize` TIL holds in the fact that during the use of the `Snapshot` TIL, an exception can be raised (and consequently a transaction can fail) if one of these three problematic cases is detected. If you choose the `Serialize` TIL, know that internally a data locking mechanism is put in place. This system is expensive as it can block the execution of other transactions since they must wait their turn before accessing the locked data. The `Snaphot` is considered *optimistic* (in the sense that we are confident that a transaction will fail rarely) while the `Serialize` approach is considered *pessimistic*.

It is up to you to choose the isolation level of your transactions by weighing the important of their success versus performance.

Transaction scope

Certain constructors of the `TransactionScope` class accept a value of the `TransactionScope-Option` enumeration which allows to determine how will behave a new scope when it is embedded in another transactional scope. The values of this enumeration are:

- `Mandatory`: A transaction must exist when the new scope is created otherwise an exception is raised.
- `NotSupported`: This new scope does not provoke the creation of a new transaction and does not modify a potential current transaction when it is created.
- `Required`: This new scope needs a transaction. It uses the current transaction if it exists or creates a new one. `Required` is the default value.
- `RequiresNew`: This new scope provokes the creation of a new transaction independently of the fact that a current transaction exists or not. If there was a current transaction, it will be cached and brought back as the current transaction when the scope is closed.
- `Supported`: This new scope does not provoke the creation of a new transaction but does take into account the current transaction when it is created.

Explicit transactions with System.Transactions

The `System.Transactions` namespace allows the use of transactions without using an instance of the `TransactionScope` class. Here is Example 20-2 rewritten using this technique:

Example 20-5
```
using System.Data.Common;
using System.Data.SqlClient;
using System.Transactions;
class Program {
   static void Main() {
```

Example 20-5

```
    string sCnx =
       "server = localhost ; uid=sa ; pwd =; database = ORGANIZATION";
    string sCmd1 =
       "INSERT INTO DEPARTMENTS VALUES ('COM','Communication')";
    string sCmd2 =
  "INSERT INTO EMPLOYEES VALUES ('COM','Smith','Adam','(123) 456-7899')";
    try {
       CommittableTransaction tx = new CommittableTransaction();
       using (SqlConnection cnx = new SqlConnection(sCnx)) {
          cnx.Open();
          // This call enlists the DB connection in the transaction.
          cnx.EnlistTransaction(tx);
          DbCommand cmd = new SqlCommand(sCmd1, cnx);
          cmd.ExecuteNonQuery();
          cmd.CommandText = sCmd2;
          cmd.ExecuteNonQuery();
       } // end using cnx.
       tx.Commit();
    } catch { /*...*/ }
  }
}
```

We will see in the next section how it is necessary to sometimes use this explicit syntax within certain asynchronous contexts. Except for this case, this practice is generally to avoid as it requires more code (since you must explicitly enroll the data sources) without offering any advantages.

Advanced usage of System.Transactions

Performing a transaction with several threads (dependent transaction)

In a multithreaded application, the current transaction defined by the `Transaction.Current` static property is only valid for the thread that created it. This implies that during the execution of a transaction by thread A, another thread B would obtain a null value through this property. If you wish to allow several threads to participate in the same transaction, it is necessary to provide the other threads *dependant transactions* of the original transaction. A dependent transaction is obtained with the `IDependantTransaction ITransaction.DependentClone(bool)` method. The `IDependantTransaction` interface, which extends the `ITransaction` method only adds the `Complete()` method. This method is used to indicate to the parent transaction that the dependent transaction has correctly completed its work. If all the dependent transactions call `Complete()` and if the parent transaction succeeds, you can then call the `Commit()` method on the transaction.

To avoid having to manage the synchronization between the calls to `Complete()` and the call to `Commit()` you can create dependent transaction by passing the `DependentCloneOption.BlockCommitUntilComplete` value to the `DependentClone(DependentCloneOption)` method. By proceeding this way, the call to `Commit()` will block until all dependant transactions have completed. If you pass the `DependentCloneOption.RollbackIfNotComplete` during the creation of a dependant transaction, the thread responsible for this dependant transaction must call the `Complete()` method before the `Commit()` be called on the parent transaction. Otherwise the whole transaction fails. Naturally, you only need that one of the transactions (dependent or parent) to fail in order for the whole transaction to fail. Here is an example which exposes the use of dependent transactions:

Example 20-6

```
using System.Data.Common;
using System.Data.SqlClient;
using System.Transactions;
using System.Threading;
class Program {
    static string sCnx =
          "server = localhost ; uid=sa ; pwd =; database = ORGANIZATION";
    static string sCmd1 =
          "INSERT INTO DEPARTMENTS VALUES ('COM','Communication')";
    static string sCmd2 =
      "INSERT INTO EMPLOYEES VALUES ('COM','Smith','Adam','(123) 456-7899')";
    static void Main() {
      try {
          using (TransactionScope txScope = new TransactionScope()) {
              using (SqlConnection cnx = new SqlConnection(sCnx)) {
                  cnx.Open();
                  DbCommand cmd = new SqlCommand(sCmd1, cnx);
                  cmd.ExecuteNonQuery();
                  DependentTransaction depTx =
                     Transaction.Current.DependentClone (
                         DependentCloneOption.BlockCommitUntilComplete );
                  ThreadPool.QueueUserWorkItem( AsyncProc, depTx);
                  txScope.Complete();
              } // end using cnx.
          } //end using txScope 'ITransaction.Commit()' is called here.
      } catch { }
    }
    static void AsyncProc(object state) {
      DependentTransaction depTx = state as DependentTransaction;
      try {
          using ( SqlConnection cnx = new SqlConnection( sCnx ) ) {
              cnx.Open();
              cnx.EnlistTransaction( depTx );
              DbCommand cmd = new SqlCommand( sCmd2, cnx );
              cmd.ExecuteNonQuery();
              depTx.Complete();
          } // end using cnx.
      } catch {
          depTx.Rollback();
      }
    }
}
```

Asynchronously completing a transaction

You can manage in an asynchronous way the completion of a transaction. This feature is useful as blocking a thread to wait for a transaction to complete can have a negative effect on performance. To use this feature, you must explicitly manage your transactions as with Example 20-5 and to call the `BeginCommit()` method instead of `Commit()`. This method takes as a parameter a delegate which will be called when the transaction is completed. Within this method, you simply need to call `EndCommit()`. This method will raise an exception if the transaction failed. You then have a chance to provide the code to execute in the case that the transaction failed by catching the exception.

Example 20-7
```
class Program {
   static void Main() {
      ...
      CommittableTransaction tx = new CommittableTransaction();
      try {
         using (SqlConnection cnx = new SqlConnection(sCnx)) {
            cnx.Open();

            cnx.EnlistTransaction(tx);
            ...
            tx.BeginCommit(OnCommited,null);
         } // end using cnx.
      } catch { /*...*/ }
      // Here, the code can be executed even though the
      // transaction is not commited.
   }
   static void OnCommited(System.IAsyncResult asyncResult) {
      CommittableTransaction tx = asyncResult as CommittableTransaction;
      try {
         using (tx) {
            tx.EndCommit(asyncResult);
         }
      } catch ( TransactionException e ) {
         // The transaction didn't commit !
      }
   }
}
```

System.Transactions and CAS

It is interesting to notice that the code that implicates the use of the DTC to manage a transaction must have the `System.Transactions.DistributedTransactionPermission` CAS permission. In the case of the promotion of a RM during the delegation of a transaction from the LTM to the DTC, it is the code responsible for the promotion which needs this permission and not the code responsible for the enrollment.

Facilities for implementing a custom RM

We will now present how you can create your own transactional RM by creating a generic class named `TxList<T>`. This class constitutes the implementation of a list where adding an element through the `TxAdd(T)` method can be done from within a transaction. You can pass several elements during a transaction. They will all be added if the transaction is committed and none of them if the transaction is rolled back. To make this possible, an instance of `TxList<T>` internally maintains the `dataToCommit` list which represents the elements waiting to be added. The two private methods `OnCommit()` and `OnRollback()` contain the implementation of the *commit* and *rollback* operations.

In order to be usable by `System.Transactions`, our `TxList<T>` must implement the `System.Transactions.ISinglePhaseNotification` interface. This interface offers the `SinglePhaseCommit()` method which is called by the TM when the concerned list is the unique RM of a transaction which is about to be completed. This interface implements the `System.Transactions.IEnlistmentNotification` interface. `IEnlistmentNotification` offers the `Prepare()`, `Commit()`, `InDoubt()` and `Rollback()` methods which are called by the TM when the concerned list is enroled in a transaction distributed across several RMs. In this case, the underlying TM (LTM or DTC) automatically manages the transaction in two phases (2PC algorithm).

Facilities for implementing a custom RM

When an element is added to an instance of `TxList<T>`, we test if it is enroled in a transaction. If this is not the case, we call the `Enlist()` method which enrols the list in the current transaction if we are in a transactional context. For this, the code of this method calls `Transaction.EnlistVolatile()` on the current transaction. This tells the TM that it will be dealing with a volatile RM.

Example 20-8

```csharp
using System;
using System.Collections.Generic;
using System.Transactions;
public class TxList<T> : List<T>, ISinglePhaseNotification {
   private Transaction m_Tx;
   private List<T> dataToCommit;
   private string m_Name;

   public TxList(string name) {
      m_Name = name;
      dataToCommit = new List<T>();
   }
   public void TxAdd(T t) {
      Console.WriteLine(m_Name + ".TxAdd(" + t.ToString() +")");
      if ( m_Tx == null )
         Enlist();
      dataToCommit.Add(t);
   }
   private void OnCommit() {
      Console.WriteLine("   "+m_Name+".OnCommit()");
      foreach (T t in dataToCommit)
         base.Add(t);
      dataToCommit.Clear();
   }
   private void OnRollback() {
      dataToCommit.Clear();
   }
   private void Enlist() {
      m_Tx = Transaction.Current;
      if (m_Tx != null) {
         Console.WriteLine("   " + m_Name + ".EnlistVolatile()");
         m_Tx.EnlistVolatile(this, EnlistmentOptions.None);
      }
   }
   public void DisplayContent() {
      Console.Write("--> Content of " + m_Name + " : ");
      foreach (T t in this)
         Console.Write( t.ToString() + ";");
      Console.Write("   dataToCommit: " );
      foreach (T t in dataToCommit)
         Console.Write(t.ToString() + ";");
      Console.WriteLine();
   }

   #region IEnlistmentNotification Members
   public void Prepare(PreparingEnlistment preparingEnlistment) {
      Console.WriteLine(m_Name + ".Prepare()");
      preparingEnlistment.Prepared();
   }
   public void Commit(Enlistment enlistment) {
```

Example 20-8

```
        Console.WriteLine(m_Name + ".Commit()");
        OnCommit();
        enlistment.Done();
    }
    public void InDoubt(Enlistment enlistment) {
        Console.WriteLine(m_Name + ".InDoubt()");
        throw new NotImplementedException();
    }
    public void Rollback(Enlistment enlistment) {
        Console.WriteLine(m_Name + ".Rollback()");
        OnRollback();
        enlistment.Done();
    }
    #endregion

    #region ISinglePhaseNotification Members
    public void SinglePhaseCommit(
                        SinglePhaseEnlistment singlePhaseEnlistment) {
        Console.WriteLine(m_Name + ".SinglePhaseCommit()");
        OnCommit();
        singlePhaseEnlistment.Committed();
    }
    #endregion
}
```

Here is a little program which uses a single instance of txList<string> in a transaction:

Example 20-9

```
using System.Transactions;
class Program {
    static void Main() {
        TxList<string> txList = new TxList<string>("List");
        using ( TransactionScope txScope = new TransactionScope() ) {
            txList.TxAdd("A");   txList.TxAdd("B");
            txScope.Complete();
            txList.DisplayContent();
        }
        txList.DisplayContent();
    }
}
```

We can easily follow the operations of this program through the console output:

```
List.TxAdd(A)
   List.EnlistVolatile()
List.TxAdd(B)
--> Content of List :    dataToCommit: A;B;
List.SinglePhaseCommit()
   List.OnCommit()
--> Content of List : A;B;    dataToCommit:
```

If we do not validate the transaction by commenting the call to txScope.Complete(), the transaction will be automatically rolled back and will display the following:

Facilities for implementing a custom RM 629

```
List.TxAdd(A)
   List.EnlistVolatile()
List.TxAdd(B)
--> Content of List :     dataToCommit: A;B;
List.Rollback()
--> Content of List :     dataToCommit:
```

Let's rewrite our program in order to manage two transactional lists within a same transaction:

Example 20-10

```
using System.Transactions;
class Program {
   static void Main() {
      TxList<string> txList1 = new TxList<string>("List1");
      TxList<string> txList2 = new TxList<string>("List2");
      using ( TransactionScope txScope = new TransactionScope() ) {
         txList1.TxAdd("A");   txList1.TxAdd("B");
         txList2.TxAdd("C");   txList2.TxAdd("D");
         txScope.Complete();
         txList1.DisplayContent(); txList2.DisplayContent();
      }
      txList1.DisplayContent(); txList2.DisplayContent();
   }
}
```

The underlying TM (LTM in this case) automatically switches to 2PC with a preparation and a validation phase. This becomes clear by looking at the display of the program:

```
List1.TxAdd(A)
   List1.EnlistVolatile()
List1.TxAdd(B)
List2.TxAdd(C)
   List2.EnlistVolatile()
List2.TxAdd(D)
--> Content of List1 :     dataToCommit: A;B;
--> Content of List2 :     dataToCommit: C;D;
List1.Prepare()
List2.Prepare()
List1.Commit()
   List1.OnCommit()
List2.Commit()
   List2.OnCommit()
--> Content of List1 : A;B;   dataToCommit:
--> Content of List2 : C;D;   dataToCommit:
```

You can also tell the TM that our RM is durable. For this, you simply need to call Transaction.EnlistDurable() instead of Transaction.EnlistVolatile() during the enrollment. The EnlistDurable() method takes as a parameter the unique identifier of the RM that the recovery service will need to call if the transaction results in an in-doubt situation.

You can alsodevelop a durable PSPE RM by implementing the System.Transaction.IPromotableSinglePhaseNotification interface rather than the ISinglePhaseNotification interface. More information on this topic as well as more general information on the development of RMs can be found in the articles named **Optimization using Single Phase Commit and Promotable Single Phase Notification** and **Implementing a Resource Manager** on **MSDN**.

21

XML

Introduction

Problems solved by XML

XML is an acronym for *eXtensible Markup Language*. XML is the response to the need for a standardized way of formatting data exchanged between heterogeneous systems. Before XML, data was exchanged in proprietary formats. Applications needed to know this proprietary format to take advantage of this and it has posed three main problems:

- **XML documents are written in text:**

  These proprietary formats base themselves on the format of the primitive types of the underlying system. But the representation of a double or a string can significantly differ from one system to another. For example, the formatting of primitive types in .NET is standardized but its use remains limited to .NET.

  In XML, an information packet is called an *XML document*. An XML document is a text file which can be read by any text editor on any platform. This problem is solved as all the data is encoded in an (initially) untyped string. We will see that we can type data contained in an XML document, in and independent way of the underlying system.

- **XML documents have the capability of self-describing their structure:**

  Another big problem with proprietary formats concerns the structure used to store data. It is normal that an application knows how to use and interpret an order number within its logic. However, it is unfortunate that the application must also know where this order number is stored in a data packet and implies that the application must know the structure of the data. We say that the packet of data received by the application is not *self-descriptive*.

  This problem is solved through a system of *Extensible Markup*. Using schemas, which describe the structure of a document, the access path to a specific piece of information within an XML document can be known by the application. This schema approach can be seen as a way to type both XML documents and data stored in it.

- **XML documents are semi-structured:**

  A third problem with proprietary formats is that quite often, they lack flexibility in the structuring of their data. If most commands contain an order number, a client identifier and a description, it is difficult to send a command without a description. Therefore, in general, we have no other choice than to determine a certain convention: if the description is *'N/A'* then it means that there is no description for this command.

  This problem is solved as XML documents are semi-structured. Furthermore, each piece of data is encapsulated in a set of markers, and a piece of data can contain several other pieces of data. If a command packet does not have a description marker, the application will simply consider that the command does not have a description. In other words, the application can obtain a piece of information (i.e. no description for this command) from the lack of information (i.e. no description markers for this command).

Unifying document world and data world

The following realization can be made: most data is stored in documents which are human readable. In fact, most information can be found in text files (.html, .doc, .txt ...).

A classic pain for developers is to automate the extraction of this information in a text document in order to process it with their software. Which developer was never tempted of extracting an order number from a HTML document simply based on the fact that it is written in blue with the Veranda font of size 14?

Since XML documents are flexible and extensible, XML document editor can at the same time provide markers for the presentation of data as well as markers for the data itself. It then becomes easy to layout the document as well as to extract the data. This vision has been becoming a reality. For example, most of *Microsoft* software in the *Office 2003* (*Word*, *Excel* ...) suite stores its data using documents in an XML format. It will become the rule with *Office 12*.

Structure of an XML document

The marker system used in XML documents is similar to the marker system used in HTML documents, with the exception that you can create as many markers as you wish, thus the notion of extensibility. Below, we will expose the content of an XML file representing an extract from the inventory of a fictitious library (this file is extract from the framework documentation):

Example 21-1 *books.xml*

```xml
<?xml version="1.0" encoding="utf-8" ?>
<bookstore>
    <book genre="autobiography" publicationdate="1981" ISBN="1-861003-11-0">
        <title>The Autobiography of Benjamin Franklin</title>
        <author>
            <first-name>Benjamin</first-name>
            <last-name>Franklin</last-name>
        </author>
        <price>8.99</price>
    </book>
    <book genre="novel" publicationdate="1967" ISBN="0-201-63361-2">
        <title>The Confidence Man</title>
        <author>
            <first-name>Herman</first-name>
            <last-name>Melville</last-name>
        </author>
        <price>11.99</price>
    </book>
    <book genre="philosophy" publicationdate="1991" ISBN="1-861001-57-6">
        <title>The Gorgias</title>
        <author>
            <name>Plato</name>
        </author>
        <price>9.99</price>
    </book>
</bookstore>
```

There are several things to note:

- There are as many different markers as there are types of data. There is a marker for the notion of library `<bookstore>`, a marker for the notion of book `<book>`, a marker for the notion of book title `<title>`... A '`<tag>data</tag>`' group is called an *XML element*. We see that an XML element can either contain data or other XML elements.

- An element which contains other elements can also contain data using the notion of *XML attributes* (note that this has nothing to do with the notion of .NET attributes). For example, the category of a book is defined in an attribute `genre` of the `<book>` elements
- The fact that an XML element can contain other elements allows the presentation of data in a hierarchical way. An application which wishes to obtain the title of books published in 1967 must first find the `<book>` elements with a `publicationdate` attribute equal to 1967 then to enumerate the corresponding `<title>` elements. No matter which order the books are stored in an XML document, the application will always be able to find the information that it needs.
- We can insert comments in an XML file using the `<!--comment-->` syntax.
- The header of an XML document can specify type of text encoding used in a document using the `encoding` attribute. We see that the `books.xml` text file is encoding using the *UTF-8* format.
- Although it is not shown in this example, certain special attributes can be used to define *XML namespaces* in an XML element. XML namespaces are used to avoid the collision of the name of elements or attributes when several XML languages are used simultaneously. We generally associate an URI (such as *http://www.smacchia.com*) to an XML namespace to ensure that the namespace is unique. Let's modify our example to use the namespace syntax:

```
...
<bookstore xmlns:SMA="http://www.smacchia.com" >
  <SMA:book genre="autobiography" publicationdate="1981"
   ISBN="1-861003-11-0">
    ...
  </SMA:book>
...
```

Introduction to XSD, XPath, XSLT and XQuery

Typing XML documents and their data with XSD schemas

From the start, the data of an XML document is not typed. The application can decide to keep the number of employees in a string. It can also decide to convert this string into an integer. In this case, the application does not necessarily know that this number cannot be negative.

To impose such constraints, you must be able to describe the schema of the data, this means to describe the type of each element (string, integer…) and the constraints on each element (positive integer, smaller than one million…). There exists several techniques to describe the schema of an XML document, and the *XSD (XML Schema Definition)* technique is the one which is used by .NET. The idea is to associate to an XML document an XSD schema describing the elements. For example, we could have associated the following XSD schema to our `books.xml` document:

Example 21-2   *books.xsd*
```
<?xml version="1.0" encoding="utf-8"?>
<xs:schema attributeFormDefault="unqualified"
           elementFormDefault="qualified"
           xmlns:xs="http://www.w3.org/2001/XMLSchema">
  <xs:element name="bookstore">
    <xs:complexType>
      <xs:sequence>
        <xs:element maxOccurs="unbounded" name="book">
          <xs:complexType>
            <xs:sequence>
              <xs:element name="title" type="xs:string" />
```

| Example 21-2 | books.xsd |

```
                    <xs:element name="author">
                      <xs:complexType>
                        <xs:sequence>
                          <xs:element minOccurs="0" name="name"
                                      type="xs:string" />
                          <xs:element minOccurs="0" name="first-name"
                                      type="xs:string" />
                          <xs:element minOccurs="0" name="last-name"
                                      type="xs:string" />
                        </xs:sequence>
                      </xs:complexType>
                    </xs:element>
                    <xs:element name="price" type="xs:decimal" />
                  </xs:sequence>
                  <xs:attribute name="genre" type="xs:string" use="required"/>
                  <xs:attribute name="publicationdate" type="xs:unsignedShort"
                                use="required" />
                  <xs:attribute name="ISBN" type="xs:string" use="required" />
                </xs:complexType>
              </xs:element>
            </xs:sequence>
          </xs:complexType>
        </xs:element>
      </xs:schema>
```

We see that we can type each element of an XML document, but this is not a requirement. The available types as well as the conversion between them and the .NET types are discussed in the article named **Data Type Support between XML Schema (XSD) Types and .NET Framework Types** on **MSDN**.

XPath

XPath is a language which allows to write queries to select nodes in an XML document. Certain have named it 'SQL for XML' as the goal of XPath to the XML data is similar to the goal of the SQL language to data stored in a relational database.

XPath allows the selection of nodes in an XML document using syntax similar to writing a file path. Here are examples of XPath expressions (in bold) applied to the `books.xml` document followed by the list of selected nodes:

```
/bookstore/book/author/first-name
<first-name>Benjamin</first-name>
<first-name>Herman</first-name>


/bookstore/book/author/*
<first-name>Benjamin</first-name>
<last-name>Franklin</last-name>
<first-name>Herman</first-name>
<last-name>Melville</last-name>
<name>Plato</name>


/bookstore/book[@publicationdate>1980]/title
<title>The Autobiography of Benjamin Franklin</title>
<title>The Gorgias</title>
```

Introduction to XSD, XPath, XSLT and XQuery 635

XSLT

The *XSLT* acronym means *eXtensible Stylesheet Language Transformation*. XSLT is a language which allows the use of the data in an XML document in order to obtain a new document. The produced document can, for example, be an HTML document, another XML document or simply any text document.

A program written in XSLT (i.e. a *stylesheet*) is an XML document. XSLT is built on a system of *templates*. During execution, XSLT selects the nodes of the source document corresponding to the *stylesheet* and then executes the body of the *template* for each selected node. The selection is done by the intermediate of an XPath expression.

The following *stylesheet* applied to the `books.xml` document illustrates this. Note the presence of the characteristic `xsl` namespace. The expressions in bold are written using XPath.

Example 21-3   *books.xslt*

```
<xsl:stylesheet version="1.0"
 xmlns:xsl="http://www.w3.org/1999/XSL/Transform">
   <xsl:template match= "/bookstore" >
      <xsl:for-each select= "book[@publicationdate>1980]" >
Title: <xsl:value-of select= "title" />
Published <xsl:value-of select= "2006 - (@publicationdate)" /> years ago
      </xsl:for-each>
   </xsl:template>
</xsl:stylesheet>
```

The document produced is the following:

```
Title: The Autobiography of Benjamin Franklin
Published 25 years ago

Title: The Gorgias
Published 15 years ago
```

XQuery

The *XQuery* language has the same goal as XSLT: transform an XML document into another text document (which is not necessarily an XML document). This functionality is also seen as a way to do requests on an XML document, hence the *XQuery* name.

XQuery is considered as more user friendly than XSLT mostly since it is not itself an XML language. The main reason for the interest in XQuery however resides in the fact that the flow of execution of its instructions is similar to the one of well known imperative languages such as C# or Java.

As with XSLT, XQuery uses the XPath language to select nodes. Here is an XQuery program which transforms our `books.xml` into a text file which enumerates autobiographies in the order of their publication:

```
for $b in document("books.xml")/book where
$b/genre="autobiography" return $b/title" sortby(publicationdate)
```

Clearly, this selection logic is closer to the one proposed by the SQL language.

XQuery 1.0 having been standardized a few months after the release of the 2.0 version of the .NET framework, thus, it unfortunately does not support this technology. We can however mention that *SQL Server 2005* does support a subset of XQuery to query XML data stored in a database.

Approaches to traverse and edit an XML document

The traversal of an XML document (i.e. the consumption of the information in an XML document by an application) can be done using two approaches:

- The **cursor** approach: The XML document is traversed using a cursor. The cursor can be seen as the position in XML document of the information being currently read. This position can designate an XML element or attribute. The program is responsible of moving the cursor from the current to the position of the next piece of information to be consumed (go to the next sibling node, go to the next child node…).

- The **tree** approach: When the XML document is loaded, an object tree is created. Each object in the tree represents an entity of the XML document. We can then use the information contained in the document by traversing the tree.

The cursor approach has several advantages over the tree approach. It does not require a pre-processing phase and the memory required to exploit the XML document does not depend on the size of the XML document. It is clear that the cursor approach is more efficient in terms of performance. However, object oriented programming makes it easier to use information contained in an object tree. Both models each have their reasons of being implemented in the .NET framework.

The operation of creation and modification of an XML document can also be done using these two approaches. The advantages and inconvenient are the same except that the pre-processing phase of the tree approach is replaced by a post-processing phase when we wish to finalize the changes.

Finally, we will explain that both approaches are not incompatible. For example, it is possible to traverse a tree loaded in memory using a cursor. In fact, we will see that you can use XPath requests on the tree in order to obtain a cursor on the set of selected nodes. The advantage of this practice resides in the fact that we can write code which manipulates data independently on the mode in which the XML data is stored. XML data is consumed in a cursor approach whether the data was pre-loaded in memory or loaded on demand from a source such as a file or a web service.

If the standard `System.Xml` framework that will present does not satisfy you on certain aspects, you can also consider using the free and open-source framework named `Mvp.Xml`. More information can be found at `http://sourceforge.net/projects/mvp-xml/`.

The cursor approach with the XmlReader and XmlWriter classes

Reading data with the XmlReader class

The `System.Xml.XmlReader` and `System.Xml.XmlWriter` abstract classes allow the traversal and modification of data stored in an XML document using a *forward only* cursor approach. A *forward only* cursor is a cursor which can only progress forward within the data.

These classes are abstract in order to separate themselves from the way that the data is stored internally. Implementation classes which derive from `XmlReader` and `XmlWriter` have the responsibility of managing the flow of XML data in read and write. The `System.Xml.XmlTextReader` and `System.Xml.XmlTextWriter` implementation classes allow the management of a flow of XML data respectively for reading and writing.

The `System.Xml.XmlNodeReader` implementation class allows to read XML data stored in a tree using a cursor type approach. The use of this class adds the inconvenience of the cursor approach (code complexity) and of the tree approach (penalty of loading all the data into memory). However, this class allows to write an XML data reading algorithm independently of the data source.

The cursor approach with the XmlReader and XmlWriter classes   637

It is recommend to not directly instantiate a classes deriving from XmlReader. In fact, several overloads to the XmlReader XmlReader.Create() method return the appropriate object based on your needs.

Based on this description, readers who are already accustomed to XML may think of XmlReader as an implementation of the *SAX* document reading protocol. This assumption is false and you can refer to the article named **Comparing XmlReader to SAX Reader** on **MSDN** to understand the differences.

Here is a program which reads the books.xml document with an instance of a class derived from XmlReader. Note the use of an indentation mechanism to expose the hierarchical structure during the display:

Example 21-4

```
using System;
using System.Xml;
class Program {
   static void Main() {
      XmlReader xtr =  XmlReader.Create(@"C:\books.xml");
      string sIndent = string.Empty;
      string sElem = string.Empty;
      while ( xtr.Read() ) {
         if ( xtr.NodeType == XmlNodeType.Element ) {
            sIndent = string.Empty;
            for (int i = 0; i < xtr.Depth; i++) sIndent += "   ";
            sElem = xtr.Name;
            if ( xtr.MoveToFirstAttribute() )
               do
                  Console.WriteLine("{0}{1} Attr:{2}" ,
                               sIndent , sElem , xtr.Value );
               while ( xtr.MoveToNextAttribute() );
         }
         else if (xtr.NodeType == XmlNodeType.Text)
            Console.WriteLine("{0}{1} Val:{2}",sIndent,sElem,xtr.Value);
      }
   }
}
```

This program displays the following:

```
bookstore Attr:http://www.contoso.com/books
   book Attr:autobiography
   book Attr:1981
   book Attr:1-861003-11-0
      title Val:The Autobiography of Benjamin Franklin
         first-name Val:Benjamin
         last-name Val:Franklin
      price Val:8.99
   book Attr:novel
   book Attr:1967
   book Attr:0-201-63361-2
      title Val:The Confidence Man
...
```

The XmlReader class offers several facilities to allow the reading of data such as the typing of the returned values, taking namespaces into account and removing spaces and comments. This is possible using several methods such as MoveToContent(), ReadContentAsBoolean(), ReadStartElement()...

Validating data while reading

To validate data while reading an XML file, you have to use one of the overloads of the `XmlReader.Create()` method which accepts an instance of the `System.Xml.XmlReaderSettings` class. This instance allows specifying the validations which must be done when data is read. Let's retake Example 21-4 by validating the input XML data against a `books.xsd` schema (the one in Example 21-2). Note the need to provide a *callback* method (in this case the `ValidatingProblemHandler()`) to retrieve any validation problems:

Example 21-5

```
...
using System.Xml.Schema;
class Program {
   static void Main() {
      XmlReaderSettings settings = new XmlReaderSettings();
      settings.Schemas.Add(String.Empty,
                           @"C:\books.xsd");
      settings.Schemas.Compile();
      settings.ValidationType = ValidationType.Schema;
      settings.ValidationEventHandler += ValidatingProblemHandler;
      settings.ValidationFlags =
         XmlSchemaValidationFlags.ReportValidationWarnings;
      XmlReader xtr = XmlReader.Create(@"C:\books.xml",settings);
      ...
   }
   static void ValidatingProblemHandler(object sender,
                                   ValidationEventArgs e) {
      if ( e.Severity == XmlSeverityType.Warning ) {
         Console.Write("WARNING: ");  Console.WriteLine(e.Message);
      } else if ( e.Severity == XmlSeverityType.Error ) {
         Console.Write("ERROR: ");    Console.WriteLine(e.Message);
      }
   }
}
```

Editing data with the XmlWriter class

In the same spirit as the `XmlReader` class, the `System.Xml.XmlTextWriter` class allows to create an XML document by specifying the elements one after the other. Here is a small example which creates an XML document (we have purposely indented the code in order to make it easier to read):

Example 21-6

```
using System.Xml;
using System.Text;
class Program {
   static void Main() {
      XmlTextWriter xtw =new XmlTextWriter(@"C:\book2.xml", Encoding.UTF8);
      xtw.Formatting = Formatting.Indented;
      xtw.WriteStartDocument(true);
        xtw.WriteStartElement("books");
          xtw.WriteStartElement("book");
            xtw.WriteAttributeString("ISBN", "10-097661322-0");
            xtw.WriteElementString("title", "Pratical .NET and C#");
          xtw.WriteEndElement();
        xtw.WriteEndElement();
```

Example 21-6

```
      xtw.WriteEndDocument();
      xtw.Flush();
      xtw.Close();
   }
}
```

Here is the created XML document:

books2.xml

```
<?xml version="1.0" encoding="utf-8" standalone="yes"?>
<books>
  <book ISBN="10-097661322-0">
    <title>Practical .NET and C#</title>
  </book>
</books>
```

The tree/DOM approach using the XmlDocument class

Loading and traversing an XML document using the XmlDocument class

The `System.Xml.XmlDocument` class represents the implementation of the W3C standard named *DOM* (*Document Object Model*). This standard describes the representation of an XML document in memory under the form of an object tree structure. This tree is built from nodes which are instances of `System.Xml.XmlNode` (for the leafs) and `System.Xml.XmlNodeList` (for groups). The `XmlDocument` class derives from the `XmlNode` node since we can always see an XML document as its root node.

Contrary to the `XmlTextReader` class, the tree is completely constructed during the loading of an XML document by a call to the `Load()` method on an instance of `XmlDocument`. It is a good idea to know the size of the document to load, as in the case of a large document, the complete loading of it in memory can be prohibitive. If the source XML document has at least one syntax error, an exception will be raised. Hence, it is recommended to call the `Load()` method within a `try/catch` block.

Here is a program which recursively traverses the structure of an `XmlDocument` document initialized from our `books.xml` document. This example displays the name, the value and the attributes of each node with the proper indentation in order to show the hierarchical structure:

Example 21-7

```
using System;
using System.Xml;
public class Program {
   static void DisplayNode(XmlNode xNode, string sIndent) {
      Console.WriteLine("{0}Node: {1}({2})",
                        sIndent, xNode.Name, xNode.Value);
      if (xNode.Attributes != null)
         foreach (XmlAttribute xAtt in xNode.Attributes)
            Console.WriteLine("{0} Attribute: {1}", sIndent, xAtt.Value);
      if (xNode.HasChildNodes)
         foreach (XmlNode _xNode in xNode.ChildNodes)
            DisplayNode(_xNode, sIndent + "   ");
   }
   static public void Main() {
      XmlDocument xDoc = new XmlDocument();
```

Example 21-7

```
        try { xDoc.Load(@"C:\books.xml"); }
        catch { }
        foreach (XmlNode xNode in xDoc.ChildNodes)
           DisplayNode(xNode, string.Empty);
     }
   }
```

Here is an extract of the output from this program:

```
Node: xml(version="1.0" encoding="utf-8")
Node: #comment(This file represents a fragment of a book store inventory database)
Node: bookstore()
  Node: book()
   Attribute: autobiography
   Attribute: 1981
   Attribute: 1-861003-11-0
     Node: title()
         Node: #text(The Autobiography of Benjamin Franklin)
     Node: author()
         Node: first-name()
             Node: #text(Benjamin)
         Node: last-name()
             Node: #text(Franklin)
     Node: price()
         Node: #text(8.99)
...
```

Editing and storing XML data with the XmlDocument class

The XmlDocument class also presents edition functionalities using methods such as InsertAfter(), InsertBefore(), AppendChild(), CreateAttribute()... You can at any time recover a string containing the XML document using the string InnerXml{get;set;} property. You can also save the XML using the different overloads of the Save() which accept various kinds of data streams or a target file name.

Validating an XML document with the XmlDocument class

The XmlDocument.Validate() method allows to validate a DOM tree based on a XSD schema. For example:

Example 21-8

```
using System;
using System.Xml;
using System.Xml.Schema;
using System.Xml.XPath;
public class Program {
   static public void Main() {
       XmlDocument xDoc = new XmlDocument();
       try { xDoc.Load(@"C:\books.xml"); } catch { }
       xDoc.Schemas.Add( string.Empty, @"C:\books.xsd");
       xDoc.Schemas.Compile();
       ValidationEventHandler validator = ValidatingProblemHandler;
       xDoc.Validate(validator);
    }
```

Example 21-8

```
    static void ValidatingProblemHandler(object sender,
                                    ValidationEventArgs e) {
      if (e.Severity == XmlSeverityType.Warning) {
         Console.Write("WARNING: "); Console.WriteLine(e.Message);
      } else if (e.Severity == XmlSeverityType.Error) {
         Console.Write("ERROR: "); Console.WriteLine(e.Message);
      }
   }
}
```

An overloaded version of the `XmlDocument.Validate()` method accepts a node of the tree in order to complete a partial verification of the tree.

Events of the XmlDocument class

The `XmlDocument` class offers the following events which allow triggering an action when a change occurs on a DOM tree:

```
public event XmlNodeChangedEventHandler NodeChanged;
public event XmlNodeChangedEventHandler NodeChanging;
public event XmlNodeChangedEventHandler NodeInserted;
public event XmlNodeChangedEventHandler NodeInserting;
public event XmlNodeChangedEventHandler NodeRemoved;
public event XmlNodeChangedEventHandler NodeRemoving;
```

Traversing and editing an XML document using XPath

Applying an XPath expression to an in-memory DOM tree

Using the `XmlNode.SelectNodes()` method it is easy to select a set of nodes using an XPath expression. Hence, the following example selects all the first names of the authors contained in the `books.xml` document:

Example 21-9

```
using System.Xml;
public class Program {
   static public void Main() {
      XmlDocument xDoc = new XmlDocument();
      try { xDoc.Load(@"C:\books.xml"); } catch { }
      XmlNodeList books = xDoc.SelectNodes(
                           @"/bookstore/book/author/first-name");
      foreach (XmlNode book in books)
         System.Console.WriteLine(book.OuterXml);
   }
}
```

This example displays:

```
<first-name>Benjamin</first-name>
<first-name>Herman</first-name>
```

Traversing an XPathDocument object using a XPathNavigator object

Instances of the `System.Xml.XPath.XPathNavigator` class allows the traversal (and eventual modification) of a DOM tree loaded in memory using XPath expressions. You can recover such an object from the `XPathNavigator CreateNavigator()` method of the `IXPathNavigable` interface. The `XmlDocument` and `System.Xml.XPath.XPathDocument` classes both implements this interface.

The `XPathDocument` class is comparable to the `XmlDocument` class as its instances allow storing a DOM tree representing an XML document. However, a DOM tree stored in an instance of `XPathDocument` can only be accessed in a read-only mode. Also, an instance of `XPathNavigator` can modify a DOM tree if it acts on a document loaded with an instance of `XmlDocument`. The implementation of `XPathNavigator` is however more apt in certain situations as it can generally bring a significant performance boost.

The following example shows how to recursively traverse, using an instance of `XPathNavigator` an XML document loaded in an instance of `XPathDocument`:

Example 21-10

```
using System;
using System.Xml;
using System.Xml.XPath;
class Program {
   static void Main() {
      XPathDocument doc = new XPathDocument(@"C:\books.xml");
      XPathNavigator navigator = doc.CreateNavigator();
      navigator.MoveToRoot();
      DisplayRecursive(navigator, string.Empty);
   }
   static public void DisplayRecursive(XPathNavigator navigator,
                                       string indent) {
      if ( navigator.HasChildren ) {
         navigator.MoveToFirstChild();
         DisplayNode(navigator,indent+"   ");
         DisplayRecursive(navigator, indent + "   ");
         navigator.MoveToParent();
      }
      while ( navigator.MoveToNext() ) {
         DisplayNode( navigator, indent );
         DisplayRecursive( navigator, indent );
      }
   }
   static private void DisplayNode(XPathNavigator navigator,string indent){
      if (navigator.NodeType == XPathNodeType.Text)
         Console.WriteLine(indent+navigator.Value);
      else if (navigator.Name != String.Empty)
         Console.WriteLine(indent + "<" + navigator.Name + ">");
   }
}
```

This example displays the following:

```
<bookstore>
   <book>
      <title>
         The Autobiography of Benjamin Franklin
      <author>
...
```

Traversing an XPath selection using a XPathNodeIterator object

An alternative to the XmlNode.SelectNodes() method to select a set of nodes using an XPath expression is to use an instance of XPathNodeIterator obtained from the XPathNodeIterator XPathNavigator.Select('XPathExpression') method. An instance of this class allows enumerating selected elements from an XPath expression. For each element, the XPathNavigator XPathNodeIterator.Current{get;} property returns a browser positioned on the current element. This is demonstrated in the following example:

Example 21-11

```
using System.Xml.XPath;
class Program {
   static void Main() {
      XPathDocument document = new XPathDocument(@"C:\books.xml");
      XPathNavigator navigator = document.CreateNavigator();
      XPathNodeIterator iterator =
         navigator.Select(@"/bookstore/book/author/first-name");
      while( iterator.MoveNext() )
         System.Console.WriteLine("<" + iterator.Current.Name + ">" +
                                  iterator.Current.Value);
   }
}
```

This program displays the following:

```
<first-name>Benjamin
<first-name>Herman
```

Editing an XmlDocument object using an XPathNavigator object

The following example shows how to use an instance of XPathNavigator in order to modify a DOM tree stored in an instance of XmlDocument. Here, we will add a new <book> element in our XmlDocument document:

Example 21-12

```
using System;
using System.Xml;
using System.Xml.XPath;
class Program {
   static void Main() {
      XmlDocument xDoc = new XmlDocument();
      try { xDoc.Load(@"C:\books.xml"); } catch { }
      XPathNavigator navigator = xDoc.CreateNavigator();
      navigator.MoveToRoot();                   // Select the root.
      if (navigator.MoveToFirstChild())         // Select <bookstore>.
         if (navigator.MoveToFirstChild())      // Select
                                                // <book>Autobiography...
            navigator.InsertElementBefore( string.Empty, "book",
                              string.Empty, "Pratical .NET and C#");
      xDoc.Save(@"C:\new_books.xml");
   }
}
```

Here is a preview of the modified books.xml file:

Books.xml

```
<?xml version="1.0" encoding="utf-8" ?>
<bookstore>
   <book>Pratical .NET and C#</book>
   <book genre="autobiography" publicationdate="1981" ISBN="1-861003-11-0">
      <title>The Autobiography of Benjamin Franklin</title>
...
```

Transforming an XML document using a XSLT stylesheet

The `System.Xml.Xsl.XslCompiledTransform` class can be used to transform an XML document using a program written using XSLT 1.0. This new class of the .NET 2 framework replaces the `XslTransform` class which is now obsolete. As its name implies, the main advantage of this class is to compile XSLT programs into MSIL code before applying a transformation. The initial cost of the compilation is quickly offset by applying only a few transformations.

The following example applies the `books.xslt` program (Example 21-3) on the `books.xml` document (Example 21-1) and displays the result on the console:

Example 21-13
```
using System.Xml.Xsl;
class Program {
   static void Main() {
      System.Xml.XmlDocument xDoc = new System.Xml.XmlDocument();
      xDoc.Load(@"C:\books.xml");
      XslCompiledTransform xTrans = new XslCompiledTransform();
      xTrans.Load(@"C:\books.xslt");
      xTrans.Transform(xDoc, null, System.Console.Out);
   }
}
```

In the last section of this chapter, we will show the features offered by *Visual Studio* to edit and debug XSLT programs.

Bridges between relational data and XML documents

Getting an XML document from a DataSet

You can easily obtain an XML document describing the data contained in the tables of a `DataSet`. For this, you need to use the `WriteXml()` method of the `DataSet` class. You can also obtain an XSD schema which describes the tables contained in a `DataSet` using the `WriteXmlSchema()` method of the `DataSet` class. Here is an example which fills a `DataSet` from the database (the one described at page 589) and then display the data and schema to the console in XML and XSD formats:

Example 21-14
```
using System.Data;
using System.Data.SqlClient;
class Program {
   static void Main() {
      string sCnx =
         "server = localhost ; uid=sa ; pwd =; database = ORGANIZATION";
      using( SqlConnection cnx = new SqlConnection( sCnx ) ) {
         using( SqlDataAdapter dataAdapter = new SqlDataAdapter() ) {
            DataSet dataSet = new DataSet();
            string sCmd = "SELECT * FROM EMPLOYEES";
            dataAdapter.SelectCommand = new SqlCommand( sCmd, cnx );
            dataAdapter.Fill( dataSet, "EMPLOYEES" );
            dataSet.WriteXml( System.Console.Out );
            System.Console.WriteLine("----------------------------");
            dataSet.WriteXmlSchema( System.Console.Out );
         } // end using SqlDataAdapter
      } // end using SqlConnection
   }
}
```

Here is an extract from the display of this program:

```
<NewDataSet>
  <EMPLOYEES>
    <EmployeeID>1</EmployeeID>
    <DepID>MKT</DepID>
    <Surname>Doo</Surname>
    <Firstname>John</Firstname>
    <Phone>(123) 456-7893</Phone>
  </EMPLOYEES>
  ...
</NewDataSet>---------------------------
<?xml version="1.0" encoding="ibm850"?>
<xs:schema id="NewDataSet" xmlns="" xmlns:xs="http://www.w3.org/2001/XMLSchema"
xmlns:msdata="urn:schemas-microsoft-com:xml-msdata">
  <xs:element name="NewDataSet" msdata:IsDataSet="true"
                                msdata:Locale="en-US">
    <xs:complexType>
      <xs:choice minOccurs="0" maxOccurs="unbounded">
        <xs:element name="EMPLOYES">
          <xs:complexType>
            <xs:sequence>
              <xs:element name="EmployeeID" type="xs:int" minOccurs="0" />
              <xs:element name="DepID" type="xs:string" minOccurs="0" />
              <xs:element name="Surname" type="xs:string" minOccurs="0" />
              <xs:element name="Firstname" type="xs:string" minOccurs="0" />
              <xs:element name="Phone" type="xs:string" minOccurs="0" />
...
```

Filling a DataSet from an XML document

It is possible to insert records in a table of a DataSet from an XML file. In the following example, we add the data of a new employee in the database described at page 589. The source data for this employee is contained in the *DataFile.xml* file:

Example 21-15

```
using System.Data;
using System.Data.SqlClient;
class Program {
    static void Main() {
        string sCnx =
            "server = localhost ; uid=sa ; pwd =; database = ORGANIZATION";
        using( SqlConnection cnx = new SqlConnection(sCnx) ) {
            using( SqlDataAdapter dataAdapter = new SqlDataAdapter() ) {
                DataSet dataSet = new DataSet();

                // Build automatically commands for updates.
                string sCmd ="SELECT * FROM EMPLOYEES WHERE EmployeeID=-1";
                dataAdapter.SelectCommand = new SqlCommand( sCmd, cnx );
                SqlCommandBuilder cmdBuilder =
                    new SqlCommandBuilder( dataAdapter );
                // Build the 'EMPLOYEES' table and insert lines from
                // the 'DataFile.xml' file.
                dataSet.ReadXml(@"C:/DataFile.xml");

                // Update the database.
```

Example 21-15
```
            dataAdapter.Update(dataSet, "EMPLOYEES");
        } // end using SqlDataAdapter
    } // end using SqlConnection
    }
}
```

Here is the *DataFile.xml* file. It is not necessary to specify the value for the `EmployeeID` field as it will be computed by the RDBMS.

Example 21-16   *DataFile.xml*
```
<?xml version="1.0" encoding="utf-8" ?>
<NewDataSet>
  <EMPLOYEES>
    <DepID>MKT</DepID>
    <Surname>Dwight</Surname>
    <Firstname>Richard</Firstname>
    <Phone>(123) 456-7883</Phone>
  </EMPLOYEES>
  <EMPLOYEES>
    <DepID>DEV</DepID>
    <Surname>Hardy</Surname>
    <Firstname>Alan</Firstname>
    <Phone>(123) 456-7885</Phone>
  </EMPLOYEES>
</NewDataSet>
```

The System.Xml.XmlDataDocument class

We have seen in the two previous sections how to transfer XML data into the tables of a `DataSet` and vice-versa. The `System.Xml.XmlDataDocument` class (which derives from `XmlDocument`) has been specially created for this task. To accomplish this, we bind an instance of `XmlDataDocument` to a `DataSet`, and we then manipulate the data through the intermediate of `XmlDataDocument` or the intermediate of a `DataSet`. You must understand that internally, the same data is manipulated. Changes made through the intermediate of `DataSet` are immediately visible through `XmlDataDocument` and vice-versa.

It is legitimate to wonder why to use the `XmlDataDocument` class while the two previous sections have shown that the `DataSet` class could manage the XML format directly. We can identify the three following reasons:

- The use of the `XmlDataDocument` class allows the completion of XPath requests on the data.

- The use of the `XmlDataDocument` class allows to remain faithful to a source XML document. If you load an XML document into a `DataSet` and then you save it, there may be formatting difference between the source and destination XML documents. With the use of the `XmlDataDocument` class, the destination XML document will be strictly identical to the source XML document (for example, spaces, the order of elements and comments will not be modified).

- The use of the `XmlDataDocument` class allows taking into account the relations between the tables of the `DataSet` during the XML formatting. Concretely, in a '*one to many*' relation, the child elements of a parent are physically included in the parent element of the XML document. The notion of relationship between the tables of a `DataSet` is discussed at page 604. With this technique, a relation is taken into account only if the `Nested` property is set to `true`, which is not the default.

XML and SQL Server

Since the 2000 version, the *SQL Server* RDBMS offers a component named *SQLXML* which allows to format the SQL request as well as its responses in an XML format. SQLXML can also be found in the IIS server. Hence, it is possible to send XML requests and receive XML responses using HTTP. In other words, this infrastructure allows the construction of basic *web services* which allows querying a database.

The SqlClient data provider of ADO.NET allows the use of SQLXML. The following example allows listing the rows of the EMPLOYEES table in an XML format. Note the addition of the FOR XML AUTO expression at the end of our XML request. This syntax is an extension of the T-SQL language and allows specifying that we wish to receive the results of the request in an XML format:

Example 21-17
```
using System.Data.Common;
using System.Data.SqlClient;
using System.Xml;
class Program {
   static void Main() {
      string sCnx =
         "server = localhost ; uid=sa ; pwd =; database = ORGANIZATION";
      string sCmd = "SELECT * FROM EMPLOYEES FOR XML AUTO";
      using (DbConnection cnx = new SqlConnection(sCnx)) {
         using (SqlCommand cmd = new SqlCommand(sCmd,
                                                cnx as SqlConnection)) {
            cnx.Open();
            System.Xml.XmlReader reader = cmd.ExecuteXmlReader();
            while ( reader.Read() )
               System.Console.WriteLine( reader.ReadOuterXml() );
            reader.Close();
         } // end using cmd.
      } // end using cnx.
      System.Console.Read();
   }
}
```

This example displays the following:
```
<EMPLOYEES EmployeeID="1" DepID="MKT" Surname="Doo" Firstname="John"
 Phone="(123) 456-7893"/>
<EMPLOYEES EmployeeID="3" DepID="DEV" Surname="Kennedy"
 Firstname="Franck" />
...
```

The 2005 version of *SQL Server* brings new features in regards to the integration of XML data in a relation database. Mainly, a column of a table can be typed as XML data. Each element of such a column is an XML document. The .NET framework type corresponding to such a column is `System.Data.SqlTypes.SqlXml`. There is also the possibility to strongly type an XML column with an XSD schema and you can accomplish *XQuery* requests on the elements of such a column. A detailed discussion of these functionalities in *SQL Server 2005* is beyond the scope of this book.

Bridges between objects and XML documents (XML serialization)

The System.Xml.XmlSerializer class

Thanks to the `System.Xml.XmlSerializer` class you have the possibility of serializing in an XML format almost any .NET object. This serialization mechanism does have a few limitations:

- `XmlSerializer` only serializes the public fields and attributes contrarily to the binary object serialization described at page 657.
- `XmlSerializer` does not take into account the `[Serializable]` attribute or the `ISerializable` interface.
- `XmlSerializer` cannot serialize an object graph which has at least one circular reference.

Here is a program which illustrates the use of the `XmlSerializer` class by saving an instance of the book class in an XML file, and by loading this state into another instance of the book class:

Example 21-18

```
using System.Xml;
using System.Xml.Serialization;
using System.IO;
public class book {
    public string genre  { get{ return m_genre; } set{ m_genre = value; } }
    private string m_genre;
    public string title  { get{ return m_title; } set{ m_title = value; } }
    private string m_title;
    public decimal price { get{ return m_price; } set{ m_price = value; } }
    private decimal m_price;
}
public class Program {
    static public void Main() {
        book b1 = new book();
        b1.genre = "autobiography";
        b1.title = "The Autobiography of Benjamin Franklin";
        b1.price = 8.99M;
        // Store the state of an instance of the 'book' class ...
        // ... in the 'book.xml' file.
        FileStream fs1 = File.OpenWrite("book.xml");
        XmlSerializer xmls = new XmlSerializer(typeof(book));
        xmls.Serialize(fs1, b1);
        fs1.Close();
        // Create an instance of the 'book' class ...
        // ... from the 'book.xml' file.
        FileStream fs2 = File.OpenRead("book.xml");
        book b2 = (book) xmls.Deserialize(fs2);
        fs2.Close();
    }
}
```

The following XML file is created:

book.xml

```
<?xml version="1.0" encoding="utf-8"?>
<book xmlns:xsi="http://www.w3.org/2001/XMLSchema-instance"
      xmlns:xsd="http://www.w3.org/2001/XMLSchema">
  <genre>autobiography</genre>
  <title>The Autobiography of Benjamin Franklin</title>
  <price>8.99</price>
</book>
```

You have the possibility of serializing information of nullable types in an XML document. In this case, the null value will be used if the element or attribute is missing in the document or if it contains an attribute xsi:nil="true". In the XSD schema, the fact that an element or attribute can be null translates itself with the nil="true" attribute present in the corresponding xs:element element.

You can serialize a generic type. This does not pose any problem during the serialization but you must be careful to specify the proper parameter types when constructing an XmlSerializer destined to deserialize the data.

XML serialization attributes

Do not confuse the notion of .NET attributes and XML attributes which are different.

You have the possibility of using .NET attributes to modify the default behavior of the serialization into an XML file. In general, we must conform ourselves to an XSD schema when we serialize an object into an XML format. For example, you could wish not to serialize the price property and to make sure that the genre be an XML attribute and not an element. Here are the .NET attributes that you can use:

- XmlRoot: Allows identifying a class or a structure as the root node. In general, we use this attribute to assign a different name of the class for the corresponding XML element.
- XmlElement: Specifies that a public field or property must be serialized as an element. As this is the default behavior, we generally use this attribute to assign a different name to the field or property in the corresponding XML element.
- XmlAttribute: Specifies that a public field or property must be serialized as an XML attribute and not as an element, which is the default behavior. We can take advantage of this attribute to specify a different name to the field or property in the corresponding XML element.
- XmlArray: Specifies that a public property or field must be serialized as an array. In general, we use this attribute to make sure that an array of objects is serialized.
- XmlArrayItem: Specifies that instances of a type can be serialized in an array.
- XmlIgnore: Indicates that this public field or property cannot be serialized.

Let's modify the book class using some of these attributes:

Example 21-19

```
...
[XmlRoot(ElementName = "livre")]
public class book {
   [XmlAttribute(AttributeName = "genre")]
   public string genre  { get{ return m_genre; } set{ m_genre = value; } }
   private string m_genre;
   [XmlElement(ElementName = "titre")]
   public string title  { get{ return m_title; } set{ m_title = value; } }
   private string m_title;
   [XmlIgnore]
   public decimal price { get{ return m_price; } set{ m_price = value; } }
   private decimal m_price;
}
...
```

Here is the XML file produced by this change:

book.xml
```
<?xml version="1.0" encoding="utf-8"?>
<livre xmlns:xsi="http://www.w3.org/2001/XMLSchema-instance"
       xmlns:xsd="http://www.w3.org/2001/XMLSchema"
       genre="autobiography">
  <titre>The Autobiography of Benjamin Franklin</titre>
</livre>
```

The sgen.exe tool

When you serialize an object into XML of a type that has not yet had any instances serialized, the XmlSerializer internally creates a new instance of a class specialized with the serialization of this type. You can improve the performance by pre-generating these XML serialization classes using the sgen.exe (*XML Serializer Generation Tool*) tool. This tool accepts as input an assembly XXX (using the /a option) and creates a new assembly XXX.XmlSerializers.dll which contains these specialized XML serialization classes. In the case of our book class in Example 21-19, a class named Microsoft.Xml.Serialization.GeneratedAssembly.bookSerializer is created and you can use it as follows:

Example 21-20
```
using Microsoft.Xml.Serialization.GeneratedAssembly;
...
public class Program {
   static public void Main() {
      ...
      FileStream fs1 = File.OpenWrite("book.xml");
      bookSerializer bookS = new bookSerializer();
      bookS.Serialize(fs1, b1);
      ...
      book b2 = (book)bookS.Deserialize(fs2);
      fs2.Close();
   }
}
...
```

The xsd.exe tool

We have showed that the use of certain .NET attributes allow ourselves to conform to an XSD schema during the serialization of an object into XML. The xsd.exe tool provided by the .NET framework goes further and allows the following operations:

- xsd.exe can generate the code of a C# class (eventually deriving from the DataSet class) from an XSD schema. At page 606 we explain how this tool can be used to create a typed DataSet.
- xsd.exe allows the generation of an XSD schema from an XML file or from the types contained in assembly.

The use of the xsd.exe is described in the article named **XML Schema Definition Tool (Xsd.exe)** on **MSDN**.

Visual Studio and XML

Creating, viewing and editing XML documents and XSD schemas

Visual Studio allows editing XML document as text documents. It also knows how to detect syntax and lexical errors in the XML document. When such errors are detected, they are underlined in the document and reported in the list of errors. It is possible to infer an XSD schema from a currently visualized XML file. For this, you simply need to go in the *XML › Create Schema* menu. The XSD schemas are themselves viewed and edited through a graphical *designer* as shown in Figure 21-1:

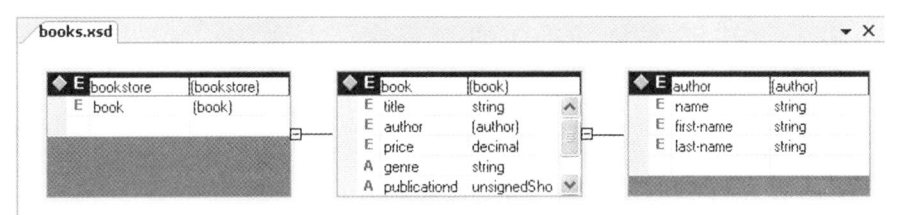

Figure 21-1: XSD schema designer

Visual Studio creates a file with an .xsx extension for each XSD schema viewed in this editor. This file contains the information used by the editor in order to organize the view of the document (coordinate of the tables, zoom level…). Note that it is always possible to return to a text view of an XSD schema.

Validating an XML document with an XSD schema

For *Visual Studio* to be able to perform such a validation, it must first have access to the related XSD schema. *Visual Studio* takes into account the XSD schemas contained in the current project and the XSD schemas stored in the [VS Install Folder]\Xml\Schemas and [VS Install Folder] \Common7\IDE\Policy\Schemas folders. You can associate an XSD schema known by *Visual Studio* to an XML document in a natural way by specifying the target namespace of the schema in the XML document. Let's review our books.xml and books.xsd example files:

Example 21-21   *books.xml*
```
<?xml version="1.0" encoding="utf-8" ?>
<bookstore xmlns ="http://www.contoso.com/books">
  <book genre="autobiography" publicationdate="1981" ISBN="1-861003-11-0">
...
```

Example 21-22   *books.xsd*
```
<?xml version="1.0" encoding="utf-8"?>
<xs:schema attributeFormDefault="unqualified"
           elementFormDefault="qualified"
           targetNamespace="http://www.contoso.com/books"
           xmlns:xs="http://www.w3.org/2001/XMLSchema">
  <xs:element name="bookstore">
...
```

You can also associate an XSD schema to an XML document through the *property › Schemas* menu of the XML document. This menu offers a help window which allows to select the schema from all the ones known by *Visual Studio*.

When an XSD schema is associated to an XML document,, *Visual Studio* not only performs the validation by detecting the errors and highlighting them, but also put in place the *intellisense* mechanism to facilitate the edition of the XML document.

Editing and debugging a XSLT schema

As with all XML documents, *Visual Studio* verifies the lexical and syntax errors when you edit an XSLT program. Also, the XML editor can verify in real-time your document against the `xslt.xsd` file which defines the schema of this object. You simply need to include the `http://www.w3.org/1999/XSL/Transform` namespace in the root element. *Visual Studio* also allows you to debug XSLT programs in two ways:

- During the debugging of a .NET program when you call the `XslCompiledTransform.Transform()` method, the debugger will directly go to the entry point of the XSLT program. This is possible only if you use the `XslCompiledTransform(bool enableDebug)` constructor with `true` in order to create your instance.

- Directly from *Visual Studio* by using the *XML > Debug XSLT* menu which is available when editing an XSLT program. To use this feature, you must have previously provided an input XML file and an output text file (which will receive the result from the XSLT transformation) in the *input* and *output* sub-menu of the *property* menu of the XSLT document.

22

.NET Remoting

Introduction

What is .NET Remoting?

We have defined the notion of AppDomain at page 71 as an assembly container during execution. We remind you that a process contains one or several AppDomains which are isolated from each other by the CLR. The `mscorlib` assembly, containing the base types of the NET platform, is physically loaded in the process outside of all AppDomains. The isolation between the AppDomains is done mostly at the level of the types, of the security and the management of exceptions. This isolation is not done at the level of threads.

If you have assimilated this notion of AppDomain, you can easily understand the definition of .NET Remoting which is:

> .NET Remoting is the infrastructure of the .NET platform which allows to objects located in different AppDomains to be able to know about each other and to communicate between them. The calling object is named the client while the called object is the server or server object.

Two different AppDomains can be found:

- in the same process;
- in two different processes on the same machine;
- in two different processes on different machines.

.NET Remoting hides to the developers these three aspects of the problem. The locating of an object is generally done after the compilation of the sources, during the installation of the application. More precisely, the *'such object is on such machine'* information cannot be part of the source code. In this case, this information is located in a configuration file which is accessible by the client of the objects.

To developers who have already used *Microsoft* technologies, let us mention that .NET Remoting can be seen as the successor to *DCOM*.

FAQ

Q: Can we choose the underlying protocol used for the communication between two objects?
A: Yes. With .NET Remoting each communication protocol is encapsulated in an object called *channel*. Channels encapsulating the HTTP, TCP as well as the communication protocol for processes on a same machine (IPC for *Inter Process Communication*) are natively implemented. You can also develop your own channels for other protocols.

Q: In which form does the data necessary to a method call transit over the network?
A: The data necessary for a method call principally contains the value of the input parameters, an identifier for the method and an identifier for the object before the call and the values of the output parameters resulting from the call. In .NET Remoting, the object responsible for the wrapping of this data are called *formatters*. The formatters which wrap the data in a binary or an XML format named SOAP are implemented natively. You can however develop your own formatters to meet your specific needs (data encryption, elimination of redundancy...).

Q: Is the architecture using these channels and formatter objects also used when the client and the server object in the same AppDomain or in the same process?
A: In these two cases, it is obviously not necessary to use a channel and .NET Remoting will automatically adopt this behavior. There is thus a specific channel for calls done within a same addressing space.

Q: How does the source code of the client, which is not in the same assembly that the classes representing the server objects, can know about these classes?
A: With .NET Remoting, at least three techniques can be considered. Either the client assembly references the server assembly during compilation. In this case, the server assembly must be installed on the client side. This technique is thus very constraining. We prefer a second technique which consists in encapsulating interfaces in a tier assembly deployed both on the client and on the server side. A third technique allows to automatically build this tier assembly from the assembly of the server. This third technique requires the use of a dedicated tool provided with the .NET framework.

Q: Would it not be simpler to retrieve a copy of the server object in the AppDomain of the client, and to work with this copy rather than using the network for each method call?
A: .NET Remoting offers this possibility and the answer to the question is: it depends. This implies that the assembly containing the class of the server object is accessible by the client and this is generally not something that we wish. Also, several server objects cannot be moved into another AppDomain. The classic reason is that the server objects contain references to other objects in the domain, which cannot be moved. For example, an instance of the Thread class can be considered as an immovable object. Finally, in the case of the recovery of an object by the client, we deprive ourselves of the possibility of being able to use the object in a concurrent way across several clients.

Q: Who is responsible for the creation of a server object? The client or the server itself?
A: The two cases can be envisioned with .NET Remoting. In the case where a server is responsible for the creation of an object, this object is identified by an URI. The client contacts this object by using this URI, in the same way as you would contact a friend using a telephone number. In this case, the object is effectively created during the first call from a client.

Q: Who is responsible for the destruction of a server object? The client or the server itself?
A: Despite an evolved ping mechanism, DCOM has shown that you must not trust the client when it comes to the destruction of a server object. DCOM has also shown that such a ping mechanism can be detrimental to performance. With NET Remoting, the server objects are automatically destroyed after a certain duration for which the object was not used. A client who tries to contact an object which does not exist anymore will receive an exception.

Q: Does .NET Remoting support asynchronous calls?
A: Yes. .NET Remoting supports the mechanism of asynchronous calls described at page 141. During an asynchronous call, you can choose to be warned by the server when it has executed your call. You can then retrieve the result relative to your processing by the server, in an asynchronous way.

Marshaling By Reference (MBR)

.NET Remoting offers two solutions which are architecturally different to allow a client to call a method on a remote object. These two solutions are named *Marshalling By Value* (*MBV*) and *Marshalling By Reference* (*MBR*). By default, the instances of a class cannot be used in a remote way.

Marshalling By Reference (*MBR*) consists into obtaining a new object called a *transparent proxy* in the AppDomain of the client. For the client code, everything happens as if the transparent proxy was a classic reference to an object, hence the notion of transparency. In fact, even the `csc.exe` compiler does not know that certain references will be transparent proxies during execution.

A necessary condition in order to use transparent proxies in an assembly instead of a reference to a type is that the metadata of this type be available during the compilation of the assembly. We will explain several ways to satisfy these conditions. At this stage, the curious readers may surely ask questions such as:

- Who is responsible of the creation of the remote object?
- Howe do we get a transparent proxy?
- How does the proxy class takes care of transiting the input and output data over the network?

The answer to all these questions will be found in this chapter. The analysis of the following program will provide a few elements to these questions. We will interest ourselves to the case where the class of the remote object and the client are in the same assembly and where the client and the remote object are in the same AppDomains.

Example 22-1   MBRTest.cs

```
using System;
using System.Runtime.Remoting.Contexts;
using System.Runtime.Remoting;
using System.Threading;

public class Foo : MarshalByRefObject {
   public void DisplayInfo(string s) {
      Console.WriteLine(s);
      Console.WriteLine("  Name of the domain: " +
                  AppDomain.CurrentDomain.FriendlyName);
      Console.WriteLine("  ThreadID    : " +
                  Thread.CurrentThread.ManagedThreadId);
   }
}

public class Program {
   static void Main() {
      // obj1
      Foo obj1 = new Foo();
      obj1.DisplayInfo("obj1:" );
      Console.WriteLine("  IsObjectOutOfAppDomain(obj1)=" +
         RemotingServices.IsObjectOutOfAppDomain( obj1 ) );
      Console.WriteLine("  IsTransparentProxy(obj1)=" +
         RemotingServices.IsTransparentProxy( obj1 ) );

      // obj2
      AppDomain appDomain=AppDomain.CreateDomain("Another AppDomain.");
      Foo obj2 = (Foo) appDomain.CreateInstanceAndUnwrap(
            "MBRTest",  // Name of the assembly that contains the type.
            "Foo");     // Name of the type.

      obj2.DisplayInfo("obj2:"); // <- Here, the client is not aware
```

Example 22-1   MBRTest.cs

```
                // that he is working with a transparent proxy.
      Console.WriteLine(" IsObjectOutOfAppDomain(obj2)=" +
         RemotingServices.IsObjectOutOfAppDomain( obj2 ) );
      Console.WriteLine(" IsTransparentProxy(obj2)=" +
         RemotingServices.IsTransparentProxy( obj2 ) );
   }
}
```

This program displays:

```
obj1:
  Name of the domain: MBRTest.exe
  ThreadID        : 6116
  IsObjectOutOfAppDomain(obj1)=False
  IsTransparentProxy(obj1)=False
obj2:
  Name of the domain: Another AppDomain.
  ThreadID        : 6116
  IsObjectOutOfAppDomain(obj2)=True
  IsTransparentProxy(obj2)=True
```

Note the use of the `IsObjectOutOfAppDomain()` and `IsTransparentProxy()` static methods of the `RemotingServices` class.

Figure 22-1 illustrates the architecture put into place by the CLR to execute this program. The notion of context is explained a little later in this chapter:

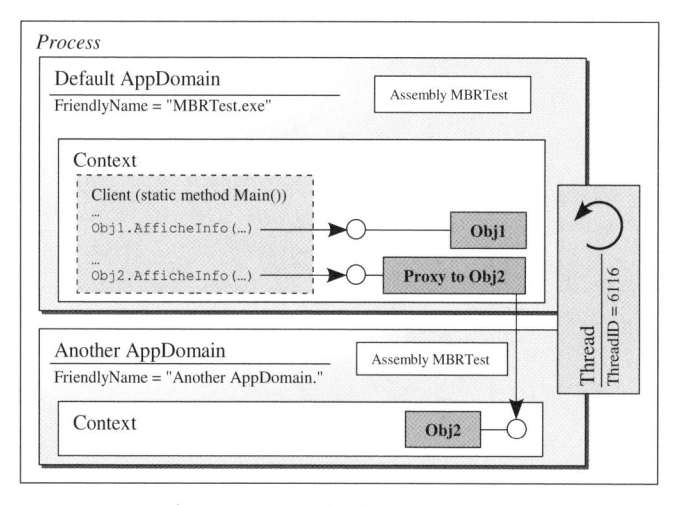

Figure 22-1: Marshalling By Reference

In the previous program, you have certainly noticed that the `Foo` class derives from the `System.MarshalByRefObject` class. When the JIT compiler encounters a reference which is typed by a class that derives from `MarshalByRefObject`, it knows that this reference can eventually be a transparent proxy. A consequence is that the JIT compiler prevents the inlining of the methods called from such a reference. Such a practice would suppose that the referenced object is not distant, which could easily be broken. This comes back to saying that to make a class derive from `MarshalByRefObject` indicates to the JIT that an instance of this class can potentially be used in a remote way using a transparent proxy. In the case where this instance and its client are in the same AppDomain, the client works with a reference to the instance and not through a transparent proxy.

Marshalling By Value (MBV) and binary serialization

Marshalling By Value (*MBV*) consists in constructing a clone of the remote object, in the same AppDomain as the client. The CLR makes it so that the clone has exactly the same state as the remote object. Let us precise that the *state of an object* at a specific point in time is the set of the value type fields of the object. Depending on the application, the state of the object also contains the state taken by the objects referenced by the reference type fields of the object.

The clone is not a remote object. The client does not need a transparent proxy to access it. Note that no constructor is called on the clone. This behavior is logical since the clone must be exactly as the original object on which a constructor has already been called.

A condition necessary to use the MBV technique is that the AppDomain of the client must be able to load the assembly containing the class of the remote object. Eventually, the client and this class can be part of the same assembly. Another necessary condition is that the original remote object must not contain references to objects which are not cloneable. Indeed, there is no sense in cloning certain objects. For example, why clone an instance of the `Thread` class outside of the process which physically contains the thread to which this instance references?

Internally, the CLR reflects the state of the object in a binary *stream* then sends this stream to the AppDomain of the client. On the client side, the CLR receives this binary *stream* and reconstructs the state of the object in the clone. These operations are called *serialization* and *deserialization* of the object. In .NET, for an object to be serializable, its class must be tagged with the `System.Serializable` attribute or (exclusive) its class must extend the `System.Runtime.Serialization.ISerializable` interface. In the first case, you tell the CLR to use the standard serialization mechanism. In the second case, you have the possibility of implementing your own serialization mechanism. By default, all primitive types are serializable.

Once the object is cloned in the AppDomain of the client, the state of the clone and of the original distant object are independent. The changes made on one are not reflected on others. The term *MBValue* takes then all its sense. Indeed, this behavior is similar to the behavior of a value type argument passed to a method. The changes made on such an argument are not reflected on the initial object in the caller. Figure 22-2 illustrates this.

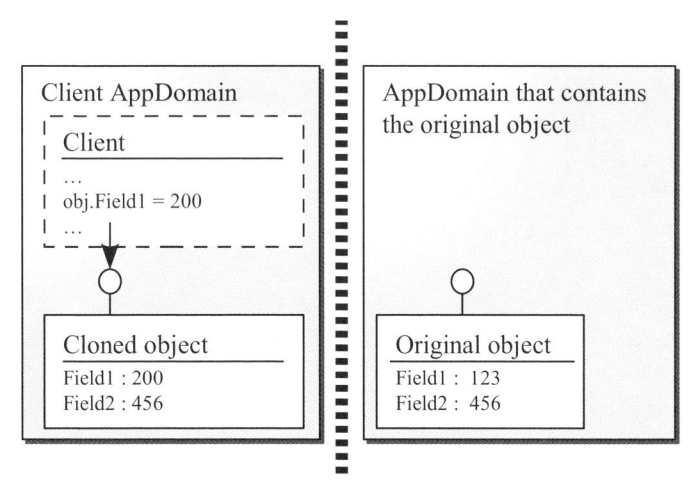

Figure 22-2: Marshalling By Value

In Example 22-1, it is interesting to notice how to modify the `Foo` class in order to make it a MBV class:

Example 22-2   MBVTest.cs

```
    ...
    [Serializable]        // <- Added
    public class Foo{    // : MarshalByRefObject  <- Commented
    ...
```

…we obtain the following results:

```
obj1:
  Nom of the domain: MBVTest.exe
  ThreadID      : 3620
  IsObjectOutOfAppDomain(obj1)=False
  IsTransparentProxy(obj1)=False
obj2:
  Nom of the domain: MBVTest.exe
  ThreadID      : 3620
  IsObjectOutOfAppDomain(obj2)=False
  IsTransparentProxy(obj2)=False
```

This proves that the remote object has in fact been cloned in a new object which is located in the AppDomain of the client.

In the chapter dedicated to generics, at page 414, we show that binary serialization knows how to handle generic types.

Version-tolerant serialization

When we use object serialization, we notice that a common problem is due to the evolution of the classes to serialize and especially the addition of new fields. In fact, after the update of the application, when we attempt to deserialize an object, an exception is raised because the new fields for the concerned class are not provided. To avoid this problem, you can tag the new fields with the `System.Runtime.Serialization.OptionalFieldAttribute` attribute. The concerned fields will then take the default values for their type.

The `System.Runtime.Serialization` namespace also contains the four following attributes which allow tagging a method in order for it to be invoked at a certain step of the serialization/deserialization process. You can take advantage of these methods in order to provide values for the new fields:

- `OnDeserializingAttribute`: The method is called before the state of the deserialized object is recovered and set.
- `OnDeserializedAttribute`: The method is called after the state of the object have been deserialized and applied.
- `OnSerializingAttribute`: The method is called before the state of the object is serialized.
- `OnSerializedAttribute`: The method is called after the state of the object has been serialized.

The ObjectHandle class

In the code of the section presenting MBR, instead of using the `CreateInstanceAndUnwrap()` method we could have written:

```
    ...
    ObjectHandle hObj2 = appDomain.CreateInstance( "Remoting1" , "Foo" );
    Foo obj2 = (Foo) hObj2.Unwrap();
    ...
```

The ObjectHandle class

An instance of the `System.Runtime.Remoting.ObjectHandle` class contains the information necessary to use a remote object. By calling the `UnWrap()` method, you recover a transparent proxy if the distant object is MBR or a clone if the distant object is MBV.

You can optimize your application by using the fact that .NET splits the operation of the retrieval of a remote object into two steps: retrieving an instance of the `ObjectHandle` class then the unwrapping of this instance. The loading of the type metadata which describes the class of the remote object is only done during the second step, during the unwrapping. If the current client does not use the remote object and only transmits it to another part of the application, it does not need to do the unwrapping. Hence we save the loading of type metadata and thus, the loading of the assembly. Here is a program which illustrates this. Note that this program takes advantage of the fact that a *class constructor* is invoked by the CLR when it loads the type metadata of the concerned class into the AppDomain.

Example 22-3 *WrapTest.cs*

```
using System;
using System.Runtime.Remoting;

[Serializable]
public class Foo {
   // Class Constructor.
   static Foo() {
      Console.WriteLine( "Loading 'Foo class' metadata in the domain : " +
                         AppDomain.CurrentDomain.FriendlyName);
   }
   // Instance Constructor.
   public Foo() {
      Console.WriteLine( "'Foo' ctor called in the domain : " +
                         AppDomain.CurrentDomain.FriendlyName);
   }
}

public class Program {
   static void Main() {
      Console.WriteLine("-->About to call CreateDomain()");
      AppDomain appDomain = AppDomain.CreateDomain( "Another AppDomain." );
      Console.WriteLine("-->About to call CreateInstance()");
      ObjectHandle hObj = appDomain.CreateInstance( "WrapTest", "Foo" );
      Console.WriteLine("-->About to call UnWrap()");
      Foo obj = (Foo) hObj.Unwrap();
      Console.WriteLine("-->UnWrap() called");
   }
}
```

Here is what the program displays:

```
-->About to call CreateDomain()
-->About to call CreateInstance()
Loading 'Foo class' metadata in the domain : Another AppDomain
'Foo' ctor called in the domain : Another AppDomain
-->About to call UnWrap()
Loading 'Foo class' metadata in the domain : WrapTest.exe
-->UnWrap() called
```

This program also illustrates the fact that no instance constructor is called during the construction of a clone. When we execute this program by making `Foo` a MBR class, the next to last line of the display did not appear. This clearly underlines that the proxy object is not of the same type than the remote object.

Object activation

If you have read the previous sections, you can enter into the core of this topic, in other words: crossing the virtual boundaries between processes and the physical boundaries between machines for your object calls in the case of MBR and for your objects in the case of MBV.

Components of a distributed architecture

In the architecture of a distributed application which uses .NET Remoting with MBR server objects, there is four main kinds of components:

- The clients, which call server objects;
- The host, which hosts the server objects;
- The type metadata of the server objects;
- The implementation of the server objects.

As a general rule, we isolate each of these components in one or several assemblies. This rule is not at all a constraint. Physically, you can mix all kind of components in a single assembly. However, using this rule offers some advantages that you will discover in the following pages. Also, we will explain why and how separating the type metadata of the type of the server objects from their implementation. Figure 22-3 illustrates the division of the assemblies in a classical distributed application.

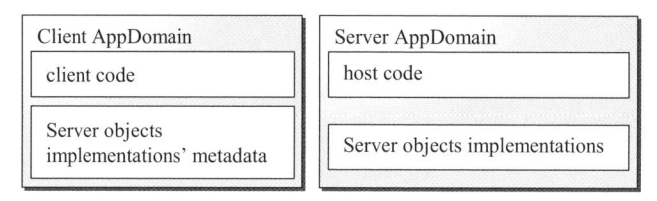

Figure 22-3: Components of a distributed architecture

Host overview

A host has several responsibilities:

- Create one or several *channels*;
- Expose classes or server objects which are accessible to the clients through the use of URIs;
- Maintain the process which contains the server objects.

It may be surprising that the host can expose not only objects but also classes. This results from the fact that a server object can be activated either by the server or by the client. In the first case, the client must know the object in order to use it while in the second case, the client must know a class in order to be able to activate an instance of this class.

Channel overview

A channel is an object which allows the communication across the network. There also exist specialized channels for the communication between processes. A channel contains three main parameters which are the network port used, the communication protocol used (TCP, HTTP, IPC) and the way that the data will be formatted in order to transit over the network (binary format, XML, SOAP standard…). By default, binary formatting is associated to the TCP and IPC protocols, and SOAP formatting is used for the HTTP protocol, but this behavior can easily be modified. To use .NET Remoting, you need two channels with the same protocol and the same data formatting: a channel on the client side and a channel on the server side. To move on with this section, you do not need to know more about channels. But we will come back to this topic a little later in the chapter in a section dedicated to channels.

Synchronous, asynchronous and one-way calls

Calls made to remote objects can by synchronous, asynchronous or asynchronous without return (one-way). It is nice to notice that the technique used to call an object in an asynchronous way is the same, whether the object is remote or not. This technique is described at page 141.

Object activation vs. object creation

Let us mention that in .NET Remoting we generally talk of *object activation* rather than the creation of an object. This comes from the fact that during the creation of an object destined to be used in a remote way, there are potentially a large number of operations which much take place between the creation request and the eventual availability of the new object. These actions are what we call the activation.

Well-Known Object activation (WKO)

An important step when we specify a distributed architecture is to define for each remote object who, of the client or the server (i.e. the host) will activate it. .NET Remoting allows client to activate a remote object on the server or to use an object which already exists on the server. Let's underline that when an object is activated by the server, the client does not need to call the|constructor of the class of the object. This aspect may be a determining factor in the choice between the server-side or client-side activation. Here we will discuss the case where the object is activated by the server and after we will discuss the case where the client activates the object.

In the case where a client uses a remote object activated by the server, it is strongly recommended to make sure that the client does not know the class of which the remote object is an instance of. For this, it is a good idea to define the interfaces supported by the class of the remote object in a special assembly for this purpose. In our global view of the components of a distributed architecture (the one in Figure 22-3), this assembly plays the role of the type metadata of the server objects. Concretely, this assembly will be present on both the client and the server AppDomains. Here is, for example, the code of such an assembly:

Example 22-4   *Interface.cs*

```
namespace RemotingInterfaces {
   public interface IAdder {
      double Add(double d1, double d2);
   }
}
```

Let's now interest ourselves to the host and the classes of the server objects. We will place these two entities in the same assembly. However, we will see that there exists standard hosts and in order to use them, the classes of the server objects must be isolated in separate assemblies. Here is the code of an assembly containing both the implementation of the server object and a custom host. Note the order of these three tasks in the code of the host: creation of a channel, activation of a server object, maintaining the process.

Example 22-5   *Server.cs*

```
using System;
using System.Runtime.Remoting;
using System.Runtime.Remoting.Channels;
using System.Runtime.Remoting.Channels.Http;
using RemotingInterfaces;

namespace RemotingServer {
   // Implementation of server objects.
```

Example 22-5   Server.cs

```csharp
   public class Adder : MarshalByRefObject, IAdder {
      public Adder() {
         Console.WriteLine( "Adder ctor" );
      }
      public double Add( double d1, double d2 ) {
         Console.WriteLine( "Adder Add( {0} + {1} )", d1, d2 );
         return d1 + d2;
      }
   }

   // Implementation of the host.
   class Program {
      static void Main() {
         // 1) Creating a HTTP channel on the port 65100.
         //    Register this channel in the current AppDomain.
         HttpChannel channel = new HttpChannel( 65100 );
         ChannelServices.RegisterChannel( channel, false );

         // 2) Register Well_Known Objects of type IAdder
         //    at the endpoint 'AddService'.
         RemotingConfiguration.RegisterWellKnownServiceType(
            typeof(Adder),
            "AddService",
            WellKnownObjectMode.SingleCall);

         // 3) Maintain the server process.
         Console.WriteLine( "Press a key to stop the server..." );
         Console.Read();
      }
   }
}
```

Note the use of the *"AddService" endpoint* associated to the activated object. By combining the information about the protocol, the machine, the port and the endpoint, we obtain an URI which completely locates the object activated by the server. In this example, this URI is *http://localhost:65100/AddService*. For this reason, we qualify of *well-known object* an object activated by the server which has an endpoint. From this point on, we will use the *WKO (Well-Known Object)* acronym to talk of an object activated by the server. When we will describe in more details the internal mechanisms of .NET Remoting, we will see that the server can publish an object that it activates without using an endpoint.

We only have the code of the client assembly left to deal with. It is necessary to create a channel and then recover a transparent proxy to the remote object associated to the *http://localhost:65100/AddService* URI. At this stage, we can use the transparent proxy which materializes itself by a reference to a non-remote object.

Example 22-6   Client.cs

```csharp
   using System;
   using System.Runtime.Remoting;
   using System.Runtime.Remoting.Channels;
   using System.Runtime.Remoting.Channels.Http;

   using RemotingInterfaces;

   namespace RemotingClient {
```

Example 22-6   Client.cs

```
    class Program {
       static void Main() {
          // Create an HTTP channel and register it in the current AppDomain
          // (the value 0 means that we delegate the choice of the port
          //  number to the CLR).
          HttpChannel channel = new HttpChannel( 0 );
          ChannelServices.RegisterChannel( channel, false );

          // Get a transparent proxy on a remote object from its URI.
          // Cast this transparent proxy to a reference of type IAdder.
          MarshalByRefObject objRef = (MarshalByRefObject)
                       RemotingServices.Connect(
                             typeof( IAdder ),
                             "http://localhost:65100/AddService" );
          IAdder obj = objRef as IAdder;

          // Invoke a method on the remote object.
          double d = obj.Add( 3.0, 4.0 );
          Console.WriteLine("Returned value:" + d);
       }
    }
}
```

We now have three C# source files, which will each allow the production of an assembly using the three following command line operations:

```
>csc.exe /target:library Interface.cs
>csc.exe Server.cs  /r:Interface.dll
>csc.exe Client.cs   /r:Interface.dll
```

We could have also used *Visual Studio* to place three separate projects in a same solution. Now, you simply need to launch Server.exe then Client.exe. Here is the display of our programs:

Server.exe display

```
Press a key to stop the server...
Adder ctor
Adder Add( 3 + 4 )
```

Client.exe display

```
Returned value:7
```

WKO single call activation vs. WKO singleton activation

In the example of the previous section, we have purposely made a single method call to the server object. Let's examine what would have been displayed if we had made two consecutive calls to Add() on the client-side:

Client.cs

```
   ...
      obj.Add( 3.0 , 4.0 );
      obj.Add( 5.0 , 6.0 );
   ...
```

Display of the server:

```
Press a key to stop the server...
Adder ctor
Adder Add( 3 + 4 )
Adder ctor
Adder Add( 5 + 6 )
```

Based on this display, it seems that the server activates an object for each call of the client since the constructor is called for each of our two calls from the client. This is indeed what happens. This behavior is taken by the server because we have declared our WKO object in *single call* mode when we wrote:

```
...WellKnownObjectMode.SingleCall...
```

There is another *call mode* for objects activated by the server which is called *singleton*. This call mode is chosen by replacing the `SingleCall` value by `Singleton`. The singleton call mode forces the server to activate an object during the first call of a client, and then to maintain this object for all the following calls of all the clients. An immediate consequence is that all the clients share the same object. Several threads of the thread pool may execute the methods of this object simultaneously. It is necessary to provide a synchronization mechanism to protect resources from concurrent accesses. Here is what the server would have displayed if we had declared our object using the singleton call mode:

```
Press a key to stop the server...
Adder ctor
Adder Add( 3 + 4 )
Adder Add( 5 + 6 )
```

Notice that the server waits for the first call from a client before activating the object in the two modes, singleton and single-call.

We prefer talking of an object activation service by the server rather than to talk about the activation of an object by the server. In fact, the client does not really have a reference to a remote object but rather a reference to a remote object activation service. Concretely, if the object used by a client is destroyed, at the next call, the client will use another object, automatically activated by the server.

Client Activated Object (CAO)

We will use the *CAO* acronym to talk of a *Client Activated Object*. To activate an object from the client, he must know the class of the object. This fact constitutes a fundamental difference compared to the architecture put in place during the activation of objects by the server. In fact, in the WKO case, the client only needs to know about the interfaces that he wishes to use on the object. In the case of a CAO object, to make the necessary type metadata of the object's class available, it is necessary to provide the assembly which contains the class of the object. This constrains might shock you, but also know that that the following section will explain how to work around it. In the meantime, let's define the C# code of an assembly which contains the `Adder` class:

Example 22-7   *ObjServer.cs*

```csharp
using System;

namespace RemotingObjServer {
   public interface IAdder {
      double Add(double d1, double d2);
   }
   // Implementation of server objects.
   public class Adder : MarshalByRefObject, IAdder {
```

Example 22-7   *ObjServer.cs*

```
      public Adder() {
         Console.WriteLine( "Adder ctor" );
      }
      public double Add( double d1, double d2 ) {
         Console.WriteLine( "Adder Add( {0} + {1} )", d1, d2 );
         return d1 + d2;
      }
   }
}
```

Now, let's interest ourselves to the source code of the assembly containing the host. This host is similar to the one we used to activate an object by the server. The only difference comes from the fact that we use the `RegisterActivatedServiceType()` static method to precise that we wish to work in CAO mode instead of the `RegisterWellKnownServiceType()` method which puts in place the WKO mode.

Example 22-8   *Server.cs*

```
using System;
using System.Runtime.Remoting;
using System.Runtime.Remoting.Channels;
using System.Runtime.Remoting.Channels.Http;

using RemotingObjServer;

namespace RemotingServer {
   class Program {
      static void Main() {
         HttpChannel channel = new HttpChannel( 65100 );
         ChannelServices.RegisterChannel( channel, false );

         // Register the Adder class as a .NET Remoting CAO class
         // in the current AppDomain.
         RemotingConfiguration.RegisterActivatedServiceType(typeof(Adder));

         Console.WriteLine("Press a key to stop the server...");
         Console.Read();
      }
   }
}
```

The client is also very similar to a client which will use an object activated by the server. The only difference comes from the fact that we use the `Activator.CreateInstance()` static method to get a transparent proxy to the object that we activate.

Example 22-9   *Client.cs*

```
using System;
using System.Runtime.Remoting;
using System.Runtime.Remoting.Channels;
using System.Runtime.Remoting.Channels.Http;
using System.Runtime.Remoting.Activation;
using RemotingObjServer;

namespace RemotingClient {
   class Program {
      static void Main() {
         HttpChannel channel = new HttpChannel( 0 );
```

Example 22-9   *Client.cs*

```csharp
            ChannelServices.RegisterChannel( channel, false );

            // Activate a remote object and get a transparent proxy
            // that references it.
            IAdder obj = Activator.CreateInstance(
               typeof(Adder),
               null,
               new Object[] { new UrlAttribute("http://localhost:65100")})
               as IAdder;

            // Invoke a method on a remote object.
            double d = obj.Add( 3.0, 4.0 );
            Console.WriteLine( "Returned value:" + d );
         }
      }
   }
}
```

We now have three C# source files which will each produce an assembly using the following three command line operations:

```
>csc.exe /target:library ObjServer.cs
>csc.exe Server.cs  /r:ObjServer.dll
>csc.exe Client.cs  /r:ObjServer.dll
```

Now, you simply need to launch `Server.exe` and then `Client.exe`. You will obtain the same display as when you used the server activation. This example is not sufficient in order to show the real difference between the client and server activation modes. However, the behavior difference with the case where the object is activated by the server in the singleton mode, is that each client will have its own object. The behavior difference with the case where the object is activated by the server in the single-call mode, is that the same object is used to serve several calls.

Activating an object with the new keyword

The previous client suffers from big disadvantages: the code does not activate the remote object with the C# syntax using the `new` keyword. Even worse, the client cannot choose which constructor of the `Adder` class the server must use. The `RemotingConfiguration.RegisterActivatedClientType()` static method allows to fix both of these problems. It allows specifying that each instance of the `Adder` in the current AppDomain be done on the server.

Example 22-10   *Client.cs*

```csharp
...
      static void Main() {
         HttpChannel channel = new HttpChannel(0);
         ChannelServices.RegisterChannel( channel, false );

         RemotingConfiguration.RegisterActivatedClientType(
            typeof(Adder),
            "http://localhost:65100");
         IAdder obj = (IAdder) new Adder();

         double d = obj.Add( 3.0, 4.0 );
         Console.WriteLine( "Returned value:" + d );
      }
...
```

Potential problems

Contrarily to the behavior of the COM/DCOM technology, the client is not responsible for the lifetime of an object that it activates. An unfortunate consequence is that a client may wish to use a remote object that he has activated but that does not exist anymore. In this case, an exception of type `System.Runtime.Remoting.RemotingException` is raised on the client-side. For this reason, the client code must always be ready for such exceptions.

The technique used by the server in order to mandate the lifetime of an object is presented a little later.

The factory design pattern and the soapsuds.exe tool

During the presentation of the Client Activated Object (CAO) technique, we have noticed that the client assembly needed to reference the assembly containing the class of the object. Let us remind you that this constraint was avoided in the WKO case since the client simply needed to know the interfaces it will interact with. However, if the class of the server object does not support interfaces, we would be forced to reference the assembly containing this class in the client assembly.

It is often unacceptable to deploy the assembly containing the implementation of the server object with the clients. This implementation often needs to remain as private as possible. In this assembly, the client only needs the type metadata for the class of the server object. There exists two solutions to this problem: the *factory design pattern* (Gof) or the `Soapsuds.exe` tool.

The factory design pattern

The idea behind the *factory design pattern* is to allow the construction of the CAO object by a WKO object. The host then only needs to expose the WKO service. As we have seen in this case, the client only needs to know of an interface and the problem is solved.

Let's modify the code presented to activate the object from the server. We must first present a new `IFactory` interface to the client:

Example 22-11 *Interface.cs*

```
namespace RemotingInterfaces {
   public interface IAdder {
      double Add( double d1, double d2 );
   }
   public interface IFactory {
      IAdder BuildANewAdder();
   }
}
```

Next, you must provide a `Factory` class which implements the `IFactory` interface and exposes a `Factory` object in singleton mode (it is better not to use the single-call mode in this case):

Example 22-12 *Server.cs*

```
...
   public class Adder : MarshalByRefObject, IAdder {
      public Adder() {
         Console.WriteLine( "Adder ctor" );
      }
      public double Add( double d1, double d2 ) {
         Console.WriteLine( "Adder Add( {0} + {1} )", d1, d2 );
         return d1 + d2;
      }
```

Example 22-12   *Server.cs*

```
   }
   public class Factory : MarshalByRefObject, IFactory {
      public IAdder BuildANewAdder() {
         return (IAdder)new Adder();
      }
   }
   class Program {
      static void Main() {
         HttpChannel channel = new HttpChannel( 65100 );
         ChannelServices.RegisterChannel( channel, false );
         RemotingConfiguration.RegisterWellKnownServiceType(
               typeof( Factory ),
               "FactoryService",
               WellKnownObjectMode.Singleton );
         Console.WriteLine( "Press a key to stop the server..." );
         Console.Read();
      }
   }
...
```

Finally, we can activate an instance of Adder from the client without knowing the Adder and Factory classes. This is exactly the goal of this approach:

Example 22-13   *Client.cs*

```
...
   class Program {
      static void Main() {
         HttpChannel channel = new HttpChannel( 0 );
         ChannelServices.RegisterChannel( channel, false );

         MarshalByRefObject tmpObj = (MarshalByRefObject)
               RemotingServices.Connect(
                     typeof( IFactory ),
                     "http://localhost:65100/FactoryService" );
         IFactory factory = tmpObj as IFactory;
         IAdder obj = factory.BuildANewAdder();

         double d = obj.Add( 3.0, 4.0 );
         Console.WriteLine( "Returned value:" + d );
      }
   }
...
```

The *design pattern* works because the Adder and Factory classes both inherit from the MarshalByRefObject class.

The soapsuds.exe tool

The Soapsuds.exe tool, provided with the .NET framework is capable of extracting the metadata of the server object class from the assembly containing this class. From this metadata, Soapsuds.exe can either construct a C# file which is ready to be compiled, or either an assembly which only contains the type metadata. Here is the command line to use in order to create an assembly named ObjectServerMetadataForClient.dll from the assembly named ObjServer.dll.

```
>soapsuds  /ia:ObjServer  /oa:ObjectServerMetadataForClient.dll
```

Here is the command line to use in order to create a C# source file named `ObjServer.cs` from this `ObjServer.dll` assembly.

```
>soapsuds  /ia:ObjServer  /gc
```

Here is an excerpt from the `ObjServer.cs` C# source file:

ObjServer.cs
```
...
public class Adder : System.Runtime.Remoting.Services.RemotingClientProxy,
                    IAdder {
   // Constructor
   public Adder() { }
   public Object RemotingReference { get { return (_tp); } }
   [SoapMethod(SoapAction = @"http://schemas.microsoft.com/clr/nsassem/
                             RemotingInterfaces.Adder/Interface#Add")]
   public virtual double Add( double d1, double d2 ) {
      return ((Adder)_tp).Add( d1, d2 );
   }
}
...
```

We in fact have a new class `Adder` presenting the same public method as the original and which derives from the `System.Runtime.Remoting.Services.RemotingClientProxy` class. We recommend that you consult the documentation relative to this class in *MSDN*, as you can use it in order to have a client authentication mechanism or to specify which proxy server to use if the client is behind a *firewall*. You can however indicate to `Soapsuds.exe` that you do not wish for the classes to derive from `RemotingClientProxy` by specifying the `/nowp` option. In this case, they will directly derive from `MarshalByRefObject`.

The `Soapsuds.exe` tool also allows you to construct the assembly containing the metadata of the server classes from a remote server which exposes an instance of this class via an HTTP channel. Here is the code of the server:

```
...
class Program {
   static void Main() {
      HttpChannel channel = new HttpChannel( 65100 );
      ChannelServices.RegisterChannel( channel, false );
      RemotingConfiguration.RegisterWellKnownServiceType(
            typeof(Adder),
            "MyDir/AddService.soap",
            WellKnownObjectMode.SingleCall);
      ...
   }
}
...
```

Here is the command line to use on the client-side:

```
>Soapsuds  /url:http://localhost:65100/MyDir/AddService.soap?wsdl
 /oa:ObjectServerMetadataForClient.dll
```

Note the `soap` extension associated to the endpoint and the use of the `?wsdl` suffix on the URL which allows to indicate to the server what we expect from him (i.e to obtain the type metadata).

Let us finally mention that the `soapsuds.exe` tool does not take into account of constructors with arguments. Therefore, the use of the *factory design pattern* is better suited to classes which must be initialized using constructors with arguments.

Life cycle of Well-Know and Client Activated Objects

The question of the lifetime of a WKO in single-call mode is pointless since the object is destroyed immediately after the first call. We will present the solution put in place by .NET Remoting to determine when an object activated by a remote entity must be destroyed. This solution rests on a mechanism of *lease*. It is important to note that this solution concerns both the CAO and the WKO objects in singleton mode. It is also important to note that all that we will explain here only applies to objects which derive from the `MarshalByRefObject` class and which are accessed by an entity from outside their AppDomain. Remember that objects which do not fall in this category have their lifetime managed by the garbage collector.

In an AppDomain, there does not exist a strong reference to an object which is accessed by an entity located outside of its AppDomain. To prevent the garbage collector from collecting such an object, the CLR makes it so that each AppDomain contains a *lease manager*. The lease manager allocates a lifetime at the moment of the activation of each MBR object used in a remote manner. The lease manage periodically checks the lease on each of these objects. The objects whose lease has expired will be automatically destroyed during the following collection by the garbage collector.

However, .NET Remoting makes this lease mechanism relatively flexible. Concretely, the duration of the lease of an object can be extended in three different ways:

- The length of the lease is automatically extended at each call to the object;
- The length of the lease can be extended directly through a call to a certain method;
- Finally, when the lease manager detects that a lease has expired, it sequentially consults the sponsors of the concerned object before making the decision to destroy it. Sponsors are objects which have the possibility of extending the lease of an object which is about to be destroyed. The class of a sponsor must derive from `MarshalByRefObject`. Sponsors can be remote objects. If the consultation of a sponsor exceeds a certain length, it will not be consulted anymore and the lease manager will move on to consult the next sponsor.

The `System.Runtime.Remoting.Lifetime` namespace contains the two interfaces named `ILease` and `ISponsor`, specially designed for the management of the mechanisms that we have just described:

```
interface System.Runtime.Remoting.Lifetime.ILease{
   // The LeaseState enumeration has values :
   //   Null       Not intialized.
   //   Initial    Currently initialized.
   //   Active     Initialized and valid.
   //   Renewing   Not valid anymore and sponsors are currently consulted.
   //   Expired    Expired.
   LeaseState   CurrentState{ get; }

   // Initial lease duration.
   // This property can be set only during lease initialization.
   TimeSpan     InitialLeaseTime{ get; set; }

   // The duration by witch a call to a remote object renews
   // the current lease time.
   TimeSpan     RenewOnCallTime{ get; set; }

   TimeSpan     CurrentLeaseTime{ get; }

   // Renew the current lease time.
   TimeSpan     Renew( TimeSpan );

   // Methods to manage sponsors of the object.
```

```
    void      Register( ISponsor );
    void      Register( ISponsor, TimeSpan );
    void      UnRegister( ISponsor ) ;

    // Maximum amount of time to wait for a sponsor to return
    // its renewal time.
    TimeSpan  SponsorshipTimeout{ get; set; }
}

interface System.Runtime.Remoting.Lifetime.ISponsor{
   Timespan Renewal(ILease);
}
```

As you can see, the use of these interfaces is intuitive. You can obtain the lease of an object by calling the `object MarshalByRefObject.GetLifetimeService()` method on the object, or by calling the `object RemotingServices.GetLifetimeService(object)` static method. For example:

```
...
ILease lease = (ILease) obj.GetLifetimeService();
lease.Renew( TimeSpan.FromSeconds(30) );
...
```

The implementation of the lease is the internal `Lease` class in `mscorlib.dll`. You do not have access to this class.

The three parameters of a lease on an object are the initial length of the lease, the extension length of the lease when a method of the object is called and the maximum wait time for the consultation of a sponsor. For a given object, these three parameters take their default values in the machine configuration file. The default durations are respectively 5 minutes, 2 minutes and 2 minutes. The static properties of the `System.Runtime.Remoting.Lifetime.LifetimeServices` class allow the configuration of these default values at the level of the current AppDomain. To set these values at the level of the instances of a class, you must override the `object MarshalByRefObject.GetLifetimeService()` virtual method. For example:

Example 22-14

```
...
using System.Runtime.Remoting.Lifetime;
...
   public class Adder : MarshalByRefObject, IAdder {
      public override object InitializeLifetimeService() {
         ILease lease = (ILease) base.InitializeLifetimeService();
         if ( lease.CurrentState == LeaseState.Initial ) {
            lease.InitialLeaseTime    = TimeSpan.FromSeconds( 50 );
            lease.RenewOnCallTime     = TimeSpan.FromSeconds( 20 );
            lease.SponsorshipTimeout  = TimeSpan.FromSeconds( 20 );
         }
         return lease;
      }
   ...
}
...
```

You have the possibility of specifying a lease of an infinite length by assigning the `TimeSpan.Zero` value to the `InitialLeaseTime` property of a lease.

You can define your own sponsor class. Let us remind you that such a class must derive from `MarshalByRefObject` and implement the `ISponsor` interface. The usefulness of a sponsor class appears during the specification of a distributed architecture, when the lifetime of an object logically depends on a condition. The most common condition is that certain client are always active You then simply need to have a sponsor for each client, which extends the lease as long as the client associated to the sponsor needs it. However, beware of this type of *ping* mechanism. The DCOM technology uses this type of mechanism and experience has proven that it is not acceptable as soon as the number of clients exceed a certain threshold based on the application.

Configuring .NET Remoting

The examples provided to expose the remote object activation mechanisms suffer from one major problem: they are not configurable. In other words, once compiled, we cannot change the port number or the name of the server machine. We will now show how to make it so that configuration parameters be readable and modifiable, as well on the server side as client side. As you might have guessed, these parameters will be specified in an XML document. To illustrate these configuration features, we will use three classes defined in a new assembly:

Example 22-15 *ObjServer.cs*

```
using System;

namespace RemotingObjServer {
   public interface IAdder {
      double Add(double d1, double d2);
   }
   public class Adder : MarshalByRefObject, IAdder {
      public Adder() {
         Console.WriteLine( "Adder ctor" );
      }
      public double Add( double d1, double d2 ) {
         Console.WriteLine("Adder Add( {0} + {1} )", d1, d2 );
         return d1 + d2;
      }
   }
   public interface IMultiplier {
      double Mult( double d1, double d2 );
   }
   public class Multiplier : MarshalByRefObject, IMultiplier {
      public Multiplier() {
         Console.WriteLine( "Multiplier ctor" );
      }
      public double Mult( double d1, double d2 ) {
         Console.WriteLine( "Multiplier Mult( {0} + {1} )", d1, d2 );
         return d1 * d2;
      }
   }
   public interface IDivider {
      double Div( double d1, double d2 );
   }
   public class Divider : MarshalByRefObject, IDivider {
      public Divider() {
         Console.WriteLine( "Divider ctor" );
      }
      public double Div( double d1, double d2 ) {
         Console.WriteLine( "Divider Div( {0} + {1} )", d1, d2 );
         return d1 + d2;
      }
   }
}
```

Configuring a host

The following XML document allows you to expose the `Adder` class in singleton WKO mode and the `Multiplier` class in single-call WKO mode. In parallel, the `Divider` class is exposed in order to be activated by remote objects. These three objects are exposed using an HTTP channel, accessible via port 65100. The `ref` attribute could have been set to one of the `tcp` or `ipc` values if you wish to use a TCP or IPC channel. In the case of IPC, we would not need to provide a port number.

Each exposed type must be prefixed with its namespace. In addition, this class name must be followed by the name of the assembly in which it is defined. If this assembly has a strong name, you must use its complete strong name:

Example 22-16   *Host.config*

```xml
<configuration>
   <system.runtime.remoting>
      <application name = "Server">
         <service>
            <wellknown type="RemotingObjServer.Adder,ObjServer"
                       mode ="Singleton" objectUri="Service1.rem" />
            <wellknown type="RemotingObjServer.Multiplier,ObjServer"

                       mode ="SingleCall" objectUri="Service2.rem" />
            <activated type="RemotingObjServer.Divider,ObjServer" />
         </service>
         <channels>
            <channel port="65100" ref="http" />
         </channels>
      </application>
   </system.runtime.remoting>
</configuration>
```

Thanks to the `void RemotingConfiguration.Configure(string)` static method which takes as a parameter the name of the XML document, the code of the host is truly reduced to its minimum:

Example 22-17   *Server.cs*

```csharp
...
   class Program {
      static void Main() {
         RemotingConfiguration.Configure( "Host.config", false );
         Console.WriteLine( "Press a key to stop the server..." );
         Console.Read();
      }
   }
...
```

Configuring a client

The following XML document allows using the two WKO services and the class exposed by the previous server:

Example 22-18   *Client.config*

```xml
<configuration>
   <system.runtime.remoting>
      <application name = "Client">
         <client>
            <wellknown type="RemotingObjServer.Adder,ObjServer"
```

Example 22-18 *Client.config*
```
                       url="http://localhost:65100/Service1.rem" />
            <wellknown type="RemotingObjServer.Multiplier,ObjServer"
                       url="http://localhost:65100/Service2.rem" />
        </client>
        <client url="http://localhost:65100/">
            <activated type ="RemotingObjServer.Divider,ObjServer"/>
        </client>
     </application>
  </system.runtime.remoting>
</configuration>
```

The specified URLs start with the `http://` access mode but they could have started with `tcp://` or `ipc://` if our receiving channel was TCP or IPC. In the case of an IPC channel, you would have to replace the host/port portion of the machine name (`localhost:65100` in this case) by the name of the underlying named pipe. This name is provided by the `portName` attribute in the channel declaration in the server configuration file.

To load the parameters from this XML file into the AppDomain of the client, we also use the `void RemotingConfiguration.Configure(string)` static method:

Example 22-19
```
...
using RemotingObjServer;
...
   class Program {
       static void Main() {
           RemotingConfiguration.Configure("Client.config", false);

           Adder objA = new Adder();
           double dA = objA.Add( 3.0, 4.0 );

           Multiplier objM = new Multiplier();
           double dM = objM.Mult( 3.0, 4.0 );

           Divider objD = new Divider();
           double dD = objD.Div( 3.0, 4.0 );
       }
   }
...
```

The calls to the constructors of the WKO objects (`objA` and `objM`) are only there to retrieve a reference (actually a transparent proxy) towards the proper type. Concretely, the do not cause any network accesses.

From a server configuration file, you can also configure the parameters of the lease manager. More information on this topic can be found in the article named **<lifetime> Element** on **MSDN**.

From the start, we cannot use interfaces since we are required to call the constructor. The *factory design pattern* cannot be applied since even in the case of the server activation, the client cannot only use an interface. You must then use the **Soapsuds.exe** tool to avoid from having to provide the assemblies containing the implementation of the server objects to the clients. However, we are about to show a trick which allows the use of interfaces in WKO mode, and thus in CAO mode using the *factory design pattern*.

Using both interfaces and configuration files

First of all, let's place the interfaces in an assembly which will be referenced both by the client and the server:

Example 22-20   *Interface.cs*

```
namespace RemotingInterfaces {
   public interface IAdder {
      double Add( double d1, double d2 );
   }
   public interface IMultiplier {
      double Mult( double d1, double d2 );
   }
   public interface IDivider {
      double Div( double d1, double d2 );
   }
   public interface IFactory {
      IAdder      BuildNewAdder();
      IMultiplier BuildNewMultiplier();
      IDivider    BuildNewDivider();
   }
}
```

Next, the trick rests on the use of a table which associates the WKO services configured by the server to the interfaces configured on the client. Here is the code of the client, who manages the table named `dicoTypes`:

Example 22-21   *Client.cs*

```
using System;
using System.Runtime.Remoting;
using System.Runtime.Remoting.Channels;
using System.Runtime.Remoting.Channels.Http;
using System.Runtime.Remoting.Activation;
using System.Collections;

using RemotingInterfaces;

namespace RemotingClient {
   class CustomActivator {
      private static bool bInit;
      // Associating interfaces with services distants WKO.
      private static IDictionary dicoTypes;

      public static Object GetObject( Type type ) {
         if ( !bInit )
            InitdicoTypes();
         WellKnownClientTypeEntry entry = (WellKnownClientTypeEntry)
                                          dicoTypes[type];
         return Activator.GetObject( entry.ObjectType, entry.ObjectUrl );
      }

      private static void InitdicoTypes() {
         bInit = true;
         dicoTypes = new Hashtable();
         foreach ( WellKnownClientTypeEntry entry in
            RemotingConfiguration.GetRegisteredWellKnownClientTypes() )
               dicoTypes.Add( entry.ObjectType, entry );
```

Example 22-21   *Client.cs*

```
      }
   }

   class Program {
      static void Main() {
         RemotingConfiguration.Configure( "Client.config", false );

         IAdder objA = (IAdder)CustomActivator.GetObject( typeof(IAdder) );
         double dA = objA.Add( 3.0, 4.0 );

         IMultiplier objM = (IMultiplier)
            CustomActivator.GetObject( typeof( IMultiplier ) );
         double dM = objM.Mult( 3.0, 4.0 );

         // Factory design pattern for a Client Activated Object.
         IFactory factory = (IFactory)
            CustomActivator.GetObject( typeof( IFactory ) );
         IDivider objD = factory.BuildNewDivider();
         double dD = objD.Div( 3.0, 4.0 );
      }
   }
}
```

The configuration file of the client will look like this:

Example 22-22   *Client.config*

```
<configuration>
   <system.runtime.remoting>
      <application name = "Client">
         <client>
            <wellknown type="RemotingInterfaces.IAdder,Interface"
                       url="http://localhost:65100/Service1.rem" />
            <wellknown type="RemotingInterfaces.IMultiplier,Interface"
                       url="http://localhost:65100/Service2.rem" />
            <wellknown type="RemotingInterfaces.IFactory,Interface"
                       url="http://localhost:65100/Service3.rem" />
         </client>
      </application>
   </system.runtime.remoting>
</configuration>
```

Understand that the interface/WKO service association table is explicitly described by this configuration file. The content is retrieved in the client code using the `RemotingConfiguration.GetRegisteredWellKnownClientTypes()` method.

The configuration file for the server presents three WKO services. Let us remind you that the third service is there to allow the use of CAO object by the mean of the *factory design pattern*:

Example 22-23   *Host.config*

```
<configuration>
   <system.runtime.remoting>
      <application name = "Server">
         <service>
            <wellknown type="RemotingServer.Adder,Server"
                       mode ="Singleton" objectUri="Service1.rem" />
```

Example 22-23   *Host.config*

```xml
            <wellknown type="RemotingServer.Multiplier,Server"

                      mode ="SingleCall" objectUri="Service2.rem" />
            <wellknown type="RemotingServer.Factory,Server"
                      mode ="SingleCall" objectUri="Service3.rem" />
        </service>
        <channels>
            <channel port="65100" ref ="http" />
        </channels>
      </application>
   </system.runtime.remoting>
</configuration>
```

Of course, the `Adder`, `Multiplier`, `Factory`, `Divider` classes can now be placed in the server code:

Example 22-24   *Server.cs*

```csharp
using System;
using System.Runtime.Remoting;
using System.Runtime.Remoting.Channels;
using System.Runtime.Remoting.Channels.Http;

using RemotingInterfaces;

namespace RemotingServer{
   public class Adder : MarshalByRefObject, IAdder { ... }
   public class Multiplier : MarshalByRefObject, IMultiplier { ... }
   public class Divider : MarshalByRefObject, IDivider { ... }
   public class Factory : MarshalByRefObject, IFactory {
      public IAdder BuildNewAdder() { return new Adder(); }
      public IMultiplier BuildNewMultiplier() { return new Multiplier(); }
      public IDivider BuildNewDivider() { return new Divider(); }
   }
   class Program {
      static void Main() {
         HttpChannel channel = new HttpChannel( 65100 );
         ChannelServices.RegisterChannel( channel, false );
         RemotingConfiguration.RegisterWellKnownServiceType(
               typeof(Factory),
               "FactoryService",
               WellKnownObjectMode.Singleton );
         Console.WriteLine( "Press a key to stop the server..." );
         Console.Read();
      }
   }
}
```

Deployment of a .NET Remoting server

During the deployment of a distributed application based on .NET Remoting, it is strongly recommended to provide at least one configuration file for each component. You then dispose of a standard way of configuring the application without having to recompile any assemblies.

Versioning problems of the server object classes can also be managed in these configuration files. In fact, when you specify a type in a `<type>` XML attribute, you can specify the strong name of its assembly. Hence, this strong name can contain the version number of the assembly.

All the hosts of this chapter are executable in console mode. In real world, we prefer using either a *Windows service* or ASP.NET to host our server objects.

Windows services

The main advantage of a *Windows* service compared to a console application resides in the fact that it is not necessary for a user to be logged onto the machine in order to execute the application hosted by the *Windows* service. Another advantage of a service is that manipulation of a service being executed can be done directly through a UI which provides the *start / stop / pause / resume / restart* commands. Another argument in favor of this approach is the fact that a service can be automatically executed after a *reboot* of the machine. We will not go into details within this book on how to create a service. Know that with the classes contained in the `System.ServiceProcess` namespace, this task is greatly simplified compared to the use of the specialized win32 functions. All this is described on **MSDN** in the article named **System.ServiceProcess Namespace**.

IIS

The use of IIS constitutes another alternative to the use of the console mode or of a *Windows* service to host your server objects. The main advantages of this choice are the following:

- You have access to the security management of IIS. Also, if your IIS server support SSL certificates, you can take advantage of data encryption services. You can also take advantage of the *Windows* authentication mechanism.

- The use of IIS relieves you of the responsibility of writing a host. Concretely, you simply need to develop your classes deriving from `MarshalByRefObject` and to provide a configuration file.

- Versioning problems are also taken into account by IIS. It will detect when you install a new version and will take care of the transition to the new version. Installing a new version simply involves replacing an assembly and a configuration file with newer ones without having to stop IIS. IIS does not block the write access to these files when they are used, as internally, IIS works with *shadow copies* of these files.

However, all these operations do come with a cost, and the principal problem of IIS is that it has a significant impact on performance. Also know that you cannot use the TCP or IPC channels when using IIS. To use IIS two steps are necessary:

1. Under `mmc` (the generic administration console of *Windows*), with the IIS snap-in, create a new *IIS virtual directory*. Let us mention that an IIS virtual directory allows to make it so that a folder on the machine be accessible from an URL. In this folder, you must place your configuration file. This file must be called `Web.Config`.

2. Create a new `bin` sub-folder in the folder created in the first step. Place the assemblies containing the classes of your server objects in this folder. Another option is to place your assemblies in the GAC folder. For this, your assemblies must have a strong name.

When you use this type of deployment, the `<application>` element of the configuration file must not have a `Name` attribute. In addition, you must not specify a port in your configuration file to avoid interfering with the port management of IIS.

Securing a .NET Remoting channel

Securing a TCP channel

If you use a TCP channel, you have the possibility of using the NTLM and Kerberos protocols in order to authenticate the *Windows* user under which the client executes and to encrypt the exchanged data. To provide this feature, the TCP channel internally uses the `NegociatedStream` class which uses the services of the win32 API relating to these protocols which is known as SSPI. These protocols as well as this class are described at page 546.

To use this feature, you simply need to set the `secure` attribute of the TCP channel to `true` in the configuration file of the client and of the server:

```
<configuration>
   <system.runtime.remoting>
      <application name = "XXX">
         <channels>
            <channel port="65100" ref="tcp" secure="true"/>
         </channels>
...
```

You can also set the value of the `secure` attribute to `true` programmatically thanks to the property list of a channel:

Example 22-25 *Client.cs*

```
...
      static void Main() {
         IDictionary properties = new Hashtable();
         properties.Add( "secure", true );
         TcpChannel channel = new TcpChannel( properties,null,null );
         ChannelServices.RegisterChannel( channel, true );
...
```

You can also set on the server side the `tokenImpersonationLevel` attribute of a TCP channel to the `Impersonation` value if you wish for the client request executes itself on the server-side with the account of the client user.

Securing an HTTP channel

If you wish to secure the data exchanged when you are using the HTTP protocol, two solutions are possible:

- Hosting the server with IIS and using the SSL protocol (thus HTTPS) at the IIS level.
- Create your own secure HTTP channel.

Proxy and message

The goal of this section is the closely analyze transparent proxies and to present the notions of real proxies and of message interceptors. Let's resume what we have already exposed in regards to transparent proxies:

- A transparent proxy is an instance of a class defined as internal in the `mscorlib.dll` assembly. Therefore, this class cannot be directly accessed.
- A transparent proxy is automatically created by the CLR to reference a remote object whose class derives from `MarshalByRefObjectet`.

- In an assembly, the internal management of the reference to an object varies depending on whether the assembly is loaded in the same AppDomain as the object or not. In the case where the assembly and the object are remote, we have a reference to a transparent proxy. In the case where they are in the same AppDomain, we have a direct reference to the object. We have seen that the `bool RemotingServices.IsTransparentProxy(object)` static method allows knowing if a reference to an object is a transparent proxy or a direct reference.

- The type metadata by which we manipulate the remote object must be loaded in the AppDomain, when the CLR builds the transparent proxy to a remote object. We have seen several ways to retrieve this metadata.

Transforming a method call to a message

As shows Figure 22-4, a call to a classic method can be seen as a transformation of the stack of the thread which triggers the call.

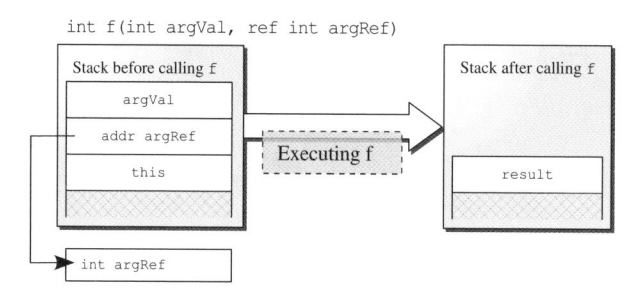

Figure 22-4: Method call = transforming the stack

This transformation is done in two steps: before the execution of the method, the CLR unstacks the arguments in order to make them local variables to the method, and after the execution, the CLR stacks the return value.

During a call to a method of a remote object, located in another AppDomain (even in another process), it is impossible to use this stack based argument passing technique. In fact, the thread which calls the method can be different than the thread which executes it. The arguments are passed using a message exchange technique, one during the call to the method (containing the information consumed by the method) and one at the end of its execution (containing the information produced by the method).

The role of a transparent proxy is to manage on the client-side the transition between the stack base parameter passing mode and the message-based parameter passing mode. An internal object to the CLR, named the *stack builder sink* completes the reverse operation on the server-side. All this is illustrated by Example 22-4.

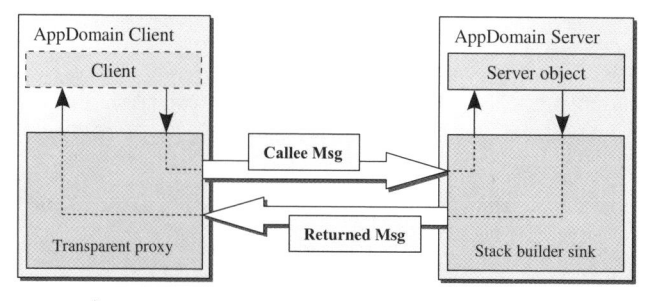

Figure 22-5: Transparent proxy and stack builder sink

The IMessage interface hierarchy

We will see in the next section that you can intercept, at different levels, the messages which are exchanged between the transparent proxy and the stack builder sink. We will notice that these messages are in fact .NET objects. Let's focus on the interfaces which allow the manipulation of these messages. Here is their hierarchy:

```
System.Runtime.Remoting.Messaging.IMessage
    System.Runtime.Remoting.Messaging.IMethodMessage
        System.Runtime.Remoting.Messaging.IMethodCallMessage
            System.Runtime.Remoting.Activation.IConstructionCallMessage
        System.Runtime.Remoting.Messaging.IMethodReturnMessage
            System.Runtime.Remoting.Activation.IConstructionReturnMessage
```

Here is the description of the `IMessage` and `IMethodMessage` interfaces:

```
using System.Runtime.Remoting.Messaging;
using System.Collections;
public interface IMessage {
   IDictionary Properties { get; }
}
public interface IMethodMessage : IMessage {
   object              GetArg( int index );
   string              GetArgName( int index );
   int                 ArgCount { get; }
   object[]            Args { get; }
   bool                HasVarArgs { get; }
   string              MethodName { get; }
   object              MethodSignature { get; }
   string              TypeName { get; }
   string              Uri { get; }
   LogicalCallContext  LogicalCallContext { get; }
   MethodBase          MethodBase { get; }
}
```

The `IMethodCallMessage` interface essentially allows the traversal of the data contained in a message constructed by a transparent proxy. The `IMethodReturnMessage` allows the traversal of the data contained in a message created by the stack builder sink.

Transparent proxy, real proxy and the ObjRef class

To not complicate our expose we have hidden so far the existence of *real proxies*. A real proxy is an object, instance of the `System.Runtime.Remoting.Proxies.RealProxy` class (or a class derived from it). For each transparent proxy object corresponds one and only one real proxy object. The transparent proxy and the real proxy share the work during a call on a remote object. As we have seen, the transparent proxy manages the transition from the *passing arguments on the stack* mode to the *passing arguments using messages* mode. The task of a real proxy is to find the proper channel to send the message created by the transparent proxy, and to send it. Another task of the real proxy is to recover from the channel the message representing the return from the method call and to transfer this return message to the transparent proxy. Contrarily to transparent proxies, you can create your own real proxy classes, as we will see a little later.

Type and real proxy

Another responsibility of a real proxy is to know the type of the remote object. The constructor of a real proxy takes as an argument a type. This type must be an interface or a class deriving from `MarshalByRefObject`; otherwise the constructor of the real proxy will raise an exception. The `Type GetProxiedType()` method is automatically called by the CLR on a real proxy, when the user casts what he thinks is a reference, but is in fact a transparent proxy.

Creating a pair transparent proxy/real proxy and the ObjRef class

In a transparent/real proxy pair, it is always the real proxy which is created first. The transparent proxy is then created by the CLR either from an instance of the `System.Runtime.Remoting.ObjRef` class, either from the locating information for a remote object. This information can contain, for example, the URI of an object activation service. Instances of the `ObjRef` class are MBV and can thus exchange information between AppDomain boundaries. An instance of `ObjRef` contains the information necessary to a real proxy to reference a remote object. This information is: the type of the remote object, the information to locate this remote object, the type of channel to use to contact the remote object and information used internally by the CLR. An instance of the `ObjRef` class referencing a remote object can be obtained in several ways.

In the case of an object activated by the client, an instance of the `ObjRef` class is effectively obtained by the client when it activates the object. This behavior concerns the use of the new keyword, the use of the `AppDomain.CreateInstance()` method or the use of the `Activator.CreateInstance()` method. We have talked at the beginning of this chapter of the `ObjectHandle` class whose instances allow wrapping an MBV object or a MBR reference. We can now specify that you can obtain this reference by calling the `ObjRef ObjectHandle.CreateObjRef(Type)` method.

In the case of a WKO object, the client does not need an instance of `ObjRef` initialized by the server. This is logical since only the knowledge of the URI of the activation service is sufficient for the client to access the service. A consequence is that, contrarily to what we may think, a call to one of the `Activator.GetObjet()` or `RemotingServices.Connect()` methods does not provoke a message to be sent over the network. In addition to optimizing the use of the network, the behavior allows the server not to have to create objects until there is a call from the client. This situation concerns both objects activated in singleton mode and in single-call mode. Understand that the implementation of this mechanism allows saving a round-trip on the network, compared to the client object activation mechanism.

Finally, know that an instance of the `ObjRef` class is returned by the server AppDomain for each return value which is a reference type and for each return parameter of a reference type. Of course, the reference type of these arguments must be either interfaces or classes deriving from `MarshalByRefObject`.

Publishing an object by using the ObjRef class

An instance of the `ObjRef` class contains all the necessary information to locate and identify a remote object. We can infer from this that by serializing such an instance to a file, we have a reference to an object. The idea is to make this file available to a client, for example, by sending an email. By deserializing the instance of the `ObjRef` class, the client now has a reference to the remote object and can use it. This practice is called *publishing an object*. Thanks to certain methods of .NET Remoting, publishing an object is an easy task to accomplish.

Here is the code of the server which serializes the reference of an object in the file named *Adder.txt*. Note that the class of the object must derive from `MarshalByRefObject`:

Example 22-26   *Serveur.cs*

```
    ...
        static void Main() {
            HttpChannel channel = new HttpChannel( 65100 );
            ChannelServices.RegisterChannel( channel, false );

            CAdditionneur obj = new CAdditionneur();
            ObjRef objRef = RemotingServices.Marshal( obj );
            FileStream fStream = new FileStream("Adder.txt", FileMode.Create);
```

Example 22-26 *Serveur.cs*
```
        SoapFormatter soapFormatter = new SoapFormatter();
        soapFormatter.Serialize( fStream, objRef );
        fStream.Close();

        Console.WriteLine( "Press a key to stop the server..." );
        Console.Read();
    }
...
```

Here is the code of the client which deserializes the reference to the remote object from the *Adder.txt* file:

Example 22-27 *Client.cs*
```
using System.IO;
using System.Runtime.Serialization.Formatters.Soap;
...
    static void Main() {
        HttpChannel channel = new HttpChannel( 0 );
        ChannelServices.RegisterChannel( channel, false );

        FileStream fStream = new FileStream( "Adder.txt",FileMode.Open );
        SoapFormatter soapFormatter = new SoapFormatter();
        IAdder obj = soapFormatter.Deserialize( fStream ) as IAdder;

        double d = obj.Add( 3.0, 4.0 );
    }
...
```

This example allows us to verify that .NET Remoting assigns a unique identity to each instance of a subclass of `MarshalByRefObject`. In other words, each remote object has a unique URI, based on a *GUID* (*Global Unique Identity*). Such an URI looks like this:

/6b03659f_0164_43e2_99cf_f36eda31adae/367459709_1.rem

When the published object is destroyed, the file which references it is of no use. This URI is communicated to the client only if the object is activated by the client or published by the server. In other words, this URI is not communicated to the client in the case of a WKO object.

The object publishing technique is then an intermediate solution between the activation of a remote object by the client (CAO) and the activation service of a remote object by the server (WKO). The object is effectively activated by the server but the client takes into account the identity of the object. We will summarize the differences of these four activation modes at the end of this chapter.

The object publishing file is built with about thirty lines of XML code which can be difficult to read. Here are a few relevant extracts:

Adder.txt
```
...
<uri id="ref-2">/6b03659f_0164_43e2_99cf_f36eda31adae/367459709_1.rem</uri>
...
<serverType id="ref-5">RemotingServer.Adder, Server,
 Version=1.0.1140.28752, Culture=neutral, PublicKeyToken=null</serverType>
...
<item id="ref-8">RemotingInterfaces.IAdder, Interface,
 Version=1.0.1138.27103, Culture=neutral, PublicKeyToken=null</item>
...
```

Adder.txt

```
<a3:CrossAppDomainData id="ref-9" xmlns:a3=
 "http://schemas.microsoft.com/clr/ns/System.Runtime.Remoting.Channels">
<_ContextID>1362648</_ContextID>
<_DomainID>1</_DomainID>
<_processGuid id="ref11">faf88595_9b2e_4f23_99ee_1d006915a98</_processGuid>
</a3:CrossAppDomainData>
...
<item id="ref-13">http://213.26.48.1:65100</item>
...
```

Message sink

To summarize, with .NET Remoting, a call to a method is done through an exchange of two messages, one which contains the information which will be consumed by the execution of the method and one which contains the information produced by the execution of the method. Each of these two messages go through some processing between the real proxy, located in the client AppDomain and the stack builder sink, located in the server AppDomain. For example, the message containing the input parameters to a method is serialized on the client-side and then deserialized on the server side. This processing is done by an object called a *message sink*. Concretely, a message sink is an instance of the class which implements the `System.Runtime.Remoting.Messaging.IMessageSink` interface and is tagged with the `Serializable` attribute:

```
public interface System.Runtime.Remoting.Messaging.IMessageSink {
  IMessageSink NextSink{get;}
  IMessage     SyncProcessMessage(IMessage request);
  IMessageCtrl AsyncProcessMessage(IMessage request,IMessageSin replySink);
}
```

Thanks to the `NextSink` property, message sinks can be chained together. As you may have guessed, the processing of a message of a synchronous call is done in the `SyncProcessMessage()` method while the processing of a message representing an asynchronous call is done in the `AsyncProcessMessage()` method. Here is an implementation where we indicate where you can place your processing code:

> You must always tag your message sink classes with the `Serializable` attribute.

```
[Serializable]
public class MonMsgSink : IMessageSink{
   private IMessageSink m_NextSink;
   public  IMessageSink NextSink{ get { return m_NextSink; } }
   public  MonMsgSink( IMessageSink nextSink ) { m_NextSink = nextSink; }

   IMessage SyncProcessMessage( IMessage msgIn ) {
      // Here, you can work on msgIn.
      IMessage msgOut = m_NextSink.SyncProcessMessage( msgIn ) ;
      // Here, you can work on msgOut.
      return msgOut;
   }
   IMessageCtrl AsyncProcessMessage(IMessage msgIn,IMessageSink replySink){
      // Here, you can work with msgIn.
      // You can also add a message sink.
      IMessageCtrl msgCtrl=m_NextSink.AsyncProcessMessage(msgIn,replySink);
      // Here, you can indicate to the CLR that it doesn't need to
      // wait more than 1 second for the asynchronous call return
```

```
        // with the line: 'msgCtrl.Cancel(1000);'
        return msgCtrl;
    }
}
```

Notice that the `SyncProcessMessage()` method can process the input and output messages while the `AsyncProcessMessage()` only deals with the input message. However, the `AsyncProcessMessage()` method has the possibility of participating in the construction of a message sink chain which will be used to process the return information of a method call. Naturally, this processing will chain itself in the reverse order from which they were initially chained.

You now know how to create message sinks. We will explain later in this chapter, how to inject your own message sinks in the message chain for a method call, and more importantly which type of advantages you can draw from doing so. But before, we will present an implementation of a custom real proxy. We will then have access to the first message sink of the message chain for a synchronous method call.

Why considering custom real proxy?

Before showing examples of how you can create your own custom real proxies, it is useful to give a few examples of how you can use a custom real proxy.

You may use a custom proxy simply to track the calls to a remote object.

You can use a custom proxy to avoid certain remote calls, which can be executed locally. You can then implement an information caching system. When information is requested from a remote object, the custom proxy first verifies if this information cannot be found locally.

You can use a custom proxy to modify the parameters to a method call in a transparent way. For example, you can translate strings passed as parameters to a method from one language to another.

You can use a custom proxy to allow the casting of a transparent proxy into a type which is not necessary the type held by the real proxy. We will not go into the details of this feature, but know that to achieve this, your custom real proxy class must implement the `System.Runtime.Remoting.IRemotingTypeInfo` interface. The description of this interface in **MSDN** should give you a good idea about how to use it.

You can also use a custom proxy to implement a *load balancing* mechanism between server machines. You simply need to regularly obtain the load of each server and to route the calls to a remote object towards the server who has the lowest load. You can also take into account the processing power of each server during the evaluation of its load. We also recommend trying randomly routing requests to various servers with a probability distribution proportional to the amount of work each server can do. This approach generally gives results equivalent to applying an algorithm which is based on the current load of each server. Let us specify that load balancing between several servers can only be done when you work with stateless remote WKO objects.

Developping a custom real proxy

It is easy to implement a custom real proxy class. You simply need to create a subclass of `RealProxy` and implements the `IMessage Invoke(IMessage)` method. This method is automatically called by the CLR during a synchronous call on the associated transparent proxy. The input message corresponds to the message created by the transparent proxy. The output message corresponds to the message representing the method return, which will be automatically passed to the transparent proxy. To transmit a synchronous call within the `Invoke()` method, you simply need to call the `IMessage.SyncProcessMessage(IMessage)` on the first message sink of the chain.

Here is an example of a custom real proxy class. In this example, the message sink that the `Invoke()` method uses is provided by the channel. However, we will see that there can be other message sinks wedged between the proxy and the channel. In the `Invoke()` method, we simply display the input parameters to the method and then the return value. Note that we place the URI of the server's object activation service in the input message. This step could be easily modified to implement a load balancing mechanism.

Example 22-28   *Client.cs*

```
using System;
using System.Runtime.Remoting;
using System.Runtime.Remoting.Channels;
using System.Runtime.Remoting.Channels.Http;
using System.Runtime.Remoting.Proxies;
using System.Runtime.Remoting.Messaging;
using System.Collections;
using RemotingInterfaces;
// You must use soapsuds.exe to le the client know
// about the 'Adder' class.
using RemotingServer;

public class CustomRealProxy : RealProxy {
   // URI for server acticvated object.
   String m_Uri;
   // References the first message sink of the HttpSender channel.
   IMessageSink m_MsgSink;

   public CustomRealProxy( Type type, String uri,
                    IChannelSender channelSender) : base(type) {
      m_Uri = uri;
      string unused;
      // Get the first message sink of 'channelSender'.
      m_MsgSink = channelSender.CreateMessageSink(m_Uri, null, out unused);
   }

   // This method is called by the CLR before any client call.
   public override IMessage Invoke( IMessage msgIn ) {
      // The URI of the remote object must be stored in msgIn.
      IDictionary d = msgIn.Properties;
      d["__Uri"] = m_Uri;

      // Display 'in parameters' stored in msgIn.
      IMethodCallMessage msgCall = (IMethodCallMessage) msgIn;
      Console.Write( "CustomRealProxy: Before calling:{0}(",
                  msgCall.MethodName );
      for ( int i = 0; i < msgCall.InArgCount; i++ )
         Console.Write(" {0}={1} ",msgCall.GetArgName(i),msgCall.GetArg(i));
      Console.WriteLine(")");

      // Perform the remote call !
      IMethodReturnMessage msgOut =
         (IMethodReturnMessage) m_MsgSink.SyncProcessMessage( msgIn );

      // Display the value returned in msgOut.
      Console.WriteLine( "CustomRealProxy: After calling:{0}() RetVal={1}",
                  msgCall.MethodName, msgOut.ReturnValue );
      return msgOut;
   }
}
```

Example 22-28   *Client.cs*

```
   }

namespace RemotingClient {
   class Program {
      static void Main() {
         HttpChannel channel = new HttpChannel( 0 );
         ChannelServices.RegisterChannel( channel, false );

         // Build a custom real proxy.
         // We initialize it with the object type, the URI of
         // the WKO service and the channel it should use.
         CustomRealProxy proxy = new CustomRealProxy(
            typeof(Adder),
            "http://localhost:65100/AddService",
            (IChannelSender) channel );
         IAdder obj = (IAdder) proxy.GetTransparentProxy();

         // Here, we haven't contacted yet the server.

         // This line triggers the first call to the server.
         double d = obj.Add(3.0, 4.0);
      }
   }
}
```

Here is the display from the client, when we use it with the adequate server:

```
CustomRealProxy: Before calling:Add( d1=3   d2=4 )
CustomRealProxy: After calling:Add() RetVal=7
```

Using a custom real proxy on all instances of a class

In the previous program, we have explicitly created the real proxy and have explicitly requested the transparent proxy. You can make it so that all instances of the Adder class each have a custom real proxy. In this case, an instance will have its own custom proxy even if it is created with the new operator and even it is used in a non-remote way. In fact, the technique that we will propose here is mostly used to obtain the benefits of such a custom real proxy on objects which are used in a non-remote way.

For this, the instances of our Adder class must derive from the System.ContextBoundObject class. We will explain the ContextBoundObject class a little later in this chapter. Then, you must define a .NET attribute class which derives from System.Runtime.Remoting.Proxies.ProxyAttribute. In this class, you will override the MarshalByRefObject ProxyAttribute.CreateInstance(Type t) virtual method in order for it to wedge a real proxy between the created object and its reference. Then, you must tag the Adder class with this attribute. Here is a program that illustrates all this:

Example 22-29

```
using System;
using System.Runtime.Remoting;
using System.Runtime.Remoting.Services;
using System.Runtime.Remoting.Messaging;
using System.Runtime.Remoting.Proxies;
using System.Runtime.Remoting.Activation;
```

Example 22-29

```csharp
public class CustomRealProxy : RealProxy {
    readonly bool m_bDisplay;
    readonly MarshalByRefObject m_TargetObj;

    public CustomRealProxy( MarshalByRefObject targetObj,
                            Type type, bool bDisplay ) : base(type) {
        m_bDisplay = bDisplay;
        m_TargetObj = targetObj;
    }

    public override IMessage Invoke( IMessage msgIn ) {
        IMessage msgOut;
        if ( msgIn is IConstructionCallMessage ) {
            IConstructionCallMessage ctorCallMsg =
                (IConstructionCallMessage) msgIn;

            // Get the default real proxy.
            RealProxy defaultRealProxy =
                RemotingServices.GetRealProxy( m_TargetObj );

            // Invoke the ctor on this real proxy
            defaultRealProxy.InitializeServerObject( ctorCallMsg );

            // Get the custom real proxy on the new object.
            msgOut=EnterpriseServicesHelper.CreateConstructionReturnMessage(
                ctorCallMsg, (MarshalByRefObject)GetTransparentProxy() );

            if ( m_bDisplay )
                Console.WriteLine( "CustomRealProxy: ctor call" );
        }
        else {
            IMethodCallMessage callMsg = (IMethodCallMessage) msgIn;

            if ( m_bDisplay )
                Console.WriteLine( "CustomRealProxy: Before calling:{0}",
                                   callMsg.MethodName );

            msgOut = RemotingServices.ExecuteMessage( m_TargetObj, callMsg );

            if ( m_bDisplay )
                Console.WriteLine( "CustomRealProxy: After calling:{0}",
                                   callMsg.MethodName );
        }
        return msgOut;
    }
}

[AttributeUsage(AttributeTargets.Class)]
public class CustomProxyAttribute : ProxyAttribute {
    bool m_bDisplay;
    public CustomProxyAttribute( bool bDisplay ) {
        m_bDisplay = bDisplay;
    }
    public override MarshalByRefObject CreateInstance( Type T ) {
```

Example 22-29

```
      MarshalByRefObject targetObj = base.CreateInstance( T );
      RealProxy realProxy = new CustomRealProxy(targetObj, T, m_bDisplay);
      return (MarshalByRefObject) realProxy.GetTransparentProxy();
   }
}

// The true params indicates that we wish that the custom real
// proxy displays info on the console.
[CustomProxyAttribute(true)]
public class Adder : ContextBoundObject {
   public int Add( int a, int b ) { return a + b; }
}

public class Program {
   static void Main() {
      Adder obj = new Adder();
      obj.Add(5, 6);
   }
}
```

This program displays the following on the console:

```
CustomRealProxy: ctor call
CustomRealProxy: Before calling:Add
CustomRealProxy: After calling:Add
```

Read and write access to method call parameters

We have seen how to read the parameters of a method from a message representing this call. We can also use a custom real proxy or a custom message sink to modify the parameters of a call. For example, you could use this feature to translate the strings passed as the parameters from one language to another. Write access to the parameters contained in a message is possible but it is not as straight as the read access, which if you remember, can be done like this:

```
...
public override IMessage Invoke( IMessage msgIn ) {
   IMethodCallMessage callMsg = (IMethodCallMessage) msgIn;
   Console.Write("CustomRealProxy: Before calling:{0}(",callMsg.MethodName);
   for(int i=0; i< callMsg.InArgCount ; i++)
      Console.Write( " {0}={1} ",callMsg.GetArgName(i),callMsg.GetArg(i) );
   Console.WriteLine( ")" );
...
```

In fact, no matter which interface we use to manipulate a message, we cannot have write access to the parameters contained in the message. In other words, each of these interfaces supports a get accessor on the parameter table but does not provide a set accessor. To achieve our goal, we propose to use the System.Runtime.Remoting.Messaging.MethodCallMessageWrapper class which has a set accessor on the parameter array. Here is a code snippet illustrating this manipulation:

```
...
public override IMessage Invoke( IMessage msgIn ) {
   IMethodCallMessage callMsg = (IMethodCallMessage) msgIn;
   MethodCallMessageWrapper callMsgWrapper =
      new MethodCallMessageWrapper( callMsg );
   object[] tmpArgs = callMsgWrapper.Args;
   tmpArgs[0] = 1; // Modifiy the first arg.
```

```
    tmpArgs[1] = 2; // Modifiy the second arg.
    callMsgWrapper.Args = methodArgs;
    callMsg = callMsgWrapper;

    msgOut = RemotingServices.ExecuteMessage( m_ObjTarget , callMsg );
...
```

Channel

Introduction

Channels are the entities which transmit the messages representing cross-AppDomain method calls. Because of this, there is at least one channel in the AppDomain of the client and one channel in the AppDomain of the server. However, an application can contain several channels and the implementation of a channel can be used by a client or a server.

A channel is an instance of a class which implements the `System.Runtime.Remoting.Channels.IChannel` interface. A channel which can only be used by a client is called a *sender channel*. By definition, a sender channel implements the `System.Runtime.Remoting.Channels.IChannelSender` interface. A channel which can only be used by a server is called a *receiver channel*. By definition, a receiver channel implements the `System.Runtime.Remoting.Channels.IChannelReceiver` interface.

The .NET framework exposes three channel implementations with the `System.Runtime.Remoting.Channels.Http.HttpChannel`, `System.Runtime.Remoting.Channels.Tcp.TcpChannel` and `System.Runtime.Remoting.Channels.Ipc.IpcChannel` classes. Each of these classes can be used both as a sender and a receiver channel.

The HTTP and TCP protocols are obviously supported respectively by the `HttpChannel` and `TcpChannel` cases. The `IpcChannel` class itself supports the notion of *named pipe*. A named pipe is a *Windows* object allowing for two *Windows* processes hosted on the same machine to communicate. You can also achieve the communication of two *Windows* processes hosted on the same matching with a network protocol such as HTTP or TCP. The advantage of named pipes resides in the fact that they are implemented at the level of the operating system and thus do not use any networking APIs. Consequently, they are more efficient when you need to allow two processes on the same machine to communicate. The *IPC* acronym means *Inter Process Communication* and is also sometimes referred to as *same-box communication*.

To register a channel in an AppDomain you can either use the `ChannelServices.RegisterChannel()` static method or to load a .NET Remoting configuration file with the `RemotingConfiguration.Configure()` static method. These two techniques have already been presented in the previous pages.

Each channel has a name and two channels in the same Appdomain cannot have the same name. By default, the name of a channel instance of `HttpChannel` is "http", the name of a channel instance of `TcpChannel` is "tcp" and the name of a channel instance of `IpcChannel` is "ipc". Here is how to assign a specific name to a channel:

```
...
static void Main() {
    IDictionary prop = new Dictionary<string,string>();
    prop["name"] = "tcp2";
    prop["port"] = "65101";
    ChannelServices.RegisterChannel( new TcpChannel( prop, null, null ) );
...
```

Each channel of HTTP or TCP type needs a port number. A port number cannot be used by several channels existing on a same machine. To avoid collision in your choice of port, you can assign the port to 0 during the creation of a channel. The CLR will then make sure to find a free port number and assign it to the channel. As you may have guessed, the *Microsoft* implementation of the HTTP and TCP channels base themselves to the use of sockets internally.

When two AppDomains are found on the same process, it would be a shame to use heavyweight mechanism for interprocess communication. For this reason, the `mscorlib.dll` assembly contains the `CrossAppDomain` internal class which is dedicated to the case where both client and server AppDomains reside in the same process. This class is automatically used by the CLR. You do not have to do anything in order to take advantage of this optimization.

Sender channels and proxies

The relationship between sender channels and proxies located in a same AppDomain is quite often misunderstood. This might lead to aberrations, such as the creation of a sender channel for each remote object!

A sender channel in an AppDomain is a message sink chain factory for the proxies. Let's come back to the program illustrating the creation of a real custom proxy (Example 22-28). The constructor of the `CustomRealProxy` class needed to know the sender channel used to contact the remote object:

```
...
    public CustomRealProxy(Type type, String uri,
                            IChannelSender channelSender): base(type){
        m_Uri = uri;
        string unused;
        // Obtain a message sink.
        m_MsgSink = channelSender.CreateMessageSink(m_Uri, null, out unused);
    }
...
```

The `IChannelSender.CreateMessageSink()` method asks to the underlying channel to create a message sink chain. This chain is configured mainly by the URI of the remote object activation service and by the port of the channel.

Receiver channels and server objects

The relationship between receiver channels and the server objects located in a same AppDomain is generally misunderstood. This might lead to aberrations such as the creation of a receiver channel for each server object.

This relationship is misunderstood in part because neither the `RemotingConfiguration.RegisterWellKnownServiceType()` method which is used to expose a WKO object activation service nor does the `RemotingConfiguration.RegisterActivatedServiceType()` method which is used to expose a class from a server, do not take a receiver channel as an argument. The reason is simple: each receiver channel of in an AppDomain can receive calls for each object of this domain that can be used in a remote way.

The call to the `RemotingConfiguration.RegisterWellKnownServiceType()` method creates an internal association between the URI of the WKO service and the WKO service itself. This service is configured by the call mode and a class. The call to the `RemotingConfiguration.RegisterActivatedServiceType()` method registers internally the fact that a certain class deriving from the `MarshalByRefObject` class can be instantiated by a remote client. Remember that each time an instance of the `ObjRef` is created to reference an object of the AppDomain, a unique URI based on a GUID is created for this object. An internal association between this URI and the real object is then created.

When a receiver channel receives a message representing a call, three cases can happen:

- The call is done on a WKO service. In this case, an object is activated if the call mode is the single-call mode. If the call mode is singleton, either an object already exists for the specified URI, either a new object is created.
- The call is done on an object of the AppDomain associated to the provided URI. If an object is effectively associated to this URI, the call is done on this object. If not, a message is sent back to the client indicating that the object does not exist anymore.
- The call is a constructor call to a CAO class. In this case, a new object is created. This object is associated with a new URI based on a new GUID. This new URI is returned to the client with the help of an instance of the `ObjRef` class.

Message sink, formatter and channel

On the server-side, a message representing a call is also processed by message sinks chained together. However a fundamental conceptual difference exists between a receiver and a sender channel. A sender channel creates a chain of message sinks for each real proxy to a remote object. A receiver channel creates a message sink chain as soon as it is created. This chain will be used by all calls which transit through this receiver channel, no matter the object concerned with the call. This difference is illustrated in Figure 22-6:

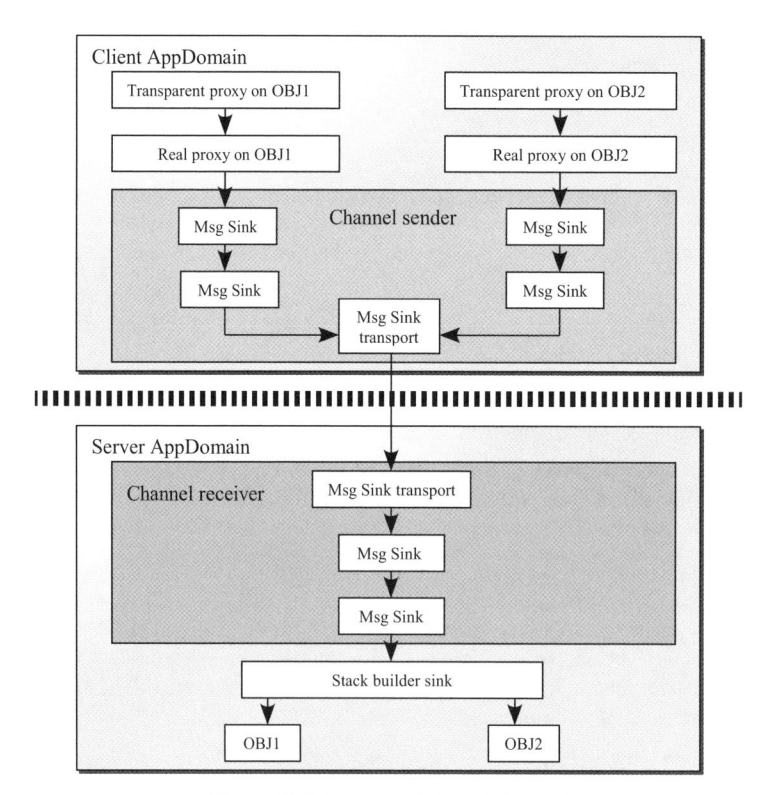

Figure 22-6: Message sink and channel

Channel sink providers

To create a message sink chains you need to harness a *channel sink provider*. A channel sink provider of a sender channel (respectively of a receiver channel) is an instance of a class which implements the `System.Runtime.Remoting.Channels.IClientChannelSinkProvider` (respectively `IServerChannelSinkProvider`) interface. Let us remind you that in a sender channel, a message sink chain is required for each real proxy while a receiver channel contains only one message sink chain.

Each of these two interfaces presents a method named `CreateSink()`. This method is called by the implementation of a channel in order to obtain a new message sink from the provider:

```
IServerChannelSink IServerChannelSinkProvider.CreateSink(
      IChannelReceiver  channel);
IClientChannelSink IClientChannelSinkProvider.CreateSink(
      IChannelSender    channel,
      String            url,
      Object            remoteChannelData);
```

In order to create a chain of such providers, each of these two interfaces offers the `Next{get;set;}` property. You can easily create such a chain in your code and supply it to a channel by using the proper constructors of the channel classes. However, we generally prefer configuring the provider chain through the use of the configuration file. This is illustrated in the following section.

Example: Displaying the size of network messages

We will create our own message sinks and our own sink providers for these message sinks. The goal is to display on the client's console, the number of bytes sent and received.

Message sink and message sink provider

We need to develop four classes for this project:

- A class named `CustomClientSink`, whose instances are message sinks. Instances of this class must be placed in the sender channel, after the formatter.

- A class named `CustomServerSink`, whose instances are message sinks. Instances of this class must be placed in the receiver channel, before the formatter.

- A class named `CustomClientSinkProvider`, whose instances are the providers for instances of `CustomClientSink`. Instances of this class must be chained after the formatter provider in the sender channel.

- A class named `CustomServerSinkProvider`, whose instances are providers for instances of `CustomServerSink`. Instances of this class must be chained before the format provider for the receiver channel.

We also develop a `Helper` static class, which provides the `GetStreamLength()` method which returns the length of a stream. This method is capable of returning this size whether or not the stream supports random access (*seek*) or not. Here is the code of all these classes:

Example 22-30 *CustomChannelSink.cs*

```
using System;
using System.Runtime.Remoting.Channels;
using System.Runtime.Remoting.Messaging;
using System.Collections;
using System.IO;

namespace CustomChannelSink {
```

Example 22-30   CustomChannelSink.cs

```csharp
      internal static class Helper {
        public static Stream GetStreamLength(Stream inStream,out long length){
          // Does 'inStream' support seek access?
          if (inStream.CanSeek) {
             length = inStream.Length;
             return inStream;
          }
          // Here 'seek acces' is not supported. We must copy 'inStream'
          // to 'outStream' to obtain the stream length.
          Stream outStream = new MemoryStream();
          byte[] buffer = new Byte[1024];
          int tmp, nBytesRead = 0;
          while ( ( tmp = inStream.Read( buffer, 0, 1024 ) ) > 0 ) {
             outStream.Write( buffer, nBytesRead, tmp );
             nBytesRead += tmp;
          }
          outStream.Seek( 0, SeekOrigin.Begin );
          length = nBytesRead;
          return outStream;
        }
      }

      //
      // Custom Client Sink.
      //
      public class CustomClientSink : BaseChannelSinkWithProperties,
                                      IClientChannelSink {
        private IClientChannelSink m_NextSink;
        public CustomClientSink( IClientChannelSink nextSink ) {
           m_NextSink = nextSink;
        }
        public IClientChannelSink NextChannelSink {
           get { return m_NextSink; }
        }
        public void AsyncProcessRequest( IClientChannelSinkStack sinkStack,
                                         IMessage msgIn,
                                         ITransportHeaders headers,
                                         Stream msgStream ) {
           long length;
           msgStream = Helper.GetStreamLength( msgStream, out length );
           Console.WriteLine(
              "CustomClientSink:Async, length of the request stream {0}",
              length );
           // Chaining message sink for async return processing.
           sinkStack.Push( this, null );
           m_NextSink.AsyncProcessRequest(sinkStack,msgIn,headers,msgStream);
        }
        public void AsyncProcessResponse(
                        IClientResponseChannelSinkStack sinkStack,
                        Object state,
                        ITransportHeaders headers,
                        Stream msgStream) {
           long length;
           msgStream = Helper.GetStreamLength( msgStream, out length );
           Console.WriteLine(
```

Example 22-30   CustomChannelSink.cs

```
         "CustomClientSink:Async, length of the response stream {0}",
         length);
      m_NextSink.AsyncProcessResponse(
                                sinkStack, state, headers, msgStream);
   }
   public Stream GetRequestStream(IMessage msg,
                                ITransportHeaders headers) {
      return m_NextSink.GetRequestStream( msg, headers );
   }

   public void ProcessMessage( IMessage msg,
                         ITransportHeaders headersIn,
                         Stream msgInStream,
                         out ITransportHeaders headersOut,
                         out Stream msgOutStream) {
      long length;
      msgInStream = Helper.GetStreamLength( msgInStream, out length );
      Console.WriteLine(
         "CustomClientSink:Sync, length of the request stream {0}",
         length);
      m_NextSink.ProcessMessage(msg, headersIn, msgInStream,
                                out headersOut, out msgOutStream);
      msgOutStream = Helper.GetStreamLength( msgOutStream, out length );
      Console.WriteLine(
         "CustomClientSink:Sync, length of the response stream {0}",
         length);
   }
}

//
// Custom Server Sink.
//
public class CustomServerSink : BaseChannelSinkWithProperties,
                                IServerChannelSink {
   private IServerChannelSink m_NextSink;
   public CustomServerSink( IServerChannelSink nextSink ) {
      m_NextSink = nextSink;
   }
   public IServerChannelSink NextChannelSink {
      get { return m_NextSink; }
   }
   public void AsyncProcessResponse(
                   IServerResponseChannelSinkStack sinkStack,
                   object state,
                   IMessage msg,
                   ITransportHeaders headers,
                   Stream msgStream) {
      long length;
      msgStream = Helper.GetStreamLength( msgStream, out length );
      Console.WriteLine(
         "CustomServerSink:Async, length of the response stream {0}",
         length);
      m_NextSink.AsyncProcessResponse(
                                sinkStack, state, msg, headers, msgStream);
   }
```

Example 22-30   CustomChannelSink.cs

```csharp
    public Stream GetResponseStream(
                    IServerResponseChannelSinkStack sinkStack,
                    object state,
                    IMessage msg,
                    ITransportHeaders headers) {
        return null;
    }

    public ServerProcessing ProcessMessage(
                    IServerChannelSinkStack sinkStack,
                    IMessage msgIn,
                    ITransportHeaders headersIn,
                    Stream msgInStream,
                    out IMessage msgOut,
                    out ITransportHeaders headersOut,
                    out Stream msgOutStream) {
        long length;
        msgInStream = Helper.GetStreamLength(msgInStream, out length);
        Console.WriteLine(
            "CustomServerSink:Sync, length of the request stream {0}",
            length);
        // Chaining message sink for return processing.
        sinkStack.Push( this, null );
        ServerProcessing svrProc = m_NextSink.ProcessMessage(
                    sinkStack, msgIn, headersIn, msgInStream,
                    out msgOut, out headersOut, out msgOutStream);
        msgOutStream = Helper.GetStreamLength(msgOutStream,out length);
        Console.WriteLine(
            "CustomServerSink:Sync, length of the response stream {0}",
            length);
        return svrProc;
    }
}

//
// Custom Client Sink Provider.
//
public class CustomClientSinkProvider : IClientChannelSinkProvider {
    private IClientChannelSinkProvider m_NextProvider;
    public CustomClientSinkProvider(IDictionary prop,
        ICollection providerData) { }
    public IClientChannelSinkProvider Next {
        get { return m_NextProvider; }  set { m_NextProvider = value; }
    }
    public IClientChannelSink CreateSink(
                    IChannelSender channel,
                    string url,
                    object remoteChannelData ) {
        IClientChannelSink next =
            m_NextProvider.CreateSink( channel, url, remoteChannelData );
        Console.WriteLine(
            "CustomClientSinkProvider:Creating a message sink.");
        return new CustomClientSink( next );
    }
```

Example 22-30   CustomChannelSink.cs

```
    }

    //
    // Custom Server Sink Provider.
    //
    public class CustomServerSinkProvider : IServerChannelSinkProvider {
       private IServerChannelSinkProvider m_NextProvider;
       public CustomServerSinkProvider( IDictionary prop,
                                        ICollection providerData) { }
       public IServerChannelSinkProvider Next {
          get { return m_NextProvider; } set { m_NextProvider = value; }
       }
       public IServerChannelSink CreateSink(IChannelReceiver canal) {
          IServerChannelSink next = m_NextProvider.CreateSink(canal);
          Console.WriteLine(
             "CustomServerSinkProvider:Creating a message sink.");
          return new CustomServerSink( next );
       }
       public void GetChannelData( IChannelDataStore channelData ) { }
    }
}
```

A few things to mention:

- In the constructors of the providers, the dictionary passed as a parameter corresponds to the properties that you wish to assign to the providers. Here, we have not taken advantage of this feature. We would simply need to add in the configuration file:

  ```
  <provider
     type = "CustomChannelSink.CustomClientSinkProvider,ChannelSink"
     Prop1="hello"/>
  ```

  You can obtain the value of the property like this:

  ```
  public CustomClientSinkProvider( IDictionary prop,
                                   ICollection providerData) {
     string s = (string) Prop["Prop1"];
     ...
  ```

  You can thus configure your provider. For example, you could specify the name of a compression or encryption algorithm for your *streams*.

- The `IServerChannelSinkStack` type used in the message sinks on the server-side relate to asynchronous calls. In fact, this stack corresponds to the message sink which will be used on the server-side to send the return message.

- The `ITransportHeaders` type, used in the message sink on both the client and server side, allows passing information concerning the message. For example, if the task of the message sink is to encrypt/decrypt a *stream*, you can specify in this header if the message is actually encrypted:

  ```
  class CustomClientSink{ ...
     public void ProcessMessage(
           IMessage              msg,
           ITransportHeaders     headersIn, ...){
        headersIn["Crypted"] ="Yes";
        ...
  ```

  This allows for the message sink in the receiver channel to test that the message was in fact encrypted before attempting to decrypt it.

```
class CustomServerSink{ ...
   public ServerProcessing ProcessMessage(
            IServerChannelSinkStack    sinkStack,
            IMessage                   msgIn,
            ITransportHeaders          headersIn,...){
      string sCrypted = (string) HeadersIn["Crypted"] ;
      if( sCrypted != null && sCrypted == "Yes") { ...
```

This receiver channel then becomes flexible and can deal with messages whether they are encrypted or not.

Server side

On the server side, all the information relative to the channels is found in the configuration file:

Server.cs
```
...
static void Main() {
   RemotingConfiguration.Configure("Server.config");
   Console.WriteLine("Press a key to stop the server...");
   Console.Read();
}
...
```

We then assign a binary formatter with an HTTP receiver channel.

Example 22-31   *Server.config*
```
<configuration>
   <system.runtime.remoting>
      <application name = "Server">
         <service>
            <wellknown type="RemotingInterfaces.Adder,Interface"
              mode ="Singleton" objectUri="Service1.rem" />
         </service>
         <channels>
            <channel port="65100" ref ="http">
               <serverProviders>
                  <provider type=
                  "CustomChannelSink.CustomServerSinkProvider,ChannelSink" />
                  <formatter ref="binary"/>
               </serverProviders>
            </channel>
         </channels>
      </application>
   </system.runtime.remoting>
</configuration>
```

Client side

On the client-side, all the relevant information is also stored in a configuration file:

Client.cs
```
...
static void Main() {
   RemotingConfiguration.Configure("Client.config",false);

   Adder objA = new Adder();
   double dA = objA.Add( 3.0 , 4.0 );
   Console.WriteLine("Returned value:" + dA);
```

Client.cs
```
        Adder objB = new Adder ();
        double dB = objB.Add( 3.0 , 4.0 );
        Console.WriteLine("Returned value:" + dB);
    }
    ...
```

Here also, we assign a binary formatter with an HTTP sender channel.

Example 22-32   *Client.config*
```
<configuration>
    <system.runtime.remoting>
        <application name = "Client">
            <client>
                <wellknown type="RemotingInterfaces.Adder,Interface"
                    url="http://localhost:65100/Service1.rem" />
            </client>
            <channels>
                <channel ref ="http">
                    <clientProviders>
                        <formatter ref="binary"/>
                        <provider type =
                        "CustomChannelSink.CustomClientSinkProvider,ChannelSink" />
                    </clientProviders>
                </channel>
            </channels>
        </application>
    </system.runtime.remoting>
</configuration>
```

Executing the example

Here is what the server displays on its console:

```
CustomServerSinkProvider:Creating a message sink.
Press a key to stop the server...
CustomServerSink:Sync, length of the request stream 155
CAdditionneur ctor
CAdditionneur Add( 3 + 4 )
CustomServerSink:Sync, length of the response stream 32
CustomServerSink:Sync, length of the request stream 155
CAdditionneur Add( 3 + 4 )
CustomServerSink:Sync, length of the response stream 32
```

Here is what the client displays on its console:

```
CustomClientSinkProvider:Creating a message sink.
CustomClientSink:Sync, length of the request stream 155
CustomClientSink:Sync, length of the response stream 32
Returned value:7
CustomClientSinkProvider:Creating a message sink.
CustomClientSink:Sync, length of the request stream 155
CustomClientSink:Sync, length of the response stream 32
Returned value:7
```

If we have chosen a SOAP formatter and not a binary formatter, the size of the call stream would have been of 574 bytes and the size of the return stream of 586 bytes.

If you dispose of a compression or encryption library, this example could have been easily tweaked to compress or encrypt the binary data transiting over the network.

.NET context

Introduction

We have seen that AppDomains allow the isolation during execution at the type, security and exception levels. There exists an entity which is more fine than the AppDomain to store .NET objects. A .NET AppDomain can contain several of these entities named *.NET context*. In the reminder of the current chapter, we will name them context as long as there is no confusion with the notion of COM+ contexts, which is different (this notion is presented at page 248). Certain author uses the *managed context* or *execution context* terms to talk of a .NET context and the term of *unmanaged context* for COM+ contexts. All .NET objects reside within a context, and there exists at least one context for each AppDomain. This context is called *default context* of the AppDomain and is created at the same time as its AppDomain. Figure 22-7 summarizes these relationships:

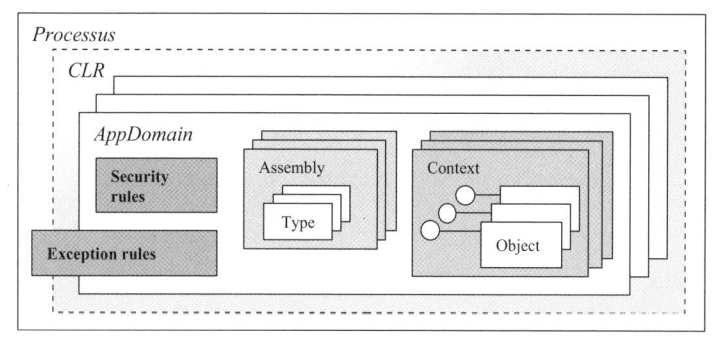

Figure 22-7: Process, AppDomain and context

The notion of context allows the interception of the calls to an object. Intercepting a call means that we can apply one or several transformations to each input or output parameters. These transformations are done using message sinks. The central idea is that when a client calls a method of an object, he is not aware that its calls are intercepted and that transformations are applied before and after the processing of the method.

Context-bound and context-agile object

Based on the previous section, a context can be seen as a zone of an AppDomain, containing objects and message sinks. Calls made to the objects of a context are transformed into messages which are intercepted and processed by message sinks. We now know that to transform a call into a message, we must go through the intermediate of a transparent proxy. Hence, we also know that the CLR only creates a transparent proxy towards an object if it is an instance of a class derived from `MarshalByRefObject` called by an entity located outside of its AppDomain. Here, we wish to benefit from the message sink mechanism for all calls, even those done from entities located in the same AppDomain. This is exactly why the `System.ContextBoundObject` class exists. An instance of a class which derives from `ContextBoundObject` is accessible only through transparent proxies. In this case, even the `this` reference used in the method of the class is a transparent proxy and not a direct reference to the object. It is logical that the `ContextBoundObject` class derives from `MarshalByRefObject`, since it reinforces the behavior of this class which is to tell the CLR that a class is potentially used through a transparent proxy.

An instance of a class deriving from `ContextBoundObject` is considered to be *context-bound*. An instance of a class which does not derive from `ContextBoundObject` is considered to be *context-agile*. A context-bound object is always executed within its context. In the case of a non-remote object, a context-agile object is always executed within the context which executes the call. All this is illustrated in Figure 22-8.

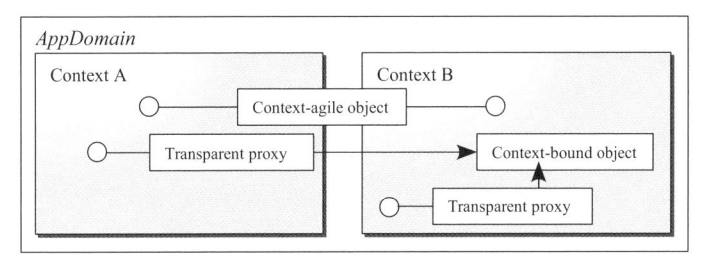

Figure 22-8: Context-bound objects vs. Context-agile objects

Context attribute and context property

Here, we will expose the technique allowing injecting message sinks at the level of the context. Let's start by introducing the notions of context attribute and context property.

Context attribute

A *context attribute* is a .NET attribute which acts on a context-bound class. A context attribute class implements the `System.Runtime.Remoting.Contexts.IContextAttribute` interface. A context-bound class can have several context attributes. During the creation of an object of this class, each context attribute of the class checks if the context of the creator of the object is appropriate. This operation is done in the method:

```
public bool IContextAttribute.IsContextOK(Context clientCtx,
                                         IConstructionCallMessage ctorMsg)
```

If at least one of the context attributes returns `false`, the CLR must create a new context to accommodate the new object. In this case, each context attribute can inject one or several context properties in the new context. These injections are done with the following method:

```
public void IContextAttribute.GetPropertiesForNewContext(
                                         IConstructionCallMessage ctorMsg)
```

Context property

A context property is an instance of a class which implements the `System.Runtime.Remoting.Contexts.IContextProperty` interface. Each context can contain several properties. The properties of a context are injected by the context attributes of the context, when it is created. Once each context attribute has injected its properties, the following method is called for each property. It is then not possible to inject an additional property in this context:

```
public void IContextProperty.Freeze( Context ctx )
```

The CLR then asks to each property is it is satisfied by the new context by calling the following method:

```
public bool IContextProperty.IsNewContextOK( Context ctx )
```

Each property of a context has a name which is defined by the `Name` property:

```
public string IContextProperty.Name{ get }
```

The methods of objects hosted in the context can have access to the properties of the context by calling the following method:

```
IContextProperty Context.GetProperty( string sPropertyName )
```

702　　　　　　　　　　　　　　　　　　　　　　　　　　　　　*Chapter 22 - .NET Remoting*

This possibility can be interesting since the objects of the context can share information and access services thanks to the properties of their context. However, the main role of context properties is not to provide this possibility: The main role of context properties is to inject message sinks, in the message sink regions of the concerned contexts.

The description of these message sink regions is the topic of the following section. Before, let's illustrate the notions of context attributes and context properties through the use of an example. For those who have read the section on channels, a context attribute plays a similar role than the configuration file which injects providers within the channel. In the same spirit, a context property plays a role similar to the message sink providers.

Example using context attribute and property

The following program defines the `LogContextAttribute` class and the `LogContextProperty` class. All instance of a class which is tagged with `LogContextAttribute` is hosted in a context that has a property of type `LogContextProperty`. Such an instance then has access to the services provided by this property. This service allows the possibility of writing a string into a file by calling the `LogContextProperty.Log(string)` method. The name of the file is a parameter of the `LogContextAttribute` attribute. We can then have a configuration file for each class. When a new instance of a class which is tagged with `LogContextAttribute` attribute is created, the `bool LogContextAttribute.IsContextOK(Context)` method allows checking if the context in which resides the entity that called the constructor already has an instance of `LogContextAttribute` with the same file name. If this is not the case, a new context must then be created. The `LogContextAttribute.GetPropertiesForNewContext(IConstructionCallMessage ctor)` method creates an instance of `LogContextProperty`. At the return of this method, the new property is automatically injected into the new context by the CLR. Here is the program:

Example 22-33

```
using System;
using System.Runtime.Remoting.Contexts;
using System.Runtime.Remoting.Activation;
using System.Threading;

public class LogContextProperty : IContextProperty {
   public LogContextProperty(string sFileName) { m_sFileName = sFileName; }
   string m_sFileName;
   public string sFileName { get { return m_sFileName; } }
   public string Name { get { return "Log"; } }
   public bool IsNewContextOK( Context ctx ) { return true; }
   public void Freeze( Context ctx ) { }
   public void Log( string sLog ) {
      // We just write logs on the console.
      Console.WriteLine( "ContextID={0} To write '{1}' in the file '{2}'",
                        Thread.CurrentContext.ContextID,
                        sLog,
                        m_sFileName);
   }
}

[AttributeUsage(AttributeTargets.Class)]
public class LogContextAttribute : Attribute, IContextAttribute {
   string m_sFileName;
   public LogContextAttribute(string sFileName){ m_sFileName = sFileName; }
   // No need to create a new context if the current one already
   // contains the proper context property.
```

Example 22-33
```
    public bool IsContextOK( Context currentCtx,
                        IConstructionCallMessage ctor) {
       LogContextProperty prop = currentCtx.GetProperty( "Log" )
                                          as LogContextProperty;
       if ( prop == null ) return false;
       return ( prop.sFileName == m_sFileName );
    }
    public void GetPropertiesForNewContext(IConstructionCallMessage ctor) {
       IContextProperty prop = new LogContextProperty( m_sFileName );
       ctor.ContextProperties.Add( prop );
    }
 }

 [LogContextAttribute("LogFoo.txt")]
 public class Foo : ContextBoundObject {
    public Foo CreateNewInst() { return new Foo(); }
    public int Add( int a, int b ) {
       string s = string.Format("Add {0}+{1}", a, b);
       Context ctx = Thread.CurrentContext;
       LogContextProperty logger = ctx.GetProperty("Log")
                                          as LogContextProperty;
       logger.Log( s );
       return a + b;
    }
 }

 public class Program {
    static void Main() {
       Foo obj1 = new Foo();
       obj1.Add(4, 5);
       Foo obj2 = new Foo();
       obj2.Add(6, 7);
       Foo obj3 = obj1.CreateNewInst();
       obj3.Add(8, 9);
    }
 }
```

This program displays:

```
ContextID=1 To write 'Add 4+5' in the file 'LogFoo.txt'
ContextID=2 To write 'Add 6+7' in the file 'LogFoo.txt'
ContextID=1 To write 'Add 8+9' in the file 'LogFoo.txt'
```

The obj1 and obj3 objects reside in the same context since obj3 was created from the context of obj1.

Message sink regions

There are four *message sink regions*, the *server* region, the *object* region, the *envoy* region and the *client* region. To understand this notion of region, you must consider the case where a context-bound object is called by an entity located in another context. This entity can be a static method or another object. In our discussion on these regions, we call the context of this entity the *calling context* and the context of the called object the *target context*. Each property of the target context has the possibility of injecting message sinks in each of these regions.

- Message sinks injected in the *server* region intercepts all incoming call messages from another context toward all objects of the target context. There is then a *server* region for each target context.
- Message sinks injected in the *object* region intercepts all the all incoming call messages from another context to a particular object of the target context. There is then an *object* context for each object in the context.
- Message sinks injected in the *envoy* region intercepts all incoming call messages from another context to a particular object of the target context. There is then an *envoy* region for each object in the context. The difference between an *envoy* region and an *object* region is that an *envoy* region is located in the calling context and not in the target context containing the object. We use *envoy* regions to transmit to the message sinks of the target context information about the calling context.
- Message sinks injected in the *client* region intercept all call messages coming from target context to objects located in other contexts. There is then a *client* region for each target context.

Figure 22-9 illustrates the notion of regions. The target context contains two objects named OBJ1 and OBJ2. We have chosen to place two objects in the target context and not one, to properly illustrate that *object* and *envoy* regions are concerned by the interception of messages at the level of the object while the *server* and *client* regions are concerned with the interception of messages at the level of the context.

We have placed two custom message sinks per region in order to properly show that a region can have zero, one or several message sinks. Concretely, all custom message sinks are injected into the regions by the properties of the target context, even when the region does not belong to the target context. Since you can define your own context property classes, you can choose which message sinks must be injected.

You notice that each region contains a system terminator sink which allows indicating to the CLR the exit of a region. Concretely, you do not need to worry about terminator sinks.

Know that when the calling context and the target context reside in the same AppDomain, the CLR uses an instance of the `CrossContextChannel` class which is internal to `mscorlib.dll`. This instance causes the `Context` property of the current thread to switch. The figure represents these instances.

Example using regions

Here is what we expose with the program in Example 22-34:

- The code of a custom context attribute (`CustomDisplayContextAttribute` class) which injects a custom context property (`CustomDisplayContextProperty` class) in a context. This context property injects custom message sinks (`CustomDisplayMessageSink` class) in the *object*, *server* and *client* regions of the target context and in the envoy *region* of the calling context.
- The modification of the behavior of the message sinks based on a parameter passed to the context attribute. Here, this parameter is a boolean which indicates to the message sinks whether or not they must display something on the console.
- The injection of message sinks in each of the four regions by a context property. The `CustomDisplayContextAttribute` attribute context makes sure to create a context for each instance of the `Foo` class. We create a first instance of `Foo` and we will call a method on this instance to go through the *envoy*, *server* and *object* region message sinks. To go through the message sinks of the *client* region, we create a second instance of `Foo` and will call it from the first instance. There are three contexts in play: the context in which the `Main()` method executes (`ContextID=0`), the context which contains the first instance of `Foo` (`ContextID=1`) and the context which contains the second instance of `Foo` (`ContextID=2`).

.NET context

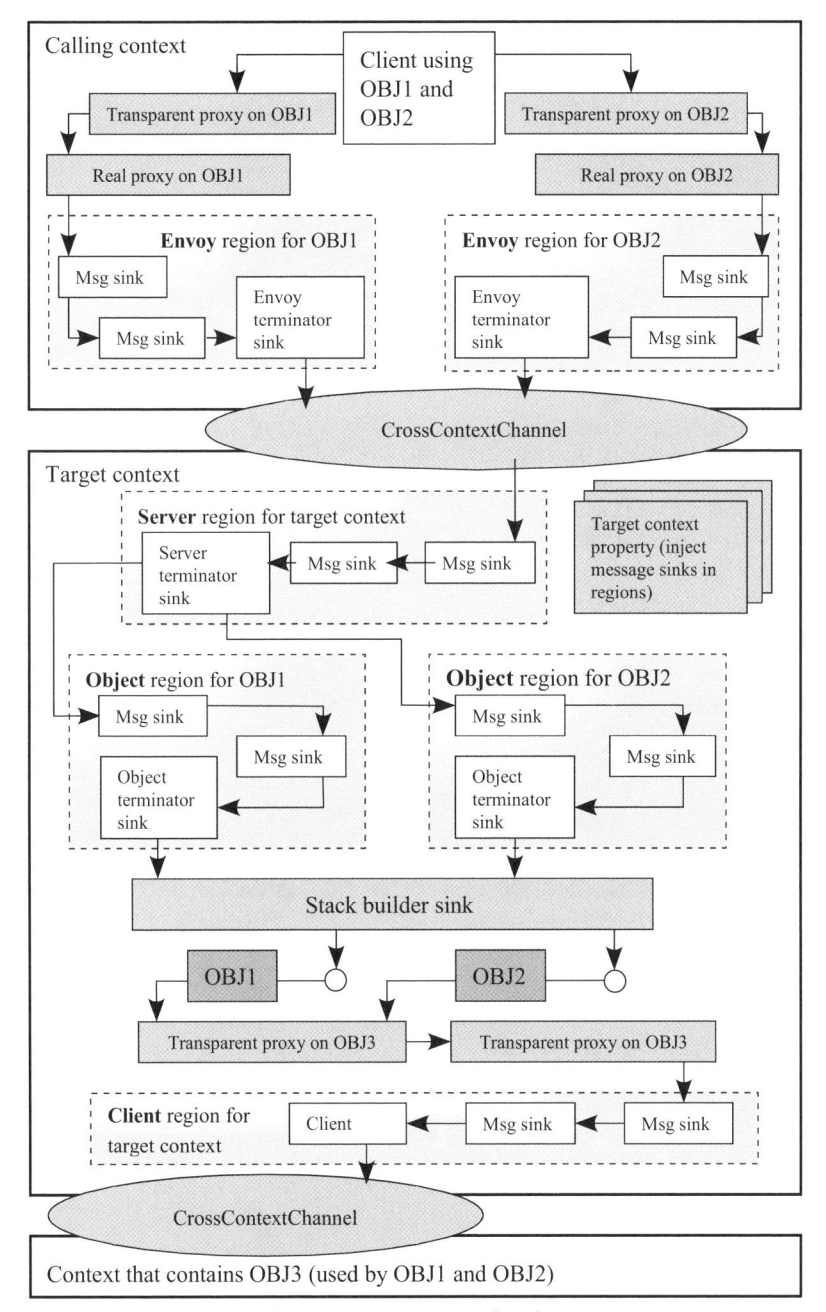

Figure 22-9: Contexts and regions

- The fact that an *intra context call* does not trigger the call of all these message sinks. This behavior is exposed when the first instance of Foo calls itself.
- The injection of several message sinks into a region (here the *client* region).
- The time when the CLR effectively injects message sinks in the regions. We clearly see that this time depends on the type of region.

Here is the program:

Example 22-34
```
using System;
using System.Runtime.Remoting.Contexts;
using System.Runtime.Remoting.Messaging;
using System.Runtime.Remoting.Activation;
using System.Threading;
using System.Collections;

//
// Instances of the context property class inject message sinks
// in all regions.
//
public class CustomDisplayContextProperty :
     IContextProperty,
     IContributeEnvoySink,
     IContributeObjectSink,
     IContributeServerContextSink,
     IContributeClientContextSink {
   public CustomDisplayContextProperty( bool bDisplay ) {
      m_bDisplay = bDisplay;
   }
   bool m_bDisplay;
   public bool bDisplay { get { return m_bDisplay; } }

   // IContextProperty
   public string Name { get { return "PropDisplay"; } }
   public bool IsNewContextOK(Context ctx) { return true; }
   public void Freeze( Context ctx ) {
      Console.WriteLine( "   Freeze ContextID={0}", ctx.ContextID );
   }

   // Inject two message sinks in the 'client' region.
   public IMessageSink GetClientContextSink( IMessageSink nextSink) {
      Console.WriteLine("   GetClientContextSink()");
      IMessageSink nextnextSink = new CustomDisplayMessageSink(
                          nextSink, "Client region1  ", m_bDisplay);
      return new CustomDisplayMessageSink(
                          nextnextSink, "Client region2  ", m_bDisplay);
   }

   // Inject a message sink in the 'server' region.
   public IMessageSink GetServerContextSink( IMessageSink nextSink) {
      Console.WriteLine("   GetServerContextSink()");
      return new CustomDisplayMessageSink(
                          nextSink, "Server region   ", m_bDisplay);
   }

   // Inject a message sink in the 'envoy' region.
   // NOTE: You can use 'mbro' to obtain a reference on the object.
   public IMessageSink GetEnvoySink( MarshalByRefObject mbro,
                                    IMessageSink nextSink) {
      Console.WriteLine("   GetEnvoySink()");
      return new CustomDisplayMessageSink(
                          nextSink, "Envoy  region   ", m_bDisplay);
   }

   // Inject a message sink in the 'object' region.
```

.NET context

Example 22-34

```
   public IMessageSink GetObjectSink( MarshalByRefObject mbro,
                                      IMessageSink nextSink) {
      Console.WriteLine("   GetObjectSink()");
      return new CustomDisplayMessageSink(
                             nextSink, "Object region   ", m_bDisplay);
   }
}

//----------------------------------------------------------------
//
// Context attribute class. It forces the creation of one context per
// object. It injects a 'CustomDisplayContextProperty' in each created
// context.
//
[AttributeUsage(AttributeTargets.Class)]
public class CustomDisplayContextAttribute : Attribute, IContextAttribute {
   bool m_bDisplay;
   public CustomDisplayContextAttribute( bool bDisplay ) {
      m_bDisplay = bDisplay;
   }
   // Forces creating a context per object.
   public bool IsContextOK( Context currentCtx,
                            IConstructionCallMessage ctor) {
      return false;
   }

   // Injects a CustomDisplayContextProperty in each created context.
   public void GetPropertiesForNewContext( IConstructionCallMessage ctor ){
      IContextProperty prop = new CustomDisplayContextProperty(m_bDisplay);
      ctor.ContextProperties.Add( prop );
   }
}


//----------------------------------------------------------------
//
// Instances of the 'CustomDisplayMessageSink' class are message sinks
// that display info on console.
//
[Serializable]
public class CustomDisplayMessageSink : IMessageSink {
   IMessageSink m_NextSink;
   // Message to display.
   string m_sDisplay;
   // Display only if 'm_bDisplay' is true.
   bool m_bDisplay;

   public IMessageSink NextSink { get { return m_NextSink; } }
   public CustomDisplayMessageSink( IMessageSink nextSink,
                                    string sDisplay,
                                    bool bDisplay) {
      m_NextSink = nextSink;
      m_sDisplay = sDisplay;
      m_bDisplay = bDisplay;
   }
   public IMessage SyncProcessMessage( IMessage msg ) {
```

Example 22-34

```
         if ( m_bDisplay )
            Console.WriteLine( "   Begin MsgSink:{0} ContextID={1}",
                               m_sDisplay, Thread.CurrentContext.ContextID);
         // Contact next message sink in the chain...
         IMessage retMsg = m_NextSink.SyncProcessMessage( msg );
         if ( m_bDisplay )
            Console.WriteLine( "   End   MsgSink:{0} ContextID={1}",
                               m_sDisplay, Thread.CurrentContext.ContextID);
         return retMsg;
      }
      public IMessageCtrl AsyncProcessMessage( IMessage msg,
                                               IMessageSink replySink) {
         return m_NextSink.AsyncProcessMessage( msg, replySink );
      }
   }
}


//-----------------------------------------------------------------------
//
// The 'Foo' class is tagged with a 'CustomDisplayContextAttribute'.
// The parameter 'true' means that message sinks
// must display info on console.
//
[CustomDisplayContextAttribute( true )]
public class Foo : ContextBoundObject {
   public Foo() { Console.WriteLine("   Foo ctor"); }
   public int Add(int a, int b) {
      Console.WriteLine( "   Add {0}+{1}", a, b );
      return a + b;
   }
   public int AddCross( Foo tmp, int a, int b ) {
      Console.WriteLine( "   Cross Add {0}+{1}", a, b );
      return tmp.Add( a, b );
   }
}


public class Program {
   static void Main() {
      Console.WriteLine( "Before constructing obj1." );
      Foo obj1 = new Foo();
      Console.WriteLine( "Before using obj1." );
      obj1.Add( 4, 5 );
      Console.WriteLine( "Before constructing obj2." );
      Foo obj2 = new Foo();
      Console.WriteLine( "Before obj1 calls obj2." );
      obj1.AddCross( obj2, 6, 7 );
      Console.WriteLine( "Before obj1 calls obj1." );
      obj1.AddCross( obj1, 8, 9 );
   }
}
```

.NET context

The execution of this program displays:

```
Before constructing obj1.
   Freeze ContextID=1
   GetServerContextSink()
   Begin MsgSink:Server region     ContextID=1
   Foo ctor
   GetEnvoySink()
   End   MsgSink:Server region     ContextID=1
Before using obj1.
   Begin MsgSink:Envoy  region     ContextID=0
   Begin MsgSink:Server region     ContextID=1
   GetObjectSink()
   Begin MsgSink:Object region     ContextID=1
   Add 4+5
   End   MsgSink:Object region     ContextID=1
   End   MsgSink:Server region     ContextID=1
   End   MsgSink:Envoy  region     ContextID=0
Before constructing obj2.
   Freeze ContextID=2
   GetServerContextSink()
   Begin MsgSink:Server region     ContextID=2
   Foo ctor
   GetEnvoySink()
   End   MsgSink:Server region     ContextID=2
Before obj1 calls obj2.
   Begin MsgSink:Envoy  region     ContextID=0
   Begin MsgSink:Server region     ContextID=1
   Begin MsgSink:Object region     ContextID=1
   Cross Add 6+7
   Begin MsgSink:Envoy  region     ContextID=1
   GetClientContextSink()
   Begin MsgSink:Client region2    ContextID=1
   Begin MsgSink:Client region1    ContextID=1
   Begin MsgSink:Server region     ContextID=2
   GetObjectSink()
   Begin MsgSink:Object region     ContextID=2
   Add 6+7
   End   MsgSink:Object region     ContextID=2
   End   MsgSink:Server region     ContextID=2
   End   MsgSink:Client region1    ContextID=1
   End   MsgSink:Client region2    ContextID=1
   End   MsgSink:Envoy  region     ContextID=1
   End   MsgSink:Object region     ContextID=1
   End   MsgSink:Server region     ContextID=1
   End   MsgSink:Envoy  region     ContextID=0
Before obj1 calls obj1.
   Begin MsgSink:Envoy  region     ContextID=0
   Begin MsgSink:Server region     ContextID=1
   Begin MsgSink:Object region     ContextID=1
   Cross Add 8+9
   Add 8+9
   End   MsgSink:Object region     ContextID=1
   End   MsgSink:Server region     ContextID=1
   End   MsgSink:Envoy  region     ContextID=0
```

Call context

You have the possibility of passing information between the message sinks executing in the calling context and a message sink executing in the target context. We use this technique mainly to pass information about the calling context to the target context (for example, if the calling context supports certain properties). This functionality has the name of *call context*. Despite its name, this functionality can be used in any message sinks, including those who are not part of a context.

For this, you must first define a class which implements the `System.Runtime.Messaging.ILogicalThreadAffinative` interface to describe the information to pass. In the code of the message sink executing in the calling context (in an *envoy* or a *client* region) we must *attach* an instance of this class to the message representing the call. In the code of the message sink executing in the target context (in an *object* or a *server* region) you must *detach* from the message representing the call, the instance of this class. These operations are done using the `IMethodMessage.LogicalCallContext` property.

Here is the code showing how to implement this technique.

Example 22-35

```
...
public class DataContext : ILogicalThreadAffinative {
   public int Data;
   public DataContext( int i ){ Data=i; }
}

[Serializable]
public class CustomEnvoyMessageSink : IMessageSink{
   public IMessage SyncProcessMessage( IMessage msg ){
      DataContext dc = new DataContext( 691 );
      // Include the data in 'msg'.
      ((IMethodMessage)Msg).LogicalCallContext.SetData( "TheDataID" , dc );
      return m_NextSink.SyncProcessMessage( msg );
   }
   ...
}

[Serializable]
public class CustomServerMessageSink : IMessageSink{
   public IMessage SyncProcessMessage( IMessage msg ){
      // Get the data from 'msg'.
      DataContext dc = (DataContext)
         ((IMethodCallMessage)Msg).LogicalCallContext.GetData(
         "TheDataID" );
      if( dc != null )
         Console.WriteLine( "   DataContext:" + dc.Data );
      IMessage retMsg = m_NextSink.SyncProcessMessage( msg );
      return retMsg;
   }
   ...
}
...
```

We have seen in the previous section that the injection of message sinks in the *client* or *envoy* sections is done after the call to the constructor of an object. A message sink in a *client* or *envoy* region cannot attach information to a message representing a call to the constructor. Hence a message sink in the *server* region potentially tries to detach information from a message representing the call of the constructor. In this case, we can attach the information in the `GetPropertiesForNewContext()` method of the context attribute:

Summary

Example 22-36

```
...
public class CustomDisplayContextAttribute : Attribute,
                                             IContextAttribute {
   public void GetPropertiesForNewContext(IConstructionCallMessage ctor) {
      DataContext dc = new DataContext( 10 );
      ctor.LogicalCallContext.SetData( "TheDataID", dc );
      IContextProperty prop = new CustomDisplayContextProperty(m_bDisplay);
      ctor.ContextProperties.Add( prop );
   }
   ...
}
```

Summary

Four ways to activate an object

We have seen four ways to activate an object, the WKO single-call mode, the WKO singleton mode, CAO and object publishing. Here is a summary table of the main differences between these modes:

	WKO single call	**WKO singleton**	**CAO**	**Publish**
When is the object activated?	At each call.	At the first call of a client	During the call of the constructor by the client	During the call of the constructor by the server
What information does the client hold to access the object?	An URI containing the endpoint.	An URI containing the endpoint.	An ObjRef obtained implicitly during the call of the constructor.	An ObjRef obtained explicitly.
Is the object shared by multiple clients?	No	Yes	No	Yes
Does the client have an instance of ObjRef on the object?	No	No	Yes	Yes
If the object is destroyed by the lease manager, will a call return an exception?	No	No	Yes, if there is no automatic reconstruction of the object	Yes, if there is no automatic reconstruction of the object
Does the client need to know the metadata of the class?	No, the client only needs the metadata of an interface	No, the client only needs the metadata of an interface	Yes, unless you use the *factory design pattern*.	Yes
Can we configure this mode using a configuration file?	Yes	Yes	Yes	No
Can we use a constructor with arguments for the activation of the object?	No	No	No, unless you use the *factory design pattern*.	Yes

Intercepting messages

We have dedicated half this chapter to expose how messages representing calls can be intercepted and for which reasons. Figure 22-10 presents a brief summary of the different possible interception levels:

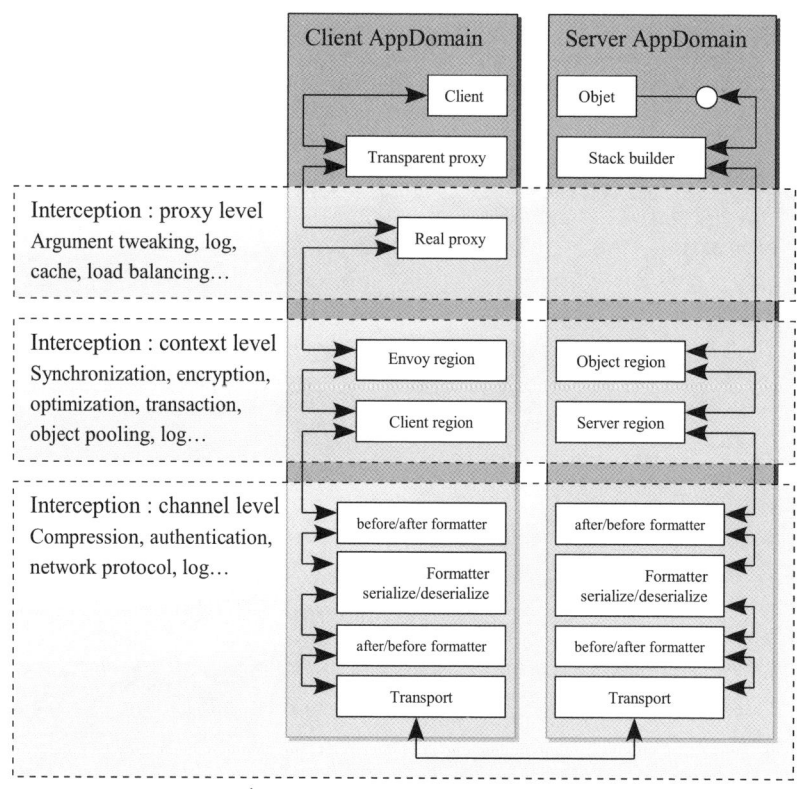

Figure 22-10: Intercepting messages

23

ASP.NET 2

Introduction

A web application is an application which sends back HTML pages in response to HTTP requests. The HTML pages are usable from the client from an application called a *browser* (such as Internet Explorer or Firefox). Browsers are specialized in the visualization of HTML pages. In 1995, *Netscape* created the first browser available to the open public. This type of software has significantly altered the daily routine of millions of individuals.

The advantages of web application over graphical applications encapsulated in an executable are numerous:

- The deployment of new versions of the application is automatic since everything is centralized on the server.
- The browser takes in consideration a big part of the complexity of managing controls.
- The creation of distributed applications is simplified. The development tools are more powerful and the underlying web protocols (HTML, HTTP…) are well known and widely adopted.

The main difference is that a graphical *Windows* application (i.e. a rich client) produces bitmaps which are displayed several times per second while a web application produces an HTML page sent back to the client on-request. Thanks to the .NET architecture which allows and fosters a high level programming approach based on the use of objects and components, the development of web clients and the development of rich clients have never been as close. We sometimes use the *unified programming* term.

History

During the 90's, the development of web applications was simplified. During the same period, web applications were more and more interactive with the introduction of controls. Information captured from the user is included within the HTTP requests. HTTP 1.1 offered seven methods to invoke a resource. The two most commonly used HTTP methods are HTTP-GET and HTTP-POST. The HTTP-GET method allows passing the parameters of a request by adding the information to the URL. The HTTP-POST method allows passing the parameters of a request in the body of the request. In this case, the parameters of the request are not visible in the URL.

The HTML pages sent back as a response to a HTTP request are less and less static. They are constructed dynamically based on the information supplied by the user. This construction is done by the code called from the HTTP server.

In the early 90's, we used *CGI* (*Common Gateway Interface*) programs to dynamically build HTML pages. With such programs, you can access databases and process data. However, the development of CGI programs is cumbersome and performance was often mediocre. Already, techniques using interpreted scripts such as *Perl* were emerging.

In 1996, Microsoft integrated the ISAPI filters to its IIS (Internet Information Server) application server to facilitate the redirection of HTTP requests. But more importantly, the same year, the Redmond giant released ASP (Active Server Page). A new thing brought by ASP was that the code was inserted inside the HTML, while with CGI, it was the HTML which was inserted in the code. Several improvements were brought to this technology from version 1 in 1996 to the version 3 in 2000. Despite its success, its main competitors, JSP and PHP were still gaining ground.

ASP vs. ASP.NET

Also, during the conception of the .NET platform, *Microsoft* decided to provide a technology named ASP.NET destined to be the successor of ASP. ASP.NET application could be written in any .NET language such as C# or VB.NET. And contrarily to ASP application, they had the peculiarity of being compiled into IL language and executed by the CLR which meant a significant performance gain as there was no more code interpretation going on.

ASP.NET was designed with a focus on addressing the major problems of the ASP technology such as:

- In ASP.NET the HTML code and the .NET code (C# or VB.NET) have the possibility of being stored in separate files to allow a better collaboration between the web site designers and the programmers.
- The ASP.NET sessions can be shared across multiple machines, for example, by storing them in a database.
- ASP.NET offers several methods to keep the state of the controls on a page up to date when reloading it. This allows avoiding a lot of cumbersome and difficult to maintain code.
- The configuration parameters of an ASP.NET application are stored in an XML file. To duplicate a configuration, you simply need to copy this configuration file. This solves the inherent problem with the use of the IIS meta-base.

ASP.NET 1.x vs. ASP.NET 2

We are now at version 2 of ASP.NET. This second version offers several improvements without changing what ASP.NET 1.x developers already know. ASP.NET 2 offers several *ready to use* components. These components address most of the recurring tasks which required effort from developers to be implemented in ASP.NET 1.x. Hence, *Microsoft* even goes as far to say that there is at best 70% less code needed in most common scenarios. Despite larger APIs and thus more information to assimilate by developers, these increase their productivity from the fact that they do not have to 'reinvent the wheel' for most common tasks.

You do not need to already have developed under ASP.NET 1.x to assimilate this chapter. If you are simply interested in the new components of ASP.NET 2, know that there are listed in the appendix at page 852 . For each of the new feature a page reference is included.

ASP.NET: The big picture

Web Forms

A *web form* is a page of a web application. During the development phase, the source code of a web form is contained in a text file with an `.aspx` extension to which will eventually be associated a .NET source file (C# or VB.NET for example) and even possibly a resource file. During execution, a web form is a .NET class derived of the `System.Web.UI.Page` class. An instance of this class is created for each request to the related page. Such an instance is responsible for the creation of an HTML page. ASP.NET collaborates with an underlying web server to make sure that this HTML page is returned to the user responsible for the request.

ASP.NET, IIS and web applications at runtime

A *web application* is the set of web forms and corresponding assemblies, located in the tree structure of the virtual folder. During execution of one or several web applications on a machine, there are two processes on the machine:

- The `INETINFO.EXE` process represents IIS. All the HTTP requests destined to web applications and services are received in this process by the code of the ISAPI filter `aspnet_isapi.dll`. The IIS security rules are then applied and the requests are transmitted to the `aspnet_wp.exe` process using a named pipe. If at the reception of a request, the `aspnet_wp.exe` process does not exist; the `aspnet_isapi.dll` ISAPI filter takes care of starting it and creating the appropriate named pipe.

- The `aspnet_wp.exe` process (wp for *Worker Process*) contains one AppDomain per web application or by web service running on the machine. No matter how many web applications or web services run on this machine, they are all executed within this process, unless a multi-processor architecture (discussed in the following pages) is present. The isolation between web applications comes from the isolation guaranteed by the CLR between AppDomains.

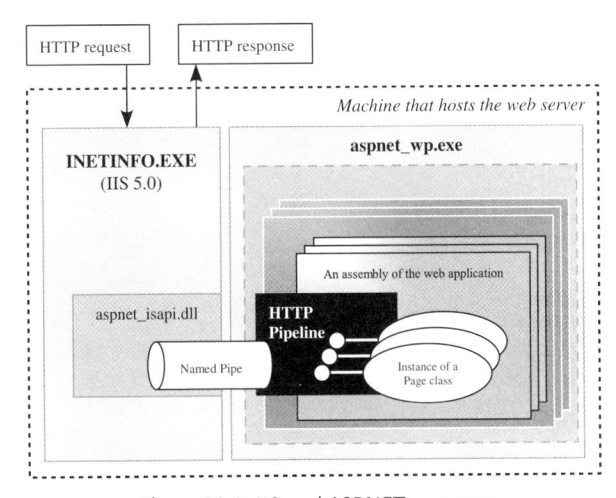

Figure 23-1: IIS and ASP.NET processes

Another architecture is implemented with IIS 6.0 under *Windows Server 2003*. In this case, IIS and ASP.NET execute within a same process named `w3wp.exe`.

ASP.NET was designed to be independent of the underlying web server. Concretely, this implies that ASP.NET can interface itself with web servers other than IIS. For example, *Visual Studio .NET 2005* is supplied with the web server named `WebDev.WebServer.EXE` allowing to test and debug your web applications during development. This web server is based on the old web server named *Cassini* which was provided freely by *Microsoft*. This is very practical since IIS is only available on the professional versions of *Windows*. It is then possible to develop a web application on a machine which only has the home edition of *Windows*. Note that you can configure *Visual Studio 2005* to interface with IIS by modifying the option *Right click on the project > Property pages > Start Options > Use custom server*.

ASP.NET does a certain number of tasks to treat the HTTP requests and responses in what we will call the *HTTP pipeline* shown in Figure 23-1. Amongst these tasks, we can mention the ASP.NET authentication of the user which initiated a request or the management of information relating to the current session for the user. Throughout this chapter we will explain these tasks in more details. We will also explain how you can extend this pipeline by injecting your own task at a specific point in the process

The execution of a request within the `aspnet_wp.exe` process is done on the same thread from end to end. For this, ASP.NET uses the I/O threads of the CLR's thread pool and can execute multiple requests simultaneously. In addition to avoiding a certain number of concurrency problems by design, this approach is generally more efficient as the reception of requests from a name pipe starts directly on an I/O thread. We then avoid the transmission of information between threads. Since there is no named pipes in IIS 6.0, things happen a little differently and in this version, ASP.NET uses several worker thread of the CLR.

It is important to note that the `aspnet_wp.exe` process is executed by default under a *Windows* user account named *ASPNET* (or *Network Service* under IIS 6.0) with restricted privileges. In fact, during development, it is possible that you do not notice certain problems from the fact that `WebDev.WebServer.EXE` executes itself by default under your user account. We will see how you can eventually configure ASP.NET so that this process executes itself under another user. Finally note that if the user initiating a request was authenticated as a *Windows* user, it is possible that the thread executing this request executes itself under the account for this user.

You can simultaneously host several web applications with ASP.NET. For example, an IIS server with the following mapped IP addresses and the following logical sites can expose the following web applications:

```
Mapped IP addresses :
    www.xyz.com
    www.smacchia.com

Logical sites :
    http://www.xyz.com
    http://www.smacchia.com

Web applications :
    http://www.xyz.com/holidays              Bank holidays
    http://www.xyz.com/holidays/mngr         Bank holidays for managers
    http://www.smacchia.com/Documents        Document publishing
    http://www.smacchia.com                  Content Introduction
```

The physical folders containing the web applications do not have any constraints in regards to their location. They can be on a local file system or even on a remote storage system. For example, the folder of the `http://www.xyz.com/holidays/mngr` web application is not required to be embedded within the folder of the `http://www.xyz.com/holidays` web application.

Finally, it is possible to make ASP.NET version 1.x coexist with a version 2 on the same machine. In this case, you will need to specify to the `aspnet_isapi.dll` ISAPI filter which version to use by using the `aspnet_regiis.exe` tool. You simply need to type the following command line with the desired version:

```
aspnet_regiis.exe -r
```

Hosting ASP.NET in your own .NET applications

The `System.Web.Hosting` namespace offers classes which allow you to host ASP.NET within any .NET application. This feature is illustrated in the following example:

Example 23-1   *AspnetHosting.cs*
```
using System;
using System.Web;
using System.Web.Hosting;
class Program {
```

Example 23-1   AspnetHosting.cs

```
      static void Main() {
         Console.WriteLine("Main Appdomain:" +
                           AppDomain.CurrentDomain.FriendlyName);
         CustomSimpleHost host = (CustomSimpleHost)
             ApplicationHost.CreateApplicationHost(
                typeof(CustomSimpleHost), @"/",
                System.IO.Directory.GetCurrentDirectory());
         host.ProcessRequest( "Default.aspx", string.Empty );
      }
   }
   public class CustomSimpleHost : MarshalByRefObject {
      public void ProcessRequest( string file , string query ) {
         Console.WriteLine( "ASP.NET AppDomain:" +
                            AppDomain.CurrentDomain.FriendlyName );
         SimpleWorkerRequest aspnetWorker =
                 new SimpleWorkerRequest( file , query , Console.Out );
         HttpRuntime.ProcessRequest( aspnetWorker );
      }
   }
}
```

We first declare our wish to host ASP.NET in the current process by calling the `ApplicationHost.CreateApplicationHost()` method which creates a new AppDomain and loads ASP.NET in it. ASP.NET then loads the assembly containing the `CustomSimpleHost` class. In this case, this assembly is the same as our application, thus `AspnetHosting.exe`. An instance of this class is then created in this new AppDomain. The `CreateApplicationHost()` method returns a reference to this instance in the initial AppDomain. This is possible because the `CustomSimpleHost` class derives from `MarshalByRefObject`. Hence, using the .NET Remoting technology, an instance of `CustomSimpleHost` can be referenced from an AppDomain different from which it resides.

The code of the `ProcessRequest` method uses an instance of the `System.Web.Hosting.SimpleWorkerProcess` class to process an HTTP GET request. Here we artificially create this request by providing the name of the request web form (`Default.aspx`), the parameters for the GET request (here there are none) and a data stream to which ASP.NET will redirect its response (in this case we use the console stream). The HTML page produced by ASP.NET from the requested `Default.aspx` web form is then displayed on the console as follows:

```
Main Appdomain:ConsoleApplication6.exe
ASP.NET AppDomain:c6ed2272-1-127654065004140000

<html xmlns="http://www.w3.org/1999/xhtml" >
   <body>
      <center>
      <form name="Form1" method="post" action="Default.aspx" id="Form1">
...
```

To execute this example, you must have a web form named `Default.aspx` in the same folder as the `AspnetHosting.exe` assembly. You can, for example use the `Default.apsx` presented a little later in Example 23-3. Also, you must duplicate the `AspnetHosting.exe` assembly in the `/bin` sub-folder of the location where the original `AspnetHosting.exe` is located. In fact, ASP.NET automatically looks in this folder for the assembly containing the `CustomSimpleHost` class to load it into the new AppDomain.

Using ASP.NET on top of HTTP.SYS

In the previous section, we have mentioned how we simulated a GET request to transmit to ASP. NET. By using a web server based on the services of the HTTP.SYS layer, it is easy to build a complete web server which hosts ASP.NET without any need for IIS. The HTTP.SYS layer is discussed at page 540. We show you example of .NET programs which use this layer using the services of the `HttpListener` class. The following program uses conjointly the hosting services of ASP.NET and of HTTP.SYS:

Example 23-2

```
using System;
using System.Web;
using System.Web.Hosting;
using System.IO;
using System.Net;
class Program {
   static void Main() {
      CustomSimpleHost host = (CustomSimpleHost)
             ApplicationHost.CreateApplicationHost(
                typeof(CustomSimpleHost), @"/",
                System.IO.Directory.GetCurrentDirectory());
      HttpListener httpListener = new HttpListener();
      string uri = string.Format("http://localhost:8008/");
      httpListener.Prefixes.Add(uri);
      httpListener.Start();
      Console.WriteLine("Waiting on " + uri);
      while (true) {
         HttpListenerContext ctx = httpListener.GetContext();
         string page = ctx.Request.Url.LocalPath.Replace("/", "");
         string query = ctx.Request.Url.Query;
         Console.WriteLine("Received request: {0}?{1}",page, query);
         StreamWriter writer = new StreamWriter( ctx.Response.OutputStream,
                                                 System.Text.Encoding.Unicode);
         host.ProcessRequest(page, query, writer);
         writer.Flush();
         writer.Close();
         ctx.Response.Close();
      }
   }
}
public class CustomSimpleHost : MarshalByRefObject {
   public void ProcessRequest(string file,string query,TextWriter writer) {
      SimpleWorkerRequest aspnetWorker =
                new SimpleWorkerRequest(file, query, writer);
      HttpRuntime.ProcessRequest(aspnetWorker);
   }
}
```

To test this web server, you simply need to use the following URL in a browser executing on the same machine:

```
http://localhost:8008/Default.aspx
```

ASP.NET application source code

Inlined-code

Each page has a single `.aspx` file and such a file corresponds to a single page. Here is the code of a web page:

Example 23-3 *Default.aspx*
```
<%@ Page Language="C#" Debug="false" Description="My First Page!" %>
<script language="C#" runat="server">
   void Btn_Click(Object sender, EventArgs e) {
      Msg.Text = "You selected : "+Color.SelectedItem.Value;
   }
</script>
<html xmlns="http://www.w3.org/1999/xhtml" >
   <body>
      <center>
      <form id="Form1" action="Default.aspx" method="post" runat="server">
         Color : <asp:dropdownlist id="Color" runat="server">
                   <asp:listitem>white</asp:listitem>
                   <asp:listitem>black</asp:listitem>
                </asp:dropdownlist>
         <br/>
         <asp:button id="Button1" text="Submit" OnClick="Btn_Click"
                   runat="server"/>
         <br/>
         <asp:label id="Msg" runat="server"/>
      </form>
      </center>
   </body>
</html>
```

This file starts with directives which supplies information to ASP.NET such as the .NET language used to code this page, compilation options or debugging options.

Besides these directives, the rest of the content resembles regular HTML code with the exception of non-HTML markers such as `<script>`, `<form>` or `<asp:button>` which are recognized by ASP. NET. A `<script>` marker contains .NET code for example written in C# or VB.NET. Here we talk of *inlined code*. ASP.NET will make sure that this code is part of the class representing the page during execution.

Other non-HTML markers contain a description of the ASP.NET controls. For now, just remember that an ASP.NET control is a field of the instance of the class for the web form which, during execution, will replace its description within the `.aspx` file with the appropriate HTML code.

Note that for a same `.apsx` page, *Visual Studio* provides two views. The design view is more commonly used by designers and the code view which presents the contents of the `.aspx` file. Understand that they are both different views of the same data and that a change in one view is automatically reflected in the other view:

Figure 23-2: Design view and source code view

Server-side script blocks

As with ASP, in ASP.NET you have the option of writing code within *server-side script blocks*, delimited by the <% and %> markers. This code must be written in the .NET language specified by the Language attribute. During the execution of the page, ASP.NET replaces this block of code by the string produced by this code. For example, this `.aspx` page produces the following HTML code:

Example 23-4 *Default.aspx*

```
<%@ Page Language="C#" Debug="true" Description="My second page!" %>
<html xmlns="http://www.w3.org/1999/xhtml" >
   <body>
      <form id="Form1" action="Default.aspx" method="post" runat="server">
         <% for(int i=4; i<8 ; i++) { %>
            <font size="<%=i%>"> Hello </font>
         <% } %>
      </form>
   </body>
</html>
```

HTML page built

```
<html xmlns="http://www.w3.org/1999/xhtml" >
   <body>
      <form method="post" action="Default.aspx" id="Form1">
...
         <font size="4"> Hello </font>
         <font size="5"> Hello </font>
         <font size="6"> Hello </font>
         <font size="7"> Hello </font>
      </form>
   </body>
</html>
```

If you execute this example, you will notice that there is extra HTML code where we placed the ellipsis (…). It is still too early in this chapter to interest ourselves in this code. Just remember that the server-side script blocks have been executed and have produced the four lines of HTML code in bold.

It is also interesting to note that the code included within the server-side scripts has been compiled into a method of the class representing this page:

```
...
private void __RenderForm1( HtmlTextWriter __w,
                           Control parameterContainer) {
   __w.Write("\r\n           ");
   for (int num1 = 4; num1 < 8; num1++) {
      __w.Write("\r\n              <font size=\"");
      __w.Write(num1);
      __w.Write("\"> Hello </font> \r\n           ");
   }
}
...
```

This method is automatically called by ASP.NET when the page is created.

Code-Behind

If you create a new C# web site using *Visual Studio* (with *File > New > Web Site…*) you will notice that when you create a new page, you can check the *Place code in separate file* option. In this case, a C# source file named [page].aspx.cs which will be associated to your new [page].aspx page. In this file, you have the possibility of defining a class which will contain members usable directly at the execution in the class representing this page. We name this a *code behind* page. Clearly, the advantages of *code behind* over *inlined code* and server-side scripts are to simplify the .aspx files to allow web designers as well as developers to collaborate more efficiently since one works more on the .aspx while the other works more with the .aspx.cs files.

To use this technique with our Btn_Click() method, you must first specify in the Default.aspx which class contains the *code behind* using the Inherits directive and indicate which source file contains this class using the CodeFile directive:

Example 23-5　　　　　　　　　　　　　　　　　　　　　　　　　　　　　　　　　*Default.aspx*
```
<%@ Page Language="C#"   Inherits="MyDefaultPage"
                         CodeFile="Default.aspx.cs" %>
<html xmlns="http://www.w3.org/1999/xhtml" >
   <body>
      <center>
         <form id="Form1" action="Default.aspx" method="post" runat="server">
            Color : <asp:dropdownlist id="Color" runat="server">
                     <asp:listitem>white</asp:listitem>
                     <asp:listitem>black</asp:listitem>
                 </asp:dropdownlist>
            <br/>
            <asp:button id="Button1" text="Submit" OnClick="Btn_Click"
                     runat="server"/>
            <br/>
            <asp:label id="Msg" runat="server"/>
         </form>
      </center>
   </body>
</html>
```

Next, you must declare the MyDefaultPage class as being partial using the partial C#2 keyword:

Example 23-6　　　　　　　　　　　　　　　　　　　　　　　　　　　　　　　　　*Default.aspx.cs*
```
using System;
public partial class MyDefaultPage : System.Web.UI.Page {
   protected void Btn_Click( Object sender , EventArgs e ) {
      Msg.Text = "You selected : " + Color.SelectedItem.Value;
   }
}
```

In fact, ASP.NET 2 offers a *code behind* model which is different than the one of ASP.NET 1.x. These two models are illustrated with the following figure:

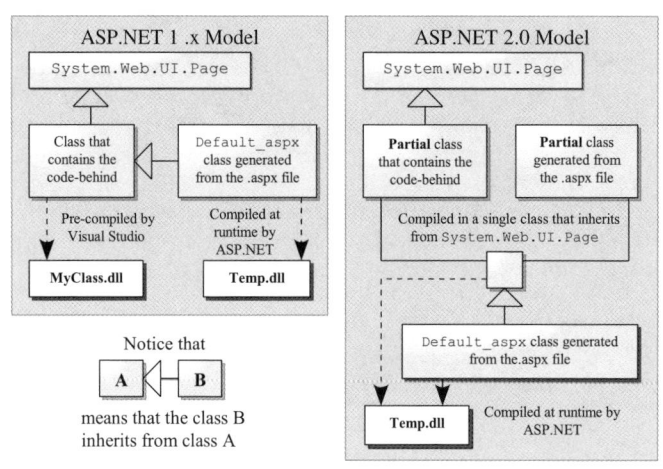

Figure 23-3: Code-behind models of ASP.NET 1.x and 2.0

We see that in ASP.NET 2, the base class containing the *code behind* has the peculiarity of being the union of two partial class definitions: our partial class definition `MyDefaultPage` and a partial class definition generated from the `.aspx` file. This model offers several advantages:

- It simplifies the definition of the class containing the *code behind* definition of several details such as the definition of controls. These details were previously generated by *Visual Studio*. They are now invisible to the developers since they are added automatically and implicitly by ASP.NET during compilation (note that the *Visual Studio* intellisense mechanism takes this into account).
- It reduces the risk of synchronization problems since the generated details are not accessible anymore by the developers.
- It facilitates the migration of ASP.NET 1.x projects by preserving the fact that the `[pageName]_aspx` derives from the class containing the *code behind* which is derived from the `Page` class.
- A same partial base class can be reused by several pages.

By curiosity, here is what the partial class and the `Default_aspx` class generated by ASP.NET in our example looks like:

```
public partial class MyDefaultPage : System.Web.UI.Page,
        System.Web.SessionState.IRequiresSessionState {
    protected System.Web.HttpApplication ApplicationInstance {
        get{ return return this.Context.ApplicationInstance; }
    }
    protected System.Web.Profile.DefaultProfile Profile {
        get { return (DefaultProfile)this.Context.Profile; }
    }
    protected System.Web.UI.WebControls.Button Button1;
    protected System.Web.UI.WebControls.DropDownList Color;
    protected System.Web.UI.HtmlControls.HtmlForm Form1;
    protected System.Web.UI.WebControls.Label Msg;
}
namespace ASP {
    public class Default_aspx : MyDefaultPage {
        public Default_aspx() {
            base.AppRelativeVirtualPath = "~/Default.aspx";
            if (!Default_aspx.__initialized) {
```

```
              string[] textArray1 = new string[2]
                 { "~/Default.aspx", "~/Default.aspx.cs" };
              Default_aspx.__fileDependencies =
                 base.GetWrappedFileDependencies(textArray1);
              Default_aspx.__initialized = true;
           }
        }
        private void __BuildControl__control2(ListItemCollection __ctrl) {
           ListItem item1 = this.__BuildControl__control3();
           __ctrl.Add(item1);
           ListItem item2 = this.__BuildControl__control4();
           __ctrl.Add(item2);
        }
        private ListItem __BuildControl__control3() { ... }
        private ListItem __BuildControl__control4() { ... }
        private Button __BuildControlButton1() { ... }
        private DropDownList __BuildControlColor() { ... }
        private HtmlForm __BuildControlForm1() { ... }
        private Label __BuildControlMsg() { ... }
        private void __BuildControlTree(Default_aspx __ctrl) { ... }
        protected override void FrameworkInitialize() {
           base.FrameworkInitialize();
           this.__BuildControlTree(this);
           base.AddWrappedFileDependencies(Default_aspx.__fileDependencies);
           base.Request.ValidateInput();
        }
        public override int GetTypeHashCode() {return 0x36b54869;}
        private static object __fileDependencies;
        private static bool __initialized;
     }
  }
```

If you use the Src directive instead of the CodeFile directive, or if you do not specify either one but that you deploy the assembly containing the *code behind* in the bin folder, you will return to the ASP.NET 1.x model and you will need to add the details such as the definition of the controls to your base class. Finally, note that the ASP.NET 1.x CodeBehind directive cannot be used anymore.

Compilation and deployment models

ASP.NET 2 offers three compilation models: the dynamic compilation (also called *full runtime compilation*), the *in-place pre-compilation* and the *deployment pre-compilation*.

Dynamic compilation

In this model, you deploy the source files on the server and ASP.NET takes care of compiling them during execution. Each source file is compiled during its first use. If a source file which was already compiled has been modified, ASP.NET detects it and recompiles the file. The main advantage of this model is to ease the work of the developers which do not need to worry about updates, deployment and compilation. However, this model slightly degrades the performance of your server as each compilation has a cost.

The notion of dynamic compilation already exists in ASP.NET 1.x since as shown in Figure 23-3, each aspx page was compiled at execution during its first request. However, with ASP.NET 1.x you needed to compile manually (or with *Visual Studio*) the classes containing the *code behind* as well as all the other classes needed by your application. If you wish to reuse classes already compiled within assemblies, you needed to place these assemblies in the [AppRootDir]/bin folder of your application (or in the GAC) and reference them during the compilation of your application.

The dynamic compilation of ASP.NET 2 has considerably evolved. You can deploy your source files in the [AppRootDir]/App_Code folder of your application (or in one of its sub-folders). This structure can contain source files eventually written in several languages such as C#, VB.NET, XSD (for typed datasets)... The classes contained in this folder can be used in the code of any page within your application. To improve the performance of the compilation, the <configuration>/ <system.web>/<compilation> element of the web.config file offers several sub-elements which allow quantifying the amount of code to compile during each compilation (also known as *batch compilation*).

The assemblies contained in the /bin do not need to be referenced in any way. The classes and other resources contained in these assemblies can be used in the code of any page of your application. ASP.NET 2 takes care of finding them during the execution.

In addition to the /App_Code and /bin folders, ASP.NET knows how to find resources other than classes in the following folders (all directly placed in the root folder of your application):

- /App_GlobalResources and /App_LocalResources for the global and local resource files to the web application (see page 791).
- /App_WebReferences for the WSDL files to be compiled into proxies.
- /App_Data for the files containing data.
- /App_Browsers for .browser files which define which features must be supported by a browser (this folder replaces the <browserCaps> element of machine.config).
- /App_Themes for .css and .skin files.

The update of any file contained in one of these folders is automatically detected and taken into account by ASP.NET 2 during execution. The update of a source file provokes its recompilation while the update of an assembly in the /bin folder causes it to be reloaded by the CLR. This reloading mechanism of an assembly uses a feature named *shadow copy* of the CLR which is described at page 88. Finally know that the aspnet_filer.dll ISAPI filter makes sure that none of the files contained in these folders can be accessed by a HTTP request.

In-place pre-compilation

This model is similar to the preceding model with the exception that you trigger the complete compilation of your application through a HTTP request on the root folder of your application followed by precompile.axd. For example:

```
http://localhost/MyWebSite/precompile.axd
```

In addition to controlling the time at which the compilation is done, the in place pre-compilation allow to encounter eventual compilation problems before they are discovered by the clients.

Deployment pre-compilation

The new tool aspnet_compiler.exe allows the complete compilation of a web application. Hence, it is possible to only deploy the DLLs with no source files. In addition to the obvious advantages for performance, this compilation and deployment model is well adapted to large scale projects. In fact, it allows the creation of a more complex compilation process (such as the use of unit tests or the use of the MSI technology) and the enforcement of intellectual property by obfuscating the assemblies. Of course, this comes at the price of a lesser flexibility for updates.

The `aspnet_compiler.exe` tool is easy to use. You specify the virtual folder containing your web application as an input using the `/m` option (or the root *Windows* folder with the `/p` option), the name of your application using the `/v` option and the output folder containing the results from the compilation.

```
aspnet_compiler.exe /m /LM/W3SVC/1/ROOT/MonSiteWeb D:/TestDeploy
aspnet_compiler.exe /v WebSite /p D:/Site/MonSiteWeb D:/TestDeploy
```

Then you simply need to copy and paste the contents of the output folder to the proper virtual folder on the server. It is interesting to note that this output folder still contains the files with `.aspx` extensions but that are emptied from their content. Your `web.config` file as well as the generated assemblies are in the `/bin` folder. You can also notice the presence of the `PrecompiledApp.config` file. The XML elements contained in this file tells ASP.NET if it is authorized to compile `.aspx` pages. Hence, the parameter of this file can prevent new `.aspx` pages added to a site to be taken into account.

Web forms and controls

Server controls

A server control is an object whose class derives from `System.Web.UI.Control`. The interest behind a server control resides in its ability to create a fragment of HTML code on-demand. For this, the `Control` class has virtual methods such as `void Render(HtmlTextControl)`. Classes which derive from `Control` have the possibility of redefining one or several of these methods. Note that the HTML code fragment generated by an ASP.NET server control can correspond to one of several HTML controls. Later on, we will say *HTML control* or *server control* when there may be a possible ambiguity.

Because of the `ControlCollection Controls{get;set;}` property of the `Control` class, each server control has the possibility of acting as a container for children server controls. For example, the `Page` class derives from `Control`. A web page is then a server control which has the peculiarity of not being a child of any other controls. Also, the `Control` class presents the `void RenderChildren(HtmlTextControl)` method which in turn calls the `Render()` method of each child control while respecting the order in which they are stores. Let us go back to the page in Example 23-5:

```
<%@ Page Language="C#" ... %>
<html xmlns="http://www.w3.org/1999/xhtml" >
    <body>
        <center>
        <form id="Form1" action="Default.aspx" method="post"
              runat="server">
            Color : <asp:dropdownlist id="Color" runat="server">
                    <asp:listitem>white</asp:listitem>
                    <asp:listitem>black</asp:listitem>
                </asp:dropdownlist>
            <br/>
            <asp:button id="Button1" text="Submit" OnClick="Btn_Click"
             runat="server"/>
            <br/>
            <asp:label id="Msg" runat="server"/>
        </form>
        </center>
    </body>
</html>
```

When ASP.NET builds the class containing this page, it will build a tree structure of server controls. This structure is illustrated in the following illustration:

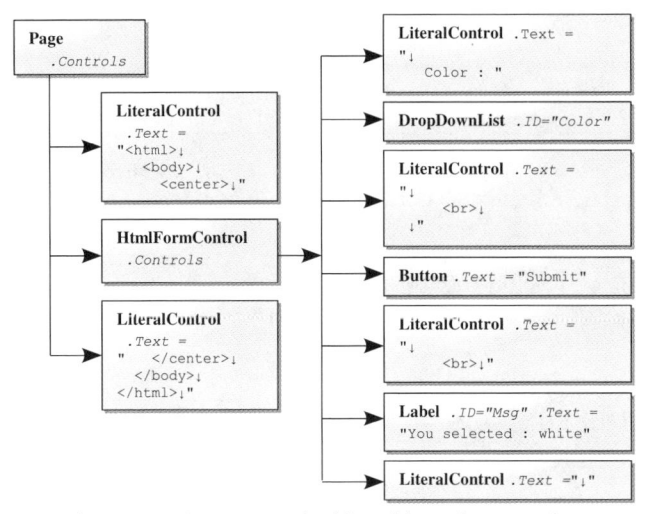

Figure 23-4: Server controls objects hierarchy at runtime

We see that the control classes `Page`, `LiteralControl`, `HtmlFormControl`, `Label`, `DropDownList` and `Button` are involved. The behavior of an instance of the `LiteralControl` is simple. During the call to its `Render()` method, such an object only adds to the page the text which is contained in the `string Text{get;set;}` property. Later on, we will have the opportunity of detailing more actively other types of controls.

Let us look again at the C# code for this page:

```
using System;
public partial class MyDefaultPage : System.Web.UI.Page {
    protected void Btn_Click( Object sender , EventArgs e ) {
        Msg.Text = "You selected : " + Color.SelectedItem.Value;
    }
}
```

Let's bring your attention on the fact that we use the two fields `Label Msg` and `DropDownList Color`. These two fields are references to objects of type `Label` and `DropDownList` in our tree structure. We also notice that their names are the same as the string specified in the `id` attribute. During our discussion on *code behind*, we had already mentioned that the declaration of these fields is automatically done by ASP.NET in the second half of our `MyDefaultPage` partial class. We can now mention that ASP.NET also generates code which is responsible for the initialization of these fields. This underlines the importance of understanding the chain of actions during the lifetime of a web page. In fact, if you try to use the `Msg` or `Color` fields before their initialization, you will obtain a `NullReferenceException` exception. We will detail a little later this chain of event, but first, let's take a look at logic in our `Default.aspx` page.

Interaction between client and serveur

Figure 23-5 illustrates the logic behind our `Default.aspx` page by listing the main steps in the client/web server interaction. The client initiates the interaction by requesting to the server the `/WebSite1/Default.aspx` page through a HTTP GET request. The server then sends back the requested HTML page. This page is built by a new instance of the `Default_aspx` class. During the first request of a client, the server controls have their initial states. For the `DropDownList` control,

Web forms and controls

the initial state is white and for the Label control, this initial state is an empty string. Once the page received, the client selects black on the HTML control corresponding to DropDownList and clicks on the button. This action causes a HTTP POST request to be sent to the server. This request contains amongst other things the state of the HTML control corresponding to the DropDownList server control. The internal ASP.NET processing of .aspx pages (in the HTTP pipeline) is capable of detecting that the POST request is due to the click of the Button1 button. Hence, it invokes the Btn_Click() method on a new instance of the Default_aspx class. In fact, this method has been associated to the 'click on Button1' event in our Default.aspx page because of the <...id=Button1...OnClick=Btn_Click...> line of code. The execution of this method sets the state of our Label control to "You selected : black". The HTML fragment added by this control is then "<span id="Msg">You selected : black</span>".

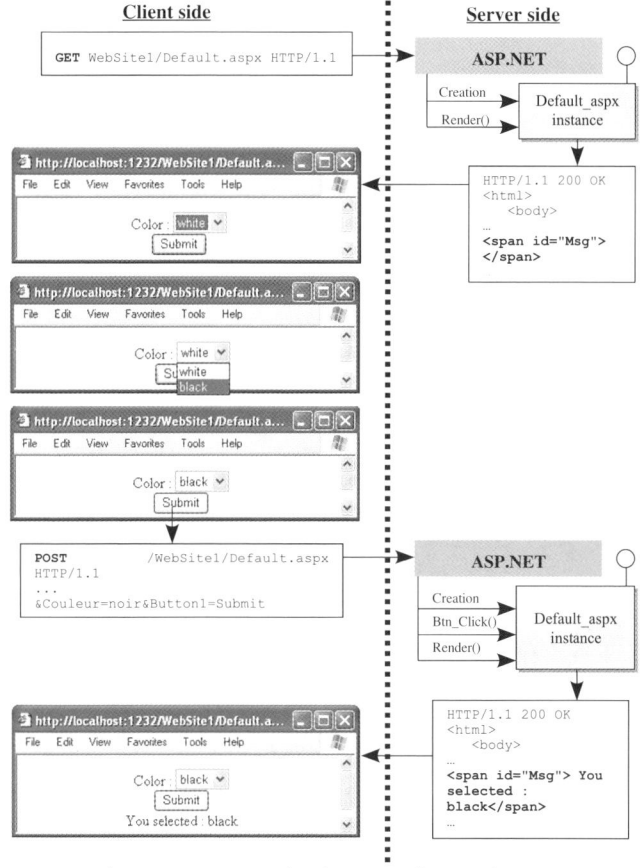

Figure 23-5: Interaction between client and server

ViewState

In the interaction between the client/server described in the previous section, you may have noticed that the black selection of the Color was retained when the client loaded the page the second time. This results from the fact that ASP.NET automatically and implicitly initializes the values of a control with values found in the POST request. Certain type of HTML controls such as the <span> control (which corresponds to a Label server control) does not have their values stored explicitly in the POST request. We see this by analyzing the POST request. Only the controls named Color, Button1 and __VIEWSTATE (which we will talk about) have their values stored in the POST request:

```
POST /WebSite1/Default.aspx HTTP/1.1
...
Content-Length: 104
__VIEWSTATE=%2FwEPDwUJOTE3ODUwMjE3ZGS%2ByRcRG2v6mOv5xTATxgcXe0GIOA%
3D%3D&Color=white&Button1=Submit
```

However, when debugging the `Btn_Click()` during a second click, we see that the server knows the content of the `Msg` control:

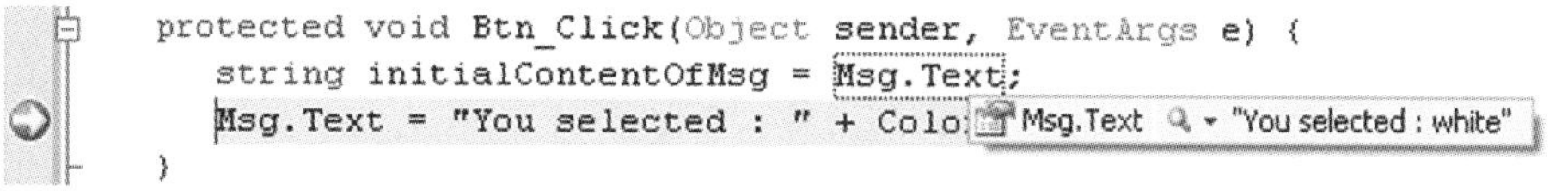

```
protected void Btn_Click(Object sender, EventArgs e) {
    string initialContentOfMsg = Msg.Text;
    Msg.Text = "You selected : " + Colo[Msg.Text  ▾ "You selected : white"]
}
```

Figure 23-6: Debugging to underline the role of the ViewState

It is important that you be convinced with this example that the server does not retain any states. The value of the `Label Msg` is then necessarily encoded implicitly in the POST request.

In fact, when the client browser builds the HTTP request, it gathers in a character string the value of all the control whose values have not been placed in a standard way in the POST request. This string is then encoded in a binary table which is then encoded into a base64 string.

It is now useful to notice that all HTML pages produced by ASP.NET include an invisible HTML control of type `Input` named `__VIEWSTATE`. To convince you, here is an extract of a HTML page produced by an instance of our `Default_aspx` class:

```
<html xmlns="http://www.w3.org/1999/xhtml" >
    <body>
        <center>
        <form method="post" action="Default.aspx" id="Form1">
<div>
...
<input type="hidden" name="__VIEWSTATE" id="__VIEWSTATE" value="/
wEPDwUJOTE3ODUwMjE3D2QWAgIBD2QWAgIFDw8WAh4EVGV4dAUfVm91cyBhdm
V6IHPDqWx1Y3Rpb25uw6kgOiBibGFuY2RkZGsF3jbEtiYP6owubOheigPWF2Fq" />
</div>
...
```

When the browser builds a HTTP request, it assigns the base64 character string to the value of the `__VIEWSTATE` HTML control. We actually find this value in the extract of our previous POST request (in bold). Hence, by decoding this information, the ASP.NET internal processing of `.aspx` pages is capable of recovering the state of all the controls.

The first time that we encounter this trick it does not appear as being a clean solution. Understand that this technique is there to work around the fact that there is no state information in a web environment. Such a behavior is useful as when we navigate from one page to another, the users expect the value of the controls to remain the same. There was no equivalent technique in the ASP technology and developers were forced to have code for each control which is expected to remember its state between requests.

Postback and non-postback events

When a user works with a HTML page in a browser, he will complete actions susceptible to trigger two types of events: The *postback events* and non-*postback* events.

Postback events cause a POST event to be sent to the server to inform it on the state of all the controls on the page. Using this information, the server can dynamically regenerate the page and send it back to the browser. Our previous example shows that the click of a button is a *postback* event.

Web forms and controls 729

Non-postback events do not cause a call to the server. A *non-postback* is saved and will be sent to the server during the next *postback* event. When the server must execute several *non-postback* events, you cannot expect a certain execution order. Typically, *non-postback* events are changes to the state of the controls of the page. Our example shows that the selection change in the combo box is a *non-postback* event. We can also mention the edition of text in a textbox. You can force a *postback* event by setting to true the AutoPostBack property of the underlying server control. For example, if we add the autopostback="true" to our Color server control, a POST request will be sent to the server each time the selection of the combo box is changed:

```
...
  <form id="Form1" action="Default.aspx" method="post"
        runat="server">
  Color : <asp:dropdownlist id="Color" runat="server" autopostback="true" >
            <asp:listitem>white</asp:listitem>
            <asp:listitem>black</asp:listitem>
          </asp:dropdownlist>
          <br/>
...
```

In this context, we can now specify that the <form> controls defines a server control of type System.Web.UI.HtmlControls.HtmlForm. All server controls which may cause a *postback* event must be declared between the <form> markers.

We have already mentioned that ASP.NET knows how to associate the Btn_Click() method of our MyDefaultPage class to the 'click on Button1' *postback* event from the fact that we have assigned Btn_Click to the OnClick attribute of Button1 in our Default.aspx page:

```
...
  <asp:button id="Button1" text="Submit" OnClick="Btn_Click"
        runat="server"/>
...
```

In fact, the System.Web.UI.WebControls.Button class offers a Click event which uses a EventHandler delegate. During the compilation of an aspx page, ASP.NET knows that the value of an OnXXX attribute corresponds to the name of a method which must be associated with the XXX event of the underlying server control. We can avoid using this feature as long as we create this association ourselves during the initialization of our instance of Default_aspx. Hence, the following page is equivalent to our original page (we will later detail the Page_Load() event which is invoked by ASP.NET when a page is loaded).

Example 23-7   *Default.aspx*

```
...
  <asp:button id="Button1" text="Submit" runat="server"/>
...
```

Example 23-8   *Default.aspx.cs*

```
using System;
public partial class MyDefaultPage : System.Web.UI.Page {
   protected void Page_Load(object sender, EventArgs e) {
      if ( IsPostBack )
         Button1.Click += Btn_Click;
   }
   protected void Btn_Click(Object sender, EventArgs e) {
      Msg.Text = "You selected : " + Color.SelectedItem.Value;
   }
}
```

Note the use of the `bool Page.IsPostBack{get;}` property which is set to `true` if the current request is a POST request. We use it as there is no need to subscribe to the `Button1.Click` event if we are not in a *postback* request.

This brings up a question: How does the ASP.NET plumbing determine which event of which control to trigger during the reception of a POST request from a client? Similar to what we have seen in regards to *viewstate*, ASP.NET adds two hidden controls named __EVENTTARGET and __EVENTARGUMENT to each generated HTML page as well as some *javascript* code to initialize them. For example, here is an extract of such an HTML page generated by an instance of our `Default_aspx` class:

```
<html xmlns="http://www.w3.org/1999/xhtml" >
  <body>
     <center>
     <form method="post" action="Default.aspx" id="Form1">
<div>
<input type="hidden" name="__EVENTTARGET" id="__EVENTTARGET" value="" />
<input type="hidden" name="__EVENTARGUMENT" id="__EVENTARGUMENT"
 value="" />
<input type="hidden" name="__VIEWSTATE" id="__VIEWSTATE" value="..." />
</div>
<script type="text/javascript">
<!--
var theForm = document.forms['Form1'];
if (!theForm) {
    theForm = document.Form1;
}
function __doPostBack(eventTarget, eventArgument) {
    if (!theForm.onsubmit || (theForm.onsubmit() != false)) {
        theForm.__EVENTTARGET.value = eventTarget;
        theForm.__EVENTARGUMENT.value = eventArgument;
        theForm.submit();
    }
}
// -->
</script>
...
```

Hence, each POST request contains in the __EVENTTARGET and __EVENTARGUMENT fields the information allowing ASP.NET to identify the HTML control responsible for the *postback*.

ContolState

A common problem encountered with ASP.NET 1.x comes from the fact that the base64 string of the *viewstate* becomes large (>10,000 characters) when it stores the content of a table such as a `DataGrid` server control. When this problem is encountered, we can choose to deactivate the *viewstate* for this control and use another way of managing its state, for example by storing the content of the table in a server-side cache and by reloading the content at every request. This brings up a second problem: for certain server controls such as `DataGrid`, the navigator uses the content of the *viewstate* for functional reasons such as the triggering of a *postback* event when data is changed. In ASP.NET 1.x we could be tempted to deactivate the *viewstate* of a control for bandwidth reasons and to activate it for functional reasons.

In ASP.NET 2 the problem of large *viewstate* blocks has been reduced because the information are stored more efficiently in the base64 string. But more importantly, ASP.NET 2 introduces the notion of *controlstate*. A server control can use the *controlstate* to store the information necessary

Web forms and controls

for the control to properly function. The following server controls can then take advantage of the *controlstate* for functional reasons but can also deactivate their *viewstate* to save on bandwidth: `CheckBoxList`, `DetailsView`, `FormView`, `GridView`, `ListControl` (and its derived classes), `LoginView`, `MultiView` and `Table`.

Know that you will not see special hidden fields in your HTML pages to store the *controlstate*. They are stored as sub-sections of the *viewstate*.

Cross-page posting

By default, all *postback* made by a page is done to itself. However, it is often necessary to change the target page during a *postback* request. This is possible by specifying the new target page with the `PostBackUrl` property of the button server controls on the source page. Let's rewrite our `Default.aspx` page so that it communicates the choice of color to another target page named `DisplayColor.aspx` specialized for the display of the color:

Example 23-9 *Default.aspx*

```
<%@ Page Language="C#" %>
<html xmlns="http://www.w3.org/1999/xhtml" >
<script language="C#" runat="server">
   private string m_SelectedColor;
   public string SelectedColor { get { return m_SelectedColor; } }
   void Btn_Click(Object sender, EventArgs e) {
      m_SelectedColor = Color.SelectedItem.Value;
   }
</script>
<body><center>
   <form id="Form1" action="Default.aspx" method="post" runat="server">
      Color : <asp:dropdownlist id="Color" runat="server">
                 <asp:listitem>white</asp:listitem>
                 <asp:listitem>black</asp:listitem>
              </asp:dropdownlist><br/>
      <asp:button id="Button1" text="Submit" OnClick="Btn_Click"
          postBackUrl ="~/DisplayColor.aspx" runat="server"/><br/>
   </form>
</center></body></html>
```

You have to understand that because the `DisplayColor.aspx` target page does not have the same server controls than the `Default.aspx` page, the data contained in our *postback* cannot be directly used. In fact, every thing happens as if we were making a GET request on the target page. Internally, the data for the *postback* request has been used by an instance of the class representing the source page. This instance can be accessed through the `PreviousPage` property of the target page. Also, you may wish to use the data of the *postback* request from the target page, it is recommended to make them accessible through the use of properties of the source page. This technique is illustrated by the `SelectedColor` of our `Default.aspx` source page and by the `DisplayColor.aspx` target page:

Example 23-10 *DisplayColor.aspx*

```
<%@ Page Language="C#" %>
<%@ previousPageType virtualpath ="~/Default.aspx" %>
<script runat="server">
void Page_Load(object sender, EventArgs e) {
  if (PreviousPage != null && PreviousPage.IsCrossPagePostBack) {
    Msg.Text = "You selected : " + PreviousPage.SelectedColor;
  } else { Msg.Text = "No color selected."; }
}
```

Example 23-10 DisplayColor.aspx
```
</script>
<html xmlns="http://www.w3.org/1999/xhtml" ><body>
<form id="form1" runat="server"><asp:label id="Msg" runat="server"/>
</form></body></html>
```

Notice that the `PreviousPage` reference takes the type of our `Default_aspx` page since we can directly invoke our `SelectedColor{get;}` property. ASP.NET could type this reference because of the use of the `<%@ PreviousPageType>` directive which indicates the origin of the source page. In certain cases, this feature can prove itself to be a limitation since it prevents a target page to have various source pages. Also, it is possible to not use this directive and thus have an untyped source page. Let's rewrite our `DisplayColor.aspx` without using the `<%@ PreviousPageType>` directive:

Example 23-11 DisplayColor.aspx
```
<%@ Page Language="C#" %>
<script runat="server">
void Page_Load(object sender, EventArgs e) {
   if (PreviousPage != null ) {
      DropDownList Color =
         PreviousPage.FindControl("Color") as DropDownList;
      if ( Color != null )
         Msg.Text = "You selected : " + Color.SelectedItem.Value;
   }
   if( Msg.Text.Length==0 ) Msg.Text = "No color selected.";
}
</script>
<html xmlns="http://www.w3.org/1999/xhtml" ><body>
<form id="form1" runat="server"><asp:label id="Msg" runat="server"/>
</form></body></html>
```

This page can then display the selected color from any page containing a `DropDownList` control named `Color`.

Another technique available since ASP.NET 1.x also allows changing pages. For this, you simply need to use the `HttpServerUtility.Transfer(string targetPage)` method as follows:

Example 23-12 Default.aspx
```
...
   void Btn_Click(Object sender, EventArgs e) {
      m_SelectedColor = Color.SelectedItem.Value;
      Server.Transfer("~/DisplayColor.aspx");
   }
...
<asp:button id="Button1" text="Submit" OnClick="Btn_Click"
   runat="server"/>
...
```

This technique has a disadvantage compared to the use of `PostBackUrl`: the URL will not change in the browser.

Finally, let's mention the presence of the `bool IsCrossPagePostBack{get;}` property. Here is a table which illustrates the value of this property depending on the context:

```
SourcePage does a postback to itself :
SourcePage.IsPostBack              true
SourcePage.IsCrossPagePostBack     false
```

Web forms and controls

```
SourcePage.PreviousPage              null
SourcePage does a postBackUrl to TargetPage:
SourcePage.IsPostBack                true
SourcePage.IsCrossPagePostBack       true
SourcePage.PreviousPage              null
TargetPage.IsPostBack                false
TargetPage.IsCrossPagePostBack       false
TargetPage.PreviousPage              references SourcePage
SourcePage does a transfer to TargetPage:
SourcePage.IsPostBack                false
SourcePage.IsCrossPagePostBack       false
SourcePage.PreviousPage              null
TargetPage.IsPostBack                false
TargetPage.IsCrossPagePostBack       false
TargetPage.PreviousPage              references SourcePage
```

HTML server controls vs. Web server controls

Until now we have only talked of server and HTML controls. Server controls are used by ASP.NET and only exist on the server-side. HTML controls are included within HTML pages and are only used by the browser on the client-side.

There are two distinct categories of server controls: *HTML server controls* and *web server controls*. To each type of HTML control corresponds a HTML server control. The reverse is not necessarily true as there are HTML server controls such as `HtmlGenericControl` which have no HTML equivalent. A HTML server control only takes care of producing the fragment of HTML code corresponding to the associated HTML control. Web server controls are more evolved and offer a more complete API. They can also generally produce HTML code fragments which contain several HTML controls. Hence, web server controls are generally preferred by developers. Actually, our `Default.aspx` page uses three web server controls (`<asp:dropdownlist>`, `<asp:button>` and `<asp:label>`) and one HTML server control (`<form>`). The advantage of HTML server controls resides in the simplicity of their declaration for the developer who knows the HTML language well. In fact, you simply need to add the `runat="server"` attribute to any HTML control of an `.aspx` page so that ASP.NET creates an associated server control. In fact, these HTML server controls are adapted to the migration from ASP to ASP.NET. Here is our `Default.aspx` page rewritten using HTML server controls:

Example 23-13 *Default.aspx*

```
<%@ Page Language="C#" %>
<script language="C#" runat="server">
   void Btn_Click(Object sender, EventArgs e) {
      Msg.InnerText = "You selected : " + Color.Value;
   }
</script>
<html xmlns="http://www.w3.org/1999/xhtml" >
   <body>
      <center>
      <form id="Form1" action="Default.aspx" method="post" runat="server" >
         Color : <select id="Color" runat="server" >
            <option value="white" />
            <option value="black" />
         </select>
         <br/>
         <input id="Button1" type="Submit" value="Submit"
                OnServerClick="Btn_Click" runat="server" />
         <br/>
```

Example 23-13   Default.aspx

```
            <span id="Msg" runat="server" />
        </form>
        </center>
    </body>
</html>
```

The list of available HTML server controls can be found in the article named **HTML Server Controls Hierarchy** on **MSDN**. These controls are all part of the `System.Web.UI.HtmlControls` namespace and also all derive from the `System.Web.UI.HtmlControls.HtmlControl` class (which is itself derived from `System.Web.UI.Control`).

The list of available web server controls can be found in the article named **Web Server Controls Hierarchy** on **MSDN**. These controls are almost all part of the `System.Web.UI.WebControls` namespace and most of them derive from the `System.Web.UI.WebControls.WebControl` class (which is itself derived from `System.Web.UI.Control`).

Page life cycle

Now that we have defined the notions of *postback* events, of *viewstate/controlstate* and of control tree, it is time to discuss the timing of events driving the processing of every requests. A good comprehension of ASP.NET cannot be achieved without a good knowledge of this life cycle. Let us remind you that the threading model behind ASP.NET associates one thread of the thread pool to process a complete request. Also, the processing of events is done one after the other on the same thread.

In the following table, each event is indexed by the name of its default method. We specify if the methods are invoked recursively on all the controls or if it is only called on the page. Most of these methods are protected and virtual, meaning that you can override them in your own implementation. In this case, it is recommended to invoke the implementation of the base class within your class to avoid causing problems with the processing of your requests. Certain of these events can be intercepted in ways other than rewriting their virtual method. For example, you can subscribe the `Control.Load` event at the page level without having to override the `OnLoad()` method. For this, you simply need to provide a method named `Page_Load()`. If you set the `AutoEventWireUp` sub-directive to `true`, ASP.NET knows how to find this method through reflection and invokes it at the appropriate time. If you do not wish to pay the cost of reflection, you can set this sub-directive to `false` and you can assign this delegate yourself or simply override the appropriate virtual methods.

To help you remember this chain of events, we have classified them by step. The events which are only triggered by a POST request have their table cells in grey. As for the new elements in ASP.NET 2, they are written in bold:

Page life cycle   735

Steps	Events and methods	Control involved	Comments
Construction	`Constructor calls`	All	Allows the initialization of fields.
Initialization	`InitializeCulture`	Page	Allows the personalization of the culture.
	`DeterminePostBackMode`	Page	Determines if a request is *postback* or not, giving you the possibility of simulating a *postback* request.
	`OnPreInit`	Page	Allows the specification of a master page or a theme.
	`OnInit`	All	Initialization of the states with the values specified in the page.
	`OnInitComplete`	Page	Gives the possibility of modifying the initial states of controls or to dynamically create controls.
Load states	`LoadPageStateFrom-PersistenceMedium`	Page	Allows the possibility of loading the *viewstate* from a different location than the page (for example, from a save done in the previous request).
	`LoadViewState`	All	Restores the states from the *viewstate* and *controlstate*.
	`LoadControlState`	All	
	`ProcessPostData`	Page	Restored the state of the control from the values specified in the *postback* parameters.
Page load	`OnPreLoad`	Page	It is here that you will do most of your actions such as the subscription to an event or obtaining a database connection.
	`OnLoad`	All	
	`OnDataBinding`	All	Load the data within controls which support databinding.
	`ProcessPostData`	Page	Called a second time in case controls are dynamically created during `OnLoad()`. Hence, their state can be restored from the parameters in the *postback* request.
	`Validate`	Page	Initiates the validation of specialized controls.
	`RaiseChangedEvent`	Page	Initiates events due to a state change (logical step after `ProcessPostData`).
	`RaisePostBackEvent`	Page	Initiates *postback* events.
	`OnLoadComplete`	Page	
Pre render	`OnPreRender`	All	Last chance to act on the control tree structure as well as their state.
	`OnPreRenderComplete`	Page	
Save states	`Page.SaveViewState`	All	Saves the states in the *viewstate* and *controlstate*.
	`SaveControlState`	All	
	`SavePageStateTo-PersistenceMedium`	Page	Allows saving the *viewstate* somewhere else than in the page. Useful to reduce the used bandwidth.
	`OnSaveStateComplete`	Page	
Render	`Render`	All	Construction of a HTML page and immediate transmission to the client.
Finalization	`UnLoad`	All	Last chance to free any unmanaged resources such as a database connection. These methods are called after the transmission of the HTML page.
	`Dispose`	All	

Handling a page request on several threads

It happens that the processing of a request implies a long wait for the thread. Typically, this happens when we access a slow web service or when we complete and expensive request on a database. In this case, the ASP.NET threading model is inefficient. In fact, the wait of a thread is not without consequences since the number of threads in the pool used to serve request is bound. If most requests imply a wait from their threads, the server will quickly find itself overloaded. We are then faced with a design bottleneck.

ASP.NET 2 offers an infrastructure to solve this problem. The idea is that the finalization of the processing of a request be accomplished on a different thread than the one that initiated the processing. Meanwhile, the access to a resource such as a web service or a database is done without holding a thread from the pool. In the case of a *SQL Server* database access, this is possible using asynchronous requests of ADO.NET 2 described at page 612. This feature allows making a request to a *SQL Server* database without using a thread from the pool while waiting for the data. The following example illustrates a page which uses the feature allowing ASP.NET 2 to process a page on multiple threads and the feature of ADO.NET 2 allowing asynchronous requests. The data recovered from the database are then presented in a `GridView`:

Example 23-14   *Default.aspx*
```
<%@ Page Language="C#" Async="true" CodeFile="Default.aspx.cs"
                                Inherits="_Default" %>
<html xmlns="http://www.w3.org/1999/xhtml" >
<body><form id="form1" runat="server">
   <asp:GridView ID="MyGridView" runat="server"
                 AutoGenerateColumns="true" />
</form></body></html>
```

Example 23-15   *Default.aspx.cs*
```
using System;
using System.Data;
using System.Data.SqlClient;
using System.Web;
using System.Web.UI;
using System.Threading;
public partial class _Default : System.Web.UI.Page {
   private SqlCommand cmd;
   private SqlConnection cnx;
   protected void Page_Load(object sender, EventArgs e) {
      Response.Write("PageLoad thread:"+
                  Thread.CurrentThread.ManagedThreadId +"<br/>");
      PageAsyncTask task = new PageAsyncTask( BeginInvoke, EndInvoke,
                                              EndTimeOutInvoke, null);
      Page.RegisterAsyncTask(task);
   }
   public IAsyncResult BeginInvoke( object sender,
                                    EventArgs e,
                                    AsyncCallback callBack,
                                    object extraData) {
      Response.Write( "BeginInvoke thread:" +
                  Thread.CurrentThread.ManagedThreadId + "<br/>");
      cnx = new SqlConnection( "async=true ; server = localhost ; " +
                               "uid=sa ; pwd =; database = ORGANIZATION");
      cmd = new SqlCommand( "SELECT * FROM EMPLOYEES", cnx );
      cnx.Open();
      return cmd.BeginExecuteReader( callBack, extraData,
                                     CommandBehavior.CloseConnection);
   }
   public void EndInvoke( IAsyncResult result ) {
      Response.Write( "EndInvoke thread:" +
                  Thread.CurrentThread.ManagedThreadId + "<br/>");
      SqlDataReader rdr = cmd.EndExecuteReader(result);
      if (rdr != null && rdr.HasRows) {
         MyGridView.DataSource = rdr;
         MyGridView.DataBind();
```

Example 23-15   Default.aspx.cs
```
      }
      rdr.Close();
   }
   public void EndTimeOutInvoke( IAsyncResult result ) {
      if (cnx != null && cnx.State != ConnectionState.Closed)
         cnx.Close();
      Response.Write("TimeOut");
      Response.End();
   }
   protected override void OnPreRender( EventArgs e ) {
      Response.Write( "OnPreRender thread:" +
                     Thread.CurrentThread.ManagedThreadId + "<br/>");
   }
   protected override void OnPreRenderComplete( EventArgs e ) {
      Response.Write( "OnPreRenderComplete thread:" +
                     Thread.CurrentThread.ManagedThreadId + "<br/>");
   }
}
```

To support this multi-threaded processing model, you must set to `true` the `Async` property of the `<%@ Page>` directive. During the `Load` event, we can create instances of the `System.Web.UI.PageAsyncTask` class. Each instance represents a processing which will occur outside of the `aspnet_wp.exe` process. No thread from the pool is used to wait for the end of the processing. This processing is represented by three delegates:

- A delegate to the method that will begin the processing of the request (i.e. the one which executes `Page_Load()`). In our example, the delegate references the `BeginInvoke()`. It is executed right after the `PreRender()` event.

- A delegate to the method which completes the processing of the work on a thread of the pool once the work is completed. In our example, our delegate references the `BeginInvoke` method. It is executed right before the `PreRenderComplete` event.

- A delegate to a method executed by a thread of the pool when the work was not completed within a certain amount of time. In this case, our delegate references the `EndTimeOutInvoke()` method.

The HTML page generated by this example starts as follows:

```
PageLoad thread:4
OnPreRender thread:4
BeginInvoke thread:4
EndInvoke thread:8
OnPreRenderComplete thread:8
...
```

If you wish to use this technique to asynchronously process a call to a web service, you can use the `IAsyncResult BeginXXX()` and `EndXXX(IAsyncResult)` methods of the proxy class generated by the `wsdl.exe` tool (see page 825).

ASP.NET application configuration (Web.Config files)

It is preferable to have assimilated the section relative to the configuration file of a .NET application at page 46 before going on.

Web.Config file organization

The configuration of an ASP.NET application is done through the use of an XML file with a .Config extension. In these files, most of the parameters relative to ASP.NET are found in the <configuration>/<system.web> section. The configuration parameters of a same ASP.NET application can be spread across the following .Config files:

- The Machine.Config file which is located in the framework installation folder C:\WINDOWS\Microsoft.NET\Framework\v2.0.50727\CONFIG\machine.config. This is the only required configuration file.
- The Web.Config file, which is located in the root folder of the sites hosted on the machine, in general C:\Inetpub\wwwroot.
- The Web.Config file, which is found in the root folder of the concerned application.
- The Web.Config file, which can be found in any sub-folder of the concerned application.

For a page stored in a [root]\Foo sub-folder of your web application, the values of the parameters defined in [root]\Foo\Web.Config mask the value of the parameters defined in [root]\Web.Config which in turn mask the values of the parameters defined in C:\Inetpub\wwwroot\Web.Config which in turn masks the parameters defined in Machine.Config. With this model, for example, it is easy to define a security policy by default common to all web applications hosted on the machine in the Machine.Config file while still being free to apply special policies for certain confidential pages stored in a special sub-folder of an application. In addition to this flexibility, this model also allows the deployment of an application as well as its configuration files by simply copying the folder structure and its files (xcopy deployment). Finally note that ASP.NET makes these configuration files inaccessible from outside.

Web.Config files sections

Here is a complete list of ASP.NET 2 configuration elements of contained in the <system.web> element. Those that are in bold have been introduced with version 2.0 of ASP.NET. We give reference to the description of their use within this book when available:

<anonymousIdentification/> seeat page 804
<authentication/> see page 797
<authorization/> see page 796
** see page 769**
****
****
see page 791
** see page 753**
****
****
see page 743
see page 744
see page 795
** see page 798**
****
see page 789
see page 739
** see page 802**

```
<protocols/>
<roleManager/> see page 800
<securityPolicy/>
<sessionPageState/>
<sessionState/> see page 747
<siteMap/> see page 793
<trace/> see page 752
<trust/>
<urlMappings/>
<webControls/>
<webParts/> see page 810
<webServices/>
<xhtml11Conformance/>
```

For more details on the configuration of a web application, we recommend you read the article named **ASP.NET Configuration** on **MSDN**.

Finally, let's add that an `<location>` element under the `<configuration>` element allows you to redefine configuration parameters for each page.

The <processModel> section

Reliability is one of the major constraints imposed by a web application. During the development of a web application, you must pay a peculiar attention to the `<processModel>` configuration element which is located in the `Machine.config` file. This element allows to setup the following features destined to solidify the reliability of a web application:

- You can indicate to ASP.NET when to restart a process which is behaving abnormally. The `requestQueueLimit` attribute specifies the maximum number of pending request. Once this number is reached, ASP.NET considers that the process is having an abnormal behavior. The `memoryLimit` attribute specifies the percentage of system memory which can be used. Once this limit is reached, ASP.NET will consider that the process is behaving abnormally. In this case, it is given the period of time specified in the `shutdownTimeout` to shutdown automatically. After this time limit, ASP.NET terminates this process and launches a new one. Note that pending requests are automatically reassigned to this new process.

- You can force ASP.NET to restart the process periodically, even is no abnormal conditions have been detected. The `timeout` attribute indicates the duration at which the process must be restarted. The `requestLimit` attribute indicates the number of processed requests at which the process will be restarted. The `idleTimeout` indicates an inactivity period at which the process will be stopped.

- The `webGarden` and `cpuMask` attributes indicate to ASP.NET how to behave itself on a multi-processor server. In fact, if a server has multiple processors, it is efficient to ensure that each processor manages only certain processes. We say that we are creating affinities between processes and processors. This technique is named *web garden*.

- The `userName` and `Password` attributes indicate the identity of the *Windows* user under which the `aspnet_wp.exe` must be executed.

Updating configuration

In ASP.NET 1.x, to update the configuration of an application you have the choice between updating the `.Config` XML file by hand or by manipulating the XML contents programmatically in an untyped way. ASP.NET 2 offers several new features to accomplish this type of operation:

- *Visual Studio 2005* assists you with intellisense during the manual edition of a configuration file.

- A new graphical web interface allows you to update the configuration directly from a browser executed locally (for security reasons). You can access it from *Visual Studio* with *Site Web > ASP. NET Configuration*.

- A new graphical interface for the update of the configuration has been inserted to the IIS configuration console.

- New base classes are supplies to programmatically manipulate in a typed way the XML content (see page 46).

Applying configuration updates at runtime

Because of the *shadow copy* mechanism, all changes made on a configuration file are taken into account by ASP.NET. Consequently, you do not need to restart the web application for the changes to be applied. This however will lead to the loss of the states maintained in the memory of the application (both session and application states). In consequence, you must avoid updating the configuration of a production web application as it could interfere with user interaction. Also, changes made to the `<processModel>` element are only taken into account when IIS is restarted.

HTTP Pipeline

Introduction

Until now, we have explained how ASP.NET processes `.aspx` page requests. During the transmission of a HTTP request between the exit of the named pile (generally coming from IIS) and the processing of the page, we had the occasion of mentioning the *HTTP pipeline* as well as the code used for the internal processing of `.aspx` pages. The HTTP pipeline is a mechanism of ASP.NET allowing mainly:

- To provide processes which work on the HTTP requests and/or the HTTP responses. Such a process is named *HTTP module*. ASP.NET has its own HTTP modules which, for example, process the session identifiers and the authentication of users. We will see how you can create your own HTTP modules.

- To provide a process which serves the HTTP requests (i.e. which fabricates a HTTP response from the request). Such a processing is called *HTTP handler*. ASP.NET has its own HTTP handlers, including the one which processes `.aspx` pages. We will see how you can create your own HTTP handlers.

Figure 23-7 illustrates the place that the HTTP pipeline as well as the HTTP module and handlers hold in ASP.NET. This figure bases itself on the IIS 5.0 process model which is different from the model used in IIS 6.0.

The HttpApplication class and the Global.asax file

Before approaching the topic of HTTP modules and handlers, it is necessary to understand the notion of HTTP application. We have already explained that the ASP.NET process maintains an AppDomain for each web application which it hosts. ASP.NET makes sure that each of these AppDomains contains an instance of the `System.Web.HttpApplication` class (or a class derived from it). This class offers events which are triggered at certain key steps, such as the launch of the application or the creation of a new session. By subscribing to certain of these events, you can execute your own tasks at the appropriate times.

HTTP Pipeline

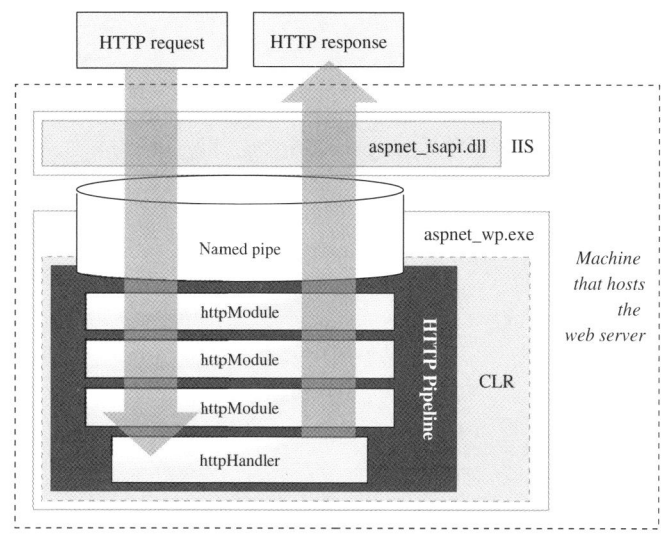

Figure 23-7: HTTP module and HTTP handler

The standard technique to subscribe to these events is to provide the code for the tasks in methods defined in a file named `Global.asax`. This file must be stored in the root of your application. ASP.NET will then compile these methods into a class named `ASP.Global_asax` which derives from `HttpApplication`. The application object will be an instance of this class during execution. Here is an example of `Global.asax`:

Example 23-16   *Global.asax*

```
<%@ Application Language="C#" %>
<script Runat="server">
protected void Application_Start(object src, EventArgs e) { /*...*/ }
protected void Application_End(object src, EventArgs e) { /*...*/ }
protected void Application_AuthenticateRequest(object src, EventArgs e)
{ /*...*/ }
protected void Application_Error(object src, EventArgs e) { /*...*/ }
protected void Session_Start(object src, EventArgs e) { /*...*/ }
protected void Session_End(object src, EventArgs e) { /*...*/ }
protected void Session_BeginRequest(object src, EventArgs e) { /*...*/ }
protected void Session_EndRequest(object src, EventArgs e) { /*...*/ }
protected void Application_PostMapRequestHandler(object src,EventArgs e)
{ /*...*/ }
/*...*/
</script>
```

We invite you to consult MSDN to get the complete list of events. It is interesting to note that ASP.NET uses reflection to associate the methods defined in the `Global.asax` file to the events of `HttpApplication`. The name of such a method starts with `Application_` or `Session_` followed by the name of the event. Consequently, you must pay attention to the name of these methods. Intellisense will not detect syntax errors. Also note that certain events such as `Application_Start()` can only be used through the `global.asax` file while other can also be exploited as any event of a .NET class.

HTTP context

An instance of the `System.Web.HttpContext` class is automatically created by ASP.NET for each HTTP request. During the processing of a request, this context object is accessible at all the levels of the HTTP pipeline by using the `Current{get;}` static property of the `HttpContext` class. During the processing of a request, we often need to store information accessible through the properties of the context object, such as the principal of the user who initiated the request (if he is authenticated), the request itself or the response that is being constructed.

HTTP module

We can now interest ourselves to the development of custom HTTP modules. A HTTP module is an instance of a class which implements the `System.Web.IHttpModule` interface:

```
public interface IHttpModule {
   void Dispose();
   void Init( HttpApplication app );
}
```

A module object is created during the launch of an ASP.NET application. After the call to the constructor of its class, ASP.NET will invoke the `Init()` method. You must take advantage of this method to subscribe your tasks to the HTTP requests and responses. In general, we subscribe to the `BeginRequest()` and `EndRequest()` of `HttpApplication` but you can also choose to subscribe to any other event. Here is an example of a simple HTTP module:

Example 23-17

```
using System;
using System.Web;
public class MyHttpModule : IHttpModule {
   public void Dispose() { }
   public void Init( HttpApplication app ) {
      app.BeginRequest += OnBeginRequest;
      app.EndRequest += OnEndRequest;
   }
   public void OnBeginRequest( object source, EventArgs args ) {
      HttpApplication app = source as HttpApplication;
      app.Response.Write( "BeginRequest : " +
                          DateTime.Now.ToLongTimeString());
   }
   public void OnEndRequest( object source, EventArgs args ) {
      HttpApplication app = source as HttpApplication;
      app.Response.Write( "EndRequest : " +
                          DateTime.Now.ToLongTimeString());
   }
}
```

This module adds the date of the start and end in the response, in this case an HTML file. Notice that in this example, the character strings added to the beginning and end of the HTML page are not included within the <html> markers but IE still displays them:

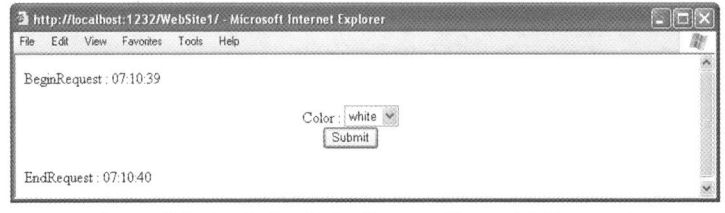

Figure 23-8: Rendering Default.aspx with our HTTP module

HTTP Pipeline

Also note that the `Init()` method of each module is only called once during the lifetime of the application. This is the same instance of the module which is responsible for processing all requests. Since several threads can be processed simultaneously by several threads, this remark is relevant as it underlines the need of proper synchronization when accessing the resources of a module.

Finally, you must know that for ASP.NET to take into account a particular module, we must specify so in the configuration file for the application as follows:

Web.Config
```
<?xml version="1.0"?>
<configuration xmlns="http://schemas.microsoft.com/.NetConfiguration/v2.0">
   <system.web>
      <httpModules>
         <add name="MyHttpModuleName" type="MyHttpModule,MyAsm"/>
      </httpModules>
...
```

The `type` attribute specifies the complete name (i.e. with namespace) of the class implementing the `IHttpModule` interface followed by a comma and then the strong name of the assembly containing the class. If the code for the class is contained in the `/App_Code` folder, you do not need to specify the assembly. If not, the assembly must be contained in the `/bin` folder. Note that the declaration of a HTTP module can be done within the `<httpModules>` marker of the `Machine.config` file in order for them to be taken into account by all the ASP.NET applications on the|machine. In this case, the assembly containing the class of the module must be located in the GAC.

You must conceive your modules to be as independent as possible as you have no control over the order in which they will be executed in the HTTP pipeline. This chaining order is in the same order as the call to the `Init()` method of the modules. Thus, Figure 23-7 is not completely exact since the processing of `EndRequest()` are called in the same order as the processing of `BeginRequest()` and not in the reverse order. Empirically, we can notice that the order in which the `Init()` are called is the same as the declaration of the `<httpModules>` markers in the configuration file but this order is not guaranteed by *Microsoft*.

HTTP handler

You can define custom HTTP handler to process your own type of resources. For this, you must define a class implementing the `System.Web.IHttpHandler` interface:

```
public interface IHttpHandler {
   bool IsReusable { get; }
   void ProcessRequest( HttpContext context );
}
```

Such a class is generally declared in a file with the `.ashx` extension. For example, the following HTTP handler is a calculator which takes an operation as well as two operands in a GET request and displays the result in the response. Note that with *Visual Studio 2005*, we now have intellisense on `.ashx` files. To keep the example simple, the response is a simple text document without the `<html>` markers:

Example 23-18   *MyCalc.ashx*
```
<%@ WebHandler Language="C#" Class=MyCalcHttpHandler %>

using System;
using System.Web;
public class MyCalcHttpHandler : IHttpHandler {
   public bool IsReusable { get { return true; } }
```

Example 23-18   *MyCalc.ashx*

```csharp
    public void ProcessRequest( HttpContext context ) {
       try {
          int a = int.Parse( context.Request["a"] );
          int b = int.Parse( context.Request["b"] );
          switch (           context.Request["op"]) {
             case "add": context.Response.Write( a + b ); break;
             case "sub": context.Response.Write( a - b ); break;
             case "mul": context.Response.Write( a * b ); break;
             case "div": context.Response.Write( a / b ); break;
             default: context.Response.Write( "Invalid op!" ); break;
          }
       } catch { context.Response.Write( "Invalid params!" ); }
    }
}
```

You can then use this calculator by typing the following GET request in your browser:

```
http://localhost:1232/WebSite1/MyCalc.ashx?a=11&b=3&op=mul
```

Note that an instance of the `MyClassHttpHandler` class is created to serve each request. Thus, the `MyCalc.ashx` resource is real as it is materialized by a file at the root of the application. ASP.NET knew how to route this request this resource and hence to the proper handler.

You can also use HTTP handlers to process request to virtual resources (i.e. not materialized by a file at the root of the application). As with what we have just seen with HTTP modules, you must specify such a HTTP handler by indicating which class implements `IHttpHandler` in a `<httpHandlers>` of the `Web.Config` file for the application as follows:

Web.Config

```xml
<?xml version="1.0"?>
<configuration xmlns="http://schemas.microsoft.com/.NetConfiguration/v2.0">
   <system.web>
      <httpHandlers>
         <add verb="GET" path="*.calc" type="MyCalcHttpHandler"/>
      </httpHandlers>
...
```

What we have mentioned earlier in regards to the format of the `type` attribute and concerning the declaration within the `Machine.config` file remains valid for HTTP handlers. However, this technique is potentially more powerful because you can, for example, route to your handler all the requests to a resource ending with the `.calc` extension. Of course, with this second technique there is no need for a `.ashx` file and you can define the `MyCalcHttpHandler` class in a C# file within the `/App_Code` folder. Here is the type of GET request which would use our handler:

```
http://localhost:1232/WebSite1/XYZ.calc?a=11&b=3&op=mul
```

This technique works perfectly with the web server of *Visual Studio*. The same is not true for a production IIS server. In fact, you must indicate to IIS that within the frame of this virtual folder, the `.calc` execution requests must be processed by ASP.NET. For this, you need to do the following modification using the IIS configuration tool:

[Right click on the concerned virtual dir] > Properties > Virtual directory > Configuration... > Add > Extension=.calc Path for executable=C:\WINDOWS\Microsoft.NET\Framework\v2.0.50727\aspnet_isapi.dll verb=GET

In the case where you use a `.ashx` file, this modification is useless as IIS is configured by default to route all these requests to ASP.NET.

In the HTTP handler development model that we have just discussed, a handler object is created by ASP.NET at the first request and is used to serve all following requests. You can modify this behavior by using the `IHttpHandlerFactory` interface. For example, you can make it so a handler object is related to serve each request to even keep a pool of recycled objects.

```
public interface IHttpHandlerFactory {
   IHttpHandler GetHandler( HttpContext context,
                            string         requestType,
                            string         url,
                            string         pathTranslated);
   void ReleaseHandler( IHttpHandler handler );
}
```

For this, you simply need to specify in the `Web.Config` file that your class implements the `IHttpHandlerFactory` interface instance of the one which implements `IHttpHandler`. The `GetHandler()` method is called by ASP.NET for the processing of each new request and the `ReleaseHandler()` is called for each transmission of a response. This gives you the freedom of deciding when your handlers are created and when they must be recycled or destroyed.

State and session management

Pages are entirely recreated at each request to a server. Because of this, we say that the web is a stateless environment. However, web applications often need to manage state information. For example, most eCommerce applications have a shopping cart to store your purchases during navigation. This allows to keep a global view of your selected items and to complete the transaction only once when you are done shopping.

There are several ways to manage states using ASP.NET. We have already covered the *viewstate/controlstate* based state management which has the peculiarity of transferring data in all requests and responses. This technique applies itself well to a small set of non-confidential information. Here are the main criteria to take into account when you decide that your application will need to manage states:

- The size of your data: It is impractical to transmit a large set of data (> 4KB) over the network. It is also impractical to store large sets of data in the memory of a process. Past a certain amount of data, the *Windows* virtual memory system will kick in, significantly affecting performance. We prefer to store this type of data inside a database.
- The required security level: It is dangerous to store confidential data on the client side (such as a credit card number). This data generally transits once over the network in an encrypted form, and then are stored on the server side.
- The desired performance: Transmitting data over the network, storing it in memory or accessing a database are all operations which have a certain cost. You must find an appropriate compromise based on your needs.

As with the management of *viewstate/controlstate*, the storage of *cookies* on the client allow the management of state data when the amount of data is small and non-confidential. This technique has the major disadvantage of not being applicable to all clients since several users deactivate cookies on their browser.

The instance of `HttpApplication` which is global to the application maintains an instance of the `System.Web.HttpApplicationState` class. This object, also global to the application, is accessible through the `Application{get;}` property offered by both the `HttpApplication` and `Page` classes. This object can be seen as a dictionary allowing the storage of data global to the application. Here is an example combining the use of this dictionary and cookies to assign a unique identifier to each client who connects itself (note the use of the `Lock()` and `UnLock()` methods to synchronize the access to the dictionary):

Example 23-19
```
using System;
using System.Web;
public partial class MyDefaultPage : System.Web.UI.Page {
    protected void Btn_Click( object sender, EventArgs e ) {
        Msg.Text = "You selected : " + Color.SelectedItem.Value;
    }
    protected void Page_Load( object src, EventArgs args ) {
        if (Application["ClientCounter"] == null) {
            Application["ClientCounter"] = 0;
        }
        HttpCookie cookie = Request.Cookies["ClientCounterCookie"];
        int clientNumber = -1;
        if ( cookie == null ) {
            Application.Lock();
            clientNumber = (int) Application["ClientCounter"] + 1;
            Application["ClientCounter"] = clientNumber;
            Application.UnLock();
            cookie = new HttpCookie( "ClientCounterCookie" );
            cookie.Value = clientNumber.ToString();
            Response.Cookies.Add( cookie );
        }
        else {
            clientNumber = Int32.Parse( cookie.Value );
        }
        Response.Write( "Client Number : " + clientNumber );
    }
}
```

In fact, we could use a similar approach to develop our shopping cart scenario. The information on the currently selected items in the cart would be stored on the server-side and indexed by the client identifier. However, this approach has a few weak points:

- If the application restarts, several clients could have the same identifier.
- A client with a browser that does not support cookies would have a different identifier at each request.
- You must write a fair amount of code in order to recover and store the information relative to each client.
- You would also need to maintain a mechanism allowing the invalidation of the client identifier after a certain time-out period.

For these reasons, we generally prefer to use the notion of ASP.NET sessions.

Session management

We will show you how to use a session to save on the server-side a history of selected colors. Our page will look like this:

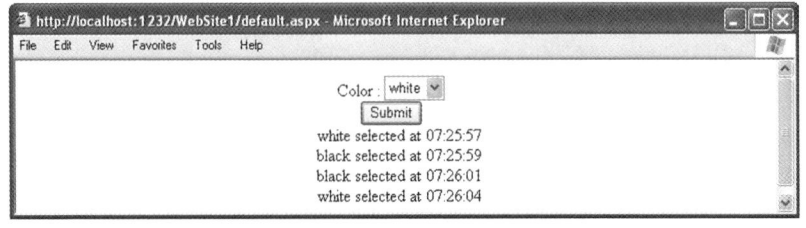

Figure 23-9: Storing selected colors in a session

State and session management 747

First, we must supply an `Item` class where each instance represents a color selection. It is important to make sure that any object stored in a session is serializable. In fact, we will see that sessions are susceptible of being serialized depending on their storage mode. Our `Item` class is serializable since it is constructed only from fields which are serializable:

Example 23-20
```
public class Item {
   public Item( string color , System.DateTime time ) {
      m_Color = color; m_Time = time;
   }
   private string m_Color;
   private System.DateTime m_Time;
   public override string ToString() {
      return  m_Color + " selected at " + m_Time.ToLongTimeString();
   }
}
```

Each time we receive a new selection, we create a new instance of `Item` that we store in the current session. Then we build the history of selections that we insert within the returned HTML page:

Example 23-21
```
...
void Btn_Click(Object sender, EventArgs e) {
   // Add a new selection Item in the session :
   System.Collections.Generic.List<Item> listItems =
      Session["ItemsSelected"] as System.Collections.Generic.List<Item>;
   listItems.Add( new Item( Color.SelectedItem.Value , DateTime.Now ) );
   Msg.Text = string.Empty;
   // Build selections historic :
   foreach( Item item in listItems )
      Msg.Text += item.ToString() + "<br/>";
}
...
```

So that you may store the data, each session maintains an internal dictionary. For our example to work, we will need at some point to initialize the "`ItemsSelected`" entry of this dictionary with a new item list. For this, we can take advantage of the `Session_Start` event that we subscribed to within the `Global.asax` file:

Example 23-22 *Global.asax*
```
<%@ Application Language="C#" %>
<script Runat="server">
   protected void Session_Start( object src, EventArgs args ) {
      Session["ItemsSelected"] = new
         System.Collections.Generic.List<Item>();
   }
</script>
```

Finally, to force ASP.NET to manage sessions, you need to add a `<sessionState>` marker to the configuration with the `mode` attribute set to something else than "`Off`" (we will detail the possible values for this attribute):

Web.Config
```
<?xml version="1.0"?>
<configuration xmlns="http://schemas.microsoft.com/.NetConfiguration/v2.0">
   <system.web>
      <sessionState mode="InProc"/>
...
```

Note that you can specify, using the `timeout` attribute, the duration in minute for which the session can remain inactive before it is destroyed by ASP.NET (the default value is 20 minutes):

```
<sessionState mode="InProc" timeout="10"/>
```

Dealing with session identifier

Internally, ASP.NET manages the sessions through an identifier mechanism. A new session identifier is created each time a new session is created. This identifier is sent back to the client who will need to send it back to the server for each request within this session. By default, this session identifier is stored in a client-side *cookie*. It is then inserted by the browser within each POST request POST. Since not all browsers support *cookies*, you can decide to configure ASP.NET so that sessions identifiers are stored within the URI. For this, you must assign `"UseUri"`to the `cookieless` attribute:

```
<sessionState mode="InProc" cookieless="UseUri"/>
```

A URI containing a session identifier looks like this:

```
http://localhost/WebSite1/(S(e53uti455tgobvi2czsh4q45))/default.aspx
```

In addition to the `"UseCookies"` (default) and the `"UseUri"` values, the `cookieless` attribute can also take the `"AutoDetect"` value. This means that ASP.NET will use a *cookie* to pass the session identifier if the browser allows if. If not, it will then fall back automatically to the URI mode. With the `"UseDeviceProfile"` value, you can tell ASP.NET to use (or not) the *cookie* mode depending on the *Device Profile* parameter in the `Machine.Config` files.

Standard implementations for storing sessions

ASP.NET offers three default modes to store server-side sessions. You tell ASP.NET which mode to use with either `"InProc"`, `"StateServer"` and `"SQLServer"` in the `mode` attribute of the configuration.

The `"InProc"` mode stores the session information in the AppDomain containing the web application. This mode is the easiest to use and most often the most efficient since it does not require any access outside of the current process. However, you should avoid using it on a production server for several reasons. First of all, if you host your application on a web farm (i.e. you application runs on several machines) you have to make sure that all the requests for a same session are processed on the same server. Next, sessions are volatile and are destroyed every time the AppDomain is unloaded. Hence, the AppDomain of a web application is susceptible to be frequently unloaded for several reasons: recompilation of a page, crash, regular restart of the process,... This means that on a production environment, it is preferable to store session information outside of the `aspnet_wp.exe` process with a mode such as `"StateServer"` or `"SQLServer"`.

The `"StateServer"` mode stores sessions within a dedicated process which can be located on the same machine hosting the web application or on another machine. You can specify this machine as well as a port using the `stateConnectionString` attribute:

```
<sessionState mode="StateServer"
    stateConnectionString="tcpip:127.0.0.1:42424"/>
```

The process containing the session presents itself as a *Windows* service named *ASP.NET State Service*. This service is installed when you install ASP.NET on a machine. By default, this service needs to be manually started. The port selected by this service to listen to session requests is stored in the registry under: `HKEY_LOCAL_MACHINE\System\CurrentControlSet\Services\aspnet_state\Parameters`.

State and session management

Although that the use of "`StateServer`" greatly improves the reliability of the session management compared to the "`InProc`" mode, sessions are still volatile and a crash of the service will cause their loss. Hence, you can opt to use the "`SQLServer`" mode which stores the sessions in a *SQL Server* database. This mode is more reliable but more expensive performance wise. This mode has the advantage of allowing you to exploit the data of expired sessions to gather statistics. To use this mode, you must provide the database connection string using the `sqlConnectionString` attribute as follows:

```
<sessionState mode="StateServer"
   sqlConnectionString="data source=127.0.0.1 ; user id=sa ;password="/>
```

Of course, you must first install the proper databases on the *SQL Server*. For this, you can use the `InstallSqlState.sql` or `InstallPersistSqlState.sql` SQL scripts depending on whether you wish to keep the sessions after they have expired. These scripts can be found in the .NET installation folder.

Providing a custom implementation for storing sessions

ASP.NET 2 allows you to provide your own session management mechanism. You may need such a mechanism if, for example, you use another RDBMS than *SQL Server*. Another possible reason could be the need to store sessions in personalized tables, different than the ones offered by default.

Internally, the session mechanism is managed by a HTTP module named "`Session`" which uses an object to manage session IDs (which implements the `System.Web.SessionState.ISessionIDManager` interface) and an object for the storage of sessions (which implements the `System.Web.SessionState.IHttpSessionState` interface). You can tell ASP.NET about your own module, your own session ID management object or your own session storage management object through the `Web.Config` file as follows:

Web.Config
```
<?xml version="1.0"?>
<configuration xmlns="http://schemas.microsoft.com/.NetConfiguration/v2.0">
   <system.web>
      <httpModules>
         <remove name="Session" />
         <add    name="Session"
                 type="MyNamespace.MyStateModuleType,MyAsm"/>
      </httpModules>
      <sessionState mode="Custom"
          sessionIDManagerType="MyNamespace.MySessionIDType,MyAsm"
          customProvider="MySessionStateProvider" >
          <providers>
             <add name="MySessionStateProvider"
                  type="MyNamespace.MySessionStateProviderType,MyAsm" />
          </providers>
      </sessionState>
   ...
```

A more complete description of how you can implement your own session management mechanism is outside the scope of this book. You can consult the articles named **Implementing a Session-State Store Provider** and **Sample Session State Store Provider** on **MSDN**.

The provider design pattern

The mechanism that we have just discussed allowing you to provide your own mechanism for the management of sessions is standard with ASP.NET. It has the name of *provider design pattern*. We will have the opportunity to see this pattern applied to other functionalities in ASP.NET such as the possibility of providing your own user and role management mechanism. The main characteristics of the *provider design pattern* are:

- The possibility of supplying several provider implementations using `<add>` elements within a `<providers>` element which is in turn contained in an element representing the functionality (in this case `<sessionState>`).
- Each provider is named using a `name` attribute.
- Each provider is implemented through a class which derives of a certain base class or interface.
- This class, as well as the assembly in which it is contained is specified using a `type` attribute.
- The implementation of a provider is totally free to choose the type of persistence which will be used to store the data. Such a persistence mode could be a relational database, an XML document, in memory, a text file, a web service...
- The functionality domain has an attribute which takes in the name of the provider to use during execution.

Let us mention that the ASP.NET 2 web interface has a *provider* tab which allows you to administrate the data providers for each functionality domain.

Error handling

There are several types of errors which can occur within an ASP.NET application:

- The network can be unavailable.
- The server may have crashed.
- The server may be overloaded.
- A client request a page which does not exist or that he is not authorized to view.
- An application process on the server-side raises an exception which is not trapped because of a bug or corrupt data.

In all these cases, a consequence of the error is that the service will not be available to the client. As a developer, only the last two types of errors are your responsibility. In the case of a page request which cannot be satisfied, you have the possibility of redirecting the user to a custom error page. In the case of an exception, ASP.NET produces by default a HTML page containing the offending code fragment as well as the state of the stack. Although that this behavior is useful to developers to fix bugs, it is somewhat cumbersome for a regular user to see this page and could introduce potential security vulnerabilities. ASP.NET offers several techniques to personalize the management of errors.

The `<system.web>` and `<customErrors>` configuration elements

You can tell ASP.NET which page needs to be sent back to the user in the case of an uncaught exception. The value of the `defaultRedirect` attribute in the `<customError>` element of the configuration file must be the name of this page. By setting the `mode` attribute to "`RemoteOnly`", you can make sure that the page specified by `defaultRedirect` is only returned to remote users. Thus, during you local tests, you can still obtain the detailed error page returned by default. The `mode` attribute can take the value of "`On`" so that the client is always redirected to the specified page even if the client is local or to "`Off`" to deactivate this service. Finally, you can also specify a page to return for each HTTP error using `<error>` elements:

Web.Config
```xml
<?xml version="1.0"?>
<configuration xmlns="http://schemas.microsoft.com/.NetConfiguration/v2.0">
   <system.web>
      <customErrors  mode="On" defaultRedirect="WebFormError.aspx">
         <error statusCode="403" redirect="MyError403.htm"/>
         <error statusCode="404" redirect="MyError404.aspx"/>
      </customErrors>
...
```

The Application_Error event

The Error event of the `HttpApplication` class is triggered by ASP.NET when an exception is not caught. You can subscribe to this event by providing an `Application_Error()` method in the `Global.asax` file. You can capture the exception and build your own response page like this:

Example 23-23   *Global.asax*
```
<%@ Application Language="C#" %>
<script Runat="server">
protected void Application_Error( object src, EventArgs args ) {
   HttpUnhandledException eHttp =
      this.Server.GetLastError() as HttpUnhandledException;
   // eApp represents the raised and not caught exception.
   Exception eApp = eHttp.InnerException;
   Response.Write( "Error : " + eApp.Message );
   Response.End();   // <- Don't forget this call!!!
}
</script>
```

For ASP.NET to properly transmit the created page, you must call the `End()` method on the current `HttpResponse` object during the execution of the `Application_Error()` method. Otherwise, the subscription to this event prevents ASP.NET from applying the standard redirection strategy in the `<customErrors>` element.

The ErrorPage property

During the processing of a page, you can at any time set the `string Page.ErrorPage{get;set;}` property. You can programmatically specify the page to which ASP.NET will redirect the client when an uncaught exception occurs.

```
<%@ Page Language="C#" %>
<html xmlns="http://www.w3.org/1999/xhtml" >
   <script language="C#" runat="server">
      void Btn_Click( Object sender, EventArgs e ) {
         this.ErrorPage = "WebFormError.aspx";
         Msg.InnerText = "You selected : " + Color.Value;
         throw new ApplicationException("An error occured !!");
      }
   </script>
...
```

For ASP.NET to properly apply this redirection, the `mode` attribute must be set to "On" within the `<customErrors>` element of the configuration file.

This technique is practical as it allows specifying an error page which is dependant of the current context. This means, for example, that if a page has several buttons, you can specify an error page for the processing of each button. Also, during an untrapped exception, ASP.NET only triggers the `HttpApplication.Error` event if the value of this property is null.

Trace, diagnostic and event management

The trace.axd HTTP handler

You can trace the behavior of an application using the `trace.axd` HTTP handler. To access this feature, you must activate the traces within the `Web.Config` file as follows:

Web.Config
```
<?xml version="1.0"?>
<configuration xmlns="http://schemas.microsoft.com/.NetConfiguration/v2.0">
   <system.web>
      <trace enabled="true" localOnly="true" />
...
```

You then have access to traces by typing an URL like this `http://[machine]/[Root]/Trace.axd` in a browser. The returned page contains a trace table, one per HTTP request processed by the server. This table is not automatically updated and you must reload the page to see the list of the most recent request. You have the possibility of displaying an information page for each trace by clicking the `View Details` link of a trace. This page is very detailed. It contains information such as the structure of server controls implicated during the processing, the states of the session and application, the information contained in POST requests, the state of internal server variables… Also, by setting the `localOnly` attribute to "true" you can prevent `Trace.axd` handler from being used remotely. We invite you to consult MSDN for more details on the attributes of the `<trace>` element.

You can use this system to include your own traces. For this, you simply need to use the object of type `System.Web.TraceContext` which can be accessed through the `Page.Trace{get;}` property as follows:

```
<%@ Page Language="C#" %>
<html xmlns="http://www.w3.org/1999/xhtml" >
   <script language="C#" runat="server">
      void Btn_Click( object sender, EventArgs e ) {
         Msg.InnerText = "You selected : " + Color.Value;
         Trace.Write( "INFO: My trace." );
         Trace.Warn( "WARN: My trace." );
      }
   </script>
...
```

In the trace page specific to a request, the traces caused by the `Warn()` method are in red while traces coming from the `Write()` are displayed in black.

ASP.NET performance counters

During the installation of ASP.NET, about fifty *Windows* performance counters are also installed. These counters include the number of current web application, the number of entries in the cache or the number of requests per second. You can find these counters in two categories named *ASP.NET Apps v 2.0.50727* and *ASP.NET v 2.0.50727*. Let us mention that the performance counters can be visualized using the `perfmon.exe` tool (accessible from *Start Menu > Run… > perfmon.exe*). Also, at page 94, we explain how you can programmatically access these counters.

ASP.NET health monitoring

ASP.NET 2 offers a framework allowing the management in a standard way of events which happen during the lifetime of a web application. The types of this framework can be found in the new namespace named `System.Web.Management`.

An event is represented by a class which derives directly (or indirectly) from the `WebManagementEvent` class. The framework offers several types of event classes by default. For example, an event of type `WebErrorEvent` happens when an exception is not caught during the processing of request while the `WebRequestEvent` event occurs at the start of the processing of each request. You can create custom classes derived from `WebManagementEvent` to supply your own type of events.

Here also, ASP.NET 2 harnesses the *provider design pattern* to implement the notion of *event provider*. Such a provider is a class deriving from `WebEventProvider`. Three providers can be used by default:

- The `EventLogWebEventProvider` provider allows the logging of events in the *Windows* log.
- The `TraceWebEventProvider` provider allows the logging of events in the ASP.NET trace.
- The `WmiLogWebEventProvider` allows the logging of events by using the *Windows* WMI framework (*Windows Management Instrumentation*).

Also, the `BufferedWebEventProvider` abstract class represents a base class allowing the development of providers which store events in memory. You can create your own event providers with classes derived from `WebEventProvider`.

You can use the `<eventMappings>` sub-element of the `<healthMonitoring>` element in the `Web.Config` file to specify which type of events ASP.NET must manage. The `<providers>` element allows you to define the event providers which can be used. Finally, the `<rules>` sub-element contains the association between events and the event provider. For example, the following `Web.Config` forces ASP.NET to log all uncaught exceptions in the ASP.NET traces:

Web.Config
```
<?xml version="1.0"?>
<configuration xmlns="http://schemas.microsoft.com/.NetConfiguration/v2.0">
    <system.web>
        <trace enabled="true"/>
        <healthMonitoring enabled="true">
            <providers>
                <add name="TraceLogProvider"
                    type="System.Web.Management.TraceWebEventProvider,
                        System.Web,Version=2.0.3600.0,Culture=neutral,
                        PublicKeyToken=b03f5f7f11d50a3a"/>
            </providers>
            <eventMappings>
                <add name="Errors"
                    type="System.Web.Management.WebErrorEvent,System.Web,
                        Version=2.0.3600.0,Culture=neutral,
                        PublicKeyToken=b03f5f7f11d50a3a" />
            </eventMappings>
            <rules>
                <add name="Errors tracing."
                    eventName="Errors"
                    provider="TraceLogProvider"/>
            </rules>
        </healthMonitoring>
    ...
```

Validation of input data

Validation controls

ASP.NET has specialized controls for the validation of the data captured by controls of type `HTMLInputText`, `HTMLTextArea`, `HTMLSelect`, `HTMLInputFile`, `TextBox`, `DropDownList`, `ListBox` and `RadioButtonList`. The following example illustrates this feature using two validation controls which work on a `TextBox`. The `RequiredFieldValidator` control makes sure that the value within `TextBox` is not empty. The `CompareValidator` control ensures that the value in the `TextBox` is an integer greater or equal to 10. Notice the use of the `ControlToValidate` property to indicate which control needs to be validated:

Example 23-24

```
<%@ Page Language="C#" %>
<html xmlns="http://www.w3.org/1999/xhtml" >
    <body>
    <form id="Form1" action="Default.aspx" method="post" runat="server">
        <asp:Button ID="MyButton" runat="server" Text="Soumettre" />
        <asp:TextBox ID="MyTextBox" runat="server" />
        <asp:RequiredFieldValidator
            ID="MyRequiredFieldValidator"      runat="server"
            ControlToValidate="MyTextBox"      SetFocusOnError="true"
            ErrorMessage="Cannot be empty!"    Display="Dynamic" />
        <asp:CompareValidator
            ID="MyCompareValidator"            runat="server"
            ControlToValidate="MyTextBox"      SetFocusOnError=" true "
            ErrorMessage="CompareValidator"    Operator="GreaterThanEqual"
            Type="Integer"                     ValueToCompare="10">
            Must be greater or equal to 10!</asp:CompareValidator>
    </form>
    </body>
</html>
```

If you execute this example, you will notice that the validation is done on the client-side. In fact, when you use these validation controls, ASP.NET automatically generates some `javascript` code used for the validation. This code is inserted into the HTML page sent to the client. If the client browser supports `javascript`, this code will be executed on the client each time a button is clicked. If the validation fails, the `javascript` code of each of the validation controls which failed generates a `<span>` tag. Such a tag displays the error message specified by the `ErrorMessage` attribute without triggering a *postback* event. You can prevent the client-side validation by setting the `EnableClientScript` property to `false`.

During the processing of a *postback* request, each validation control also makes its validation on the server-side. These validations are done independently of the validation done by the `javascript` code on the client's browser. If the validation fails, the page is returned to the client. On such a page, the validation controls which detected a problem insert their error message in the page. Despite this validation guarantee on the server-side, we recommend to always activate the client-side validation to avoid useless *postback* events.

Each type of validation control implements the `IValidator` interface which exposes the `bool IsValid{get;set;}` property. The `Page` class also offers a `bool IsValid{get;}` property. The server-side validation is done when ASP.NET calls the `Page.Validate()` method. This step sets the value of the `IsValid` properties of the page and of the validation controls. While presenting ASP.NET page life cycle, we saw that this validation is done after the call to `Page_Load()`. Consequently, you must either manually call `Page.Validate()` during the execution of `Page_Load()` or you should not test the value of any `IsValid` properties in this method.

Validation of input data

In the previous example, we have set the `Display` property of the `MyRequiredFieldValidator` validation control to `Dynamic`. This means that when the control completed its validation successfully, it will not use any space on the page. This allows us to properly treat the case where an other validation control physically placed after `MyRequiredFieldValidator` that validates the same `MyTextBox` has failed its validation. In fact, the text of this second validation control will be physically placed right next to `MyTextBox`.

In addition to the `RequiredFieldValidator` and `CompareValidator` controls that we have just demonstrated, ASP.NET offers the `RangeValidator` and `RegularExpressionValidator` controls. These four controls derive from the `BaseValidator` base class.

- Using the `ValidationDataType Type{get;set;}`, `string MaximumValue{get; set;}` and `string MinimumValue{get;set;}` properties of the `RangeValidator` class, you can ensure that the value in a control is within a specific range. The possible types defined in the `ValidationDataType` enumeration are `String`, `Integer`, `Double`, `Date` and `Currency`.

- Using the `string ValidationExpression{get;set;}` property of the `RegularExpressionValidator` class, you can provide a regular expression to validate the data. Regular expressions are described at page 517.

- In regards to the `CompareValidator` class, we attract your attention to the fact that the available types are also in the `ValidationDataType` enumeration. Also, rather than comparing the captured data to a fixed value as in out example, you can compare it to another control value by using the `string ControlToCompare{get;set;}` property.

It is common to use a control of type `RequiredFieldValidator` in addition to one of these other three validation controls since non of them detect a problem if the captured data is empty.

ASP.NET 2 has a property named `bool SetFocusOnError{get;set;}` which is present in all validation controls. It allows specifying if the focus must be put on the control to be validated when its data is invalid. The effect of this property is done independently of whether the validation failed on the client-side or the server-side.

Implementing custom validation

If the validation offered by the four default classes does not fit your needs, you can supply your own logic by using a `CustomValidator` control. The following example demonstrates this feature by testing if an integer input is a multiple of five. The `MultipleOfFive_Clnt()` function is written in `javascript` and is destined to be executed on the client-side. The `MultipleOfFive_Svr()` method is written in C# and is destined to be executed on the server-side:

Example 23-25
```
<%@ Page Language=»C#»  %>
<script language=»JavaScript»>
   function MultipleOfFive_Clnt( source, args) {
      if( args.Value % 5 == 0 )
         args.IsValid = true;
      else
         args.IsValid = false;
   }
</script>
<script language="C#" runat="server">
   void MultipleOfFive_Svr(object source, ServerValidateEventArgs e) {
      e.IsValid = false;
      int num;
      if ( Int32.TryParse( e.Value, out num ) )
         if ( num % 5 == 0 )
            e.IsValid = true;
   }
```

Example 23-25
```
  </script>
  <html xmlns="http://www.w3.org/1999/xhtml" >
    <body>
      <form id="Form1" action="Default.aspx" method="post" runat="server">
        <asp:Button ID="MyButton" runat="server" Text="Submit" />
        <asp:TextBox ID="MyTextBox" runat="server" />
        <asp:CustomValidator
            ID="MyCustomValidator" runat="server"
            ControlToValidate="MyTextBox"
            ClientValidationFunction="MultipleOfFive_Clnt"
            OnServerValidate="MultipleOfFive_Svr"
            ErrorMessage="Must be a multiple of 5!"
            ValidateEmptyText="False" />
      </form>
    </body>
  </html>
```

ASP.NET 2 introduces the `bool CustomValidator.ValidateEmpty{get;set;}` property which lets you specify if an empty value must be validated.

Validation groups

ASP.NET 2 introduces the notion of *validation groups*. This feature solves a common problem encountered with ASP.NET 1.x. By default, for each event, all validation controls are executed. It is common that on a same page we can trigger an event without necessarily needing to validate all the captured data. For example, a form may contain a '*Search the web*' button whose action has nothing to do with the capture of data on the form.

Using the new `string ValidationGroup{get;set;}` property offered by the validation controls, the `Button` class and controls classes supporting validation, you can partition the set of controls of a page into several groups. A click of a button will only trigger the validation of the controls within its group. This feature is used in the following example which exposes a page with two validation groups, each containing a button, a `TextBox` and a `RequiredFieldValidator` control:

Example 23-26
```
  <%@ Page Language="C#"  %>
  <html xmlns="http://www.w3.org/1999/xhtml" >
    <body>
      <form id="Form1" action="Default.aspx" method="post" runat="server">
        <asp:Button   ID="MyButton1"      runat="server"
                      Text="Submit 1"     ValidationGroup="Group1"/>
        <asp:TextBox  ID="MyTextBox1"     runat="server"
                      ValidationGroup="Group1"/>
        <asp:RequiredFieldValidator ID="MyRequiredFieldValidator1"
            ControlToValidate="MyTextBox1" runat="server"
            ValidationGroup="Group1"        ErrorMessage="Field 1 empty!"/>
        <br/>
        <asp:Button   ID="MyButton2"      runat="server"
                      Text="Submit 2"     ValidationGroup="Group2"/>
        <asp:TextBox  ID="MyTextBox2"     runat="server"
                      ValidationGroup="Group2"/>
        <asp:RequiredFieldValidator ID="MyRequiredFieldValidator2"
            ControlToValidate="MyTextBox2" runat="server"
            ValidationGroup="Group2"        ErrorMessage="Field 2 empty!"/>
      </form>
    </body>
  </html>
```

You can initiate the validation of a group on the server-side using the new void Validate(string validationGroup) method of the Page class.

Controls without a group are implicitly placed by ASP.NET into a global group, ensuring backward compatibility with ASP.NET 1.x.

The ValidationSummary class

In a form with a lot of data to capture, you may wish to unite all the error messages from your validation controls together in a same place. This is possible by using the ValidationSummary validation control. Such a control displays a list of error messages for the validation of controls in his group. You can choose the way that the error messages are listed using the Validation SummaryDisplayMode DisplayMode{get;set;} property. Also, rather than displaying this list in a <span> element on your page, you can choose to display the errors in a message box by using the bool ShowMessageBox{get;set;} and bool ShowSummary{get;set;} properties.

User controls

ASP.NET allows you to define your own server controls. Such a control is called a *user control*. A user control is generally defined through a file with an .ascx extension which starts with the <%@ Control> directive. This file is compiled by ASP.NET into a class deriving from the Control class. The name of this class is defined by the ClassName sub-directive. Here is an example of a simple user control:

Example 23-27 *MyUserCtrl.ascx*
```
<%@ Control Language="C#" ClassName=MyUserCtrl %>
<% Response.Write("HTML rendered by the control."); %>
```

Here is an example of a page which uses this control. We see that a <%@ Register%> directive is necessary to import the name of the class, the name of the .ascx file with defines it as well as a prefix which plays the role of a namespace:

Example 23-28 *MyUserCtrlClient.aspx*
```
<%@ Page Language=»C#» %>
<%@ Register TagPrefix="PRACTICAL" Src="~/MyUserCtrl.ascx"
             TagName="UserCtrl" %>
<html xmlns="http://www.w3.org/1999/xhtml" >
   <body>
      <% Response.Write("HTML rendered by the page."); %>
      <PRACTICAL:UserCtrl runat="server" />
   </body>
</html>
```

We generally want to have user controls which are configurable. For this, we use properties presented by the class which represents our control:

Example 23-29 *MyUserCtrl.ascx*
```
<%@ Control Language="C#" ClassName="MyUserCtrl" %>
<script language="C#" runat="server">
   private string m_Color;
   public string Color{ get{ return m_Color;} set{ m_Color = value; } }
   private string m_Text;
   public string Text { get{ return m_Text; } set{ m_Text = value;  } }
</script>
<p><font color="<%= Color %>"><%= Text %></font></p>
```

Example 23-30   *MyUserCtrlClient.aspx*
```
<%@ Page Language=»C#» %>
<%@ Register TagPrefix=»PRACTICAL" Src="~/MyUserCtrl.ascx"
            TagName="UserCtrl" %>
<html xmlns="http://www.w3.org/1999/xhtml" >
  <body>
    <PRACTICAL:UserCtrl runat="server" Color="red" Text="hello red"/>
    <PRACTICAL:UserCtrl runat="server" Color="green" Text="hello green"/>
  </body>
</html>
```

You can define yourself the class representing the user control without needing to define an .ascx file. In this case, each page using such a control must include the namespace sub-directive in the <@ Register> directive to specify the namespace containing the class:

Example 23-31   *MyUserCtrl.cs*
```
using System.Web.UI;
namespace MyUserCtrls {
   public class MyUserCtrl : Control {
      private string m_Color;
      public string Color{ get{return m_Color;} set{m_Color = value;}}
      private string m_Text;
      public string Text { get{return m_Text; } set{m_Text = value; }}
      protected override void Render(HtmlTextWriter writer) {
         writer.Write("<p><font color=\"" + m_Color +
                      "\">" + m_Text + "</font></p>");
      }
   }
}
```

Example 23-32   *MyUserCtrlClient.aspx*
```
<%@ Page Language=»C#» %>
<%@ Register TagPrefix=»PRACTICAL" namespace="MyUserCtrls" %>
<html xmlns="http://www.w3.org/1999/xhtml" >
  <body>
    <PRACTICAL:MyUserCtrl runat="server" Color="red" Text="hello red"/>
    <PRACTICAL:MyUserCtrl runat="server" Color="green" Text="hello green"/>
  </body>
</html>
```

Composite user controls

We often harness user controls to display a same form on multiple pages. Also, as with all controls, a user control can have children server controls. Note that you can use the *design* mode of *Visual Studio* to edit such a user control:

Example 23-33   *MyUserCtrl.ascx*
```
<%@ Control Language="C#" ClassName="MyUserCtrl" %>
<script language="C#" runat="server">
   void Btn_Click(Object sender, EventArgs e) {
      Msg.Text = "You selected : " + Color.SelectedItem.Value;
   }
</script>
 Color : <asp:dropdownlist id="Color" runat="server">
            <asp:listitem>white</asp:listitem>
            <asp:listitem>black</asp:listitem>
         </asp:dropdownlist>
```

Example 23-33 *MyUserCtrl.ascx*
```
<asp:button id="Button1" text="Submit" OnClick="Btn_Click" runat="server"/>
<asp:label id="Msg" runat="server"/>
```

Example 23-34 *MyUserCtrlClient.aspx*
```
<%@ Page Language=»C#»  %>
<%@ Register TagPrefix=»PRACTICAL» Src=»~/MyUserCtrl.ascx»
             TagName=»UserCtrl» %>
<html xmlns=»http://www.w3.org/1999/xhtml» >
   <body>
      <form id=»Form1» action=»Default.aspx» method=»post» runat=»server»>
         <PRACTICAL:UserCtrl ID=»UserCtrl1» runat=»server» /><br/>
         <PRACTICAL:UserCtrl ID=»UserCtrl2» runat=»server» />
      </form>
   </body>
</html>
```

Also, ASP.NET will automatically rename during execution the child controls by prefixing them with the name of the parent control followed by a _ (i.e. an underscore). This prevents several controls on the same page from having the same name.

User controls events

You have the possibility of creating your own events in a user control and you can subscribe to them from a page using the On[NameOfEvent] syntax which is illustrated by the following example:

Example 23-35 *MyUserCtrl.ascx*
```
<%@ Control Language="C#" ClassName="MyUserCtrl" %>
<script language="C#" runat="server">
   public event EventHandler WhiteSelected;
   void Btn_Click(Object sender, EventArgs e) {
      if ( Color.SelectedItem.Value == "white" )
         WhiteSelected(this, EventArgs.Empty);
   }
</script>
Color : <asp:dropdownlist id="Color" runat="server">
            <asp:listitem>white</asp:listitem>
            <asp:listitem>black</asp:listitem>
         </asp:dropdownlist>
<asp:button id="Button1" text="Submit" OnClick="Btn_Click" runat="server"/>
```

Example 23-36 *MyUserCtrlClient.aspx*
```
<%@ Page Language=»C#»  %>
<%@ Register TagPrefix=»PRACTICAL» Src=»~/MyUserCtrl.ascx»
             TagName=»UserCtrl» %>
<script language=»C#» runat=»server»>
   void WhiteSelectedHandler(Object sender, EventArgs e) {
      Msg.Text = «White selected!»;
   }
</script>
<html xmlns=»http://www.w3.org/1999/xhtml» >
   <body>
      <form id=»Form1» action=»Default.aspx» method=»post» runat=»server»>
         <PRACTICAL:UserCtrl ID=»UserCtrl1» runat=»server»
                      OnWhiteSelected="WhiteSelectedHandler"/>
```

Example 23-36 *MyUserCtrlClient.aspx*
```
            <asp:label id="Msg" runat="server" EnableViewState="false"/>
        </form>
    </body>
</html>
```

User control state

A user control can use the *viewstate* to maintain its state between requests from a same user. The following example illustrates this feature by rewriting our `MyUserCtrl` user control with a stateless class (i.e. without a field). The `Color` and `Text` states are maintained between the requests using the *viewstate*. Note that they are not initialized by the client during the first request:

Example 23-37 *MyUserCtrl.cs*
```
using System.Web.UI;
namespace MyUserCtrls {
   public class MyUserCtrl : Control {
      public MyUserCtrl() {
         ViewState["Color"] = string.Empty;
         ViewState["Text"] = string.Empty;
      }
      public string Color {
         get { return ViewState["Color"] as string; }
         set { ViewState["Color"] = value; }
      }
      public string Text {
         get { return ViewState["Text"] as string; }
         set { ViewState["Text"] = value; }
      }
      protected override void Render(HtmlTextWriter writer) {
         writer.Write("<p><font color=\"" + ViewState["Color"] +
                     "\">" + ViewState["Text"] + "</font></p>");
      }
   }
}
```

Example 23-38 *MyUserCtrlClient.aspx*
```
<%@ Page Language="C#" %>
<%@ Register TagPrefix="PRACTICAL" namespace="MyUserCtrls" %>
<script language="C#" runat="server">
   void Page_Load(Object sender, EventArgs e) {
      if ( !IsPostBack ) {
         MyUserCtrl1.Color = "red";
         MyUserCtrl1.Text = "hello red";
      } else {/* No need for initialization */}
   }
</script>
<html xmlns="http://www.w3.org/1999/xhtml" >
   <body>
      <form id="Form1" action="Default.aspx" method="post" runat="server">
         <PRACTICAL:MyUserCtrl ID="MyUserCtrl1" runat="server" />
         <asp:button ID="Button1" runat="server" text="Submit" />
      </form>
   </body>
</html>
```

Note the necessity to initialize the required entries of the *viewstate* in the constructor of our user control. We can rewrite our `get` accessors as follows:

User controls

Example 23-39 — MyUserCtrl.cs

```
...
    public string Color {
        get {
            string s = ViewState["Color"] as string;
            return (s == null) ? string.Empty : s;
        }
        set { ViewState["Color"] = value; }
    }
    public string Text {
        get {
            string s = ViewState["Text"] as string;
            return (s == null) ? string.Empty : s;
        }
        set { ViewState["Text"] = value; }
    }
...
```

We can also overload the `LoadViewState()` and `SaveViewState()` methods of the `Control` class to maintain the state of a user control in the *viewstate*. Here is our `MyUserCtrl` rewritten to use this technique:

Example 23-40 — MyUserCtrl.cs

```
using System.Web.UI;
namespace MyUserCtrls {
    public class MyUserCtrl : Control {
        private string m_Color;
        public string Color { get{return m_Color;} set{ m_Color=value;} }
        private string m_Text;
        public string Text { get{return m_Text;} set{ m_Text=value;} }
        protected override object SaveViewState() {
            object[] state = new object[2];
            state[0] = m_Color;
            state[1] = m_Text;
            return state;
        }
        protected override void LoadViewState(object _state) {
            if (_state != null) {
                object[] state = _state as object[];
                if (state[0] != null) m_Color = state[0] as string;
                if (state[1] != null) m_Text = state[1] as string;
            }
        }
        protected override void Render(HtmlTextWriter writer) {
            writer.Write("<p><font color=\"" + m_Color +
                        "\">" + m_Text + "</font></p>");
        }
    }
}
```

Know that you can also use the *controlstate* to maintain states between requests. For this, you must override the `Control.LoadControlState()` and `Control.SaveControlState()` methods in addition of declaring that this control supports the use of *controlstate* by calling the `Page.RegisterRequiresControlState()` method:

Example 23-41 — MyUserCtrl.cs

```
using System.Web.UI;
namespace MyUserCtrls {
```

Example 23-41   MyUserCtrl.cs

```
    public class MyUserCtrl : Control {
        ...
        protected override void OnInit(System.EventArgs e) {
            Page.RegisterRequiresControlState(this);
            base.OnInit(e);
        }
        protected override object SaveControlState() {
            ...
        }
        protected override void LoadControlState(object _state) {
            ...
        }
        ...
    }
}
```

User controls and design-time support in Visual Studio

ASP.NET offers facilities to enhance the integration of a user control with the *design* mode of *Visual Studio*. The description of these features is outside the scope of this book and we invite you to consult the article named **Attributes and Design-Time Support** on **MSDN**.

Caching

ASP.NET offers a *caching* service which allows to significantly improve the performance by keeping in memory expensive and frequently used data. In the case of a web application, a lot of data satisfies these two properties. In addition, the generation of HTML pages requires server-side resources. Clients often request the same pages, which contain the same data. Objects such as instance of `DataSet`, disconnected from the database are expensive to obtain and are good candidates for caching. The caching system of ASP.NET comes in three flavors: caching multiple versions of a page, caching page fragments and data caching.

Page caching

The following example shows how to tell ASP.NET that it must cache a page for one minute by using the `OutputCache` directive:

Example 23-42

```
<%@ Page Language="C#"  %>
<%@ OutputCache Duration="60" VaryByParam="none" %>
<html xmlns="http://www.w3.org/1999/xhtml" >
    <body>
        <% Response.Write("Page generated at : " + DateTime.Now); %>
    </body>
</html>
```

The page is generated a first time and cached for one minute. Here, it is easy to verify that the page is being cached since it contains the time and date at which it was generated.

You can go without using the `OutputCache` directive and programmatically configure caching by using the various methods of the `System.Web.HttpCachePolicy` class. In fact, the `Page` class maintains an object of this type which can be accessed through the `Cache{get;}` property:

Example 23-43

```
<%@ Page Language="C#" %>
<html xmlns="http://www.w3.org/1999/xhtml" >
   <body>
      <% Response.Write("Page generated at: " + DateTime.Now); %>
   </body>
   <script language="C#" runat="server">
      void Page_Load(Object sender, EventArgs e) {
          Response.Cache.SetExpires( DateTime.Now.AddSeconds(60) );
          Response.Cache.SetCacheability( HttpCacheability.Public );
          Response.Cache.SetSlidingExpiration(true);
      }
   </script>
</html>
```

In this example, we set a sliding expiration policy using a call to `SetSlidingExpiration()` with the `true` argument. This means that one minute delay on which the cached page will be destroyed is reset after each request to the page. The sliding expiration policy is very useful as it allows guaranteeing that only commonly used resources remain in the cache. However, know that you cannot declare a sliding expiration policy through the `OutputCache` directive. It must be done programmatically.

The call to the `SetCacheability()` method allows to communicate where a page can be cached. In fact, the HTTP 1.1 protocol knows the notion of cache. It allows caching a page directly on the client or in a transparent proxy which places itself between the client and the server. With the cache maintained by ASP.NET, this makes three possible caches where a page can be stored. Refer to the description of the `HttpCacheability` enumeration on **MSDN** to see the different possible options. Also know that you can use the `Location` sub-directive of `OutputCache` to indicate the locations where a page can be cached.

Finally, know that when sliding expiration is activated, each request to the server triggers the regeneration of the page. This technique is only useful if you have caches other than the one maintained by ASP.NET.

Caching multiple versions of a page

You can cache several versions of a same page depending on the value of the parameters contained in the GET and POST requests. For this, you need to tell ASP.NET the set of parameters used with the `VaryByParam` sub-directive of `OutputCache`. Here are the different values that the `VaryByParam` sub-directive can take:

- The presence of the `VaryByParam` sub-directive is mandatory. If you do not wish to use this feature, you must provide the "none" value.
- If you wish to use multiple parameters, you must separate their names using commas. In this case, ASP.NET will cache a page for each value in the matrix of provided parameters.
- If you wish to use all the parameters, you can use the "*" value.

The following example bases itself on Example 23-3. It shows how to cache two versions of this page: one when a client selects the `black` value, the other when you select the `white` value.

Example 23-44

```
<%@ Page Language="C#" %>
<%@ OutputCache Duration=60  VaryByParam="Color" %>
<html xmlns="http://www.w3.org/1999/xhtml" >
...
   <body>
```

Example 23-44

```
        <% Response.Write("Page generated at : "+DateTime.Now); %> <br/>
...
        Color : <asp:dropdownlist id="Color" runat="server">
                    <asp:listitem>white</asp:listitem>
                    <asp:listitem>black</asp:listitem>
                </asp:dropdownlist>
...
```

Understand that you should not use this feature with parameters susceptible of varying for each client, such as the name of clients. This would be inefficient since the cache would be filled with several pages which are rarely used.

There is also a `VaryByControl` sub-directive with a behavior similar to `VaryByParam`. In fact, by specifying the identifier of a control in `VaryByControl`, several versions of a page can be cached based on the value provided by the client for this control. Hence, the following example has a similar behavior to the previous example (note that the presence of the `VaryByControl` sub-directive makes the use of the `VaryByParam` sub-directive optional):

Example 23-45

```
<%@ Page Language="C#"  %>
<%@ OutputCache Duration=60   VaryByControl="Color" %>
...
<html xmlns="http://www.w3.org/1999/xhtml" >
   <body>
       <% Response.Write("Page generated at : "+DateTime.Now); %> <br/>
...
        Color : <asp:dropdownlist id="Color" runat="server">
                    <asp:listitem>white</asp:listitem>
                    <asp:listitem>black</asp:listitem>
                </asp:dropdownlist>
...
        <asp:label id="Msg" runat="server"/>
...
```

Understand that ASP.NET bases itself on the state of the control as provided by the client and not the state assigned to the control during the generation of the page. A consequence is that this example would not work if we had used `VaryByControl="Msg"`.

You can also use the `VaryByHeader` sub-directive to tell ASP.NET to cache several versions of a same page based on the content of the header of client requests. For example, the language desired by the client is put in the `Accept-Language` header. Hence, several versions of the following page can be cached, one for each language requested by the client:

Example 23-46

```
<%@ Page Language=»C#»  %>
<%@ OutputCache Duration=»60»
              VaryByParam=»none» VaryByHeader="Accept-Language" %>
<html xmlns="http://www.w3.org/1999/xhtml" >
   <script language="C#" runat="server" >
      void Page_Load(Object sender, EventArgs e) {
         if ( !IsPostBack ) {
            switch ( Request.UserLanguages[0] ) {
               case "fr": Response.Write( "Bonjour!" ); break;
               case "de": Response.Write( "Guten tag!" ); break;
               default: Response.Write( "Hello!" ); break;
            }
```

Example 23-46
```
            }
        }
    </script>
    <body>
        <% Response.Write("Page generated at : " + DateTime.Now); %>
    </body>
</html>
```

Finally, you can use the `VaryByCustom` sub-directive to tell ASP.NET that it can cache several versions of a page based on your own criteria. These criteria are generally relative to the type of browser that the client uses. If you wish to cache a page based on the type/version of the browser, you can set this sub-directive to "Browser". If not, you must override the `GetVaryByCustomString()` method of the `HttpApplication` class to create your own parameter tests.

The following example expose a page which is generated differently based on whether or not the client browser supports bold characters. We create our own parameter named `SupportsBold`. For each request, ASP.NET will know the value of this parameter by asking our code in the `GetVaryByCustomString()` method.

Example 23-47
```
<%@ Page Language="C#"  %>
<%@ OutputCache Duration="60" VaryByParam="none"
                VaryByCustom="SupportsBold" %>
<html xmlns="http://www.w3.org/1999/xhtml" >
    <script language="C#" runat="server" >
        void Page_Load( Object sender, EventArgs e ) {
            if ( Request.Browser.SupportsBold )
                Response.Write("<B> Hello! </B>");
            else
                Response.Write("Hello! ");
        }
    </script>
    <body>
        <% Response.Write( "Page generated at : " + DateTime.Now ); %>
    </body>
</html>
```

Example 23-48   Global.asax
```
<%@ Application Language="C#" %>
<script Runat="server">
    public override string GetVaryByCustomString(
                            HttpContext ctx, string custom) {
        if( custom  == "SupportsBold" )
            return "SupportsBold=" + ctx.Request.Browser.SupportsBold;
        return string.Empty;
    }
</script>
```

Page fragment caching

It is quite common that only part of a page be specific to each client. For example, on an eCommerce site, the portion displaying the shopping cart will vary for each client while the rest of a product detail page will remain the same. ASP.NET allows you to cache HTML fragments. More precisely, you have the possibility of keeping in the cache only the HTML fragments resulting from user controls. This is possible through the use of the `OutputCache` directive during the definition of a user control within an `.ascx` file:

Example 23-49 *MyUserCtrl.ascx*

```
<%@ Control Language="C#" ClassName="MyUserCtrl" %>
<%@ OutputCache Duration=60 VaryByParam=none %>
<br/>
<% Response.Write("Fragment generated at : " + DateTime.Now); %>
```

For example, the following page uses the `MyUserCtrl` control. By executing this example, you will see that the page is generated at each request while the HTML fragment generated by the user control is reused.

Example 23-50 *MyUserCtrlClient.aspx*

```
<%@ Page Language="C#" %>
<%@ Register TagPrefix="PRACTICAL" Src="~/MyUserCtrl.ascx"
             TagName="UserCtrl" %>
<html xmlns="http://www.w3.org/1999/xhtml" >
   <body>
      <% Response.Write("Page generated at : " + DateTime.Now); %>
      <form runat="server">
         <PRACTICAL:UserCtrl runat="server" />
      </form>
   </body>
</html>
```

In this context, you can store several HTML fragments generated by a same user control. Here also, the `VaryByParam`, `VaryByControl` and `VaryByCustom` sub-directives can be used within the `OutputCache` directive. However, you cannot use the `VaryByHeader` and `Location` sub-directives in this context.

If you control has public properties, ASP.NET will store them automatically in the cache of an HTML fragment generated for each value of the vector composed of these properties. In order to use this feature, property values must be provided statically during the declaration of the control in the page. For example:

Example 23-51 *MyUserCtrl.ascx*

```
<%@ Control Language="C#" ClassName=MyUserControl %>
<%@ OutputCache Duration=60 VaryByParam=none   %>

<script runat="server">
   private string m_Color;
   public  string Color { get { return m_Color; } set { m_Color = value; } }
</script>
<br/>
<% Response.Write( "Color : " + Color ); %>
<br/>
<% Response.Write( "Fragment generated at : " + DateTime.Now ); %>
```

Example 23-52 *MyUserCtrlClient.aspx*

```
...
   <PRACTICAL:UserCtrl Color="white" runat="server" />
...
```

Finally, be aware that a control which produces HTML fragments that are potentially cached cannot be manipulated programmatically. In fact, when ASP.NET decides to reuse a cached HTML fragment, it does not create the underlying control and the reference to the control is null.

Post-cache substitution

ASP.NET 2 allows you to regenerate only certain portions of a cached page. This technique is called *post-cache substitution*. This allows addressing the problem of semi-dynamic pages in a way which is complementary to the use of cached page fragments. However, post-cache substitution cannot be used from cached user controls or master pages.

Caching

To use post-cache substitution, you simply need to use the `<asp:Substitution>` control. This control takes a parameter named `MethodName` which is the name of a static method which returns a string. The control sends back the string as the HTML fragment. For example:

Example 23-53
```
<%@ Page Language="C#"  %>
<%@ OutputCache Duration=60 VaryByParam=none %>
<html xmlns="http://www.w3.org/1999/xhtml" >
  <script runat="server">
    public static string Fct( HttpContext ctx ) {
      return "Substitution given at : " + DateTime.Now;
    }
  </script>
  <body>
    <% Response.Write("Page generated at : " + DateTime.Now); %> <br/>
    <asp:Substitution Id="Substitution1" MethodName="Fct" runat="server"/>
  </body>
</html>
```

You can also use post-cache substitution through the `HttpResponse.WriteSubstitution()` method.

Data caching

To cache HTML pages or HTML fragments, ASP.NET internally uses its own cache engine. You can take advantage of this cache engine to store your own data. The following example caches an instance of `DataView` created from a `DataSet` which was filled from the `ORGANIZATION` database. This database is described at page 589:

Example 23-54
```
<%@ Page Language="C#" %>
<%@ Import Namespace ="System.Data" %>
<%@ Import Namespace ="System.Data.Common" %>
<%@ Import Namespace ="System.Data.SqlClient" %>
<script runat="server">
protected void Page_Load(object sender, EventArgs e) {
   DataView dv = Cache["Employees"] as DataView;
   if ( dv == null ) {
      using ( DbDataAdapter dAdapter = new SqlDataAdapter(
        "SELECT * FROM EMPLOYEES",
        "server = localhost ; uid=sa ; pwd =; database = ORGANIZATION") ) {
         DataSet ds = new DataSet();
         dAdapter.Fill( ds );
         dv = ds.Tables[0].DefaultView;
         dv.AllowDelete = false;
         dv.AllowEdit = false;
         dv.AllowNew = false;
         Cache["Employees"] = dv;
      } // end using dAdapter.
   }
   else Response.Write( "Loaded from cache!" );
   MyList.DataSource = dv;
   MyList.DataTextField = "SurName";
   DataBind();
}
</script>
<html xmlns="http://www.w3.org/1999/xhtml" >
```

Example 23-54
```
    <body>
        <form id="Form1" runat="server">
            <asp:ListBox ID="MyList" runat="server"/>
        </form>
    </body>
</html>
```

The implementation of the data cache is done in a global way to the web application. This means that this technique of data caching is similar to the use of the `HttpApplicationState` global dictionary. There are however two differences that you will need to note:

- During the recovery of data from the cache, there is no guarantee that the data will still be present. As with our example, you must always provide a mechanism to get the data from another source than the cache in case the data has been destroyed.
- The update philosophy of the cache data is different than with global data. The copy stored in a data cache must not be modified. If the data is changed, you must provide a mechanism which destroys the expired copy to replace it with an up-to-date copy. Know that internally, the access to the data stored in a cache is synchronized using an instance of `ReaderWriterLock`.

Cache dependencies

ASP.NET has a dependency mechanism to address the expired data problem that we have just discussed. Concretely, during the insertion of data in the cache, you can couple the data with a dependency. For this, the `System.Web.Caching.Cache` class has several overloads of the `Insert()` method which accept an instance of `System.Web.Caching.CacheDependency`.

A dependency can be used during the insertion of one or several pieces of data in the cache. A same instance of `CacheDependency` can represent a dependence to zero, one or several files, zero, to one or several folders, to one or several other dependencies. If the state of any of these entities changes, the concerned dependency detects this and makes sure that its associated cached data is destroyed.

The following example illustrates the caching of the content of a text file. The page displays the content of this file by recovering it from the cache. Using dependence to the file, we can guarantee that the client will always see the latest version of this content:

Example 23-55
```
<%@ Page Language="C#" %>
<html xmlns="http://www.w3.org/1999/xhtml" >
    <body>
    <% string content = this.Cache["Content"] as string;
        if( content == null ) {
            Response.Write(@"Loaded in the cache.<br/>");
            content = System.IO.File.ReadAllText( @"D:\Temp\Test.txt" );
            CacheDependency dep = new CacheDependency( @"D:\Temp\Test.txt" );
            Context.Cache.Insert( "Content", content, dep );
        }
        Response.Write( @"Content of the file D:\Temp\Test.txt:" + content );
    %>
    </body>
</html>
```

The `CacheDependency` class offers several constructors allowing you to communicate the entities associated with a dependency.

Also, the `Cache.Insert()` method offers an overload which takes as a parameter a value from the `CacheItemPriority` enumeration. This value allows you to give more or less importance to your cached data. Of course, the cache purging algorithm of ASP.NET takes this priority into account. This overload of the `Cache.Insert()` also takes a delegate parameter of type `CacheItemRemovedCallback`. This gives you a way to be warned when the data in the cache is destroyed.

SQL server cache dependencies

ASP.NET 2 also offers the `SqlCacheDependency` class which allows to create dependencies to tables or rows of a *SQL Server* database. Such a dependency can cause the destruction of the associated cache data when the data of a table has been modified. Here is how to modify Example 23-54 to create dependency on the EMPLOYEES table:

Example 23-56

```
...
     dv.AllowNew = false;
     Cache.Insert( "Employees", dv,
        new SqlCacheDependency( "DbORGANIZATION","EMPLOYEES" ) );
  } // end using dAdapter.
...
```

Naturally, you must specify to which database corresponds the DbORGANIZATION alias like this:

Web.config

```
<?xml version="1.0"?>
<configuration xmlns="http://schemas.microsoft.com/.NetConfiguration/v2.0">
   <connectionStrings>
      <add name="CnxStrORGANIZATION"
           connectionString="Data Source=localhost;
                Integrated Security=SSPI;Initial Catalog=ORGANIZATION"
           providerName="System.Data.SqlClient"/>
   </connectionStrings>
   <system.web>
      <caching>
         <sqlCacheDependency enabled="true">
            <databases>
               <add name="DbORGANIZATION"
                    connectionStringName="CnxStrORGANIZATION"
                    pollTime="500"/>
            </databases>
         </sqlCacheDependency>
      </caching>
...
```

If you use SQL Server 2005 as your RDBMS, you can also depend on the update of certain rows in a table. You can specify the rows using a SELECT command like this:

Example 23-57

```
...
     dv.AllowNew = false;
     SqlConnection cnx = new SqlConnection(
        "server = localhost ; uid=sa ; pwd =; database = ORGANIZATION" );
     SqlCommand cmd = new SqlCommand(
        "SELECT * FROM EMPLOYEES WHERE EmployeeID=6 OR EmployeeID=7", cnx);
     Cache.Insert( "Employees", dv, new SqlCacheDependency(cmd) );
  } // end using dAdapter.
...
```

The database dependency feature is also useable when you cache a page or the fragment of a page through the `SqlDependency` sub-directive of the `<%@ OutputCache>` directive:

```
<%@ OutputCache Duration=60 VaryByParam="none"
                SqlDependency="DbORGANIZATION:EMPLOYEES" %>
```

Internally, the mechanism used to detect changes is different based on the version of *SQL Server* you are using.

- In the case of *SQL Server 2005*, the mechanism of *Query Notification* is used. Internally, an ADO.NET 2 dependency is created on the table or the concerned rows. This dependency is triggered by this mechanism as soon as an update takes place.

- In the case of a version previous to *SQL Server 2005* (7 or 2000), a polling approach is used on the ASP.NET server-side. A background thread is used regularly to detect if the data of a table has been modified. The interval used is defined in milliseconds by the `pollTime` attribute of the `caching\sqlCacheDependency\databases` element. The default value is of five seconds. A certain amount of preparation using the `aspnet_regsql.exe` command line tool is needed to activate this mechanism. You must first tell your RDBMS which databases support this mechanism (ed for `enable database`):

```
>aspnet_regsql.exe -S <host> -U <usr> -P <pwd> -d <database> –ed
```

After, you must use this tool to activate one by one the tables which will support this mechanism (et for `enable table`):

```
>aspnet_regsql.exe -S <host> -U <usr> -P <pwd> -d <database> -t <table> –et
```

Internally, this tool creates stored procedures, triggers and the necessary tables to activate this mechanism.

Custom cache dependencies

ASP.NET 2 offers the option of providing dependencies to your own type of resources. For this, you must provide a class which derives from `CacheDependency` which will check the state of the resource. An instance of this class must call the `NotifyDependencyChanged()` method when it detects a state change. The caching engine will then destroy the cached data associated to this instance and will call the `DependencyDispose()` method to give it a chance to free its own resources.

All this is illustrated by the following example which implements a skeleton for a class derived from `CacheDependency`. We use a timer of type `System.Timers.Timer` to periodically monitor the state of a fictitious resource:

Example 23-58

```
using System;
using System.Web.Caching;
using System.Timers;
public class CustomCacheDependency : CacheDependency {
    private Timer m_Timer = new Timer();
    private string m_ResourceId;
    public CustomCacheDependency( int pollIntervalSec, string resourceId ) {
        m_ResourceId = resourceId;
        m_Timer.Interval = pollIntervalSec * 1000;
        m_Timer.Elapsed += this.CheckDependencyHandler;
        m_Timer.Start();
    }
    private void CheckDependencyHandler(object sender, ElapsedEventArgs e) {
        // Here, insert the code that detects any change on the
        // state of the resource indexed by m_ResourceId.
```

Example 23-58
```
      bool resourceHasChanged = false;
      if ( resourceHasChanged )
         NotifyDependencyChanged(this, EventArgs.Empty);
   }
   protected override void DependencyDispose() {
      m_Timer.Stop();
   }
}
```

Data sources

Binding programmatically controls and data sources

In the previous section, Example 23-54 (at page 767) shows how to use an ASP.NET control of type `ListBox` to present the data of column contained in a `DataView`. For this, you need to supply the `DataView` through the `object ListBox.DataSource{set;}` property and to supply the name of the column to display through the `string ListBox.DataTextField{set;}` property and then call the `DataBind()` method on the object representing the current page. This method is a member of the `Control` class and is consequently also offered by the `Page` class and all other classes representing pages as well as all server controls. The default implementation of the method essentially calls `DataBind()` on all of its child controls.

Only certain type of server controls such as `ListBox` effectively implement this method. This implementation recovers an internal copy of all the data that the object provides through the `DataSource` property. This data is then used by the `Render()` method of the control to display them in the HTML page.

The class representing a data source must implement one of these interfaces:

- `System.ComponentModel.IListSource` (implemented by the `DataSet` and `DataTable` classes).
- `IEnumerable` (implemented by the `DataView`, `ArrayList`, `List<>`, `Dictionary<,>` classes).
- `IDataReader` (implemented by the `DbDataReader` as well as the classes deriving from it).

In Example 23-54, the data was already present in the underlying `DataSet` during the call to `DataBind`. This implies that there exist three copies of this data: in the `DataSet`, in the `ListBox` after the call to `DataBind()` and in the `__VIEWSTATE` section of the rendered HTML page. If you can, you may want to deactivate the use of the storage of the control data in the `__VIEWSTATE`. Also, certain data sources such as `DataReader` do not internally keep a copy of the data. They only represent a means to access the data. Hence, in the following example, there is only one copy of the data, the copy created in the `ListBox` object during the call to the `DataBind()` method.

Example 23-59
```
<%@ Page Language="C#" %>
<%@ Import Namespace ="System.Data" %>
<%@ Import Namespace ="System.Data.Common" %>
<%@ Import Namespace ="System.Data.SqlClient" %>
<script runat="server">
protected void Page_Load(object sender, EventArgs e) {
   string sCnx =
      "server = localhost ; uid=sa ; pwd =; database = ORGANIZATION";
   string sCmd = "SELECT * FROM EMPLOYEES";
   using (DbConnection cnx =new SqlConnection(sCnx)) {
      using (DbCommand cmd =new SqlCommand(sCmd, cnx as SqlConnection)){
         cnx.Open();
         using ( DbDataReader rdr = cmd.ExecuteReader() ) {
```

Example 23-59
```
            MyList.DataSource = rdr;
            MyList.DataTextField = "SurName";
            DataBind();
            MyList.EnableViewState = false;
         } // end using rdr.
      } // end using cmd.
   } // end using cnx.
}
</script>
<html xmlns="http://www.w3.org/1999/xhtml" >
   <body>
      <form id="Form1" runat="server">
         <asp:ListBox ID="MyList" runat="server" />
      </form>
   </body>
</html>
```

Consequently, you can see three practices which can be used to improve performance during the use of data sources.

- Either we limit the number of copies of the data to a minimum as with our previous example.
- Either we only load the data during the first use of a page and then use the *viewstate* to store them.
- Either we allow ourselves to keep a copy in memory (at the cache, session of application level) as with Example 23-54.

Depending on the context, one of these techniques will give you optimal performance.

Binding declaratively controls and data sources

ASP.NET 2 introduces several new server controls allowing the declarative binding to a data source. This relieves the developer from having to write code which manipulates the ADO.NET API necessary to gather and modify the data from a database. The following example is equivalent to Example 23-59:

Example 23-60
```
<%@ Page Language="C#" %>
<html xmlns="http://www.w3.org/1999/xhtml" >
   <body>
     <form id="Form2" runat="server">
       <asp:SqlDataSource ID="DataSrc" runat="server" ConnectionString=
           "server = localhost ; uid=sa ; pwd =; database = ORGANIZATION"
           SelectCommand="SELECT * FROM EMPLOYEES"
           DataSourceMode="DataReader" />
       <asp:ListBox ID="MyList" DataSourceID="DataSrc" runat="server"
           DataTextField="SurName" EnableViewState="False" />
     </form>
   </body>
</html>
```

We see that a data source control of type `SqlDataSource` needs to know the connection to the database, the SQL command which gathers data and optionally a data recovery mode: connected (`DataReader` value for the `DataSourceMode` property) or disconnected (`DataSet` value). The `DataSet` value is chosen by default. This example does not show that the `SqlDataSource` server control has several other options such as the caching of data (`EnableCaching`, `CacheDuration`, `CacheExpirationPolicy` properties) or the filtering of data.

The following example shows how to use this notion in order to only display the employees which belong to a department. The department is chosen from a dropdown list filled with the `DataSrc1`

Data sources 773

data source. Each time the selection of this list is changes, a *postback* event is triggered. On the server side, we use a `ControlParameter` control to recover the selected department to the SELECT SQL command of the data source used to fill the list:

Example 23-61
```
<%@ Page Language="C#" %>
<html xmlns="http://www.w3.org/1999/xhtml" >
  <body>
    <form id="Form1" runat="server">
      <asp:SqlDataSource ID="DataSrc1" runat="server" ConnectionString=
         "server = localhost ; uid=sa ; pwd =; database = ORGANIZATION"
         SelectCommand=
            "SELECT DISTINCT DepId FROM EMPLOYEES ORDER BY DepId" />
      <asp:DropDownList ID="ListDep" DataSourceID="DataSrc1"
         DataTextField="DepId" Autopostback="true" runat="server" />
      <asp:SqlDataSource ID="DataSrc2" runat="server" ConnectionString=
         "server = localhost ; uid=sa ; pwd =; database = ORGANIZATION"
         SelectCommand="SELECT * FROM EMPLOYEES WHERE DepId=@ParamDepId">
         <SelectParameters>
            <asp:ControlParameter Name="ParamDepId" ControlID="ListDep"
                                  PropertyName="SelectedValue" />
         </SelectParameters>
      </asp:SqlDataSource>
      <asp:ListBox ID="MyList" DataSourceID="DataSrc2" runat="server"
         DataTextField="SurName" />
    </form>
  </body>
</html>
```

The execution of this page looks like this:

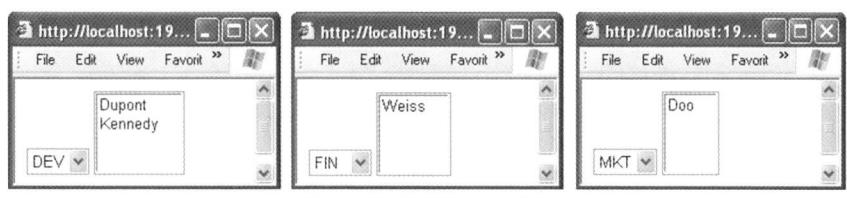

Figure 23-10: Filtering data

We will see that a server-side data source control can be used for the modification of the data (insertion, update, deletion). We will also see that the server controls which use data source controls support features such as data paging and sorting.

Flat data sources vs. hierarchical data sources

There are mainly two types of data sources: flat data sources and hierarchical data sources. Flat data sources are for example the tables of a relational data source or a list of objects. The server controls which allow the use of such sources derive from the `DataSourceControl` class. Here is the list (these classes are all in the `System.Web.UI.WebControls` namespace):

- The `SqlDataSource` class that we have just presented. It can be used for all type of RDBMS since it supports the *SQL Server*, *ODBC* and *OleDB* data providers.
- The `ObjectDataSource` class that we will describe in the next section.

Hierarchical data sources are used to exploit data within XML documents. Server controls allowing the use of such data sources are `XmlDataSource` and `SiteMapDataSource`. These classes derive from `HierarchicalDataSourceControl`. The `SiteMapDataSource` class allows the use of special XML documents which represent the structure of a site. It is described further at page 794. Also, we will come back to the notion of hierarchical data sources a little later at page 785.

The ObjectDataSource class

The `ObjectDataSource` class allows you to use your object as a flat data source. Contrarily to other data sources which encourage the use of a 2-tier architecture by binding the graphical data controls directly to the data source, this class allows the elaboration of a 3-tier architecture. For example, let's suppose that the following data object class named `Employee` represents employees. You can use the `ObjectDataSource` class to link an employee collection to a presentation control such as a `ListBox`. For this, you must provide a stateless class (i.e. without instance fields) presenting a public method which returns the employee collection. The public method, in our case `ICollection GetData()`, is known by the data source through the value of the `SelectMethod` property and is then called by reflection. This method can be either static or not. This is illustrated by the following listings:

Example 23-62
```
using System.Collections;
using System.Collections.Generic;
public class Employee {
   private int m_EmployeeID = -1;
   private string m_SurName;
   private string m_FirstName;
   public int EmployeeID {
      get{ return m_EmployeeID; } set{ m_EmployeeID=value; }
   }

   public string SurName {
      get{ return m_SurName; }    set{ m_SurName = value; }
   }
   public string FirstName{
      get{ return m_FirstName; }  set{ m_FirstName = value; }
   }
}
public class Helper {
   private static List<Employee> list = new List<Employee>();
   static Helper() {
      Employee emp = new Employee();
      emp.EmployeeID = 1;
      emp.SurName = "Doo";
      emp.FirstName = "John";
      list.Add(emp);
      emp = new Employee();
      emp.EmployeeID = 2;
      emp.SurName = "Dupont";
      emp.FirstName = "Anne";
      list.Add(emp);
   }
   static public ICollection GetData() { return list; }
}
```

Example 23-63
```
<%@ Page Language="C#" %>
<html xmlns="http://www.w3.org/1999/xhtml" >
   <body>
   <form id="Form2" runat="server">
      <asp:ObjectDataSource ID="ObjDataSrc" runat="server"
                         SelectMethod="GetData" TypeName="Helper"/>
      <asp:ListBox ID="MyList" DataSourceID="ObjDataSrc"
```

Example 23-63
```
                        DataTextField="SurName" runat="server" />
    </form>
  </body>
</html>
```

Harnessing a data sources in order to update data

The `ObjectDataSource` class also allows the modification of data. For this, you simply need that the intermediate *helper* class offers the insertion, update and/or deletion methods. You need to specify these methods in the declaration of the `ObjectDataSource` using the `InsertMethod`, `UpdateMethod` and `DeleteMethod` properties These methods are respectively called when one of the methods `IEnumerable Select()`, `int Update()`, `int Insert()` and `int Delete()` methods are called on the `ObjectDataSource` control. The update of data is illustrated in the following example. By taking the preceding example, this page allows the update of the name of an employee:

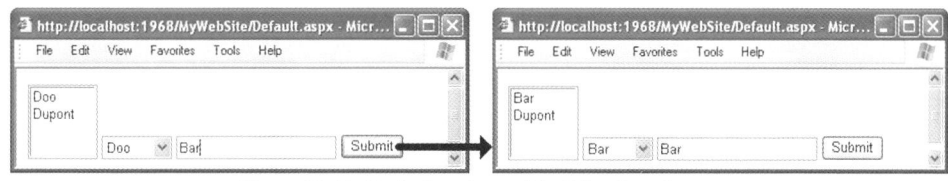

Figure 23-11: Updating data with ObjectDataSource

Example 23-64
```
...
public class Employee { ... }
public class Helper {
...
   static public void UpdateName( string oldName, string newName ) {
      foreach ( Employee emp in list )
         if ( emp.SurName == oldName )
            emp.SurName = newName;
   }
}
```

Example 23-65
```
<%@ Page Language="C#" %>
<script language="C#" runat="server">
   void Btn_Click(Object s, EventArgs e) { ObjDataSrc.Update(); }
</script>
<html xmlns="http://www.w3.org/1999/xhtml" >
   <body>
      <form id="Form2" runat="server">
         <asp:ObjectDataSource ID="ObjDataSrc" runat="server"
                               TypeName="Helper" SelectMethod="GetData"
                               UpdateMethod="UpdateName" >
            <UpdateParameters>
               <asp:ControlParameter name="oldName" type="String"
                                     controlid="OldName"
                                     propertyname="SelectedValue" />
               <asp:FormParameter Name="newName" formfield="NewName"
                                  Type="String" />
            </UpdateParameters>
         </asp:ObjectDataSource>
```

Example 23-65
```
        <asp:ListBox ID="MyList" DataSourceID="ObjDataSrc"
                    DataTextField="SurName" runat="server" />
        <asp:DropDownList ID="OldName" runat="server"
            DataTextField="SurName" DataSourceID="ObjDataSrc"   />
        <asp:TextBox ID="NewName" runat="server"/>
        <asp:Button  ID="Button1" runat="server" Text="Submit"
                    OnClick="Btn_Click" />
    </form>
  </body>
</html>
```

Note the way that the parameters coming into the `UpdateName()` method are tied to the `OldName` and `NewName` controls within a `<UpdateParameters>` section. Naturally, for the selection, insertion and destruction you can also use the equivalent `<SelectParameters>`, `<InsertParameters>` and `<DeleteParameters>` sections. These sections contain the declaration of the server controls allowing you to capture the entry parameter for the processing. For example, the `ControlParameter` control allows retrieving a value from the property of another control while `FormParameter` allows the retrieve a parameter contained in a `TextBox`. All these controls derive from the `Parameter` control. You can find a complete list by consulting the article named **Parameter Hierarchy** on **MSDN**.

Viewing and editing data

ASP.NET 2 introduces a new hierarchy of server controls allowing the presentation and edition of data from a data source:

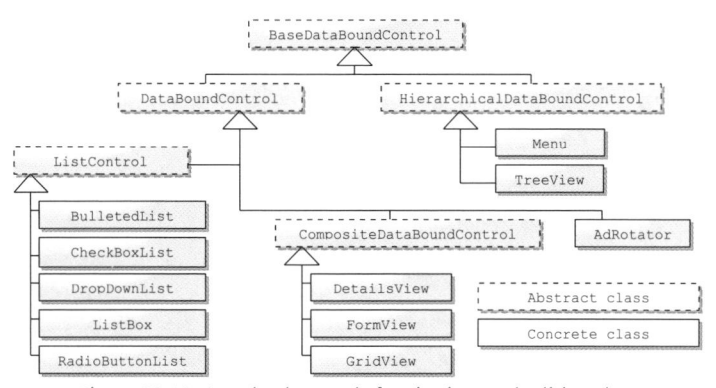

Figure 23-12: Standard controls for viewing and editing data

If you already know ASP.NET 1.x, you will notice the lack of a `DataGrid` control. This control is still present in the .NET 2 framework for backward compatibility reasons. However it is recommended that you use its successor, the `GridView` control which is more powerful.

In the examples from the previous sections, we had the opportunity of using the `ListBox` and `DropDownList` controls as well as the ability of being bound to a data source.

The `Menu` and `Treeview` controls can be used to present a hierarchical data source as described at page 794 when we will use them to display the structure of a site.

The `AdRotator` control allows to randomly display general ad banner. We invite you to consult **MSDN** for more details on this control.

Here, we will mostly interest ourselves to the `GridView`, `DetailsView` and `FormView` controls particularly adapted to the presentation and the edition of data from a flat data source.

The GridView control

As with its predecessor the `DataGrid` control, the new `GridView` control allows the presentation and edition of data in a table. In addition to several functional improvements, the power of this control resides mostly in its efficiency and ease of use when it comes to work with data sources. To prove this, here is the code of a page allowing filling a `GridView` with the data from a database table:

Example 23-66

```
<%@ Page Language="C#" %>
<html xmlns="http://www.w3.org/1999/xhtml" >
   <body>
   <form id="Form1" runat="server">
      <asp:SqlDataSource ID="DataSrc" runat="server" ConnectionString=
          "server = localhost ; uid=sa ; pwd =; database = ORGANIZATION"
          SelectCommand="SELECT * FROM EMPLOYEES" />
      <asp:GridView ID="Grid" DataSourceID="DataSrc" runat="server" />
   </form>
   </body>
</html>
```

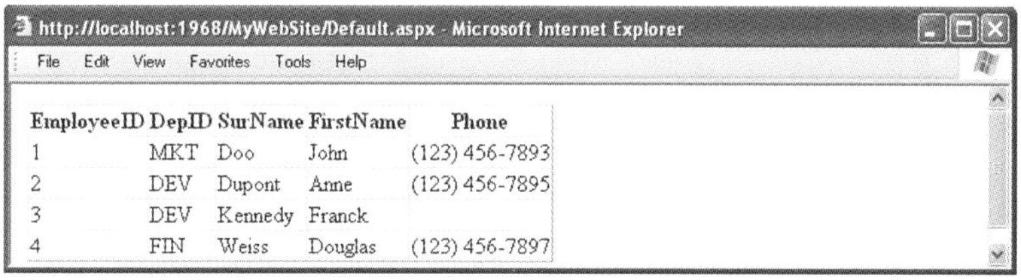

EmployeeID	DepID	SurName	FirstName	Phone
1	MKT	Doo	John	(123) 456-7893
2	DEV	Dupont	Anne	(123) 456-7895
3	DEV	Kennedy	Franck	
4	FIN	Weiss	Douglas	(123) 456-7897

Figure 23-13: Simple use of a GridView

Behind this simplicity of use is hidden one of the most complex server controls in ASP.NET 2. For length reasons, we will limit ourselves to only presenting some of its main functionalities. Also, do not hesitate to consult **MSDN** for more information.

The `bool AllowPaging` property of the `GridView` control allows specifying if you wish to page the data presented over several pages. By default, paging is done on 10 rows but you can change this value using the `PageSize` property. You can obtain or set the index of the page displayed using the `int PageIndex` property. When more that one page is necessary for the display of data, the `GridView` controls generates a row specialized for the navigation of the pages. You can personalize this row by accessing the object of type `PagerSettings` which can be accessed through the `GridView.PagerSettings{get;}` property. A significant improvement in the paging behavior of `GridView` versus `DataGrid` is that only the data displayed on the current page are stored within the *viewstate*.

The `bool AllowSorting` property allows you to specify if you wish to allow the user to sort the data based on the content of a column. The activation of this feature makes it so that the header for the columns becomes hyperlinks. Sorting is done on the server-side and is returned to the client when such a request is made.

You can easily edit the data of a row and even delete such a row when using a `GridView`. For this, the underlying data source must support these operations and you must set to `true` the `AutoGenerateEditButton` and `AutoGenerateDeleteButton` properties. The following example illustrates this:

Example 23-67

```
<%@ Page Language="C#" %>
<html xmlns="http://www.w3.org/1999/xhtml" >
  <body>
    <form id="Form1" runat="server">
      <asp:SqlDataSource ID="DataSrc" runat="server" ConnectionString=
          "server = localhost; uid=sa ; pwd =; database = ORGANIZATION"
          SelectCommand="SELECT * FROM EMPLOYEES"
          UpdateCommand= "UPDATE EMPLOYEES SET
                          DepID = @DepID, SurName = @SurName,
                          FirstName = @FirstName, Phone = @Phone
                          WHERE EmployeeId = @Original_EmployeeId"
          DeleteCommand= "DELETE EMPLOYEES WHERE
                          EmployeeId = @Original_EmployeeId" />
      <asp:GridView ID="MyGrid" DataSourceID="DataSrc" runat="server"
          AutoGenerateEditButton="true"
          AutoGenerateDeleteButton="true"
          DataKeyNames="EmployeeId"/>
    </form>
  </body>
</html>
```

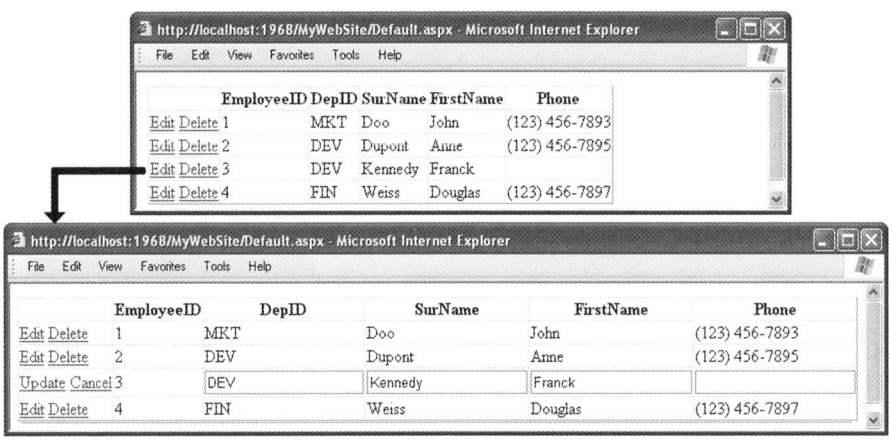

Figure 23-14: Editing/Deleting data with the GridView control

The `GridView` control offers events such as `RowDeleting` or `RowDeleted` allowing you to call a server-side method right before or after a modification. The insertion of rows required the use of the `DetailsView` control which we will detail in the next section.

You can also act on the way the data is displayed in the grid by modifying the displayed columns. ASP. NET 2 provides several built-in column styles using types which derive from `DataControlField` class such as `ButtonField` or `BoundField`. However, by using the `TemplateField` type, you can define the exact HTML code contained in a cell. This is illustrated by the following example which displays a grid composed of:

- A column of type `ButtonField` containing buttons which display the names of the employees. When such a button is clicked, the `Grid_RowCommand()` method is invoked and changes the content of `Msg` label.

- A column of type `TemplateField` which contains `CheckBox` controls. A `CheckBox` is checked only if the name of the employee contains the letter 'o'.

- A column of type `BoundText` containing the name of the employees.

Example 23-68
```
<%@ Page Language="C#" %>
<script language="C#" runat="server">
    void Grid_RowCommand(Object sender, GridViewCommandEventArgs e) {
        if (e.CommandName == "Hello") {
            int index = Convert.ToInt32(e.CommandArgument);
            GridViewRow selectedRow = Grid.Rows[index];
            TableCell cell = selectedRow.Cells[2];
            string surname = cell.Text;
            Msg.Text = "You selected " + surname + ".";
        }
    }
</script>
<html xmlns="http://www.w3.org/1999/xhtml" >
  <body>
    <form id="Form1" runat="server">
      <asp:SqlDataSource ID="DataSrc" runat="server" ConnectionString=
          "server = localhost ; uid=sa ; pwd=; database = ORGANIZATION"
          SelectCommand="SELECT * FROM EMPLOYEES" />
      <asp:GridView ID="Grid" DataSourceID="DataSrc" runat="server"
          AutoGenerateColumns="False" OnRowCommand="Grid_RowCommand" >
        <Columns>
          <asp:ButtonField DataTextField="SurName" ButtonType="Button"
                    HeaderText="Click..." CommandName="Hello"/>
          <asp:TemplateField HeaderText="The name contains the 'o' char">
            <ItemTemplate>
              --<asp:CheckBox runat="server" Enabled="False"
                Checked=<%# ((string)Eval("SurName")).Contains("o") %>  />--
            </ItemTemplate>
          </asp:TemplateField>
          <asp:BoundField DataField="SurName" HeaderText="SurName" />
        </Columns>
      </asp:GridView>
      <asp:Label ID="Msg" runat="server"></asp:Label>
    </form>
  </body>
</html>
```

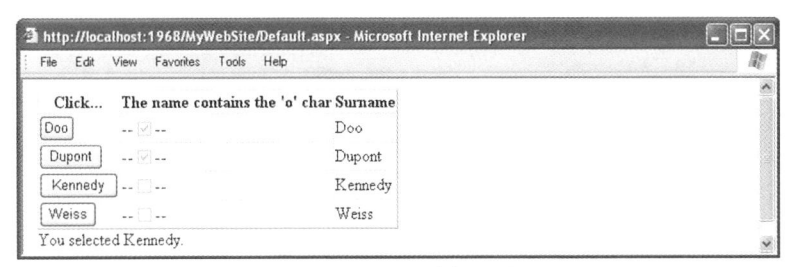

Figure 23-15: Customizing columns

Templates

In the previous example, you may have noticed this block of code which resembles to a code block:

<%# ((string)Eval("SurName")).Contains("o") %>

We name such a block a *template*. This template replaces itself by `false` or `true` depending on whether the name of the employee on the current row contains an 'o'. Template is a way to allow you to decide how the content is displayed. The data presentation server controls which use templates are `GridView`, `DetailsView`, `FormView`, `LoginView`, `TreeView`, `Repeater`, `DataList` and `DataGrid`. Contrarily to code blocks, templates are evaluated when the data binding is done (i.e. during the call to `DataBind()` on the control). Each template is evaluated once per row.

Internally, each template introduces a child control to the presentation control in which it is defined. These child controls are of type `DataBoundLiteralControl`. During compilation, ASP.NET adds to the class representing the current page a method which is subscribed to the `DataBinding` event of the control. This event is triggered for each row retrieved during the call to `DataBind()` for the parent presentation control. The following method has been generated for our example:

```
public void __DataBinding__control6(object sender, EventArgs e) {
   CheckBox box1 = (CheckBox) sender;
   IDataItemContainer container1 =
      (IDataItemContainer) box1.BindingContainer;
   box1.Checked = ( (string) DataBinder.Eval(
      container1.DataItem,"SurName") ).Contains("o");
}
```

The `BindingContainer` property of the `CheckBox` control returns a reference to the row currently being processed. This row is materialized by a control of type `GridViewRow` which implements the `IDataItemContainer` interface. Finally, the `Eval()` method of the `DataBinder` is capable, through reflection, of extracting the name of the current employee.

Although not present in the new presentation control hierarchy of ASP.NET 2, we want to mention the possibility of using two control types particularly adapted to the use of templates: the `Repeater` and `DataList` controls. Their use is illustrated in the following example:

Example 23-69

```
<%@ Page Language="C#" %>
<html xmlns="http://www.w3.org/1999/xhtml" >
  <body>
    <form id="Form1" runat="server">
      <asp:SqlDataSource ID="DataSrc" runat="server" ConnectionString=
          "server = localhost; uid=sa ; pwd =; database = ORGANIZATION"
        SelectCommand="SELECT EmployeeId, SurName, Phone FROM EMPLOYEES"/>
      <i>Repeater:</i><br/>
      <asp:Repeater ID="MyRepeater" DataSourceID="DataSrc"
            runat="server">
        <ItemTemplate>
          SurName: <b><%# Eval("SurName") %></b>
          Phone: <b><%# Eval("Phone") %></b><br/>
        </ItemTemplate>
      </asp:Repeater>
      <br/><i>DataList:</i><br/>
      <asp:DataList ID="MyDataList" DataSourceID="DataSrc"
          runat="server" RepeatColumns="3" RepeatDirection=Vertical>
        <ItemTemplate>
          SurName:<b><%# Eval("SurName") %></b>
          Phone:<b><%# Eval("Phone") %></b><br/>
        </ItemTemplate>
      </asp:DataList>
    </form>
  </body>
</html>
```

Viewing and editing data   781

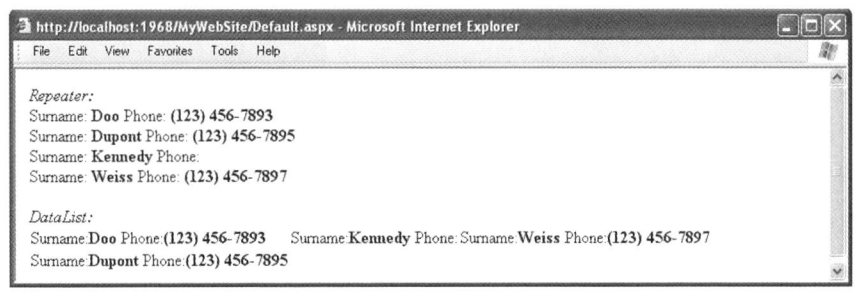

Figure 23-16: Repeater and DataList controls and Templates

There are three other types of templates in addition to the Eval template:

```
<%# Eval( "Column|Property|Field" [,"format"] ) %>
<%# Bind( "Column|Property|Field" [,"format"]) %>
<%# XPath( "Expression-XPath" [,"format"]) %>
<%# XPathSelect( "Expression-XPath") %>
```

The optional format string allows to format the string which represents the evaluated data (see page 310 for more detail on the use of string formatting).

A template of type Bind is used in the same way as the Eval template. However, such a template allows the recovery of information input by the user and communicates it to the parent presentation control. Typically, templates of type Bind are used when you activate the edition mode on a presentation control. Such a template is used a little later in Example 23-73 when we will explain the edition mode of a FormView control. For more information on Bind templates, read the article named **Two-Way Data Binding Syntax** on **MSDN**.

Templates of type XPath and XPathSelect are used on hierarchical data structures described a little later.

The DetailsView control

The DetailsView control allows you to present a detailed view of each row. As illustrated in the following example, it is easy to use a DetailsView control to navigate the various rows of a flat data source:

Example 23-70
```
<%@ Page Language="C#" %>
<html xmlns="http://www.w3.org/1999/xhtml" >
  <body>
    <form id="Form1" runat="server">
      <asp:SqlDataSource ID="DataSrc" runat="server" ConnectionString=
          "server = localhost; uid=sa ; pwd =; database = ORGANIZATION"
          SelectCommand="SELECT * FROM EMPLOYEES" />
      <asp:DetailsView ID="Details" DataSourceID="DataSrc" runat="server"
          AllowPaging="True" >
        <PagerSettings Mode="NextPreviousFirstLast" />
      </asp:DetailsView>
    </form>
  </body>
</html>
```

Figure 23-17: Using a DetailsView control

The DetailsView control is complementary to the GridView control. Also, it is common to use a combination of both controls to obtain what is called a *master detail view* of a flat data source. To obtain such a view, it is necessary to activate the selection of a row on the GridView using the AutoGenerateSelectButton. Moreover you have to define two data sources: one used by the GridView which presents the set of rows and one used by the DetailsView which presents the currently selected row. This second data source uses the FilterExpression property to determine which row is currently selected:

Example 23-71
```
<%@ Page Language="C#" %>
<html xmlns="http://www.w3.org/1999/xhtml" >
  <body>
    <form id="Form1" runat="server">
      <asp:SqlDataSource ID="DataSrc1" runat="server" ConnectionString=
         "server = localhost; uid=sa ; pwd =; database = ORGANIZATION"
         SelectCommand="SELECT * FROM EMPLOYEES" />
      <asp:GridView ID="MyGrid" DataSourceID="DataSrc1" runat="server"
                    DataKeyNames="EmployeeId" SelectedIndex="0"
                    AutoGenerateSelectButton="true" />


      <asp:SqlDataSource ID="DataSrc2" runat="server" ConnectionString=
           "server = localhost; uid=sa ; pwd =; database = ORGANIZATION"
           SelectCommand="SELECT * FROM EMPLOYEES"
           FilterExpression="EmployeeId={0}">
         <FilterParameters>
            <asp:ControlParameter Name="EmployeeId" ControlID="MyGrid"
                                  PropertyName="SelectedValue" />
         </FilterParameters>
      </asp:SqlDataSource>
      <asp:DetailsView ID="MyDetails" DataSourceID="DataSrc2"
                       runat="server" DataKeyNames="EmployeeId" />
    </form>
  </body>
</html>
```

Viewing and editing data 783

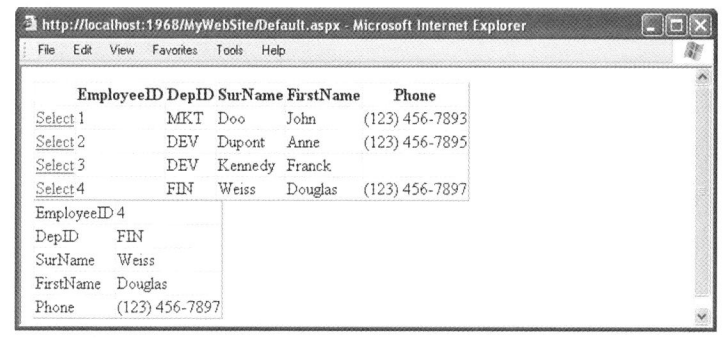

Figure 23-18: Master details view

A master detail view represents the optimal alternative for the edition and insertion of data for each row. As the following example shows, to obtain such a view, you simply need to activate the insertion and edition features on the `DetailsView` data source as well as on the `DetailsView` itself:

Example 23-72
```
<%@ Page Language="C#" %>
<html xmlns="http://www.w3.org/1999/xhtml" >
   <body>
   <form id="Form1" runat="server">
      <asp:SqlDataSource ID="DataSrc1" runat="server" ConnectionString=
         "server = localhost; uid=sa ; pwd =; database = ORGANIZATION"
         SelectCommand="SELECT * FROM EMPLOYEES" />
      <asp:GridView ID="MyGrid" DataSourceID="DataSrc1" runat="server"
                 DataKeyNames="EmployeeId" SelectedIndex="0"
                 AutoGenerateSelectButton="true" />

      <asp:SqlDataSource ID="DataSrc2" runat="server" ConnectionString=
         "server = localhost; uid=sa ; pwd =; database = ORGANIZATION"
         SelectCommand="SELECT * FROM EMPLOYEES"
      UpdateCommand= "UPDATE EMPLOYEES SET
                 DepID = @DepID, SurName = @SurName,
                 FirstName = @FirstName, Phone = @Phone
                 WHERE EmployeeId = @Original_EmployeeId"
      DeleteCommand="DELETE EMPLOYEES WHERE EmployeeId=@Original_EmployeeId"
      InsertCommand="INSERT INTO EMPLOYEES (DepID,SurName,FirstName,Phone)
                 VALUES(@DepID,@SurName,@FirstName,@Phone)"
         FilterExpression="EmployeeId={0}"
      OnDeleted="OnChgData" OnInserted="OnChgData" OnUpdated="OnChgData" >
         <FilterParameters>
            <asp:ControlParameter Name="EmployeeId" ControlID="MyGrid"
                           PropertyName="SelectedValue" />
         </FilterParameters>
      </asp:SqlDataSource>
      <asp:DetailsView ID="MyDetails" DataSourceID="DataSrc2"
                 runat="server" DataKeyNames="EmployeeId"
                 AutoGenerateDeleteButton="True"
                 AutoGenerateEditButton="True"
                 AutoGenerateInsertButton="True"/>
   </form>
   </body>
</html>
<script language="C#" runat="server">
   void OnChgData(Object sender, EventArgs e) { MyGrid.DataBind(); }
</script>
```

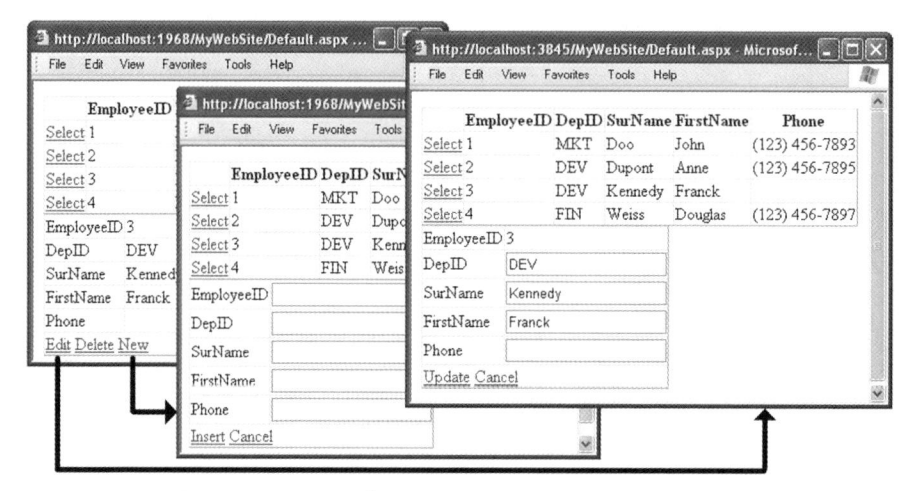

Figure 23-19: Editing/Inserting data with a master details view

Note the need to use the `DataBind()` method on our `GridView` each time the data is updated through the `DetailsView`. Without this step, the data within the `GridView` would not be automatically updated.

The `DetailsView` control offers several configuration properties as well as several events which are useful. We invite you to consult **MSDN** for more information. At page 570 we show how you can obtain this type of view within a *Windows Forms* application.

The FormView control

The `FormView` server control is similar to the `DetailsView` control with the exception that it is specially adapted to the personalization of the presentation and edition of the data of a row. Contrarily to the `DetailsView` control, the `FormView` control does not provide default code for the presentation of data. It is necessary to provide your own code within the `<ItemTemplate>`, `<EditItemTemplate>` and `<InsertItemTemplate>` sections. As shows the following example, the use of templates is extremely useful within these sections:

Example 23-73

```
<%@ Page Language="C#" %>
<html xmlns="http://www.w3.org/1999/xhtml" >
  <body>
    <form id="Form1" runat="server">
      <asp:SqlDataSource ID="DataSrc" runat="server" ConnectionString=
          "server = localhost; uid=sa ; pwd =; database = ORGANIZATION"
          SelectCommand="SELECT EmployeeId, SurName, Phone FROM EMPLOYEES"
          UpdateCommand= "UPDATE EMPLOYEES SET Phone = @Phone WHERE
                          EmployeeId = @Original_EmployeeId"/>
      <asp:FormView ID="Details" DataSourceID="DataSrc" runat="server"
                    DataKeyNames="EmployeeId"  AllowPaging="True" >
        <ItemTemplate>
            SurName: <%# Eval("SurName") %> <br/>
            Phone: <%# Eval("Phone") %> <br/>
            <asp:Button ID="BtnEdit" runat="server" CommandName="Edit"
              Text="Edit phone number"/>
        </ItemTemplate>
        <EditItemTemplate>
```

Viewing and editing data 785

Example 23-73
```
                SurName: <%# Eval("SurName") %> <br/>
                Phone: <asp:TextBox ID="EditPhone" runat="server"
                                    Text=<%# Bind("Phone") %> /> <br/>
                <asp:Button ID="BtnUpdate" CommandName="Update"
                            Text="Update phone number." runat="server" />
                <asp:Button ID="BtnCancel" CommandName="Cancel"
                            Text="Cancel update" runat="server" />
            </EditItemTemplate>
        </asp:FormView>
    </form>
  </body>
</html>
```

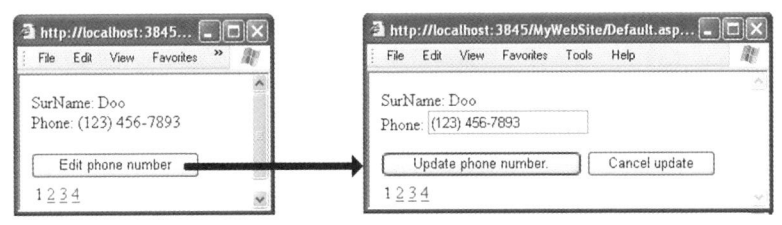

Figure 23-20: Using the FormView control

Displaying XML data

Here, we will not discuss the `TreeView` and `Menu` hierarchical data presentation controls. Know that we will briefly detail them at page 793.

We will rather focus our attention on the fact that hierarchical data sources can be used by presentation controls originally meant to be bound to flat data sources. In this case, such a control presents the first level of data hierarchy. The advantage is that you can use another data presentation control embedded in the first one in order to access the second level of hierarchy. For example, consider the following XML document which contains books and a list of chapters for each book:

Example 23-74 *books.xml*
```
<?xml version="1.0" encoding="utf-8" ?>
<bookstore>
   <book title="The unbearable lightness of being"
         author="Kundera" publicationdate="1985" >
      <chapter name="Lightness and weight"/>
      <chapter name="Soul and body"/>
   </book>
   <book title="Practical .NET 2 and C#2"
         author="Patrick Smacchia" publicationdate="2006" >
      <chapter name="Introduction to .NET"/>
      <chapter name="Assembly, module, IL language"/>
   </book>
   <book title="The New York Trilogy"
         author="Paul Auster" publicationdate="2002" >
      <chapter name="City of glass"/>
      <chapter name="Ghosts"/>
      <chapter name="The locked room"/>
   </book>
</bookstore>
```

The following page allows the presentation of books published after the year 2000 as well as the list of chapters for each book. Notice the use of the `XPath` and `XPathSelect` templates to select an attribute and to select several nodes. Also note that the use of the two embedded `Repeater` controls to present the two levels of hierarchy. Finally note the use of an `XPath` request at the level of the data to select only the books published after the year 2000:

Example 23-75

```
<%@ Page Language="C#" %>
<html xmlns="http://www.w3.org/1999/xhtml" >
  <body>
    <form id="Form1" runat="server">
      <i>List of books published after 2000:</i><br/>
      <asp:XmlDataSource id="MySrc" DataFile="~/App_Data/books.xml"
                         XPath="/bookstore/book[@publicationdate>2000]"
                         runat="server"/>
      <asp:Repeater id="ListBook" DataSourceId="MySrc" runat="server">
         <ItemTemplate>
  Title: <b><%# XPath("@title") %></b>
  Author:<b><%# XPath("@author") %></b>
  Publication date:<b><%# XPath("@publicationdate")%></b><br/>
           <asp:Repeater id="ListChapter" runat="server"
                         DataSource='<%# XPathSelect("chapter") %>' >
              <ItemTemplate>- <%# XPath("@name")%><br/></ItemTemplate>
           </asp:Repeater>
         </ItemTemplate>
      </asp:Repeater>
    </form>
  </body>
</html>
```

Here is the content of this page:

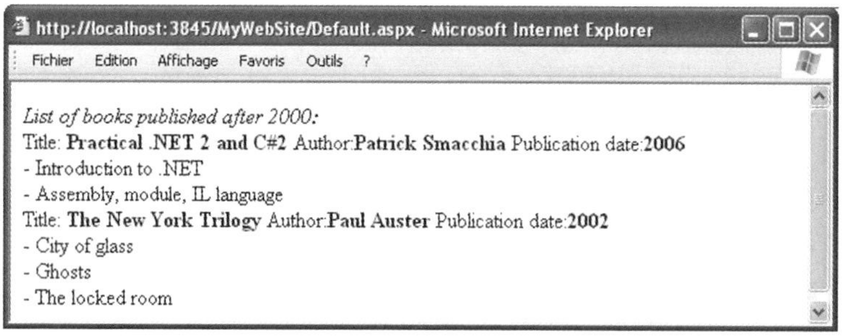

Figure 23-21: Presenting XML data

Master pages

Master page and content page

To guarantee the visual consistency of a web site, it is common that all its pages present similar parts such as the headers and footers. With ASP.NET 1.x, you needed to use user control to provide and reuse similar parts. This approach has the drawback of forcing the developer to create several user controls, for example for the header and footer of a page. Also, you needed to copy the declaration of these controls into every page of this site which would cause update nightmares.

Master pages

ASP.NET 2 introduces the notion of *master page* which allows the reuse of a page design on all the pages of a site. The use of such a model is illustrated by the following figure:

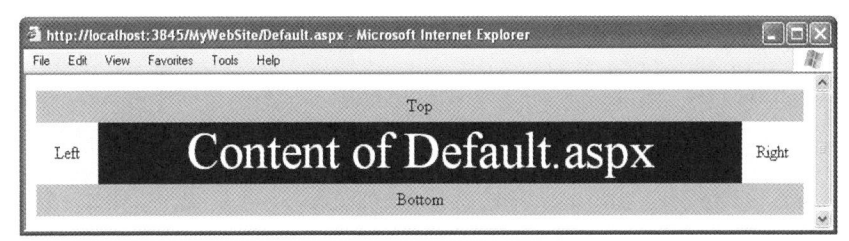

Figure 23-22: A master page

A master page presents itself as a file with a `.master` extension that begins with the `<%@ master%>` directive. The content of such a file is similar to the one of an `.aspx` with the exception that it can contain controls of type `<asp:ContentPlaceHolder>`. Such a control defines the location where the pages of a site can place their own content. Here is the code for the master page illustrated in our figure:

Example 23-76 *MyMasterPage.master*

```
<%@ master language="C#" %>
<html><body><form id="Form1" runat="server">
   <table id="Tbl1" width="100%" height="30px"
                    cellspacing="0" cellpadding="0">
      <tr><td width="100%" align="center" bgcolor="silver">Top</td></tr>
   </table>
   <table id="Tbl2" width="100%" height="50%"
                    cellspacing="0" cellpadding="0">
      <tr>
         <td width="60px" align="center" bgcolor="yellow">Left</td>
         <td align="center">
            <asp:contentplaceholder id="MyContentPH" runat="Server">
            </asp:contentplaceholder>
         </td>
         <td width="60px" align="center" bgcolor="yellow">Right</td>
      </tr>
   </table>
   <table id="Tbl3"  width="100%" height="30px"
                    cellspacing="0" cellpadding="0">
      <tr><td width="100%" align="center" bgcolor="silver">Bottom</td>
      </tr>
   </table>
</form></body></html>
```

Here is the code of an `.aspx` page which uses the `MyMasterPage.master` master page. We say that such a page is a *content page*:

Example 23-77 *Default.aspx*

```
<%@ Page Language="C#" MasterPageFile="~/MyMasterPage.master"  %>
<asp:content id="MyContent" contentplaceholderid="MyContentPH"
             runat="server" >
   <asp:label id="lbl"         Height="100%"    Width="100%"
              BackColor="Black" ForeColor="White" runat="server"
              Font-Size="XX-Large">Content of Default.aspx</asp:label>
</asp:content>
```

You can notice that we specify the master page to use with the `MasterPageFile` sub-directive of `<%@ Page%>`. A content page cannot have root elements other than `<asp:Content>` controls. The `ContentPlaceHolderId` of such a control is mandatory. It must be initialized with the identifier of the corresponding `<asp:ContentPlaceHolder>` control in the master page. This means that the content defined within a `<asp:Content>` control will be injected during the execution of the master page in the place of the associated `<asp:ContentPlaceHolder>` control.

Know that such a content page does not need to necessarily associate a `<asp:Content>` control to each `<asp:ContentPlaceHolder>` control of the master page. Moreover, the definition of a master page can contain `<asp:Content>` controls associated to its own `<asp:ContentPlaceHolder>` controls. The content of such a `<asp:Content>` control will be injected in the place of the `<asp:ContentPlaceHolder>` control by default when a page does not provide a corresponding `<asp:Content>` control.

An interesting feature of master pages is that *Visual Studio .NET 2005* is capable of displaying, in read-only mode, the content of the page design during the edition of a page using a master page.

During execution, a master page is materialized by an instance of the `System.Web.UI.MasterPage` class. This class itself derives from the `UserControl` class. A content page compiles just as with a `.aspx` page. However, the `get` accessor of the `MasterPage Master{get;set;}` property on a content page returns a reference to the object representing the corresponding master page. The ASP.NET 2 engine takes care of constructing the structure of the control rendered by the page. For this, it combines the control structure defined in the master page user control and the control structure defined in each `<asp:Content>` controls of the content page.

A consequence of the fact that ASP.NET implements the notion of master page as user controls is that the page cache feature that we have discussed earlier can be used within a content page.

Nested master page

You have the possibility of encapsulating a master page within another master page. This feature is illustrated by the page bellow:

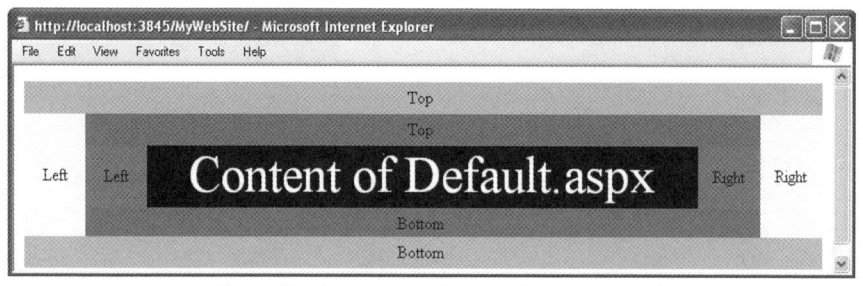

Figure 23-23: Example of a nested master page

To reproduce this page, you need to build in our solution a new master page named `MyMasterPageNested.master` which is associated to our initial `MyMasterPage.aspx` master page using the `MasterPageFile` sub-directive of `<%@ master%>`. As with a content page, an encapsulated master page can contain `<asp:Content>` controls. However, these controls can themselves contain `<asp:ContentPlaceHolder>` controls.

Example 23-78   *MyMasterPageNested.master*
```
<%@ master language="C#" MasterPageFile="~/MyMasterPage.master"%>
<asp:Content ContentPlaceHolderID=MyContentPH runat="server">
   <table id="Tbl1" width="100%" height="30px"
                   cellspacing="0" cellpadding="0">
     <tr><td width="100%" align="center" bgcolor="olive">Top</td></tr>
```

Master pages

Example 23-78   *MyMasterPageNested.master*

```
      </table>
      <table id="Tbl2" width="100%" height="50%"
                  cellspacing="0" cellpadding="0">
        <tr>
            <td width="60px" align="center" bgcolor="red">Left</td>
            <td align="center">
                <asp:contentplaceholder id="MyContentPH2" runat="Server">
                </asp:contentplaceholder>
            </td>
            <td width="60px" align="center" bgcolor="red">Right</td>
        </tr>
      </table>
      <table id="Tbl3" width="100%" height="30px"
                  cellspacing="0" cellpadding="0">
        <tr> <td width="100%" align="center" bgcolor="olive">Bottom</td>
        </tr>
      </table>
</asp:Content>
```

A content page can be associated to a nested master page in the same way as if it wasn't nested:

Example 23-79   *Default.aspx*

```
<%@ Page Language="C#" MasterPageFile="~/MyMasterPageNested.master" %>
<asp:content id="MyContent" contentplaceholderid="MyContentPH2"
            runat="server" >
   <asp:label id="lbl"          Height="100%"       Width="100%"
              BackColor="Black" ForeColor="White" runat="server"
              Font-Size="XX-Large">Content of Default.aspx</asp:label>
</asp:content>
```

Note that *Visual Studio 2005* can't provide design mode support when you are using nested master pages.

Configuring master page

In large sites, with a large number of pages, the simple fact of having to put the `MasterPageFile` sub-directive in every content page can be cumbersome for maintenance reasons. You can use the `masterPageFile` of the `<pages>` configuration element in order to tell ASP.NET that all the pages affected by this element are associated with a certain master page. Only pages which do not contain their own `MasterPageFile` sub-directive will be affected.

Web.Config

```
<?xml version="1.0"?>
<configuration xmlns="http://schemas.microsoft.com/.NetConfiguration/v2.0">
   <system.web>
       <pages masterPageFile="~/MyMasterPage.master"/>
...
```

In order to use these two static association techniques (i.e. during compilation) of master pages to content pages, you can also dynamically (i.e. during execution) choose which master page a content page will use. For this, you simply need to set the `string MasterPageFile{get;set;}` property of a content page during the `OnPreInit()` event.

Example 23-80   *Default.aspx*

```
<%@ Page Language=»C#» %>
<asp:content id=»MyContent» contentplaceholderid="MyContentPH"
            runat="server" >
```

Example 23-80 *Default.aspx*
```
    <script language="C#" runat="server">
    protected override void OnPreInit(EventArgs e) {
        this.MasterPageFile ="~/MyMasterPage2.master";
        base.OnPreInit(e);
    }
    </script>
    <asp:label id="lbl"         Height="100%"    Width="100%"
            BackColor="Black" ForeColor="White" runat="server"
            Font-Size="XX-Large">Content of Default.aspx</asp:label>
</asp:content>
```

This technique can be very powerful for certain large sites but we recommend to use it sparingly because of the constraints that it introduces. Notably, it makes you responsible of the maintenance of the correspondence between the identifiers for the `<asp:ContentPlaceHolder>` controls as it prevents the *de facto* verification by the compiler.

Accessing a master page from a content page

It can be useful to be able to access the controls of the master page directly from the code of a content page. To illustrate this possibility, let's modify our `MyMasterPage` master page in order to introduce a new server control which represents the header:

Example 23-81 *MyMasterPage.master*
```
<%@ master language="C#" %>
    <script language="C#" runat="server">
    public HtmlTableCell CellHeader {
        get { return _CellHeader; } set { _CellHeader = value; }
    }
    </script>
<html>
<body>
<form id="Form1" runat="server">
    <table id="Tbl1" width="100%" height="30px"
                    cellspacing="0" cellpadding="0" >
        <tr>
            <td id="_CellHeader" runat="server" width="100%"
                align="center" bgcolor="silver" >Top</td>
        </tr>
    </table>
...
```

Based on the way that master pages are compiled by ASP.NET, it is clear that we can have access to this `_CellHeader` control from our content page as follows:

Example 23-82 *Default.aspx*
```
<%@ Page Language="C#" MasterPageFile="~/MyMasterPage.master" %>
<asp:content id="MyContent" contentplaceholderid="MyContentPH"
            runat="server" >
    <script language="C#" runat="server">
    void Page_Load(object sender, EventArgs e) {
        HtmlTableCell cell =
            Master.FindControl("_CellHeader") as HtmlTableCell;
        cell.BgColor = "white";
    }
    </script>
    <asp:label id="lbl"         Height="100%"    Width="100%"
            BackColor="Black" ForeColor="White" runat="server"
```

Example 23-82   *Default.aspx*
```
              Font-Size="XX-Large">Content of Default.aspx</asp:label>
</asp:content>
```

Understand that in this example, we create a late binding between the code of the `Page_Load()` method in the content page and the object representing the control responsible for the rendering of the header cell in the master page. The late binding introduces a certain flexibility to the detriment of performance and static verifications.

In the case where the master page is defined statically in a `MasterPageFile` sub-directive of the content page, we do not need the flexibility of late binding. In fact, in this case we know during compilation the type of the master page used. Hence, you can use the `<%@ MasterType%>` directive in the content page in order to tell the compiler which type of master page you wish to use. This can be done by using a `VirtualPath` sub-directive which specifies the file name containing the master page or through a `TypeName` sub-directive which directly names the class representing the master page. The compiler will make sure that type of the `Master{get;set;}` property of the content page be correct. You can then use early binding on this master page.

To make best use of this feature, it is recommended to supply public properties on the class of the master page which give access to the controls susceptible of being used from a content page (as with what we have done with the `CellHeader` property defined in our master page):

Example 23-83   *Default.aspx*
```
<%@ Page Language="C#" MasterPageFile="~/MyMasterPage.master" %>
<%@ MasterType VirtualPath="~/MyMasterPage.master" %>
<asp:content id="MyContent" contentplaceholderid="MyContentPH"
             runat="server" >
   <script language="C#" runat="server">
      void Page_Load(object sender, EventArgs e) {
         Master.CellHeader.BgColor = "white";
      }
   </script>
   <asp:label id="lbl"         Height="100%"    Width="100%"
              BackColor="Black" ForeColor="White" runat="server"
              Font-Size="XX-Large">Content of Default.aspx</asp:label>
</asp:content>
```

ASP.NET 2 and localization

Before starting the current section, we must first assimilate the notions relating to the localization of a .NET application which is the topic of the section named Internationalization/localization and satellite assemblies at page 27.

In the case of an *ASP.NET 2* application, *Visual Studio 2005* offers facilities to edit several localized versions of a same web page. When you select a `XXX.aspx` page in design mode, you can select the *Tools › Generate Local Resources* menu item. A `XXX.aspx.resx` file is then added to the /App_LocalResources folder of the web application. This file contains the values relative to the neutral culture of the resources for this web page. You can then add resource files relating to other cultures by doing the following: `App_LocalResources` folder › *Add New Item › Assembly Resource File* › `XXX.yy-ZZ.resx`. By editing this file, you can modify the value of resources for the version of the page relative to the yy-ZZ culture. Note that all this also applies to user controls (i.e. files with an .ascx extension) and to master pages (i.e. files with a .master extension).

It is interesting to note that the ASP.NET code of a localized page is different. Most importantly, the values of localized server controls are not present anymore since they are contained in the resource file associated to the page. This means that each control contains a `meta:resourcekey="XXX"` attribute where XXX designates a string used to identify the control within the resource file.

The value of the `CurrentUICulture` of the thread which processes a web request is determined during the call to the `Page.InitializeCulture()` virtual method at the beginning of the lifecycle of the request. By default, the culture of the client is sent by the browser with each request and is used by ASP.NET 2 for this request. You can change this behavior by rewriting the `InitializeCulture()` method.

To test a page against different cultures either:

- You can modify the culture of your browser. Under *Internet Explorer* you simply need to go in the *Tools › Internet options › General › Languages › provide a list of cultures*, they will be processed in order of priority by ASP.NET.
- You can set the `UICulture` property of the page to the desired culture. Remember to put this value back to **Auto** once the page has been tested.

You can supply a default culture to all pages located (recursively) in a folder through the use of the `culture` and `uiCulture` attributes of the `<globalization>` section of the `Web.Config` file. This culture will be used to process a request which does not specify a culture or to process a request where the requested culture isn't supported.

Finally note that you can place global resource files for your web application in the `/App_GlobalResources` folder.

Site navigation

ASP.NET 2 offers an extensible infrastructure allowing the insertion in your pages of site navigation controls. Site navigation can be mainly done using three types of controls: the `TreeView`, the `Menu` and the `SiteMapPath`. They are all illustrated by the following screenshots:

Figure 23-24: Navigation with a TreeView

Figure 23-25: Navigation with a Menu

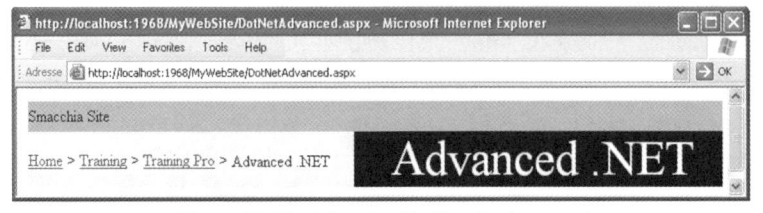

Figure 23-26: Using the SiteMapPath control

Site navigation

To benefit from site navigation, you must first add a file with a `.SiteMap` extension to your web site. This XML describes the organization of a site using an XML structure where each node represents a page:

Example 23-84   *App.SiteMap*
```xml
<?xml version="1.0" encoding="utf-8" ?>
<siteMap>
  <siteMapNode title="Home" url="~/Default.aspx">
    <siteMapNode title="Training" url="~/Trainings.aspx">
      <siteMapNode title="Training Pro" url="~/TrainingPro.aspx">
        <siteMapNode title=".NET 2.0" url="~/DotNet2.aspx"/>
        <siteMapNode title="Advanced .NET" url="~/AdvancedDotNet.aspx"/>
        <siteMapNode title="ASP.NET 2.0" url="~/ASPDotNet2.aspx"/>
      </siteMapNode>
    </siteMapNode>
    <siteMapNode title="Articles" url="~/Articles.aspx">
      <siteMapNode title=".NET2.0 News" url="~/DotNet2News.aspx"/>
    </siteMapNode>
    <siteMapNode title="Contact" url="~/Contact.aspx"/>
  </siteMapNode>
</siteMap>
```

Next, you must communicate to ASP.NET our wish to use the site navigation facilities by using a `<siteMap>` element in the configuration file:

Web.Config
```xml
<?xml version="1.0"?>
<configuration xmlns="http://schemas.microsoft.com/.NetConfiguration/v2.0">
    <system.web>
        <pages masterPageFile="~/MyMasterPage.master"/>
        <siteMap defaultProvider="MySiteMapProvider" enabled="true"  >
            <providers>
                <add type="System.Web.XmlSiteMapProvider"
                    name="MySiteMapProvider"
                    siteMapFile= "App.SiteMap"/>
            </providers>
        </siteMap>
...
```

Here is the notion of *SiteMap provider*. You configure such a provider by creating a class which derives from `System.Web.SiteMapProvider` and a data source containing the organization of the site. Here, we will use the `System.Web.XmlSiteMapProvider` class and our `App.SiteMap` file. This is another example of use for the *provider design pattern* presented at page 750.

A same site can contain several sitemap providers. In addition, the organization of a site can be stored in several `.SiteMap` files. These two features are the topic of the article named **How to: Configure Multiple Site Maps and Site-Map Provider** on **MSDN**.

You can create your own sitemap provider by using a proprietary class derived from `SiteMapProvider`. For example, you can wish to store the organization of a site in a database or dynamically modify the structure presented to the client. The construction of such a class is exposed in the article named **SiteMapProvider Class (System.Web)** on **MSDN**.

Once you have configured a sitemap provider, you must add to each page containing a site navigation control a control of type `<asp:SiteMapDataSource>` bound to this provider. You can then use server controls of type `<asp:Menu>` `<asp:TreeView>` and `<asp:SiteMapPath>` to provide site navigation. By placing such controls in master pages, we can easily develop a powerful page design for a site. Of course, each of these controls offers several properties that allow you to modify the way they are rendered.

The following example illustrates the use of a `<asp:Menu>` control within a master page:

Example 23-85   *MyMasterPage.master*

```
<%@ master language="C#" %>
<html><head runat="server"/><body>
<form id="Form1" runat="server">
   <table id="Tbl1" width="100%" height="30px"
                   cellspacing="0" cellpadding="0" >
       <tr> <td width="100%" bgcolor="silver">Smacchia Site</td> </tr>
   </table>
   <table id="Tbl2" width="100%" height="50%"
                   cellspacing="0" cellpadding="0">
       <tr>
           <td width="30%"  bgcolor="yellow">
              <asp:SiteMapDataSource ID="MySiteMapDataSource" runat="server"/>
              <asp:Menu ID="Menu1" runat="server" Orientation="Horizontal"
                   DataSourceID="MySiteMapDataSource" >
              </asp:Menu>
           </td>
           <td align="center">
              <asp:contentplaceholder id="MyContentPH" runat="Server">
              </asp:contentplaceholder>
           </td>
       </tr>
   </table>
</form></body></html>
```

Security

It is recommended to have assimilated the concepts presented in chapter 6 dedicated to security before reading this section.

The management of security is particularly important in the case of a web application. In fact, when an application is accessible from the internet, you must restrict access to certain server critical resources to non-authorized users. We then need an authentication mechanism, allowing identifying the entity at the origin of a request. We also need an authorization mechanism allowing specifying which resources are accessible during the execution of a request based on the identity at the origin of the request.

Authenticating Windows users with IIS

IIS offers an authentication mechanism independent from the mechanisms of ASP.NET. You can choose to activate the authentication only at the IIS level, only at the ASP.NET level or activating both.

To configure IIS authentication for a specific virtual folder, you must accomplish the following modification with the IIS configuration tool: *[right click on the concerned virtual directory click] › Properties › Security of directory › Anonymous connection and authenticating control › Modify.* You will then obtain the following window:

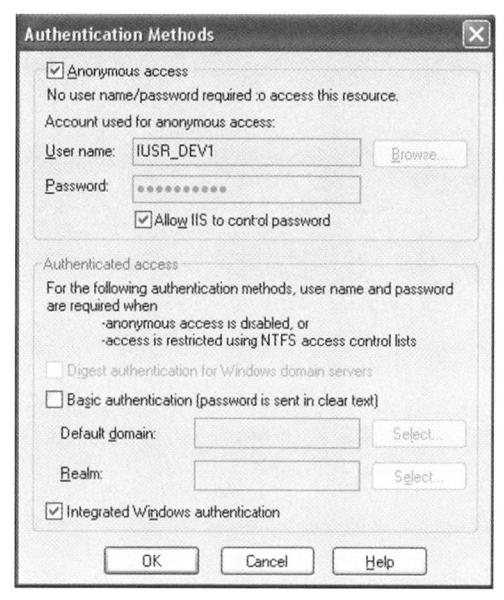

Figure 23-27: IIS authentication methods

IIS offers four authentication modes: anonymous access, digest authentication, base authentication and *Windows* integrated authentication. They are all based on the concept of *Windows* user.

- The *anonymous access* mode offers no authentication control. It implies that all clients can access the application. In the case where this mode is activated with other IIS authentication modes, all will happen as if only the anonymous access mode was active. You have the possibility of providing a *Windows* account which represents anonymous users. This account must have a non-empty password.
- The *digest authentication* mode sends a hashing value of the password of a *Windows* user rather than the password itself. This technique has the advantage of avoiding the transit of the password over the network. However, this technique is not still supported by all browsers.
- The *base authentication* mode is not really secure. In fact the name of the user as well as his password are sent to the server in an unencrypted way. The base-64 encoding technique is used to encode the data. You can however use the HTTPS mode in order to encrypt this data.
- The *Windows integrated authentication* uses an encrypted data exchange system with the client. This mode is only supported by .NET clients and the *Internet Explorer* browser.

At the level of an ASP.NET application, the IIS authentication mechanism is not taken into account unless you activate the *impersonation* mechanism as follows:

Web.Config
```
<?xml version="1.0"?>
<configuration xmlns="http://schemas.microsoft.com/.NetConfiguration/v2.0">
   <system.web>
      <identity impersonate = "true" />
...
```

At page 173, we explain that the impersonation system allows to assign an authenticated *Windows* user to the security context of an unmanaged thread. In this case, it is the *Windows* user that has been authenticated by IIS and the unmanaged thread underneath the managed thread which handles requests in the ASP.NET process. Let us remind you that *Windows* verifies the validity of the access to all *Windows* resources (files, folders …) made by threads. For this, it bases itself on the user account associated to the thread and the security descriptor of the resource (seeAt page 174). By default, the ASP.NET process and each of its threads execute themselves within the context of the *Windows* user specified in the `<processModel>` section of the `Machine.Config` file (see page 739).

You can also programmatically control the belonging of a *Windows* user to a role that is associated to the current thread as follows:

```
...
    IPrincipal p = Thread.CurrentPrincipal ;
    if( p.IsInRole(@"BUILTIN\Administrators") ){
        // Here, you can execute administrator operations.
    }
...
```

ASP.NET allows to considerably simplify this verification operation. In fact, in the configuration file for the application, you can define a list of *access rules* that ASP.NET must apply to each requests. A rule is a permission which allows or denies the request, based on the principal or on the roles played by the principal. For example, to only allow *Joe*, *Bob* and local administrators to make requests, you need to write the following in the configuration file:

Web.Config
```
<?xml version="1.0"?>
<configuration xmlns="http://schemas.microsoft.com/.NetConfiguration/v2.0">
    <system.web>
        <authentication mode="Windows" />
        <authorization>
            <allow users = "Bob,Joe" />
            <allow roles = "BUILTIN\Administrators" />
            <deny  users = "*" />
        </authorization>
...
```

The "*" user name represents all users and "?" represents the anonymous user.

For each rule, you can also specify a verb which specifies the set of allowed HTTP methods. For example, you can authorize all users to use the HTTP-GET but restrict access to the HTTP-POST method only for administrators by using the following:

Web.Config
```
...
        <authorization>
            <allow users = "*" verb = "GET" />
            <allow roles = "BUILTIN\Administrators" verb = "POST" />
            <deny  users = "*" />
        </authorization>
...
```

As you can see, the algorithm used to apply these rules is very simple: the list of rules is traversed linearly and as soon as a rule is satisfied by the current principal, it is applied. Note that the list of rules is made from the combination of the list of rules specified in each configuration file. Hence, this list starts with the list of rules in the current sub-folder within the current application and ends with the list of rules within the machine configuration file.

ASP.NET authentication

ASP.NET supports authentication by the intermediate of a software layer called an *authentication provider*. Currently, ASP.NET supported the *Windows*, *Forms* and *Passport* authentication providers but you can also develop your own.

To configure the ASP.NET authentication provider that a web application must use, you simply need to set the mode attribute of the <authentication> element of the application configuration file:

```
<configuration>
   <system.web>
      <authentication mode="Windows|Form|Passport|none" />
...
```

In practice, we generally use the *Windows* authentication provider in an intranet environment where the *Windows* accounts are centralized on a server. We prefer using the *Passport* and *Forms* authentication provider within the context of applications accessible through the internet. In the first case, the application uses the *Microsoft Passport* authentication mechanism while in the second case, the application must manage user account itself, generally using a database. We will focus ourselves on the *Forms* authentication provide but we invite you to read the article named **The Passport Authentication Provider** on **MSDN** for more details on the use of the *Passport* authentication provider.

The Forms authentication provider

The *Forms* authentication provider allows applications to present their own user interface to capture the necessary data for the authentication, in the form of a standard .aspx page. The internal method used to authenticate from this data is the responsibility of the web application. When an unauthorized client attempts to access a page, ASP.NET will automatically redirect him to the authentication page. Once authenticated, ASP.NET automatically redirects the user to the requested page. To avoid that the client need to authenticate himself explicitly for each request, a cookie is created by ASP.NET during the authentication process. This cookie contains a key which is only valid for a certain amount of time. This cookie is communicated to the client browser which stores it and uses it for any subsequent requests. The following page illustrates a minimal implementation of this scenario:

Example 23-86   *Login.aspx*

```
<%@ Page Language="»C#» %>
<script runat="»server»>
      void Btn_Click(Object sender, EventArgs e) {
         // Generally, here you need to access a database for
         // users authenticatiion.
         if (Usr.Text == "pat" && Pwd.Text == "pwd")
            FormsAuthentication.RedirectFromLoginPage(Usr.Text, true);
         else
            Msg.Text = "Invalid login, please retry.";
      }
</script>
<html xmlns="http://www.w3.org/1999/xhtml" >
<body>
      <form id="form1" runat="server">
         <asp:Label ID="Lbl1" runat="server" Text="User:"/>
         <asp:TextBox ID="Usr" runat="server"/>
         <asp:Label ID="Lbl2" runat="server" Text="Password:"/>
         <asp:TextBox ID="Pwd" runat="server" TextMode="Password"/>
```

Example 23-86   Login.aspx

```
            <asp:Button ID="Button1" runat="server" Text="Login"
                        OnClick="Btn_Click"   /><br/>
            <asp:Label ID="Msg" runat="server"/>
        </form>
    </body>
</html>
```

You must of course tell ASP.NET that anonymous requests (i.e. without an authentication cookie) must be redirected to this page:

Web.Config

```
<?xml version="1.0"?>
<?xml version="1.0"?>
<configuration xmlns="http://schemas.microsoft.com/.NetConfiguration/v2.0">
    <system.web>
        <authorization>
            <deny users="?"/>
        </authorization>
        <authentication mode="Forms">
            <forms loginUrl="Login.aspx" />
        </authentication>
    ...
```

The simple call to the `RedirectFromLoginPage()` is sufficient for ASP.NET to create a cookie, send it to the client and redirect him to the origin page. We see that ASP.NET stores the page that the client must be redirected to in the URL used for the redirection to the authentication page:

```
http://localhost:1968/MyWebSite/...
... Login.aspx?ReturnUrl=%2fMyWebSite%2fdefault.aspx
```

The `<form>` section contains several attributes which allow naming the cookie, protecting the contained information and assigning it a validity period.

As with what we have seen at page 748 in regards to the management of a session without a cookie, the management of authentication can also be done without a cookie. As with the `<sessionState>` element, the `<forms>` element has an attribute named `cookieless`. You can use this attribute to constrain or leave to ASP.NET the choice of using an URI to store the key representing the evidence that the user is authenticated. Here is what such an URI would look like:

```
http://localhost:1968/MyWebSite/(F(Xd6tEmGNyNKdZ-Df9B69q4F2JUXxLd-
7fk8QzQt1qhqWk1FLyUX2_gw31a5XeP18YdR-YzYxEm6kuareBQqgjw2))/default.aspx
```

Be aware that in our example, the password is not encrypted in the authentication request. To avoid this confidentiality problem, you must use HTTPS to encrypt this request. As we have just seen, all other requests do not need to be encrypted since they do not contain the password.

We will now take a look at other security features added to ASP.NET 2. You can now manage the user and their membership to a role in a standard way using a database. In addition, new server controls have been added to greatly simplify the creation of ASP.NET applications which support authentication.

Managing users

ASP.NET 2 offers a framework to standardize the management of user accounts, for example, in a database. This framework was conceived to be independent from forms based authentication. However, the integration of user management and authentication using forms present an extremely flexible and powerful way allowing you to rewrite Example 23-86 in four lines of C# code:

Example 23-87   *Login.aspx*
```
<%@ Page Language=»C#» %>
<script runat=»server»>
    void Btn_Click(Object sender, EventArgs e) {
        if ( Membership.ValidateUser( Usr.Text , Pwd.Text ) )
            FormsAuthentication.RedirectFromLoginPage( Usr.Text, true );
        else
            Msg.Text = "Invalid login, please retry.";
    }
</script>
...
```

Of course, for this example to work, you must tell ASP.NET where is stored the user data and how to access it. For this, you need to use a *membership provider* that we define in the configuration file:

Web.Config
```
<?xml version="1.0"?>
<configuration xmlns="http://schemas.microsoft.com/.NetConfiguration/v2.0">
    <connectionStrings>
        <add name="MyLocalSqlServer"
            connectionString="Data Source=localhost;Integrated
                    Security=SSPI ;Initial Catalog=MyWebSiteUsers;" />
    </connectionStrings>
    <system.web>
        <membership defaultProvider="MyMembershipSqlProvider" >
            <providers>
                <add    name="MyMembershipSqlProvider"
                        type="System.Web.Security.SqlMembershipProvider,
                            System.Web, Version=2.0.0.0, Culture=neutral,
                            PublicKeyToken=b03f5f7f11d50a3a"
                        connectionStringName="MyLocalSqlServer" />
            </providers>
        </membership>
    ...
```

The data relative to the users of this site are stored in a database named `MyWebSiteUsers`. This database is located in a RDBMS of type *SQL Server*. To build such a database, you simply need to use the `aspnet_regsql.exe` tool described at page 770:

```
>aspnet_regsql.exe -S <host> -U <usr> -P <pwd> -d <database> –ed
```

Since our user data is stored in a relational database, we have told ASP.NET to use the `System.Web.Security.SqlMembershipProvider` membership provider. A membership provider is a class which derives from `System.Web.Security.MembershipProvider`. You can create your own provider by writing such a class. Note that ASP.NET 2 also provides the `System.Web.Security.ActiveDirectoryMembershipProvider` membership provider. This is another example of the use of the *provider design pattern* presented at page 750.

In Example 23-87, the `bool ValidateUser(string username,string password)` static method of the `System.Web.Security.Membership` class is capable of verifying if a user exists by using the membership provider defined for the application. This class presents other static methods whose meaning and use is intuitive:

```csharp
MembershipUser CreateUser(string username, string password);
MembershipUser CreateUser(string username, string password, string email);
bool DeleteUser(string username);
bool DeleteUser(string username, bool deleteAllRelatedData);
MembershipUserCollection FindUsersByEmail(string emailToMatch);
MembershipUserCollection FindUsersByName(string usernameToMatch);
string GeneratePassword(int length, int numOfNonAlphanumericCharacters);
MembershipUserCollection GetAllUsers();
int GetNumberOfUsersOnline();
MembershipUser GetUser(); // Return the current user.
MembershipUser GetUser(string username);
string GetUserNameByEmail(string emailToMatch);
void UpdateUser(MembershipUser user);
bool ValidateUser(string username, string password);
```

Instances of the `MembershipUser` class represent validated users during execution. This class contains a few properties allowing you to obtain the name, email, creation date, last login date, the last requested page, the security question to use if the user lost its password and a few methods allowing you to change the password and the associated question. You may notice that only the information relative to authentication is stored in an instance of `MembershipUser`. We will see in the next section how to extend this mechanism to associate personal information to a user such as his address, phone number and even purchase history.

Know that a lock-out mechanism is provided in the case there are too many unsuccessful login attempts. In this case, the `Membership.ValidateUser()` method cannot return `true` while the lock-out has not been deactivated on the user through a call to `MembershipUser.UnlockOut()`. You can configure this mechanism with the `passwordAttemptThreshold` and `passwordAttemptWindows` integer attributes which are placed in the `<membership>` configuration element. The lock-out is automatically put in place if more that `passwordAttemptThreshold` failed login attempts are made within `passwordAttemptWindows` minutes.

Managing roles

In general, it is more practical to use the notion of role to validate user permissions within your code. Also, ASP.NET 2 has a framework which allows the management of roles as well as the membership of users to these roles. To use this framework, you must use a *role provider* that we define in the configuration file:

Web.Config
```xml
<?xml version="1.0"?>
<configuration xmlns="http://schemas.microsoft.com/.NetConfiguration/v2.0">
   <connectionStrings>
      <add name="MyLocalSqlServer"
           connectionString="Data Source=localhost;Integrated
                    Security=SSPI ;Initial Catalog=MyWebSiteUsers;" />
   </connectionStrings>
   <system.web>
      <roleManager defaultProvider="MyRoleSqlProvider" enabled="true" >
         <providers>
            <add     name="MyRoleSqlProvider"
                     type="System.Web.Security.SqlRoleProvider,
                        System.Web, Version=2.0.0.0, Culture=neutral,
                        PublicKeyToken=b03f5f7f11d50a3a"
                     connectionStringName="MyLocalSqlServer" />
         </providers>
      </roleManager>
...
```

Security

As you can see, the notion of role provider is defined in the same way as the membership provider since it also uses the notion of *provider design pattern* discussed at page 750. A role provider is a class that derives from `System.Web.Security.RoleProvider`. ASP.NET 2 includes the `SqlRoleProvider`, `AuthorizationStoreRoleProvider` and `WindowsTokenRoleProvider` classes but you can create your own provider by creating a class which derives from `RoleProvider`.

In the same way that we used the static methods of `MembershipUser` to manipulate user accounts, we use the static methods of the `System.Web.Security.Roles` class to manipulate roles. Here also, the names of these methods as well as their signatures which are self-descriptive:

```
void AddUsersToRole(string[] usernames,string roleName);
void AddUsersToRoles(string[] usernames,string[] roleNames);
void AddUserToRole(string username,string roleName);
void AddUserToRoles(string username,string[] roleNames);
void CreateRole(string roleName);
bool DeleteRole(string roleName);
bool DeleteRole(string roleName,bool throwOnPopulatedRole);
string[] FindUsersInRole(string roleName,string usernameToMatch);
string[] GetAllRoles();
string[] GetRolesForUser();
string[] GetRolesForUser(string username);
string[] GetUsersInRole(string roleName);
bool IsUserInRole(string roleName);
bool IsUserInRole(string username,string roleName);
void RemoveUserFromRole(string username,string roleName);
void RemoveUserFromRoles(string username,string[] roleNames);
void RemoveUsersFromRole(string[] usernames,string roleName);
void RemoveUsersFromRoles(string[] usernames,string[] roleNames);
bool RoleExists(string roleName);
```

Finally, notice that we can define access rules by basing ourselves on roles in the `<authorization>` configuration element:

Web.Config
```xml
<?xml version="1.0"?>
<configuration xmlns="http://schemas.microsoft.com/.NetConfiguration/v2.0">
   <system.web>
      <authorization>
         <allow roles="admin"/>
         <deny  roles="simpleUser"/>
      </authorization>
...
```

Security server controls

ASP.NET 2 offers several evolved server controls which implement the common tasks in regards to the management of users on a site:

- The `CreateUserWizard` control takes charge of the creation of users with password verification and the possibility of supplying an email and question/answer pair in case of the loss of a password. This control is highly configurable with a regular expression for the password, another for the email, customizable error messages for all type of errors.
- The `Login` control allows a user to authenticate itself by entering a user name and password. This is generally the page containing this control which must be designated in the `loginUrl` attribute.

- The `LoginStatus` allows inserting in the current page a link which varies whether the current user is authenticated or not. In general, we use it to display *Login* when a user is not authenticated and *Logout* otherwise.
- The `LoginView` is similar to the `LoginStatus` with the exception that is allows the display of a different set of controls depending on whether the current user is authenticated or not.
- The `LoginName` allows inserting in the current page a string containing the name of the currently authenticated user.
- The `PasswordRecovery` allows sending an email containing a lost password to the email address associated with the user account. This control bases itself on the question/answer system. If the password is encrypted in an unrecoverable way, ASP.NET builds a new password for the user.
- The `ChangePassword` control allows a user to change his password.

Controls such as `CreateUserWizard`, `ChangePassword` or `Login` which directly use the membership provider have an attribute named `MembershipProvider` to specify it.

Let's also mention that the ASP.NET 2 graphical web interface has a security tab which allows administrating users, roles as well as the access rules for a web application.

Personalization and user profiles

Profile provider and the management of user data

ASP.NET 2 offers a framework which allows to store and manipulate in a standard way profile data for each user. Here again, to specify the mode used to store the data, ASP.NET uses the *provider design pattern*. ASP.NET 2 only offers a single *profile provider* class, `SqlProfileProvider`. This class uses a database which has been previously prepared using the `aspnet_regsql.exe` tool. Of course, you can create your own profile provider by creating a class which derives from `System.Web.Profile.ProfileProvider`.

Web.Config
```xml
<?xml version="1.0"?>
<configuration xmlns="http://schemas.microsoft.com/.NetConfiguration/v2.0">
   <connectionStrings>
      <add name="MyLocalSqlServer"
           connectionString="Data Source=localhost;Integrated
                    Security=SSPI ;Initial Catalog=MyWebSiteUsers;" />
   </connectionStrings>
   <system.web>
      <profile enabled="true" defaultProvider="MyProfileSqlProvider">
         <providers>
            <add     name="MyProfileSqlProvider"
                     type="System.Web.Profile.SqlProfileProvider,
                        System.Web, Version=2.0.0.0, Culture=neutral,
                        PublicKeyToken=b03f5f7f11d50a3a"
                     connectionStringName="MyLocalSqlServer" />
         </providers>
         <properties>
            <add name="CompanyName" type="System.String" />
            <add name="Birthday" type="System.DateTime" />
            <add name="RequestCount" type="System.Int32" defaultValue="0"/>
         </properties>
      </profile>
...
```

Personalization and user profiles 803

The <profile> section is dedicated to personalization. The <properties> sub-property allows the definition of custom parameters. Each of these parameters is named, typed and can have a default value.

These parameters can be used programmatically from the Profile class. The compiles makes sure that the ProfileCommon has a read/write property for each of the specified parameters. To access this property, you simply need to write Profile.PropertyName:

```
...
   void Page_Load(Object sender, EventArgs e) {
      Profile.RequestCount += 1;
      LabelRequestCount.Text = Profile.RequestCount.ToString();
   }
...
```

The ASP.NET compiler interprets this as an access to a hidden instance to the ProfileCommon class. This hidden instance contains the data for the user currently logged in. If no user is currently logged in, an exception is raised.

The profile data for a user is only loaded during the first access to data during the processing of a request. The data will be saved at the end of the processing of the request. This means that you do not need to write any code to handle the loading and saving of the profile data.

However, it can be efficient not to load all the profile data for each request as they may represent a large volume of data but we only increment the RequestCount counter at each request. ASP.NET 2 allows you to partition this data into groups. When we access the data from a group, only this data is loaded in memory:

Web.Config

```
...
    <properties>
        <add name="RequestCount" type="System.Int32" defaultValue="0"/>
        <group name="ProfessionalInfo">
           <add name="CompanyName" type="System.String"/>
           <add name="ProfessionalEmail" type="System.String"/>
        </group>
    </properties>
...
```

A group cannot contain other groups. The access to the data within a group is done through a property with the same name as the name of the group:

```
...
   void Page_Load(Object sender, EventArgs e) {
      LblCompanyName.Text = Profile.ProfessionalInfo.CompanyName;
   }
...
```

You can type a piece of profile data with any type which can be serialized into XML or binary, including collections such as System.Collections.Specialized.StringCollection. It is interesting to examine the content of the tables created by aspnet_regsql.exe to discover that the profile data is stored in a serialized way. However, you cannot use generic types within the profile data.

Anonymous identification

It may be desirable to store data relative to an anonymous user. For example, most eCommerce sites will authorize you to start shopping without authenticating yourself. The authentication process being made only when you need to provide personal information in order to complete your purchase.

ASP.NET 2 has facilities to allow the implementation of this scenario. You must specify that you wish to be able to identify an anonymous user using the <anonymousIdentification> section. The idea is that a new user is automatically created for each anonymous user which makes a request. ASP.NET gives this user a new unique identifier which is known by the client's browser and is reused for each request. This is accomplished by either a cookie or a URI parameter. The <anonymousIdentification> element accepts a cookieless attribute which can take one of the values described at page 748.

Each of the profile parameters susceptible of being stored for an anonymous user must be marked with the allowAnonymous attribute. Here is what our configuration file would look like:

Web.Config
```
<?xml version="1.0"?>
<configuration xmlns="http://schemas.microsoft.com/.NetConfiguration/v2.0">
    <connectionStrings>...</connectionStrings>
    <anonymousIdentification enabled="true" cookieless="AutoDetect"/>
    <system.web>
        <profile enabled="true" defaultProvider="MyProfileSqlProvider">
            <providers>...</providers>
            <properties>
                <add name="RequestCount" type="System.Int32"
                    defaultValue="0" allowAnonymous="true" />
                ...
            </properties>
        </profile>
...
```

To correctly implement the scenario of an anonymous user which will eventually authenticate itself, you must provide a way to migrate the data from the anonymous user account to the real user account. For this, you simply need to insert your migration code in the Profile_MigrationAnonymous() method of the Global.asax file:

Example 23-88 *Global.asax*
```
<%@ Application Language="C#" %>
<script Runat="server">
protected void Profile_MigrateAnonymous(object sender,
                                        ProfileMigrateEventArgs e) {
    ProfileCommon anonymousProfile = Profile.GetProfile(e.AnonymousId);
    if (anonymousProfile != null) {
        Profile.LoginCount += anonymousProfile.LoginCount;
    }
}
</script>
```

Personalization vs. Session

As you might have noticed, the concepts of session and profile are close since they both provide a way to store user data in a way that remains between requests. Thus, it is important to underline the semantic difference between sessions and profiles (or personalization):

- The personalization/profile mechanism is intended to store **intrinsic data relative to a user** such as their birth date, their address or even their credit card number.
- The session mechanism is intended for the storage of **temporary data relative to a user** such as a shopping cart.

Also, the personalization mechanism is more thought out and is easier to use:

- The names and types of the parameters are verified during compilation and not during the execution.
- The profile data for a user is loaded on-demand contrarily to session data which is loaded at every request.

Styles, Themes and Skins

CSS styles, and controls

Most web browsers take in consideration the `style` property of a HTML control to modify its appearance. For example, the following HTML page contains a styled text edit zone:

```
<html><body>
  <input type="text" style="font: 34pt times; background-color:yellow;
         border-style:dashed; width:500 ; border-color:blue;"
         value="Enter your text here." />
</body></html>
```

Figure 23-28: Applying style

The `style` property contains a list of *CSS* (*Cascading Style Sheet*) attributes separated be semi-colons. Another syntax can be used to refactor a same style over several controls:

```
<html><head><style>
    .inputstyle  { font: 34pt times; background-color:yellow;
                   border-style:dashed; width:500 ; border-color:blue; }
</style></head>
<body>
  <input type="text" class="inputstyle"
         value="Enter your text here." />
</body></html>
```

The `HtmlControl` class, and consequently all HTML server controls, have the `CssStyleCollection Style{get}` property which allows you to store a dictionary where the keys represent the name of CSS attributes.

The base class common to all web server controls, the `WebControl` class, has the `string CssClass{get;set;}` property which allows specifying the name of a style to apply (such as `inputstyle`). It presents also a few strongly typed attributes which are common to all web server controls such as `BackColor` or `BorderWidth`. The `System.Web.UI.Controls` namespace as well as all its sub-namespaces contain several style definitions which derive from the `System.Web.UI.Controls.Style`. These classes such as `TableStyle`, `PanelStyle`, `TitleStyle` or `TreeNodeStyle` are used to specify the styling of every server control or a part of each web control. The properties of theses styles can be initialized in the definition of a control as follows:

```
<asp:Calendar ...>
   <TitleStyle BorderColor="green" BorderWidth="3" ... />
</asp:Calendar>
```

...or like this:

```
<asp:Calendar ...
   TitleStyle-BorderColor="green"
   TitleStyle-BorderWidth="3" ... />
```

Themes

Despite the possibility of factoring styles in a `<header>` element, the need for a more powerful mechanism allowing the configuration of the global appearance of a site forced the ASP.NET 2 designers to come up with the notion of *themes*. A theme is the definition of all styles which can be statically or dynamically applied to the controls of the pages of a site. The modification of the styles within a theme causes all the pages which use the style to automatically modify their appearance.

A theme materializes itself by the content of a folder. The name of the theme is simply the name of the folder. A theme can be local to an application or even shared across all the applications on a machine. In the first case, the theme folder must be a sub-folder of `/App_Theme` for the application. In the second case, the folder of the theme is either a sub-folder of the ASP.NET installation folder (which is `%WINDIR%\Microsoft.NET\Framework\<version>\ASP.NETClientFiles\Themes`) or a sub-folder of `Inetpub\wwwroot\aspnet_client\system_web\<version>\Themes` in the case of web applications hosted by IIS.

There are several ways to apply a theme to the pages of an ASP.NET application:

- By using the `theme` attribute of the `<pages>` section in the configuration file. In this case, this theme is applied to all pages affected by this configuration file:

   Web.Config
   ```
   <?xml version="1.0"?>
   <configuration xmlns="http://schemas.microsoft.com/.NetConfiguration/v2.0">
      <system.web>
         <pages theme="NameOfTheTheme" >
   ...
   ```

- By using the `Theme` sub-directive of `<@ Page>` in the concerned `.aspx` pages. This feature allows to override a global theme specified in the `<page>` configuration section:

   PagesXXX.aspx
   ```
   <%@ Page Theme="NameOfTheTheme" %>
   ...
   ```

- By using the `StyleSheetTheme` sub-directive of `<@ Page>` for the concerned `.aspx` pages. You must know that for the controls of a page, the styles are chosen in an increasing order of priority: styles defined by the `StyleSheetTheme` sub-directive; styles defined directly in the declaration of the controls, styles defined in the `<page>` configuration element and the styles defined with the `Theme` sub-directive.

   PagesXXX.aspx
   ```
   <%@ Page StyleSheetTheme="NameOfTheTheme" %>
   ...
   ```

- Dynamically by specifying the type in a method subscribed to the `PreInit` for the page. Typically, this feature is used when we wish to let the user select the theme of their choice:

PagesXXX.aspx

```
<%@ Page Language=»C#» %>
<script runat=»server»>
  protected void Page_PreInit(){
    if (Profile.IsAnonymous == false)
       Page.Theme = Profile.Theme;
  }
</script>
...
```

Finally, you can deactivate the application of the style of a theme for a control simply by setting its `EnableTheming` to `false`. This property is implemented by the `Control` class.

Skins

A theme folder contains one or several files with a `.skin` extension, zero, one or several files with a `.css` extension and eventually sub-folders which contains resources referenced by the styles such as images. The *stylesheets* of a theme, defined in files with a `.css` extension will be applied to the concerned pages.

Files with a `.skin` extension contain the definition of skins. The definition of a skin resembles the definition of a control with the exception that only certain properties can be set. These are the properties which relate to the style for this type of control. You can recognize them be looking at the definition of a control as they are marked with the `System.Web.UI.ThemeableAttribute` (`true`) attribute. Here is an example of the definition of a `.skin` file:

Example 23-89   *BigText.skin*

```
<asp:Label Font-Bold="true" Font-Size="20" runat="server" />
<asp:TextBox Font-Bold="true" Font-Size="20" runat="server" />
```

Here is a page on which we apply the `ThemeBig` theme which only contains the `BigText.skin` file:

Example 23-90   *Default.aspx*

```
<%@ Page Language="C#" Theme="ThemeBig" %>
<html xmlns="http://www.w3.org/1999/xhtml">
<body>
   <form id="form1" runat="server">
      <asp:Label ID="Lbl1" runat="server" Text="Label 1" /><br/>
      <asp:Label ID="Lbl2" runat="server" Text="Label 2" Font-Size="10"/>
      <br/>
      <asp:Label ID="Lbl3" runat="server" Text="Label 3"
                  EnableTheming=false  /><br/>
      <asp:TextBox ID="TextBox1" runat="server" Text="TextBox"/>
   </form>
</body>
</html>
```

Finally, here is a screenshot of this page. We see that only the number 3 `Label` is not affected by the theme because we have set its `EnableTheming` property to `false`:

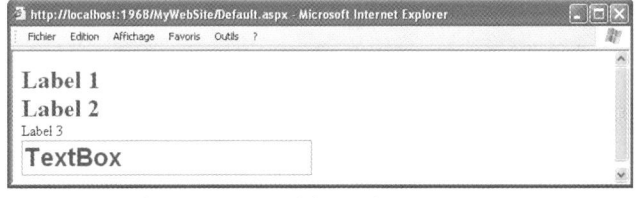

Figure 23-29: Applying a theme to a page

Named skins

During the definition of a skin, you have the possibility of naming it with the `SkinId` attribute. We can thus define several skins for a same type of control within a theme. Of course, a theme cannot contain several skins with the same name nor can it contain more than one anonymous skin.

As we can guess, we can use a named skin on a control through the use of the `SkinId` attribute. If during the execution, a named skin does not exist in the current theme, ASP.NET will not apply any skin to this control. Also it is recommended to redefine all the skins used in all of your themes.

WebParts

ASP.NET 2 has a framework dedicated to the creation of *webParts*. This notion of webParts allows a user to personalize the set of services which may be offered by a page. For example, we could imagine that a user would have the choice between the services: latest IT news, latest stock exchange quotations, the local weather, the television schedule for the evening... Each of these services is materialized on the page by a control we name a webPart. A web application which supports this level of personalization is named a *web portal*. Until now, in the *Microsoft* world, only the *SharePoint* technology was dedicated to the creation of portals. ASP.NET 2 webParts, essentially allow you to:

- Present one or several zones on a same page which each contains one or several webParts. Each of these zones is a server control of type `WebPartZone`. The webParts contained in a zone can be aligned horizontally or vertically.

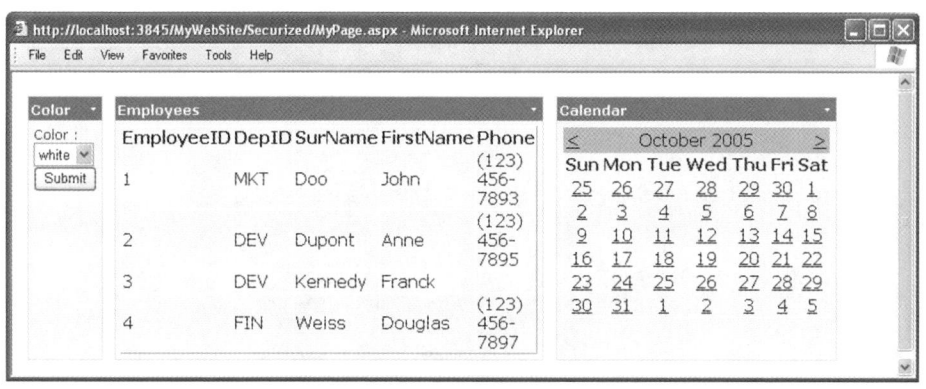

Figure 23-30: A page with three webParts

- To define the order in which are defined the webParts within a zone.

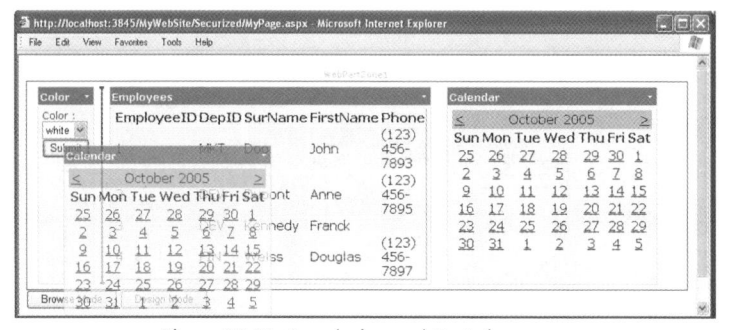

Figure 23-31: Reordering webParts in a zone

WebParts

- To chose the webParts which are contained in a zone through the use of a webParts catalog. A default catalog is provided by the site but the user can import his own webParts stored in an XML file on his hard disk.

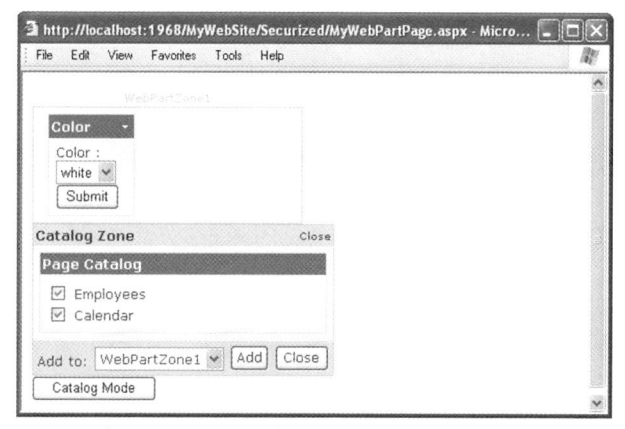

Figure 23-32: Selecting a webPart in the catalog

- The content of a webPart is displayed in a special window that we name *chrome*. For each webPart, the user can define the appearance of the chrome, the actions offered by the chrome, the title displayed by the chrome... Note that actions offered by a chrome are named *verbs*.

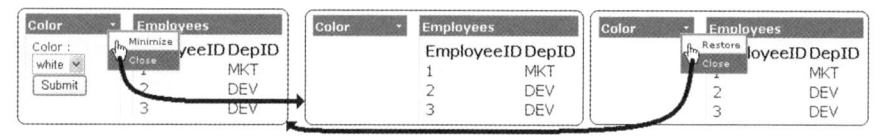

Figure 23-33: Chrome menu

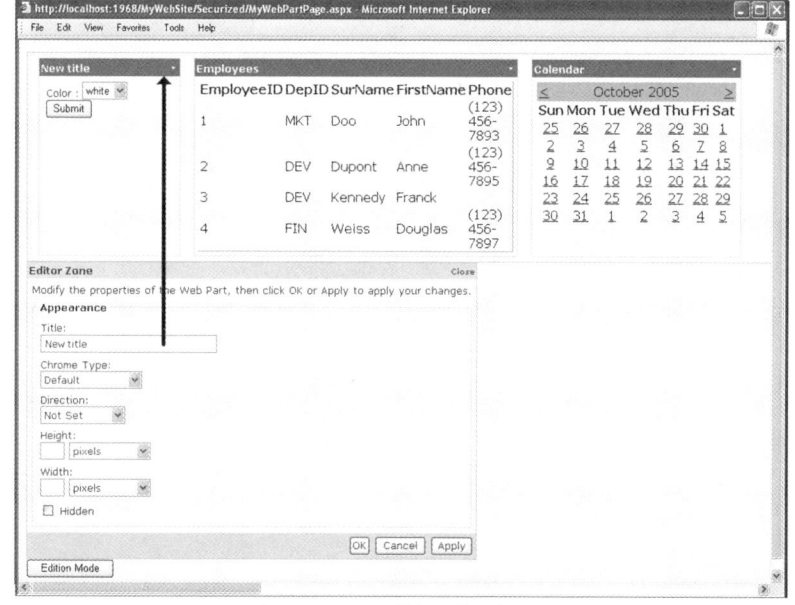

Figure 23-34: Editing the chrome

- To connect two webParts. In this case, one webPart plays the role of data producer as little like a data source while the other plays the role of a consumer.

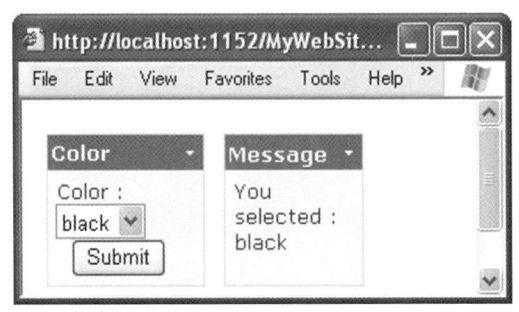

Figure 23-35: Connecting two webParts

A user can modify the webParts of a page if he is currently authenticated. In fact, each modification results in a POST request, which in turn causes the server-side to save the current state of the webParts for the authenticated user.

Creating a page that contains webPart

A webPart can contain a standard server control or a user control. A webPart is materialized on the server-side by an instance of a class which derives from `System.Web.UI.WebControls.WebParts.WebPart`. ASP.NET 2 automatically and implicitly uses an instance of the `GenericWebPart` class to contain a standard control or a user control defined in a `.ascx` file. A user control defined directly in C# (such as the one in Example 23-31) must itself be a webPart. Consequently, to be used as a webPart its class must derive from the `WebPart` rather than the `Control` class.

As we have seen, to allow the modification of webParts on a page, a user must be authenticated. This is not sufficient to save the state of the webParts. You must provide a webParts provider in the configuration file as follows:

Web.Config
```
<?xml version="1.0"?>
<configuration xmlns="http://schemas.microsoft.com/.NetConfiguration/v2.0">
   <connectionStrings>
      <add name="MyLocalSqlServer"
           connectionString="Data Source=localhost;Integrated
                    Security=SSPI ;Initial Catalog=MyWebSiteUsers;" />
   </connectionStrings>
   <system.web>
      <webParts>
         <personalization defaultProvider="MyWebPartsSqlProvider">
            <providers>
               <add     name="MyWebPartsSqlProvider"
       type="System.Web.UI.WebControls.WebParts.SqlPersonalizationProvider,
                    System.Web, Version=2.0.0.0, Culture=neutral,
                    PublicKeyToken=b03f5f7f11d50a3a"
                    connectionStringName="MyLocalSqlServer" />
            </providers>
         </personalization>
      </webParts>
   ...
```

Since the *provider design pattern* is used, you can of course supply your own webParts provider with classes that derive from `System.Web.UI.WebControls.WebParts.PersonalizationProvider`.

WebParts

Hence, the data relative to the state of webParts of the pages accessible by a user can be stored in another location than the user's profile information.

For a page to display webParts, it must contain a server control of type `WebPartManager` before the declaration of all server controls relative to webParts. Then comes the notion of *webPartsZone*. A webPartsZone is a server control which has the particularity of being able to contain webParts. Let us precise that a webParts must be contained within a webPartsZone. The following page contains one webPartsZone which contains three webParts: one webPart contains a user control (the one defined in Example 23-33), one webPart which contains a `GridView` server control and one webPart which contains a server control of type `Calendar`:

Example 23-91
```
<%@ Page Language="C#" %>
<%@ Register TagPrefix="PRACTICAL" Src="~/Securized/MyUserCtrl.ascx"
            TagName="UserCtrl" %>
<html xmlns="http://www.w3.org/1999/xhtml" >
<body>
    <form id="Form1" runat="server">
        <asp:SqlDataSource ID="DataSrc" runat="server" ConnectionString=
            "server = localhost ; uid=sa ; pwd=; database = ORGANIZATION"
         SelectCommand="SELECT * FROM EMPLOYEES" />
        <asp:WebPartManager ID="WebPartManager1" runat="server"/>
        <asp:WebPartZone ID="WebPartZone1" runat="server"
                      LayoutOrientation="Horizontal">
          <ZoneTemplate>
            <PRACTICAL:UserCtrl ID="UserCtrl1" runat="server" />
            <asp:GridView ID="Grid" DataSourceID="DataSrc" runat="server"/>
            <asp:Calendar ID="Calendar1" runat="server"></asp:Calendar>
          </ZoneTemplate>
        </asp:WebPartZone>
    </form>
</body>
</html>
```

Figure 23-30 shows a screen capture of this page. Note that we have chosen the "professional style" to display the webParts. Here are the changes that such a style implies in the code of our page. For more clarity, we will omit the code necessary for styles in the following listings. Also, you will rarely need to access the code of pages containing webParts since the *Visual Studio* designer is quite efficient for this task:

Example 23-92
```
<%@ Page Language="C#" %>
...
<body>
    ...
        <asp:WebPartZone ID="WebPartZone1" runat="server"
                  LayoutOrientation="Horizontal" BorderColor="#CCCCCC"
                  Font-Names="Verdana" Padding="6">
          <ZoneTemplate> ... </ZoneTemplate>
          <PartChromeStyle BackColor="#F7F6F3" BorderColor="#E2DED6"
                        Font-Names="Verdana" ForeColor="White" />
          <MenuLabelHoverStyle ForeColor="#E2DED6" />
          <EmptyZoneTextStyle Font-Size="0.8em" />
          <MenuLabelStyle ForeColor="White" />
          <MenuVerbHoverStyle BackColor="#F7F6F3" BorderColor="#CCCCCC"
              BorderStyle="Solid" ForeColor="#333333" BorderWidth="1px" />
          <HeaderStyle Font-Size="0.7em" ForeColor="#CCCCCC"
```

Example 23-92
```
                    HorizontalAlign="Center" />
        <MenuVerbStyle BorderColor="#5D7B9D" BorderStyle="Solid"
                    BorderWidth="1px" ForeColor="White" />
        <PartStyle Font-Size="0.8em" ForeColor="#333333" />
        <TitleBarVerbStyle Font-Size="0.6em" Font-Underline="False"
                    ForeColor="White" />
        <MenuPopupStyle BackColor="#5D7B9D" BorderColor="#CCCCCC"
                    BorderWidth="1px" Font-Names="Verdana"
            Font-Size="0.6em" />
        <PartTitleStyle BackColor="#5D7B9D" Font-Bold="True"
                    Font-Size="0.8em" ForeColor="White" />
    </asp:WebPartZone>
...
</body>
```

The screen shot in Figure 23-33 shows that at this stage, we can minimize/restore or close a webPart. The state of the chrome for each webPart (minimized/restored, opened/closed) is saved for the authenticated user in the database specified by the webParts provider. Upon returning to this page, the user will find the chrome for each of the webParts in the same states that he left them.

A question may come up: how can you define the attributes of a webPart such as its title or description which must be displayed in the tooltip? In fact, in our .aspx page our three controls are implicitly contained in a control of type `GenericWebPart`. Since we do not have access to these controls, we cannot configure them. Two solutions exist to this problem:

- In the case of standard controls or .aspx, we are obligated to set the attributes which will be used by the `GenericWebPart` as the following example shows:

```
...
<ZoneTemplate>
    <PRACTICAL:UserCtrl title="Color" ID="UserCtrl1" runat="server" />
    <asp:GridView title="Employees" ID="Grid" DataSourceID="DataSrc"
                runat="server"/>
    <asp:Calendar title="Calendar" ID="Calendar1"
                runat="server"></asp:Calendar>
</ZoneTemplate>
...
```
    We note that intellisense does not know these attributes and that the compiler will generate a warning.
- In the case of a user control, you can implement the `IWebPart` interface which defines the attributes as properties.

Design mode

The mode of a page containing webParts is defined by the `DisplayMode{get;set;}` of the `WebPartManager` control for the page. By default, this mode is set to `BrowseDisplayMode` which does not allow the user to minimize/restore and closing webParts. If you switch to the `DesignDisplayMode` mode, it now becomes possible to change the order of webParts (as illustrated in Figure 23-31). Here also, every change made results into a *postback* event which allows saving the new state of the webParts.

Example 23-93

```
<%@ Page Language="C#" %>
...
<script runat="server">
   protected void ButtonBrowse_Click( object sender, EventArgs e ) {
      WebPartManager1.DisplayMode = WebPartManager.BrowseDisplayMode;
   }
   protected void ButtonDesign_Click( object sender, EventArgs e ) {
      WebPartManager1.DisplayMode = WebPartManager.DesignDisplayMode;
   }
</script>
<html xmlns="http://www.w3.org/1999/xhtml" >
<body>
   <form id="Form1" runat="server">
      ...
      <asp:Button ID="ButtonBrowse" runat="server"
                  OnClick="ButtonBrowse_Click" Text="Browse Mode" />
      <asp:Button ID="ButtonDesign" runat="server"
                  OnClick="ButtonDesign_Click" Text="Design Mode" />
   </form>
</body>
</html>
```

WebParts catalog

We have seen that the chrome allows making a webPart invisible when selecting the *Close* verb. You can use a server control of type `PageCatalogPart` to make visible one or several webParts which were closed. Such a control displays the list of closed webParts that the page contains. This control must be contained within a `CatalogZone` control which is only displayed when the display mode is set to `CatalogDisplayMode`:

Example 23-94

```
<%@ Page Language="C#" %>
...
<script runat="server">
   protected void ButtonCatalog_Click(object sender, EventArgs e) {
      WebPartManager1.DisplayMode = WebPartManager.CatalogDisplayMode;
   }
</script>
<html xmlns="http://www.w3.org/1999/xhtml" >
<body>
   <form id="Form1" runat="server">
      ...
      <asp:CatalogZone ID="CatalogZone1" runat="server">
         <ZoneTemplate>
            <asp:PageCatalogPart ID="part1" runat="server"/>
         </ZoneTemplate>
      </asp:CatalogZone>
      <asp:Button ID="ButtonCatalog" runat="server"
                  OnClick="ButtonCatalog_Click" Text="Catalog Mode" />
   </form>
</body>
</html>
```

The notion of catalog goes much further than the simple reactivation of closed webParts. You can declare a control catalog that the user can potentially add to your page through a control of type

DeclarativeCatalogPart. This type of control contains definitions of webParts, a little like a WebPartZone.

Using controls of type ImportCatalogPart, you can even authorize a user to import webParts defined in an XML document. Reference the **MSDN** documentation to get more information on the format of such a file.

These two controls allow to dynamically add webParts. Note that internally, on the server-side, a unique identifier is assigned to every webPart. WebParts which are added dynamically offer the Delete which allows the user to destroy them. As shows the following page, it is possible to dynamically add webParts from code:

Example 23-95

```
<%@ Page Language="C#" %>
<script runat="server">
   private static int calendarID = 0;
   protected void ButtonAdd_Click(object sender, EventArgs e) {
      Calendar calendar = new Calendar();
      calendar.ID = "Calendar_" + calendarID++;
      GenericWebPart wrapper = WebPartManager1.CreateWebPart(calendar);
      WebPartManager1.AddWebPart(wrapper, WebPartZone1, 0);
   }
</script>
<html xmlns="http://www.w3.org/1999/xhtml" >
<body>
   <form id="Form2" runat="server">
      <asp:SqlDataSource ID="DataSrc" runat="server" ConnectionString=
         "server = localhost ; uid=sa ; pwd=; database = ORGANIZATION"
       SelectCommand="SELECT * FROM EMPLOYEES" />
      <asp:WebPartManager ID="WebPartManager1" runat="server"/>
      <asp:WebPartZone ID="WebPartZone1" runat="server"
                       LayoutOrientation="Horizontal"/>
      <asp:Button id="ButtonAdd" runat="server"
            Text="Add a calendar" OnClick="ButtonAdd_Click"/>
   </form>
</body>
</html>
```

Edit mode

The edit mode allows modifying all the attributes of a webParts in a page. For this, you must switch to the EditDisplayMode mode. The controls contained within the controls of type EditorZone are then visible. They can be of type:

- AppearanceEditorPart (illustrated in Figure 23-34): Allows the edition of the visual properties of a webPart such as its title or size.
- BehaviorEditorPart: Allows to edit behavioral properties of a webPart such verbs available from its chrome.
- LayoutEditorPart: Allows to edit the organization of webParts like, for example, the display order of the webParts within a zone. This editor is useful as certain browsers do not support drag-and-drop facilities.

The following page shows how to declare a control within an EditorZone:

WebParts

Example 23-96

```
<%@ Page Language="C#" %>
...
<script runat="server">
   protected void ButtonEdit_Click(object sender, EventArgs e) {
      WebPartManager1.DisplayMode = WebPartManager.EditDisplayMode;
   }
</script>
<html xmlns="http://www.w3.org/1999/xhtml" >
<body>
   <form id="Form1" runat="server">
      ...
      <asp:EditorZone ID="EditorZone1" runat="server">
        <ZoneTemplate>
          <asp:AppearanceEditorPart ID="AppearanceEditorPart1"
                                    runat="server" />
        </ZoneTemplate>
      </asp:EditorZone>
      <asp:Button ID="ButtonEdit" runat="server"
                  OnClick="ButtonEdit_Click" Text="Edition Mode" />
   </form>
</body>
</html>
```

Connecting webParts

You have the possibility of creating connections between two webParts. This type of connection is asymmetrical: while one webPart plays the role of producer, the other plays the role of consumer. Let's illustrate this feature by using a page which uses a producer user server control which allows the selection of a color and a consumer server control which displays the selected color. This page is illustrated by Figure 23-35:

Example 23-97 *MyProviderCtrl.ascx*

```
<%@ Control Language="C#"  CodeFile="~/Securized/MyProviderCtrl.ascx.cs"
             Inherits="MyUserCtrl" %>
Color : <asp:dropdownlist id="Color" runat="server">
           <asp:listitem>white</asp:listitem>
           <asp:listitem>black</asp:listitem>
        </asp:dropdownlist>
<asp:button id="Button1" text="Submit" OnClick="Btn_Click"
   runat="server"/>
```

Example 23-98 *MyProviderCtrl.ascx.cs*

```
using System.Web.UI;
using System.Web.UI.WebControls.WebParts;
public interface IColor { string SelectedColor { get;set; } }
public partial class MyProviderCtrl : UserControl, IColor {
   private string m_SelectedColor;
   public string SelectedColor {
      get { return m_SelectedColor; }
      set { m_SelectedColor = value; }
   }
   protected void Btn_Click(System.Object sender, System.EventArgs e){
      m_SelectedColor = Color.SelectedItem.Value;
   }
```

Example 23-98   *MyProviderCtrl.ascx.cs*

```
    [ConnectionProvider("TestProviderConsumer")]
    public IColor ProvideColor() { return this;  }
}
```

The server control which presents the producer webPart (in this case `MyProviderCtrl`) must support an interface known by the consumer server control (in this case `MyProviderCtrl`). The `IColor` interface plays the role of an intermediate:

Example 23-99   *MyConsumerCtrl.ascx*

```
<%@ Control Language="C#"  ClassName="MyConsumerCtrl" %>
<script runat="server">
    [ConnectionConsumer("TestProviderConsumer")]
    public void Consume(IColor colorProvider){
        Msg.Text = "You selected : " + color.SelectedColor;
    }
</script>
<asp:Label ID="Msg" runat="server" />
```

We see that you must use the `ConnectionProvider` attribute to indicate the method that ASP.NET must use to obtain the object representing the producer webPart. Also, we indicate the method of the consumer control that ASP.NET must invoke through the `ConnectionConsumer` attribute. At this stage, if you build a page with these two controls contained in two webParts, nothing will happen. To enable webParts communication, you must create a connection between them. You can create such a connection through a `WebPartConnection` control as follow:

Example 23-100

```
<%@ Page Language="C#" %>
<%@ Register TagPrefix="PRACTICAL" Src="~/Securized/MyProviderCtrl.ascx"
             TagName="ProviderCtrl" %>
<%@ Register TagPrefix="PRACTICAL" Src="~/Securized/MyConsumerCtrl.ascx"
             TagName="ConsumerCtrl" %>
<html xmlns="http://www.w3.org/1999/xhtml" >
<body>
   <form id="Form1" runat="server">
      <asp:WebPartManager ID="WebPartManager1" runat="server">
         <StaticConnections>
            <asp:WebPartConnection ID="MyCnx"
               ConsumerID="ConsumerCtrl1" ProviderID="ProviderCtrl1"/>
         </StaticConnections>
      </asp:WebPartManager>
      <asp:WebPartZone ID="WebPartZone1" runat="server"
                       LayoutOrientation="Horizontal">
         <ZoneTemplate>
            <PRACTICAL:ProviderCtrl ID="ProviderCtrl1" runat="server" />
            <PRACTICAL:ConsumerCtrl ID="ConsumerCtrl1" runat="server" />
         </ZoneTemplate>
      </asp:WebPartZone>
   </form>
</body>
</html>
```

This page illustrates a statically built connection. You can also allow your users to dynamically create connections. For this, you must switch to the `ConnectDisplayMode` mode and provide a `ConnectionZone` control:

Example 23-101
```
<%@ Page Language="C#" %>
...
<script runat="server">
   protected void ButtonBrowse_Click(object sender, EventArgs e) {
      WebPartManager1.DisplayMode = WebPartManager.BrowseDisplayMode;
   }
   protected void ButtonCnx_Click(object sender, EventArgs e) {
      WebPartManager1.DisplayMode = WebPartManager.ConnectDisplayMode;
   }
</script>
<html xmlns="http://www.w3.org/1999/xhtml" >
<body>
   <form id="Form1" runat="server">
      <asp:WebPartManager ID="WebPartManager1" runat="server"/>
      ...
      <asp:ConnectionsZone ID="ConnectionsZone1" runat="server"/>
      <asp:Button ID="ButtonBrowse" runat="server"
                  OnClick="ButtonBrowse_Click" Text="Browse Mode" />
      <asp:Button ID="ButtonDesign" runat="server"
                  OnClick="ButtonCnx_Click" Text="Connexion Mode" />
   </form>
</body>
</html>
```

If the user wishes to create a connection which implicates a webPart, he simply needs to select the Connect verb on this webPart. Based on the presence of the ConnectionProvider or ConnectionConsumer attributes, ASP.NET knows to recognize if a webPart is a producer or consumer. The ConnectionZone control is then displayed and offers to the user the webPart to which our first webPart will be connected to. Here again, a large part of the interest behind this technique resides in the fact that the existences of connections created dynamically are saved on the server-side for each user.

24 Introduction to web services development with .NET

Introduction

SOA: Service Oriented Architecture

The Service Oriented Architecture (*SOA*) is a recent complement to Object Oriented Programming (*OOP*). The notion of *service* is simple: a service is an application that we interact with through the use of messages. A service has clients which send request messages to which the service can return response messages. A service can also be the client of another service. SOA is founded on four key principles:

- The **boundaries** of a service are **explicit**:
  Each message sent to or received from a service represents a cost in terms of performance since it requires generally the use of a network. The different distributed object technologies (such as .NET Remoting or Java RMI) hide to the developer the fact that an object is distant by implicitly converting a call to one of its methods into a message which is sent over the network. The approach behind SOA is the opposite as it requires the developer to be aware of the sending and reception of messages. We will see that this approach allows for different message exchange models rather than the traditional request/response model used to simulate calls to remote objects.

- A service is an **autonomous entity**:
  The notion of autonomous entity derives from radically different rules than standard OOP paradigms. The **deployment** and evolution of a service is done independently from its clients. It is the client's responsibility to adapt themselves to a new **version** of a service. This way, the topology of a set of services adapts itself naturally to new needs. This also allows putting in evidence the importance of **error management** since errors are bound to happen. In the same way, we cannot avoid implementing a serious **security** management policy since services are generally accessible from public network such as the *Internet*.

- The **use structure** of a service is **unambiguously defined** by a **unique contract presented by the service to its clients**:
  The evolution of object languages illustrated the increasing importance of the dissociation between abstraction and implementation. In fact, the notion of interface is now a privileged component of modern languages such as C# or Java which isn't the case for example in C++. The SOA model goes further by formalizing the use of a service in a unique contract which presents itself in the form of an XML document. This contract specifies the structure of the information contained in messages using some XSD schemas. This contract can contain comments and thus inform human users of the structure of use of the service. This contract can also be used by a program, for example, to generate classes which will be used by the client to send messages to the service. The fact that the reception of a message by the service triggers internally the call to certain methods of certain classes is an implementation detail of the service and is not part or its contract.

- The **use semantics** of a service is also called **policy** and is **defined without ambiguity** in the contract presented by the service to its clients:
Most object oriented languages do not present any simple mechanisms to indicate to the clients of an interface what are the pre and post-conditions for its use. These conditions are verified within the implementations of the interface and if they aren't rigorously documented, the client has no way to know them precisely. In SOA, this use semantics takes integral part of the contract presented to its clients. For example, a service can declare policy where it will only accept an incoming message if it is encoded using a certain technique. A service can declare in a policy that it is only accessible from 8h to 22h GMT or that it supports a certain transactional protocol. As with the contract, policies are also stored in an XML file meaning that they can be consumed by a framework to prevent developers from having to code the specified logic (for example, a message will be automatically encrypted in a certain way by the client side by such a framework if it is required by the policy of the target service).

SOAP and WSDL

Web services represent today's preferred way to implement the notion of service as we have defined it. Web services have two essential characteristics:

- **Execution platform independence of the client and web service**: All has been done so that messages exchanged between a web service and its clients are independent of the platform on which they are executed. Web services constitute the best means by which to transmit information in a heterogeneous way. A web service implemented in Java functions the same way with a client written in C# or Java. This is called interoperability.

- **Independence to the protocol used to transport the messages**: A web service will behave the same way when messages are transmitted using various protocols such as HTTP, HTTPS, TCP/IP, UDP/IP or SMTP. In consequence to this, the web service does not make any assumptions about the characteristics of the underlying protocol (such as HTTPS data encryption or TCP reliability). We will see how most of the transport protocol characteristics can be obtained at the level of the message exchange, independently from the underlying transport protocol. Finally, the expression *web service* contains the word *web* because the HTTP protocol (which is the web protocol) is the most commonly used in the world. Being able to place yourself in the footsteps of the phenomenal success of the web definitely constitutes a decision making point for the adoption of web services.

To obtain interoperability, web services base their foundation on two simple and normalized XML languages. At page 631, we discuss how one of the major advantages of XML is its ability to encode data in a platform independent way:

- The XML language named **SOAP** (*Simple Object Access Protocol*) is used to compose the **messages** exchanged between services. Specifications exist for each network protocol which describes how the transport of messages must be accomplished.

- The XML language named **WSDL** (*Web Service Definition Language*) is used to define the **contracts** presented by services to their clients. We will see that this language also allows you to define the links between a contract and its implementation (in other words, indicating which method of which class must be invoked to handle a particular message). This means that the contract presented by a service to its clients only constitutes a part of a WSDL document since it also contains information which does not need to be consumed by the clients.

WS-I Basic profiles

One of the main characteristics of the SOAP and WSDL languages is that they are extensible. The big names in the market such as *Microsoft*, *IBM* and *BEA* united together within an organization named *WS-I* (*Web Service Interoperability*) to produce a set of specifications which allow the extension of these languages. This set of specifications is named *WS-** (pronounced *WS Star*) as

Introduction

the name of these specifications start with *WS-* and end with an expression illustrated the design. For example, the *WS-Security* specification allows the introduction of a certain level of security in the exchange of messages. Here are the major topics covered currently (end of 2005) by the *WS-** specifications:

- **Security**: Many WS-* specifications allow the implementation of various security facets such as authentication, confidentiality of data or secure conversation.
- **Description**: The WSDL is extended by several WS-* specifications which allow the creation of more precise contracts. For example the *WS-SecurityPolicy* specification allows the contract of a service to specify if a message is to be accepted when encrypted in a certain manner.
- **Discovery**: Some specifications describe the implementation of search mechanisms of web services through a network based on certain criteria. Hence a client can discover the set of services which meet a certain need. When the client decides to take advantage of a service, he only has to look at its contract in order to learn how to use it.
- **Message delivery**: Some WS-* specifications allow certain guarantees in regards to message delivery. This allows remedying the fact that the underlying network protocol is not necessarily reliable. For example, the UDP protocol does not provide acknowledgment facilities. The message delivery domain also address issues related to sending messages to multiple destinations (*broadcasting*) as well as problem related to the consumption of a same message by multiple services working in a chain.
- **Coordination and transaction**: Some WS-* specifications allow the coordination of the activities of several services in order to obtain proper global behavior. The notion of distributed transactions between multiple services constitutes an example of such coordination.

A very interesting aspect of the WS-* specifications is that they allows combining protocols. If two protocol goals are orthogonal, then they can be used together in an independent manner. For example, a security protocol destined to make messages confidential by encrypting them can optionally be used conjointly with a delivery protocol ensuring the client that messages are received by the service.

However, understand that the independence in the combination of protocols is made when possible. The WS-* specifications act at different levels of the architecture. It is not uncommon that a WS-* specification interacts with another specification at a lower level. For example, the distributed transaction algorithms work on the assumption that messages are received in the same order that they are sent.

Message Exchange Pattern (MEP)

Because they allow cross-platform interoperability and the fact that they abstract themselves from the characteristics of the underlying network protocols, we have seen that web services represent a major evolution in regards to other application information exchange mechanisms. Contrary to most of these technologies, the notion of service makes elaborate message exchange models a reality (also called *Message Exchange Pattern* or *MEP*). In fact, up until now, developers were restricted by these technologies to use a synchronous request/response model. This model was popularized by a technology named RPC (*Remote Procedure Call*). This technology simulates from the client-side a call to a local procedure by encapsulating the incoming data into a request message sent through the network and then waiting for a response with the output data. The SOAP and WSDL languages of web services allow to implement all MEP possible such as:

- RPC style **synchronous request/response** model that we have just described.
- An **asynchronous request/response** model. The difference with the previous model is that the client thread which is responsible for sending the request message resumes its execution after the message is sent. The client must mobilize some resources in order to ensure the reception of the response message. This model is adapted to the management of request which can take a certain time to be serviced.

- The **request/response polling** model. The difference with the previous model is that after the request message is sent, the client periodically request a response from the service by the use of a request/response until it obtains a response or an error.
- The **one way** model. In this model, the client does not wait for any information from the service and only sends a one-way message. This model is adapted for sending non crucial information such as logging information.
- The **broadcast** model allows sending a same message simultaneously to multiple services. Variants of this model allow the client to expect one or multiple responses from the contacted services.
- The **event** model allows a client to subscribe to a service. It will then receive the messages constructed by the service to satisfy its needs. Several variants to this model exist to specify how the service is notified that a client wishes to unsubscribe.

These models represent most of the common message exchange approaches but many other more or less complex models can be imagined and implemented.

Developing a simple web service

Developing a simple web service without using Visual Studio

A simple web service is a service which only supports the RPC style message exchange model on top of the HTTP protocol and which does not exploit any of the WS-* specifications. *Visual Studio* provides facilities to develop such services. Note that it is good to have assimilated the notions of ASP.NET development before continuing.

With .NET, the source code of a web service is a file with an .asmx execution stored in a folder hosting the service. For example, this directory will be named `localizationcorp`. The source code contained in .asmx files will automatically be compiled before execution thanks to ASP.NET. An assembly will be produced in the `bin` sub-folder.

In this chapter, we will base ourselves on a geo-localization web service which presents a unique operation: the possibility of obtaining a town/country pair based on a latitude/longitude coordinate. The operation clearly only needs a synchronous RPC style model of message exchange. Also, the concept of a class method fits perfectly to the implementation. A method which represents the implementation of such a service is generally called a *web method*. Understand that the implementation of other message exchange models may not be as simple.

To keep things simple, we will limit our implementation to the town of Nice/France. Here is the code for the web service:

Example 24-1   Localizer.asmx

```
<%@ WebService language="C#" class="LocalizationCorp.Localizer" %>

using System;
using System.Web.Services;
using System.Xml.Serialization;
namespace LocalizationCorp {
   public class Localizer : WebService {
      [XmlRoot(Namespace="http://localizationcorp.com/documents/data/")]
      public class Town {
         public string Name;
         public string Country;
      }
      [WebMethod]
      public Town GetTownFromLatLon( double lat, double lon ) {
```

Example 24-1　　　　　　　　　　　　　　　　　　　　　　　　　　　　　　　　　　　　　Localizer.asmx
```
      Town town = new Town();
      if (lat < 43.44 && lat > 43.39 && lon < 7.18 && lon > 7.10) {
         town.Name = "Nice"; town.Country = "France";
      } else {
         town.Name = "Unkown"; town.Country = "Unkown";
      }
      return town;
   }
  }
}
```

The first line indicates to ASP.NET that this file describes a web service. During execution, a web service is in fact an instance of the class specified at the first line using the `class` attribute, in this case the `LocalizationCorp.Localizer` class. Such an instance is created by ASP.NET to deal with each request. Here, we talk about a stateless environment since a same object cannot service multiple requests. Understand that depending on your needs you can always store persistent states between requests on the server side, for example, using a database.

In this first line, we indicate to ASP.NET the .NET language used to write this class using the `Language` attribute, in this case the C# language. As with an ASPX page, you can separate the source code of ASMX pages. We explain this in more details at page 721.

Notice that our class derives from the `System.Web.Services.WebService` class. Note that a class representing a service does not need to necessarily derive from the `WebService` class. However, doing so allows access to several functionalities such as the management of states from one page to another. A class representing a web service must satisfy the following constraints:

- The class must be public and have a public default constructor.
- All of the web methods must be marked with the `System.Web.Services.WebMethod` attribute. The properties of this attribute configure the functionalities accessible to this method such as its behavior in relation to sessions. The `Description` property allows supplying a human-readable description of the method. Take a look at the article named **WebMethodAttribute Members** on **MSDN** for more details.

The `Namespace` property of the `WebService` class allows you to name in a unique way a web service. In general, we supply a URL for this property but this is not a requirement. If we do not specifically supply an URL, *http://tempuri.org/* will be used by default. In all cases, the resources located at the URL (if it exists) will never be accessed. The fact of using an URL which belongs to you gives you the possibility to guarantee that no other web service in the world will use the same as yours. Here is how we could have written our web service to use this property:

Example 24-2
```
...
namespace LocalizationCorp {
   [WebService(Namespace="http://localizationcorp.com/localizer")]
   public class Localizer : WebService {
      ...
```

You may notice that there is no WSDL file present in the folder hosting the web service. To obtain this document, you simply need to type the URL of our service in a web browser followed by ?wsdl. In our example this will give: `http://localhost/localizationcorp/localizer.asmx`**`?wsdl`**.

A bit further, we will dedicate a section on the description of WSDL documents. You can already notice that our data class `LocalizationCorp.Town` has been converted into an XSD schema which is included inside the WSDL document and is defined with the `http://localizationcorp.com/documents/data/` namespace.

Developing a simple web service with Visual Studio

Visual Studio offers several features to help you build a simple ASP.NET web service.

To create a web service using *Visual Studio* you simply need to do the following: *File › New › Web Site… › ASP.NET Web Service › Location* = http://localhost/localizationcorp › *OK*. Our service is hosted on the local machine since we have specified localhost.

You can now rename the file Service1.asmx to localizer.asmx and copy the C# code of Example 24-1 into the localizer.asmx.cs file (accessible by right clicking on localizer.asmx › *View code*).

Testing and debugging a web service

Testing a web service

Because of ASP.NET, you can test a web service without having to write a client. You simply need to open a web browser and navigate to the asmx using the following URL http://localhost/localizationcorp/localizer.asmx. A HTML page is constructed automatically from the WSDL document presenting the operations of the service. You can then select the GetTownFromLatLon operation which will bring up a new HTML page which allows you to input information that will be consumed by the operation, in this case a latitude and longitude. If you type in the geographical coordinates of the town of Nice (such as latitude=43.42 and longitude=7.15) you will obtain an HTML page containing the following XML document:

```xml
<?xml version="1.0" encoding="utf-8" ?>
<Town xmlns:xsd="http://www.w3.org/2001/XMLSchema"
      xmlns:xsi="http://www.w3.org/2001/XMLSchema-instance"
      xmlns="http://localizationcorp.com/documents/data/">
  <Name>Nice</Name>
  <Country>France</Country>
</Town>
```

This test feature uses the Documentation method to generate the HTML pages. If you deactivate this method, you will not have access to this testing facility through your web browser. This remark will be especially pertinent when we will explain how the WSE development platform depends on the HttpSoap method to accomplish its work. This means that all WSE processing cannot be tested from the Documentation method.

In a production environment, you may wish to increase security by deactivating all methods other than HttpSoap. This deactivation can be done by adding the following lines to the web.config file of your service or to your machine.config (which can be found in the .NET installation folder C:\WINDOWS\Microsoft.NET\Framework\v2.0.50727\CONFIG):

```xml
<configuration>
  <system.web>
    <webServices>
      <protocols>
        <add name="HttpSoap1.2" />
        <add name="HttpSoap" />
        <remove name="HttpPost" />
        <remove name="HttpGet" />
        <remove name="HttpPostLocalhost"/>
        <remove name="Documentation"/>
...
```

Debugging a web service

Visual Studio allows you to debug a web service as with any other .NET application. If you select *Debug > Start Debugging* you will obtain the same HTML test page. You can then debug your service by sending messages to it using the HTML pages or through any other client.

Creating a .NET client of a web service

Creating a .NET client of a web service without Visual Studio

In general, to develop the client of a web service whose operations use a RPC style model, we use a *proxy* class adapted to the concerned service. This class is directly accessed by the source code of the client. For each web method of the service, the proxy class exposes a method with the same name and even accepts and returns the same arguments. The proxy class takes care of the construction and transmission of SOAP request messages in addition of taking care of receiving and parsing the SOAP response messages.

If your client is developed with .NET, you will use the `wsdl.exe` tool supplied with *Visual Studio* to generate such a proxy class. This tool is capable of generating a proxy class in C#, VB.NET or JScript directly from the WSDL contract for the service. For example, this command generates the following proxy class:

```
wsdl.exe /out:LocalizerProxy.cs /language:C#
```

LocalizerProxy.cs
```
//------------------------------------------------------------
// <auto-generated>
//     This code was generated by a tool.
//     Runtime Version:2.0.50727
//
//     Changes to this file may cause incorrect behavior and will be lost
//     if the code is regenerated.
// </auto-generated>
//------------------------------------------------------------
using System;
using System.ComponentModel;
using System.Diagnostics;
using System.Web.Services;
using System.Web.Services.Protocols;
using System.Xml.Serialization;

[System.Diagnostics.DebuggerStepThroughAttribute()]
[System.ComponentModel.DesignerCategoryAttribute("code")]
[System.Web.Services.WebServiceBindingAttribute(
  Name="LocalizerSoap", Namespace="http://tempuri.org/")]
public partial class Localizer :
    System.Web.Services.Protocols.SoapHttpClientProtocol {
   ...
   public Localizer() {
      this.Url = "http://localhost/LocalizationCorp/Localizer.asmx";
   }

   [System.Web.Services.Protocols.SoapDocumentMethodAttribute(
      "http://tempuri.org/GetTownFromLatLon",
```

LocalizerProxy.cs

```csharp
            ...)]
    [return: System.Xml.Serialization.XmlElementAttribute(
       Namespace="http://localizationcorp.com/documents/data/",
       IsNullable=true)]
    public Town GetTownFromLatLon(double lat, double lon) {
       object[] results = this.Invoke("GetTownFromLatLon", new object[] {
               lat,
               lon});
       return ((Town)(results[0]));
    }

    public System.IAsyncResult BeginGetTownFromLatLon(
               double lat, double lon,
               System.AsyncCallback callback, object asyncState) {
       return this.BeginInvoke("GetTownFromLatLon", new object[] {
               lat, lon}, callback, asyncState);
    }

    public Town EndGetTownFromLatLon(System.IAsyncResult asyncResult) {
       object[] results = this.EndInvoke(asyncResult);
       return ((Town)(results[0]));
    }

    public void GetTownFromLatLonAsync(double lat, double lon) {
       this.GetTownFromLatLonAsync(lat, lon, null);
    }

    public void GetTownFromLatLonAsync(double lat, double lon,
                               object userState) {
       if ((this.GetTownFromLatLonOperationCompleted == null)) {
          this.GetTownFromLatLonOperationCompleted =
             new System.Threading.SendOrPostCallback(
                this.OnGetTownFromLatLonOperationCompleted);
       }
       this.InvokeAsync("GetTownFromLatLon", new object[] {
               lat,
               lon}, this.GetTownFromLatLonOperationCompleted,
               userState);
    }

    private void OnGetTownFromLatLonOperationCompleted(object arg) {
       if ((this.GetTownFromLatLonCompleted != null)) {
          System.Web.Services.Protocols.InvokeCompletedEventArgs
             invokeArgs =
             ((System.Web.Services.Protocols.InvokeCompletedEventArgs)
                (arg));
          this.GetTownFromLatLonCompleted(this,
             new GetTownFromLatLonCompletedEventArgs(
                invokeArgs.Results, invokeArgs.Error,
                invokeArgs.Cancelled, invokeArgs.UserState));
       }
    }

    public new void CancelAsync(object userState) {
       base.CancelAsync(userState);
```

Creating a .NET client of a web service

LocalizerProxy.cs

```
    }

    public event GetTownFromLatLonCompletedEventHandler
        GetTownFromLatLonCompleted;

}

[System.SerializableAttribute()]
[System.Xml.Serialization.XmlTypeAttribute(
    Namespace="http://localizationcorp.com/documents/data/")]
public partial class Town {
    private string nameField;
    private string countryField;
    public string Name {
        get { returnthis.nameField;} set {this.nameField = value;}
    }
    public string Country {
        get {return this.countryField;} set {this.countryField = value;}
    }
}
...
```

It is interesting to notice that the Town class has been regenerated from the XSD schema contained in the WSDL file for the service. Certain documentations suggest removing this definition from the generated file and encapsulating this data class in a library referenced by both the service and the client. We do not agree with this practice as it goes against a fundamental principle of SOA: **a service and its clients only share a contract**.

Note that the proxy class derives from SoapHttpClientProtocol. This offers a certain number of features such as the configuration of authentication methods to use.

You can now create an assembly which references the System.Web.Services.dll standard assembly and which is made of the LocalizerProxy.cs file as well as the following C# source file:

Example 24-3

```
using System;
class Program {
    static void Main() {
        Localizer proxy = new Localizer();
        Town town = proxy.GetTownFromLatLon(43.42, 7.15);
        Console.WriteLine("Town:"+town.Name+" Country:"+town.Country);
    }
}
```

Creating a .NET client of a web service with Visual Studio

To use a web service from an application developed with *Visual Studio*, you simply need to add a web reference to the web service you wish to use. To accomplish this, you need to right click on the project and select *Add Web Reference*. A service search window will appear from which you can select a local or remote web service. When the reference is added, *Visual Studio* uses automatically the wsdl.exe tool to construct the C# proxy class. This new file is hidden from the solution browser to prevent you from editing it. You can verify that the file is in fact there in the project folder for the client.

Note that *Visual Studio* uses the UDDI technology to search for remote web services. We will detail this technology a bit later in this chapter.

Asynchronous calls and Message Exchange Patterns

Notice that for each web method which can be invoked, the proxy class also presents a method for asynchronous calls (named `Begin[method]`) and a method (named `End[method]`) to recover the results of an asynchronous call for each web method. This type of asynchronous call is described at page 141.

For each web method, another asynchronous call model is supplied using `[method]Async()`, `On[method]OperationCompleted()` and the `[method]CompletedEventHandler` event. This model allows the cancellation of all asynchronous of this type using the `CancelAsync()` method.

Understand that this approach does not follow the spirit of SOA. With SOA the client/server paradigm is replaced with the idea of a sender/receiver pair for each message. Also, in the exchange of request/response messages (synchronous or asynchronous), the roles of sender/receiver are reversed depending on our point of view:

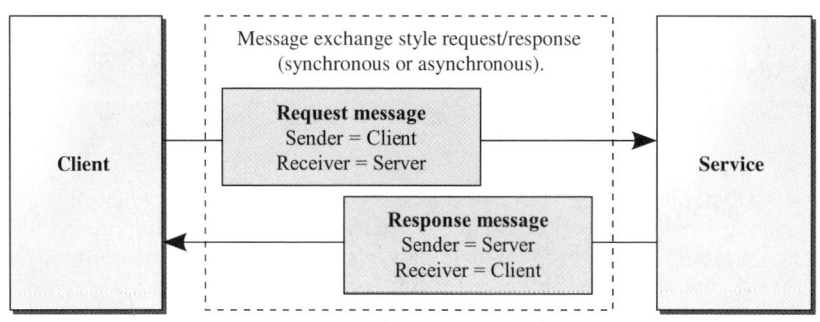

Figure 24-1: Client/Server vs. Sender/Receiver

In other words, to be capable of receiving a response, or more generally to support any message exchange model, the client must also be a service. The rest of this chapter will not make use of message exchange models other than the traditional RPC style.

Using a web service from a .NET Remoting client

You can consume a simple web service using the .NET Remoting technology. For this, you simply need to use the type metadata produced by the tool named `soapsuds.exe` (described at page 668). So that `soapsuds.exe` can consume a web service, it must support the RPC formatting which is not recommended. This formatting, as well as its disadvantages is described in the next section dedicated to SOAP. You must use the `SoapRpcService` attribute of the class containing the web methods of our service. The web service of Example 24-1 must be rewritten as follows to be consumed by `soapsuds.exe`:

Example 24-4   *localizer.asmx*

```
...
namespace LocalizationCorp {
   [System.Web.Services.Protocols.SoapRpcService()]
   public class Localizer : WebService {
      ...
```

You can now obtain metadata which is exploitable by .NET Remoting in the `ProxyLocalizationCorp.dll` assembly by typing the following command line. Note that to execute this command on a service hosted by IIS, you must deactivate the integrated *Windows* authentication on the virtual folder of the service. If you execute the web service with the *Visual Studio 2005* web server you must also deactivate the integrated authentication by using following menu *Project properties › Start Options ›* Uncheck *NTLM Authentication* option:

```
soapsuds.exe /url:http://localhost:80/LocalizationCorp/Localizer.asmx?wsdl /oa:
ProxyLocalizationCorp.dll
```

The following program, which must be compiled by referencing the ProxyLocalizationCorp.dll and System.Runtime.Remoting.dll assemblies, uses the web service using .NET Remoting. A .NET Remoting client does not need for the web service to support RPC formatting meaning that you can now remove the SoapRpcService attribute by reverting to Example 24-1. Note that the LocalizerSoap and Town classes are in the InteropNS namespace:

Example 24-5

```
using System;
using System.Runtime.Remoting;
using System.Runtime.Remoting.Channels;
using System.Runtime.Remoting.Channels.Http;
class Program {
   static void Main() {
      HttpChannel canalHttp = new HttpChannel(0);
      ChannelServices.RegisterChannel( canalHttp, false );

      MarshalByRefObject obj = (MarshalByRefObject)
         RemotingServices.Connect(
         typeof(InteropNS.LocalizerSoap),
         "http://localhost:80/LocalizationCorp/Localizer.asmx");
      InteropNS.LocalizerSoap proxy = obj as InteropNS.LocalizerSoap;

      InteropNS.Town town = proxy.GetTownFromLatLon(43.42, 7.15);
      Console.WriteLine("Town:"+town.Name+" Country:"+town.Country);
   }
}
```

After this incursion into the practical aspect of web services, it is time to be a little more theoretical on the SOAP and WSDL languages.

SOAP messages

Before we start this section let us remind you the three main characteristics of SOAP as seen in the introduction:

- The possibility of extending the SOAP language to implement new communication protocols (encryption, authentication, transactional…).
- Messages coded using the SOAP language can be transmitted by any network protocols such as HTTP, TCP, UDP or SMTP.
- SOAP allows for any type of message exchange model.

Introduction

Version 1.0 of SOAP was designed for use with distributed object technologies. Version 1.1 of SOAP has been used for many years mostly within web services. This means that the *Object* word of the SOAP acronym has lost its meaning. Also, since version 1.2 of SOAP, the term SOAP is not considered as an acronym anymore.

WSE 3.0 now works using version 1.2 of SOAP by default. From now on we will base ourselves on version 1,2. You can obtain a complete history of the evolution of SOAP 1.1 to 1.2 in this article http://www.idealliance.org/papers/xmle02/dx_xmle02/papers/02-02-02/02-02-02.html. The complete specification for SOAP 1.2 is divided into three documents available at http://www.w3.org/TR/soap12-part0/, http://www.w3.org/TR/soap12-part1/ and http://www.w3.org/TR/soap12-part2/.

A SOAP message contains a root element named <Envelope>. This element optionally contains a <Header> element at the beginning and must contain a <Body> element at the end. This means that a SOAP message may looks as follows:

```
<soap:Envelope xmlns:soap="http://schemas.xmlsoap.org/soap/envelope/">
   <soap:Header> <!-- optional -->
      <!- Contains message transport data. -->
   </soap:Header>
   <soap:Body> <!-- mandatory -->
      <!-- Contains business data. -->
   </soap:Body>
</soap:Envelope>
```

The <body> element contains business data encoded as XML. For example, here is what a SOAP message would look like for a request sent by a client to the `localizer` service:

```
<soap:Envelope xmlns:soap="http://schemas.xmlsoap.org/soap/envelope/">
   <soap:Body>
      <GetTownFromLatLon xmlns="http://tempuri.org/">
         <lat>43.42</lat>
         <lon>7.15</lon>
      </GetTownFromLatLon>
   </soap:Body>
</soap:Envelope>
```

The <Header> element contains data encoded in XML format, fabricated and consumed by SOAP extensions such as WS-* specification implementation. The SOAP language does not define sub-elements to <Header>. Only the WS-* specifications define the sub-elements for <Header>. Each specification involved in the transmission of a message adds its sub-elements. It is because of this mechanism that the extensibility of the SOAP language is achieved.

Here is a SOAP message which contains a security token in the form of a user/password added by an implementation of the WS-Security specification. It also contains information on the source of the messages that were added by an implementation of WS-Addressing:

```
<soap:Envelope xmlns:soap="http://schemas.xmlsoap.org/soap/envelope/"
   xmlns:wsa="http://schemas.xmlsoap.org/ws/2003/03/addressing"
   xmlns:wsse="http://schemas.xmlsoap.org/ws/2002/12/secext/">
   <soap:Header>
      <!-- WS-Addressing data -->
      <wsa:From>
         <wsa:Address>http://smacchia.com/client</wsa:Address>
      </wsa:From>
      ...
      <!-- WS-Security data -->
      <wsse:Security soap:mustUnderstand="1">
         <wsse:UserName>psmacchia</wsse:UserName>
         <wsse:Password wsse:Type="wsse:PasswordDigest">
            yH/*kiGGdsdujg5%16?LHRVhbg...
         </wsse:Password>
         ...
      </wsse:Security>
      ...
   </soap:Header>
   <soap:Body>
      ...
   </soap:Body>
</soap:Envelope>
```

Defining and processing SOAP headers

Although the SOAP language does not define sub-elements for the <header> element, it defines a set of rules to treat these header elements. The WS-* specification must then follow these rules. To explain what these rules are we have to go a little deeper with SOAP terminology.

A *SOAP node* is a software agent which emits or receives SOAP messages. For a specific SOAP message, we distinguish the origin node (also named expeditor node that is the client of the service) and the final node (also named the destination node, which is the service). As illustrated by the following figure, between these two nodes a same message can be received and then resent by intermediate nodes. The intermediate nodes as well as the final node are also considered as path nodes. Naturally, all SOAP node topologies aren't necessarily this sophisticated and may not use different protocols between the nodes:

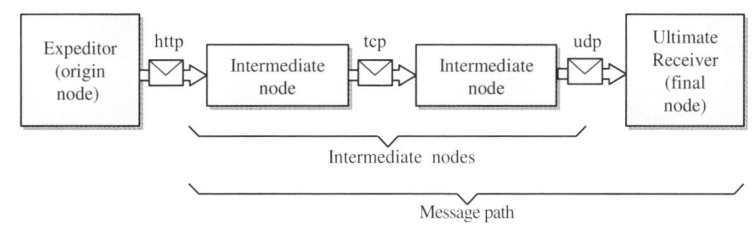

Figure 24-2: SOAP nodes

Only the final node is qualified to deal with the business data within the <body> element. However, a header element can be handled by any node on the path. The processing on these elements is defined by the WS-* specifications. SOAP supplies a mechanism to determine which path node must deal with a specific element of the header using three XML attributes role, mustUnderstand and relay.

Each path node plays one or multiple *roles*. A header element informs the SOAP node if it can process it using the role attribute. If the URI specified by this attribute defines one of the roles played by the SOAP node then this node can potentially process it. In fact, such a SOAP node is obligated to process a header element only if it contains the mustUnderstand="1" (or mustUnderstand='true') attribute. If an intermediate node processes one or multiple elements of the header, it must remove these elements from the message before passing it on to the next node. An element of the header which corresponds to the role of an intermediate node but is not treated can either be removed from the message or passed to the next node if it contains the relay="1" (or relay='true') attribute.

SOAP 1.2 only defined three roles: the Next role is played by all intermediate nodes while the UltimateReceiver role is only played by the final node. The None role is not played by any node. The data in a header element that has this role is then purely informative. These three roles are respectively represented by the following URIs "http://www.w3.org/2003/05/soap-envelope/role/next", "http://www.w3.org/2003/05/soap-envelope/role/ultimateReceiver" and "http://www.w3.org/2003/05/soap-envelope/role/none". The WS-* specifications are free to extend the SOAP language by defining new roles.

It is interesting to note that only the header elements that must be processed (those with the mustUnderstand attribute set to true) can cause a break condition. In other words, if a path node encounters a problem during processing such a header element, it is obligated to produce an error which will prevent the processing of the message's body be the final node. This error can eventually be transmitted to the origin node through a new error SOAP message.

Encoding SOAP messages bodies

The data contained within the body of a SOAP message (i.e. in the `<body>` element) generally presents itself as an XML document whose schema is specified in the contract of the service. This approach is also known as *document/literal* since the data is formatted in an XML *document* that *literally* satisfies an XSD schema.

The object oriented history of the SOAP language that we have mentioned brings forth an alternative to how the data in the body of a SOAP message can be encoded. This other approach is known as *RPC/encoded*. This technique is more adapted to the exchange of synchronous request/response messages of RPC type. The encoding is part of the SOAP specification and describes how to serialize in XML the input and output arguments of a method based on a set of rules. These rules specify the way that objects, tables, structures and object graphs are to be serialized.

SOAP is now mainly used for the encoding of messages exchanged between services. As we have mentioned, the RPC style request/response message exchange is now only one model amongst others. There is then no reason to privilege this model. Also, the different implementations of web services such as ASP.NET/WSE use the *document/literal* rather than the *RPC/encoded* model.

SOAP error messages

We have seen that the processing of a header element by a SOAP node part of the path can generate an error which will be returned to the origin node through a new SOAP message. This is possible because the SOAP language allows the definition of error messages. A SOAP error message is like other messages but the body only contains a single `<Fault>` element. The SOAP language specification explains how to encode within this message the cause of the error, the SOAP role which caused the error, the node that generated the error etc. It also specifies certain error codes such as the `MustUnderstand` code which means that a header element with the `mustUnderstand` attribute could not be processed.

SOAP and underlying transport protocols

For each network protocol which could be used to transport SOAP messages, there is a specification explaining in details how the message must be transmitted. In general, this does not pose any problems as most of the protocols have a notion of what is a message.

The 1.2 SOAP specification only describes the relationship with the HTTP protocol. It establishes a natural correspondence with the synchronous request/response message exchange model of HTTP.

Web services contracts and the WSDL language

We have introduced *WSDL* (*Web Service Description Language* pronounced *Wizdil*) as an extensible XML language used to define service contracts. We will now look at this language in more details.

What can you express with WSDL?

The WSDL language is composed of a root element called `<definitions>` and of seven sub-elements which can be classified into two categories:

- The `<types>`, `<message>`, `<operation>` and `<portType>` elements are used to describe the contract presented by a web service.
- The `<binding>`, `<port>` and `<service>` elements are used to specify the links between a contract and its implementation. In addition to linking the web methods to specific operations of the service, these links describe other aspects of the implementation such as the network protocol or the encoding of data within a SOAP message.

Web services contracts and the WSDL language

Hence, certain information described by the second category is not useful to a client of the web serviced and is not part of the contract.

The WS-Policy specification describes how to extend the WSDL language to create policies. The policies are clauses of the contract allowing you to improve their precision and semantic. For example, the WSDL language does not specify how to enforce that the messages sent to a service must be encrypted. For this, you must add security policies to the contract. Hence, only part of the contract is effectively written in WSDL:

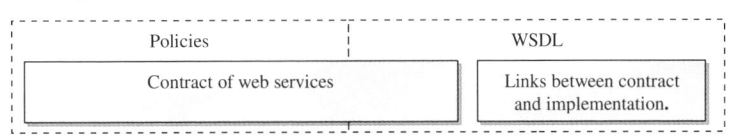

Policies	WSDL
Contract of web services	Links between contract and implementation.

Figure 24-3: WSDL and contracts

Dissecting a WSDL document

Here is the WSDL file for our `localizer` service:

```xml
<?xml version="1.0" encoding="utf-8" ?>
<definitions
    xmlns:s1="http://localizationcorp.com/documents/data/"
    xmlns:http="http://schemas.xmlsoap.org/wsdl/http/"
    xmlns:soap="http://schemas.xmlsoap.org/wsdl/soap/"
    xmlns:s="http://www.w3.org/2001/XMLSchema"
    xmlns:s0="http://tempuri.org/"
    xmlns:soapenc="http://schemas.xmlsoap.org/soap/encoding/"
    xmlns:tm="http://microsoft.com/wsdl/mime/textMatching/"
    xmlns:mime="http://schemas.xmlsoap.org/wsdl/mime/"
    targetNamespace="http://tempuri.org/"
    xmlns="http://schemas.xmlsoap.org/wsdl/">
  <types>
    <s:schema elementFormDefault="qualified"
              targetNamespace="http://tempuri.org/">
      <s:import namespace="http://localizationcorp.com/documents/data/" />
      <s:element name="GetTownFromLatLon">
        <s:complexType>
          <s:sequence>
            <s:element minOccurs="1" maxOccurs="1" name="lat"
                       type="s:double" />
            <s:element minOccurs="1" maxOccurs="1" name="lon"
                       type="s:double" />
          </s:sequence>
        </s:complexType>
      </s:element>
      <s:element name="GetTownFromLatLonResponse">
        <s:complexType>
          <s:sequence>
            <s:element minOccurs="1" maxOccurs="1"
              ref="s1:GetTownFromLatLonResult" />
          </s:sequence>
        </s:complexType>
      </s:element>
    </s:schema>
    <s:schema elementFormDefault="qualified"
              targetNamespace="http://localizationcorp.com/documents/data/">
```

```xml
            <s:element name="GetTownFromLatLonResult" nillable="true"
                       type="s1:Town" />
          <s:complexType name="Town">
            <s:sequence>
              <s:element minOccurs="0" maxOccurs="1" name="Name"
                         type="s:string" />
              <s:element minOccurs="0" maxOccurs="1" name="Country"
                         type="s:string" />
            </s:sequence>
          </s:complexType>
        </s:schema>
     </types>
     <message name="GetTownFromLatLonSoapIn">
        <part name="parameters" element="s0:GetTownFromLatLon" />
     </message>
     <message name="GetTownFromLatLonSoapOut">
        <part name="parameters" element="s0:GetTownFromLatLonResponse" />
     </message>
     <portType name="LocalizerSoap">
        <operation name="GetTownFromLatLon">
          <input message="s0:GetTownFromLatLonSoapIn" />
          <output message="s0:GetTownFromLatLonSoapOut" />
        </operation>
     </portType>
     <binding name="LocalizerSoap" type="s0:LocalizerSoap">
        <soap:binding transport="http://schemas.xmlsoap.org/soap/http"
          style="document" />
        <operation name="GetTownFromLatLon">
          <soap:operation soapAction="http://tempuri.org/GetTownFromLatLon"
             style="document" />
          <input>
             <soap:body use="literal" />
          </input>
          <output>
             <soap:body use="literal" />
          </output>
        </operation>
     </binding>
     <service name="Localizer">
        <port name="LocalizerSoap" binding="s0:LocalizerSoap">
          <soap:address
             location="http://localhost/localizationcorp/localizer.asmx" />
        </port>
     </service>
  </definitions>
```

The <definitions> element

The <definitions> element is the root of all WSDL document. This element includes all the standard namespaces used (SOAP, XSD etc) as well as eventual proprietary namespaces.

The <Types> element

We see that the <types> element contains the XSD schema for the data that will be contained in the <Body> of the exchanged SOAP messages. Note that the <types> is mandatory but it can be empty if you import the XSD schemas in a <import> root element:

```xml
<?xml version="1.0" encoding="utf-8" ?>
<import namespace="http://localizationcorp.com/documents/data/"
        location="http://localizationcorp.com/documents/data/schema.xsd" >
<definitions>
  <types />
  ...
</definitions>
```

The <message> element

Each `<message>` element defines an input, output or error SOAP message. Each `<part>` of a `<message>` element references a data schema. Since a SOAP message can contain multiple parts, a `<message>` element may contain multiple `<part>` entries.

The <operation> element

Each `<operation>` element defines the SOAP messages supported by each operation of the web service. In our simple `localizer` web service, the only operation is defined as a synchronous RPC style message exchange presenting both an input and output message. An operation supporting another message exchange model could only define an input or an output message. An operation also has the possibility of presenting an error message by containing a `<fault>` element.

The name of an operation defined in the `soap:operation` element is prefixed by default with the `http://tempuri.org/` namespace. Example 24-2 shows how to customize this namespace.

The <portType> element

A `<portType>` element defines the set of operations presented by a service. In the case of our example, the operations have the possibility of being defined directly in a `<portType>` element. They can also be defined outside of this element and then referenced as follows:

```xml
...
    <operation name="GetTownFromLatLon">
        <input message="s0:GetTownFromLatLonSoapIn" />
        <output message="s0:GetTownFromLatLonSoapOut" />
    </operation>
    <portType name="LocalizerSoap">
      <operation name="GetTownFromLatLon" />
    </portType>
...
```

If we think in terms of object oriented language, types of the `<types>` elements relate to structures, the `<message>` element relate to the method signatures, the `<operation>` elements relate to the methods and the `<portType>` relate to interfaces. Let us now take a look at the WSDL elements which allow you to establish a link between a contract and an implementation.

The <binding> element

The `<binding>` element allows to specify information on the implementation of a service. This information contains:

- The encoding protocols for the SOAP messages with the `<soap:body>` element;
- The name of the web methods to use for each operation using the `<soap:operation>` elements;
- The underlying network protocol using the `<soap:binding>` element.

Understand that, for example, the `<soap:operation>` and `<operation>` elements are different as they do not belong to the same namespace. Although that some of this information may be useful to the clients to consume a service, they do not contain any information in regards to the semantics of the service.

The <port> element

The `<port>` element allows to make a link between a `<binding>` element and an implementation of a service through the use of a `<soap:address>` element. It is interesting that this information is not part of the `<binding>` element as it gives the liberty of redirecting SOAP message to other implementations.

The <service> element

The `<service>` element is simply a collection of `<port>` elements.

Introduction to WSE and to WS-* specifications

Introduction to WSE

The facilities offered by *Visual Studio* and ASP.NET for the development of a web service do not allow the implementation of basic features such as the use of message encryption and the use of a transport protocol other than HTTP. On the other hand only certain of the WS-* have been finalized. Since 2003, to allow .NET developers to build web services using these finalized specifications, *Microsoft* freely supplies a development platform named *WSE* (*Web Service Enhancement* pronounced *Wizi*).

WSE is principally constructed of a configuration editor integrated in *Visual Studio* and the `Microsoft.Web.ServiceXX.dll` assembly (XX designates the version of WSE). The WSE configuration editor allows to specify the parameters of a project using WSE. This editor works by parsing and updating the code within the configuration file of the application (`web.config` in the case of a service and `app.config` in the case of the client of a service). You may choose not to use this editor and modify these files by hand.

The `Microsoft.Web.ServiceXX.dll` assembly must be referenced by each assembly which uses WSE and is distributed with every WSE based application. This assembly contains code which modifies SOAP messages sent and received according to the supported WS-* specifications. It can be used both on the service and client side.

The .NET 2 platform is only compatible with 3.0+ version of WSE. You must know that the major versions of WSE (1.0, 2.0, 3.0 etc) are not compatible between each other. However, the deliverables of WSE do not necessarily coincide with deliverables of the framework. This liberty taken by *Microsoft* allows for certain flexibility in the evolution of WSE.

You may be hesitant investing into a technology which does not offer backward compatibility. However know that WSE constitutes the most efficient alternative to implement services using the .NET platform as of today. It is clear that you will benefit from this as you approach future more evolved development platforms such as the *Windows Communication Foundation*.

Specifications supported by WSE 3.0

WSE 3.0 supports the following specifications:

- *WS-Policy*: for the development of strategies.
- *WS-Security* for authentication and encryption of messages.
- *WS-SecureConversation* to establish secured message exchange sessions (similar to the SSL protocol).
- *WS-SecurityPolicy* for the description of security policies.
- *WS-Trust* to obtain security tokens.
- *WS-Addressing* to support message exchange models other than RPC style messages.
- *MTOM* (*Message Transmission Optimization Mechanism*) for the transmission of large sets binary data.

Introduction to WSE and to WS-* specifications   837

In addition to HTTP, WSE 3.0 allows the use of the TCP protocol and an optimized transport model for when the service and its client reside in the same process. In these two cases, it is obvious that the use of ASP.NET or a web server such as IIS is pointless.

Installing WSE

WSE can be downloaded for free on the *Microsoft* website. In addition to the WSE configuration editor and the `Microsoft.Web.ServiceXX.dll` you will find in the installation folder some additional tools, some documentation and sample projects using WSE.

The X509 certificate technology (described in the section at page 191) is largely used in the security domain for applications developed using WSE. The *X509 Certificate Tool* supplied with WSE facilitates the manipulation of X509 certificates. WSE comes with two X509 certificates that you can use to test the samples supplied as well as your own code.

WSE is also delivered with the *Policy Wizard* tool which simplifies the process of generating olicies.

Once WSE has been installed on your development machine you can easily activate it in your *Visual Studio* (ASP.NET or not). You simply need to right click on your project in the solution explorer and select *WSE Settings 3.0...*. The editor will then display itself and you only need to select *Enable this project for Web Services Enhancements*. In the case of an ASP.NET project, you will need to select *Enable Microsoft Web Services Enhancements Soap Extensions*.

How does WSE work thanks to SOAP extension?

In the case of an ASP.NET project, WSE exploits the *SOAP extensions*. A SOAP extension is a class capable of accessing a message before it is used by the service. To be recognized as a SOAP extension, a class must derive from the abstract class `System.Web.Services.SoapExtension`.

A detailed description of SOAP extensions is beyond the scope of this book. However, you may reference the MSDN documentation for the `SoapExtension` class. In fact, this documentation contains an example of a SOAP extension especially instructive which allows you to save in a log all the input and output SOAP messages. To make this example work, you must take three precautions:

- Make sure that the *Windows* user which executes the ASP.NET process (ASPNET by default) has all access rights on the folder in which the web application is located so it can create and modify the log files.
- Use a client developed using a proxy class. In fact, if you use a browser to test your service, the `HttpSoap` method will not be accessible and in this case SOAP extensions will not be used.
- Add the following in your `web.config` file in order to activate SOAP extensions.

```
<configuration>
   <system.web>
      <webServices>
         <soapExtensionTypes>
            <add type="NameOfTheClassNamespacesIncluded,
                       NameOfTheAssemblyWhichContainsTheClass",
                 priority="1" group="0" />
         </soapExtensionTypes>
         ...
```

Note that you may decide to apply a SOAP extension only to certain web methods. In this case, you must not make the modification to your `web.config` file but mark each method with the proper SOAP extension attribute. More information on this topic is available on the MSDN documentation for the `SoapExtensionAttribute` class.

In the case of a non ASP.NET project, the WSE configuration editor creates a new proxy class with a name ending by Wse. In our example, there are then two proxy classes: `Localizer` and `LocalizerWse`. The `Localizer` class derives from `System.Web.Services.Protocols.SoapHttpClientProtocol` while the `LocalizerWse` derives from `Microsoft.Web.Services3.WebServicesClientProtocol`. Of course, you only get the WSE services if you use the `LocalizerWse` proxy class to access the service.

First test with WSE diagnostics

You can easily test WSE on a project (ASP.NET or not) by activating the SOAP message log in the *Diagnostics* tab of the WSE configuration editor. It is instructive to notice the modifications which are made to the `web.config` file (or `app.config` in the case of a non ASP.NET project). Here again, the test will only work correctly if the precautions from the previous section are taken into account.

WS-* specifications not yet supported by WSE

WS-PolicyAttachment and WS-MetadataExchange

It is not yet possible for a client to automatically obtain the *WS-Policy* expressions which apply to the operations of a service developed with WSE. The responsible party of a service may always communicate the file containing these expressions somehow to the client but this solution is less than satisfying as it is non-standard. Also, there exists the *WS-PolicyAttachment* which describes how to assign an expression to the operations of a service directly into a WSDL contract. There is also the *WS-MetadataExchange* specification which describes how a client consumes expressions referenced by WS-PolicyAttachment.

WS-ReliableMessage

The *WS-ReliableMessage* specification allows dealing with the absence of delivery guarantee on certain network protocols. For example, the UDP network protocol does not provide any reception acknowledgement mechanism nor does it guarantee the delivery or the order of delivery of messages. Of course the WS-ReliableMessage specification places itself at the lowest level of the WS-* and will implicitly be managed by the execution environment.

UDDI and WS-Discovery

The *UDDI* (*Universal Description Discovery and Integration*) and the *WS-Discovery* specifications allow the discovery of web services. While UDDI defines a centralized system based on subscriptions and directory searches, the WS-Discovery specification exploits broadcasting mechanisms and can work without a centralized directory.

The UDDI directories can be published externally or internally to an enterprise. Each entry in the directory corresponds to a service provider. Part of this entry is dedicated to the presentation of the service provider (activity domain, contacts, fees etc). A second part is dedicated to the abstract description of the offered web services (the `<types>`, `<import>`, `<message>`, `<portType>` and `<binding>` elements of the WSDL contract). The document representing the abstract description of the services is named *Types Models* (*tModel*). The search for a service is essentially done by requesting from the directory which services support certain tModel. Finally, each entry in the directory contain a third part which stores the links to the implementation of the services (the `<import>` and `<service>` elements of the WSDL contract).

WS-Discovery defines two messages *'hello'* and *'bye'* which allow a service to add or remove itself from the directory when it connects and disconnects from the network. These messages are relayed through broadcasting to reach all potential clients of the service. The clients also have at their disposition two messages called *'probe'* and *'resolve'* to launch the search of a service on the network. To limit excessive use of broadcast bandwidth, WS-Discovery allows the implementation of special services called *discovery proxy* to base itself on a certain centralization of list of services available on the network.

WS-Federation

The *WS-Federation* specification extends the WS-Trust to refine the authentication model between different trust domains. WS-Federation allows a same user to navigate between various federated domains without having to explicitly authenticate each time. WS-Federation mainly defines the SOAP messages which will be exchanged to make this navigation possible. From a practical point of view, this specification aims to address several problems commonly encountered within organizations and companies such as:

- The difficulty in obtaining the authorization of an agent within a collaborating organization within the scope of a specific operation.
- The difficulty of authenticating a same person through multiple email addresses (professional, personal…).
- The difficulty in determining the level of sensitivity of personal information within the context of an operation.

WS-Coordination

The *WS-Coordination* specification allows for multiple web services to coordinate their operations in the context of a task that must be realized in common. Each task is identified by a unique identifier called a coordination context. This identifier ends up in the SOAP header entries for each message exchanged within the context of this task. WS-Coordination defines these headers as well as their meaning (request to complete an operation, refusal or impossibility to complete the operation, terminating an operation…). Take note that certain common tasks such as 2PC transactions require the presence of a service which plays the role of coordinator. Some other tasks do not need such a coordinator. WS-Coordination manages these two kinds of tasks and the set of possible tasks is open. This extension translates into other WS-* specifications such as WS-AtomicTransaction which bases themselves on WS-Coordination to define specific tasks.

WS-AtomicTransaction and WS-BusinessActivity

The *WS-AtomicTransaction* specification uses features from the WS-Coordination specification to perform volatile or durable ACID transactions distributed over multiple services. For this, WS-AtomicTransaction takes advantage of 2PC style algorithms. This specification will be implemented by the DTC (Distributed Transaction Coordinator) which will be part of *Windows Vista*. It supports both the notion of volatile and durable transactions.

The *WS-BusinessActivity* specification uses features from the WS-Coordination specification to accomplish long transactions distributed over several services. Long transactions come to work around the impossibility of locking certain resources during an ACID transaction. Also, such a resource is updated as soon as the long transaction begins. If such a transaction happens to fail, the coordinator will inform each participant which are free to complete a corrective action to restore the resources into their initial state. A consequence of this approach is that we loose the notion of isolation between multiple long transactions. Consequently, this means that a participant may not be able to restore the state of a resource as it may have been modified during another transaction.

WS-Enumeration

The *WS-Enumeration* allows a client to request large amounts of information from a service. Such a demand translates itself by the creation of a WS-Enumeration session which takes care of managing the sequence of messages sent to the requester. The tracking of the cursor on the data to be transmitted can be done on either the client or the service. This tracking can even be handed off, for example, from the server to the requester to free the server from the management of this tracking when it detects that latency between messages becomes prohibitive.

WS-Eventing

The *WS-Enumeration* specification allows the implementation in a standard way of subscription/event messages as described at page 822.

WS-Management

The *WS-Management* specification aims to promote the uniformity of information systems. Note that the information system term must be taken broadly and includes both *software* (such as an IIS server or an operating system) and *hardware* (such as a *SmartPhone* or a *Pocket PC*). WS-Management defines SOAP messages modeling the operations required by all supervision solution. Amongst these operations, let us mention the discovery of supervision resources, the parameterization of these resources, the sharing of resources and the requesting of information regarding the current state of a system. WS-Management is support by the main players in the market such as *Microsoft*, *Intel*, *AMD*, *Dell* and Sun.

Introduction to WCF (Windows Communication Framework)

WCF (*Windows Communication Framework* previously codenamed *Indigo*) is a framework which will take an integral part of *Windows Vista* (but will also be made available for *Windows XP*). This framework aims to unify all the different communication technologies created by *Microsoft* until today, that is: ASMX, .NET Remoting, COM+/Enterprise Services, System.Messaging, MSMQ and WSE. The compatibility between these technologies will allow for each enterprise to migrate towards WCF at their own rhythm.

WCF allows the establishment of communications between *WCF endpoints*. Each endpoint is characterized by three components:

- Its address allows it to be located.
- Its binding information defines the type of protocols it can communicate with.
- Its contracts as defined in this chapter (structure and use semantics).

The WCF architecture makes sure to separate each of these components. As a developer, you will mostly be concerned with the contract component since the notion of address and protocol information are only significant during the deployment and maintenance.

WCF will support most not-yet implemented WS-* specifications that we have discussed. The design behind WCF takes care of hiding the complexities of these specifications from developers. Also, you will have access to all these features through the use of simple configuration file parameters and you will rarely hear about the underlying WS-* specifications.

Appendix

Appendix A: keywords of the C#2 language

Here is the list of C#2 keywords:

- Bold keywords do not exist in C++
- Italic keywords exist in C++ but have a different use or signification.
- The *C#2* term is used for a keyword which has been introduced with this version of the language. Few keywords have been added compared to the amount of new features.

Note that several keywords have multiple significations (`using`, `delegate`, `new`, `fixed`...).

A keyword cannot be used as an identifier. However, a keyword prefixed with the @ character can be an identifier but you should avoid this practice.

Keyword	Reference
abstract	A solution: abstract classes and abstract methods page 375
as	The as operator page 385
base	Class inheritance page 368
bool	The bool type page 297
break	The break and continue instructions page 277
	The switch instruction page 274
byte	Integer types page 295
case	The switch instruction page 274
catch	Introduction to exception management in C# page 424
char	The char type page 297
checked	Dealing with overflows page 299
class	Class definition page 328
	Reference\Value type constraint page 395
const	Constant fields page 330
continue	The break and continue instructions page 277
decimal	Real types page 296
default	The switch instruction page 274
	The default operator page 401
delegate	Delegate classes and delegate objects page 313
	Introduction to C#2 anonymous methods page 436
do	The while and do/while loops page 276
double	Real types page 296
else	Use of if/else page 273
enum	Enumerations page 304
event	Events page 340

Keyword	Reference
explicit	Cast operator overloading page 361
extern	The DllImport attribute page 219
extern alias C#2	Extern aliases page 268
false	The bool type page 297
finally	Catch and finally blocks page 428
fixed	Pinned object page 420 Fixed arrays page 422
float	Real types page 296
for	The for loop page 276
foreach	Iterating through the items of a collection with the 'foreach' and 'in' keywords page 469
get	Properties page 337
global C#2	Global qualifiers page 267
goto	The goto instruction page 278
if	Use of if/else page 273
implicit	Cast operator overloading page 361
in	Iterating through the items of a collection with the 'foreach' and 'in' keywords page 469
int	Integer types page 295
interface	Interfaces page 377
internal	Visibility of members page 345 The protected and internal protected visibility levels page 369
is	The is operator page 384
lock	The lock C# keyword page 122
long	Integer types page 295
namespace	The namespaces page 257
new	Accessing constructors when creating objects page 349 Disabling polymorphism page 374 Default constructor constraint page 393
null	Understanding references page 284 Evolution of the C# syntax: Nullable<T> is the null keyword page 320
object	The System.Object class page 287
operator	Operator overloading page 358
out	Out parameters page 334
override	A solution: virtual methods and polymorphism page 372
params	The params keyword page 335
partial C#2	Partial types page 324
private	Visibility of members page 345
protected	Visibility of members page 345 The protected and internal protected visibility levels page 369
public	Visibility of members page 345
readonly	Constant fields page 330
ref	Passing any argument by reference page 332
return	Out parameters page 334
sbyte	Integer types page 295
sealed	Sealed classes page 371
set	Properties page 337
short	Integer types page 295
sizeof	The sizeof operator page 419

Appendix A: keywords of the C#2 language   843

Keyword	Reference
stackalloc	Allocating memory on the stack with the stackalloc keyword page 422
static	Static members page 356
string	Strings page 307
struct	Structures page 303
	Reference\Value type constraint page 395
switch	The switch instruction page 274
this	Indexer page 339
	The this keyword page 347
throw	Introduction to exception management in C# page 424
true	The bool type page 297
try	Introduction to exception management in C# page 424
typeof	Precise a type page 199
uint	Integer types page 295
ulong	Integer types page 295
unchecked	Dealing with overflows page 299
unsafe	Declaring unsafe code in C# page 418
ushort	Integer types page 295
using	Harnessing resources declared in a namespace page 258
	The IDisposable interface and its Dispose() method page 351
	Creating an alias on namespaces and types page 266
value	The set accessor page 338
virtual	A solution: virtual methods and polymorphism page 372
volatile	Volatile fields page 119
void	Pointer casting page 420
where	Derivation constraint page 393
while	The while and do/while loops page 276
yield break C#2	The yield break keyword page 454
yield return C#2	The keyword yield return page 451

Appendix B : .NET 2 enhancements

Assembly

The use of the `AssemblyKeyFile` attribute to sign an attribute is to be avoided. It is now preferred that you use the `/keycontainer` and `/keyfile` options of the `csc.exe` or the new project properties of *Visual Studio 2005* (page 24).

The new `System.Runtime.CompilerServices.InternalsVisibleToAttribute` attribute allows you to specify assemblies which have access to non-public types within the assembly to which you apply the attribute. We discuss this notion of friend assemblies at page 22.

The `ildasm.exe` 2 tool offers by default the possibility of obtaining statistics in regards to the byte size of each section of an assembly and the display of its metadata. With `ildasm.exe` 1.x you needed to use the `/adv` command line option (page 18).

Application localization

The `resgen.exe` tool can now generate C# or VB.NET code which encapsulates access to resources in a strongly typed manner (page 28).

Application build process

The .NET platform is now delivered with a new tool called `msbuild.exe`. This tool is used to build .NET applications and is used by *Visual Studio 2005* but you can use it to launch your own build scripts (page 39).

Application configuration

The .NET 2 platform features a new strong typed management of your configuration parameters (page 48). *Visual Studio 2005* also contains a configuration parameter editor which generates the code needed to take advantage of this feature (page 50).

Application deployment

The new deployment technology named *ClickOnce* allows a fine management of the security, updates as well as on-demand installation (page 62) of applications. *Visual Studio 2005* offers some practical facilities to take advantage of this technology (page 66).

CLR

A major bug with version 1.x of the CLR which made it possible to modify signed assemblies has been addressed in version 2 (page 22).

The `System.GC` class offers two new methods named `AddMemoryPressure()` and `RemoveMemoryPressure()` which allow you to give the GC an indication in regards to the amount of unmanaged memory held (page 101). Another method `CollectionCount(int generation)` allows you to know the number of collections applied to the specified generation (page 101).

New features have been added to the `ngen.exe` tool to support assemblies using reflection and to automate the update of the compiled version of an assembly when one of its dependencies has changed (page 93).

Appendix B : .NET 2 enhancements

The `ICLRRuntimeHost` interface used from unmanaged code to host the CLR replaces the `ICorRuntimeHost` interface. It allows access to a new API permitting the CLR to delegate a certain number of core responsibilities such as the loading of assemblies, thread management or the management of memory allocations. This API is currently only used by the runtime host for *SQL Server 2005* (page 81).

Three new mechanisms named *constrained execution region* (CER), *critical finalizer* and *critical region* (CR) allow advanced developers to increase the reliability of applications such *SQL Server 2005* which are likely to deal with a shortage of system resources (page 102, page 105 and page 106).

A memory gate mechanism can be used to evaluate before an operation if sufficient memory is available (page 104).

You can now quickly terminate a process by calling the `FailFast()` static method which is part of the `System.Environment` class. This method bypasses certain precautions such as the execution of finalizers or the pending `finally` blocks (page 112).

Delegate

A delegate can now reference a generic method or a method that is part of a generic type. We then see appearing the notion of generic delegates (page 407).

With the new overloads of the `Delegate.CreateDelegate(Type, Object, MethodInfo)` method, it is now possible to reference a static method and its first argument from a delegate. The calls to the delegates then do not need this first argument and is similar to the use of instance method calls (page 448).

In addition, the invocation of methods through the use of delegates is now more efficient.

Threading/Synchronization

You can easily pass information to a new thread that you created by using the new `ParametrizedThreadStart` delegate. Also, new constructors of the `Thread` class allow you to set the maximum size of the thread stack size in bytes (page 114).

The `Interlocked` class offers new methods and allows to deal with more types such as `IntPtr` or `double` (page 119).

The `WaitHandle` class offers a new static method named `SignalAndWait()`. In addition, all classes deriving from `WaitHandle` offer a new static method named `OpenExisting()` (page 126).

The `EventWaitHandle` can be used instead of its subclasses `AutoResetEvent` and `ManualResetEvent`. In addition, it allows to name an event and thus share it amongst multiple processes (page 128).

The new class `Semaphore` allows you take advantage of win32 semaphores from your managed code (page 129).

The new method `SetMaxThreads()` of the `ThreadPool` class allows to modify the maximal number of threads within the CLR thread pool from managed code (page 138).

The .NET 2 framework offers new classes which allow to capture and propagate the execution context of the current thread to another thread (page 149).

Security

The `System.Security.Policy.Gac` class allows the representation of a new type of evidence based on the presence of an assembly in the GAC (page 156).

The following new permission classes have been added:
`System.Security.Permissions.KeyContainerPermission`,
`System.Net.NetworkInformation.NetworkInformationPermission`,
`System.Security.Permissions.DataProtectionPermission`, `System.Net.Mail.SmtpPermission`,
`System.Data.SqlClient.SqlNotificationPermission`,
`System.Security.Permissions.StorePermission`, `System.Configuration.UserSettingsPermission`,
`System.Transactions.DistributedTransactionPermission` and
`System.Security.Permissions.GacIdentityPermission`.

The `IsolatedStorageFile` class presents the following new methods: `GetUserStoreForApplication()`, `GetMachineStoreForAssembly()`, `GctMachineStoreForDomain()` and `GetMachineStoreForApplication()` (page 170).

The .NET 2 framework allows to launch a child process within a different security context than the parent process (page 110).

The .NET 2 framework offers new types within the `System.Security.Principal` namespace allowing the representation and manipulation of *Windows* security identifiers (page 172).

The .NET 2 framework presents new types within the `System.Security.AccessControl` namespace to manipulate *Windows* access control settings (page 174).

The .NET 2 framework offers new hashing methods within the `System.Security.Cryptography` namespace.

The .NET 2 framework offers several classes giving access to the functionality offered by the *Windows* Data Protection API (DAPI) (page 187).

The `System.Configuration.Configuration` class allows the easy management of the application configuration file. In particular, you can use it to encrypt your configuration data (page 189).

The .NET 2 framework offers new types within the `System.Security.Cryptography.X509Certificates` and `System.Security.Cryptography.Pkcs` namespaces which are specialized for the manipulation of *X.509* and *CMS/Pkcs7* certificates (page 191).

The new namespace named `System.Net.Security` offers the new classes `SslStream` and `NegociateStream` which allow the use of the SSL, NTLM and Kerberos security protocols to secure data streams (page 546).

Reflection/Attribute

You now have the possibility of loading an assembly in *reflection only* mode (page 197). Also, the `AppDomain` class offers a new event named `ReflectionOnlyAssemblyResolve` triggered when the resolution of an assembly fails in the reflection-only context (page 75).

The .NET 2 framework introduces the notion of conditional attribute. Such an attribute has the particularity of being taken into consideration by the C#2 compiler only when a certain symbol is defined (page 212).

Interoperability

The notion of function pointer and delegates are now interchangeable using the new GetDelegateForFunctionPointer() and GetFunctionPointerForDelegate() methods of the Marshal class (page 224).

The HandleCollector class allows you to supply to the garbage collector an estimate on the number of *Windows handle* currently held (page 229).

The new SafeHandle and CriticalHandle classes allow to harness *Windows handles* more safely than with the IntPtr class (page 229).

The tlbimp.exe and tlbexp.exe tools present a new option named /tlbreference which allow the explicit definition of a type library without having to go through the registry. This allows the creation of compilation environments which are less fragile.

Visual Studio 2005 offers features to take advantage of the *reg free COM* technology of *Windows XP* within a .NET application. This technology allows the use of a COM class without needing to register it into the registry (page 237).

The structures relatives to the COM technology such as BINDPTR, ELEMDESC or STATDATA have been moved from the System.Runtime.InteropServices namespace to the new System.Runtime.InteropServices.ComTypes namespace. This namespace contains new interfaces which redefine certain standard COM interfaces such as IAdviseSink or IConnectionPoint.

The new namespace named System.Runtime.InteropServices contains new interfaces such as _Type, _MemberInfo or _ConstructorInfo which allow unmanaged code to have access to reflection services. Of course, the related managed classes (Type, MemberInfo, ConstructorInfo...) implement these interfaces.

C#2

Chapter 13 is dedicated to the highlight feature in .NET 2 and C#2: generics.

C#2 allows the declaration of anonymous methods (page 436).

C#2 presents a new syntax to define iterators (page 451).

The csc.exe compiler offers the following new options /keycontainer, /keyfile, /delaysign (page 27), /errorreport and /langversion.

C#2 brings forth the notions of namespace alias qualifier (page 266), of global:: qualifier (page 267) and of external alias (page 268) to avoid certain identifier conflicts.

C#2 introduces the new compiler directives #pragma warning disable and #pragma warning restore (page 263).

The C#2 compiler is now capable of inferring a delegation type during the creation of a delegate object (page 314). This makes source code more readable.

The .NET 2 framework introduces the notion of nullable types which can be exploited through a special C#2 syntax (page 318).

C#2 now allows you to spread the definition of a same type across multiple source files within a same module (page 324). This new feature is called *partial type*.

C#2 allows the assignment of a different visibility to the accessor of a property or indexer (page 347).

C#2 allows the definition of static classes (page 358).

C#2 now allows the definition of a table field with a fixed number of primitive elements within a structure (page 422).

Visual Studio 2005 intellisense feature now uses the XML information contained within /// comments (page 270).

Visual Studio 2005 allows you to build UML-like classes diagrams in-sync with your code (page 369).

Exceptions

The `SecurityException` class and *Visual Studio 2005* have been improved to allow you to more easily test and debug your mobile code (page 169).

The *Visual Studio 2005* debugger offers a practical wizard to obtain a complete set of information relating to an exception (page 424).

Visual Studio 2005 allows you to be notified when a problematic event known by the CLR occurs. These events sometime provoke managed exception (page 434).

Collection

The whole set of the collection types within the .NET framework have been revised in order to account for generic types. These new types are discussed in chapter 15. At page 496 we overview a comparison chart between the `System.Collections` and `System.Collections.Generic` namespaces.

The `System.Array` class has no generic equivalent and is still current. Indeed, since the beginning of .Net the collection model proposed by this class support a certain level of genericity. It presents new methods such as `void Resize<T>(ref T[] array, int newSize)`, `void ConstrainedCopy(...)` and `IList<T> AsReadOnly(T[] array)` (page 476)

Debugging

The `System.Diagnostics` namespace provides new attributes `DebuggerDisplayAttribute`, `DebuggerBrowsable`, `DebuggerTypeProxyAttribute` and `DebuggerVisualizerAttribute` which allow you to customize the display of the state of your objects while debugging (page 510).

.NET 2 allows indicating through attributes the assemblies, modules or zones of code that you do not wish to debug. This feature is known as *Just My Code* (page 512).

C#2 programmers now have access to the *Edit And Continue* feature allowing them to modify their code while debugging it.

.NET 2 presents the new enumeration named `DebuggableAttribute.DebuggingModes` which is a set of binary flags on the debugging modes we wish to use (page 512).

Base classes

The primitive types (integer, boolean, floating point numbers) now expose a method named `TryParse()` which allow to parse a value within a string without raising an exception in the case of failure (page 298).

Appendix B : .NET 2 enhancements   849

The .NET 2 framework offers several implementations derived from the `System.StringComparer` abstract class which allows to compare strings in a culture and case sensitive manner (page 487).

The new `Sytem.Diagnostics.Stopwatch` class provided especially to accurately measure elapsed time (page 213).

The new `DriveInfo` class allows the representation and manipulation of volumes (page 504).

The .NET 2 framework introduces the notion of trace source allowing a better management of traces (page 514). Also, the following trace listener classes have been added: `ConsoleTraceListener`, `DelimitedListTraceListener`, `XmlWriterTraceListener` and `WebPageTraceListener`. (page 513).

Several new functionalities have been added to the `System.Console` class in order to improve the data display (page 520).

IO

The .NET 2 framework offers the new class `System.Net.HttpListener` which allows to take advantage of the HTTP.SYS component of *Windows XP SP2* and *Windows Server 2003* to develop a HTTP server (page 540).

In .NET 2, the classes part of the `System.Web.Mail` namespace are now obsolete. To send mail, you must use the classes within the `System.Net.Mail` namespace. This new namespaces now contains classes to support the MIME standard (page 542).

New methods now allows you to read and write a file in a single call (page 525).

New classes are now available to compress/decompress a data stream (page 545).

A new unmanaged version `System.IO.UnmanagedMemoryStream` of the `MemoryStream` class allows you to avoid the copying of data onto the CLR's object heap and is thus more efficient (page 545).

The new `System.Net.FtpWebRequest` class implements a FTP client (page 540).

The new namespace `System.Net.NetworkInformation` contains types which allow to query the network interfaces available on a machine in order to know their states, their traffic statistics and to be notified on state changes (page 537).

Web resource caching services are now available in the new `System.Net.Cache` namespace (page 540).

The new `System.IO.Ports.SerialPort` class allows the use of a serial port in a synchronous or event based manner (page 545).

Windows Forms 2

Visual Studio 2005 takes advantage of the notion of partial classes in the management of *Windows Forms*. Hence, it will not mix anymore the generated code with our own code in the same file (page 555).

Windows Forms 2 offers the `BackgroundWorker` class which standardize the development of asynchronous operations within a form (page 560).

The appearance (i.e. the visual style) of controls is better managed by *Windows Forms 2* as it does not need to use the `comctl32.dll` DLL to obtain a *Windows XP* style (page 563).

A quick overview of the new controls in *Windows Forms 2* can be found at page 564.

Windows Forms 2 and *Visual Studio 2005* contains a framework and development tools for the quick and easy development of presentation and edition windows for data (page 570).

Windows Forms 2 presents the new classes `BufferedGraphicsContext` and `BufferedGraphics` which allow a fine control on a double buffering mechanism (page 583).

ADO.NET 2

ADO.NET 2 presents new abstract classes such as `DbConnection` or `DbCommand` in the new namespace `System.Data.Common` which implements the `IDbConnection` or `IDbCommand` interfaces. The use of these new classes is now preferred to the use of the interfaces (page 590).

ADO.NET 2 offers an evolved architecture of abstract factory classes which allow decoupling the data access code from the underlying data provider (page 590).

ADO.NET 2 presents new features to construct connection strings independently of the underlying data provider (page 594).

ADO.NET 2 offers a framework allowing the programmatic traversal of a RDBMS schema (page 596).

The indexing engine used internally by the framework when you use instances of the `DataSet` and `DataTable` classes have been revised in order to be more efficient during the loading and manipulation of data.

Instances of the `DataSet` and `DataTable` classes are now serializable into a binary form using the new `SerializationFormat RemotingFormat{get;set;}` property. You can achieve a gain of 3 to 8 times in relation to the use of XML serialization.

The `DataTable` class is now less dependant from the `DataSet` class as the XML features of this one (described at page 644) have been added.

The new method `DataTable DataView.ToTable()` allow the construction of a `DataTable` containing a copy of a view (page 606).

ADO.NET 2 now offers a bridge between the connected and disconnected modes which allow the `DataSet/DataTable` and `DataReader` classes to work together (page 609).

Typed `DataSet` directly takes into account the notion of relationships between tables. Now, thanks to partial types, the generated code is separated from your own code (page 606). Finally, the new notion of `TableAdapter` allows you to create some sort of typed SQL requests directly usable from your code (page 608).

ADO.NET 2 allows to store data updates in a more efficient manner thanks to batch updates (page 603).

ADO.NET 2: SQL Server data provider (SqlClient)

You now have the possibility of enumerating *SQL Server* data sources (page 594).

You have more control on connection pooling (page 596).

The `SqlClient` data provider of ADO.NET 2 allows the execution of commands in an asynchronous way (page 612).

Appendix B : .NET 2 enhancements

You can harness the bulk copy services of the *SQL Server* tool `bcp.exe` using the `SqlBulkCopy` class (page 613).

You can obtain statistics about the activity of a connection (page 614).

There is a simplified and freely distributed version of *SQL Server 2005* which offers several advantages over the previous *MSDE* and *Jet* products (page 614).

Transaction

The new namespace named `System.Transactions` (contained in the `Systems.Transactions.dll`) offers at the same time a unified transactional programming model and a new transactional engine which has the advantage of being extremely efficient on certain type of lightweight transactions (page 615).

XML

The performance of all classes involved in XML data handling have been significantly improved (by a factor of 2 to 4 in classic use scenarios according to *Microsoft*).

The new `System.Xml.XmlReaderSettings` class allows to specify the type of verifications which must be done when using a subclass of `XmlReader` to read XML data (page 637).

It is now possible to partially validate a DOM tree loaded within an instance of `XmlDocument` (page 641).

It is now possible to modify a DOM tree stored in an `XmlDocument` instance through the `XPathNavigator` cursor API (page 643).

The `XslCompiledTransform` class replaces the `XslTransform` class which is now obsolete. Its main advantage is to compile XSLT programs into MSIL code before applying a transformation. According to *Microsoft*, this new implementation improves performance by a factor of 3 to 4 (page 644). Moreover, *Visual Studio 2005* can now debug XSLT programs (page 652).

Support for the XML `DataSet` class has been improved. You can now load XSD schemas with names repeated in different namespaces and load XML data containing multiple schemas. Also, XML load and save methods have been added to the `DataTable` class (page 652).

The 2005 version of *SQL Server* brings forth new features in regards to the integration of XML data inside a relational database (page 647).

XML serialization can now serialize nullable information and generic instances. Also, a new tool named `sgen.exe` allow the pre-generation of an assembly containing the code to serialize a type (page 648).

.NET Remoting

The new `IpcChannel` channel is dedicated to the communication between different processes on a same machine. Its implementation is based on the notion of *Windows* named pipe (page 690).

If you use a channel of type TCP, you now have the possibility of using the NTLM and Kerberos protocols to authenticate the *Windows* user under which the client executes to encrypt the exchanged data and impersonate your requests (page 679).

New attributes of the `System.Runtime.Serialization` namespace allow the management of problems inherent to the evolution of a serializable class (page 658).

It is possible to consume an instance of a closed generic type with the .NET Remoting technology whether you are in CAO or WKO mode (page 415).

ASP.NET 2

Visual Studio .NET 2005 is now supplied with a web server which allows the testing and debugging of your web applications during development (page 715).

It is now easy to use the HTTP.SYS component to build a web server which hosts ASP.NET without needing to use IIS (page 718).

ASP.NET 2 presents a new model for the construction of the classes representing web pages. This model is based on partial classes and is different than the one offered in ASP.NET 1.x (page 721).

The `CodeBehind` directive of ASP.NET v1.x is no longer supported (page 723).

In ASP.NET 2, the model used for the dynamic compilation of your web application has significantly improved and is now based on several new standard folders (page 723). In addition, ASP.NET 2 offers two new pre-compilation modes: the in-place pre-compilation (page 724) and the deployment pre-compilation (page 724).

To counter the effects of large *viewstate* in ASP.NET 1.x, ASP.NET 2 stores information in a base64 string more efficiently and introduces the notion of *controlstate* (page 730).

ASP.NET 2 introduces a new techniques which allows to postback a page to another page (page 731).

Certain events have been added to the lifecycle of a page (page 734).

ASP.NET 2 offers an infrastructure to allow the process of a same request across multiple threads of the pool. This allows us to avoid running out of threads within the pool when several long requests are executed at the same time (page 735).

New events have been added to the `HttpApplication` class (see the MSDN documentation).

The manipulation of configuration files has been simplified because of the *Visual Studio 2005* intellisense, a new web interface, a new UI integrated in IIS and because of new base classes (page 739).

ASP.NET 2 offers a framework allowing the standard management of events occurring during the life of a web application (page 753).

You can now configure ASP.NET 2 so that it can detect whether it is possible to store session identifier in a client-side *cookie* or if it should automatically switch over to the URI mode if cookies are not supported (page 748).

ASP.NET 2 now allows you to supply your own session or session ID management mechanism (page 749).

The cache engine of d'ASP.NET 2 offers interesting new features. You can now use the `VaryByControl` sub-directive in your pages (page 764). You can substitute dynamic fragments within your cached pages (page 766). You can associate your cached data dependencies towards tables and rows of a *SQL Server* data source (page 769). Finally, you can create your own type of dependencies (page 770).

ASP.NET 2 offers new server controls allowing the declarative binding to a data source (page 772).

ASP.NET 2 offers a new hierarchy of server-side controls for the presentation and the edition of data. These controls have the peculiarity of being able to use a data source control to read and write data (page 776).

ASP.NET 2 offers a simplified template syntax (page 779).

ASP.NET 2 adds the notion of *master page* which allows the easy reuse a page design across all pages of a website (page 787).

ASP.NET 2 now offers an extensible architecture to allow the insertion of navigational controls within your site (page 792).

With ASP.NET 2 you can use the Forms authentication mode without being forced to use *cookies* (page 798).

ASP.NET 2 allow the management of the user authentication data as well of the roles to which they may belong through the use of a database (page 798 and page 800). Hence, several new server-side controls have been added to greatly simplify the development of ASP.NET applications which support authentication (page 801).

ASP.NET 2 presents a new framework allowing the storage and access of users profile (page 802).

ASP.NET 2 offers a framework facilitating the management and maintenance of the overall appearance of a site thanks to the notions of theme and skin (page 806).

ASP.NET 2 also offers a framework dedicated to the creation of web portals through the use of what is called *webParts* (page 808).

ASP.NET 2 offers a framework allowing the modification of the rendered HTML code if the initiating HTTP request comes from a system with a small screen such as a mobile phone. Concretely, the rendering of each server control is done in a way to use less screen space. This modification is done through the use of adapter objects which are requested automatically and implicitly by ASP.NET during the rendering of the page. The **Inside the ASP.NET Mobile Controls** article on **MSDN** offers a good starting point on this newASP.NET 2 feature.

Web service

The proxy classes generated by `wsdl.exe` now offer a new asynchronous model which allows cancellation (page 828).

Appendix C: Introduction to design patterns

The notion of *pattern* has appeared in the 1970's in the domain of classic architecture (i.e. buildings). Since then, it has been popularized in the domain of Object Oriented Programming at the end of the 90's by this reference title:

Design Patterns, Elements of Reusable Object-Oriented Software

ADDISON-WESLEY 1994

Erich Gamma, Richard Helm, Ralph Johnson, John Vlissides

ISBN : 0-201-63361-2

This book is often quoted as the *Gof* book (*Gang of Four*). It presents two dozens interaction patterns between classes and between objects. Since then, the notion of *pattern* has weaved itself into other domains of software design such as distributed application architectures. The following title exposes patterns in the management of persistence and the exchange of data between the tiers of a distributed application:

Patterns of Enterprise Application Architecture

ADDISON-WESLEY 2002

Martin Fowler, David Rice, Matthew Foemmel, Edward Hieatt, Robert Mee, Randy Stafford

ISBN: 0-321-12742-0

Microsoft has interested itself for a few years into software design patterns. The company reports its findings through a workgroup named *Pattern & Practices* (*PAG*). More information on this topic can be found at `http://msdn.microsoft.com/practices/`.

Seasoned developers who think in terms of *patterns* can generally quickly conceive architectures of better quality. In addition, their communication and abstraction skills are improved because of the fact that the patterns are named. Every developer has an interest in learning and using them. Each *pattern* defines a behavior which is more of less flexible, and responds to one or many frequent problem within software design. Here are a few examples of problems introduced in this title that are solved using some well known patterns:

- The creation of objects without explicitly specifying their concrete class (**Abstract factory**). This pattern is used by the *ADO.NET* technology to avoid coupling an application with a specific data provider (see page 592). A variant of this pattern is also used by the .NET Remoting technology to avoid exporting the implementation of server objects to the client side (see page 667).
- The interception of the calls to an object (**Proxy**). More details are available at page 679.
- The definition of a *one-to-many* relationship between objects such as each dependant object is notified when the state of the target object changes (**Observer**). The notion of .NET/C# events constitutes an excellent alternative to implement this pattern (see page 340).
- The possibility of choosing the implementation of a feature after the code has been compiled through the use of a configuration file (**Provider**). This pattern is widely used by *ASP.NET*, most notably in allowing you to supply your own extensions to the framework (see page 750). In the same spirit, you can delay the choice of an implementation until execution through the use of late binding (**Plugin**). At page 205 we show you a practical example of its use.
- The possibility of accessing the elements of a collection in a sequential manner without having to worry about the physical representation of the elements (**Iterator**). C#2 offers features which allow an elegant implementation of this pattern (page 451).
- Allow objects which do not know about each other to interact through the use of a class encapsulating these interactions (**Mediator**). This pattern is used by the *Windows Form* technology to facilitate the development of forms (page 553).

Appendix C: Introduction to design patterns 855

- The control of the number of instances of a class (**Singleton**). The notion of class constructors facilitate the implementation of this pattern (see page 357).
- The addition of responsibilities to an object during execution (**Decorator**). This pattern is used by the .NET framework to add services to a data stream (see page 543).
- Create objects at whim based on a known prototype through an interface which contains a cloning method (**Prototype**). The `System.ICloneable` interface of the framework presented at page 290 is essentially dedicated to this role.
- Maintain the list of changes made during an operation and coordinate the persistence of these changes by managing eventual concurrency problems (**Work unit**). This pattern is used to save the changes made to the data within `DataSet` in the ADO.NET technology (see page 602).
- Obtaining a *thread-safe* implementation of a class (**SyncRoot**). More details are available at page 122.

You can complete this lecture by reading the article named **Discover the Design Patterns You're Already Using in the .NET Framework** by *Rob Pierry* in the July 2005 issue of **MSDN Magazine**: `http://msdn.microsoft.com/msdnmag/issues/05/07/DesignPatterns/default.aspx`.

Appendix D: Tools for the .NET 2 platform

You can consult the web site located at http://sharptoolbox.com which maintains an impressive list of hundreds of tools available to .NET developers. Here is a list of the tool that we use within this book

Assembly

ildasm.exe page 16
Reflector page 19
resgen.exe page 28
al.exe page 30 and page 54
ilasm.exe page 33
ILMerge page 12

Build/Deployment

msbuild.exe page 39
GACUtil.exe page 53
mage.exe page 62
mageui.exe page 62
fuslogvw.exe page 86
ngen.exe page 93

Profiling

CLR Profiler page 98

Security

caspol.exe page 162
mscorcfg.msc page 162
permview.exe page 169
certmgr.exe page 192
permcalc.exe page 67

Interoperability

regsvr32.exe page 242
regasm.exe page 242
tlbimp.exe page 230
tlbexp.exe page 239
guidgen.exe page 15
regsvcs.exe page 252
oleview.exe page 239

C#

csc.exe page 264
NDoc page 271

Windows Forms

HTML Help WorkShop page 562

XML serialization and typed datasets

xsd.exe and typed datasets page 606
xsd.exe and XML serialization page 650
sgen.exe page 650

Object/Relational mapping

Links to popular tools can be found at page 611

SQL Server

bcp.exe page 613

.NET Remoting

soapsuds.exe page 668

ASP.NET 2

aspnet_regiis.exe page 716
aspnet_compiler.exe page 724
aspnet_regsql.exe page 770

Web service

wsdl.exe page 825
X509 Certificate Tool page 837
Policy Wizard page 837

Diagnostic

perfmon.exe page 752 and page 94

Aspect Oriented Programming (AOP)

AspectDNG page 386

Static code analyses

Finally, we mention the existence of the **NDepend** tool. This tool statically analyzes the compiled code of any .NET application and is non-intrusive. In addition to computing most standard code metrics, it can detect a certain number of code design problems. This tool is a good complement to the **FxCop** tool.

Index

Symbols

#pragma managed 226
#pragma unmanaged 226
#pragma warning disable 263
#pragma warning restore 263
.NET Framework Configuration 88
2PC
    See 2 Phase Commit
2 Phase Commit 616
AssemblyRef (type metadata table) 14
business exception 434
Directory
    See System.IO.Directory
I/O thread 138
identity comparison 288
lazy evaluation pattern 459
MemberRef (type metadata table) 15
ModuleRef (type metadata table) 14
pessimistic (transaction management) 603
plugin 205
provider design pattern 801
StringComparer
    See System.StringComparer
System.Reflection.ConstructorInfo 201
System.Reflection.MethodInfo 204
System.StringComparer 487
System.Type 201
TypeRef (type metadata table) 15

A

abstract class 375
abstract factory 592
abstraction 375
abstract methods 375
Access Control Element 175
Access Control List 175
accessor (event) 341
accessor (property) 337
access rights 174
access rules (ASP.NET) 796
ACE
    See Access Control Element
ACID (properties) 615
ACL
    See Access Control List
Activator
    See System.Activator
ActiveDirectoryMembershipProvider
    See System.Web.Security.
        ActiveDirectoryMembershipProvider
active object (garbage collector) 96
add (event accessor) 341
al.exe 30

alias 266
alias namespace qualifier 267
allocation 281
AllowPartiallyTrustedCallersAttribute
    See System.Security.
        AllowPartiallyTrustedCallersAttribute
anonymous methods 436
AOP
    See aspect oriented programming
AppDomain
    See application domain
AppDomains
    loaded domain neutral 78
AppDomainSetup
    See System.AppDomainSetup
AppearanceEditorPart 814
AppLaunch.exe 67
application 109
application deployment 51
ApplicationDirectory
    See System.Security.Policy.ApplicationDirectory
application domain 71
application domain recycling 103
application exception 102
ApplicationScopedSettingAttribute 49
ApplicationSettingsBase
    See System.Configuration.ApplicationSettingsBase
arenas 98
array 287
ArrayList
    See System.Collections.ArrayList
as (keyword) 385
ASCII 524
Aspect Oriented Programming 386
aspnet_isapi.dll 715
aspnet_regiis.exe 716
aspnet_regsql.exe 770, 799, 802
aspnet_wp.exe 715
AssemblyDef (manifest table) 13
assembly loader 83
AsyncCallback
    See System.AsyncCallback
asynchronous call 141
asynchronous call (.NET Remoting) 828
asynchronous delegate 141
asynchronous exceptions 102, 434
atomic (operation) 119
Attachment
    See System.Net.Mail.Attachment
attribut
    AttributeTargets 207
Attribute
    See System.Attribute; See System.Attribute
attribute
    ConditionalAttribute 261
attributs 206
AuthenticatedStream
    See System.Net.Security.AuthenticatedStream
authentication provider 797
Authenticode 59, 191
authorization

See permission
auto-reset event 128
AutoEventWireUp 734
Automation 89
AutoResetEvent 126
    See System.Threading.AutoResetEvent

B

base (keyword) 370
Base64 (encoding) 28
base class 368
Basic String
    See BSTR
bcp.exe 613
BehaviorEditorPart 814
big-endian 525
binary flag 307
binary operator 359
BinaryReader
    See System.IO.BinaryReader
BinaryWriter
    See System.IO.BinaryWriter
BindingList<T>
    See System.ComponentModel.BindingList<T>
BindingNavigator 571
bindingRedirect 86
BindingSource 573
BitArray
    See System.Collections.BitArray
Bitmap
    See System.Drawing.Bitmap
BitVector32
    See System.Collections.Specialized.Bitvector32
blind trust (CAS) 164
blittable type 221
bool (keyword) 297
bootstrapper 63
boxing 292
branches 272
break (keyword) 277
browser 713
BSTR 235
buffer 526
BufferedStream
    See System.IO.BufferedStream
BufferedWebEventProvider 753
byte (keyword) 295
bytecode 33

C

C 611
C++/CLI 225
CA
    See Certificate Authorities
cab file 57
cab files 57
Cache
    See System.Web.Caching.Cache
CacheDependency
    See System.Web.Caching.CacheDependency
caching (ASP.NET) 762
callback method 142, 528, 533
callback procedure 551
call context 710
CallingConvention
    See System.Runtime.InteropServices.
    CallingConvention
call mode (WKO) 664
CamelCase 272
CAO 664
capacity (class List<T>) 481
capacity (StringBuilder class) 311
Cascading Style Sheet 805
Cassini 715
catch (keyword) 425
CategoryAttribute 568
cctor. See class constructor
Cdecl 220
CER
    See constrained execution regions
certificate 191
Certificate Authorities 191
Certificate Store 192
certmgr.exe 192
CGI 713
ChangePassword 802
channel 690
channel sink providers 693
char (keyword) 297
checked 299
checked exception 428
child process 110
chrome (WebParts) 809
CIL
    See IL
class 327
class (keyword) 328
class constructor 357
class inheritance 368
class instance 327
ClassInterface
    See System.Runtime.InteropServices.
    ClassInterface
class interface 241
class loader 89, 158
CLI 106
Client Activated Object
    See CAO
closed generic type 390
closure 446
CLR Profiler 98
CLS 106
CLSCompliantAttribute
    See System.CLSCompliantAttribute
CMS/Pkcs7 191
code-bloat 391
CodeAccessPermission
    See System.Security.CodeAccessPermission
codebase 86
code behind 721

codepage 525
COFF
    See PE/COFF
collection (GC) 96
COM+ application 249
commit 615
Common Langage Runtime (CLR) 71
Common Language Infrastructure
    See CLI
Common Type System
    See CTS
Comparer<T>
    See System.Collections.Generic.Comparer<T>
Comparison<T>
    See System.Comparison<T>
comparison operators 363
Compilation 260
component (graphical) 553
COMVisible
    See System.RunTime.InteropServices.COMVisible
conditional attribute 212
conditionals 272
configuration section 48
configuration section handler 49
connection pool 595
connection string 594
Console
    See System.Console
Console Application 551
ConsoleColor
    See System.ConsoleColor
const (keyword) 330
Constrained Execution Regions 103
Constraint
    See System.Data.Constraint
constraint (generics) 392
constraints (DB) 604
constructor (of a class) 349
ConstructorInfo
    See System.Reflection.ConstructorInfo
content page 787
context (security) 138
ContextBoundObject
    See System.ContextBoundObject
continuation 460
continue (C# keyword) 277
contravariance 402, 408
Control
    See System.Web.UI.Control
controls (graphical) 553
controlstate 730, 761
cookies 539
cooperative multitasking 82, 113
copy constructor 292
coroutine 460
covariance 402, 408, 474
CR
    See critical region
CreateUserWizard 801
creator object 134
critical finalizer 105

CriticalFinalizerObject
    See System.Runtime.ConstrainedExecution.CriticalFinalizerObject
Critical Region 106
critical section 120
CrossAppDomain 691
CrossAppDomainDelegate
    See System.CrossAppDomainDelegate
CryptoStream
    See System.Security.Cryptography.CryptoStream
csc.exe 16, 264
CSS
    See Cascading Style Sheet
ctor
    See constructor
CTS 285
culture 27
CurrentCulture 33
CurrentUICulture 30
cursor (data stream) 523
custom attribute 209

D

DACL
    See Discretionary Access Control List
DataGrid 776
DataList 780
Data Protection API
    See DPAPI
data slot 146
Data Source Name
    See DSN
DataView
    See System.Data.DataView
DataViewManager
    See System.Data.DataViewManager
DbCommandBuilder
    See System.Data.Common.DbCommandBuilder
DbConnectionStringBuilder
    See System.Data.Common.DbConnectionStringBuilder
DbProviderFactories
    See System.Data.Common.DbProviderFactories
DbProviderSupportedClasses
    See System.Data.Common.DbProviderSupportedClasses
deadlocks 118
deallocation 281
Debug
    See System.Diagnostics.Debug
decimal (keyword) 296
DeclarativeCatalogPart 814
decorator 543
deep copy 291
default (keyword) 401
default application domain 71
default constructor 349
DeflateStream 545
delayed signature 26
delaysign (csc.exe option) 27

delegate 138
delegate (keyword) 313
delegate class 313
delegate objects 313
delegate types 287
dependentAssembly 86
dependent transaction 624
deployment module 55
deployment pre-compilation 723
derived class 368
DES
    See Digital Encryption Standard
destructors 350
DetailsView 781
deterministic 120
devenv.exe 39
dfsvc.exe 67
Digital Encryption Standard 182
digital signature 185
digital signatures 23
directory 504
DirectoryInfo
    See System.IO.DirectoryInfo
discovery proxy 839
Discretionary Access Control List 175
Dispose()
    See System.IDisposable
distributed transaction 615
Distributed Transaction Coordinator 618
DistributedTransactionPermission
    See System.Transactions.
    DistributedTransactionPermission
division by zero 299
DLL hell 52
DllImport
    See System.Runtime.InteropServices.DllImport
Dns
    See System.Net.Dns
DOM (Document Object Model) 639
domain neutral assembly 71
Domain Specific Language 3
DOS (Disk Operating System) 551
dotnetfx.exe 70
double (keyword) 296
double buffering 583
double linked list 482
double pointer 333
downcast 374
download cache 69
DPAPI 187
drive 504
DriveInfo
    See System.IO.DriveInfo
DSL
    See Domain Specific Language
DSN 595
DTC
    See Distributed Transaction Coordinator
due time 140
durable (RM) 619
dynamic allocation 282

dynamic binding 197

E

ECMA 4, 23
elementary types
    See primitive type
encapsulation 345
end point 662
enregistration 92
enterprise server 249
entropy 187
enum (keyword) 305
enumerable 448
enumerations 287
enumerator 448
Environment
    See System.Environment
equivalence comparison 288
equivalence relation 289
escalation policy 106
European Computer Manufacturer's Association
    See ECMA
event 128
event (keyword) 341
EventDef 14
EventLogWebEventProvider 753
event provider 753
EventResetMode
    See System.Threading.EventResetMode
events 340
EventWaitHandle
    See System.Threading.EventWaitHandle
Evidence
    See System.Security.Policy.Evidence
evidences 158
exclusive access rights (synchronization domain) 133
execution unit. See thread
Exit() 111
explicit (keyword) 361
explicit cast operator 361
explicit loading 89
ExportedTypeDef (manifest table) 14
extern (keyword) 219
extern alias 268
eXtreme Programming 3

F

factory (design pattern) 667
FailFast() 112
fiber 82
FieldDef 14
FieldOffset
    See System.Runtime.InteropServices.FieldOffset
FieldPtr (type metadata table) 15
FIFO 483
file 505
File (classe)
    See System.IO.File
FileDef (manifest table) 13

F

FileInfo
    See System.IO.FileInfo
FileStream
    See System.IO.FileStream
FileSystemInfo
    See System.IO.FileSystemInfo
FileSystemWatcher
    See System.IO.FileSystemWatcher
FileWebRequest
    See System.Net.FileWebRequest
FileWebResponse
    See System.Net.FileWebResponse
finalized class 371
finalizer 97, 350
finally (keyword) 428
firewall 669
flag enum 307
float (keyword) 296
focus 559
for (keyword) 276
foreach (keyword) 277
ForeignKeyConstraint
    See System.Data.ForeignKeyConstraint
forms 552
FormsIdentity
    See System.Web.Security.FormsIdentity
FormView 784
forward-only (data stream) 523
Fragile Base Class 386
Framework Configuration 88
FreeBSD Unix 5
friend assemblies 22
friend assembly 347
friends (C++
   classes and methods) 328
FTP 538
FtpWebRequest
    See System.Net.FtpWebRequest
FtpWebResponse
    See System.Net.FtpWebResponse
full runtime compilation 723
Fully trusted assemblies 164
functional languages 446
functional unit
    See process
functor 446, 493
functors (C++) 358
fusion 83
fuslogvw.exe 86

G

GAC 51
Gac (class)
    See System.Security.Policy.Gac
GACUtil.exe 53
garbage collector 78, 95, 282
GC
    See System.GC
GCHandle
    See System.Runtime.InteropServices.GCHandle
generation (garbage collector) 96
generic method 404
generics 387
generic type 389, 390
GenericWebPart 810
getter 337
global (keyword) 268
Global.asax 741
Global Assembly Cache
    See GAC
global assembly cache 93
globalization (culture) 27
Gof book 854
goto (keyword) 278
growth factor 481
GUID 683
Guid
    See System.RunTime.InteropServices.Guid
guidgen.exe 15
GZipStream 545

H

handle (C++/CLI) 227
Hash
    See System.Security.Policy.Hash
hashing value 157, 185
hash value 13
heap fragmentation 95
HRESULT 236
HtmlControl
    See System.Web.UI.HtmlControls.HtmlControl
HtmlForm
    See System.Web.UI.HtmlControls.HtmlForm
HTML server controls 733
HTTP.SYS 540
HttpApplication
    See System.Web.HttpApplication
HttpApplicationState
    See System.Web.HttpApplicationState
HttpCachePolicy
    See System.Web.HttpCachePolicy
HttpChannel
    See System.Runtime.Remoting.Channels.http.HttpChannel
HTTP handler 740
HttpListener
    See System.Net.HttpListener
HttpListenerContext
    See System.Web.HttpListenerContext
HTTP module 740
HTTP pipeline 740
HttpWebRequest
    See System.Net.HttpWebRequest

I

IAsyncResult
    See System.IAsyncResult
IBindingList 574
IChannel

863

See System.Runtime.Remoting.Channels.
  IChannel
IChannelReceiver
  See System.Runtime.Remoting.Channels.
  IChannelReceiver
IChannelSender
  See System.Runtime.Remoting.Channels.
  IChannelSender
IClientChannelSinkProvider
  See System.Runtime.Remoting.Channels.
  IClientChannelSinkProvider
ICollection<T>
  See System.Collections.Generic.ICollection<T>
IComparable
  See System.Collections.IComparable
IComparable<T>
  See System.Collections.Generic.IComparable<T>
IComparer
  See System.Collections.IComparer
IComparer<T>
  See System.Collections.Generic.IComparer<T>
identity permission 159
IDictionary<K,V>
  See System.Collections.Generic.IDictionary<K,T>
IDispatch 89
IDisposable
  See System.IDisposable
idle process 114
IEnlistmentNotification
  See System.Transactions.IEnlistmentNotification
IEnumerable
  See System.Collections.IEnumerable
IEnumerator
  See System.Collections.IEnumerator
IHttpHandler
  See System.Web.IHttpHandler
IHttpModule
  See System.Web.IHttpModule
IJW 225
IL 33
ilasm.exe 33
ildasm.exe 16, 90
ILease
  See System.Runtime.Remoting.Lifetime.ILease
IList<T>
  See System.Collections.Generic.IList<T>
IListSource
  See System.ComponentModel.IListSource
ILogicalThreadAffinative
  See System.Runtime.Remoting.Messaging.
  ILogicalThreadAffinative
Image
  See System.Drawing.Image
ImageFormat
  See System.Drawing.Imaging.ImageFormat
IMessageSink
  See System.Runtime.Remoting.Messaging.
  IMessageSink
immutable 308
imperative languages 446
impersonation 173, 795

implicit (keyword) 361
implicit cast operator 361
implicit late binding 197
implicit loading 89
ImportCatalogPart 814
In
  See System.Runtime.InteropServices.In
in-place pre-compilation 723
incremental construction 43
indexers 339
Indigo
  See Windows Communication Framework
INETINFO.EXE 715
InetInfo.exe 715
Initialization Vector 182
inlined code 719
inlining 92, 277
instance members 356
InsufficientMemoryException 104
int (keyword) 295
interface (keyword) 377
interface extension 378
Interlocked
  See System.Threading.Interlocked
Intermediate Language
  See IL
internal 346
internal call 219
internal protected 346, 369
InternalsVisibleToAttribute
  See System.Runtime.CompilerServices.
  InternalsVisibleToAttribute
internationalization 27
IP 530
IP address 530
IPC
  See Inter Process Communication
IpcChannel
  See System.Runtime.Remoting.Channels.Ipc.
  IpcChannel
IPermission
  See System.Security.IPermission; See System.
  Security.IPermission
IPromotableSinglePhaseNotification
  See System.Transaction.
  IPromotableSinglePhaseNotification
IRemotingTypeInfo
  See System.Runtime.Remoting.
  IRemotingTypeInfo
is (keyword) 384
ISA 368
IServerChannelSinkProvider
  See System.Runtime.Remoting.Channels.
  IServerChannelSinkProvider
ISinglePhaseNotification
  See System.Transactions.ISinglePhaseNotification
ISponsor
  See System.Runtime.Remoting.Lifetime. ISponsor
ISynchronizeInvoke
  See System.ComponentModel.ISynchronizeInvoke
iterator (design pattern) 449

It Just Works
    See IJW
IXPathNavigable 642

J

Jet 614
JIT 91
JMC
    See Just My Code
jumps 272
Just In Time
    See JIT
Just My Code 512

K

Kerberos 546
kernel mode 112
keyboard (management of) 559
keycontainer (csc.exe option) 24
keyfile (csc.exe option) 24

L

late binding 197, 198
LayoutEditorPart 814
lease 670
lease manager 670
lexical environment 446
LifetimeServices
    See System.Runtime.Remoting.Lifetime.
        LifetimeServices
LIFO 484
lightweight process 71
lightweight thread 82
Lightweight Transaction Manager 619
LinkedList<T>
    See System.Collections.Generic.LinkedList<T>
LinkedListNode<T>
    See System.Collections.Generic.
        LinkedListNode<T>
list 480
List<T>
    See System.Collections.Generic.List<T>
little-endian 525
load balancing 685
load factor 487
LocalDataStoreSlot
    See System.LocalDataStoreSlot
LocalFileSettingsProvider
    See System.Configuration.
        LocalFileSettingsProvider
localization (culture) 27
log 513
logical thread 82
Login 801
LoginName 802
LoginStatus 802
LoginView 802
long (keyword) 295

long weak reference 100
loops 272, 276
LTM
    See Lightweight Transaction Manager

M

machine.config 593, 738
mage.exe 62
mageui.exe 62
MailAddress
    See System.Net.Mail.MailAddress
MailMessage
    See System.Net.Mail.MailMessage
Main 278
main thread 109
managed heap 95
managed thread 112
ManifestResourceDef (manifest table) 14
manual-reset event 128
ManualResetEvent 126
    See System.Threading.ManualResetEvent
Marshal
    See System.Marshal.InteropServices.Marshal
MarshalAs
    See System.Runtime.InteropServices.MarshalAs
master detail view 782
MasterPage
    See System.Web.UI.MasterPage
master page 787
math (functions) 497
MD5 (hashing algorithm) 24
members 328
Membership
    See System.Web.Security.Membership
MembershipProvider
    See System.Web.Security.MembershipProvider
membership provider 799
MembershipUser 800, 801
MemberwiseClone() 291
MemoryFailPoint
    See System.Runtime.MemoryFailPoint
memory gates 104
memory leak 282
MemoryStream
    See System.IO.MemoryStream
MEP
    See Message Exchange Pattern
Message Exchange Pattern 821
message sink 684
Message Transmission Optimization Mechanism 836
metadata token 37
MethodCallMessageWrapper
    See System.Runtime.Remoting.Messaging.
        MethodCallMessageWrapper
MethodDef (type metadata table) 14
MethodInfo
    See System.Reflection.MethodInfo
MethodPtr (type metadata table) 15
MFC 552
Microsoft.Win32.RegistryKey 509

Microsoft SQL Server Desktop Engine 614
MIME. See Multipurpose Internet Mail Exchange
modal (dialog) 558
modeless 559
ModuleDef (type metadata table) 14
Monitor
    See System.Threading.Monitor
Mono 5
Moore (law) 112
mouse (management of) 559
msbuild.exe 39
mscoree.dll 78
mscorlib 18
mscorlib.dll 76
mscorsvr.dll 76
mscorwks.dll 76
MSDE
    See Microsoft SQL Server Desktop Engine
MSIL
    See IL
MTOM
    See Message Transmission Optimization
    Mechanism
multiple inheritance 368
Multipurpose Internet Mail Exchange 543
Mutex 126

N

named mutex 127
named parameter 211
named pipe 690
namespace 257
    namespace alias 258
Nant 39
native image cache 53, 93
Native Image Generator
    See ngen.exe
native images 93
NDepend 857
NegociateSteam
    See System.Net.Security.NegociateSteam
nested type 345
NetworkChange
    See System.Net.NetworkInformation.
    NetworkChange
NetworkInterface
    See System.Net.NetworkInformation.
    NetworkInterface
new (keyword) 350, 374
ngen.exe 93
NHibernate 611
nodes 482
NotifyFilters
    See System.IO.NotifyFilters
No Touch Deployment 68
NTD
    See No Touch Deployment
NT Lan Manager 546
NTLM. See NT Lan Manager
null (keyword) 285

Nullable<T>
    See System.Nullable<T>
nullable types 319

O

object 327
object activation 661
ObjectDataSource 774
ObjectDisposedException
    See System.ObjectDisposedException
ObjectHandle 200
    See System.Runtime.Remoting.ObjectHandle
object oriented programming (OOP) 327
Object Space 612
ObjRef
    See System.Runtime.Remoting.ObjRef
OEM 525
oleview.exe 239
one to many (relationship) 601
OneWay
    See System.Runtime. Remoting.Messaging.
    OneWay
one way asynchronous call 145
open generic type 390
operator (keyword) 359
optimistic (transaction management) 603
OptionalFieldAttribute
    See System.Runtime.Serialization.
    OptionalFieldAttribute
Out
    See System.Runtime.InteropServices.Out
overflow 299
overloading 336
override (keyword) 372

P

P/Invoke 219
P/Invoke Marshalling 220
PAG
    See Pattern & Practices
Page
    See System.Web.UI.Page
PageCatalogPart 813
PAL 5
ParamArrayAttribute
    See System.ParamArrayAttribute
parameter type 389
ParamPtr (type metadata table) 15
parent process 110
partial (keyword) 324
partial collection (GC) 97
Partially trusted assemblies 164
partial trust (CAS) 164
partial type 324
    See type defined over several source file
PascalCase 272
passing arguments by reference 331
passing arguments by value 331
Passport 172, 797

PassportIdentity
    See System.Web.Security.PassportIdentity
PasswordRecovery 802
path
    absolute path 506
    relative paths 506
Path (classe)
    See System.IO.Path
paths 506
Pattern & Practices 854
PE. See PE file
perfmon.exe 94, 752
permcalc.exe 67
permission 158
PermissionSet
    See System.Security.PermissionSet
PersonalizationProvider
    See System.Web.UI.WebControls.WebParts.PersonalizationProvider
Ping
    See System.Net.NetworkInformation.Ping
ping 672
pinvokeimpl 226
pipeline pattern 461
pitching 92
Platform Abstraction Layer
    See PAL
Platform Invoke. See P/Invoke
pointer 287
Policy
    See System.Security.Policy
policy 820
Policy Wizard 837
polymorphic class 372
polymorphism 197, 372
port (IP) 530
portable binary code 90
post-cache substitution 766
postback events 728
preemptive multitasking 82, 113
Preprocessing 260
preprocessor directives 260
primary thread
    See main thread
primitive types 287
principal 171
PrincipalPermission
    See System.Security.Permissions.PrincipalPermission
principal policy (security) 179
priority of operators 300
private 346
private key 184
privileges
    See permission
probing 85
procedural programming 327
process 76, 109
ProcessStartInfo
    See System.Diagnostics.ProcessStartInfo
producer/consumer 463

ProfileProvider
    See System.Web.Profile.ProfileProvider
ProgId
    See System.RunTime.InteropServices.ProgId
program entry point 279
promotable enlistment 620
Promotable Single Phase Enlistment 619
PropertyDef 14
protected 346, 369
ProtectedData
    See System.Security.Cryptography.ProtectedData
    See System.Security.Cryptography.ProtectedMemory
prototype (design pattern) 292
provider design pattern 750, 793, 799, 802
proxy (web service) 825
ProxyAttribute
    See System.Runtime.Remoting.Proxies.ProxyAttribute
pseudo-attributes 206
PSPE
    See Promotable Single Phase Enlistment
public 346
public key 184
public key token 24
Publisher
    See System.Security.Policy.Publisher
publisherPolicy 86
publisher policy assembly 54
publishing an object 682
pure virtual
    See abstract method

Q

quantum 113, 120
Query Notification 770
queue 483
Queue<T>
    See System.Collections.Generic.Queue<T>

R

race conditions 118
RAD 570
random number 499
Rapid Application Development
    See RAD
readonly (keyword) 330
RealProxy
    See System.Runtime.Remoting.Proxies.RealProxy
real proxy 681
receiver channel 690
recovery service 617
reference (of an object onto another) 329
reference type 283
Reflection Only 197
regasm.exe 242
regedit.exe 508
regedt32.exe 508
RegEx

See System.Text.RegularExpressions.RegEx
regex
    See regular expression
regexp
    See regular expression
registry 508
RegistryKey
    See Microsoft.Win32.RegistryKey
regsvr32.exe 242
regular expression 517
relative URI 539
Remote Procedure Call 821
RemotingClientProxy
    See System.Runtime. Remoting.Services. RemotingClientProxy
RemotingException
    See System.Runtime.Remoting. RemotingException
remove (event accessor) 341
Repeater 780
RequestCacheLevel
    See System.Net.Cache.RequestCacheLevel
RequestCachePolicy
    See System.Net.Cache.RequestCachePolicy
resgen.exe 28
resource file 27
ResourceManager 615
    See System.Resources.ResourceManager
resxgen.exe 28
return (keyword) 334
reverse engineering 18
rights
    See permission
RM
    See Resource Manager
role 171
RoleProvider
    See System.Web.Security.RoleProvider
role provider 800
Roles
    See System.Web.Security.Roles
rollback 615
root certificates 192
Rotor
    See Shared Source CLI
RPC
    See Remote Procedure Call
RSA 185
RTTI
    See RunTime Type Information
Rule
    See System.Data.Rule
RuntimeHelpers
    See System.Runtime.CompilerServices. RuntimeHelpers
runtime host 77
runtime host of an AppDomain 158
RunTime Type Information 384

S

S/MIME
    See Secure/Multipurpose Internet Mail Extensions
SACL
    See System Access Control List
SAFEARRAY 235
safe point 98
same-box communication
    See Inter Process Communication
satellite assemblies 27
SAX 637
sbyte (keyword) 295
scheduler 113
scheme (URI) 538
scope resolution operator 328, 356
SD
    See security descriptor
SDDL
    See Security Descriptor Definition Language
sealed (keyword) 371
sealed method 372
Secure/Multipurpose Internet Mail Extensions 191
secure session 184
Secure Socket Layer 546
SecureString
    See System.Security.SecureString
SecurityAction
    See System.Security.Permissions.SecurityAction
security descriptor 175
Security Descriptor Definition Language 172
security identifier 172
security policy 160
Security Support Provider Interface 546
security token 171
seek 523
SEH 433
self-descriptive (format) 631
Semaphore
    See System.Threading.Semaphore
semaphore 129
sender channel 690
sequence 478
SerialPort
    See System.IO.Ports.SerialPort
server-side script blocks 720
service 819
Service Oriented Architecture 819
session key 184
session logon 171
setter 337
SettingsProvider
    See System.Configuration.SettingsProvider
sgen.exe 650
SHA-1 (hashing algorithm) 24
shadow copy 88, 740
shallow copy 291
shared assembly 51
shared key 184
shared members 356
Shared Source CLI 5
SharePoint 808
ShFusion.dll 52

shim 78
short (keyword) 295
short weak reference 100
SID
    See security identifier
side-effect 331
side by side 52
sieve of Eratosthène 465
simple inheritance 368
SimpleWorkerProcess
    See System.Web.Hosting.SimpleWorkerProcess
single call 664
singleton 349
singleton (call mode WKO) 664
Site
    See System.Security.Policy.Site
SiteMapProvider
    See System.Web.SiteMapProvider
SiteMap provider 793
Smalltalk 347
SmtpClient
    See System.Net.Mail.SmtpClient
sn.exe 23
SOA
    See Service Oriented Architecture
SoapExtension
    See System.Web.Services.SoapExtension
SOAP extensions 837
SOAP node 831
SOAP roles 831
Soapsuds.exe 668
Socket
    See System.Net.Sockets.Socket
socket 530
software interrupt 113
SqlBulkCopy
    See System.Data.SqlClient.SqlBulkCopy
SqlDataSource 773
SqlMembershipProvider
    See System.Web.Security.SqlMembershipProvider
SqlProfileProvider 802
SQL Server 2005 Express Edition 614
SQLXML 647
SSCLI
    See Shared Source CLI
SSL
    See Secure Socket Layer
SslStream
    See System.Net.Security.SslStream
SSPI
    See Security Support Provider Interface
stack 281, 484
stack (IL) 34
Stack<T>
    See System.Collections.Generic.Stack<T>
stack frames 35, 220
stack overflow 104
standard deviation 598
state machine 278
state of the object 328
static allocation 282

static class 358
static constructor 357
StdCall 220
STL 493
stored procedure 598
Stream
    See System.IO.Stream
StreamReader
    See System.IO.StreamReader
StreamWriter
    See System.IO.StreamWriter
string 287
string (keyword) 308
StringCollection
    See System.Collections.Specialized.
    StringCollection
string encoding 524
StringReader
    See System.IO.StringReader
StringWriter
    See System.IO.StringWriter
StrongName
    See System.Security.Policy.StrongName
strong name 22
StrongNamePublicKeyBlob
    See System.Security.Permissions.
    StrongNamePublicKeyBlob
struct (keyword) 303
StructLayout
    See System.Runtime.InteropServices.StructLayout
Structured Exception Handling. See SEH
structures 287
stub 91
stub (of a method) 198
Style
    See System.Web.UI.Controls.Style
stylesheet 807
subroutine 460
subscriber (to an event) 340
super class 368
SuppressUnmanagedCodeSecurity
    See System.Security.
    SuppressUnmanagedCodeSecurity
SuppressUnmanagedCodeSecurityAttribute
    See System.Security.
    SuppressUnmanagedCodeSecurityAttribute
symmetric algorithm 181
symmetric algoritms 183
Synchronization (attribute)
    See System.Runtime.Remoting.Contexts.
    Synchronization
syntactic sugar 324
System.Activator 200, 201
System.AppDomain 72, 201
System.AppDomainSetup 73
System.AsyncCallback 143
System.Attribute 209
System.Boolean 297
System.Byte 295
System.Char 298
System.CLSCompliantAttribute 107

System.Collections.ArrayList 480
System.Collections.BitArray 477
System.Collections.Generic.ICollection<T> 478
System.Collections.Generic.IComparable<T> 490
System.Collections.Generic.IComparer<T> 490
System.Collections.Generic.IDictionary<K,V> 484
System.Collections.Generic.IEqualityComparer<T> 488
System.Collections.Generic.IList<T> 479
System.Collections.Generic.KeyValuePair<K,V> 489
System.Collections.Generic.LinkedList<T> 482
System.Collections.Generic.LinkedListNode<T> 482
System.Collections.Generic.List<T> 480
System.Collections.Generics.Queue<T> 483
System.Collections.IComparable 490
System.Collections.IComparer 490
System.Collections.IEnumerable 448
System.Collections.IEnumerator 448
System.Collections.Specialized.BitVector32 478
System.Collections.Specialized.StringCollection 483
System.Comparison<T> 490
System.ComponentModel.BindingList<T> 482
System.ComponentModel.Component 553
System.ComponentModel.IListSource 771
System.ComponentModel.ISynchronizeInvoke 148
System.Configuration.ApplicationSettingsBase 49
System.Configuration.LocalFileSettingsProvider 50
System.Configuration.SettingsProvider 50
System.Console 520
System.ConsoleColor 521
System.CrossAppDomainDelegate 74
System.Data.Common 591
System.Data.Common.DbCommandBuilder 602
System.Data.Common.DbConnectionStringBuilder 594
System.Data.Common.DbProviderFactories 592
System.Data.Common.DbProviderSupportedClasses 593
System.Data.Constraint 604
System.Data.DataView 604
System.Data.DataViewManager 606
System.Data.ForeignKeyConstraint 604
System.Data.Rule 604
System.Data.SqlClient.SqlBulkCopy 613
System.Data.SqlTypes.SqlXml 647
System.Data.UniqueConstraint 604
System.DateTime 499
System.Decimal 296
System.Deletage 317
System.Deployment 65
System.Diagnostics.Debug 513
System.Diagnostics.Process 110
System.Diagnostics.ProcessStartInfo 110
System.Diagnostics.Trace 513
System.Diagnostics.TraceListener 513
System.Diagnostics.TraceSource 514
System.Double 296
System.Drawing.Bitmap 579
System.Drawing.Image 579
System.Drawing.Imaging.ImageFormat 579
System.Enum 306
System.Environment 111
System.EventArgs 340

System.EventHandler 555
System.Exception 426
System.GC 100
System.Globalization 499
System.IAsyncResult 142
System.IDisposable 351
System.Int16 295
System.Int32 295
System.Int64 295
System.IO 503, 523
System.IO.BinaryReader 524
System.IO.BinaryWriter 524
System.IO.BufferedStream 544
System.IO.Compression 545
System.IO.Directory 504
System.IO.DirectoryInfo 504
System.IO.DriveInfo 504
System.IO.File 505
System.IO.FileInfo 505
System.IO.FileStream 526
System.IO.FileSystemInfo 504
System.IO.FileSystemWatcher 506
System.IO.MemoryStream 545
System.IO.NotifyFilters 507
System.IO.Path 506
System.IO.Ports.SerialPort 545
System.IO.Stream 523
System.IO.StreamReader 524, 527
System.IO.StreamWriter 524, 527
System.IO.StringReader 524
System.IO.StringWriter 524
System.IO.TextReader 524
System.IO.TextWriter 524
System.IO.UnmanagedMemoryStream 545
System.LocalDataStoreSlot 146
System.Marshal.InteropServices.Marshal 235
System.Math 497
System.MulticastDelegate 313
System.Net.Cache.RequestCacheLevel 540
System.Net.Cache.RequestCachePolicy 540
System.Net.Dns 533
System.Net.FileWebRequest 539
System.Net.FileWebResponse 539
System.Net.FtpWebRequest 539
System.Net.FtpWebResponse 539
System.Net.HttpListener 540
System.Net.HttpWebRequest 539
System.Net.Mail.Attachment 543
System.Net.Mail.MailAddress 543
System.Net.Mail.MailMessage 543
System.Net.Mail.SmtpClient 542
System.Net.Mime 543
System.Net.NetworkInformation.NetworkChange 538
System.Net.NetworkInformation.NetworkInterface 537
System.Net.NetworkInformation.Ping 537
System.Net.Security 546
System.Net.Security.AuthenticatedStream 546
System.Net.Security.NegociateSteam 546
System.Net.Security.SslStream 546
System.Net.Sockets.Socket 530
System.Net.Sockets.TcpClient 531

Index

System.Net.Sockets.TcpListener 531
System.Net.WebClient 539
System.Nullable<T> 319
System.ObjectDisposedException 353
System.ParamArrayAttribute 335
System.Random 499
System.Reflection.Emit 212
System.Resources.ResourceManager 30
System.Runtime.CompilerServices.
    InternalsVisibleToAttribute 22
System.Runtime.CompilerServices.
    RuntimeHelpers 103, 104, 357
System.Runtime.ConstrainedExecution.
    CriticalFinalizerObject 105
System.Runtime.InteropServices. 219
System.Runtime.InteropServices.
    CallingConvention 220
System.Runtime.InteropServices.ClassInterface 241
System.RunTime.InteropServices.COMVisible 241
System.Runtime.InteropServices.DllImport 219
System.Runtime.InteropServices.FieldOffset 223
System.Runtime.InteropServices.GCHandle 227
System.RunTime.InteropServices.Guid 241
System.Runtime.InteropServices.In 224
System.Runtime.InteropServices.MarshalAs 224
System.Runtime.InteropServices.Out 224
System.RunTime.InteropServices.ProgId 243
System.Runtime.InteropServices.StructLayout 223
System.Runtime.MemoryFailPoint 104
System.Runtime.Remoting.Channels.http.
    HttpChannel 690
System. Runtime.Remoting.Channels.IChannel 690
System.Runtime.Remoting.Channels.
    IChannelReceiver 690
System.Runtime.Remoting.Channels.
    IChannelSender 690
System.Runtime.Remoting.Channels.
    IClientChannelSinkProvider 693
System.Runtime.Remoting.Channels.Ipc.
    IpcChannel 690
System.Runtime.Remoting.Channels.
    IServerChannelSinkProvider 693
System.Runtime.Remoting.Channels.Tcp.
    TcpChannel 690
System.Runtime.Remoting.Contexts.
    Synchronization 124
System.Runtime.Remoting.IRemotingTypeInfo 685
System.Runtime.Remoting.Lifetime.ILease 670
System.Runtime.Remoting.Lifetime.ISponsor 670
System.Runtime.Remoting.Lifetime.
    LifetimeServices 671
System.Runtime.Remoting.Messaging.AsyncResult 142
    See System.Runtime.Remoting.Messaging.
    AsyncResult
System.Runtime.Remoting.Messaging.
    ILogicalThreadAffinative 710
System.Runtime.Remoting.Messaging.
    IMessageSink 684
System.Runtime.Remoting.Messaging.
    MethodCallMessageWrapper 689
System.Runtime. Remoting.Messaging.OneWay 144

System.Runtime.Remoting.ObjectHandle 659
System.Runtime.Remoting.ObjRef 682
System.Runtime.Remoting.Proxies.ProxyAttribute 687
System.Runtime.Remoting.Proxies.RealProxy 681
System.Runtime.Remoting.RemotingException 667
System.Runtime.Remoting.Services.
    RemotingClientProxy 669
System.Runtime.Serialization.
    OptionalFieldAttribute 658
System.SByte 295
System.Security.AccessControl 127, 175
System.Security.
    AllowPartiallyTrustedCallersAttribute 164
System.Security.CodeAccessPermission 158
System.Security.Cryptography.CryptoStream 549
System.Security.Cryptography.ProtectedData 187
System.Security.Cryptography.ProtectedMemory 188
System.Security.IPermission 167
System.Security.Permissions. PrincipalPermission 180
System.Security.Permissions.SecurityAction 168
System.Security.Permissions.
    StrongNamePublicKeyBlob 156
System.Security.PermissionSet 165
System.Security.Policy 155
System.Security.Policy.ApplicationDirectory 156
System.Security.Policy.Evidence 157
System.Security.Policy.Gac 156
System.Security.Policy.Hash 157
System.Security.Policy.Publisher 156
System.Security.Policy.Site 156
System.Security.Policy.StrongName 156
System.Security.Policy.Url 156
System.Security.Policy.Zone 156
System.Security.Principal.WindowsIdentity 172
System.Security.SecureString 189
System.Security.SecurityZone 156
System.Security.SuppressUnmanagedCodeSecurity 220
System.Security.
    SuppressUnmanagedCodeSecurityAttribute 166
System.Single 296
System.Text.RegularExpressions.RegEx 518
System.Text.StringBuilder 311
System.Threading.AutoResetEvent 128
System.Threading.EventResetMode 128
System.Threading.EventWaitHandle 128
System.Threading.Interlocked 119
System.Threading.ManualResetEvent 128
System.Threading.Monitor 120
System.Threading.Semaphore 129
System.Threading.ThreadPool 137
System.Threading.Timer 140
System.Threading.WaitHandle 126
System.ThreadStaticAttributes 145
System.Timers.Timer 139
System.Transaction.
    IPromotableSinglePhaseNotification 629
System.Transactions.
    DistributedTransactionPermission 626
System.Transactions.
    IEnlistmentNotification.IEnlistmentNotification 626
System.Transactions.ISinglePhaseNotification 626

System.Transactions.TransactionScope 621
System.Type 199
System.UInt16 295
System.UInt32 295
System.UInt64 295
System.Uri 539
System.WeakReference 99
System.Web.Caching.Cache 768
System.Web.Caching.CacheDependency 768
System.Web.Hosting.SimpleWorkerProcess 717
System.Web.HttpApplication 740
System.Web.HttpApplicationState 745
System.Web.HttpCachePolicy 762
System.Web.HttpContext 742
    See System.Web.HttpContext
System.Web.HttpListenerContext 541
System.Web.IHttpHandler 743
System.Web.IHttpModule 742
System.Web.Management 753
System.Web.Profile.ProfileProvider 802
System.Web.Security.
    ActiveDirectoryMembershipProvider 799
System.Web.Security.FormsIdentity 172
System.Web.Security.Membership 799
System.Web.Security.MembershipProvider 799
System.Web.Security.PassportIdentity 172
System.Web.Security.RoleProvider 801
System.Web.Security.Roles 801
System.Web.Security.SqlMembershipProvider 799
System.Web.Services.SoapExtension 837
System.Web.Services.WebMethod 823
System.Web.Services. WebService 823
System.Web.SiteMapProvider 793
System.Web.TraceContext 752
System.Web.UI.Control 725
System.Web.UI.Controls.Style 805
System.Web.UI.HtmlControls.HtmlControl 734
System.Web.UI.HtmlControls.HtmlForm 729
System.Web.UI.MasterPage 788
System.Web.UI.Page 714
System.Web.UI.WebControls.WebControl 734
System.Web.UI.WebControls.WebParts.WebPart 810
System.Web.UI System.Web.UI.WebControls.WebParts.
    PersonalizationProvider 810
System.Web.XmlSiteMapProvider.
    XmlSiteMapProvider 793
System.Windows.Forms.Control 553
System.Windows.Forms.Timer 141
System.Xml.XmlDataDocument 646
System.Xml.XmlDocument 639
System.Xml.XmlNode 639
System.Xml.XmlNodeList 639
System.Xml.XmlNodeReader 636
System.Xml.XmlReader 636
System.Xml.XmlReaderSettings 638
System.Xml.XmlSerializer 648
System.Xml.XmlTextReader 636
System.Xml.XmlTextWriter 636, 638
System.Xml.XmlWriter 636
System.Xml.XPath.XPathDocument 642
System.Xml.XPath.XPathNavigator 642, 643

System.Xml.Xsl.XslCompiledTransform 644

T

TableAdapter 608
task manager 109
TCP/IP 530
TcpChannel
    See System.Runtime.Remoting.Channels.Tcp.
    TcpChannel
TcpClient
    See System.Net.Sockets.TcpClient
TcpListener
    See System.Net.Sockets.TcpListener
template 779
template (C++/CLI) 227
templates (C++) 391
TextReader
    See System.IO.TextReader
TextWriter
    See System.IO.TextWriter
theme 806
this (keyword) 347
thread 109
   Multiple Apartment Thread 137
   Single Apartment Thread 137
thread-safe 123
thread local storage 146
ThreadPool
    See System.Threading.ThreadPool
thread pool 137, 528
ThreadStaticAttributes
    See System.ThreadStaticAttributes
ThreadStore 112
throw (keyword) 427
TIL
    See Transaction Isolation Level
timeout 118
Timer 582
    See System.Threading.Timer
time slices
    See quantum
tlbexp.exe 239
TLS
    See thread local storage
tModel
    See Types Models
Trace
    See System.Diagnostics.Trace
trace.axd 752
TraceContext
    See System.Web.TraceContext
TraceListener
    See System.Diagnostics.TraceListener
TraceSource
    See System.Diagnostics.TraceSource
trace source 514
TraceWebEventProvider 753
transaction 615
Transaction Isolation Level 622
transaction manager 616

TransactionScope
    See System.Transactions.TransactionScope
Transport Layer Security 546
trusted site 156
try (keyword) 425
Type
    See System.Type
typed DataSet 606
TypeDef (type metadata table) 14
type defined over several source files 324
typeof (keyword) 199
Types Models 838

U

UDDI
    See Universal Description Discovery and Integration
UDP/IP 530
UDT
    See User Defined Type
uint (keyword) 295
ulong (keyword) 295
unary operator 359
UnBoxing 294
UNICODE 525
union 223
UniqueConstraint
    See System.Data.UniqueConstraint
Universal Description Discovery and Integration 838
unmanaged function pointer 224
UnmanagedMemoryStream
    See System.IO.UnmanagedMemoryStream
untrusted site 156
URI 538
URL 84
Url
    See System.Security.Policy.Url
user control (ASP.NET) 757
User Defined Type 611
user groups 171
user mode 112
UserScopedSettingAttribute 49
ushort (keyword) 295
using (keyword) 266, 352
UTF 525
UTF-8 525, 633

V

validation group 756
value (keyword) 338
value type 283
variable 327
variance 598
VARIANT 235
verb (WebParts) 809
verbatim 506
verbatim (string) 309
virtual (keyword) 372
virtual machine 71

virtual memory 110
virtual method 372
visibility levels 346
void (keyword) 334
volatile (keyword) 119
volatile (RM) 619
VSHost 67

W

W3C 4, 639
w3wp.exe 715
WaitHandle
    See System.Threading.WaitHandle
WCF
    See Windows Communication Framework
WCF endpoints 840
WeakReference
    See System.WeakReference
weak reference 99
web.config 593
web application 715
WebClient
    See System.Net.WebClient
WebControl
    See System.Web.UI.WebControls.WebControl
WebDev.WebServer.EXE 715, 716
web form 714
web garden 739
WebManagementEvent 753
WebMethod
    See System.Web.Services.WebMethod
web method 822
WebPart
    See System.Web.UI.WebControls.WebParts.WebPart
WebParts 808
webPartsZone 811
web server controls 733
WebService
    See System.Web.Services. WebService
Web Service Enhancement 836
Web Service Interoperability 820
web services 820
well-known object 662
while (keyword) 276, 841, 843
Win32 220
Windows Application 551
Windows application reference 67
Windows Communication Framework 840
WindowsIdentity
    See System.Security.Principal.WindowsIdentity
Windows Management Instrumentation 753
Windows messages 551
Windows Socket API 540
Winsock 540
WKO 662
WM_TIMER 141
WMI
    See Windows Management Instrumentation
WmiLogWebEventProvider 753

worker thread 138
WS-Addressing 836
WS-AtomicTransaction 617, 839
WS-BusinessActivity 618, 839
WS-Coordination 618, 839
WS-Discovery 838
WS-Enumeration 840
WS-Federation 839
WS-I
    See Web Service Interoperability
WS-Management 840
WS-MetadataExchange 838
WS-Policy 836
WS-PolicyAttachment 838
WS-ReliableMessage 838
WS-SecureConversation 836
WS-Security 836
WS-SecurityPolicy 836
WS-Trust 836
WSDL 832
wsdl.exe 825
WSE
    See Web Service Enhancement
WYSIWYG 552

X

X.509 191
X509 Certificate Tool 837
XA (transaction) 617
XCopy (deployment) 51
XML 631
XML attribute 633
XmlDataDocument
    See System.Xml.XmlDataDocument
XML document 631
XmlDocument
    See System.Xml.XmlDocument
XML element 632
XmlNode
    See System.Xml.XmlNode
XmlNodeList
    See System.Xml.XmlNodeList
XmlNodeReader
    See System.Xml.XmlNodeReader
XmlReader
    See System.Xml.XmlReader
XmlReaderSettings
    See System.Xml.XmlReaderSettings
XmlSerializer
    See System.Xml.XmlSerializer
XmlSiteMapProvider
    See System.Web.XmlSiteMapProvider
XmlTextReader
    See System.Xml.XmlTextReader
XmlTextWriter
    See System.Xml.XmlTextWriter; See System.Xml.XmlTextWriter
XmlWriter
    See System.Xml.XmlWriter
XP
    See eXtreme Programming
XPath 634
XPathDocument
    See System.Xml.XPath.XPathDocument
XPathNavigator
    See System.Xml.XPath.XPathNavigator
XPathNodeIterator 643
XQuery 635
XSD 633
xsd.exe 606, 650
XslCompiledTransform
    See System.Xml.Xsl.XslCompiledTransform
XSLT 635

Y

yield return (keyword) 451

Z

zone 156